Special Edition

Using Java™ 2

Standard Edition

Brian Keeton

Chuck Cavaness

Geoff Friesen

201 West 103rd Street
Indianapolis, Indiana 46290

Contents at a Glance

Special Edition Using Java™ 2, Standard Edition

International Standard Book Number: 0-7897-2468-5

Library of Congress Catalog Card Number: 00-108362

Printed in the United States of America

First Printing: December 2000

03 02 01 4 3 2

Trademarks

All terms mentioned in this book that are known to be trademarks or service marks have been appropriately capitalized. Que cannot attest to the accuracy of this information. Use of a term in this book should not be regarded as affecting the validity of any trademark or service mark.

Java and JavaBeans are registered trademarks of Sun Microsystems, Inc.

Warning and Disclaimer

Every effort has been made to make this book as complete and as accurate as possible, but no warranty or fitness is implied. The information provided is on an "as is" basis. The authors and the publisher shall have neither liability nor responsibility to any person or entity with respect to any loss or damages arising from the information contained in this book.

Associate Publisher
Dean Miller

Acquisitions Editor
Todd Green

Development Editors
Victoria Elzey
Sean Dixon

Technical Editors
Mark Roth
Mike Stevenson
Alan Moffet

Managing Editor
Thomas F. Hayes

Project Editor
Linda Seifert

Copy Editor
Julie A. McNamee

Indexer
Erika Millen

Proofreader
Harvey Stanbrough

Team Coordinator
Cindy Teeters

Media Developer
Michael Hunter

Interior Designer
Ruth Lewis

Cover Designers
Dan Armstrong
Ruth Lewis

Editorial Assistant
Angela Boley

Production
Mark Walchle

Contents

II User Interface

Appendixes

About the Authors

Chuck Cavaness is a senior Java Architect for NetVendor, a B2B supplier-enablement Internet company. He specializes in full J2EE architecture design and construction for B2C and B2B Internet solutions. His experiences include development of several multithreaded CORBA and EJB Internet solutions, including the development of a couple of full Object-to-Relational frameworks using JDBC. He is certified in several Java Technologies and is involved heavily in developing Internet Auction components for the Internet.

Geoff Friesen is heavily involved with Java technology. He has written numerous Java-based articles for *JavaWorld*—ranging from internationalization to Java Plug-In to the future of Java—and an introductory Java book called *Java 2 by Example*. Furthermore, he's taught university-level and college-level introductory Java courses. Geoff is currently serving as the moderator to the Java Beginner discussion group at *ITworld.com*.

Brian Keeton is a software engineer at NetVendor, where he develops server-side Java components to support B2B trading using EJB. He is a Sun Certified Java programmer and developer with 10 years of professional software development experience. He spent five years developing object-oriented applications in C++ for the defense industry before transitioning to Java business application development using Swing, CORBA, and EJB.

Dedication

To my wife Tracy, who labored more than I ever did on this book to give me two great boys, Josh and Zachary. Thanks for all of the support. —Chuck Cavaness

To my parents, Bill and Mary; my sister, Sharon Larsen; her husband, Richard Larsen; and their children, Eric, Ryan, and Rebecca. —Geoff Friesen

To my wife Rebeccah and daughter Emily—my two Joys. —Brian Keeton

Acknowledgments

Chuck Cavaness I would like to give thanks to the many people who participated in the process of putting this book together. The act of writing the content for a book is so very important, but is such a small part of putting it together.

I would like to thank the entire editorial staff led by Victoria Elzey, who provided the necessary prodding and poking to ensure that the work was of quality and on time.

I imagine that Victoria's technical vocabulary must have increased 100-fold with all the great questions and deep curiosity that she exhibited during the editing process. I can also imagine Sun's technical support calls will drop by half now that you don't have to call them to help clarify anything.

A special thanks needs to be given to the technical editors who kept me in line and on target and provided enough suggestions to almost fill another entire book. I appreciate the work you have done to increase the quality of the material and give the reader more insight.

Finally, I owe a special debt to my family, who had to put up with the long hours with me off in a room with the door closed. The support that you have provided me is dearly appreciated.

Geoff Friesen My contribution to this book represents the culmination of a long journey into the realm of computer technology—a journey that began 20 years ago. Along the way, I've been privileged to meet many people who've been a source of inspiration. This is my way of saying thanks.

Many thanks to my parents, my sister, and her family. I hope you enjoy this book (even if you only think of Java as coffee).

Back in my university days, I was fortunate to be taught by two excellent professors: Dr. George E. McMaster and Dr. Gwynfor Richards. Thanks for your inspiration, and for teaching me about the need to achieve excellence in computer programming. (By the way, I don't throw chalk at my students; they might throw chalk brushes back at me.)

My sincere thanks goes to a very classy lady by the name of Yvonne Baert, who secured my Java teaching position at a local college. Even though I've been contacted by other IT recruiters, you'll always be the number one IT recruiter in my books!

Many other people have been an inspiration to me. They include Jerry Goebel, Chris Goudy, Glen Beer, Helen Stroud, Chris Stroud, Dave Stearns, David Fisher, Diana Smith, Hilda Sydor, Clark Sydor, Eileen Miller, Belinda Jeanne Teichgrab, Lorne Cooper, Pastor and Mrs. Joe MacDonald, Steven and Shannon MacDonald, Carol Wilkinson, Mark and Tamara Stropko, Ted and Sheila Vidler, Dino and Shannon Sylvestri, Jane Eidse, Pierre Cho, Chris Ashley, Yolande Cates, Manuel Santos, Robert Lapensee, Jack Stephenson, Marc Caron, Robert Paquin, and the late Father Lucian Kemble.

Finally, I would like to thank Todd Green, my editor for *Java 2 by Example* and this book. I appreciate all your patience with me, especially in light of my tendency to miss deadlines.

Brian Keeton I first want to thank my NetVendor colleague Chuck Cavaness, and Todd Green, our acquisitions editor at Que, for getting me involved in this project. Contributing to this book has been an experience I would never want to have missed. A special note of gratitude also goes to Joe Weber and Mark Wutka for their work on the previous edition that served as a solid foundation for this effort. I have great respect for your ability to create from a blank page.

Much of the credit for this final product goes to the editors who helped turn my drafts into what you'll find in my chapters that follow. Victoria Elzey led the way with her big-picture insight that allowed her to skillfully merge the contributions of three authors into one cohesive work. Also, Julie McNamee's keen eye for grammar and consistency was a tremendous help (I hope to never again say *may* when I should have said *might*). For the clarity of the text and the quality of the examples, I owe much to the technical editors. I especially want to thank Alan Moffet for the insights he provided and his attention to detail.

Most importantly, I want to thank my wife Rebeccah for her support and patience through these long hours. You're the best!

Tell Us What You Think!

As the reader of this book, *you* are our most important critic and commentator. We value your opinion and want to know what we're doing right, what we could do better, what areas you would like to see us publish in, and any other words of wisdom you're willing to pass our way.

As an associate publisher for Que, I welcome your comments. You can fax, email, or write me directly to let me know what you did or didn't like about this book—as well as what we can do to make our books stronger.

Please note that I cannot help you with technical problems related to the topic of this book, and that due to the high volume of mail I receive, I might not be able to reply to every message.

When you write, please be sure to include this book's title and author as well as your name and phone or fax number. I will carefully review your comments and share them with the author and editors who worked on the book.

Fax: 317-581-4666

Email: `feedback@quepublishing.com`

Mail: Associate Publisher
Que
201 West 103rd Street
Indianapolis, IN 46290 USA

INTRODUCTION

In this introduction

Welcome to the amazing and dynamic world of Java! If you are brand new to Java, get ready for a solid introduction to the hottest programming technology in the industry. Java is an extremely rich language that is relatively simple and easy to learn, especially when compared to some of the languages from which its inventors drew. Java gives you unprecedented support for even the most complex of tasks through its powerful API.

What is Java? Java is a revolutionary programming language that was introduced by Sun Microsystems in June 1995. Since then, hundreds of thousands of programmers have picked up books just like this one and have realized just how powerful the language is.

Java is an object-oriented programming language, which means that programmers using Java can develop complex, yet maintainable, programs more easily than programmers attempting to do the same with procedural languages. In addition, Java has built-in support for threads, networking, and a variety of other tools that allow you to focus more on the true requirements of your programs and less on the low-level infrastructure that you need.

A note about version numbers: This book supports the Java 2 Platform, which was first introduced with the release of SDK 1.2 and subsequently upgraded with Java™ 2 SDK, version 1.3. Both of these SDK versions are referred to as Java 2. This book specifically points out the enhancements found in the SDK 1.3 release to give you the most up-to-date understanding of the latest Java 2 Platform.

Note

Throughout this book, there are references to the SDK and sometimes the JDK. Sun Microsystems originally referred to (and registered) the platform as the Java Development Kit–JDK. However, according to a Sun marketing representative, with the release of version 1.2 Sun switched from using JDK to the more general name of Software Development Kit–SDK. For a complete explanation of this name change and how it affects parts of the Java platform, check out the marketing information on Sun's site at the following URL:

`http://java.sun.com/products/jdk/1.2/java2.html`

Another change in the packaging of Java by Sun has been to introduce the concept of multiple editions of the language. The editions are all based on the same core API and do not compete with each other in any way, but they allow developers to focus more easily on the technology that supports their particular needs. This book addresses the Java 2 Standard Edition (J2SE), which is the core of the language. Every Java developer makes use of the J2SE functionality, and it is definitely the starting point for learning the language. Sun also provides the Java 2 Enterprise Edition (J2EE), which supports distributed application development using technologies such as Java Server Pages (JSP) and Enterprise JavaBeans (EJB), and the Java 2 Micro Edition (J2ME), which supports the development of small, embedded programs for portable devices.

This Book Is for You

If you're new to Java, this book is for you. Don't be intimidated by the size of this book. It contains a vast amount of rich information about every facet of the Standard Edition of the Java programming language, along with easy-to-follow chapters that are designed to get you started. If you're already a Java expert, this book will become an often-used reference item on your shelf. Actually, it may never leave your desk. This book puts into one source a complete reference and set of examples on every aspect of the J2SE. Between the covers of this book, you'll find examples and explanations that will make your life as a programmer immensely easier.

How This Book Is Organized

This book is organized into six parts. Each part covers a significant number of related topics that have been organized to build your knowledge of the Java language as you progress through the book.

Part I, "The Java Language," teaches you the syntax of Java and how to build correctly formed classes and interfaces. The fundamental aspects of Java are found in its language syntax. Every program is built using the fundamentals of the language, and this part walks you through each segment. For the beginner, each of the chapters has been structured to help you become familiar with Java programming. For the expert, the individual aspects of the language are explored in great detail, making Part I a great reference as well as a learning tool. This part concludes with more advanced discussions of the Java collections framework and the language's built-in support for multi-threaded applications.

Part II, "User Interface," teaches you the details of building a graphical user interface in Java, from both the AWT and Swing perspectives. In addition to exploring these Java Foundation Classes (JFC) APIs, Part II explores the JFC accessibility, Java 2D, and Drag and Drop APIs. Furthermore, because of its closeness to the JFC, the Java Media Framework is explored in Part II.

Part III, "I/O," walks you through reading and writing data from your Java applications. The part begins by teaching you the fundamental components and techniques of streaming and reading files. Then you learn how to use Java's serialization for sending and retrieving whole Java objects. This part concludes with the information needed to build networked applications using Java and to build applications for international use.

Part IV, "Databases," provides the details of one of the most important aspects of building modern business applications. Databases are the core to almost all business applications, and Java's JDBC (Java Database Connectivity) eases the burden of communicating between your Java applications and the database. In this part, you are introduced to how Java allows you to access and use databases to develop powerful and portable applications in a short amount of time. Welcome to the world of platform-independent and DBMS-independent systems!

Part V, "Component Development," shows you how to make the development cycle faster and easier. Component-based development has been around for many years now, but it has never been as easy to do as with Java. In this part, you learn how to use JavaBeans, which is Java's platform-independent component model. This section is preceded by coverage of the Reflection API, which supports JavaBeans and any other class discovery that you may need to perform at runtime in a Java application.

The appendixes give you the detailed instructions you need to get up and running with a Java development environment and start writing your own programs. Refer to the appendixes when you begin the early examples if you have any difficulty compiling and running your code. This part also covers the performance enhancements introduced in SDK 1.3 and provides you with a list of resources you can explore to learn even more about Java.

Conventions Used in This Book

This book uses various stylistic and typographic conventions to make it easier to use.

Note

When you see a note in this book, it indicates additional information that may help you avoid problems or that should be considered in using the described features.

Tip

Tips suggest easier or alternative methods of executing a procedure. Tips introduce techniques applied by seasoned developers to simplify a task or to make design and implementation decisions that produce robust and maintainable systems.

Caution

Cautions warn you of hazardous procedures (for example, activities that delete files).

Look for this icon throughout the book wherever Java 2 features and enhancements that were introduced in SDK 1.3 are described.

Special Edition Using Java 2 uses cross references to help you access related information in other parts of the book.

→ **See** " Interfaces," **p. 197**

Each chapter ends with a "Troubleshooting" section that provides solutions to some of the common problems that might crop up regarding a particular topic. Throughout the main chapter text, cross references like these appear directing you to the appropriate heading within the "Troubleshooting" section to address these problems.

PART I

The Java Language

CHAPTER 1

Object-Oriented Programming

In this chapter

by Brian Keeton

OBJECT-ORIENTED PROGRAMMING: A DIFFERENT WAY OF THINKING

Even if you have never programmed in an object-oriented language, you have almost certainly heard the term *object-oriented programming* (OOP) used widely in the software development industry. Although not a new concept (the first object-oriented languages came into existence in the '70s), OOP did not come to the forefront until the '90s. The limitations of early CPUs and the initial high cost of memory slowed the acceptance of OOP, but now, for most programmers, the choice has been made and there is no turning back.

Although similar to structured programming in many ways, object-oriented programming is a completely different approach that requires a different mindset. The similarities between OOP and structured programming tend to be syntax related and can often be seen when comparing statements that perform arithmetic and control flow functions. The differences, on the other hand, appear when the bigger picture of overall design and code structure is considered. If you have a background in structured programming, you will definitely find familiar constructs and syntax in OOP languages such as Java (there are only so many ways to write a `for` loop, after all). Although true that OOP languages do add some entirely new functionality, the primary difference is in the thought process that goes into designing and implementing an object-oriented system. It is not so much learning the syntax of an OOP language as it is learning to apply it correctly that matters more when moving from a structured programming background to Java.

Whether your background is in structured programming or you have never programmed at all, the possibilities offered by OOP will become apparent as you build your knowledge of its basic concepts. If you have programmed in other object-oriented languages, the capabilities offered by Java will likely strengthen your ties to this approach as your preferred method for developing robust and maintainable systems.

A SHORT HISTORY OF PROGRAMMING

To understand why object-oriented programming is of such great benefit to you as a programmer, it's useful to look at the history of programming as a technology.

In the early days of computing, programming was an extremely labored process. Each step the computer needed to take had to be meticulously (and flawlessly) programmed. The early languages were known as machine languages, which later evolved to assembly languages. *Machine language programming* required programmers to code CPU instructions to manipulate individual memory locations to achieve a desired result. *Assembly language programming* provided a minimal level of abstraction by combining commonly used sequences of instructions into higher-level instructions that could be referred to by name.

The painstaking detail required to program this way can be seen in an example of evaluating a simple expression. Consider a case in which you need to evaluate (4 * 5) + 7 and assign the result to a variable. In a higher-level language, this requires you to write a statement of the form "c = 4 * 5 + 7." However, to achieve the same result using machine code, you would have to write individual instructions that communicate steps such as set register A to 4, set register B to 5, multiply register A by B storing the result in C, set register A to 7, add register A and C, and store in memory location 15234.

Considering the number of instructions you would need to perform this simple computation, you can probably get a good idea of what machine and assembly language programming were like for a typical programmer. The instructions were a bit more cryptic than those you are accustomed to working with in modern languages and meticulous specification of detail was a must (computers are not forgiving at all when presented with imprecise directions).

PROCEDURAL LANGUAGES

Assembly languages were easier to work with than machine languages, but programmers soon saw the need to move beyond CPU instructions and work at a higher level of abstraction. This abstraction was achieved through procedural languages, which provided the programmer with functions and data types that could be manipulated without so much concern for the underlying machine instructions. These functions, or procedures, acted like black boxes that each implemented some useful task. For instance, you might create a procedure to write something to the screen, such as `writeln` in Pascal or `printf` in C. The initial purists of this type of programming believed that you could always write these functions without modifying any data that existed external to them. As an example, you clearly would not expect a call to `printf` or `writeln` to modify the string you pass in after printing it to the screen. In essence, the perceived ideal was not only to build a black box that hid implementation details, but also one that had no side effects related to the parameters passed into it.

For procedures that perform simple tasks, such as outputting information to the screen, this principle of not modifying external data is easy to satisfy. However, as you can imagine, applying this constraint when more complex operations are involved is difficult at best. Designing a system so that functions only introduce data changes through their return values is a significant restriction, so this goal was, for the most part, abandoned. This brought about increased flexibility, but with tradeoffs. As functions began changing data outside their scope (for example, by declaring C functions that accept pointers as arguments), problems with coupling began to surface. Because the functions were now changing data outside of their scope, testing became increasingly difficult. Coupling between a function and the code that called it meant that each function had to be tested not only individually, but also within the context of its usage to make sure that variable changes it introduced through its parameters were not corrupting other parts of a program. Individual black boxes weren't so black anymore because changes to their implementations required other functions that used them to be retested as well to make sure data updates were still handled correctly. This complexity grew dramatically with increasing program size and added to the need for the automated software testing industry of today.

STRUCTURED DEVELOPMENT

Most early programming efforts were judged solely on whether they worked for their originally intended use. Not until software applications began to increase in size and complexity was attention focused on how well code was actually written and how well it could be maintained. This led to the implementation of structured development practices. Structured development didn't necessarily change the languages that were being used, but rather provided a new process for designing and writing software. Under a structured development philosophy, programmers were expected to plan 100% of a program before writing a single line of code. When a program was planned for development, huge schematics and flow charts were produced showing the interaction of each function with every other and how each piece of data would eventually flow through the program. This heavy precode work proved to be effective in some cases, but limiting for most. The shortcomings here might have resulted in large part from an emphasis on good documentation and not necessarily great design.

In addition, when programmers were pushed to predesign all their code before actually writing any of it, some flexibility and support for creative solutions were lost. Programming became institutionalized. Good programs tend to result from experimentation in some areas built upon a foundation of a solid underlying design. Structured development limited this by requiring complete specification of implementation details up front.

Even with that said, you should not think that current development approaches overlook the importance of the design phase. The opposite is, in fact, true. The difference is that most current methods stress that the design and construction phases of a software project should be iterative. Unlike structured development, current methods specifically allow developers to refine a design as requirements solidify and new solutions (or problems) are uncovered.

OBJECT-ORIENTED PROGRAMMING

Object-oriented analysis, design, and programming have now come into prominence as a successor to structured development. This did require some language changes to support the associated constructs, but the more significant impact has been to change the way developers think about the problems they must solve with software and the associated systems they must design. The resulting programming technique goes back to procedural development (by emphasizing black boxes), continues the advancements made through structured development, and, most importantly, encourages creative programming design.

Using an OOP paradigm, the objects associated with a problem and its software solution are represented as true entities in a system, not just corresponding data structures. Objects aren't just numbers, like integers and characters; they also contain the functions, or methods in Java terminology, which relate and manipulate the numbers. In OOP programming, rather than passing data around a system openly (such as to a globally accessible function), messages are passed to and from objects via method calls that instruct an object to perform a certain task using the data it is provided.

As stated earlier, object-oriented programming really isn't all that new; it was developed in the 1970s by the same group of researchers at Xerox Parc that brought the world GUI (graphical user interface) technology, Ethernet, and a host of other products that are commonplace today. Why did OOP take so long to gain wide acceptance? For one thing, OOP requires a paradigm shift in development, and the inertia found in development organizations and their existing systems is a challenge for any new technology to overcome. In addition, the available hardware at the time OOP was introduced was not up to the job. For programming languages, less abstraction tends to correspond to less memory and CPU usage. Hardware capabilities continue to grow in leaps and bounds; however, while limited capabilities were more of a concern, procedural languages remained an attractive option. Now, increases in available (and affordable) memory and CPU horsepower have made development cost and maintainability much more significant drivers in architecture and design choices than the hardware requirements for a system.

The question now is where to start. Perhaps the first, and most significant, concept each programmer who wants to do OOP design and development must understand is the object itself. An *object* is a robust bundle that contains both data and the methods that operate on that data. This bundling provides significant advantages, such as code isolation, over alternate approaches. Instead of worrying about innumerable potential uses, a programmer can define an object's methods with complete knowledge of the data upon which it will work. Besides this careful control over method use, the nature of OOP allows methods to be reused and selectively replaced as object hierarchies are built up to satisfy increasingly complex requirements.

A LESSON IN OBJECTS

As you work, you interact with objects all the time. Phones, computers, fax machines, handheld devices, and cars are all examples of objects in the real world. When you deal with these objects, you don't separate an object from its attributes and its operations. For example, when you drive your car, you don't think about its attributes (such as its current speed of travel) apart from the operations (such as accelerating in response to increased pressure on the gas pedal). You put your car in gear, adjust the speed using the gas pedal, and drive. Every aspect is part of a single, cohesive package.

By using object-oriented programming, you can approach the same simplicity of use. A structured programmer is accustomed to creating data structures to hold attributes and then defining separate functions to manipulate this data. Objects, however, combine the data with the code that manipulates it. This results in self-contained units that hold everything necessary to define an object's state and work with it.

To continue the preceding example, when you describe a car and its current state, there are a number of important physical attributes: the speed it is traveling, the amount of horsepower the engine has, the drag coefficient associated with its body, the number of doors it has, and so on. In addition, the car has several associated functions: It accelerates, decelerates, turns, and shifts gears. Neither the physical nor the functional definitions alone complete the definition of a car—it is necessary to define them both.

TRADITIONAL PROGRAM DESIGN

To manipulate information about cars using a traditional programming approach, you might define a data structure called `MyCarData` that looks something like this:

```
public class MyCarData {
  float speed;
  int hp;
  double dragCoef;
  int numDoors;
}
```

Then you would create a set of functions to operate on the data that is completely separate from the declaration for `MyCarData`:

```
  public void speedUp(MyCarData m){
    ...
  }

  public void slowDown(MyCarData m){
    ...
  }

  public void stop(MyCarData m){
    ...
  }
```

Here the only link between these functions and the data they operate on is through a function parameter. Whenever changes to `MyCarData` are required, a programmer must search for all such uses of the data structure because there is no natural grouping imposed by the structure of the code. It is also difficult for a programmer working on `MyCarData` to know if all its attributes are even needed by the programs that use it because of this separation.

THE OOP WAY

In OOP, the attributes maintained for a car and the methods needed to work with it are combined into a single object:

```
public class Car {
  float speed;
  int hp;
  double dragCoef;
  int numDoors;

  public void speedUp() {
    speed += 1;
  }

  public void slowDown() {
    speed -= speed * dragCoef;
  }
```

```
  public void stop() {
    speed=0;
  }
}
```

Here the variables and methods are grouped together to form a single view of a car and what can be done with it in a program. Within each of these methods, there is no need to pass in a reference to a data structure variable. The methods implicitly know about the variables of their own class and have full access to them.

Extending Objects Through Inheritance

Many of the benefits of OOP are achieved when objects are defined so that they inherit the functionality of objects that already exist. Given this, the next step in this overview of developing objects is to create multiple objects based on one super object. Return to the preceding car example. A Saturn SL 2 is a car, and yet certainly it has several attributes that not all cars have. When building a car, manufacturers don't typically start from scratch. They know their cars are going to need several things: tires, doors, steering wheels, and more. Frequently, the same parts can be used between cars. Wouldn't it be nice to start with a generic car, build up the specifics of a Saturn, and from there (because each Saturn has its own peculiarities) build up the SL 2?

Inheritance is a feature of OOP programming that enables you to do just that. By inheriting all the general features of a car into a Saturn, it isn't necessary to reinvent the common functionality and attributes every time a new model of car is needed. The details of inheritance in Java are described in Chapter 7, "Classes," but you'll get just enough information here to give you a head start toward thinking in an object-oriented way.

By inheriting a car's features into the Saturn—through an added benefit called polymorphism—it can be treated generically as a car whenever the unique features that make it a Saturn are unimportant. Now that might seem obvious, but the implications of that fact are enormous. Under traditional programming techniques, you would have to separately deal with each type of car—Fords here, GMCs there, and so on. Under OOP, the features that all cars have are encapsulated within the `Car` object. When you inherit `Car` into Ford, GMC, and Saturn, you can reuse the common functionality provided by `Car` without any extra work or redundant programming.

> **Note**
>
> When you use inheritance to build a more specific type of object, such as `Saturn`, from a general type, such as `Car`, you can describe the relationship using the terminology "Saturn inherits from Car" or "Saturn extends Car."

For example, assume you have a racetrack program. On the racetrack, you have a green light, yellow light, and red light. Now, each racecar driver comes to the track with a different type of car. Each driver has accessible to him each of the peculiarities of his individual car (such as a CD player in a Saturn SL2, or some fancy accelerator found in a Lamborghini Diablo). As you put each car on the track, you provide a reference to the car to the track itself. The track controller doesn't need access to any methods that access that fancy Lamborghini accelerator or the Saturn's CD player; those methods are individual to each of the cars. However, the person sitting in the control tower does want to be able to tell every driver to slow down when the yellow light is illuminated. Because this requirement is common to all car types, the associated functionality can be defined in `Car`, inherited by each of the particular car makes, and used by the control tower program accordingly. Look at this hypothetical code.

Here are two types of cars with their unique features defined:

```
class LamborghiniDiablo extends Car {
  public void superCharge() {
    for (int x=0; x<infinity; x++)
      speedUp();
  }
}

class SaturnSL2 extends Car {
  CDPlayer cd;

  public void goFaster() {
    while(I_Have_Gas) {
      speedUp();
    }
  }

  public void entertain() {
    cd.turnOn();
  }
}
```

Here is the race track itself:

```
class RaceTrack {
  Car theCars[] = new Car[3];
  int numberOfCars = 0;

  public void addCar(Car newCar) {
    theCars[numberOfCars]=newCar;
    numberOfCars++;
  }

  public void yellowLight() {
    for (int x=0; x<numberOfCars; x++)
      theCars[x].slowDown();
  }
}
```

Here is the program that puts it all together:

```
class RaceProgram {
  LamborghiniDiablo me = new LamborghiniDiablo();
  SaturnSL2 you = new SaturnSL2();
  RaceTrack rc = new RaceTrack();

  public void start() {
    rc.addCar(me);
```

```
      rc.addCar(you);
      while(true) {
        if (somethingIsWrong)
          rc.yellowLight();
      }
    }
}
```

This works because in the `RaceProgram` class, you created two different objects: `me` (of type `LamborghiniDiablo`) and `you` (of type `SaturnSL2`). You can call `rc.addCar`, which takes a `Car` as a parameter type, because of polymorphism (see Chapter 7). Because both of the cars extended `Car`, they can be used as `Cars` as well as their individual types. This means that if you create yet another type of car (`VolvoS80`), you could call `rc.addCar(theVolvo)` without having to make any changes to `RaceTrack` whatsoever. Notice that this is true even though `SaturnSL2` effectively is a different structure because it now also contains a `CDPlayer` variable.

Objects as Multiple Entities

One of the pitfalls for procedural programmers is that of thinking of a data structure in a program as representing a single entity. A perfect example of this is the display screen. Usually, procedural programs tend to write something to the (one) screen. The problem with this method is that when you switch to a windowing environment and have to write to multiple screens, the whole program is in jeopardy. It takes a lot of work to go back and change the program so that the correct data is written to the appropriate window.

In contrast, OOP programming simplifies the task of treating the screen not as *the* screen but as *a* screen. Adding windows is as simple as telling an output method which screen object to use.

This demonstrates one of the aspects of OOP that has the potential to save a great deal of programming time. OOP programmers think of the problems they are solving with software in the context of a relevant set of objects. No matter if you're working with 1 or 100 objects of a single type, it doesn't affect how a program interacts with any one of those objects at all. If you're not familiar with OOP programming, this might not make sense yet. You might be thinking "If I have two screens, when I print something to the screen, I need to position it on the correct screen, and then handle user interaction with each screen separately."

The key point here is that OOP removes the need to constantly address this multiplicity of objects in your code. After the elements of a window or screen are abstracted sufficiently, you can write an output method that writes to the window it's directed to without being concerned about which one it is. The window object referenced by the method takes care of the details of providing the required output functionality. Now, obviously there is still the need to implement some controller functionality that determines which window to direct an output method to use, and to handle any interaction between windows. However, this functionality can be written once and maintained independently of the window objects and output methods. The knowledge of multiple entities is completely decoupled from the entities themselves.

MODULARITY AND CODE ORGANIZATION

The maintainability of a program is largely determined by how well the code is organized. Typical programs are large enough that no single programmer can focus on the details of an entire program at once. Instead, it is necessary to concentrate on a particular functional area while ignoring the implementation details of the remainder of the system. If a program is written using a few long and highly coupled functions, this task is nearly impossible for anyone other than the original programmer. On the other hand, when OOP is applied correctly, a modular design with minimal coupling is achievable. In general, this modularity is the result of two key factors:

- When used correctly, OOP forces you to break your code down into many manageable pieces. Even in the simple examples so far, you have seen small code modules result from the definition of the object types needed to solve a particular problem.
- By using OOP, each piece is organized naturally, without you having to actually think about the organization. In the car example, the organization of the code wasn't consciously considered; it simply resulted from the thought process used to represent the entities of the problem domain.

RELATING OBJECTS TO JAVA CLASSES

So far, the term *object* has been treated somewhat generically and it has been used a little loosely when referring to the code examples. Now classes need to be brought into the discussion to make it more concrete with respect to Java. Object data types are defined in Java using classes, like the `Car` class shown previously. In the software realm, objects are instances of those classes.

A class can be thought of as a template for creating an object. In the car example, `SaturnSL2` is a class, not an object. It is a template for creating car objects that are of that type (a particular make and model in this case). If you go to a car dealership and ask to see a Saturn SL2, you are using a type (the class) to describe what variety of car you want, but you are not yet referring to a particular object. Once the dealer takes you to the SL2 section of the car lot, the cars you see are the objects. They are each unique, but they were created from the same template, or class. The red SL2 with a tan interior that you select to test drive and purchase is an object that is an instance of the `SaturnSL2` class.

BUILDING A HIERARCHY: STEPS IN OOP DESIGN

When setting out to develop an OOP program for the first time, it is often helpful to have an ordered set of steps to follow. Developing good OOP structures is like most work that you do in that the outcome is largely determined by the analysis of the problem that you do before attempting a solution. In the case of OOP, the goal here is to first decide what classes and objects are required to support a program before doing any coding. This section introduces several steps to guide you through that process.

DECOMPOSE THE PROBLEM INTO ENTITIES

When writing an OOP program, it's first necessary to figure out the types of objects that are needed. As an example, if you were writing an adventure video game, you would need to figure out everything in that game, such as the main character, the opponents to battle, power pieces to adjust the abilities of the main character, ammunition, and so on. A common approach to creating such a list is to write out a description of what a program must do, and look for the nouns that appear in that description. For example, part of a description of a video game might state, "The user controls the movement of the main character, who can pick up ammunition and use that ammunition to inflict damage on one or more opponents." When you use this approach, every noun that you find is not a part of the problem domain that needs to be represented in your program, but those nouns that appear often and are involved in key actions are definitely the candidates to consider.

After you have identified the significant parts of the problem domain, you need to break them down into individual entities, both data and functional. For this example, you might create a list like this for the four items:

Game Part	Data and Functional Needs
Main Character	Capability to receive commands from the user; capability to move around the maze according to these commands; attack capability; location; power level; and size
Opponents	Location; size; power level; attack capability; and maneuverability
Power Pieces	Appearance when drawn; location; and power level
Ammunition	Capability to be fired; damage level; and quantity

LOOK FOR COMMONALITY BETWEEN ENTITIES

A strength of OOP is the exploitation of common behavior to achieve code reuse. After the entities required by a program have been identified, a frequent next step is to look for common characteristics across entities. Perhaps the most obvious commonality in this example is an easy one to overlook at first: the capability for each entity to be drawn on the screen. This capability is so obvious you might just miss it. Remember to consider low-level functionality that might be considered obvious, because it often carries a big payback in reduced development time.

The game entities also have higher-level characteristics in common. From the data and functional needs identified in the list of game parts, you can see that the main character, the opponents, and the power pieces all have a location. It is also true that the main character and the opponents have a size, a power level, and an attack capability. You can quickly see here that significant code reuse could be achieved by writing the code to control attributes such as location, power, and size once, and then sharing that code through inheritance.

LOOK FOR DIFFERENCES BETWEEN ENTITIES

Making sure that you uncover the areas that truly differentiate entities is equally as important as identifying commonality. For this program, one example of a key difference is that the power pieces remain in a fixed location until consumed, but a piece of ammunition moves after it is fired toward the main character or an opponent. When performing this exercise, you are looking for qualities and behavior that either unite or separate entities in your program.

Significant to note here is that the primary difference between the main character and the opponents within the game (aside from how they look) is who controls each. Namely, the computer controls the opponents, and the user controls the main character. It would be a great advantage if you could write most of the code for both the opponents and the main character once, and then write only the code that moves them separately. Treating objects this way is exactly what the OOP paradigm is all about.

DESIGN A HIERARCHY USING ABSTRACTION AND INHERITANCE

The point of identifying entity commonality and differences is to use it to define a class hierarchy. One approach to this is to start by focusing on the greatest common characteristic across the entities in your program. Looking at the game example, what do you see that all four objects have in common? A quick list might include, at a minimum, size and location attributes. Also, remember that the low-level requirement to be drawn on the screen is shared by every entity.

With these entities, you could create a class called `DrawnObject` to take advantage of the commonality identified. This class would contain the attributes and behavior related to size, location, and the common screen drawing requirements.

The next step is to continue to group objects that still have common characteristics together (after you have eliminated the aspects that were just grouped into the previous class). You can use these commonalties to produce another level of classes, each of which inherits from `DrawnObject` to take advantage of the highest level of commonality.

Going back to the example, at this point the power pieces and the ammunition probably split from the opponents and the main character because they have nothing in common beyond what can be captured in `DrawnObject`. You can now take the remaining objects and repeat the steps of the design procedure again.

Going through the next iteration, you find that the only real difference between the power pieces and the ammunition is their size and how fast they move (the power pieces at speed 0). Even though these are primarily minor differences, you could choose to create a `Powerup` class to define the shared behavior and inherit `Ammunition` and `PowerPiece` classes from it to address the differences.

When you look at the opponents and the main character, you see that they are not the same, but they do have much in common. Here you can define a `GameCharacter` class to hold the shared attributes and behavior and inherit `Opponent` and `MainCharacter` classes from it. The major difference between `Opponent` and `MainCharacter` would be in the control of entity movement.

The resulting class hierarchy from this approach is shown in Figure 1.1. Try this process on your own. There are countless variations to the design developed here that depend on how the various tradeoffs are addressed.

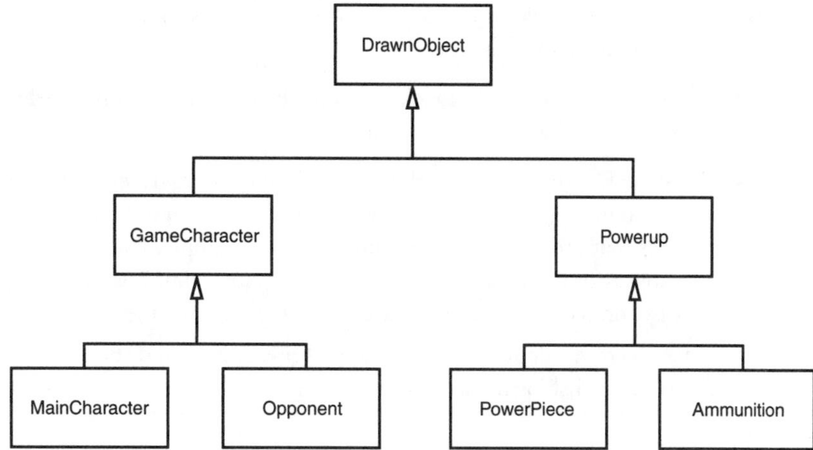

Figure 1.1
Building a class hierarchy for your game enables you to save a lot of coding.

OOP AND THE UML

When you are first learning an object-oriented language such as Java, your initial focus is likely to be solely on the mechanics of writing code in that particular language. This is perfectly reasonable as you start out, but you will quickly realize, if you have not already, that object-oriented development has brought many changes to the software design process in addition to those related to coding syntax. The guidelines of structured development and artifacts such as flowcharts have proved themselves inadequate for properly supporting the development of object-oriented systems. This has led to the establishment of many analysis and design methods created specifically to drive OOP development efforts.

The focus of this book is on programming in Java, so the detailed coverage of any object-oriented analysis and design method won't be presented here. There are numerous books already available to address such topics. However, as a Java programmer, you will no doubt encounter design information that is specified based on a particular method, or at least a particular notation. Specifically, the Unified Modeling Language (UML) developed by Grady Booch, Ivar Jacobson, and James Rumbaugh has become the de facto standard notation for communicating the design of an object-oriented system. This section provides enough UML overview to allow you to interpret a subset of the UML diagrams most closely associated with class design.

UML in Brief

UML is not a design method itself, but a means of modeling the results produced from applying one of the available methods. UML is independent of the design process you use, but it allows you to communicate the artifacts of the design to others using a common notation. Prior to its introduction, each method tended to have its own modeling notation. Although the notations were often similar, expecting developers to communicate in competing modeling languages was quickly seen as counterproductive. The common ground provided by UML is a major advance that allows designers to now focus on system design and not diagramming subtleties.

UML is not a single type of model, but actually a set of diagrams in which each diagram addresses a different aspect of a design:

- Use Case Diagrams capture the interactions of users (referred to as actors) with a software system. The intent is to describe the system requirements in terms of concrete features that are needed by the end user. For example, "Submit Order" is an appropriate subject for a use case in an order entry system, but "Validate Username" likely isn't because, on its own, it doesn't satisfy any real need of the user.
- Class Diagrams depict the classes found in a system and the relationships among them. These relationships include both inheritance relationships and associations between classes.
- Sequence Diagrams depict the object interactions required to carry out the tasks required by a single use case. These interactions are represented as messages between objects (method calls) that are shown in a top to bottom flow that indicates their time ordering.
- Collaboration Diagrams depict the same type of information as sequence diagrams, but the layout is not restricted to a vertical stacking of object messages. The sequence of messages is instead indicated with numbers, which allows the diagram to be laid out in a way that can include other information.
- State Diagrams show the allowed states of an object and the events that cause state transitions to occur. Viewing system behavior in terms of state transitions is a long used practice that remains just as significant in OOP as it was in earlier programming techniques.
- Deployment Diagrams go beyond the logical elements of a design and address the physical mapping of software components onto the target hardware.

This list doesn't cover every aspect of UML, but it should be enough to give you an appreciation for the breadth of this approach to modeling. The various diagrams cover every step from capturing system requirements through deployment. As far as the coverage here, the focus is only on class diagrams and sequence diagrams. Mastering the basics of these two diagrams will give you a head start toward developing Java programs using formal design procedures.

CLASS DIAGRAMS

As the name implies, a class diagram provides information about the classes in a system. When a design has been completed, the resulting class diagrams are the major drivers in defining the actual code that must be written. These diagrams identify each class in a system and define the required attributes and methods. Unlike some UML diagrams, such as use cases, class diagrams are very much technical in nature and are intended for use solely by a development team and not the eventual users. Of course, this might not hold true if the eventual users are other developers intending to build on the software whose design is defined in the diagrams.

ASSOCIATIONS AND INHERITANCE

Class diagrams also illustrate the inheritance hierarchies and inter-class associations found among the classes they include. These diagrams communicate inheritance relationships by identifying the parent of each class that extends another class. The modeling of associations is somewhat more complicated because associations have a corresponding cardinality, and they can be defined as either bidirectional or unidirectional.

The cardinality of an association defines the number of class instances that can be involved in the relationship. For example, if a `Car` class is related to a `Tire` class, the association is referred to as one-to-many because each `Tire` is related to one `Car` and a `Car` has many `Tires` (strictly speaking, "many" means any value greater than one). If `Car` is also associated with `SteeringWheel`, this reflects a one-to-one association because a `Car` can only have one `SteeringWheel` (and a `SteeringWheel` is owned by exactly one `Car`). The remaining cardinality option is referred to as many-to-many. A many-to-many relationship indicates a situation in which class instances are associated in a non-exclusive manner. In this case, neither side owns the other.

For an association to be useful, at least one of the objects involved must be able to access, or navigate to, the other. You can use a class diagram to indicate whether both sides of a relationship or only one can be navigated.

NOTATION

The first step in working with class diagrams is to learn the notation so that you can interpret design information produced by other developers. Figure 1.2 shows a representative diagram that includes the major components of this type of diagram.

The example in Figure 1.2 is a subset of the classes that might be designed to support an order-entry system that allows a customer to order one or more products from a catalog. This diagram includes an inheritance relationship and associations of each of the three cardinality types. Walking through this example will give you a good introduction to the notation used within this part of UML.

First of all, the example in Figure 1.2 shows that two types of `Products` can be ordered in this system, objects typed by either `ClothingItem` or `Appliance`. These classes are each defined in terms of their attributes, such as the `size` field associated with `ClothingItem`. In a system such as this, different product types can have unique attributes, but the bulk of the handling of products is independent of this specific detail. Using good OOP techniques, this is best addressed with inheritance. The open-arrow drawn from `ClothingItem` and `Appliance` to `Product` indicates that `Product` is the parent class for each of these specific product classes. The model for the parent class `Product` also shows how method signatures can be included for a class in addition to attribute definitions.

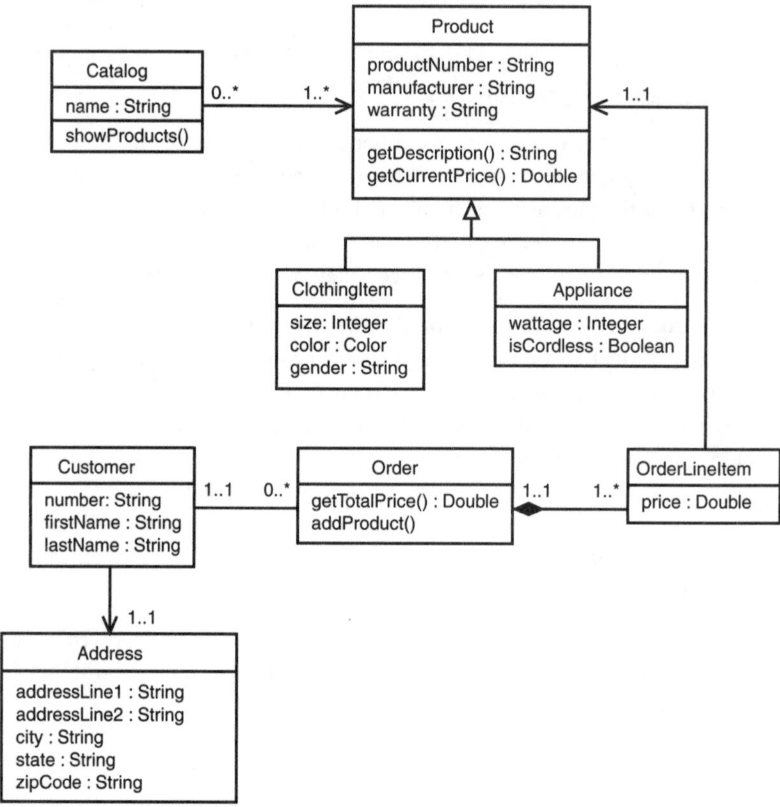

Figure 1.2
Class diagrams illustrate class attributes, methods, and associations.

Each `Product` that can be ordered might appear in one or more `Catalogs`. This relationship is drawn as a many-to-many association between the two classes. Notice how the cardinality is indicated with numbers placed adjacent to the line drawn between the classes. Cardinality can be expressed as either a single value or a range of values. An asterisk is a special value that can be used either alone or as the upper value in a range. Used alone, an asterisk indicates an association to zero or more instances of a class. When used in a range, an asterisk represents some number greater than or equal to the corresponding lower bound. Here, a `Catalog` must reference at least one `Product`, but there is no upper bound expressed. Similarly, a `Product` can be in any number of `Catalogs`, but it might also be left out of all the `Catalogs` given that the lower bound of this part of the relationship is zero.

Note

The asterisks used in the upper bounds of the association between `Catalog` and `Product` are the only indications in Figure 1.2 that the design is intended to support multiple catalogs and multiple products. Cardinality information in a class diagram is intended to describe how two classes are related, but it often provides additional information about the overall design as well.

Also, note that the line drawn between `Catalog` and `Product` has an arrowhead at one end. An arrowhead on one end of an association line indicates unidirectional navigation. Here, a `Catalog` knows the `Products` it contains, but a `Product` has no knowledge of the `Catalogs` that include it. Instead of including arrowheads at both ends, bidirectional associations are shown without any arrows to avoid cluttering the diagram.

The rest of the diagram can be interpreted in similar fashion. A `Customer` in the system has a single associated address and some number of `Orders`. An `Order` is associated with a single `Customer` and one or more `OrderLineItems`. The filled diamond shown on the association between `Order` and `OrderLineItem` indicates a special type of association known as *composition*. This notation indicates that an `Order` is composed of `OrderLineItems` that are wholly owned by their order (composition is the one type of association that implies ownership of one object by another). This implies that the removal of an order also removes its line items. Each `OrderLineItem` references a single `Product`. Notice that no cardinality value is shown on the `OrderLineItem` side of this association. Often when a relationship is unidirectional, the specification of this value is omitted because it can be assumed that an object that has no knowledge of the objects that reference it can be referenced by many of them. This is, in effect, a unidirectional one-to-many relationship.

SEQUENCE DIAGRAMS

Sequence and collaboration diagrams are collectively referred to as interaction diagrams because they both focus on how objects interact to perform a requested operation. A sequence diagram is used for the example here given the two are so similar. Where class diagrams are geared toward static relationships that show how classes are linked, sequence diagrams provide a dynamic view that illustrates how associations are created and then used to perform meaningful work. The work shown in a particular sequence diagram is typically the set of steps required to satisfy a single use case.

MESSAGES

As discussed previously in this chapter, method calls made on a class instance can be thought of as messages being passed to an object. Basically, a method call is a request passed to an object that instructs it to do something specific and then return control to the caller. The goal of creating a set of sequence diagrams for a system is to capture all the object interactions that are needed to satisfy the system's functional requirements. The messages identified by these diagrams then provide a basis for defining the complete set of class methods that must be implemented.

NOTATION

Just like class diagrams, sequence diagrams have their own notation that must be learned. Figure 1.3 shows an example sequence diagram that builds on the previous class diagram to indicate some of the steps necessary to select a product from a catalog and order it.

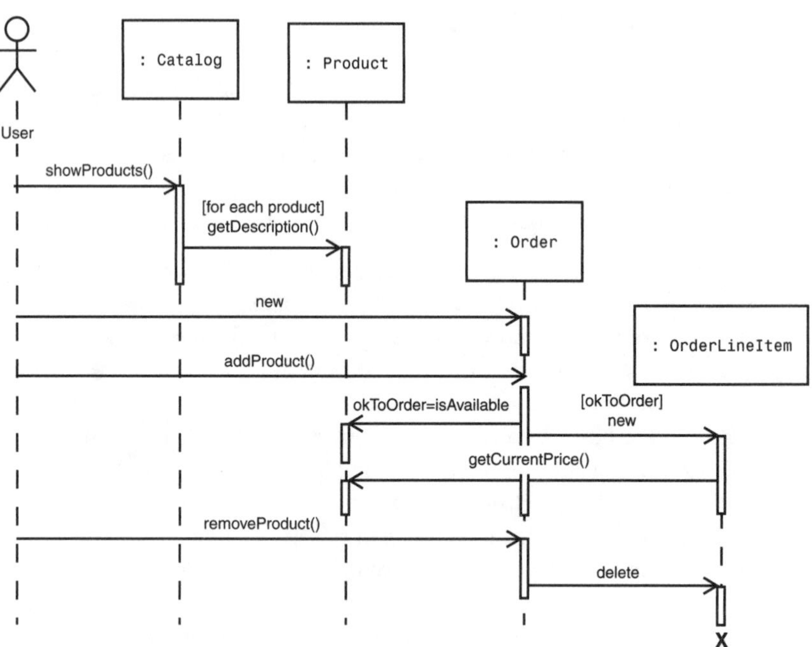

Figure 1.3
Sequence diagrams illustrate object interactions using time-ordered messages.

Each box along the top of a sequence diagram is an object (not a class, but a single instance). An object is identified by its class name preceded by a colon that might optionally be preceded by an object name. The inclusion of object names is necessary if more than one object of a particular class type participates in the sequence of events, but it is usually omitted otherwise. The order of the objects across the top of the diagram is unimportant; you should, however, select an order that places the objects with the most interaction near each other to reduce clutter in the diagram.

The vertical line that extends beneath each object in a sequence diagram is a lifeline. A lifeline begins when an object is created and ends when it is destroyed. If a lifeline begins at the top of the diagram (just beneath an object box), the associated object exists before the task described by the diagram starts. Similarly, if a lifeline extends to the bottom of a diagram, the associated object still exists when the task is completed. The horizontal arrows between lifelines indicate messages being passed to objects as execution control is transferred. The rectangles drawn along the lifelines are known as *activations*. An activation indicates that the associated object is either performing work at that time or waiting for another object to return control to it after being sent a message. Activation rectangles are often omitted from sequence diagrams that do not include any concurrent processing by the objects involved. In those cases, the transitions of object activity coincide with the message arrow locations.

Sequence diagrams borrow a bit of notation from use case diagrams in that they typically include an actor (denoted as `User` in Figure 1.3) that initiates the sequence of events. In this example, the first event is a `showProducts` message sent to a `Catalog`. This message represents a request to view the items available for purchase. The `Catalog` responds by iterating through its associated `Products` and sending a `getDescription` message to each one to obtain information that can be returned to the `User`. Although multiple `Products` participate in this activity, only one representative object is needed in the diagram because there is no interaction between `Products` and no two `Products` are active simultaneously.

After the `Product` descriptions are collected by the `Catalog`, control returns to the `User`. UML notation includes the concept of a return action that is indicated by a dashed horizontal line between lifelines, but you only need to include that indication if the return is unclear. Here, the activation rectangles indicate that the `Catalog` stops processing prior to the `new` message from the `User` to an `Order`, so the return is implied.

The `new` message from the `User` causes the creation of an `Order` object (note the start of the object's lifeline). A request to add a product to the order is then submitted. The actual definition of the `addProduct` message would at least need to include an input parameter to identify the selected `Product`, but showing the message parameters in a sequence diagram is optional. Here, an `Order` would have to be told what `Product` to add, so including the parameter in the diagram wouldn't add any information that wasn't already implied by the context.

The response of the `Order` to an `addProduct` message demonstrates the use of a conditional in a sequence diagram. The `Order` checks the availability of the requested `Product`, and then creates an `OrderLineItem` only if the `Product` is currently available. If an `OrderLineItem` is created, it gets the price of the `Product` and control is returned to the `User`.

The preceding steps would normally complete a use case corresponding to a simple product order scenario, but an additional action is included to illustrate how a sequence diagram indicates the deletion of an object. When the `User` requests that a `Product` be removed from an `Order`, the corresponding `OrderLineItem` is deleted. The end of an object's lifeline is denoted with a large "X."

UML Guidelines

The preceding UML examples covered the fundamentals you need to interpret class and sequence diagrams created by other developers and begin using the notation to express your own designs. However, UML is a complex topic with numerous books dedicated to it alone, so you should view what you have been equipped with so far as a foundation upon which to build as you gain experience in OOP. To conclude this section, here are several guidelines to keep in mind as that occurs:

- Always remember that object modeling is intended to be an iterative process. For other than trivial applications, you shouldn't expect the first set of sequence and class diagrams produced for a system to fully capture all the requirements or even reflect the best design to satisfy the requirements that are known. One of the strengths of UML is that it supports the communication of proposed designs between developers so that they might be improved upon through iteration.
- As pointed out in the examples, UML includes notation to cover a variety of circumstances that can (and often should) be omitted when that notation doesn't add to the reader's understanding of a diagram. The goal of a UML diagram is to clearly communicate some aspect of a system's requirements or design; any details that do not add to what is being communicated might be unnecessary clutter.
- If you choose to use UML to document your designs, use the standard notation consistently and correctly. The primary benefit of this standard notation is that the readers of your diagrams who are familiar with UML can spend their time focused on the information you are providing rather than learning the mechanisms by which you are trying to convey it.

Is Java a Magic OOP Bullet?

The focus of this chapter has been to introduce the concepts of good OOP and to outline some of the standard notation used to document object-oriented designs. The chapter has intentionally avoided complicated coding implementations; the rest of this book will help you build the knowledge to do that.

Now that you have seen many of the fundamentals of OOP programming, at least at a high level, it should be pointed out why it was important to cover these topics before getting into the specifics of Java programming. Java isn't a magic bullet for creating OOP programs. Although Java embraces the OOP paradigm, it is still possible (and not unusual) for programmers to write structured programs using Java. Unfortunately, it's not unusual to see Java programs written that do not exploit any of the key OOP tools just covered, such as polymorphism.

By introducing OOP at this stage, hopefully you can avoid the bad habits of structured programming instead of having to break them later. You need to remember that OOP is as much a different way of thinking as it is a different way of programming. After you have covered the example applications and applets throughout this book and gained a better understanding of OOP, run through the concepts pointed out in this chapter again to help keep some of the justification for the language features provided in mind as you begin to develop your own programs.

CHAPTER

HelloWorld: Your First Java Program

by Brian Keeton

In this chapter

HELLOWORLD APPLICATION

When you're learning a new programming language, it is often useful to jump in headfirst, learn how to write a short application, and then step back and learn the rest of the fundamentals. In this chapter, you do just that, and by the end you'll be able to write simple Java programs of your own.

Let's get started with an example application. Listing 2.1 shows the complete source code for the well-known HelloWorld program as written in Java.

LISTING 2.1 THE HELLOWORLD APPLICATION

```
/**
* My first program demonstrates displaying
* a string on the screen
*/
public class HelloWorld {
  public static void main(String args[]){
  System.out.println("Hello World!");
  }
}
```

As you can see, there really isn't a lot to this program, which makes it a good place to start. The syntax might look unfamiliar to you at this point, but you can probably gather by looking at the code that the purpose of this program, just like any other HelloWorld program, is to write a simple message to the screen. You'll see the details of the code later, but first follow the steps in the next few sections to create your own copy of the source file and compile and run the program.

CREATE THE FILE

The first step in creating the HelloWorld application is to copy the text from Listing 2.1 into a file called `HelloWorld.java` using your favorite text editor (Windows Notepad, or SimpleText on the Macintosh will work if you don't have another). It is very important to call the file `HelloWorld.java`, because the compiler expects the filename to match the class identifier (see "Declaring a Class" later in this chapter). Java is case sensitive, so you must also be careful to name the file `HelloWorld.java` and not `helloworld.java`, `HELLOWORLD.JAVA`, or any other variation.

Caution

If you use a program such as Microsoft Word to create your source file, make sure you save the file as text only. If you save it as a Word document, the compiler will have problems with the extra formatting information in the file.

COMPILE THE CODE

To compile the program, you must have the SDK installed. If you do not, refer to Appendix A, "Installing the SDK and Getting Started," for step-by-step instructions on obtaining a current copy of the SDK and configuring your development environment. You can then use the javac program to compile your source file into a form that the Java virtual machine can load and execute. To run javac on a Macintosh, drag the source file over the javac icon. On any other computer, type the following at a command prompt set to the directory containing the source file:

```
javac HelloWorld.java
```

The javac program creates a file called HelloWorld.class from the HelloWorld.java file. HelloWorld.class is referred to as a *class file*. A class file represents a Java class and contains bytecodes, which are instructions that can be run by the Java interpreter. If you get a compiler error when running javac, go back and make sure you typed in the file exactly as it is shown in Listing 2.1, and make sure that you named the file HelloWorld.java.

➔ **See** Appendix A, "Installing the SDK and Getting Started," **p. 1027**

RUN THE PROGRAM

Now that you have compiled the program, you can run it by typing the following at the command prompt:

```
java HelloWorld
```

Note

The HelloWorld used in the command java HelloWorld is not HelloWorld.class or HelloWorld.java, just the name of the class.

After you do this, the computer should print the following to the screen:

```
Hello World!
```

If instead of seeing the Hello World! *message, you get a* java.lang.NoClassDefFoundError, *you might have a problem with your classpath. See "*NoClassDefFoundError*" in the "Troubleshooting" section at the end of this chapter for help in resolving this error.*

UNDERSTANDING HELLOWORLD

The result you get from running HelloWorld might not seem very interesting, but then it's a simple program. There is a good bit to be learned from the code, however. After you understand each piece, you'll be much closer to being able to write any program you want.

COMMENTS

The HelloWorld source code begins with a comment that describes the purpose of the program:

```
/**
* My first program demonstrates displaying
* a string on the screen
*/
```

Given enough time, another programmer reading your code can usually understand what it does, but comments allow you to explain why you implemented a program in a certain way, or even how you intend for it to be used. Java supports several styles of comments that are described in Chapter 3, "Data Types and Other Tokens." This example is a simple one, but the sooner you develop the habit of commenting your code, the better.

→ **See** "Comments," **p. 65**

DECLARING A CLASS

Java is a language built on classes, so the first task when creating any Java program is to create a class. Look at the first line of the HelloWorld application that follows the comment:

```
public class HelloWorld {
```

This declares a class called `HelloWorld`. The compiler would allow the class to be named almost anything, but remember to use descriptive class names so their purposes will be clear to other programmers.

→ **See** "Classes in Java," **p. 136**

Note

Although the compiler doesn't require it, it is considered good style to always begin class names with a capital letter and use mixed case to separate words. There are also a number of limitations on the names you can assign to a class, but you'll learn more about that later in Chapter 7, "Classes."

Sun's "Code Conventions for the Java Programming Language" includes these class naming guidelines along with many other elements of proper Java coding style. You can access this document at `http://java.sun.com/docs/codeconv/html/CodeConvTOC.doc.html` to help you adopt good style conventions while you're learning the language.

Next, notice the brace ({) that is located after the class name. If you look at the end of the class, there is also a closing brace (}). The braces tell the compiler where your class definition begins and ends. Any code between those two braces is considered part of the `HelloWorld` class.

Braces are used to delimit blocks, which are covered in more detail in Chapter 4, "Methods and Exceptions."

A closing brace closes the open brace closest to it. In the case of the HelloWorld program, there are two open braces and two closing braces, one to close the `main` method and one to close the class.

THE `main` METHOD

Now look again at the next line of HelloWorld:

```
public static void main(String args[]){
```

This line declares a method named `main` within the `HelloWorld` class. Methods are equivalent to functions or procedures in other languages. Each method performs some of the tasks of a program. The `main` method is special because it is the first method called when a Java application starts. When you run `java HelloWorld`, the Java interpreter starts executing at the first line of the main method. A Java application stops running after the main method and any user threads started by it have finished executing.

When creating any Java application, you need to create a main method as shown. In Chapter 4, you'll learn more about the different parts of a method declaration, such as the meaning of the public access specifier and static modifier used here. For now, consider only the method return type and the args parameter. Notice that the return type is specified to be void, which means that nothing is returned by the main method. Unlike some languages, a Java program does not return a value to the process that launched it using a method return value. However, you can return a value with a special statement that is used to force a program to exit:


```
System.exit(0);
```

You can terminate a Java program at any point by calling System.exit and passing an integer status code. Passing zero as shown in the preceding example indicates a normal exit condition. You should pass a nonzero code if your program is exiting abnormally because of an error condition.

Now look at the single method parameter, String args[], that is part of the declaration. This parameter declaration means that the main method must be passed as an array of zero or more String objects when it is called. String is the Java class used to represent text strings (see Chapter 8, "Using Strings and Text"). When main is called, the method parameter represents any command line arguments that are passed to the java program when the application is started. When you run java HelloWorld, the only string given to the java program is the name of the class that starts your application. The class name does not count as a command line argument, so in this case the args array passed to main is an empty array (that is, an array of length zero). If you instead type java HelloWorld hello, main is called with an args array that contains the string "hello" as its first element. Chapter 3, "Data Types and Other Tokens," contains more details of how arrays are used in Java.

WRITING TO THE SCREEN

How does the text Hello World! appear when you run the HelloWorld program? The answer (as you have probably guessed) lies in the next line of the program:

```
System.out.println("Hello World!");
```

This line outputs the string specified within the quotation marks. You can replace the "Hello World!" text with any text you would like to display.

Now you've seen all the steps necessary to make HelloWorld work. With your first Java program behind you, you're ready to learn more about System.out, its counterpart System.in, and how to use them to write more interesting programs.

System.out AND System.in

You have just seen how System.out.println is used to print text to the screen. In fact, System.out.println can be used at any time to print text to what is known as *Standard Out*.

Standard Out is typically the screen but you can also redirect it elsewhere (for example, to a text file) by supplying a new destination through the `System.setOut` method. `System.out` refers to an instance of the `PrintStream` class that is a standard part of Java (see Chapter 21, "Streams, Files, and Serialization").

Chapter 21 describes streams in more detail, but fundamentally a stream is an object that represents a supplier or a receiver of data, such as a keyboard, a printer, or a file. In the case of a data receiver, `println` is a `PrintStream` method that sends the parameter passed to it to the associated output stream.

This method serves roughly the same purpose as `writeln` in Pascal, `printf` in C, or `cout` in C++.

`println` VERSUS `print`

There is one minor variation on `println` that is also commonly used: `print("Hello World!")`. The difference between `println` and `print` is that `print` does not add a line separator at the end of the line. Strictly speaking, `print` is the true parallel to `printf` and `cout` for C/C++ programmers.

To demonstrate this, expand your HelloWorld example a little by copying Listing 2.2 into a file called `HelloWorld2.java` and compiling it with the line `javac HelloWorld2.java`.

LISTING 2.2 A HELLOWORLD PROGRAM WITH TWO PRINTOUTS

```
public class HelloWorld2 {
  public static void main(String args[]){
    System.out.println("Hello World!");
    System.out.println("Hello World Again!");
  }
}
```

To run the program, type `java HelloWorld2`.

You should see output that looks like the following:

```
Hello World!
Hello World Again!
```

Notice that each phrase appears on its own line. Now, for comparison, try the program again using `print` instead of `println`. Copy Listing 2.3 into a file called `HelloWorld3`, compile, and run it.

LISTING 2.3 A HELLOWORLD OUTPUT USING `print` STATEMENTS

```
public class HelloWorld3 {
  public static void main (String args[]){
    System.out.print ("Hello World!");
    System.out.print ("Hello World Again!");
  }
}
```

You should notice that the output looks like this because of the lack of line separators:

```
Hello World!Hello World Again!
```

GETTING INFORMATION FROM THE USER WITH `System.in`

Having a means for output is balanced by having a similar means for input. `System.out` is used to write to a stream, and `System.in` is used to read from one.

REQUESTING INPUT FROM THE USER

Use `System.in.read` when you want to get a character from the user. This is not covered in too much depth here because `System.in` isn't used that often in Java programs. Typical applications that require user input are graphical, Swing-based applications that use more sophisticated means for accepting user input. Also, as you learn in the upcoming section "HelloWorld as an Applet," `System.in` does not apply to applets. Nevertheless, Listing 2.4 shows an example of a Java application that reads a character from the user and echoes it to the screen.

LISTING 2.4 `ReadHello`—AN APPLICATION THAT READS INPUT FROM THE USER

```
import java.io.*;

public class ReadHello {
  public static void main (String args[]){
    int inChar;
    System.out.println("Enter a Character:");
    try {
      inChar = System.in.read();
      System.out.print("You entered ");
      System.out.println(inChar);
    }
    catch (IOException e){
      System.out.println("Error reading from user");
    }
  }
}
```

You've probably already noticed that there is a lot more to this code than there was to the last one. Before that's explained, you should compile the program and prove to yourself that it works. After compiling, execute the program by typing `java ReadHello`, enter an `A` as the character to be read, and you should see the following result displayed onscreen:

```
Enter a Character:
A
You entered 65
```

You probably noticed that this program printed a number instead of the character you typed. Let's look more closely at the example to see why.

In this example, the code you are most interested in is the line that reads:

```
inChar = System.in.read();
```

`System.in.read()` is a method that accepts a single character from an input stream (associated with the keyboard in this case) and returns that character so that it can be used in an expression or assigned to a variable.

In the case of `ReadHello`, the character returned by `System.in.read` is assigned to a variable called `inChar`.

Following the input of a character, the program calls `System.out.println` to display what was typed.

Note

It isn't necessary to assign the result of `System.in.read` to a variable. If you prefer, you can print it out directly in the second `System.out` call by changing it to the following:

```
System.out.println(System.in.read());
```

The program displays a number instead of a character for what you entered because the `read` method of `System.in` returns an integer code between -1 and 255, not an actual character.

The code represents a character in the ASCII character set or –1 if the end of the stream has been reached.

To convert the number that is returned from `System.in.read` into a character, you must use a cast. Casting converts a given data type to another one. Change `ReadHello` to look like Listing 2.5.

LISTING 2.5 `ReadHello2`—AN APPLICATION THAT READS IN A CHARACTER FROM THE USER

```
import java.io.*;

public class ReadHello2 {
  public static void main (String args[]){
    char inChar;
    System.out.println("Enter a Character:");
    try {
      inChar =(char) System.in.read();
      System.out.print("You entered ");
      System.out.println(inChar);
    }
    catch (IOException e){
      System.out.println("Error reading from user");
    }
  }
}
```

Notice the differences from the original version. In Listing 2.5, `inChar` is now declared as a character instead of an integer and a cast operator, `(char)`, has been inserted before the `read` call. The cast operator causes the integer returned from the `read` method to be treated as a character. The result of the cast is a character that is assigned to `inChar`.

THE REST OF THE CODE: `try` AND `catch` What does the rest of the code do? The input and output calls are contained inside what is called a `try-catch` block.

A `try-catch` block provides a simple mechanism for handling errors or exceptional conditions. In some programming languages, when a problem occurs during execution, there is no way for you as a programmer to intercept it and try to handle it gracefully.

Java, along with languages such as C++ and Ada, supports what is known as exception handling. Most error conditions in a Java program will cause an exception that can be "caught" and handled. You place statements that might cause an exception inside a `try` block and follow that with a `catch` statement to intercept exceptions that occur. `System.in.read` will cause an `IOException` if an error occurs reading from an input stream, so, as shown in this example, it must be placed inside a `try` block.

→ **See** "Catching and Throwing Exceptions," **p. 84**

HELLOWORLD AS AN APPLET

One of the features of Java that first drew public attention was its capability to add dynamic content to HTML pages using applets. Applets are Java classes that you can execute in a Java-enabled browser such as Netscape Navigator or Internet Explorer. Before applets were introduced, Web sites consisted solely of static HTML content.

Several differences exist between applets and applications. Most of these differences will be explained in Part II, "User Interface." For the HelloWorld example, the most important difference in the source code is that applets must define a subclass that inherits from the SDK's `java.applet.Applet` class (or its `javax.swing.JApplet` subclass if you're developing a Swing applet). For now, it's enough to say that you have to extend `Applet` for a class to be executed in a browser instead of as a standalone application.

→ **See** "Applets Versus Applications," **p. 323**

MODIFYING AND COMPILING THE SOURCE CODE

One of the simplest applets is the HelloWorld applet, the source code for which is shown in Listing 2.6. Right away, you should see that the applet HelloWorld is quite different from the HelloWorld application in Listing 2.1. You'll get more detail about the meaning of the source code a little later in this chapter. For now, copy Listing 2.6 into a file called `HelloApplet.java` and compile it.

LISTING 2.6 HELLOWORLD AS AN APPLET

```
import java.applet.Applet;
import java.awt.Graphics;
public class HelloApplet extends Applet {
  public void paint (Graphics g) {
     g.drawString ("Hello World!",0,50);
  }
}
```

CREATING AN HTML FILE

When you created the HelloWorld application in Listings 2.1 through 2.5, you ran them using the Java interpreter. Applets, however, don't run from the command line; they are executed within a browser. So, how do you tell the browser to open the applet?

If you have ever created a Web page, you are familiar with HTML. HTML uses a set of tags to define Web content that can be displayed by a browser. Just as you use the `<TABLE>` tag to insert a table into an HTML page, you use the `<APPLET>` tag to instruct a browser to load and execute an applet you have created.

The simplest HTML file for the `HelloApplet` class is shown in Listing 2.7. Although most browsers are forgiving when certain closing tags are omitted in an HTML file, don't forget to include the closing `</APPLET>` tag, or your applet might not be loaded correctly. Copy this text into a file called `HelloApplet.html`.

→ **See** "Applets," **p. 306**

> **Note**
>
> With Java files, the filename must be the same as the class name. There is usually only one class per source file. This is not necessary with the HTML file. In fact, a single HTML file can contain several `<APPLET>` tags.

LISTING 2.7 `HelloApplet.html`**—HTML FILE THAT LOADS AN APPLET**

```
<HTML>
<BODY>
<APPLET CODE="HelloApplet.class" WIDTH = 200 HEIGHT=200> </APPLET>
</BODY>
</HTML>
```

RUNNING THE PROGRAM IN APPLETVIEWER

The simplest way to run an applet is to use the AppletViewer program located in the `bin` directory of your SDK installation. AppletViewer is a scaled-down browser that looks for `<APPLET>` tags in a specified HTML file and opens a new window for each of them.

> **Note**
>
> If you are using Sun's SDK 1.3, the directory that holds the AppletViewer program is typically `c:\jdk1.3\bin`. Other development environments place this executable in other locations. You can always locate the program by searching for `appletviewer.exe`.

→ **See** "AppletViewer," **p. 1038**

To run `HelloApplet` using AppletViewer, type `appletviewer HelloApplet.html` on the command line. AppletViewer produces output such as that shown in Figure 2.1.

Figure 2.1
AppletViewer opens a new window and runs HelloApplet in it.

RUNNING HELLOWORLD IN INTERNET EXPLORER

AppletViewer provides a simple test environment for your applets, but you really should execute the applet inside a full-featured browser that recognizes the `<APPLET>` tag, such as Microsoft's Internet Explorer. To open `HelloApplet` in Internet Explorer, choose File, Open, and then select the `HelloApplet.html` file, as shown in Figure 2.2.

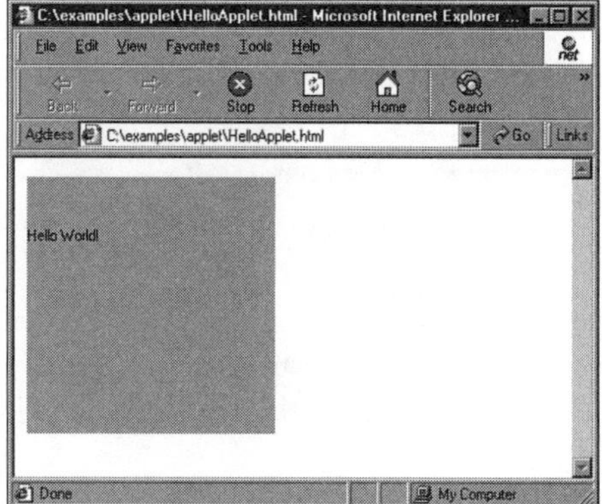

Figure 2.2
HelloApplet can also be run using Internet Explorer.

Now that you have seen how to run HelloApplet, you can see how the program works in the following sections.

IMPORTING OTHER CLASSES

Notice the first two lines of the `HelloApplet.java` file:

```
import java.applet.Applet;
import java.awt.Graphics;
```

The `import` statement is a new one. It enables you to use other classes. If you are familiar with the C/C++ `#include` directive, the import statement is similar (see "Packages" in Chapter 7).

→ **See** "Packages," **p. 167**

HelloApplet uses two additional classes. The first is the java.applet.Applet class, which, as was stated before, is the parent of every class that runs in a browser as an applet. This class provides the basic functionality required for an applet to interface with the browser. Reusing the methods implemented by this class frees you from having to work with the details of how a browser loads and displays an applet.

The second class that is imported into HelloApplet is the java.awt.Graphics class, which provides the capability to draw to the screen or any other output device. A Graphics object lets you draw primitive shapes (lines, rectangles, and so on), display text, fill areas, specify clipping regions, select colors, and select fonts. In the case of an applet, its appearance is defined by method calls made on a Graphics object when the applet is loaded.

DECLARING AN APPLET CLASS

The main difference, other than the class name, between the class declarations for HelloApplet and HelloWorld is that HelloApplet extends Applet. Remember in the last chapter how you learned about building a class structure? extends is the keyword that indicates that a class inherits from another class in a class hierarchy.

→ **See** "Extending Objects Through Inheritance," **p. 13**

Because you imported the Applet class, you can refer to it as Applet in the extends clause. If you had not imported java.applet.Applet, you could still have extended it using its full name:

```
public class HelloApplet extends java.applet.Applet {
```

APPLET paint METHOD

Perhaps the biggest difference between the implementations of HelloApplet and HelloWorld is that HelloApplet doesn't have a main method. Instead, this class only has a paint method. How is this possible given that the main method is the starting point when a class is loaded to start an application?

The answer lies in the fact that applets don't run in a standalone fashion like Java applications do. They are added to an already running program (the browser). The browser starts an applet and controls its execution by calling the methods defined in java.awt.Applet. One of these methods is paint:

```
public void paint (Graphics g) {
```

The browser calls the paint method any time the applet needs to be displayed on the screen. The paint method accepts a Graphics object that you can use to draw anything you want onto the screen space allocated to the applet. HelloApplet's paint method makes a call to the drawString method of Graphics to display "Hello World!" within the browser window.

```
g.drawString ("Hello World!",0,50);
```

THE BRIEF LIFE OF AN APPLET

The `paint` method is not the only applet method that the browser calls, but the default implementations of those methods in `java.awt.Applet` work in the example without being overridden.

When the applet is loaded, the browser calls the `init` method to perform any work that needs to be done before the applet is displayed the first time. This method is only called once no matter how many times you return to the same Web page within a browser session. After `init`, the `start` method is called and then `paint`.

The `start` method is called every time an applet's parent Web page is accessed. This means that if you leave a page and then click the browser's Back button, the `start` method is called again. The `stop` method is called when you leave the applet's page, and `destroy` is called when the browser exits altogether.

Note

> Notice that unlike the `paint(Graphics g)` method, the `init()`, `start()`, `stop()`, and `destroy()` methods do not take any parameters.

Let's look at how far you've come. You have now learned how to write a simple Java application and a corresponding applet. You have written to the screen and read from the keyboard using some of the core features of the language. You have also seen some of the exception handling capabilities that allow you to intercept and gracefully handle problems that might occur during execution of your programs. This chapter concludes with the introduction of two topics that will help you build on this knowledge to write more complex and useful programs.

KEYWORDS

Before you set off on a more in-depth exploration of each of the topics discussed in this chapter, there are a few other basic concepts that need to be introduced.

The most important of these is the use of keywords in Java. There are certain sequences of characters, called keywords, which have special meaning in Java. The following is a list of the 51 keywords defined as part of the language. After you learn the implications and proper use of these terms, you will have a solid understanding of the Java fundamentals.

```
abstract     boolean       break        byte        case
catch        char          class        const       continue
default      do            double       else        extends
false        final         finally      float       for
goto         if            implements   import      instanceof
int          interface     long         native      new
null         package       private      protected   public
return       short         static       strictfp    super
switch       synchronized  this         throw       throws
transient    true          try          void        volatile
while
```

Note

The keywords `const` and `goto` are reserved words that have no meaning in Java. `goto` is reserved just so it can never be used in a Java program, even as an identifier name.

The reason you care about keywords is that these terms have specific meaning in Java; you cannot use them as identifiers for anything else. If `HelloApplet` were on the list, the compiler would have reported an error when compiling that class for you. Besides class names, keywords cannot be used as variables, constants, method names, and so on. However, they can be used as part of a longer token, for example:

```
public int abstractInt;
```

Because Java is case sensitive, you can add one or more uppercase letters to a keyword and use it as an identifier if you are determined to do so. Although this is possible, it would do nothing but cause confusion to others reading your code. You should always treat the reserved words as reserved and keep your identifier names distinct.

THE JAVA 1.3 API

As you progress through this book, you will become familiar with the meanings of the Java keywords and their uses. You will also become familiar with the functionality provided in the SDK class library.

One of the reasons for Java's success is the rich class library provided through the Java Application Programmer Interface, or API. The Java API is a set of classes developed by Sun for use with the Java language. It is designed to assist you in developing your own classes, applets, and applications. With these classes already written for you, you can write an application that is only a few lines long, as opposed to the hundreds of lines that would be necessary to develop the same functionality from scratch. The simple implementation of this chapter's `HelloApplet` example is only possible because of the functionality provided by `java.applet.Applet` and `java.awt.Graphics`. Even the HelloWorld examples relied heavily on the stream classes accessed through `System.out` and `System.in`.

Although it's unlikely that you will have great success understanding the API until you have finished reading several more chapters, it's important to start looking at it now. A key measure of proficiency in Java is based on knowing what is available in the API and how to use it. Remember that Java provides a lot of functionality to you out of the box, and you should build up your knowledge of the API so you don't end up reinventing the wheel.

You can access a hyperlink version of the API documentation on Sun's site at `http://java.sun.com/j2se/1.3/docs/api/index.html`. If you download the documentation as part of your SDK install, you can also access the API documentation by opening `index.html` in the `docs/api` subdirectory of your install directory.

When exploring the API, you should notice how various classes inherit from others using the `extends` keyword. Sun has done a great deal of work to keep you from having to write nearly as much code; you must learn to make good use of the classes that are already there.

TROUBLESHOOTING

`Source File Must Be Named to Match a Public Class`

You get a compiler error stating that a public class must be declared in a file with a certain name.

When you declare a public class, such as `HelloWorld` or `HelloApplet` in the examples found in this chapter, the name of the source file that contains the class must match the class name. For example, a public class named `HelloWorld` must be stored in a file named `HelloWorld.java`.

`NoSuchMethodError: main`

You get a runtime error identifying a `NoSuchMethodError` *related to the* `main` *method.*

When you execute a Java application, the interpreter attempts to call the `main` method on the class identified as the starting point for the program. This error indicates that either the class specified in the `java` command does not contain a `main` method or the method it contains is not declared correctly. Your `main` method must be declared using the following syntax:

```
public static void main(String args[]){
```

`NoClassDefFoundError`

You attempt to run a program and you get an error stating that the class definition cannot be found.

The Java interpreter executes a program by first loading the class file corresponding to the name you provide to the `java` command. For example, when you type `java HelloWorld`, `HelloWorld.class` is loaded and executed. A `NoClassDefFoundError` indicates that the specified class file cannot be located in the current classpath. First, locate the class file and make sure that you spelled the class name correctly and typed it using the proper case. If this is correct, it is likely that class file is not in your classpath. Refer to Appendix A, "Installing the SDK and Getting Started," for more information on setting the classpath.

➔ **See** " The CLASSPATH Environment Variable," **p. 1035**

`IOException`

You get a compiler error stating that `java.io.IOException` *must be caught or declared to be thrown.*

If you are calling `System.in.read` within one of this chapter's examples, the call must be placed inside a `try-catch` block that handles `java.lang.IOException`. Refer to Listing 2.4 for the proper syntax of this `try-catch` block.

CHAPTER 3

Data Types and Other Tokens

In this chapter

by Brian Keeton

JAVA DATA TYPES

Every program you write deals with data in some form. Java has several types of data it can work with, and this chapter covers some of the most important.

Although Java is a language based on classes and all Java programs are built from classes, not all data types in Java are classes. In Java, there are two categories into which data types have been divided using this distinction:

- Primitives
- Reference types

PRIMITIVES

Primitives are data types whose state represents a number, a character, or a true/false indication.

Primitive types are not class types; they do not provide any behavior associated with the type-appropriate values they hold. Java has eight primitive types that should look familiar to you from other languages:

- `boolean`
- `byte`
- `char`
- `double`
- `float`
- `int`
- `long`
- `short`

As you proceed through this chapter, each of these types is covered in detail. For now, take a look at Table 3.1, which shows the numerical limits associated with each type.

TABLE 3.1 PRIMITIVE DATA TYPES IN THE JAVA LANGUAGE

Type	Description
`boolean`	`true` or `false`.
`byte`	8-bit twos-complement integer with values between -2^7 and 2^7-1 (–128 to 127).
`short`	16-bit twos-complement integer with values between -2^{15} and $2^{15}-1$ (–32,768 to 32,767).
`char`	16-bit Unicode characters from \u0000 to \uFFFF. For alphanumerics, these are the same as ASCII with the high byte set to 0.
`int`	32-bit twos-complement integer with values between -2^{31} and $2^{31}-1$ (–2,147,483,648 to 2, 147,483,647).

TABLE 3.1 CONTINUED

Type	Description
`long`	64-bit twos-complement integer with values between -2^{63} and $2^{63}-1$ (–9,223,372,036,854,775,808 to 9,223,372,036,854,775,807).
`float`	32-bit single precision floating-point numbers using the IEEE 754-1985 standard (+/– about 10^{39}).
`double`	64-bit double precision floating-point numbers using the IEEE 754-1985 standard (+/– about 10^{317}).

You might have heard Java described as a platform-independent language. The values shown in Table 3.1 are language features that support that statement. Unlike some languages, a given primitive type in Java is always represented using the same number of bits and the same supported range regardless of the platform. You will never be concerned about a 2-byte `int` versus a 4-byte `int` in Java because a Java `int` is always 4 bytes. Porting your program from one platform to another will not change how your primitive type variables are allocated and used.

Note

Although you should always declare a variable using a type that is sufficiently large to hold its possible values, the storage size associated with the primitive types should otherwise be transparent to you. Unlike C/C++, Java does not use pointers and pointer arithmetic to locate contiguously stored variables based on their size. Notice that Java has no equivalent to the C/C++ `sizeof` operator to support such usage.

REFERENCE TYPES

Classes, interfaces, and arrays are known as *reference types* in Java. When you declare a variable of a reference type, you are specifying that the variable will refer, or point, to an object instead of holding a single value as in the case of a primitive.

This makes sense for classes because class instances are objects that have associated behavior and state that can be represented with many values as opposed to one. However, it might seem strange to you to see arrays in the same category. You'll get a closer look at the details a little later in this chapter, but arrays in Java are true objects whose elements can be either primitives or references to other objects.

WORKING WITH VARIABLES

Data types come into play when you need to declare variables to hold values that are important to your program. Variables can be either primitives or reference types. They are always declared within a class but a variable might be associated with the class as a whole or its scope might be limited to a method or a block of statements within a method.

DECLARING A VARIABLE

Here's a simple example of declaring an integer variable:

```
int maxLoginAttempts = 3;
```

When you create a variable in Java, you must know a few things:

- You must know what data type you are going to use. In this case, that was the `int` primitive.
- You must know what you want to call the variable (`maxLoginAttempts`).
- You might also want to know the value with which the variable should be initialized. In this case, an initial value of 3 was assigned as part of the declaration. If you do not specify an initial value when you declare a variable as an attribute of a class, the Java compiler automatically assigns a default (`0` in the case of `int`). Variables declared within a method are not assigned default values, so you must explicitly set them before you can use them.

You can create any variable in Java in the same way as was just shown:

1. State the data type that you will be using (`int`).
2. State the name the variable will be called (`maxLoginAttempts`).
3. Assign the variable a value (`=3`).
4. As with every other statement in Java, terminate the declaration with a semicolon (;).

IDENTIFIERS: THE NAMING OF A VARIABLE

Refer to the first example:

```
int maxLoginAttempts = 3;
```

How does Java use the characters that make up the string `maxLoginAttempts`?

`maxLoginAttempts` is called an *identifier* in programming terminology. Identifiers are important because they are used to represent a whole host of things. In fact, identifiers are any names chosen by the programmer to represent variables, constants, classes, objects, labels, or methods. After an identifier is created, it represents the same object in any other place it is used in the same code block.

There are several rules you must obey and points to consider when creating an identifier:

- The first character of an identifier must be a letter, an underscore (_), or a currency symbol ($, £, and so on). Subsequent characters can be any of these or numerals.

Note

Although it is allowed, Sun's "Code Conventions for the Java Programming Language" advises against using an underscore or currency symbol to begin an identifier. This is a non-standard practice that results in identifiers that are difficult to read and that can easily be mistyped.

- The characters do not need to be Latin letters or numerals; they can be from any alphabet. Because Java is based on the Unicode standard, identifiers can be in any language, such as Arabic-Indic, Devanagari, Bengali, Tamil, Thai, or many others.
- In Java, as in C/C++ and many other modern languages, identifiers are case sensitive and language sensitive.

  This means that `maxLoginAttempts` is not the same as `MaxLoginAttempts`. Changing the case changes the identifier so that it cannot refer to the same variable. To aid the reader in distinguishing identifiers, it is standard practice in Java to name variables using identifiers that start with a lowercase letter and use mixed case to separate words.

Note

> The language sensitivity of Java means that language differentiates identifiers in the same way case does. Identifiers are unique between languages even if the characters appear the same visually.

- An identifier cannot be the same as one of the Java reserved words listed in Chapter 2, "HelloWorld: Your First Java Program."
- Make your identifier names long enough to be descriptive. Most application developers walk the line between choosing identifiers that are short enough to be quickly and easily typed and those that are long enough to be descriptive and easily read. Remember that the time spent reading source code to maintain it is typically many times greater than that spent to develop it. Meaningful identifiers will always add to the clarity of your work.

Table 3.2 shows several examples of legal and illegal identifiers based on the preceding rules. Example causes of illegal identifiers include starting an identifier with a numeral, using a special character, or embedding whitespace. Notice the last example that contains a hyphen. Java would try to treat this as an expression containing two identifiers that are being subtracted.

TABLE 3.2 EXAMPLES OF LEGAL AND ILLEGAL IDENTIFIERS

Legal Identifiers	Illegal Identifiers
`HelloWorld`	`9HelloWorld`
`counter`	`count&add`
`HotJava$`	`Hot Java`
`_65536`	`65536`
`userInterface`	`user-interface`

THE boolean PRIMITIVE

The simplest data type available to you in Java is the primitive type `boolean`. A `boolean` variable has only two possible values, `true` or `false`, which are represented with reserved words. In some other languages, Boolean types take on values of `0` or `1`; or, as in C/C++, `0` represents `false` and all other numbers are interpreted as `true`. Java treats `boolean` in a strict and type-safe manner by tightly restricting its allowed values. A `boolean` can never be treated as an integer or vice versa.

`boolean` variables are often used when you want to keep track of the state of a simple object attribute. For instance, if you are writing a flight scheduling application, whether a given flight is on time is important to you. You might declare a variable like this:

```
boolean onTime = true;
```

In Chapter 6, "Control Flow," you see how `boolean` variables can be used to direct the behavior of a program. For instance, if a flight is on time, your program proceeds normally, but if a flight is late, it sends a message to the departure gate for each connecting flight to alert someone that passengers will be arriving late.

You can change the value of a `boolean` variable in several ways. The first way to do this is explicitly. For instance, you can change the `onTime` status of flight by typing

```
onTime = false;
```

You can also assign the value of one `boolean` variable to another:

```
onTime = arrivedOnSchedule;
```

This only works if `arrivedOnSchedule` is also declared as a `boolean` (it's a compiler error otherwise). If so, `onTime` will only be assigned a value of `true` or `false` because those are the only values possible for `arrivedOnSchedule`.

The previous two examples changed the value of `onTime` using a `boolean` literal and another `boolean` variable. Although you are now familiar with variables, you might wonder what a literal is. A *literal* is a source-code representation of a value, in this case, the value `false`.

The main point is that the right side of an assignment statement for a `boolean` variable must evaluate to a `boolean`. In addition to using a single value or variable, you can also write logical expressions that meet this criterion. For instance, the following line would update `onTime` based on the supporting times:

```
onTime = (estimatedArrivalTime <= scheduledArrivalTime);
```

The equation on the right will evaluate to either `true` or `false` depending on the specific time values. You learn more about this type of equation later in Chapter 6.

Note

Boolean types are a feature in Java not found in languages such as C. To some, this stricter adherence to typing might seem oppressive. However, the ambiguity and potential typecasting abuses that it prevents are well in line with the goals of making Java a safer and more reliable language.

THE FLAVORS OF INTEGER

The next set of primitive types in Java contains what are known as the integer types:

- `byte`
- `int`
- `long`
- `short`

The types of integer differ only in the range of values they can hold. For instance, a `byte` cannot hold any number that is greater than 127, but a `long` can easily hold the world's population count (many times over actually).

Why are there so many types of integer? Couldn't you just declare every integer variable you need as a `long` and not worry about size restrictions? Although this would work in many cases, it is a confusing and inefficient use of a limited resource, namely the memory available to execute your programs. When you specify a meaningful integer type for a variable, you are providing information about the expected use of that variable to other programmers. For instance, storing the number of months of financing selected in a car loan program as a `long` would be confusing, or at least appear careless to others.

Besides clarity, you should also be concerned about the memory footprint required by your programs. A careful assignment of variable types prevents a program from requiring more memory to load and run than it actually needs to do its work. Programmers of embedded systems should be especially cautious.

LIMITS ON INTEGER VALUES

Table 3.3 summarizes the supported ranges for each of the integer types. It also defines the default value assigned to an integer attribute of a class if it isn't explicitly initialized as part of its declaration.

TABLE 3.3 INTEGER TYPES AND THEIR LIMITS

Integer Type	Minimum Value	Default Value	Maximum Value
`byte`	–128	0	127
`short`	–32,768	0	32,767
`int`	–2,147,483,648	0	2,147,483,647
`long`	–9,223,372,036,854,775,808	0	9,223,372,036,854,775,807

Notice there is no concept of an `unsigned int` in Java. The integer types in Java are always treated as signed values.

Note

If an operation or assignment produces a value outside the allowed limits for an integer type, no overflow or exception occurs. Instead, the twos-complement value is the result. This produces a wrapping effect. For example, assigning 127+1 to a `byte` results in a stored value of –128. Assigning 127+2 would result in –127 and so on. You must be careful when assigning types to make sure that variables are sufficiently large for their use because you will not be notified at either compile time or runtime if this wrapping occurs.

DECLARING INTEGER VARIABLES

You declare variables of any of the integer types in basically the same way. The following lines show how to create a variable of each type:

```
byte myFirstByte = 10;

short myFirstShort = 1000;

int myFirstInt = 1000000;

long myFirstLong = 1000000000;
```

Notice that the form of a declaration for an integer variable is nearly identical to what you already looked at for a `boolean`. The declaration for a Java primitive always consists of the type, an identifier, and an optional initial value. The initial value for an integer variable can be any whole number within the supported range of the specific type.

OPERATIONS ON INTEGERS

You can perform a wide variety of operations on integer variables. Table 3.4 shows a complete list. C and C++ programmers should find these very familiar.

TABLE 3.4 OPERATIONS ON INTEGER EXPRESSIONS

<table>
<tr><th>Operation</th><th>Description</th></tr>
<tr><td>=, +=, –=, *=, /=</td><td>Assignment operators</td></tr>
<tr><td>==, !=</td><td>Equality and inequality operators</td></tr>
<tr><td><, <=, >, >=</td><td>Relational operators</td></tr>
<tr><td>+, –</td><td>Unary sign operators</td></tr>
<tr><td>+, –, *, /, %</td><td>Addition, subtraction, multiplication, division, and remainder operators</td></tr>
<tr><td>+=, –=, *=, /=</td><td>Addition, subtraction, multiplication, division, and assign operators</td></tr>
<tr><td>++, ––</td><td>Increment and decrement operators</td></tr>
<tr><td><<, >>, >>></td><td>Bitwise shift operators</td></tr>
<tr><td><<=, >>=, >>>=</td><td>Bitwise shift and assign operators</td></tr>
<tr><td>~</td><td>Bitwise logical negation operator</td></tr>
<tr><td>&, |, ^</td><td>Bitwise AND, OR, and exclusive or (XOR) operators</td></tr>
<tr><td>&=, |=, ^=</td><td>Bitwise AND, OR, exclusive or (XOR), and assign operators</td></tr>
</table>

Later in Chapter 6, you learn about the equality, inequality, and relational operators that produce Boolean results. For now, let's concentrate on the arithmetic operators.

OPERATORS

You apply operators to integer variables to change a value or evaluate an expression for other use. The operators that apply to integers are described here in several related categories. Those not discussed in this section are covered in Chapter 5, "Using Expressions," and Chapter 6.

ARITHMETIC OPERATORS

Arithmetic operators are used to perform standard mathematical operations on variables. These operators include:

+	Addition operator
–	Subtraction operator
*	Multiplication operator
/	Division operator
%	Remainder operator (gives the remainder of a division)

The only operator in this list that you might not be familiar with is the remainder operator. The remainder of an operation is the remainder of the divisor divided by the dividend. In other words, in the expression `10 % 5`, the remainder is `0` because `10` is evenly divisible by `5`. However, the result of `11 % 5` is `1` because `11` divided by `5` is `2` remainder `1`. This operator works equally well with floating-point operands. For example, `12.5 % 1.5` yields the result `0.5`.

Although a familiar operator, the division operator exhibits some special behavior of which you must be aware. If the result of dividing two integers is not a whole number, Java always truncates the result (rather than rounding) to produce a whole number result. For example, `10 / 3` evaluates to `3`, and `-10 / 3` evaluates to `-3`.

You should also note that an `ArithmeticException` occurs if the right-side operand of either `/` or `%` evaluates to 0 (see "Catching and Throwing Exceptions" in Chapter 4, "Methods and Exceptions").

Listing 3.1 shows examples of the arithmetic operators in use with integers.

LISTING 3.1 EXAMPLES USING ARITHMETIC OPERATORS

```
int j = 60;
int k = 24;
int l = 30;
int m = 11;
int result = 0;

result = j + k;              // result = 84: (60 plus 24)
```

LISTING 3.1 CONTINUED

```
result = result / m;          // result = 7: (truncated result of 84 divided by 11)
result = j - (2*k + result); // result = 5: (60 minus (48 plus 7))
result = k % result;          // result = 4: (remainder 24 divided by 5)
```

ASSIGNMENT OPERATORS

The simplest assignment operator is the standard equals sign operator:

= Assignment operator

This operator assigns the value of the expression on the right side to the variable on the left side. For example, `x = y+3` evaluates the expression `y+3` and assigns the result to `x`.

The assignment operator can also be used to make a series of assignments in a single statement. For example, `x = y = z` assigns the value of `z` to `y` and then the value of `y` to `x`. Notice that the assignments are performed from right to left.

The other Java assignment operators are known as *arithmetic assignment operators*. These operators provide a shortcut for assigning a value. When the previous value of a variable is a factor in determining the value that you want to assign, the arithmetic assignment operators are often more efficient:

+= Add and assign operator

-= Subtract and assign operator

*= Multiply and assign operator

/= Divide and assign operator

%= Remainder and assign operator

The arithmetic assignment operators are best explained by example. For instance, the following two lines are equivalent:

```
x += 5;
x = x + 5;
```

These operators instruct the interpreter to use the operand on the left (`x` in this case) as the left-side operand in an expression with the right-side operand (`5` in this case). The operator that precedes the equals sign determines the operation performed between the two entities. The result of this operation is then assigned to the operand on the left (`x`).

When using an arithmetic assignment operator, the operand on the left is evaluated only once. This distinction is unimportant if the operand is a simple variable like that shown in the preceding example. However, if that operand contains an expression that modifies another variable, the use of the arithmetic assignment operator might not produce the same results as that obtained without it. This is most likely to occur if the left operand contains an increment or decrement operator as discussed in the following section.

Listing 3.2 shows more examples of the assignment operators in use.

Listing 3.2 Examples Using Arithmetic Assignment Operators

```
byte j = 60;
short k = 24;
int l = 30;
long m = 12L;
long result = 0L;

result += j;                    // result = 60: (0 plus 60)
result += k;                    // result = 84: (60 plus 24)
result /= m;                    // result = 7: (84 divided by 12)
result -= l;                    // result = -23: (7 minus 30))
result = -result;               // result = 23: (-(-23))
result %= m;                    // result = 11: (remainder 23 divided by 12)
```

Increment/Decrement Operators

The increment and decrement operators are used with a single operand (they are known as unary operators):

++ Increment operator

-- Decrement operator

For instance, the increment operator (++) adds one to its operand, as shown in the next line of code:

```
x++;
```

This is the same as:

```
x += 1;
```

The increment and decrement operators behave differently based on which side of the operand they are placed. When the increment operator is placed before its operand (for example, ++x), it is known as the *pre-increment* operator. This means that the increment occurs before the expression is evaluated. For example, after execution of the following two statements, both x and y have the value 6:

```
int x = 5;
int y = ++x;
// x and y are now both 6
```

This is because x is incremented before the right side is evaluated and assigned to y.

When the increment operator appears after its operand, it is known as the *post-increment* operator and the increment does not occur until after the expression has been evaluated. In the following modified lines of code, x is still incremented to 6 but only after y has been assigned the original value 5:

```
int x=5;
int y = x++;
// x is now 6 and y is 5
```

Similarly, you can use the decrement operator (--) in both *pre-decrement* and *post-decrement* fashion to subtract one from its operand.

CHARACTER VARIABLES

A feature of Java that makes it unique is its built-in support for internationalization (see Chapter 24, "Using Internationalization"). A key component of this support is the storage of characters as 16-bit values rather than a typical 8-bit representation. The `char` primitive type holds a 16-bit Unicode character. The Unicode standard allows the use of languages with alphabets that cannot be represented with only 256 characters. Although different from what you might be accustomed to, Java's representation of characters is transparent to you as a programmer. As a convenience, `char` variables that represent the Latin alphabet, numerals, and punctuation symbols have the same values as the ASCII character set (these characters have values between `0` and `255` with the upper byte set to `0`).

The syntax to create a character variable is the same as for the other primitives:

```
char myChar = 'b';
```

In this example, the `myChar` variable has been assigned the value of the letter `'b'`. Character literals must be expressed within single quotes as shown here.

Variables of type `char` can also be converted to the integer primitive types. When viewed as an integer, a `char` can hold values between `0` and `65,535`. It is unique in that its values are treated as unsigned (a negative index into a character set wouldn't be too meaningful).

FLOATING-POINT VARIABLES

Floating-point numbers are the last category of primitive types that need to be covered. Floating-point numbers are used to represent numbers that have a decimal point in them (such as 5.3 or 99.234). Whole numbers can also be represented, but as a floating point, the number 5 is actually 5.0.

In Java, floating-point numbers are represented by the types `float` and `double`. Both of these follow a standard floating-point specification: IEEE Standard for Binary Floating-Point Arithmetic, ANSI/IEEE Std. 754-1985 (IEEE, New York). The fact that these data types follow this specification—no matter what machine an application or applet is running on—is one of the details that makes Java so portable. In other languages, floating-point operations are defined for the floating-point unit (FPU) of the particular machine the program is executing on. For example, this means that the representation of 5.0 on an IBM PC might not be the same as on a DEC VAX.

Table 3.5 summarizes the numeric ranges supported for each of the floating-point types. It also defines the default value assigned to a `float` or `double` attribute of a class if it isn't explicitly initialized as part of its declaration.

TABLE 3.5 FLOATING-POINT TYPES AND THEIR SUPPORTED RANGES

Floating-Point Type	Minimum Positive Value	Default Value	Maximum Value
`float`	`1.40239846e-45f`	`0`	`3.40282347e+38f`
`double`	`4.94065645841246544e-324d`	`0`	`1.7976931348623157e+308d`

In addition to representing normal floating-point numbers, there are five unique states that can be assigned to `float` and `double` variables:

- Negative infinity
- Positive infinity
- Positive zero
- Negative zero
- Not-a-Number (NaN)

These states are required, by definition of the IEEE 754-1985 standard, in part to account for rollover. For instance, adding one to the maximum number that can be stored in a floating-point type results in a positive infinity result. When an operation results in a number too small to be represented, this is an underflow condition that is represented by a zero state. Unlike some integer operations, floating-point arithmetic never results in an exception. Dividing by zero produces a positive infinity or negative infinity result depending on the sign of the non-zero operand (NaN results if both operands are zero). Positive or negative infinity also results if a positive operand is divided by a positive or negative zero, respectively. The `Float` wrapper class introduced in Chapter 7, "Classes," provides several useful methods for working with these special states.

Most of the operations that can be applied to integers have an analogous operation for floating-point numbers. The exceptions are the bitwise operations. The operators that can be used in expressions of type `float` or `double` are given in Table 3.6.

TABLE 3.6 OPERATIONS ON `float` AND `double` EXPRESSIONS

Operation	Description
=, +=, −=, *=, /=	Assignment operators
==, !=	Equality and inequality operators
<, <=, >, >=	Relational operators
+, −	Unary sign operators
+, −, *, /, %	Addition, subtraction, multiplication, division, and remainder operators
+=, −=, *=, /=	Addition, subtraction, multiplication, division, and assign operators
++, −−	Increment and decrement operators

LITERALS: ASSIGNING VALUES

When you learned about assigning a literal value to a `boolean` variable, there were only two possibilities: the reserved words `true` and `false`. For integers, the values are nearly endless. In addition, there are many ways an integer value can be represented using literals.

The easiest way to assign a value to an integer value is by specifying a traditional numeral:

```
int j = 3;
```

However, what happens when you want to assign a number that is represented in a different form, such as hexadecimal? To tell the computer that you are giving it a hexadecimal number, you need to use a hexadecimal integer literal. For a number such as 3, this doesn't make much difference—the value is the same in decimal as it is in hexadecimal—but consider the number 11. Interpreted as hexadecimal (0x11), it has a value of 17! Certainly, you need a way to make sure the computer understands which you mean.

The following statements contain examples of assignments using literals:

```
boolean systemReady = true;
int j = 0;
long grainsOfSandOnTheBeach = 1L;
short mask1 = 0x007f;
char TIBETAN_NINE = '\u1049';
float accountBalance = 101.23F;
String buttonLabel = "Cancel";
```

Clearly, there are several types of literals. In fact, there are six major types of literals in the Java language:

- Boolean
- Integer
- Character
- Floating-point
- String
- Null

Note

Similar to the Boolean literals `true` and `false`, `null` is known as the *null literal*. It is a special value assigned to a reference type variable to indicate that the variable does not refer to any object.

You've already learned about the two Boolean literals, so take a look at the other types in the following sections.

INTEGER LITERALS

Integer literals are used to represent specific integer values. Because integers can be expressed as decimal (base 10), octal (base 8), or hexadecimal (base 16) numbers in Java, each representation has its own form of literal. In addition, integer literals can also be expressed with an uppercase L (`'L'`) or lowercase L (`'l'`) at the end to instruct the compiler to treat the number as a long (64-bit) integer.

As with C and C++, Java identifies any number that begins with a non-zero digit and does not contain a decimal point as a decimal integer literal (for example, any number between 1 and 9). To specify an octal literal, you must precede the number with a leading 0 (for example, 045 is the octal representation of 37 decimal). As with any octal representation, these literals can only contain the numerals 0 through 7. Hexadecimal integer literals are known by their distinctive `'zero-X'` at the beginning of the token.

Note

Tokens are the identifiers, keywords, literals, separators, and operators of Java. In short, they are every element of your source code other than whitespace and comments, which are described later in this chapter. Of the token types, only the separators have not been introduced. As the name implies, these tokens serve the purpose of separating other elements of your code. The separators consist of

`( ) {} [ ] ; , .`

Hex numbers are composed of the numerals 0 through 9 plus the Latin letters A through F (case is not important).

The following shows the largest and smallest values for integer literals in each of the three supported formats:

Largest 32-bit integer literal	2147483647
	017777777777
	0x7fffffff
Most negative 32-bit integer literal	–2147483648
	020000000000
	0x80000000
Largest 64-bit integer literal	9223372036854775807L
	0777777777777777777777L
	0x7fffffffffffffffL
Most negative 64-bit integer literal	–9223372036854775808L
	01000000000000000000000L
	0x8000000000000000L

Caution

Attempts to represent integers outside the range shown in this table using literals result in compile-time errors.

CHARACTER LITERALS

Character literals are enclosed in single quotation marks.

Any printable character, other than a backslash (\), can be specified as the single character itself enclosed in single quotes. Some examples of these literals are `'a'`, `'A'`, `'9'`, `'+'`, `'_'`, and `'~'`.

Some characters, such as the backspace, cannot be written out like this, so these characters are represented by escape sequences. Escape sequences, like all character literals, are enclosed within single quotes. They consist of a backslash followed by one of the following:

- A single character (b, t, n, f, r, ", ', or \)
- An octal number between 000 and 377
- A u followed by four hexadecimal digits specifying a Unicode character

The escape sequences built from single characters are shown in Table 3.7.

TABLE 3.7 ESCAPE SEQUENCES

Escape Sequence	Unicode	Meaning
`'\b'`	`\u0008`	Backspace
`'\t'`	`\u0009`	Horizontal tab
`'\n'`	`\u000a`	Linefeed
`'\f'`	`\u000c`	Form feed
`'\r'`	`\u000d`	Carriage return
`'\"'`	`\u0022`	Double quotation mark
`'\''`	`\u0027`	Single quotation mark
`'\\'`	`\u005c`	Backslash

Caution

Don't use the Unicode format to express an end-of-line character. Use the `'\n'` or `'\r'` characters instead.

The octal values allowed in character literals support the Unicode values from `'\u0000'` to `'\u00ff'` (the traditional ASCII range). Table 3.8 shows some examples of octal character literals.

TABLE 3.8 OCTAL CHARACTER LITERALS

Octal Literal	Unicode	Meaning
'\007'	\u0007	Bell
'\101'	\u0041	'A'
'\141'	\u0061	'a'
'\071'	\u0039	'9'
'\042'	\u0022	Double quotation mark

You can use Unicode sequences anywhere in your Java code, not just as character literals. As indicated earlier, identifiers can be composed of any Unicode character. In fact, comments, identifiers, and the contents of character and string literals can all be expressed using Unicode. You must use caution, however, because they are interpreted early by the compiler. For example, if you were to use the Unicode representation for a linefeed ('\u000a') as part of a print statement, it would cause a compiler error. This is because the compiler would see this as an actual linefeed in your source code that occurs before the closing single quote of a character literal. This is the reason for the earlier caution to always use '\n' and '\r' for line termination literals.

For an example of using Unicode, look at the following statements that declare and reference a variable using an identifier specified with a Unicode sequence:

```
int \u0074\u0065\u0073\u0074 = 3;
System.out.println( test );
System.out.println( \u0074\u0065\u0073\u0074 );
```

This code probably looks strange to you, but the first statement in this example declares and initializes an integer variable named `test` ('\u0074' equates to 't', '\u0065' equates to 'e', and so on). Although quite different in appearance, both println statements are equivalent; they each display the value assigned to `test` when executed.

Now look at two attempts to output a linefeed using different representations:

```
System.out.print( "\n" );       // OK
System.out.print( '\u000a' );   // a compiler error
```

The first statement is valid and is the equivalent of calling `System.out.println()`. The second statement, however, causes a compiler error. As mentioned previously, the Unicode sequence is interpreted early, and it appears to the compiler that the argument to `print` is a character literal that is prematurely terminated by a linefeed.

FLOATING-POINT LITERALS

Floating-point numbers can be represented in a number of ways. The following are all legitimate floating-point numbers:

1003.45	.00100345e6	100.345E+1100345e–2
1.00345e3	0.00100345e+6	

Floating-point literals have several parts, which appear in the following order as shown in Table 3.9.

TABLE 3.9 FLOATING-POINT LITERAL REQUIREMENTS

Part	Is It Required?	Examples
Whole Number	Not if fractional part is present.	0, 1, 100, 1003
Decimal Point	Not if exponent is present; must be there if there is a fractional part.	
Fractional	Cannot be present if there is no decimal point; must be there if there is no whole number part.	0, 1, 1415927
Exponent	Only if there is no decimal point.	e23, E–19, E6, e+307, e–1
Type Suffix	No. The number is assumed to be double precision in the absence of a type suffix.	f, F, d, D

The following representations illustrate the ways you can specify a floating-point literal that is consistent with the requirements in Table 3.9:

1.234	(Whole Number) . (Fractional)
1E2	(Whole Number)(Exponent)
1.234F	(Whole Number) . (Fractional)(Type Suffix)
1E2D	(Whole Number)(Exponent)(Type Suffix)

The following restrictions apply to floating-point literals:

- Single precision floating-point literals produce compile-time errors if their values are non-zero and have an absolute value outside the range 1.40239846e–45f through 3.40282347e+38f.
- Double precision floating-point literals produce compile-time errors if their values are non-zero and have an absolute value outside the range 4.94065645841246544e–324 through 1.79769313486231570e+308.

If you have trouble assigning floating-point literals to variables of type `float`, see "Floating-Point Literal Loss of Precision Error," in the "Troubleshooting" section at the end of this chapter.

STRING LITERALS

The `char` primitive supports variables that represent a single character. Sequences of characters are not represented by a primitive type in Java, but by a reference type, the `String` class, instead. This class is discussed in Chapter 8, "Using Strings and Text," but you need to know a little about strings now to finish the discussion of literals. String literals contain zero or more characters enclosed in double quotation marks. These characters can include the escape sequences listed in the "Character Literals" section earlier in this chapter. Both double quotation marks must appear on the same line of the source code, so strings cannot directly contain a new line character. To achieve the new line effect, you must use an escape sequence such as `\n` within the string. The double-quotation mark (") and backslash (\) characters must also be represented using escape sequences (`\"` and `\\`) within a string literal.

Some examples of string literals include

```
"Java"
"Hello World!\n"
"The Devanagari numeral for 9 is \u096f "
```

ARRAYS

Now that you have an understanding of the primitive types, let's turn our attention to one of the reference types. Recall the three reference types in Java:

- Classes
- Interfaces
- Arrays

Classes and interfaces are complex enough to earn their own chapters, but arrays are comparatively simple, so they are covered here with the primitive types.

An array is simply a way to maintain a sequence of items. Arrays are objects that hold a fixed number of variables of the same type. Arrays can hold primitive types, other objects, or even references to other arrays. If you have data that can be easily indexed and the number of data elements is known in advance, you should definitely consider using an array. Alternatives to arrays are described in Chapter 10, "Data Structures and Java Utilities."

As an example of array usage, suppose you collect a rainfall measurement at five different locations around a city and need to manipulate those values. An array would work well in this case. An example might be

```
float rainfall[] = {0.01F, 0.012F, 0.0F, 0.222F, 0.5F};
```

In this example, an array of floating point variables has been created and initialized with values corresponding to the rainfall measurements at the five locations.

Array elements are accessed using the indexing operator ([]) to specify an index into the array. As in the case of C and C++, Java array indices start at 0 rather than 1. The next line shows an example of accessing the measurement taken at the third location (index 2):

```
float thirdMeasurement = rainfall[2];
```

The result of this statement is that the value `0.0F` is assigned to `thirdMeasurement`.

Arrays in Java are different than those in most other languages because they are treated as objects. This might be confusing at first, but it does provide advantages. For example, every array has a length attribute that can be checked to determine its allocated size. In the example, the following would set `numMeasurements` to `5`:

```
int numMeasurements = rainfall.length;
```

The `length` attribute is especially useful when looping through the elements of an array. The maximum array index is always the value of the `length` attribute minus 1. (Remember that the index of an array has an origin of 0.) Although the `length` attribute can be used to get the size of an array, it cannot be set to change the size of an array. An array's size is determined when it is created and it cannot be changed.

Because Java arrays are reference types, there are several steps to creating an array and assigning its elements:

1. Declare the array. An array declaration must contain a pair of brackets, but the compiler allows you to choose between placing the brackets after the data type or after the identifier that names the array. The following two lines produce the same result:

   ```
   int[] myIntArray;
   int myIntArray[];
   ```

   Although both forms are allowed, you should pick one syntax and use it consistently. Most programmers opt for the form that places the brackets after the data type. In the preceding example, this form makes it instantly clear that the variable is an integer array.

   Also notice from these declarations that a Java array must contain elements that are of a single type only. Here, `myIntArray` cannot contain anything other than `int` primitives.

2. Create space for the array and define its length. To do this, you must use the keyword `new`, followed by the variable type and the number of elements:

   ```
   myIntArray = new int[500];
   ```

   The `new` operator is discussed in Chapter 7. Its purpose is to instantiate the objects associated with reference type variables. Before space is allocated for an array in this manner, it has a length of zero.

Caution

> **Forgetting to use the `new` operator before you attempt to assign a primitive or an object to an array element results in a NullPointerException. This is because an array of length zero cannot hold anything.**

There is a slight variation of using the `new` operator with arrays that allows you to create an *anonymous array*. These are called anonymous because they are created without being declared with a name. For example, the following expression creates an anonymous array of integers that could be used in an assignment statement or as a parameter in a method call:

```
new int[] { 1, 2, 3 }
```

3. Place data in the array. For arrays of primitive types (such as those in this chapter), the array values are all initialized to `0`, `false`, or `'\u0000'` as appropriate. The next line shows how to set the fifth element in the array:

   ```
   myIntArray[4] = 467;
   ```

In the rainfall example, you might have noticed that you were able to create the five-element array and assign it values at the same time. This example took advantage of a shortcut.

You can declare the initial values of the array by placing the values between braces ({,}) on the initial declaration line. The number of values provided determines the number of array elements allocated. This bulk assignment of values can only be done as part of an array's declaration. After an array has been declared, attempting to assign values this way causes a compiler error.

In addition to the preceding example that demonstrated the declaration of an array of primitives, you can also initialize an array of object references when you declare it. An example of this is shown in the following:


```
String dayAbbreviation[] = {"Sun", "Mon", "Tues", "Wed",
  "Thurs", "Fri", "Sat"};
```

The preceding declaration allocates an array of seven `String` references and assigns references to the array elements using a list of `String` literals.

Array declarations are composed of the following parts:

Array modifiers	Optional	The keywords `public`, `protected`, `private`, or `synchronized` (see Chapter 7)
Type name	Required	The name of the type or class being arrayed
Brackets	Required	[]
Initialization	Optional	See Chapter 7 for more details about initialization
Semicolon	Required	;

Java supports multidimensional arrays, which are simply arrays of arrays. The declaration of a multidimensional array includes a set of brackets for each dimension. When you create space for a multidimensional array using `new`, you do not have to specify the size for each dimension, only the leftmost one (and any to the left of any other dimensions you specify). The following declarations are all valid:

```
int[][] xyData1 = new int[5][10];
int[][] xyData2 = new int[5][];
int[][][] xyzData1 = new int[5][10][15];
int[][][] xyzData2 = new int[5][10][];
int[][][] xyzData3 = new int[5][][];
```

A unique aspect of multidimensional arrays in Java is that they can be nonrectangular. If you continue to think of a multidimensional array as an array of arrays, this makes sense. Each element of the main array references an array whose size is independent of the arrays referenced by the other elements. Consider the following example:

```
int[][] pyramid = { {0}, {1, 2}, {3, 4, 5} };
System.out.println(pyramid[0][0]);  // 0
System.out.println(pyramid[1][0]);  // 1
System.out.println(pyramid[1][1]);  // 2
System.out.println(pyramid[2][0]);  // 3
System.out.println(pyramid[2][1]);  // 4
System.out.println(pyramid[2][2]);  // 5
```

Listing 3.3 shows several more examples of using arrays.

Listing 3.3 Examples of Declaring Arrays

```
long primes[] = new long[1000000];      // Declare an array and assign
                                        // some memory to hold it.
long[] evenPrimes = new long[1];        // Either way, it's an array.
evenPrimes[0] = 2;                      // Populate the array.

// Now declare an array with an implied 'new' and populate.
long fibonacci[] = {1,1,2,3,5,8,13,21,34,55,89,144};

long perfects[] = {6, 28};              // Creates a two element array.

// Declare a two-dimensional array and populate it.
long towerOfHanoi[][]={{10,9,8,7,6,5,4,3,2,1},{},{}};

long[][][] threeDTicTacToe;             // Uninitialized 3D array.
```

There are several additional points about arrays that you need to know:

- Array indexes must either be type `int` (32-bit integer) or be able to be cast as an `int` (if you use a `short`, `byte`, or `char`, the compiler promotes it to an `int` automatically). As a result, the largest possible array size is 2,147,483,647. Most Java installations would fail with arrays anywhere near that size, but that is the maximum defined by the language.
- Java automatically provides runtime bounds checking for arrays. If a statement attempts to access an invalid array index, it causes an `ArrayIndexOutOfBoundsException`.

If you have trouble accessing array elements, see "`ArrayIndexOutOfBoundsException`," in the "Troubleshooting" section at the end of this chapter.

- The `System.arraycopy` method provides the means to copy the elements of one array into another. If you assign one array variable to another, you have not created two copies of the array elements, only two references to the same set of elements.

Non-Token Input Elements

Now that you've seen the various types of tokens in Java, let's complete the discussion with a look at the only input elements in your source code that aren't classified as tokens. As was stated when tokens were defined previously, whitespace and comments are the two non-token element types.

WHITESPACE

Of some importance to most languages is the use of whitespace. Whitespace is any character that is used just to separate text—a space, tab, form feed, line feed, or carriage return.

In Java, whitespace can be inserted almost anywhere within an application's source code without affecting the meaning of the code to the compiler. The only place that whitespace cannot be used is within an identifier, such as a variable or class name. Put simply, the following two lines are not the same to a Java compiler:

```
int myInt;
int my   Int;  // compiler error
```

Proper use of indentation, blank lines, and spaces in your source code makes your code easier to read and understand. Little or inconsistent use of whitespace makes your code harder to maintain than necessary. Take a look at the ever-popular HelloWorld application written with minimal use of whitespace:

```
public class HelloWorld{public static void main(String args
[]){System.out.println("Hello World!!");}}
```

Clearly, it is a little harder to determine what this application does or even if the code is correct. You should choose a consistent pattern of whitespace use and stick with it.

COMMENTS

Comments are an important part of any language. Comments enable you to describe the purpose of your code, any assumptions it relies on, and the rationale behind its implementation approach. You should always comment the aspects of your code that aren't obvious, even if it's only for your own use later. When you do add comments, however, be certain to keep them up-to-date with changes to the surrounding code. Perhaps the only situation worse than maintaining code without comments is maintaining code with comments that are obsolete or just plain wrong.

Java supports three styles of comments:

- Traditional (the type found in C)
- C++ style
- javadoc (a unique approach for Java class documentation)

TRADITIONAL COMMENTS

A traditional comment is a C-style comment that begins with a slash-star (/*) and ends with a star-slash (*/). Take a look at Listing 3.4, which shows four traditional comments.

LISTING 3.4 AN EXAMPLE CONTAINING FOUR TRADITIONAL COMMENTS

```
/* Set up the desired loan parameters
 * and call the method that computes
 * the monthly payment amount
 */
int numPayments = 3 * 12;        /* 3 years of monthly payments */
double interestRate = 0.08 / 12; /* 8% annual interest paid monthly */

double payment = computePayment( interestRate, numPayments,
  5000.0 /* hard code the loan amount for now */ );
```

As you can see, comments of this sort can span many lines or can be contained within a single line (outside a token). Traditional comments cannot be nested. Thus, if you try to nest them, the opening `/*` of the inner one is not detected by the compiler and the closing `*/` of the inner one ends the comment. The subsequent text, including the `*/` of the outer comment, is then interpreted as part of your source code and causes a compiler error. Listing 3.5 shows how this can become very confusing.

LISTING 3.5 AN EXAMPLE OF A SINGLE COMMENT THAT LOOKS LIKE TWO

```
/* This opens the comment
/* That looked like it opened another comment but it is the same one
* This will close the entire comment                                      */
```

Traditional comments are extremely useful when you are debugging your code. This style of comment makes it easy to quickly comment out blocks of code as you work to isolate the source of an error.

C++ STYLE COMMENTS

The second style of comment begins with a slash-slash (`//`) and ends when the current source code line ends. These comments are especially useful for describing the intended meaning of a single line of code. Listing 3.6 demonstrates the use of this style of comment.

LISTING 3.6 AN EXAMPLE USING C++ STYLE COMMENTS

```
// entry point for the application
public static void main(String[] args) {
  if (args.length < 1) {  // application requires a command-line argument
    System.out.println("<usage> java ClassName InputString");
    System.exit(-1);  // exit the program
  }

  String inputString = args[0];  // get command-line argument
  System.out.println(inputString);
}
```

JAVADOC COMMENTS

The final style of comment in Java is a special type specifically intended for defining descriptions of your code that can be read by the javadoc tool (see Appendix B, "SDK Tools"). These comments look very much like traditional comments except that they begin with `/**` instead of `/*`. These comments have the properties of traditional comments, including the capability to span multiple lines. By using these comments in an appropriate manner, you can use javadoc to automatically create documentation pages similar to those of the Java API. Listing 3.7 shows a javadoc comment (see Appendix B for a description of the javadoc tags `@param`, `@return`, and `@throws used in this example`).

LISTING 3.7 AN EXAMPLE OF A `javadoc` COMMENT

```
/**
 * This method computes the payment for a loan based on
 * the interest rate, the number of payment periods, and
 * the loan amount.
 *
 * @param rate         The interest rate per payment period
 * @param numPayments The total number of payment periods
 * @param loanAmount  The present value of the loan
 * @return             The computed payment amount
 *
 * @throws InvalidLoanParameterException If one of the
 *           arguments is <= 0
 */
public static double computePayment( double rate, int numPayments,
  double loanAmount ) throws InvalidLoanParameterException {
  // compute and return the payment amount
  ...
}
```

Caution

This style of comment should only be used for information that should be extracted by javadoc. Other use will produce confusing documentation of your classes.

TROUBLESHOOTING

FLOATING-POINT LITERAL LOSS OF PRECISION ERROR

The compiler reports as error stating that your assignment of a floating-point literal to a variable of type `float` might result in a loss of precision.

When you assign a floating-point literal to a `float` variable, you must explicitly specify the type suffix. When you omit the suffix, the compiler assumes that the literal is of type `double`, which cannot be assigned to a `float` without an explicit cast. The following two statements illustrate a correct and an incorrect assignment statement:

```
float myFirstFloat = 1.0;    // compiler error
float mySecondFloat = 2.0F; // correct
```

`ArrayIndexOutOfBoundsException`

An `ArrayIndexOutOfBoundsException` *occurs at runtime when you attempt to access an array's elements.*

Remember that the first index in a Java array is 0 and the last valid index is one less than the length of the array. For example:

```
// create an array to hold two integer values
int[] dataArray = new int[2];

// several correct data assignment statements
dataArray[0] = 23;  // valid assignment to first index
dataArray[1] = 43;  // valid assignment to last index
dataArray[dataArray.length-1] = 50;  // valid assignment to last index

// runtime errors
dataArray[2] = 55;                   // ArrayIndexOutOfBoundsException
dataArray[dataArray.length] = 55;  // ArrayIndexOutOfBoundsException
```

CHAPTER 4

Methods and Exceptions

In this chapter

by Brian Keeton

DECLARING A METHOD

Methods are truly the heart and soul of Java programs. They serve the same purpose in Java that functions do in C, C++, and Pascal—only the terminology is different. All execution that takes place in any application or applet takes place within a method. It is only by combining multiple dynamic methods that large-scale Java applications are written.

Like C++ functions, Java methods are the essence of each class and are responsible for managing all the tasks that can be performed. It is also true that methods exist only within classes in Java. There is no concept of a global function in Java that exists outside of a class.

Look at the parts of a method as shown in the following simple example:

```
void simpleMethod(){
  System.out.println("Inside simpleMethod");
}
```

A method has two parts: a signature and a body. A *method signature* specifies a method's name, its return type, its modifiers and access specifiers, the list of parameters it requires, and the types of exceptions it can throw. Unlike C++, Java methods are defined in one place rather than having a separate header file that declares the method signatures for a class. You also do not have to be concerned about defining method prototypes like some languages require you to do if you want to call a method from code that is declared before the method. The Java compiler does not place any restriction on the order of method declarations.

Although the actual implementation of a method is contained within its body (see "Blocks and Statements" later in this chapter), a great deal of important information is defined in the method signature. Using the preceding example, the simplest form of a method signature looks like this:

```
void simpleMethod()
```

At the very least, a method signature specifies what the method will return, and the name by which the method will be known. As you will soon see, there are several more options that are available. In general, method signatures take the form

```
access_specifier modifiers return_value nameOfMethod (parameters) throws
ExceptionList
```

where everything in italics is optional.

ACCESS SPECIFIERS

You use methods by calling them from other methods. Remember how the HelloWorld application in Chapter 2, "HelloWorld: Your First Java Program," demonstrated that the Java interpreter calls the `main` method of an application to start its execution. The `main` method then calls other methods to perform the work of the application. The `simpleMethod` example performs its undemanding task by calling the `println` method of the `PrintStream` class.

The first option available within a method signature addresses the fact that a method can place restrictions on who can call it. Given that methods are only called by other methods and methods only exist within classes, the "who" here refers to the classes that can call a method. The access specifier in a method signature determines how visible a method is to other classes. At a minimum, any method is accessible to the other methods in the same class. You can, however, exercise control over access beyond that by selecting an appropriate specifier. By choosing to accept the default access level, or to instead declare a method as `public`, `protected`, or `private`, you determine a great deal about how that method can be used.

`public`

The `public` modifier is the least-restrictive modifier for a method. When you declare a method as `public`, you can access it from any other class regardless of inheritance or any other class relationships. A `public` method's signature looks like this:

```
public void toggleStatus()
```

You should reserve this modifier for methods that make up the external interface you want to expose for a class. The set of public methods declared by a class determines how it is seen and used by the rest of the world.

`protected`

The `protected` modifier raises the subject of packages, which are discussed later in Chapter 7, "Classes." For now, think of a *package* as a group of related classes. Because classes in a package are intended to form a cohesive unit, you have the option to allow less-restrictive method access between classes in the same package. Any class in the same package, or any class that extends the current class, regardless of package, can access a `protected` method. For instance, the class `java.awt.Component` has a `protected` method named `paramString`. This method is used in subclasses such as `java.awt.Button`, but it is not accessible to any class that you might create that does not extend `Component`. You declare a protected method like the following:

```
protected void toggleStatus()
```

→ **See** Chapter 7, "Packages," **p. 167**

When you attempt to use a `protected` method, or any other restricted method, that you do not have access to from the current scope, the compiler reports an error. This error might be difficult to diagnose at first because of the way inaccessible methods are hidden from the compiler. Instead of getting an error that tells you that you are attempting to violate an access restriction, you get an error telling you that there is no such method as the one you are attempting to call. Such an error resembles the following:

```
method paramString() not found in class java.awt.Button
```

This makes sense after you think about it. As far as the compiler is concerned, `protected` methods do not exist unless you have sufficient access to call them. They are literally hidden by the accompanying encapsulation.

DEFAULT

You might have noticed that the `simpleMethod` declaration did not include an access specifier. When the specifier is omitted, the default access restrictions are imposed. The default access type is sometimes referred to as *friendly* or *package* access. Methods declared in this manner are only accessible to other classes within the same package. Consider the following class declarations:

```
package abc;
public class NetworkSender {
  void sendInfo(String mes) {
    System.out.println(mes);
  }
}

package abc;
public class NetworkSenderTest {
  String mes = "test";
  void informOthers(String mes) {
    NetworkSender messenger;
    messenger = new NetworkSender();
    messenger.sendInfo(mes); // this is legal
  }
}
package xyz;
import abc.NetworkSender;
public class NetworkSenderTest2 extends NetworkSender{
  String mes = "test";
  void informOthers(String mes) {
    NetworkSender messenger;
    messenger = new NetworkSender();
    messenger.sendInfo(mes); // this is NOT legal
  }
}
```

In this example, `NetworkSender` in the `abc` package declares a `sendInfo` method with default access. The `informOthers` method of `NetworkSenderTest` is allowed to call `sendInfo` because this class is also in the `abc` package. However, the same call is illegal in `NetworkSenderTest2` because this class is in a different package. This is true even though `NetworkSenderTest2` is a subclass of `NetworkSender`. Such a call would be legal if `sendInfo` had instead been declared as `protected`.

`private`

The `private` modifier assigns the highest degree of protection available to a method. A `private` method is only accessible to methods in the same class. Even classes that extend the current class cannot access a `private` method. Just like the other specifiers, a `private` method's signature takes the form:

```
private void toggleStatus()
```

You might not immediately see the need for `private` methods. After all, why declare a method that no other class can use? The answer is that `private` methods allow you to factor the work a class does into smaller, more manageable methods while still hiding the implementation details. This access level is well suited for utility or intermediate methods that support the work of other methods in a class but do not offer any general usefulness outside the class.

MODIFIERS

Modifiers are similar to access specifiers in how they are used within method declarations. They do serve a different purpose, however. In fact, each of the method modifiers (`static`, `abstract`, `final`, `native`, and `synchronized`) serves a different purpose altogether. Some of these modifiers will make more sense to you after you get to Chapter 7, but you'll get enough details now to make this discussion of the method signature complete.

`static`

The `static` modifier was briefly introduced in the HelloWorld application in Chapter 2 when you looked at the signature of the `main` method for an application:

```
public static void main(String args[])
```

When you declare a method as `static`, you are stating that the method belongs to a class and not to an instance of a class, which would represent an individual object. Static methods are often referred to as class methods, as opposed to instance methods, for this reason. Instance methods operate on instance variables to access and maintain the state of a particular object. A static method, on the other hand, has no knowledge of an individual object's state. It is intended to provide a service that is independent of a class instance.

The difference between instance and class methods can best be demonstrated with an example. Listings 4.1 and 4.2 show examples of both method types used within a pair of cooperating classes. The complete details of class declarations are covered in Chapter 7, so for now, the focus is only on the method implementations that are shown.

LISTING 4.1 `AccountManager.java`—ACCOUNT MANAGER EXAMPLE WITH A STATIC METHOD

```
public class AccountManager {

  // account numbers are validated simply based on length
  private static int MIN_ACCOUNT_NUM_LENGTH = 8;
  private static int MAX_ACCOUNT_NUM_LENGTH = 9;

  public static boolean validAccountNumber(String accountNum) {
    // make sure length is ok
    if ( (accountNum.length() < MIN_ACCOUNT_NUM_LENGTH) ||
     (accountNum.length() > MAX_ACCOUNT_NUM_LENGTH) ) {
      return false;
    }

    // make sure every character is a digit
    for (int i=0; i<accountNum.length(); i++) {
      if ( !Character.isDigit( accountNum.charAt(i) ) ) {
```

LISTING 4.1 CONTINUED

```
        return false;
      }
    }
    // passed all the tests
    return true;
  }
}
```

LISTING 4.2 Account.java—ACCOUNT EXAMPLE WITH INSTANCE METHODS

```
public class Account {
  private String accountNumber;
  private float balance;

  public String getAccountNumber() {
    return accountNumber;
  }

  public void setAccountNumber(String num) {
    // call static method of AccountManager class to validate
    // the account number
    if ( AccountManager.validAccountNumber( num ) ) {
      accountNumber = num;
    }
  }

  public void deposit(float amount) {
    balance += amount;
  }

  public void withdraw(float amount) {
    balance += amount;
  }
}
```

In Listing 4.1, `AccountManager` is declared as a class without any instance variables or methods. This means that an instance of the class has no state to maintain. The `validAccountNumber` method is declared as `static` because it is not tied to any particular instance of `AccountManager`. You could have 100 instances of the class in your application and still get the same result from the method no matter which instance you use to call the method. `Account`, in Listing 4.2, on the other hand, has both instance variables and methods. Each instance of an `Account` has its own account number and balance that cannot be managed by static methods because the associated values are always attached to a particular instance.

The `setAccountNumber` method of `Account` calls the `static validAccountNumber` method of `AccountManager` to make sure the account number it is passed is acceptable to use. Notice that this method call is stated using the class name instead of a variable name before the dot and the method name. The `validAccountNumber` method in turn uses the `static` variables declared in `AccountManager` and the `static isDigit` method of the `Character` class to do its work. A static method can access any static variables or other static methods defined in its class, but attempting to reference an instance variable or method causes a compiler error. However, in the reverse situation, it is perfectly legal for an instance method to access static variables and methods in addition to instance ones.

An important concept to note here is that you never even need to create an instance of a class to access the `static` methods and variables that it defines. Here, the `Account` class does not create an `AccountManager`, but it makes use of the class's functionality nonetheless.

Note

The conventional way to access a `static` method is to specify the class name followed by a dot and the method name. If you have an instance of a class with a `static` method, you can also use that instance identifier to access the method. Although legal, this is not as clear to someone reading your code because it does not make it obvious that a `static` method is being used.

`abstract`

An `abstract` method is a method that is declared but not implemented in the current class. The responsibility for defining the body of the method is passed on to the subclasses of the current class. This type of method is useful when you know that a certain behavior will be implemented in a hierarchy of classes, but there is no default implementation of that behavior. An `abstract` method serves as a placeholder for the behavior in the parent class. The ability to define `abstract` methods is a key part of object-oriented design. The value will be more obvious to you when polymorphism and `abstract` classes are discussed in Chapter 7.

An `abstract` method declaration takes the form

```
access_specifier modifiers return_value nameOfMethod (parameters) throws
ExceptionList;
```

where everything in italics is optional. Unlike the previous use of this declaration template, this actually defines a complete method. The semicolon at the end of an `abstract` method's signature takes the place of the method body.

There are a couple of restrictions associated with the `abstract` modifier. First, a class that contains one or more `abstract` methods must also be declared as `abstract` itself. Also, you cannot declare a `static` method, class constructor, or `final` method to be `abstract`.

`final`

By placing the keyword `final` in front of a method declaration, you prevent any subclasses of the current class from overriding the method. This is your way to dictate that this implementation of a method is the only implementation to be allowed by the compiler. It makes your intent regarding the use of the method decisively clear.

In C++, you must declare a method as `virtual` to allow it to be overridden. In contrast, all methods in Java can be overridden by default. The `final` modifier is your way to turn off this default behavior for a specific method.

Tip

Besides providing control over how your methods are used, the `final` and `static` modifiers and the `private` specifier offer an additional performance advantage. A method declared using any of these attributes cannot be overridden, so any calls to it can be bound at compile time. This saves the time that would otherwise be spent at runtime performing a dynamic lookup.

`native`

Native methods are methods that you want to use, but do not want to write in Java. They are most commonly written in C or C++ and can provide several benefits, such as faster execution time, reuse of existing code, or access to features unique to a platform. Similar to `abstract` methods, you declare a `native` method by placing the modifier `native` in front of the method declaration and substituting a semicolon for the method body. It is important to remember that this declaration informs the compiler of the return type, name, and arguments associated with a method. Even though you do not define a method body here, you must make the signature consistent with its implementation.

Use of `native` methods is not that common for most programmers. If you find it necessary to implement part of a class this way, refer to Sun's documentation of the Java Native Interface (JNI). JNI provides the functionality required to load a `native` method implementation at runtime and associate it with a Java class.

`synchronized`

One of the most powerful features of Java is the built-in support it provides for developing multi-threaded applications. Declaring a method as `synchronized` signals that incorrect results might occur if use of the method by multiple threads is not guarded. When a `synchronized` method is being executed, no other thread can call that method, or any other `synchronized` method, in the same class until the method returns.

→ **See** "Thread Synchronization" **p. 275**

RETURNING INFORMATION

When a method completes its execution, it can return a primitive value, an object reference, or nothing at all to the method that called it. The return type in a method signature defines what, if anything, is returned. Methods that do not return anything must be declared with a return type of `void`.

Although returning information is an important part of what a method can do, there is actually little to discuss on this subject. A method returns a value or reference with a `return` statement that includes an expression that evaluates to the appropriate type. A `void` method uses a `return` statement without an expression. In fact, the use of a `return` is optional in this situation unless there is a condition that requires the method to exit before its last statement is executed.

The compiler requires that any `return` statement in a method be consistent with the declared return type. If a method is not declared `void`, it must have at least one corresponding `return` statement.

For example, the following method is declared to return a value of type `boolean`. The return is accomplished by executing one of the two `return` statements:

```
public boolean inOrder(int x, int y) {
  if (x<y) {
    return true;
  }
  else {
    return false;
  }
}
```

As a simplification, a `return` statement with an expression can be substituted:

```
public boolean inOrder(int x, int y) {
  return x<y;
}
```

METHOD NAME

A method signature includes the method name. The rules regarding method names are simple and are the same as any other Java identifier. A method name must begin with a letter, underscore, or currency symbol. The remaining characters in the name can be any of these characters or a digit. To follow standard naming conventions, you should start method names with a lowercase letter and use mixed case to separate words.

PARAMETERS

Simply put, the parameter list in a method signature is the list of information that will be passed to the method whenever it is called. A parameter list takes the following form and can consist of as many parameters as you want:

```
(DataType variableName, DataType variableName,...)
```

If you have no parameters, Java requires that you leave the parentheses empty. (This is unlike other languages that permit you to omit a parameter list, or C, which requires the keyword `void`.) Therefore, a method that takes no parameters has a signature resembling the following:

```
public void reset()
```

The strong typing and compile-time checking of Java result in a number of restrictions on parameter lists. There is no direct support for variable length parameter lists or default parameter values. Each call to a method has to include each parameter declared for the method and provide them in the correct order. The type of each parameter does not have to match exactly as long as those that differ can be implicitly converted to the type required. The concepts of variable parameter lists and default values are best handled in Java by using sets of overloaded methods. You might also consider replacing individual arguments with an array, or one of the collection classes introduced later in Chapter 10, "Data Structures and Java Utilities." The following example demonstrates an overloaded method that does the equivalent of assigning a default parameter value:

```
public void setFont(String fontName) {
  // no point size specified using this method,
  // so default to 12
  setFont(fontName, 12);
}

public void setFont(String fontName, int pointSize) {
  // use the two method parameters to set the font
  ...
}
```

Here, `setFont` is overloaded so that it can be called either with or without a `pointSize` parameter. If this argument is omitted, the single-parameter version of the method is called. This method calls the other version to do the real work by supplying a default value of `12` for the missing argument. A key point here is that methods such as this should be chained together as shown instead of being implemented by copying and pasting the same code into each one.

For the most part, the name of a method parameter can be any valid Java identifier. One restriction is that a parameter name cannot be the same as a parameter to a `catch` clause, which is described later in this chapter when exception handling is discussed.

Caution

The Java compiler does not place any restriction on the number of parameters you include in a method declaration, but a long parameter list is often an indication of a poorly designed method. When you find yourself passing a lot of parameters to a method, you might be trying to do too much within a method that should really be broken out into smaller pieces. If this is not the issue, grouping some of the parameters into a class might be an alternative that will simplify your design.

PASS BY REFERENCE OR PASS BY VALUE?

An important concept to understand about any programming language is whether variables passed to a method as arguments are passed by value or by reference. If a language uses pass by reference, when you pass a variable into a method and the method changes the variable's value, the change is seen in the calling method as well. On the other hand, if a language uses pass by value, changes made to a parameter inside a method are never seen by the calling method. Here, pass by value literally means that only a value is passed into the method and not an associated variable that can be modified in such a way that changes are reflected outside the method. A parameter in this case is like a local variable of the method that gets its initial value from the calling method instead of being known in advance.

Some languages allow you to specify when you want to pass by value and when you want to pass by reference. For example, in Pascal the `var` keyword allows you to distinguish parameters that are passed by reference from those that are not. C++ provides similar flexibility allowing you to attach the `&` operator to a parameter's declaration so that it is interpreted as a reference. Java, on the other hand, always treats parameters in a consistent fashion.

The short answer is that Java always passes parameters by value. This does not give you the complete story however, and probably sounds confusing given that objects in Java are always handled by reference. First, consider the simple case. Primitive types (`byte`, `short`, `char`, `int`, `long`, `float`, `double`, and `boolean`) are passed by value and any modifications made to them in a method are seen only by that method and not by the caller. You cannot change the value of a primitive variable by passing it into another method.

Objects are also passed by value when used as method arguments, but the interpretation is different. It is the object reference that is passed by value, not the object itself. That might sound like a play on words, but the implications of this are significant. You cannot change an object reference within a method call, but you can change the state of the object that is being referenced. When you pass an object to a method, a reference to the object is passed and not a copy of the object and its attributes. You are free to modify the attributes of an object within the method and those changes will be seen by the calling method as well. What you cannot do is assign a different object reference to the parameter and have that change reflected in the calling method.

Listing 4.3 demonstrates the basic differences between passing primitives and passing object references. As shown here, if you pass an `int` to a method and that method changes the `int`, the calling class still sees the original value. However, when a class instance is passed and a variable within it is changed, the change is visible in the calling method as well.

LISTING 4.3 `PassingDemo.java`—**THE DIFFERENCE BETWEEN PASSING AN OBJECT AND A PRIMITIVE TYPE**

```
public class PassingDemo {

  public void first() {
    xObject o = new xObject();
    // initialize an object and a primitive
    o.x   = 5;
    int x = 5;

    // pass them to another method and then recheck their values
    changeThem(x, o);
    System.out.println();
    System.out.println("Back in the original method");
    System.out.println("The value of o.x is now "+o.x);
    System.out.println("But, The value of x is still "+x);
  }

  public void changeThem (int x, xObject o) {
    x   = 9;
    o.x = 9;
```

LISTING 4.3 CONTINUED

```
    System.out.println("In the changeThem method");
    System.out.println("The value of o.x was changed to "+o.x);
    System.out.println("The value of x was changed to "+x);
  }

  public static void main(String args[]) {
    PassingDemo myDemo = new PassingDemo();
    myDemo.first();
  }
}


class xObject {
  public int x;
}
```

The resulting output from this code is

```
In the changeThem method
The value of o.x was changed to 9
The value of x was changed to 9
Back in the original method
The value of o.x is now 9
But, The value of x is still 5
```

That example shows how you change the value of an object attribute. Now look at Listing 4.4 where the meaning of not being able to change a reference is demonstrated. Here, the code might at first appear to be swapping the two references passed by the calling method. However, references are passed by value, so the attempted swap has no real effect.

LISTING 4.4 SwapAttempt.java—A METHOD CANNOT CHANGE A REFERENCE PASSED AS A PARAMETER

```
public class SwapAttempt {

  public static void swap( String s1, String s2 ) {
    // these statements are legal but they have no
    // effect on the variables in the calling method
    String temp = s1;
    s1 = s2;
    s2 = temp;
  }

  public static void main( String args[] ) {
    String s1 = "First String";
    String s2 = "Second String";
    swap(s1, s2);
    // the object references are unchanged
    System.out.println("After the swap");
    System.out.println("s1 is " + s1);
    System.out.println("s2 is " + s2);
  }
}
```

The output of this program isi

```
After the swap
s1 is First String
s2 is Second String
```

HOLDER CLASSES

There might be situations in which you want to change a reference within a method. In particular, you might want a method to create an object if an existing one is not supplied by an argument. A variable of a class, array, or interface type does not always refer to a valid object. It might instead point to nothing, which is indicated by the reserved word `null`. If you pass a `null` argument to a method, the method cannot create an object and assign it to the variable used in the method call. This is the same issue as in the string-swapping example; references are passed by value and cannot be changed.

A common solution to this limitation is to wrap the argument in what is known as a *holder class*. A holder class is declared with a single attribute of the type that the argument of your method would normally be. If you pass a non-`null` holder class instance to a method, the method can create an object of the wrapped type and assign it to the holder. This changes an attribute of the method parameter and not the reference to the parameter, so the new object can be accessed in the calling method. This approach can also be used to correct the string swapper, as shown in Listing 4.5.

LISTING 4.5 `StringSwap.java`—**A METHOD CAN CHANGE THE REFERENCES STORED BY A HOLDER CLASS**

```
public class StringSwap {

  public static void swap( StringHolder s1, StringHolder s2 ) {
    // swap two strings wrapped using a holder class
    String temp = s1.myString;
    s1.myString = s2.myString;
    s2.myString = temp;
  }

  public static void main( String args[] ) {
    StringHolder s1 = new StringHolder();
    StringHolder s2 = new StringHolder();
    s1.myString = "First String";
    s2.myString = "Second String";
    swap(s1, s2);
    // the string object references are now swapped
    System.out.println("After the swap");
    System.out.println("s1 is " + s1.myString);
    System.out.println("s2 is " + s2.myString);
  }

  static class StringHolder {
    public String myString;
  }
}
```

The output of this program is

```
After the swap
s1 is Second String
s2 is First String
```

You will become quite familiar with holder classes if you ever develop CORBA applications using Java. CORBA requires that methods be able to return references to new objects through variables in their parameter lists. Holder classes are the mechanism used to do this in Java.

EXCEPTIONS

The last part of a method signature is the list of exceptions that can be thrown during execution. Exceptions are discussed in detail later in this chapter, but a method must declare any checked exceptions that it might throw by listing them after the `throws` keyword. (Checked exceptions are also described later.) Identifying exceptions in a method declaration tells any calling method what potential problems it might need to handle.

BLOCKS AND STATEMENTS

The method body is where the work of a method is performed. This body is defined by a block of statements, which is a series of statements enclosed within curly braces {}. You can substitute a block of statements anywhere you can use a single statement.

The simplest block, `{}`, is shown in the following example:

```
public void emptyMethod() {
}
```

The next example is only slightly more complex:

```
public void simpleMethod(){
    int test;
    test = 5;
}
```

Code blocks are essential for defining the body of a method, but they can also be used in a variety of locations throughout your code. One very important aspect of a block is that it is treated lexically as one instruction. This means that you can put together large blocks of code that will be treated as one instruction line. You will see this used often in Chapter 6, “Control Flow,” where control constructs such as the `if` and `while` statements are introduced. These control directives determine whether, and how many times, a statement is executed, but the associated statement is most often a block.

There is nothing in the Java specification that prevents you from breaking your code into blocks even when they are not specifically called for, but this is seldom done. Unless separating out a segment of code adds to its readability as a unit, you should use blocks only when they are required to achieve correct execution of your code.

Tip

Although there is no limit to the number of statements included in a block, you should break your code down into relatively short methods that are each focused on a specific task. A long body typically results in a method that is difficult, if not impossible, to reuse because it is performing a sequence of tasks needed by a specific application instead of splitting the work into more manageable pieces. There is no strict guideline to follow, but if you define a method that cannot be printed on a single piece of paper, you should consider breaking some of the functionality out into smaller supporting methods.

LABELED STATEMENTS

You can assign a label to a statement as a way to reference it from other parts of a method. Any statement in Java can have a label, which consists of an identifier followed by a colon. The identifier part is like any other identifier in that its name must only contain the allowed characters, it cannot be the same as any reserved word, and it cannot be the same as any already declared local identifier. If a label has the same name as a variable, method, or type name that is available to the block that contains it, the label takes precedence within that block and hides the outside variable, method, or type. A labeled statement looks like the following:

```
myLabel: System.out.println("This is a labeled statement");
```

Labels are used only by the `break` and `continue` statements that are discussed in Chapter 6.

SCOPE

Another use of blocks is to control what is known as the *scope* of a variable. When you declare a variable within a method, it is only available for use within the code block that contains the declaration. For instance, consider the following code fragment:

```
{
   int x = 5;
}
System.out.println("x is =" + x); // This line is not valid.
```

The last line of this code is not valid. The variable `x` is created for use within the block that declares it and discarded when the end of the block is reached. The variable is no longer within scope when the `println` is attempted.

LOCAL VARIABLE INITIALIZATION

Some programming languages automatically assign an initial value, such as zero, to a variable when it is declared but not explicitly initialized. Unfortunately, some languages will also allow you to use an uninitialized variable without assigning any consistent default value to it. In this case, you might unintentionally access a garbage value attached to a variable.

In Java, local variables declared within a method are not assigned an initial value, but they cannot be used before an explicit assignment is made. As a habit, you should normally go ahead and assign an initial value to a local variable as part of its declaration. If you don't do this, and the compiler sees any possibility of a variable being referenced prior to an assignment, it will report an error.

METHODS AND THE UML SEQUENCE DIAGRAM

The UML overview in Chapter 1, "Object-Oriented Programming," introduced the practice of using sequence diagrams to depict method calls between objects, which can be thought of as message passing. Figure 4.1 shows a sequence diagram for a simplified scenario for withdrawing a sum of money from a bank account. Here, the actor in the system sends a message to the `AccountController` that then interacts with an `Account` and an `AccountTransaction` to satisfy the request.

In a formal design process, using an approach like this is precisely how the set of methods you need to implement for a class gets defined. If you know that a system must support a withdrawal operation, you can focus on the classes that will be involved and the required interaction between their instances. This allows you to discover the methods that are needed and eventually specify their exact signatures. From a design standpoint, the functionality introduced in this chapter relating to return types and parameter lists is the most important. After you move into implementation on the basis of the methods discovered in your sequence diagrams, other factors such as the access specifiers and modifiers associated with your methods become significant.

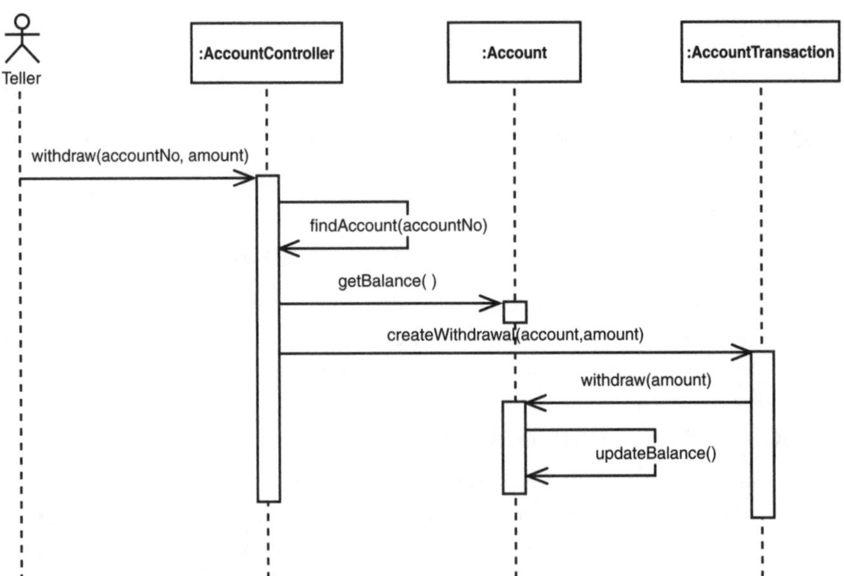

Figure 4.1
A sequence diagram depicts method calls between objects.

CATCHING AND THROWING EXCEPTIONS

When you write programs using Java, sooner or later (and probably much sooner) you're going to run into exceptions. An *exception* is a special type of object that is created when something goes wrong in a method. The rest of your program is notified about a problem when a method performs an action called throwing an exception. When an exception is thrown, it's up to your program to catch the exception and handle it.

USING `try/catch/finally`

In some of the previous chapters, you've gotten a quick look at exceptions and how they are handled in a program. An exception is thrown when a method call cannot complete successfully. You can prevent some exceptions by guarding actions that have the potential to cause an error. Examples of this are making sure you don't try to access an invalid array index or divide an integer by zero. Other potential errors are beyond your control, such as the possibility of losing a database connection or encountering an error when reading from an input stream. As an example, many common I/O operations can result in an `IOException` being thrown:

```
try {
  int c = System.in.read();
}
catch (IOException e) {
  System.out.println(e.getMessage());
}
```

The `System.in.read` method throws an `IOException` if it cannot complete correctly. As you can see in this example, you place any code that might cause an exception inside a `try` block, and the corresponding exception-handling code inside a `catch` block. Whenever an exception is thrown, Java ignores the rest of the code inside the current `try` block, if there is one, and jumps to the corresponding `catch` block, where the program handles the exception.

When a `catch` block is entered, it is passed an object of the corresponding exception type, much like a method parameter. Methods can be called on this exception object to obtain a description of the error or a stack trace that can be displayed as an aid to the user or programmer. If a `try` block executes successfully, its `catch` block is skipped.

Besides a `catch` block, a `try` block can also be followed by a `finally` block. The code you put inside a `finally` block will always be executed, no matter what happens inside the `try` block. Look at a slightly modified version of the example:

```
try {
  int c = System.in.read();
}
catch (IOException e) {
  System.out.println(e.getMessage());
}
finally {
  System.out.println("Will always execute this statement");
}
```

When this code is executed, the last `println` will always be performed, whether an exception is thrown or not. A `try` block does not have to be followed by a `finally` block, but every `try` must be followed by at least one `catch` or `finally` block.

The preceding examples focused only on IOException, but Java defines many exception objects that can be thrown by the various methods in the API. How do you know which exceptions you have to handle? In these examples, a compiler error would have resulted if the read method call had not been placed inside a try block that handles IOException (see Figure 4.2). Compiler errors are one way to determine the exception handling required within your programs.

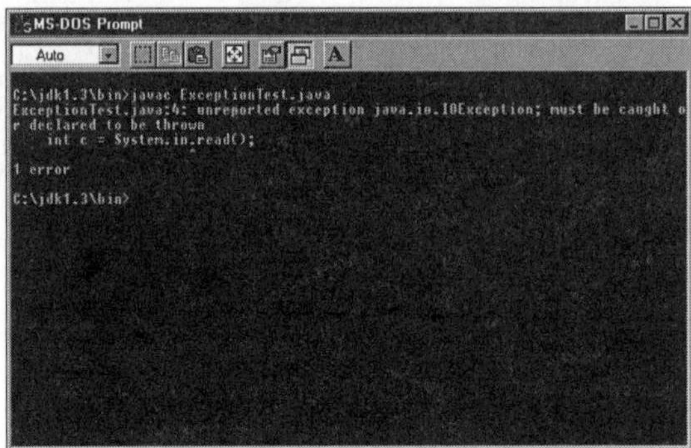

Figure 4.2
The Java compiler gives you an error message if you fail to handle an exception.

Compiler errors will always alert you when you have neglected to handle a specific exception, but you shouldn't rely solely on this passive approach. Earlier in this chapter, you saw that part of each method signature is a list of any exceptions that can be thrown by the method. This information lets you as a programmer know in advance which exceptions, if any, you must handle when you call a particular method. The documentation generated by the javadoc tool for a class also includes the possible exceptions in its description of each method. Figure 4.3 shows an example from the Java API documentation with the exceptions noted for a specific method.

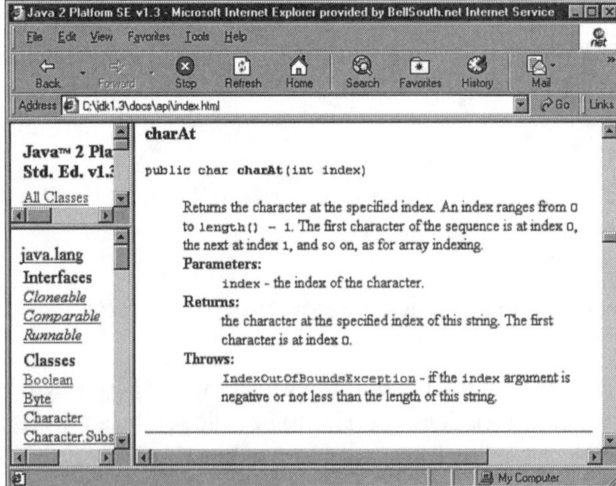

Figure 4.3
Java's API documentation lists the exception objects that can be thrown by methods in a class.

THROWING AN EXCEPTION

In the `IOException` example, a `try-catch` block was used to handle an exception right in the method where it might occur. No other method would ever know that this exception occurred because the code segment fully encapsulated the exception handling. There might be times when this behavior is not desirable. Because a method does not know how it is being used by the rest of your program, it might not have enough knowledge to respond appropriately to an exception. In some situations, it might be acceptable to log an exception and continue. In others, the same exception might be a fatal error that requires a program to exit.

If you don't know what to do with an exception, you might not want to catch it. In that case, Java enables you to pass the buck, so to speak, by throwing the exception up the method chain. The following code fragment shows one way you might do this with an `IOException`:

```
void myMethod() {
  try {
    doRead();
  }
  catch (IOException e) {
    System.out.println(e.getMessage());
  }
}

void doRead() throws IOException {
  int c = System.in.read();
}
```


The `System.in.read` method call in `doRead` might throw an `IOException`, so you could have called it within a `try-catch` block. However, the responsibility can also be passed up the chain by including `IOException` in the `throws` clause of `doRead`'s declaration. The compiler allows you to defer the handling of an exception by including it in a method declaration in this way. This does not, however, relieve you from handling the exception eventually. Notice that in this example, the exception gets handled in `myMethod`. This method could have also passed the buck and declared the exception in a `throws` clause instead of handling it.

In short, you can handle an exception in two ways:

- Write `try` and `catch` blocks right where you call a method that might generate an exception.
- Declare that a method might throw an exception that must be handled somewhere up the chain of method calls.

Note

The Java compiler requires you to provide a `catch` block or `throws` clause for the exceptions that might occur in a method, but any exceptions that you list must have the potential to occur. If you list an exception in a `catch` or `throws` clause that cannot possibly occur in the corresponding `try` block or method, the compiler will issue an error.

A COMBINED APPROACH

There might be situations in your programs where you want to both catch an exception in your code and pass it on to the calling method. Java enables you to construct your code so that different parts of a program can handle an exception as appropriate while still reporting the exception to the caller. To use this combined approach to exception handling, you include both a `try-catch` block within a method and also a `throws` clause in its declaration. This is referred to as rethrowing an exception. Listing 4.6 shows an example of this technique.

LISTING 4.6 CODE THAT HANDLES AND RETHROWS AN EXCEPTION

```
protected void myMethod() throws IOException {
  try {
    doRead();
  }
  catch (IOException e) {
    System.out.println(e.getMessage();
    throw e;
  }
}
```

Listing 4.6 demonstrates the use of the keyword `throw`. A `throw` statement allows you to generate your own occurrence of an exception. When you rethrow an exception using `throw`, you are not limited to passing the same exception object up the chain. You might also create a new exception object that can be of the same or a different exception type. For example, a method might be able to report a more specific exception that provides the caller with a better understanding of the actual problem that occurred. You'll learn how to define your own exception classes for this purpose a little later.

As you've seen in the last few examples, exception objects can do a lot of traveling. They are passed from method to method, up the chain of method calls until they are finally handled. If an exception makes its way up to the Java system, the system handles it in some default manner, usually by generating an error message and exiting.

TYPES OF EXCEPTIONS

Java defines many different exception objects. So many in fact that if you were to set up a `catch` block for every possible exception that a method call could produce, you would find yourself doing little more than writing exception handling code. The truth is you are not required to handle every exception that might occur. Java divides exceptions into two categories, referred to as *checked* and *unchecked* exceptions.

A checked exception, such as `IOException`, is an exception you must always handle or declare in the `throws` clause of your method when you make a call that can produce it. These exceptions represent problems that might occur in a perfectly correct program. Even though there might be nothing wrong with your code, your program might not be able to perform a certain I/O operation, load a required class file, or execute some other similar task at runtime. Because these errors are beyond your control, the Java compiler requires you to provide a way to handle them if they do occur. Like all exceptions, the checked exceptions are subclasses of `java.lang.Exception`.

The unchecked exceptions are subclasses of `java.lang.RuntimeException`, which is itself a subclass of `java.lang.Exception`. An unchecked exception, such as `NullPointerException` or `ClassCastException`, should never occur in a correct program. For this reason, you are not required to handle or declare an unchecked exception in a method's `throws` clause. You might choose to handle them anyway, but this is not typical.

Table 4.1 and 4.2 list some common exceptions that you should become familiar with as you gain experience programming with exceptions. Table 4.1 contains checked exceptions and Table 4.2 provides some examples of unchecked exceptions.

TABLE 4.1 COMMON JAVA CHECKED EXCEPTIONS

Exception	Caused By
`AWTException`	An error in an AWT user interface method
`ClassNotFoundException`	An attempt to load a class file that cannot be located by the class loader
`FileNotFoundException`	An attempt to access a nonexistent file
`IOException`	General I/O failures, such as inability to read from a file
`ParseException`	Inability to parse a string, such as when trying to convert a string into a date object
`SQLException`	A database access error

TABLE 4.2 COMMON JAVA UNCHECKED EXCEPTIONS

Exception	Caused By
`ArithmeticException`	Math errors, such as division by zero
`ArrayIndexOutOfBoundsException`	Bad array indexes
`ArrayStoreException`	A program trying to store the wrong type of data in an array
`NullPointerException`	Referencing a null object
`NumberFormatException`	A failed conversion between strings and numbers
`SecurityException`	A security violation detected by the security manager, such as an attempt by an applet to perform an action not allowed by the browser's security setting
`StringIndexOutOfBoundsException`	A program attempting to access a nonexistent character position in a string

The `Exception` superclass for all Java exceptions is a subclass of `java.lang.Throwable`. The `Throwable` class defines three useful methods that you can call to get information about an exception:

- **`getMessage()`**—Returns a string that describes the exception that occurred.
- **`toString()`**—Returns a string made up of the specific exception class name and the error message.
- **`printStackTrace()`**—Displays the sequence of method calls that led to the exception to the standard error stream.

Listing 4.7 shows a `catch` clause that calls these various methods and Figure 4.4 shows the corresponding output.

LISTING 4.7 `ExceptionOutput.java`—CALLING METHODS ON A `Throwable` SUBCLASS

```
public class ExceptionOutput {

  public static void main( String args[] ) {
    try {
      int testInt = Integer.parseInt("abc");
    }
    catch ( NumberFormatException e ) {
      System.out.println();
      System.out.println("Output of getMessage():");
      System.out.println("--------------");
      System.out.println( e.getMessage() );
      System.out.println();
      System.out.println("Output of toString():");
      System.out.println("-------------");
      System.out.println( e.toString() );
      System.out.println();
      System.out.println("Here's the stack trace:");
      System.out.println("-----------");
      e.printStackTrace();
    }
  }
}
```

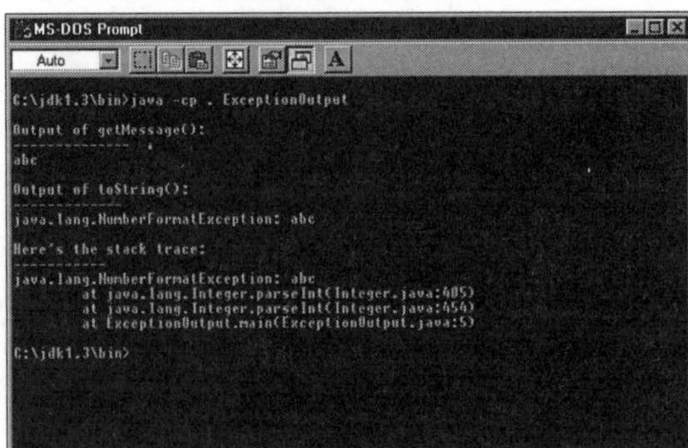

Figure 4.4
Here's the output generated by the catch block in Listing 4.7.

HANDLING MULTIPLE EXCEPTIONS

In the previous examples, each try block was followed by a single catch block that handled a specific exception class. You actually have more flexibility when defining catch blocks. First, you can take advantage of the class hierarchy formed by exception classes to handle exceptions in either very specific or general terms. Remember that all exceptions are subclasses of java.lang.Exception. Beneath this class, there are many other inheritance relationships between exceptions. When you define a catch clause, you can specify the name of a specific exception type or any of its parent classes. As an example, the following two code segments are equivalent:

```
try {
  int c = System.in.read();
}
catch ( java.io.IOException e ) {
  e.printStackTrace();
}

try {
  int c = System.in.read();
}
catch ( java.lang.Exception e ) {
  e.printStackTrace();
}
```


Although, these blocks behave in the same way, the former version that uses IOException provides a clearer picture of what is happening in the code and is normally the preferred approach. The use of a parent exception class such as Exception is useful when multiple exception types can occur in a try block and the response to any of them is the same.

Besides using parent exception classes in catch clauses, you also have the option to define more than one catch block for a single try block. This allows you to handle more than one exception type without using a common parent exception and thus giving up the clarity obtained by identifying the specific exceptions. When you define more than one catch block, you are even allowed to have overlapping exception types (for example, IOException and Exception). In this case, an exception is handled by the most specific catch that matches it. With this, you have the option to handle a few exceptions in a specific way while providing a catch all response for others. When you do this, the order of the catch blocks does matter. You must always define specific catch blocks before more general ones.

Caution

Although handling exceptions is a powerful tool for creating reliable and robust programs, you should only use them in situations in which you have little control over the cause of the exception, such as when dealing with user input or an external system. A try block itself adds little overhead to your code, but the act of throwing an exception is relatively slow. As a general rule, you should never implement a method that generates an exception as a normal part of its execution. Exceptions should not be viewed as a flow control mechanism. There are, however, a few special uses of exceptions related to threads that are discussed later in Chapter 11.

CREATING YOUR OWN EXCEPTION CLASSES

Although Java provides exception classes for just about every general error you can imagine, the designers of the language could not possibly know what type of code you are going to write and what kinds of errors that code might experience. You should extend the standard exception classes whenever you need to report and handle a problem not addressed by an existing exception type. For example, you might write a method that sums two numbers within a specific range. If the user enters a value outside the selected range, your program could throw a custom exception called something like `NumberRangeException`.

To create and throw your own custom exceptions, you must first define a class for the exception. Usually, you derive this class from Java's `Exception` class. Listing 4.8 shows how you might define the aforementioned `NumberRangeException` class.

LISTING 4.8 `NumberRangeException.java`—**THE** `NumberRangeException` **CLASS**

```
public class NumberRangeException extends Exception {

  public NumberRangeException( String msg ) {
     super(msg);
  }

}
```

As you can see, defining a new exception requires little work. You'll learn about the details of class constructors in Chapter 7, but for now, note that a *constructor* is a special initialization method that has the same name as its class. You can create a new exception by creating a constructor for the class that accepts an error message string as a parameter. This error message should then be passed on to the parent exception class constructor using the `super` keyword.

After you define your own exception class, whenever you determine that your custom exception condition has occurred, you can create and throw an object of your exception class using a statement like the following:

```
throw new NumberRangeException("An out of range value was specified");
```

EXCEPTIONS VERSUS RETURN VALUES

If you normally program in languages that do not support the concept of exceptions, you are probably accustomed to using method return values to indicate the occurrence of an error in a method. As you are likely aware, this approach has many drawbacks. Chief among these is that there is no way to force a method caller to check the return value for an error after a call is completed. Such a scheme also leads to an assortment of error code values that must be carefully maintained so that a consistent interpretation of errors is possible. Although some programmers might view exception handling as costly from a performance standpoint, the advantages in maintainability and robustness of code built around solid exception handling cannot be underestimated. The performance impact is minor compared to the benefits of such a framework.

JAVA'S ERROR CLASSES

So far, you've had a look at the exception classes you can handle in your own programs. Java also defines a set of error classes that are really little more than special types of exceptions. These error classes are subclasses of `Error`, which, like `Exception`, is a subclass of `Throwable`.

Java's error classes represent serious errors, such as running out of memory or encountering an internal error in the virtual machine. Just as with unchecked exceptions, you are not required to handle the errors that might be thrown by a method. The rationale is quite different in this case however. Remember that unchecked exceptions should never occur in a correctly written program. Errors represented by the `Error` subclasses, however, might very well occur in a correct program, but they are so severe that there is no assumption by the compiler that you can handle them. After all, if you totally run out of memory or overflow the stack, it's likely too late to do anything about it.

Table 4.3 gives some examples of the error classes. All but `AWTError` are defined in `java.lang`.

TABLE 4.3 EXAMPLES OF THE JAVA ERROR CLASSES

Exception	**Caused By**
`AbstractMethodError`	Attempting to call an abstract method
`AWTError`	A problem in an AWT user interface method
`ClassFormatError`	An attempt to load a class file that is malformed
`InstantiationError`	An attempt to instantiate an abstract class or an interface
`InternalError`	A problem in the virtual machine
`NoClassDefFoundError`	An inability to locate and load a class file that was present when the class that depends on it was compiled
`OutOfMemoryError`	Having insufficient memory to create an object
`StackOverflowError`	Recursion so deep that it overflows the stack
`VirtualMachineError`	A flaw in the virtual machine or its inability to allocate the resources it needs to operate

TROUBLESHOOTING

REFERENCING `this` FROM A STATIC CONTEXT

I get a compiler error that says I'm attempting to reference `this` *from a static context.*

This compiler error results from an attempt to access an instance field or method from a `static` method. This commonly occurs when you try to reference instance members within the `main` method. Make sure you declare all fields and methods `static` that should be, and then use a class instance to access any others from `static` methods.

Abstract Methods Cannot Have a Body

I get a compiler error that says I have an abstract method with a body.

You cannot declare a body for a method, and this includes an empty body, `{}`. When you declare an `abstract` method, make sure you replace the curly braces for the body with a semicolon.

Returning a New Object Using a Method Parameter

I passed an object reference to a method and assigned a new or different object to it in the method, but the calling method does not see the change.

Object references are passed by value to a method, which means you cannot change a parameter reference within methods. To create a new object or reassign a reference within a method, you need to return the new object as the method's return value, or pass the object into the method using a holder class.

Field Shadowing

I changed the value of a field but the change won't hold.

The Java compiler allows you to shadow identifiers based on variable scoping. Make sure that you are not reusing a field identifier as a parameter or local variable name in a method without using the `this` specifier each time the field name is referenced.

Local Variable Initialization

I get a compiler error that says a local variable might not have been initialized.

Unlike fields, local variables are not assigned a default initial value if you do not explicitly initialize them as part of their declaration. The compiler complains if it cannot guarantee that a local variable is assigned a value before it is accessed. Assign an initial value in the declaration to avoid this error completely.

Exception Must Be Caught or Thrown

I get a compiler error that says a specific exception must be caught or thrown by my method.

When you call a method that is declared to throw a checked exception, you must place the method call inside a `try-catch` block that catches the exception (or one of its superclasses), or declare it in the `throws` clause of your method declaration.

No Error Information When a Problem Occurs

My program is not working correctly, but I'm not getting any exception messages.

Make sure that whenever you catch an exception that you do something with it. An empty `catch` body satisfies the compiler that a checked exception is being handled, but it is often a cause of difficulty in debugging a program. Make sure that in every `catch` block, your implementation at least writes out the associated error message or the stack trace so that you can quickly track down any exceptions that occur.

CHAPTER 5

Using Expressions

In this chapter

by Brian Keeton

WHAT IS AN EXPRESSION?

Expressions—combinations of operators and operands—are one of the key building blocks of the Java language, as they are of most any programming language. Expressions allow you to perform arithmetic calculations, compare values, perform logical operations, and manipulate objects. Without expressions, a programming language would be of little use to you.

You've already seen some expressions, mostly fairly simple ones, in other chapters in this book. Chapter 3, "Data Types and Other Tokens," showed you that the operators used in expressions form one of the main classifications of Java tokens, along with others such as keywords, comments, and so on. In this chapter, you get a closer look at how you can use operators to build expressions—in other words, how to put operators to work for you.

You can define what an expression is in technical terms, but at its simplest, an expression is a sequence of one or more operands and operators that are evaluated by the Java interpreter when your code is executed, or by the compiler if the result can be computed in advance. An expression might be used simply to state the value of a variable or a literal without the use of any operators. However, expressions are more interesting when they contain operators that manipulate variables and do work for you. Table 5.1 shows several legal Java expressions.

TABLE 5.1 EXAMPLES OF JAVA EXPRESSIONS

Name of Expression	Example
Primary expression	`x`
Additive expression	`x + 5`
Assignment expression	`x = 5`
Array indexing	`sizes[11]`
Method invocation	`triangle.rotateLeft(50)`

HOW EXPRESSIONS ARE EVALUATED

When an expression is simple, like those shown in Table 5.1, figuring out its evaluated result is easy. When expressions become more complex and multiple operators are used, following what they do gets a little more complicated.

The examples of expressions in Chapter 3 showed you that expressions are just combinations of operators and operands. And although that definition is true, it's not always very helpful. Sometimes you need to create and use complex expressions—maybe to perform a complicated calculation or some other involved manipulation of multiple variables. To do this, you need a deeper understanding of how Java expressions are created and evaluated. In this section, you look at three major tools that will help you in your work with Java expressions: operator associativity, operator precedence, and order of evaluation.

Operator Associativity

The easiest of the expression rules is associativity. All the arithmetic operators are said to associate left to right. This means that if the same operator appears more than once in an expression—such as the plus sign in `a+b+c`—then the leftmost occurrence is evaluated first, followed by the one to its right, and so on. Consider the following assignment statement:

```
x = a+b+c;
```

In this example, the value of the expression on the right of the `=` operator is calculated and assigned to the variable `x` on the left. In calculating the value on the right, the fact that the `+` operator associates left to right means that the value of `a+b` is calculated first, and the result is then added to `c`. The result of that second calculation is assigned to `x`. So if you were to write it using explicit parentheses, the line would read:

```
x=((a+b)+c);
```

The concept of associativity holds true for the other arithmetic operators in the same way. You would use the associativity rule in evaluating the right sides of each of the following assignment statements:

```
volume = length * width * height;

orderTotal = subTotal + freight + tax;

subTotal = orderTotal - freight - tax;

perOrderPerUnit = purchase / orders / units;
```

You probably remember from your early math classes that multiplication and addition are associative operations. This means that the order of the two operands used with either of these operators can be switched without affecting the result of an expression. Simply put, `a+b` is the same as `b+a` and `c*d` is the same as `d*c`. Subtraction and division are not associative however. Clearly, `a-b` and `c/d` are not the same as `b-a` and `d/c`. With this in mind, expressions that use subtraction and division rely on a correct ordering of operands to produce a correct result. Using the example for `perOrderPerUnit`, this expression would be evaluated as


```
(purchase / orders) / units
```

If the intent, however, is to get the result of

```
purchase / (orders / units)
```

the expression must be written as

```
purchase / orders * units
```

or parentheses must be added to control the order of evaluation. As with other languages, operations inside parentheses in Java are evaluated prior to being used within a surrounding expression.

Note

Unlike the arithmetic operators, the unary and assignment operators associate right to left. This means that it is possible to chain assignment statements such as `a=b=c` where values are successively assigned to the operand to the left of the rightmost `=` operator.

OPERATOR PRECEDENCE

When you have an expression that involves more than one type of operator, the associativity rule isn't enough to determine the order of evaluation. Now the precedence, or relative priority, of operators must be considered also.

Precedence determines which operator acts first in an expression. If you wanted to evaluate `A+B*C`, by standard mathematics you would first multiply `B` and `C` and then add the result to `A`. Operator precedence accomplishes the same thing in your programs. The multiplicative operators (*, /, and %) have higher precedence than the additive operators (+ and –). So, in a compound expression that incorporates both multiplicative and additive operators, the multiplicative operators are evaluated first.

Consider the following assignment statement, which is intended to convert a Fahrenheit temperature to Celsius:

```
Celsius = Fahrenheit - 32 * 5 / 9;
```

To correctly convert between these two scales, you take a temperature measured in degrees Fahrenheit, subtract 32 from it, multiply the result by 5, and divide that result by 9. However, because the * and / operators have higher precedence than the – operator, the subexpression 32*5/9 would be evaluated first (yielding the result 17) in the preceding equation. That value would then be subtracted from the Fahrenheit variable giving an incorrect result.

The solution to problems like this is a simple one. As in the case of associativity, you can use parentheses to control the order of evaluation of operators in an expression. To perform the correct conversion for the preceding example, you would write the equation as:

```
Celsius = ( Fahrenheit - 32 ) * 5 / 9;
```

Interestingly, there are some computer languages that do not use rules of precedence. Some languages, such as APL for example, use a straight left-to-right or right-to-left order of evaluation, regardless of the operators involved.

Use of parentheses also helps the following examples be evaluated correctly:

```
newAmount = (savings + cash) * exchangeRate;
```

```
totalConsumption = (distance2 - distance1) * consumptionRate;
```

Although the multiplicative operators have high precedence, the unary operators, which are those that act on a single operand, take precedence over even them. In the following example, you multiply the value –5 times the value of `height` instead of multiplying 5 times `height` and negating the result (although the results are the same in this case):

```
offset = -5 * height;
```

Table 5.2 is what is known as the precedence table. The operators with the highest precedence are at the top. Operators on the same line are of equal precedence.

The majority of these operators associate left to right. The exceptions to this rule are the unary operators, assignment operators, and the conditional operator. For any single operator, operand evaluation is strictly left to right, and all operands are evaluated before operations are performed. The implications of this are explained in the next section.

Table 5.2 The Java Operator Precedence Table

Description	Operators
Postfix Operators	. [] () expr++ expr--
Prefix Unary Operators	+ - ~ ! ++expr --expr
Creation or Cast	new (type)expr
Multiplicative	* / %
Additive	+ -
Shift	<< >> >>>
Relational	< <= >= > > instanceof
Equality	== !=
Bitwise AND	&
Bitwise XOR	^
Bitwise OR	|
Conditional-AND	&&
Conditional-OR	||
Conditional	?:
Assignment	= operator=

Order of Evaluation

Many people, when they first learn a language, confuse the issue of operator precedence with order of evaluation. The two are actually quite different. The precedence rules help you determine which operators act first in an expression. This effectively determines what the operands are for a specific operator. For example, in the following line of code, the operands of the * operator are `a` and `(b+c)`:

```
d = a * (b+c);
```

The order-of-evaluation rules, on the other hand, help you to determine not when *operators* are evaluated, but when *operands* are evaluated. Now, with a simple operand such as `a`, the concept of evaluating an operand doesn't seem to mean much. In this case, the operand evaluates to the value of the variable `a`. The operand `(b+c)` is more interesting, but still simple. First, `b` and `c` are operands of the `+` operator, so they must be evaluated to their corresponding values. These values are then added to produce the evaluated result of `(b+c)`. At this point, with the values of both operands known, the * operator can be invoked.

Here are three rules (in no particular order) that should help you remember how an expression is evaluated:

- For any binary operator (one with two operands), the left operand is evaluated before the right operand. In the preceding example, a is evaluated before `(b+c)`.
- Operands are always evaluated fully before the operator is evaluated. Again, a and `(b+c)` are evaluated before any multiplication takes place.
- If a number of arguments are supplied in a method call separated by commas, the arguments are evaluated strictly left to right.

The following shows how this works with something more complicated. This isn't an example of good, or even acceptable programming style, but see if you can correctly evaluate the results of the following code segment.

```
int[] x = {0,0,0};
int y = 1;
int z = 3;

x[y++] = y = z * --y;
```

This might look more like a compiler error to you than a useful example, but the rules already covered here enable you to work this out. After this code is executed, both `y` and `x[1]` are equal to 3 (the other elements of `x` are still 0).

The way to approach a statement like this is to divide and conquer. Without any parentheses present, first determine what the operands are for each operator. Given that unary operators take precedence over multiplication, and multiplication takes precedence over assignment, this determination is actually straightforward. The operands of the * operator are `z` and `--y`. Assignment is performed from right to left, so the second = operator is assigning `z * --y` to the variable `y`. The first = operator is then assigning this value of `y` to `x[y++]`. The equation could then be viewed as

```
x[y++] = (y = (z * (--y)))
```

Now it gets tricky. The important point to remember here is that although operators in an expression act according to precedence, the individual operands are evaluated from left to right. This matters most in a case like this where operands that produce side effects (++ and --) are present. So, with this rule in mind, the first step is to evaluate `x[y++]`. Because a post-decrement is being used, this operand evaluates to `x[1]` and then has the side effect of incrementing `y` to 2 afterward. The operand `y` (to the left of the second = operator) evaluates to the variable `y`. That leaves you with `(z * (--y))`. The operator precedence has already been represented by adding the parentheses, so the first step is to decrement `y`. This occurs before the operand is evaluated this time because it's a pre-decrement. Because `y` was already incremented to 2, this takes it back down to 1. The `z * --y` operand is then fully evaluated as 3 * 1 or 3. The assignment operations are then performed, so `y` is assigned this value of 3 and `x[1]` is assigned this new value of `y`.

Go through this example until each step makes sense to you. Acquiring a solid understanding of these rules early on will reduce your chances of being surprised by an unexpected evaluation of a statement deep within your code someday. If nothing else, you will gain an appreciation for programmers who use parentheses to make their expressions clear.

OF SPECIAL INTEREST TO C PROGRAMMERS

Because Java is an evolutionary outgrowth of C and C++, the expression syntax for the three languages is similar in many ways. If you have programmed in either of the other two languages, you've no doubt seen functionality in Java by now that is identical to what you've used before. You have also seen cases where Java has added functionality not found elsewhere. It is also likely that you've noticed some of the cases where Java has intentionally taken away functionality because it proved itself to be troublesome or error-prone elsewhere. It takes time to get used to these additions and deletions, but at least deletions are easy to keep track of because the compiler will quickly let you know when you try to use a feature that doesn't exist. Learning the new features added by Java is part of what you're doing right now, so that will come with time. The hardest part is the case that's left. You will often use syntax in Java that looks the same as that of another language but does not function in the same way. This is where an attention to detail and a good knowledge of Java fundamentals are key.

One difference to consider is that order of evaluation is guaranteed in Java, and is generally undefined or implementation-specific in C. There are also differences in how operators can be applied. In Java, the remainder (%), increment (++), and decrement (--) operators are defined for all primitive data types (except `boolean`); in C, they are defined only for integers.

There is also a slight difference related to how you might be accustomed to using expressions. It isn't necessary for the result of an expression in C/C++ to be used. For example,

```
x + y;
```

is a perfectly valid C++ statement, assuming `x` and `y` have been declared. This syntax is used when the side effects introduced by the evaluation of the operands are useful, but the value of the overall expression is not. This is a compiler error in Java; the result of an expression like this must be used as part of an assignment statement or as a method parameter.

You have already seen that Java's strong typing is employed heavily for the `boolean` type. Relational and equality operators in Java produce a `boolean` result; in C, they produce results of type `int`. Furthermore, the logical operators in Java are restricted to only work with `boolean` operands.

In C, using the right-shift operator (>>) on a signed quantity results in implementation-specific behavior. As discussed in the next section, Java avoids this confusion by using two different right-shift operators: one that preserves the sign bit and another that treats it like any other bit.

BITWISE OPERATORS

Depending on the types of programs you write, the bitwise operators are either very important or completely unimportant to you. If you write typical business applications, you will find little need to employ these operators. However, if you develop engineering applications that interface with hardware systems or binary files, the opposite is likely true. When you need a bitwise operator, it is rarely the case that you can substitute any other operation to easily reproduce the same results. However, most of the work you do probably won't put you in this position in the first place.

Bitwise operators work at the fundamental level of how values are stored in a computer. This is probably remedial, but, for completeness, it should be covered here. Computers store everything using values stored as sequences of on and off, known as bits, which are most often translated to the binary digits 1 and 0. For example, 32 of these 1s and 0s are required to store a variable of type `int`. Most of the time, you will manage the value held by an `int` variable using assignment statements and the various unary and arithmetic operators. Bitwise operators give you the additional option of manipulating the bits used to store a variable directly.

Consider a simple example using bytes. A byte comprises 8 bits of memory. Each of the 8 bits can have the value of 0 or 1, and the value of the whole quantity is determined by using base-2 arithmetic, meaning that the rightmost bit represents a value of 0 or 1; the next bit represents the value of 0 or 2; the next represents the value 0 or 4; and so on. The overall value represented by a sequence of bits is just the sum of these individual values. Table 5.3 shows the binary representation of several numbers as an example.

TABLE 5.3 SOME BASE-10 VALUES AND THEIR BASE-2 EQUIVALENTS

Base-10 Value	128 (2^7)	64 (2^6)	32 (2^5)	16 (2^4)	8 (2^3)	4 (2^2)	2 (2^1)	1 (2^0)
17	0	0	0	1	0	0	0	1
63	0	0	1	1	1	1	1	1
75	0	1	0	0	1	0	1	1
131	1	0	0	0	0	0	1	1

To find the base-10, or decimal, value of a number in Table 5.3, you add the numbers at the top of each column that contains a 1 for a given row. These columns represent the bits that are set in the number's base-2, or binary, representation. For instance, the first row shows that the binary number 00010001 is equivalent to

```
16+1 = 17
```

Twos-Complement

The numeric quantities in Table 5.3 are all positive integers, and that is intentional. Negative numbers are a little more difficult to represent. For any integer quantity in Java, except a `char`, the leftmost bit is reserved for the sign bit. If the sign bit is 1, the value is negative. The rest of the bits in a negative number are also interpreted a little differently using what is known as twos-complement. When using twos-complement, a negative number is represented by inverting each bit of the binary representation of the number's magnitude and adding 1. You can see this illustrated in these examples of binary representations:

```
 1 = 0...0001
-1 = 1...1111
 2 = 0...0010
-2 = 1...1110
```

The addition of 1 to the inverted bit sequence might sound arbitrary, but it is significant because it avoids having two representations for zero. Without this adjustment, both all 0s and all 1s would be interpreted as zero (positive zero and negative zero, strictly speaking). Instead, all 0s represents zero and all 1s represents –1 in twos-complement.

Now that you've seen examples of bit representations, the results of applying the bitwise operators are more intuitive. The bitwise operators perform the logical operations of AND, OR, Exclusive OR (sometimes called XOR), and Complement (or NOT) on each bit in turn. The operators are

- Bitwise AND: &
- Bitwise OR: |
- Bitwise Exclusive OR: ^
- Bitwise Complement: ~

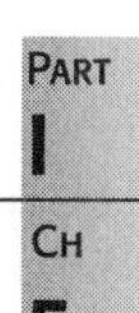

The &, |, and ^ operators are binary operators and ~ is a unary operator. To determine the result of applying a bitwise operator, it is necessary to view each of the operands in its base-2 representation (a sequence of 1s and 0s). For each bit position in the operands, a bitwise operator sets the corresponding bit in the result based on what is known as the operator's truth table. Each of the operators has a different truth table as shown in the following:

First Value (a)	Second Value (b)	Result (a & b)
0	0	0
0	1	0
1	0	0
1	1	1

First Value (a)	Second Value (b)	Result (a | b)
0	0	0
0	1	1

<table>
<tr><th>First Value (a)</th><th>Second Value (b)</th><th>Result (a | b)</th></tr>
<tr><td>1</td><td>0</td><td>1</td></tr>
<tr><td>1</td><td>1</td><td>1</td></tr>
</table>

First Value (a)	Second Value (b)	Result (a ^ b)
0	0	0
0	1	1
1	0	1
1	1	0

Value (a)	Result (~a)
0	1
1	0

The operands of the bitwise operators can be any integer type. Booleans can also be operands to each of the bitwise operators with the exception of the complement operator. When you apply &, |, or ^ to two booleans, the result is the same as that given in the preceding truth table if you substitute a value of true for each 1 and false for each 0.

If integer operands are used, each operand is promoted to at least an `int` and the result is an `int`. If one operand is a `long`, the other is promoted to a `long` if necessary, and the result is returned as a `long`. These rules are true for any of the operators applied to integers. If a `boolean` operand is used, both operands must be `boolean` and the result is a `boolean`.

Table 5.4 shows the results of applying each of the bitwise operators to two arbitrary values. First, you see the binary representations of the two decimal numbers 11309 and 798, and then the resulting bit sequences after the various operators are applied.

TABLE 5.4 BITWISE OPERATION EXAMPLES

<table>
<tr><th>Expression</th><th>Binary Representation</th></tr>
<tr><td>11309</td><td>0010 1100 0010 1101</td></tr>
<tr><td>798</td><td>0000 0011 0001 1110</td></tr>
<tr><td>11309 & 798</td><td>0000 0000 0000 1100</td></tr>
<tr><td>11309 | 798</td><td>0010 1111 0011 1111</td></tr>
<tr><td>11309 ^ 798</td><td>0010 1111 0011 0011</td></tr>
<tr><td>~798</td><td>1111 1100 1110 0001</td></tr>
</table>

Similar to the arithmetic assignment operators, the bitwise operators are also supported as shorthand assignment operators. You can use &=, |=, or ^= to perform a bitwise operation and assign the result back to the left operand.

SHIFT OPERATORS

There are three shift operators in Java:

- Left Shift: <<
- Signed Right Shift: >>
- Unsigned Right Shift: >>>

The shift operators move (shift) all the bits in a number to the left or the right. The left operand is the value to be shifted and the right operand specifies the number of bit positions to shift. You can apply these operators to any integer type, but both operands are promoted to at least an `int`. In fact, you should limit your use of the shift operators to variables of type `int` or `long` to avoid any bit truncation effects resulting from promotions of intermediate values in your expressions.

Note

> The right operand of a shift operator can be any integer value, but this can be misleading. Any shift value larger than the number of bits allocated to the result of the operation is moduloed down by this same number of bits. For example, requesting a shift of an `int` (32-bit operand will yield a 32-bit result) by 33 bits is the same as requesting a shift of 1 bit (33 % 32 = 1). Similarly, any request to shift a `long` by more than 64 bits will be moduloed down by 64. This results from the use of only the 5 (for an `int`) or 6 (for a `long`) lowest order bits of the right operand of a shift operator.

LEFT SHIFT

The << operator shifts the left operand to the left by the number of bits given by the right operand. For example, consider the expression:

```
17 << 2
```

Remember that integer literals are interpreted as type `int`, so the value 17 is treated as a 32-bit number. However, the upper 24 bits of 17 are all 0s, so only consider the lower 8 bits:

```
00010001
```

The << operator inserts 0s into the lower bits as it shifts and drops the same number of upper bits (all 0s here). This is equivalent to multiplying the left operand by 2^n where n is the right operand. Shifting the value by 2 yields

```
01000100
```

which is the decimal value 68 ($17 * 2^2 = 68$).

Caution

The twos-complement representation used for negative numbers makes it possible for the left shift operator to change positive numbers into negative and vice versa when dealing with large left operands or shift values. For example, left shifting –17 by 27 bits produces a positive number.

SIGNED RIGHT SHIFT

The >> operator shifts the left operand to the right by the number of bits given by the right operand. In this case, it is the lower bits that are lost as a value is shifted. This operator differs from that found in C/C++ in how the upper bits are treated. The signed right shift operator applies *sign extension*, meaning that the upper bits that are inserted as a value is shifted are either all 0s or all 1s. The bit value inserted is the same as the uppermost bit of the left operand. Remember that in twos-complement, a 1 in the uppermost bit signifies a negative number. The result is that applying >> always produces a value that has the same sign as the original value.

UNSIGNED RIGHT SHIFT

Although the integer types in Java are signed, the >>> operator allows you to shift values as if they were unsigned. This operator behaves identically to the C/C++ right shift operator and ignores the fact that the uppermost bit is a sign bit. When a value is shifted, the lower bits are lost and 0s are inserted into the upper bits.

The following table shows two 8-bit quantities, 31 and –17, and the results of applying each of the three shift operators to them:

Quantity	x	x<<2	x>>2	x>>>2
31	00011111	01111100	00000111	00000111
–17	11101111	10111100	11111011	00111011

Note

The shift operators, just like the bitwise operators, support shorthand assignment. You can use <<=, >>=, or >>>= to perform a shift operation and assign the result back to the left operand. You should never use the >>>= operator with a `byte` or `short` because it will promote the operand to an `int` and then assign a truncated result back into the original operand.

TYPE CONVERSIONS

A critical part of understanding data types in a programming language is knowing how expressions that contain different types are evaluated. For example, how does the language handle situations where a `float` is assigned to a `double` or a `byte` is added to an `int`? Java is a strongly typed language, so issues like this are resolved at compile time. Extensive type checking is performed (to help detect programmer errors) and strict restrictions are imposed on which values can be converted from one type to another.

There are really two different kinds of conversions:

- Implicit conversions occur any time a value is of a different type than that required in an expression and the compiler can safely convert it to what is required. This happens without any intervention on your part.
- Explicit conversions occur when you deliberately change the data type of a value. This is called *casting*.

Note

In C, almost any data type can be converted to almost any other across an assignment statement. This is not the case in Java, and implicit conversions between numeric data types are only performed if they do not result in loss of precision or magnitude. Any attempted conversion that would result in such a loss produces a compiler error, unless you use an explicit cast.

IMPLICIT CONVERSIONS

Java performs a number of implicit type conversions when evaluating expressions that contain primitives. The rules for these conversions are highly restrictive, which actually makes them simpler to understand than those in C or even C++. The fundamental rule for implicit conversions is that they must be *widening* conversions as opposed to *narrowing* ones. This means that an implicit conversion can only convert a primitive type to one with a larger bit representation. For example, implicit conversions include `byte` to `int`, `int` to `long`, and `float` to `double`. A notable exception is that `char` cannot be converted to `short`. Both types are 16-bit, but remember that the integer equivalent for a `char` is treated as an unsigned value, so it can only be converted to a 32-bit or greater representation.

Implicit conversions for unary operators (such as ++ or --) are simple: Operands of type `byte`, `short`, or `char` are converted to `int`, and all others are left alone.

For binary operators, the situation is only slightly more complex. For operations involving only integer operands, if either of the operands is `long`, the other is converted to `long`; otherwise, both operands are converted to `int`. The result of the expression is an `int` unless its magnitude requires a `long` for storage. For operations involving at least one floating-point operand, if either of the operands is `double`, the other is also converted to `double` and the result of the expression is a `double`; otherwise, both operands are converted to `float`, and the result of the expression is also a `float`. Consider the expressions in Listing 5.1.

LISTING 5.1 EXPRESSIONS SHOWING IMPLICIT TYPE CONVERSIONS

```
short width;
long length, area;
double totalCost, costPerFoot;
```

LISTING 5.1 CONTINUED

```
// In the multiplication below, width will be converted to a
// long, and the result of the calculation will be a long.
area = length * width;

// In the division below, area will be converted to a double,
// and the result of the calculation will be a double.
costPerFoot = totalCost / area;
```

In addition to expressions, implicit conversions might also take place as part of method calls. This happens when a parameter is not of the same type specified in the method signature. Again, all widening conversions of primitive types are supported implicitly.

Implicit conversions safely take place at compile time without any effort on your part. If the compiler cannot perform an implicit conversion, you will get a compiler error that you can usually address with an explicit conversion.

EXPLICIT CONVERSIONS USING THE CAST OPERATOR

Sometimes an implicit conversion might not be supported within an expression you need to evaluate, or you might need to force a type conversion for a specific need. Here you need to perform an explicit conversion using the cast operator. It is sometimes even helpful from a maintenance standpoint to use a cast where an implicit conversion would be performed anyway just to make the intent of the code more obvious.

The cast operator doesn't look like other operators, but it can be described in the same way. It is a unary operator that comes before its operand and consists of a type name inside parentheses. Casting an operand is an operation with high precedence that produces a variable of the type specified by the cast. This variable has the value of the original operand. The following example shows an example of a cast:

```
float x = 2.0;
float y = 1.7;
x = ( (int)(x/y) * y);
```

When `x` is divided by `y` in this example, the type of the result is a floating-point number. However, the value of `x/y` is explicitly converted to type `int` by the cast operator, resulting in a 1, not 1.2. So, the end result of this equation is that `x` equals 1.7. It wasn't an issue in this example, but truncation is always used instead of rounding when you cast a floating-point value to an integer. Also, note that you can cast a literal value in the same way a variable was cast in this example.

Unlike implicit conversions, narrowing conversions are allowed in addition to widening ones when casting. Narrowing conversions result in a loss of bits, so you should use them with caution. Narrowing conversions between integer types will lose data if the upper bits of a value are nonzero. Also, casting an integer to a `float` or `double` might also lose precision just as casting a `double` to a `float` likely will.

Explicit conversions are generally allowed between any primitives, but the compiler will reject some casts as illegal. In particular, you cannot cast a `boolean` to any other type or cast any other type to a `boolean`.

The cast operator applies to classes (see Chapter 7, "Classes") and interfaces (see Chapter 9, "Interfaces") in addition to primitives. An object can be cast to a superclass or any interface that it implements. An interface can be cast to any other interface that it extends.

→ **See** "Casting and Converting Reference Types," **p. 164**
→ **See** "Referencing Interfaces," **p. 210**

Note

Because casting involves an unconditional type conversion (if the conversion is legal), it is also sometimes known as *type coercion*.

CHARACTER CONVERSIONS

Characters can be implicitly converted to `int`, `long`, `float`, or `double`, or be cast to any primitive type other than `boolean`. However, casting a `char` to a type smaller than `int` might cause a loss of data.

Note

If you are using the Han character set (Chinese, Japanese, or Korean), you can lose data by casting a `char` into a `short`. Although both are 16-bit types, the upper bit of a `short` is reserved for the sign bit.

SPECIAL OPERATOR SUPPORT FOR STRINGS

Before leaving the subject of operators, it is important to cover a special use of the addition operator as it relates to the `String` class discussed later in Chapter 8, "Using Strings and Text."

In general, Java, unlike C++, does not support operator overloading. There is one exception, however. Java does allow the concatenation of `String` objects using the + and += operators. The behavior of these operators with `String` objects is just what you would expect if you are familiar with C++. The `String` operands are concatenated to produce a new `String` that contains the values of both. In the following expression, the resulting string would be "Hello World":

```
"Hello" + " World"
```

If one of the operands used with these operators is not a `String`, its string representation is implicitly obtained and used in the expression. This means, for example, that a numeric value can be added to a `String`. The numeric value is converted to an appropriate sequence of characters, which are concatenated to the original `String`. All the following are legal concatenations:

```
"Wizard" + " of " + "Oz"
"Emily's birthday is " + "December " + 19
"Answer is: " + true
```

Note

This might seem like a contradiction that Java does not allow you to overload operators, yet it provides such support as a built-in feature for `Strings`. Although viewed as a powerful feature in C++, operator overloading can make code difficult to read because it is not always obvious when an operator in an expression is tied to a class method. The use of overloaded operators also adds to the maintenance required for a class because each such method must be updated whenever attributes are added to or removed from a class. Java made an exception for the `String` class because almost every program you write will require simple manipulation of text like that supported by these operators.

TROUBLESHOOTING

EXPRESSION SYNTAX ERRORS

The compiler reports a `')' expected` *error in an expression.*

Syntax errors often result from mismatched parentheses in an expression. When an expression cannot be compiled, verify that the parentheses are correctly paired. If an expression is so complex that this is difficult to do, consider separating it into multiple statements that assign intermediate results to variables that are then used to compute the desired result. This approach will reduce the likelihood of syntax errors and improve the maintainability of your code.

UNEXPECTED EXPRESSION RESULTS

An expression produces a numeric result other than what you expected.

First, review the precedence of Java operators in Table 5.2 to determine if the expression operators are being evaluated in an order other than what you intended. If this is the case, add parentheses to the expression as needed to correctly identify the desired operands. Also, examine the expression for any integer division that might introduce unintended truncation of intermediate results.

POSSIBLE LOSS OF PRECISION

You get a compiler error warning you that a statement might result in a loss of precision.

This error results from an attempt to perform a narrowing conversion, such as assigning the result of an expression that operates on `double` values to a `float` variable, without an explicit cast. You can address this error by explicitly casting the expression result to the type of the target variable in the assignment. However, you should only do this if you are certain that the target variable can hold the magnitude of the result and that the resulting precision is acceptable. For example, you should not cast a `long` result to an `int` if the magnitude of the result might exceed the storage capacity of an `int`. You should instead change the type of the target variable to support what is required.

CHAPTER 6

Control Flow

In this chapter

by Brian Keeton

CONTROLLING THE FLOW OF EXECUTION

Controlling the flow of execution is perhaps the most important aspect of any programming language. Control flow allows you to direct the execution of your program down different paths in response to the inputs to your system. A proper construction of loops and branches in your code provides your program a map to follow as it performs its work.

You can also think about control flow like a stoplight. The logic in a traffic system directs the flow of traffic based on the current conditions and the timing mechanism that drive it. Your programs must also have the capability to start, stop, and direct their flow of execution. Without the variety of control constructs found in modern programming languages, you would be limited to developing simple applications, or developing complex ones using an abundance of redundant and inefficient code. This chapter introduces you to the control mechanisms available in Java and describes how you use them to develop dynamic programs.

BOOLEAN OPERATORS

Most control flow expressions in Java direct program execution based on a computed `true` or `false` value. For instance, as you'll see later in this chapter, an `if (`*`expression`*`)` statement causes the next statement to be executed only if *`expression`* evaluates to `true`. You can actually write something like `if (true)`, but this is not very useful in general (except for concepts such as conditional compilation, which you'll learn about later). Instead, control mechanisms such as the `if` statement are usually driven by a Boolean expression.

Note

The use of the term *Boolean* in this chapter refers to Boolean logic in general and not the `Boolean` class found in Java. The expressions used in flow control typically evaluate to the `true` and `false` literals associated with the `boolean` primitive type and not to an object reference. Boolean and `boolean` are used somewhat interchangeably throughout this chapter depending on the context, but from a Java implementation standpoint, they are referring to the same type of data or expression.

Operators in Java have particular meanings when used in Boolean expressions. Many of these operators are used with the other primitive types as arithmetic and bitwise operators. In most cases, the Boolean meanings are a natural extension from the operations performed on integer types. Table 6.1 shows the operations that can be performed on Booleans.

TABLE 6.1 OPERATIONS ON BOOLEAN EXPRESSIONS

Operation	Name	Description
=	Assignment	As in `lightOn = true;`.
==	Equality	This produces a `true` if the two `boolean` operands have the same value (`true` or `false`). It produces `false` otherwise. This is equivalent to `NOT EXCLUSIVE OR` (`NXOR`).

Table 6.1 Continued

<table>
<tr><th>Operation</th><th>Name</th><th>Description</th></tr>
<tr><td>!=</td><td>Inequality</td><td>This produces a true if the two boolean operands have different values (one true, the other false). It produces false otherwise. This is equivalent to EXCLUSIVE OR (XOR).</td></tr>
<tr><td>!</td><td>Logical NOT</td><td>A unary operator. If the operand is false, the result is true, and vice versa.</td></tr>
<tr><td>&</td><td>AND</td><td>Produces a true if and only if both operands are true. For non-boolean operands, it is interpreted as a bitwise operator.</td></tr>
<tr><td>|</td><td>OR</td><td>Produces a false if and only if both operands are false. For non-boolean operands, it is interpreted as a bitwise operator.</td></tr>
<tr><td>^</td><td>XOR</td><td>Produces true only if exactly one (EXCLUSIVE OR) operand is true. For non-boolean operands, it is interpreted as a bitwise operator.</td></tr>
<tr><td>&&</td><td>Logical AND</td><td>Same result for boolean operands as described for &.</td></tr>
<tr><td>||</td><td>Logical OR</td><td>Same result for boolean as described for |.</td></tr>
<tr><td>?:</td><td>if-then-else</td><td>Uses a boolean expression before the question mark to determine which of two expressions to evaluate.</td></tr>
</table>

The Relational Operators

The most intuitive comparative operators are those that fall into a category known as relational operators. Relational operators include the standard greater-than and less-than symbols you learned about back in third grade. Conveniently enough, they work the same in Java as they did back in third grade, too. For instance, you know that if you write (3>4), you have written something wrong (a false statement). On the other hand, (3<4) is correct (a true statement). These examples use literal values, which makes them easy to evaluate, but not very useful in a program because their result is known in advance, and it is always the same. Fortunately, in Java and other languages, you are not limited to comparing constants when you use relational operators; you are free to use variables, so the statement `(accountBalance > minimumBalance)` is also a valid relational expression that provides much more potential for use in a flow control statement. These expressions are built using the operators shown here:

Operator	Boolean Result
<	Less than
<=	Less than or equal to
>	Greater than
>=	Greater than or equal to

The precedence of the relational operators is below that of the arithmetic operators, but above that of the assignment operator. Thus, the following two assignment statements produce identical results:

```
result1 = a+b < c*d;
result2 = ((a+b) < (c*d));
```

The associativity of relational operators is left-to-right, but this aspect really is not an issue because they can be used only with non-`boolean` operands. It might not be immediately obvious what this implies, so consider the following (illegal) expression:

a < b < c

Using left-to-right associativity, the expression `a < b` is evaluated first to produce a `boolean` value of either `true` or `false`. This value would then have to be compared to `c`. What does it mean to ask if `true` (or `false`) is less than some other operand? Unlike some languages, a `boolean` in Java is not the same as a 0 or 1 or any other number, so a relational comparison with a `boolean` has no meaning. An expression like this results in the compiler generating a syntax error.

In C and C++, the relational operators produce an integer value of 0 or 1, which can be used in any expression expecting an integer. Expressions such as the following are legal in C or C++ if the variables are declared accordingly, but they generate compiler errors in Java:

```
dailyRate = rateArray [ dayOfWeek < 4 ];
newValue = oldValue + ( newRate > oldRate ) * interest;
```

Try a basic program to test some of what you have just learned. Listing 6.1 includes some simple print statements that demonstrate the use of the relational operators with literals.Another convenient fact of Java is used here: You can concatenate `boolean` values with a string using the `+` or `+=` operator and the string `true` or `false` will be displayed in the output.

LISTING 6.1 `QuickTest.java`—A SIMPLE LESSON FROM THE THIRD GRADE

```
public class QuickTest
{
     public static void main(String args[]){
          System.out.println("5 is greater than 6:"+(5>6));
          System.out.println("6 is greater than or equal to 3:"+(6>=3));
          System.out.println("8 is less than 10:"+(8<10));
     }
}
```

To run this program, first copy Listing 6.1 to a file called `QuickTest.java`. As discussed in previous chapters, it's important the file be called `QuickTest.java` with all capitalization the same. Next, compile the program using `javac`:

```
javac QuickTest.java
```

After the file is compiled, you're ready to run it:

```
java QuickTest
```

As you might have already guessed, the output you get should look like this:

```
5 is greater than 6:false
6 is greater than or equal to 3:true
8 is less than 10:true
```

THE EQUALITY OPERATORS

The equality operators are the next set of Boolean operators in Java. Equality operators enable you to compare one value to another to determine if they are the same. In third grade, you might have written an equality statement such as (3=3). Unfortunately, in Java, this statement would cause the compiler to attempt to use the assignment operator rather than evaluate it as a Boolean expression.

The problem is that this is not the result you are looking for. It is also a compiler error when using literal values because you cannot assign a new value to the number 3, even if it is the value 3. To solve this problem, a separate two-character operator (==) is used to distinguish equality comparisons from assignments. In Java then, you would write the expression as `(3==3)`. This would be read as "three equals three" and would produce a `true` result when evaluated. Similarly, the expression `(3==4)` would evaluate to `false`.

The two equality operators are very similar to the relational operators, with slightly lower precedence:

Operator	Boolean Result
`==`	Is equal to
`!=`	Is not equal to

The equality operators take operands of virtually any type and always produce a `boolean` result. If the operands are primitive data types, the values of the operands are compared to evaluate the expression. However, if the operands are object references, the purpose of these operators is to determine if both operands refer to exactly the same object. Consider the following example:

```
string1 == string2
```


In this expression, `string1` and `string2` must refer to the same string—not to two different strings that happen to contain the same sequence of characters—for the expression to evaluate to `true`. Consider the lines shown in Listing 6.2.

LISTING 6.2 `ObjectEquals.java`—COMPARING OBJECTS IN JAVA

```
public class ObjectEquals
{
     public static void main(String args[]){
          String string1 = new String("Hi Mom");
          String string2 = new String("Hi Mom");
```

LISTING 6.2 CONTINUED

```
        //At this point string1 is not equal to string2
        System.out.println("string1 == string2 :"+(string1==string2));

        String string3=string1;
        //Now string1 is equal to string3
        System.out.println("string1 == string3 :"+(string1==string3));
    }
}
```

Given this sequence, `string1==string2` returns `false` after the first two lines despite the fact that the two objects being referenced are initialized using equivalent string literals. What matters here is that they are not the same object. On the other hand, `string1==string3` returns `true` because these two variables refer to exactly the same object. So as you might have already guessed, the output of this program is as follows:

```
string1 == string2 :false

string1 == string3 :true
```

Note

If you want to compare `string1` to `string2` based on the text they contain rather than what objects they refer to, you can use the `equals` method of `String`. This would be written `string1.equals(string2)`, which would evaluate to `true` in this case. The `equals()` method compares the strings character by character. This method is an overridden version of the one defined in the `Object` class that is introduced later in Chapter 7, "Classes."

The associativity of the equality operators is again left-to-right. You have seen that the associativity of the relational operators is really not meaningful to you as a programmer. The associativity of the equality operators is only slightly more useful. Take a look at the following example:

```
startTemp == endTemp == lastRace
```

Here, the variables `startTemp` and `endTemp` are compared first to produce a `boolean` result. This result becomes the left operand for a comparison with `lastRace`. A `boolean` can only be compared with another `boolean` for equality, so a compiler error results here if `lastRace` is any other data type.

Caution

Although this expression is valid if the far right operand is a `boolean`, you should avoid writing code that requires such a careful examination by the reader to determine its correctness. Even if you understand it completely when you write it, chances are you'll be as mystified as everyone else when you try to read it a few weeks or months later. Try to use constructs in your code that are easily read. If there is some reason that you must use an expression like the one just given, be sure to use comments to explain how the expression operates and, if possible, why you have chosen to implement your algorithm that way.

LOGICAL EXPRESSIONS

Logical expressions work a bit differently than the previous operators and are probably not something you covered in your third-grade math class. These expressions either operate on a pair of Booleans or manipulate the individual bits of integer variables or literals. This distinction divides the logical operators into two categories:

- ***Boolean operators***—Only operate on `boolean` operands.
- ***Bitwise operators***—Operate on each bit in a pair of integer operands.

You have already seen in Chapter 5, "Using Expressions," how bitwise operators work. This chapter covers only the Boolean, or conditional, half of the logical expression operators. However, it is interesting to note that, with some minor exceptions, bitwise operators and conditional operators produce the same result if the operands are `boolean`.

CONDITIONAL-AND AND CONDITIONAL-OR OPERATORS

There are two primary Boolean operators:

- Conditional-AND, `&&`
- Conditional-OR, `||`

These operators obey the same truth table that was constructed in Chapter 5 for the bitwise operators, but have lower precedence. For your convenience, the truth tables for AND and OR are reproduced here:

When A is	And B is	(A && B)	(A || B)
false	false	false	false
false	true	false	true
true	false	false	true
true	true	true	true

These operators provide an additional feature related to efficiency. The operands of a conditional-OR or a conditional-AND expression are evaluated left-to-right; if the value of the expression can be determined after evaluating only the left operand, the right operand will not be evaluated. So, in the following example, if `x` is indeed less than `y`, then `m` and `n` are not compared:

```
(x<y) || (m>n)
```

If the left side of this expression produces the Boolean value `true`, then the result of the whole expression is `true`, regardless of the result of the comparison `m>n`. The right operand is only evaluated if the left operand is `false`. This behavior is the reason `||` and `&&` are referred to as "conditional" operators. Note that in the following expression, if you instead used the bitwise form of the operator, `m` and `n` are compared regardless of the values of `x` and `y`:

```
(x<y) | (m>n)
```

The `&&` operator behaves similarly to `||`. If the left operand of a conditional-AND expression is `false`, then the result of the expression is obviously `false`. The right operand is only evaluated if the left operand evaluates to `true`.

The conditional-AND and conditional-OR operators are often referred to as short-circuit operators because they short-circuit the evaluation of the right operand if it's unnecessary. You should normally use them instead of the bitwise form. The only exception would be cases in which the right operand produces a side effect by calling a method or applying another operator that changes the value of a variable or does some other work. Here you should use the bitwise form to make sure the work of the right operand is performed.

Note

You might have noticed that there is no conditional-XOR operator defined as part of this set. This is because both sides of an XOR comparison must always be evaluated to determine the result of an expression.

THE LOGICAL NEGATION OPERATOR

The logical negation, or NOT, operator (!), is a unary operator that evaluates the opposite value of a Boolean expression. For example, `!true` evaluates to `false`. Recall that the bitwise complement operator (~) described in Chapter 5 cannot be applied to a Boolean expression. You must use the negation operator to obtain an opposite value when working with Booleans.

The negation operator has high precedence, equivalent to that of the other unary operators. Take a look at the following example, which shows a combination of logical negation and the conditional-AND:

```
if (!done && inputString.equals("exit") )
```

Here, assume `done` is a `boolean` variable that indicates that some required processing has finished. Because the logical negation operator has higher precedence, it is evaluated before the conditional-AND. The method call in the right operand is only performed if `done` is `false` in this example. This is a good use of a short-circuit operator, especially if this statement is inside a loop or a method that gets called often because string comparisons are relatively slow.

THE CONDITIONAL OPERATOR

The conditional operator is unique because it is the one ternary, or triadic, operator in Java. This distinction means that it is the only operator that acts on three operands in an expression (instead of the typical one or two). It functions in Java as it does in C and C++, and takes the following form:

```
expression1 ? expression2 : expression3
```

In this syntax, `expression1` must evaluate to a Boolean value. If this value is `true`, then `expression2` is evaluated, and its result is the value of the conditional. If `expression1` is `false`, then `expression3` is evaluated, and its result is the value of the conditional. You can look at the ternary operator just as if it were a typical `if-else` statement:

```
if (expression1) {
  expression2;
}
else {
  expression3;
}
```

Consider the following examples. The first uses the conditional operator to determine the maximum of two values; the second determines the minimum of two values; the third determines the absolute value of a quantity.

```
bestReturn = stockReturn > bondReturn ? stockReturn : bondReturn;
lowSales = juneSales < julySales ? juneSales : julySales;
distance = site1-site2 > 0 ? site1-site2 : site2-site1;
```

The purpose of the ternary operator is not only to cause a specific operand to be evaluated, but to produce a result that can be assigned to a variable or used in another expression or a method call. Remember that the result of any Java expression must be used or a compiler error results.

```
// this statement causes a compiler error because the result
// of the expression is not used
stockReturn > bondReturn ? stockReturn : bondReturn;
```

In reviewing these examples, think about the precedence rules and convince yourself that none of the three examples requires any parentheses to be evaluated correctly. You might want to use parentheses to make code that uses the conditional operator easier to read, but this operator has very low precedence, so its operands are obvious to the compiler.

BOOLEANS IN CONTROL FLOW STATEMENTS

As you have already seen, Java is very strict when it comes to use of the `boolean` type. This strong typing also holds `true` in the restrictions placed on expressions that are allowed in the conditional clause of a control statement. These expressions are limited to variables (or literals) of the primitive type `boolean` and expressions that evaluate to a `boolean` result. Examples are shown in the following code fragments:


```
boolean testVal = false;
int intVal = 1;
...
if (testVal) {} else {}
if (intVal != 1) {} else {}
...
while (testVal) {}
while (intVal == 0) {}
...
do {} while (testVal)
```

```
do {} while (intVal == 0)
for (int j=0; testVal; j++) {}
for (int j=0; intVal < 5; j++) {}
```

Here, the conditionals used by the various control statements are demonstrated with both a `boolean` variable and a Boolean expression built from a comparison of the integer `intVal` with an integer constant. Naturally, much more complicated Boolean expressions could be used in the same way.

A key point to make here is that this restriction to Boolean expressions is very much unlike C and C++. These languages allow a variety of data types and expressions to be used to direct control statements. Typical examples are the use of an integer variable or a pointer. Here, a non-zero integer or a non-null pointer is treated the same as a value of `true`. The following examples demonstrate the differences:

```
int myInt = 3;
String myString = null;
...
// compiler error
if (myInt) {} else {}
// can use this instead
if (myInt != 0) {} else {}
...
// compiler error
if (myString) {} else {}
// can use this instead
if (myString != null) {} else {}
```

CONTROL FLOW FUNCTIONS

Control flow is the heart of any program. It is the capability to adjust (control) the way that a program progresses (flows). By directing the paths of execution that your code takes, you build programs that behave dynamically based on their inputs. Without control flow, programs would not be able to do anything more than several sequential operations.

`if` STATEMENTS

The simplest form of control flow is the `if` statement. An `if` statement checks its conditional expression (typically derived through any of the means described in the first half of this chapter) and, if the value is `true`, directs the interpreter to execute the next block of code. The general syntax for the `if` statement is as follows:

```
if (expression)
  statement;
```

If the expression evaluates to `false`, the computer skips the following statement and continues on. An example of an `if` statement is shown in the following code fragment:

```
if (userNameIsRebeccah)
  System.out.println("Hi Rebeccah");
System.out.println("Welcome to the system");
```

If the value of userNameIsRebeccah is true, the computer prints out the following when this fragment runs:

```
Hi Rebeccah
Welcome to the system
```

However, if the value is false, the program skips over the line after the if and the result is as follows:

```
Welcome to the system
```

In many situations, you will want to execute more than one line of code based on a condition. To do this, you can place a code block, which is a series of statements inside a pair of curly braces, after the if statement. The following code fragment shows just such an example:

```
int transferAmount = 100;
if (checkingAccount.transferApproved(transferAmount)) {
  checkingAccount.withdraw(transferAmount);
  savingsAccount.deposit(transferAmount);
  System.out.println("Transfer completed");
}
System.out.println("After transfer request");
```

Although the use of braces is only required when you define a block that contains more than one statement, it is common practice to also use braces for single-statement blocks to improve the readability of your code. Notice that in the first example given here, the only indication that the if statement applies only to the first statement following it is an arbitrary use of whitespace. This code executes the same even if this indentation is removed because all whitespace is ignored by the compiler. You should always use indentation even if you choose not to use braces, but as you'll see in the next section, indentation alone can be deceiving if it isn't applied carefully.

Note

> Although the preceding examples used boolean variables or expressions as conditions, you can also use boolean literals. The result of such a control statement is obviously known in advance, so this provides one possible way to simulate conditional compilation. Any code that is tied to a false condition at compile time will not be included in the compiled class file.

if-else STATEMENTS

Only slightly more advanced than a simple if, the if-else statement evaluates a condition and then, if the condition is true, executes the statement (or block) after the if. Otherwise the statement (or block) after the else is executed. Only one or the other set of code is run. The general syntax for an if-else is as follows:

```
if (expression)
  statement1;
else
  statement2;
```

Our earlier example can be expanded slightly to use an `if-else` statement as follows:

```
int transferAmount = 100;
if (checkingAccount.transferApproved(transferAmount)) {
  checkingAccount.withdraw(transferAmount);
  savingsAccount.deposit(transferAmount);
  System.out.println("Transfer completed");
}
else {
  System.out.println("Transfer refused");
}
System.out.println("After transfer request");
```

The `if-else` statement complicates the issue of `if` statement readability further if indentation, or preferably, braces, are not properly used. This can be seen when looking at how `else` blocks are evaluated when there are nested `if` statements. Consider the following code:

```
if (firstVal==0)
   if (secondVal==1)
      firstVal++;
else
   firstVal--;
```

When is the `else` executed? The indentation implies that it is executed whenever `firstVal` is not equal to 0. However, the rules governing `if-else` statements are independent of any use of whitespace. An `if-else` expression forms a single statement, so an `else` always belongs to the most recent `if`.

This means that, in this example, the `else` is executed whenever `firstVal` is 0 and `secondVal` is not 1. The following two code fragments show better ways to write this example:

```
// better to at least get the indentation right
if (firstVal==0)
   if (secondVal==1)
      firstVal++;
   else
      firstVal--;

// still better to use braces
if (firstVal==0) {
   if (secondVal==1) {
      firstVal++;
   }
   else {
      firstVal--;
   }
}
```

The use of braces also allows you to control which `if` statement an `else` is associated with as shown in the following:

```
if (firstVal==0) {
   if (secondVal==1) {
      firstVal++;
   }
}
else {
```

```
    firstVal--;
}
```

Because a block counts as a single statement, the `else` is now associated with the first `if`.

Another variation on the `if-else` statement is known as the compound `if`:

```
if (firstVal==0)
   if (secondVal==1)
      firstVal++;
   else if (thirdVal==2)
      firstVal--;
```

In this example, `firstVal` is only decremented when `firstVal` is 0, `secondVal` is not 1, and `thirdVal` is 2. Follow this last example through to verify to yourself that this is the case.

Note

Some languages use a separate keyword, `ELSIF` for example, to represent a compound `if` statement. Java does not add a keyword but instead uses both the `else` and `if` keywords as part of the same statement.

switch STATEMENTS

The next type of control flow is the `switch` statement. The `switch` statement is the first control flow statement that does not require a Boolean evaluation. A `switch` statement consists of a control expression and a block of statements delineated by `case` labels. The control expression is evaluated and the resulting value determines which `case` will be executed. Each `case` is labeled with a unique constant expression that is used in making this determination. Control is passed to the `case` whose expression matches the value of the control expression. If there is no match, control passes to the `default` label. If there is no `default` label, control passes to the first statement after the `switch` block.

An example of a `switch` statement is as follows:

```
switch (expression){
  case C1:
    statement1;
    break;
  case C2:
    statement2;
    break;
  default:
    statementD;
}
```


The control expression that drives a `switch` statement and the label values for each `case` must evaluate to a `byte`, `short`, `char`, or `int`. It is an error to have duplicate case labels, so the compiler must be able to verify that the labels are unique at compile time. For this reason, only constants or constant expressions are allowed in the labels. This is also the reason for the restriction on the data types that are allowed.

The break statement serves an important purpose in a switch. When the block of statements associated with a case has finished executing, execution will continue with the statements for the next case unless a break is encountered. This is useful if you need to perform the same work for multiple values of the switch expression. The order of the case statements is not restricted, so you can arrange them to best support reuse of the same statements. However, if you do not want this behavior, proper use of the break statement is a must. Take a look at the following example:

```
switch (1){
  case 1:
    System.out.println ("one");
  case 2:
    System.out.println ("two");
  case default:
    System.out.println("Default");
}
```

In this example, the resulting output would be

```
one
two
Default
```

This happens because execution falls through each case after the match of case 1 occurs. It is likely, however, that this code was not intended to print all three results. The break statement can be used to only produce the one desired output. To do this, the code should be changed to the following:

```
switch (1){
  case 1:
    System.out.println ("one");
    break;
  case 2:
    System.out.println ("two");
    break;
  case default:
    System.out.println("Default");
    break;
}
```

Note

Notice that blocks are not required for the statements associated with each case because a label identifies the start of each one and a break statement marks the end. Braces can still be used if they aid in readability, but they are purely optional.

It is not necessary for a case to specify any statements at all if it's only intended to execute the statements defined for another case that follows. The next example demonstrates how statements are reused for multiple case labels:

```
switch (strike) {
  case 0:
  case 1:
    System.out.println("Got a 0 or 1, want to do the same thing");
    break;
```

```
    case 2:
      System.out.println("Got a 2, do something different");
      break;
    default:
      System.out.println("Value out of range");
}
```

You should adopt the practice of always defining a `default` label for your `switch` statements. Even if you do not need to perform any processing for values that do not match the other cases, a `default` label with an appropriate comment makes this intent clear to anyone reading your code. If you never expect to see values that do not match a `case`, a `default` label is essential so that you can throw an exception or at least write out a warning message if it happens. Although the `default` label is typically specified last in a `switch` statement, it can appear anywhere in the sequence of cases.

ITERATION STATEMENTS

Programmers use iteration statements to control sequences of statements that are repeated according to runtime conditions.

Java supports three types of iteration statements:

- `while`
- `do`
- `for`

`while` LOOPS

The `while` statement tests an expression and, if it's `true`, executes the next statement or block repeatedly until the expression becomes `false`. When the variable or expression is `false`, control is passed to the next statement after the `while` statement. The syntax for a `while` loop looks very similar to that of an `if` statement:

```
while (expression)
  statement;
```

The following example shows a while loop in action:

```
boolean done = false;
// read characters from the keyboard until an x is typed
while (!done) {
  int c = System.in.read();
  done = (c == 'x');
}
```

In this example, the condition evaluates to `true` initially, so the loop is entered. The loop continues until a specific value of the variable `c` causes the state of the control expression to change. A `while` loop will never execute if the condition evaluates to `false` the first time it is checked.

`while` loops can execute indefinitely, either intentionally or by accident. It is common to use a loop like the following to run a program until it is terminated externally or by an embedded `break` statement:

```
// an intentional "infinite" loop
while (true) {
  statement;
}
```

do LOOPS

The `do` statement is similar to the `while` statement. In fact, it has a `while` clause at the end. Like the `while` expression in the previous section, the expression here must be a Boolean. A `do` loop executes its statement(s) and then evaluates the `while` expression. If the `while` expression is `true`, execution returns to the `do` statement and the loop continues to iterate until the expression becomes `false`. The complete syntax for a `do-while` loop is as follows:

```
do
  statement;
while (expression)
```

The primary reason a programmer chooses to use a `do` statement instead of a `while` statement is that the statement will always be executed at least once, regardless of the value of the expression. This is also known as post-evaluation.

for LOOPS

The most complicated of the iteration statements is the `for` loop. The `for` statement gives the programmer the capabilities of each of the other iteration statements. The complete syntax of a `for` loop is as follows:

```
for (initialization; expression; step)
  statement;
```

The `for` loop first runs the initialization code (like a `do`) and then evaluates the expression (like an `if` or `while`). If the expression is `true`, the statement is executed and then the step is performed. A `for` loop will not execute any iterations if the expression is `false` when it is first evaluated. A `for` loop can also be written as a `while` loop as follows:

```
initialization;
while (expression){
  statement;
  step;
}
```

An example of a `for` loop appears in the following code fragment:

```
// for loop that limits a batter to 10 pitches
for (int balls=0, strikes=0, pitches=0; (balls<4) && (strikes<3) && (pitches<10);
pitches++) {
  pitcher.pitch();
  player.swing();
  // do something that updates the ball and strike counts
  ...
}
```

This example demonstrates the fact that the initialization clause can include a variable declaration statement that creates and initializes several local variables.

You can only specify a single declaration statement here, so multiple variables can only be declared if they are of a single type. Integer literals are used in this example, but you can also use expressions to initialize `for` statement variables. If you do use an expression here and it terminates abruptly, the `for` statement completes abruptly as well. Any variables declared in the initialization clause have scope limited to the `for` statement block and the expression and statement portions of the `for` clause. They are no longer accessible after the loop completes executing.

You are not required to provide an expression for any of the three sections of a `for` loop. You can also use empty statements for any or all of them in situations where the loop is controlled by the statements it executes. An *empty statement* is a semicolon without any associated expression to evaluate. For example, our previous infinite loop example can be rewritten as:

```
// an intentional "infinite" loop
for (;;) {
  statement;
}
```

JUMP STATEMENTS

In addition to the more common control flow functions, Java also has three kinds of jump statements: `break`, `continue`, and `return`.

The `break` and `continue` statements optionally include a label to identify their target statement. A *label* is any valid identifier prefixed to a statement or block of statements as shown in the following:

```
myLabelName: statement;
```

Java does not support a `goto` operator, but you can use labels to direct execution within nested loops using a `break` or `continue`. As you'll see in the next sections, labels are meant to allow you to specify which loop you are referencing with one of these jump statements. They do not, however, give you the ability to jump anywhere in your code like the much maligned `goto` does.

Note

In some respects, you can view the `throw` statement used to raise an exception as a jump statement because it causes an abrupt transfer of control. However, this statement is intended to handle error conditions rather than anticipated processing like that associated with the statements discussed in this section. You should never throw an exception (or intentionally perform an operation that causes one to be thrown) to direct program flow when processing is proceeding normally. Exception throwing is an expensive operation in terms of performance that should be reserved for error handling. See Chapter 4, "Methods and Exceptions," for a description of `throw`.

break STATEMENTS

The substatement (or inner) blocks of loops and switch statements can be terminated using the break statement. You will often find situations where a certain condition occurs that makes it unnecessary or undesirable to continue executing a loop or a switch statement case. You have seen the importance of break with a switch statement already. An unlabeled break statement passes control to the next line after the current (innermost) iteration (while, do, for, or switch statement). Consider the example in Listing 6.3.

LISTING 6.3 BreakTest.java—USING break INSIDE A while LOOP

```
public class BreakTest {
  public static void main(String[] args) {
    try {
      // loop forever until an x is typed
      while (true) {
        int c = System.in.read();
        if (c == 'x')
          break;
      }
    }
    catch (java.io.IOException e) {
      e.printStackTrace();
    }
    finally {
      System.out.println("Will do this before leaving the loop");
    }

    System.out.println("Started here after break was called");
  }
}
```

In this example, the while loop iterates on a condition that will never be false, but a break statement provides an escape when the character x is read from the keyboard. Because the break is inside a try block, the finally block is executed before control transfers to the last print statement. It is possible for a finally block to redirect control by throwing an exception or executing a return statement.

→ **See** "Catching and Throwing Exceptions," **p. 84**, for a discussion of try-catch-finally

You can include a label as part of a break statement to pass control to a labeled statement within the current method. This is typically used with nested loops as shown in the following example:

```
outerLoop: for (int i=0; i<10; i++) {
  System.out.println("Iterate outer loop");
  innerLoop: while (true) {
    System.out.println("Iterate inner loop");
    int c = System.in.read();
    if (c == 'x')
      break;  // exit while loop and iterate for loop
    else if (c == 'q')
      break outerLoop;  // exit for loop
  }
}
```

`continue` STATEMENTS

Instead of leaving a loop, a `continue` statement requests that the remaining statements in an iteration be skipped and that the loop start its next iteration. This is typically a replacement for one or more `if` statements that would otherwise be required to prevent execution of some statements during an iteration. A `continue` may only appear within the substatement block of a `while`, `do`, or `for` statement. As with `break`, the optional label parameter allows you to end an iteration of an outer loop if necessary.

If there is a `finally` clause for a currently open `try` statement within the indicated level of nesting, that clause is executed before control is transferred due to a `continue`.

The following example demonstrates the use of the `continue` statement:

```
int[] data = {2,0,5,1,0,3};
for (int i=0; i<data.length; i++) {
  if (data[i]==0)
    continue;
  // now do processing that is only necessary for non-zero data
}
```

`return` STATEMENTS

A `return` statement passes control to the caller of the method, constructor, or static initializer containing the `return` statement. Unless the `return` statement is in a class constructor or a method that is declared `void`, it must include a parameter of the same type specified in the method declaration.

If a `return` statement is encountered inside a `try` block, the `finally` clause associated with the block, if there is one, will be executed before control is transferred.

TROUBLESHOOTING

TWO EQUIVALENT OBJECTS ARE NOT EQUAL

An equality comparison between two object references using == fails even though the objects are equivalent.

When used with reference types, the == operator returns `true` only if the two references point to the same object. To test for object equivalence, you must use the `equals` method as declared in the associated class instead of ==. If `equals` has not already been overridden for the class, you must implement an override that returns `true` if two instances of the class are equivalent relative to the needs of your program. For example, `equals` is overridden for `String` to return `true` if two `String` objects hold the same sequence of characters.

MISMATCHED `if` AND `else` STATEMENTS

The blocks executed within an `if-else` statement are not those you intended.

This error typically results from a mismatch of `if-else` pairs in a control statement. Remember that indentation plays no role in how `else` statements are matched with `if` statements. Place braces around the statement blocks associated with each `if` and `else` statement you are examining to clearly identify how they should be matched.

INCOMPATIBLE TYPE FOR CONDITIONAL CLAUSE OF A CONTROL STATEMENT

The compiler reports an error stating that the variable or expression you have specified in the conditional clause of a control statement, such as an `if` *or* `while` *statement, is of an incompatible type.*

The Java compiler is exceedingly strict regarding the use of `boolean` expressions. The expression you supply to a conditional clause must evaluate to a `boolean` result. If you are attempting to control execution based on an integer value or an object reference, build your control expression by comparing the integer variable for equality with 0 or the object reference with null instead of attempting to use either directly.

`for` OR `while` LOOP NEVER EXECUTES

The block associated with a `for` *or* `while` *loop never executes although you expected it to execute at least once.*

The conditional clause of a `for` or `while` loop is evaluated prior to the first iteration of the loop. If this condition is `false`, the loop is never entered. You should use a `do` loop if you require a loop to execute once regardless of the value of the conditional expression.

CHAPTER 7

Classes

In this chapter

by Brian Keeton

WHAT ARE CLASSES?

Classes are the building blocks of an object-oriented system, so it's important to define them and talk about how they relate to objects before you learn to declare and use them. On one hand, objects are relatively easy to define because they surround you. Obviously, this book you're reading and the keyboard on which you type are both objects. The concreteness of objects makes the concept simple to grasp—objects are specific things (persons, places, ideas, and so on if you want to be complete). Turning to classes, however, you must trade this concrete view for the abstract.

In nearly every aspect of life, from simple conversation to scientific research, people have found it easier to understand objects and work with them after they have been put into categories that make similarities and differences clear. The world is too complex otherwise. Imagine Henry Ford trying to explain his plans for the Model T when there was no such abstraction as a "car" from which to start. When an automaker introduces a new model today, you might be anxious to see what it looks like but no one has to tell you what it does. When abstractions are used to group objects, the key is to focus on what they have in common and ignore the ways in which they differ when those differences are unimportant in a given context.

So how does this relate to classes? A class defines an abstraction using a set of attributes and behavior that represents what is common among objects in a group. From a programming standpoint, these attributes are variables that represent state and you define methods to act on these variables as a way to model behavior. With proper adherence to encapsulation, these methods define everything that is allowed in terms of accessing, using, and changing the state of an object. Any behavior that is important to the system you're building should be found in the classes you design.

Before going any further, consider this simple example: Suppose you have to design a system to coordinate the stoplights in a busy section of town as a way to ease traffic congestion. You look at the problem and right away know that the stoplights found at the affected intersections are the primary objects that need to be represented in your system. There might be tens or even hundreds of individual stoplights, but based on your problem, they're all the same when it comes to state and behavior. With this in mind, you decide you need a class named `StopLight`. The first step is to define variables to hold the state of a `StopLight`. As an initial pass, you decide that the color of the light is the only state of a `StopLight` that the rest of your system needs to know. To represent this state, you select a single integer variable named `greenYellowRed` that will hold the value of the light color. Java offers a much better way than using an integer here but you'll learn about that a little later. Given these design choices, here's an example class declaration:

```
public class StopLight{
  /* 0 -> Green
     1 -> Yellow
     2 -> Red
   */
  int greenYellowRed;
}
```

This class declaration is valid but it isn't very interesting and it doesn't do anything to model the behavior of a stoplight. This is where methods are needed. In the case of a `StopLight` class, it is likely that you would have a method called `changeLight()`, which would cause the light to change from red to green (probably by changing the `greenYellowRed` variable). The following modified declaration of `StopLight` shows how this behavior is incorporated into the class:

```
public class StopLight{
  int greenYellowRed;
  void changeLight(){
    greenYellowRed = ++greenYellowRed % 3;
  }
}
```

Note

To distinguish class variables with variables that are parts of methods, class variables are often referred to as *fields*, or class scope variables. In the previous example, the `greenYellowRed` variable would be a field of the `StopLight` class.

WHY USE CLASSES?

When dealing with classes, it's important to remember that classes do not enable programmers to do anything more than they would be able to do without them. Although it might be significantly more work, you could write all OOP programs structurally.

Classes are used for the same reason large companies are divided into departments and those departments are divided into subdepartments. When a company is faced with organizing hundreds of people around hundreds of tasks, a divide and conquer strategy is the only way to survive. A departmental architecture divides tasks into manageable, and hopefully related, pieces that can be addressed by an appropriate group of staff. If you're in the engineering department, you care about getting your paycheck on time, but you're probably not concerned with how the payroll system knows how to handle paid holidays. If you're in the payroll department, however, you might care a great deal. As far as the rest of the company is concerned, the processing of paychecks has been fully encapsulated within the payroll department. Taking this same idea and moving it into the software arena is what OOP does when responsibility is divided among classes. As with a company department, each class should be able to do one thing and do it well so the rest of the system can be assured that the assigned tasks are carried out.

In OOP, encapsulation is achieved by enclosing data and methods in classes. When done properly, this isolates information so that state can be carefully managed, and it insulates the rest of a program from the details of class implementation. After you have developed a complete class that performs a certain task, you can effectively forget the intricacies of that task and use the class and the methods it provides. Because the class mechanisms are hidden within its methods, even significant changes to the inner workings of the class that might be necessary later do not require you to modify the rest of your program unless the method signatures change.

Beyond encapsulation, classes allow you to change how you think about the elements of your programs. By writing classes that enclose everything associated with particular tasks or entities, you can build types that have meaning in the problem domains in which you work. You are not limited to describing your program elements as integers, Booleans, or any other native data type. Instead of using these relatively indistinct mechanisms and relying on unattached functions to interpret their values appropriately, you can build software with class types that help describe the problem being solved. In the preceding payroll example, a procedural approach could be implemented that maintains holidays as integer day and month values that are compared against the dates in a pay period whenever a paycheck amount is calculated. However, think of how much more expressive a class-based approach could be. Using a `Calendar` class, holidays could be maintained as a collection of `Date` objects. To produce a paycheck, each day during a pay period could also be represented as a `Date` that is queried for whether it's a weekend day or holiday relative to the current `Calendar`. The processing that must be performed doesn't change significantly between the two approaches, but a system built on classes allows responsibility to be clearly divided and produces entities that support the thought process required to solve the problem.

Although encapsulation frees developers who use a class from having to know the implementation details, it is also a powerful means of preventing accidental corruption of the data. When access to the data members of a class is managed through methods, relationships between members can be maintained so that invalid states do not occur.

Encapsulation and the capability to create your own descriptive types are strong arguments for object-oriented programming, but they're not the only ones. A great deal of the appeal of OOP is in its support for inheritance. You'll learn more about the mechanics of inheritance a little later, but for now think of it as a way to pull common behavior out of multiple classes and implement that behavior in a separate class so that it can be shared.

As an example of inheritance, consider a program that manages the accounts at a bank. Assume the bank offers both checking and savings accounts to its customers. Viewing each type separately, you could write independent code to support the required functionality. However, this is unnecessary effort and a maintenance headache waiting to happen given the common features checking and savings accounts share. A better approach is to factor out the common attributes and behavior shared by the account types and define a class to represent them. You can define a class called `GeneralAccount` for this purpose with an account balance attribute and methods to check the balance, make a deposit, and make a withdrawal. You won't use this `GeneralAccount` class to represent an actual account object but you can use it to simplify the development of `CheckingAccount` and `SavingsAccount` classes. If checking accounts at this bank do not pay interest, you can inherit the functionality of `GeneralAccount` when declaring `CheckingAccount` and be finished. You can then declare `SavingsAccount` to inherit from `GeneralAccount` and add a method to compute an interest payment and add it to the current account balance. With this approach, you can focus only on how the account types differ and reflect those differences in the methods you write. Inheritance allows you to build class hierarchies that simplify the task of representing complex structures in a software system.

Note

When new classes inherit the properties of another class, they are referred to as child classes or *subclasses*. The class from which they are derived is then called a parent or *superclass*.

Also, with inheritance comes the concept of *polymorphism*, which is the true mark of an object-oriented programming language. To understand this aspect of OOP, first think of an object's type not as a specific class implementation, but as the set of messages it understands (that is, the methods to which it can respond). Using this definition, objects of the same type can be implemented by different classes. Each of these classes can respond to the same set of messages, but every one can respond with different behavior through its own distinct method implementations. Polymorphism allows you to treat instances of these classes as instances of a type without regard to their particular implementation. For this to work, the classes must share a common superclass that defines the methods that relate them. Code that makes use of a polymorphic type makes method calls on a reference to the superclass and the behavior that results is determined by the particular subclass implementation.

The classic example of polymorphism uses a set of classes found in a simple drawing program. In this example, the program provides a tool palette with circle and rectangle drawing tools. The user selects a tool from the palette, clicks a screen location, and drags the mouse to size and shape a figure when adding to a drawing. In a structured program, the application displays the drawing using a loop that checks each figure created by the user and calls a specific function that knows how to draw that type of shape. This approach works reasonably well until the program users add a requirement that a triangle must also be supported as a drawing tool. A programmer must then locate the drawing loop, and every other place shapes are treated differently based on their type, and update the code to understand triangles. This update is not too burdensome in this simple example, but it illustrates a maintenance and reliability drawback that can get out of hand quickly in a system with any true complexity. With OOP, encapsulation comes into play first as a better approach to this program. The functions for drawing different shape types should be located in the code that defines each shape, namely within `CircleShape`, `RectangleShape`, and `TriangleShape` classes. The drawing functionality should be implemented as a `draw` method that holds all the knowledge required to draw the associated shape on the screen. This is already an improvement because the behavior of each shape is now encapsulated within the definition of the shapes themselves. This encapsulation significantly reduces the number of places code must be modified if the drawing requirements for a particular shape are later changed.

There's still more, however. A drawback in our system so far is that although the `draw` methods are encapsulated within classes, the program still has to call a separate method for each shape type when the screen needs to be displayed. This is unnecessary effort because the program does not care about the shape types; it only wants them to be drawn correctly. The capability for a shape to be drawn correctly is a common behavior found in each of the shape classes (`CircleShape`, `RectangleShape`, and `TriangleShape`).

This is where polymorphism comes into play. Instead of defining three unrelated classes, you can factor out the common behavior that, in this case, is the capability for a shape to draw itself. The example becomes a true OOP implementation when a `GenericShape` class with a `draw` method is defined as a superclass for each of the three shape classes. A `GenericShape` does not correspond to any real shape, so it has no implementation for its `draw` method. However, this class does serve a significant purpose by declaring that its subclasses must support a `draw` method. With this change, the program can keep track of its shapes as `GenericShape` instances rather than a collection of `CircleShape`, `RectangleShape`, and `TriangleShape` instances. This works because the program doesn't need to know the difference, provided that it can direct a shape of any type to draw itself. When it's time to draw the screen, the `draw` method of each `GenericShape` can be called and, through polymorphism, the `draw` method of the specific shape type is called.

Note

The dynamic behavior possible with polymorphism is the result of a process known as *late binding*. When the Java compiler encounters a call to a method, it doesn't bind the call to a particular method implementation until runtime (unless the method is declared `static` or `final`, which would mean that the implementation is known at compile-time). This is in contrast to *early binding*, which binds a method call to a specific implementation during compilation.

Caution

In the previous example, although every circle and rectangle is also a shape, a given shape is not necessarily a circle or a rectangle. Thus, although the `CircleShape` and `RectangleShape` classes can be treated just like the `GenericShape` class in Java, you cannot perform an operation such as `getRadius` that is reserved for the `CircleShape` class on an instance of the `GenericShape` class.

CLASSES IN JAVA

As stated at the beginning of this chapter, classes are the building block in an object-oriented language such as Java. In fact, Java, unlike C++, goes so far as to make it impossible to define any variables or methods outside a class. Everything you do in Java is based on designing and implementing classes.

The Java Platform

Java itself is built from classes that are made available to the public in the SDK. These classes, known as the Java platform, provide a powerful set of common functionality typically found only in third-party add-ons to other languages. Although there are some limitations, a large number of the classes that make up the Java platform can themselves be extended. By doing this, you can tailor the classes in the Java API library—especially those that support user interface development—to meet your particular needs.

Before you start creating programs, you must first learn how to create classes. In terms of syntax, there are two parts to a class in Java: the declaration and the body. Listing 7.1 is a simple class that fulfills some of the requirements of the simple bank account example discussed in the previous section.

Examine this listing to get an idea of what constitutes a class. You can refer to this listing again later as your understanding of classes grows.

LISTING 7.1 `GeneralAccount.java`—A GENERAL CLASS FOR MAINTAINING A BANK ACCOUNT

```
/**
 * A simple class used to implement common behavior for various
 * types of bank accounts. It should be extended to implement
 * behavior for specific accounts.
 */
public class GeneralAccount {

  // unique account identifier
  private String accountNumber;

  // this will hold the current account balance
  protected float balance;

  public GeneralAccount( String accountNum ) {
    accountNumber = accountNum;
  }

  public String getAccountNumber() {
    return accountNumber;
  }

  public float getBalance() {
    return balance;
  }

  public void makeDeposit( float amount ) {
    balance += amount;
  }

  public void makeWithdrawal( float amount ) {
    balance -= amount;
  }
}
```

Take a quick look through this class. The first part of any class is the class declaration. Most class declarations you write will look similar to that for `GeneralAccount`:

```
public class GeneralAccount
```

Declaring a class states several things, but probably the most important one is the name of the class (`GeneralAccount`). In the case of any public class, the name of the class must also match the name of the file that contains it. In other words, this class must appear in the file `GeneralAccount.java`.

Caution

Remember that Java is a case-sensitive language. This case sensitivity applies to filenames also. In the preceding example, naming the source file that contains the `GeneralAccount` class `generalAccount.java` or anything else other than `GeneralAccount.java` results in a compiler error.

The next part of the class is the opening brace. You should notice that there is a brace ({) at the beginning of the class, and if you look all the way down at the bottom there, is also a closing brace (}). The braces define the area in the file where the class definition will exist. Also, note that there is no semicolon at the end of the final closing brace like you find in C++.

A bit farther down, you will see several comments. As you learned in "Comments" (Chapter 3, "Data Types and Other Tokens"), comments can exist anywhere in the file and are ignored by the compiler, but they help you leave messages for yourself or other programmers. Next, you will see several fields declared. Each of these variables is accessible from any of the methods in the class. When you change them in one method, all the other methods will see the new value.

DECLARING A CLASS

In general, Java class declarations take the form

```
AccessSpecifier Modifiers class NewClass extends SuperclassName
  implements InterfaceName
```

where everything in italics is optional. As you can see, there are five properties of the class that can be defined in the declaration:

- Access Specifier
- Modifiers
- Class name
- Superclass
- Interfaces implemented

→ **See** Chapter 9, "Interfaces," **p. 197**

ACCESS SPECIFIERS

The access specifier in a class declaration determines how visible a class is to other classes. The specifiers that apply to classes are similar to the method access specifiers discussed in Chapter 4, "Methods and Exceptions." Although specifiers are not of primary importance while developing an individual class, they become very important when you decide to create other classes, interfaces, and exceptions that use that class.

For now, focus on top-level classes (that is, those not defined within another class declaration). Classes that are not top-level classes are known as *inner classes* and are discussed later in this chapter. When declaring a top-level class, you can state that the class has `public` access, which is what you have seen in the examples so far, or you can omit the access specifier and accept the default access restrictions.

PUBLIC CLASSES

Using the `public` specifier in a class declaration makes the class accessible to all other classes. A public class can be used (for example, as a data type for a class variable or a type for a method parameter) or extended by any class. Here's an example:

```
public class PictureFrame
```

Also, remember that public classes must be defined in a file called `ClassName.java` (for example, `PictureFrame.java` for the preceding declaration).

A second restriction relates to the contents of an individual source file, which has not been discussed yet. Java allows you to define more than one top-level class in a single file as long as no more than one of those classes is declared as public.

PACKAGE CLASSES

If you do do not explicitly declare a class to be `public`, it will be assigned package access by default.

Packages are the subject of a later section, but you need a quick introduction here to make the definition of package access clear. A *package* in Java is a grouping of classes defined by the programmer. Packages provide a way to organize your code by placing related classes together. Access restrictions are less stringent between classes within the same package because the intent is for these classes to work together as a cohesive unit. With that said, package access can be distinguished from public access. Whereas any class can use a public class, by omitting the `public` modifier, you can declare a class for use only by classes within the same package.

Remember that although `package` is a keyword in Java, you do not use it (or any other access specifier) in a declaration for a class with package access. Here's an example declaration:

```
class PictureFrame
```

Note

Package access is also known as "default" or "friendly" access. "Default" access is an appropriate description given that this level of access is the default assigned when the `public` specifier is not present. "Friendly" reflects the fact that package access is not as restrictive as that associated with the `private` specifier, but also not as accessible as `protected`.

MODIFIERS

In addition to an access specifier, you can precede the class name in a declaration with one of two optional modifiers. These modifiers, `final` and `abstract`, control the use of a class in an inheritance hierarchy. Note that both modifiers cannot be used in a single class declaration. The reason for this will be clear after the supported modifiers are defined.

> **Note**
>
> There is a third modifier, `strictfp`, that you can include in a class, interface, or method declaration. This rarely needed modifier instructs the compiler to use the IEEE 754 standard for all floating-point operations. This standard was the default prior to Java 2, but it is not as fast as other implementations that are the default for current JVMs. The one disadvantage of these other implementations is that there is a slight chance of them producing different results across platforms. If you require identical results across all JVMs and platforms, include the `strictfp` modifier in your declarations.

FINAL CLASSES

The `final` modifier prevents a class from being extended (that is, having any subclasses).

The reason for declaring final classes might not be evident at first. You might be wondering why you would want to prevent other classes from extending your class, especially since inheritance is supposed to be one of the appeals of object-oriented programming.

It is important to remember that the object-oriented approach effectively enables you to create alternate versions of a class (by creating children that inherit its properties and change it somewhat). Consequently, if you create a class to serve as a complete implementation of some particular function (for example, a class that will handle network communications using a specific protocol), you don't want to allow other classes to modify parts of this function because the original intent will be lost. Thus, by making the class final, you eliminate this possibility and ensure consistency. The `final` modifier gives you a precise way to make your intent clear to other programmers regarding the use of a class.

In addition, the compiler can carry out a number of performance optimizations on a final class that otherwise would not be possible. Polymorphism allows you to write flexible code, but the associated dynamic method calls degrade performance somewhat. If you write code that calls a method on a non-final class instance, the compiler must allow for the possibility that the instance encountered at runtime will actually be an instance of a subclass. This means that the method must be looked up when the code is executed rather than being known when the class is compiled. If, instead, you use a final class, the method call is fully defined during compilation because there is no possibility of a subclass instance being used. Of course, the `final` modifier should only be used when a class should have no subclasses. The performance advantage is a side effect only, but you should use this as incentive to consider whether your classes should allow subclasses when you are declaring them.

Here's an example declaration for a final class:

```
final class PictureFrame
```

Access specifiers and modifiers can be used in any order within a class declaration. The following two declarations are the same to the compiler:

```
public final class PictureFrame
final public class PictureFrame
```

Abstract Classes

You can view the `abstract` modifier as the opposite of `final`. Whereas final classes cannot be extended, abstract classes must be extended before an instance can be created. The `abstract` modifier indicates that a class implementation is incomplete and must be added to before it can represent an actual object. A declaration for an abstract class takes the following form:

```
abstract class PictureFrame
```

A class that you have completely written and compiled can be incomplete depending on how common behavior is isolated and reused in an inheritance hierarchy. The superclass that contains the common behavior in such a hierarchy often does not contain enough behavior to represent a valid object. For example, consider a grammar-checking program that must support multiple written languages. You could proceed by defining an `EnglishChecker`, a `FrenchChecker`, and a `SpanishChecker` class in which each defines the required functionality for a given language. Knowing that some of the methods you need are independent of the language, you define a `GrammarChecker` class as a common superclass that contains these methods rather than repeating them in each class. This alone does not produce an abstract class, because even though `GrammarChecker` does not implement all you need for a language, it is nonetheless a complete implementation of the methods it does provide. The advantage in making `GrammarChecker` an abstract class is to take advantage of polymorphism.

Here, assume that each of your language-specific classes has a `checkPunctuation()` method that validates the punctuation found in a string. To prevent your program from having to know which language is being used each time you make a call to `checkPunctuation()`, this method can be declared in `GrammarChecker` without an implementation (that is, an abstract method), and the language-specific subclasses can provide an appropriate implementation in each case. Having an abstract method forces `GrammarChecker` to be declared as an abstract class. Even though an instance of `GrammarChecker` itself cannot be created, it is still a key component of the flexible design needed for this example. This structure supports a clean separation of the language-dependent and language-independent functionality of the program. If a programmer later needed to add a `GermanChecker` class, a perfect starting point would be to look at the list of abstract methods in `GrammarChecker` to gain an understanding of what behavior has to be provided to support a new language.

Note

Although most abstract classes contain at least one abstract method, this is not required. You might find cases in which you define a class that has no abstract methods but still does not represent an object that should be instantiated. You can declare the class abstract and require subclassing just as in the preceding example.

Class Name

The name of a Java class must adhere to the same rules as any other identifier. Specifically, class names must

- Begin with a letter, an underscore (_), or a currency symbol ($, £, and so on)
- Contain only letters, digits, underscores, and currency symbols
- Not be the same as any Java keyword (such as `void` or `int`)

Also, it is accepted practice to capitalize the first letter in the name of a class and use mixed case instead of underscores to separate words (for example, `MyClassName`).

Although only required for public classes, it is generally a good practice to name the file in which `NewClass` is defined `NewClass.java`. Doing so helps the compiler find `NewClass`, even if `NewClass` has not been compiled yet.

SUPERCLASSES—EXTENDING ANOTHER CLASS

One of the most important aspects of OOP is the capability to use the methods and fields of a class you have already built. This can be done by declaring a member variable that is a reference to another class (this is known as either *aggregation* or *composition*) or it might involve building upon another class through inheritance and subclassing (this is known as *derivation*).

To define an inheritance relationship, you include an `extends` clause in the declaration of a class, making it a subclass of the named parent class.

> **Note**
>
> Even if you omit the `extends` clause in a class declaration, any class you declare is still a subclass. The `java.lang.Object` class, discussed a little later, is at the root of the Java class hierarchy and is the superclass of any class declared without an explicit superclass.

By extending a class, you gain all the functionality of a superclass while providing yourself the opportunity to add new behavior or even modify existing behavior. If you declare a subclass without defining any fields or methods (and use the same access specifier and modifier, if any), the new class will behave identically to its superclass and only differ by its name. The subclass would not be very interesting but it would be a valid class, and it would have all the fields and methods declared in or inherited by it superclass.

> **Note**
>
> Multiple-inheritance is not supported in Java. Thus, unlike C++, Java classes can extend only one class. Interfaces provide Java with a more flexible alternative to multiple inheritance that focuses on behavior rather than a class hierarchy.

How Much Inheritance Is Too Much?

A common mistake in object-oriented programming is to overuse inheritance. Although inheritance is a powerful feature, a class hierarchy can become rigid if inheritance is taken to the extreme. A standard rule of thumb is to apply the "is-a" versus "has-a" test.

For example, a Ford *is a* car, so a class hierarchy that defines a `Ford` class as a subclass of a `Car` class makes sense. This example strictly follows an "is-a" definition, because there is nothing that a `Ford` does that a generic `Car` does not do. A `Ford` is a unique classification of `Car` that has its own implementation of automotive behavior, but you don't need to add some new capability, such as floating on water, when you declare a `Ford` class.

Slightly different from an "is-a" justification for inheritance is the "is-like-a" test. In this case, you make use of inheritance to declare a subclass that is similar enough to its superclass to share its interface, but it is also dissimilar in that it requires additional methods to represent its behavior completely. This design is not as clean an approach because treating the subclass as its superclass doesn't allow you to exercise all its functionality, but it can be useful.

If two classes cannot be described as having an "is-a" or "is-like-a" relationship, you should not inherit one from the other. For example, a car *has an* engine, but it isn't an engine, so `Car` should not be a subclass of an `Engine` class. A composition approach should be used here so that `Car` contains a reference to an `Engine` and delegates all functionality related to powering the vehicle to that instance.

The appropriate use of inheritance in these simple examples is obvious, but this is not always the case. You should exercise caution when considering inheritance and more often stress composition and delegation in your class designs to make them more flexible and better able to adapt to new requirements during their lifecycles.

VARIABLES—DEFINING STATE

Obviously, variables are an integral part of programs and, thus, classes as well. In Chapter 3, you examined the various types of variables, but now you must also consider how they are employed in your programs and the different roles they can assume.

When creating variables, whether they are as simple as integers or as complex as derived classes, you must consider how they will be used, what code will require access to the variables, and what degree of protection you want to provide to these variables.

The capability to access a given variable is dependent on two things: the access specifier used when creating the variable and the location of the variable declaration within a class.

→ **See** "Literals: Assigning Values," **p. 56**

Fields Versus Method Variables

Everything in Java is declared within a class, but variables within a class fall into two categories based on their scope. A class definition can include variables that belong to the class itself and also variables that belong to specific methods.

Those variables declared outside of any methods, but within a given class (usually immediately after the class declaration and before any methods), are referred to as fields of the class. Fields are accessible within all methods of the class. Non-private fields are also accessible to other classes.

You can also declare variables within a method. These variables are local to the method and can only be accessed within that method and not by any other class. Consequently, there is no need for access specifiers when declaring a method variable, so they are not allowed by the compiler.

Although it is possible to make every field accessible to every class, this is not a prudent practice. First of all, you would be defeating a great deal of the purpose of creating your program from classes. You choose appropriate class names instead of `class1`, `class2`, `class3`, and so on to create a clean program that is easy to code, follow, and debug. For the same reason, by creating various levels of protection, you encapsulate your code into self-sufficient and more logical chunks.

Furthermore, because OOP encourages and facilitates the reuse of code that you have written beforehand, careful assignment of access restrictions to code you write now prevents you from later doing something that you shouldn't.

(Keep in mind that preventing access to a field does not prevent the use of it.) For example, if you were creating a `Circle` class, there would most likely be several fields that would keep track of the properties of the class, such as radius, area, border color, and so on—many of which might be dependent on each other. Although it might seem logical to make the radius field public (accessible by all other classes), consider what would happen if a few weeks later you decided to write the code shown in Listing 7.2.

LISTING 7.2 `Circle.java`**—CODE FRAGMENT SHOWING DIRECT ACCESS TO A FIELD**

```
import java.awt.*;

public class Circle {
  public int radius, area;
  public Color borderColor;
...
}

class GraphicalInterface {
  Circle ball;
  ...
  void animateBall() {
    for (int updateRadius = 0; updateRadius <= 10; updateRadius++){
      ball.radius = updateRadius;
      paintBall(ball.area, ball.borderColor);
      ...
    }
  }

  void paintBall(int area,Color color){
    ...
  }
}
```

This code would not produce the desired result. Although the

```
ball.radius = updateRadius;
```

statement would change the radius, it would not affect the area field (remember that the area of a circle is a function of the radius and is equal to π times the radius squared). As a result, you would be supplying the `paintBall()` method with incorrect information.

Because the area field depends on the radius, it should be updated whenever the radius is changed. Your first thought might be to ask why area is a field at all instead of just being the return value of an area() method that is computed based on the radius when needed. Using a field that is derived from one or more other fields is a common approach when addressing performance. Assume, in this case, that performance is critical when the area of the circle is needed. Calling a method that computes the area each time is extra overhead if the radius has not changed since the last call. Declaring a field to hold the area offers a better solution when the radius and area fields are properly protected as shown in Listing 7.3.

LISTING 7.3 Circle.java—PROVIDING ACCESS TO THE CIRCLE FIELDS THROUGH METHODS

```
import java.awt.Color;

class Circle {
  public Color borderColor;
  private int radius;
  private double area;

  public void setRadius (int rad){
    if ( rad != radius ) {
      radius = rad;
      area =  Math.PI * radius * radius;
    }
  }

  public int getRadius(){
    return radius;
  }

  public double area (){
    return area;
  }
}

class GraphicalInterface {
  Circle ball;
//   ...

  void animateBall() {
    for (int updateRadius = 0; updateRadius <= 10; updateRadius++){
      ball.setRadius (updateRadius);
      paintBall(ball.area(), ball.borderColor);
      ...
    }
  }
}
```

As shown in the preceding listing, the area and radius fields cannot be directly manipulated from outside the class because they have private access. When the radius is changed through a call to setRadius(), which is the only way it can be changed from outside the class, the area field is updated accordingly. This way the area of the circle is always correctly represented by the field and is never computed unnecessarily.

Although it is important to consider the level of access that other objects will have to your fields, it is also important to consider the scope of the fields and method variables within your class. *Scope* describes the part of a program within which a variable can be referred to using its simple name. In general, every variable is within scope only within the block (delimited by the curly braces { and }) in which it is declared. However, there are some slight exceptions to this rule. Examine Listing 7.4.

LISTING 7.4 `CashRegister.java`—**VARIABLES HAVE SCOPE BASED ON WHERE THEY ARE DECLARED**

```
public class CashRegister {
  public int total;
  int salesValue[];
  Outputlog log;

  void printReceipt(int totalSale) {
    Tape.println("Total Sale = $"+ totalSale);
    Tape.println("Thank you for shopping with us.");
  }

  void sellItem(int value) {
    log.sale(value);
    total += value;
  }

  int totalSales() {
    int numSales, total = 0;
    numSales = log.countSales();

    for (int i = 1; i <= numSales; i++) {
      total += salesValue[i];
    }
    return total;
  }
}
```

Now examine some of the variables and their scope:

Variable Name	Declared As	Scope
`total`	Field of `CashRegister` class	Entire class
`total`	Local to `totalSales()` method	Within `totalSales()`
`log`	Field of `CashRegister` class	Entire class

Variable Name	Declared As	Scope
`value`	Parameter to `sellItem()`	Within `sellItem()`
`i`	Local to `totalSales()` within `for` loop	Within the `for` loop

There are several things to note from the table. Start with the simplest variable, `log`. `log` is a field of the `CashRegister` class and is, therefore, visible throughout the entire class.

Every method in the class (as well as other classes in the same package) can access `log`. The method parameter `value` is local to the method `sellItem()` in which it is declared. All statements in `sellItem()` can access `value` but it can't be accessed by any other methods. The variable `i` is similar, but has a different scope based on where it is declared within the method that contains it. Like `log` and `value` that exist only within the block in which they are defined, `i` exists only within the `for` statement in which it is defined. In fact, if you consider a complex `for` loop like that shown in the following example, `i` is recreated (in this case, 10 times):

```
for (int x = 0; x<10 ;x++){
  for (int i =0;i < numSales; i++ )
    ...
}
```

To understand why this is the case, consider how this code might look if you "unwound it" into a `while` loop as in the following:

```
{
  int x = 0; //declare x and set its initial value
  while (x <10) {
    { //start the next for loop
      int i = 0; //declare i and set its initial value
      while (i < numSales) {
        ... //do whatever is in the inner for loop
        i++; //perform the increment of i
      }
    }
    x++; //increment x
  }
}
```

As you can see, even though the `for` loop looks simple, the scope of the variables is actually complicated if you add all the implied braces.

The remainder of the scope table is complicated by the presence of two `total` variables with overlapping scope. Although the `total` field is accessible to all methods, the use of `total` might seem confusing in the `totalSales()` method. In Java, a locally declared variable takes precedence over a field relative to scope resolution. This is known as *class variable hiding*.

So in this case, the identifier `total` in `totalSales()` refers only to the local variable and not to the field. This means that after exiting the `totalSales()` method, the `total` class variable is unchanged. In such a situation, you can access the class variable by using the `this` keyword that is discussed later in more detail. For now, know that you could set the class variable `total` to the value of the local variable `total` with this statement:

```
this.total = total;
```

Although using the same identifier as both a field and a method variable name is supported, it is confusing to other programmers working with your code and is arguably error prone. It is preferable to choose a different (and more descriptive) identifier. The local variable in `totalSales()` could just as easily been named `totalSales` and any confusion would have been avoided.

ACCESS SPECIFIERS

Similar to class and method declarations, access specifiers for field declarations determine how accessible variables are to other classes. It is important to remember that access specifiers for variables apply only to fields. It makes little sense to speak of access specifiers for variables within methods because they exist only while the method is executing. Afterwards, they are collected to free up memory for other variables.

Why Not Make All Local Variables Fields?

Given that all class variables (fields) are accessible to all methods in a class, why not make all variables within a class fields?

The first reason is that you would be wasting a great deal of memory. Although local variables (those variables declared within the methods themselves) exist only while the method is executing, fields must exist for the lifetime of a class instance. Consequently, allocating memory for variables needed only by individual methods at the class level is a poor use of resources.

The second reason is that declaring all your variables as fields would make your class declarations cumbersome and hard to follow. If you are going to be using a counter only in one method, why not declare it in that method? Matching a variable's declaration to its logical scope makes the intent of that variable's use much more clear. Using local variables within methods is a way to encapsulate information. There is no reason to expose the details of a method's implementation to the rest of the class.

DEFAULT

If no access specifier is included in a field declaration, the field is assigned a default level of access. This default level makes fields accessible within the current class and to classes within the same package. No access is granted to classes outside the package, including subclasses. An example default access declaration follows:

```
int size;
```

`public`

Identical to the `public` access specifier for methods, the `public` specifier makes fields visible to all classes, regardless of their package. For example:

```
public int size;
```

You should make an effort to limit public fields and provide methods for controlled manipulation instead.

protected

The `protected` specifier is an extension of the default access level that differs only in how subclasses are treated. Protected fields can be accessed by all classes within the same package and by all subclasses, including those declared in other packages. For example:

```
protected int size;
```

private

The highest degree of protection is achieved with the `private` specifier. Private fields are only accessible to methods within the current class. They are not accessible to any other classes, including subclasses of the current class. For example:

```
private int size;
```

MODIFIERS

Field declarations can also include modifiers that affect their use. These optional modifiers are `static`, `final`, `transient`, and `volatile`.

static

As with methods, placing the `static` modifier in front of a field declaration makes the field static. Static fields are shared by all instances of a class rather than having an individual copy allocated to each instance. Consequently, changing a static field affects the state of that field seen by all instances of a class. Static fields can be modified in both static and non-static methods. For example:

```
static int size;
```

➔ **See** Chapter 4, "Methods and Exceptions," **p. 69**

final

The `final` modifier tells the compiler that the value of a variable can be assigned only once, making it a constant. Typically, you will assign the value of a final variable as part of the declaration. For example:

```
final int MAX_LOGIN_FAILURES = 3;
```

Java also supports the concept of a *blank final* where a final variable is declared without a value assignment and is initialized later before its first use.

transient

It is common for the programs you write to require that certain information be persisted, or saved, for later use by another program or another execution of the same program. This persistence can be accomplished in several ways, including writing to a database or making use of Java's support for the serialization of objects as discussed in Chapter 22, "Object Serialization." Regardless of the method chosen, persistence of a class instance is accomplished by saving the states of the class fields so they can be later retrieved and used to create an equivalent instance. However, it is possible that not all the fields need to be saved to accomplish this. Remember the earlier example of a `Circle` class with radius and area fields. Here the value of the area field is derived from the radius and only exists as a separate field for performance purposes. Saving the value of the area field when a `Circle` instance is persisted is unnecessary overhead because it isn't needed to restore the instance. Instead, the area field can be declared as `transient`. The `transient` modifier lets the compiler know that a given field does not need to be persisted. For example:

```
private transient double area;
```

volatile

The `volatile` modifier indicates that multiple threads can modify a variable and that certain compiler optimizations should be prevented to ensure that changes to the variable are handled properly.

Instance Fields

This chapter introduced the term "field" when referring to a variable defined within a class. You should also be familiar with the term *instance field*, which is used to describe a non-static field of a class. Instance field is meant to imply that a field belongs to a single instance of a class. When an instance field is modified, the change in state is seen only by the associated class instance. Because instance fields exist only within the context of a class instance, they cannot be accessed by static class methods.

> **Caution**
>
> A common error is to attempt to access an instance field within the `main()` method of a class. Although the `main()` method is a special case because of the entry point it provides for an application, it is nonetheless a static method. It is typical for a `main()` method to create an instance of its enclosing class and then use the fields and methods of that instance to perform its work.

Initialization

You can explicitly initialize an instance field as part of its declaration or it will be assigned a default value automatically. If you do not specify an initial value, reference types are set to `null` and primitives are initialized to zero or false, as appropriate. If you declare a field with an initialization statement, that statement is executed after the superclass constructor is called for the object but before its own constructor. Initialization statements can include method calls but only if the call cannot throw an exception that must be handled.

You also have the option of using an instance initializer block to initialize instance fields. This is a block of code enclosed in curly braces that can appear anywhere in a class declaration that a field declaration can appear. The code in an instance initializer is executed whenever any constructor in the class is called just as if it had been included at the beginning of each constructor. This mechanism is useful when you need to perform an initialization that is too complex to be done as part of a field declaration. Rather than placing this code in every constructor (or a method called by every constructor), you can place an instance initializer block next to the fields it initializes. An example initializer block is shown in the following code segment that initializes an array with 100 random numbers:

```
...
  private double[] randomValue = new double[100];
  {
    for (int i=0; i<randomValue.length; i++) {
      randomValue[i] = Math.random();
    }
  }
...
```

CLASS FIELDS

Class fields are the complement to instance fields. A *class field* is a field defined with the `static` modifier. As discussed previously when this modifier was introduced, `static` fields are shared by all instances of a class. A class field belongs to the class as a whole and not to a particular instance. A common example of a class field is a counter that keeps track of the number of instances of a class that have been instantiated. The class constructors each increment this field when called as a way to maintain information related to the class as a whole. A public class field is the closest Java gets to the concept of a global variable.

Given that class fields are not associated with a class instance, they cannot be initialized in a constructor or an instance initializer block. For most applications, you can initialize a class field as part of its declaration. You might also make use of one or more static initializer blocks within the class declaration as shown in the following example:

```
...
static Circle specialCircle;
...
static {
  specialCircle = new Circle();
  specialCircle.setRadius(3);
  specialCircle.borderColor = Color.blue;
}
...
```

A static initializer block is enclosed in curly braces just like an instance initializer, but it is preceded by the `static` modifier. Because these initializers affect only static fields, they are executed once during class initialization rather than being executed as part of each constructor call.

Note

Because class fields are not associated with a particular class instance, it isn't necessary for a class instance to be created before the class fields can be accessed from other classes. The normal access rules apply, so this only works for non-private class fields.

DECLARING A CONSTANT

A constant is a field whose value cannot change during program execution. Although `const` is a reserved word in Java, it plays no part in the declaration of constants within your programs (actually it isn't used for anything). Also, unlike C and C++, the Java compiler does not use a preprocessor so there is no support for an equivalent to `#define` statements. Instead, constants in Java are class fields declared with both the `static` and `final` modifiers. As discussed previously, applying the `final` modifier to a field prevents its value from being changed. This alone is sufficient to create a constant, but when the declaration is at a class level instead of within a method, it is also standard practice to define the field as `static`. The value of a constant cannot change, so declaring it as `static` avoids the unnecessary overhead of maintaining a copy per class instance. Here's an example constant declaration:

```
public static final int NUM_ADDRESS_LINES = 3;
```

If the value of a constant cannot change, why not use the value itself within the program? The answer to this question is twofold:

- Although you cannot change the value of a constant during execution, as a programmer, you might later realize that an assigned value was not as constant as you thought. If program requirements change and the value of a constant needs to be updated, changing the assignment statement in one place is far simpler than searching for all occurrences of a hard-coded value and changing each one.
- By using constants, your code becomes cleaner and easier to follow. Although the literal "3" might make perfect sense to you when you first code a `for` loop, using `NUM_ADDRESS_LINES` instead increases the likelihood that the code will make sense to another developer or even you several months later.

Note

By convention, constants are named with all capital letters and underscores are used to separate multiple words.

IMPLEMENTING AN ENUMERATED TYPE

An enumerated type provides a way to restrict the values of a variable to a well-defined set. You can think of the values allowed by a particular enumerated type as a set of constants. Java provides no direct support for enumerated types, so you have to do some work to create your own using a class as shown in Listing 7.5.

LISTING 7.5 `StopLightColor.java`—**A CLASS THAT REPRESENTS AN ENUMERATED TYPE**

```
public class StopLightColor {

  // declare static instances to represent all allowed states
  public static final StopLightColor GREEN = new StopLightColor("Green");
  public static final StopLightColor YELLOW = new StopLightColor("Yellow");
  public static final StopLightColor RED = new StopLightColor("Red");

  private String color;

  // constructor is private to prevent any extraneous values
  private StopLightColor(String colorName) {
    color = colorName;
  }

  public String toString() {
    return color;
  }
}
```

Listing 7.5 shows a way to improve the previous example of a class that represents a stoplight. In the `StopLight` class, an integer field named `greenYellowRed` represented the state of the light with values between 0 and 2 used to indicate the current light color. Using an integer value is not intuitive in this case and requires careful coding to prevent the assignment of invalid values. A better approach is to use a reference to a `StopLightColor` instance to represent this state. There are several characteristics of `StopLightColor` to notice. First, three static instances of the class are defined as fields of the class itself. This might look strange but it is common practice to provide access to constant class instances using this approach. Second, notice that the constructor, which is a special method described in the next section, for the class is declared as private. A constructor is the method called when a class instance is created. Given that a private method can only be called by the class that defines it, this constructor definition makes it impossible to create any instances of `StopLightColor` other than those created within the class itself. Therefore, the only instances that can ever exist are the `GREEN`, `YELLOW`, and `RED` instances defined as public constants. If you were to now change the `greenYellowRed` field in `StopLight` from an `int` to a `StopLightColor`, you would prevent the possibility of an invalid state being assigned while making the class easier to understand as well.

METHODS—DEFINING BEHAVIOR

Although variables define the state of a class instance, methods define the associated behavior that controls that state and do the actual work that takes place in your programs. Methods support access specifiers and modifiers in a similar manner to fields. The details of method declarations and syntax were discussed previously in Chapter 4. This section extends that discussion to look at some special uses of methods.

CONSTRUCTORS

A constructor is a special method that is called when a class instance is created. A constructor provides a place for you to define any initialization code you want executed for a new class instance. A constructor is named the same as the class and its declaration looks like a typical method declaration because it can include an access specifier and a parameter list. However, a constructor declaration cannot contain a modifier, a return type, or a `throws` clause. For example, the constructor for the earlier `GeneralAccount` class was

```
public GeneralAccount( String accountNum ) {
  accountNumber = accountNum;
}
```

Caution

Be careful when you declare a constructor to omit the return type found in regular method signatures. Even if you insert a return type of `void`, the compiler will interpret what you implement as a normal method and not a constructor.

THE DEFAULT CONSTRUCTOR

Look again at the `StopLight` class example:

```
public class StopLight{
  /* 0 -> Green
     1 -> Yellow
     2 -> Red
   */
  int greenYellowRed;
}
```

This is a complete and valid class declaration but notice that it does not contain a constructor declaration. If a constructor is called when a class instance is created, what is called when a `StopLight` instance is created? The answer is that the compiler is doing some of your work for you in this case. When you declare a class without any constructors, the compiler automatically generates a default constructor that takes no arguments and performs no operations. Consequently, the original `StopLight` declaration is equivalent to

```
public class StopLight{
  /* 0 -> Green
     1 -> Yellow
     2 -> Red
   */
  int greenYellowRed;

  public StopLight(){
  }
}
```

You should remember, however, that the compiler only generates a default constructor when no constructors are defined. If you declare a constructor, even one that takes one or more arguments, the default no-argument constructor will not exist unless you explicitly define it.

If you have trouble accessing a no-argument constructor. See "No-Argument Constructor Not Found in Superclass," in the "Troubleshooting" section at the end of this chapter.

CONSTRUCTION SEQUENCE

The construction of an object involves more than the execution of a single constructor. When an object is created, constructor calls are chained so that a constructor for each superclass of the object is also called. Constructors for the superclasses are executed first, so a subclass constructor can access superclass fields with the assurance that any initialization defined for them in their corresponding constructor has been performed. Before the constructor for a class is executed, any initialization statements found in its instance field declarations or instance initializer blocks are performed.

ASSIGNING DEFAULT VALUES USING MULTIPLE CONSTRUCTORS

Defining multiple constructors enables you to create an object in several different ways. As with regular methods, you can overload constructors by declaring multiple versions in which each accepts a different set of parameters. This practice is prevalent in the Java libraries themselves. As a result, you can create most data types (such as `java.lang.String` and `java.net.Socket`) while specifying varying degrees and types of information.

If you make use of multiple constructors, try to reuse any common initialization code that you write. Because Java does not support variable parameter lists or default parameter values in method calls, multiple constructors that reuse common code are often implemented to address this need. One constructor can call another using the `this` keyword as long as it is done as the first statement in the method. For example, the following two constructors could be used to create class instances either with or without default parameter values:

```
public Point() {
  // no initial position specified, use default of (0,0)
  this(0,0);
}

public Point(int initialX, int initiallY) {
  x = initialX;
  y = initiallY;
}
```

IMPLEMENTING A SINGLETON USING A PRIVATE CONSTRUCTOR

The classic text on object-oriented design patterns (*Design Patterns*, Erich Gamma et al, Addison-Wesley, 1995) introduced the `Singleton` pattern among many others. The purpose of this often-used pattern is to provide a common way to ensure that only one instance of a class exists in a program and that it is globally accessible. A `Singleton` is typically used for a class that encapsulates access to an external resource (for example, a relational database connection) in which the creation of multiple instances would be costly and possibly error prone. Listing 7.6 shows an approach for implementing a `Singleton` in Java.

LISTING 7.6 DatabaseConnection.java—A Singleton CLASS

```
public class DatabaseConnection {

  private static DatabaseConnection singleton;

  private DatabaseConnection() {
    // do steps to establish connection to database
    ...
  }

  // only access to an instance of DatabaseConnection
  public static DatabaseConnection getInstance() {
    if ( singleton == null ) {
      singleton = new DatabaseConnection();
    }
    return singleton;
  }
}
```

The definition of `DatabaseConnection` ensures that the class is instantiated only once and that this instance is made accessible to all classes through the public `getInstance()` method. The `getInstance()` method also demonstrates *lazy instantiation* in that the Singleton instance is not created until it is needed.

OVERRIDING METHODS

Creating two methods within the same class that have both the same name and the same parameter list is illegal. It would be impossible for the compiler to associate a call with one method instead of the other. However, you have already seen an example of a subclass declaring a method that has the same signature as one in its superclass in the discussion of polymorphism. This reuse of a method signature is called *overriding* a method. For an example, start with the `Elevator` class shown in Listing 7.7.

LISTING 7.7 Elevator.java—A SIMPLE Elevator CLASS

```
class Elevator {
  ...
  private boolean running = true;
  ...
  public void shutDown() {
    running = false;
  }
}
```

At some point, you realize that this elevator just isn't very safe, so you decide to create a safer one. You want to extend the old `Elevator` class and maintain most of its properties, but change some of its behavior as well. Specifically, you want to check to make sure the elevator car is empty before stopping, so you override the `shutDown()` method as shown in Listing 7.8.

LISTING 7.8 `SaferElevator.java`—**A SAFER ELEVATOR THAT EXTENDS** `Elevator`

```
class SaferElevator extends Elevator {
  ...
  public void shutDown() {
    if ( isEmpty() )
      running = false;
    else
      printErrorMessage();
    }
}
```

Note that overriding is accomplished only if the new method has the same name and parameter list as the method in the parent class. If the parameter signature is not the same, the new method will overload the parent method, not override it. For example, look at Listing 7.9.

LISTING 7.9 `SaferElevator.java`—**SAFER ELEVATOR WITH AN OVERLOADED** `shutDown()`, **NOT AN OVERRIDDEN ONE**

```
class SaferElevator extends Elevator {
  ...
  public void shutDown(int delay) {
    if ( isEmpty() )
      running = false;
    else
      printErrorMessage();
  }
}
```

In this case, the `shutDown` method from the `Elevator` class is still used for instances of `SaferElevator` if a shutdown is requested without a specified delay. Adding the integer `delay` parameter to the method changes the method signature so it is not an override. The new `shutDown` method is still valid, however, and can be called, but it has merely overloaded the original `shutDown`, as you learned in Chapter 4.

Note

When you override a method, you can't change its name or parameter list but you do have some flexibility with the access specifier and the `throws` clause, if there is one. An overriding method can be more accessible than its parent (for example, a protected method can be overridden as public but not as private). Also, if a method declaration includes a `throws` clause, an overriding method can be implemented so that all exceptions are handled and no `throws` clause is needed or the listed exceptions are subclasses of those specified in the parent class.

These two options might seem confusing at first so look at the implications. The key here is that polymorphism is only possible if subclass instances can be treated as instances of a common parent class. If it were possible for a subclass to override a public method in a parent class as private, the compiler would accept a call to the method using a reference to the parent class. However, if this reference were to point to an instance of the subclass at run time, it would be impossible for the call to the private override of the method to take place. Now consider the declaration of thrown exceptions. A method is required to handle or throw any exceptions declared in the `throws` clause of each method it calls. If a subclass were to throw exceptions not declared as being thrown by the parent class, it would be impossible for a method that uses a reference to the parent class to know what exceptions to handle.

When you override a method, you might need to replace the behavior implemented in the superclass or you might only need to add to it. The `super` keyword allows you to do this by calling a superclass method from within a subclass. For example:

```
public void reset() {
  // reset instance fields
  counter = 0;
  ...

  // reset superclass state
  super.reset();
}
```

The call to a superclass method can occur anywhere within a subclass method.

Note

Unlike C++, Java does not allow a specific superclass to be named as part of a method call. In Java, superclass calls are always made to the immediate parent class.

The `super` keyword also applies when you are defining a constructor for a subclass. Although calling a superclass constructor is not much different from calling any other method, its syntax might seem confusing at first:

```
public CheckingAccount(String accountNum) {
  super(accountNum);

  // perform subclass initialization
  ...
}
```

There are two points to take note of here:

- A call to a superclass constructor must appear as the first statement in a subclass constructor if it is explicitly included.
- If a subclass constructor does not explicitly call a superclass constructor, the compiler automatically inserts a call to the no-argument constructor of the superclass.

Caution

A common error in the use of superclass constructors occurs when a parent class has at least one constructor defined with one or more arguments and doesn't have a no-argument constructor declared. In this case, the compiler will not generate a no-argument constructor automatically. Therefore, all subclass constructors must explicitly call a superclass constructor because there is no default constructor for the compiler to use in an automatically generated call.

Using Methods to Provide Guarded Access

Although it might be preferable to restrict access to certain fields in your class, it is typically necessary to provide some form of access to those fields. Access to fields is regularly provided through methods that are less restricted than the fields. An example of this approach was shown previously in the `Circle` class of Listing 7.3. These access methods are often referred to as *set* and *get* methods.

Class Methods

Static methods are referred to as *class methods*. As in the case of class fields, the implication of this term is that static methods are associated with a class as a whole and not a particular instance. Class methods can access class fields but not instance fields without referring to an instance of a class.

Creating an Instance of a Class

To use a class you have defined, you need to create an instance of that class. An instance is an object whose data type is the class. Any class you create can be instantiated, just like any other reference data type in Java.

The `new` Operator

Declaring a reference to an object in Java does not actually create an object.

The following declaration creates a reference to a `Circle` but does not create a `Circle`:

```
Circle myCircle;
```

Following this declaration, `myCircle` is a null reference if it's a field, or it is undefined if it's a method variable. Objects are created using the `new` operator as shown here:

```
Circle myCircle = new Circle();
```

The `new` operator is followed by the signature of the constructor to call for initialization of the object. In the preceding example, the created `Circle` instance is constructed using the no-argument constructor for the class. The new operator returns a reference to the newly created `Circle` that is assigned to the `myCircle` variable. A compiler error occurs if there is no constructor corresponding to the signature used with the `new` operator. As you might have noticed, the primary difference between declaring a reference type, such as `Circle`, and a primitive type, such as `int`, is the use of `new`.

You might be wondering how a Java application or applet starts running when you don't have any way to actually instantiate a class to start the execution. The answer lies with the virtual machine.

When the Java program is run to start an application or a browser encounters an `<APPLET>` tag, the virtual machine does a few things for you. In the case of an application, when you type `java MyClass`, the virtual machine calls the static `main()` method in `MyClass`. This does not create an instance of `MyClass`, but, because `main()` is a static method, an instance is not necessary. As pointed out previously, you will typically create an instance of your class in the `main()` method. In the case of an applet, the browser creates an instance of `MyClass` when it encounters `<APPLET CODE="MyClass">` and automatically calls the `init()` method.

GARBAGE COLLECTION

Although Java uses the C++ concept of a constructor, it does not support the complementary destructor method. A major advantage of Java is that you, as a programmer, are not directly responsible for freeing the memory that has been dynamically allocated using the `new` operator. Hence, Java does not include a `delete` operator. This automatic reclaiming of memory provided by Java is referred to as *garbage collection*.

An object is available for garbage collection when there are no longer any references to that object. Garbage collection occurs at intervals determined by the virtual machine, so objects that are available for collection are not immediately reclaimed. You can call `System.gc()` to request that garbage collection take place but this is merely a suggestion to the virtual machine that it is not obligated to obey.

Caution

A common problem in Java programs is the existence of extraneous references to objects that are no longer needed. These references prevent the associated objects from being reclaimed and result in memory leaks during execution. You need to pay careful attention to setting references to unneeded objects to `null`, especially in memory-intensive programs.

REFERRING TO CLASS ELEMENTS

Classes become useful when they work together to build more complex functionality. Java classes often contain references to other classes.

The fields and methods of these referenced classes are accessed using the standard dot notation used in most OOP languages. If a `Circle` class has a `borderColor` field and a `getArea()` method that are publicly accessible, another class with a `Circle` instance named `myCircle` could access them as shown in the following:

```
myCircle.borderColor = Color.blue;
double area = myCircle.getArea();
```

You have seen how to refer to other classes but how does a class refer to itself? Although the reasons to do so might not seem so obvious at first, self-reference by a class is an important capability. In general, there are three situations where this need arises:

- When a parameter or local variable in a method has the same name as a field of the class.
- When a class needs to pass itself as an argument to a method.
- When a class needs to return a reference to itself as the result of a method call. This is particularly helpful in building method calls that can be chained together as a single statement.

Self-reference within a class is supported by the `this` keyword. In addition to the preceding uses for `this`, you also saw its use previously when calling one constructor from another. Here's an example of a common use for `this` in distinguishing a field named `width` from a parameter with the same name:

```
public void setWidth(int width) {
  this.width = width;
}
```

The `Object` Class

The `java.lang.Object` class sits at the root of the Java class hierarchy and is therefore a superclass of every class you create. `Object` is unique in that it is the only class in Java without a superclass. The methods implemented by `Object` provide a framework for several general-purpose operations. You saw one of these methods, the `toString()` method, earlier in the `StopLightColor` class (refer to Listing 7.5). You can override `toString()` in the classes you declare to define a text representation of a class instance. Whenever your program has a need to display a value for an object, `toString()` is called to find out what to display. This is how a method such as `System.out.println()` can accept an `Object` as a parameter in place of a string. In this case, the text sent to the console is the return value from the object's `toString()` method.

The usefulness of `toString()` is also evident when you are building a Swing application. Instead of looping through a set of objects and manually populating a component such as a `JList` with strings that represent each instance, you can add the objects themselves to the list and let the component do the work for you. When this type of Swing component needs to display its entries, it makes calls to the `toString()` methods of the objects without requiring you to do anything. The use of `toString()` also ensures that objects are always represented the same way when they are displayed in this manner. The `Object` class provides a default implementation for `toString()`, but you should normally override this to make the returned string more meaningful.

Object Equality

When two objects are compared using the == operator, the comparison is actually a test of whether the two object references are pointing to the same object. The `equals()` method defined in `Object` performs this same comparison, but the intent is to allow you to override this method and provide your own definition of equality for a given class. The `equals()` method is commonly overridden to return true if two objects are of the same class type and have equivalent values for each instance field.

Copying a Class Instance

The fact that Java always works with objects by reference complicates the issue of copying an object to some degree. Consider the following example:

```
Circle firstCircle = new Circle();
Circle secondCircle = firstCircle;
```

The execution of these two statements creates a single `Circle` object with two references, `firstCircle` and `secondCircle`, pointing to it. The assignment of `firstCircle` to `secondCircle` does not copy the state of the `Circle` referred to by `firstCircle` into a second instance; it copies a reference to the single object that exists. To copy an object, you use the `clone()` method defined in the `Object` class:

```
Circle firstCircle = new Circle();
Circle secondCircle = (Circle)firstCircle.clone();
```

Now, the execution of these modified statements results in two unique objects having the same state. The implementation might seem simple, but there are some other details under the hood to consider. First, the `clone()` method defined in `Object` performs a simple byte-by-byte shallow copy. Because the purpose of clone() is to duplicate the state of an object, this copying process is not preceded by the invoking of a constructor or any initializer blocks. A shallow copy is sufficient in the example here, but, if `Circle` were a more complicated class that included references to other objects, its class declaration would have to override `clone()` to provide a suitable deep-copy implementation. Also, `Circle` must be declared to implement the `Cloneable` marker interface (see Chapter 9). This restriction prevents `clone()` from being called for a class that the programmer has not explicitly stated can support the operation correctly.

Note

A *shallow copy* of an object produces a copy of its primitive attributes and its references to other objects, but it does not create copies of those referenced objects. A *deep copy* produces copies of the referenced objects, any objects they reference, and so on until all the references are exhausted.

CLEANING UP IN THE `finalize()` METHOD

Although Java classes do not need a destructor to free allocated memory, there is support for cleaning up any associated resources before an object is garbage collected. The `Object` class defines a `finalize()` method for this purpose. Empty by default, this method is called by the Java runtime system during the process of garbage collection and can be used to clean up any ongoing processes before the object is destroyed. For example, in a class that deals with sockets, it is a good practice to close all sockets opened by an object before it is destroyed. You could place the code to close the sockets in an overridden version of the `finalize()` method that would be invoked when the instance is no longer being used in the program.

For example, take a look at the `finalize()` method in Listing 7.10.

LISTING 7.10 `NetworkSender.java`—**USING** `finalize()`

```
import java.io.*;
import java.net.*;
public class NetworkSender
{
```

LISTING 7.10 CONTINUED

```
  private Socket me;
  private OutputStream out;

  public NetworkSender(String host, int port) {
    try {
      me = new Socket(host,port);
      out = me.getOutputStream();
    }
    catch (Exception e) {
      System.out.println(e.getMessage());
    }
  }

  public void sendInfo(char signal) {
    try {
      out.write(signal);
      out.flush();
    }
    catch (Exception e) {
      System.out.println(e.getMessage());
    }
  }

  public void disconnect() {
    System.out.println("Disconnecting...");
    try {
      me.close();
    }
    catch (Exception e) {
      System.out.println("Error on Disconnect" + e.getMessage());
    }
    System.out.println("done.");
   }

  // override finalize() to make sure the socket is closed
  protected void finalize() {
    disconnect();
    try {
      super.finalize();
    }
    catch (Throwable t) {
      t.printStackTrace();
    }
  }
}
```

Note

`finalize()` is declared to be protected in `java.lang.Object`, so it must remain protected or become less restricted. Unlike the case of constructors, the compiler does not automatically insert calls to superclass `finalize()` methods. These calls must be explicitly coded as shown previously in Listing 7.10.

Caution

Although the `finalize()` method is a legitimate tool, it should not be relied upon too heavily because garbage collection is not a predictable process. Garbage collection runs in the background as a low-priority thread and might occur only when a program has totally run out of memory. Consequently, it is a good practice to perform such clean-up tasks elsewhere in your code.

CASTING AND CONVERTING REFERENCE TYPES

Classes and arrays are known as reference types in Java. These types are always handled with references. Unlike C/C++, you cannot dereference an object to work with it by value instead. When you are using reference types, it is often necessary to cast or convert an object to another type.

One strength of inheritance is that you can treat an instance of a subclass the same as an instance of its parent class. You typically see this when you pass an object to a method that expects a parameter whose type is that of the object's superclass. This might look like a parameter mismatch in your code but the compiler automatically handles the use of a subclass in place of one of its superclasses by converting the reference. This is not true when you attempt to use a reference declared to be of a superclass type as one of its subclasses. In this case, you need to explicitly cast the reference to the expected type as shown in the following:

```
public void myMethod(MyParentClass myObject) {
  if (myObject != null) {
    MySubClass childInstance = (MySubClass)myObject;
    childInstance.specialMethod();
  }
}
```

COMPILE-TIME VERSUS RUNTIME TYPE CHECKING

If you look carefully at the preceding example, you will notice that there is nothing in place to guarantee that `myObject` really refers to an instance of `MySubClass`. Why does the compiler allow this? The answer lies in the difference between compile-time and runtime type checking. In this example, although it is possible that `myObject` does not refer to the correct instance type, it is also possible that it does. The compiler trusts you to provide a correct instance and thus defers type checking to runtime when the cast is actually performed. If `myMethod` is called with an instance that is not a `MySubClass`, the cast operation will cause a `ClassCastException`.

USING THE `instanceof` OPERATOR

The `instanceof` operator allows you to check the class of an object during execution of your program. This operator is commonly used before a cast is performed to ensure that the cast will not throw an exception. For example, here is a safer version of `MyMethod`:

```
public void myMethod(MyParentClass myObject) {
  // perform an operation if the object passed to the method is
```

```
    // an instance of a particular subclass
    if (myObject instanceof MySubClass) {
      // myObject is a MySubClass instance, so this cast is safe
      MySubClass childInstance = (MySubClass)myObject;
      childInstance.specialMethod();
    }
  }
```

Caution

The `instanceof` operator is useful but you should not use it excessively. If you find yourself coding `instanceof` conditionals in many of your methods, you should probably re-evaluate your class design. In the preceding example, `myMethod` would be cleaner and easier to maintain if `specialMethod` were defined in `MyParentClass` with a do-nothing implementation (it could also be abstract if `MyParentClass` happened to be abstract already). The `MySubClass` implementation of the method would then be an override. With this change, `myMethod` would no longer need to implement special behavior based on the specific subclass type. You could call `specialMethod` directly on `myObject` and polymorphism would take care of the rest. Behavior like that in the original `myMethod` implementation is sometimes necessary, but it is difficult to maintain a method that might need to be updated whenever a new subclass is defined.

INNER CLASSES

Beginning with JDK 1.1, Java has supported the concept of nested, or inner, class declarations. Inner classes aren't found in most other programming languages, so its usefulness might not be clear to you at first. This section describes why inner classes exist and what purposes they serve.

INNER CLASSES DEFINED

Inner classes are classes that are declared within the body of another class. In fact, you can even declare a class within the body of a method. You might wonder why you would ever want to declare one class inside another. You are never required to use inner classes when you develop in Java, but in certain situations they provide you with the ability to organize your code in a more understandable fashion, and, occasionally, they provide the compiler with a means to further optimize your code.

REASONS TO USE INNER CLASSES

The best way to demonstrate the usefulness of inner classes is by example. Interfaces are described in detail in Chapter 9, but for now think of an interface as a set of methods that a class must implement to provide some behavior needed by another class. No matter how many methods an interface defines, a class that supports it must provide an implementation for each one. It often happens that a class does not need to implement any behavior for one or more of an interface's methods. The class must still include a do-nothing implementation for each of these methods. If you write a class that has a lot of methods that don't do anything, the class declaration will begin to look cluttered and the purpose of the class will become less obvious to another programmer reading through the method implementations.

You can avoid the declaration of do-nothing implementations of interface methods if you use an adapter class. An *adapter class* implements an interface by providing a do-nothing implementation for each method. On its own, an adapter class isn't useful, but to a class that wants to implement an interface without implementing all the methods, it provides a clean approach. A class uses an adapter class by extending it and then overriding only those methods that have behavior that needs to be implemented.

This relates to inner classes because a class that extends an adapter class is often limited to a specific use given that it only implements a subset of an interface's methods. If such a class is too specific to reuse, using an inner class reduces the overhead of the class declaration by defining it within the only class that needs that particular implementation. Adapter classes provided within the Swing packages are commonly used as shown in Listing 7.11.

LISTING 7.11 `MyFrame.java`—USE OF ADAPTER CLASSES

```
import java.awt.event.*;
import javax.swing.*;

public class MyFrame extends JFrame {

  public MyFrame() {

    // declare an inner class that extends an adapter class
    class MyWindowAdapter extends WindowAdapter {
      // only do something when the window is closing
      public void windowClosing(WindowEvent e) {
        System.out.println("Window about to close");
        System.exit(0);
      }
    }
    this.addWindowListener( new MyWindowAdapter() );

    // use an anonymous adapter class instead
    this.addWindowListener( new WindowAdapter() {
      // only do something when the window is activated
      public void windowActivated(WindowEvent e) {
        System.out.println("Window is active");
      }
    } );
  }

  public static void main(String[] args) {
    MyFrame frame = new MyFrame();
    frame.setVisible(true);
  }
}
```

Notice in Listing 7.11 that the `WindowAdapter` class is used in two different ways. The `windowClosing` method is implemented within the declaration of the `MyWindowAdapter` inner class that extends `WindowAdapter`. Multiple instances of `MyWindowAdapter` could be declared if

`MyFrame` required it. Now examine the inner class that implements `windowActivated`. There is no name because this declaration demonstrates the use of an *anonymous inner class*. An anonymous inner class is an unnamed class declared for a single use. There is no need for it to have a name because it will never be referred to outside its declaration. You will see anonymous inner classes used extensively in Swing applications.

HOW INNER CLASSES WORK

Under Java 1.0, inner classes were not available. Java designers were able to make the programs that you write using inner classes work with virtual machines that were designed from the 1.0 specification because inner classes aren't really new. When you write a class with an inner class inside it, the compiler takes the inner class outside of the containing class and adjusts the compiled result.

PACKAGES

When you start creating a large number of classes for a program, having a way to organize them becomes important. A clutter of class files is not unlike how your hard drive would look without subdirectories or folders. Imagine if all the files on your hard drive were placed in a single folder. You would have thousands of files without any obvious associations among them and you would have to make sure that no two files had the same name.

Class files without any organization cause similar problems. To overcome this, Java has a system called packages. A package contains a group of classes just as a subdirectory contains a group of files. You have already seen how a number of packages are used in the Java API. For example, `java.awt` and `java.lang` are commonly used packages. The `java.` prefix is reserved by Sun to indicate packages that are part of the SDK. When you create your own packages, the recommended naming convention is to use the reverse of your Internet domain name. For example if you work at a company whose Web site is `www.mycompany.com`, you would start your package names with `com.mycompany`.

A package should contain classes that are related in some way. For example, you might have a package called `com.mycompany.Transportation` that contains classes such as `Car`, `Boat`, `Airplane`, and `Train`. Programmers of applications that deal with modes of transportation could easily access classes of interest to them by using this package.

Packages create namespaces so that duplicate class names can be resolved.

Obviously more than one person will write a `Car` class at some point. However, placing a class in a package is equivalent to prepending the package name to the name of the class. With this, `com.mycompany.Transportation.Car` is easily distinguishable from any other `Car` class.

To make a class a member of a package, you must declare it using the package statement:

```
package Transportation;
```

If you declare a class without a package statement, it is placed in a default package. Use of the package statement is restricted as follows:

- For a class to be included in a package, its source code must be in the same directory as the rest of the package files.
- The package statement must be the first statement in a source file, appearing before any import statements and the first line of any class declaration. You can have comments and whitespace before the package statement, but nothing else.

USING PACKAGES TO ORGANIZE YOUR CODE

Packages are a way of keeping things organized. You could never navigate the large number of classes that are provided with Java if they were not organized into packages. Table 7.1 summarizes some of the top-level packages included with SDK 1.3.

TABLE 7.1 STANDARD JAVA PACKAGE EXAMPLES

Package	Description
`java.applet`	Classes needed to create Java applets that run under Java-compatible browsers.
`java.awt`	Classes helpful in writing platform-independent graphic user interface (GUI) applications.
`java.beans`	Classes that support JavaBeans development.
`java.io`	Classes such as streams for performing input and output.
`java.lang`	Contains the essential Java classes, such as Object and System.
`java.net`	Classes used for creating network applications. These are used in tandem with `java.io` for reading and writing data from a network.
`java.rmi`	The root package of classes used in remote method invocation.
`java.security`	Classes needed to build upon Java's security framework.
`java.sql`	Classes used for accessing a database.
`java.text`	Classes helpful for supporting language-independent applications.
`java.util`	Contains other tools and data structures, such as encoding, decoding, vectors, stacks, and more.

When you separate your classes into packages, you make it easier for other programmers to understand and reuse what you have developed. You could nevertheless place every class developed for a program into a single package. This is allowed and, for sufficiently small programs, perhaps even preferable. It is more likely, however, that you will want to use packages. Nearly every program you develop will require some classes that are useful to other programs also. Separating these classes into packages simplifies their reuse, just like what has been done with the standard Java packages.

Packages and Your File System

When you place the classes you develop into packages, you must store the source files using a subdirectory structure that matches the elements of the package name. For example, the classes in the example `Transportation` package should be stored in a `com/mycompany/Transportation` subdirectory located underneath your working directory or in a path relative to the `CLASSPATH`.

If you have trouble compiling classes in a package. See "Compiler Unable to Locate Source Files," in the "Troubleshooting" section at the end of this chapter.

Importing a Class from Another Package

Packages play a key role in how the compiler locates the other classes referenced by a class you create. When the compiler encounters a reference to another class, it checks to see if that class can be found within the same package as the class being compiled. If you declare a class that references only classes within the same package, you do not have to do anything to help the compiler locate them. If, however, you reference classes outside the package, you have to help the compiler by using the `import` statement. A programmer working in another package could reference your `Car` class by including the following statement in a source file:

```
import com.mycompany.Transportation.Car;
```

This `import` statement tells the compiler what package to look in to locate the `Car` class. A source file can include any number of `import` statements but they must appear after the `package` statement if there is one, and before the first line of any class declaration.

Importing an Entire Package

It is also possible to import all the classes in a package with a single import statement. You have probably already seen this done with some of the SDK classes such as those in `java.awt`. To import an entire package, replace the individual class name with an asterisk:

```
import java.awt.*;
```

This is a convenient replacement for multiple imports from the same package, such as

```
import java.awt.Graphics;
import java.awt.Image;
import java.awt.Button;
import java.awt.Canvas;
```

Importing an entire package is simple, but it does havea slight drawback. When you import using a wildcard, class dependencies are not as obvious to others reading your code. If a class makes use of only a few classes in another package, explicit imports of those individual classes make the dependencies immediately evident. Similarly, when a class from another package is referenced, an explicit import makes it easier for someone reading the code to locate the source file or documentation for that class because the package assignment for it is stated as part of the import.

Note

An import of `java.awt` does not also import `java.awt.event` because package imports are not recursive.

USING A CLASS WITHOUT IMPORTING IT

It is actually not necessary to import a class before you use it. You can instead use the full class name when declaring the instance. If you want to declare an instance of your `Car` class in another package without using an import, you can declare the instance as a `com.mycompany.Transportation.Car`.

IMPLICIT IMPORT OF `java.lang`

You might have noticed from reading the code examples throughout this book that there are certain classes within the SDK that you can use without importing them or referring to them using their full names. The classes in the `java.lang` package are used so frequently that the compiler implicitly imports them for you. This means that you can directly use the `java.lang.System` class in statements like this:

```
System.out.println("System can be used without an import statement");
```

This is convenient, but it can be confusing until you become familiar with the classes defined in the `java.lang package`.

WRAPPING THE PRIMITIVE TYPES IN CLASSES

You saw in Chapter 3, that although Java is a language based on classes, it does support a set of primitive data types that includes `int`, `boolean`, and `float` among others. These types are used extensively, but there are situations in which treating primitives as true Java objects would be more useful. In fact, the `java.lang` package includes a set of wrapper classes for the primitive data types to serve this purpose. This set consists of `Boolean`, `Byte`, `Character`, `Double`, `Float`, `Integer`, `Long`, and `Short`. Each of these classes provides an immutable object representation of its corresponding primitive type. The methods defined by the classes consist mainly of conversion and comparison operations. Each class also overrides `toString()` and `equals()` to provide an intuitive text representation and a simple equality check for wrapped values.

USING THE STANDARD MATHEMATICAL FUNCTIONS

Java provides standard mathematical functions through the static methods of the `java.lang.Math` and `java.lang.StrictMath` (new in SDK 1.3) classes. These methods support absolute value calculation, trigonometry, exponentiation, min/max determination, rounding, random number generation, and other utilities. The `java.lang.Math` implementation won't necessarily produce identical results on different platforms. These differences are in the least-significant bits and are unimportant for most applications. However, SDK 1.3

added `java.lang.StrictMath`. This implementation does not perform as well as `java.lang.Math`, but its methods are guaranteed to produce platform-independent results.

BUILDING A UML CLASS DIAGRAM

Now that you have built up your understanding of classes, look again at how class designs can be communicated to other developers. As discussed in Chapter 1, "Object-Oriented Programming," class diagrams are the UML mechanism for identifying class fields and methods and depicting associations between classes. The first step in building a class diagram is to identify the relevant classes and their inheritance relationships. Field and method declarations can be included in the diagram if that level of detail is needed to support the information you are trying to convey. Perhaps the most useful information, however, is that conveying the associations and relationships between classes.

Figure 7.1 depicts a class diagram extrapolated from the previous `Car` examples.

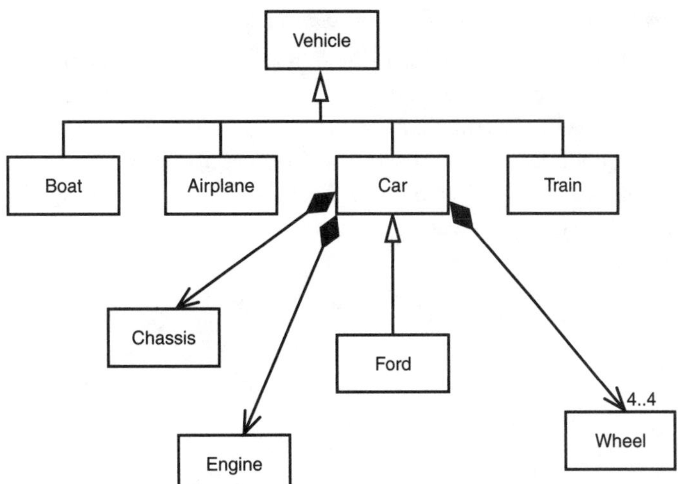

Figure 7.1
A class diagram for the transportation package depicts inheritance and class associations.

TROUBLESHOOTING

NO-ARGUMENT CONSTRUCTOR NOT FOUND IN SUPERCLASS

You get a compiler error stating that the superclass for a class you are compiling does not have a no-argument constructor.

Every class constructor (other than the constructor for `java.lang.Object`) calls one of the constructors for its immediate superclass. This call is an implicit call to the no-argument constructor for the superclass unless you explicitly call another constructor using the `super` keyword with the required parameter list. If the no-argument superclass constructor is being called, the compiler reports an error if this constructor does not exist or is declared private.

Every class has a no-argument constructor by default unless it declares one or more constructors (that accept parameters) without explicitly declaring the no-argument version. If the no-argument constructor for the class you are extending was lost inadvertently, define it explicitly to correct this compiler error. Otherwise, you must include an explicit call to a valid superclass constructor as the first line of each subclass constructor using the `super` keyword.

INCONSISTENT CLASS STATE

You encounter a situation in which the state of an object, as defined by its fields, is inconsistent.

A strength of OOP is the support it provides for encapsulation. If you have fields in a class that are interdependent, you should encapsulate them by declaring them as private. You can then control access to them using public **get** and **set** methods. Each set method should update any fields dependent on the field it modifies to maintain a consistent object state.

COMPILER UNABLE TO LOCATE SOURCE FILES

You are unable to compile classes that are assigned to packages.

When you assign a class to a package, you must store the source file in a subdirectory structure that parallels the package hierarchy. For example, a public class named `Car` declared to be in package `com.transportation.vehicle` must be stored as `Car.java` in a `com/transportation/vehicle` subdirectory underneath the root directory from which `javac` is run. Note that you must compile from a directory one level above the root package directory when compiling classes assigned to packages.

CHAPTER 8

Using Strings and Text

In this chapter

by Chuck Cavaness

INTRODUCING STRINGS

String handling in C or C++ (the languages that inspired Java) is infamously clunky. Java solves that problem the same way many C++ programmers do: by creating a `String` class. Java's `String` class enables your programs to manage text strings effortlessly, using statements similar to those used in simpler languages, such as BASIC or Pascal.

You can probably find many instances of the `String` class in most Java applications, especially business type applications. They are used extensively. So, what exactly is a Java `String` class anyway? In its simplest form, a string is nothing more than one or more text characters arranged consecutively in memory. You can think of a string as an array of characters, with this array having an index that starts at zero. (That is, the first character in the string is at array index 0.)

Note

> The beginning index of a Java `String` is 0, not 1. This is very important and will make it very hard to find bugs if you are not aware of it and use 1 as the beginning index of a string. Many things in Java start with 0 instead of 1. This is just one more.

If you are having trouble with String indexes, see "One Off Index Error," in the "Troubleshooting" section at the end of this chapter.

Unfortunately, few computer languages deal with strings in such a simple form. This is because a program needs to know where a string ends, and there are several different solutions to the length problem. Pascal, for example, tacks the length of the string onto the front of the characters, whereas C++ expects to find a null character (a zero) at the end of the string. A Java `String` is an object, rather thing just being a primitive or an array of primitives. This comes in handy, as you will see later.

In Java, strings can be represented by one of two classes:

- `String Best` is used for string constants—that is, for strings that are not going to change after they're created.
- `StringBuffer` is used for strings that require a lot of manipulation, such as overriding a Class's `toString` method to provide a more meaningful display string for the class.

You'll learn more about the `StringBuffer` class later in this chapter. For now, concentrate on the `String` class itself.

Note

With the `String` class, you can do operations such as find, compare, and concatenate characters, but you cannot insert new characters into the string or change the length of the string. (Concatenating might seem like it is simply inserting new characters; however, in actuality it is creating an entirely new string.) This inability to modify an existing string is known as *immutability*.

Within an object of the `String` class, Java creates an array of characters much like that used for strings in C++ programs. Because this character array is hidden within the class, however, it cannot be accessed except through the class's methods. This data encapsulation (a key feature of object-oriented programming, by the way) ensures that the string will be maintained properly and will be manipulated in accordance with the rules of the class. You work with the `String` through the public methods of the class and can't modify the internal data structure.

The alternative to this approach would be to actually use an array of characters to represent a `String`. This is how several other languages handle `Strings`. The problem with that approach is that all code that modifies or works with the `String` must be careful not to misuse the `String`. The other problem is that the internal data structure of the `String` is exposed. That is, the client code using the array of characters is aware that the `String` is stored in an array. This is a violation of data encapsulation that is fundamental in object-oriented design and programming. In contrast, a Java `String` encapsulates how the actual `String` is stored. It could be stored in a different data structure, and because the client uses the public methods of the `String` class, the client does not need to know how it's stored internally. This is a good thing.

Figures 8.1 and 8.2 illustrate this concept. In Figure 8.1, a conventional C++ string is left hanging in memory where the program can manipulate it at will, regardless of whether the manipulation makes sense or results in a fatal error. In Figure 8.2, the string is protected by the methods of the class—the only way the program can access the string.

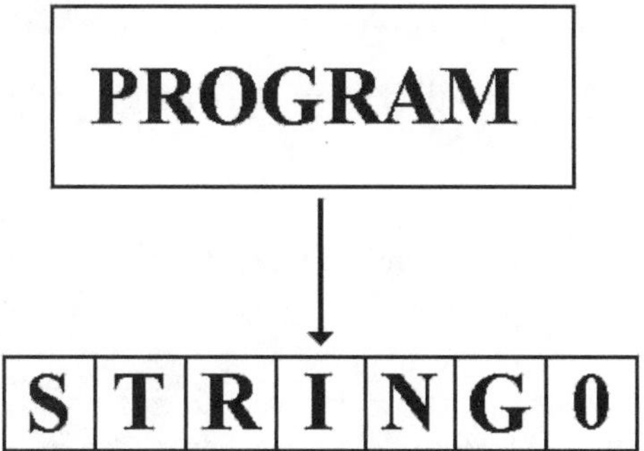

Figure 8.1
In conventional programs, strings can be accessed directly by the program, leading to complications and errors.

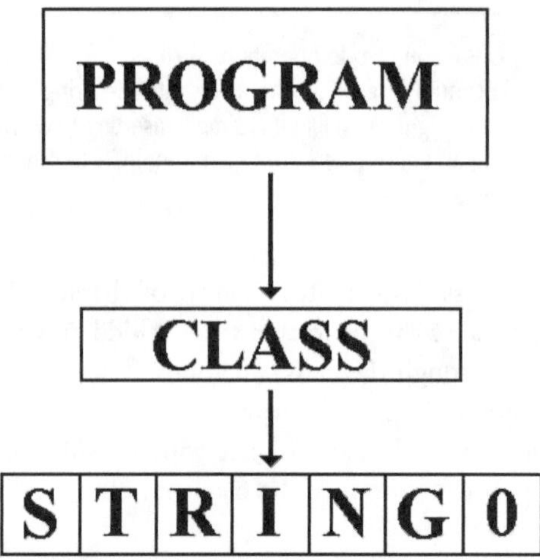

Figure 8.2
By using a `String` class, the string can be accessed only through the class's methods, which eliminates many potential errors.

Using the `String` Class

In Java, you create strings by creating an instance of the `String` class. This `String` object can be created implicitly or explicitly depending on how the string is being used in the program. To create a string implicitly, you just place a string literal in your program, and Java automatically creates a `String` object for the string. This is because, even internally, Java uses `String` objects to represent string literals. Look at this line, for example:

```
String fullName = new String( "Mr. John Doe" );
```

Java implicitly creates a `String` object for the string literal `"Mr. John Doe"`. Every time you refer to a string this way in a Java program, you're creating a `String` object.

The other way to create a `String` object is to explicitly instantiate an object of the `String` class. The `String` class has nine `constructors`, so there are plenty of ways to explicitly create a `String` object, the most obvious way being this:

```
String str = new String("This is a string");
```

You can also declare a `String` object and then set its value later in the program, like this:

```
String str = null;
str = "This is a string";
```

Finally, any of the following lines creates a null string:

```
String str = new String();
String str = "";
```

Caution

There's a big difference between a null `String` object reference and a null string. When you declare a `String` object with a line such as `String str = null`, you are declaring an object of the `String` class that has not yet been instantiated. That is, there is not yet a `String` object associated with the variable `str`. When you create a `String` object with a line such as `String str = ""`, you are creating a fully instantiated `String` object whose string contains no characters (has a string length of zero). This is called a null or an empty string.

Although the preceding examples are the most common ways of explicitly creating `String` objects, the `String` class offers several alternatives. The nine constructors in the `String` class look like this:

```
public String()
public String(byte[] bytes)
public String(byte[] bytes, int offset, int length)
public String(byte[] bytes, int offset, int length, String enc)
public String(byte[] bytes, String enc)
public String(char[] value)
public String(char[] value, int offset, int count)
public String(String value)
public String (StringBuffer buffer)
```

These constructors create, respectively, the following:

- Null string
- A `String` object by converting the byte array using the default encoding
- A `String` object by converting the byte array using the default encoding starting at offset for length bytes
- A `String` object by converting the byte array using the encoding passed in starting at offset for length bytes
- A `String` object by converting the byte array using the passed in encoding
- `String` from an `array` of characters
- `String` from a `subarray` of characters
- A `String` object using the string passed in to copy it from
- `String` from a `StringBuffer` object

GETTING INFORMATION ABOUT A String OBJECT

After you have your `String` object constructed, you can call upon the methods in the `String` class to obtain information about the string. To get the length of the string, for example, you can call the `length` method, like this:

```
String str = "This is a string";
int len = str.length();
```

The value of the `len` variable should be 16, which is the length of the string (including spaces, of course).

If you want to know whether a string starts with a certain prefix, you can call the `startsWith` method, like this:

```
String str = "This is a string";
boolean result = str.startsWith("This");
```

Here, the boolean variable result is equal to `true`, because `str` does indeed start with `This`. In the following example, `result` is `false`:

```
String str = "This is a string";
boolean result = str.startsWith("is");
```

A similar method is `endsWith`, which determines whether the `String` object ends with a given set of characters. You use that method as follows:

```
String str = "This is a string";
boolean result = str.endsWith("string");
```

In this example, `result` ends up equal to `true`, whereas the following code segment sets `result` equal to `false`:

```
String str = "This is a string";
boolean result = str.endsWith("This");
```

If you're setting up a table for strings that you want to be able to locate quickly, you can use a hash table. To get a hash code for a string, you can call the `hashCode` method:

```
String str = "This is a string";
int hashcode = str.hashCode();
```

If you want to find the location of the first occurrence of a character within a string, use the `indexOf` method:

```
String str = "This is a string";
int index = str.indexOf('a');
```

In this example, index is equal to 8, which is the index of the first a in the string.

Note

Remember that the first position in a `String` has an index of 0 and the last position in a `String` has an index of length –1.

To find the location of subsequent characters, you can use two versions of the `indexOf` method. To find the first occurrence of `i`, for example, you might use these lines:

```
String str = "This is a string";
int index = str.indexOf('i');
```

This gives `index` a value of `2`. To find the next occurrence of `i`, you can use a line similar to this:

```
index = str.indexOf('i', index+1);
```

By including the `index+1` as the method's second argument, you're telling Java to start searching at `index` 3 in the string (the old value of `index`, plus 1). This results in `index` being equal to 5, which is the location of the second occurrence of `i` in the string. If you called the previous line again, `index` would be equal to 13, which is the location of the third `i` in the string.

You can also search for characters backward through a string, using the `lastIndexOf` method:

```
String str = "This is a string";
int index = str.lastIndexOf("i");
```

Here, `index` is equal to 13. To search backward for the next `i`, you might use a line like this:

```
index = str.lastIndexOf('i', index-1);
```

Now, `index` is equal to 5, because the `index-1` as the second argument tells Java where to begin the backward search. The variable `index` was equal to 13 after the first call to `lastIndexOf()`, so in the second call, `index-1` equals 12.

There are also versions of `indexOf` and `lastIndexOf` that search for substrings within a string. The following example sets `index` to 10, for instance:

```
String str = "This is a string";
int index = str.indexOf("string");
```

Listing 8.1 is a small application that gives you a chance to experiment with the `indexOf` method. When you run the application, you provide two strings on the command line. The first string is the string that you want to search through and the second is the substring that you are looking for.

LISTING 8.1 `IndexOfExample.java`—AN APPLICATION THAT SEARCHES FOR SUBSTRINGS

```
public class IndexOfExample
{
  // Default Constructor
  public IndexOfExample()
  {
    super();
  }

  // Method that actually performs the search
  public int doSearch( String str, String subStr )
  {
    return str.indexOf( subStr );
  }

  // Main Method
  public static void main( String[] args )
  {
    if ( args.length != 2 )
    {
      System.out.println( "Usage: java IndexOfExample <String> <Substring>" );
      System.exit( 0 );
    }

    // Create an instance of the example
    IndexOfExample example = new IndexOfExample();
    // Get the strings passed in from the command line
    String str = args[0];
    String subStr = args[1];
```

LISTING 8.1 CONTINUED

```
    // Inform the user what is going on
    System.out.println( "Searching string: " + str + " for: " + subStr );

    // perform the search
    int index = example.doSearch( str, subStr );

    // check the result
    if ( index != -1 )
    {
      System.out.println( "Found the substring at position " + index );
    }
    else
    {
      System.out.println( "Did not find the substring" );
    }
  }
}
```

Here is what the output looks like when you run the application in Listing 8.1:

```
C:\jdk1.3se_book\classes>java IndexOfExample "An apple a day" day
Searching string: An apple a day for: day
Found the substring at position 11

C:\jdk1.3se_book\classes>
```

Notice that quotes had to be put around the command line argument `"An apple a day"` in the search query so that the entire quote would be considered as a single argument.

COMPARING STRINGS

Often, you need to know when two strings are equal. For example, you might want to compare a string entered by the user to another string in your program or compare data returned by the database for a particular value. There are three general ways you can compare strings:

- Calling the `equals()` method
- Calling the `equalsIgnoreCase()` method
- Using the normal comparison operator `==`

The `equals` method returns `true` when the argument is non-null and the argument string represents the same set of characters as the source string. Otherwise, it returns `false`. Here's an example:

```
String str = "This is a string";
boolean result = str.equals("This is a string");
```

Here, the boolean variable `result` is equal to `true`. Because strings of exactly the same set of characters will represent the same reference in memory, you could also do something similar using the comparison, or double-equals, operator:

```
String str = "This is a string";
if (str == "This is a string")
    result = true;
```

This also results in `result` being `true`. Remember that for this to be `true`, it must be exactly the same literal string.

Although these two methods are the easiest ways to compare strings, the `String` class gives you many other options. The `equalsIgnoreCase` method compares two strings without regard for upper- or lowercase letters. That is, the following code sets result to `false` because `equals` considers the case of the characters in the string:

```
String str = "THIS IS A STRING";
boolean result = str.equals("this is a string");
```

This code fragment, however, sets `result` to `true`:

```
String str = "THIS IS A STRING";
boolean result = str.equalsIgnoreCase("this is a string");
```

If you want to know more than just whether the strings are equal, you can call on the `compareTo` method, which returns a value less than zero when the `String` object is less than the given string, zero when the strings are equal, and greater than zero if the `String` object is greater than the given string. The comparison is done according to lexicographic ordering. So, this code segment sets result to a value greater than zero because `THIS IS A STRING` is greater than `ANOTHER STRING`:

```
String str = "THIS IS A STRING";
int result = str.compareTo("ANOTHER STRING");
```

Note

With "Lexicographic ordering," if two strings are different, then either they have different characters at some index that is a valid index for both strings, or their lengths are different, or both.

If they have different characters at one or more index positions, then the string whose character at the closest position to `0` has the smaller value compared to the string at the same index position, as determined by using the < operator, lexicographically precedes the other string.

If there is no index position at which they differ, then the shorter string lexicographically precedes the longer string.

In the following comparison, however, `result` is set to a value less than zero, because `THIS IS A STRING` is less than `ZZZ ANOTHER STRING`:

```
String str = "THIS IS A STRING";
int result = str.compareTo("ZZZ ANOTHER STRING");
```

Finally, the following comparison results in zero because the strings are equal:

```
String str = "THIS IS A STRING";
int result = str.compareTo("THIS IS A STRING");
```

C and C++ programmers should be familiar with this form of string comparison.

The `regionMatches` method is another comparison method that you can use to compare part of one string with part of another. Here's an example:

```
String str = "THIS IS A STRING";
boolean result = str.regionMatches(10, "A STRING", 2, 6);
```

The `regionMatches()` method's four arguments are as follows:

- Where to start looking in the source string
- The string to compare to
- The location in the comparison string at which to start looking
- The number of characters to compare

The preceding example sets `result` to `true`. In this case, Java starts looking in `THIS IS A STRING` at the tenth character (starting from 0), which is the `S` in `STRING`. Java also starts its comparison at the second character of the given string `A STRING`, which is also the `S` in `STRING`. Java compares six characters starting at the given offsets, which means it is comparing `STRING` with `STRING`, a perfect match.

There's also a version of `regionMatches` that is not case sensitive. The following example sets `result` to `true`:

```
String str = "THIS IS A STRING";
boolean result = str.regionMatches(true, 10, "A string", 2, 6);
```

The first argument in this version of `regionMatches` is a boolean value indicating whether the comparison should not be case sensitive. A parameter value of `true` tells the method to ignore the case of the characters. A value of `false` tells the method to use a case-sensitive comparison. This is the same as you get with the four-argument version of `regionMatches`.

Listing 8.2 is an application that gives you a chance to experiment with the `compareTo` method. When you run the application, you need to provide two strings that will be compared against one another.

LISTING 8.2 `StringCompareExample.java`—**AN APPLICATION COMPARING TWO STRINGS**

```
public class StringCompareExample
{
  // Default Constructor
  public StringCompareExample()
  {
    super();
  }

  // Method that actually performs the comparison
  public int compareStrings( String str1, String str2 )
  {
    return str1.compareTo( str2 );
  }
```

LISTING 8.2 CONTINUED

```
  // Main Method
  public static void main( String[] args )
  {
    if ( args.length != 2 )
    {
      System.out.println(
          "Usage: java StringCompareExample <String1> <String2>" );
System.exit( 0 );
    }

    // Create an instance of the example
    StringCompareExample example = new StringCompareExample();
    // Get the strings passed in from the command line
    String str1 = args[0];
    String str2 = args[1];

    // Inform the user what is going on
    System.out.println(
        "Comparing string: '" + str1 + "' with: '" + str2 + "'");

    // perform the comparison
    int result = example.compareStrings( str1, str2 );

    // check the result for a negative
    if ( result < 0 )
    {
      System.out.println( "String 1 is less than String 2" );
    }
    else if ( result > 0 )
    {
      System.out.println( "String 1 is greater than String 2" );
    }
    else
    {
      System.out.println( "String 1 and String 2 are equal" );
    }
  }
}
```

Here is the output when you run the example from Listing 8.2:

```
C:\jdk1.3se_book\classes>java
➥StringCompareExample "All good things" "Must come to an End"
Comparing string: 'All good things' with: 'Must come to an End'
String 1 is less than String 2

C:\jdk1.3se_book\classes>java
➥StringCompareExample "All good things" "All good people"
Comparing string: 'All good things' with: 'All good people'
String 1 is greater than String 2

C:\jdk1.3se_book\classes>
```

String Extraction

There might be occasions in your programs when you want to extract portions of a string. The String class provides this functionality with a set of methods for just that purpose. You can determine the character at a given position in the string, for example, by calling the charAt method, like this:

```
String str = "This is a string";
char chr = str.charAt(6);
```

In these lines, the character variable chr ends up with a value of s, which is the fifth character in the string. Why didn't chr become equal to i? Remember that in Java, you start counting array elements at zero rather than one.

A similar method, getChars(), enables you to copy a portion of a String object to a character array:

```
String str = "This is a string";
char chr[] = new char[20];
str.getChars(5, 12, chr, 0);
```

In this code sample, the character array chr ends up containing the characters is a st. The getChars method's arguments are the index of the first character in the string to copy, the index of the last character in the string, the destination array, and where in the destination array to start copying characters.

The method getBytes does the same thing as getChars, but uses a byte array as the destination array:

```
String str = "This is a string";
byte byt[] = new byte[20];
str.getBytes(5, 12, byt, 0);
```

Another way to extract part of a string is to use the substring method:

```
String str1 = "THIS IS A STRING";
String str2 = str1.substring(5);
```

In this case, the String object str2 ends up equal to the substring IS A STRING. This is because substring()'s single argument is the index of the character at which the substring starts. Every character from the index to the end of the string is extracted.

Note

Remember that Strings are immutable. Therefore, all these methods that extract or otherwise seem to work on an existing String really just return a new String object and do not change the original String.

If you don't want to extract all the way to the end of the string, you can use the second version of the substring method, whose arguments specify the beginning and ending indexes:

```
String str1 = "THIS IS A STRING";
String str2 = str1.substring(5, 9);
```

These lines set str2 to the substring IS A.

Listing 8.3 is an application that enables you to experiment with the `substring` method. When you run the application, you need to provide a `String` and two numbers. The first number is the starting index and the second number is the ending index.

LISTING 8.3 `SubstringExample.java`—**AN APPLICATION THAT EXTRACTS SUBSTRINGS**

```
public class SubstringExample
{
  // Default Constructor
  public SubstringExample()
  {
    super();
  }

  // Method that actually performs the extraction
  public String extractSubstring( String str1, int beginIndex, int endIndex )
  {
    return str1.substring( beginIndex, endIndex );
  }

  // Main Method
  public static void main( String[] args )
  {
    if ( args.length != 3 )
    {
      System.out.println(
            "Usage: java StringCompareExample <String1> <String2>" );
System.exit( 0 );
    }

    String str = args[0];
    String beginIndexStr = args[1];
    String endIndexStr = args[2];
    int beginIndex = 0;
    int endIndex = 0;

    // Make sure the arguments are valid
    try
    {
      beginIndex = Integer.parseInt( beginIndexStr );
      endIndex = Integer.parseInt( endIndexStr );
    }
    catch( NumberFormatException ex )
    {
      System.out.println( "The arguments are invalid" );
    }

    // Create an instance of the example
    SubstringExample example = new SubstringExample();
    // Get the strings passed in from the command line

    // Inform the user what is going on
    System.out.println(
    "Extracting from string: '" + str + "' starting at: " + beginIndex +
  ➥" endIndex: " + endIndex );
```

LISTING 8.3 CONTINUED

```
    // perform the comparison
    String newSubstring =
        example.extractSubstring( str, beginIndex, endIndex );

    System.out.println( "Substring: " + newSubstring );
  }
}
```

Here is the output when you run the example from Listing 8.3 using some sample `Strings`:

```
C:\jdk1.3se_book\classes>java SubstringExample "Now is the time for all" 4 15
Extrating from string: 'Now is the time for all' starting at: 4 endIndex: 15
Substring: is the time

C:\jdk1.3se_book\classes>
```

STRING MANIPULATION

Although the `String` class is used for string constants, the class does provide some string manipulation methods that "modify" the `String` object. The word modify is in quotation marks here because as stated earlier, these string manipulation methods don't actually change the original `String` object, but rather create an additional `String` object that incorporates the requested changes. A good example of this is the `replace()` method, which enables you to replace any character in a string with another character:

```
String str1 = "THIS IS A STRING";
String str2 = str1.replace('T', 'X');
```

If the code fragment above were to be executed, `str2` would contain the `String` `XHIS IS A SXRING` after execution because the call to `replace` requests that every occurrence of a `T` be replaced with an `X`. Note that `str1` remains unchanged and that `str2` is a brand new `String` object.

If you want to be certain of the case of characters in a string, you can rely on the `toUpperCase` and `toLowerCase` methods, each of which returns a string whose characters have been converted to the appropriate case. Look at these lines, for example:

```
String str1 = "THIS IS A STRING";
String str2 = str1.toLowerCase();
```

After execution of this code fragment, `str2` is `this is a string` because the `toLowerCase` method converts all characters in the string to lowercase. The `toUpperCase` method, of course, does just the opposite—converting all characters to uppercase.

Sometimes you have strings that contain leading or trailing spaces. The `String` class features a method called `trim` that removes both leading and trailing whitespace characters. You use it like this:

```
String str1 = "   THIS IS A STRING   ";
String str2 = str1.trim();
```

In this example, str2 would contain the string THIS IS A STRING, missing all the spaces before the first T and after the G.

Concatenating Strings

Another way you can manipulate strings is to concatenate (in other words, join) them. So, when you concatenate two strings, you get a new string that contains both of the original strings. Look at these lines of Java source code, for example. There are several ways to concatenate Strings together. The first is the concat method on the String class.

```
String str1 = "This is one string";
String str2 = str1.concat(" and this is another.");
```

If this code fragment was executed, str2 would contain This is one string and this is another and str1 would remain unchanged. As you can see, the concat method's single argument is the string to concatenate with the original string.

To make things simpler, the String class defines an operator, the plus sign (+), for concatenating strings. By using this operator, you can join strings in a more intuitive way. Here's an example:

```
String str1 = "This is one string";
String str2 = str1 + " and this is another.";
```

This code segment results in exactly the same strings as the preceding concat example. Note that you can use the concatenation operator many times in a single line, like this:

```
String str = "This " + "is " + "a test";
```

As you'll see in the StringBuffer section shortly, there is another alternative to using the concat method or the "+" operator when you need to concatenate many Strings together.

Converting Objects to Strings

As you learned in one of the earlier chapters, the Class Object implements a basic toString, which every class that inherits from Object will be able to use. The behavior in the Object class for the method just returns a String that is the name of the class, followed by the @ symbol, and a unsigned hexadecimal value of the hash code for the object.

You should most always override the toString method for your Java classes to provide a user-friendly String representation of the instance of the object. Listing 8.4 shows an example class that overrides the toString method to print out a more user-friendly representation of the instance.

If you are not seeing the correct display string for one or more of your Java Classes, see "Incorrect String *Representation," in the "Troubleshooting" section at the end of this chapter.*

LISTING 8.4 `Customer.java`—**AN** `Example` **CLASS THAT OVERRIDES THE** `toString()` **METHOD**

```
public class Customer
{
  // Default Constructor
  public Customer()
  {
    super();
  }

  // Private Instance Variables
  private String id;
  private String name;
  private String city;
  private String state;
  private String zip;

  // Public Accessors
  public String getId()
  {
    return id;
  }

  public void setId( String custId )
  {
    id = custId;
  }

  public void setName( String newName )
  {
    name = newName;
  }

  public String getName()
  {
    return name;
  }

  public void setCity( String city )
  {
    this.city = city;
  }

  public String getCity()
  {
    return city;
  }

  public void setState( String state )
  {
    this.state = state;
  }

  public String getState()
  {
    return state;
```

Listing 8.4 Continued

```
  }

  public void setZip( String zip )
  {
    this.zip = zip;
  }

  public String getZip()
  {
    return zip;
  }

  // Override the default toString method to output something of your own
  public String toString()
  {
    StringBuffer buf = new StringBuffer();
    buf.append( "ID: " );
    buf.append( getId() );
    buf.append( " Name: " );
    buf.append( getName() );
    buf.append( " City: " );
    buf.append( getCity() );
    buf.append( " State: " );
    buf.append( getState() );
    buf.append( " Zip: " );
    buf.append( getZip() );

    return buf.toString();
  }
}
```

If you had an instance of the `Customer` class, called the `toString` method on it, and sent it out to the console like this

```
System.out.println( customer.toString() );
```

the output would look this:

```
ID: 12 Name: Bryan Daniel City: Atlanta State: California Zip: 11111
```

This is much easier to read than the default, which might look like this:

```
Customer@1e85
```

You should always override the `toString` method for your classes if you need to. It will also help when debugging.

Converting Primitives to Strings

Just as you can convert an `Object` representation into a `String`, you can also explicitly convert a primitive into a `String`. There are several ways that this can be done, but by far the easiest is to use the `String` class's `valueOf()` method. The `valueOf` method can be used to convert just about any type of data object to a `String`, thus enabling you to display the `Object`'s value onscreen. The following lines convert an integer to a string, for example:

```
int value = 10;
String str = String.valueOf( value );
```

Notice that `valueOf` is a static method, meaning that it can be called by referencing the `String` class directly, without having to instantiate a `String` object. Of course, you can also call `valueOf` through any object of the `String` class, like this:

```
int value = 10;
String str1 = "";
String str2 = str1.valueOf( value );
```

USING THE StringBuffer CLASS

The `StringBuffer` class enables you to create `String` objects that can be changed in various ways, unlike the `String` class, which are immutable. When you modify a string of the `StringBuffer` class, you're not creating a new `String` object, but rather operating directly on the original string itself. For this reason, the `StringBuffer` class offers a different set of methods than the `String` class, all of which operate directly on the buffer that contains the string.

CREATING A StringBuffer OBJECT

The `StringBuffer` class offers several constructors that enable you to construct a `StringBuffer` object in various ways. Those constructors look like this:

```
StringBuffer()
StringBuffer(int length)
StringBuffer(String str)
```

These constructors create an empty `StringBuffer`, an empty `StringBuffer` of the given length, and a `StringBuffer` from a `String` object (or string literal), respectively.

APPENDING TO A StringBuffer

You saw earlier that the `concat` method or the `"+"` operator can be used to concatenate string objects. To append strings using a `StringBuffer`, you just pass the string to be appended as an argument to the `append` method on the `StringBuffer` Class. The following code shows how easy it is to concatenate multiple `String` objects:

```
StringBuffer buf = new StringBuffer();
buf.append( "This is " );
buf.append( "another way " );
buf.append( "to join " );
buf.append( 5 );
buf.append( " strings together" );
```

Notice that you can also append numbers with the strings. In fact, the `StringBuffer` class has an append method that supports all the Java primitives. A neat feature about the append method is that you can chain multiple append methods together like this:

```
StringBuffer buf = new StringBuffer();
buf.append( "This is another " ).append( "StringBuffer object" );
```


Note

When you use the "+" operator to concatenate `String` objects, the compiler actually uses a `StringBuffer` internally to perform the concatenation. Whether you use a "+" operator or a `StringBuffer` instance should depend on how many strings you are appending and which way makes it easier to read for the reader of the code.

CONVERTING A StringBuffer OBJECT TO A String

To produce the `Result` string from the `StringBuffer` instance, just call the `toString` method on the `StringBuffer` instance like this:

```
StringBuffer buf = new StringBuffer();
buf.append( "This is " );
buf.append( "another way " );
buf.append( "to join " );
buf.append( 5 );
buf.append( " strings together" );
return buf.toString();
```

You've already had some experience with string extraction when you learned about the `String` class. The `StringBuffer` class has two of the same methods for accomplishing this task. Those methods are `charAt` and `getChars`, both of which work similarly to the `String` versions. Here's an example of using `charAt`:

```
StringBuffer str = new StringBuffer("String buffer");
char ch = str.charAt(5);
```

And here's an example of using `getChars`:

```
StringBuffer str = new StringBuffer("String buffer");
char ch[] = new char[20];
str.getChars(7, 10, ch, 0);
```

In addition, you can also obtain a `subString` from a `StringBuffer`, just like with the `String` class as shown in the next example:

```
StringBuffer str = new StringBuffer("String buffer");
String buffer = str.subString(8);
String rin = str.subString(3,6);
```

MANIPULATING A StringBuffer OBJECT

You can modify the string that's stored in a `StringBuffer` object in several ways. Unlike the string modification methods in the `String` class, which create a new string, the methods in the `StringBuffer` class work directly on the buffer in which the original string is stored. The first thing you can do with a string buffer is set its length. You do this by calling the `setLength` method:

```
StringBuffer str = new StringBuffer("String buffer");
str.setLength(40);
```

This method's single argument is the new length. If the new length is greater than the old length, both the string and buffer length are increased, with the additional characters being filled with zeros. If the new length is smaller than the old length, characters are chopped off the end of the string, but the buffer size remains the same.

If you want to be guaranteed a specific buffer size, you can call the `ensureCapacity` method, like this:

```
StringBuffer str = new StringBuffer("String buffer");
str.ensureCapacity(512);
```

The `ensureCapacity` method's argument is the new capacity for the buffer.

You can change a character in the string buffer by calling the `setCharAt` method:

```
StringBuffer str = new StringBuffer("String buffer");
str.setCharAt(3, 'X');
```

The `setCharAt` method's arguments are the index of the character to change and the new character. In the preceding example, the string buffer becomes `StrXng buffer`. You can also replace sections of the `String` with `Strings` or other native types using the `replace` methods. The set of `replace` methods works similar to `setCharAt`, only instead of requiring a character, you can replace sections of the other string types as well. Notice in the following example, that with `insert` you must provide the beginning and ending index of the characters to replace, instead of just the single character index you need with `setCharAt`:

```
StringBuffer str = new StringBuffer("String buffer");
str.replace(3,6, 'XYZ');
```

You can add characters to the end of the string with the `append` method and insert characters anywhere in the string with the `insert` method. Both of these methods come in several versions that enable you to handle many different types of data. To add a character version of an integer to the end of the string, for example, do something like this:

```
StringBuffer str = new StringBuffer("String buffer");
int value = 15;
str.append(value);
```

After this code executes, `str` contains `String buffer15`. Similarly, you insert characters like this:

```
StringBuffer str = new StringBuffer("String buffer");
int value = 15;
str.insert(6, value);
```

This code results in a string of `String15 buffer`. The two arguments in the previous version of `insert` are the index at which to insert the characters and the data object to insert.

You can also delete characters from the `StringBuffer` using `deleteCharAt` and the `delete` method. `deletCharAt` requires the index of the character you want to delete, whereas `delete()` requires the start (inclusive) index and the end (exclusive) index, as shown in the next example:

```
StringBuffer str = new StringBuffer("String buffer");
str.deleteCharAt(6);
str.delete(3,6);
```

USING THE StringTokenizer CLASS

There are times when you are dealing with Strings that must be broken up into pieces or into multiple Strings. Where the strings are broken apart depends on which delimiters are specified for the tokenization process. By default, a space is used to separate the strings, but you can also use any other character to separate the tokens.

Imagine if you had to parse through a text file of words and separate each word so that later you could perform a query and determine if a particular word was in your search list and how many times it appeared. As you can see, searching through a large String and looking for beginnings and endings of words could be tedious and take some effort. Fortunately for Java developers, you get this feature free with the StringTokenizer class.

The StringTokenizer class is in the java.util package. You must import the util package or at least the StringTokenizer class into your application if you plan to use it. You can construct a StringTokenizer object in several ways, but the easiest is to supply the string you want to tokenize as the constructor's single argument, like this:

```
StringTokenizer tokenizer = new StringTokenizer("One Two Three Four Five");
```

This type of string tokenizer uses space characters as the separators (called *delimiters*) between the tokens. You can also supply a different delimiter for the tokens to be separated by. To get a token, you call either the nextElement or the nextToken methods. The nextElement method returns an Object, whereas the nextToken returns a String. The following is an example of getting the next token as a String:

```
String token = tokenizer.nextToken();
```

Each time you call nextToken, you get the next token in the string. Usually, you extract tokens using a while loop. To control the while loop, you call the hasMoreTokens method, which returns true as long as there are more tokens in the string. A typical tokenizer loop might look like this:

```
while ( tokenizer.hasMoreTokens() )
{
   String token = tokenizer.nextToken();
}
```

As you might have guessed, the StringTokenizer maintains the what the current position it is at in the String that it is tokenizing. Certain methods like nextToken advance the current position on to the next position. The tokenizer takes a substring of the String that it is tokenizing and returns it back from the nextToken method. The original String is not modified during this process.

You can also determine how many tokens are in the string by calling the countTokens() method:

```
StringTokenizer tokenizer = new StringTokenizer("One Two Three Four Five");
int count = tokenizer.countTokens();
```

In this example, count equals 5.

GETTING ALL THE TOKENS FROM A FILE

Listing 8.5 shows a Java application that opens and reads from a file and searches for all the strings that are within the file that match a string that you pass in on the command line.

LISTING 8.5 `WordSearchExample.java`—**A APPLICATION THAT TOKENIZES STRINGS**

```
import java.util.StringTokenizer;
import java.io.*;

public class WordSearchExample
{
  private String fileName = null;

  // Default Constructor
  public WordSearchExample( String fileName )
  {
    super();
    this.fileName = fileName;
  }

  // Private Accessor
  private String getFilename()
  {
    return fileName;
  }

  // Method that actually performs the search
  public int doSearch( String word )
  {
    LineNumberReader reader = null;
    int count = 0;
    StringTokenizer tokenizer = null;
    String currentString = null;
    String tempString = null;
    try
    {
      reader = new LineNumberReader( new FileReader( getFilename() ) );
      while( (currentString = reader.readLine()) != null )
      {

        // No sense tokenizing an empty string
        if ( currentString.equals( "" ) )
          continue;

        System.out.println(
            "Searching through string: " + currentString );

        tokenizer = new StringTokenizer( currentString );
        while( tokenizer.hasMoreTokens() )
        {
          tempString = tokenizer.nextToken();
          if ( !tempString.equals("") && tempString.equals( word ))
          {
            System.out.println(
         "Found on line " + reader.getLineNumber() + ": " + currentString );
            count++;
```

LISTING 8.5 CONTINUED

```
          }
        }
      }
    }
    catch( IOException ex )
    {
      System.out.println(
            "Problem locating or opening the file: " + getFilename() );
    }

    // return the number of instances that were found
    return count;
  }

  // Main Method
  public static void main( String[] args )
  {
    if ( args.length != 2 )
    {
      System.out.println( "Usage: java WordSearchExample <Filename>" );
      System.exit( 0 );
    }

    // Get the strings passed in from the command line
    String fileName = args[0];
    String word = args[1];

    // Create an instance of the Example Class
    WordSearchExample example = new WordSearchExample( args[0] );

    int count = example.doSearch( word );
    System.out.println (
         count + " instances of the word: " + word + " found!" );
  }
}
```

Here is the output when the word `String` is searched for in the text file using the `WordSearchExample` from Listing 8.5:

```
C:\jdk1.3se_book\classes>java WordSearchExample c:\\jdk1.3se_book\sample.txt
String
Searching: String handling in C or C++ (the languages that inspired Java) is
infamously clunky.
Found on line 1: String handling in C or C++ (the languages that inspired Java)is
infamously clunky.


Searching: Java solves that problem the same way many C++ programmers do: by
creating a String class.
Found on line 2: Java solves that problem the same way many C++ programmers do: by
creating a String class.


Searching: Java's String class enables your programs to manage text strings
effortlessly, using
```

```
Found on line 3: Java's String class enables your programs to manage text strings
effortlessly, using


Searching: statements similar to those used in simpler languages such as BASIC or
Pascal. Java
Searching: also makes it easy to handle fonts, which determine the way that your
text strings
Searching: appear onscreen.
3 instances of the word: String found!

C:\jdk1.3se_book\classes>
```

Play around with this example. You can also extend it to search for multiple words in a file. You could also easily extend it to search for strings using case insensitivity and even search substrings with little modification to the source code.

STRINGS AND THE COMPILER

As mentioned earlier, there's no escaping strings in Java programs. In fact, you should embrace them. There is, however, an issue of having too many `String` instances around in an application, just like there's an issue of having too much of any objects around in memory. If you have ever used a performance tool on a Java application, you have definitely noticed the large number of objects and especially `String` in the application. Of course, this is entirely dependent on the application and the circumstance. Having too many instances alive in memory and relying on the garbage collection process to clean them up is not the best approach. Just be aware that because a `String` is an object just like any other, it takes up memory and therefore will cause performance issues if there are too many instances being used without the proper cleanup.

TROUBLESHOOTING

ONE OFF INDEX ERROR

The first item from the `String` is not being used or printed.

Remember that like other things in the Java language, the index for a `String` starts at zero, not one. As you can no doubt figure out, the last `index` of a String is length –1. This does not affect the actual length of the `String`. It remains at exactly the number of characters that are in the `String`.

INCORRECT `String` REPRESENTATION

When I print out an `Object`, I see something that looks like this: `classname@8e41`.

To get a better `String` representation for an object to print out, you must override the `toString()` method for the class you are trying to print. Otherwise, the default `toString()` method will be used that is defined on the `Object` class.

CHAPTER

INTERFACES

In this chapter

by Brian Keeton

WHAT ARE INTERFACES?

A Java interface is a set of constants and method declarations without an implementation, as shown in Listing 9.1.

LISTING 9.1 `Steerable.java`**—AN INTERFACE FOR STEERABLE VEHICLES**

```
public interface Steerable {

  String NORTH_DIRECTION = "North";
  String SOUTH_DIRECTION = "South";
  String EAST_DIRECTION  = "East";
  String WEST_DIRECTION  = "West";

  void turnLeft();
  void turnRight();
  String getCurrentDirection();
}
```

This concept might not sound too impressive at this point, but interfaces are a powerful feature of the Java language. Successful object-oriented programming depends on separating the functionality needed by one part of your system from how that functionality is ultimately implemented by another part. Interfaces are the way to achieve that separation.

In the preceding example, the `Steerable` interface defines three operations that a class responsible for sending steering commands to some type of vehicle in a system cares about. Notice that there is nothing in the interface that references any details about a particular type of vehicle or what it has to do to respond to a steering command. A vehicle that wants to allow itself to be steered in this manner must provide an implementation for these methods, but it does not have to supply any details about this implementation or any other part of its operation.

You should think of an interface as a contract. The `Steerable` contract is satisfied when both sides agree to its terms. A class that wants to steer a vehicle does this by using only those methods in the interface to issue its commands. A vehicle class that can be steered is obligated to provide a valid implementation for each one. By doing this, a class is said to *implement* the interface. A vehicle class that can only turn left cannot satisfy this contract, unless maybe it implements a right turn as a series of three left turns. This wouldn't be very efficient, but the `Steerable` interface only cares that a vehicle be able to make a right turn, not that it be able to do it in any particular way. If the behavior of this class later changed so that its implementation of the method needed to be modified, any code that relied on the interface would be unaffected. Placing your implementations behind interfaces gives you the freedom to change them without breaking the contract agreed upon in advance.

To summarize, interfaces allow you to focus on behavior without being concerned about implementation details. They also allow you to relate classes with similar behavior without forcing a class inheritance hierarchy. This aspect is key in developing flexible designs.

DOESN'T EVERY CLASS ALREADY HAVE AN INTERFACE?

The idea of interfaces is similar to encapsulation and implementation hiding in general. Through the proper use of access restrictions, you can already limit other classes from having knowledge of how the behavior of a class is implemented within its methods. This typically includes restricting the use of any intermediate and utility methods that are part of a class implementation. From this perspective, every class already has a well-defined interface. All the fields and methods of a class that are accessible to other classes make up its interface in this sense. There is a significant difference between this concept and the use of a Java interface however. The interface defined by the fields and methods of a class is specific to an implementation. This is true even if most of the details of that implementation are hidden. A declared interface, such as the `Steerable` example, decouples you from any particular implementation because it, in fact, has no implementation.

MULTIPLE INHERITANCE

A class can extend only one class in Java, but it can implement multiple interfaces. This is the closest Java comes to the true multiple inheritance found in languages such as C+. Java was designed to build on the strengths of C++ and at the same time, avoid some of its features that proved troublesome.

In practice, multiple inheritance typically produces less glamorous results than it does in theory. This is especially true when class hierarchies result such that a class appears twice in the inheritance chain for a subclass. For example, if classes `B` and `C` both inherit from `A`, and class `D` is declared to inherit from `B` and `C`, how do you deal with the two versions of the superclass `A`? Careful design can prevent these situations, but designs that favor composition over complex inheritance hierarchies tend to produce much more scalable and robust solutions. A common problem for programmers new to an object-oriented language is to go overboard with inheritance. When a class implements an interface, it is stating that it supports a specific behavior, not that it is a subtype of some other type. Implementing multiple interfaces allows a class to provide a robust set of behavior without being tied to any superclass hierarchy whatsoever.

DEFINING AN INTERFACE

You define an interface using syntax very similar to that of a class definition. However, there are a few exceptions. Namely, an interface cannot define any implementation for its methods and its fields are always `public`, `static`, and `final`.

An example interface is shown in Listing 9.2. It is followed by a set of classes declared to implement the interface in Listing 9.3 through Listing 9.5.

LISTING 9.2 `Sellable.java`—**SELLABLE PRODUCT INTERFACE**

```
public interface Sellable {
  String getDescription();
  String getUnits();
  double getPricePerUnit();
  double getWeight();
}
```

LISTING 9.3 `JavaBook.java`—**PROGRAMMING LANGUAGE BOOK CLASS**

```
public class JavaBook implements Sellable {
  public String getDescription() {
    return "Java Book";
  }

  public String getUnits() {
    return "Each";
  }

  public double getPricePerUnit() {
    return 39.95;
  }

  public double getWeight() {
    return 4.5;
  }
}
```

LISTING 9.4 `AbstractAircraft.java`—**ABSTRACT SUPERCLASS FOR AN AIRCRAFT PRODUCT**

```
public abstract class AbstractAircraft {
  protected long weight;
  protected int wingspan;
  protected String manufacturer;
  protected String model;

  public abstract float computeFuelRequirement(
    float cargoWeight, int numPassengers);
}
```

LISTING 9.5 `Boeing767.java`—**A SPECIFIC AIRCRAFT PRODUCT**

```
public class Boeing767 extends AbstractAircraft implements Sellable {
  public Boeing767() {
    manufacturer = "Boeing";
    model = "767-300";
    weight = 395000;
    wingspan = 156;
  }

  public float computeFuelRequirement(float cargoWeight,
```

Listing 9.5 Continued

```
      int numPassengers) {
      // implementation for this specific aircraft would know how to
      // compute its fuel requirements, let's just use a constant
      return 24000;
    }

    public String getDescription() {
      return manufacturer + " " + model;
    };

    public String getUnits() {
      return "Each";
    }

    public double getPricePerUnit() {
      return 100000000.00;
    }

    public double getWeight() {
      return weight;
    }
}
```


In the preceding listings, `Sellable` is an interface that defines a set of basic methods needed by an application that displays a description and price for any product offered for sale. The application does not care about any product details other than those referenced in the interface. `JavaBook` implements `Sellable` to describe a programming language book that can be sold. `Boeing767` is a concrete implementation of `AbstractAircraft` that also implements `Sellable`. The value of interfaces can be seen even in this simple, and somewhat contrived, example. A book and a commercial airliner have nothing in common. The fact that they can both be described by a string and sold is not enough to justify deriving them from a common superclass. By instead using an interface, their common behavior relative to product sales can be captured without affecting the class hierarchy.

The Declaration

Interface declarations take the general form

`public` `interface NameOfInterface` *`extends InterfaceList`*

where everything in italics is optional.

Public Interfaces

Just like classes, interfaces are defined within a package. If you declare an interface in a source file without a package statement, the compiler places it in the default package just as it would a class. The benefits of namespace management discussed in Chapter 7, "Classes," apply equally to interfaces, so you should avoid leaving your interfaces in the default package.

The optional `public` modifier in an interface declaration allows classes outside an interface's package to implement it and use it in variable and method declarations. If you omit the modifier, only classes within the same package can use the interface. You will usually declare your interfaces as `public`.

INTERFACE NAME

The rules for an interface name are identical to those for classes. The only requirements on the name are that it begin with a letter, an underscore character, or a currency symbol; contain only these characters and digits; and not be the same as any Java keyword (such as `extends` or `int`). Again, like classes, it is accepted practice to capitalize the first letter of an interface name and use mixed case to separate words rather then underscores.

> **Note**
>
> Just like public classes, public interfaces must be defined in a file named `NameOfInterface.java`. Although not required for non-public interfaces, it is a good practice to use this same naming convention for those also. This enables both you and the Java compiler to quickly find the source code for your interfaces.

EXTENDING OTHER INTERFACES

If an interface inherits from one or more other interfaces, its declaration identifies each super-interface using the `extends` keyword. This sub-interface inherits all the methods and fields of its super-interfaces, just as subclasses inherit the fields and methods of their superclasses. When extending more than one interface, separate them in the `extends` clause using commas.

You extend an interface for purposes similar to those for extending a class, but the implications are quite different. With the exception of purely abstract classes, you can take advantage of previously defined behavior when you extend a class. This reuse of method implementations is one of the strengths of inheritance. However, interfaces have no method bodies, so there can be no reuse of implementation when you extend them. What do you gain from extending an interface then? Declaring an interface is all about specifying a contract for a set of behavior on which other classes in your system can rely. In the previous example, a `Sellable` interface was defined to use in a sales application. You might find a need in the same program or another to treat `Sellable` products that exhibit some other unrelated behavior differently. Rather than duplicate the behavior defined by `Sellable` in another interface that includes the new requirements, you can extend `Sellable` to create a new contract that reuses the original interface through inheritance.

> **Note**
>
> Interfaces cannot extend classes even though the same `extends` keyword is used in their declaration. If an interface were to extend a class, it would be inheriting behavior unless the class were purely abstract. Even in this case, the interface would be coupled to a specific class implementation, which defeats the purpose of separating the two.

When a class implements an interface that extends another interface, it must provide an implementation for all the methods in the interfaces, or be declared abstract.

THE BODY

The body of an interface contains the declarations for its methods and constants. Like a class, an interface body is enclosed in braces.

METHODS

The main purpose of interfaces is to declare abstract methods that will be implemented in other classes. These method declarations take the form

```
public returnType nameOfMethod(parameters) throws ExceptionList;
```

where everything in italics is optional. As you can see, the syntax for declaring a method in an interface is nearly identical to declaring a method in a class, but a method in an interface cannot possess a body, even one that performs no operations. Just like an abstract method in a class, an interface method consists of only a declaration. For example, the following two method declarations are complete if they are defined in an interface:

```
public double getPricePerUnit();
public void showState();
```

However, in a class, they would require method bodies unless they were declared as abstract:

```
public double getPricePerUnit() {
  return price;
}

// do-nothing implementation may not be useful
// but an empty-bodied method declaration is valid
// when there is no return value
public void showState() {
}
```

When you declare an abstract method in a class, you must use the `abstract` keyword in the declaration. This makes your intent obvious to other programmers by clearly distinguishing abstract methods from those with empty bodies. An interface method declaration does not require the `abstract` keyword because an interface method has to be abstract. Using the keyword in the declaration would be redundant, so the compiler does not require it. Similarly, the `public` modifier is also assumed if you omit it. This differs from class methods where the default is package access if no modifier is specified.

Note

Although the compiler does not care whether you use the `public` and `abstract` modifiers when declaring interface methods, common practice is to include `public` but omit `abstract`.

A method declaration does not determine how a method will behave; it only defines what, if any, information it needs in the form of a parameter list and what, if any, information will be returned. An implementation of an interface method in a class must have the same properties as you define in the interface. This makes it important to carefully consider factors such as return type and parameter lists when defining an interface.

> **Note**
>
> Although optional, `public` and `abstract` are the only modifiers allowed in an interface method declaration. It is illegal to use any of the other standard modifiers (including `native`, `static`, `synchronized`, `final`, `private`, or `protected`) when declaring a method in an interface. If an `abstract` method were `private`, it would be impossible for it to ever be implemented because only the current class can reference `private` methods. Similarly, a `final` method cannot be overridden. This is in direct conflict with an `abstract` method, which must be overridden. Several of the others (`native`, `static`, and `synchronized` in particular) involve implementation details, so they are out of place in an interface.

FIELDS

Although interfaces are most often talked about in terms of their method declarations, they are also valuable for the constants they define. Declarations of constant interface fields take the form

```
public static final type FIELD_NAME = someValue;
```

where everything in italics is optional. As with class fields, an interface field must be declared with a type and a valid identifier name. It might seem strange to you to see the specific modifiers `public`, `static`, and `final` listed as optional parts of the declaration. When you declare a class field, modifiers are optional in the declaration, but they are not restricted to such a narrow set of choices. These modifiers are listed as optional for interface fields, but the only optional part is whether you explicitly state them. Interface fields are required to be `public`, `static`, and `final`, so the compiler does not require you to include the modifiers. It is, however, a common practice to explicitly include the modifiers to remind yourself (and other programmers) of this fact.

As seen in the `Steerable` interface, interface fields—just like `final static` fields in classes—are used to define constants that can be accessed by all classes that implement the interface:

```
public interface Steerable {

  // define constants for directions to make sure
  // that they are used consistently
  String NORTH_DIRECTION = "North";
  String SOUTH_DIRECTION = "South";
  String EAST_DIRECTION  = "East";
  String WEST_DIRECTION  = "West";

  void turnLeft();
  void turnRight();
  String getCurrentDirection();
}
```

Note

Unlike final class fields, you cannot declare an interface field using a blank final. Given that an interface has no method implementations, you have nowhere to assign the value to an interface field other than as part of its declaration. You are not prevented from using an expression, or even a method call, to perform this assignment, however. It is even legal for you to use an expression that assigns a different value each time your program is run. Remember that a constant is only required to maintain the same value throughout a single execution and not across executions. An interface's fields are initialized only once no matter how many instantiated objects implement it.

Some confusion over interface fields can occur when a class implements multiple interfaces that define a field with the same name. There is clearly a conflict because each interface could assign a different value to the same identifier name. In this case, you must reference the field using the interface name as a prefix, such as `Steerable.NORTH_DIRECTION`.

It is also possible for a class to inherit a field more than once if, for example, two of its super-interfaces extend the same class. In this case, an implementing class only has one copy of the field as far as the compiler is concerned, so it does not create any ambiguity.

MARKER INTERFACES

Although the interface declarations used in the examples so far contain at least one method, an interface is not required to declare any methods or fields. The following two interfaces are among the most important found in the Java API:

```
package java.lang;
public interface Cloneable {
}


package java.io;
public interface Serializable {
}
```

Interfaces like these are called *marker interfaces*. Typically, an interface defines method signatures that impose a requirement on an implementing class to provide some associated behavior. Marker interfaces do not carry any requirements for behavior, but instead serve as an indicator that certain operations on a class are allowed.

The `Cloneable` interface demonstrates the use of a marker interface well. Remember that all classes, even those without an `extends` clause in their declarations, are a subclass of `Object`. `Object` defines a `clone` method that creates and returns a shallow copy of a class instance using a byte-by-byte copy of attribute values. If a class has only simple attributes, such as all primitive fields, this implementation is a valid one. However, a class that includes object references among its fields typically requires a more sophisticated procedure to create a deep copy of its instances. The `Cloneable` interface allows you, as the programmer, to state whether a valid `clone` implementation exists for a class you write. If you declare a class without stating that it implements `Cloneable`, a `CloneNotSupportedException` is thrown if the `clone` method in `Object` is called for one of its instances.

The serialization of class instances is discussed later in Chapter 22, "Object Serialization," but the Serializable interface is similar to Cloneable in that it identifies classes that support specific operations. Such a marker allows a class to be treated a certain way with some assurance that it will behave correctly.

IMPLEMENTING AN INTERFACE

Now that you know how to create interfaces, look at how they are used in developing classes. Look again at the JavaBook class that implements our Sellable interface:

```
public class JavaBook implements Sellable {
  public String getDescription() {
    return "Java Book";
  }

  public String getUnits() {
    return "Each";
  }

  public double getPricePerUnit() {
    return 39.95;
  }

  public double getWeight() {
    return 4.5;
  }
}
```

This class satisfies the contract of the interface by providing an implementation for each method. As with classes, implementing abstract methods from an interface is referred to as overriding the methods. The JavaBook class is not restricted from defining methods other than those in the Sellable interface, but it must at least implement those to avoid being declared abstract. If a class has methods other than those in an interface it implements, they are unaffected by the interface. An advantage of interfaces is that they typically can be associated with a class by adding methods that have no effect on the other behavior already required for the class.

Note

Overriding the methods defined by an interface is not enough to implement the interface. When you intend for a class to implement an interface, you must include an implements clause in the class declaration that names the interface. This enables the compiler to verify that the required method overloads are present in the class definition. If you attempt to use an object whose class is not explicitly declared to implement a particular interface as an implementation of that interface, a compiler error is reported, or a ClassCastException results at runtime. This is true even if the class properly overrides every method of the interface.

OVERRIDING THE METHODS

A class implements an interface by overriding its method declarations with concrete implementations. Remember that if you want to fully implement an interface, you are required to override every method declared in the interface or in any of its super-interfaces. Failure to do so will require you to declare your class abstract.

It might sound bad to end up with an abstract class when working with interfaces, but an abstract interface implementation is actually a good design approach in many cases. It is more common than you might initially think to create an abstract class that provides default behavior for only a portion of an interface's methods. You can then extend this class when you want to create a specific implementation for the behavior that remains. For example, this approach is used widely in the Swing classes in the Java API. Many of the abstract classes found there are partial implementations of interfaces.

MODIFIERS

As discussed in Chapter 7, you can change the access specifier in a method override only if you change it to one that makes the method more accessible. For example, a `protected` method can be overridden as `public`. This simplifies your choices when you implement an interface method because there is nothing more accessible than `public`, which is the access specifier given to all interface methods. Consequently, all implementations of interface methods must be assigned the `public` access modifier. Remember that in the class implementation, this modifier must be explicitly assigned because, unlike in an interface declaration, methods in a class do not default to `public`. This is one reason to go ahead and include the `public` modifier in the interface declaration. If you do, the method signatures in the interface and the implementing classes will look the same.

Of the remaining modifiers that can be applied to methods, only `native` and `abstract` can be applied to methods originally declared in interfaces. You might wonder why `abstract` is allowed given that an `abstract` override of a method is the same as not overriding it at all. The advantage is in code readability; declaring an `abstract` override for a method you do not implement makes it clear to programmers why the resulting class is `abstract`.

PARAMETER LIST

Interface method declarations optionally define a set of parameters that must be passed to the method when it is called. Any attempt to implement a method without declaring the same parameter list results in an overloaded version of the method (at best). A class that implements an interface must declare each overridden method using a parameter list that references the same data types in the same order as the interface declaration. There is nothing wrong with including overloaded methods in your implementation if you need them, but declaring the correct overrides must be your first priority.

BODY

The whole point in implementing an interface is to provide a concrete set of behavior that satisfies the contract defined by the interface. As with any class, behavior is defined through method body implementations. Unless you decide to make a method `native`, it is necessary to create the body for every method originally declared in your interface if you do not want to make your new class abstract.

The actual implementation code in the body of your new method is entirely up to you. This is one of the benefits of using interfaces. Although the interface ensures that—in a non-abstract class—its methods will be defined and will return an appropriate data type, the interface places no further restrictions or limitations on the method bodies.

EXCEPTIONS

For a method to throw a checked exception, the exception type (or one of its superclasses) must be listed in the exception list in the method declaration. This is no different for exceptions thrown from interface methods. Here are the rules for overriding methods that throw exceptions:

- The exception list in a method override can only contain exceptions listed in the original exception list, or subclasses of the originally listed exceptions.
- The exception list in a method override does not need to contain any exceptions, regardless of the number listed in the original exception list. This is because the original list is implicitly assigned to the method override.
- The method override can throw any exception listed in the original exception list or derived from an exception in the original list, regardless of its own exception list.

In general, the exception list of the method as declared in the interface determines which exceptions can and cannot be thrown. In other words, when a method override changes the exception list, it cannot add any exceptions that are not included in the original interface declaration.

Examine the interface and method declarations in Listing 9.6. These code fragments show both legal and illegal attempts to change the exception list in a method override.

LISTING 9.6 ALTERNATE EXCEPTION LISTS

```
interface Example {
  public int getPrice(int id) throws java.lang.RuntimeException;
}

class User implements Example {
  public int getPrice(int id) throws java.awt.AWTException {
    // Illegal -
    // java.awt.AWTException is not a subclass of
    //java.lang.RuntimeException
  }
```

LISTING 9.6 CONTINUED

```
  public int getPrice(int id) {
    if (id == 6) {
      throw new java.lang.IndexOutOfBoundsException();
      // Legal -
      // IndexOutOfBoundsException is derived from RuntimeException
    }
  }

  public int getPrice(int id) throws java.lang.IndexOutOfBoundsException {
    // Legal -
    // IndexOutOfBoundsException is derived from
    //RuntimeException
    if (id == 6) {
      throw new java.lang.ArrayIndexOutOfBoundsException();
        // Legal -
        // ArrayIndexOutOfBoundsException is derived from
        //     IndexOutOfBoundsException
    }
  }
}
```


INTERFACE METHOD COLLISIONS

One of the strengths of interfaces is the flexibility you get from declaring a class to implement multiple interfaces. Taking advantage of common behavior without restricting yourself to a rigid class hierarchy reduces redundancy in your code without sacrificing implementation independence. However, you must exercise some caution when you design a system based on multiple interface implementation. Look at the following two interface declarations for an example of a problem that might arise when multiple interfaces are implemented:

```
public interface IOne {
  /**
   * Perform my operation
   * @return an integer result
   * @throws IOException if the operation fails
   */
  public int myMethod() throws java.io.IOException;
}


public interface ITwo {
  /**
   * Perform my operation
   * @return a floating point result
   * @throws ParseException if the operation fails
   */
  public float myMethod() throws java.text.ParseException;
}
```

The interfaces `IOne` and `ITwo` each declare a single method that accepts no parameters. You can declare a class to implement either of these interfaces by providing a corresponding override of myMethod. This works without any problem until you need to declare a class that implements the behavior declared by both IOne and ITwo. Notice that the two declarations of myMethod differ only in return type and the thrown exceptions. It is impossible for a class to implement both interfaces because a class cannot declare two methods with the same name and parameter list even if their return types or thrown exceptions are different. A collision of method declarations between the two interfaces has occurred.

Both the method return type and the exception list cause problems in this example, but the return type difference is the more severe. There is nothing you can do in a class declaration to resolve a discrepancy in return type when a method collision occurs. A difference in exception lists has an impact, but you might be able to work around it. Suppose that ITwo were instead declared as

```
public interface ITwo {
  /**
   * Perform my operation
   * @return an integer result
   * @throws ParseException if the operation fails
   */
  public int myMethod() throws java.text.ParseException;
}
```

With the return types now the same, you can implement both interfaces in a class if the thrown exceptions satisfy the requirements for overriding both versions of the method declaration. The way to do that in this case is to handle any exceptions in the implementation and not declare any as thrown. The following class declaration shows a valid implementation that uses this approach:

```
public class OneTwo implements IOne, ITwo {
  public int myMethod() {
    // do some processing and return the result
    return 0;
  }
}
```

You can now use class OneTwo as either interface type, but you have given up the ability to throw exceptions from your implementation of myMethod. If the exception lists in IOne and ITwo were the same, the method collision would never have occurred and a single implementation of the method in a class would satisfy the requirements of both interfaces.

When programmers exercise due caution, method collisions between interfaces are fortunately rare. You will not encounter them when using the Java API unless you declare an interface that reuses a method name already found there. The main guideline related to method collisions is to strive to avoid them. If you select appropriate method names for your interface declarations that precisely describe their purpose, collisions are unlikely.

Referencing Interfaces

You have learned how to create interfaces and build classes based on interfaces. However, interfaces are not useful unless you can develop classes that will either employ the derived classes or the interface itself.

ACCESSING CONSTANTS

Although the fields of an interface must be both `static` and `final`, they can be extremely useful in your code.

The following example demonstrates that any constant from an interface can be referenced using the same dot notation you use with classes. This means that you can use constants from your own interfaces or those in the Java API such as `java.awt.image.ImageConsumer.COMPLETESCANLINES` and `java.awt.Event.MOUSE_DOWN` in your code. Listing 9.7 shows an example of another `ImageConsumer` field being used.

LISTING 9.7 USING THE CONSTANT FIELDS OF AN INTERFACE

```
import java.awt.image.*;
public class MyImageHandler {
  /* The java.awt.image.ImageConsumer interface defines certain
     constants to serve as indicators. STATICIMAGEDONE, which
     is set to equal 3, informs the consumer that the image is complete.
   */
  ImageConsumer picture;

  void checkStatus(boolean done) {
    if (done)
      picture.imageComplete(ImageConsumer.STATICIMAGEDONE);
  }
}
```

DESIGN TO AN INTERFACE RATHER THAN AN IMPLEMENTATION

The most important concept to take away from a discussion of interfaces is that you should develop a mindset of designing your systems based on contracts specified by interfaces rather than specific class hierarchies and implementations. If you establish the interfaces in your system early in the design process, you greatly reduce the likelihood of rewriting the implementations as a result of incompatibilities between system components. Establishing the interfaces is a way to clearly draw the lines of responsibility between classes.

When you design and develop using interfaces, you are creating reference types that can be used as any other data type even though an interface will never itself be instantiated. An interface variable can be used just as you would a variable of any class type, except that you cannot use a `new` statement, or any other means of object creation, on an interface type.

AN INTERFACE AS A PARAMETER TYPE

In Listing 9.8, you create a simple application that employs the `JavaBook` class developed earlier. Because the `JavaBook` class implements the `Sellable` interface, you can deal with an instance of this class either as a `JavaBook` object or as an object that implements the `Sellable` interface. Although both approaches produce the same results when the methods accessed are all from the underlying interface, accessing the instance through the `Sellable` interface provides you with a more flexible approach. Here an instance of `Boeing767`, or any other `Sellable` class, could just as easily be passed to the `getPrice` method. This method doesn't care if it is working with a commercial airliner or a book, so there is no reason to restrict its use by specifying a particular class implementation the way the `getInfo` method does.

LISTING 9.8 USING THE SELLABLE INTERFACE AS A PARAMETER TYPE

```
public class Store {
  static JavaBook programmersGuide;

  public static void init() {
    programmersGuide = new JavaBook();
  }

  public static void main(String argv[]) {
    init();
    getInfo(programmersGuide);
    getPrice(programmersGuide);
  }

  public static void getInfo(JavaBook item) {
    System.out.println("Product Description: "+ item.getDescription());
  }

  public static void getPrice(Sellable item) {
    System.out.println("Price: "+ item.getPricePerUnit());
  }
}
```

Notice that in treating `programmersGuide` as an instance of the `Sellable` interface, you are asking the compiler to perform an implicit type conversion for you. This can be done at compile time because `JavaBook` implements `Sellable`. A class instance can always be converted to any interface it implements or one of its superclasses. You could explicitly cast `programmersGuide` to `Sellable` in the call to `getPrice`, but it would be redundant and a potential runtime error if the class and interface relationships were to change later.

Although it is not necessary to use the `Sellable` type as your argument in this simplistic example, the advantages of its use become apparent when you have a large number of classes that implement an interface. A method should accept parameters of as general a type as possible so that it can be more easily reused. This example would quickly become unwieldy if a different version of `getPrice` had to be created for each type of product encountered by the system.

CHOOSING BETWEEN AN INTERFACE AND AN ABSTRACT CLASS

Interfaces and abstract classes provide similar functionality, so it is important to know when to select one over the other as you design a system. In general, you should choose interfaces over abstract classes. The use of an interface separates your design from any implementation details. Even if you declare a purely abstract class without any method implementations, you must inherit from it to define classes that share the behavior defined by its methods. Given that Java only supports single inheritance, this requirement is a significant one. If you define your required method signatures in an interface instead, you place no restrictions on the class hierarchy in your system.

If you have default behavior that could be shared by several classes, you might be tempted to base your design on an abstract class instead of an interface. The main point to remember is that the two choices are not mutually exclusive. You can design using an interface and then provide a class that implements the default behavior that you need. This class can be an abstract implementation of the interface that you extend, or a collection of method implementations that you delegate a portion of the method responsibility to in your interface implementations. This latter approach is often preferred because it places no inheritance requirements on your class design.

The use of interfaces is not without its drawbacks, however. In particular, trying to change an interface after code has been developed with it is not always easy. If you add a method to an existing interface, every class that previously implemented it is now a compiler error waiting to happen. Each implementation must be updated to include any method additions or changes in method signature. Because of this, it is typically a better idea in this situation to create a new interface that extends the original one and adds any new methods that are now required. Code that depends on the new methods can be written to reference the new interface without impacting the existing implementations.

Depicting Interfaces in UML

Figure 9.1 shows the relationships between the `Sellable` interface and its two implementations. Notice that interfaces in UML can be depicted in two different ways in a class diagram. The `Sellable` interface is shown very much like a class description with only the addition of the `<<Interface>>` stereotype to differentiate it. This form is useful when you want to include the details of an interface contract. As a slight change to our earlier example, the `JavaBook` class is also shown to implement the `Cloneable` interface. This interface is shown using a notation that does not include any details of the interface. This form is appropriate when the interface details are not needed to convey information about the class design. For example, marker interfaces and interfaces that are part of the Java API are good candidates for this notation.

You can see in Figure 9.1 that it is not necessary to list the `getDescription`, `getUnits`, `getPricePerUnit`, and `getWeight` methods in the class entries for `Boeing767` and `JavaBook`. The indication that they implement the `Sellable` interface is sufficient information to let a reader know that these methods must be implemented in these classes. The notation used to show the interface dependencies mirrors that of an inheritance relationship in this diagram. Interface implementation is often indicated with a dashed line rather than a solid one to emphasize the difference.

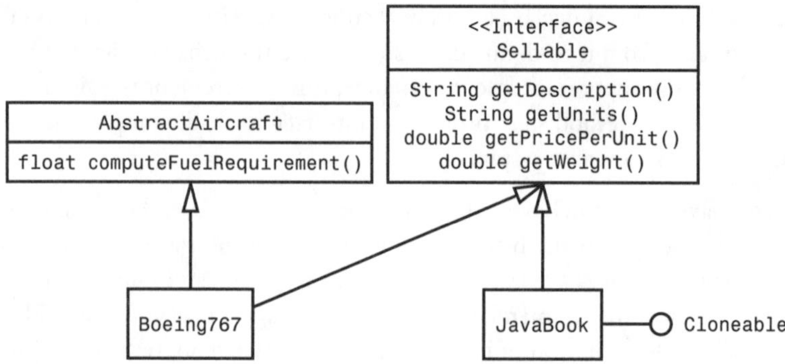

Figure 9.1
A class diagram depicts common behavior defined through interfaces.

→ **See** "OOP and the UML," **p. 19**

TROUBLESHOOTING

CLASS SHOULD BE DECLARED ABSTRACT

The compiler reports that a class should be declared abstract because it does not implement a particular method.

A class that is declared to implement an interface must explicitly be declared as `abstract` if it does not implement every method defined by that interface and its super-interfaces. If you don't intend for the class to be `abstract`, examine the signature for the method named in the compiler error to determine why your implementation does not match. To correctly override an interface method, you must define a method with the exact same name and parameter list.

INVALID METHOD IMPLEMENTATION BECAUSE OF A THROWN EXCEPTION

The compiler reports that a method in your class cannot implement an interface method because that interface method does not throw a particular exception.

When you override an interface method, the exception list in its `throws clause` can only contain exceptions found in the interface's declaration of the method, or subclasses of those exceptions. For example, you cannot declare a method to throw `java.lang.Exception` if the interface method it is intended to override is declared to only throw `java.io.IOException`. You would instead have to handle any exceptions other than `java.io.IOException` and its subclasses. Resolve this error by comparing the exception list of the interface method declaration to that found in your implementation.

INVALID METHOD IMPLEMENTATION BECAUSE OF RETURN TYPE

The compiler reports that a method in your class cannot implement an interface method because the return type is different.

As with any method override, the implementation of an interface method must not change the return type. Resolve this error by comparing the return type of the interface method declaration to that stated in your implementation.

`ClassCastException` When Casting to an Interface

A `ClassCastException` occurs when an attempt is made to cast an object to a particular interface even though you have overridden each of the interface methods in the object's class.

A class can only implement an interface if its declaration includes an `implements` clause that names the interface. Add the necessary `implements` clause to your class and recompile it to correct this problem.

CHAPTER 10

Data Structures and Java Utilities

In this chapter

by Brian Keeton

COLLECTION AND UTILITY CLASSES

The `java.util` package contains a number of useful classes that support important functionality as part of the Java API. These classes provide basic utilities that you frequently end up either writing yourself or purchasing from a third party when you are working in other languages. The creators of Java tried to capture the best concepts from several programming languages, and the results of this are clearly seen in the collection and utility classes. This aspect of Java was in particular influenced by Smalltalk, which is a pure object-oriented language highly regarded for its abundance of utility classes.

This chapter walks you through the majority of the `java.util` classes with examples and guidelines on their uses. Those classes that are not covered here relate to threads, event handling, and internationalization and are covered in later chapters where their purposes can be more clearly demonstrated.

The `java.util` package focuses mostly on collection objects—that is, objects that contain or hold other objects. In addition to the collections, the package also adds support for property files, dates, bit manipulation, random number generation, and a carryover from Smalltalk called observables.

> **Note**
>
> Smalltalk was the first object-oriented language to become popular. It was developed in the '70s at Xerox's Palo Alto Research Center and demonstrates many of the strengths of OOP. Everything in Smalltalk is an object, and all operations are performed by passing messages between objects. The language is highly integrated with its development environment, which has served as a model for both operating systems and development tools that have followed.

THE COLLECTIONS FRAMEWORK

A significant design change introduced in the Java 1.2 API and updated somewhat in the Java 1.3 release relates to how collections of objects are created and manipulated. Earlier versions of the language provided the `Vector`, `Hashtable`, and `Stack` classes for limited collection functionality, but Java 1.2 increased this support dramatically. Collections are now supported by a number of interfaces and classes in the `java.util` package known as the Java collections framework.

A *collection* is nothing more than a type of data structure, which refers to a grouping of multiple data elements. You already saw the simplest Java collection, the array, back in Chapter 3, "Data Types and Other Tokens." Collections can vary in complexity, but ultimately their goal is always to hold and manipulate primitives or objects.

Some collections, such as arrays, keep data in one long list. Others, such as trees, keep the data sorted in non-linear storage compartments. Each type of collection has its advantages and disadvantages. For instance, trees are extremely efficient at finding and inserting sorted data; hash tables are even more efficient at finding data, but at the cost of more memory usage.

Before collections, converting between one data structure and another required a lot of work. However, the collection framework provides a uniform mechanism for doing this. In addition, the framework is designed to allow characteristics, such as the ordering of an object, to be used in many types of structures.

COLLECTION INTERFACES

As you saw in Chapter 9, "Interfaces," Java interfaces provide a way to reduce dependencies, or coupling, between classes. When you code to an interface rather than a specific class implementation, you allow for the possibility of multiple classes being available to implement the behavior you need. The collection framework is built on a set of fundamental interfaces. This allows you to choose the proper data structure based on its performance characteristics, without having to worry about the implementation details. The collection framework includes at least one implementation for each of its interfaces, but it also allows you to create your own special purpose collection classes if the need arises.

Note

An interface cannot enforce any requirements on the constructors defined by the classes that implement it, only on the overridden methods. However, classes that implement the collection framework interfaces should, at a minimum, declare a no-argument constructor and a "copy" constructor that accepts another collection as an argument. This copy constructor should build a new collection that contains the same objects as its argument.

`Collection`

The `Collection` and `Map` interfaces sit at the root of the collection framework. `Collection` focuses on groups of objects, whereas `Map`, which is discussed later, focuses on groups of associations between objects. The goal of the `Collection` interface is to identify the common set of methods applicable to any type of object collection. This interface is generic in that it does not dictate whether the contained objects are held in a particular order. It also does not prevent a collection from containing multiple references to the same object. These details are deferred to the sub-interfaces of `Collection`.

Note

The `java.util` interfaces and classes that make up the collection framework apply only to objects, not the primitive types. If you need to store a primitive in a collection, you must first wrap it in one of the classes introduced in "Wrapping the Primitive Types in Classes" in Chapter 7, "Classes." For example, to create a collection of `int` variables, you would wrap each one in an instance of `Integer`.

It is possible for a class that implements `Collection` (or `Map`) to not support every method defined in the interface. A collection class is allowed to choose to not support a method and instead throw an `UnsupportedOperationException` if the method is ever called. Although the `Collection` methods are general, there might be cases where one of the methods does not make sense for a specific implementation. Not supporting an interface method is not the same as not providing an implementation. Remember that a concrete class that implements an interface must implement every method of the interface or the compiler will reject it. However, there are no restrictions on what a method implementation does. To the compiler, an implementation that does nothing but throw an exception is perfectly valid. Of course, certain methods must be supported for a collection to be of any use. The API documentation for the collection framework interfaces clearly identifies each method that is not mandatory as an "optional operation."

As you might expect, the `Collection` interface defines methods for inserting objects into a collection. There are two such methods in the interface. The first allows you to insert a single element, and the second allows you to add all the elements in another collection:

```
boolean add(Object o)
boolean addAll(Collection c)
```

Each of these methods returns true if the collection changes as a result of the call. Some collections do not allow duplicate objects, so a request to add an object that is already contained is ignored and `false` is returned. When you call one of these methods and it returns `true` without throwing an exception, you are guaranteed that the object is included in the collection. Some implementations might place restrictions on the objects allowed in the collection, such as not supporting `null` entries or only allowing objects of a certain type. In these cases, the method implementations are required to throw an exception when an insert is refused rather than returning `false` because the collection will not include the object after the call completes.

You also have several options for removing objects from a collection. A call to `clear` will empty a collection entirely. You can also remove a single object with the `remove` method, which will only remove one occurrence of an object even if it is held multiple times by the collection. Multiple objects can be removed selectively using `removeAll` and `retainAll`, which both accept a collection as a parameter. After calling `removeAll`, a collection will not contain any of the objects specified by the parameter. The `retainAll` method will instead remove all objects that are not found in the specified collection. The following signatures define the set of object removal methods:

```
void clear()
boolean remove(Object o)
boolean removeAll(Collection c)
boolean retainAll(Collection c)
```

The primary reason you build a collection is to access its elements and use them either individually or as a set. To access what you've placed in a collection, you can choose from three methods. Two of these return the elements of a collection as an array of objects. This points out an important issue with collections in Java. The generic nature of the collection framework requires that the elements held by a collection be treated as references to the ultimate superclass `Object`. When you retrieve the contents of a collection, you will typically have to cast it to its actual type before using it. This is unlike some languages that implement collections using templates that handle any typing issues. The remaining retrieval method returns an `Iterator` for a collection, which is the most used access mechanism. You'll see how `Iterator` works later in this chapter. The following signatures define the collection access methods:

```
Object[] toArray()
Object[] toArray(Object[] a)
Iterator iterator()
```

Notice that the second version of `toArray` accepts an array as a parameter. This parameter determines the type of the resulting array. Also, if the input array is long enough to hold the output of the method, it is used for that purpose as well.

The final set of `Collection` methods allows you to query a collection in several ways. When you need to determine if a collection holds one or more objects, you can find out by calling either `contains` or `containsAll`. The `isEmpty` and `size` methods allow you to query the collection regarding the number of objects it currently contains. Calling `isEmpty` is equivalent to calling `size` and comparing the result to zero, but it makes your code a little more readable. These query methods are declared as follows:


```
boolean contains(Object o)
boolean containsAll(Collection c)
boolean isEmpty()
int size()
```

The `Collection` interface is implemented by several classes described throughout this chapter, so you'll find examples of how to use each of these methods later.

List

The `Collection` interface is extended and specialized with two direct sub-interfaces: `List` and `Set`. The `List` interface represents a collection that stores its objects in order. Like `Collection`, `List` places no restriction on allowing duplicate objects in a collection.

Note

> The introduction of the `java.util.List` interface created a name conflict with `java.awt.List`. If you import both `java.awt.*` and `java.util.*` into a single source file, you will have to do some extra work to differentiate the use of the name `List` when working with collections. You can do this in two ways: by importing `java.util.List` specifically, or by using the fully qualified name `java.util.List` wherever the interface is referenced.

The primary extension that `List` adds to `Collection` is the concept of an index. The fact that the objects in a `List` are ordered allows you to access an element by referring to its position in the collection using an integer index. `List` adds several methods that deal with this concept.

`List` includes overloaded versions of `add` and `addAll` that allow you to specify the index at which objects are inserted into a collection. Like arrays, index values for a `List` are zero-based. When you call `add` with an index, the specified object is inserted into the position given by the index, and any element currently at that position is shifted down by one position, along with any subsequent elements. Similarly, the overloaded `addAll` method inserts the elements of a collection in the order given by their iterator at the specified index. In addition, you can replace an object at a particular index in a `List` using the `set` method. This method returns a reference to the object that is replaced. The following signatures define the object insertion methods unique to `List`:

```
void add(int index, Object element)
boolean addAll(int index, Collection c)
Object set(int index, Object element)
```

Caution

> The ability to specify indexes when working with a `List` places an additional burden on you as a programmer. You must always ensure that any index you pass to a `List` method is greater than or equal to zero, and less than or equal to the size of the collection minus one. Each `List` method that accepts an index throws an `IndexOutOfBoundsException` at runtime when this is not the case.

`List` also provides a new way to remove an object from a collection. An overloaded version of `remove` that accepts an integer index instead of an object reference allows you to remove an object based solely on its position in the collection. This method shifts any subsequent elements up one position and returns a reference to the removed object:

```
Object remove(int index)
```

The ordering inherent in a `List` allows you to access its members in several additional ways. First, you can retrieve a single object by calling `get` with the desired index. The other two additional methods return a new iterator called a `ListIterator`, which supports bidirectional movement through a collection. These two methods provide you with either an iterator for an entire collection or one that includes only the elements beginning with a specified index. The following signatures define the element access methods unique to `List`:

```
Object get(int index)
ListIterator listIterator()
ListIterator listIterator(int index)
```

The querying methods added in `List` provide information on the index where an element is positioned within a collection. These two methods will return either the index where the element is stored, or, if the element is not found, a `-1`. The first of these methods returns the first index where a specified object is found within the collection; the second returns the last index where the object can be found:

```
int indexOf(Object o)
int lastIndexOf(Object o)
```

There are situations where you might want to work only with a portion of a list. The `subList` method returns a view of a portion of a list as determined by a beginning and an ending index:

```
List subList(int fromIndex, int toIndex)
```

The `toIndex` parameter to this method is treated as exclusive, so the returned list consists of the objects with indexes `fromIndex` through `toIndex-1`.

Describing the `List` returned by `subList` as a view is an important distinction. This method does not create a new `List` that holds references to the same objects; it simply provides a convenient way to work with the underlying list. If you modify the `List` reference returned by `subList`, any changes you make are reflected in the original list. For example, the following code removes a range of elements from `mainList`:

```
public static void removeRange( List mainList, int startIndex,
 int endIndex ) {
  List killList = mainList.subList( startIndex, endIndex );
  // remove all the elements in the specified range
  killList.clear();
}
```

If you experience runtime exceptions when accessing a `List`, see "`IndexOutOfBoundsException`," in the "Troubleshooting" section at the end of this chapter.

Set AND SortedSet

Just like `List`, `Set` extends directly from `Collection` to refine the interface for more specific use. From a mathematical standpoint, a *set* is a group of unordered values that does not contain any duplicates. The `Set` interface imposes these same characteristics on a collection of objects. The objects held in a `Set` are unordered, so there is no concept of an index as in the case of `List`. In fact, `Set` adds only restrictions to a collection and not any additional functionality, so it defines no methods beyond those already found in the `Collection` interface.

Given that `Set` does not add any methods to its parent interface, what does it do? Previously, in Chapter 9, an interface was described as a contract that defines a set of behavior that one class can expect from another. What the `Set` interface does is add stipulations to the contract defined by `Collection`. Any class that implements `Set` must agree to disallow duplicate objects within its collection. In practice, this means the constructors and the `add` and `addAll` methods for a class that implements `Set` must check for duplicates and reject them.

`SortedSet` is an extension of the `Set` interface that adds another stipulation to the `Set` contract and several more methods. A class that implements `SortedSet` guarantees that its iterator method returns an `Iterator` that traverses the elements of the collection in order. It is intended that the order used by a `SortedSet` be determined in one of two ways. First, the elements in the collection can be sorted in their *natural ordering* if they implement the `java.lang.Comparable` interface. Alternatively, a `SortedSet` implementation should provide a constructor that accepts a `Comparator` that defines the sort mechanism for the collection. Both the `Comparable` and `Comparator` interfaces are discussed later in this chapter in the "Sorting a Collection" section.

Map AND SortedMap

The `Map` interface represents a different concept from the collection types covered so far. It is a root-level interface, like `Collection`, that holds key-value pairs. You have encountered this type of association before if you have ever dealt with hash tables. Basically, a `Map` allows you to insert an object into a collection using an associated key, and then use that key as your means of retrieving the object later. For example, you might store `Employee` objects in a

Map using an Integer or String key that holds the value of the corresponding employee's Social Security Number.

Not unlike the other collection framework interfaces, Map places restrictions on the classes that implement it. Chief among these is that a key object in a Map must not be duplicated. This restriction guarantees that each key maps to only a single value object. There is no such restriction on the value objects. In addition, it is strongly advised, although not required, that you use immutable objects for keys. The behavior of a Map when its keys change is not defined by the interface.

To insert an association into a Map, you must provide both the key and the value. For a single association, you accomplish this using the put method. If the key you specify is already mapped, the put method returns the value object from the previous mapping. A Map can also insert multiple associations with a single method call, but, unlike the other collections, this cannot be done using a Collection as a parameter. This isn't possible because a Map must have a key to associate with each object. Therefore, the putAll method is declared to instead accept a reference to another Map. The two methods for inserting associations into a Map are declared as follows:

```
Object put(Object key, Object value)
void putAll(Map t)
```

If you experience runtime exceptions when inserting elements into a Map, see "NullPointerException," in the "Troubleshooting" section at the end of this chapter.

Like inserting a new element into a Map, the removal of a single element is done via the key value, not the element itself. The remove method extracts a single object from a Map and returns the associated value object as the method's return value. A return value of null indicates that either the specified key was not found in the Map, or the key was mapped to a value of null. Just as with Collection, Map also declares a clear method that removes all its elements with a single call. The following signatures declare Map's element removal methods:

```
Object remove(Object key)
void clear()
```

You retrieve an object from a Map using its key. The get method accepts a key object as a parameter and returns the corresponding value object, or null if the key is not mapped:

```
Object get(Object key)
```

Map also provides access to three views of its contents. Again, the term "view" here implies that any changes made to the objects or mappings retrieved in this manner affect the underlying Map. The keySet method returns the key objects as a Set. A Set is used here because, by definition, the collection of keys in a Map cannot contain duplicates. The interface's values method returns the value objects held by a Map as a Collection. A generic Collection is used here because the value objects can be duplicated. The third view provided by a Map is returned by the entrySet method. The Set returned by this method represents each element in the Map using a Map.Entry. Map.Entry is a nested interface of Map that allows you to query the key and value for each association and replace the value object if desired. The following signatures declare the three view methods:

```
Set keySet()
Collection values()
Set entrySet()
```

Note

Chapter 9 focused on the methods and fields declared within interfaces, but `Map.Entry` illustrates that an interface can also declare another interface as a member. A nested interface is useful when a set of methods has meaning only within a particular context. The methods declared by `Map.Entry` relate to a single association, but this association is only meaningful as part of a `Map`.

The remaining `Map` methods allow you to query information from the collection. These methods include the same `isEmpty` and `size` methods found in `Collection`. In addition, `containsKey` and `containsValue` allow you to determine if a Map holds a particular key or value object. The following signatures define the query methods:


```
boolean isEmpty()
int size()
boolean containsKey(Object key)
boolean containsValue(Object value)
```

The `SortedMap` interface extends `Map` to identify implementations that return the results of `entrySet`, `keySet`, and `values` sorted based on the keys. As with `SortedSet`, the sort order of a `SortedMap` is determined either by a `Comparator` provided when the map is constructed, or by the natural ordering of key objects that implement `java.lang.Comparable`.

You can access the lowest and highest keys of a `SortedMap` using the `firstKey` and `lastKey` methods:

```
public Object firstKey()
public Object lastKey()
```

`SortedMap` also provides the `headMap`, `tailMap`, and `subMap` methods that return views of portions of the underlying map. The `headMap` method returns a view of that part of the map that is less than the specified key. Conversely, `tailMap` returns a view of the elements with keys greater than its argument. You can retrieve any arbitrary portion of the map using `subMap`. The following signatures declare the three view methods:

```
public SortedMap headMap(Object toKey)
public SortedMap tailMap(Object fromKey)
public SortedMap subMap(Object fromKey, Object toKey)
```

IN THE BEGINNING

The collection framework introduced with the Java 1.2 API provided much needed new functionality, but several collection classes have been a part of the language since the beginning. Namely, the `Vector`, `Stack`, and `Hashtable` classes and the `Enumeration` interface have been around since the 1.0 API. With the release of Java 1.2, `Vector` and `Hashtable` were retrofitted to implement `List` and `Map`, respectively. This was done to integrate them into the collection framework, but, beyond that, their functionality has remained unchanged.

This section provides an overview of how these classes are used because it is likely you will see them in practice for some time to come. You should view them as legacy classes only, however. When you are developing new classes that will operate with a Java 1.2 or higher virtual machine, you should always prefer the newer collection classes to these. However, if you are restricted to an earlier Java release for any reason, these classes are your only option for object containers.

Vector

The `Vector` class represents an ordered collection of objects that can be referenced using indexes, and can grow and shrink in size. Since the release of the 1.2 API, `Vector` has extended `AbstractList`, which implements the `List` interface in the collections framework. The major difference between `Vector` and other implementations of `List` is that the methods of `Vector` are implemented as `synchronized` to provide thread-safe access, whether your application requires it or not. The majority of the `Vector` methods correspond to equivalent `List` methods, although there are differences in some of the method names. `Vector` also provides a few convenience methods that the designers of the collections framework decided not to make a part of the `List` interface.

If you are limited to JDK 1.1.x, you should use `Vector` for the type of collection it supports. Otherwise, you should use `ArrayList`, which is a standard implementation of `List` discussed later in this chapter. If you require synchronization, the `Collections` class contains a utility method that returns a synchronized view of a `List`. This functionality is covered a little later also.

Just like `List`, the intent of `Vector` has been to provide an alternative to the array. Java arrays perform well and are truly useful, but they don't always fit your needs. Sometimes you might prefer to put items into an array, but, at the point you need to allocate the array, you don't know how many items you will eventually have to store. One way to solve this is to create an array larger than you think you'll need. This is an approach sometimes used in C programming. A `Vector` is similar to an array in that it holds multiple objects and you can retrieve the stored objects using an index value. However, the primary difference between an array and a `Vector` is that a `Vector` automatically grows when its capacity is exceeded. A `Vector` also provides extra methods for adding and removing elements that you would normally have to do manually in an array, such as inserting an element between two others. Effectively, a `Vector` is an extensible array.

When you create a `Vector`, you can specify its initial capacity and how much it should grow each time its capacity is reached. You can also just set one of these values, or neither, and rely on the class defaults. If you have an idea of how many elements a specific `Vector` will typically store, you can improve its performance by specifying the initial capacity and capacity increment accordingly. To accomplish these various forms of initialization, the JDK 1.1.x `Vector` class defines three constructors:

```
public Vector()
public Vector(int initialCapacity)
public Vector(int initialCapacity, int capacityIncrement)
```

JDK 1.2 added one more constructor to support the collections framework. This constructor accepts a `Collection` as a parameter and initializes the `Vector` to hold each of the objects found in the specified collection:

```
public Vector(Collection c)
```

The remainder of this section focuses on how `Vector` differs from the `List` interface. To use `Vector` in a JDK 1.1.x application, you should consult the API documentation for the exact details of the supported methods. In particular, this section omits any discussion of `Vector` methods that are declared by the `List` interface, such as `contains`, `indexOf`, `isEmpty`, and `size`.

`Vector` provides `addElement` and `insertElementAt` methods to either add an object to the end of its collection or insert one at a specified index. These methods are functionally equivalent to the two overloaded `add` methods in the `List` interface:

```
public final synchronized void addElement(Object newElement)
public final synchronized void insertElementAt(Object newElement, int index)
```


You can change the object at a specific position in a `Vector` with the `setElementAt` method, which is equivalent to `set` in the `List` interface:

```
public final synchronized void setElementAt(Object ob, int index)
```

`Vector` allows you to retrieve an object based on its index using the `elementAt` method, which is equivalent to `get` in the `List` interface:

```
public final synchronized Object elementAt(int index)
```

You can also access the first and last elements in a `Vector` with its `firstElement` and `lastElement` methods, which were not carried over when `List` was defined:

```
public final synchronized Object firstElement()
public final synchronized Object lastElement()
```

From a performance standpoint, you might want to use a `Vector` to build up a container of objects but then convert the `Vector` into an array after all the objects, or at least the number of objects, are known. `Vector` provides the `copyInto` method for this purpose, which is similar to the `toArray` methods of `List`:

```
public final synchronized void copyInto(Object[] obArray)
```

`Vector` defines three methods that are not a part of the `List` interface for removing one or more objects from its collection. These are `removeAllElements`, which is equivalent to `clear`, and `removeElement` and `removeElementAt`, which are equivalent to the two overloaded `remove` methods:

```
public final synchronized void removeAllElements()
public final synchronized boolean removeElement(Object ob)
public final synchronized void removeElementAt(int index)
```

A `Vector` has two notions of size—the number of elements it currently holds and the currently allocated capacity. The capacity method tells you how many objects the `Vector` can hold before having to grow:

```
public final int capacity()
```

You can increase the capacity of a `Vector` using the `ensureCapacity` method:

```
public final synchronized void ensureCapacity(int minimumCapacity)
```

This method tells the `Vector` that it should allocate more space if its current capacity is less than `minimumCapacity`. Using this method improves performance by avoiding a lot of small capacity adjustments when the eventual size requirement for a `Vector` is known. Conversely, if you want to reduce the the capacity, use the `trimToSize` method:

```
public final synchronized void trimToSize()
```

This method reduces the capacity of a `Vector` down to the number of elements it is currently storing.

You can use the `setSize` method to change the current number of elements:

```
public synchronized final void setSize(int newSize)
```

If the new size is less than the old size, the elements at the end of the `Vector` are lost. If the new size is greater than the old size, new elements set to `null` are added. Calling `setSize(0)` is the same as calling `removeAllElements` or `clear`.

THE ENUMERATION INTERFACE

If you want to cycle through all the elements in a `Vector`, you can use the `elements` method to get a corresponding `Enumeration` object. An `Enumeration` is responsible for accessing elements in a collection sequentially. It contains two methods, `hasMoreElements` and `nextElement`:

```
public abstract boolean hasMoreElements()
public abstract Object nextElement()
```

`hasMoreElements` returns true while there are still more elements to access. `nextElement` returns a reference to each element in turn as the collection is traversed. If there are no more elements to access when you call `nextElement`, you get a `NoSuchElementException`. You should always use `hasMoreElements` when working with an `Enumeration` to avoid this exception.

As an example, the following code fragment uses the `Enumeration` interface to examine every object in a `Vector`:

```
Enumeration vectEnum = myVector.elements();     // get the vector's enumeration

while ( vectEnum.hasMoreElements() ) {    // while there's something to get...
  Object nextOb = vectEnum.nextElement();       // get the next object
  // do whatever you want with the next object
}
```

The `Enumeration` interface is the preferred approach for traversing a `Vector` in a JDK 1.1.x application; however, for JDK 1.2 and above, you should obtain a `ListIterator` from one of the overloaded `listIterator` methods of `List` instead.

STACK

A *stack* is a data structure that inserts and retrieves objects in a last-in-first-out (LIFO) manner. In other words, when you ask a stack to give you the next item, it hands back the most recently added item.

The `Stack` class is implemented as a subclass of `Vector` that is created with a no-argument constructor:

```
public Stack()
```

To add an item to the top of the stack, you push it onto the stack:

```
public Object push(Object newItem)
```

The `pop` method removes the top item from the stack:

```
public Object pop()
```


If you try to pop an item off an empty stack, you get an `EmptyStackException`. You can find out which item is on top of the stack without removing it by using the `peek` method:

```
public Object peek()
```

The `empty` method returns `true` if there are no items on the stack:

```
public boolean empty()
```

The `search` method tells you how far an object is from the top of the stack:

```
public int search(Object ob)
```

If the object is not on the stack at all, `search` returns `-1`.

As with its superclass `Vector`, `Stack` is a legacy class. With JDK 1.2 and above, you should use `LinkedList` instead. This class is discussed in the "General-Purpose Implementations" section later in this chapter.

Hashtable

The `Hashtable` class holds mappings between keys and value objects. The benefit of using this structure over a simple collection of objects is in the efficiency of object retrieval. When you can associate a key with an object, it is much faster to locate that object in a `Hashtable` than to iterate through a collection searching for it. If you have not used this type of construct before, you should definitely add it to your toolkit as a programmer.

With JDK 1.2, `Hashtable` was updated to implement the `Map` interface. With this in mind, the same basic comments apply to `Hashtable` as did to `Vector`. You should prefer `HashMap`, the true collection framework implementation of `Map`, to `Hashtable` if you are working with JDK 1.2 or above. `Hashtable` differs from `HashMap` in that it is synchronized and does not allow `null` for either a key or value. This synchronization results in unnecessary overhead if your application does not require it. Beyond this, the differences between the two are mostly limited to method naming.

Effectively, you can think of Hashtable as a class that uses the hash codes of its key objects to perform lookups for the associated objects. A *hash code* refers to associating an integer value with an object to help distinguish it from other objects. The Object class defines the hashCode method to support the concept. The particular value of a hash code is unimportant, but it must remain the same for an object during a single execution of an application unless the object changes significantly. Also, any objects that are equal must report the same hash code value. Objects that are not equal are not required to have different hash codes, but the performance of any lookup that uses hash codes is greatly improved when they do.

A Hashtable groups its keys into "buckets" based on their hash codes. When it needs to locate a key, it queries the key's hash code, uses the hash code to find the correct bucket, and then searches the bucket for the correct key. Usually, the number of keys in a bucket is small compared to the total number of keys in the Hashtable, so the number of comparisons performed is much smaller than what is required in a collection such as Vector for a similar search.

A Hashtable has a capacity, which defines the number of buckets it uses, and a load factor, which is the ratio of the number of entries it holds to the number of buckets. When you create a Hashtable, you can specify a load factor threshold value. When the current load factor exceeds this threshold, the capacity is increased by its protected rehash method. The default load factor threshold is 0.75, but you can specify any load factor threshold greater than 0 and less than or equal to 1. A smaller threshold means a faster lookup because there will be few keys per bucket (maybe no more than one), but the table will have far more buckets than elements, so there is some wasted space. A larger threshold means the possibility of slower lookups, but the number of buckets is closer to the number of elements.

The JDK 1.1.x Hashtable class has three constructors that support various options related to initial capacity and load factor. You have the flexibility to specify both of these parameters, to accept a default value for either one, or both:

```
public Hashtable()
public Hashtable(int initialCapacity)
public Hashtable(int initialCapacity, float loadFactorThreshold)
```

JDK 1.2 added one more constructor to support the collections framework. This constructor accepts a Map as a parameter and initializes the Hashtable to hold each of the associations found in the specified Map:

```
public Hashtable(Map m)
```

The remainder of this section focuses on how Hashtable differs from the Map interface. To use Hashtable in a JDK 1.1.x application, you should consult the API documentation for the exact details of the supported methods.

The Map interface defines the containsKey and containsValue methods for querying a Map on whether it holds a specific key or value object. The original implementation of Hashtable supported the containsValue operation with a method named contains. The functionality is equivalent, only the name is less clear. This method is declared as follows:

```
public synchronized boolean contains(Object value)
```

The `keySet` and `values` methods of `Map` return a map's keys and value objects as a `Set` and a `Collection`, respectively. `Hashtable` also allows these objects to be retrieved through an `Enumeration` using its `keys` and `elements` methods:

```
public abstract Enumeration elements()
public abstract Enumeration keys()
```

GENERAL-PURPOSE IMPLEMENTATIONS

Fortunately, Sun did not stop with the definition of interfaces when the collections framework was established. The Java API includes seven concrete implementations of the various interfaces found within the framework. These general-purpose implementations will typically suffice when you need a particular collection or map class to support a program. Even if you find a need for a more specialized implementation, you will likely find it easier to use one of the classes in this hierarchy as a starting point rather than implementing one of the interfaces from scratch.

If you experience runtime exceptions when using collection classes other than the general-purpose implementations, see "`UnsupportedOperationException`," in the "Troubleshooting" section at the end of this chapter.

The implementations discussed in this section provide the basic functionality required by the corresponding interfaces. They are unsynchronized; they do not restrict the elements that can be contained; and the iterators they produce fail quickly and cleanly if any illegal concurrent modification is detected. These implementations are complete in that they support all the optional operations defined by the interfaces.

In an example of good design that you should also adopt, the general-purpose implementations are built from a group of abstract classes that provide partial implementations of the collection framework interfaces. You will find that interfaces often define methods that could easily be supported with default implementations. Given that an interface cannot define any implementation details, the best way to handle this from a design approach is to capture that behavior in an abstract class that can then be extended by multiple concrete implementations. The collections framework does just that with `AbstractCollection`, `AbstractSet`, `AbstractList`, `AbstractSequentialList`, and `AbstractMap`. These classes, for the most part, implement the required interface operations and throw an `UnsupportedOperationException` for the optional ones. If no default behavior exists at this level for a required operation, the corresponding method is declared as `abstract` in these classes.

A common comment about these implementations is that, unlike the legacy collection classes introduced earlier, they are not synchronized to support access by multiple threads. This is not a drawback, however. The later section "Collection Utilities and Wrappers" describes how to obtain synchronized versions of these classes when you require them. This aspect of the general-purpose implementations is actually a feature. When using these classes, you have the flexibility to select between synchronized and unsynchronized implementations. You should avoid the overhead of synchronized collections when your application does not require it.

ArrayList

ArrayList is a resizable implementation of List based on an array that is the collection framework replacement for Vector. Its functionality is much like Vector, but it is not synchronized. It supports all the optional methods of Collection and List and allows all values, including null, as elements. When the capacity of an ArrayList is exceeded, it is recreated to grow as necessary. The use of an underlying array gives ArrayList much better performance for retrieving objects by index than that obtained with LinkedList. The tradeoff is that ArrayList does not perform as well when inserting and removing elements.

An ArrayList can be constructed with no arguments, an initial capacity, or a Collection to copy:

```
public ArrayList()
public ArrayList(int initialCapacity)
public ArrayList(Collection c)
```

ArrayList extends AbstractList, which in turn extends AbstractCollection. Part of the basic List functionality that is required is provided through this inheritance hierarchy. The ArrayList implementation overrides the abstract and optional methods found in AbstractList.

ArrayList also defines the ensureCapacity and trimToSize methods to allow better management of its internal mechanisms. You should call ensureCapacity prior to adding a large number of items to an ArrayList to prevent the possibility of multiple internal reallocations. You can use trimToSize to minimize the amount of memory required by an ArrayList after its maximum size is determined These methods are declared with the following signatures:

```
public void ensureCapacity(int minCapacity)
public void trimToSize()
```

Listing 10.1 shows example calls to many of the methods implemented by ArrayList.

LISTING 10.1 ArrayListExample.java—CALLS TO THE VARIOUS ArrayList METHODS

```
import java.util.ArrayList;

public class ArrayListExample {

  public void doExample() {
    ArrayList myList = new ArrayList(5);  // set initial array capacity to 5
    // load the list with integers 0-4 wrapped in Integer
    for ( int i=0; i<5; i++) {
      myList.add( new Integer(i) );
    }
    System.out.println( "List contains " + myList.size() + " elements" );

    // locate a specific object in the list
    Integer int2 = new Integer(2);
    System.out.println( "List contains Integer(2): " +
      myList.contains(int2) );
    System.out.println( "Integer(2) is at index " + myList.indexOf(int2) );
```

LISTING 10.1 CONTINUED

```
    // replace an object and then locate it by index
    myList.set(2, new Integer(99));
    System.out.println( "Get element at index 2: " + myList.get(2) );

    // add 5 more elements - capacity will grow automatically
    for ( int i=5; i<10; i++) {
      // add by specifying the index
      myList.add( i, new Integer(i) );
    }

    // add 5 more elements, but increase the capacity first
    myList.ensureCapacity(15);
    for ( int i=10; i<15; i++) {
      myList.add( new Integer(i) );
    }

    // take the last 5 elements back out and reduce the capacity
    myList.subList(10,15).clear();
    myList.trimToSize();

    // create another list and copy it into the original one
    ArrayList otherList = new ArrayList();
    otherList.add( new String("otherList 1") );
    otherList.add( new String("otherList 2") );
    myList.add(7,otherList);

    // display the list elements
    System.out.println(myList);
  }

  public static void main( String args[] ) {
    new ArrayListExample().doExample();
  }

}
```

If you execute the code in Listing 10.1, you get the following output:

```
List contains 5 elements
List contains Integer(2): true
Integer(2) is at index 2
Get element at index 2: 99
[0, 1, 99, 3, 4, 5, 6, [otherList 1, otherList 2], 7, 8, 9]
```


LinkedList

The array-based `List` implementation provided by `ArrayList` works well when you need random access to a collection of objects. Of course, there are always tradeoffs to consider. `ArrayList` is well suited for accessing objects by index, but at the price of reduced performance when inserting and removing elements. This is where the value of an interface-based collection framework comes into play. `LinkedList` also implements the `List` interface, but it is optimized instead for sequential data access and fast insertions and removals. By way of class hierarchy, LinkedList extends AbstractSequentialList, which extends AbstractList. AbstractSequentialList partially implements List in a manner that favors sequential access.

As with the other general-purpose implementations, LinkedList implements all the optional List methods and allows all values, including null. LinkedList supports its operations based on a doubly linked list implementation, which is a concept you have likely seen, or even implemented yourself, in other languages. In this construct, each element in the list maintains a reference to the element before it and the element after it. When a new element is inserted, only the references associated with the new element and the two existing elements between which it is inserted are changed. The removal of an element is just as easy. The tradeoff between LinkedList and ArrayList is in accessing an element by its index. A LinkedList must be traversed sequentially to locate a specific object, so it will never have the performance of an ArrayList when random access is required.

Note

If you have worked with linked lists in other languages, you are probably accustomed to working with pointers to maintain the links. As in all cases, Java works only with object references and not pointers. There is nothing within the implementation of LinkedList, or any other Java class, that relies on pointer arithmetic.

A LinkedList can be constructed with no arguments, or a Collection to copy:

```
public LinkedList()
public LinkedList(Collection c)
```

The elements in the middle of a LinkedList are slow to retrieve, but those at the beginning and end are easily accessible. The class provides two methods beyond those defined by List to simplify this further:

```
public Object getFirst()
public Object getlast()
```

The storage mechanism used by LinkedList also readily supports adding to, or removing from, the beginning or end of a list, so convenience methods are provided for that also:

```
public void addFirst(Object o)
public void addLast(Object o)
public Object removeFirst()
public Object removeLast()
```

The two removal methods return the object that is removed from the collection. These methods throw a NoSuchElementException if called when the list is empty, so you should also check isEmpty before using either of them.

The ease of inserting and removing elements from a LinkedList make it the preferred choice for stack and queue implementations. Where ArrayList is the framework's replacement for Vector, LinkedList is a similar replacement for Stack. Again, LinkedList is not synchronized, but you can obtain a synchronized version using a static method of the Collections class.

Listing 10.2 shows how a `LinkedList` can be used to implement a stack using the same method signatures as the `Stack` class.

LISTING 10.2 `LinkedListStack.java`—A STACK BUILT FROM A `LinkedList`

```
import java.util.LinkedList;
import java.util.EmptyStackException;

public class LinkedListStack {

  private LinkedList listDelegate = new LinkedList();

  public boolean empty() {
    return listDelegate.isEmpty();
  }

  // return the element on top of the stack without removing it
  public Object peek() {
    if ( !this.empty() ) {
      return listDelegate.getFirst();
    }
    throw new EmptyStackException();
  }

  // return the element on top of the stack and remove it
  public Object pop() {
    if ( !this.empty() ) {
      return listDelegate.removeFirst();
    }
    throw new EmptyStackException();
  }

  // place an object on top of the stack
  public Object push(Object item) {
    listDelegate.addFirst(item);
    return item;
  }

  // look for an object in the stack
  public int search(Object item) {
    return listDelegate.indexOf(item);
  }

  public static void main( String args[] ) {
    LinkedListStack stack = new LinkedListStack();
    // push 5 elements onto the stack
    for ( int i=0; i<5; i++ ) {
      stack.push( new Integer(i) );
    }

    System.out.println("Peek at the top of the stack: " + stack.peek() );

    // empty the stack
    while ( !stack.empty() ) {
      System.out.println("Pop: " + stack.pop() );
    }
```

LISTING 10.2 CONTINUED

```
    }

}
```

If you execute the code in Listing 10.2, you get the following output:

```
Peek at the top of the stack: 4
Pop: 4
Pop: 3
Pop: 2
Pop: 1
Pop: 0
```

Listing 10.2 defines a fairly simple class, but, in addition to showing the use of `LinkedList`, it also demonstrates an important design concept. `LinkedListStack` could have been implemented by extending `LinkedList` instead of holding a `LinkedList` object as a class member. Instead, the approach shown here is one of delegation, which focuses on composition rather than class inheritance. To reflect a good object-oriented design, `LinkedListStack` should reuse the functionality of `LinkedList` in a way that leaves it encapsulated and clearly divides responsibility between the cooperating classes. Inheriting from `LinkedList` would have achieved some of the same benefits, but it would have locked `LinkedListStack` into a class hierarchy without providing any advantages. If a better underlying implementation for a stack were to come along later, `LinkedListStack` could be modified internally to use it without requiring any externally visible changes.

HashMap

Just as `Vector` and `Stack` have their replacements in `ArrayList` and `LinkedList`, `Hashtable` has a replacement in `HashMap`. `HashMap` extends `AbstractMap` to implement the `Map` interface using an internal hashtable representation. It makes no guarantee about the storage order of its associations, and, similar to the other general-purpose implementations, it supports the optional methods of `Map`, allows `null` (as either a key or a value), and is not synchronized.

A `HashMap` can be constructed with no arguments, an initial capacity, a capacity and a load factor, or a `Map` to copy:

```
public HashMap()
public HashMap(int initialCapacity)
public HashMap(int initialCapacity, float loadFactor)
public HashMap(Map m)
```

The hash table basis for `HashMap` supports good performance of both its `put` and `get` operations. Performance of the class is driven, for the most part, by the assigned capacity and load factor. The tradeoffs related to these parameters are mostly based on competition between iteration speed and element insertion time. The capacity of a `HashMap` is the number of buckets it uses to hold keys, and the load factor is a weighting used to determine how full the map can get before the capacity is automatically increased.

Whenever the number of elements stored in a HashMap exceeds the product of its capacity and load factor, the rehash method is called to double the capacity and restructure the map. You can reduce the occurrences of this operation by setting the initial capacity sufficiently high, but the time to iterate through a HashMap grows when you do this. The load factor defaults to 0.75, which is regarded as a good balance between access time and storage space costs. If you isolate a performance bottleneck to the use of a HashMap, you should experiment with other values for the initial capacity.

Listing 10.3 shows example calls to many of the methods implemented by HashMap.

Listing 10.3 HashMapExample.java—Calls to Various HashMap Methods

```
import java.util.HashMap;

public class HashMapExample {

  public void doExample() {
    HashMap myMap = new HashMap(2);

    Employee emp = new Employee( "123-45-6789", "Smith", "John" );
    myMap.put( emp.getSocialSecurityNumber(), emp );
    emp = new Employee( "987-65-4321", "Doe", "Jane" );
    myMap.put( emp.getSocialSecurityNumber(), emp );

    if ( myMap.containsKey("123-45-6789") ) {
      System.out.println("Found by key: " + myMap.get("123-45-6789"));
    }

    if ( myMap.containsValue(emp) ) {
      System.out.println("Map contains value: " +
        myMap.get(emp.getSocialSecurityNumber()));
    }

    // clear the list and verify that it's empty
    myMap.clear();
    System.out.println("Map is now " +
      (myMap.isEmpty() ? "Empty" : "Not Empty"));
  }

  public static void main( String args[] ) {
    new HashMapExample().doExample();
  }
}

class Employee {
  private String socialSecurityNumber;
  private String lastName;
  private String firstName;

  public Employee( String ssn, String lname, String fname ) {
    socialSecurityNumber = ssn;
    lastName = lname;
    firstName = fname;
  }
```

LISTING 10.3 CONTINUED

```
  // the SSN can be retrieved, but is immutable, which
  // is best for an object used as a key
  public String getSocialSecurityNumber() {
    return socialSecurityNumber;
  }

  public String toString() {
    return socialSecurityNumber + " " + lastName + ", " + firstName;
  }
}
```

If you execute the code in Listing 10.3, you get the following output:

```
Found by key: 123-45-6789 Smith, John
Map contains value: 987-65-4321 Doe, Jane
Map is now Empty
```

TreeMap

`TreeMap` implements `SortedMap` by extending `AbstractMap` and using a Red-Black tree to maintain its keys in sorted order. This sorting results in performance of the `containsKey`, `get`, `put`, and `remove` operations that remains logarithmically proportional to the number of entries in the map. Although this is relatively efficient, you should rely on `HashMap` if you do not require sorting functionality.

A `TreeMap` can be constructed with no arguments, a `Map` or a `SortedMap` to copy, or a `Comparator`:

```
public TreeMap()
public TreeMap(Map m)
public TreeMap(SortedMap m)
public TreeMap(Comparator c)
```

Remember that a `SortedMap` must be told how to sort its keys. This can be accomplished by either providing a `Comparator` or using keys that implement `java.lang.Comparable`. The constructor that accepts a `Comparator` obviously relies on this first method for sorting its keys. If you construct a `TreeMap` without any arguments or with a `Map`, the keys must implement `Comparable`. If you supply a `SortedMap`, a new map is created using the same sort mechanism.

You use a `TreeMap` exactly like you use `HashMap`, only you have access to the additional methods defined by `SortedMap` that rely on the ordering of the keys.

WeakHashMap

The `WeakHashMap` provides a hash table–based implementation of `Map` just as in the case of `HashMap`, but it does it using weak references to the keys. Prior to Java 1.2, the garbage collector would reclaim the memory allocated to an object only when no references to that object remained. The Java 1.2 release introduced the `java.lang.ref` package to allow you to make use of references that release their association to an object when certain events occur. In particular, you can establish a `WeakReference` to an object that is automatically cleared when the garbage collector detects that no other references to the object exist. Basically, it's your way of telling the compiler that you care about an object, but only as long as some other part of your program is using it too.

When you create a `WeakHashMap`, you can associate information with each key object that is only maintained as long as that key is in use elsewhere. After all other references to the object are released, the garbage collector will mark it as unused and remove it from the hash table.

Just like a `HashMap`, a `WeakHashMap` can be constructed with no arguments, an initial capacity, a capacity and a load factor, or a `Map` to copy:

```
public WeakHashMap()
public WeakHashMap(int initialCapacity)
public WeakHashMap(int initialCapacity, float loadFactor)
public WeakHashMap(Map m)
```

The `WeakHashMap` constructor that accepts a `Map` was added in the Java 1.3 release. The primary purpose was to make it consistent with `HashMap` and to follow the `Map` interface decree that each implementation implement a copy constructor of this type.

HashSet

`HashSet` provides a basic implementation of `Set` by extending `AbstractSet` and making use of an underlying `HashMap` instance. A `HashSet` does not maintain any particular order of its elements, but it does implement the optional methods of `Set` and allow `null` as an element. When you need a collection that does not allow duplicate elements and does not have to be ordered, `HashSet` can supply the appropriate functionality and produce quick lookup times given its `HashMap` backing.

A `HashSet` can be constructed with no arguments, an initial capacity, a capacity and a load factor, or a `Collection` to copy:

```
public HashSet()
public HashSet(int initialCapacity)
public HashSet(int initialCapacity, float loadFactor)
public HashSet(Collection c)
```

The capacity and load factor parameters in the `HashSet` constructors are used to construct the supporting `HashMap`.

TreeSet

`TreeSet` implements `SortedSet` by extending `AbstractSet` and using an underlying `TreeMap` instance. The use of `TreeMap` keeps the performance of the `add`, `contains`, and `remove` operations logarithmically proportional to the number of entries in the set. `HashSet` is a better choice if you do not require sorting functionality.

A `TreeSet` can be constructed with no arguments, a `Collection` or a `SortedSet` to copy, or a `Comparator`:

```
public TreeSet()
public TreeSet(Collection c)
```

```
public TreeSet(SortedSet s)
public TreeSet(Comparator c)
```

As with `SortedMap`, a `SortedSet` must be told how to sort its elements. This can be accomplished by either providing a `Comparator` or only storing `Comparable` objects. If you construct a `TreeSet` without any arguments or with a `Collection`, the elements must implement `Comparable`. If you supply a `SortedSet`, a new set is created using the same sort mechanism.

You use a `TreeSet` exactly like you use `HashSet`, only you have access to the additional methods defined by `SortedSet` that rely on the ordering of the elements.

SORTING A COLLECTION

One of the drawbacks of `Vector` when it was first introduced was that it provided no way to sort its elements. You were left to either write your own sort routines or incorporate a set of third-party classes to provide what is typically a key function in most applications. Fortunately, the collections framework addressed the issue of sorting directly and provided the functionality as part of the API.

THE COMPARABLE INTERFACE

Throughout this chapter, classes have been discussed that make use of the *natural ordering* of objects. A class has a natural ordering when it implements the `java.lang.Comparable` interface:

```
public interface Comparable {
  public int compareTo(Object o);
}
```

The `compareTo` method of this interface is implemented by a class to compare the current object with the object passed in as a parameter for order. The method returns a positive integer if the `Object` argument is less than the current object, zero if they are equal, or a negative integer if the argument is greater. You should implement this interface for any class you write whose instances can be sorted or ordered. The ordering produced by this interface is referred to as natural because it is the order decided internally by the class without any knowledge of how it might be used.

Many of the core API classes implement `Comparable` to simplify the display of their instances. This list of classes includes, among others, `Character`, `File`, `Long`, `Short`, `String`, `Float`, `Integer`, `Byte`, `Double`, `BigInteger`, `BigDecimal`, and `Date`.

THE `Comparator` INTERFACE

You might also find it necessary to sort objects that do not have a natural ordering, or to impose a different sorting algorithm on a class that does. The `Comparator` interface allows you to sort a collection regardless of its natural ordering. This interface declares two methods, of which `compare` is the more important:

```
public interface Comparator {
```

```
  public int compare(Object o1, Object o2);
  public boolean equals(Object obj);
}
```

The `compare` method of `Comparator` accepts two `Object` arguments and returns an integer value that defines their sort order. This return value must be a negative value if the first object is less than the second, a zero if they are equal, or a positive value if the first object is greater. Normally, you will allow the `Object` implementation of `equals` to satisfy the remainder of the interface. The only reason to override `equals` would be if a particular implementation could improve performance in cases where the method gets called often.

Tip

Although not required, you should declare any comparators you write to implement `java.io.Serializable`. If you assign a `Comparator` to a `TreeMap` or `TreeSet`, it must be `Serializable` to allow its associated container to be serialized.

The preceding section listed `String` as an example of a `Comparable` class. Java's natural ordering for `String` is case sensitive, which might not always be desirable. If you want to sort a collection of strings and ignore case, the `String` class holds a class field named `CASE_INSENSITVE_ORDER` that is a case-insensitive implementation of `Comparator`. This is one case where the usefulness of being able to override the natural ordering of a class is easy to see.

USING `Collections.sort()`

The `Collections` class in the `java.util` package consists solely of `static` utility methods that simplify working with collection classes. Included among these are two sorting operations for lists:

```
public static void sort(List list)
public static void sort(List list, Comparator c)
```

The single-argument version sorts a `List` based on the natural ordering of its elements, and the other uses a specified `Comparator`. You can apply these methods to any `List` that is modifiable as long as its elements are *mutually comparable*. This means that the `compareTo`, or `compare`, method must not throw a `ClassCastException` when attempting to compare any two elements.

The `Collections` class also provides another interesting method related to sorting:

```
public static Comparator reverseOrder()
```

The `reverseOrder` method returns a `Comparator` that sorts a collection of objects that implement `Comparable` in the reverse of its natural ordering. If you want to sort a group of `Integer` or `String` instances in reverse order, this method, combined with the sort method of `Collections` that accepts a `Comparator`, provides a simple and efficient way to do it.

Listing 10.4 shows an example of sorting a class that implements `Comparable` using its natural ordering, and using a `Comparator`.

LISTING 10.4 AuctionBid.java—Comparable AND Comparator SORTING

```
import java.util.*;
import java.text.NumberFormat;
public class AuctionBid implements Comparable {

  // class holds the bidder's name and the amount bid
  String bidder;
  int amount;

  public AuctionBid(String name, int bid) {
    bidder = name;
    amount = bid;
  }

  public String toString() {
    // get a currency formatter to make the output look nice
    NumberFormat formatter = NumberFormat.getCurrencyInstance();
    return bidder + " bid " + formatter.format(amount);
  }

  // implement Comparable interface
  public int compareTo( Object other ) {
    // this method defines the natural ordering of
    // the class to be based on ascending bid amount
    AuctionBid otherBid = (AuctionBid)other;
    if ( otherBid == null ) {
      return 1;
    }
    if ( this.equals(otherBid) || (amount == otherBid.amount) ) {
      return 0;
    }
    return ( otherBid.amount < amount ) ? 1 : -1;
  }

  // define a Comparator that instead sorts on the bidder's name
  static class BidComparator implements Comparator, java.io.Serializable {
    public int compare(Object o1, Object o2) {
      AuctionBid firstBid = (AuctionBid)o1;
      AuctionBid secondBid = (AuctionBid)o2;
      if ( (firstBid == null) || (firstBid.bidder == null) ) {
        return ((secondBid == null) || (secondBid.bidder == null)) ? 0 : -1;
      }
      if ( (secondBid == null) || (secondBid.bidder == null) ) {
        return 1;
      }
      // String implements Comparable, so let it do the work
      return firstBid.bidder.compareTo(secondBid.bidder);
    }
  }

  public static void main( String args[] ) {
    // fill a list with 5 bids
    ArrayList bidList = new ArrayList();
    for ( int i=0; i<5; i++ ) {
      // generate a random number 0-100 for a bid amount
      bidList.add( new AuctionBid("Bidder" + i, (int)(Math.random()*100)) );
```

LISTING 10.4 CONTINUED

```
    }

    // sort the bids in natural order and display them
    Collections.sort( bidList );
    System.out.println("Natural order sort by bid amount");
    System.out.println( bidList );

    // impose a different sort using a Comparator
    Collections.sort( bidList, new BidComparator() );
    System.out.println("Comparator sort by bidder name");
    System.out.println( bidList );
  }
}
```


The code in Listing 10.4 generates random numbers for bids, but, if you execute it, you'll get output similar to the following:

```
Natural order sort by bid amount
[Bidder1 bid $15.00, Bidder2 bid $44.00, Bidder3 bid $56.00,
Bidder4 bid $79.00, Bidder0 bid $83.00]
Comparator sort by bidder name
[Bidder0 bid $83.00, Bidder1 bid $15.00, Bidder2 bid $44.00,
Bidder3 bid $56.00, Bidder4 bid $79.00]
```

ITERATING A COLLECTION

The collections framework introduced the concept of iterators to take the place of the `Enumeration` interface for traversing the elements of a collection. The iterators are defined using interfaces just like `Enumeration`, but they differ in their method names, and they optionally allow you to remove elements from a collection while it is being iterated.

THE `Iterator` INTERFACE

An `Iterator` can be obtained for any object that implements the `Collection` interface. This interface defines three methods for traversing a collection:

```
boolean hasNext()
Object next()
void remove()
```

These methods allow you to check the iteration for more elements, retrieve the next element, and remove the last retrieved element from the collection. The `next` method throws a `NoSuchElementException` if called when the iteration has completed, which makes it important to always check `hasNext` first. The `remove` method is optional; it throws an `UnsupportedOperationException` if it is not a part of the `Iterator` being used.

Listing 10.5 shows a typical block of code used with an iterator. As you can see, obtaining and using an `Iterator` instance is simple. You do need to be aware of the object types held by a collection, however. The code shown here relies on the collection holding only instances of Address. A more robust implementation would check the type of each object before performing the cast operation.

LISTING 10.5 Address.java—ITERATING A COLLECTION

```
import java.util.*;
public class Address {

  public String addressLine1;
  public String addressLine2;
  public String city;
  public String state;
  public String zip;

  public Address( String line1, String line2, String city,
   String state, String zip ) {
    addressLine1 = line1;
    addressLine2 = line2;
    this.city = city;
    this.state = state;
    this.zip = zip;
  }

  public static void main( String args[] ) {
    HashSet set = new HashSet();
    set.add( new Address("123 Peachtree St", "", "Atlanta", "GA", "30305") );
    set.add( new Address("100 Main St", "", "Any Town", "NY", "10101") );

    // retrieve an iterator from the collection
    Iterator iter = set.iterator();
    while ( iter.hasNext() ) {  // loop while elements remain
      // elements are returned as Object so cast to subtype
      Address add = (Address)iter.next();
      System.out.println( add.zip );
    }
  }
}
```

THE ListIterator INTERFACE

An Iterator makes no assumptions about the underlying behavior of the collection it iterates, so it is limited to the basic functionality shown in the preceding example. For more interesting operations, a List has the capability to provide a more specific form of the Iterator. The ListIterator takes advantage of the indexing in the List to allow you to perform several additional operations.

To start with, a ListIterator allows you to insert a new object into a List, or replace an existing one during its iteration. The add method inserts a new object immediately before the one that would be returned by a call to next. The set method replaces the last object returned by the iterator with the one specified. Both of these methods are optional and rely on the associated List being modifiable:

```
void add(Object o)
void set(Object o)
```

The methods defined by `Iterator` allow you to move only forward through a collection. A `ListIterator` also allows you to move backward through a list using `hasPrevious` and `previous` the same way you use `hasNext` and `next`:

```
boolean hasPrevious()
Object previous()
```

Finally, because you're looking at a `List`, you can also get the index values of the next or previous elements:

```
int nextIndex()
int previousIndex()
```

EFFICIENT SEARCHING

Iterating a collection is useful when you need to do something with each element it contains, but it is not an efficient way to locate a particular object. If you have a sorted `List`, you can take advantage of the `binarySearch` methods provided by the `Collections` class to efficiently locate a specific object in a collection. One form of `binarySearch` relies on the natural ordering of the elements, and the other allows you to associate a `Comparator`:

```
static int binarySearch(List list, Object key)
static int binarySearch(List list, Object key, Comparator c)
```

These methods perform a binary search, or—if the `List` implements `AbstractSequentialList`—a sequential search, to locate the specified key.

COLLECTION UTILITIES AND WRAPPERS

Besides the methods already introduced, the `Collections` class provides a number of other useful support functions. This section outlines some of the more commonly used utilities and the `Collections` methods that wrap the general-purpose collection implementations with special features.

UTILITY METHODS AND FIELDS

In addition to searching for a specific object in a collection, you can use `Collections` to locate the maximum or minimum object based either on natural ordering or a `Comparator`:

```
public static Object max(Collection coll)
public static Object max(Collection coll, Comparator c)
public static Object min(Collection coll)
public static Object min(Collection coll, Comparator c)
```

You can reorder the elements in a `List` by reversing or randomly shuffling them:

```
public static void reverse(List l)
public static void shuffle(List l)
public static void shuffle(List l, Random rnd)
```

You can copy from one `List` into another:

```
public static void copy(List src, List, dest)
```

You can replace each element in a `List` with a specific object:

```
public static void fill(List list, Object o)
```

You can create a new `List` with a specified number of copies of a single object:

```
publis static List nCopies(int n, Object o)
```

Even when you use the collection framework interfaces and classes, you might need to interface with an API that relies on the `Enumeration` interface instead of the preferred `Iterator`. You can create an `Enumeration` for any `Collection`:

```
public static Enumeration enumeration(Collection c)
```

The `Collections` class defines three publicly accessible fields in addition to its methods. `EMPTY_LIST`, `EMPTY_MAP`, and `EMPTY_SET` represent immutable, empty implementations of the corresponding interfaces. When you need to return an empty collection from a method, for example, you can reference one of these fields and avoid the overhead of creating a new one. `EMPTY_MAP` was added as part of the Java 1.3 release.

SINGLETONS

`Collections` provides several methods you can use to create an immutable collection or map that holds one and only one element:

```
public static Set singleton(Object o)
public static List singletonList(Object o)
public static Map singletonMap(Object key, Object value)
```

The `singleton` method was part of the original collections framework, but `singletonList` and `singletonMap` were not added until Java 1.3.

SYNCHRONIZED COLLECTIONS

The description of the general-purpose implementations of the collections framework interfaces pointed out that these classes, unlike their legacy counterparts, are not thread safe. When you do not require a container to be synchronized, these implementations offer an efficient solution with no extra overhead. However, when you do need synchronization, these classes are not sufficiently capable on their own. Rather than including a second set of classes to provide synchronization, the framework relies on a set of `Collections` methods that returns a wrapped version of a specified collection that is thread safe:

```
public static Collection synchronizedCollection(Collection c)
public static Set synchronizedSet(Set s)
public static SortedSet synchronizedSortedSet(SortedSet s)
public static List synchronizedList(List l)
public static Map synchronizedMap(Map m)
public static SortedMap synchronizedSortedMap(SortedMap m)
```

You must follow two guidelines to use these wrapped collections correctly. First, all access to a collection must be done through the wrapper version returned by one of these methods to guarantee synchronized thread access to the underlying collection. Also, you must manually synchronize the wrapper collection using a synchronized block whenever you iterate through it. See Chapter 11, "Threads," for details.

Unmodifiable Collections

A feature of the general-purpose collection interface implementations is that they support all the optional operations defined by their corresponding interfaces. A result of this is that these collections are modifiable. The `Collections` class provides wrappers to give you read-only views of a collection if you need to ensure that it is not modified:

```
public static Collection unmodifiableCollection(Collection c)
public static Set unmodifiableSet(Set s)
public static SortedSet unmodifiableSortedSet(SortedSet s)
public static List unmodifiableList(List l)
public static Map unmodifiableMap(Map m)
public static SortedMap unmodifiableSortedMap(SortedMap m)
```


Which Collection Class to Use?

Given the number of collection classes, the difficulty is sometimes in deciding which one to use for a particular need. The following guidelines outline some recommendations you should consider when making this choice:

- Use the general-purpose implementations in the collections framework instead of `Vector`, `Stack`, and `Hashtable`, unless you are restricted to a JDK 1.1.x version.
- Use `ArrayList` for ordered collections (instead of `Vector`).
- Use `HashSet` for unordered collections.
- Use `HashMap` for key-value associations (instead of `Hashtable`).
- Use `ArrayList` when random access of the elements is more important than the time required to perform inserts and removals in the middle of the list.
- Use `LinkedList` when the performance of inserts and removals is more important than that of locating specific elements.
- Use `TreeMap` when you need to iterate over a set of key-value pairs in sorted key order.
- Use `TreeSet` when you need to maintain a set of objects in sorted order.
- Use the synchronized wrappers provided by the `Collections` class if thread safety is an issue; avoid their overhead if it isn't.

Array Utilities

The `java.util` package focuses on supporting the collections framework classes, but the simple array is not overlooked either. The `Arrays` class provides a number of `static` methods useful in manipulating arrays just as the `Collections` class supports the more sophisticated containers.

THE Arrays CLASS

The Arrays class consists solely of static methods that operate on an array, or compare two arrays for equality. Nearly all the methods are for searching, comparing, filling, or sorting an array. The one exception is the asList method, which provides a List view of an underlying array:

```
public static List asList(Object[] a)
```

You can iterate an array using the reference returned by asList and even modify the array through the List methods if desired.

SEARCHING AN ARRAY

The Arrays class defines nine overloaded versions of its binarySearch method. You can use one of these methods to efficiently locate a specific primitive value or object within an array. In general, the signature of each method expects an array of a specific data type followed by a value or object to locate. Before using one of these methods, you must sort the array into ascending order or its natural order, or apply a Comparator to it. The sort methods defined by the class make this easy to do.

COMPARING TWO ARRAYS

The nine overloaded equals methods compare two arrays for equality and return a boolean result. For two arrays to be considered equal, they must contain the same elements in the same order. The overloaded methods support each of the primitive types and Object.

FILLING AN ARRAY

The fill methods assign a single value or object to either every element in an array or a range that you specify. The 18 overloaded versions support full or partial filling for each of the primitive types and Object.

SORTING AN ARRAY

Similar to fill, Arrays provides 18 versions of its sort method to support sorting an array of primitives or Object. You have the option of sorting an entire array or only a specific range of elements.

CONFIGURING AN APPLICATION USING THE Properties CLASS

The Properties class is an extension of Hashtable that restricts its keys and value objects to being strings. The intended use is to support a set of properties that can be easily read from and written to a stream, such as a text file. The System class uses this functionality to store system properties, but you can also use it to create and maintain your own property sets. A common use of this class is in maintaining a file of properties used to configure an application when it is launched.

You can create a new empty Properties object with the no-argument constructor:

```
public Properties()
```

You can also create a Properties object with a set of default properties. If the Properties object cannot find a requested property in its table, it searches the default properties table. The default properties are maintained independently and are not changed if you modify a corresponding entry in the Properties instance that refers to it. This means that multiple Properties objects can safely share the same default Properties object. To create a Properties object with a set of defaults, just pass the default Properties object to the constructor:

```
public Properties(Properties defaultProps)
```

SETTING Properties

Because Properties extends Hashtable, it is possible to insert entries using the put and putAll methods. However, this allows for the possibility of non-string keys or values being used. You should instead use the setProperty method, which restricts its arguments to strings:

```
public Object setProperty(String key, String value)
```

QUERYING Properties

The getProperty method returns the string corresponding to a property name, or null if the property is not set:

```
public String getProperty(String key)
```

If the key is not found and you have assigned a default Properties object, that set is also checked for a match before returning. You can also call getProperty and specify a default value to be returned if the specified property is not set:

```
public String getProperty(String key, String defaultValue)
```

This default value is only returned if the property cannot be found in the Properties object or its default properties, if any are assigned.

In addition to requesting the value of a specific property, you can also retrieve an Enumeration of all the property names in a Properties object, including the default properties, with the propertyNames method:

```
public Enumeration propertyNames()
```

SAVING AND RETRIEVING Properties

You can maintain a set of application properties in a text file using the store and load methods of Properties. You should consider this approach for initialization parameters and user preferences that can be pulled out of your code and placed in a file. Providing access to configuration information in such a manner is an important part of making your programs flexible.

You save a properties file using the `store` method (the previously supported `save` method was deprecated when Java 1.2 was released):

```
public void store(OutputStream out, String header) throws IOException
```

This method saves the properties to the specified stream, which is typically an instance of `FileOutputStream`. The header string is written to the stream before the contents of the `Properties` object to, for example, identify the purpose of the file.

You read a properties file using the corresponding `load` method:

```
public void load(InputStream in) throws IOException
```

The `load` method treats `#` and `!` as comment characters and ignores anything after them on a line. You can use the `\` character as a line continuation indicator to split a property value string across multiple lines in a file.

The following lines show an example set of properties created using the `store` method:

```
#Sample Properties File
#Wed Aug 16 13:59:42 EDT 2000
root=\\projects\\deploy\\
colorScheme=red, green, blue, yellow
password=1234
username=jsmith
```

Although the `colorScheme` property in this example appears to have four values, the `load` method assigns a single string with the value `"red, green, blue, yellow"` to this property. This format allows you to associate a set of values with a property, but you must parse the string yourself.

The `list` methods of `Properties` are similar to `store`, but they output the properties in a more readable form. They produce a format that works well for debug use. These methods have the following signatures:

```
public void list(PrintStream out)
public void list(PrintWriter out)
```

WORKING WITH DATES

The utilities provided by Java are by no means limited to data containers. Part of the Java API consists of a number of classes useful for creating and manipulating dates. When Java's support for internationalization was introduced with the 1.1 release, the date-related classes in the language were obviously impacted significantly. For this reason, most of the discussion of dates is held until Chapter 24, "Using Internationalization." However, this section covers the `Date` class in particular, which provides some useful functionality for representing a specific instant in time and comparing two such values.

THE `Date` CLASS

The `Date` class represents a specific date and time. It is centered around the Epoch, which is midnight GMT on January 1, 1970. If you look at the API documentation for this class, you will see that the majority of its constructors and methods are deprecated. Prior to the Java 1.1 release, `Date` provided functionality for formatting dates and separating them out into year, month, day, hour, and so on. The existing functionality did not support the need for internationalization, so these responsibilities were transferred to the `Calendar` and `DateFormat` classes introduced later in Chapter 24. This section instead focuses on the non-deprecated operations of the class.

You can create a `Date` object that represents the current date and time by calling its no-argument constructor:

```
public Date()
```

You can also create a `Date` object using the number of milliseconds from the Epoch, which is the same kind of value returned by `System.currentTimeMillis()`:

```
public Date(long millis)
```


COMPARING DATES

The nondeprecated methods of `Date`, other than `clone` and `toString`, relate to comparing two `Date` instances. As is true with all classes, you can compare two dates for object equality with the `equals` method. The `Date` class also provides methods for determining whether one date comes before or after another. The `after` method returns true if a date instance comes after the date passed to the method as an argument:

```
public boolean after(Date when)
```

Similarly, the `before` method tells whether a date instance occurs before a date passed to the method:

```
public boolean before(Date when)
```

`Date` also provides two overloaded implementations of `compareTo` whose signatures differ only in the type of the method parameter. `Date` implements `Comparable` so one of these methods is declared to accept a parameter of type `Object`. The other specifically declares its parameter to be a `Date`. These methods function equivalently, except that the second version throws a `ClassCastException` if the method argument is not a `Date` instance:

```
public int compareTo(Date otherDate)
public int compareTo(Object o)
```

CONVERTING DATES TO STRINGS

`Date` was originally created with several methods for returning a string representation, but all other than `toString` have been deprecated. This method converts a `Date` to a `String` of the form:

```
dow mon dd hh:mm:ss zzz yyyy
```

→ **See** Chapter 24, "Using Internationalization," **p. 865**

CHANGING DATE ATTRIBUTES

You can change the date and time represented by a `Date` instance by calling the `setTime` method and passing a new offset from the Epoch:

```
public void setTime(long time)
```

THE BitSet CLASS

To shift gears further, `java.util` includes the `BitSet` class as a convenient way to maintain and manipulate a set of bits. A `BitSet` instance can grow as needed, so you can create an empty set with the no-argument constructor as a starting point:

```
public BitSet()
```

If, on the other hand, you have an idea of how many bits you will need, you should create the `BitSet` with a specific initial size instead:

```
public BitSet(int numberOfBits)
```

Each bit in a `BitSet` is represented by a `boolean` value that can be examined, set, or cleared. Using an index value, you can set an individual bit to either true or false with the `set` or `clear` method, respectively:

```
public void set(int whichBit)
public void clear(int whichBit)
```

A `BitSet` automatically grows to accommodate its highest set bit. For example, if you create a bit set of 20 bits and then call the `set` method on bit 45, the bit set automatically grows to contain at least 46 bits. Other than the bit at index 45, the new bits are all cleared initially. The `size` method tells you how many bits are in the current bit set, and `length` reports the highest set index plus one:

```
public int size()
public int length()
```

You can test to see whether a bit is set or cleared using the `get` method, which returns a `boolean` result:

```
public boolean get(int whichBit)
```

`BitSet` also defines four methods that operate jointly on two bit sets. These operations manipulate the current bit set using bits from a second bit set. Corresponding bits are matched to perform the operation. In other words, bit 0 in the current bit set is compared to bit 0 in the second bit set. The bitwise operations are

- The `or` operation sets the bit in the current bit set if either the current bit or the second bit is set. If neither bit is set, the current bit remains cleared.
- The `and` operation sets the bit in the current bit set only if the current bit and the second bit are set. Otherwise, the current bit is cleared.
- The `and not` operation clears the bit in the current bit set if the second bit is set.

- The `xor` operation sets the bit in the current bit set if only one of the two bits is set. If both are set, the current bit is cleared.

The signatures of these bitwise operations are

```
public void or(Bitset bits)
public void and(Bitset bits)
public void andNot(Bitset bits)
public void xor(Bitset bits)
```

GENERATING RANDOM NUMBERS

The `java.util.Random` class provides a pseudorandom number generator that is more flexible than the one in the `Math` class. Actually, the random number generator in the `Math` class just uses one of the methods in the `Random` class to produce its results. Because the methods in the `Random` class are not `static`, you must create an instance of `Random` to use it. You can do this with the no-argument constructor or the one that accepts a seed:


```
public Random()
public Random(long seed)
```

Note

"Random" numbers generated by a mathematical algorithm are not truly random, but are instead well-distributed values taken from a sequence that is defined by the algorithm. This distinction is why `java.util.Random` is described as a *pseudorandom* number generator.

If you define the seed for an instance of `Random`, you can duplicate a series of random numbers by using the same seed at a later time. The capability to generate the same series of numbers might not be useful for writing games or some other application that relies on randomness across executions, but it is useful when writing simulations where you want to replay the same sequences repeatedly. The no-argument constructor uses `System.currentTimeMillis` to seed the random number generator.

You can change the seed of the random number generator at any time using the `setSeed` method:

```
public synchronized void setSeed(long newSeed)
```

The `Random` class can generate random numbers in five different data types:

- **`public int nextInt()`**—Generates a 32-bit random number that can be any legal `int` value.
- **`public long nextLong()`**—Generates a 64-bit random number that can be any legal `long` value.
- **`public float nextFloat()`**—Generates a random float `value` between 0.0 and 1.0, although always less than 1.0.

- **`public double nextDouble()`**—Generates a random `double` value between 0.0 and 1.0, always less than 1.0. This is the method used by the `Math.random` method.
- **`public boolean nextBoolean()`**—Generates a `boolean` value of either true or false with equal probability.

There is also a special variation of random number that has some interesting mathematical properties. This variation is called `nextGaussian`, as declared in the following line:

```
public synchronized double nextGaussian()
```

This method returns a random `double` value that can be any legal `double` value. The mean (average) of the values generated by this method is 0.0, and the standard deviation is 1.0. This means that the numbers generated by this method are usually close to zero and that very large numbers are possible but rare.

MONITORING STATE CHANGES USING `Observer/Observable`

As you will see in later chapters, Java relies heavily on the Model-View-Controller (MVC) paradigm. MVC stresses that data (a model) should be unaware of how it is used and displayed (by views), and that a third party (a controller) should coordinate their interaction. This chapter serves as a prelude to those concepts by introducing observables and observers.

THE `Observable` CLASS

The `Observable` class allows an object to notify other objects when it changes. The concept of observables is borrowed from Smalltalk. In Smalltalk, an object can express interest in another object, meaning that it would like to know when the other object changes.

When building user interfaces, you might have multiple ways to change a piece of data, and changing that data might cause several different parts of the display to update. For instance, suppose that you want to create a scrollbar that changes an integer value and, in turn, that integer value is displayed on some sort of graphical meter. You want the meter to update as the value is changed, but you don't want the meter to know anything about the scrollbar. If you are wondering why the meter shouldn't know about the scrollbar, what happens if you decide you don't want a scrollbar, but instead want the number entered from a text field? You shouldn't have to change the meter every time you change the input source.

In this example, you would be better off creating an integer variable that is observable. This observable integer could notify any interested objects (called *observers*) of changes in its value without being concerned about how many or what type of objects are interested in this information. In the case of the graphical meter, it would be informed that the value changed and would query the integer variable for the new value and then redraw itself. This allows the meter to display the value correctly, no matter what mechanism is used to change the value.

From an MVC standpoint, the integer variable can be classified as a model. The graphical meter is an example of a view. The scrollbar is both a controller and a view because it modifies the value as it is moved, and it depicts the current value using the scrollbar position.

You create an observable object using a subclass of `Observable`. You can then register and report changes using the `setChanged` and `notifyObservers` methods. The `setChanged` method marks the observable as having been changed:

```
protected synchronized void setChanged()
```

This method sets an internal changed flag that is used by the `notifyObservers` method. It is automatically cleared when `notifyObservers` is called, but you can also clear it manually with the `clearChanged` method:

```
protected synchronized void clearChanged()
```

The `notifyObservers` method checks to see whether the changed flag has been set, and if so, sends a notification to each registered observer:


```
public void notifyObservers()
```

The `notifyObservers` method can also be called with an argument to pass additional information about the change, such as the new value assigned to the observable:

```
public void notifyObservers(Object arg)
```

You can determine whether an observable has changed by calling the `hasChanged` method:

```
public synchronized boolean hasChanged()
```

Observers register interest in an observable by calling the `addObserver` method:

```
public synchronized void addObserver(Observer obs)
```

Observers de-register interest in an observable by calling `deleteObserver`:

```
public synchronized void deleteObserver(Observer obs)
```

An observable can also clear out its list of observers by calling the `deleteObservers` method:

```
public synchronized void deleteObservers()
```

The `countObservers` method returns the number of observers registered for an observable:

```
public synchronized int countObservers()
```

Listing 10.6 shows an example implementation of an `ObservableInt` class.

LISTING 10.6 `ObservableInt.java`—EXAMPLE OF AN OBSERVABLE

```
import java.util.*;

public class ObservableInt extends Observable {
  int value;     // The value everyone wants to observe

  public ObservableInt() {
  }
```

LISTING 10.6 CONTINUED

```
  public ObservableInt(int newValue) {
    value = newValue;
  }

  public synchronized void setValue(int newValue) {
    //
    // Check to see that this call is REALLY changing the value
    //
    if (newValue != value) {
      value = newValue;
      setChanged();
      notifyObservers();
    }
  }

  public synchronized int getValue() {
    return value;
  }
}
```

THE Observer INTERFACE

The `Observable` class has a companion interface called `Observer`. Any class that wants to receive updates about a change in an observable needs to implement the `Observer` interface. This interface consists of a single method called `update` that is called when an object changes:

```
public abstract void update(Observable obs, Object arg);
```

The `Object` argument is a value passed by the observable when it called `notifyObservers`. If `notifyObservers` is called with no arguments, this reference is `null`.

Listing 10.7 shows an example of a `JLabel` class that implements the `Observer` interface so that it can be informed of changes in an integer variable and update itself with the new value.

LISTING 10.7 IntLabel.java—AN EXAMPLE OBSERVER

```
import javax.swing.*;
import java.util.*;

public class IntLabel extends JLabel implements Observer {
  private ObservableInt intValue;     // The value being observed

  public IntLabel(ObservableInt theInt) {
    intValue = theInt;

    // Tell intValue you're interested in it
    intValue.addObserver(this);

    // Initialize the label to the current value of intValue
    setText( "" + intValue.getValue() );
  }
```

LISTING 10.7 CONTINUED

```
  // Update will be called whenever intValue is changed, so just update
  // the label text.
  public void update(Observable obs, Object arg) {
    setText( "" + intValue.getValue() );
  }
}
```

TROUBLESHOOTING

`IndexOutOfBoundsException`

I get a runtime error reporting an `IndexOutOfBoundsException` *when I call a collection method.*

Java provides automatic bounds checking for collections just as it does for arrays. This exception means you have passed in invalid index value to a `List`. Remember that an index must be greater than or equal to zero and strictly less than the number of elements in the list.

`NullPointerException`

I get a runtime error reporting a `NullPointerException` *when I call a Map method.*

Support for `null` key and value objects in a `Map` is optional. A `Map` implementation that does not allow `null` values in one or the other throws a `NullPointerException` if you attempt to insert one.

`UnsupportedOperationException`

I get a runtime error reporting an `UnsupportedOperationException` *when I call a collection method.*

The collections framework interfaces define a number of methods as optional, particularly those that modify a collection after it has first been created. A class that does not support an optional method throws an `UnsupportedOperationException` if it is called. The general-purpose implementations support all optional operations, but other implementations might not. If you require the functionality provided by an unsupported method, consider using a different implementation that is more complete.

JDK 1.1.X USE

I am restricted to a JDK 1.1.x runtime environment and cannot use the general-purpose collection classes.

JDK 1.1.x supports only the `Vector`, `Stack`, and `Hashtable` containers. You cannot use the general-purpose implementations in this environment.

DEPRECATED METHOD WARNINGS FOR `Date`

The compiler reports deprecation warnings when I use the methods of the `Date` *class.*

Most of the methods of `Date` are deprecated due to their inability to properly support internationalization. Most operations related to dates must be performed using the `Calendar` and `DateFormat` classes instead.

THREAD SAFETY

I get errors resulting from simultaneous access to a collection by multiple threads.

A primary difference between the collections framework classes and the legacy classes is that the collections classes are not synchronized. If multiple threads have access to a collection, you must obtain a synchronized wrapper for it using the `Collections` class and then perform all access to the collection through that wrapper. You must also manually synchronize any iterations through the collection.

POOR PERFORMANCE

The time required to add to, remove from, or search a collection is excessive.

The different collection classes offer different strengths and weaknesses when it comes to performance. Refer to the "Which Collection Class to Use?" section for an overview of these differences.

CHAPTER 11

THREADS

In this chapter

by *Chuck Cavaness*

WHAT ARE THREADS?

A unique property of Java is its built-in support for threads. *Threads* allow you to do many tasks simultaneously, or at least it seems that the tasks are working simultaneously. As you'll see later in this chapter, most of the time, there is actually only one thread running at a time. A thread is really nothing but a sequential flow of control within a program. In *multithreaded* programs, there are multiple flows of control. For the purposes of this chapter, a "flow of control" is referred to as a task.

If an application could only perform a new task when another task was completed, your applications would be severely limited. Fortunately, Java has built-in thread support that allows programmers to schedule multiple tasks to work together concurrently to accomplish the overall goal of the application. This chapter covers how threads can be used in Java programs to increase the performance and scalability of your applications.

Think of a typical application. There are usually screens to view and capture information from the user. There might be a need to retrieve and store that information in some form of persistent store such as a database. And usually, other system-type services are happening in the background that the end-user might not be aware of. Imagine how the application would perform if one task had to finish completely before any other tasks could begin. This obviously would not be efficient and probably would cause big problems with performance and scalability.

Fortunately, this is not how things really work. Operating systems, the Java Virtual Machine (JVM), and multithreaded programming combine their efforts to allow Java developers to create multiple threads to seemingly accomplish many tasks simultaneously.

With some hardware systems, you might only have a single processor, and that single processor has to take on all these tasks. Even with multiple processors, true parallelism might never be fully appreciated. To manage these multiple tasks or threads, a concept called multitasking was invented. In reality, the processor is still only doing one thing at any one time, but it switches among them so fast that it seems like it is doing them all simultaneously. Fortunately, modern computers work much faster than human beings, so you hardly even notice that this is happening.

Think about it in this way: Each program is assigned a process. That program then breaks up its tasks into threads. Although you might not have realized it at the time, you have already worked with threads. When you wrote your first program back in Chapter 1, "Object-Oriented Programming," you were actually using your first thread. Of course, you didn't have to do anything special because you actually wrote a program that contained a single thread. When you started the HelloWorld program, a main thread of control was created for you. This is shown in Figure 11.1.

Sometimes, the term *lightweight process* is also used instead of thread. A thread and a process are similar in that both are a sequential flow of control. A thread is considered lightweight because it is started from a process. This does not mean that a thread must have a process always associated with it; it's just started from a process. There are ways to have a thread running without a process. This will be explained along with daemon threads later in this chapter. For now, it's worthwhile to know that a thread needs to be started by a program and must share the resources allocated to it by the operating system. Each thread occupies some private space, however. This allows the thread to act independently of the other threads running (see Figure 11.2).

Figure 11.1
Here is a single thread within a program.

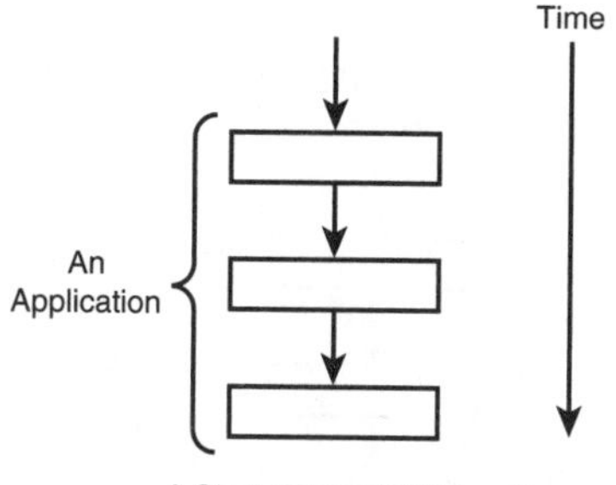

Figure 11.2
Two running threads can act concurrently within a program.

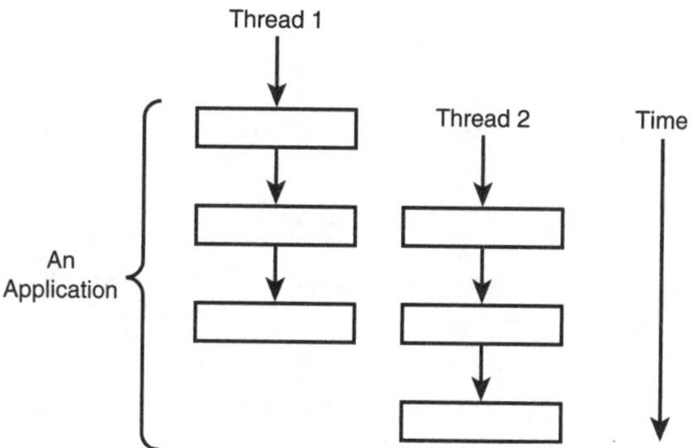

As stated earlier, when you have a multithreaded program, the threads might not really be running at the same time. Putting aside multiple CPUs and parallel processing for a moment, there is really only one thread running at all times. The reason is that each thread is given a little amount of time to execute by the CPU and then it has to wait while another thread is allowed to run. Each operating system or Java Virtual Machine can handle this differently. Sometimes the thread might get to run to completion and then another thread can run. This is known as *non-preemptive*. Other times, a thread will be interrupted so that other threads can run. This is known as *preemptive*. There is also the case in which only higher threads can preempt other threads. This material is slightly below the needs of this discussion, but you should be aware that a thread might have to compete for CPU time against the other threads that are running. This situation is shown in Figure 11.2. The good news is that the speed at which this happens is so fast, it gives the appearance that multiple threads are running at the same time.

The most important point to take from all this is that threads will be interrupted from time to time to allow for other threads to run. Later in this chapter, you will see how this affects Java programs and what interesting problems arise from this and how you can manage these problems. Figure 11.3 shows two separate threads competing for execution time.

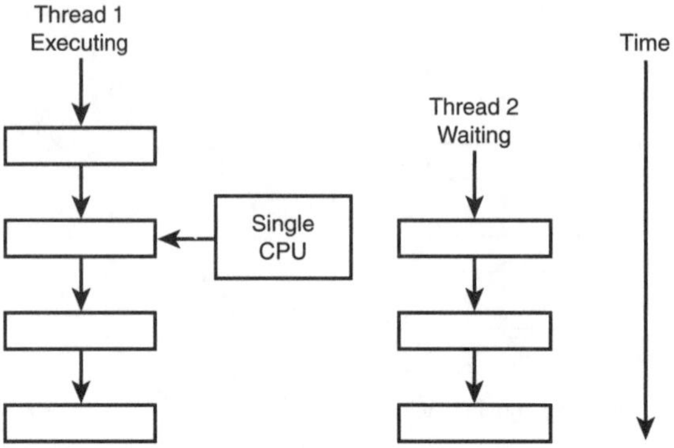

Figure 11.3
Here, two threads are competing for processor time.

Thread 1 Executing

Thread 2 Waiting

Single CPU

Time

WHY USE THREADS?

Understanding how threads work is important for building better-performing, scalable applications. It's also important for supporting multiple users using a single application and having the application seem responsive to the user's requests.

Another good reason to understand multithreading is because one of the great advances Java makes over other programming languages is its built-in, native support for threading. By using threading, you can avoid long pauses between what your users do and when they see things happen. Better yet, you can send tasks such as printing off into the background while other threads concentrate on handling new requests.

HOW TO MAKE YOUR CLASSES THREADABLE

There are two approaches to making your classes behave as threads:

- Extending the `Thread` class
- Implementing the `Runnable` interface

Which approach you choose depends on your application's needs and the constraints placed on it. Giving your class the capability to run as a thread does not automatically make it run as such. When a class is called runnable, that means it has the ability to act as a separate thread, but not necessarily that it *is* running as a separate thread. The reason for this is that the `start` method that is defined in the `Runnable` interface must be called to start the thread running. You'll learn more about the `start` method later in this chapter.

EXTENDING Thread

You can make your class runnable as a thread by extending the class java.lang.Thread. This gives the class direct access to all the thread methods defined in the Thread class. The Thread class defines a run method that you will need to override because the run method in the Thread class does not do anything but return void. The run method is empty and will not do any work for you. You must override the run method and provide the implementation for the particular application.

Listing 11.1 shows the class SimpleThread, which extends the Thread class and overrides the parent's run method.

LISTING 11.1 SOURCE CODE FOR SimpleThread.java

```
public class SimpleThread extends Thread
{

// Default Constructor
  public SimpleThread()
  {
     super();
  }

  // Override the parent's run method to get the work done
  public void run()
  {
     // Do the thread work here
  }
}
```


Note

As stated earlier, just because the Thread class has been extended in the sample code does not mean it will run as a thread if the SimpleThread class is instantiated. As you will see, the start method must be called to start the thread running as a thread.

IMPLEMENTING Runnable

The second way to cause classes to behave as threads is to have those classes implement the java.lang.Runnable interface. A second method is available because extending the Thread class will not work in all cases. This is because Java does not allow for a class to be a subclass of more than one direct parent class. Other languages such as C++ do allow this, but Java does not. For example, the SimpleThread class shown previously could not extend Thread and Date classes simultaneously.

If you need to create a new class that acts as a thread and this new class already extends a different class, the alternative is to have the new class implement the Java Runnable interface instead. The Runnable interface defines a single interface operation, the run method.

Therefore, if you have a class implement the Runnable interface, it must implement the run method. All the work the class will do when running as a thread goes in the run method. Listing 11.2 shows the alternative approach.

LISTING 11.2 SOURCE CODE FOR SimpleThread2.java

```
public class SimpleThread2 extends java.util.Date implements Runnable
{
  private String threadName = null;

  // Default Constructor
  public SimpleThread2( String name )
  {
    super();
    threadName = name;
  }

  // Private accessor for the instance variable
  private String getThreadName()
  {
    return this.threadName;
  }

  // Implement the run method required from the Runnable interface
  public void run()
  {
    // Do the thread work here
    this.setTime( System.currentTimeMillis() );
    System.out.println( getThreadName() + ": " + this.toString() );
  }
}
```

This class can now be used as a parameter to the Thread constructor. When that thread instance is started, the run method is executed. Listing 11.3 shows the source code for the test class that uses the SimpleThread2 from Listing 11.2. This is a simple run method that prints out a date instance and then quits, but it gives you the necessary idea on how to use the Runnable interface.

If you are having trouble with starting a thread, see "Thread Does Not Start," in the "Troubleshooting" section at the end of this chapter.

LISTING 11.3 SOURCE CODE FOR SimpleThread2Main.java

```
public class SimpleThread2Main
{
  public static void main(String[] args)
  {
    // Create an instance of our new class that implements the
    // Runnable interface
    SimpleThread2 simpleThread = new SimpleThread2( "SimpleThread2" );

    // Create a new instance of a thread using our Runnable class
    // as the target and tell it to use "SimpleThread2" as the name
    Thread newThread = new Thread( simpleThread, "SimpleThread2" );
```

LISTING 11.3 CONTINUED

```
    // Start the thread
    newThread.start();
  }
}
```

Here is the output when you run the `SimpleThread2Main` class from the previous listing:

```
C:\jdk1.3se_book\classes>java SimpleThread2Main
SimpleThread2: Wed Apr 26 21:27:53 PDT 2000
C:\jdk1.3se_book\classes>
```

Notice that the only thing printed out is the text from the `println` method in the `run` method as expected. The second parameter to the `Thread` constructor sets up a name for the thread. This is mainly for display purposes. When using the `Runnable` interface approach, there isn't an easy way to get access to the thread that it's running within. That's why a private variable was added in the `SimpleThread2` class to hold onto the name. When extending the `Thread` class, the variable is already defined and you can use the `getName` method to retrieve the name of the `Thread`.

> **Note** The `Thread` class actually already implements the `Runnable` interface itself. The `Runnable` interface has only one method: `run`. Any time you make a class implement `Runnable`, you need to have a `run` method in your class. In the `run` method, you actually do all the work you want to have done by that particular thread.

Listing 11.4 shows another example of a new `Thread` class. In this example, the first method of extending the `Thread` class is used rather than the `Runnable` interface. In fact, the `SimpleThread` class from before is used to do a little more work.

LISTING 11.4 SOURCE CODE FOR `SimpleThread.java`

```
public class SimpleThread extends Thread
{
  // Default Constructor
  public SimpleThread( String threadName )
  {
    // Set the name of the thread for display purposes
    setName( threadName );
    System.out.println( threadName + " has been created" );
  }

  // Override the parents run method to get the work done
  public void run()
  {
    // Do the thread work here
    System.out.println( getName() + " entered run method" );
    try
    {
      System.out.println( getName() + " going to sleep..." );
      // Tell this thread to go to sleep for 3,000 milliseconds
```

LISTING 11.4 CONTINUED

```
        sleep( 3000 );
      }
      catch( InterruptedException ex )
      {
        // Do nothing for now when this exception is raised
      }
      System.out.println( getName() + "  woke up from sleep" );
    }
  }
```

Listing 11.5 shows the main class used for testing the `SimpleThread.java` class.

LISTING 11.5 SOURCE CODE FOR `TestMain.java`

```
public class TestMain
{
  public static final int NUMBER_OF_THREADS = 5;

  public static void main(String[] args)
  {
    SimpleThread[] threads = new SimpleThread[NUMBER_OF_THREADS];
    for( int i = 0; i < NUMBER_OF_THREADS; i++ )
    {
      String name = "Thread: " + i;
      SimpleThread newThread = new SimpleThread( name );
      threads[i] = newThread;
    }

    for ( int i = 0; i < NUMBER_OF_THREADS; i++ )
    {
      threads[i].start();
    }
  }
}
```

In this example, the class called `SimpleThread` has been expanded. It extends the `Thread` class and overrides the `run` method that it inherits from the `Thread` class. In the `run` method, it prints some basic information to the screen to let you know what's going on. In the constructor of the class, the name for this thread is passed in as a parameter to the constructor and you set the name for this instance.

The `name` property on a `Thread` class is used for identification purposes. The name is not required to be unique, but it might get confusing if you are using the names somewhere and you use the same names for different threads. If you don't assign a name to a thread, the VM will set one for you automatically. You only need to give it a name if you will be interested in that name later.

The other thing to notice in this simple example is the `sleep` method being called in the `run` method. The `sleep` method causes the thread to temporarily cease execution for the specified amount of milliseconds set in the parameter. Notice that the `java.lang.InterruptedException` must be caught even if you aren't interested in doing anything with that exception. The `InterruptedException` will be thrown if another thread interrupts this one. It will not be called when the thread comes out of the sleep.

The `TestMain` class is used to test the new `SimpleThread` class. This class has a public static final `int` variable called `NUMBER_OF_THREADS` that you can change to see the different behavior as you vary the number of threads being created. The `TestMain` class uses an array to instantiate the number of threads that the `NUMBER_OF_THREADS` variables declare and after all the threads are instantiated and stored in the array, it goes through the array and tells each thread to start. It was done this way so that you could get each thread to enter the `run` method as fast as possible for the purpose of this example. An instance of the `SimpleThread` class could have been instantiated and at the same time its start method called, but this way there is less lag time between the instantiation and the start of the `run` method being called.

If you run the previous example from the command line, the output looks something like this:

The following text shows the output when `TestMain.java` from Listing 11.5 is executed:

```
C:\jdk1.3se_book\classes>java TestMain
Thread-0 entered run method
Thread-0 going to sleep...
Thread-1 entered run method
Thread-2 entered run method
Thread-3 entered run method
Thread-4 entered run method
Thread-1 going to sleep...
Thread-2 going to sleep...
Thread-3 going to sleep...
Thread-4 going to sleep...
Thread-0  woke up from sleep
Thread-1  woke up from sleep
Thread-2  woke up from sleep
Thread-4  woke up from sleep
Thread-3  woke up from sleep

C:\jdk1.3se_book\classes>
```


Note

If your output looks similar to this, but not in the same order, don't worry. This is a good example of not being guaranteed which thread will be doing what when. Play around with changing the number of threads created by adjusting the `NUMBER_OF_THREADS` constant in the `TestMain` class. Also, change the sleep time and see how the output varies. You should also notice that the first `Thread` is number 0. This is because the `Threads` are being stored in an array and the first position of an array is 0.

If you are having trouble with seeing all of your threads starting, check "One Off Error," in the "Troubleshooting" section at the end of this chapter.

THE LIFE CYCLE OF A THREAD

A thread can undergo one of any five states during the complete life cycle (see Figure 11.4). The five states are

- New
- Runnable
- Running
- Not Runnable
- Dead

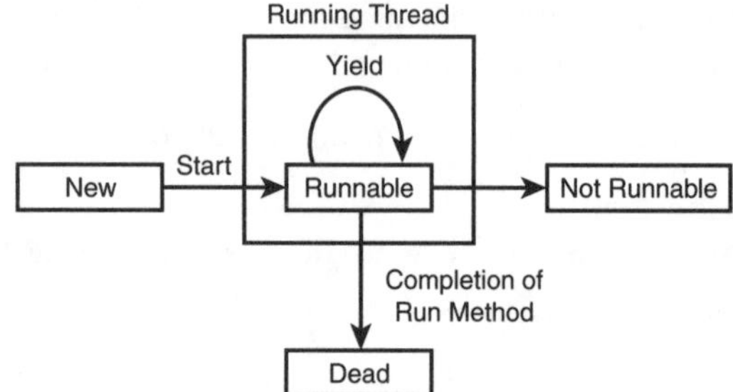

Figure 11.4
The life cycle of a thread can illustrate all five states.

When the `SimpleThread` class was instantiated in the previous section, the thread was in the New state. No system resources are allocated to a thread in the New state. The only method that can be called on a new thread is the `start` method; otherwise an `IllegalThreadStateException` will be thrown.

When the `start` method is called on a new thread, the thread enters the Runnable state and is considered to be running. This does not mean that the thread is actually executing instructions. This is where thread scheduling comes in. After `start` is called, the new thread is set to the Runnable state and is scheduled for running. When the scheduler decides it is time for the new thread to get some CPU time, it gives control over to the thread. After the scheduler decides the thread has had enough of the CPU or another thread with a higher priority comes along, the scheduler causes the thread to yield. You will learn about priorities later in this chapter. Keep in mind that this scheduling is dependant on many factors, such as operating system, CPU manufacturer, and which Java VM is being used. If the operating system does not having a thread-scheduling algorithm, the Java VM will use its own implementation to schedule threads instead of the operating system.

There are three conditions that cause a thread not to be runnable:

- The `sleep` method is called.
- The thread called the `wait` condition.
- The thread is waiting on I/O.

After sleep is called, the thread is considered not Runnable, even if there are no other threads available. After the thread comes out of the sleep, the thread is put back into the Runnable state and ready for scheduling to give it to the CPU.

If one thread needs to communicate or work with another thread, it can call the wait method and wait for the other thread to catch up. After the second thread is ready, it can notify the first thread through the notify method. You will learn more about this when thread synchronization is explained later in this chapter.

The final condition when a thread is considered not Runnable is if a thread is waiting for I/O. In this case, it's up to the thread to finish the I/O and get back into the Runnable state.

Notice in the SimpleThread example from the previous section that nothing special was done in the run method to terminate the thread. It's normally up to the thread to terminate itself. It does this by letting the run method finish. In Listing 11.4,the thread was put to sleep and then a few statements were printed out when it woke up. After that, the thread was free to exit the run method, which actually stopped that thread. It's very common to have an infinite loop in a thread and some exit condition that causes the thread to exit gracefully. Listing 11.6 shows a small example illustrating using a while loop in the run method and checking an exit condition before allowing the thread to exit:

LISTING 11.6 SOURCE CODE FOR InfiniteLoopThread.java

```
public class InfiniteLoopThread extends Thread
{
  // Default Constructor
  public InfiniteLoopThread()
  {
    super();
  }

  // Override the parents run method
  public void run()
  {
    // variable for exit condition - default to false
    boolean timeToExit = false;

    // Keep the thread going until time to exit is true
    while( !timeToExit )
    {
      // Do some work here that might cause the exit
      // condition to change
    }

    // Thread is exiting. Clean up any open resources
  }
}
```

Notice that after the thread exits the while loop, it will exit the run method and will be considered a dead thread.

The isAlive method is a way for you to determine the state of the thread. If the isAlive method returns true, then the thread's start method has been called and the thread is not yet dead. You can't determine if the thread is currently running with this method, but you can determine whether it has been killed yet. If the isAlive method returns false, then you know that the thread is either a new thread and the start method has not been called or the thread has been terminated.

USING Thread LOCAL VARIABLES

The ThreadLocal and InheritableThreadLocal are two classes that most Java developers might not use properly or even know exist. These classes provide a mechanism to set up an object that can be associated with a specific thread and have the thread access its copy of the object. In other words, it's a way to associate a state with a thread. The ThreadLocal class can hold onto objects only, not primitives.

You might be asking, how is this different than declaring a private variable within a thread class. That's an important question. Normally, a ThreadLocal object is declared as a private static variable in some class. You'll remember that this means all instances of this class have access to it. Every time a new thread accesses this object by using the getter or setter, the thread is accessing its copy of the object. The first time a thread uses the get or set method on a ThreadLocal instance, a new copy of the object is associated with that particular thread. From that point on, the thread will access its own copy of the object and not any other instance that belongs to other threads in the system. You can kind of think of this as a hash table in which the key is the thread and the value is the object that is associated with just that thread.

The good news is most of the maintenance is handled by the ThreadLocal implementation itself. All the developer has to do is create a single static instance of the ThreadLocal object, optionally assigning an initial value for the object, and then any thread that accesses the static ThreadLocal object gets an implicit reference to its copy of the object. The initialValue method is called one time per thread. The initial Value method in the ThreadLocal class initializes the object that the ThreadLocal instance holds onto to a null value. If there is a need for an initial value other than null, the ThreadLocal class must be overridden. The thread holds onto its reference of the ThreadLocal object as long as the thread is alive and the ThreadLocal object is accessible.

The use of this still might be confusing, so take a look at a simple example to see how to use this class. Listing 11.7 shows a class that extends the ThreadLocal class as an inner class inside a new Thread class.

LISTING 11.7 SOURCE CODE FOR ThreadLocalExample.java

```
public class ThreadLocalExample extends Thread
{
  // Static instance for all threads to use
  private static MyThreadLocal threadLocal = new MyThreadLocal();
// Holds which thread number this instance is. Used for display only
```

LISTING 11.7 CONTINUED

```
  private int threadCount = 0;

  // Default Constructor
  public ThreadLocalExample( String threadName, int threadCount )
  {
    super( threadName );
    this.threadCount = threadCount;
  }

  // Use an inner class to declare your new class
  static private class MyThreadLocal extends ThreadLocal
  {
    // If this is the first time the get or set is used,
    // this method will be called automatically
    protected Object initialValue()
    {
      // Initialize a new Double object
      return new Double (Math.random() * 1000.0);
    }
  }

  // Override the parent's run method
  public void run()
  {
    // Print out the initial value for the ThreadLocal Object
    System.out.println( getName() + " - Initial Value: " + this.threadLocal.get()
);
// Change the value for this thread only
    this.threadLocal.set( new Integer( threadCount ) );
// Print out the value, so you can be sure that only your instance changed
    System.out.println( getName() + " - Current Value: " + this.threadLocal.get()
);
  }
}
```

Listing 11.8 shows a class called `ThreadLocalMain` that can be used to test the `ThreadLocalExample` class.

LISTING 11.8 SOURCE CODE FOR ThreadLocalMain.java

```
public class ThreadLocalMain
{

  public ThreadLocalMain()
  {
  }

  public static void main(String[] args)
  {
    ThreadLocalExample ex1 = new ThreadLocalExample( "Thread 1", 1 );
    ThreadLocalExample ex2 = new ThreadLocalExample( "Thread 2", 2 );
    ex1.start();
    ex2.start();
  }
}
```

Running the `ThreadLocalMain` class from Listing 11.8, here's the output:

```
C:\jdk1.3se_book\classes>java ThreadLocalMain
Thread 1 - Initial Value: 412.2123189553676
Thread 1 - Current Value: 1
Thread 2 - Initial Value: 51.71279074374135
Thread 2 - Current Value: 2

C:\jdk1.3se_book\classes>
```

Notice that when the value for thread 1 was changed, it did not modify the value for thread 2. Only when the value for thread 2 was actually changed, did it in fact change. The `ThreadLocal` object does maintain a copy of the object for each thread.

The `InheritableThreadLocal` class subclasses the `ThreadLocal` class and provides a way for a parent thread to pass along the initial value of the `ThreadLocal` object to any child threads that are created from the parent thread. By default, the child thread gets a copy of the `ThreadLocal` object that is equal to the parent's value. It's not the same reference, but a clone of the actual value. If the child's copy of the `ThreadLocal` object needs to modify the initial value that was passed down from the parent, it can override the method `childValue` on the `InheritableThreadLocal` class and do whatever needs to be done on the initial value. The `InheritableThreadLocal` is preferred over the `ThreadLocal` class when the per-thread object must be passed from the parent thread to any child threads created.

CHANGING THREAD PRIORITIES

As mentioned previously, multiple threads compete for CPU time. There are various algorithms used by the operating system and Java VM when figuring out which thread should be executed next. Thread scheduling can be divided into two main types: preemptive and non-preemptive. Java native threads usually support the preemptive model. This means that the schedule interrupts the current thread when its time for the processor runs out. With Java green threads, the non-preemptive model is normally used. This model allows the thread to continue until the thread yields control. However, even with the non-preemptive model, if a higher priority thread is ready to execute, the current thread has to give up the CPU.

The discussion of these different algorithms is beyond this book, but it's safe to say that a thread with a higher priority will get more attention than a thread with a lower priority. This can cause problems sometimes if a developer is not careful. If there is a thread in an application doing some background work occasionally and there are a bunch of higher priority threads doing work all the time, there is a possibility that the lower priority thread will never get the attention of the processor. This is known as thread *starvation*.

There are no hard and fast rules for how to set priorities for threads in your application. Each application has different constraints placed on it. However, most Java developers will agree that for threads doing mundane tasks that need to happen every so often, it's best to set their priorities low so they will execute when all the other threads have finished or are not running. For tasks in which something depends on the thread's completion, it's better to set the priorities of these threads high so they can execute and finish their tasks. An example of this might be a thread that checks a directory for a file and reads in the file if it exists. These types of threads should have a higher priority because another part of the application is probably depending on that data from the file.

To set the priority of a thread, use the `setPriority` method defined in the `Thread` class. The parameter to the `setPriority` method is an integer value that you want the new priority to be. The `Thread` class defines a minimum and maximum value for a thread priority. If the new priority is not between those ranges, an `IllegalArgumentException` will be thrown. Also, if the `setPriority` method was called by an outside thread instance and that thread did not have permission to change the priority, a `SecurityException` will be thrown.

Note

If you are creating `Applets` and the `Applet` attempts to change the priority of a `Thread`, a `SecurityException` will be thrown.

To determine what the current priority of a thread is, use the `getPriority` method defined on the `Thread` class. It returns an `int` value for the priority of that thread. The `Thread` class defines three constant's priority levels: minimum priority, normal priority, and maximum priority. Your applications can use them like this:

```
setPriority( Thread.MIN_PRIORITY );
```

Note

Most applications should always use one of the predefined constants. Using these constants ensures that you never set the priority outside the valid ranges.

Go back to the `SimpleThread` example from Listing 11.4 and change the priority of the last thread that gets started and see how the output is affected. Set the priority of the last thread to the maximum and all the other threads to the minimum. Hopefully you are imagining the outcome. All you have to do is create a new test main class and reuse the same `SimpleThread` class. Listing 11.9 shows the new class used to test setting the priorities of threads. Only the `test` class had to change. You can use the `SimpleThread` class as before.

LISTING 11.9 SOURCE CODE FOR `TestMainPriority.java`

```
public class TestMainPriority
{
  public static final int NUMBER_OF_THREADS = 5;

  public static void main(String[] args)
  {
    SimpleThread[] threads = new SimpleThread[NUMBER_OF_THREADS];
    for( int i = 0; i < NUMBER_OF_THREADS; i++ )
    {
      String name = "Thread: " + i;
      SimpleThread newThread = new SimpleThread( name );
      threads[i] = newThread;
```

LISTING 11.9 CONTINUED

```
      // If this is the last thread, set it's priority to the maximum
      // otherwise set the priority of the thread to the minimum
      if ( i == NUMBER_OF_THREADS )
      {
        newThread.setPriority( Thread.MAX_PRIORITY );
      }
      else
      {
        newThread.setPriority( Thread.MIN_PRIORITY );
      }
    }

    for ( int i = 0; i < NUMBER_OF_THREADS; i++ )
    {
      threads[i].start();
    }
  }
}
```

All you are doing in this class is just checking for the last thread defined by the constant `NUMBER_OF_THREADS` and when it is hit in the loop, you set the priority to the maximum constant defined in the `Thread` class. All the other threads get set to the minimum. Here's the output:

```
C:\jdk1.3se_book\classes>java TestMainPriority
Thread-0 entered run method
Thread-0 going to sleep...
Thread-1 entered run method
Thread-2 entered run method
Thread-1 going to sleep...
Thread-3 entered run method
Thread-4 entered run method
Thread-2 going to sleep...
Thread-3 going to sleep...
Thread-4 going to sleep...
Thread-0  woke up from sleep
Thread-1  woke up from sleep
Thread-2  woke up from sleep
Thread-3  woke up from sleep
Thread-4  woke up from sleep

C:\jdk1.3se_book\classes>
```

Notice that after all the threads have been created, the last thread enters the `run` method first and then the rest of the threads enter the `run` method in a sort of random order. This is because the last thread has the maximum priority, so it will get the attention of the processor the most. So the results agree with what should have happened. Play around with changing some of the other priorities to different values and inspect the different results.

Tip

Remember that the priority value must be between the minimum and maximum constants defined in the `Thread` class. It's a good idea to try to use these values when setting priorities to prevent the `IllegalArgumentException` from being thrown.

THREAD SYNCHRONIZATION

Up to this point in the discussion, the threads haven't needed to interact with other threads. However, there are many cases in which threads need to work together to perform a larger task. For example, if you have two threads, one is creating or "producing" data and the other thread needs to read or "consume" that data. This problem is commonly known as the producer/consumer problem. One thread is the producer of the data and the second thread is considered the consumer. As you learned previously, there is no guarantee which thread will be running at any given instance of time. In fact, the producer thread can be right in the middle of creating some data and be interrupted by the consumer thread. What would the data look like? It's really undeterminable. The problem here is really one of accessing shared data.

The other problem to consider occurs when one thread is faster than the other thread or is getting more processor attention. What happens if the producer thread is able to create data faster than the consumer thread can consumer it? Some of the data might be missed if it can't be persisted somehow until the consumer is ready to read more. In this case, the threads must communication better. The consumer thread should tell the producer thread that it's ready to read more. You'll see a solution for this problem later in this section. For now, take a look at how you can solve the problem of ensuring that a single thread will not be interrupted by another thread until it has completed a certain task.

The sections of an application that are accessed by separate threads are known as "*critical sections*." In these areas, programmers must be cautious to protect multiple threads from interrupting each other too early. That protection can be achieved in Java by using the `synchronized` keyword. There are two ways that the keyword `synchronized` can be placed in Java, one is on a method and the second is by synchronizing a section or block of code. Placing `synchronized` on a method looks like this:

```
public synchronized void writeSharedData( Object data )
{
  // Work to write the shared data
}
```

Notice the `synchronized` keyword added to the method signature. When a class defines a method as being synchronized, the Java VM associates a lock with each instance of the class that is instantiated. When a thread calls a synchronized method on a particular instance, no other thread can access that method or any other synchronized method defined in that class. The thread that calls and enters the critical section gets the lock on the object. This ensures that the first thread continues to execute until it completes with that method before allowing other threads to access it. Other threads are still free to access any non-synchronized method on the instance, just not the ones declared as synchronized. The tricky part when developing the application is identifying which parts of the code are the critical sections. For example, if there were a corresponding `get` method for the shared data object, you would want to protect that with a synchronized method like this:

```
public synchronized Object readSharedData()
  {
    // Work to read and return the shared data
  }

  public synchronized void writeSharedData( Object data )
  {
    // Work to write the shared data
  }
```

Caution

Make sure you protect all critical sections in your application to ensure that multiple threads are not accessing shared data simultaneously.

The other way the synchronized keyword can be used in Java is by synchronizing on a block of code. Here is an example of this:

```
public String getValue()
{
   // No lock acquired yet so other threads can access this instance
   // while the other thread is doing this work

   synchronized( this )
   {
     // A lock is obtained here by the calling thread and will remain until the
     // thread leaves this block of code
   }

   return value;
}
```

The parameter to the synchronized block is the object on which the lock will be obtained. You can, of course, use any instance here, but in most cases the object that will need to be locked will be the current instance object.

The reason for this alternative method of synchronization revolves around the concept of *deadlocks*. Remember that when you synchronize a method, no other threads can enter that or any other synchronized method on that same instance until the thread with the lock is finished. If the thread with the lock needed to access another object that was locked by a different thread, each thread would be waiting on each other and neither one would be able to do anything. This is known as a deadlock condition, which you want to avoid at all costs. Preventing your application from entering a deadlock condition will be easier than detecting when you are in this condition and recovering from it gracefully.

Let's take a look at a complete example of synchronizing threads. The following example uses a shared object that each thread will need to access. The producer thread will need to write to the shared object, and the consumer thread will need to read from it. For now, just ignore what happens if either one of the threads works faster or slower than the other. You'll learn how to deal with that later in this section when the discussion turns to communication among threads using the `notify` and `wait` methods. For now, concentrate on synchronizing access to a share object or data.

Listing 11.10 shows the code you will work with for a while. The `SharedObject` class is the shared object data that both the producer and consumer will communicate with. Notice that the `get` and `set` methods are synchronized to protect two threads from accessing the shared data at the same time.

LISTING 11.10 SOURCE CODE FOR `SharedObject.java`

```
public class SharedObject
{
  // The private shared data variable
  private Integer sharedData = null;

  // Default Constructor
  public SharedObject( int initialValue )
  {
    super();
    // Initialize the shared object value to something
    sharedData = new Integer( initialValue );
  }

  // The producer will call this method to update the data
  public synchronized void setSharedData( int newData )
{
    System.out.println( "Shared Object - New Value Set: " + newData );
    sharedData = new Integer( newData );
  }

  // The consumer will call this method to get the new data
  public synchronized Integer getSharedData()
  {
    return sharedData;
  }
}
```

Listing 11.11 shows the class for the producer thread. It is initialized with the reference to the shared data object and a maximum number of writes that it should do. For this example, a loop is used to go from 1 up to the maximum and an `Integer` object wrapper is created around the loop counter. Notice that you don't have to do anything special when dealing with synchronization. All that was handled in the shared data class.

LISTING 11.11 SOURCE CODE FOR SharedObjectProducer.java

```
public class SharedObjectProducer extends Thread
{
  int maxCounter = 0;
  SharedObject sharedObject = null;

  public SharedObjectProducer( SharedObject obj, int maxWrites )
  {
    super();
    sharedObject = obj;
    maxCounter = maxWrites;
  }

  public void run()
  {
    for( int counterValue = 1; counterValue <= maxCounter; counterValue++ )
    {
      System.out.println( "Producer - Writing New Value: " + counterValue );
      sharedObject.setSharedData( counterValue );
    }
  }
}
```

Listing 11.12 shows the counterpart to the producer, the consumer of the shared data. It is initialized with a reference to the same shared data object as the producer, and with a maximum number of times to read from it. These classes could have been designed to figure out when to stop writing and reading in many different ways. The point here is to see an example of synchronizing shared data between threads. Notice again that you don't have to do anything special to detect for other threads accessing the shared data. All of it was handled by using the `synchronized` keyword in the `SharedObject` class.

LISTING 11.12 SOURCE CODE FOR SharedObjectConsumer.java

```
public class SharedObjectConsumer extends Thread
{
  // The reference to the shared data
  SharedObject sharedObject = null;
  // How many reads of the shared data should happen
  int numberOfReads = 0;

  public SharedObjectConsumer( SharedObject obj, int numberOfTimesToRead )
  {
    super();
    sharedObject = obj;
    numberOfReads = numberOfTimesToRead;
  }

  private int getNumberOfReads()
  {
    return numberOfReads;
  }

  public void run()
```

LISTING 11.12 CONTINUED

```
  {
    int maxCounter = getNumberOfReads();
    for( int counter = 1; counter <= maxCounter; counter++ )
    {
      Integer intObj = sharedObject.getSharedData();
      System.out.println( "Consumer - Getting New Value: " + intObj.intValue() );
    }
  }
}
```

Listing 11.13 shows the class that gets it all started in testing these classes. Its job is to help you test the producer and consumer classes. The class creates a single instance of the `SharedObject` class and a single instance of both the producer and consumer classes. It then starts the produced and consumer threads.

LISTING 11.13 SOURCE CODE FOR `SharedObjectMain.java`

```
public class SharedObjectMain
{
  public static void main(String[] args)
  {
    int MAX_COUNTER = 5;
    SharedObject sharedObject = new SharedObject( 0 );

    SharedObjectProducer producer =
 new SharedObjectProducer( sharedObject, MAX_COUNTER );

    SharedObjectConsumer consumer =
new SharedObjectConsumer( sharedObject, MAX_COUNTER );

    producer.start();
    consumer.start();
  }
}
```

Running the `SharedObjectMain` class, here is what the output should look like:

```
C:\jdk1.3se_book\classes>java SharedObjectMain
Producer - Writing New Value: 1
Shared Object - New Value Set: 1
Producer - Writing New Value: 2
Shared Object - New Value Set: 2
Producer - Writing New Value: 3
Shared Object - New Value Set: 3
Producer - Writing New Value: 4
Shared Object - New Value Set: 4
Producer - Writing New Value: 5
Shared Object - New Value Set: 5
Consumer - Getting New Value: 5
Consumer - Getting New Value: 5
Consumer - Getting New Value: 5
Consumer - Getting New Value: 5
Consumer - Getting New Value: 5
```

```
Consumer - Getting New Value: 5

C:\jdk1.3se_book\classes>
```

If the output does not match exactly with yours, don't worry. Again, this is due to the randomness of threads, operating systems, and other features of where you are running this example. This example demonstrates when multiple threads needs to access the same object, the critical sections needs to be synchronized. There is a really interesting thing in this output however. Notice the first data value that the consumer reads and prints out. Looking at the output in the previous code sample, you see that the first value is 5!

Hopefully you are asking what happened to 1, 2, 3, and 4. What happened is that because the producer thread got started first and maybe got a little more attention than the consumer thread, the producer thread just went right along writing values without ever checking to see that the consumer got them. This can be a big problem in applications if all the data needed to be sent to the consumer. You solve this problem with thread communication, which is discussed next.

COMMUNICATING BETWEEN THREADS

As you saw in the last example, the consumer thread and the producer thread were not really aware of each other. And because they were not aware of each other and had no idea when one was writing and one was reading, they were not able to communicate. You need a way for the producer thread to notify the consumer thread that a new value has been written. You also need a way for the consumer thread to wait on a new value to be written and then signal to the producer thread that the new value has been read. Fortunately, Java has is able to do this with the `wait` and `notify` methods that exist on the `Object` class.

The `wait` method on the `Object` class causes the current thread to wait until another thread invokes the `notify` or `notifyAll` method on the current object. There are three variations of the `wait` method, the second and third take parameters that specify how long to wait, whereas the `wait` method with no parameters will wait indefinitely. When another thread calls the `notify` or `notifyAll` methods, an `InterruptedException` will be thrown. Therefore, you must be sure to catch this exception to know when another thread has signaled.

The `nofityAll` method wakes up all threads that are waiting on the lock for this object. The thread(s) that are notified when this method is called are not allowed to access the object until the current thread relinquishes control by getting out of the synchronized method or block. At that point, if there are multiple threads wanting access to the critical section, they must compete for it in the usual way by calling the synchronized method and acquiring a lock.

Caution

> Only a thread that has acquired a lock on an object is able to call these methods. If a thread, which does not have a lock on the object, attempts to call one of the variations of these methods, a `IllegalMonitorStateException` will be thrown. A thread acquires the lock through the synchronization techniques discussed earlier.

Extend the previous example by creating a new class called `BetterSharedObject`. You can extend the previous `SharedObject` class to make it easier on yourself and to gain a little reuse. Listing 11.14 shows the new class.

LISTING 11.14 SOURCE CODE FOR BetterSharedObject.java

```
public class BetterSharedObject extends SharedObject
{

  // The private shared data variable
  private Integer sharedData = null;
  private boolean dataAvailable = false;

  // Default Constructor
  public BetterSharedObject( int initialValue )
  {
    super( initialValue );
    // Initialize the shared object value to something
    sharedData = new Integer( initialValue );
  }

  // The producer will call this method to update the data
public synchronized void setSharedData( int newData )
  {
    if ( dataAvailable )
    {
      try
      {
        wait();
      }
      catch( InterruptedException ex )
      {}
    }

    System.out.println( "Shared Object - New Value Set: " + newData );
    sharedData = new Integer( newData );
    System.out.println( "Send notification that it is ok to read data" );
dataAvailable = true;
    notifyAll();
  }

  // The consumer will call this method to get the new data
  public synchronized Integer getSharedData()
  {
    if ( !dataAvailable )
    {
      try
      {
        wait();
      }
      catch( InterruptedException ex )
      {
        System.out.println( "Got notification that it was ok to read data" );
      }
    }
    dataAvailable = false;
```

LISTING 11.14 CONTINUED

```
      notifyAll();
      return sharedData;
   }
}
```

There are really three changes that you should note with the new class. One is the new instance variable called `dataAvailable`. This boolean variable is used to provide an additional message between the two threads about when data is actually present in the `sharedObject`. If you just depended on the `wait` and `notifyAll` methods in this class because both the get and set methods need to wait in the beginning of the methods, neither would do anything. They would just sit and wait on each other. This is a case of deadlock. However, when you add the `dataAvailable` flag and initialize it to false, the set method, which is called by the producer thread, sees that there is no data available and jumps down past the `wait` method and sets the data. It then calls the `notifyAll` method to signal all the threads that the lock is being released and they can come after the `sharedData`.

You need to change the `SharedObjectMain` class to use the `BetterSharedObject` rather than the `SharedObject` class. When you run the `SharedObjectMain`, the output looks like this:

```
C:\jdk1.3se_book\classes>java SharedObjectMain
Producer - Writing New Value: 1
Shared Object - New Value Set: 1
Send notification that its ok to read new data
Producer - Writing New Value: 2
Consumer - Getting New Value: 1
Shared Object - New Value Set: 2
Send notification that its ok to read new data
Producer - Writing New Value: 3
Consumer - Getting New Value: 2
Shared Object - New Value Set: 3
Send notification that its ok to read new data
Producer - Writing New Value: 4
Consumer - Getting New Value: 3
Shared Object - New Value Set: 4
Send notification that its ok to read new data
Producer - Writing New Value: 5
Consumer - Getting New Value: 4
Shared Object - New Value Set: 5
Send notification that its ok to read new data
Consumer - Getting New Value: 5

C:\jdk1.3se_book\classes>
```

Notice that even though the producer is writing the new value, the shared object does not show that new value being sent until after the consumer has retrieved the previous value. This is because in the set method, it first checks to see if data from the previous set is still there. If it is, it calls the `wait` method until the consumer signals using the `notifyAll` method. This informs the producer thread that it's okay to write the next value. That's when you see the print statement from the SharedObject that the new value has been set.

Notice again that each of these two methods have to be synchronized as well so that each thread will have exclusive access to the object.

CHANGING THE RUNNING STATE OF A THREAD

Threads have a number of possible states as you saw previously in "The Life Cycle of a Thread." Take a look at how to change the state of a thread and cause it to enter these states and what the effects are. The methods covered here are

- `sleep(long)`, `sleep(long,int)`
- `yield()`
- `destroy()`

You have already briefly looked at the `sleep` method in the `SimpleThread` example from the previous section. Putting a thread to sleep essentially tells the VM, "I'm done with what I am doing right now; wake me up in a little while." By putting a thread to sleep, you are allowing lower-priority threads a chance to get a shot at the processor. This is especially important when very low-priority threads are doing tasks that, although not as important, still need to be done periodically. Without stepping out of the way occasionally, your thread can put these threads into starvation. As stated earlier, this is where one or more threads never get a chance to execute because other threads are using the CPU too much and won't give it up.

The `sleep` method comes in two varieties. The first is `sleep(long)`, which tells the interpreter that you want to go to sleep for a certain number of milliseconds:

```
thisThread.sleep(100);
```

The only problem with this version is that a millisecond, although only an instant for humans, is a long time for a computer. Even on a 486/33 computer, this is enough time for the processor to do 25,000 instructions. On high-end workstations, hundreds of thousands of instructions can be done in 1 millisecond.

As a result, there is a second incantation: `sleep(long,int)`. With this version of the sleep command, you can put a thread to sleep for a number of milliseconds, plus a few nanoseconds:

```
thisThread.sleep(99,250);
```

Note

You might notice something strange if you look at the Sun API's for the `sleep` methods. Notice that these two methods are static. That means that you should be able to do something like this: `Thread.sleep(3000)`. If you call `sleep` on a thread instance object, only the current thread will sleep. You can't tell an outside thread to sleep from a different thread.

The `yield` method is very similar to the `sleep method`. With `yield`, you're telling the interpreter that you want to get out of the way of the other threads, but when they are done, you want to pick back up. `yield` does not require a `resume` to start back up when the other threads have stopped, gone to sleep, or died.

Caution

You may see older Java code that uses the `suspend` or the `resume` method when dealing with threads. Both of these methods have been deprecated by Sun and can be very dangerous to use.

The last method to change a thread's running state is the `destroy` method. In general, don't use this method. The `destroy` method doesn't do any cleanup on the thread; it just destroys it. However, if you read the Sun API for this method, you will see that they say this method is not implemented. So, you really should never try to use this method anyway.

THREAD GROUPS

The `ThreadGroup` class can be used to establish some thread security and authorization constraints on threads. It is also a way to group threads together so that actions can be performed on an entire set of threads. For example, you can start or stop all the threads within a `ThreadGroup`. After a thread is inserted into a `ThreadGroup`, it can't be put into a different `ThreadGroup`.

Most Java developers don't use `ThreadGroups`. That is, they just create new threads and accept whatever `ThreadGroup` the default is and put the new thread into that group. By default, all threads that are created belong to the default `ThreadGroup` of the main thread or a `ThreadGroup` called `main`. This is the same `ThreadGroup` in which the `main` thread is running.

`Threads` that belong to a particular `ThreadGroup` are not allowed to access or change the state of other threads that are in a different `ThreadGroup`. This restriction includes the parent `ThreadGroup` of the `ThreadGroup` or any other `ThreadGroup` that exists. The `ThreadGroup` class itself does not enforce this restriction, but rather relies on the `SecurityManager` that is installed for the running application. The `ThreadGroup` object works with the `SecurityManager` that is installed for the running application and together they determine what access is granted and what access is restricted.

`ThreadGroups` can form trees in which one `ThreadGroup` can be the parent or child of another `ThreadGroup`. By creating a custom `ThreadGroup` and assigning your new threads to this `ThreadGroup` object, you are locking down your thread's capability to access information about other threads outside of its `ThreadGroup`.

Caution

If a thread attempts to access another thread that belongs to a different `ThreadGroup` and the `SecurityManager` has not granted this access, a `SecurityException` will be thrown.

Take a look at an example using ThreadGroups. This example isn't too complicated, but it shows how to create a new ThreadGroup other than the default and assign threads into the group. This examples uses a thread called WorkerThread to perform some repetitive task that might need to be performed. The idea here is that there are multiple worker threads created, each one doing something for the overall application. In this case, it's just going to print out that the thread is running. This could have been something like checking a directory for a file, or listening on a socket for a request. This example is simple because the only purpose is to understand the ThreadGroups. Listing 11.15 shows the source for the WorkerThread that belongs to a ThreadGroup.

LISTING 11.15 SOURCE CODE FOR WorkerThread.java

```
public class WorkerThread extends Thread
{
  // Boolean flag that keeps state about when the thread should stop
  boolean keepRunning = true;

  // Default Constructor
  public WorkerThread( ThreadGroup group, String threadName )
  {
    super( group, threadName );
  }
  // Override the parents run method to do something special
  public void run()
  {
    // While the thread should keep running
    while( getKeepRunning() )
    {
      System.out.println( "Thread " + getName() + " is Running" );
      try
      {
        // Sleep for a time
        sleep( 3000 );
      }
      catch( Exception ex )
      { /* Don't do anything here */ }
    }
    // Let the user know that this thread is exiting
    System.out.println( "Thread: " + getName() + " is stopping" );
  }
  // public setting method to stop the thread
  public synchronized void setKeepRunning( boolean trueOrFalse )
  {
    keepRunning = trueOrFalse;
  }
  // public accessor for getting the state of this thread
  public synchronized boolean getKeepRunning()
  {
    return keepRunning;
  }
}
```

The boolean flag `keepRunning` is similar to the one from the synchronization section. Its used by the worker thread to know when it's time to quit. It needs to be synchronized because both the `HandlerThread` and the `WorkerThread` need to access it.

The next class in this example is the handler thread that is responsible for creating the worker threads and also informing them when it's time to stop. Listing 11.16 shows the `HandlerThread`. The main method is located inside the `HandlerThread` to keep this example compact

LISTING 11.16 SOURCE CODE FOR `HandlerThread.java`

```
public class HandlerThread extends Thread
{
  // The default constructor for the HandlerThread
  public HandlerThread( ThreadGroup ownerGroup, String threadName )
  {
    super( ownerGroup, threadName );
  }
  // Override the parents run to do something different
  public void run()
  {
    // How many worker threads to start up
int numberOfChildren = 3;
    // Declare the reference outside of the loop for better performance
    WorkerThread childThread = null;
    // Loop through and start up the worker threads
    for( int i = 1; i <= numberOfChildren; i++ )
    {
      childThread = new WorkerThread( getThreadGroup(),
                                      "Thread" + String.valueOf(i) );
      childThread.start();
    }
    // Go to sleep for 3 seconds and let the worker threads do something
try
    {
      sleep( 3000 );
    }
    catch( InterruptedException ex )
    {
      /* Don't need to handle this for now */
    }

    // Get the thread group that I belong to
    ThreadGroup myGroup = getThreadGroup();
    // how many active threads are in my group that I need to stop
    int activeEstimatedThreadCount = myGroup.activeCount();
    Thread[] activeThreads = new Thread[ activeEstimatedThreadCount ];
    // Get the count of active threads
    int activeThreadCount = myGroup.enumerate( activeThreads );
    // Declare the reference outside of the loop for performance
    Thread thread = null;
    // Loop through all the active threads and signal them to quit
    for( int counter = 0; counter < activeThreadCount; counter++ )
    {
      // Get one of the active threads out of the array
```

LISTING 11.16 CONTINUED

```
      thread = activeThreads[counter];
      // Make sure it's a worker thread. There may be others active
      // If it is a worker thread, tell it to stop running
      if ( thread instanceof WorkerThread )
        ((WorkerThread)thread).setKeepRunning(false);
    }
  }

  public static void main( String args[] )
  {
    // Create a new ThreadGroup
    ThreadGroup threadGroup = new ThreadGroup( "MyNewGroup" );
    // Start the handler, which will start the worker threads
    HandlerThread handler = new HandlerThread( threadGroup, "HandlerThread" );
    // Start the handler thread running
    handler.start();
  }
}
```

OBTAINING THE NUMBER OF RUNNING THREADS

You saw in the `ThreadGroup` class that the method `activeCount` returned an estimate of the number of threads running within that `ThreadGroup`. The `Thread` class itself also has a method called `activeCount`. It is a static method that returns the number of threads that are running within the thread's `ThreadGroup`. Using this method, you don't have to get the `ThreadGroup` for the thread and ask it.

YIELDING TO OTHER THREADS

You learned earlier about thread starvation. To refresh, thread starvation occurs when one or more threads are not getting enough attention from the CPU. There are several reasons this might occur:

- Incorrect thread priorities
- Staying too long in a `sleep` method
- Other threads not yielding correctly

The first two possible reasons have already been discussed in previous sections of this chapter, so now focus on the third possibility: incorrect yielding. You can think of a thread yielding as "being a good citizen." Just because a thread has been given a high prioritydoes not mean that it should always have access to the CPU for performing its tasks. It sometimes needs to back away and let other threads have a chance. When the higher priority thread really needs to do something, it can gain control again through normal preemptive or non-preemptive means.

What this means is that as you are creating new thread classes and implementing the `run` method; keep in mind that you might need to insert some places where your thread manually gives up control if any other thread needs the control. You can do this by using the `yield` method in the `Thread` class. The `yield` method is a static method that causes the currently executing thread to temporarily pause and allow other threads of the same priority a chance to execute. If there are no other threads that are the same priority and are runnable, the original thread gains control and continues on. Again, it's up to each developer that is creating the thread to use the `yield` method properly and in the correct situation.

Now that you understand a little better what the `yield` is for, you might not have to use it all. The `yield` method is actually a hint to the Java Virtual Machine. It tells the JVM that if there are any threads that are runnable and the same priority, now is a good time to run them. If the operating system that you are using uses a preemptive scheduling technique, the JVM might completely ignore the yield suggestion. Remember, preemptive means that each thread has an amount of time that it can run before it is automatically interrupted. So in reality, the JVM or actually the scheduler might decide that it knows best and choose to ignore the suggestion. It's best to know how the operating system that the thread is executing on deals with threads. Just to be safe, it also a good idea to get in the habit of using the `yield` method. For one, Java is portable and the application might end up on an operating system that doesn't support preemptive.

Listing 11.17 shows a sample of how to incorporate the `yield` method into your thread class. Only the `run` method from a thread class is being shown in this example, not the entire thread class.

LISTING 11.17 SOURCE CODE FOR AN EXAMPLE `run` METHOD

```
public void run()
  {
    // Condition to determine when the thread should stop running
    boolean keepRunning = true;

    // While the condition says keep going
    while( keepRunning )
    {
      // Some time intensive operation or calculation
      if ( Math.random() < 0.1 )
      {
        keepRunning = false;
      }

      // Call yield here so that other threads of equal priority have an
      // opportunity to execute
      Thread.yield();
    }
  }
```

Notice how the `yield` is called after the calculation to give other threads a chance to run.

DAEMON THREADS

Threads can be one of two types: a user thread or a daemon thread.

So what is a *daemon*? Well, Webster's Dictionary says it is "…an attendant spirit," or "…an inferior deity."

In a sense, Webster's is right in both cases with respect to daemon threads. *Daemon* threads usually perform a valuable service for the application by doing some task that the rest of the application doesn't really want to do. This may be personifying an application, but daemon threads usually end up performing tasks that, although important, are somewhat less critical to the application.

Daemon threads are also inferior to normal user threads. This is because as long as a user thread is running, the JVM will not stop an application. If there are only daemon threads running in an application, the JVM will stop the application.

Two methods in `java.lang.Thread` deal with the daemonic state assigned to a thread:

- `isDaemon()`
- `setDaemon(boolean)`

The first method, `isDaemon`, is used to test the state of a particular thread. Occasionally, this is useful to an object running as a thread so that it can determine whether it is running as a daemon or a regular thread. `isDaemon` returns `true` if the thread is a daemon, and `false` otherwise.

The second method, `setDaemon(boolean)`, is used to change the daemonic state of the thread. To make a thread a daemon, you indicate this by setting the input value to `true`. To change it back to a user thread, you set the boolean value to `false`.

Here's an example of using a daemon thread. Listing 11.18 is a class that implements the `Runnable` interface. In the `run` method, it has an infinite loop that prints out a line of text each time through the loop. This would normally be a bad idea, but because a thread is being started up as a daemon, the application should not run forever because there are only daemon threads running. The JVM should detect that there are only daemon threads running and stop the entire application.

LISTING 11.18 SOURCE CODE FOR `MyDaemon.java`

```
public class MyDaemon implements Runnable
{
  // Default Constructor
  public MyDaemon()
  {
    super();
  }

  // Implement the required method from the Runnable interface
  public void run()
  {
    // Go into an infinite loop. This is normally not a good idea
    while( true )
    {
      // Print this out each time through the loop
      System.out.println( "Still Running..." );
    }
  }
}
```

Listing 11.19 is the main class used to start the daemon thread running.

LISTING 11.19 SOURCE CODE FOR DaemonThreadMain.java

```
public class DaemonThreadMain
{
  public DaemonThreadMain()
  {
  }

  // Main method that starts it all
public static void main(String[] args)
  {
    // Create a new thread using the MyDaemon class as the runnable target
    Thread thread = new Thread( new MyDaemon(), "My Daemon Thread" );
    // Set the thread up as a daemon thread
    thread.setDaemon( true );
    thread.start();
  }
}
```

Here's the output from the example:

```
C:\jdk1.3se_book\classes>java DaemonThreadMain
Still Running...
Still Running...
Still Running...
Still Running...
Still Running...
Still Running...
Still Running...
Still Running...
Still Running...
Still Running...
Still Running...
C:\jdk1.3se_book\classes>
```

Notice that even though there was an infinite loop in the `run` method, the application exited. It did make it several times through the loop, but exited when the JVM realized it was only daemon threads running.

USING THE `Timer` AND `TimerTask` CLASSES

The `Timer` and `TimerTask` classes are brand new to SDK 1.3. Most developers would admit to having created classes similar to these two classes time and time again in their applications. So, it's nice to see them being included in the core API.

The `Timer` class provides a facility for threads to schedule tasks to be completed in the future by a background thread. The tasks can be scheduled for a one-time execution or repeated execution at some interval cycle. A system might create multiple `Timer` instances, each one having a thread that runs in the background executing the tasks one by one. If the task was set up to execute just once, then after that task completed, it would no longer be executed by the Timer thread. By default, the Timer thread does not run as a daemon thread. So, the Timer thread would keep an application running, as it is an actual user thread by default. You can, of course, make the Timer thread a daemon thread. This would allow the application to exit if it was the only thread running.

One of the nice features about the Timer class is that it is thread-safe. Multiple threads can share a single Timer object without having to have any synchronization of its own.

The partner to the Timer class is the TimerTask. This is the task that is scheduled with the Timer object. The TimerTask class provides an abstract run method that must be overridden and include the behavior to execute when the task is scheduled to run. There is also a cancel method on the TimerTask that will cause the task to stop executing. If the task has not executed yet or scheduled with the Timer object, the cancel method guarantees that it will never run. If it is a repeating task, then it will never run, unless it is in the middle of execution. In that case, after execution is completed, it is guaranteed never to run again. The cancel method returns a boolean value. If the canceling of the task prevented at least one execution from happening, then the return value will be true. If the cancel method was called after the task has completed and it was a one-time execution, the return value will be false.

Listing 11.20 shows an example of extending the TimerTask class.

LISTING 11.20 SOURCE CODE FOR MyTask.java

```
import java.util.Date;
import java.util.Timer;
import java.util.TimerTask;

public class MyTask extends TimerTask
{
  int maxNumberOfTimesToRun = 0;
  // A reference to a date object
  Date currentDateTime = null;
  static int counter = 1;
  Timer myTimer = null;

  // Default Constructor
  public MyTask( int maxCounter, Timer aTimer )
  {
    super();
    maxNumberOfTimesToRun = maxCounter;
    myTimer = aTimer;
  }

  // Override the abstract method  run()
  public void run()
  {
    if ( MyTask.counter <= maxNumberOfTimesToRun )
    {
      System.out.println( MyTask.counter );
      // Create a current date instance
      currentDateTime = new Date( System.currentTimeMillis() );
      // Display the current date object as a string
```

LISTING 11.20 CONTINUED

```
      System.out.println( "MyTask: " + currentDateTime.toString() );
      MyTask.counter++;
    }
    else
    {
      // Since we reached the counter max, cancel the task
      cancel();
      // Also cancel the timer since I'm the only one using it.
      // This might not be true in all cases
      myTimer.cancel();
    }
  }
}
```

Listing 11.21 is the main class that creates the `Timer` object, schedules the `MyTask` class from Listing 11.20 with the `Timer`, and starts the `Timer` moving.

LISTING 11.21 SOURCE CODE FOR `MyTaskMain`

```
import java.util.Timer;

public class MyTaskMain
{
  // This is the main method that starts the Timer. Notice we did not have to
  // call a start method on the Timer. It actually associates a thread with
  // each Timer instance
  public static void main(String[] args)
  {
    Timer timer = new Timer();
    MyTask task = new MyTask( 5, timer );
    // Schedule the task to run every 3,000 millisecs or 3 seconds starting
    // right from the beginning.
    timer.schedule( task, 0, 3000 );
  }
}
```

Here's the output from running the `MyTaskMain` class in Listing 11.21:

```
C:\jdk1.3se_book\classes>java MyTaskMain
1
MyTask: Mon Jul 03 22:19:58 PDT 2000
2
MyTask: Mon Jul 03 22:20:01 PDT 2000
3
MyTask: Mon Jul 03 22:20:04 PDT 2000
4
MyTask: Mon Jul 03 22:20:07 PDT 2000
5
MyTask: Mon Jul 03 22:20:10 PDT 2000

C:\jdk1.3se_book\classes>
```

MAKING YOUR APPLICATION THREAD-SAFE

Many new concepts were covered in this chapter, from deadlocks to thread scheduling algorithms. Probably the most important concept to walk away from this chapter with, other than understanding the Thread API, is the concept of a critical section.

As stated earlier, a critical section is a part or multiple parts of an application that can be accessed simultaneously from multiple threads. If an application has more than a single thread running and there is shared data that can be accessed, this area has to be protected. By using the keyword `synchronized`, these critical sections can be made safe to allow multiple threads in an application to share the data. One of the most important things to remember when making your applications thread-safe is to look for any way that a thread has access to the shared data. Usually this is through the `get` and `set` methods for a member variable. However, there usually are other methods that make it possible for shared data to be accessed. You must either protect these as well, or remove them from public access.

Finally, remember that an entire method does not have to be synchronized in all cases. You have the ability to synchronize a block or section of code. This is sometimes more efficient and helps in preventing deadlock conditions.

TROUBLESHOOTING

THREAD DOES NOT START

My thread never starts to run.

A `Thread` is started by calling the `start` method, not the `run` method. Whether you are implementing the `Runnable` interface or extending the `Thread` class, you must always call the `start` method to start the `Thread`.

ONE OFF ERROR

The first or last thread in a array of Threads is not starting up.

Remember that like other things in the Java language, the index for a array starts at zero, not one. As you can no doubt figure out, the last `index` of a array is length –1. This does not affect the actual length of the array. Ensure that if you are using an array that you are indexing it correctly.

PART II

User Interface

CHAPTER 12

Introduction to Java Foundation Classes

by Geoff Friesen

In this chapter

What Is the JFC?

Java Foundation Classes (JFC) provides a framework for developing Java programs with user interfaces. This framework can be conveniently divided into five major APIs: AWT (Abstract Windowing Toolkit), Swing, Accessibility, Java 2D, and Drag and Drop. AWT is the foundation of the JFC, whereas Swing is built on top of the AWT. Accessibility is mainly built into Swing, although it is also being added to the AWT—this is a work in progress. Finally, Java 2D and Drag and Drop are built into the AWT.

AWT

Since its inclusion with the first Java development kit, the AWT has provided developers with the means to create event-driven graphical user interfaces (GUIs) for their Java programs. The AWT also supports primitive graphics operations (such as drawing text and shapes, displaying images, manipulating colors, and choosing fonts). Furthermore, the AWT makes it possible to create flicker-free animations, process images, and print graphics.

Although the AWT generated a lot of excitement when it was first released, developers soon became aware of its limitations. These limitations include the following:

- The AWT relies on the host computer's operating system (OS) to provide visual and interactive GUI components. Therefore, it isn't easy to create a GUI with a consistent look and feel across all OSes that support the Java Virtual Machine. For example, suppose you want to use the AWT to develop a program with IBM's OS/2 graphical look and event-driven feel. Furthermore, you want to run this program under another OS (such as Windows 2000) and have its users perceive this program as one that looks and feels like a program running under OS/2. Unfortunately, this scenario is not easy to achieve under the AWT.
- The AWT uses the lowest-common denominator components and component features to ensure that an AWT-based Java program will work under all OSes that support the JVM. As an example of the first situation, not all OSes supported table and tree components when the AWT was initially released. Therefore, the AWT could not support tables or trees. As an example of the second situation, the AWT does not support Motif's tear-off menu feature because this feature is not implemented by the menu components of any Windows OS. Because tear-off menus are not in the lowest-common denominator of menu features, they are not part of the AWT.
- The AWT's graphics capabilities are very limited in what they can do. For example, it is not possible to control either the thickness or the style (such as dashed or dotted) of a shape's borders.

→ **See** Chapter 13, "Beginning AWT," **p. 335**

Swing

Swing was developed to address the AWT's GUI limitations. With Swing, it is possible to create GUIs that are richer than their AWT counterparts in appearance and capabilities.

The classes and interfaces that constitute Swing provide new components (such as trees, tables, and split panes). Swing also introduces a concept known as pluggable look and feel. *Pluggable look and feel* makes it possible to design a GUI that looks and feels the same on every platform, or that adapts its look and feel to a specific platform. For example, a program could choose to look and feel like a Motif program when run under Unix, Windows and MacOS, or it could choose to look and feel like a Motif program when run under Unix, a Windows program when run under Windows, and a MacOS program when run under MacOS. (The latter case is accomplished by giving Swing programs access to the system look and feel.) Swing also provides access to its own default cross-platform look and feel, known as Metal (or Java).

Note

You might be wondering where Swing got its name. Swing was christened at the 1997 JavaOne conference in San Francisco. Swing engineers used a music-based demonstration to showcase Swing components. Among the jokes that were passed back and forth, one of the engineers suggested that Swing was being considered the "in" sound in music. Because the Swing classes did not yet have a name and because its engineers felt that it would be the "in" GUI development technology for Java, they decided to call this unnamed technology Swing. After all, for many developers and users of Java technology, "GUIs don't mean a thing if they ain't got that Swing."

→ **See** Chapter 16, "Building a GUI: Swing Style," **p. 519**

Accessibility

People who are afflicted with varying physical challenges (such as blindness or diminished loss of vision, loss of limbs, and so on) can find software usage either impossible or next to impossible. And then there are times (such as when driving a car with both hands on the wheel) when an individual who is not physically challenged might find it difficult to use software. In either situation, software accessibility is beneficial.

Accessibility includes support for alternative input and output devices (such as speech recognition/synthesis devices, Braille keyboards, and screen magnifiers). The accessibility portion of the JFC makes it almost transparent for software to support these devices.

Accessibility provides the mechanism by which automation software can be created. This software can automatically send keystrokes, mouse clicks, and mouse movements to a program for testing, screen magnification, and other purposes.

→ **See** Chapter 17, "Accessibility," **p. 599**

Java 2D

Java 2D was developed to address the AWT's graphics limitations. For example, AWT's rectangle, arc, and polygon shapes are not sufficient for an automotive designer who needs access to advanced shapes (such as Bézier curves) for modeling curved surfaces.

Java 2D offers many features that are not part of the AWT's graphics package. These features include

- The ability to decide the width and style (dashed, dotted, solid) of the pen used to draw a shape's outline
- The ability to fill the interior of an arbitrary shape with a solid color or pattern
- The ability to determine what happens when two shapes overlap
- The ability to transform a shape through scaling, rotation, translation, or some other operation
- The ability to clip to an arbitrary shape
- The ability to detect mouse clicks in an arbitrary shape through advanced hit detection
- The ability to use any available font to display text
- A sophisticated printing model for complex documents
- Improved image processing capabilities

→ **See** Chapter 18, "Java 2D," **p. 633**

DRAG AND DROP

Drag and Drop supports the dragging and dropping of objects between Java programs, or between Java and non-Java programs. For example, it is possible to create a Java program that functions as a file manager. A user can select a graphical image (such as a file icon) and drag this image off of the file manager program and onto a Linux word processor program or a Macintosh trash can icon. As a result, Drag and Drop helps improve application interoperability.

→ **See** Chapter 19, "Drag and Drop," **p. 703**

HISTORY OF THE JFC

Now that you understand what it is all about, it's time to see how the JFC came into existence, and find out if there are any competing frameworks.

AWT 1.0

The first release of Java—in the fall of 1995—included AWT 1.0. In hindsight, this AWT was noted for its poor performance and a very restrictive event model. These failings led Sun Microsystems developers to create a new version of the AWT that incorporated a greatly improved event model and offered superior performance.

INTERNET FOUNDATION CLASSES

Netscape had its own ideas regarding the direction AWT should take. On December 11, 1996, Netscape unveiled a user interface framework completely written in Java—the Internet Foundation Classes (IFC).

The IFC allowed for the creation of Java programs that are independent of OS-specific windows and user interface controls—Netscape's term for GUI components. The IFC framework included window hierarchies, integrated drag and drop, and basic controls.

Many developers have used the IFC and this framework is still available for use, although it is being downplayed in favor of the JFC.

APPLICATION FOUNDATION CLASSES

Not to be outdone, Microsoft announced in January 1997 that it would release its own foundation class framework, dubbed the Application Foundation Classes (AFC). Companies were given a look at the AFC in March of that same year. And in April, an early version of the AFC was released to developers.

Although Microsoft's AFC was completely written in Java, its architecture was based on the C++ Microsoft Foundation Classes (MFC). Many developers with MFC experience adopted this framework.

However, Microsoft was never happy with Java, and saw this technology as a threat to its Windows-everywhere vision. Therefore, Microsoft evolved the AFC into the Windows Foundation Classes (WFC), a Windows platform-specific framework. The WFC made it possible for Java developers to write Win32 applications in Java as opposed to C++, and was incorporated into Microsoft's Visual J++ 6.0 compiler.

The Java community was not impressed with Microsoft's move, because they saw Visual J++ 6.0 and the WFC to be a threat to the cross-platform nature of Java. Sun took Microsoft to court, claiming that Microsoft had violated Sun's license agreement, and won an injunction against Microsoft's continued involvement with its own brand of Java. As to the future of the AFC and the WFC, this issue is clouded and only time will tell.

JAVA FOUNDATION CLASSES

Around the time that Microsoft first announced the AFC, Sun and Netscape jointly announced the development of a new framework called the Java Foundation Classes (JFC). This framework would be based on Netscape's IFC. IBM, Apple, and several other companies were invited to contribute to the JFC.

The JFC was first introduced on July 8, 1997. It incorporated a comprehensive set of GUI components and foundation services that were designed to simplify development of Internet, intranet and desktop applications.

Many developers associate Swing with the JFC, because the Swing API has undergone the most changes. This has prompted several releases of the JFC. The current version of the JFC, bundled as part of SDK 1.3, has matured to the point where this framework is your best bet for developing quality user interfaces.

VISION OF THE FUTURE

So, what comes next for the JFC? It is possible that Sun will incorporate Java media—Java 3D, television, movies, and so on—into the JFC. After all, the JFC is all about creating user interfaces, and media has an important role to play in the development of these interfaces.

JFC APPLICATIONS

In previous chapters, you were exposed to non-JFC applications (that is, Java applications that don't make use of graphics or GUIs). It's time to see what a JFC application looks like. To that end, you're going to have an opportunity to examine a pair of AWT and Swing skeletal JFC applications.

A TASTE OF JFC'S AWT APPLICATIONS

An AWT application uses the AWT API. This application contains a class that either inherits from the AWT's `Frame` class or creates an instance of the `Frame` class in its `main` method.

Note

A *frame* is a window that provides a title bar, window decorations (such as a system menu, minimize and maximize buttons, borders, and so on), a menu bar, and an area to place GUI components.

An AWT application often incorporates a skeletal structure that looks similar to the code in Listing 12.1.

LISTING 12.1 THE `AppAWTSkeleton` APPLICATION SOURCE CODE

```
// AppAWTSkeleton.java

import java.awt.*;
import java.awt.event.*;

class AppAWTSkeleton extends Frame
{
   AppAWTSkeleton (String title)
   {
      super (title);

      addWindowListener (new WindowAdapter ()
                         {
                             public void windowClosing (WindowEvent e)
                             {
                                System.exit (0);
                             }
                         });

      // Build GUI here.

      pack ();
      setVisible (true);
   }

   public static void main (String [] args)
   {
      new AppAWTSkeleton ("Title goes here");
   }
}
```

As Listing 12.1 shows, this AWT application's sole class extends the `Frame` class. Its `main` method creates an instance of this class and invokes the constructor. A title is passed to this constructor, which is further passed to one of `Frame`'s constructors, via the `super (title)` method call. This title will be displayed in the frame's title bar.

After taking care of the title, the constructor registers a window listener that responds to window closing events. To register this listener, the `addWindowListener` method is called with a reference to an object created from an anonymous subclass of the `WindowAdapter` class. In this subclass, the `windowClosing` method is overridden to allow the application to exit when the user selects the Close box from the frame. (Behind the scenes, this method is called when the user selects the frame's Close box.)

Now that the constructor has taken care of the frame's title and window closure registration, it can proceed to construct a GUI. Once the GUI has been built, the `pack` method is called to establish the size of the frame (by determining the preferred sizes of all contained components). Finally, the `setVisible` method is called, with a Boolean `true` value argument, to ensure that the frame is visible.

Tip

As an alternative to `pack`, a program can also call the `setSize` method to explicitly specify the frame's horizontal and vertical sizes.

The constructor exits, along with the main thread. However, the program does not exit because background threads that manage the frame are still running.

To get an idea of what an AWT application's output looks like, take a look at Figure 12.1. This figure illustrates the output from the `PNViewer1` AWT application. (Although not shown in this chapter, `PNViewer1`'s source code is included with the rest of this book's source code.)

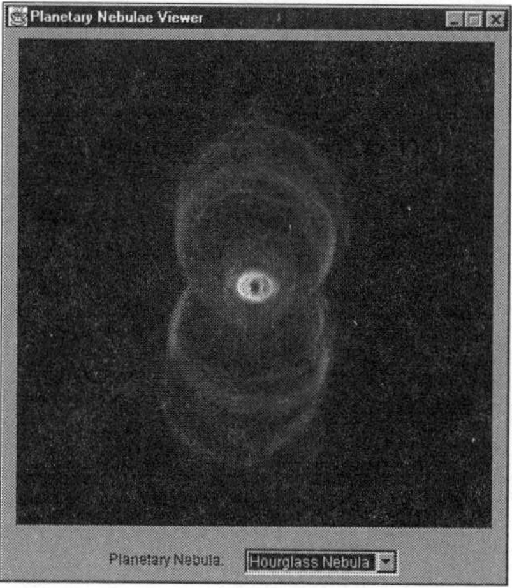

Figure 12.1 The `PNViewer1` application presents an AWT GUI consisting of a planetary nebula image (displayed in a custom `Picture` component) and a `Choice` component.

Note

Planetary nebulae are gaseous clouds surrounding those stars that shed their outer layers through violent explosions. When viewing an image of a planetary nebula, keep in mind that the star located at the center of the nebula is the source of the explosions that formed the nebula. (The star still exists: it just "hiccupped.")

If you study `PNViewer1`'s source code, you'll find that there is a lot of code required to construct this application. However, most of this code is involved in building the GUI. You might also notice a similarity between `PNViewer1`'s skeletal structure and `AppAWTSkeleton`'s structure. This is no accident: I tend to use this skeletal structure in many of my AWT applications.

You'll get a chance to study the various elements that contribute to `PNViewer1` and other AWT applications when you get to Chapters 13, "Beginning AWT," and 14, "Building a GUI: AWT Style."

Suppose you want to create an AWT application that generates an audible beep when something important happens. You don't want to go to all the bother of loading and playing a sound file. (In fact, you don't want to have to distribute a sound file with your program.) Is there a simple way to generate this beep? The answer is yes. To see how this is done, check out "Beeping the System Speaker" in the "Troubleshooting" section at the end of this chapter.

A Taste of JFC's Swing Applications

In contrast to AWT applications, a Swing application uses the Swing API. It can also take advantage of the AWT API, although discernment is required in choosing what portions of this API to use.

Each Swing application contains a class that either inherits from Swing's `JFrame` class or creates an instance of the `JFrame` class in its `main` method. Swing applications incorporate skeletal structures that look similar to the code in Listing 12.2.

Listing 12.2 The `AppSwingSkeleton` Application Source Code

```
// AppSwingSkeleton.java

import javax.swing.*;
import java.awt.event.*;

class AppSwingSkeleton extends JFrame
{
   AppSwingSkeleton (String title)
   {
      super (title);

      setDefaultCloseOperation (EXIT_ON_CLOSE);

      // Build GUI here.

      pack ();
      setVisible (true);
   }
```

LISTING 12.2 CONTINUED

```
   public static void main (String [] args)
   {
      new AppSwingSkeleton ("Title goes here");
   }
}
```

As Listing 12.2 shows, a Swing application's skeletal structure is similar to the skeletal structure of an AWT application. However, there are differences—besides extending `JFrame` instead of `Frame`.

The first difference can be found in the imports section. Whereas an AWT application contains an `import java.awt.*;` import, a Swing application contains an `import javax.swing.*;` import. Although not required in `AppAWTSkeleton` and `AppSwingSkeleton`, both AWT and Swing applications often contain an `import java.awt.event.*;` import, so they can register objects that listen for various events.

The second difference is the manner by which a window listener is registered to listen for window closing events. Unlike AWT applications, a Swing application doesn't need to call `Frame`'s `addWindowListener` method with an argument that references an object created from an anonymous subclass of the `WindowAdapter` class. Instead, a Swing application calls `JFrame`'s `setDefaultCloseOperation` method with an `EXIT_ON_CLOSE` argument to register this intent.

To get an idea of what a Swing application's output looks like, take a look at Figure 12.2. This figure illustrates the output from the `PNViewer2` Swing application. (Although not shown in this chapter, `PNViewer2`'s source code is included with the rest of this book's source code.)

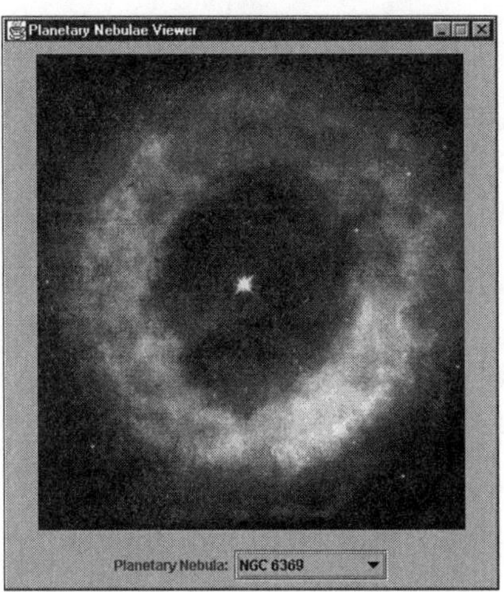

Figure 12.2 The `PNViewer2` application presents a Swing GUI consisting of an image (displayed in a `JLabel` component) and a `JComboBox` component.

For those who study `PNViewer2`'s source code, you'll notice that it was designed to be as similar to the `PNViewer1` source code as possible (for comparison purposes). Once you've learned about Swing, you'll be in a good position to understand the differences between these two programs.

You'll get a chance to study the various elements that contribute to `PNViewer2` and other Swing applications when you get to Chapters 15, "And Then There Was Swing," and 16, "Building a GUI: Swing Style."

APPLETS

Applications aren't the only kind of Java programs that can make use of the JFC. *Applets*—Java programs that run in the context of a Web browser—can also benefit from the JFC APIs. In fact, applets are intimately connected to the JFC, by virtue of inheriting capabilities from important JFC classes.

WHAT IS AN APPLET?

An *applet* is a Java program that runs in the context of a Web browser. At various times, the Web browser calls certain applet methods to perform applet-specific tasks, and these methods respond appropriately.

The Web browser reserves a rectangular portion of its main window as a display area for each applet that requires a place in which to draw its output. The Web browser also arranges for an applet to receive input from either the keyboard or the mouse.

The Web browser subjects applets to security restrictions. These restrictions prevent rogue applets from causing damage to a user's computer (such as stealing passwords or deleting files). For example, an applet is not normally given access to the local file system or printer. It must first be granted access.

Note

> The topic of granting access to the file system, printer, and other sensitive aspects of a computer system is beyond the scope of this chapter, and is not covered in this book. For more information, please consult the SDK 1.3 documentation.

APPLETS AND THE WORLD WIDE WEB

When you start your Web browser and select a site to visit, the Web browser attempts to locate this site. If successful, the Web browser will attempt to connect to the server that hosts this site and request that the server send it an *HTML document*—a file containing literal text and tags. *Tags* instruct the Web browser as to what additional files are required and how to render a Web page.

After the Web browser has received this document, it might close its connection to the server, unless it leaves this connection open for performance reasons. It then parses the document in preparation to displaying the resultant Web page. During parsing, the Web browser examines the document for special HTML tags (such as `<IMG>` or `<APPLET>`). For each occurrence of these tags, the Web browser establishes a new connection to the server (unless a persistent connection was established) and requests an appropriate file, such as a GIF/JPEG file in the case of an <IMG> tag or a JAR (Java archive)/class file in the case of an <APPLET> tag.

Caution

Although a JAR file has the same architecture as a ZIP file, this could change in the future. Therefore, it's good to think of JAR and ZIP files as separate entities.

If an <APPLET> tag is encountered, this tag is parsed to identify the JAR file and/or main class file that constitutes an applet. If a JAR file is present, the Web browser requests this file from the server. Otherwise, only the main class file is requested.

Assuming that a JAR file is retrieved, the Web browser makes sure the main class file is extracted from the JAR file. In any event, the Web browser starts the JVM by loading its library into memory. It then passes the main class file to the JVM.

The JVM's class loader loads the class file, and its bytecode verifier ensures that all bytecode instructions are properly formed so that they will not cause problems for the JVM. As the JVM encounters references to other classes, via internal import directives, the JVM makes requests, via the Web browser, to the server for additional class files.

Figure 12.3 illustrates the process by which the Web browser requests class files from a server.

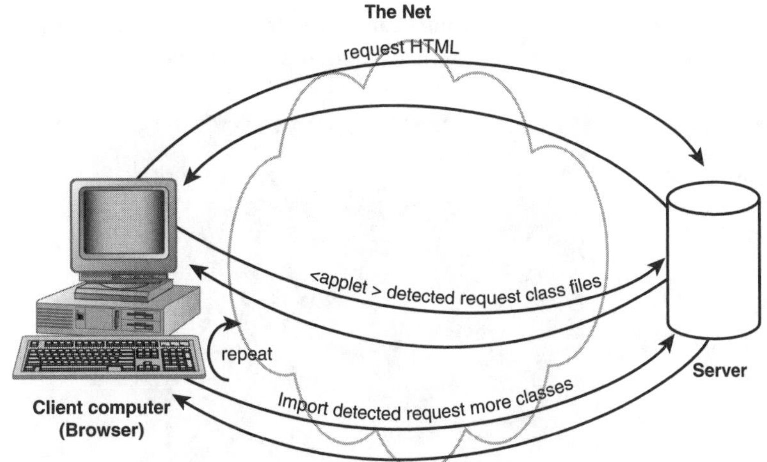

Figure 12.3
The Web browser and server continue to interact until all class files have been obtained.

AWT APPLETS

An AWT applet inherits capabilities from the AWT's `Applet` class (located in the `java.applet` package). Because `Applet` is ultimately derived from the `java.awt.Component` class, AWT applets are first-class GUI components. Figure 12.4 shows the `PNViewer3` AWT applet—that mirrors the `PNViewer1` AWT application—running in the Netscape Communicator Web browser. (Although not shown in this chapter, `PNViewer3`'s source code is included with the rest of this book's source code.)

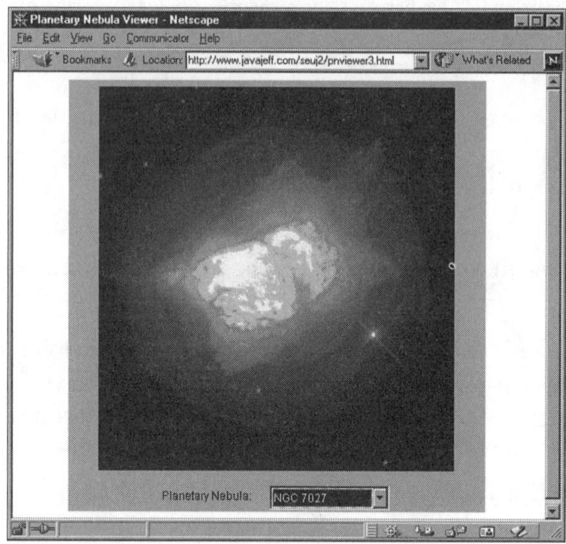

Figure 12.4
The `PNViewer3` applet runs in the Netscape Communicator Web browser.

To illustrate that an AWT applet can be run in multiple Web browsers, Figure 12.5 shows `PNViewer3` running in the Internet Explorer Web browser.

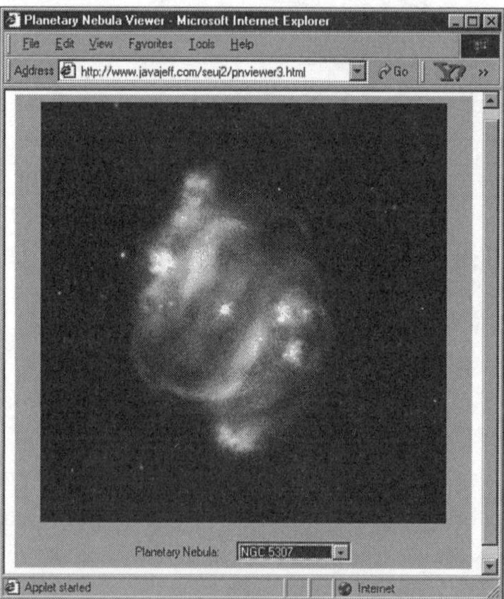

Figure 12.5
The `PNViewer3` applet runs in the Internet Explorer Web browser.

SDK 1.3 comes with an Applet Viewer program for running AWT applets. This program takes a single argument that identifies an HTML document. For example, the following code fragment shows how to run `PNViewer3` with the `pnviewer3.html` file. (Although not shown in this chapter, `pnviewer3.html` is included with the rest of this book's files.)

```
appletviewer pnviewer3.html
```

An AWT applet consists of one or more classes. However, one of these classes (the main class) must be declared `public` and must extend the `Applet` class, in the `java.applet` package. Listing 12.3 shows what this looks like, via an applet called `MyApplet1`.

LISTING 12.3 `MyApplet1`—THE WORLD'S SIMPLEST AWT APPLET

```
public class MyApplet1 extends java.applet.Applet
{
}
```

The `MyApplet1` applet appears to be a simple applet. After all, it occupies just three lines of source code. However, looks are deceiving. In reality, `MyApplet1` is inheriting more than 200 methods and field variables from ancestor classes. The hierarchy of these classes (along with `MyApplet1`) is shown in the following inheritance tree:

```
java.lang.Object
   |
   +----java.awt.Component
           |
           +----java.awt.Container
                   |
                   +----java.awt.Panel
                           |
                           +----java.applet.Applet
                                   |
                                   +----MyApplet1
```

Because `MyApplet1` inherits from `Applet`, `MyApplet1` is an AWT applet. Also, because `Applet` inherits from `Panel`, `MyApplet1` is a kind of panel. Furthermore, because `Panel` inherits from `Container`, `MyApplet1` is a kind of container. Finally, because `Container` inherits from `Component`, `MyApplet1` is a kind of component. You can see that `MyApplet1` is deeply connected to the JFC, because of the presence of `Component`, `Container`, and `Panel` in this hierarchy.

→ **See** Chapter 14, "Building a GUI: AWT Style," **p. 419**

Tip

Mastering the JFC requires a time investment to understand the class hierarchies (along with methods and fields) that make up the five major APIs. However, this investment will richly pay off. Not only will this organizational knowledge speed development, it will also help speed the process of debugging faulty JFC programs.

The `Applet` class contains many useful methods for your applets, and some of these methods are designed to be overridden. You'll have a chance to see some of these methods in action, as you progress through this chapter. To get a head start, check out Table 12.1.

TABLE 12.1 THE METHODS IN THE `Applet` CLASS

Method	Description
`destroy ()`	This method is called by the Web browser prior to reclaiming applet memory. Code would be placed in this method to cleanup global resources.
`getAccessibleContext ()`	Returns a reference to an accessible context object. This object is used in conjunction with the Accessibility API (discussed in a later chapter).
`getAppletContext ()`	Returns a reference to an object that implements the `AppletContext` interface. The applet might call methods defined by this interface to query and affect its environment. (Contexts will be discussed later in this chapter.)
`getAppletInfo ()`	Returns a reference to a `String` object containing applet information (such as author name and copyright). Some Web browsers use this information, although many do not.
`getAudioClip (URL url)`	Returns a reference to an object that implements the `AudioClip` interface. This object is associated with the `URL` (Uniform Resource Locator) argument `url`, which specifies the location and name of an audio file. The applet might call methods defined by this interface to play audio. This method returns immediately, regardless of the audio file's existence. The first attempt to play the audio file causes this file to be downloaded.
`getAudioClip (URL url, String file)`	This method concatenates the location of an audio file (specified by `url`) and its name (specified by `file`) into a single entity, and then calls `getAudioClip (URL url)`.
`getCodeBase ()`	Returns a reference to a `URL` object that identifies the location from which this applet was downloaded.
`getDocumentBase ()`	Returns a reference to a `URL` object that identifies the location from which this applet's HTML document was downloaded.
`getImage (URL url)`	Returns a reference to an `Image` object. This object is associated with `url`, which specifies the location and name of an image file. This method returns immediately, regardless of the image file's existence. The first attempt to draw this image will cause this file to be downloaded.
`getImage (URL url, String file)`	This method concatenates the location of an image file (specified by `url`) and its name (specified by `file`) into a single entity, and then calls `getImage (URL url)`.

Table 12.1 Continued

Method	Description
`getLocale ()`	Returns a reference to the current `Locale` object. With this object, an applet can tailor its output (such as text, sound, formatting, and so on) to the conventions of a particular country or region.
`getParameter (String p)`	Returns a reference to a `String` object containing the value of a parameter, whose name is specified by `p`, or `null` if this parameter cannot be found. (Parameters will be discussed later in this chapter.)
`getParameterInfo ()`	Returns a reference to a three-column by `n`-row table of `String` objects, in which each row contains the name, type, and description of a parameter. Some Web browsers use this information, although many do not. However, various Java tools (such as Integrated Development Environments) tend to use this information. (Parameter information helps Web page authors learn how to configure the applet.)
`init ()`	This method is called by the Web browser prior to any other method (except `setStub`), to give the applet a chance to initialize.
`isActive ()`	Returns a Boolean `true` value if the applet is active. An applet is made active just prior to a call to its `start` method and inactive just prior to a call to its `stop` method.
`newAudioClip (URL url)`	Returns a reference to an object that implements the `AudioClip` interface. This object is associated with `url`, which specifies the location and name of an audio file. Because `newAudioClip` is the only `static` method in `Applet`, applications can call this method to return objects implementing `AudioClip`, and then call `AudioClip` methods through these objects to play audio.
`play (URL url)`	This method plays the audio file whose location and name are specified by `url`. Nothing happens if this audio file cannot be found.
`play (URL url, String file)`	This method concatenates the location of an audio file (specified by `url`) and its name (specified by the `file` argument) into a single entity, and then calls `play (URL url)`.
`resize (Dimension d)`	This method requests that the applet's display area be resized to the width and height contained in `d`. This request is typically ignored by Web browsers.
`resize (int w, int h)`	This method requests that the applet's display area be resized to the width and height contained in `w` and `h`, respectively. This request is typically ignored by Web browsers.

TABLE 12.1 CONTINUED

Method	Description
`setStub (AppletStub as)`	This method is called by a Web browser to set an applet's stub to `as`. (Stubs will be discussed later in this chapter.)
`showStatus (String msg)`	This method requests that the contents of `msg` be displayed in the Web browser's status bar window.
`start ()`	This method is called by the Web browser to inform the applet that it should start its execution.
`stop ()`	This method is called by the Web browser to inform the applet that it should stop its execution.

Suppose you want to create a simple JFC application that plays an audio clip *(audio data stored in a sound file). To see how this task is accomplished, check out "Playing Audio Clips from a JFC Application in the "Troubleshooting" section at the end of this chapter.*

AWT APPLET HTML

AWT applets are identified to a Web browser by including the HTML `<APPLET>` tag in an HTML document. Each AWT applet is introduced with its own `<APPLET>` tag and terminated with a `</APPLET>` tag. `<APPLET>` contains several attributes that characterize an applet. These attributes include `CODE`, `WIDTH`, and `HEIGHT`.

The `CODE` attribute identifies the name of an applet's main class file. The `WIDTH` attribute identifies the width (in pixels or as a percentage) of the applet's display area. Finally, the `HEIGHT` attribute identifies the height (in pixels or as a percentage) of the applet's display area. To demonstrate an `<APPLET>` tag and its attributes, Listing 12.4 presents `MyApplet1.html`. This HTML document contains an `<APPLET>` tag for the `MyApplet1` applet.

LISTING 12.4 `MyApplet1.html`

```
<applet code="MyApplet1.class" width=100 height=100>
</applet>
```

Caution

As with other HTML tags, the `<APPLET>` and `</APPLET>` tags and their attribute names (such as `CODE`) are not case sensitive. However, attribute values are. When providing the `CODE` attribute's value, you must specify the main class file's name using the appropriate case of each letter. For example, the previously presented `MyApplet1` class requires an uppercase letter `M` and an uppercase letter `A` in its name. All the other letters are required to be lowercase. As a result, an attempt to specify the tag `<applet code="MYAPPLET1.class" width=100 height=100>` would most likely cause an error, because the Web browser's JVM would probably not be able to find a class file called `MYAPPLET1.class`.

Although CODE, WIDTH, and HEIGHT are the more commonly specified attributes, <APPLET> supports several additional attributes. All attributes are listed and described in Table 12.2.

TABLE 12.2 ATTRIBUTES FOR THE <APPLET> TAG

Attribute	Value	Description
CODE+	Class name	Defines the name of the class file that extends either java.applet.Applet or javax.swing.JApplet. Note: Either a CODE attribute or an OBJECT attribute must be specified.
WIDTH*	Number	Width (in pixels or a percentage) of the applet's display area.
HEIGHT*	Number	Height (in pixels or a percentage) of the applet's display area.
HSPACE	Number	Horizontal space (in pixels) between the applet and the rest of the HTML. Behaves identically to the <IMG> tag's HSPACE attribute value.
VSPACE	Number	Vertical space (in pixels) between the applet and the rest of the HTML. Behaves identically to the <IMG> tag's VSPACE attribute value.
ALIGN	Any of LEFT, RIGHT, TOP, TEXTTOP, MIDDLE, ABSMIDDLE, BASELINE, BOTTOM, ABSBOTTOM	Indicates the alignment of the applet in relation to the rest of the HTML. These values work the same as their <IMG> tag counterparts.
ALT	String	Specifies alternate text to be displayed by the browser if it is unable to display the actual applet. This attribute is only used if the browser understands the <APPLET> tag but is unable to display the applet. Otherwise, any HTML between the <APPLET> and </APPLET> tags is displayed.
ARCHIVE	Archive list	Contains a list of JAR files and other resources that should be "preloaded" by the Web browser before it begins execution.
OBJECT+	Serialized	Contains the name of the file that has a serialized representation of the applet. When reconstituting the applet, the init method will not be called because it is presumed to have been called on the serialized applet. However, the start method will be called. Note: Either a CODE attribute or an OBJECT attribute must be specified.
CODEBASE	URL	Identifies the directory that contains an applet's class files. If this attribute is not specified, the HTML document's URL is used.

** Required*
+ Either attribute (but not both) is required.

Suppose you need to design an applet that launches a separate window frame, in response to a button press. Later, you want to be able to close this frame and continue working with the applet. To see how this task is accomplished, check out "Launching a Frame from an Applet" in the "Troubleshooting" section at the end of this chapter.

SWING APPLETS

A Swing applet inherits capabilities from Swing's `JApplet` class (located in the `javax.swing` package). Like `Applet`, `JApplet` is ultimately derived from the `java.awt.Component` class. Therefore, Swing applets are also first-class GUI components. Figure 12.6 shows the `PNViewer4` Swing applet—that mirrors the `PNViewer2` Swing application—running in the Netscape Communicator Web browser. (Although not shown in this chapter, `PNViewer4`'s source code is included with the rest of this book's source code.)

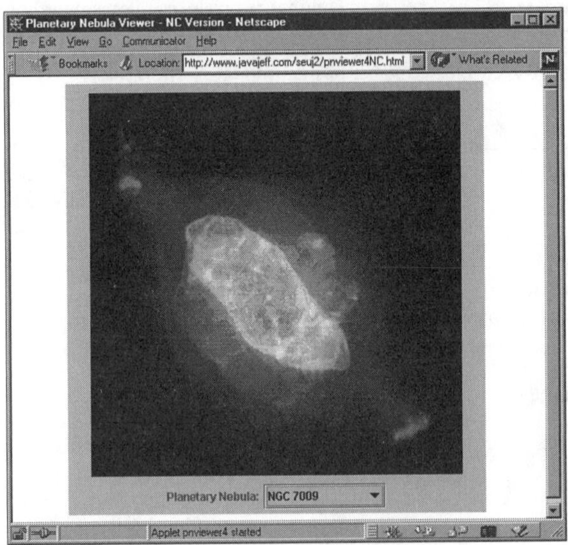

Figure 12.6
The `PNViewer4` applet runs in the Netscape Communicator Web browser.

To illustrate that a Swing applet can be run in multiple Web browsers, Figure 12.7 shows `PNViewer4` running in the Internet Explorer Web browser.

SDK 1.3's Applet Viewer program can also be used to run Swing applets. For example, the following code fragment shows how to run `PNViewer4` with the `pnviewer4IE.html` file. (Although not shown in this chapter, `pnviewer4IE.html` is included with the rest of this book's files.)

```
appletviewer pnviewer4IE.html
```

As with AWT applets, a Swing applet consists of one or more classes. However, one of these classes (the main class) must be declared `public` and must extend the `JApplet` class, in the `javax.swing` package. Listing 12.5 shows what this looks like, via an applet called `MyApplet2`.

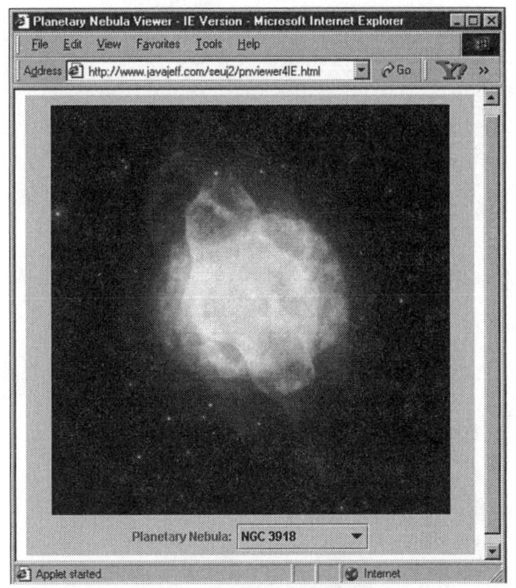

Figure 12.7
The PNViewer4 applet runs in the Internet Explorer Web browser.

LISTING 12.5 MyApplet2—THE WORLD'S SIMPLEST SWING APPLET

```
public class MyApplet2 extends javax.swing.JApplet
{
}
```

As with `MyApplet1`, the `MyApplet2` applet appears to be a simple applet. However, it also inherits more than 200 methods and field variables from ancestor classes. The hierarchy of these classes (along with `MyApplet2`) is shown in the following inheritance tree:

```
java.lang.Object
   |
   +----java.awt.Component
           |
           +----java.awt.Container
                   |
                   +----java.awt.Panel
                           |
                           +----java.applet.Applet
                                   |
                                   +----javax.swing.JApplet
                                           |
                                           +----MyApplet2
```

The only difference between this and the previous inheritance trees is the presence of the `javax.swing.JApplet` class. `MyApplet2` inherits `JApplet` methods that establish a Swing-based GUI environment for the Swing applet. This involves using different kinds of panes. Until panes are discussed in a later chapter, it's sufficient to think of *panes* as being analogous to the AWT's panels.

One item to note in the preceding inheritance tree is that `JApplet` inherits from `Applet`. This means that all of `Applet`'s methods (described in Table 12.1) are available to Swing applets.

Unlike AWT applets, Swing applets can use menu bars with drop-down menus. This is accomplished by constructing a `JMenuBar` object, constructing one or more `JMenu` objects, constructing one or more `JMenuItem` objects for each `JMenu` object, adding the `JMenuItem` objects to the appropriate `JMenu` objects, adding the `JMenu` objects to the `JMenuBar` object, and finally calling `JApplet`'s `setJMenuBar` method to establish the menu bar. To demonstrate this concept, Listing 12.6 shows the source code to the Swing-based `MenuApplet`.

LISTING 12.6 THE `MenuApplet` APPLET SOURCE CODE

```
// MenuApplet.java

import javax.swing.*;

public class MenuApplet extends JApplet
{
   public void init ()
   {
      JMenuBar menubar = new JMenuBar ();

      JMenu menuFile = new JMenu ("File");

      JMenuItem openItem = new JMenuItem ("Open");
      menuFile.add (openItem);

      JMenuItem saveItem = new JMenuItem ("Save");
      menuFile.add (saveItem);

      menubar.add (menuFile);

      JMenu menuHelp = new JMenu ("Help");

      JMenuItem aboutItem = new JMenuItem ("About");
      menuHelp.add (aboutItem);

      menubar.add (menuHelp);

      setJMenuBar (menubar);
   }
}
```

Don't worry about understanding Swing menus, because they will be discussed in a later chapter.

➔ **See** Chapter 16, "Building a GUI: Swing Style," **p. 519**

For now, note the `setJMenuBar (menubar)` method call. This method call is responsible for adding the menu bar to `MenuApplet`.

Listing 12.7 presents the HTML code for the `MenuApplet` applet. (Keep in mind that a Web browser will not properly run `MenuApplet` using this tag, because current Web browser implementations of JVMs do not recognize Swing. However, you can use Applet Viewer to run `MenuApplet` with this HTML.)

LISTING 12.7 THE MenuApplet APPLET HTML CODE

```
<applet code="MenuApplet.class" width=275 height=100>
</applet>
```

Now that you've seen MenuApplet's source and HTML code, check out Figure 12.8. As you can see, it's possible for Swing applets to contain menu bars with drop-down menus.

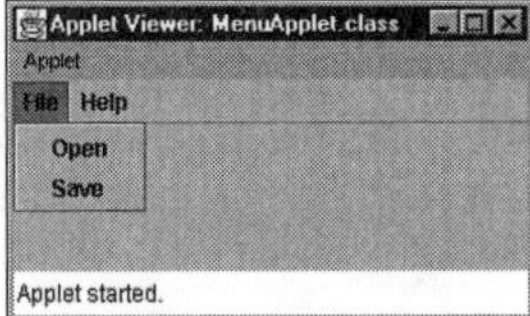

Figure 12.8 Menu bars with drop-down menus are possible with Swing applets.

SWING APPLET HTML

In the early days of Java and Web browsers, Sun would release a new version of Java and vendors would continually play catch-up by incorporating this version in the next release of their Web browsers. Because of the time lag between the release of a new Java version and the next release of Web browsers supporting this version, developers were often inconvenienced. They had to wait before they could take advantage of new Java features (or even use features that were previously bug-ridden but now fixed). And if developers were inconvenienced, users relying on the work of those developers were also inconvenienced. This problem reached its climax when Microsoft decided not to completely support Java 1.1 in Version 4 of its Internet Explorer Web browser.

Sun remedied this problem by creating a product called Java Plug-in. Java Plug-in takes advantage of a Web browser's plug-in architecture and serves as a bridge between the Web browser and Java runtime software. As a result, it is possible to run more advanced AWT applets and Swing applets in a Web browser environment.

Java Plug-in works in partnership with Netscape's <EMBED> tag and Microsoft's <OBJECT> tag. These tags make it possible to embed either an advanced AWT applet or a Swing applet in the context of the appropriate Web browser.

Listing 12.8 shows the HTML code required to run the PNViewer4 applet in the Netscape Communicator Web browser. This code makes use of Netscape's <EMBED> tag.

LISTING 12.8 THE PNViewer4 APPLET NETSCAPE COMMUNICATOR HTML CODE

```
<html>
  <head>
    <title>Planetary Nebula Viewer - NC Version</title>
  </head>

  <body>
    <embed code="PNViewer4.class"
       height=450
```

LISTING 12.8 CONTINUED

```
        width=450
        pluginspage="http://java.sun.com/products/plugin/1.3/plugin-install.html"
        type="application/x-java-applet;version=1.3">
    <noembed>
  </body>
</html>
```

Listing 12.9 shows the HTML code required to run the `PNViewer4` applet in the Internet Explorer Web browser. This code makes use of Microsoft's `<OBJECT>` tag.

LISTING 12.9 THE `PNViewer4` APPLET INTERNET EXPLORER HTML CODE

```
<html>
  <head>
    <title>Planetary Nebula Viewer - IE Version</title>
  </head>

  <body>
    <object classid="clsid:8AD9C840-044E-11D1-B3E9-00805F499D93"
            height=450
            width=450
            codebase="http://java.sun.com/products/plugin/1.3/
                      jinstall-12-win32.cab@Version=1,3,0,0">
      <param name="code" value="PNViewer4.class">
      <param name="type" value="application/x-java-applet;version=1.3">
    </object>
  </body>
</html>
```

If you want to learn more about Java Plug-in (including the `<EMBED>` and `<OBJECT>` tags), check out the *JavaWorld* article "*Plug into Java with Java Plug-in.*" This article is located at `http://www.javaworld.com/javaworld/jw-06-1999/jw-06-plugin.html`.

Netscape Communicator does not recognize the `<OBJECT>` tag and Internet Explorer does not recognize the `<EMBED>` tag. To create an HTML document that supports both Web browsers, you might think it a simple matter to specify both tags and let each Web browser ignore the inappropriate tag. Unfortunately, it's not a simple thing to support both tags. In fact, Sun has created a utility called HTML Converter to facilitate supporting multiple tags. For more information, visit Sun's HTML Converter Web page at `http://java.sun.com/products/plugin/1.3/features.html`.

SDK 1.3's Applet Viewer program can run Swing applets, as well as AWT applets, via an HTML document that contains an `<APPLET>` tag. Furthermore, because Applet Viewer "understands" several tags in addition to `<APPLET>`, you can take the HTML from either Listing 12.8 or 12.9 and run it using Applet Viewer.

Tip

It's a good idea to test your applet in both the Internet Explorer and Netscape Communicator Web browsers. This ensures that people viewing your applet in either Web browser will share the same experience–and guarantees correct HTML.

ARCHITECTURE

By now, you probably realize that AWT and Swing applets share a common architecture. The only real difference is the `JApplet` class—inherited by Swing applets. In this section, we'll take a look at some of this commonality.

STUBS AND CONTEXTS

How does the Web browser create a working applet from the `MyApplet1` class? Internally, the Web browser begins by creating an object from this class, as follows:

```
// Create an AWT applet.

MyApplet1 someName1 = new MyApplet1 ();
```

Note

Although `someName1` is shown for illustrative purposes, the Web browser is free to choose an appropriate name for the applet objects.

If you recall, no constructor was declared in the `MyApplet1` class. Instead, a default no-argument constructor is created by the compiler. This `MyApplet1 ()` constructor calls the `Applet ()` constructor to initialize the applet object. (This constructor call is not the same as calling the `init` method.) After the applet object is created, the Web browser calls the applet's `setStub` method, passing a reference to a *stub* (that is, an object that implements the `AppletStub` interface). The stub provides the means by which an applet interfaces with the Web browser. Several `Applet` methods (such as `isActive` and `getDocumentBase`) call corresponding `AppletStub` methods, via this stub.

One of `AppletStub`'s methods is `getAppletContext`. This method returns an applet's *context* (that is, a reference to an object that implements the `AppletContext` interface). This context corresponds to the HTML document that contains the applet. As with `AppletStub`, some of `Applet`'s methods (such as `getAudioClip` and `getImage`) call corresponding `AppletContext` methods.

After the stub has been set, the applet's life cycle begins.

LIFE CYCLE

Each AWT and Swing applet has a life cycle. The applet is initialized, started and stopped one or more times, and finally destroyed. The Web browser controls this life cycle by calling four methods (inherited from `Applet` and usually overridden): `init`, `start`, `stop`, and `destroy`.

The `init` method is called immediately after `setStub` and prior to any other method, and gives an applet a chance to initialize itself. `init` is the perfect place for the applet to construct its GUI. It will never again be called during the life of the applet.

The `start` method is called immediately after `init` and each time a Web page containing the applet is revisited. This method is the perfect place to start threads.

The `stop` method is called whenever a Web page containing the applet is replaced by another Web page, or just prior to a call to the `destroy` method. This method is the perfect place to stop threads.

The `destroy` method is called when a Web browser is terminating. This method is the perfect place to clean up any resources acquired during the `init` method call. Obviously, `destroy` will never again be called.

To demonstrate an applet's life cycle, Listing 12.10 provides the source code to an applet called `LifeCycle`.

LISTING 12.10 THE `LifeCycle` APPLET SOURCE CODE

```
// LifeCycle.java

public class LifeCycle extends java.applet.Applet
{
   public void init ()
   {
      System.out.println ("init () called");
   }

   public void start ()
   {
      System.out.println ("start () called");
   }

   public void stop ()
   {
      System.out.println ("stop () called");
   }

   public void destroy ()
   {
      System.out.println ("destroy () called");
   }
}
```

`LifeCycle` overrides `Applet`'s four life cycle methods. When each method is called, a string is sent to the standard output device. Depending on where this applet is run, this device corresponds to either a Web browser's *Java console* (a special window that is accessed from a Web browser's menu and displays any information sent to the standard output device) or an OS-specific command window.

> **Note**
>
> The `LifeCycle` class has been placed in a file called `LifeCycle.java`, and the spelling of the filename is identical to the spelling of the class name. This is no accident. Whenever source code specifies a `public` class, this source code must be saved to a file with the same name (including uppercase/lowercase sensitivity). Otherwise, the Java compiler will report an error. (Only one `public` class can be specified in any given source file.)

Before you can run `LifeCycle` (or any other applet), its source code must be compiled. Compiling applets is identical to compiling applications.

You will need some HTML code to "glue" this applet to a Web browser. Listing 12.11 shows a simple `<APPLET>` tag for running `LifeCycle`. The width and height of this applet have been set to zero because this applet does not output anything to its display area. (The standard output device, to which strings are sent, does not correspond to the applet's display area.)

LISTING 12.11 THE `LifeCycle` APPLET HTML CODE

```
<applet code="LifeCycle.class" width=0 height=0>
</applet>
```

Figure 12.9 shows Applet Viewer running `LifeCycle` and `LifeCycle`'s output being sent to a Windows 98 command window.

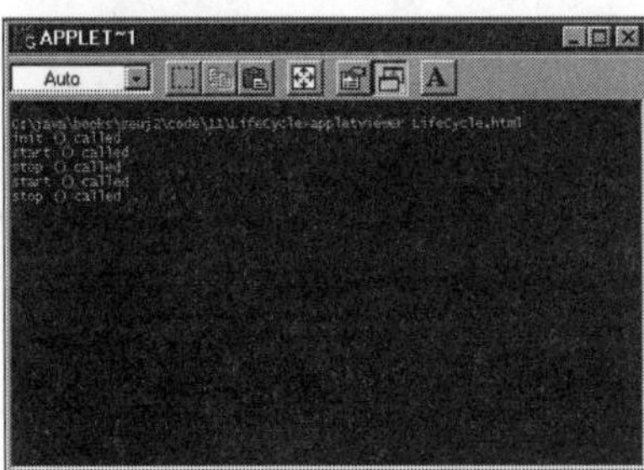

Figure 12.9
The `LifeCycle` applet output is sent to the Windows 98 command window.

You don't see the string `destroy () called` in the command window because Applet Viewer is still running. As soon as it terminates, `destroy () called` will be output to the command window.

CONFIGURING APPLETS

The Planetary Nebula Viewer programs (`PNViewer1`, `PNViewer2`, `PNViewer3`, and `PNViewer4`) have a design problem. The names of the images and image files are hard-wired into the source code. To view arbitrary images, you must make changes to each program's code and recompile.

As far as the Planetary Nebula Viewer applets (`PNViewer3` and `PNViewer4`) are concerned, it would be much better to specify the image descriptions and filenames using HTML, and allow the applet to dynamically load these descriptions and their associated image files. In other words, it should be possible to dynamically configure an applet.

The `<APPLET>` and `<OBJECT>` tags support dynamic configuration, via the optional `<PARAM>` tag. Each `<PARAM>` tag denotes a single parameter to the applet. (The `<EMBED>` tag does not make use of `<PARAM>` tags. Instead, parameters are treated as `<EMBED>` tag attributes.) If present, `<PARAM>` is situated between `<APPLET>` and `</APPLET>` or `<OBJECT>` and `</OBJECT>`.

The format of the `<PARAM>` tag is

```
<param name="some name" value="some value">
```

The name of the parameter is identified by `some name` and the value is identified by `some value`. (The double quote characters surrounding `some value` are not required if `some value` is a number.) For example, `<param name="image" value="orion.jpg">` specifies a parameter called `image` with a value set to `orion.jpg` whereas `<param name="age" value=23>` specifies a parameter called `age` with a value set to `23`.

If you recall from Table 12.1, the `Applet` class contains a method called `getParameter`. This method's `String` argument corresponds to the value of the `NAME` attribute in a `<PARAM>` tag. If a `<PARAM>` tag exists whose `NAME` attribute matches this argument, the value of the `VALUE` attribute is returned. Otherwise, `null` is returned. For example, using `<param name="image" value="orion.jpg">`, `getParameter ("image")` would return `orion.jpg`, whereas `getParameter ("image1")` would return `null`.

To get a feel for parameters, Listing 12.12 shows the source code to a `ShowPage` applet. When run, this applet causes the Web browser to load a Web page from a server located at the specified URL.

LISTING 12.12 THE `ShowPage` APPLET SOURCE CODE

```
// ShowPage.java

import java.applet.Applet;
import java.net.*;

public class ShowPage extends Applet
{
   public void init ()
   {
      String defaultURL = "http://www.javajeff.com";

      String url = getParameter ("url");
      if (url == null)
          url = defaultURL;

      try
      {
         getAppletContext ().showDocument (new URL (url));
      }
```

LISTING 12.12 CONTINUED

```
      catch (MalformedURLException e)
      {
         System.out.println ("DEBUG: " + url + " is malformed.");
      }
   }
}
```

The `init` method calls `getParameter ("url")` to obtain the value of a `<PARAM>` tag whose name matches `url`. If not found, `null` is returned and the default URL is used.

Earlier, you were introduced to the `AppletContext` interface and the `getAppletContext` method. (To recap, this method returns an object that implements `AppletContext`.) `AppletContext`'s `showDocument` method attempts to redirect the applet's Web page to the Web page associated with its URL argument. If this URL is not properly formed, `showDocument` throws a `MalformedURLException` object.

Listing 12.13 shows the HTML code for this applet.

LISTING 12.13 THE ShowPage APPLET HTML CODE

```
<applet code="ShowPage.class" width=0 height=0>
  <param name="URL" value="http://www.cnn.com">
</applet>
```

Note the value of the `<PARAM>` tag's `NAME` attribute: `URL`. This value is specified in uppercase, whereas the argument passed to `getParameter`—`url`—is specified in lowercase. This isn't a problem because `getParameter` treats `URL` and `url` as the same parameter.

APPLETS VERSUS APPLICATIONS

Many people associate applets with Java. They see graphical (and possibly audible) applets and conclude that this is what Java is all about. Nothing could be further from the truth. As useful and interesting as applets are, they are by no means all there is to Java. Java applications are just as important as applets. In fact, for many situations, applications are even more important.

When you plan to deploy a JFC-based program, you'll be faced with a major decision: Should this program be deployed as an applet or as an application? Understanding the architectural differences between these program categories can simplify this decision. And knowing how to convert between applications and applets can make this decision seem like child's play.

ARCHITECTURAL DIFFERENCES

Applications and applets have many differences. Applications are designed as standalone programs, whereas applets are designed to rely exclusively on a Web browser.

Note Sun's HotJava Web browser is a Java application that's capable of running applets.

Some of the differences between application and applet architectures include the following:

- An application's main class contains a special `static` method called `main`. This `main` method serves as the execution entry point for applications. Applets do not normally have a `main` method.
- When an application starts to run, no application object exists. In contrast, an applet cannot run until an applet object has been created.
- An applet's main class contains inherited or overridden life cycle methods. These methods are called by the Web browser at various times during an applet's life. Applications have no notion of a life cycle.
- By default, applications are not subjected to security restrictions, although a security manager can be installed. In contrast, applets are at the "mercy" of a Web browser's security manager. They can only carry out tasks that the security manager allows.
- Unlike applets, applications do not require an HTML document.

CONVERTING BETWEEN APPLETS AND APPLICATIONS

Due to architectural differences, the task of converting between applets and applications is not trivial. There are many things to think about. To assist you in this undertaking, take a look at the hybrid applet/application that's shown in Listing 12.14.

LISTING 12.14 THE `AppletAndApp` APPLET SOURCE CODE.

```
// AppletAndApp.java

import java.applet.*;
import java.awt.*;
import java.awt.event.*;
import java.io.*;
import java.net.*;
import java.util.*;

public class AppletAndApp extends Applet implements ActionListener
{
   static AppletAndApp aa;
   static Stub s;

   Image im;

   public void init ()
   {
      System.out.println ("Code base = " + getCodeBase ());
      System.out.println ("Document base = " + getDocumentBase ());

      System.out.println ("\ninit () called");
      System.out.println ("isActive () returns " + isActive ());
```

LISTING 12.14 CONTINUED

```
      // Create simple GUI.

      Button b = new Button ("Visit CNN");
      b.addActionListener (this);
      add (b);

      b = new Button ("Audio");
      b.addActionListener (this);
      add (b);

      // Obtain an Image object in preparation for loading.

      String imageName = getParameter ("image");

      if (imageName != null)
          im = getImage (getCodeBase (), imageName);
   }

   public void start ()
   {
      System.out.println ("start () called");
      System.out.println ("isActive () returns " + isActive ());
   }

   public void paint (Graphics g)
   {
      // Load and draw an image.

      if (im != null)
          g.drawImage (im, 0, 0, this);
   }

   public void actionPerformed (ActionEvent e)
   {
      if (e.getActionCommand ().equals ("Audio"))
      {
          String soundName = getParameter ("audio");

          if (soundName != null)
          {
              AudioClip ac = getAudioClip (getDocumentBase (),
                                           soundName);

              ac.play ();
          }

          return;
      }

      try
      {
          URL u = new URL ("http://www.cnn.com");
          getAppletContext ().showDocument (u);
      }
      catch (MalformedURLException exc) { System.out.println (e); }
   }
```

LISTING 12.14 CONTINUED

```
   public void stop ()
   {
      System.out.println ("stop () called");
      System.out.println ("isActive () returns " + isActive ());
   }

   public void destroy ()
   {
      System.out.println ("destroy () called");
      System.out.println ("isActive () returns " + isActive ());
   }

   public static void main (String [] args)
   {
      Frame frame = new Frame ("AppletAndApp as an Application");

      aa = new AppletAndApp ();

      frame.add (new Panel ().add (aa));

      // Create the frame's peer.  Peer is not visible.

      frame.addNotify ();

      aa.setStub (s = new Stub (args));
      aa.init ();

      frame.setSize (300, 200);
      frame.setVisible (true);

      s.setActive (true);
      aa.start ();

      frame.addWindowListener (new WindowAdapter ()
                               {
                                   public void windowClosing
                                                       (WindowEvent w)
                                   {
                                      s.setActive (false);
                                      aa.stop ();
                                      aa.destroy ();
                                      System.exit (0);
                                   }
                               });
   }
}

// The Stub class provides a mechanism for obtaining information from
// the run-time environment.  Typically, this environment is maintained
// by a Web browser.  For this program, a Web browser environment is
// being simulated.

class Stub implements AppletStub
{
   private boolean active = false;
```

Listing 12.14 Continued

```
private Hashtable ht = new Hashtable ();

private Context c;

// Create a new Stub object.  The application's array of command
// arguments are passed to this constructor, where they are saved
// in a Hashtable object, for later retrieval by the getParameter
// method.

Stub (String [] args)
{
   c = new Context (); // Create an applet context.

   // Make sure an even number of arguments has been passed.

   if ((args.length & 1) != 0)
       return;

   for (int i = 0; i < args.length; i += 2)
        ht.put (args [i], args [i + 1]);
}

// Return the current state of an applet.  During initialization,
// the applet is not active (and this method returns false).  The
// applet's active state is set to true just before the start
// method is called.

public boolean isActive ()
{
   return active;
}

// Return the complete URL of the HTML document containing the
// applet.  This URL includes the name of the document's file.
// NOTE: The code in this method could be improved.

public URL getDocumentBase ()
{
   URL u = null;

   try
   {
      u = new URL ("file:///" + (new File (".").getAbsolutePath ()) +
                   "/x.html"); // Use a fake document.
   }
   catch (MalformedURLException e) {}

   return u;
}

// Return the complete URL of the applet's .class file(s).  This
// method is often used with the getImage and getAudioClip
// methods to load image/audio files relative to the .class files.
// NOTE: The code in this method could be improved.
```

LISTING 12.14 CONTINUED

```
   public URL getCodeBase ()
   {
      URL u = null;

      try
      {
          u = new URL ("file:///" + new File (".").getAbsolutePath ());
      }
      catch (MalformedURLException e) {}

      return u;
   }

   // Return the value of the applet parameter, identified by the
   // name argument.  If not present, null is returned.  The Applet
   // class contains a getParameter method that calls this method.

   public String getParameter (String name)
   {
      return (String) ht.get (name);
   }

   // Return a reference to the applet's context.  The Applet class
   // contains a getAppletContext method that calls this method.

   public AppletContext getAppletContext ()
   {
      return c; // Return current applet context.
   }

   // Resize the applet.  The Applet class contains a pair of resize
   // methods that call this method. Note: Web browsers don't permit
   // applets from being resized.

   public void appletResize (int width, int height)
   {
   }

   // The following method is an extra method that is called to set
   // the value of the private active variable.

   public void setActive (boolean active)
   {
      this.active = active;
   }
}

// The Context class provides a mechanism to control the environment
// in which the program is running.  Typically, this environment is
// maintained by a Web browser.  For this program, a Web browser
// environment is being simulated.

class Context implements AppletContext
{
   // Load the file located by the url argument.  The Applet
```

Listing 12.14 Continued

```
// class contains a pair of getAudioClip methods that call
// this method.

public AudioClip getAudioClip (URL url)
{
   return Applet.newAudioClip (url);
}

// Prepare to load the image located by the url argument.  The
// image is loaded when needed (by one of Graphics' drawImage
// methods).  The Applet class contains a pair of getImage
// methods that call this method.

public Image getImage (URL url)
{
   Toolkit tk = Toolkit.getDefaultToolkit ();
   return tk.getImage (url);
}

// Fetch the Applet (identified by name) from the current HTML
// document.

public Applet getApplet (String name)
{
   return null;
}

// Return an enumeration to all Applets located on the current HTML
// page.

public Enumeration getApplets ()
{
   return null;
}

// Show the HTML document, located by the url argument, in the
// current Web browser window.

public void showDocument (URL url)
{
   System.out.println ("Showing document " + url);
}

// Show the HTML document, located by the url argument, in the
// Web browser window, identified by the frame argument.

public void showDocument (URL url, String frame)
{
   try
   {
      showDocument (new URL (url.toString () + frame));
   }
   catch (MalformedURLException e) {}
}

// Show a status message, identified by the message argument, in
```

```
    // the Web browser's status bar.  The Applet class contains a
    // showStatus method that calls this method.

    public void showStatus (String message)
    {
       System.out.println (message);
    }
}
```

AppletAndApp is designed to run in one of two modes. It runs in applet mode when run from either a Web browser or the Applet Viewer and it runs in application mode when run from the Java interpreter program.

AppletAndApp consists of three classes: AppletAndApp, Stub, and Context. Apart from the main method and a pair of field variables, all the logic in AppletAndApp is what you would expect from an applet. The Stub and Context classes support this logic when AppletAndApp is run in application mode. (Although functionality has been added to the Stub and Context classes, more work is required.)

If you want to experiment with this applet, you'll need an HTML document—for use with applet mode. Listing 12.15 shows the HTML code for AppletAndApp.

LISTING 12.15 THE AppletAndApp APPLET HTML CODE

```
<applet code="AppletAndApp.class" width=300 height=200>
  <param name="image" value="shuttle.jpg">
  <param name="audio" value="landing.au">
</applet>
```

To run AppletAndApp in applet mode, use the Applet Viewer AppletAndApp.html command. However, if you want to run this program in application mode, use java AppletAndApp image shuttle.jpg audio landing.au. (The image and sound files are included with the rest of this book's files.)

Note

When you run this program from Applet Viewer, pressing the button doesn't do anything. However, if you press this button from a Web browser, it takes you to the CNN Web site. (Applet Viewer is not a Web browser for viewing Web pages.)

Figure 12.10 shows AppletAndApp being run as an application.

Figure 12.10
The AppletAndApp program displays an image of the space shuttle, along with a pair of buttons.

When you run AppletAndApp in either mode, you'll notice a curious thing. The isActive method does not always work as expected. In application mode, isActive follows the behavior specified in the SDK documentation. However, in applet mode, this method does not work as advertised: It never seems to return a true value. (This strange behavior appears to be the result of a bug in the Netscape Communicator/Applet Viewer implementation of isActive, although there might be some other reason.)

Note

Further research into the isActive problem has led to the discovery of an entry in Sun's Bug database (located at http://developer.java.sun.com/developer/bugParade/bugs/4179136.html) for this method. This entry suggests that the SDK documentation should be modified to state "An applet is marked active just AFTER its start method is called. It becomes inactive just before its stop method is called." It would appear that either the documentation or the Netscape Web browser/Applet Viewer code for the isActive method should be changed. I'll leave it up to you to decide how you feel isActive should work in AppletAndApp.

TROUBLESHOOTING

BEEPING THE SYSTEM SPEAKER

How do I generate a beep from the system speaker?

The Toolkit class (located in the java.awt package) contains a beep method. You call this method to beep the system speaker, as demonstrated by the following Audio1 application.

```
// Audio1.java

import java.awt.*;

class Audio1
{
   public static void main (String [] args)
   {
      Toolkit tk = Toolkit.getDefaultToolkit ();
      tk.beep ();
      System.exit (0);
   }
}
```

The System.exit (0) method call is needed to ensure that this application terminates. It doesn't terminate because the Toolkit.getDefaultToolkit method call results in the AWT library being loaded, and a couple of threads starting. Even though the thread executing the main method terminates, these other threads continue to run, which keeps this program "alive." System.exit kills all threads, allows the application to "die."

PLAYING AUDIO CLIPS FROM A JFC APPLICATION

How do I create an application that plays audio clips?

The `Applet` class contains a `newAudioClip` method that can be called to load an audio clip. Once this audio clip has been loaded, `AudioClip`'s `play` and `stop` methods can be called to play this audio clip, and stop playing when necessary. The following `Audio2` application demonstrates using `newAudioClip` to load an audio clip, which is subsequently played.

```
// Audio2.java

import java.applet.*;
import java.net.*;

class Audio2
{
   public static void main (String [] args)
   {
      if (args.length != 1)
      {
          System.out.println ("usage: java Audio2 url");
          return;
      }

      try
      {
          URL url = new URL ("file:" + args [0]);

          AudioClip ac = Applet.newAudioClip (url);

          ac.play ();

          System.out.println ("Press any key to exit.");

          System.in.read ();

          ac.stop ();

          System.exit (0);
      }
      catch (Exception e)
      {
          System.out.println (e);
      }
   }
}
```

Suppose you have an audio clip file called `laugh.wav`. You can play this file by issuing the following command:

```
java Audio2 laugh.wav
```

LAUNCHING A FRAME FROM AN APPLET

How do I create an AWT applet that opens a frame when I press an applet button, and then closes the frame when I press a frame button?

In the applet's `init` method, you construct a GUI consisting of a single button. You then register an object to listen for button press events. When such an event occurs, you create and display a frame.

The frame is created with its own button that, when pressed, closes the frame. This is accomplished by registering an object that listens for press events from this button. In response, the listener calls the `dispose` method (inherited from `Frame`'s `Window` class parent) to close the frame. The following `MyApplet3` applet demonstrates this technique.

```
// MyApplet3.java

import java.awt.*;
import java.awt.event.*;

public class MyApplet3 extends java.applet.Applet
                       implements ActionListener
{
   Button b;

   public void init ()
   {
      b = new Button ("Open frame");
      b.addActionListener (this);
      add (b);
   }

   public void actionPerformed (ActionEvent e)
   {
      b.setEnabled (false);
      new MyFrame ("MyFrame", b);
   }
}

class MyFrame extends Frame implements ActionListener
{
   private Button launch;

   MyFrame (String title, Button launch)
   {
      super (title);

      // Assign launch argument to launch field.

      this.launch = launch;

      Button b = new Button ("Close Frame");
      b.addActionListener (this);

      Panel p = new Panel ();
      p.add (b);

      add (p);

      setSize (200, 80);
      setVisible (true);
   }
```

```
   public void actionPerformed (ActionEvent e)
   {
      dispose ();
      launch.setEnabled (true);
   }
}
```

If you would like to launch multiple frames, comment out the `b.setEnabled (false)` method call (in `MyApplet3`'s `actionPerformed` method) and the `launch.setEnabled (true)` method call (in `MyFrame`'s `actionPerformed` method). These two method calls are responsible for disabling the button prior to launching a frame, and enabling the button after disposing this frame. As a result, these method calls ensure that only one frame is launched at a time.

Why would you want to launch a frame from an applet? Suppose you need to construct an image gallery applet. You have a complex GUI that you want to display in the applet's display area, but you also need to be able to display images of various sizes. Instead of trying to figure out appropriate sizes for the `<APPLET>` tag's `WIDTH` and `HEIGHT` attributes, you could choose to display the GUI (minus the image) in the display area, and the image in a frame that is displayed from this GUI. Each time the frame is displayed, it might be given a new size, to match the size of the image it's displaying.

CHAPTER 13

Beginning AWT

In this chapter

by Geoff Friesen

WHAT IS THE AWT?

The *AWT* is a windowing framework that abstracts commonality from diverse platform-specific windowing systems (such as Windows GDI and UNIX Motif). Developers target the AWT and let each platform's Java runtime software handle the details of connecting the AWT to the platform's windowing system. This is in keeping with Java's portability mantra: "Write Once, Run Anywhere." (In other words, you should need to write your AWT code only once and have it run under the windowing system of any platform that supports Java.)

Perhaps the best way to start learning the AWT is to take a brief look at those Java packages that comprise this framework. Table 13.1 presents the names and contents of these packages.

TABLE 13.1 JAVA'S AWT PACKAGES

Package	Contents
`java.applet`	Interfaces and a class for constructing AWT applets. This functionality is also available to Swing applets.
`java.awt`	Classes and interfaces for constructing user interfaces, graphics contexts, and images, and obtaining information about the graphics environment.
`java.awt.color`	Classes for working with sophisticated color spaces.
`java.awt.datatransfer`	Classes and interfaces for transferring data between and within applications.
`java.awt.dnd`	Classes and interfaces for implementing drag and drop.
`java.awt.event`	Classes and interfaces for working with different kinds of events.
`java.awt.font`	Classes and interfaces for advanced font manipulation. (Used in the construction of portable software from an international perspective.)
`java.awt.geom`	Classes and an interface for working with Java 2D shapes.
`java.awt.im`	Classes and interfaces for working with the input method framework. (Used in the construction of portable software from an international perspective.)
`java.awt.im.spi`	Interfaces that enable the development of input methods for use in any Java environment. (Used in the construction of portable software from an international perspective.)
`java.awt.image`	Classes and interfaces for creating images, filtering images, and working with color models.
`java.awt.image.renderable`	Classes and interfaces for creating rendering-independent images.
`java.awt.print`	Classes and interfaces for printing.

The AWT packages contain nearly 300 classes and interfaces, which is a solid foundation on which to build. In fact, other JFC APIs—Swing, Accessibility, Java 2D, and Drag and Drop—are built on the AWT.

Because Java 2D and Drag and Drop are closely related to the AWT (from an architectural perspective), their classes and interfaces are stored in packages under the `java.awt` umbrella. A portion of Java 2D is stored in `java.awt.geom`, whereas the rest of this API is stored in other packages under `java.awt`. Furthermore, although most of Drag and Drop is stored in `java.awt.dnd`, some of this API is stored in `java.awt.datatransfer`.

GRAPHICS

One of the most enticing aspects of a computer is its capability to render graphical content. Right now, you're probably eager to use the AWT to create some graphics. However, before you can let your imagination and creativity run rampant, you first need to learn about the AWT's approach to drawing.

THE FUNDAMENTALS OF DRAWING

In the last chapter, you learned that JFC applets (or just applets for short) are assigned rectangular display areas in which to draw their output. These display areas (also known as *drawing surfaces*) are implemented as objects created from subclasses of the AWT's abstract `Component` class. Although `Component` will not be discussed until the next chapter, its influence is pervasive throughout the AWT. Keep this influence in mind as you read this chapter.

Note

Applications can also use drawing surfaces. However, because applications do not default to using these surfaces, you must explicitly create an application with a drawing surface in mind. Such applications are known as JFC applications. You will learn how to create JFC applications in later chapters.

Each drawing surface consists of small colored dots called *picture elements* (*pixels*) or *points*. The exact number of pixels on a drawing surface is controlled by that surface's width and height.

Tip

The `Component` class provides a `getSize` method that returns an object created from the `Dimension` class. This class contains two public field variables of type `int`—`width` and `height`—that represent a drawing surface's width and height (measured in pixels). Applets always inherit this method.

A drawing surface is mapped out with a two-dimensional coordinate system that locates each pixel on its surface. The pixel is identified by a coordinate pair—a pair of integer numbers that identify the horizontal and vertical distances (measured in pixels) from the origin (the pixel located in the upper-left corner of the drawing surface) to a pixel.

The horizontal distance from the origin is known as an *x-coordinate*, whereas the vertical distance from the same origin is known as a *y-coordinate*. The x-coordinate increases through positive values from left to right, whereas the y-coordinate increases through positive values from top to bottom.

Pixels are written out using the (`x`, `y`) format: `x` identifies the x-coordinate and `y` identifies the y-coordinate. The origin is written out as (`0`, `0`).

Figure 13.1 illustrates the AWT's coordinate system.

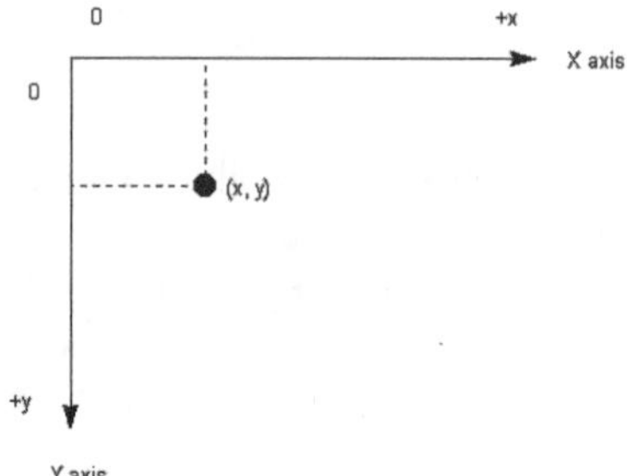

Figure 13.1
The AWT's coordinate system locates each pixel on a drawing surface.

A drawing surface is associated with an object that represents either a physical device (such as a video display or a printer) or a virtual device (such as an image memory buffer), and is capable of manipulating the appearance of this device's surface through a variety of method calls. This object is known as a *graphics context*. In essence, drawing on a drawing surface takes place by having the drawing surface object call graphics context methods, via the graphics context object, to render content on the underlying device's surface.

Graphics contexts are created by the AWT from subclasses of its abstract `Graphics` class. This class is located in the `java.awt` package.

The AWT uses a callback mechanism to handle drawing. Whenever a drawing surface must be updated, the AWT's drawing thread calls the drawing surface's `paint` method (either directly or indirectly) and passes a graphics context as an argument to this method. Code placed in `paint` calls graphics context methods, via this argument, to update the drawing surface.

In the previous chapter, you were briefly introduced to the `paint` method by way of two Planetary Nebula Viewer programs. The following code fragment provides another example of this method.

```
public void paint (Graphics g)
{
   g.drawString ("Hello World!", 10, 30);
}
```

In this example, the AWT calls the `paint` method to update the drawing surface. In response, `paint` calls the `drawString` method, via `Graphics` argument `g`, to draw the string `Hello World!` `10` pixels from the left-hand side and `30` pixels from the top of the drawing surface.

Caution

> The y-coordinate passed to `drawString` represents the location of an imaginary line on which the drawn characters (obtained from `drawString`'s `String` argument) rest. Because these characters are drawn upwards from this line (toward lower y-coordinates), you must exercise caution when choosing a y-coordinate. For example, if you were to choose 0 as the y-coordinate (as in `g.drawString ("Hello World!", 10, 0);`), you would not see `drawString`'s characters displayed on the drawing surface. After all, the characters would be drawn upwards, from y-coordinate 0 toward negative y-coordinates, and the AWT *clips* (doesn't draw) pixels located at negative x-/y-coordinates.

DRAWING TEXT

Normally, when it comes to drawing graphics, the first thing many people want to draw is *text* (characters organized into meaningful groups—such as words and sentences). A Java program can store text in `byte` arrays, `char` arrays, or `String` objects. These data structures contain only the 7-bit ASCII numbers (`byte` arrays) or 16-bit Unicode numbers (`char` arrays or `String` objects) that are associated with these characters. When text is displayed, these numbers are used in partnership with a graphics context's current font and color attributes the text's “look.” (Font and color are examined in more detail under the “Fonts ;” section, later in this chapter.)

provides several methods for drawing text. Each method takes advantage of an line on which the text rests. This line is known as a *baseline*. Although most char- ” on this baseline, the bottom parts of certain characters, such as `j` and `g`, drop s baseline. (Baseline is used when measuring fonts. Font measurement will be d later in this chapter.) These methods include

- `wBytes`
- `drawChars`
- `drawString`

The `drawBytes` method draws text from all or part of an array of bytes. This method has the following signature:

```
void drawBytes (byte [] text, int offset, int length, int x, int y)
```

Specifically, the text contained in the `byte` array is drawn using the graphics context's current font and color. The first text character is located at `text [offset]` and the number of text characters is specified by `length`. The leftmost text character is located `x` pixels from the left edge of the drawing surface. The baseline of these text characters is located `y` pixels from the top edge of the drawing surface.

Tip

> The capability to draw text from an array of bytes is useful when displaying files of information created by legacy programs. (Legacy programs typically use ASCII to store text.) When `drawBytes` is used to display this text, no conversion from ASCII to Unicode is required, which results in a performance boost.

The drawChars method draws text from all or part of an array of characters. This method has the following signature:

```
void drawChars (char [] text, int offset, int length, int x, int y)
```

The text contained in the char array is drawn using the graphics context's current font and color. The first text character is located at text [offset] and the number of text characters is specified by length. The leftmost text character is located x pixels from the left edge of the drawing surface. The baseline of these text characters is located y pixels from the top edge of the drawing surface.

Finally, the drawString method draws text from a String object. This method has the following signature:

```
void drawString (String text, int x, int y)
```

The text is drawn using the graphics context's current font and color. The leftmost text character is located x pixels from the left edge of the drawing surface. The baseline of these text characters is located y pixels from the top edge of the drawing surface.

Listing 13.1 presents source code to the DrawTextDemo applet. This applet illustrates the text drawing methods.

LISTING 13.1 THE DrawTextDemo APPLET SOURCE CODE

```
// DrawTextDemo.java

import java.awt.*;
import java.applet.Applet;

public class DrawTextDemo extends Applet
{
   public void paint (Graphics g)
   {
      byte [] barray = { 0x41, 0x42, 0x43 };

      char [] carray = { 'x', 'y', 'z' };

      String s = "Even more text!";

      g.drawBytes (barray, 0, barray.length, 10, 30);

      g.drawChars (carray, 0, carray.length, 10, 60);

      g.drawString (s, 10, 90);
   }
}
```

Note

Please refer to the previous chapter to learn how to execute an applet.

The DrawTextDemo applet displays all text contained in barray, carray, and s on its drawing surface. The default font and color of graphics context g controls the appearance of this text.

The y-coordinate of each baseline—30, 60, and 90—is chosen so one line of text will not overwrite the next line. (A better mechanism to control the baseline's location will be presented when font metrics are discussed.) Figure 13.2 shows `DrawTextDemo` running in the Applet Viewer.

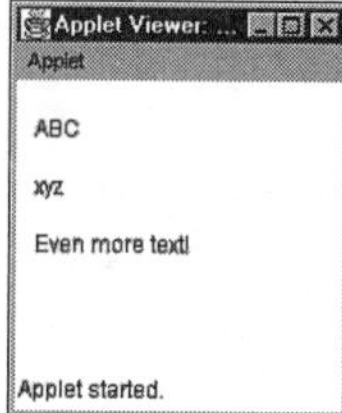

Figure 13.2
The `DrawTextDemo` applet shows text displayed using a graphics context's text drawing methods.

Caution

Be careful when choosing the starting array index and length passed to either `drawBytes` or `drawChars`. Each method adds the length to the starting array index. If this sum is negative or equals/exceeds the length of the array, either an `ArrayIndexOutOfBoundsException` object or a `StringIndexOutOfBoundsException` object will be thrown. (The same exceptions are thrown if the starting array index is negative or equals/exceeds the array's length.)

DRAWING SHAPES

Many graphics-based computer programs require various shapes to be drawn. For example, computer-assisted drafting programs (often referred to as CAD programs) make extensive use of lines and rectangles. The AWT's `Graphics` class provides methods for drawing several useful shapes. These shapes can be divided into the following categories:

- Lines and points
- Rectangles
- Ovals
- Arcs
- Polygons

LINES AND POINTS

In addition to text, lines and points are probably the most commonly drawn entities. To accomplish this task, `Graphics` provides a method called `drawLine`. This method has the following signature:

```
void drawLine (int x1, int y1, int x2, int y2)
```

A line of pixels is drawn using the graphics context's current color. This line starts at (`x1`, `y1`) and continues to (`x2`, `y2`). However, a point is drawn instead of a line if `x1` equals `x2` and `y1` equals `y2`.

To illustrate drawing lines and points, Listing 13.2 presents source code to an applet called DrawLinePointDemo.

LISTING 13.2 THE DrawLinePointDemo APPLET SOURCE CODE

```
// DrawLinePointDemo.java

import java.awt.*;
import java.applet.Applet;

public class DrawLinePointDemo extends Applet
{
   public void paint (Graphics g)
   {
      // Get the width and height of the applet's drawing surface.

      int width = getSize ().width;
      int height = getSize ().height;

      g.drawLine (0, 0, width - 1, height - 1);
      g.drawLine (0, height - 1, width - 1, 0);

      int centerX = width / 2;
      int centerY = height / 2;

      for (int row = -5; row < 5; row++)
           for (int col = -5; col < 5; col++)
                g.drawLine (centerX + col, centerY + row,
                            centerX + col, centerY + row);
   }
}
```

The DrawLinePointDemo applet displays two intersecting diagonal lines on its drawing surface. A rectangular bull's-eye is drawn around this intersection. Figure 13.3 shows DrawLinePointDemo running in the Applet Viewer.

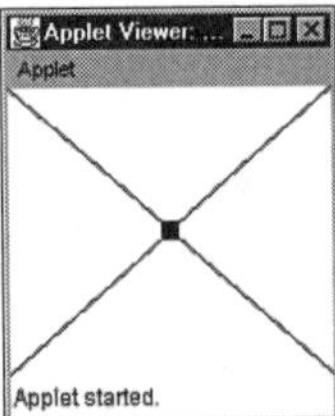

Figure 13.3
The DrawLinePointDemo applet shows lines and points displayed using a graphics context's drawLine method.

Caution

DrawLinePointDemo introduces a pair of for loops in its paint method to draw the bull's-eye. However, in most situations, loops should not be placed in paint. The reason for this restriction has to do with performance.

A drawing surface's paint method is called whenever it needs updating. This can occur if the drawing surface was partially or completely covered by some other window and is now being made visible. If `paint` takes too long to execute, you'll notice a decrease in your program's performance. To be responsive, the `paint` method (or methods) should execute as quickly as possible. Large loops slow down this execution.

RECTANGLES

Rectangles can be drawn by using the `drawLine` method. However, this is not necessary because `Graphics` provides several methods for drawing and filling various kinds of rectangles. Except for `clearRect`, each method draws either a solid rectangle or the outline of a rectangle using a graphics context's current color. These methods include

- `drawRect`
- `fillRect`
- `clearRect`
- `drawRoundRect`
- `fillRoundRect`
- `draw3DRect`
- `fill3DRect`

The `drawRect` method draws the outline of a rectangle. This method has the following signature:

```
void drawRect (int x, int y, int width, int height)
```

The rectangle is drawn with an upper-left corner located at (`x`, `y`) and a lower-right corner located at (`x + width`, `y + height`).

In contrast, the `fillRect` method draws a solid rectangle. This method has the following signature:

```
void fillRect (int x, int y, int width, int height)
```

The rectangle is drawn with an upper-left corner located at (`x`, `y`) and a lower-right corner located at (`x + width - 1`, `y + height - 1`). The filled rectangle is one pixel smaller to the right and bottom than requested. (This is standard practice for several rectangle and non-rectangle methods.)

Note

It might interest you to know that the practice of creating a filled rectangle, one pixel smaller to the right and bottom than requested, originated in drawing 3D objects with polygons (multi-sided shapes). The idea was to avoid drawing the same pixel twice, because many graphics routines place filled rectangles next to each other.

The `clearRect` method draws a solid rectangle by filling it with the drawing surface's current background color. (This color is NOT the same as a graphics context's current color.)

This method is commonly used to clear all pixels from a drawing surface, and has the following signature:

```
void clearRect (int x, int y, int width, int height)
```

The rectangle is drawn with an upper-left corner at (x, y), and a lower-right corner at (x + width - 1, y + height - 1).

The drawRoundRect method draws the outline of a rectangle with rounded corners. This method has the following signature:

```
void drawRoundRect (int x, int y, int width, int height,
                    int arcWidth, int arcHeight)
```

The rectangle is drawn with an upper-left corner located at (x, y) and a lower-right corner located at (x + width, y + height). The horizontal diameter of each corner arc is specified by arcWidth and the vertical diameter of each arc is specified by arcHeight.

Figure 13.4 illustrates a rounded rectangle with various dimensions, including height, width, and arc width/height diameters (for its rounded corners).

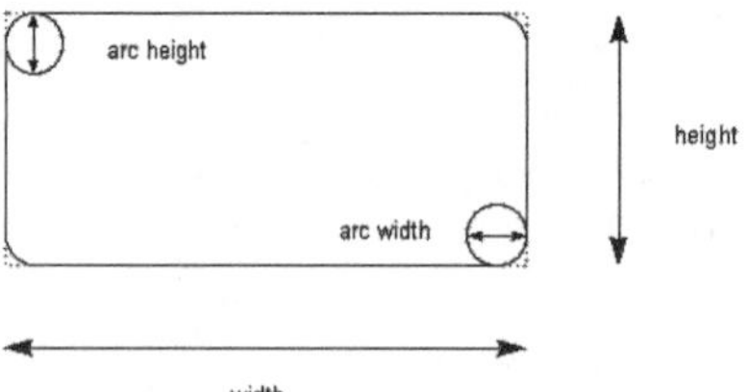

Figure 13.4
A rounded rectangle's four corners have the same arc widths and the same arc heights. However, the arc width can differ from the arc height.

The fillRoundRect method draws a solid rectangle with rounded corners. This method has the following signature:

```
void fillRoundRect (int x, int y, int width, int height,
                    int arcWidth, int arcHeight)
```

The rectangle is drawn with an upper-left corner located at (x, y) and a lower-right corner located at (x + width - 1, y + height - 1). The horizontal diameter of each corner arc is specified by arcWidth and the vertical diameter of each arc is specified by arcHeight.

Tip

The drawRoundRect and fillRoundRect methods can be used to draw circles or ellipses by making arcWidth the same as width and arcHeight the same as height. However, Graphics provides other methods better suited to this task.

The draw3DRect method draws the outline of a rectangle with a 3D appearance. This method has the following signature:

```
void draw3DRect (int x, int y, int width, int height, boolean raised)
```

The rectangle is drawn with an upper-left corner located at (x, y) and a lower-right corner located at (x + width, y + height). The edges of the rectangle are highlighted so that they appear to be beveled and lit from the upper-left corner. The rectangle appears raised if raised is true or sunken if raised is false. If the current color is black, raised has no effect.

Finally, the fill3DRect method draws a solid rectangle with a 3D appearance. This method has the following signature:

```
void fill3DRect (int x, int y, int width, int height, boolean raised)
```

Apart from drawing a solid rectangle with a 3D appearance (and the fact that the resulting rectangle is one pixel narrower and one pixel shorter), this method is basically the same as draw3DRect.

Listing 13.3 presents source code to the DrawRectangleDemo applet. This applet illustrates the rectangle methods.

LISTING 13.3 THE DrawRectangleDemo APPLET SOURCE CODE

```
// DrawRectangleDemo.java

import java.awt.*;
import java.applet.Applet;

public class DrawRectangleDemo extends Applet
{
   public void paint (Graphics g)
   {
      // Get the width and height of the applet's drawing surface.

      int width = getSize ().width;
      int height = getSize ().height;

      int rectWidth = (width - 50) / 3;
      int rectHeight = (height - 70) / 2;

      int x = 5;
      int y = 5;

      g.drawRect (x, y, rectWidth, rectHeight);

      g.drawString ("drawRect", x, rectHeight + 30);

      x += rectWidth + 20;

      g.fillRect (x, y, rectWidth, rectHeight);

      // Calculate a border area with each side equal to 25% of
      // the rectangle's width.

      int border = (int) (rectWidth * 0.25);

      // Clear 50% of the filled rectangle.
```

LISTING 13.3 CONTINUED

```
        g.clearRect (x + border, y + border,
                     rectWidth - 2 * border, rectHeight - 2 * border);

        g.drawString ("fillRect/clearRect", x, rectHeight + 30);

        x += rectWidth + 20;

        g.drawRoundRect (x, y, rectWidth, rectHeight, 15, 15);

        g.drawString ("drawRoundRect", x, rectHeight + 30);

        x = 5;
        y += rectHeight + 40;

        g.fillRoundRect (x, y, rectWidth, rectHeight, 15, 15);

        g.drawString ("fillRoundRect", x, y + rectHeight + 25);

        x += rectWidth + 20;

        g.setColor (Color.yellow);
        for (int i = 0; i < 4; i++)
             g.draw3DRect (x + i * 2, y + i * 2,
                           rectWidth - i * 4, rectHeight - i * 4, false);
        g.setColor (Color.black);

        g.drawString ("draw3DRect", x, y + rectHeight + 25);

        x += rectWidth + 20;

        g.setColor (Color.yellow);
        g.fill3DRect (x, y, rectWidth, rectHeight, true);
        g.setColor (Color.black);

        g.drawString ("fill3DRect", x, y + rectHeight + 25);
    }
}
```

The `DrawRectangleDemo` applet divides its drawing surface into six regions. A separate kind of rectangle is drawn in each region. For the rectangle created by `fillRect`, `clearRect` is used to clear 50% of this rectangle.

Because a 3D rectangle's effects cannot be seen with a black color, `DrawRectangleDemo` changes the current color of its graphics context to yellow. Figure 13.5 shows `DrawRectangleDemo` running under Applet Viewer.

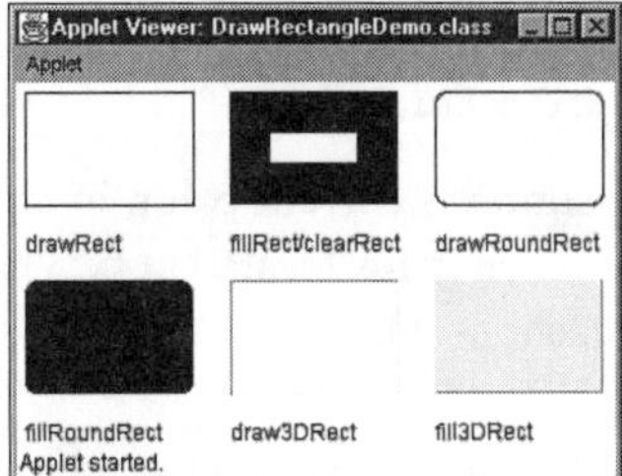

Figure 13.5
The `DrawRectangle Demo` applet shows various kinds of rectangles displayed using a graphics context's rectangle methods.

OVALS

There is a lot to be said for curved shapes. After all, cars wouldn't drive very well with rectangular wheels. A perfectly curved and closed shape is an *oval*.

It is important to make a distinction between two kinds of ovals: circles and ellipses. A *circle* is an oval with a single center. This occurs when the oval's width and height are identical. An *ellipse* is an oval with two centers. If the width is greater than the height, a short and fat oval results. However, if the height is greater than the width, a tall and skinny oval results.

Tip

On some video displays, because of screen curvature, an oval might look like a circle when viewed in certain spots, and an ellipse when viewed in other spots. If you notice this behavior, try adjusting your video display's screen adjustment controls.

`Graphics` provides a pair of methods for drawing ovals:

- `drawOval`
- `fillOval`

The `drawOval` method draws the outline of an oval. This method has the following signature:

```
void drawOval (int x, int y, int width, int height)
```

The outline is drawn, using the graphics context's current color, in an imaginary bounding rectangle. The upper-left corner of this rectangle is located at (`x`, `y`) and the lower-right corner is located at (`x + width`, `y + height`). Figure 13.6 illustrates an oval drawn in a bounding rectangle.

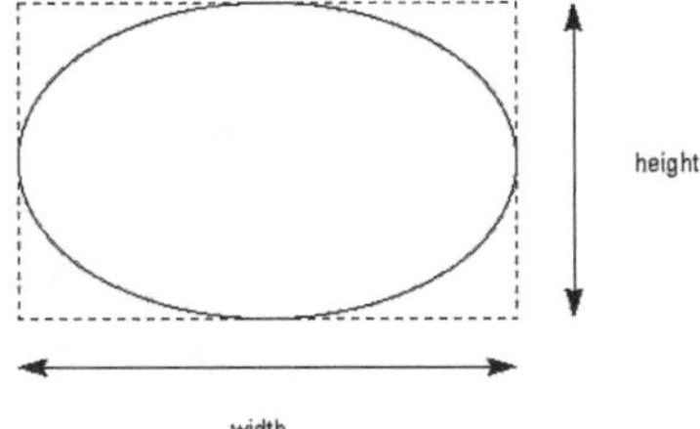

Figure 13.6
An oval is drawn inside an imaginary bounding rectangle.

The `fillOval` method draws a solid oval. This method has the following signature:

```
void fillOval (int x, int y, int width, int height)
```

The solid oval is drawn, using the graphics context's current color, in an imaginary bounding rectangle. The upper-left corner of this rectangle is located at (x, y) and the lower-right corner is located at (`x + width - 1`, `y + height - 1`).

Note

There is no technical reason for the `fillOval` method filling a solid oval in a rectangular area one pixel smaller horizontally and vertically than the area defined by the `drawOval` method. In fact, the `fillOval` method could have been designed to draw from `(x, y)` to `(x + width, y + height)`. However, because `fillOval` was designed to behave in a manner consistent with the other "fill" methods, it adopts the same behavior.

To illustrate these methods, Listing 13.4 presents source code to the `DrawOvalDemo` applet.

LISTING 13.4 THE `DrawOvalDemo` APPLET SOURCE CODE

```
// DrawOvalDemo.java

import java.awt.*;
import java.applet.Applet;

public class DrawOvalDemo extends Applet
{
   public void paint (Graphics g)
   {
      // Get the width and height of the applet's drawing surface.

      int width = getSize ().width;
      int height = getSize ().height;

      g.drawOval (0, 0, width - 1, height - 1);

      g.fillOval (0, width / 4, width / 2, height / 2);
      g.fillOval (width / 2, width / 4, width / 2, height / 2);
   }
}
```

The `DrawOvalDemo` applet displays an oval outline with two solid ovals inside this outline. Figure 13.7 shows `DrawOvalDemo` running in the Applet Viewer.

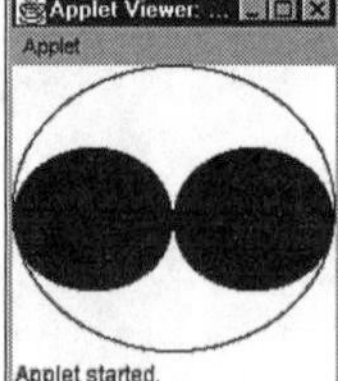

Figure 13.7
The `DrawOvalDemo` applet shows ovals displayed using a graphics context's oval methods.

ARCS

An *arc* is a piece of an oval. `Graphics` provides two methods for drawing arcs:

- `drawArc`
- `fillArc`

The `drawArc` method draws the outline of an arc. This method has the following signature:

```
void drawArc (int x, int y, int width, int height, int startAngle,
              int endAngle)
```

The outline is drawn, using the graphics context's current color, in an imaginary bounding rectangle. The upper-left corner of this rectangle is located at (`x`, `y`) and the lower-right corner is located at (`x + width`, `y + height`). The arc begins at `startAngle` and continues for `arcAngle` degrees. A `startAngle` of 0 degrees represents the three o'clock position. A positive `arcAngle` value causes the arc to be drawn in a counter-clockwise rotation, whereas a negative value causes the arc to be drawn in a clockwise rotation. Figure 13.8 illustrates an arc drawn in a bounding rectangle.

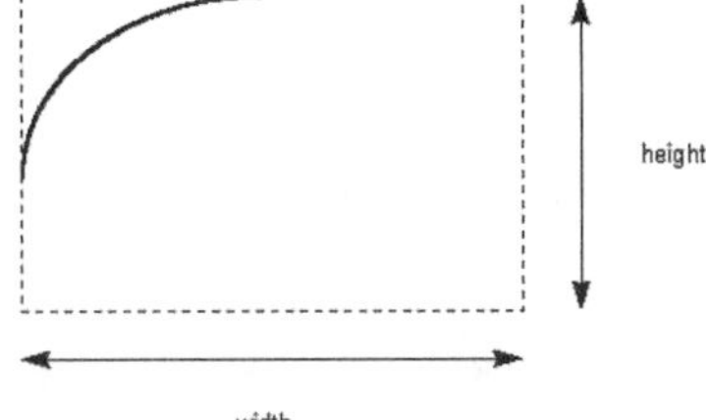

Figure 13.8
An arc is drawn inside an imaginary bounding rectangle.

The `fillArc` method draws a solid arc—a pie-shaped wedge—by filling all pixels from the arc to the origin of its bounding rectangle. This method has the following signature:

```
void fillArc (int x, int y, int width, int height, int startAngle,
              int endAngle)
```

The solid arc is drawn, using the graphics context's current color, in an imaginary bounding rectangle. The upper-left corner of this rectangle is located at (`x`, `y`) and the lower-right corner is located at (`x + width - 1`, `y + height - 1`). Apart from the facts that a solid arc is being drawn and that the rectangle's lower-right corner is one pixel closer to the upper-left corner, `fillArc` behaves identically to `drawArc`.

Listing 13.5 presents source code to a `DrawArcDemo` applet that illustrates these methods.

LISTING 13.5 THE `DrawArcDemo` APPLET SOURCE CODE

```
// DrawArcDemo.java

import java.awt.*;
import java.applet.Applet;
```

Listing 13.5 Continued

```
public class DrawArcDemo extends Applet
{
   public void paint (Graphics g)
   {
      // Get the width and height of the applet's drawing surface.

      int width = getSize ().width;
      int height = getSize ().height;

      g.drawArc (0, 0, width, height, 0, 90);

      g.fillArc (0, 0, width, height, 90, 90);
   }
}
```

This applet displays an arc outline rotated counter-clockwise from three o'clock to twelve o'clock and a solid arc rotated counter-clockwise from twelve o'clock to nine o'clock. Figure 13.9 shows `DrawArcDemo` running in the Applet Viewer.

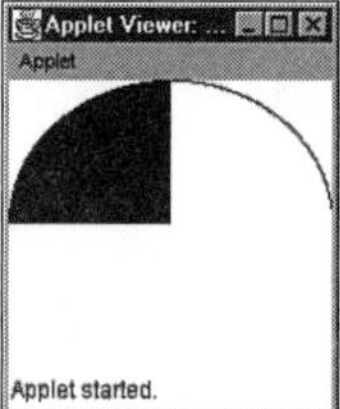

Figure 13.9
The `DrawArcDemo` applet shows arcs displayed using a graphics context's arc methods.

Polygons

Computer games (such as flight simulators) make extensive use of *polygons* (multisided shapes). Polygons are drawn by connecting line segments to a sequence of points laid out in some kind of path.

There are two varieties of polygons: closed polygons and open polygons. A closed polygon has a line segment connecting the final point to the first point, whereas an open polygon does not have this connection.

`Graphics` provides the following methods for drawing and filling polygons:

- `drawPolyline`
- `drawPolygon`
- `fillPolygon`

The `drawPolyline` method draws the outline of an open polygon. This method has the following signature:

```
void drawPolyline (int [] xPoints, int [] yPoints, int numPoints)
```

The `xPoints` and `yPoints` arrays identify coordinates of points that lie on the polygon's path. The number of points is identified by `numPoints`. The path is drawn, using the graphics context's current color, by connecting these points with line segments. The polygon is left open.

The `drawPolygon` method draws the outline of a closed polygon. This method has the following signature:

```
void drawPolygon (int [] xPoints, int [] yPoints, int numPoints)
```

This method is identical to the previous method except that the polygon is automatically closed by drawing a line segment from the last point to the first point.

The `fillPolygon` method draws a solid polygon. This method has the following signature:

```
void fillPolygon (int [] xPoints, int [] yPoints, int numPoints)
```

This method is identical to `drawPolygon` except that it also fills in the polygon's interior with the graphics context's current color.

To illustrate polygons, Listing 13.6 presents source code to an applet called `DrawPolygonDemo`.

LISTING 13.6 THE `DrawPolygonDemo` APPLET SOURCE CODE

```
// DrawPolygonDemo.java

import java.awt.*;
import java.applet.Applet;

public class DrawPolygonDemo extends Applet
{
   public void paint (Graphics g)
   {
      // Get the width and height of the applet's drawing surface.

      int width = getSize ().width;
      int height = getSize ().height;

      int [] xp1 = { 30, 120, 70 };
      int [] yp1 = { 90, 30, 110 };

      g.drawPolygon (xp1, yp1, xp1.length);

      int [] xp2 = { 90, 170, 130 };
      int [] yp2 = { 150, 120, 150 };

      g.drawPolyline (xp2, yp2, xp2.length);

      int [] xp3 = { 130, 170, 150 };
      int [] yp3 = { 50, 90, 120 };

      g.fillPolygon (xp3, yp3, xp3.length);
   }
}
```

The DrawPolygonDemo applet displays a pair of closed and open polygon outlines along with a filled polygon. Figure 13.10 shows DrawPolygonDemo running in the Applet Viewer.

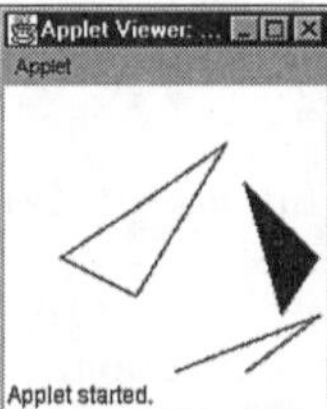

Figure 13.10 The DrawPolygonDemo applet shows polygons displayed using a graphics context's polygon methods.

Caution

Care is required when creating polygon arrays. If either array does not have numPoints elements, an ArrayIndexOutOfBoundsException object is thrown.

UTILITY CLASSES AND INTERFACES

The AWT provides several utility classes and one interface that simplify working with graphics. These include

- Point
- Dimension
- Rectangle
- Polygon
- Shape

Point

The Point class (located in the java.awt package) encapsulates the coordinates of a point. This class is commonly used by methods that return a pair of coordinates.

Table 13.2 presents Point's fields and methods (except for a handful of overridden Java 2D methods) that are publicly accessible.

TABLE 13.2 INSIDE THE AWT'S Point CLASS

Member	Description
x	This int field specifies the point's x-coordinate.
y	This int field specifies the point's y-coordinate.
Point ()	Initializes a Point object to (0, 0).
Point (int x, int y)	Initializes a Point object to (x, y).
Point (Point p)	Initializes a Point object to the contents of p.

TABLE 13.2 CONTINUED

Member	Description
`equals (Object o)`	Compares the current `Point` object with `o` (which must be a `Point`) for equality. A Boolean `true` value is returned if they are equal.
`getLocation ()`	Returns a copy of the current `Point` object.
`move (int x, int y)`	Moves the x-coordinate to `x` and the y-coordinate to `y`.
`setLocation (int x, int y)`	This method is identical to `move`.
`setLocation (Point p)`	Sets the current `Point` object to the contents of `p`.
`toString ()`	Returns a `String` object containing a representation of the current `Point` object.
`translate (int dx, int dy)`	Translates the coordinates of the current `Point` object by adding `dx` to the x-coordinate and `dy` to the y-coordinate.

`Dimension`

The `Dimension` class (located in the `java.awt` package) encapsulates the width and height dimensions of a shape.

Table 13.3 presents `Dimension`'s fields and methods (except for a handful of overridden Java 2D methods) that are publicly accessible.

TABLE 13.3 INSIDE THE AWT'S `Dimension` CLASS

Member	Description
`width`	This `int` field specifies the shape's width dimension.
`height`	This `int` field specifies the shape's height dimension.
`Dimension ()`	Initializes a `Dimension` object to a height and width of zero.
`Dimension (Dimension d)`	Initializes a `Dimension` object to the contents of `d`.
`Dimension (int w, int h)`	Initializes a `Dimension` object to a width of `w` and a height of `h`.
`equals (Object o)`	Compares the current `Dimension` object with `o` (which must be a `Dimension`) for equality. A Boolean `true` value is returned if they are equal.
`getSize ()`	Returns a copy of the current `Dimension` object.
`setSize (Dimension d)`	Sets the size of the current `Dimension` object to the contents of `d`.
`setSize (int w, int h)`	Sets the size of the current `Dimension` object to a width of `w` and a height of `h`.
`toString ()`	Returns a `String` object containing a representation of the current `Dimension` object.

Rectangle

The `Rectangle` class (located in the `java.awt` package) encapsulates the coordinates and dimensions of a rectangular shape.

Table 13.4 presents `Rectangle`'s fields and methods (except for a handful of overridden and implemented Java 2D methods) that are publicly accessible.

TABLE 13.4 INSIDE THE AWT'S `Rectangle` CLASS

Member	Description
`x`	This `int` field specifies the shape's upper-left corner x-coordinate.
`y`	This `int` field specifies the shape's upper-left corner y-coordinate.
`width`	This `int` field specifies the shape's width dimension.
`height`	This `int` field specifies the shape's height dimension.
`Rectangle ()`	Initializes a `Rectangle` object to an upper-left corner at (0, 0), a width of zero, and a height of zero.
`Rectangle (Dimension d)`	Initializes a `Rectangle` object to an upper-left corner at (0, 0) and a width/height specified by the contents of `d`.
`Rectangle (int w, int h)`	Initializes a `Rectangle` object to an upper-left corner at (0, 0), a width of `w` and a height of `h`.
`Rectangle (int x, int y, int w, int h)`	Initializes a `Rectangle` object to an upper-left corner at (`x`, `y`), a width of `w` and a height of `h`.
`Rectangle (Point p)`	Initializes a `Rectangle` object to an upper-left corner specified by the contents of `p`, a width of zero, and a height of zero.
`Rectangle (Point p, Dimension d)`	Initializes a `Rectangle` object to an upper-left corner specified by the contents of `p` and a width/height specified by the contents of `d`.
`Rectangle (Rectangle r)`	Initializes a `Rectangle` object to the contents of `r`.
`add (int x, int y)`	Adds the point specified by (`x`, `y`) to the current `Rectangle` object. The resulting rectangle is the smallest rectangle containing the original rectangle and point.
`add (Point p)`	Adds the point specified by `p` to the current `Rectangle` object. The resulting rectangle is the smallest rectangle containing the original rectangle and point.

TABLE 13.4 CONTINUED

Member	Description
`add (Rectangle r)`	Adds the rectangle specified by `r` to the current `Rectangle` object. The resulting rectangle is the union of the two rectangles.
`contains (int x, int y)`	Returns a Boolean `true` value if the point specified by (`x`, `y`) lies inside the boundaries of the current `Rectangle` object.
`contains (int x, int y, int w, int h)`	Returns a Boolean `true` value if the rectangle specified by (`x`, `y`), width `w`, and height `h` lies inside the boundaries of the current `Rectangle` object.
`contains (Point p)`	Returns a Boolean `true` value if the point specified by `p` lies inside the boundaries of the current `Rectangle` object.
`contains (Rectangle r)`	Returns a Boolean `true` value if the rectangle specified by `r` lies inside the boundaries of the current `Rectangle` object.
`equals (Object o)`	Compares the current `Rectangle` object with `o` (which must be a `Rectangle`) for equality. A Boolean `true` value is returned if they are equal.
`getBounds ()`	Returns a copy of the current `Rectangle` object.
`getDimension ()`	Returns a `Dimension` object containing the width and height of the current `Rectangle` object.
`getLocation ()`	Returns a `Point` object containing the upper-left corner coordinates of the current `Rectangle` object.
`grow (int h, int v)`	Grows the current `Rectangle` object by `h` units on both the left and right sides and `v` units on both the top and bottom. The new upper-left corner is located at (`x - h`, `y - v`), the new `width` is `2 * h` plus the old `width`, and the new `height` is `2 * v` plus the old `height`. If negative values are supplied for `h` and `v`, the rectangle shrinks accordingly.
`intersection (Rectangle r)`	Returns a new `Rectangle` object that contains the intersection of the current `Rectangle` object with `r`.
`intersects (Rectangle r)`	Returns a Boolean `true` value if the current `Rectangle` object and `r` intersect.
`setBounds (int x, int y, int w, int h)`	Sets the bounds of the current `Rectangle` object to `x`, `y`, `w`, and `h`.
`setBounds (Rectangle r)`	Sets the bounds of the current `Rectangle` object to the contents of `r`.

TABLE 13.4 CONTINUED

Member	Description
`setLocation (int x, int y)`	Sets the location of the current `Rectangle` object's upper-left corner to the location specified by (x, y).
`setLocation (Point p)`	Sets the location of the current `Rectangle` object's upper-left corner to the contents of `p`.
`setSize (Dimension d)`	Sets the size of the current `Rectangle` object to the width and height specified by `d`.
`setSize (int w, int h)`	Sets the size of the current `Rectangle` object to the width specified by `w` and height specified by `h`.
`toString ()`	Returns a `String` object containing a representation of the current `Rectangle` object.
`translate (int dx, int dy)`	Translates the coordinates of the current `Rectangle` object by adding `dx` to the x-coordinate and `dy` to the y-coordinate of its upper-left corner.
`union (Rectangle r)`	Returns a new `Rectangle` object that contains the union of the current `Rectangle` object with `r`.

`Polygon`

The `Polygon` class (located in the `java.awt` package) encapsulates two arrays of point coordinates that connect the line segments comprising a polygon.

Table 13.5 presents those fields and methods (except for a handful of implemented Java 2D `Shape` methods) that are publicly accessible.

TABLE 13.5 INSIDE THE AWT'S `Polygon` CLASS

Member	Description
`npoints`	This `int` field specifies the number of elements in both the `xpoints` and `ypoints` array.
`xpoints`	This `int` array field specifies the x-coordinate of each point making up this polygon.
`ypoints`	This `int` array field specifies the y-coordinate of each point making up this polygon.
`Polygon ()`	Initializes an empty `Polygon` object.
`Polygon (int [] xp, int [] yp, int n)`	Initializes a `Polygon` object to `n` points where the x-coordinates are stored in the `xp` array and the y-coordinates are stored in the `yp` array.

TABLE 13.5 CONTINUED

Member	Description
`addPoint (int x, int y)`	Adds the point specified by (x, y) to the current `Polygon` object.
`contains (int x, int y)`	Returns a Boolean `true` value if the point specified by (x, y) lies inside the boundaries of the current `Polygon` object.
`contains (Point p)`	Returns a Boolean `true` value if the point specified by `p` lies inside the boundaries of the current `Polygon` object.
`getBounds ()`	Returns a `Rectangle` object that contains the smallest rectangle parallel to the x and y axes and completely enclosing the polygon represented by the current `Polygon` object.
`translate (int dx, int dy)`	Translates the coordinates of each point making up the polygon by adding `dx` to the point's x-coordinate and `dy` to the point's y-coordinate.

You've already seen some of `Graphic`'s polygon methods. However, there are two other methods specially designed for use with the `Polygon` class. These methods take a single `Polygon` argument, and have the following signatures:

```
void drawPolygon (Polygon)

void fillPolygon (Polygon)
```

Listing 13.7 presents source code for the `DrawPolygonDemo2` applet that demonstrates these methods.

LISTING 13.7 THE `DrawPolygonDemo2` APPLET SOURCE CODE

```
// DrawPolygonDemo2.java

import java.awt.*;
import java.applet.Applet;

public class DrawPolygonDemo2 extends Applet
{
   public void paint (Graphics g)
   {
      // Get the width and height of the applet's drawing surface.

      int width = getSize ().width;
      int height = getSize ().height;

      int [] xp1 = { 30, 120, 70 };
      int [] yp1 = { 90, 30, 110 };

      Polygon p = new Polygon (xp1, yp1, xp1.length);
      g.drawPolygon (p);

      p = new Polygon ();
```

LISTING 13.7 CONTINUED

```
      p.addPoint (90, 180);
      p.addPoint (180, 120);
      p.addPoint (130, 200);

      g.drawPolygon (p);

      int [] xp2 = { 130, 170, 150 };
      int [] yp2 = { 50, 90, 120 };

      g.fillPolygon (new Polygon (xp2, yp2, yp2.length));
   }
}
```

`Shape`

The `Shape` interface provides methods that are used by objects representing geometric shapes. With the exception of `getBounds`, these methods are designed to be implemented by Java 2D shapes. `getBounds` returns a `Rectangle` object whose upper-left corner coordinates and dimensions completely enclose a shape. (You might have noticed that `Polygon` and `Rectangle` have a `getBounds` method. This is no coincidence; these classes implement `Shape`.)

UTILITY METHODS

The `Graphics` class provides a number of utility methods for accomplishing tasks related to drawing text and shapes. These tasks include

- Clipping
- Copying regions
- Selecting drawing modes

CLIPPING

Clipping is the technique of restricting graphics drawing to a specific region on a drawing surface. Usually, this region has a rectangular shape, although nonrectangular shapes are also possible (with Java 2D). `Graphics` provides several methods for defining and determining clipping regions. These methods include

- `clipRect`
- `getClipBounds`
- `setClip`
- `getClip`

The `clipRect` method reduces the clipping region to the intersection of the current clipping region and its argument values. You can never enlarge the clipping region. This method has the following signature:

```
void clipRect (int x, int y, int width, int height)
```

The desired clip rectangle has an upper-left corner located at (x, y), and a lower-right corner located at (x + width - 1, y + height - 1). However, if the current clip rectangle is smaller, the new clip rectangle will be the intersection of this rectangle and the desired clip rectangle. If no previous clip rectangle was established, the new clip rectangle will be the desired clip rectangle.

The getClipBounds method returns a Rectangle object containing the bounds of the current clip rectangle. This method has the following signature:

```
Rectangle getClipBounds ()
```

The setClip method sets the clipping region to the intersection of the current clipping region and its argument values. This method has the following signature:

```
void setClip (int x, int y, int width, int height)
```

The desired clip rectangle has an upper-left corner located at (x, y), and a lower-right corner located at (x + width - 1, y + height - 1).

Graphics provides a variation of setClip that takes a single argument. This argument is an object whose class implements the Shape interface. The alternate setClip has the following signature:

```
void setClip (Shape clip)
```

The clipping region is restricted to that specified by clip. For non-Java 2D work, the object implementing Shape must be of type Rectangle.

The getClip method returns an object that implements the Shape interface and specifies the clipping region. This method has the following signature:

```
Shape getClip ()
```

Listing 13.8 presents source code to a ClipDemo applet that demonstrates clipping.

LISTING 13.8 THE ClipDemo APPLET SOURCE CODE

```
// ClipDemo.java

import java.awt.*;
import java.applet.Applet;

public class ClipDemo extends Applet
{
   public void paint (Graphics g)
   {
      g.drawString (g.getClipBounds ().toString (), 10, 30);

      g.clipRect (10, 40, getSize ().width - 20, getSize ().height - 80);

      g.fillOval (0, 0, getSize ().width, getSize ().height);

      String newClip = g.getClipBounds ().toString ();

      g.setClip (0, 0, getSize ().width, getSize ().height);
```

LISTING 13.8 CONTINUED

```
      g.drawString (newClip, 10, getSize ().height - 10);
   }
}
```

The `ClipDemo` applet displays a pair of text strings and a clipped oval. These strings represent the contents of `Rectangle` objects returned from calls to `getClipBounds`. In essence, they show the size of the clip region before and after a clip rectangle is established. Figure 13.11 shows Applet Viewer running `ClipDemo`.

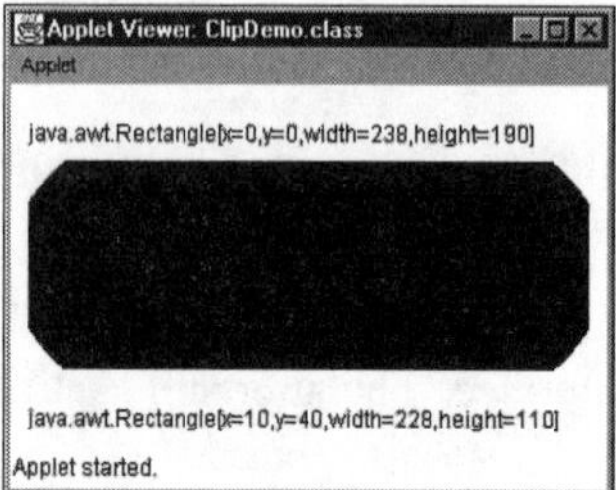

Figure 13.11 The `ClipDemo` applet shows the results of using a graphics context's clipping methods.

COPYING REGIONS

Sometimes, you might want to copy a region of graphics from one area on the drawing surface and paste this copy to another area (perhaps for tiling or scrolling purposes). To simplify this task, `Graphics` provides the `copyArea` method. This method has the following signature:

```
void copyArea (int x, int y, int width, int height, int dx, int dy)
```

The region to be copied is bounded by an upper-left corner at (`x`, `y`) and a lower-right corner at (`x + width`, `y + height`). This region is copied to a target area with an upper-left corner at (`x + dx`, `y + dy`) and a lower-right corner at (`x + width + dx`, `y + height + dy`). The target area can lie partially/completely outside the clipping region.

Listing 13.9 presents source code to a `CopyDemo` applet that demonstrates copying regions.

LISTING 13.9 THE `CopyDemo` APPLET SOURCE CODE

```
// CopyDemo.java

import java.applet.*;
import java.awt.*;

public class CopyDemo extends Applet
{
   public void paint (Graphics g)
   {
      g.fillArc (5, 15, 50, 75, 25, 165);
```

Listing 13.9 Continued

```
        g.copyArea (5, 15, 50, 75, 50, 50);
    }
}
```

The CopyDemo applet draws a solid arc and copies this region to another area on the drawing surface. Figure 13.12 shows CopyDemo running in the Applet Viewer.

Figure 13.12 The CopyDemo applet shows the results of using a graphics context's copyArea method.

Selecting Drawing Modes

Normally, when you draw a shape over a previously drawn shape, the new shape's pixels completely replace the old shape's pixels. This default drawing mode is known as *paint mode*. However, there is an alternate mode that you can use: *XOR mode*.

XOR mode dates back several years to a time when it was commonly used to achieve animation. This is how it works: When XOR mode is in effect, whatever shape is drawn changes the background colors to something quite different. Then, when the same shape is drawn a second time, the original background colors are restored. (This mode works by exclusive ORing pixel color values on the binary digit level. Repeating the same operation twice in a row restores the original color.)

Nowadays, XOR mode is often used to draw the selection rectangle in painting programs. This rectangle (which is typically displayed with a dashed or dotted outline) is drawn over the background, to show the portion of a drawing that has currently been selected. XOR mode is used to draw (and later remove) this rectangle. When the rectangle is removed, that part of the drawing hidden by the rectangle is restored, thanks to XOR mode.

Graphics provides a pair of methods for switching to either paint mode or XOR mode:

- setPaintMode
- setXORMode

The setPaintMode method switches the drawing mode to paint mode. Because paint mode is the default drawing mode, you would only use this method to switch from XOR mode back to paint mode. This method has the following signature:

```
void setPaintMode ()
```

In contrast, the `setXORMode` method switches the drawing mode to XOR mode, and has the following signature:

```
void setXORMode (Color c)
```

`Color` argument `c` is known as an XOR color. This color is usually the drawing surface's background color, but it can be any color. For each subsequently drawn pixel, the XOR color will be XORed with the color of the pixel being overwritten and the graphics context's current color.

Listing 13.10 presents source code to an applet called `ModeDemo` that demonstrates paint and XOR modes.

LISTING 13.10 THE ModeDemo APPLET SOURCE CODE

```
// ModeDemo.java

import java.awt.*;
import java.applet.Applet;

public class ModeDemo extends Applet
{
   public void paint (Graphics g)
   {
      int w = getSize ().width;
      int h = getSize ().height;

      int midW = w / 2;

      g.drawString ("Use XOR", 0, 30);
```

```
        g.drawOval (7, 37, 50, 50);

        g.setXORMode (Color.white);

        for (int i = 0; i < 15; i += 3)
        {
             g.drawOval (10 + i - 3, 40 + i - 3, 50, 50);

             g.drawOval (10 + i, 40 + i, 50, 50);
        }

        g.setPaintMode ();

        g.drawString ("No XOR", midW, 30);

        g.drawOval (midW + 7, 37, 50, 50);

        for (int i = 0; i < 15; i += 3)
        {
             g.drawOval (midW + 10 + i - 3, 40 + i - 3, 50, 50);

             g.drawOval (midW + 10 + i, 40 + i, 50, 50);
        }
    }
}
```

When you run `ModeDemo`, you'll see the applet's drawing surface divided into two halves: Both halves display identical sequences of circles. However, because the left half uses XOR mode, only the final circle in this sequence is displayed. In contrast, the right half uses paint mode, and displays the entire sequence. Figure 13.13 shows `ModeDemo` running in the Applet Viewer.

Figure 13.13
The `ModeDemo` applet divides its drawing surface into two halves, with the left half demonstrating XOR mode and the right half demonstrating paint mode.

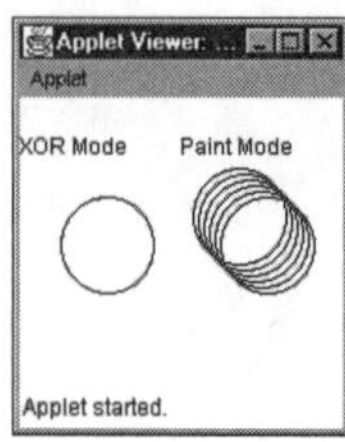

FONTS AND COLORS

Fonts and colors are important attributes of JFC programs. Fonts give text an aesthetic quality and make it easier to read. Colors offer excitement and information. Without color, images would be dull and warning messages would be harder to convey. Because of their importance, Java simplifies the task of working with fonts and colors.

GETTING TO KNOW FONTS

Fonts are nothing more than sets of type. Each font has a size and *face* (style). Size is measured in *points* (units of type that are approximately 1/72 of an inch). Faces include Bold, Italic, Bold and Italic, or neither Bold nor Italic (Plain). When a program draws text, this text always appears in a specific font.

A font is given a *face name* that identifies its typographic design and face. For example, Courier New Bold identifies a font that has the Courier New typographic design and a Bold face.

Each font belongs to a family of fonts, and each family's fonts are related in that they share a common typographic design and a common *family name*. For example, Times New Roman Bold and Times New Roman Italic share the common Times New Roman family name.

Before you create a font, it's a good idea to find out what fonts are available. Prior to Java 2, you would enumerate the family names of available fonts by calling the `getFontList` method in the AWT's `Toolkit` class. (This method returns an array of `String` objects in which each object contains a family name.) The `getFontList` method was deprecated in Java 2 because a much better technique was introduced.

→ **See** "Environments, Devices, and Configurations" in Chapter 18, "Java 2D," **p. 633**

Under Java 1.0, `getFontList` returned Times Roman, Helvetica, Courier, Dialog, DialogInput, and ZapfDingbats as the family names of available fonts. For copyright and portability reasons, Java 1.1 changed Times Roman to Serif (with serifs), Helvetica to Sans Serif (without serifs), and Courier to Monospaced. (The actual fonts didn't change, just their names.) Furthermore, Zapf Dingbats was dropped from Java 1.1 because this font's characters were given official Unicode mappings in the range `\u2700` to `\u27ff`. (The Java 1.1 family names are still available for use in Java 2 programs.)

The AWT's font family names are virtual family names. They are virtual because these names are mapped to the family names of physical fonts on each Java platform. As long as you use virtual family names, your font code will be portable.

CREATING FONTS

You create a font by instantiating an object from the AWT's `Font` class (located in the `java.awt` package). To demonstrate font creation, the following code fragment creates a 12-point Dialog Bold `Font` object:

```
Font f = new Font ("Dialog", Font.BOLD, 12);
```

`Font.BOLD` is a read-only class field (declared in the `Font` class) that identifies a font family's Bold face. `Font` also declares `PLAIN` and `ITALIC` fields to identify a font family's Plain and Italic faces.

`Font.BOLD` and `Font.ITALIC` can be combined to achieve a Bold Italic face by using either the addition operator (+) or the bitwise OR operator (|). This is demonstrated by the following code fragment:

```
Font f = new Font ("Serif", Font.ITALIC | Font.BOLD, 36);
```

After a `Font` object has been created, the drawing surface needs to be "told" to use this new `Font`. `Graphics` provides a `setFont` method to carry out this task. This method takes a `Font` argument and sets the drawing surface's current font to this argument. To complement `setFont`, `Graphics` also provides a `getFont` method that returns the drawing surface's current `Font`.

To see how these concepts apply, check out Listing 13.11 which presents source code to an applet called `FontNamesDemo`.

LISTING 13.11 THE FontNamesDemo APPLET SOURCE CODE

```
// FontNamesDemo.java

import java.awt.*;
import java.applet.*;

public class FontNamesDemo extends Applet
{
   public void paint (Graphics g)
   {
      Font f = new Font ("Serif", Font.PLAIN, 12);
      g.setFont (f);
      g.drawString ("Serif - PLAIN - 12", 10, 30);

      f = new Font ("Sanserif", Font.ITALIC, 10);
      g.setFont (f);
      g.drawString ("Sanserif - ITALIC - 10", 10, 60);

      f = new Font ("Monospaced", Font.BOLD | Font.ITALIC, 14);
      g.setFont (f);
      g.drawString ("Monospaced - BOLD and ITALIC - 14", 10, 90);
```

LISTING 13.11 CONTINUED

```
        f = new Font ("Dialog", Font.PLAIN, 12);
        g.setFont (f);
        g.drawString ("Dialog - PLAIN - 12", 10, 120);

        f = new Font ("DialogInput", Font.BOLD + Font.ITALIC, 10);
        g.setFont (f);
        g.drawString ("DialogInput - BOLD and ITALIC - 10", 10, 150);
    }
}
```

`FontNamesDemo` creates a `Font` object based on each of the virtual font family names. The `setFont` method is then called to establish this font as the drawing surface's current font. Finally, text is displayed using this font. Figure 13.14 shows the Applet Viewer running `FontNamesDemo`.

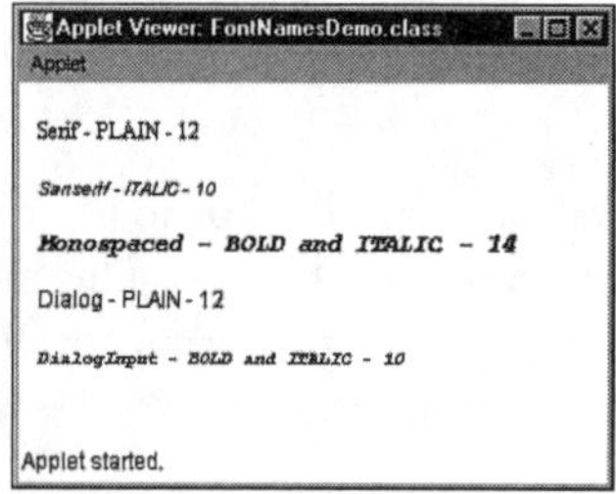

Figure 13.14
The `FontNamesDemo` applet shows text displayed using the AWT's virtual font family names.

Sometimes, changing the font in the `paint` *method causes the contents of a drawing surface to flicker. If this problem is bothering you, see "A Flicker-Free Drawing Surface," in the "Troubleshooting" section at the end of this chapter.*

To learn more about the `Font` class, check out Table 13.6. This table presents commonly used `Font` methods.

TABLE 13.6 INSIDE THE AWT'S `Font` CLASS

Method	Description
`Font (String name, int style, int size)`	Initializes a `Font` object to a specific family `name`, `style`, and `size`
`equals (Object o)`	Compares the current `Font` object with `o` (which must be a `Font`) for equality. A Boolean `true` value is returned if they are equal
`getFamily ()`	Returns a `String` object containing the current `Font` object's family name
`getFontName ()`	Returns a `String` object containing the current `Font` object's face name

TABLE 13.6 CONTINUED

Method	Description
getSize ()	Returns an int containing the current Font object's size
getStyle ()	Returns an int containing the current Font object's style
isBold ()	Returns a Boolean true value if the current Font object contains the Bold style
isItalic ()	Returns a Boolean true value if the current Font object contains the Italic style
isPlain ()	Returns a Boolean true value if the current Font object uses the default Plain style
toString ()	Returns a String object containing a representation of the current Font object

MEASURING FONTS

After you've created a font, how do you determine various font measurements, such as a character's height or the average width of characters in a proportional font? The answer is to use the FontMetrics class (located in the java.awt package).

FontMetrics, like Graphics, is an abstract class. Therefore, you cannot create objects from FontMetrics. Instead, you must call Graphics' getFontMetrics method to return an object created from a subclass of FontMetrics. This object is associated with the graphics context's current font. The following code fragment shows how to call this method:

```
public void paint (Graphics g)
{
   FontMetrics fm = g.getFontMetrics ();
}
```

Tip

You can also obtain a FontMetrics object for a specific font by calling java.awt.Toolkit's getFontMetrics method, as demonstrated by the following code fragment:

```
Font f = new Font ("Serif", Font.PLAIN, 10);
FontMetrics fm;
fm = Toolkit.getDefaultToolkit ().getFontMetrics (f);
```


Each time you set a graphics context's current font, a new FontMetrics subclass object is automatically created. This new object replaces the previous object. Therefore, you need to call getFontMetrics after setting a new font before you can obtain measurements. This is shown in the following code fragment:

```
public void paint (Graphics g)
{
```

```
      FontMetrics fm1 = g.getFontMetrics ();
      g.setFont (new Font ("Dialog", Font.PLAIN, 12));
      FontMetrics fm2 = g.getFontMetrics ();
   }
```

Each font is associated with certain measurements. These measurements are illustrated in Figure 13.15.

Figure 13.15
Every font is associated with certain measurements.

> **Note**
>
> In Java, measurements are always made from a font's baseline. The portion of a character that appears below the baseline is known as a *descent*, whereas the portion of a character appearing above the baseline is known as an *ascent*. Some characters have extra visual information (such as an acute) appearing above the ascent. This extra information is known as *leading* (pronounced ledding). The combination of descent, ascent, and leading is known as *height*. Finally, the width of the current character plus any inter-character space is known as *advance width*.

Listing 13.12 presents source code to an applet called `FontMetricsDemo`. This applet demonstrates various `FontMetrics` methods.

LISTING 13.12 THE `FontMetricsDemo` APPLET SOURCE CODE

```
// FontMetricsDemo.java

import java.awt.*;
import java.applet.Applet;

public class FontMetricsDemo extends Applet
{
   String the = "The ";

   String [] msgs =
   {
      " method is handy for centering text.",
      " method is handy for spacing between rows of text.",
      " method returns the maximum ascent of any character.",
      " method returns the maximum descent of any character."
   };

   String [] methods =
   {
      "stringWidth",
      "getHeight",
```

LISTING 13.12 CONTINUED

```
        "getMaxAscent",
        "getMaxDescent"
    };

    public void paint (Graphics g)
    {
        // Create a Bold Serif font, establish this font
        // as the graphics context font, and obtain font
        // metrics for this font.

        Font f1 = new Font ("Serif", Font.BOLD, 12);
        g.setFont (f1);
        FontMetrics fm = g.getFontMetrics ();

        // Create an array to hold method name widths.

        int [] wMethod = new int [methods.length];

        // For each method name in the methods array,
        // compute its width (in pixels) when displayed
        // using the Bold font.

        for (int i = 0; i < wMethod.length; i++)
             wMethod [i] = fm.stringWidth (methods [i]);

        // Establish a Plain Serif font as the graphics
        // context font.

        Font f2 = new Font ("Serif", Font.PLAIN, 12);
        g.setFont (f2);
        fm = g.getFontMetrics ();

        // Calculate the width (in pixels) of the string
        // referenced by the, when displayed using Plain
        // Serif.

        int wThe = fm.stringWidth (the);

        // Calculate a width array for all messages.

        int [] wMsg = new int [msgs.length];

        // Compute each message's display width based on
        // Plain Serif.

        for (int i = 0; i < wMsg.length; i++)
             wMsg [i] = fm.stringWidth (msgs [i]);

        // For each message, determine the horizontal
        // start position so that the message can be
        // horizontally centered.  Then, obtain the
        // current display row (taking baseline into
        // account), and draw the message.  Change
        // fonts (accordingly) so that method names
        // appear in Bold Serif and the rest of the
```

LISTING 13.12 CONTINUED

```
        // text appears in Plain Serif.

        for (int i = 0; i < msgs.length; i++)
        {
             int x = getSize ().width - wThe - wMethod [i] - wMsg [i];
             x  >>= 1; // A faster way of dividing by 2.

             int y = fm.getHeight () * (i + 1);

             g.drawString (the, x, y);
             x += wThe;

             g.setFont (f1);

             g.drawString (methods [i], x, y);
             x += wMethod [i];

             g.setFont (f2);
             fm = g.getFontMetrics ();

             g.drawString (msgs [i], x, y);
        }
    }
}
```

`FontMetricsDemo` displays horizontally centered lines of text that are properly positioned vertically. Each line consists of one word that is displayed using the Bold style, whereas the rest of the line is displayed using the Plain style. Figure 13.16 shows `FontMetricsDemo` running in the Applet Viewer.

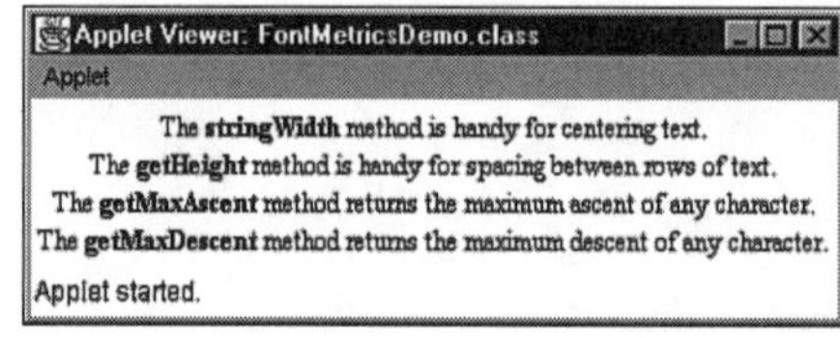

Applet Viewer: FontMetricsDemo.class
Applet
The stringWidth method is handy for centering text.
The getHeight method is handy for spacing between rows of text.
The getMaxAscent method returns the maximum ascent of any character.
The getMaxDescent method returns the maximum descent of any character.
Applet started.

Figure 13.16
The `FontMetricsDemo` applet shows text centering and positioning.

Right-justifying text can seem like an impossible endeavor, especially when proportional fonts are involved. If you are having trouble with this task, see "Right-Justifying Text," in the "Troubleshooting" section at the end of this chapter.

To learn more about the `FontMetrics` class, check out Table 13.7. This table presents commonly used `FontMetrics` methods.

TABLE 13.7 INSIDE THE AWT'S `FontMetrics` CLASS

Method	Description
`getAscent ()`	Returns an `int` containing the font ascent of the `Font` associated with the current `FontMetrics`
`getDescent ()`	Returns an `int` containing the font descent of the `Font` associated with the current `FontMetrics`
`getHeight ()`	Returns an `int` containing the standard height (leading plus ascent + descent) of the `Font` associated with the current `FontMetrics`
`getLeading ()`	Returns an `int` containing the leading of the `Font` associated with the current `FontMetrics`
`getMaxAdvance ()`	Returns an `int` containing the maximum advance width of any character in the `Font` associated with the current `FontMetrics`
`getMaxAscent ()`	Returns an `int` containing the maximum ascent of any character in the `Font` associated with the current `FontMetrics`
`getMaxDescent ()`	Returns an `int` containing the maximum descent of any character in the `Font` associated with the current `FontMetrics`
`stringWidth (String s)`	Returns an `int` containing the combined advance width of all characters in `s`, based on the `Font` associated with the current `FontMetrics`
`toString ()`	Returns a `String` object containing a representation of the current `FontMetrics`

A DASH OF COLOR

Colors are represented by objects created from the AWT's `Color` class (located in the `java.awt` package). Each color can be based on either the default RGB (Red, Green, Blue) *color space* (a mathematical model for representing colors) or a color space created from a subclass of the abstract `ColorSpace` class (located in the `java.awt.color` package).

The RGB color space requires a color to be specified by providing three primary color components (red, green, and blue) that range from 0 to 255 (0 is darkest and 255 is brightest). Furthermore, an *alpha component* (a measure of transparency) can be specified, but this is optional. If specified, its value ranges from 0 (completely *transparent*—the background shows through) to 255 (completely *opaque*—the background does not show through). (Alpha components are used with images and not with graphics drawn via `Graphics`'s methods—such as `drawLine`.) The following code fragment demonstrates the creation of a `Color` object (based on RGB) that represents the color orange.

```
// Create a Color object representing orange (based on RGB).

Color c = new Color (255, 200, 0);
```

Three integers are passed to the constructor. The integer 255 is the red component, the integer 200 is the green component, and the integer 0 is the blue component of the resulting orange color.

For commonly used colors, the AWT predefines the following `Color` constants: `black`, `blue`, `cyan`, `darkGray`, `gray`, `green`, `lightGray`, `magenta`, `orange`, `pink`, `red`, `white`, and `yellow`. Assigning these constants to `Color` variables is straightforward, as illustrated by the following code fragment.

```
Color c = Color.green; // Assign predefined Color green to c.
```

You can extract the red, green, blue, and alpha components from a `Color` object by calling `Color`'s `getRed`, `getGreen`, `getBlue`, and `getAlpha` methods. To demonstrate, the following code fragment extracts the components from the `Color.pink` object.

```
int red = Color.pink.getRed ();
int green = Color.pink.getGreen ();
int blue = Color.pink.getBlue ();
int alpha = Color.pink.getAlpha ();
```

After a `Color` object has been created, the drawing surface needs to be "told" to use this new `Color`. `Graphics` provides a `setColor` method to carry out this task. This method takes a `Color` argument and sets the drawing surface's current color to this argument. To complement `setColor`, `Graphics` also provides a `getColor` method that returns the drawing surface's current `Color`.

To see how these concepts apply, check out Listing 13.13, which presents source code to an applet called `ColorDemo`.

LISTING 13.13 THE ColorDemo APPLET SOURCE CODE

```
// ColorDemo.java

import java.awt.*;
import java.applet.Applet;

public class ColorDemo extends Applet
{
   public void paint (Graphics g)
   {
      int w = getSize ().width;
      int h = getSize ().height;

      g.setColor (Color.red);
      g.fillRect (0, 0, w - 1, h - 1);

      g.setColor (Color.black);
      g.fillOval (0, 0, w - 1, h - 1);

      g.setColor (new Color (60, 190, 175));

      FontMetrics fm = g.getFontMetrics ();
      String s = "This text is aquamarine.";
      int x = (w - fm.stringWidth (s)) / 2;
```

Listing 13.13 Continued

```
      g.drawString (s, x, h / 2);

      System.out.println ("Red = " + g.getColor ().getRed ());
      System.out.println ("Green = " + g.getColor ().getGreen ());
      System.out.println ("Blue = " + g.getColor ().getBlue ());
      System.out.println ("Alpha = " + g.getColor ().getAlpha ());
   }
}
```

`ColorDemo` uses predefined `Color` constants—and a newly created `Color` object that represents aquamarine—as drawing colors. The `setColor` method is called to establish each color as the drawing surface's current color and the `getColor` method is called to return the current color's `Color` object. This object's `getRed`, `getGreen`, `getBlue`, and `getAlpha` methods are called to extract the red, green, blue, and alpha components, which are subsequently printed. Figure 13.17 shows Applet Viewer running `ColorDemo`.

Figure 13.17 The `ColorDemo` applet shows the use of color.

HSB (hue, saturation, brightness) is another commonly used color space. Hue represents the base color, saturation represents the color's purity, and brightness represents the luminance level. The `Color` class provides methods for converting between RGB and HSB. If you're interested in working with HSB, consult the SDK documentation for more information on these methods.

To learn more about the `Color` class, check out Table 13.8. This table presents commonly used `Color` methods.

Table 13.8 Inside the AWT's `Color` Class

Method	Description
`Color (int rgb, boolean hasAlpha)`	Initializes a `Color` object to the red, green, and blue color components specified by `rgb`. Bits 16–23 contain the red, bits 8–15 contain the green, and bits 0–7 contain the blue components. If `hasAlpha` is `true`, bits 24–31 contain the alpha component. If `hasAlpha` is `false`, the alpha component defaults to 255 (completely opaque).

TABLE 13.8 CONTINUED

Method	Description
`Color (int r, int g, int b)`	Initializes a `Color` object to a specific amount of red (`r`), green (`g`), and blue (`b`). A default value of 255 is assigned to the color's alpha component. Each color component must range from 0 to 255.
`Color (int r, int g, int b, int a)`	Initializes a `Color` object to a specific amount of red (`r`), green (`g`), blue (`b`), and alpha (`a`). Each color component must range from 0 to 255.
`brighter ()`	Returns a `Color` object containing a brighter version of the current `Color` object's color.
`darker ()`	Returns a `Color` object containing a darker version of the current `Color` object's color.
`equals (Object o)`	Compares the current `Color` object with `o` (which must be a `Color`) for equality. A Boolean `true` value is returned if they are equal.
`getAlpha ()`	Returns an `int` containing the alpha component of the current `Color` object.
`getBlue ()`	Returns an `int` containing the blue component of the current `Color` object.
`getGreen ()`	Returns an `int` containing the green component of the current `Color` object.
`getRed ()`	Returns an `int` containing the red component of the current `Color` object.
`getRGB ()`	Returns an `int` containing the alpha, red, green, and blue components of the current `Color` object. Bits 24–31 contain the alpha, bits 16–23 contain the red, bits 8–15 contain the green, and bits 0–7 contain the blue components.
`toString ()`	Returns a `String` object containing a representation of the current `Color` object.

SYSTEM COLORS

You can create JFC programs that automatically adapt their colors to the current desktop color theme, used by the underlying windowing system. For example, under Windows 98, you can choose a theme in which a button's color changes from black text on a gray background to white text on a black background. These theme colors are known as *system colors*. By taking advantage of system colors, your JFC programs will be more user friendly.

The `SystemColor` class (located in the `java.awt` package) contains a number of constants that represent various system colors. The following code fragment shows how you would access these colors.

```
public void paint (Graphics g)
{
   g.setColor (SystemColor.control);
   g.fillRect (0, 0, getSize ().width, getSize ().height);
}
```

If you investigate `SystemColor`, you'll notice that there are two sets of constants: The first set consists of `int` constants that you will never need to use. They are the symbolic names of indexes into the internal system color lookup table. The second set consists of `SystemColor` constants. These are the constants that you will use.

This second set of constants is declared `public static final`. Although you cannot modify their values, the AWT can indirectly modify these values by changing the internal representation of a system color when it receives notification that the corresponding desktop color has changed. As a result, you should not compare regular `Color` objects with `SystemColor` objects by using the `equals` method. Instead, you call the `getRGB` methods in both classes to ensure that the current color values are being compared. This is demonstrated by the following code fragment.

```
if (Color.red.getRGB () == SystemColor.desktop.getRGB ())
{
    // whatever
}
```

IMAGES

Images are an exciting part of modern user interfaces and "enjoy" AWT support. This support is manifested through the AWT's facilities for image loading, drawing, animation, production, consumption, and filtering. Before exploring this support, some essential concepts need to be understood. These concepts include

- Definition of an image
- The producer, consumer, and image observer model
- Color models

An *image* is one or more rectangular grids of colored pixels. Each grid is known as a *frame*. JPEG files can only contain a single frame, whereas GIF files can contain one or more frames. A GIF file containing multiple frames is known as an *animated GIF*.

Each image is associated with an object created from a subclass of the AWT's abstract `Image` class (located in the `java.awt` package). This class contains a number of constants and methods of importance to images. Various `Image` methods will be mentioned throughout the remainder of this chapter. (Check out the SDK documentation for a complete description of `Image` members.)

The AWT's support rests on a producer, consumer, and image observer model. A *producer* is an object that produces an image. Producing this image might involve loading a GIF, JPEG, or another image format file, reading memory, or filtering pixels. Regardless, the producer sends an image's pixels to a *consumer* object that consumes these pixels. Consuming an image might involve saving the pixels to a file, storing the pixels in a memory buffer, storing the pixels in preparation for display, or filtering pixels. Consumers register/de-register their interest in producers by calling producer methods and producers send image information to consumers by calling consumer methods. Producers and consumers are usually (but not always) hidden deep inside the AWT. Furthermore, they work in partnership with image observers.

An *image observer* is a drawing surface that is notified when the producer has produced image information (such as width, height, or pixels). Pixels are never sent to an image observer: They are always sent to a consumer. As a frame becomes available, the producer calls the image observer which, in turn, "asks" the AWT to render the consumer's pixels (making up the frame) on the drawing surface.

To be an image observer, an object's class must implement the `ImageObserver` interface (located in the `java.awt.image` package). Because all drawing surfaces descend from `Component` and because `Component` implements `ImageObserver`, all drawing surfaces are image observers.

`ImageObserver` declares several flag constants and a method that is called by the producer. This method, known as `imageUpdate`, has the following signature:

```
boolean imageUpdate (Image im, int flags, int x, int y, int width, int height)
```

The `im` argument is a reference to an `Image` subclass object. (It is possible to determine the producer for this image by calling `Image`'s `getSource` method.) The `flags` argument is a set of `ImageObserver` flags that have been ORed together. These flags specify information about `im` that is now available. The meaning of the `x`, `y`, `width`, and `height` arguments depends on `flags`. After a frame has loaded, these arguments identify the upper-left corner location and dimensions of this frame. The `imageUpdate` method returns a Boolean `true` value to the producer if it needs more information. After the last frame has finished loading, `false` is returned.

You're probably wondering about the rationale for this model. Why not load images directly without using producers, consumers, and image observers? There is one good reason for this model's existence: applets.

A Web browser loads an applet's class and resource files (including image files) from a remote computer over a network. This can take time. In fact, back in 1995 when Java was first unveiled, slow modems were the order of the day. Loading even small images took time. If an applet was forced to wait until its images were completely loaded, users would get fed up and not want anything to do with the applet. However, because of the producer, consumer, and image observer model, an applet can get work done while loading images. In other words, it can be more responsive. (This idea carries over to JFC applications.)

Figure 13.18 illustrates the relationship between producers, consumers, and image observers.

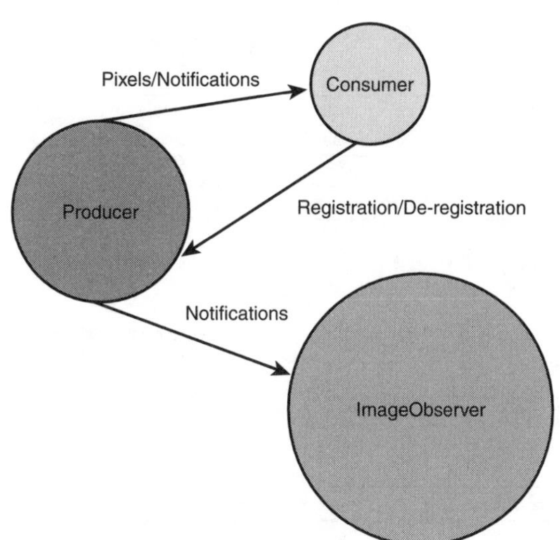

Figure 13.18
Under the producer, consumer, and image observer model, consumers register their interest in receiving pixels and notifications from producers, and producers notify image observers to inform programs when significant image information has been sent to consumers.

An image's pixels are nothing more than colors. How these colors are represented depends on the image's color model. A *color model* is a mechanism that associates an image's pixel colors with their storage representation. There are two commonly used color models: direct and index.

The *direct color model* uses color numbers to directly store pixel color information. A *color number* is an integer that encodes a color's alpha, red, green, and blue components in a `0xAARRGGBB` format. This requires 32 bits of storage per color number (8 bits per component). For example, a 500×500 pixel image consisting of 32-bit color numbers would require 1,000,000 bytes of storage. That's a lot of storage!

Years ago, memory was expensive and it was not practical to directly store color numbers in images consisting of many pixels. Therefore, an alternative to the direct color model was commonly used: the index color model.

The *index color model* uses color indexes to indirectly store pixel color information. A *color index* is an integer that refers to an entry in a lookup table. Each entry contains a color number. A program can obtain a color number by indexing this table via the color index. Instead of requiring 32 bits of storage per pixel, fewer bits can be used. For example, a 500×500 pixel image consisting of 8-bit color indexes would require 250,000 bytes of storage. This is a 75% storage savings over the direct color model. However, an 8-bit color index can only reference a maximum of 256 entries in the lookup table. As a result, it's impossible to simultaneously display more than 256 colors. There is always a tradeoff!

Figure 13.19 illustrates the direct and index color models.

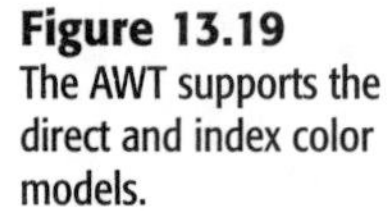

Figure 13.19
The AWT supports the direct and index color models.

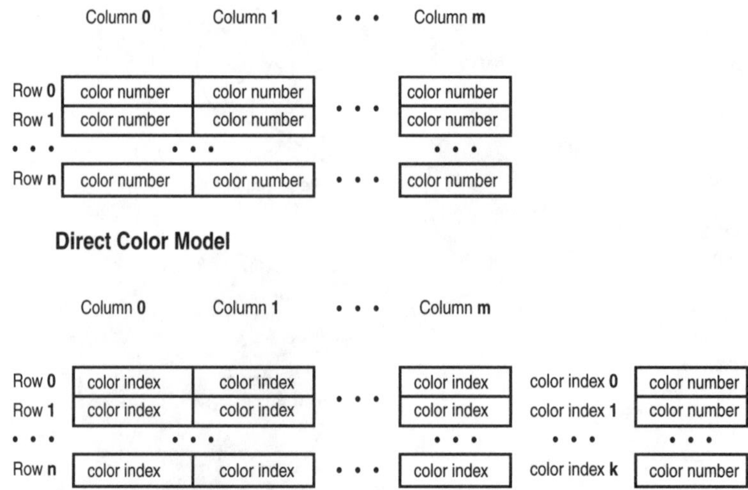

The AWT supplies an abstract `ColorModel` class (located in the `java.awt.image` package) that serves as the parent for its `DirectColorModel` and `IndexColorModel` subclasses. A producer can create objects from either subclass to represent the direct and index color models. Table 13.9 describes some of `ColorModel`'s methods.

TABLE 13.9 INSIDE THE AWT'S `ColorModel` CLASS

Method	Description
`ColorModel (int bits)`	Initializes a subclass object to the number of required bits per pixel. The maximum value for `bits` is 32 because `bits` is an `int`. (Normally, 32 bits would be used to represent the direct color model and anything less would be used to represent the index color model.)
`getAlpha (int pixel)`	Returns an `int` containing the alpha component of `pixel`. Its range is between 0 and 255, where 0 means completely transparent and 255 means completely opaque.
`getBlue (int pixel)`	Returns an `int` containing the blue component of `pixel`. Its range is between 0 and 255, where 0 means no blue and 255 means blue at its maximum intensity.
`getGreen (int pixel)`	Returns an `int` containing the green component of `pixel`. Its range is between 0 and 255, where 0 means no green and 255 means green at its maximum intensity.
`getPixelSize ()`	Returns an `int` containing the number of required bits per pixel, as passed to the constructor.
`getRed (int pixel)`	Returns an `int` containing the red component of `pixel`. Its range is between 0 and 255, where 0 means no red and 255 means red at its maximum intensity.

TABLE 13.9 CONTINUED

Method	Description
`getRGB (int pixel)`	Returns an `int` containing the color number of `pixel`. If a subclass changes the ordering or size of the different color components (from the `0xAARRGGBB` format), this method will still return `pixel` as a color number.
`getRGBdefault ()`	Returns either a direct color model object or an index color model object that directly or indirectly uses color numbers to represent pixel colors.

LOADING AND DRAWING IMAGES

Images are normally loaded by calling `getImage` methods. After it's loaded, an image can be drawn by using any one of several `drawImage` methods. Some of these `drawImage` methods can manipulate an image prior to drawing by performing scaling, flipping, and cropping operations.

EXPLORING THE LOADING AND DRAWING PROCESS

Applets and applications load images in a similar manner. However, applets usually load images from remote computers on a network, whereas applications typically load images from a computer's file system. Regardless, they do share one thing in common: `getImage`.

The `Applet` class provides two overloaded `getImage` methods. These methods take one or two arguments that identify the location and name of an image file. When called, they create a producer and an object from a subclass of the abstract `Image` class. A reference to the producer is stored in this "`Image`" object. Each `getImage` method returns immediately with a reference to the "`Image`" object. The producer is not yet started.

After `getImage` has been called, the applet can call one of `Graphics`' `drawImage` methods to start the production and drawing process. An internal consumer is also created. Each `drawImage` method returns immediately and the producer begins to produce the image. Pixels are sent from the producer to the consumer.

To see an example of an applet that obtains and displays an image, check out the source code to `ImageApplet` in Listing 13.14.

LISTING 13.14 THE `ImageApplet` APPLET SOURCE CODE

```
// ImageApplet.java

import java.awt.*;
import java.applet.Applet;

public class ImageApplet extends Applet
{
   Image im;

   public void init ()
```

LISTING 13.14 CONTINUED

```
   {
      im = getImage (getDocumentBase (), "sojourner.jpg");
   }

   public void paint (Graphics g)
   {
      g.drawImage (im, 0, 0, this);
   }
}
```

Note

The image file `sojourner.jpg` (as with all other image files in this and other chapters) is included with this book's source code.

`ImageApplet` calls `getImage` in its `init` method. This method creates a producer. It records the location (as specified by `getDocumentBase`'s return value) and name of the image file (`sojourner.jpg`) in this producer. An `Image` subclass object is created and a reference to the producer is stored in this object.

The `Image` subclass object is returned from `getImage` and its reference is assigned to `im`. When the applet needs to update its drawing surface, the drawing surface's `paint` method is called. In turn, this method calls `drawImage` to start the producer and create a consumer. `im` is passed as an argument to `drawImage` so that `drawImage` can obtain a reference to the producer. Java's `this` keyword is passed as an argument to `drawImage` so that the newly created producer "knows" which image observer to contact. An internal consumer is also created and registered with the producer. (Of course, this activity takes place during the first call to `drawImage`.)

The producer starts loading the image and periodically calls the image observer's `imageUpdate` method when information has been obtained. The image observer "asks" the AWT to call `paint` when either part of the image or the entire image has been loaded, and `paint` calls `drawImage`. On this and subsequent calls, `drawImage` obtains the consumer's pixels and renders them onto the drawing surface. The result is shown in Figure 13.20.

Figure 13.20 `ImageApplet` shows an image of the Sojourner rover on Mars.

Tip

> When an animated GIF is displayed, the AWT takes care of the animation on your behalf. For example, in `ImageApplet`, you could replace `sojourner.jpg` with the name of an animated GIF file and watch the resulting animation.

The application approach to obtaining and drawing images is similar to the applet approach. However, instead of using `Applet`'s `getImage` methods, an application calls one of `Toolkit`'s `getImage` methods. (`Toolkit` will be examined in the next chapter.) These methods works in a similar manner to `Applet`'s `getImage` methods.

For an example of an application that loads and draws an image, check out the source code to `ImageApp` in Listing 13.15.

LISTING 13.15 THE `ImageApp` APPLICATION SOURCE CODE

```
// ImageApp.java

import java.awt.*;
import java.awt.event.*;

class ImageApp extends Frame
{
   ImageApp (String title)
   {
      super (title);

      addWindowListener (new WindowAdapter ()
                         {
                             public void windowClosing (WindowEvent e)
                             {
                                System.exit (0);
                             }
                         });

      add (new Picture ("sojourner.jpg"));

      pack ();

      setResizable (false);

      setVisible (true);
   }

   public static void main (String [] args)
   {
      new ImageApp ("Image Application");
   }
}

class Picture extends Canvas
{
   private Image image;

   Picture (String imageFileName)
```

LISTING 13.15 CONTINUED

```
   {
      Toolkit tk = Toolkit.getDefaultToolkit ();
      image = tk.getImage (imageFileName);
   }

   public Dimension getPreferredSize ()
   {
      return new Dimension (256, 248);
   }

   public void paint (Graphics g)
   {
      g.drawImage (image, 0, 0, this);
   }
}
```

Don't worry about not understanding the GUI aspects of this code. After you've had a chance to explore AWT GUI concepts in the next chapter, come back and review `ImageApp`. You'll find that the GUI code makes more sense.

> **Note**
>
> You might be wondering why this chapter has focused solely on applets (until now) to present AWT features. The reason is that applets require no special GUI setup before they can be used. In contrast, JFC applications require this setup—as evidenced by `ImageApp`. Rather than get sidetracked into discussing their GUI setup, JFC applications have been avoided. This will change in the next chapter, where the GUI side of the AWT is discussed.

If you examine the `Graphics` class, you'll discover six overloaded `drawImage` methods. Each method handles drawing-related tasks in different ways. For example, some versions render transparent pixels in a specified color (as opposed to leaving the original pixel colors unchanged), whereas other versions provide scaling, cropping, and flipping features. Regardless of differences, each method's approach to working with producers/consumers is the same, and each method returns a Boolean `true` value after the image has been completely loaded.

SCALING IMAGES

Several `drawImage` methods can be called to perform scaling prior to drawing an image. To demonstrate how this works, Listing 13.16 presents source code to an `ImageScale` applet. This applet draws an original image along with a scaled down version of the image.

LISTING 13.16 THE `ImageScale` APPLET SOURCE CODE

```
// ImageScale.java

import java.awt.*;
import java.applet.Applet;
import java.awt.image.ImageObserver;

public class ImageScale extends Applet
```

LISTING 13.16 CONTINUED

```
{
   Image im;

   public void init ()
   {
      im = getImage (getDocumentBase (), "twain.jpg");
   }

   public void paint (Graphics g)
   {
      if (g.drawImage (im, 0, 0, this))
      {
          int width = im.getWidth (this);
          int height = im.getHeight (this);

          g.drawImage (im, width, 0, width + width / 2, height / 2,
                       0, 0, width, height, this);
      }
   }
}
```

`ImageScale` takes advantage of `drawImage` returning a Boolean `true` value after the original image is completely loaded. After it's loaded, the width and height of this image are obtained by calling `Image`'s `getWidth` and `getHeight` methods. These methods take an `ImageObserver` argument—an object that implements the `ImageObserver` interface—and return -1 until the producer has produced the width/height information. Because they are not called until `drawImage` returns `true`, `getWidth` and `getHeight` are guaranteed to return the image's width and height. A second version of `drawImage` (with 10 arguments) is called to load and draw the scaled image.

Scaling is achieved by dividing the target image's lower-right corner coordinates by a specified value. `ImageScale` divides these coordinates by 2. The result is shown in Figure 13.21.

Figure 13.21 `ImageScale` shows original and scaled down images of Mark Twain (an early American author and humorist).

Tip

The `Image` class provides the `getScaledInstance` method for generating a prescaled version of an image. Instead of calling a `drawImage` method to scale and then draw, you can call `getScaledInstance` to prescale and then a `drawImage` method to only draw. This is useful in situations in which calling `drawImage` to scale and then draw results in a degraded appearance (because scaling takes time).

CROPPING AND FLIPPING IMAGES

Several `drawImage` methods can be called to achieve cropping and flipping prior to drawing an image. Listing 13.17 presents source code to an `ImageCropFlip` applet that demonstrates drawing an original image along with a cropped and flipped version of the image.

LISTING 13.17 THE `ImageCropFlip` APPLET SOURCE CODE

```
// ImageCropFlip.java

import java.awt.*;
import java.applet.Applet;

public class ImageCropFlip extends Applet
{
   Image im;

   public void init ()
   {
      im = getImage (getDocumentBase (), "lions.jpg");
   }

   public void paint (Graphics g)
   {
      if (g.drawImage (im, 0, 0, this))
      {
          int width = im.getWidth (this);
          int height = im.getHeight (this);

          g.drawImage (im, width, height + 10, 0, 2 * height - 40,
                       0, 0, width, height - 50, this);
      }
   }
}
```

Cropping is achieved by modifying the original image coordinates. `ImageCropFlip` crops vertically by subtracting 50 from the height of the original image. Flipping is achieved by swapping the target image coordinates. `ImageCropFlip` flips the image horizontally by swapping the x-coordinates of the target image's upper-left and lower-right corners. Instead of having an upper-left corner at (`0`, `height + 10`) and a lower-right corner at (`width`, `2 * height - 40`), the target image is given an upper-left corner at (`width`, `height + 10`) and a lower-right corner at (`0`, `2 * height - 40`). The result is shown in Figure 13.22.

Figure 13.22 `ImageCropFlip` shows original and cropped/flipped images of lions.

ANIMATION

Animation has come a long way since Walt Disney's original black and white Mickey Mouse cartoons debuted in the early part of the last century. The central idea behind animation is to draw a frame of pixels, display this frame, pause for a certain length of time, draw the next frame, and so on. (You can change this order to pause, draw a frame, display this frame, and so on—as long as there is a pause between the display of two frames.)

The AWT makes it easy to achieve animation. To see an example, check out the `TypeWriter` applet source code in Listing 13.18.

LISTING 13.18 THE `TypeWriter` APPLET SOURCE CODE

```
// TypeWriter.java

import java.awt.*;
import java.applet.Applet;

public class TypeWriter extends Applet implements Runnable
{
   Thread t;
   String text = "Java makes typing fun!";

   int index;
   final int len = text.length ();

   public void start ()
   {
      if (t == null)
      {
          t = new Thread (this);
```

LISTING 13.18 CONTINUED

```
            t.start ();
        }
    }

    public void stop ()
    {
      t = null;
    }

    public void run ()
    {
       Thread current = Thread.currentThread ();

       while (t == current)
       {
          try
          {
             Thread.sleep (200);
          }
          catch (InterruptedException e) {}

          repaint ();

          index++;
          if (index >= len)
              index = 0;
       }
    }

    public void paint (Graphics g)
    {
       g.setColor (Color.blue);

       String s = text.substring (0, index + 1);
       g.drawString (s, 10, 30);
    }
}
```

`TypeWriter` mimics the effect of a typewriter typing a message, one character at a time. It follows a standard pattern that Java applets use to achieve animation. With a few modifications, this pattern also can be used by JFC applications.

A `Thread` variable is required to reference a `Thread` object that controls the animation. This object is created and the animation thread is started in the applet's `start` method. The `Thread` object is marked for garbage collection in the applet's `stop` method when `null` is assigned to the `Thread` variable.

The `Thread` constructor used to initialize the `Thread` object requires a single argument. This argument must be an object that implements the `Runnable` interface. Because `this` is passed as the argument, the object implementing `Runnable` is the current applet object. To implement `Runnable`, the applet must provide a `run` method. It is in this method that the animation loop is placed.

The animation loop runs for as long as the Web page containing the applet is the currently displayed Web page. As soon as the user switches to another Web page, it is important to stop this loop. Otherwise, the animation thread keeps running. To know when to stop, a reference to the current `Thread` object must be obtained. Then, for each iteration of the animation loop, the current thread reference is compared to the original `Thread` object reference. If they differ, the animation loop "knows" that the applet's `stop` method was called, and the `run` method terminates.

Each iteration of the animation loop does three things: First, it pauses for 200 milliseconds by calling `Thread.sleep`. Then, it calls the AWT's `repaint` method. This method asks the AWT to draw the next frame by calling `paint`. (More will be said about `repaint` in the next chapter.) Finally, an index variable is updated for determining what gets drawn in the next frame. This index can be thought of as the frame number.

ANIMATING GRAPHICS AND IMAGES

Earlier, you were cautioned against using large `for` loops in a `paint` method. This restriction can be a problem if you need to draw quite a bit of graphical content (such as a star field consisting of several hundred stars). Fortunately, there is a solution—the animation process. All you need to do is restructure the original `for` loop idea into the animation idea of frames. Check out the `StarField1` applet source code in Listing 13.19 to see how this is accomplished.

LISTING 13.19 THE `StarField1` APPLET SOURCE CODE

```
// StarField1.java

import java.awt.*;
import java.applet.Applet;

public class StarField1 extends Applet implements Runnable
{
   Thread t;
   int counter;

   Color starColors [] = { Color.white, Color.darkGray, Color.lightGray,
                           Color.blue, Color.yellow };

   public void start ()
   {
      if (t == null)
      {
          t = new Thread (this);
          counter = 0;
          t.start ();
      }
   }

   public void stop ()
   {
      t = null;
   }
```

LISTING 13.19 CONTINUED

```
public void run ()
{
   Thread current = Thread.currentThread ();

   while (t == current)
   {
      // Draw frame

      repaint (); // This method causes the update method to be called.

      // Pause

      try
      {
         Thread.sleep (50);
      }
      catch (InterruptedException e) {}

      // Manipulate counter

      if (++counter > 500)
          counter = 0;
   }
}

public void paint (Graphics g)
{
   // The following getClipBounds method call returns
   // a rectangle that contains the dimensions of the
   // clip (a rectangular portion of the drawing
   // surface that must be redrawn, because of
   // damage). Damage represents a "hole" in the
   // drawing surface. It occurs when a window
   // partially (or completely) obscures the drawing
   // surface and then is removed. Because the
   // surface's obscured pixels were replaced by the
   // overlapping window, they must be redrawn.
   // Rather than redraw the entire drawing surface,
   // only the clip should be redrawn - which also
   // improves drawing performance.


   Rectangle r = g.getClipBounds ();

   // Redraw the clip area by filling all pixels with
   // the color black. Any stars in this area will be
   // wiped out.

   g.setColor (Color.black);
   g.fillRect (r.x, r.y, r.width, r.height);
}

// Return a random integer from 0 through limit - 1.
```

LISTING 13.19 CONTINUED

```
    int rnd (int limit)
    {
       return (int) (Math.random () * limit);
    }

    public void update (Graphics g)
    {
       // When there are enough stars, redraw the background
       // and erase visible stars.

       if (counter == 0)
           paint (g);

       // Set the next star's color and draw this star.

       g.setColor (starColors [rnd (starColors.length)]);

       int x = rnd (getSize ().width);
       int y = rnd (getSize ().height);

       g.drawLine (x, y, x, y);    }
}
```

`StarField1` is an animation program that displays a constantly changing star field on a black background. To achieve animation, `StarField1` uses the same multithreading technique as `TypeWriter`. However, `StarField1` also makes use of a clipping rectangle and distributes the painting task between its `paint` and `update` methods. To understand why this is done, it's important to learn about the AWT's painting process.

Painting is initiated in one of two ways: system-controlled and program-controlled. System-controlled painting occurs when the AWT directly calls the `paint` method. This usually happens when a window that either completely or partially obscures the program's drawing surface is removed, or the program's drawing surface is resized. When either scenario happens, the colors of those pixels occupying the previously obscured portion of the drawing surface (or the entire drawing surface—if resized) will be changed to a default background color (such as white). (These pixels are said to be damaged.) This situation is not desirable for `StarField1`, whose background must be black. As a result, this program's `paint` method takes care of setting background pixels to black. Before this is done, `paint` calls the `getClipBounds` method to return a clipping rectangle. The clipping rectangle's coordinates and dimensions identify the region of damage (either those drawing surface pixels that were obscured or all pixels—if the drawing surface was resized). `StarField1`'s `paint` method uses the clipping rectangle in conjunction with the `fillRect` method to ensure that only damaged pixels are colored black.

Tip

Although it's possible to set all drawing surface pixels to an appropriate background color (such as black), this is rather wasteful when only a few pixels have been obscured. However, if your program's `paint` method is designed to modify only pixels that lie in the clipping rectangle, it will achieve a better drawing performance, than if it always modifies all drawing surface pixels.

The problem with the approach that `StarField1` uses to repair damage to its background is that any stars displayed in the damaged region are erased. The technique of double buffering (discussed later in this chapter) solves this problem.

Program-controlled painting results from the program calling the `repaint` method. In response, the AWT calls the program's `update` method. Because `StarField1` was designed to erase all stars after 500 stars have been displayed (otherwise the star field looks cluttered), it only calls `paint` to clear the star field whenever the `counter` variable is zero. (This variable is reset to zero when it reaches 500.) The only other task performed by `update` is to generate a new color and position for a star, and to draw this star.

Note

Like `paint`, `update` is called by the AWT and is used to update a drawing surface. However, the inherited version of `update` clears the drawing surface's background to a default color (such as white) before calling `paint`. This method is overridden to prevent this clearing to a default color, and to control when the background is cleared to black. As with `repaint`, `update` will be more fully discussed in the next chapter.

Figure 13.23 `StarField1` shows one frame of an animated star field.

Now that you've seen animated graphics, you're probably eager to see how images are animated. As you'll discover, there isn't a lot of difference between animating graphics and images.

Listing 13.20 presents source code to the `Animator1` applet. This applet takes advantage of HTML parameters to animate images.

Listing 13.20 The `Animator1` Applet Source Code

```
// Animator1.java

import java.awt.*;
import java.net.URL;
```

LISTING 13.20 CONTINUED

```
import java.applet.Applet;

public class Animator1 extends Applet implements Runnable
{
   Thread t;
   int frameNo;
   Image imArray [];

   public void init ()
   {
      String prefix = getParameter ("imageprefix");
      if (prefix == null)
      {
          System.out.println ("image prefix parameter missing");
          return;
      }

      String ext = getParameter ("imageext");
      if (ext == null)
      {
          System.out.println ("image extension parameter missing");
          return;
      }

      String nimages = getParameter ("numimages");
      if (nimages == null)
      {
          System.out.println ("number of images parameter missing");
          return;
      }

      int numImages = Integer.parseInt (nimages);

      if (numImages < 0)
      {
          System.out.println ("number of images < 0");
          return;
      }

      imArray = new Image [numImages];

      URL u = getDocumentBase ();

      for (int i = 0; i < numImages; i++)
      {
           imArray [i] = getImage (u, prefix + i + ext);
           showStatus ("Loading frame " + i);
      }
   }

   public void start ()
   {
      if (t == null)
      {
          t = new Thread (this);
```

LISTING 13.20 CONTINUED

```
           frameNo = 0;
           t.start ();
       }
   }

   public void stop ()
   {
     t = null;
   }

   public void run ()
   {
      Thread current = Thread.currentThread ();

      while (t == current)
      {
         repaint ();

         try
         {
            Thread.sleep (50);
         }
         catch (InterruptedException e) {}

         frameNo++;
         if (frameNo >= imArray.length)
             frameNo = 0;
      }
   }

   public void paint (Graphics g)
   {
      g.drawImage (imArray [frameNo], 0, 0, this);

      showStatus ("Showing frame " + frameNo);
   }
}
```

Much of `Animator1`'s code is pretty straightforward. You've already seen most of these techniques in prior applets. One item that will be new to you is the `showStatus` method. This method, inherited from `Applet`, displays a string of text in a browser's (or the Applet Viewer's) status bar. It is useful for providing updates of what is happening.

As you scan through the `init` method, you'll discover several calls to the `getParameter` method. This method allows `Animator1` to be more adaptable. Three parameters are used by `Animator1`: `imageprefix` provides the name of an image file, `imageext` provides the file's extension (such as `.gif` or `.jpg`), and `numimages` provides a count of image files. To create an image filename, `Animator1` concatenates the extension to a number ranging from zero through one less than the `numimages` value, which in turn is concatenated to the prefix. For example, assuming a prefix of `sts`, an extension of `.jpg`, and a `numimages` value of `506`, `Animator1` will generate filenames ranging from `sts0.jpg` through `sts505.jpg`. Listing 13.21 provides an example of what the HTML code looks like to run this applet.

LISTING 13.21 THE Animator1 APPLET HTML CODE

```
<applet code="Animator1.class" width=175 height=135>
<param name="imageprefix" value="sts">
<param name="imageext" value=".jpg">
<param name="numimages" value="506">
</applet>
```

The `Animator1` HTML is configured to animate 506 image frames of a Space Shuttle landing. (The space shuttle is also known as the Space Transport System or STS.) When run, this applet looks like a tiny TV set. Figure 13.24 shows `Animator1` displaying one of these frames.

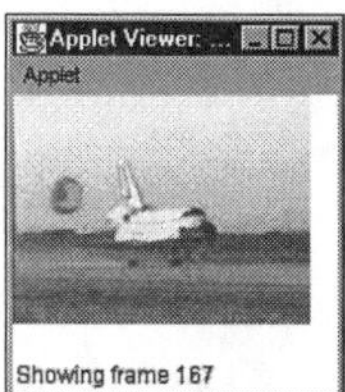

Figure 13.24 `Animator1` shows one frame of a Space Shuttle landing animation.

TRACKING MEDIA

When you run `Animator1`, you'll notice a lot of flicker. Part of the flicker has to do with the absence of an `update` method. Without this method, the background is cleared between each frame. This clearing causes momentary jitters that are picked up by the human eye. The rest of this flicker has to do with the animation starting before all frames are loaded.

The AWT provides the `MediaTracker` class (located in the `java.awt` package) to track media loading. Contrary to its name, `MediaTracker` only tracks image loading—audio loading is not tracked.

To use `MediaTracker`, you create a `MediaTracker` object, call one of its methods to add each image file (whose loading you want to track) to `MediaTracker`'s internal data structure, and call a method to wait until `MediaTracker` has loaded all files. To see what this looks like, check out the `Animator2` source code in Listing 13.22.

LISTING 13.22 THE Animator2 APPLET SOURCE CODE

```
// Animator2.java

import java.awt.*;
import java.net.URL;
import java.applet.Applet;

public class Animator2 extends Applet implements Runnable
{
   Thread t;
   int frameNo;
   Image imArray [];
```

LISTING 13.22 CONTINUED

```
public void init ()
{
   String prefix = getParameter ("imageprefix");
   if (prefix == null)
   {
       System.out.println ("image prefix parameter missing");
       return;
   }

   String ext = getParameter ("imageext");
   if (ext == null)
   {
       System.out.println ("image extension parameter missing");
       return;
   }

   String nimages = getParameter ("numimages");
   if (nimages == null)
   {
       System.out.println ("number of images parameter missing");
       return;
   }

   int numImages = Integer.parseInt (nimages);

   if (numImages < 0)
   {
       System.out.println ("number of images < 0");
       return;
   }

   imArray = new Image [numImages];

   URL u = getDocumentBase ();

   MediaTracker mt = new MediaTracker (this);

   for (int i = 0; i < numImages; i++)
   {
        imArray [i] = getImage (u, prefix + i + ext);
        mt.addImage (imArray [i], 0);
        showStatus ("Loading frame " + i);
   }

   showStatus ("Waiting for load completion");

   try
   {
      mt.waitForID (0);
   }
   catch (InterruptedException e) {}
}

public void start ()
```

LISTING 13.22 CONTINUED

```
    {
       if (t == null)
       {
           t = new Thread (this);
           frameNo = 0;
           t.start ();
       }
    }

    public void stop ()
    {
      t = null;
    }

    public void run ()
    {
       Thread current = Thread.currentThread ();

       while (t == current)
       {
          repaint ();

          try
          {
             Thread.sleep (50);
          }
          catch (InterruptedException e) {}

          frameNo++;
          if (frameNo >= imArray.length)
              frameNo = 0;
       }
    }

    public void paint (Graphics g)
    {
       g.drawImage (imArray [frameNo], 0, 0, this);

       showStatus ("Showing frame " + frameNo);
    }

    public void update (Graphics g)
    {
       paint (g);
    }
}
```

A MediaTracker object is created in the init method. Its addImage method is called to add an image to its data structure. Upon examination, you'll notice that zero is passed as an argument to this method. This number identifies an image and is used for grouping purposes. (Different numbers can be assigned to different groups of images to facilitate management.) Finally, MediaTracker's waitForID method is called. Zero is passed as an argument to this method. As a result, waitForID forces the applet thread to wait until all image files associated with group code zero have loaded.

If you don't want to use MediaTracker, there is an alternative. This alternative involves two methods inherited from Component—prepareImage and checkImage—and is somewhat faster than MediaTracker. (MediaTracker internally uses these methods but is slowed down by some internal bookkeeping.)

The prepareImage method is called to start the producer associated with its Image argument, whereas checkImage checks to see if the image has loaded and returns a combination of status flags. These flags are represented by constants in the ImageObserver interface. For example, the ALLBITS constant means the image has completely loaded.

The following code fragment shows how you might modify the init method in Animator1 to use this alternative. (This code fragment was taken from the Animator3 applet, included with this book's source code.)

```
for (int i = 0; i < numImages; i++)
{
     imArray [i] = getImage (u, prefix + i + ext);
     prepareImage (imArray [i], this);
     showStatus ("Loading frame " + i);
}

showStatus ("Waiting for load completion");

for (int i = 0; i < numImages; i++)
     while ((checkImage (imArray [i], this) &
             ImageObserver.ALLBITS) != ImageObserver.ALLBITS)
     {
        // Occasionally, yield control to other threads.
        // This makes the system more responsive.

        Thread.yield ();
     }
}
```

DOUBLE BUFFERING

Some animations are complicated. They require multiple overlapping images to be drawn via drawImage. Furthermore, other Graphics methods might need to be called to add effects. Despite overriding update and using MediaTracker, flicker can still occur because of the time required to render all of this information, and the human eye observes part of this process. A solution to this problem was devised some years ago, and is known as double buffering.

Double buffering is the technique of creating a buffer, rendering all graphics and images to the buffer, and drawing the buffer on the drawing surface. It takes advantage of the createImage and getGraphics methods.

The Component class provides a pair of createImage methods that are inherited by every drawing surface. One of these methods takes a pair of int arguments that represents the size of the buffer (in pixels), and returns a reference to an `Image` subclass object. For example, the following code fragment creates a buffer of 100 horizontal by 200 vertical pixels:

```
Image buffer;
// ...
buffer = createImage (100, 200);
```

The `Image` class provides a method called `getGraphics`. This method returns a graphics context associated with `Image`—as long as `Image` represents a buffer. Otherwise, `null` is returned. The following code fragment shows how to extract this context from the buffer in the previous code fragment:

```
Graphics bkContext = buffer.getGraphics ();
```

You perform all your drawing operations using this graphics context. The following code fragment illustrates this concept by building on the previous code fragments:

```
bkContext.setColor (Color.red);
bkContext.drawLine (10, 10, 30, 30);
```

Finally, in the `paint` method, you dump the contents of the buffer to the drawing surface. Bringing together all the previous code fragments results in the following logic:

```
Image buffer;
Graphics bkContext;

public void init ()
{
   buffer = createImage (100, 200);
   bkContext = buffer.getGraphics ();
}

public void run ()
{
// ... setup code

   bkContext.setColor (Color.red);
   bkContext.drawLine (10, 10, 30, 30);

   repaint ();

// ... additional code
}

public void paint (Graphics g)
{
   // You can manipulate the buffer from any method, including paint.

   g.drawImage (buffer, 0, 0, this);
}
```

When you use double buffering, the idea is to prepare a single frame of animation at a time. This frame consists of a buffer's contents—built using a wide variety of `Graphics` method calls. You want all this work to occur in the `run` method and only display the buffer in the `paint` method.

Note

A `StarField2` applet is included with this book's source code. This program uses double-buffering to ensure that no stars are erased when the user obscures or resizes the applet's drawing surface. (If you recall, this was a problem with `StarField1`.)

PRODUCING IMAGES

A producer is responsible for passing image data to a consumer. To be a producer, an object's class must implement the `ImageProducer` interface. (It's good to understand this interface in the event that you want to create your own producer.) One of the color models that the producer might use to represent pixel colors is the direct color model. The producer can work with the direct color model by using the `DirectColorModel` class. Instead of creating your own producers, you can take advantage of the AWT's `MemoryImageSource` class.

THE `ImageProducer` INTERFACE

Any object implementing the `ImageProducer` interface (located in the `java.awt.image` package) is known as a producer. A consumer can call this interface's methods to register itself with a producer and request image data. These methods include

- `addConsumer`
- `isConsumer`
- `removeConsumer`
- `requestTopDownLeftRight`
- `startProduction`

The `addConsumer` method registers a consumer with the producer. It has the following signature:

```
void addConsumer (ImageConsumer ic)
```

The consumer is represented by `ic`. It will be notified when image data becomes available.

The `isConsumer` method determines if a given consumer is currently registered with the producer. It has the following signature:

```
boolean isConsumer (ImageConsumer ic)
```

The consumer is represented by `ic`. A Boolean `true` value is returned if `ic` is registered with the producer.

The `removeConsumer` method de-registers a consumer from the producer. It has the following signature:

```
void removeConsumer (ImageConsumer ic)
```

The consumer is represented by `ic`. After it is de-registered, the consumer is no longer eligible to receive image data.

The `requestTopDownLeftRight` method requests the producer to resend image data. It has the following signature:

```
void requestTopDownLeftRight (ImageConsumer ic)
```

The consumer, represented by `ic`, requests the producer to resend image data in top/down/left/right order so that higher quality conversion algorithms (dependent on this order) can create a better rendered version of the image.

The `startProduction` method registers a consumer with the producer and requests that image data immediately be sent to the consumer. It has the following signature:

```
void startProduction (ImageConsumer ic)
```

The consumer is represented by `ic`.

THE DirectColorModel CLASS

The `DirectColorModel` class (located in the `java.awt` package) is used to create objects representing direct color models. Each pixel is represented by a 32-bit color number.

`DirectColorModel` inherits methods from `ColorModel`, and provides a few methods of its own. These methods include

- constructors
- `getAlphaMask`
- `getBlueMask`
- `getGreenMask`
- `getRedMask`

The first of `DirectColorModel`'s constructors has the following signature:

```
DirectColorModel (int bits, int redMask, int greenMask, int blueMask,
                  int alphaMask)
```

This constructor initializes a `DirectColorModel` object to a model that uses `bits` to represent the total number of bits per pixel. This value is less than or equal to 32. The `redMask`, `greenMask`, `blueMask`, and `alphaMask` arguments state where in a pixel's bits each color component exists. Each of the bit masks must be contiguous (for example, green cannot occupy only the first and eighth bits) and should not exceed 8 bits in size. When joined together, the numbers of mask bits should sum to the value specified by `bits`.

The color number-based direct color model can be created by using the following code fragment:

```
DirectColorModel dcm = new DirectColorModel (32, 0x00ff0000, 0x0000ff00,
                                             0x000000ff, 0xff000000);
```

An `IllegalArgumentException` object is thrown if the bits in a mask are not contiguous, the number of mask bits exceeds `bits`, or mask bits overlap (that is, the same bit appears in two or more masks).

The second `DirectColorModel` constructor has the following signature:

```
DirectColorModel (int bits, int redMask, int greenMask, int blueMask)
```

This constructor calls the previous constructor. It passes an alpha mask of `0x00000000`, which means that this color model will not have a transparency component. All colors will be fully opaque with an alpha value of 255.

The `getAlphaMask`, `getBlueMask`, `getGreenMask`, and `getRedMask` methods return the alpha, blue, green, and red component masks, respectively. In all cases, the returned values ranges from 0 through 255. These methods have the following signatures:

```
int getAlphaMask ()

int getBlueMask ()

int getGreenMask ()

int getRedMask ()
```

THE `MemoryImageSource` CLASS

The `MemoryImageSource` class (located in the `java.awt.image` package) is used to create producers that produce images from arrays of pixels. Basically, you create an array of pixel data and pass this array along with a color model to a `MemoryImageSource` constructor. The resulting object becomes a producer for this image. It passes the pixel and color model information to a consumer. In addition to the `ImageProducer` methods, `MemoryImageSource` provides six constructors and several of its own methods.

`MemoryImageSource`'s constructors include

```
MemoryImageSource (int w, int h, ColorModel cm, byte [] pixels,
                   int off, int scan)

MemoryImageSource (int w, int h, ColorModel cm, byte [] pixels,
                   int off, int scan, Hashtable prop)

MemoryImageSource (int w, int h, ColorModel cm, int [] pixels,
                   int off, int scan)

MemoryImageSource (int w, int h, ColorModel cm, int [] pixels,
                   int off, int scan, Hashtable prop)

MemoryImageSource (int w, int h, int [] pixels, int off, int scan)

MemoryImageSource (int w, int h, int [] pixels, int off, int scan,
                   Hashtable properties)
```

The `w` and `h` arguments specify the width and height of the image (in pixels). The `cm` argument specifies the color model. If not present, `ColorModel`'s `getRGBDefault` method is called to supply the default color number-based direct color model. The `pixels` argument specifies an array of pixels. This is either a `byte` array (for use with the index color model) or an `int` array (for use with the direct color model). The `off` argument specifies the offset of the first pixel in the array. This is usually zero. The `scan` argument specifies the number of pixels per row and is usually equal to `w`. The `prop` argument specifies a `Hashtable` of properties (such as copyright information) to be associated with the image. If this argument isn't present, no properties are assumed.

Listing 13.23 presents source code to a `ColorBlend1` applet that demonstrates using `MemoryImageSource`.

LISTING 13.23 THE `ColorBlend1` APPLET SOURCE CODE

```
// ColorBlend1.java

import java.awt.*;
import java.awt.image.*;
import java.applet.Applet;

public class ColorBlend1 extends Applet
{
   Image im;

   public void init ()
   {
      int width = getSize ().width;
      int height = getSize ().height;

      int [] pixels = new int [width * height];

      int index = 0;

      for (int y = 0; y < height; y++)
      {
           int numerator = y * 255;
           int b = numerator / height;
           int r = 255 - numerator / height;

           for (int x = 0; x < width; x++)
           {
                int g = x * 255 / width;
                pixels [index++] = (255 << 24) | (r << 16) | (g << 8)
                                   | b;
           }
      }

      im = createImage (new MemoryImageSource (width, height, pixels,
                                               0, width));
   }

   public void paint (Graphics g)
   {
      g.drawImage (im, 0, 0, this);
   }
}
```

`ColorBlend1` creates an image from a blend of the primary colors. `MemoryImageSource` is used to produce this image and the default color number-based direct color model is the color model.

The image is created as follows: An array of pixels is allocated. The size of this array is equal to the width and height of the applet. For each pixel, the intensity of its blue component is chosen to be weak toward the top of the image and increase toward the bottom. In contrast, the intensity of red is chosen to be strong toward the top and decrease toward the bottom. Toward the left side, the intensity of green is chosen to be weak and increase toward the right. All pixels are completely opaque. This results in a pleasant blend of colors. Figure 13.25 shows `ColorBlend1`'s output. (The colors are not shown in the figure. To see these colors, please run `ColorBlend1`.)

Figure 13.25 `ColorBlend1` shows a color-blended image.

Because `MemoryImageSource` supports animation, it is possible to pass multiple frames to consumers using this producer. This feature mimics animated GIFs. To accomplish this task, `MemoryImageSource` provides the `setAnimated`, `setFullBufferUpdates`, and several overloaded `newPixels` methods. The idea is to call `setAnimated` and `setFullBufferUpdates` immediately after creating a `MemoryImageSource` object. Then, when it comes time to do the actual animation, you keep calling one or more of the `newPixels` methods to send partial or complete frames to the consumer. (For more information, check out the SDK documentation.)

Note

For an example of a program that uses this kind of animation, check out the source code to the `ColorBlend2` applet. (This source code is included with the rest of this book's source code.)

If you are having trouble trying to extract an image's properties (assuming that it has properties), see "Extracting Property Values," in the "Troubleshooting" section at the end of this chapter.

Consuming Images

Consumers complement producers. A consumer receives image data from a producer and is responsible for storing or manipulating this data. To be a consumer, an object's class must implement the `ImageConsumer` interface. (If you ever want to create your own consumer, you'll need to understand this interface.) One of the color models that the consumer might have to work with is the index color model. This color model is the result of the producer creating an object from the `IndexColorModel` class. Instead of creating your own consumers, you can take advantage of the AWT's `PixelGrabber` class.

THE `ImageConsumer` INTERFACE

Any object implementing the `ImageConsumer` interface (located in the `java.awt.image` package) is known as a consumer. A producer can call this interface's methods to send notifications and data to a consumer. These methods include

- `imageComplete`
- `setColorModel`
- `setDimensions`
- `setHints`
- `setPixels`
- `setProperties`

The `imageComplete` method is called when a complete image has been transferred to the consumer. It has the following signature:

```
void imageComplete (int status)
```

This method provides the consumer with status information, via the `status` argument. This argument tells the consumer why the producer has finished producing an image, and is represented by one of the following `ImageConsumer` constants:

- **`IMAGEABORTED`**—The producer had to abort production. A retry might succeed.
- **`IMAGEERROR`**—The producer had to abort production because of a serious error (such as invalid pixel data). A retry will not succeed.
- **`SINGLEFRAMEDONE`**—A frame apart from the last frame has completed loading. There are additional frames to produce.
- **`STATICIMAGEDONE`**—The final frame has completed loading. There are no more frames to produce.

The `setColorModel` method informs the consumer about the color model being used for the majority of the image's pixels. It has the following signature:

```
void setColorModel (ColorModel model)
```

The `model` argument can be used to optimize the image. However, because each call to `setPixels` is given its own `ColorModel` argument, `model` is only advisory.

The `setDimensions` method passes the actual dimensions of an image to the consumer. It has the following signature:

```
void setDimensions (int width, int height)
```

The `width` and `height` arguments contain the actual dimensions. The consumer will perform scaling and resizing as appropriate.

The `setHints` method provides hints for optimally rendering an image. It has the following signature:

```
void setHints (int hints)
```

This method is called prior to `setPixels`. The `hints` argument is formed by ORing together the following `ImageConsumer` constants:

- **`COMPLETESCANLINES`**—Each call to `setPixels` will deliver at least one complete scan line of pixels.
- **`RANDOMPIXELORDER`**–The pixels are not provided in any particular order. As a result, optimization that depends on pixel delivery order cannot be performed by the consumer.
- **`SINGLEFRAME`**—The image consists of a single frame. An example of an image that does not consist of a single frame is a GIF89a image.
- **`SINGLEPASS`**—Expect each pixel to be delivered once and only once. (Certain image formats, such as JPEG, deliver an image in several passes, with each pass yielding a much clearer image.)
- **`TOPDOWNLEFTRIGHT`**–Expect the pixels to arrive in a top/down/left/right order.

The first of two overloaded `setPixels` methods has the following signature:

```
void setPixels (int x, int y, int width, int height, ColorModel cm,
                byte [] pixels, int off, int scan)
```

This method delivers pixels to the consumer as a rectangle of bytes. The `x`, `y`, `width`, and `height` arguments specify the upper-left corner and dimensions of this rectangle. These dimensions are relative to the actual size of the image. The color model is passed via `cm`. The pixels are taken from the array `pixels`. The location of the first pixel is found at `pixels [off]`. The length of an array scan line is specified by `scan`. Usually, `scan` equals `width`. To determine the location of pixel (`a`, `b`), use the following formula: `((b - y) * scan + (a - x) + off)`. (This method is usually called when the index color model is used.)

The second overloaded `setPixels` method has the following signature:

```
void setPixels (int x, int y, int width, int height, ColorModel cm,
                int [] pixels, int off, int scan)
```

This method is similar to the other `setPixels` method except that `pixels` is specified as an array of `int`s. This is necessary when there are more than 8 bits of data per pixel. (This method is usually called when the direct color model is used.)

The `setProperties` method passes image properties to the consumer. It has the following signature:

```
void setProperties (Hashtable properties)
```

Properties might include copyright, cropping, or comment information. These properties can be retrieved at a later time by calling `Image`'s `getProperty` method. (Many images do not have properties.)

THE `IndexColorModel` CLASS

The `IndexColorModel` class is used to create objects representing index color models. This model uses a lookup table (also known as a color map) with a maximum size of 256 entries.

Each entry holds a color number. A pixel is represented by an index into the lookup table and is no more than 8 bits in size.

`IndexColorModel` inherits methods from `ColorModel`, and provides a few methods of its own. These methods include

- constructors
- `getAlphas`
- `getBlues`
- `getGreens`
- `getMapSize`
- `getReds`
- `getTransparentPixel`

The first of `IndexColorModel`'s constructors has the following signature:

```
IndexColorModel (int bits, int size, byte [] cmap, int start,
                 boolean hasAlpha, int transparent)
```

The number of bits used to represent each pixel is specified by `bits`. This number must not exceed 8. The number of elements in the internal color map is specified by `size` and must not be less than the number 2 raised to the power of `bits`. If `hasAlpha` is true, the color map's color numbers include alpha components. If the image will have a transparent pixel, `transparent` is the index of this pixel in the color map. Otherwise, `transparent` should be set to -1.

The color map is specified by `cmap` and `start` is the index at which this map begins—prior elements are ignored. Each map entry consists of 3 or 4 consecutive bytes. If `hasAlpha` is `true`, this entry consists of 4 bytes and contains a 32-bit color number. Otherwise, this entry consists of 3 bytes and contains a 24-bit color number. (There is no alpha component.)

If `bits` is greater than 8, `size` is greater than 2 to the power of `bits`, or `cmap` is too small to hold the color map, an `ArrayIndexOutOfBoundsException` object is thrown.

Note

A *transparent pixel* is a pixel with an index in the color map that refers to a color number whose alpha component is ignored. Transparent pixels are commonly used with GIF files. A transparent pixel can be used by color models that either ignore transparency levels in other entries (when `hasAlpha` is `false`) or support these levels (when `hasAlpha` is `true`).

The second `IndexColorModel` constructor has the following signature:

```
IndexColorModel (int bits, int size, byte [] cmap, int start, boolean hasAlpha)
```

This constructor calls the previous constructor with `transparent` set to –1.

The third `IndexColorModel` constructor has the following signature:

```
IndexColorModel (int bits, int size, byte [] red, byte [] green, byte [] blue,
                 int transparent)
```

Instead of a single color map array, this constructor uses three arrays to represent the red, green, and blue components. These arrays must each be at least `size` elements in length. A pixel with index `i` has a red component at `red [i]`, a green component at `green [i]`, and a blue component at `blue [i]`.

If `bits` is greater than 8, `size` is greater than 2 to the power of `bits`, or the `red`, `green`, and `blue` arrays are too small to hold the color map, an `ArrayIndexOutOfBoundsException` object is thrown.

The fourth `IndexColorModel` constructor has the following signature:

```
IndexColorModel (int bits, int size, byte [] red, byte [] green, byte [] blue)
```

This constructor calls the previous constructor with `transparent` set to –1.

The final `IndexColorModel` constructor has the following signature:

```
IndexColorModel (int bits, int size, byte [] red, byte [] green, byte [] blue,
                 byte [] alpha)
```

This constructor is similar to the previous two constructors except an `alpha` array is used instead of a transparent pixel. This allows you to determine the amount of transparency for each individual color number.

If `bits` is greater than eight or `size` is greater than two to the power of `bits` or the `red`, `green`, `blue` and `alpha` arrays are too small to hold the color map, an `ArrayIndexOutOfBoundsException` object is thrown.

The `getAlphas` method returns an array of all alpha components in the color map. It has the following signature:

```
void getAlphas (byte [] alphas)
```

Space must be pre-allocated for `alphas`, so that this array is capable of holding at least `size` elements.

The `getBlues` method returns an array of all blue components in the color map. It has the following signature:

```
void getBlues (byte [] blues)
```

Space must be pre-allocated for `blues`, so that this array is capable of holding at least `size` elements.

The `getGreens` method returns an array of all green components in the color map. It has the following signature:

```
void getGreens (byte [] greens)
```

Space must be pre-allocated for `greens`, so that this array is capable of holding at least `size` elements.

The `getMapSize` method returns the number of entries in the color map. It has the following signature:

```
int getMapSize ()
```

The `getReds` method returns an array of all red components in the color map. It has the following signature:

```
void getReds (byte [] reds)
```

Space must be pre-allocated for `reds`, so that this array is capable of holding at least `size` elements.

The `getTransparentPixel` method returns the index of the color map entry that represents the transparent pixel. It has the following signature:

```
int getTransparentPixel ()
```

If there is no transparent pixel, -1 is returned.

THE `PixelGrabber` CLASS

The `PixelGrabber` class (located in the `java.awt.image` package) is used to create consumers that consume images and place the pixels in arrays. These consumers are the opposite of `MemoryImageSource` producers and can be used to extract image pixels for storage in files. To recreate an image, load the pixels into an array and pass this array to a `MemoryImageSource` producer. In addition to the `ImageConsumer` methods, `PixelGrabber` provides the following:

- constructors
- `abortGrabbing`
- `getColorModel`
- `getHeight`
- `getPixels`
- `getStatus`
- `getWidth`
- `grabPixels`
- `startGrabbing`

The first `PixelGrabber` constructor has the following signature:

```
PixelGrabber (ImageProducer ip, int x, int y, int width, int height,
              int [] pixels, int off, int scan)
```

The `PixelGrabber` object uses `ip` as its producer. This producer stores the image whose upper-left corner is (`x`, `y`) and dimensions are (`width`, `height`) in the `pixels` array beginning at `pixels [off]`. Each row starts at `scan` increments. The default color number-based direct color model is used.

The second PixelGrabber constructor has the following signature:

```
PixelGrabber (Image im, int x, int y, int width, int height, int [] pixels,
              int off, int scan)
```

This constructor extracts the producer by calling im.getSource and then calls the previous constructor.

The final PixelGrabber constructor has the following signature:

```
PixelGrabber (Image im, int x, int y, int width, int height, boolean forceRGB)
```

No array needs to be pre-allocated. This constructor takes care of that task. The forceRGB argument determines whether the original or the default color number-based direct color model is used.

The abortGrabbing method causes pixel grabbing to stop. It has the following signature:

```
void abortGrabbing ()
```

Any thread waiting for pixel data via grabPixels is interrupted and grabPixels throws an InterruptedException object.

The getColorModel method retrieves the color model. It has the following signature:

```
ColorModel getColorModel ()
```

This method returns null until pixel grabbing has finished.

The getHeight method retrieves the image's height. It has the following signature:

```
int getHeight ()
```

This method returns -1 until pixel grabbing is finished.

The getPixels method retrieves the image's pixels as an array. It has the following signature:

```
Object getPixels ()
```

This method returns null until pixel grabbing is finished.

The getStatus method provides information on whether pixel grabbing succeeded. It has the following signature:

```
int getStatus ()
```

The return value is a set of flags specified by ImageObserver. These flags can be ORed together. ALLBITS and FRAMEBITS indicate success. ABORT and ERROR indicate production problems.

The getWidth method retrieves the image's width. It has the following signature:

```
int getWidth ()
```

This method returns -1 until pixel grabbing is finished.

The grabPixels method starts the pixel grabbing process. It has the following signature:

```
boolean grabPixels ()
```

This method starts storing pixel data. It doesn't return until all pixels have been stored. A Boolean `true` value is returned if all pixels were obtained. An `InterruptedException` object is thrown if the thread waiting for pixel data is interrupted.

The `startGrabbing` method makes it possible to asynchronously retrieve image data. It has the following signature:

```
void startGrabbing ()
```

This method immediately returns. You should call the `getStatus` method to find out when grabbing is complete.

Listing 13.24 presents source code to a `Negative` applet that demonstrates using `PixelGrabber` with `MemoryImageSource`.

LISTING 13.24 THE `Negative` APPLET SOURCE CODE

```
// Negative.java

import java.awt.*;
import java.awt.image.*;
import java.applet.Applet;

public class Negative extends Applet
{
   Image im, imInv;
   int width;

   public void init ()
   {
      MediaTracker mt = new MediaTracker (this);
      im = getImage (getCodeBase (), "tiger.jpg");
      mt.addImage (im, 0);

      try
      {
         mt.waitForID (0);
      }
      catch (InterruptedException e) {}

      width = im.getWidth (this);
      int height = im.getHeight (this);

      int [] pixels = new int [width * height];

      PixelGrabber pg = new PixelGrabber (im, 0, 0, width, height,
                                          pixels, 0, width);

      try
      {
         pg.grabPixels ();
      }
      catch (InterruptedException e) {}

      int size = width * height;
      for (int i = 0; i < size; i++)
```

Listing 13.24 Continued

```
            pixels [i] = pixels [i] ^ 0xffffff;

        imInv = createImage (new MemoryImageSource (width, height,
                                                     pixels, 0, width));
    }

    public void paint (Graphics g)
    {
        g.drawImage (im, 0, 0, this);
        g.drawImage (imInv, width, 0, this);
    }
}
```

`Negative` displays an image of a Bengal tiger together with a negative of this image. `PixelGrabber` grabs all pixels of the tiger image and stores them in `pixels`. Each pixel's color is negated by XORing the red, green, and blue components with `0xffffff`. (Any alpha information is preserved.) Figure 13.26 shows `Negative`'s output.

Figure 13.26
`Negative` shows original and negative images.

If you are having trouble using `PixelGrabber` to save the contents of an image to a Microsoft BMP file, see "Saving Images as Bitmap Files," in the "Troubleshooting" section at the end of this chapter.

Filtering Images

What does an image sent to Earth from a distant spacecraft and an old black and white photograph have in common? The answer is deterioration. In many cases, an image sent to Earth has its pixels corrupted by solar radiation. Also, photographs tend to fade with time (with a resulting loss of detail). In either situation, image-processing techniques can recover lost details and render a higher-quality image.

The AWT provides the `FilteredImageSource` and `ImageFilter` classes, along with a variety of `ImageFilter` subclasses, to support image processing. Various filters can be constructed to perform tasks, ranging from sharpening and blurring images, to modifying colors and embossing. Filters can be cascaded together to achieve some truly powerful effects (with minimal extra coding).

THE FilteredImageSource AND ImageFilter CLASSES

The `FilteredImageSource` class (located in the `java.awt.image` package) is a producer that works with an `ImageFilter` class (also located in the `java.awt.image` package) and its subclasses to filter images.

`FilteredImageSource` works with another producer, an intermediate `ImageFilter` consumer, and an ultimate consumer. The other producer generates pixel data for an original image and sends it to `FilteredImageSource`. `FilteredImageSource` takes this data and sends it to an `ImageFilter` consumer for modification. (The data is modified so that the resulting image appears scaled, grayed, rotated, cropped, and so on.) `FilteredImageSource` then takes the data and sends it to an ultimate consumer. Figure 13.27 illustrates the relationship between these entities.

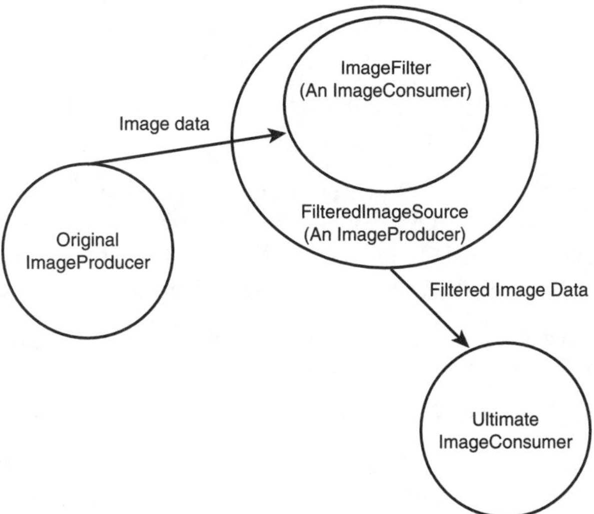

Figure 13.27
A `FilteredImageSource` producer works with other entities to create filtered images.

The default `ImageFilter` is known as a "null" filter because it doesn't modify an image. To accomplish anything useful, this class must be subclassed. Assuming you have a class that subclasses `ImageFilter`, the following code fragment illustrates how you would create and draw a filtered image.

```
Image im;
Image imFiltered;

public void init ()
{
   im = getImage (getDocumentBase (), "tiger.jpg");
   imFiltered = createImage (new FilteredImageSource (im.getSource (),
                                                      new Filter ()));
}

public void paint (Graphics g)
```

```
{
   g.drawImage (imFiltered, 0, 0, this);
}
```

FILTER CLASSES

For common filtering tasks, the AWT provides a variety of `ImageFilter` subclasses. These subclasses include

- `RGBImageFilter`
- `CropImageFilter`
- `ReplicateScaleFilter`
- `AreaAveragingScaleFilter`

All these classes are located in the `java.awt.image` package. With the exception of `RGBImageFilter`, the names of these classes reflect their purpose.

`RGBImageFilter` (located in the `java.awt.image` package) is an abstract subclass of `ImageFilter`. This class makes it possible to create filters that independently change pixels based on their position and color.

If the filtering algorithm does not depend on a pixel's position, the AWT can use an optimization for images that use the index color model. Instead of filtering individual pixels, only the color map is filtered. To tell the AWT to use this optimization, a constructor that sets `RGBImageFilter`'s `canFilterIndexColorModel` variable to `true` can be provided.

When creating an `RGBImageFilter` subclass, the only method you need to override is the abstract `filterRGB` method. This method has the following signature:

```
int filterRGB (int x, int y, int rgb)
```

The `x` and `y` arguments identify the pixel's position. If a color table entry is being filtered instead of a pixel (by setting `canFilterIndexColorModel` to `true`), -1 is passed in each of `x` and `y`. The `rgb` argument provides the existing color. The filtered `rgb` value is returned.

To see what an `RGBImageFilter` subclass looks like, check out the source code to `GrayFilter` in Listing 13.25.

LISTING 13.25 THE `GrayFilter` SOURCE CODE

```
// GrayFilter.java

import java.awt.image.*;

public class GrayFilter extends RGBImageFilter
{
   public GrayFilter ()
   {
      canFilterIndexColorModel = true;
   }
```

LISTING 13.25 CONTINUED

```
   public int filterRGB (int x, int y, int rgb)
   {
      int gray = (((rgb & 0xff0000) >> 16) +
                  ((rgb & 0x00ff00) >> 8) +
                  (rgb & 0x0000ff)) / 3;

      return (0xff000000 | (gray << 16) | (gray << 8) | gray);
   }
}
```

`GrayFilter` converts the RGB colors of an image to equivalent shades of gray. This filter can be used in conjunction with `FilteredImageSource`.

Listing 13.26 presents source code to a `GrayFilterDemo` applet that uses `GrayFilter`.

LISTING 13.26 THE `GrayFilterDemo` APPLET SOURCE CODE

```
// GrayFilterDemo.java

import java.awt.*;
import java.awt.image.*;
import java.applet.Applet;

public class GrayFilterDemo extends Applet
{
   Image im, imGray;

   public void init ()
   {
      im = getImage (getCodeBase (), "tiger.jpg");

      GrayFilter gf = new GrayFilter ();

      imGray = createImage (new FilteredImageSource (im.getSource (),
                                                     gf));
   }

   public void paint (Graphics g)
   {
      if (g.drawImage (im, 0, 0, this));
          g.drawImage (imGray, im.getWidth (this), 0, this);
   }
}
```

Figure 13.28 shows `GrayFilterDemo`'s output.

Figure 13.28
`GrayFilterDemo` shows original and grayed images.

CASCADING FILTERS

Complex filtering tasks can be simplified by chaining multiple filters together. For example, suppose you wanted to perform gray filtering followed by negative filtering. In other words, you would first like to convert RGB colors to shades of gray and then generate a negative. This is a perfect situation in which to cascade filters.

To demonstrate cascading, you will need a filter for generating a negative. The source code to a filter that accomplishes this task is presented in Listing 13.27.

LISTING 13.27 THE `NegativeFilter` SOURCE CODE

```
// NegativeFilter.java

import java.awt.image.*;

public class NegativeFilter extends RGBImageFilter
{
   public NegativeFilter ()
   {
      canFilterIndexColorModel = true;
   }

   public int filterRGB (int x, int y, int rgb)
   {
      return rgb ^ 0x00ffffff;
   }
}
```

`NegativeFilter` flips the RGB components of an image to achieve a negative. As with `GrayFilter`, this filter can be used with `FilteredImageSource`.

Listing 13.28 presents source code to a `CascadeFilterDemo` applet that uses the previous `GrayFilter` to convert an image to shades of gray, followed by `NegativeFilter` to generate a negative.

LISTING 13.28 THE `CascadeFilterDemo` APPLET SOURCE CODE

```
// CascadeFilterDemo.java

import java.awt.*;
import java.awt.image.*;
import java.applet.Applet;

public class CascadeFilterDemo extends Applet
{
   Image im, im2;

   public void init ()
   {
      im = getImage (getCodeBase (), "tiger.jpg");

      GrayFilter gf = new GrayFilter ();

      Image imTemp;
      imTemp = createImage (new FilteredImageSource (im.getSource (),
                                                      gf));

      NegativeFilter nf = new NegativeFilter ();

      im2 = createImage (new FilteredImageSource (imTemp.getSource (),
                                                   nf));
   }

   public void paint (Graphics g)
   {
      if (g.drawImage (im, 0, 0, this));
          g.drawImage (im2, im.getWidth (this), 0, this);
   }
}
```

Finally, the moment of truth is at hand. Figure 13.29 shows `CascadeFilterDemo`'s output. As you can see, the image to the right is both grayed and negated.

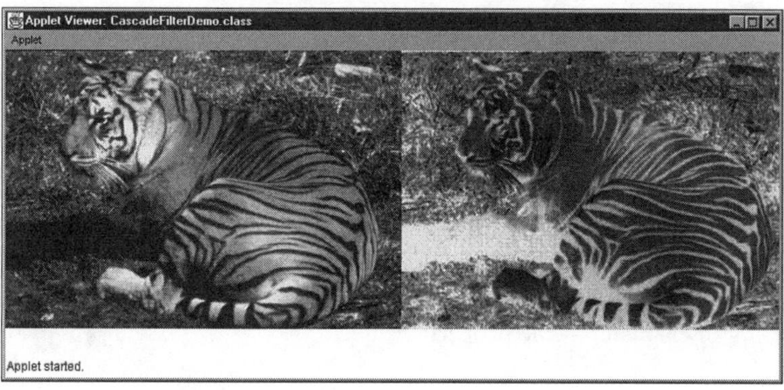

Figure 13.29 `CascadeFilterDemo` shows original and grayed/negative images.

TROUBLESHOOTING

A FLICKER-FREE DRAWING SURFACE

Whenever I try to change the font from inside a drawing surface's `paint` *method, the contents of the drawing surface flicker. What's going on?*

The problem originates from calling the wrong `setFont` method. Instead of calling `setFont` via the `Graphics` argument, you are calling the inherited `setFont` method from the `Component` class. When you call this method, a recursive loop is established and the drawing surface flickers. Here is a code fragment that demonstrates incorrectly and correctly setting the font:

```
public void paint (Graphics g)
{
   // The following method call is incorrect:
   setFont (new Font ("Serif", Font.PLAIN, 14));

   // The following method call is correct:
   g.setFont (new Font ("Serif", Font.PLAIN, 14));
}
```

EXTRACTING PROPERTY VALUES

I've heard about image property values but I'm not sure how to extract these values.

Earlier, you learned that `Image` has a method called `getProperty`. This method returns the value of an image property when it is passed a valid property name. The following code fragment (which would be placed in an applet's `init` method) shows how to extract and display (via standard output) the comment property value for a hypothetical `coffee.gif` file.

```
im = getImage (getDocumentBase (), "coffee.gif");

MediaTracker mt = new MediaTracker (this);
mt.addImage (im, 0);

try
{
   mt.waitForID (0);
}
catch (InterruptedException e) {}

System.out.println (im.getProperty ("comment", this));
```

If the producer has not yet obtained the property (or the property cannot be found) when `getProperty` is called, this method returns `Image`'s `UndefinedProperty` constant. If you try to display this constant, you'll see something like `java.lang.Object@4cce3c`. (This is due to `UndefinedProperty` being defined as type `Object`.) If everything is successful, you'll see a string of characters—the property value.

RIGHT-JUSTIFYING TEXT

If you've ever had to right-justify text when creating columns, you probably know something about frustration. When proportional fonts are involved, right-justifying text can be very difficult.

`FontMetrics` comes to the rescue with its `stringWidth` method. Using this method, you can determine the width (in pixels) of each text item. After you know the longest width, you can subtract the widths of other items and determine the starting x-coordinate for each item. As a result, you right-justify your text. The following code fragment shows you how to achieve this goal:

```
String [] num =
{
   "Price",
   "------------",
   "1.23",
   "689.32",
   "1867.00",
   "------------",
   "Total = 2557.55"
};

public void paint (Graphics g)
{
   g.setFont (new Font ("Serif", Font.PLAIN, 18));

   FontMetrics fm = g.getFontMetrics ();

   int longestWidth = 0;

   for (int i = 0; i < num.length; i++)
   {
        int width = fm.stringWidth (num [i]);
        if (width > longestWidth)
            longestWidth = width;
   }

   for (int i = 0, y = 30; i < num.length; y += fm.getHeight (), i++)
        g.drawString (num [i], 10 + longestWidth - fm.stringWidth (num [i]), y);
}
```

As a rule, it's a good idea to stay away from placing `for` loops in the `paint` method. However, for small loops, this should not be a problem.

SAVING IMAGES AS BITMAP FILES

I would like to save an image file in the Microsoft bitmap file format but I don't know how.

JavaWorld published an article titled "Java Tip 60: Saving Bitmap Files in Java." This article explains how to use `PixelGrabber` to grab an image's pixels, and then shows how to save these pixels to a Microsoft BMP file. The article is located at `http://www.javaworld.com/javaworld/javatips/f_jw-javatip60_p.html`.

CHAPTER 14

Building a GUI: AWT Style

In this chapter

by Geoff Friesen

INTRODUCING THE WINDOWING TOOLKIT

In the previous chapter, you explored the AWT's support for graphics, fonts, colors, and images. In this chapter, you'll explore the AWT's support for GUIs. This support is manifested by way of the AWT's windowing toolkit.

The *windowing toolkit* is a combination of entities and code that binds these entities to the underlying windowing system. Entities include components, containers, layout managers, events, and listeners.

Components lie at the heart of a GUI. They range from buttons, labels, and text fields to lists, choices, menus, and scrollbars. By using either the mouse or keyboard, a user can interact with most of these components to accomplish useful tasks.

Containers (such as frames and panels) organize components into meaningful groups. Because containers are also components, it is possible to nest containers in other containers. This nesting process can lead to sophisticated GUI layouts (and continue until memory is exhausted).

Layout managers automatically lay out GUIs by choosing appropriate positions and sizes for their components. As a result, a GUI can look good under any windowing system and video resolution. Without layout managers, you would have to manually take care of layout tasks. Although the resulting GUI might look okay when viewed under some windowing systems/video resolutions, it would probably look awful under others. This is not your fault! Without access to every supported windowing system and video resolution, how could you be expected to properly test your GUI?

Events are fired when users interact with components and containers. *Listeners* register themselves with these entities to "listen" for events. When an event is fired, the windowing toolkit contacts a listener and the listener takes appropriate action. For example, suppose a user presses a button. This activity results in an event being fired. Information describing this button press event is stored in an event object. The windowing toolkit passes this object to a listener and the listener handles the event.

The relationship between the windowing toolkit's components, containers, layout managers, events, and listeners is illustrated in Figure 14.1.

Over the years, the AWT's windowing toolkit has been criticized for the lackluster GUIs that it creates. Although a certain amount of criticism is justified, the windowing toolkit is able to create some nice-looking GUIs, if given a chance. By the time you reach the end of this chapter, you'll find that the windowing toolkit can meet a lot of your GUI-building needs. To give you some idea of what is possible, check out the GUI presented in Figure 14.2. This GUI was produced by the `TellTime` application, which is used to teach young children how to tell the time. (`TellTime`'s source code is included with the rest of this book's source code—available from this book's Web site at www.mcp.com.)

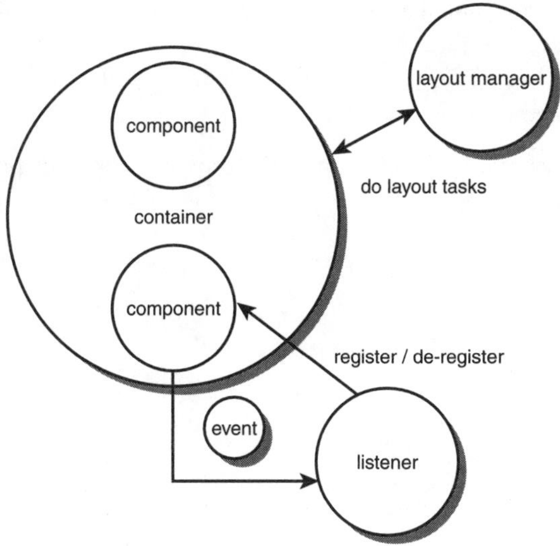

Figure 14.1
The windowing toolkit relates components, containers, layout managers, events, and listeners to each other.

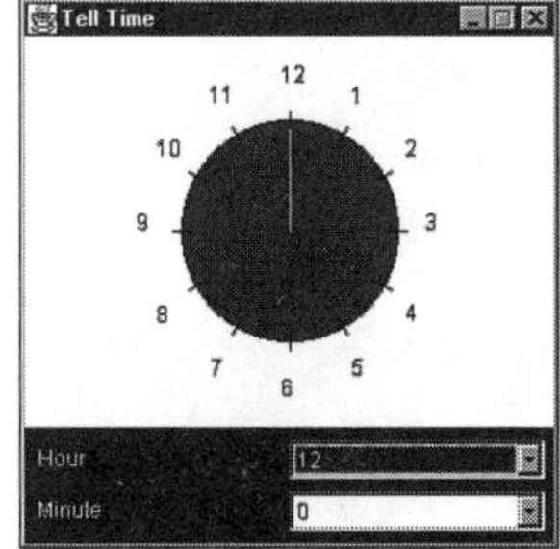

Figure 14.2
TellTime's GUI is a sample of the windowing toolkit's abilities.

BUILDING A GUI: COMPONENTS, CONTAINERS, AND LAYOUT MANAGERS

In the first phase of the GUI building process, the focus is on the look of a GUI. To achieve this look, you'll work with the windowing toolkit's components, containers, and layout managers. However, before exploring these entities, you should have a basic understanding of the system toolkit and peers.

EXPLORING THE SYSTEM TOOLKIT

The windowing toolkit (along with the rest of the AWT) interacts with the system toolkit to carry out windowing system-specific tasks on its behalf. Tasks range from acquiring system-specific details (such as system color model, system clipboard, system event queue, screen size, font metrics, print jobs, and so on) to beeping the speaker and getting images.

The system toolkit is represented by an object created from a subclass of the abstract `Toolkit` class (located in the `java.awt` package). Call `Toolkit`'s `getDefaultToolkit` method to obtain this object. (You can also retrieve the system toolkit by calling any component object's `getToolkit` method.)

To show some of the system toolkit's features, the source code to an application called `SystemInfo` is presented in Listing 14.1. This application retrieves the system toolkit and then calls some of its methods.

LISTING 14.1 THE `SystemInfo` APPLICATION SOURCE CODE

```
// SystemInfo.java

import java.awt.*;

class SystemInfo
{
   public static void main (String [] args)
   {
      Toolkit tk = Toolkit.getDefaultToolkit ();

      System.out.println ("Color model = " +
                          tk.getColorModel ());

      System.out.println ("Menu shortcut key mask = " +
                          tk.getMenuShortcutKeyMask ());

      System.out.println ("AWT.control = " +
                          tk.getProperty ("AWT.control", ""));

      System.out.println ("Screen resolution = " +
                          tk.getScreenResolution ());

      Dimension d = tk.getScreenSize ();
      System.out.println ("Screen width = " + d.width);
      System.out.println ("Screen height = " + d.height);

      System.out.println ("System clipboard = " +
                          tk.getSystemClipboard ());

      System.out.println ("System event queue = " +
                          tk.getSystemEventQueue ());

      tk.beep ();

      System.exit (0);
   }
}
```

Note

SystemInfo concludes by calling System.exit. Without this method call, SystemInfo would appear to "hang." In other words, it would not return to its caller. The reason for this strange behavior is as follows: The system toolkit is created when getDefaultToolkit is called. During toolkit creation, the windowing system-specific AWT library is loaded and a pair of threads is created to manage this library. (One of these threads handles events and the other thread handles screen maintenance.) Both threads enter infinite loops. Because neither thread is a daemon thread, SystemInfo will not terminate when the thread that executes its main method terminates. However, by calling System.exit, all threads (including AWT threads) are forced to terminate. SystemInfo exits!

System toolkit methods are called either directly or behind the scenes. One of these methods (often called by JFC applications) is getImage. Because a JFC application cannot call Applet's getImage methods, it must call Toolkit's getImage methods as shown in the previous chapter. (For more information on Toolkit, check out the SDK documentation.)

Exploring Peers, Heavyweights, and Lightweights

Components and containers are managed by objects on the AWT "side of the fence" and *peers* (native code and data) on the host operating system/windowing system side. In other words, each component and container is the integration of an object and its peer. The relationship between these entities is managed by the windowing toolkit, and is illustrated in Figure 14.3 by way of a Button object (created from the Button class, which is located in the java.awt package) and its corresponding peer.

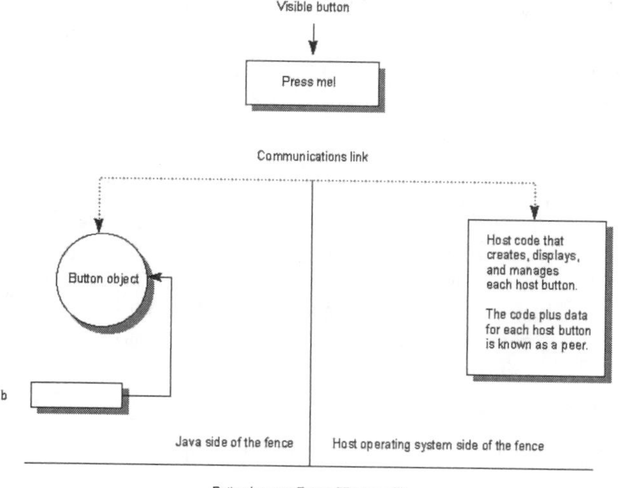

Figure 14.3
A button component consists of a Button object and its button peer.

When Java is ported to a new windowing system, a special set of classes is included in the port. These classes are known as *peer classes* because their methods communicate directly (by way of the Java Native Interface, JNI) with windowing system peers.

Each peer class implements a peer interface (located in the `java.awt.peer` package). This interface identifies those methods that a peer class is obligated to implement, and that a component object will call to do its work. For example, the `Button` class contains a `setLabel` method for setting a button's label. When this method is called via a `Button` object, `setLabel` calls—via a peer object—the `setLabel` method (as specified by the `ButtonPeer` interface) that's implemented in `Button`'s peer class. In turn, the peer class' `setLabel` method uses JNI to call into the windowing system so that this label is displayed on the button peer.

A component that has its own peer, with an opaque native window (another name for drawing surface), is known as a *heavyweight component*. For example, when you create a visible button, what you see on the screen is the peer's opaque native window. The windowing system is responsible for creating and maintaining (such as painting) this window. (All windowing toolkit components are heavyweight.)

There are a couple of problems with heavyweight components:

- Heavyweight components consume windowing system resources because each heavyweight component requires its own native window.
- A heavyweight component's native window is opaque so transparent areas cannot be implemented, resulting in heavyweight components that can only have rectangular appearances.

In contrast, a *lightweight component* is a component that reuses the opaque native window of its closest heavyweight ancestor. For example, if you create a class that inherits from the `Component` class, and then create an object from this subclass, you've created a lightweight component. This component will reuse the opaque native window of `Component`'s peer class—its closest heavyweight ancestor—and will perform all drawing on this window.

Note

The AWT does not include any lightweight components. Therefore, you'll need to create your own (if you're in need of such components). Sun provides an example of a lightweight round button component, by creating a `RoundButton` class that inherits from the `Component` class. This example is part of an article called "Java AWT: Lightweight UI Framework"–located at `http://java.sun.com/products//jdk/1.2/docs/guide/awt/designspec/lightweights.html`.

Lightweight components solve a heavyweight component's problems:

- Lightweight components don't consume as many windowing resources as their heavyweight siblings because lightweight components share a single opaque native window.
- Lightweight components don't have to appear rectangular because they can incorporate transparent areas.

It is usually not a good idea to mix heavyweight and lightweight components, because the heavyweight component is always displayed on top of the lightweight component when these components overlap. This can lead to confusing problems, especially if you mix heavyweight AWT components with lightweight Swing components.

Note

If you would like more information on heavyweight versus lightweight components, and mixing these components, please read The Swing Connection's "Mixing heavy and light components" article—located at `http://java.sun.com/products/jfc/tsc/articles/mixing/index.html`.

EXPLORING COMPONENTS

Choosing appropriate components is the first step in building a GUI. You should explore the windowing toolkit's components and find out what they have to offer, before making these choices.

The abstract `Component` class (located in the `java.awt` package) is the ultimate parent class of nonmenu component classes. Getting to know `Component` requires a fair bit of studying because it offers more than 160 methods! However, you'll discover that many of these methods are designed to be used by the windowing toolkit and not by you. As a result, you only need to become familiar with some of these methods. This study begins by examining those methods that govern a component's color, *cursor* (an icon that identifies the appearance of the mouse pointer), font, and *locale* (a combination of region, country, and language codes). Table 14.1 presents these methods.

TABLE 14.1 `Component`'S COLOR, CURSOR, FONT, AND LOCALE METHODS

Method	Description
`getBackground ()`	Returns a `Color` object containing the component's background color. If there is no background color, the parent's background color is returned.
`getCursor ()`	Returns a `Cursor` object identifying the component's cursor. If there is no cursor, the parent's cursor is returned.
`getFont ()`	Returns a `Font` object containing the component's font. (This would be the font used for displaying text, if the component displays text.) If there is no font, the parent's font is returned.
`getFontMetrics ()`	Returns a `FontMetrics` subclass object that describes the metrics for the component's font.
`getForeground ()`	Returns a `Color` object containing the component's foreground color. If there is no foreground color, the parent's foreground color is returned.

TABLE 14.1 CONTINUED

Method	Description
`getGraphics ()`	Returns a `Graphics` subclass object that represents the component's graphics context. Because the peers of most components are responsible for managing graphics contexts, their `getGraphics` methods throw an `InternalError` object when called. (`Canvas` is one of the few components that returns a graphics context when this method is called.)
`getLocale ()`	Returns a `Locale` object containing the component's locale. If there is no locale, the parent's locale is returned.
`setBackground (Color c)`	Sets the component's background color to `c`. If `null` is passed, the parent's background color is used.
`setCursor (Cursor c)`	Sets the component's cursor to `c`. If `null` is passed, the parent's cursor is used.
`setFont (Font f)`	Sets the component's font to `f`. If `null` is passed, the parent's font is used.
`setForeground (Color c)`	Sets the component's foreground color to `c`. If `null` is passed, the parent's foreground color is used.
`setLocale (Locale l)`	Sets the component's locale to `l`. If `null` is passed, the parent's locale is used.

As you work your way through Table 14.1, you'll come across a few references to a component's parent. This parent is the container that contains the component. To retrieve this parent, call `Component`'s `getParent` method.

The appearance of a mouse pointer depends on the cursor assigned to the component over which the mouse pointer is hovering. As Table 14.1 indicates, `Component`'s `setCursor` method can be called to set the component's cursor and its `getCursor` method can be called to return the component's cursor. These methods work with objects, created from the `Cursor` class, that represent cursors.

The `Cursor` class (located in the `java.awt` package) identifies a variety of predefined cursors by way of various constants. For example, `Cursor.HAND_CURSOR` identifies a hand-shaped (or equivalent) cursor, whereas `Cursor.WAIT_CURSOR` identifies an hourglass-shaped (or equivalent) cursor. Call `Cursor.getPredefinedCursor` to retrieve one of these cursors. You can then pass this cursor to `setCursor` for a given component object. When the mouse pointer moves over the object's peer, the appearance of this pointer will change to the cursor's icon. This is demonstrated in the following code fragment, by way of a `Button` object:

```
Button b = new Button ("Hand Cursor");
b.setCursor (Cursor.getPredefinedCursor (Cursor.HAND_CURSOR));
```

In addition to `color`, `cursor`, `font`, and `locale` methods, `Component` provides methods for positioning and sizing a component. Many of these methods are called by the windowing toolkit (behind the scenes) when working with a layout manager to lay out components.

(With the exception of `getSize`, you wouldn't normally call any of these methods, unless you are creating your own layout manager.) Table 14.2 presents some of `Component`'s positioning and sizing methods.

TABLE 14.2 `Component`'S POSITIONING AND SIZING METHODS

Method	Description
`getBounds ()`	Returns a `Rectangle` object that identifies the upper-left corner of the component's bounding box in the parent's coordinate space, along with its width and height.
`getLocation ()`	Returns a `Point` object that identifies the upper-left corner of the component's bounding box in the parent's coordinate space.
`getMaximumSize ()`	Returns a `Dimension` object that identifies the maximum width and height of the component's bounding box.
`getMinimumSize ()`	Returns a `Dimension` object that identifies the minimum width and height of the component's bounding box.
`getPreferredSize ()`	Returns a `Dimension` object that identifies the preferred width and height of the component's bounding box.
`getSize ()`	Returns a `Dimension` object that identifies the current width and height of the component's bounding box.
`setBounds (Rectangle r)`	Sets the upper-left corner (in the parent's coordinate space) along with the width and height of the component's bounding box to the contents of `r`. However, the layout manager might not allow this change to take place. If the change is made, the component's container is invalidated, so the container's layout manager can re-layout the container's components. (This method indirectly calls `Component`'s `reshape` method.)
`setLocation (Point p)`	Sets the upper-left corner (in the parent's coordinate space) of the component's bounding box to the contents of `p`. (This method indirectly calls `setBounds`.)
`setSize (Dimension d)`	Sets the width and height of the component's bounding box to the contents of `d`. (This method indirectly calls `setBounds`.)

To be useful, a component might need pixels rendered on its drawing surface. Rendering is a two-step process (because a component is a combination of a peer and an object). First, the peer renders its own pixels. This presents the unadorned component. After the peer is finished, the windowing system notifies the AWT. Second, the AWT's windowing toolkit calls the object's `paint` method. Code placed in this method calls the methods of its `Graphics` argument to render a layer of pixels on top of the peer's pixels, customizing the component for the Java program's own use.

Consider the following example. A button peer will render its pixels when first made visible, resized, or it sustains damage. (Damage occurs when a container that partially or completely obscured a component is removed so that the hidden portion of the component is now exposed.) It's possible to subclass the button's `Button` class and override its `paint` method. As a result, a layer of pixels can be rendered on top of the button peer's pixels. To see how this is done, Listing 14.2 presents source code to the `MangledButtonDemo` application. This application draws pixels on top of a button peer's pixels.

Note

Don't worry about those portions of the program that have not yet been explained. (They are explained in later sections of this chapter.) What's important is to see how a layer of pixels can be rendered on top of a peer's existing pixels.

LISTING 14.2 THE `MangledButtonDemo` APPLICATION SOURCE CODE

```
// MangledButtonDemo.java

import java.awt.*;
import java.awt.event.*;

class MangledButtonDemo extends Frame
{
   MangledButtonDemo (String title)
   {
      super (title);

      addWindowListener (new WindowAdapter ()
                         {
                            public void windowClosing (WindowEvent e)
                            {
                               System.exit (0);
                            }
                         });

      add (new MangledButton ("OK"));

      setSize (200, 100);
      setVisible (true);
   }

   public static void main (String [] args)
   {
      new MangledButtonDemo ("Mangled Button");
   }
}

class MangledButton extends Button
{
   MangledButton (String label)
   {
      super (label);
   }
```

LISTING 14.2 CONTINUED

```
   public void paint (Graphics g)
   {
      g.setColor (Color.red);

      int w = getSize ().width - 1;
      int h = getSize ().height - 1;

      g.drawLine (0, 0, w, 0);
      g.drawLine (w, 0, w, h);
      g.drawLine (w, h, 0, h);
      g.drawLine (0, h, 0, 0);

      g.drawLine (0, 0, w, h);
      g.drawLine (w, 0, 0, h);
   }
}
```

When you run `MangledButtonDemo`, you'll see some red lines drawn over the button peer's pixels. The button is first rendered by the peer. In response to a notification from the windowing system, the windowing toolkit calls `paint` to render a layer of pixels (consisting of diagonal lines) over the peer's pixels. The result is shown in Figure 14.4.

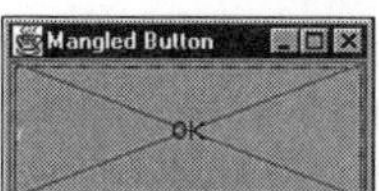

Figure 14.4
Combining peer and object drawing results in a mangled button.

The `paint`, `repaint`, and related methods originate in the `Component` class and form the basis of the windowing toolkit's painting model. Table 14.3 presents some of these methods.

TABLE 14.3 `Component`'S PAINTING MODEL METHODS

Method	Description
`paint (Graphics g)`	Renders a layer of pixels on a drawing surface via calls to `Graphics` argument `g`'s rendering methods. The default version of `paint` does nothing: You override this method in a subclass (such as an `Applet` subclass) to do something useful.
`repaint ()`	Asks the screen maintenance thread to call `update` as soon as possible.
`update (Graphics g)`	Allows a program to render output in an incremental fashion. The default version of `update` first clears the component's background (if the component is a canvas, dialog, frame, panel, or window), and then calls the component's `paint` method.

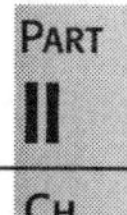

It's necessary to distinguish between system-triggered painting and application-triggered painting, to understand the painting model. *System-triggered painting* occurs when the system requests a component to render a layer of pixels on its drawing surface. This is accomplished by the screen maintenance thread calling the component's `paint` method. System-triggered painting occurs when a component is first made visible, a component is resized, or a component has sustained damage that must be repaired.

In contrast, *application-triggered painting* occurs when an application (or applet) "asks" the windowing toolkit to render a layer of content. In other words, the application/applet initiates the painting request. This is accomplished by the program calling one of the component's overloaded `repaint` methods. In response, the screen maintenance thread calls the component's `update` method at its earliest convenience. Application-triggered painting occurs when the program has "decided" to update a component's drawing surface due to a change in the component's internal state.

The default implementation of `update` first clears a component's drawing surface (if the component is a canvas, dialog, frame, panel, or window) and then calls `paint`. Regardless of `paint` being called by the system or by `update`, its `Graphics` argument is initialized to a current color that is obtained from the component's foreground color, a current font that is obtained from the component's font, and a clipping rectangle that is calculated to encompass the area of the component that needs to be rendered.

Tip

> It is usually not a good idea to place rendering code in any method apart from `paint` or `update`. The reason is that this code might be called at inappropriate times. For example, it could be called prior to a component becoming visible or prior to it having access to a valid graphics context. If you need to update a component from some method apart from `paint` or `update`, call one of the component's `repaint` methods.

The `update` method is a hook that a program can use to handle the application-triggered painting request differently from a system-triggered painting request. Whereas a program assumes that a call to `paint` implies damage to the component's drawing surface, this assumption cannot be made when `update` is called. As a result, a program can perform *incremental painting* (the capability to render graphics in a sequence of steps). This is useful when only rendering newly generated graphics (for performance reasons) and keeping existing graphics displayed. Incremental painting can be demonstrated by the `IncPaintDemo` applet. Its source code is presented in Listing 14.3.

LISTING 14.3 THE `IncPaintDemo` APPLET SOURCE CODE

```
// IncPaintDemo.java

import java.awt.*;
import java.util.*;
import java.applet.Applet;

public class IncPaintDemo extends Applet implements Runnable
{
```

Listing 14.3 Continued

```
private Thread animator;
private int pointsPainted;
private Vector v = new Vector ();

public void start ()
{
   if (animator == null)
   {
       animator = new Thread (this);
       animator.start ();
   }
}

public void stop ()
{
   animator = null;
}

public void run ()
{
   int w = getSize ().width;
   int h = getSize ().height;

   Thread cur = Thread.currentThread ();

   while (cur == animator)
   {
      v.add (new Point ((int) (Math.random () * w),
                        (int) (Math.random () * h)));

      repaint ();

      try
      {
         Thread.sleep (15);
      }
      catch (InterruptedException e) {}
   }
}

public void paint (Graphics g)
{
   int np = v.size ();
   pointsPainted = 0;
   for (int i = 0; i < np; i++)
        draw (g, i);
}

public void update (Graphics g)
{
   for (int i = pointsPainted; i < v.size (); i++)
        draw (g, i);
}
```

LISTING 14.3 CONTINUED

```
   private void draw (Graphics g, int index)
   {
      Point p = (Point) v.elementAt (index);
      g.drawLine (p.x, p.y, p.x, p.y);
      pointsPainted++;
   }
}
```

IncPaintDemo uses a background thread to create Point objects and add them to a Vector data structure. This thread calls repaint every 15 milliseconds. In response, the screen maintenance thread calls update to render only the most recently added point (or points if several points are created before update gets called). It's important to note that only new points are rendered by update. If a user moves a window over IncPaintDemo's drawing surface, the windowing toolkit calls the paint method. In response, paint renders all points.

A component exists in one or more states. These states include valid, visible, showing, and enabled. To be *valid*, the windowing system must know the component's size. If the component is a container, its layout manager must be aware of all components that belong to the container and these components must already have been laid out. If a component's size has changed since the last time it was displayed, it becomes invalid. If the component is a container and any of its components become invalid, the container also becomes invalid. To be *visible*, a component must be added to a container (whether or not the container is visible). To be *showing*, the component must be seen by a user. (A component is showing after it and its container are visible.) Finally, to be *enabled*, the component must be able to accept input from a user. Table 14.4 presents some of Component's state methods.

TABLE 14.4 Component'S STATE METHODS

Method	Description
invalidate ()	Sets the component's valid state to false, nullifies its preferred and minimum sizes, and calls its parent's invalidate method (assuming this component has a valid parent). This method is called by Component's setFont, setLocale, setComponentOrientation, addNotify, reshape, hide, and (one of its) show methods.
isEnabled ()	Returns a Boolean identifying the component's enabled state. A true value means the component is enabled.
isShowing ()	Returns a Boolean identifying the component's showing state. A true value means the component is showing.
isValid ()	Returns a Boolean identifying the component's valid state. A true value means the component is valid. (If the component's peer has not yet been created, this method returns false.)

TABLE 14.4 CONTINUED

Method	Description
`isVisible ()`	Returns a Boolean identifying the component's visible state. A `true` value means the component is visible.
`setEnabled (boolean e)`	Sets the component's enabled state to `e`. A `true` value means the component is enabled.
`setVisible (boolean v)`	Sets the component's visible state to `v`. A `true` value means the component is visible. (To do its job, `setVisible` calls one of `Component`'s `show` methods. In turn, this `show` method either calls the other `show` method or calls the `hide` method, depending on the value of `v`.)
`validate ()`	If the component is not valid, this method updates its peer's font (if there is a peer and the peer's existing font differs from the component's current font) and sets the component's valid state to `true`.

When you are creating dialogs, the concept of *focus* (the ability to receive keyboard input) becomes important. You need to be able to determine which component has the current focus and how to transfer this focus from one component to another. Table 14.5 presents `Component`'s focus methods.

TABLE 14.5 `Component`'S FOCUS METHODS

Method	Description
`isFocusTraversable ()`	Returns a Boolean identifying whether the component can receive the focus. If the component has a peer, the peer is "asked" if it can receive focus. A `true` value is returned if the peer can receive the focus. If not (or there is no peer), `false` is returned.
`requestFocus ()`	Requests the component be given the focus. (If `isFocusTraversable` returns `false`, the component will not get the focus.)
`transferFocus ()`	Transfers focus from the current component to the next component in the container. (This will be the next component to which `isFocusTraversable` returns `true`.)

To wind up this investigation, `Component` provides several useful methods (ranging from pop-up menu support to debugging) that fall into a miscellaneous category. Table 14.6 presents some of these methods.

TABLE 14.6 `Component`'S MISCELLANEOUS METHODS

Method	Description
`add (PopupMenu pm)`	Adds a pop-up menu component (created from the `PopupMenu` class) to the component. If the user right-clicks the component, the menu specified by `pm` will be displayed. (Some windowing systems might ignore this request because they already use predefined pop-up menus.) The pop-up menu is displayed by calling its `show` method.
`getName ()`	Returns a `String` object containing the component's name.
`list ()`	Lists the contents of the component's fields to the standard output device. This is useful for debugging.
`remove (MenuComponent pm)`	Removes a pop-up menu component that is attached to the component. If there is no pop-up menu, nothing happens. (`PopupMenu` extends `MenuComponent`.)
`setName (String name)`	Sets the name of the component to `name`.
`toString ()`	Returns a `String` object containing a representation of the component. (The `list` method calls `toString` to obtain the component's string representation, which it sends to standard output via `System.out.println`.)

Although quite a few methods have been presented, there are still many other methods provided by `Component`. Keep this in mind when examining its subclasses. If you cannot find a method in one of these subclasses, there's a good chance this method is located in `Component`.

The abstract `MenuComponent` class (located in the `java.awt` package) is the ultimate parent class of menu component classes (such as `PopupMenu`). These components range from simple pop-up menus to menu bars with drop-down menus. (`MenuComponent` does not inherit from `Component`.)

Unlike `Component`, `MenuComponent` has far fewer methods. These methods include `getFont` and `setFont` for getting and setting the font used to display menu text, as well as methods dedicated to event handling. If you need to obtain the menu component's parent, you can call `MenuComponent`'s `getParent` method. (For more information on `MenuComponent`, check out the SDK documentation.)

Now that you've been introduced to `Component` and `MenuComponent`, it's time to explore their subclasses. The windowing toolkit organizes these subclasses in a hierarchical fashion as shown in Figure 14.5. (`Component` and `MenuComponent` are shown in gray because they are abstract classes.)

Before exploring the classes that belong to this hierarchy, take a look at Figure 14.6. This figure shows the Windows 98 peers associated with the objects created from these classes. (Menu short cuts and separators are also shown. These concepts will be explained when menus are discussed.)

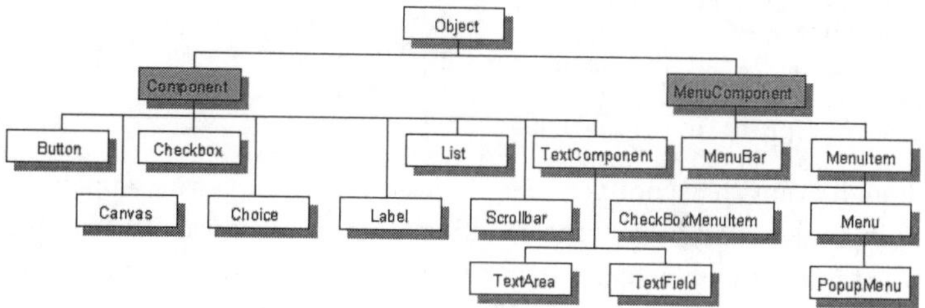

Figure 14.5
The windowing toolkit organizes component classes into a hierarchy.

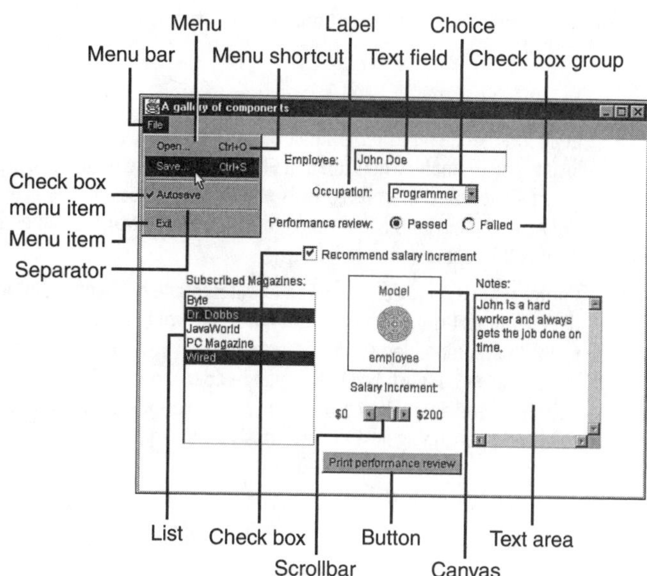

Figure 14.6
The windowing toolkit provides a gallery of components.

BUTTONS

Of all the various components, buttons are probably the most familiar. For example, dialog boxes often contain `OK` and `Cancel` buttons. These buttons give users the ability to close a dialog box with changes either saved (when `OK` is clicked) or discarded (when `Cancel` is clicked).

Objects created from the `Button` class (located in the `java.awt` package) represent buttons. Call the `Button ()` constructor to create a button with no label. If you want a button to be created with a label, call the `Button (String label)` constructor. The `label` argument contains the characters that will appear on the button peer's label.

At any time, you can add a label by calling `setLabel` or retrieve the current label by calling `getLabel`. To see some of `Button`'s methods in action, check out the following code fragment:

```
Button b1 = new Button ("OK");
Button b2 = new Button ();
// some time later in the program …
b2.setLabel ("Cancel");
System.out.println (b1.getLabel ());
```

Although events have not yet been discussed, `Button` provides a pair of methods that are used in conjunction with event handling: `setActionCommand` and `getActionCommand`. Call `setActionCommand` to assign a string-based command identifier to a button. This identifier uniquely identifies that button. When a button-related event occurs, call `getActionCommand` to return the identifier assigned to the button that triggered the event. (If `setActionCommand` is not called for some button, `getActionCommand` returns the button's label instead of an identifier.)

Tip

In an internationalized program, a button's label consists of text obtained from a user's locale. For example, when run in a French locale, the button's text consists of French characters. In contrast, this text consists of German characters when run in a German locale. If `setActionCommand` is not called to assign an arbitrary identifier, `getActionCommand` returns this locale-dependent text.

Complex decision logic is required to differentiate between a pair of buttons when locale-dependent text is involved. For example, you would need to compare a button's German text with an embedded string of German text (when your code detects that German is the current locale), French text with an embedded string of French text (if a French locale is detected), and so on. When `setActionCommand` is used, you can detect a button with a single comparison against the previously assigned identifier.

CANVASES

Down through the centuries, impressionists and other artists have expressed their creativity by applying paint to canvas. Although computer art has replaced paint with light, the canvas concept is still prevalent. Therefore, it's not surprising to discover that the windowing toolkit provides a `Canvas` class (located in the `java.awt` package) for modeling canvases.

You will never work directly with `Canvas` because its `paint` method is inherited from `Component` and does nothing. You must subclass `Canvas` and override `paint` to achieve something interesting. When you create this subclass, you will also override `getPreferredSize` (inherited from `Component`) to specify the dimensions of your canvas. The following code fragment shows how you would declare a subclass that represents a more useful canvas:

```
class Surface extends Canvas
{
   public Dimension getPreferredSize ()
   {
      return new Dimension (100, 100);
   }

   public void paint (Graphics g)
   {
      Dimension d = getSize ();
```

```
      g.setColor (Color.red);
      g.drawLine (0, 0, d.width, d.height);
      g.drawLine (d.width, 0, 0, d.height);
   }
}
```

Objects created from the `Surface` class represent specialized canvases. The following code fragment creates a `Surface` object:

```
Surface s = new Surface ();
```

A `Surface` canvas occupies a region with dimensions of 100×100 pixels. These dimensions are used behind the scenes, by a layout manager, to ensure that at least this much room is reserved for this component.

CHECK BOXES AND CHECK BOX GROUPS

GUIs use check box components to give users a choice between two possibilities. When the user clicks a check box, either a check mark appears to indicate a Boolean true state (the item represented by the check box has been chosen) or the check mark vanishes to indicate a Boolean false state (the item is no longer chosen). Check boxes are often associated with labels (displayed beside them) to identify the items they represent.

Objects created from the `Checkbox` class (located in the `java.awt` package) represent check boxes. Call the `Checkbox ()` constructor to create a check box with no label. The initial state of this component is false and no check mark is displayed. If you want to provide a label when creating a check box, call the `Checkbox (String label)` constructor. As with the previous constructor, no check mark is displayed. Finally, if you want to display a label and a check mark during check box creation, call the `Checkbox (String label, boolean state)` constructor. Passing `true` as the `state` argument's value causes a check mark to be displayed.

You can specify a label by calling `setLabel` and retrieve the current label by calling `getLabel`. Furthermore, you can set the check box state by calling `setState` and retrieve its current state by calling `getState`. The following code fragment shows how to create check boxes and call some of these methods:

```
Checkbox cb1 = new Checkbox ("Married");
Checkbox cb2 = new Checkbox ();
System.out.println (cb1.getState ());
cb2.setLabel ("Single");
cb2.setState (true);
```

At times, you want to group multiple check boxes to achieve a this-or-that scenario. In effect, you want to create a group of *radio buttons*. Only one of the buttons in this group can be selected at any point in time.

The `CheckboxGroup` class (located in the `java.awt` package) works with `Checkbox` to achieve the effect of radio buttons. You call the `CheckboxGroup ()` constructor to create a grouping object and then add `Checkbox` objects to this group. However, only check boxes created by calling a `Checkbox` constructor with a `CheckboxGroup` argument can be placed in a group. The following code fragment demonstrates grouping three check boxes into one group:

```
CheckboxGroup cbg = new CheckboxGroup ();
Checkbox cb1 = new Checkbox ("Left justify", true, cbg);
Checkbox cb2 = new Checkbox ("Center justify", false, cbg);
Checkbox cb3 = new Checkbox ("Right justify", false, cbg);
```

Any check box belonging to a group can be selected by calling `CheckboxGroup`'s `setSelectedCheckbox` method. If you want to know which check box is currently selected, call `getSelectedCheckbox`. The following code fragment builds on the previous fragment to illustrate these methods:

```
if (cbg.getSelectedCheckbox () == cb1)
    cbg.setSelectedCheckbox (cb2);
```

CHOICES

Choices are drop-down lists of textual items. One of these items is displayed along with a down arrow button. When this button is clicked, a scrollable window appears from which a user can make a choice. This window disappears after an item has been selected. As a result, choices conserve GUI space.

Objects created from the `Choice` class (located in the `java.awt` package) represent choices. Call the `Choice ()` constructor to create a choice with an initially empty list.

To add items to a choice, call either of `Choice`'s `add` or `insert` methods. The `add` method appends an item to the end of a choice's list whereas `insert` adds an item at a specified position in this list. In contrast, you can remove an item by calling either of `Choice`'s two overloaded `remove` methods. If you want to remove all items, call `removeAll`.

Each item is associated with a zero-based integer index. You can retrieve an item at a specified index by calling `getItem`. You can find out how many items are currently maintained in the choice's list by calling its `getItemCount` method. Furthermore, you can specify which item is currently selected by calling either of two overloaded `select` methods. One of these methods requires the index of the item to be selected.

When a selection event originates from a choice, you can find out which item was selected by calling `getSelectedItem`. This method returns `null` if there are no items in the choice's list. If you are more concerned about the selected item's index, call `getSelectedIndex`. This method returns `-1` if there are no items in the choice's list. The following code fragment shows how to create a `Choice` object and demonstrates calls to some of its methods:

```
Choice countries = new Choice ();
countries.add ("Albania");
countries.add ("Algeria");
countries.add ("Bahrain");
countries.add ("China");
// and so on ...
System.out.println (countries.getItemCount ());
countries.insert ("Canada", 2); // Canada precedes China in AZ order.
```

To perform an insert, the index passed to the `insert` method must be the index of an item that immediately precedes the item being inserted. (`Bahrain` is assigned index `2` and immediately precedes `Canada`.)

Caution

If you don't use care when specifying indexes, an `IllegalArgumentException` object will be thrown. Valid indexes range from zero through one less than `getItemCount`'s return value.

LABELS

Labels exist to identify the purposes of other components. For example, a label can be used to identify a text field as a place to enter a person's name. Without this label, would the text field refer to a name or an address, or something else?

You've already seen two kinds of dedicated labels: button labels and check box labels. However, the `Label` class (located in the `java.awt` package) makes it possible to create generic labels that identify any kind of component.

`Label` declares three read-only class fields called `LEFT`, `CENTER`, and `RIGHT`. These fields are useful for aligning a label's text against the left-hand side, center, or right-hand side of its window. (The default alignment is `LEFT`.)

Call the `Label ()` constructor to create a label with no text and a default `LEFT` alignment. To create a label with predefined text, call the `Label (String text)` constructor. Once again, `LEFT` alignment is the default. Finally, to specify a label's text and alignment during construction, call the `Label (String text, int alignment)` constructor.

You can change a label's text by calling `setText` and you can retrieve this text by calling `getText`. A label's alignment can be changed by calling `setAlignment` and retrieved by calling `getAlignment`. The following code fragment shows how to create `Label` objects and demonstrates these text and alignment methods:

```
Label l1 = new Label ();
Label l2 = new Label ("Center aligned", Label.CENTER);
l1.setText ("Right aligned");
l1.setAlignment (Label.RIGHT);
System.out.println (l1.getAlignment ());
System.out.println (l2.getText ());
```

LISTS

Lists and choices are similar components. They give a user the ability to select textual items from a scrollable window. However, unlike a choice, a list's window does not drop down. Instead, it displays items in a certain number of onscreen rows (one item per row). If there are more items than onscreen rows, a scrollbar is displayed to allow a user to scroll non-displayed items into view. Furthermore, a list allows users to select multiple items (which is not possible with choices). This capability is governed by a list's selection mode: single selection (only one item can be selected at a time) or multiple selection (more than one item can be selected at a time).

The List class (located in the java.awt package) creates objects that represent lists. Call the List () constructor to create a list that displays four visible rows of items and does not allow multiple items to be selected. You can increase the number of visible rows by calling the List (int rows) constructor. As with the previous constructor, multiple items cannot be selected. If you want control over both the number of visible rows and whether or not the user can select multiple items, call the List (int rows, boolean multipleMode) constructor. Passing a true value as the multipleMode argument will allow a user to select multiple items.

Note

You can determine if a list is operating in multiple selection mode by calling the isMultipleMode method; you can change a list from single selection mode to multiple selection mode by calling setMultipleMode.

After you've created a List object, call either of its two overloaded add methods to add items either to the end of the list or at some position in the list. You can also remove an item by calling either of List's two overloaded remove methods. To remove all items, call removeAll.

As with choices, each list item is associated with a zero-based integer index. Given a valid index, the getItem method retrieves an item at this index. If you want to know how many items are currently maintained by a list, call getItemCount. You can select one or more items (depending on the selection mode) by calling the select method. To deselect an item, call deselect. If you want to know whether an item has been selected, call the isIndexSelected method.

When a selection event originates from a list, you can find out which item was selected by calling getSelectedItem. If there are no items in the list, this method returns null. If you are more concerned about the selected item's index, call getSelectedIndex. This method returns -1 if there are no items in the list. (These methods assume that the list is operating in single selection mode. In multiple selection mode, you would call getSelectedItems and getSelectedIndexes.) The following code fragment shows how to create a List object and demonstrates calls to some of its methods:

```
List magazines = new List ();
magazines.add ("Byte");
magazines.add ("Dr. Dobbs");
magazines.add ("Javaworld");
// and so on ...
System.out.println (magazines.getItemCount ());
magazines.setMultipleMode (true);
```

MENUS

The windowing toolkit supports the creation of menu-driven GUIs. These GUIs have a menu bar situated at the top of a window with a list of menu names appearing on this bar. Selecting one of these names causes a menu to drop down. This menu consists of one or more menu items that are text-based commands for handling tasks. Some of these menu items can be checked to represent state. For example, a ruler menu item might be checked to indicate that a ruler should be displayed in a word processor program. A special keystroke combination can be assigned to a menu item to speed up access. This keystroke combination is known as a *menu shortcut*.

The following classes (all located in the `java.awt` package) work together to implement menus:

- `MenuBar`
- `Menu`
- `MenuItem`
- `CheckboxMenuItem`
- `MenuShortcut`

The `MenuBar` class creates objects that represent menu bars. Call the `MenuBar ()` constructor to create a menu bar.

Menus are added to a menu bar by calling `MenuBar`'s `add` method and removed by calling either of its two overloaded `remove` methods. To obtain a specific menu, call `getMenu`. If you need to know how many menus have been added, call `getMenuCount`.

Menu bars typically display a special Help menu on their extreme right. Call `setHelpMenu` to designate the Help menu. To find out which menu is the Help menu, call `getHelpMenu`.

`MenuBar` provides a `shortcuts` method that conveniently enumerates all menu shortcuts assigned to menu items. Given a menu shortcut, you can obtain the associated menu item by calling `MenuBar`'s `getShortcutMenuItem` method. If you want to remove a shortcut, call `deleteShortcut`.

A menu bar doesn't accomplish very much without menus. Menus are represented by objects created from the `Menu` class. Call the `Menu ()` constructor to create a menu without a label.

Caution

> If a label is not specified and the menu is added to a menu bar, the menu will not appear on the bar. However, in Windows, the menu can still be accessed by pressing F10 to activate the menu bar and using the left- and right-arrow keys to navigate.

In most cases, you'll want to assign a label (such as `File`, `Edit`, `View`, and so on) to a menu. This can be accomplished by calling the `Menu (String label)` constructor.

After you have a menu, you need to add menu items. This is done by calling the `add (String label)` method, with the menu item's text specified by `label`. If the menu item is a checked menu item, call the `add (MenuItem mi)` method to add menu item `mi` to the menu. (This method is called because a checked menu item is created from the `CheckboxMenuItem` class and you cannot pass a `CheckboxMenuItem` object to the `add (String label)` method.) Both `add` methods append the menu item to the end of a menu. If you need to insert a menu item between existing menu items, call either of two overloaded `insert` methods. When you want to remove a menu item, call either of `Menu`'s two overloaded `remove` methods.

Sometimes, you want to separate menu items into logical groups. This can be accomplished by adding *separators* (horizontal lines that divide menu items into visible groups) to menus. Call `addSeparator` to append a separator to a menu or `insertSeparator` to insert a separator between two menu items.

When you are dynamically creating menus, you'll probably call `getItem` to obtain a menu item and `getItemCount` to find out how many menu items have been added to a menu. To create menu items, you'll need to work with the `MenuItem` class.

Objects created from the `MenuItem` class represent menu items. Call the `MenuItem ()` constructor to create an object with no label or menu shortcut. If you want a label (which is normally the case), call `MenuItem (String label)`. To specify both a label and a menu shortcut, call `MenuItem (String label, MenuShortcut s)`.

You can assign a label at a later time by calling `setLabel` and you can assign a menu shortcut by calling `setShortcut`. To retrieve the current label, call `getLabel`. To retrieve the current menu shortcut, call `getShortcut`.

Menu items can be enabled or disabled. When disabled, they appear grayed out and don't respond to keyboard/mouse input. Call `setEnabled` with an appropriate Boolean argument value to control this state. If you want to determine a menu item's current state, call `isEnabled`.

As with buttons, call `setActionCommand` to assign a string-based command identifier to a menu item. This identifier uniquely identifies that menu item. When a menu-related event occurs, call `getActionCommand` to return the identifier assigned to the menu item that triggered the event. (If `setActionCommand` is not called for some menu item, `getActionCommand` returns the menu item's label instead of an identifier.)

Objects created from the `CheckboxMenuItem` class represent check box menu items. Call the `CheckboxMenuItem ()` constructor to create a check box menu item without a label and a state that is initially unchecked. To specify a label, call `CheckboxMenuItem (String label)`. If you also want to specify an initial checked state, call `CheckboxMenuItem (String label, boolean checked)` and pass a `true` value as the `checked` argument.

You can change a check box's label or retrieve its current label by calling the `setLabel` and `getLabel` methods, respectively. These methods are inherited from `MenuItem`. You can also change the checked state by calling `setState` and you can retrieve this state by calling `getState`.

Objects created from the `MenuShortcut` class represent menu shortcuts. Call the `MenuShortcut (int key)` constructor to create a menu shortcut using the specified `key`. (Key constants can be found in the `KeyEvent` class.) Alternatively, call `MenuShortcut (int key, boolean useShiftModifier)` to create a menu shortcut that uses a combination of a `Shift` key along with `key`. (This modifier is only chosen if `useShiftModifier` is `true`.)

The shortcut key can be returned by calling `getKey` and the shift modifier state can be returned by calling `usesShiftModifier`. The following code fragment demonstrates the use of these classes in setting up the menu shown earlier in Figure 14.6 (the last line calls the setMenuBar method, which adds a menu bar to a container):

```
Menu file = new Menu ("File");

MenuItem mi = new MenuItem ("Open...",
                            new MenuShortcut (KeyEvent.VK_O));
file.add (mi);

mi = new MenuItem ("Save...", new MenuShortcut (KeyEvent.VK_S));
file.add (mi);

file.addSeparator ();

mi = new CheckboxMenuItem ("Autosave", true);
file.add (mi);

file.addSeparator ();

mi = new MenuItem ("Exit");
file.add (mi);

MenuBar mb = new MenuBar ();
mb.add (file);
setMenuBar (mb);
```

POP-UP MENUS

AWT applets do not support menu bars. Therefore, the previously discussed menu capabilities can only be used by AWT applications. However, it is possible to incorporate the windowing toolkit's pop-up menu support into either AWT applets or AWT applications.

Objects created from the PopupMenu class (located in the java.awt package) represent pop-up menus. Call the PopupMenu () constructor to create a pop-up menu.

Because PopupMenu inherits from Menu, you have access to all of Menu's methods, including its add methods for adding menu items to the pop-up menu.

When it comes times to show the pop-up menu, call PopupMenu's show (Component origin, int x, int y) method. This method shows a pop-up menu at the (x, y) position relative to the coordinates of the origin component. (origin and its parent must both be showing for this method to work.)

Pop-up menus are meant to be used in conjunction with events and listeners. Therefore, an example of creating and using a pop-up menu will be deferred until these entities are discussed.

SCROLLBARS

Scrollbars are used with containers to select a portion of a large component for display. For example, a user can adjust a scrollbar to view a portion of a large image that is displayed in a component created from a subclass of Canvas. Scrollbars are also used (by themselves) to select a specific value from a large range of values. For example, three scrollbars can be used to allow a user to choose the red, green, and blue components of a color.

Scrollbars come in two flavors: horizontal and vertical. Figure 14.7 illustrates both kinds of scrollbars.

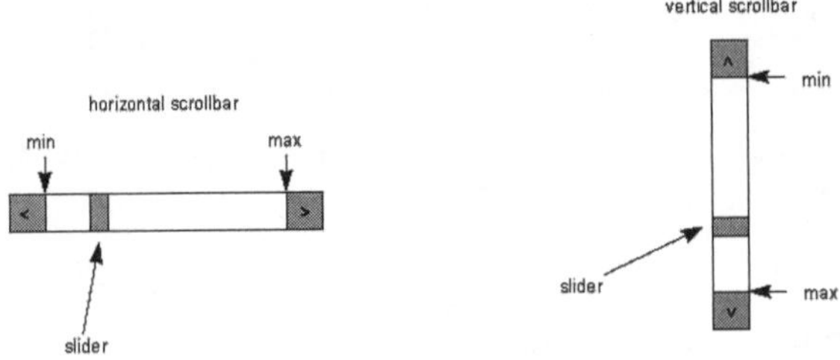

Figure 14.7
Scrollbars come in two flavors: horizontal and vertical.

Objects created from the `Scrollbar` class (located in the `java.awt` package) represent scrollbars. Call `Scrollbar (int orientation)` to create either a horizontal or a vertical scrollbar. You can choose either of `Scrollbar`'s `HORIZONTAL` or `VERTICAL` constants as the `orientation` argument's value.

A scrollbar has a minimum position, a maximum position, and a current position that is indicated by a slider. Furthermore, the width of this slider can be specified. To create a more customized scrollbar that incorporates this information, call the `Scrollbar (int orientation, int value, int visible, int minimum, int maximum)` constructor. The `value` argument specifies the current position of the slider, whereas `visible` specifies the slider's width. The `minimum` and `maximum` arguments specify the minimum and maximum range, represented by the scrollbar.

You can change a scrollbar's orientation by calling `setOrientation`. The scrollbar's current slider value can be set by calling `setValue` and its width set by calling `setVisibleAmount`. Also, the minimum and maximum values can be set by calling `setMinimum` and `setMaximum`. To reduce the number of method calls, the scrollbar's current value, width, minimum, and maximum can be specified in a single call to `setValues`.

Note

Conversely, you can call `getOrientation` to retrieve the current orientation, `getValue` to retrieve the current value, `getVisibleAmount` to retrieve the current width, `getMinimum` to retrieve the current minimum value, and `getMaximum` to retrieve the current maximum value.

The following code fragment shows how to create a `Scrollbar` object and demonstrates calling some of its methods:

```
Scrollbar sb = new Scrollbar (Scrollbar.HORIZONTAL, 0, 1, 0, 50);
System.out.println (sb.getOrientation ());
System.out.println (sb.getValue ());
System.out.println (sb.getVisibleAmount ());
System.out.println (sb.getMinimum ());
System.out.println (sb.getMaximum ());
Scrollbar sb2 = new Scrollbar (Scrollbar.VERTICAL);
sb2.setValues (0, 1, 0, 50);
```

TEXT

GUIs often require users to enter one or more lines of text. To accomplish these tasks, the windowing toolkit provides text field and text area components. (A single line of text is entered in a text field component and multiple lines are entered in a text area component.) Because these components share much in common, the windowing toolkit has factored this commonality into an abstract class called `TextComponent` (located in the `java.awt` package).

`TextComponent` provides methods for getting and setting a text component's text (`getText` and `setText`), getting and setting the background color used in the display of this text (`getBackground` and `setBackground`), getting and setting the *caret*—text input indicator—(`getCaretPosition` and `setCaretPosition`), getting and setting a region of selected text (`getSelectionEnd`, `getSelectionStart`, `setSelectionEnd`, and `setSelectionStart`), and getting and setting the editable state of the component (`isEditable` and `setEditable`). These methods are inherited by the `TextField` and `TextArea` classes (both located in the `java.awt` package).

Caution

You cannot call `setCaretPosition` until the text component is showing. Prior to this moment, an `IllegalComponentStateException` object is thrown.

Objects created from the `TextField` class represent text fields. Call `TextField (int columns)` to create an initially empty text field that can display at least `columns` characters using the average character width of the current font. Call `TextField (String text)` to display text in the text field and choose an appropriate number of columns. You can also call `TextField (String text, int columns)` to initialize the text field to `text` and its displayable width to `columns` characters.

Text fields are designed with passwords in mind. Instead of displaying a password's characters, a different character (such as an asterisk) is echoed to the screen for each password character that is typed. To take advantage of this feature, call `setEchoChar` to set the echo character and `getEchoChar` to retrieve this character. To determine if echoing is in effect, call `echoCharIsSet`.

`TextField` overrides its inherited `getText` and `setText` methods. You can call these methods to get or set a text field's text. Also, if you want to get or set the number of displayable columns, call `getColumns` and `setColumns`. The following code fragment shows the creation of two `TextField` objects along with calls to some of their methods:

```
TextField t = new TextField ("Enter a name.", 20);
t.setBackground (Color.cyan);
System.out.println (t.getText ());

TextField password = new TextField (20);
password.setEchoChar ('*');
```


Objects created from the `TextArea` class represent text areas. Call `TextArea (int rows, int columns)` to create an initially empty text area that can display at least `rows` by `columns` characters. Scrollbars are automatically displayed. To initialize a text area with some text, call `TextArea (String text)`. (An appropriate number of rows and columns is selected. Scrollbars are also displayed.) You can also call `TextArea (String text, int rows, int columns)` to initialize the text area to `text` and a displayable area capable of displaying at least rows×columns characters. Scrollbars are automatically displayed. Finally, if you want to control whether or not scrollbars are displayed, call the `TextArea (String text, int rows, int columns, int scrollbars)` constructor.

Note

One of `TextArea`'s `SCROLLBARS_BOTH`, `SCROLLBARS_HORIZONTAL_ONLY`, `SCROLLBARS_VERTICAL_ONLY`, or `SCROLLBARS_NONE` constants can be passed as the `scrollbars` value.

To change the current number of displayable rows and columns, call `setRows` and `setColumns`. You can also obtain the current number of rows by calling `getRows` and the current number of columns by calling `getColumns`. If you need to know what scrollbars are in use, call `getScrollbarVisibility`.

Text can be appended by calling the `append` method and inserted by calling `insert`. If you want to replace a range of text, call `replaceRange`. The following code fragment shows how to create a `TextArea` object and demonstrates calls to some of its methods:

```
TextArea ta = new TextArea (5, 5);

// Rows/columns passed to constructor subject to the container's size.

ta.setText ("Initial text");
ta.insert ("ized", 7);    // Insert ized after the l in Initial.
ta.setSelectionStart (4); // Highlight text in positions 4 and 5 only.
ta.setSelectionEnd (6);
```

EXPLORING CONTAINERS

Choosing appropriate containers is the second step in building a GUI. Before making a choice, you need to explore the windowing toolkit's containers and find out what they have to offer.

The `Container` class (located in the `java.awt` package) is the ultimate parent class for all containers. The windowing toolkit extends `Container` with subclasses that represent specific containers. `Frame` and `Dialog`, which represent frames and dialog boxes, are examples of these subclasses.

When added to a container, components are stored in an internal data structure—in a front-to-back *tab order* (the order in which components receive the focus when the `Tab` key is pressed). The component at the head of the data structure is first in tab order, whereas the component at the tail of this data structure is last in tab order.

Some of `Container`'s methods are presented in Table 14.7. Except for `getInsets` and `validate`, you call these methods when working with containers.

TABLE 14.7 Container'S METHODS

Method	Description
`add (Component c)`	Adds component `c` to the end of the container.
`add (Component c, int index)`	Adds component `c` to the container at the position specified by `index`.
`add (Component c, Object const)`	Adds component `c` to the end of the container and calls the layout manager's `addLayoutComponent` method with the constraints specified by `const`.
`add (Component c, Object const, int index)`	Adds component `c` to the container at the position specified by `index` and calls the layout manager's `addLayoutComponent` method with the constraints specified by `const`.
`getInsets ()`	Returns an `Insets` object that denotes the size of a border to appear around the container's edge.
`getLayout ()`	Returns the container's current layout manager.
`invalidate ()`	Invalidates the container by calling its layout manager's `invalidateLayout` method. This method then calls `Component`'s `invalidate` method. (Don't forget: `Container` is derived from `Component`.) `Container`'s `invalidate` method is called from `Container`'s `add`, `remove`, `removeAll`, and `setLayout` methods.
`remove (Component c)`	Removes component `c` from the container.
`remove (int index)`	Removes the component located at position `index` from the container.
`removeAll ()`	Removes all components from the container.
`setLayout (LayoutManger m)`	Sets the container's layout manager to `m`.
`validate ()`	If the container is not valid, `validate` lays out its components, and recursively lays out the components in all child containers. If a non-container component is encountered during validation, `Component`'s `validate` method is called for that component.

Suppose you need to create a GUI with several windows of similar components, but you don't want a lot of peers (which consume native system resources) to be created. You would really like to create a few components that can be reused on different windows of your GUI. Is there some way to dynamically add and remove components? The answer is yes. For more information, check out "Dynamically Adding and Removing Components" in the "Troubleshooting" section at the end of this chapter.

Containers support the concept of *insets* (margins—measured in pixels—that occupy the top, bottom, right, and left sides of a container). These insets are taken into account by many (but not all) layout managers when components are being laid out. The idea is to provide a border area between the container's borders and its components.

The windowing toolkit provides an `Insets` class (located in the `java.awt` package) that encapsulates these four margins as integer values. When you create your own container (by extending an existing container's class), you can choose to override its inherited `getInsets` method and return an object, created from `Insets`, that describes these margins. The following code fragment demonstrates creation of a container subclass along with overriding its inherited `getInsets` method to create a margin of 5 pixels around each side:

```
class myContainer extends Container
{
   public void Insets getInsets ()
   {
      return new Insets (5, 5, 5, 5);
   }
}
```

Now that you've been introduced to `Container`, it's time to explore its subclasses. The windowing toolkit organizes these subclasses in a hierarchical fashion and Figure 14.8 illustrates this hierarchy. `Component` is shown in gray because it's an abstract class. Furthermore, because `Component` is shown as the parent class of `Container`, this illustration reinforces the fact that each container is also a component.

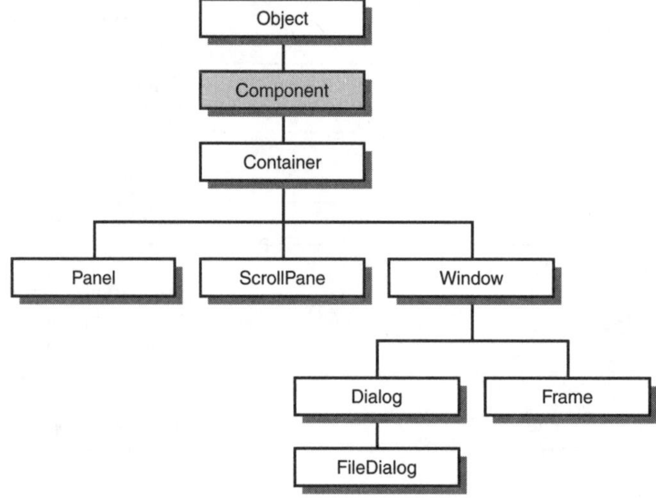

Figure 14.8
The windowing toolkit organizes container classes into a hierarchy.

The windowing toolkit offers five kinds of containers: dialogs, frames, panels, scroll panes, and windows. Dialogs are the basis for user interaction, frames serve as top-level windows for AWT applications (and contain title bars, menu bars, and various adornments), panels are the simplest of all containers and are used by AWT applets, scroll panes make it possible to scroll the contents of a container, and windows are designed to be used if the other containers do not meet a program's requirements (which is hard to imagine).

DIALOGS

A dialog implements a pop-up window. This window displays a message along with button (and possibly other) components to a user, and allows this user to interact with these components. The window displays a title bar along with minimize, maximize, and close buttons. Dialogs are useful for entering or editing data. These windows normally contain a button labeled `OK` that is clicked to save changes and a button labeled `Cancel` that is clicked to discard changes.

Dialogs exist in two flavors: modal and modeless. A *modal dialog* forces a user to close the dialog before she can interact with the rest of the GUI. It does not display minimize and maximize buttons. A dialog that forces a user to finish entering configuration information before this user can interact with the rest of the GUI is an example of a modal dialog. In contrast, a *modeless dialog* allows a user to continue working with a GUI while interacting with the dialog. It displays minimize and maximize buttons. An example of a modeless dialog is a search dialog. While searching for a particular piece of text, a user can make adjustments to each found occurrence while the search dialog is still displayed.

Dialogs are represented by objects created from the `Dialog` class (located in the `java.awt` package). This class provides several constructors for creating these objects. Call the `Dialog (Frame parent, String title)` constructor to create an initially invisible modeless dialog whose title bar will display `title` (when the dialog is visible). This dialog is owned by the `parent` frame. If you want to create a modal dialog, call `Dialog (Frame parent, String title, boolean modal)`. Pass a `true` value in the `modal` argument to force this dialog to be modal.

After a dialog has been created, either its inherited `add (Component c, Object const)` method can be called to add a component (identified by `c`) to the dialog (subject to the constraints that are specified by `const`) or its inherited `add (Component c)` method can be called to add a component (identified by `c`) to the dialog (subject to a default constraint). The following code fragment demonstrates creating a dialog and adding three buttons to this container:

```
Dialog d = new Dialog (this, "Are you sure?", true);
d.add (new Button ("Yes"), "West");
d.add (new Button ("No"));
d.add (new Button ("Don't know"), "East");
```

This code fragment assumes that the current container is a frame. The reserved word `this` is passed to the dialog's constructor to represent this frame as the dialog's parent. The `"West"` and `"East"` literal strings identify constraints that constrain the `OK` button to the western area of the dialog and the Cancel button to the eastern area. If no literal string is specified, "Center" is assumed. This literal string means that its associated component should be constrained to the center area.

You can call setTitle to set the text that appears in a dialog's title bar and retrieve this text by calling getTitle. You can also change a dialog's modality (after being created) by calling setModal. To find out if the dialog is currently modal, call isModal.

Dialogs default to being resizable. You can change this policy by calling setResizable. To find out if a dialog is resizable, call its isResizable method.

After a dialog has been created and added to a container, you can call its show method to make it visible. This call will not return until either the dialog's hide method or its dispose method is called. The following code fragment continues from the previous code fragment to display a dialog:

```
d.show ();
```

To see what a dialog looks like, check out the source code to DialogDemo in Listing 14.4. (Press Ctrl+C, or the equivalent, to terminate this program.)

LISTING 14.4 THE DialogDemo APPLICATION SOURCE CODE

```
// DialogDemo.java

import java.awt.*;

class DialogDemo
{
   public static void main (String [] args)
   {
      Frame f = new Frame ("Dialog Demo");
      f.setSize (200, 100);
      f.setVisible (true);

      Dialog d = new Dialog (f, "Is the sky blue?", true);

      Panel p = new Panel ();
      p.add (new Button ("Yes"));
      p.add (new Button ("No"));
      d.add (p);

      d.setSize (200, 100);
      d.setResizable (false);
      d.show ();
   }
}
```

Figure 14.9 shows the frame and dialog that are displayed when DialogDemo is run.

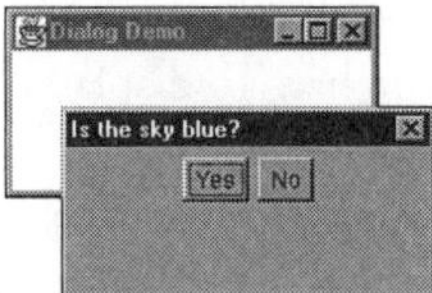

Figure 14.9 `DialogDemo` presents a dialog with `Yes` and `No` buttons.

You can create dialogs by using the approach presented in Listing 14.4, or you can subclass `Dialog` and create a dialog from the subclass. This is shown in the following code fragment:

```
class YesNo extends Dialog
{
   YesNo (Frame f, String title)
   {
       super (f, title);
       Panel p = new Panel ();
       p.add (new Button ("Yes"));
       p.add (new Button ("No"));
       add (p);

       setSize (200, 100);
       setResizable (false);
   }
}

// In some other method ...

Frame f = new Frame ();
YesNo yn = new YesNo (f, "Is the sky blue?");
yn.show ();
```

To remove a dialog, call its `dispose` method in response to an event—which is typically a button press event. (You'll see how to dispose of a dialog when events and listeners are discussed.)

`Dialog` serves as the parent to the `FileDialog` class (located in the `java.awt` package). Objects created from this class represent dialogs for selecting files in response to an open or save operation. However, you must provide the actual open/save code. Furthermore, because files are involved, `FileDialog` can only be used with AWT applications. (For security reasons, AWT applets are not allowed to work with files.)

`FileDialog` contains two constants that indicate the mode in which a file dialog is being used. These constants are `LOAD` and `SAVE`. The `LOAD` constant "tells" `FileDialog` to select appropriate load text that will appear on the file dialog's load button. (The same idea holds for `SAVE`, except that appropriate save text is selected to appear on the save button.)

`LOAD` and `SAVE` also discriminate between mode-specific operations. For example, in load mode, the file dialog might not allow a filename to be chosen if the file does not exist. Furthermore, in save mode, the file dialog might prompt to choose if an existing file should be replaced.

Call `FileDialog (Frame parent)` to create a file dialog that is owned by `parent`. This dialog defaults to load mode and it displays no text in its title bar. To display a title, call `FileDialog (Frame parent, String title)`. As before, load mode is the default. To control the mode in addition to specifying a title, call `FileDialog (Frame parent, String title, int mode)` and pass either `LOAD` or `SAVE` as the value of the `mode` argument. (You can call `getMode` to retrieve the current mode and `setMode` to change this mode.)

Before the file dialog is displayed, call `setDirectory` to specify the initial directory, `setFile` to specify the default file, and `setFileNameFilter` to specify the current *filter* (an object that identifies the types of files that are visible, such as `.jpg`, `.bmp`, `.doc`, and so on). After the file dialog is closed, you can call `getDirectory` to retrieve the file dialog's current directory, `getFile` to retrieve the current file selection (which is `null` if the `Cancel` button was pressed), and `getFileNameFilter` to return the current filter choices. The following code fragment demonstrates creating a file dialog to be used in load mode, displaying this file:

```
FileDialog file = new FileDialog (new Frame (), "Open file", FileDialog.LOAD);
file.show ();
System.out.println (file.getFile ());
System.out.println (file.getDirectory ());
```

For more information on `FileDialog`, consult the SDK documentation.

FRAMES

A frame serves as an AWT application's top-level container. Unlike a window, a frame has a title bar, a menu bar, and various adornments (such as maximize, minimize, and close buttons).

Frames are represented by objects created from the `Frame` class (located in the `java.awt` package). Call the `Frame (String title)` constructor to create a frame that displays `title` in its title bar.

After a frame has been created, its inherited `add (Component c, Object const)` method can be called to add a component (identified by `c`) to the frame, subject to the constraints that are specified by `const`. The following code fragment demonstrates creating a frame and adding a pair of buttons to this frame:

```
Frame f = new Frame ("Demo");
f.add (new Button ("Hello"), BorderLayout.WEST);
f.add (new Button ("Goodbye"), BorderLayout.EAST);
```

The `BorderLayout` class provides several constants that are used to constrain the location of a button. In the code fragment, `WEST` constrains one button to the western area of the frame and `EAST` constrains the other button to eastern area.

You can change a frame's title by calling `setTitle` and retrieve its current title by calling `getTitle`. Furthermore, a frame can be associated with a menu bar. Call `setMenuBar` to set its menu bar and `getMenuBar` to retrieve the current menu bar. (You can remove this menu bar either by calling `remove` or by passing `null` to `setMenuBar`.)

Frame declares two constants that represent its state: ICONIFIED (the frame has been minimized) and NORMAL (the frame is displayed at its regular size). Call setState to set the frame's state and getState to retrieve the current state.

You can associate an icon image with a frame. This image is displayed when the frame is minimized. Call setIconImage to set this icon's image and getIconImage to retrieve the current icon.

It is possible to create either a resizable or a nonresizable frame. A nonresizable frame prevents a user from wreaking havoc with an otherwise nice-looking layout. Call setResizable with a Boolean true value if the frame can be resized or a false value if the frame has a fixed size. (The default is resizable.) If you want to know if a frame is resizable, call isResizable.

Listing 14.5 presents source code to a FrameDemo1 application: It serves as a template for creating a frame-based GUI. (Press Ctrl+C, or the equivalent, to terminate this program.)

LISTING 14.5 THE FrameDemo1 APPLICATION SOURCE CODE

```
// FrameDemo1.java

import java.awt.*;

class FrameDemo1 extends Frame
{
   FrameDemo1 (String title)
   {
      super (title); // Pass the title to the Frame layer.

      Button b = new Button ("Hello");
      add (b, BorderLayout.WEST);

      b = new Button ("Goodbye");
      add (b, BorderLayout.EAST);

      pack ();

      setResizable (false);

      setVisible (true);
   }

   public static void main (String [] args)
   {
      new FrameDemo1 ("Frame Demo 1");
   }
}
```

FrameDemo1 adds a pair of buttons to its GUI. It calls pack (inherited from Window) to resize the frame to the preferred size of these buttons, ensures that the frame is not resizable, and displays the frame. The resulting GUI is shown in Figure 14.10.

Figure 14.10
FrameDemo1's GUI consists of a pair of buttons.

A frame can incorporate panels for controlling the size of its components. Without panels, these components would occupy the entire frame. (More will be said about panels very shortly.) Listing 14.6 presents source code to FrameDemo2 that demonstrates this situation. (Press Ctrl+C, or the equivalent, to terminate this program.)

LISTING 14.6 THE FrameDemo2 APPLICATION SOURCE CODE

```
// FrameDemo2.java

import java.awt.*;

class FrameDemo2 extends Frame
{
   FrameDemo2 (String title, boolean usePanel)
   {
      super (title); // Pass the title to the Frame layer.

      Button b1 = new Button ("Hello");
      Button b2 = new Button ("Goodbye");

      if (usePanel)
      {
          Panel p = new Panel ();
          p.add (b1);
          p.add (b2);
          add (p);
      }
      else
      {
          add (b1, BorderLayout.WEST);
          add (b2, BorderLayout.EAST);
      }

      setSize (100, 100);

      setResizable (false);

      setVisible (true);
   }

   public static void main (String [] args)
   {
      boolean usePanel = (args.length == 1) ? true : false;

      new FrameDemo2 ("Frame Demo 2", usePanel);
   }
}
```

FrameDemo2 builds on FrameDemo1, but allows you to choose between panels or no panels (via the presence or absence of one or more command line arguments, respectively). Furthermore, instead of calling pack to resize the frame, FrameDemo2 calls its inherited setVisible method. Figure 14.11 shows FrameDemo2's GUI when no arguments are specified.

Figure 14.11 FrameDemo2's GUI shows enlarged buttons.

When a component (such as a button) is added directly to a frame, the frame's default layout manager tends to "grow" this component so that it occupies as much of the frame as it can. (This is subject to the component's constraints.) However, if you add the component to a panel and then add the panel to a frame, the component will be displayed using a more natural size. The reason is that the panel's default layout manager will work in concert with the frame's layout manager to achieve this size. Figure 14.12 shows the difference that a panel makes.

Figure 14.12 FrameDemo2's GUI shows normal-sized buttons.

PANELS

A panel is often used by other containers (and applets) to arrange components. Panels do not have visible borders and are represented by objects created from the Panel class (located in the java.awt package) by calling the Panel () constructor.

After a panel has been created, its inherited add (Component c) method can be called to add a component (identified by c) to the panel. The following code fragment demonstrates creating a panel and adding a button to this panel.

```
Panel p = new Panel ();
p.add (new Button ("Cancel"));
```

When you study the SDK documentation, you'll discover that Applet extends the Panel class. In other words, every applet is also a panel. This implies that you can use this panel as both a drawing surface and a container in which to add components. To see how this works, check out the source code to the PanelDemo1 applet in Listing 14.7.

LISTING 14.7 THE `PanelDemo1` APPLET SOURCE CODE

```
// PanelDemo1.java

import java.awt.*;
import java.applet.Applet;

public class PanelDemo1 extends Applet
{
   public void init ()
   {
      Button b = new Button ("Ok");
      add (b);
   }

   public void paint (Graphics g)
   {
      int width = getSize ().width;
      int height = getSize ().height;

      g.setColor (Color.red);
      g.drawLine (0, 0, width - 1, height - 1);
      g.drawLine (0, height - 1, width - 1, 0);
   }
}
```

As you read through `PanelDemo1`'s source code, you'll notice that a button is created in its `init` method. This is the perfect place to create an applet's GUI. However, there is also a problem with this GUI: The button can hide part of the graphics that are rendered on the applet's panel. This is shown in Figure 14.13.

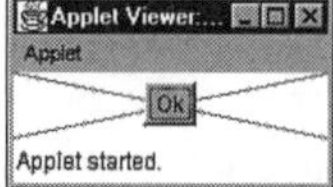

Figure 14.13 `PanelDemo1`'s GUI shows a button hiding graphics.

> **Note**
>
> If you compile `PanelDemo1` and run this program with `AppletViewer`, you will need to resize `AppletViewer`, to demonstrate the button hiding the line.

The problem stems from using a panel as a place for simultaneously rendering pixels and storing a component. A solution to this problem is to render graphics on a canvas and add this canvas (along with the button) to the applet's panel. `PanelDemo2` provides a demonstration. Check out its source code in Listing 14.8.

LISTING 14.8 THE `PanelDemo2` APPLET SOURCE CODE

```
// PanelDemo2.java

import java.awt.*;
import java.applet.Applet;
```

Listing 14.8 Continued

```
public class PanelDemo2 extends Applet
{
   public void init ()
   {
      Button b = new Button ("Ok");
      add (b);

      add (new Surface ());
   }
}

class Surface extends Canvas
{
   public Dimension getPreferredSize ()
   {
      return new Dimension (50, 50);
   }

   public void paint (Graphics g)
   {
      int width = getSize ().width;
      int height = getSize ().height;

      g.setColor (Color.red);
      g.drawLine (0, 0, width - 1, height - 1);
      g.drawLine (0, height - 1, width - 1, 0);
   }
}
```

The canvas is guaranteed to occupy no more than 50 pixels by 50 pixels. You can resize `PanelDemo2` all you want and the button will never hide the graphics drawn on the canvas. Figure 14.14 shows the result of using this canvas. (If you are creating an applet and only plan to draw, you can go ahead and draw on the panel.)

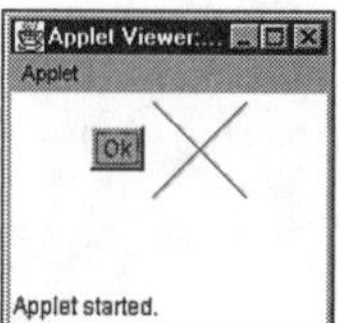

Figure 14.14 `PanelDemo2`'s GUI shows a canvas containing graphics that cannot be hidden.

Scroll Panes

A scroll pane makes it possible to scroll a very large component (such as a canvas displaying a large image) in a container. Only one component can be placed in a scroll pane. However, this component can be a container that holds several other components.

Scroll panes use policies that determine whether scrollbars will be displayed. These policies are represented by three constants that are found in the `ScrollPane` class (located in the `java.awt` package). The `SCROLLBARS_ALWAYS` constant forces scrollbars to always be displayed, even if the component stored in the scroll pane does not require scrollbars. The `SCROLLBARS_AS_NEEDED` constant only allows horizontal/vertical scrollbars to be displayed if the component's size exceeds the scroll pane's size in one or both directions. Finally, `SCROLLBARS_NEVER` prevents scrollbars from being displayed, even if they are needed.

To create a scroll pane with an "as needed" policy, call the `ScrollPane ()` constructor. To create a scroll pane and specify a policy, call `ScrollPane (int policy)` and pass one of the previously discussed policy constants as the `policy` argument.

After a scroll pane has been created, its inherited `add (Component c)` method can be called to add component `c` to the scroll pane. The following code fragment demonstrates creating a scroll pane and adding a panel of buttons to this scroll pane:

```
ScrollPane sp = new ScrollPane ();
Panel p = new Panel ();

for (int i = 0; i < 5; i++)
     p.add (new Button ("Button" + i));

sp.add (p);
```

You can scroll the scroll pane by calling one of two overloaded `setScrollPosition` methods and you can return the current scroll position by calling `getScrollPosition`. There are several other methods that can be called to obtain status information (such as scrollbar width or height and view port size). (For more information, check out the SDK documentation.)

Listing 14.9 presents source code to the `ScrollPaneDemo` application. This application adds a canvas—displaying an image of the International Space Station—to a scroll pane, and automatically displays scrollbars using the as needed policy. (Press `Ctrl+C`, or the equivalent, to terminate this program.)

LISTING 14.9 THE `ScrollPaneDemo` APPLICATION SOURCE CODE

```
// ScrollPaneDemo.java

import java.awt.*;

class ScrollPaneDemo extends Frame
{
   ScrollPaneDemo (String title)
   {
      super (title);

      // Create a MediaTracker object to track image loading.

      MediaTracker mt = new MediaTracker (this);

      // Applications require a Toolkit for image loading.

      Toolkit tk = Toolkit.getDefaultToolkit ();

      // Get the next image.
```

LISTING 14.9 CONTINUED

```
        Image im = tk.getImage ("iss.jpg");

        // Add image to MediaTracker object.

        mt.addImage (im, 0);

        // Force image to load.

        try
        {
            mt.waitForID (0);
        }
        catch (InterruptedException e) {}

        // Create a scroll pane container.

        ScrollPane sp = new ScrollPane ();

        // Create picture component.

        Picture pic = new Picture ();

        // Add picture to scroll pane.

        sp.add (pic);

        // Draw image.

        pic.draw (im);

        // Add scroll pane to frame (in center of its border layout).

        add (sp);

        // Set frame background (around scroll pane component/container)
        // to light gray.

        setBackground (Color.lightGray);

        // Set frame size to 400 by 400 pixels.

        setSize (400, 400);

        // Ensure that frame is visible.

        setVisible (true);
    }

    public static void main (String [] args)
    {
        new ScrollPaneDemo ("Scroll Pane Demo");
    }
}
```

LISTING 14.9 CONTINUED

```
class Picture extends Canvas
{
   private Image image;     // The current image.

   public void draw (Image image)
   {
      this.image = image;  // Save the current image.
      repaint ();          // Draw the image (update is called).
   }

   public Dimension getPreferredSize ()
   {
      // When the layout manager calls picture's getPreferredSize ()
      // method, this method will return a Dimension object that
      // tells the layout manager how much room to reserve for the
      // picture component. Because the iss image is 640×481,
      // these dimensions are returned.

      return new Dimension (640, 481);
   }

   public void paint (Graphics g)
   {
      // Determine the upper-left image corner (x, y) coordinates so
      // that the image will be centered.

      int x = (getSize ().width - image.getWidth (this)) / 2;
      int y = (getSize ().height - image.getHeight (this)) / 2;

      // Draw the image.

      g.drawImage (image, x, y, this);
   }
}
```

Figure 14.15 shows `ScrollPaneDemo's` output—the International Space Station in all its glory. Try moving the scrollbars, and see different parts of this space station.

Tip

You could also cheat and see the entire image, by clicking the maximize button on the frame's title bar.

WINDOWS

A *window* is a generic container that serves as the parent for dialogs, file dialogs, and frames. It encapsulates the commonality between these containers. Although surrounded by a visible border, a window has no title bar, menu bar, or minimize, maximize, and close buttons. In AWT 1.0, windows were used to implement pop-up menus. This is no longer necessary

Figure 14.15 `ScrollPaneDemo` presents a scroll pane that contains an image of the International Space Station.

A window is represented by an object created from the `Window` class (located in the `java.awt` package). This object is created by calling the `Window (Frame parent)` constructor, which implies that a window belongs to another container—a frame. This frame is the window's `parent`.

The `Window` class provides several useful methods that are inherited by its `Frame` and `Dialog` subclasses. These methods include `pack` (resize the container to the preferred size of its components and then validate the container), `dispose` (release the container's resources and hide/remove the container's peer), `toFront` (bring the container's peer to the foreground), `toBack` (bring the container's peer to the background), and `isShowing` (determine whether the container's peer is visible).

Exploring Layout Managers

The third step in building a GUI is to choose appropriate layout managers. This is probably the hardest step in the five-step building process. After all, choosing an appropriate layout manager often requires quite a bit of trial and error. Sometimes, multiple layout managers must be combined to produce the right effect. Although this process sounds intimidating, it is actually not that difficult, after you gain some experience.

Layout managers are closely associated with containers (with the sole exception of a scroll pane, which doesn't use a layout manager). Although each container (except for scroll pane) has a default layout manager, a new layout manager can be specified by calling the container's `setLayout` method. (Attempting to call this method on a scroll pane causes an `AWTError` object—containing the message `ScrollPane controls layout`—to be thrown.) After a layout manager has been specified (or the default is being used), `Container`'s `add` methods are called to add components to the container. (Depending on the layout manager, some of these methods are more appropriate than others.)

Note

Each add method works in harmony with the current layout manager (except in the case of scroll pane) to ensure that it lays out the component as specified by the layout manager's *constraints* (restrictions that govern where a component might appear and what its size will be when displayed).

Suppose there was no layout manager. In this case, you would be forced to lay out components by specifying your own positions and sizes. Listing 14.10 presents source code to an NLDemo application that demonstrates absolute positioning and sizing. (Press Ctrl+C, or the equivalent, to terminate this program.)

LISTING 14.10 THE NLDemo APPLICATION SOURCE CODE

```
// NLDemo.java

import java.awt.*;

class NLDemo extends Frame
{
   NLDemo (String title)
   {
      super (title);

      setLayout (null);

      Label l = new Label ("Enter your name:");
      add (l);
      l.setBounds (new Rectangle (10, 40, 100, 40));

      TextField t = new TextField (30);
      add (t);
      t.setBounds (new Rectangle (10, 80, 120, 30));

      setSize (250, 120);

      setVisible (true);
   }

   public static void main (String [] args)
   {
      new NLDemo ("No layout manager demo");
   }
}
```

Passing null to setLayout specifies no layout manager. After this is done, the setBounds method must be called to perform positioning and sizing. However, it's not a good idea to perform your own positioning and sizing, because your GUI will not be portable to different windowing systems and video resolutions.

With one exception, all the windowing toolkit's layout manager classes support the concept of horizontal and vertical *gaps* (reserved regions that surround a component and separate it from surrounding components). Each gap is measured in pixels. You can retrieve these horizontal and vertical gaps by calling the layout manager's `getHgap` and `getVgap` methods. You can also set the gaps, either in a call to a layout manager constructor or by calling its `setHgap` and `setVgap` methods.

BORDERS

A border layout manager divides its container into five regions: north, south, east, west, and center. One and only one component can be placed in each region. However, this limitation can be overcome by adding a container—with multiple components—to the region. The last component added to a region will appear in that region. The border layout manager is the default layout manager for dialog, file dialog, frame, and window containers.

Objects created from the `BorderLayout` class (located in the `java.awt` package) represent border layout managers. Call the `BorderLayout ()` constructor to create a border layout manager that does not allow horizontal or vertical gaps to appear between regions. However, if you want the layout manager to use gaps, call `BorderLayout (int hgap, int vgap)`. The following code fragment shows how to create and establish a border layout manager as a panel's default layout manager:

```
Panel p = new Panel ();
p.setLayout (new BorderLayout ());
```

Now that you've assigned a newly created border layout manager to a container, you need to add components. If you recall, Table 14.7 presented several of `Container`'s `add` methods for adding components to a container. When working with a border layout manager, you can call `add (Component c)` to add component `c` to the container and notify the border layout manager that this component is to be laid out in its center (the default). Conversely, you can call `add (Component c, Object const)` to add component `c` to the container, subject to `const`—the border layout manager's north, south, east, west, and center constraints. The following code fragment shows how this is done, assuming the previous code fragment has just been executed:

```
add (new Button ("OK"));                          // Add button to the center (default).
add (new Button ("Cancel"), "North");             // Add button to the north.
add (new Label ("Press me"), BorderLayout.WEST);  // Add label to the west.
```

As you can see, there are two ways to specify constraints. You can either use the literal strings—`"North"`, `"South"`, `"East"`, `"West"`, and `"Center"`— or use the `BorderLayout` constants—`NORTH`, `SOUTH`, `EAST`, `WEST`, and `CENTER`.

Caution

> The `"North"`, `"South"`, `"East"`, `"West"`, and `"Center"` literal strings are case-sensitive. Attempting to specify `"NORTH"`, `"center"`, or some other case mangling will result in an `IllegalArgumentException` object being thrown from the `add` method.

There is one other way to specify constraints. This way involves calling `Container`'s `add (String name, Component comp)` method, as demonstrated by the following code fragment:

```
add ("North", new Choice ());
```

The SDK documentation advises against this form of the add method because it is being phased out. Therefore, get into the habit of calling the alternate versions of add. (You might come across this form of add in some of the program listings that appear in an earlier chapter.)

Listing 14.11 presents source code to the BLDemo application that demonstrates the border layout manager. (Press Ctrl+C, or the equivalent, to terminate this program.)

LISTING 14.11 THE BLDemo APPLICATION SOURCE CODE

```
// BLDemo.java

import java.awt.*;

class BLDemo extends Frame
{
   final static int NOGAPS = 0;
   final static int GAPS = 1;

   BLDemo (String title, int gapsOption)
   {
      super (title);

      if (gapsOption == GAPS)
          setLayout (new BorderLayout (10, 10));
      else
          setLayout (new BorderLayout ());

      add (new Button ("North"), "North");
      add (new Button ("South"), BorderLayout.SOUTH);
      add (new Button ("Center"), "Center");
      add (new Button ("West"), BorderLayout.WEST);
      add (new Button ("East"), "East");

      setSize (250, 250);
      setVisible (true);
   }

   public static void main (String [] args)
   {
      int option = NOGAPS;

      for (int i = 0; i < args.length; i++)
           if (args [i].equalsIgnoreCase ("GAPS"))
               option = GAPS;
           else
           if (args [i].equalsIgnoreCase ("NOGAPS"))
               option = NOGAPS;

      new BLDemo ("BorderLayout Demo", option);
   }
}
```

`BLDemo` can be run without any command arguments. If none are specified, it assumes that no gaps will appear between buttons. However, if you specify gaps when running this program (as in `java BLDemo gaps`), you'll see space between each button. Figure 14.16 shows `BLDemo`'s output when gaps are specified.

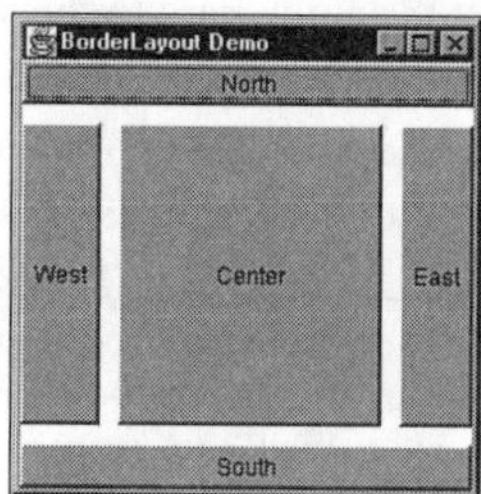

Figure 14.16
`BLDemo` lays out its components in five separate regions.

CARDS

A card layout manager differs from the other layout managers in that it treats a container as a series of cards—similar to tabs in a tabbed dialog. Only one component can be placed on a card. However, it's possible to add a container (containing multiple components) to a card, so this really isn't a limitation.

Objects created from the `CardLayout` class (located in the `java.awt` package) represent card layout managers. Call the `CardLayout ()` constructor to create a card layout manager that does not allow horizontal or vertical gaps to appear between the currently displayed component and the borders of its container. If you prefer, you can specify gaps by calling `CardLayout (int hgap, int vgap)`. The following code fragment shows how to create and establish a card layout manager as a frame's default layout manager:

```
Frame f = new Frame ();
f.setLayout (new CardLayout ());
```

Card layout managers require a name to be specified when adding a component to a container. This name identifies the card on which a component appears. To add a component, call `Container`'s `add (Component c, Object const)` method. The component is identified by `c` and the card's name is identified by `const`. (Constraints are very versatile.) The following code fragment demonstrates adding a button to a card called `Card1`. The previously created frame is assumed:

```
f.add (new Button ("OK"), "Card1");
```

You can specify the card on which a component is currently displayed by calling the card layout manager's `show` method. For example, you could call `((CardLayout) getLayout ()).show (f, "Card1");` to show the `Card1` card using the previous frame. You can also call the `first`, `last`, `next`, and `previous` methods to navigate from card to card. Each method requires an argument that identifies the layout manager's container. If the container does not use a card layout manager, an `IllegalArgumentException` object is thrown. `CardLayout`'s navigation methods are presented in Table 14.8. (In all cases, `parent` refers to the container whose layout manager was set to the card layout manager.)

TABLE 14.8 CardLayout's CARD NAVIGATION METHODS

Method	Description
`first (Container parent)`	Set the visible card to the first card managed by the card layout manager.
`last (Container parent)`	Set the visible card to the last card managed by the card layout manager.
`next (Container parent)`	Set the visible card to the next card managed by the card layout manager. If there is no next card, the first card is shown.
`previous (Container parent)`	Set the visible card to the previous card managed by the card layout manager. If there is no previous card, the last card is shown.
`show (Container parent, String name)`	Set the visible card to the card identified by `name`.

Listing 14.12 presents source code to the `CLDemo` application that demonstrates the card layout manager. (Press `Ctrl+C`, or the equivalent, to terminate this program.)

LISTING 14.12 THE CLDemo APPLICATION SOURCE CODE

```
// CLDemo.java

import java.awt.*;
import java.awt.event.*;

class CLDemo extends Frame implements ActionListener, ItemListener
{
   final static int NOGAPS = 0;
   final static int GAPS = 1;

   CLDemo (String title, int gapsOption)
   {
      super (title);

      if (gapsOption == GAPS)
          setLayout (new CardLayout (10, 10));
      else
          setLayout (new CardLayout ());

      Panel p1 = new Panel ();
      Button b = new Button ("Press Me");
      b.addActionListener (this);
      p1.add (b);
      add (p1, "First");

      Panel p2 = new Panel ();
      Checkbox cb = new Checkbox ("Check or Uncheck Me");
      cb.addItemListener (this);
      p2.add (cb, "Second");
      add (p2, "Second");

      setSize (200, 100);
      setVisible (true);
```

LISTING 14.12 CONTINUED

```
   }

   public void actionPerformed (ActionEvent e)
   {
      // Switch to the other card.

      ((CardLayout) getLayout ()).next (this);
   }

   public void itemStateChanged (ItemEvent e)
   {
      // Switch to the other card.

      ((CardLayout) getLayout ()).next (this);
   }

   public static void main (String [] args)
   {
      int option = NOGAPS;

      for (int i = 0; i < args.length; i++)
           if (args [i].equalsIgnoreCase ("GAPS"))
               option = GAPS;
           else
           if (args [i].equalsIgnoreCase ("NOGAPS"))
               option = NOGAPS;

      new CLDemo ("CardLayout Demo", option);
   }
}
```

`CLDemo` can be run without any command arguments. If none are specified, it assumes that no gaps will appear between the regions. However, if you specify gaps when running this program (as in `java CLDemo gaps`), you'll see extra space above the component on each card. Figure 14.17 shows `CLDemo`'s output when no gaps are specified.

Figure 14.17 `CLDemo` lays out its components on separate cards.

FLOWS

A flow layout manager divides its container into one or more rows and adds components to these rows in a left-to-right and top-to-bottom fashion. Components can be aligned with the container's left edge, right edge, or center. The flow layout manager is the default layout manager for panel containers.

Objects created from the `FlowLayout` class (located in the `java.awt` package) represent flow layout managers. This class provides three constants that control alignment: `LEFT`, `RIGHT`, and `CENTER`. Call the `FlowLayout ()` constructor to create a flow layout manager with default horizontal and vertical gaps of five pixels and a left alignment. You can change this alignment by calling `FlowLayout (int alignment)` and these gaps by calling `FlowLayout (int alignment, int hgap, int vgap)`. (You can retrieve the current alignment by calling `getAlignment` and set the alignment by calling `setAlignment`.) The following code fragment shows how to create and establish a flow layout manager as a frame's default layout manager:

```
Frame f = new Frame ();
f.setLayout (new FlowLayout ());
```

Now that you've assigned a newly created flow layout manager to a container, you need to add components. This is done by calling the container's `add (Component c)` method. The following code fragment calls this method to add an `OK` button to the previously created frame container; this button is then managed by the flow layout manager:

```
add (new Button ("OK"));
```

Listing 14.13 presents source code to the `FLDemo` application that demonstrates the flow layout manager. (Press `Ctrl+C`, or the equivalent, to terminate this program.)

LISTING 14.13 THE `FLDemo` APPLICATION SOURCE CODE

```
// FLDemo.java

import java.awt.*;

class FLDemo extends Frame
{
   final static int NOGAPS = 0;
   final static int GAPS = 1;

   FLDemo (String title, int gapsOption, int alignOption)
   {
      super (title);

      if (gapsOption == GAPS)
          setLayout (new FlowLayout (alignOption));
      else
          setLayout (new FlowLayout (alignOption, 0, 0));

      for (int i = 0; i < 10; i++)
           add (new Button ("Button " + i));

      setSize (250, 250);
      setVisible (true);
   }

   public static void main (String [] args)
   {
      int option1 = NOGAPS;
      int option2 = FlowLayout.LEFT;

      for (int i = 0; i < args.length; i++)
           if (args [i].equalsIgnoreCase ("LEFT"))
               option2 = FlowLayout.LEFT;
           else
```

LISTING 14.13 CONTINUED

```
            if (args [i].equalsIgnoreCase ("RIGHT"))
                option2 = FlowLayout.RIGHT;
            else
            if (args [i].equalsIgnoreCase ("CENTER"))
                option2 = FlowLayout.CENTER;
            else
            if (args [i].equalsIgnoreCase ("GAPS"))
                option1 = GAPS;
            else
            if (args [i].equalsIgnoreCase ("NOGAPS"))
                option1 = NOGAPS;

        new FLDemo ("FlowLayout Demo", option1, option2);
    }
}
```

FLDemo can be run without any command arguments. If none are specified, it assumes that no gaps will appear between components and that left alignment is in effect. However, if you specify gaps when running this program (as in `java FLDemo gaps`), you'll see extra space between components. You can also change the alignment (as in `java FLDemo right` or `java FLDemo center`). Furthermore, you can combine gaps and alignment arguments in any order (as in `java FLDemo center gaps`). Figure 14.18 shows FLDemo's output—buttons centered and separated by gaps.

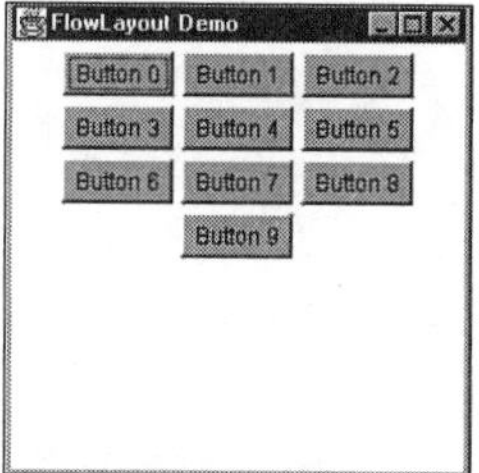

Figure 14.18
FLDemo lays out its components in a left-to-right flow.

GRIDS

A grid layout manager divides its container into a grid of rows and columns. The intersection of each row and column is known as a *cell*. A component is laid out in a cell and each cell has the same size. Row and column numbering is zero-based (that is, the first row and column numbers are zeroes).

Objects created from the `GridLayout` class (located in the `java.awt` package) represent grid layout managers. Call the `GridLayout ()` constructor to create a grid layout manager that divides a container into one row by as many columns as required—and no gaps. You can change the number of rows and columns by calling `GridLayout (int rows, int columns)`. As before, there are no gaps. However, you can specify gaps in addition to rows and columns by calling `GridLayout (int rows, int columns, int hgap, int vgap)`.

Note

You can retrieve the current number of rows by calling `getRows` and the current number of columns by calling `getColumns`. You can also set the number of rows by calling `setRows` and the number of columns by calling `setColumns`.

The following code fragment shows how to create and establish a 3-row by 5-column grid layout manager as a panel's default layout manager:

```
Panel p = new Panel ();
p.setLayout (new GridLayout (3, 5));
```

As with flow layout manager, you add components to a container managed by a grid layout manager by calling the container's `add (Component c)` method. The following code fragment shows how this is done, assuming the previous code fragment has just been executed:

```
add (new Button ("OK"));
```

When you add components, the grid layout manager keeps track of the next row and column in which to place the component. For example, using a 3-row by 2-column layout, the first component would be placed at row 0 and column 0, the second at row 0 and column 1, the third at row 1 and column 0, the fourth at row 1 and column 1; and so on.

Listing 14.14 presents source code to the `GLDemo` application that demonstrates the grid layout manager. (Press `Ctrl+C`, or the equivalent, to terminate this program.)

LISTING 14.14 THE `GLDemo` APPLICATION SOURCE CODE

```
// GLDemo.java

import java.awt.*;

class GLDemo extends Frame
{
   final static int NOGAPS = 0;
   final static int GAPS = 1;

   GLDemo (String title, int gapsOption)
   {
      super (title);

      if (gapsOption == GAPS)
          setLayout (new GridLayout (3, 3, 10, 10));
      else
          setLayout (new GridLayout (3, 3));

      for (int i = 0; i < 9; i++)
           add (new Button ("Button " + i));

      setSize (250, 250);
      setVisible (true);
   }

   public static void main (String [] args)
   {
      int option = NOGAPS;
```

LISTING 14.14 CONTINUED

```
      for (int i = 0; i < args.length; i++)
           if (args [i].equalsIgnoreCase ("GAPS"))
               option = GAPS;
           else
           if (args [i].equalsIgnoreCase ("NOGAPS"))
               option = NOGAPS;

      new GLDemo ("GridLayout Demo", option);
   }
}
```

GLDemo can be run without any command arguments. If none are specified, it assumes that no gaps will appear between the cells. However, if you specify gaps when running this program (as in `java GLDemo gaps`), you'll see extra space surrounding each cell. Figure 14.19 shows GLDemo's output when no gaps are specified

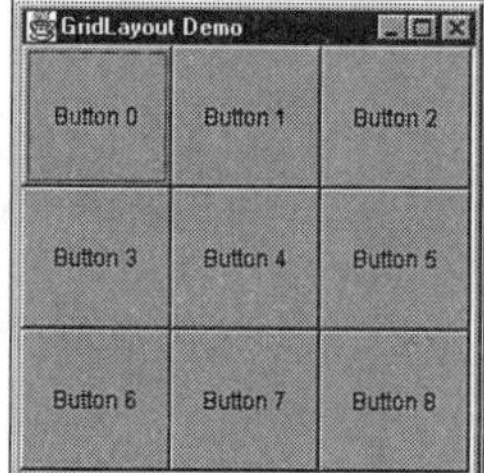

Figure 14.19 GLDemo lays out its components in equal-size regions.

GRID-BAGS

The windowing toolkit provides a sophisticated grid-bag layout manager. This layout manager makes it possible to create a grid (as with the grid layout manager). However, instead of each cell being the same size, a single cell might occupy multiple columns and multiple rows. This can lead to very sophisticated layouts.

Grid-bag layout managers are created from the `GridBagLayout` class (located in the `java.awt` package). This is the only layout manager that does not support gaps. However, it works in partnership with the `GridBagConstraints` class (also located in `java.awt`) to allow a greater precision in positioning and sizing.

If you want to learn more about this layout manager, please consult the SDK documentation.

COMBINING LAYOUT MANAGERS

You can combine multiple layout managers to achieve the desired effect for your GUI. For example, the grid layout manager and border layout manager can be combined to create a calculator GUI. To demonstrate this effect, Listing 14.15 presents source code to a `Calc` applet.

LISTING 14.15 THE Calc APPLET SOURCE CODE

```
// Calc.java

import java.awt.*;
import java.applet.Applet;

public class Calc extends Applet
{
   public void init ()
   {
      setLayout (new BorderLayout ());

      add (new Label ("0", Label.RIGHT), BorderLayout.NORTH);

      Panel p = new Panel ();
      p.setLayout (new GridLayout (4, 4));

      String [] btnNames =
      {
         "7", "8", "9", "/", "4", "5", "6", "x",
         "1", "2", "3", "-", "0", ".", "C", "+"
      };

      for (int i = 0; i < btnNames.length; i++)
           p.add (new Button (btnNames [i]));

      add (p, "Center");
   }
}
```

To achieve the calculator layout, Calc's default flow layout manager must be changed to a border layout manager. The calculator's display is then added to the north region of Calc's inherited panel. A panel is created and assigned a 4-row by 4-column grid layout manager. A total of 16 buttons are added to this panel, and the panel is then added to the south region of Calc's panel. Figure 14.20 shows the resulting GUI.

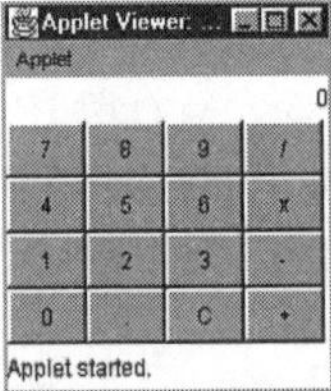

Figure 14.20 Layout managers can be combined to achieve an appropriate layout for a calculator GUI.

BUILDING A GUI: EVENTS AND LISTENERS

In the second phase of the GUI building process, the focus is on the feel of a GUI. To achieve this feel, you'll work with the windowing toolkit's events and listeners. After you've integrated this feel with a GUI's look, you're almost finished. (All that is left is to test your GUI.)

EXPLORING EVENTS

An event is fired when a user presses a button, scrolls through a list of textual items, makes a selection from a menu, moves the mouse, presses a key, and so on. These events originate with the component's peer and are forwarded by the windowing toolkit to a corresponding object. This object is understood to be the *source* of the event.

The windowing toolkit associates events with objects that provide descriptive information about what happened, and are created from subclasses of the abstract `AWTEvent` class (located in the `java.awt` package). Getting to know `AWTEvent` and its subclasses is the fourth step in building a GUI.

The event class hierarchy is shown in Figure 14.21. (`AWTEvent` and `InputEvent` appear in gray because they are abstract classes.)

Figure 14.21
The windowing toolkit organizes event classes into a hierarchy.

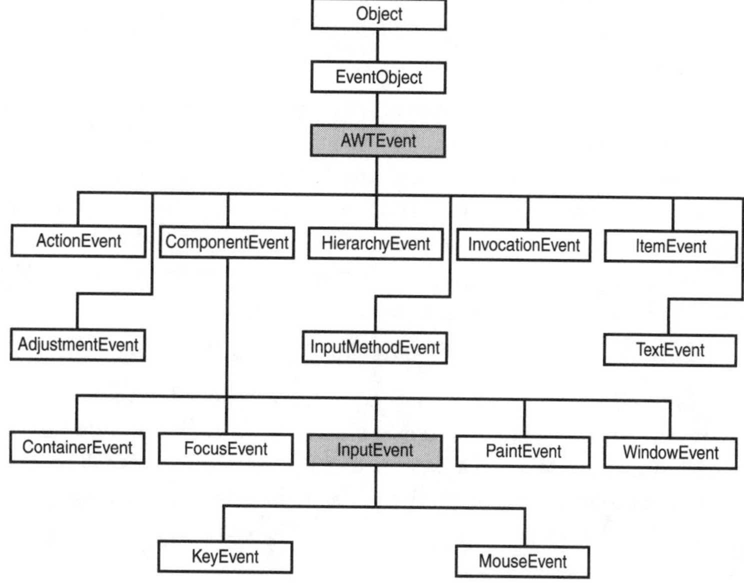

If you look carefully, you'll notice that `AWTEvent` inherits from the `EventObject` class (located in the `java.util` package). This class encapsulates the concept of being a source, and provides a `getSource` method that returns an event's source.

NEW TO 1.3

The `HierarchyEvent` class is new to the Java 2 Platform Standard Edition, Version 1.3. Objects created from this class represent events that are fired when a change is made to the component and container hierarchy. For example, a hierarchy event is fired when a panel is added to another container (such as a frame). These events are provided for notification purposes only, because the windowing toolkit automatically takes care of these changes.

`AWTEvent` provides several constants (such as `ACTION_EVENT_MASK`) that are useful when processing events without using listeners. These constants are used in conjunction with `Component`'s `enableEvents` method. `AWTEvent` also provides methods for use with peers.

Event objects are typically created behind the scenes, by calling a constructor in the appropriate event class. Normally, you will not be creating these objects. For this reason, these constructors will not be discussed when some of the more common event classes are explored. (To explore all the event classes in detail, consult the SDK documentation.)

ACTION EVENTS

Action events are generated by components when component-specific actions occur. For example, an action occurs when a user presses a button or selects a menu item. This results in an action event being generated. Objects representing action events are created from the `ActionEvent` class (located in the `java.awt.event` package).

When an action event occurs, it is possible that a user might be holding down the `Alt`, `Ctrl`, `Meta`, or `Shift` key. This key can be used to modify the purpose of the action event. For example, a simple button press might accomplish one thing, whereas pressing the `Alt` key in conjunction with a button press might accomplish something slightly different. For this reason, these four keys are known as *modifiers*.

`ActionEvent` provides the `getModifiers` method to return an integer value that identifies all pressed modifiers. To distinguish between multiple modifiers, you need to use one of the four constants provided by `ActionEvent`—`ALT_MASK`, `CTRL_MASK`, `META_MASK`, and `SHIFT_MASK`—in conjunction with the bitwise AND operator. A nonzero result means the modifier was pressed when the action event occurred. The following code fragment shows how to isolate a modifier by using a mask. This code fragment determines whether `Alt` was pressed. (An `ActionEvent` object referenced by `e` is assumed.)

```
if (e.getModifiers () & ActionEvent.ALT_MASK) { }
```

If you are writing an internationalized program, you will want to identify the button that was pressed or the menu item that was selected. You can simplify this task by using nonlocalized identifiers. When a component object is created, you call its `setActionCommand` method to assign an identifier. When the action event occurs, call `getActionCommand` to retrieve this identifier.

FOCUS EVENTS

Focus events occur when a component either gains or loses focus. For example, when a user is tabbing from one component to another in a dialog, one of these components gains focus, whereas the other loses focus. Objects representing focus events are created from the `FocusEvent` class (located in the `java.awt.event` package).

A focus change can be temporary or permanent. For example, when a window appears in front of another, this is a temporary change of focus. In contrast, a permanent change of focus occurs when the mouse is used to click in a text field or the `Tab` key is used to switch to another component. `FocusEvent`'s `isTemporary` method returns a Boolean `true` value if the focus change is temporary and a Boolean `false` value if this change is permanent.

ITEM EVENTS

Item events occur when a user selects a check box, check box menu item, choice item, or list item (or items). Objects representing item events are created from the `ItemEvent` class (located in the `java.awt.event` package).

Whereas `ItemEvent`'s inherited `getSource` method returns the source of the event, this source can be narrowed down to the actual item (for choices and lists) or items (for lists), by calling the `getItemSelectable` method, which returns a reference to an object implementing the `ItemSelectable` interface (located in the `java.awt` package). Call `ItemSelectable`'s `getSelectedItems` method to fetch an array of all selected items. (Remember, lists can operate in multiple selection mode, allowing a user to select more than one item.)

Item events are fired when an item is selected or deselected. These two states are represented by the `SELECTED` and `DESELECTED` constants in the `ItemEvent` class. Furthermore, to discover whether an item was selected or deselected, call `ItemEvent`'s `getStateChange` method.

KEY EVENTS

Key events occur when a user presses or releases a key, and fall into three categories: key pressed, key released, and key typed. A key pressed event occurs when a user presses a key and a key released event occurs when a user releases the key. The key that was pressed/released is represented by a *key code* (a 32-bit `int`) and each key on the keyboard is assigned its own unique key code. A key typed event occurs when one or more keys are pressed to generate a single Unicode character (a 16-bit `char`). For example, pressing the `A` key results in a key typed event that represents a lowercase letter `a`, whereas simultaneously pressing both the `A` key and either `Shift` key results in a key typed event that represents an uppercase letter `A`. Keep in mind that the order of events is key pressed followed by key typed followed by key released.

For every key typed event, there is at least one key pressed event. For example, when you press the `A` key by itself, a single key pressed event is fired, which is followed by a single key typed event. Now, if you press either `Shift` key and then press the `A` key, a key pressed event is fired for the `Shift` key. This is followed by a key pressed event being fired for the `A` key. Finally, a key typed event is fired that represents an uppercase letter `A`. Some key pressed events do not result in any key typed events. For example, if you press a `Shift` key, a key pressed event is fired. However, a key typed event is not fired because a `Shift` key does not represent a character.

Objects representing key events are created from the `KeyEvent` class (located in the `java.awt.event` package).

`KeyEvent` provides a variety of constants (such as `VK_ENTER`, `VK_A`, and `VK_ALT`) that identify key codes. These key codes are also known as *virtual keys* because they are independent of any windowing system. To retrieve a key code from a key event object, call `KeyEvent`'s `getKeyCode` method. This method returns the `VK_UNDEFINED` constant if called for a key typed event.

You can compare getKeyCode's return value against one of the virtual key constants to determine which key was pressed. The following code fragment demonstrates this comparison. (A KeyEvent object referenced by e is assumed.)

```
if (e.getKeyCode () == KeyEvent.VK_ENTER) { }
```

In the case of a key typed event, you are more interested in a character. You can obtain this character by calling getKeyChar. This method returns KeyEvent's CHAR_UNDEFINED constant if there is no character associated with the key code.

You can compare getKeyChar's return value against a character literal to determine which character is represented by the event. The following code fragment demonstrates this comparison. (A KeyEvent object referenced by e is assumed.)

```
if (e.getKeyChar () == 'A') { }
```

MOUSE EVENTS

Mouse events occur when a user presses a mouse button, releases a mouse button, or moves the mouse pointer. Objects representing mouse events are created from the MouseEvent class (located in the java.awt.event package).

MouseEvent's getX and getY methods return the coordinates of the mouse pointer. These coordinates are relative to the coordinates of the source. Instead of retrieving these coordinates separately, you can retrieve them together as one Point object by calling getPoint.

When working with pop-up menus, you will need to call MouseEvent's isPopupTrigger method. This method retrieves the pop-up trigger setting (a Boolean value that is true when a user has chosen to activate a pop-up menu). This is demonstrated in the following code fragment. (A MouseEvent object referenced by e is assumed. Furthermore, a pop-up menu component identified by popup is assumed.)

```
if (e.isPopupTrigger ())
    popup.show (e.getComponent (), e.getX (), e.getY ());
```

The getComponent method (inherited from the ComponentEvent class) identifies the component to which a pop-up menu is attached. Its coordinate system is used in partnership with the returned values from getX and getY to identify the upper-left corner of the pop-up menu.

TEXT EVENTS

Text events occur when the contents of a text area or a text field change, or a user presses Return when a text field has the focus. A change happens by pressing keys (when this component has the focus) or by calling the component's setText method. Objects representing text events are created from the TextEvent class (located in the java.awt.event package).

WINDOW EVENTS

Window events occur when a window is activated, deactivated, opened, closing, closed, iconified, or deiconified. Objects representing window events are created from the

WindowEvent class (located in the java.awt.event package). To identify the container window—dialog, file dialog, or frame—that fired the event, call WindowEvent's getWindow method.

Exploring Listeners

There is hardly any point in firing an event when there is no one around to listen for that event and take appropriate action. The ability to create and register listeners is the final step in the GUI building process.

A listener object registers itself with a source. The source will then call the listener when an event occurs. Figure 14.22 illustrates the process of sending an event from a component peer to its object (via the AWT), and then forwarding the event object from this source to a registered listener.

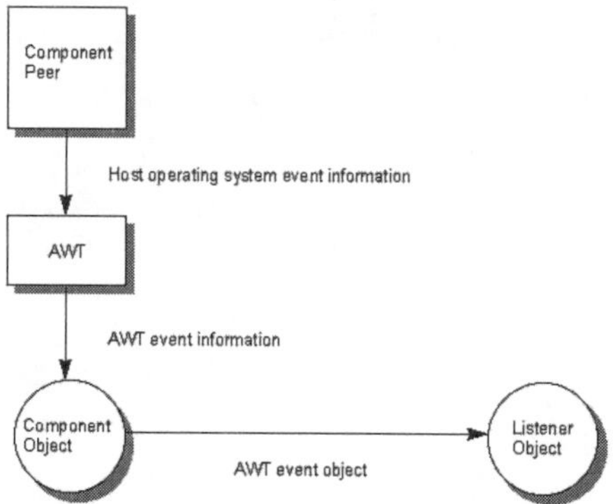

Figure 14.22 An event is fired from a component peer to a component object, and then forwarded to a listener.

To become a registered listener to a source's events, an object must be created from a class that implements a listener interface and must also call a source registration method.

The HierarchyListener interface is new to the Java 2 Platform Standard Edition, Version 1.3. Objects created from classes that implement this interface can register themselves as listeners for hierarchy events.

Action Listeners

Action listeners listen for action events. They are represented by objects implementing the ActionListener interface (located in the java.awt.event package).

ActionListener specifies a single method that must be implemented by an action listener's class. This method has the following signature:

```
public abstract void actionPerformed (ActionEvent e)
```

The actionPerformed method is called when a button is pressed or a menu item is selected.

To register with an action source, an action listener must call the source's `addActionListener` method. (To de-register, an action listener would call the source's `removeActionListener` method.)

Listing 14.16 presents the source code to an `ActionListenerDemo1` applet that demonstrates listening for action events.

LISTING 14.16 THE ActionListenerDemo1 APPLET SOURCE CODE

```
// ActionListenerDemo1.java

import java.awt.*;
import java.applet.*;
import java.awt.event.*;

public class ActionListenerDemo1 extends Applet
                                 implements ActionListener
{
   public void init ()
   {
      String [] cursorNames =
      {
         "DEFAULT_CURSOR",
         "CROSSHAIR_CURSOR",
         "TEXT_CURSOR",
         "WAIT_CURSOR",
         "HAND_CURSOR",
         "MOVE_CURSOR",
         "N_RESIZE_CURSOR",
         "S_RESIZE_CURSOR",
         "E_RESIZE_CURSOR",
         "W_RESIZE_CURSOR",
         "NE_RESIZE_CURSOR",
         "NW_RESIZE_CURSOR",
         "SE_RESIZE_CURSOR",
         "SW_RESIZE_CURSOR"
      };

      int [] cursorTypes =
      {
         Cursor.DEFAULT_CURSOR,
         Cursor.CROSSHAIR_CURSOR,
         Cursor.TEXT_CURSOR,
         Cursor.WAIT_CURSOR,
         Cursor.HAND_CURSOR,
         Cursor.MOVE_CURSOR,
         Cursor.N_RESIZE_CURSOR,
         Cursor.S_RESIZE_CURSOR,
         Cursor.E_RESIZE_CURSOR,
         Cursor.W_RESIZE_CURSOR,
         Cursor.NE_RESIZE_CURSOR,
         Cursor.NW_RESIZE_CURSOR,
         Cursor.SE_RESIZE_CURSOR,
         Cursor.SW_RESIZE_CURSOR
      };
```

LISTING 14.16 CONTINUED

```
      for (int i = 0; i < cursorNames.length; i++)
      {
           Button b = new Button (cursorNames [i]);
           b.setActionCommand ("" + i);
           b.setCursor (Cursor.getPredefinedCursor (cursorTypes [i]));
           b.addActionListener (this);
           add (b);
      };
   }

   public void actionPerformed (ActionEvent e)
   {
      String id = e.getActionCommand ();
      AudioClip ac = getAudioClip (getDocumentBase (), id + ".au");
      ac.play ();
   }
}
```

`ActionListenerDemo1` displays a GUI consisting of several buttons. Each button contains the name of a constant in the `Cursor` class. When you move the mouse pointer over a button, its icon changes to reflect the button's cursor. Figure 14.23 shows this GUI.

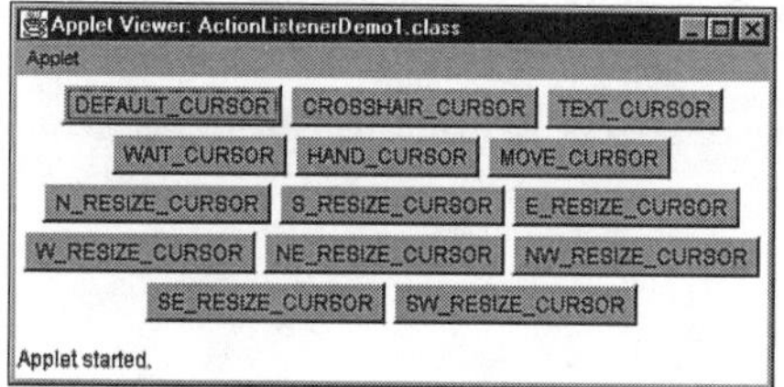

Figure 14.23 `ActionListenerDemo1` demonstrates action events—and more.

`ActionListenerDemo1` implements the `ActionListener` interface by providing an `actionPerformed` method. It establishes a GUI in its `init` method. As part of this process, buttons are created. For each button, the `setActionCommand` method is called to give this button a unique ID. Then, the `setCursor` method is called to establish the cursor that will appear when the mouse pointer is moved over this button. The button's `addActionListener` method is called to register the applet as a listener for action events that originate from this button. Finally, the button is added to the applet's panel container. When an action event occurs, `actionPerformed` is called. To handle this event, `actionPerformed` calls `getActionCommand` to retrieve the button's ID. It uses this ID to choose an appropriate sound file, which is subsequently played.

Applets and applications are capable of producing sounds by calling one of two overloaded `getAudioClip` methods (for applets) and the `newAudioClip` method (for applications). These methods are located in the `Applet` class and require a URL argument that identifies the location and name of a sound file. (The following sound file formats are supported: AIFF, AU, MIDI, RMF, and WAV.)

Each method returns an object that implements the `AudioClip` interface (located in the `java.applet` package). This object is known as an *audio clip*. `AudioClip` specifies three methods that the audio clip's class implements. These methods are presented in Table 14.9.

TABLE 14.9 `AudioClip`'S METHODS

Method	Description
`loop`	Play an audio clip in a continuous loop.
`play`	Play an audio clip once.
`stop`	Stop an audio clip that is currently playing.

When you click one of `ActionListenerDemo1`'s buttons, you will hear a voice identifying the cursor. If you click another button before this sound finishes, a new sound will begin and can be simultaneously heard with the other sound.

`ActionListenerDemo1` integrates GUI presentation and the handling of events. However, by separating these tasks, you can simplify your GUI and promote reusable code. Listing 14.17 presents the source code to an `ActionListenerDemo2` application that demonstrates event handling/presentation separation, along with action events from an application perspective. (Press `Ctrl+C`, or the equivalent, to terminate this program.)

LISTING 14.17 THE `ActionListenerDemo2` APPLICATION SOURCE CODE

```
// ActionListenerDemo2.java

import java.awt.*;
import java.net.*;
import java.applet.*;
import java.awt.event.*;

class MakeSomeNoise implements ActionListener
{
   public void actionPerformed (ActionEvent e)
   {
      try
      {
         String id = e.getActionCommand ();
         URL url = new URL ("file:" + id + ".au");
         AudioClip ac = Applet.newAudioClip (url);
         ac.play ();
      }
      catch (MalformedURLException e2) {}
   }
}

public class ActionListenerDemo2 extends Frame
{
   ActionListenerDemo2 (String title)
   {
      super (title);

      String [] cursorNames =
```

Listing 14.17 Continued

```
        {
           "DEFAULT_CURSOR",
           "CROSSHAIR_CURSOR",
           "TEXT_CURSOR",
           "WAIT_CURSOR",
           "HAND_CURSOR",
           "MOVE_CURSOR",
           "N_RESIZE_CURSOR",
           "S_RESIZE_CURSOR",
           "E_RESIZE_CURSOR",
           "W_RESIZE_CURSOR",
           "NE_RESIZE_CURSOR",
           "NW_RESIZE_CURSOR",
           "SE_RESIZE_CURSOR",
           "SW_RESIZE_CURSOR"
        };

        int [] cursorTypes =
        {
           Cursor.DEFAULT_CURSOR,
           Cursor.CROSSHAIR_CURSOR,
           Cursor.TEXT_CURSOR,
           Cursor.WAIT_CURSOR,
           Cursor.HAND_CURSOR,
           Cursor.MOVE_CURSOR,
           Cursor.N_RESIZE_CURSOR,
           Cursor.S_RESIZE_CURSOR,
           Cursor.E_RESIZE_CURSOR,
           Cursor.W_RESIZE_CURSOR,
           Cursor.NE_RESIZE_CURSOR,
           Cursor.NW_RESIZE_CURSOR,
           Cursor.SE_RESIZE_CURSOR,
           Cursor.SW_RESIZE_CURSOR
        };

        Panel p = new Panel ();
        for (int i = 0; i < cursorNames.length; i++)
        {
             Button b = new Button (cursorNames [i]);
             b.setActionCommand ("" + i);
             b.setCursor (Cursor.getPredefinedCursor (cursorTypes [i]));
             b.addActionListener (new MakeSomeNoise ());
             p.add (b);
        };
        add (p);

        setSize (450, 200);

        setVisible (true);
    }

    public static void main (String [] args)
    {
        new ActionListenerDemo2 ("Action Listener Demo2");
    }
}
```

FOCUS LISTENERS

Focus listeners listen for focus events. They are represented by objects implementing the `FocusListener` interface (located in the `java.awt.event` package).

`FocusListener` specifies two methods that must be implemented by a focus listener's class. These methods have the following signatures:

```
public abstract void focusGained (FocusEvent e)
public abstract void focusLost (FocusEvent e)
```

When the very first focus event occurs, `focusGained` is called for the component that receives focus. (This would be the very first component added to a container that is capable of receiving focus.) For each subsequent focus event, `focusLost` is called for the component losing focus and then `focusGained` is called for the component receiving focus.

To register with a focus source, a focus listener must call the source's `addFocusListener` method. (To de-register, a focus listener would call the source's `removeFocusListener` method.)

Listing 14.18 presents the source code to a `FocusListenerDemo` application that demonstrates listening for focus events. (Press `Ctrl+C`, or the equivalent, to terminate this program.)

LISTING 14.18 THE `FocusListenerDemo` APPLICATION SOURCE CODE

```
// FocusListenerDemo.java

import java.awt.*;
import java.awt.event.*;

class FocusListenerDemo extends Frame implements FocusListener
{
   TextField numField;

   FocusListenerDemo (String title)
   {
      super (title);

      Panel p = new Panel ();
      p.add (new Label ("Please enter a number:"));
      numField = new TextField (20);
      numField.addFocusListener (this);
      p.add (numField);
      add (p, "North");

      p = new Panel ();
      p.add (new Label ("Please enter a name:"));
      TextField nameField = new TextField (20);
      nameField.addFocusListener (this);
      p.add (nameField);
      add (p, "South");

      setSize (350, 100);
```

LISTING 14.18 CONTINUED

```
      setVisible (true);
   }

   public void focusGained (FocusEvent e)
   {
      Component c = (Component) e.getSource ();
      System.out.println ("GAIN: " + c.getName ());
   }

   public void focusLost (FocusEvent e)
   {
      Component c = (Component) e.getSource ();
      System.out.println ("LOST: " + c.getName ());

      if (e.getSource () == numField)
          try
          {
             int i = Integer.parseInt (numField.getText ());
          }
          catch (NumberFormatException e2)
          {
             numField.requestFocus ();
          }
   }

   public static void main (String [] args)
   {
      new FocusListenerDemo ("Focus Listener Demo");
   }
}
```

`FocusListenerDemo` displays a GUI consisting of a pair of labels and two text fields. One of these text fields is used to input a number, whereas the other text field is used to input a name.

As you know, users don't necessarily do what a program asks. For example, a user might try to enter a name in the number field and then move to the name field. To prevent this from happening, you can force the user to remain in the number field until a valid number is entered. This is accomplished in part by listening for focus change events. When a focus event occurs, `focusLost` will be called when the number field loses focus. After displaying the name of the component losing focus, the code checks to see if this component is the number field. If it is, the code tries to convert the contents of that field to an integer, by calling `Integer.parseInt`. This method throws a `NumberFormatException` object if it cannot parse these contents into an integer. If this should happen, the `requestFocus` method for the number field object is called in the exception handler. This method call immediately transfers focus back to the number field. As a result, the user is not allowed to exit this field until a valid number has been entered. `FocusListenerDemo`'s GUI is shown in Figure 14.24.

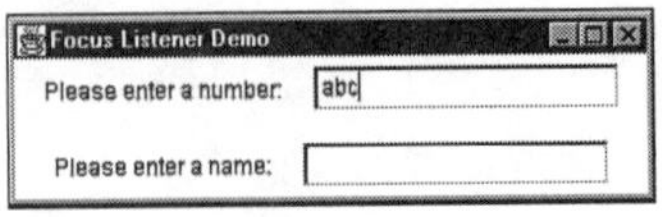

Figure 14.24
FocusListener Demo demonstrates focus events.

ITEM LISTENERS

Item listeners listen for item events. They are represented by objects implementing the `ItemListener` interface (located in the `java.awt.event` package).

`ItemListener` specifies a single method that must be implemented by an item listener's class. This method has the following signature:

```
public abstract void itemStateChanged (ItemEvent e)
```

The `itemStateChanged` method is called when the state of a check box, check box menu item, choice, or list changes. For example, selecting an item from a list—by clicking that item—changes the state of that component.

To register with an item source, an item listener must call the source's `addItemListener` method. (To de-register, an item listener would call the source's `removeItemListener` method.)

For an example of an item listener, please review the source code to Chapter 12's `PNViewer1` AWT application.

Note

Although `PNViewer1` is mentioned in Chapter 12, its source code is not listed in the chapter. Instead, `PNViewer1`'s fully-commented source code is included with the rest of this book's source code. You will need to download `PNViewer1`'s source code (along with the rest of this book's source code) from MacMillan's Web site.

KEY LISTENERS

Key listeners listen for key events. They are represented by objects implementing the `KeyListener` interface (located in the `java.awt.event` package).

`KeyListener` specifies three methods that must be implemented by a key listener's class. These methods have the following signatures:

```
public abstract void keyPressed (KeyEvent e)
public abstract void keyReleased (KeyEvent e)
public abstract void keyTyped (KeyEvent e)
```

The `keyPressed` method is called when a key pressed event occurs, the `keyReleased` method is called when a key released event occurs, and the `keyTyped` method is called when a key typed event occurs.

To register with a key source, a key listener must call the source's `addKeyListener` method. (To de-register, a key listener would call the source's `removeKeyListener` method.)

Listing 14.19 presents the source code to a KeyListenerDemo application that demonstrates listening for key events. (Press Ctrl+C, or the equivalent, to terminate this program.)

LISTING 14.19 THE KeyListenerDemo APPLICATION SOURCE CODE

```
// KeyListenerDemo.java

import java.awt.*;
import java.awt.event.*;

class KeyListenerDemo extends Frame implements KeyListener
{
   KeyListenerDemo (String title)
   {
      super (title);

      addKeyListener (this);

      setSize (100, 100);

      setVisible (true);
   }

   public void keyPressed (KeyEvent e)
   {
      System.out.println ("Key pressed: virtual key code = "
                          + e.getKeyCode ());
   }

   public void keyReleased (KeyEvent e)
   {
      System.out.println ("Key released: virtual key code = "
                          + e.getKeyCode ());
   }

   public void keyTyped (KeyEvent e)
   {
      System.out.println ("Key typed: character = "
                          + e.getKeyChar ());
   }

   public static void main (String [] args)
   {
      new KeyListenerDemo ("Key Listener Demo");
   }
}
```


KeyListenerDemo sends messages to the standard output device when key events occur. For example, when Shift and then A is pressed, the following is output:

```
Key pressed: virtual key code = 16
Key pressed: virtual key code = 65
Key typed: character = A
Key released: virtual key code = 65
Key released: virtual key code = 16
```

Caution

You might see multiple key pressed, key released, and key typed lines because of a keyboard's auto-repeat feature—which is triggered when you keep pressing a key past a minimum amount of time.

MOUSE LISTENERS

Mouse listeners listen for mouse events. Mouse button-related events are represented by objects implementing the `MouseListener` interface (located in the `java.awt.event` package). In contrast, mouse movement-related events are represented by objects implementing the `MouseMotionListener` interface (also located in the `java.awt.event` package). This separation makes it easy to ignore mouse motion events (which happen quite frequently and can slow down performance).

`MouseListener` specifies five methods that must be implemented by a mouse listener's class. These methods have the following signatures:

```
public abstract void mouseClicked (MouseEvent e)
public abstract void mouseEntered (MouseEvent e)
public abstract void mouseExited (MouseEvent e)
public abstract void mousePressed (MouseEvent e)
public abstract void mouseReleased (MouseEvent e)
```

The `mouseClicked` method is called when a user clicks a mouse button (that is, when a mouse button is pressed and then released). The `mouseEntered` method is called when the mouse pointer first enters the boundaries of a component and the `mouseExited` method is called when the mouse pointer leaves these boundaries. The `mousePressed` method is called when a user presses a mouse button and the `mouseReleased` method is called when this button is released.

To register with a mouse source, a mouse listener must call the source's `addMouseListener` method. (To de-register, a mouse listener would call the source's `removeMouseListener` method.)

`MouseMotionListener` specifies two methods that must be implemented by a mouse listener's class. These methods have the following signatures:

```
public abstract void mouseDragged (MouseEvent e)
public abstract void mouseMoved (MouseEvent e)
```

The `mouseDragged` method is called when the mouse moves while one of its buttons is pressed. The source of this event is the component that lies under the mouse pointer. The `mouseMoved` method is called when the mouse moves within the bounding area of a component (and no mouse button is pressed).

To register with a mouse motion source, a mouse listener must call the source's `addMouseMotionListener` method. (To de-register, a mouse listener would call the source's `removeMouseMotionListener` method.)

Listing 14.20 presents the source code to a `MouseListenerDemo` application that demonstrates listening for mouse events. (Press `Ctrl+C`, or the equivalent, to terminate this program.)

Listing 14.20 The `MouseListenerDemo` Application Source Code

```
// MouseListenerDemo.java

import java.awt.*;
import java.awt.event.*;

class MouseListenerDemo extends Frame
                        implements MouseListener, MouseMotionListener
{
   PopupMenu popup;

   MouseListenerDemo (String title)
   {
      super (title);

      popup = new PopupMenu ("Hello");
      popup.add (new MenuItem ("First"));
      popup.add (new MenuItem ("Second"));
      popup.addSeparator ();
      popup.add (new MenuItem ("Third"));

      add (popup);

      addMouseListener (this);
      addMouseMotionListener (this);

      setSize (100, 100);

      setVisible (true);
   }

   public void mouseEntered (MouseEvent e)
   {
      System.out.println ("Mouse Entered");
   }

   public void mouseExited (MouseEvent e)
   {
      System.out.println ("Mouse Exited");
   }

   public void mousePressed (MouseEvent e)
   {
      System.out.println ("Mouse Pressed");

      if (e.isPopupTrigger ())
          popup.show (e.getComponent (), e.getX (), e.getY ());
   }

   public void mouseReleased (MouseEvent e)
   {
      System.out.println ("Mouse Released");

      if (e.isPopupTrigger ())
          popup.show (e.getComponent (), e.getX (), e.getY ());
   }
```

LISTING 14.20 CONTINUED

```
   public void mouseClicked (MouseEvent e)
   {
      System.out.println ("Mouse Clicked");
   }

   public void mouseMoved (MouseEvent e)
   {
      System.out.println ("Mouse Moved");
   }

   public void mouseDragged (MouseEvent e)
   {
      System.out.println ("Mouse Dragged");
   }

   public static void main (String [] args)
   {
      new MouseListenerDemo ("Mouse Listener Demo");
   }
}
```

`MouseListenerDemo` sends messages to the standard output device when mouse events occur. You'll notice that code to detect whether a user has triggered a pop-up menu is placed in both the `mousePressed` and `mouseReleased` methods. When run under Windows 98, a pop-up menu is triggered by a mouse button release. Therefore, `e.isPopupTrigger` returns true when called from the `mouseReleased` method. (It does not return true when called from `mousePressed`.) Under another operating system, a pop-up menu might be triggered by a mouse button press instead of a mouse button release. Therefore, to achieve portability, it is a good idea to place pop-up menu triggering code in both methods.

TEXT LISTENERS

Text listeners listen for text events. They are represented by objects implementing the `TextListener` interface (located in the `java.awt.event` package).

`TextListener` specifies a single method that must be implemented by a text listener's class. This method has the following signature:

```
public abstract void textValueChanged (TextEvent e)
```

The `textValueChanged` method is called when a text component's contents are changed as a user types or when the `setText` method is called to specify this text.

To register with a text source, a text listener must call the source's `addTextListener` method. (To de-register, a text listener would call the source's `removeTextListener` method.)

Listing 14.21 presents the source code to a `TextListenerDemo` application that demonstrates listening for text events. (Press `Ctrl+C`, or the equivalent, to terminate this program.)

LISTING 14.21 THE `TextListenerDemo` APPLICATION SOURCE CODE

```
// TextListenerDemo.java

import java.awt.*;
import java.awt.event.*;

class TextListenerDemo extends Frame implements TextListener
{
   TextListenerDemo (String title)
   {
      super (title);

      Panel p = new Panel ();
      p.setLayout (new FlowLayout (FlowLayout.LEFT));
      p.add (new Label ("Please enter a name (8 chars maximum):"));
      TextField nameField = new TextField (10);
      nameField.addTextListener (this);
      p.add (nameField);
      add (p, "North");

      setSize (400, 100);

      setVisible (true);
   }

   public void textValueChanged (TextEvent e)
   {
      TextField tf = (TextField) e.getSource ();
      String text = tf.getText ();

      if (text.length () > 8)
      {
          int cp = tf.getCaretPosition ();
          tf.setText (text.substring (0, text.length () - 1));
          tf.setCaretPosition (cp);
      }
   }

   public static void main (String [] args)
   {
      new TextListenerDemo ("Text Listener Demo");
   }
}
```

`TextListenerDemo` displays a GUI consisting of a single label and a text field. As a user types, text events are generated and the `textValueChanged` method is called. The current text is retrieved and its length is compared to a maximum of eight. If the length exceeds this limit, the last character of text is removed, and the text field is reset to all characters except this character. The caret position is preserved so that a user can continue typing from where he left off.

Sometimes, you might want to restrict the actual characters that a user can type. For example, you might want to prevent a user from entering lowercase letters. If you aren't sure how to solve this problem, see "Restricting Text Characters" in the "Troubleshooting" section at the end of this chapter.

Window Listeners

Window listeners listen for window events. These events include opening a window, closing a window, window closed, iconifying a window, deiconifying a window, activating a window, and deactivating a window. Each window listener is represented by an object that implements the `WindowListener` interface (located in the `java.awt.event` package).

`WindowListener` specifies seven methods that must be implemented by a window listener's class. These methods have the following signatures:

```
public abstract void windowOpened (WindowEvent e)
public abstract void windowClosing (WindowEvent e)
public abstract void windowClosed (WindowEvent e)
public abstract void windowIconified (WindowEvent e)
public abstract void windowDeiconified (WindowEvent e)
public abstract void windowActivated (WindowEvent e)
public abstract void windowDeactivated (WindowEvent e)
```

The `windowOpened` method is called when a window is initially opened. When a user tries to close a window, `windowClosing` is called. The `windowClosed` method is called after the window has closed. When a window is being iconified (minimized), the `windowIconified` method is called. When a user deiconifies the window (by returning it to its normal size), `windowDeiconified` is called. The `windowActivated` method is called when the window is brought to the front of a stack of windows. Finally, when the window is removed from the front (through iconfication, closing, or another window becoming activated), `windowDeactivated` is called.

To register with a window source, a window listener must call the source's `addWindowListener` method. (To de-register, a window listener would call the source's `removeWindowListener` method.)

Listing 14.22 presents the source code to a `WindowListenerDemo` application that demonstrates listening for window events.

Listing 14.22 The `WindowListenerDemo` Application Source Code

```
// WindowListenerDemo.java

import java.awt.*;
import java.awt.event.*;

class WindowListenerDemo extends Frame implements WindowListener
{
   WindowListenerDemo (String title)
   {
      super (title);

      addWindowListener (this);

      setSize (100, 100);

      setVisible (true);
   }
```

LISTING 14.22 CONTINUED

```
   public void windowOpened (WindowEvent e)
   {
      System.out.println ("window opened");
   }

   public void windowClosing (WindowEvent e)
   {
      System.out.println ("window closing");
      dispose ();
   }

   public void windowClosed (WindowEvent e)
   {
      System.out.println ("window closed");
      System.exit (0);
   }

   public void windowIconified (WindowEvent e)
   {
      System.out.println ("window iconified");
   }

   public void windowDeiconified (WindowEvent e)
   {
      System.out.println ("window deiconified");
   }

   public void windowActivated (WindowEvent e)
   {
      System.out.println ("window activated");
   }

   public void windowDeactivated (WindowEvent e)
   {
      System.out.println ("window deactivated");
   }

   public static void main (String [] args)
   {
      new WindowListenerDemo ("Window Listener Demo");
   }
}
```

`WindowListenerDemo` sends messages to the standard output device (via window listener method calls when window events occur) in a certain order. For example, under Windows 98, the following order is observed: When a window is first displayed, `windowActivated` is called followed by `windowOpened`. When the window is iconified, `windowIconified` is called followed by `windowDeactivated`. When the window is deiconified, `windowActivated` is called, followed by `windowDeiconified`, followed by `windowActivated`. When another window is moved over `WindowListenerDemo`'s window, `windowDeactivated` is called. When `WindowListenerDemo`'s window is brought back to the front, `windowActivated` is called. Finally, when the user selects the window's close box, `windowClosing` is called, followed by `windowClosed`.

Placing a `System.exit` call in `windowClosing` would not cause the `windowClosed` method to be called. If you want this method called, you should call `dispose` from `windowClosing`. You can then call `System.exit` from `windowClosed`. (If you are not concerned with any code being executed in `windowClosed`, you can call `System.exit` from `windowClosing`—which is done by most of the programs in this chapter.)

The `dispose` method is also useful for closing dialog windows in response to a user pressing some appropriate button (such as `OK` or `Cancel`). This behavior can be demonstrated by the `DisposeDialogDemo` application, whose source code is presented in Listing 14.23.

LISTING 14.23 THE `DisposeDialogDemo` APPLICATION SOURCE CODE

```
// DisposeDialogDemo.java

import java.awt.*;
import java.awt.event.*;

class DisposeDialogDemo
{
   public static void main (String [] args)
   {
      Frame f = new Frame ("Dialog Demo");
      f.setSize (200, 100);
      f.setVisible (true);

      AreYouSure ays = new AreYouSure (f, "Is the sky blue?");

      if (ays.getState () == true)
          System.out.println ("Yes, the sky is blue.");
      else
          System.out.println ("No, the sky is not blue.");

      System.exit (0);
   }
}

class AreYouSure extends Dialog implements ActionListener
{
   private boolean state;

   AreYouSure (Frame f, String title)
   {
      super (f, title, true); // Ensure dialog is modal

      Panel p = new Panel ();

      Button b = new Button ("Yes");
      b.addActionListener (this);
      p.add (b);

      b = new Button ("No");
      b.addActionListener (this);
      p.add (b);
```

LISTING 14.23 CONTINUED

```
      add (p);

      setSize (200, 100);
      setResizable (false);
      setVisible (true);
   }

   public void actionPerformed (ActionEvent e)
   {
      if (e.getActionCommand ().equals ("Yes"))
          state = true;
      else
          state = false;

      dispose ();
   }

   public boolean getState ()
   {
      return state;
   }
}
```

If you look carefully at the source code, you'll see that this program exits via a call to `System.exit`. This method is required in `DisposeDialogDemo` for the same reason that it was required in `SystemInfo`, `MangledButton`, and `WindowListenerDemo`—the background AWT threads must be terminated before the program can exit.

Note

When you run `DisposeDialogDemo`, you'll discover that its parent frame is also displayed, even though the frame's `setVisible` method wasn't called. This proves that a container is also made visible when one of its contained components is made visible. (When you run this program, you might have to move the dialog so you can see the parent frame.)

ADAPTERS

Suppose you are implementing `MouseListener`, `WindowListener`, or another listener interface with more than one method. It can be a real pain to have to implement those methods that aren't going to be used. (You end up stubbing out these other methods.) The windowing toolkit has a solution to this problem—adapters.

An *adapter* is a class that implements a listener interface. All methods in this class are stubbed out. To use an adapter, you must create a subclass and override the method (or methods) of interest. You then create an object from your subclass and pass its reference to an appropriate registration method.

Listing 14.24 presents the source code to a `WindowAdapterDemo1` application that demonstrates listening for window closing events (only), via an object created from a subclass of `WindowAdapter`.

LISTING 14.24 THE `WindowAdapterDemo1` APPLICATION SOURCE CODE

```
// WindowAdapterDemo1.java

import java.awt.*;
import java.awt.event.*;

class myWindowAdapter extends WindowAdapter
{
   public void windowClosing (WindowEvent e)
   {
      System.exit (0);
   }
}

class WindowAdapterDemo1 extends Frame
{
   WindowAdapterDemo1 (String title)
   {
      super (title);

      myWindowAdapter mwa = new myWindowAdapter ();
      addWindowListener (mwa);

      setSize (100, 100);
      setVisible (true);
   }

   public static void main (String [] args)
   {
      new WindowAdapterDemo1 ("Window Adapter Demo1");
   }
}
```

Caution

When working with adapters, be sure to specify the exact signature(s) of the method(s) being overridden. If you don't specify an exact signature, the compiler will "think" you've created a new method, instead of overriding an inherited method. The compiler won't warn you, and the only way you'll know that something is wrong is when your program doesn't work as expected. For example, in `WindowAdapterDemo1`'s, `myWindowAdapter` class, `windowClosing` is overridden. If this method had been spelled `WindowClosing`, the compiler would not have overridden `windowClosing`. Instead, it would have introduced a new method called `WindowClosing`. The only way you would know about this problem is when you tried to close the window, and found out that it wouldn't close.

Having to introduce a new class and figure out a name that does not conflict with an existing class name can be bothersome. In this kind of situation, you can use an anonymous inner class. Listing 14.25 presents the source code to a `WindowAdapterDemo2` application that demonstrates listening for window closing events (only), via an object created from an anonymous subclass of `WindowAdapter`.

LISTING 14.25 THE `WindowAdapterDemo2` APPLICATION SOURCE CODE

```
// WindowAdapterDemo2.java

import java.awt.*;
import java.awt.event.*;

class WindowAdapterDemo2 extends Frame
{
   WindowAdapterDemo2 (String title)
   {
      super (title);

      addWindowListener (new WindowAdapter ()
                         {
                             public void windowClosing (WindowEvent e)
                             {
                                System.exit (0);
                             }
                         });

      setSize (100, 100);
      setVisible (true);
   }

   public static void main (String [] args)
   {
      new WindowAdapterDemo2 ("Window Adapter Demo2");
   }
}
```

CUSTOMIZING THE WINDOWING TOOLKIT

It's possible to customize the windowing toolkit by building new components, containers, layout managers, events, and listeners. All that customization could fill another entire book, so here only customized containers and layout managers will be discussed. If you would like to create your own lightweight components and learn about the AWT's lightweight UI framework, please visit the following Web site:

`http://java.sun.com/j2se/1.3/docs/guide/awt/designspec/lightweights.html`

BUILDING YOUR OWN CONTAINERS

You can create new containers that are lightweight (as opposed to the existing heavyweight dialog, file dialog, frame, scroll pane, and window containers). These new containers do not have corresponding peers, so they don't use up system resources. The simplest way to create a lightweight container is to subclass the `Container` class. This is shown in the following code fragment:

```
public class myContainer extends Container
{
}
```

Because lightweight containers do not have associated peers, they must be contained by heavyweight containers. The following code fragment creates an object from the myContainer class and adds it to a Frame object:

Caution

Because the new container does not have a layout manager, one must be specified. Otherwise, you'll never see the added components.

```
myContainer panel = new myContainer ();
panel.setLayout (new FlowLayout ());
panel.add (new Button ("Hello"));
Frame f = new Frame ();
f.add (panel);
f.setSize (200, 200);
f.setVisible (true);
```

BUILDING YOUR OWN LAYOUT MANAGERS

If you're dissatisfied with the existing layout managers provided by the windowing toolkit, you can create your own. To create a layout manager, you need to construct a class that implements the LayoutManager interface. This interface provides the following five methods:

```
void addLayoutComponent (String name, Component comp)

void removeLayoutComponent (Component comp)

Dimension preferredLayoutSize (Container parent)

Dimension minimumLayoutSize (Container parent)

void layoutContainer (Container parent)
```

The following method is called by a container's add (String name, Component comp) method. The name is used to provide constraint information, such as a position in which to place comp—north, south, left, right, top, bottom, and so on. In response, this method saves name and comp in an internal data structure. If the layout manager does not use constraints, this method can be stubbed out, forcing the container to store comp.

```
void addLayoutComponent (String name, Component comp)
```

The following method is called by the container's remove and removeAll methods. Information previously stored in internal data structures by addLayoutComponent should be removed at this time. If addLayoutComponent is stubbed out, this method can be stubbed out as well.

```
void removeLayoutComponent (Component comp)
```

The following method is called by the container's getPreferredSize method to determine the size of the parent container. If you don't care about placing space around a component, call parent.getSize ().

```
Dimension preferredLayoutSize (Container parent)
```

The following method is called by the container's `getMinimumSize` method to determine the minimum size of the `parent` container. To determine this minimum size, you will typically call the `getMinimumSize` method of each component contained in the container. As with the `preferredLayoutSize` method, you can call `parent.getSize ()`.

```
Dimension minimumLayoutSize (Container parent)
```

The following method is called when the `parent` container is displayed for the first time, and whenever this container is resized. It takes care of laying out `parent`'s components. To obtain these components, you can call `parent`'s `getComponents` method, or refer to previously saved components. Call each component's `setBounds` method to position and size the component (as long as it is visible).

```
void layoutContainer (Container parent)
```

Listing 14.26 presents source code to a debugging layout manager called `DebugLayout`. In addition to providing debugging messages (to show what is happening), this layout manager also attempts to lay out its components by assuming that the width and height of each component are the same.

Caution

This assumption leads to a technique that really needs to be improved, because the technique usually results in components along the right side and the bottom being partially hidden.

LISTING 14.26 THE `DebugLayout` SOURCE CODE

```
// DebugLayout.java

import java.awt.*;

class DebugLayout implements LayoutManager
{
   public void addLayoutComponent (String name, Component comp)
   {
      System.out.println ("addLayoutComponent called");
      System.out.println ("name = " + name);
      System.out.println ("comp = " + comp);
   }

   public void removeLayoutComponent (Component comp)
   {
      System.out.println ("removeLayoutComponent called");
      System.out.println ("comp = " + comp);
   }

   public Dimension preferredLayoutSize (Container parent)
   {
      System.out.println ("preferredLayoutSize called");
      System.out.println ("parent = " + parent);
      return parent.getSize ();
   }
```

LISTING 14.26 CONTINUED

```
   public Dimension minimumLayoutSize (Container parent)
   {
      System.out.println ("minimumLayoutSize called");
      System.out.println ("parent = " + parent);
      return parent.getSize ();
   }

   public void layoutContainer (Container parent)
   {
      System.out.println ("layoutContainer called");
      System.out.println ("parent = " + parent);

      Component [] c = parent.getComponents ();

      if (c.length == 0)
          return;

      Dimension size = parent.getSize ();
      Insets in = parent.getInsets ();

      // Compute actual width and height by subtracting parent's
      // insets.

      int width = size.width - in.left - in.right;
      int height = size.height - in.top - in.bottom;

      // Each component will be laid out as a square.

      int cxy = (int) (Math.sqrt (width * height / c.length));

      int x = in.left;
      int y = in.top;

      for (int i = 0; i < c.length; i++)
      {
           if (c [i].isVisible ())
               c [i].setBounds (x, y, cxy, cxy);

           x += cxy;
           if (x >= width)
           {
               x = in.left;
               y += cxy;
           }
      }
   }
}
```

To see `DebugLayout` in action, Listing 14.27 presents source code to the `UseDebugLayout` application. This application sets a frame's layout manager to a debug layout manager and then adds 100 buttons to its container.

LISTING 14.27 THE `UseDebugLayout` APPLICATION SOURCE CODE

```
// UseDebugLayout.java

import java.awt.*;
import java.awt.event.*;

class UseDebugLayout extends Frame
{
   UseDebugLayout (String title)
   {
      super (title);

      addWindowListener (new WindowAdapter ()
                         {
                             public void windowClosing (WindowEvent e)
                             {
                                System.exit (0);
                             }
                         });

      setLayout (new DebugLayout ());
      for (int i = 0; i < 100; i++)
           add ("squished", new Button ("" + i));

      setSize (200, 200);

      setVisible (true);
   }

   public static void main (String [] args)
   {
      new UseDebugLayout ("Use Debug Layout");
   }
}
```

AWT 1.1 introduced the `LayoutManager2` interface to make up for shortcomings with `LayoutManager`. For example, `LayoutManager2` provides an `addLayoutComponent (Component comp, Object const)` method that is called when a container's `add (Component comp, Object const)` method is called. As an exercise (for those so inclined), read up on `LayoutManager2` and modify `DebugLayout` so it also implements this interface. Then, try calling `add (Component comp, Object const)` from `UseDebugLayout` instead of `add (String name, Component comp)`.

TROUBLESHOOTING

RESTRICTING TEXT CHARACTERS

How can I restrict the characters that a user enters in a text field or a text area?

Restricting what characters a user can input is accomplished in a manner that is very similar to restricting the total number of characters that are input—as shown in the

TextListenerDemo application. To see how this is accomplished, the following textValueChanged method prevents a user from entering lowercase letters:

```
public void textValueChanged (TextEvent e)
{
   TextField tf = (TextField) e.getSource ();
   StringBuffer text = new StringBuffer (tf.getText ());

   int cp = tf.getCaretPosition ();
   if (cp == 0)
       return;

   char ch = text.charAt (cp - 1);
   if (Character.isLowerCase (ch))
   {
       ch = Character.toUpperCase (ch);
       text.setCharAt (cp - 1, ch);
       tf.setText (text.toString ());
       tf.setCaretPosition (cp);
   }
}
```

DYNAMICALLY ADDING AND REMOVING COMPONENTS

How do I dynamically add components to and remove components from a GUI?

You can call any one of Container's overloaded add methods to add components, and call its remove method to remove components. This situation is demonstrated in the following source code to the CARDemo application.

```
// CARDemo.java

import java.awt.*;
import java.awt.event.*;

class CARDemo extends Frame implements ActionListener
{
   final static int USE_BUTTON = 0;
   final static int USE_LIST = 1;
   final static int USE_TEXTAREA = 2;
   final static int USE_TEXTFIELD = 3;

   int use = USE_TEXTAREA;

   Component c;

   CARDemo (String title)
   {
      super (title);

      addWindowListener (new WindowAdapter ()
                         {
                             public void windowClosing (WindowEvent e)
                             {
                                System.exit (0);
                             }
                         });
```

```
      switch (use)
      {
         case USE_BUTTON:
            c = new Button ("Ok");
            break;

         case USE_LIST:
            c = new List ();
            ((List) c).add ("First");
            ((List) c).add ("Second");
            ((List) c).select (0);
            break;

         case USE_TEXTAREA:
            c = new TextArea ();
            break;

         case USE_TEXTFIELD:
            c = new TextField ();
      }

      add (c);

      MenuBar mb = new MenuBar ();

      Menu m = new Menu ("File");
      m.addActionListener (this);

      m.add ("Add");
      m.add ("Remove");
      m.addSeparator ();
      m.add ("Exit");

      mb.add (m);
      setMenuBar (mb);

      pack ();
      setVisible (true);
   }

   public void actionPerformed (ActionEvent e)
   {
      if (e.getActionCommand ().equals ("Exit"))
          System.exit (0);

      if (e.getActionCommand ().equals ("Add"))
      {
          add (c);
          c.requestFocus ();
      }
      else
          remove (c);
   }

   public static void main (String [] args)
   {
      new CARDemo ("Component Add/Remove Demo");
   }
}
```

`CARDemo` presents a GUI with a `File` menu and either a button, list, text area, or text field component (depending on which "`USE`" constant is assigned to the `use` variable). If `Add` is selected from the `File` menu, the appropriate component is added to the GUI by calling the `add` method. However, if `Remove` is selected, the component is removed by calling the `remove` method.

When `add` is called, it (internally) removes the component from the container. This is why you don't see multiple copies of the newly added component. The component's `requestFocus` method is then called to ensure that the added component has the focus.

Note

When you add a text area to the GUI, you might notice a `NullPointerException` object being thrown. This exception is related to internal logic and appears to be the result of a Java bug (because this exception is never thrown when either a button, list, or text field component is added). However, the thrown `NullPointerException` object doesn't disrupt execution of `CARDemo`.

If you run `CARDemo`, type some text in either the text area or text field component (depending on which component is identified by the `use` variable), remove this component, and then add the component; you'll notice that the text reappears. This proves that component removal results in only removing its peer: The component's object still exists. When the component is added at a later time, the information in this object is used to restore the peer to previous settings.

CHAPTER 15

And Then There Was Swing

In this chapter

by Geoff Friesen

WHAT IS SWING?

Swing is a windowing framework that adds new capabilities to the AWT. For example, Swing introduces a wide assortment of lightweight components (from lightweight buttons to lightweight trees and tables). These components are completely managed by Java and not by peers. (Some of the containers into which Swing's components are placed are associated with heavyweight peers. After all, at some point, Swing must ensure that the underlying windowing system displays these components.)

Because Swing's components are rendered and managed by Java, they look nicer and have more capabilities (such as tooltips) than their AWT counterparts. Furthermore, these components can have either a consistent look and feel across windowing systems, or take on any desired (and available) look and feel. (In contrast, AWT components are "forced" to adopt the look and feel of the underlying windowing system. Look and feel will be explored in the next chapter.)

Perhaps the best way to start learning Swing is to take a brief look at those Java packages that comprise this framework. Table 15.1 presents the names and contents of these packages.

TABLE 15.1 JAVA'S SWING PACKAGES

Package	Contents
`javax.swing`	Classes and interfaces that describe a set of lightweight (all-Java) components
`javax.swing.border`	Classes and an interface that make it possible to draw borders around Swing components
`javax.swing.colorchooser`	Classes and an interface that are used by the `JColorChooser` component
`javax.swing.event`	Classes and interfaces that describe Swing-specific events and listeners
`javax.swing.filechooser`	Classes that are used by the `JFileChooser` component
`javax.swing.plaf`	Classes and an interface that Swing uses to provide its pluggable look-and-feel capabilities
`javax.swing.plaf.basic`	Classes and an interface that Swing uses to provide a basic look and feel foundation, on which other look and feels are built
`javax.swing.plaf.metal`	Classes that Swing uses to provide a metal look and feel (also known as the Java look and feel)
`javax.swing.plaf.multi`	Classes that Swing uses to provide an auxiliary look and feel—a combination of a custom look and feel with the default look and feel
`javax.swing.table`	Classes and interfaces that are used by the `JTable` component
`javax.swing.text`	Classes and interfaces that are used by editable and read-only text components

TABLE 15.1 CONTINUED

Package	Contents
`javax.swing.text.html`	Classes for creating HTML text editors
`javax.swing.text.html.parser`	Classes and an interface for creating an HTML parser
`javax.swing.text.rtf`	A single class for creating a rich-text editor
`javax.swing.tree`	Classes and interfaces that are used by the `JTree` component
`javax.swing.undo`	Classes and interfaces for supporting undo/redo capabilities in an application (such as a text editor)

One of Swing's more important features is its pluggable look-and-feel. This feature makes it possible to create a GUI that looks the same on any windowing system. You can also change a GUI's look and feel on-the-fly. (Pluggable look-and-feel is discussed in Chapter 16, "Building a GUI: Swing Style.")

Swing (as with the rest of the JFC) is an evolving API. Each new version offers new features and fixes bugs. If you are asked to create a Swing-based program that requires a certain version of Swing, you must be able to determine the version. A solution to this problem is demonstrated by the `Version` application, whose source code is presented in Listing 15.1.

LISTING 15.1 THE `Version` APPLICATION SOURCE CODE

```
// Version.java

import javax.swing.*;

class Version
{
   public static void main (String [] args)
   {
      JLabel l = new JLabel ();

      Package p = Package.getPackage ("javax.swing");
      if (p != null)
      {
          System.out.print ("Swing Version: ");
          System.out.println (p.getSpecificationVersion ());
      }

      p = Package.getPackage ("java.awt");
      if (p != null)
      {
          System.out.print ("AWT Version: ");
          System.out.println (p.getSpecificationVersion ());
      }
   }
}
```

`Version` obtains the current version of Swing and the AWT by using the `Package` class, along with its `getPackage` and `getSpecificationVersion` methods. The `getPackage` method returns a reference to a `Package` object that corresponds to its package name argument, provided that at least one class belonging to the package has been loaded. (By creating a dummy `JLabel` object, it's possible to obtain `Package` objects corresponding to `javax.swing` and `java.awt`.) After a `Package` object has been obtained, `getSpecificationVersion` is called to return a `String` object containing the package's assigned version number. And there you have it—the current version of Swing and the AWT.

Swing's startup performance has been significantly improved in Java 2 Platform Standard Edition, version 1.3. This has been accomplished by minimizing the number of classes that are loaded at startup.

COMPARING SWING TO THE AWT

Although you won't be exploring Swing until the next chapter, you might want to see an example of how Swing compares to the AWT. AWT and Swing versions of a small application are presented here. The first version is called `AWTHello`, and its source code is presented in Listing 15.2.

LISTING 15.2 THE `AWTHello` APPLICATION SOURCE CODE

```
// AWTHello.java

import java.awt.*;
import java.awt.event.*;

class AWTHello extends Frame implements ActionListener
{
   Button b;

   static String [] labels =
   {
      "Hello! Welcome to AWT!",
      "You cannot assign icons to AWT buttons."
   };

   int nextLabel;

   AWTHello (String title)
   {
      super (title);

      addWindowListener (new WindowAdapter ()
                         {
                             public void windowClosing (WindowEvent e)
                             {
                                System.exit (0);
                             }
                         });

      Panel p = new Panel ();
      b = new Button (labels [nextLabel++]);
      b.addActionListener (this);
```

LISTING 15.2 CONTINUED

```
      p.add (b);
      add (p);

      setSize (300, 100);
      setVisible (true);
   }

   public void actionPerformed (ActionEvent e)
   {
      b.setLabel (labels [nextLabel++]);
      validate ();
      nextLabel %= labels.length;
   }

   public static void main (String [] args)
   {
      new AWTHello ("Hello, AWT Version");
   }
}
```

`AWTHello` builds a GUI consisting of a single button. This button is initialized to some default text, which changes when the button is pressed. Figure 15.1 shows `AWTHello`'s GUI.

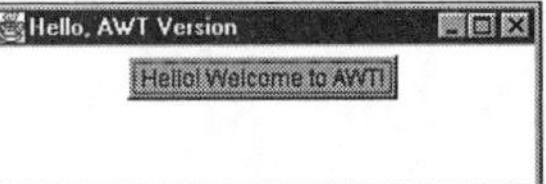

Figure 15.1 `AWTHello`'s GUI consists of a button initialized to default text.

Much of `AWTHello`'s source code should make sense (now that you've worked your way through the previous chapter). However, you might be wondering why `validate` is called in `actionPerformed`.

The `validate` method is called to inform the container's current layout manager that it must re-layout all components added to the container. If `validate` is not called, the button's new label will be displayed using the existing dimensions of the button. A large label would be truncated at the button's edges. By informing the layout manager that something has changed (by calling `validate`), it will have a chance to resize the button to a more appropriate size. (If you don't call `validate`, you'll only see a resized button by physically resizing the button's frame container.)

To see what the Swing equivalent of this program looks like, check out Listing 15.3, which presents `SwingHello`'s source code.

LISTING 15.3 THE `SwingHello` APPLICATION SOURCE CODE

```
// SwingHello.java

import javax.swing.*;
import java.awt.event.*;
```

LISTING 15.3 CONTINUED

```
class SwingHello extends JFrame implements ActionListener
{
   JButton b;

   static String [] labels =
   {
      "Hello! Welcome to Swing!",
      "You can assign icons to Swing buttons."
   };

   int nextLabel;

   SwingHello (String title)
   {
      super (title);

      addWindowListener (new WindowAdapter ()
                         {
                             public void windowClosing (WindowEvent e)
                             {
                                System.exit (0);
                             }
                         });

      JPanel p = new JPanel ();
      b = new JButton (labels [nextLabel++],
                       new ImageIcon ("bullet.gif"));
      b.addActionListener (this);
      p.add (b);
      setContentPane (p);

      setSize (300, 100);
      setVisible (true);
   }

   public void actionPerformed (ActionEvent e)
   {
      b.setText (labels [nextLabel++]);
      nextLabel %= labels.length;
   }

   public static void main (String [] args)
   {
      new SwingHello ("Hello, Swing Version");
   }
}
```

Caution

When running `SwingHello` under version 1.2.2 of the Java 2 Platform Standard Edition on Windows 2000, you must explicitly specify the path to `bullet.gif`.

As with `AWTHello`, `SwingHello` also builds a GUI consisting of only one button. This GUI is shown in Figure 15.2.

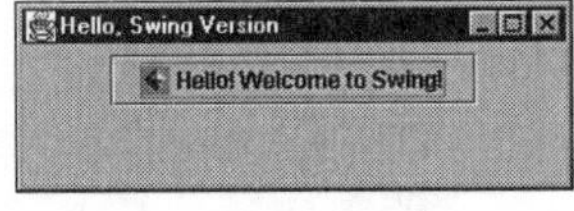

Figure 15.2 Like `AWTHello`, `SwingHello`'s GUI consists of a button initialized to default text.

Compare Figures 15.1 and 15.2. It's easy to see the differences. Among these differences, there's an icon on the Swing button, which is something that cannot be done with AWT buttons. You've compared GUIs, so now compare `SwingHello`'s source code to `AWTHello`'s source code.

To begin, notice that instead of an `import java.awt.*;` directive, `SwingHello` begins with an `import javax.swing.*;` directive. After you start to create Swing programs, you'll use this directive to import Swing classes and interfaces.

`SwingHello` extends the `JFrame` class, instead of extending `Frame`. This turns `SwingHello` into a Swing application. (If you check the SDK documentation, you'll discover that `JFrame` extends `Frame`.)

`AWTHello` references `Button` and `Panel` classes, whereas `SwingHello` references `JButton` and `JPanel` classes. If you look through the SDK documentation, you'll find that all the AWT's component/container classes have equivalent Swing classes. (The letter `J` differentiates Swing classes from AWT classes and stands for Java.)

Unlike the AWT's `Button` class, Swing's `JButton` class allows you to attach an icon to a button. This is accomplished by creating an instance of Swing's `ImageIcon` class, and passing this instance to one of `JButton`'s constructors.

`AWTHello` allows you to add a panel directly to its AWT frame container. You cannot do this with `SwingHello`. Instead, you add the panel to its Swing frame's content pane. This pane serves as an intermediate container that is part of a Swing GUI's layered architecture.

The `Button` class declares a method called `setLabel` for setting an AWT button's text. However, this method is marked deprecated by `JButton`'s `AbstractButton` superclass. Therefore, you must call `JButton`'s `setText` method (inherited from this superclass) to set a Swing button's text.

Finally, you'll notice that the `validate` method is not called in `SwingHello`'s `actionPerformed` method. Unlike the AWT, Swing ensures that the current layout manager is called when a component's size and/or position changes.

As you've just seen, Swing and AWT programs are very similar. By building onto the AWT's architecture, Swing's designers made it easy for AWT developers to migrate over to Swing. Although it's not a good idea to include the AWT's components and containers in a Swing program, there is no reason why you cannot use the AWT's layout managers, events, and listeners.

Mixing Heavyweight and Lightweight Components

In Chapter 14, "Building a GUI: AWT Style," you learned that it's not a good idea to mix AWT heavyweight components with lightweight Swing components. Now, you're going to see what happens when this advice is ignored. To demonstrate what can go wrong, several Swing programs will be presented. Don't be concerned about not understanding their collective source code. After you've read the next chapter, come back and study this code. You'll find that it makes more sense.

The first program—`MixedDemo1`—demonstrates what happens when a lightweight label is placed into the same container as a heavyweight label. The result is shown in Figure 15.3 and source code is presented in Listing 15.4.

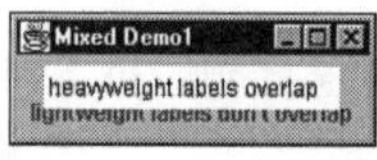

Figure 15.3
`MixedDemo1`'s GUI shows a heavyweight label overlapping a lightweight label.

Listing 15.4 The `MixedDemo1` Application Source Code

```
// MixedDemo1.java

import java.awt.*;
import java.awt.event.*;
import javax.swing.*;

class MixedDemo1 extends JFrame
{
   MixedDemo1 (String title)
   {
      super (title);

      addWindowListener (new WindowAdapter ()
                         {
                             public void windowClosing (WindowEvent e)
                             {
                                System.exit (0);
                             }
                         });

      JPanel jp = new JPanel ();
      JLabel jl = new JLabel ("lightweight labels don't overlap");
      jp.add (jl);
      getContentPane ().add (jp, BorderLayout.SOUTH);

      jp = new JPanel ();
      Label l = new Label ("heavyweight labels overlap");
      l.setBackground (Color.white);
      jp.add (l);
      getContentPane ().add (jp, BorderLayout.CENTER);
```

LISTING 15.4 CONTINUED

```
      setSize (200, 70);
      setVisible (true);
   }

   public static void main (String [] args)
   {
      new MixedDemo1 ("Mixed Demo1");
   }
}
```

The second program—MixedDemo2—demonstrates what happens when a lightweight component and a heavyweight component are placed into the same container, and then this container is added to a Swing scroll pane container. The result is shown in Figure 15.4 and source code is presented in Listing 15.5.

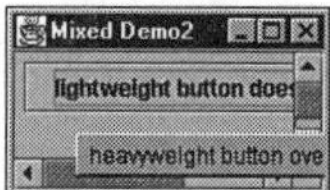

Figure 15.4 MixedDemo2's GUI shows a heavyweight button overlapping a scroll pane and scrollbars.

LISTING 15.5 THE MixedDemo2 APPLICATION SOURCE CODE

```
// MixedDemo2.java

import java.awt.*;
import java.awt.event.*;
import javax.swing.*;

class MixedDemo2 extends JFrame
{
   MixedDemo2 (String title)
   {
      super (title);

      addWindowListener (new WindowAdapter ()
                         {
                             public void windowClosing (WindowEvent e)
                             {
                                System.exit (0);
                             }
                         });


      JPanel jp = new JPanel ();
      jp.setLayout (new BorderLayout ());

      JPanel jp1 = new JPanel ();
      JButton jb = new JButton ("lightweight button doesn't overlap");
      jp1.add (jb);
      jp.add (jp1, BorderLayout.NORTH);
```

LISTING 15.5 CONTINUED

```
      jp1 = new JPanel ();
      Button b = new Button ("heavyweight button overlaps");
      jp1.add (b);
      jp.add (jp1, BorderLayout.SOUTH);

      JScrollPane jsp = new JScrollPane (jp);

      getContentPane ().add (jsp);

      setSize (175, 100);
      setVisible (true);
   }

   public static void main (String [] args)
   {
      new MixedDemo2 ("Mixed Demo2");
   }
}
```

The third program—`MixedDemo3`—demonstrates what happens when a lightweight component is placed into a Swing internal frame container; a heavyweight component is placed into a second internal frame; both frames are added to a Swing desktop pane container; both frames overlap; and the frame with the lightweight component is shown in front of the frame with the heavyweight component. The result is shown in Figure 15.5 and source code is presented in Listing 15.6. (If you compile and run this program, you'll have to drag the internal frame with the lightweight component over the internal frame with the heavyweight component, to see the heavyweight component overlapping the internal frame with the lightweight component.)

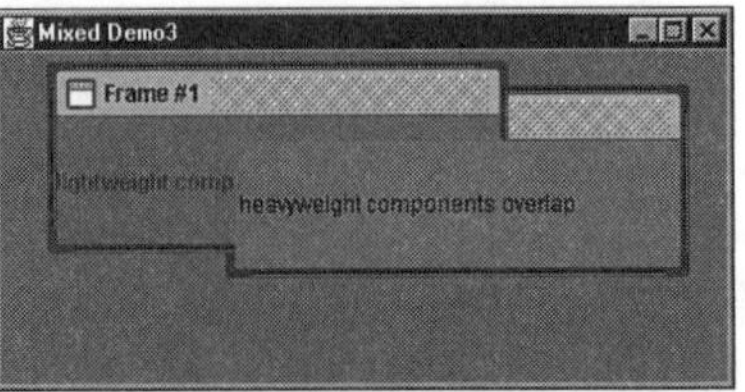

Figure 15.5 `MixedDemo3`'s GUI shows a heavyweight component in an internal frame overlapping a lightweight component in another internal frame.

LISTING 15.6 THE `MixedDemo3` APPLICATION SOURCE CODE

```
// MixedDemo3.java

import java.awt.*;
import java.awt.event.*;
import javax.swing.*;

class MixedDemo3 extends JFrame
```

LISTING 15.6 CONTINUED

```
{
   JDesktopPane desktop;

   MixedDemo3 (String title)
   {
      super (title);

      addWindowListener (new WindowAdapter ()
                         {
                             public void windowClosing (WindowEvent e)
                             {
                                System.exit (0);
                             }
                         });

      desktop = new JDesktopPane ();

      JInternalFrame jf1 = new JInternalFrame ("Frame #1");
      JLabel jl = new JLabel ("lightweight components don't overlap");
      jf1.getContentPane ().add (jl);
      jf1.setSize (250, 100);
      jf1.setVisible (true);
      desktop.add (jf1);

      JInternalFrame jf2 = new JInternalFrame ("Frame #2");
      Label l = new Label ("heavyweight components overlap");
      jf2.getContentPane ().add (l);
      jf2.setSize (250, 100);
      jf2.setVisible (true);
      desktop.add (jf2);

      setContentPane (desktop);

      desktop.setVisible (true);

      setSize (400, 200);
      setVisible (true);
   }

   public static void main (String [] args)
   {
      new MixedDemo3 ("Mixed Demo3");
   }
}
```

Finally, the fourth program—`MixedDemo4`—demonstrates what happens when a lightweight Swing combo box component and a heavyweight component are placed into the same container, and the combo box's pop-up menu is displayed. The result is shown in Figure 15.6 and source code is presented in Listing 15.7.

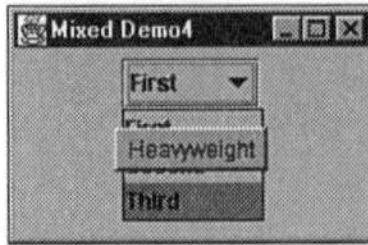

Figure 15.6
MixedDemo4's GUI shows a heavyweight button overlapping a combo box's pop-up menu.

LISTING 15.7 THE MixedDemo4 APPLICATION SOURCE CODE

```
// MixedDemo4.java

import java.awt.*;
import java.awt.event.*;
import javax.swing.*;

class MixedDemo4 extends JFrame
{
   MixedDemo4 (String title)
   {
      super (title);

      addWindowListener (new WindowAdapter ()
                         {
                             public void windowClosing (WindowEvent e)
                             {
                                System.exit (0);
                             }
                         });

      JPanel p = new JPanel ();

// JPopupMenu.setDefaultLightWeightPopupEnabled (false);

      JComboBox cb = new JComboBox ();

// cb.setLightWeightPopupEnabled (false);

      cb.addItem ("First");
      cb.addItem ("Second");
      cb.addItem ("Third");
      p.add (cb);
      getContentPane ().add (p, BorderLayout.NORTH);

      p = new JPanel ();
      p.add (new Button ("Heavyweight"));
      getContentPane ().add (p, BorderLayout.CENTER);

      setSize (200, 125);
      setVisible (true);
   }

   public static void main (String [] args)
   {
      new MixedDemo4 ("Mixed Demo4");
   }
}
```

In MixedDemo4, two lines are commented out. If you uncomment either line, recompile, and run the program, you'll discover that the heavyweight button does not overlap the lightweight combo box when its pop-up menu is displayed.

Any Swing component that displays a pop-up menu (such as a combo box) has a Boolean lightWeightPopupEnabled property. If this property is true (the default), the pop-up menu component is placed in a lightweight Swing container. When activated, any heavyweight component in the vicinity can overlap this pop-up menu. However, when this property is set to false, the pop-up menu is placed in a heavyweight panel container. The heavyweight component can no longer overlap the pop-up menu. You can set this property to true for all pop-up menu components by calling JPopupMenu's setDefaultLightWeightPopupEnabled class method. If you're more concerned with a single pop-up menu, you can call the component's setLightWeightPopupEnabled method.

Although it's usually not a good idea to mix lightweight and heavyweight components, you might not always have a choice. If you are very careful, it's possible to successfully mix these components. MixedHello demonstrates this successful mixing by combining lightweight and heavyweight buttons into a single GUI. The result is shown in Figure 15.7 and source code is presented in Listing 15.8.

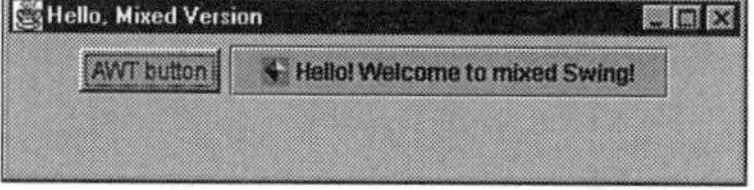

Figure 15.7 MixedHello's GUI shows a mixture of heavyweight and lightweight button components.

LISTING 15.8 THE MixedHello APPLICATION SOURCE CODE

```
// MixedHello.java

import java.awt.*;
import javax.swing.*;
import java.awt.event.*;

class MixedHello extends JFrame implements ActionListener
{
   Button b1;
   JButton b2;

   static String [] labels =
   {
      "Hello! Welcome to mixed Swing!",
      "This program mixes an AWT button with a Swing button.",
      "You cannot assign icons to AWT buttons.",
      "You can assign icons to Swing buttons."
   };

   int nextLabel;
```

LISTING 15.8 CONTINUED

```
   MixedHello (String title)
   {
      super (title);

      addWindowListener (new WindowAdapter ()
                         {
                             public void windowClosing (WindowEvent e)
                             {
                                System.exit (0);
                             }
                         });

      Panel p = new Panel ();
      b1 = new Button ("AWT button");
      b1.addActionListener (this);
      p.add (b1);
      b2 = new JButton (labels [nextLabel++],
                        new ImageIcon ("bullet.gif"));
      b2.addActionListener (this);
      p.add (b2);
      setContentPane (p);

      setSize (400, 100);
      setVisible (true);
   }

   public void actionPerformed (ActionEvent e)
   {
      b2.setText (labels [nextLabel++]);
      nextLabel %= labels.length;
   }

   public static void main (String [] args)
   {
      new MixedHello ("Hello, Mixed Version");
   }
}
```

CONVERTING FROM THE AWT TO SWING

If you are presented with the task of creating a Swing program that replaces an existing AWT program, it's important that you first learn some Swing basics (like you will learn in the next chapter). Then, convert the AWT program to its Swing-based equivalent, and then add new capabilities and/or remove/replace existing capabilities. When you are ready to convert from the AWT to Swing, keep the following tips in mind:

- Back up your code.
- Remove all `java.awt` package/subpackage references.
- Remove all `java.applet` package references (for applets only).
- Add an import `javax.swing.*;` directive.

- Watch out for threading problems. (Chapter 16, "Building a GUI: Swing Style," explains Swing's threading issues and discusses workarounds.)
- Convert AWT components to Swing equivalents.
- Rewrite calls that add components to containers.
- Move all painting code out of any `paint` and `update` methods.
- Let the compiler find any other required changes.
- Run the converted program.
- Make any additional improvements offered by Swing (such as using its capability to right justify a `JTextField` component's text, which is not possible in a `TextField` component).
- Clean up any AWT code hacks and bug workarounds

These tips are summarized—and paraphrased—from the conversion tips offered by the online Java Tutorial located at `http://www.javasoft.com/tutorial`. For more details, please visit this tutorial and check out its AWT to Swing conversion section.

If you're converting an AWT program that uses list and text components to Swing, you might notice that when you run the Swing version of this program, its list and text components don't have scrollbars. See "List and Text Component Scrollbar Differences," in the "Troubleshooting" section for more information.

TROUBLESHOOTING

LIST AND TEXT COMPONENT SCROLLBAR DIFFERENCES

Why is it that scrollbars never appear when working with Swing's list and text components?

Unlike their AWT cousins, Swing's list and text components don't have automatic scrollbars. If you want scrollbars, you must add either component to Swing's scroll pane container. Chapter 16, "Building a GUI: Swing Style," will show you how to accomplish this task.

CHAPTER 16

Building a GUI: Swing Style

In this chapter

by Geoff Friesen

A SWINGING TOOLKIT

Chapter 13, "Beginning AWT," introduced you to the AWT's windowing toolkit. As you learned, this toolkit consists of components, containers, layout managers, events, and listeners. In an effort to overcome the limitations of these entities, Sun's engineers extended the AWT's windowing toolkit into a much more capable product—the Swing windowing toolkit.

> **Note**
>
> Swing's windowing toolkit is vast. Because of space limitations, this chapter omits many details. To learn more about this toolkit, please consult both the SDK's documentation, and the Java Tutorial at `http://java.sun.com/docs/books/tutorial/`.

One of the main features that Swing offers is a superb collection of lightweight components. (This is the reason for not presenting an example of a lightweight component in Chapter 14.) Because no peers are involved, Swing's components are completely managed and rendered in Java.

> **Note**
>
> Swing's `JApplet`, `JDialog`, `JFrame`, and `JWindow` classes represent heavyweight container components. They are heavyweight so that their associated peers can render the appearances of lightweight Swing components and containers in native windows. Furthermore, the peers propagate events from the native windowing system to lightweight components and containers. (Because these are the only heavyweight Swing containers, and all other components are lightweight, Swing uses fewer system resources than the AWT.)

MODEL-VIEW-CONTROLLER ARCHITECTURE

Swing's components and containers weren't designed to work in the same manner as AWT components and containers. Instead, they were designed to be much more flexible. This flexibility results from supporting the Model-View-Controller (MVC) architecture.

MVC (developed by Xerox PARC in the late 1970s for use with its Smalltalk windowing system) factors a component into a model, one or more views, and a controller.

The *model* maintains a component's state. For a button component, a model would probably contain button press information. For a text field component, the model might contain the text field's characters. When some models are changed, they notify their associated views. With other models, corresponding controllers notify these views on each model's behalf.

The *view* provides a visual representation of a component's model. Views give components their "look." For example, a button view could receive button press information, either from the button's model or from its controller. In turn, the view would render an appropriate appearance for the button.

The *controller* determines if a component should respond to input events that originate from input devices (such as keyboards and mice). Controllers give components their "feel." For example, a mouse button press (while the mouse pointer is positioned over a button) would cause the controller to notify the model and/or all views for the underlying button component.

Figure 16.1 illustrates a generic component by way of its model, view, and controller.

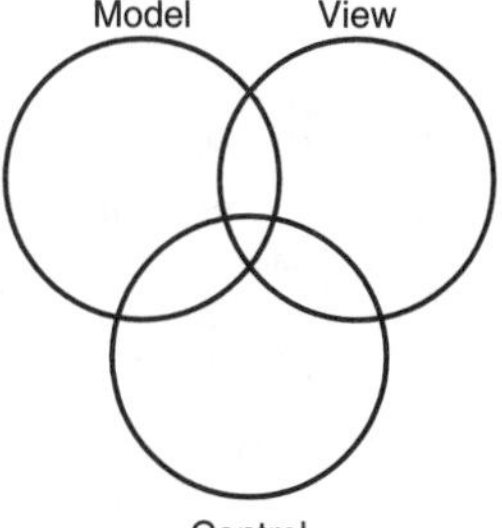

Figure 16.1
MVC architecture factors a component into a model, one or more views, and a controller.

Each Swing component has a default model. However, this model can be changed by calling the component's `setModel` method. For example, the `JButton` class creates Swing button components. If you investigate its `setModel` method (which is located in its `AbstractButton` superclass), you'll discover that `setModel` requires a `ButtonModel` argument—an object created from a class that implements the `ButtonModel` interface. The various methods in this interface manage the button's model. (Furthermore, this interface is also used to create models for check boxes and radio buttons—which are special kinds of buttons.)

Because it is easier to manage an integrated controller and view, many modern windowing toolkits (including Swing) tend to collapse the controller and view into a single entity—known as a *UI (User Interface) delegate*. UI delegates and models are completely separate: They communicate by way of events. As a result, a UI delegate can be associated with more than one model, and a model can be associated with more than one UI delegate. A generic component is illustrated in Figure 16.2, by way of its model and UI delegate.

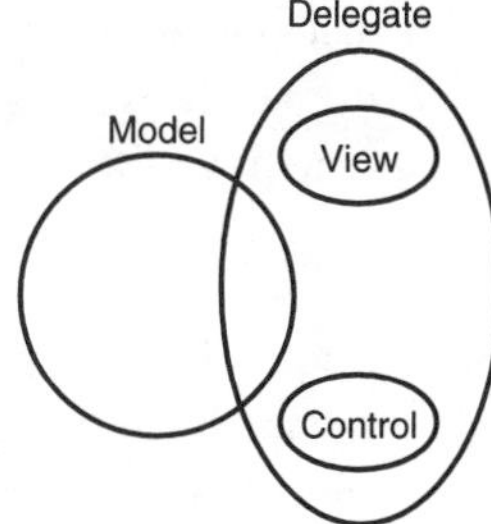

Figure 16.2
The Swing windowing toolkit collapses a view and controller into a UI delegate.

Each Swing component has a separate UI delegate and each delegate is derived from the abstract `ComponentUI` class (located in the `javax.swing.plaf`) package. `ComponentUI`'s methods provide a basic communication link between a UI delegate and its component.

Each Swing component has a `setUI` method that can be called to set the UI delegate for that component. Furthermore, some components have a `getUI` method that returns this delegate. You will rarely (if ever) need to call these methods, because they are designed to be used by Swing's pluggable look and feel capability.

PLUGGABLE LOOK AND FEEL

A set of UI delegates (one per component) is known as a *look and feel.* Swing provides a mechanism for choosing between a variety of look and feels. By using this mechanism, a look and feel can be plugged into a GUI at any time. For this reason, a look and feel is also known as a *pluggable look and feel* or PLAF.

The classes making up a PLAF are stored in a unique package. One of these classes is the PLAF's main class, and extends the abstract `LookAndFeel` class (located in the `javax.swing` package). The following PLAFs are available:

- The Basic PLAF is an abstract PLAF that serves as a foundation for other PLAFs. Its main class is `BasicLookAndFeel` (located in the `javax.swing.plaf.basic` package).
- The Java PLAF (also known as the Metal PLAF) is a cross platform PLAF that serves as the default PLAF. `MetalLookAndFeel` (located in the `javax.swing.plaf.metal` package) is the main class.
- The Motif PLAF provides the look and feel of Unix's Motif. Its main class is `MotifLookAndFeel` (located in the `com.sun.java.swing.plaf.motif` package).
- The Windows PLAF provides the look and feel of Windows. Its main class is `WindowsLookAndFeel` (located in the `com.sun.java.swing.plaf.windows` package). For trademark reasons, this PLAF is only available on Windows machines.
- The Macintosh PLAF provides the look and feel of the MacOS. Its main class is `MacLookAndFeel` (located in the `com.sun.java.swing.plaf.mac` package). For trademark reasons, this PLAF is only available on Macintosh machines.
- The multiplexing PLAF provides multiple look and feels that can be simultaneously associated with a GUI. Its main class is `MultiLookAndFeel` (located in the `javax.swing.plaf.multi` package). Each multiplexing UI delegate is designed to manage its child UI delegates. (This PLAF is primarily intended for use with accessibility PLAFs.)

The `UIManager` class (located in the `javax.swing` package) provides the means to choose any of these PLAFs. To establish the new PLAF, pass the fully qualified name of the PLAF's main class to `UIManager`'s `setLookAndFeel` method. The following code fragment shows how to accomplish this task:

```
public static void main (String [] args)
{
   try
   {
       UIManager.setLookAndFeel
("com.sun.java.swing.plaf.motif.MotifLookAndFeel");
```

```
    }
    catch (Exception e) { }

    new SwingApplication (); // Create and show the GUI.
}
```

The code fragment establishes Motif as the current PLAF. If the `MotifLookAndFeel` class cannot be found, `setLookAndFeel` throws a `ClassNotFoundException` object. An `InstantiationException` object is thrown if an instance of this class cannot be created. If the class is not public (or is located in some other package), an `IllegalAccessException` object is thrown. Finally, `setLookAndFeel` calls `UIManager`'s `isSupportedLookAndFeel` method to find out if this look and feel is supported on the current platform. If this method returns a Boolean `false` value, `setLookAndFeel` throws an `UnsupportedLookAndFeelException` object. (A PLAF is not supported for trademark reasons.) Figure 16.3 shows an application's GUI, rendered using the Motif PLAF.

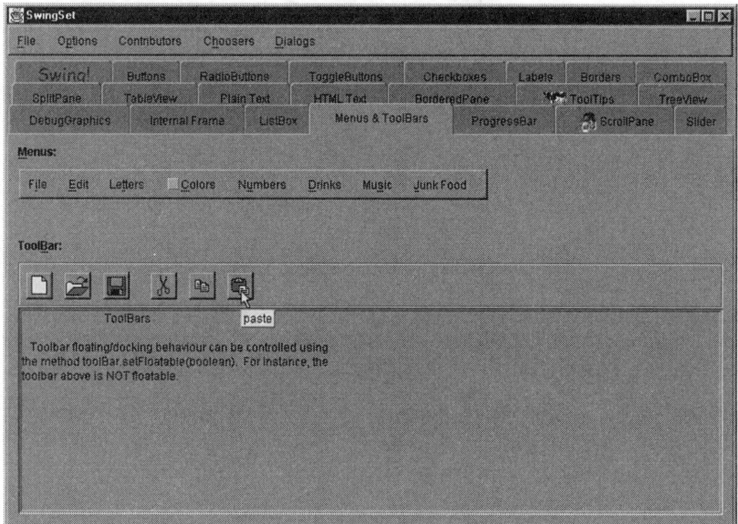

Figure 16.3
An application's GUI, rendered by the Motif PLAF, has a rather dark appearance.

`UIManager` provides a `getCrossPlatformLookAndFeelClassName` method, as a convenience in identifying the Java PLAF. (This method might not be much of a convenience, considering the length of its name. However, `getCrossPlatformLookAndFeelClassName` is recommended for applications to use because it allows applications to be extensible if the default look and feel package changes in the future.) The following code fragment shows how you would call this method to retrieve the name of the Java PLAF's main class, and then pass this name to the `setLookAndFeel` method to establish the Java PLAF as the current PLAF.

```
public static void main (String [] args)
{
    try
    {
        String name = UIManager.getCrossPlatformLookAndFeelClassName();
        UIManager.setLookAndFeel (name);
```

```
   }
   catch (Exception e) { }

   new SwingApplication (); // Create and show the GUI.
}
```

Figure 16.4 shows an application's GUI, rendered using the Java PLAF.

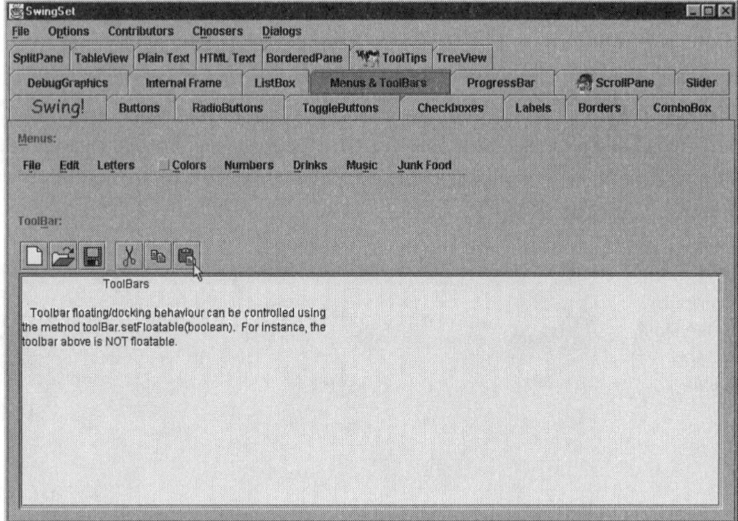

Figure 16.4
An application's GUI, rendered by the Java PLAF, has a subtle 3D appearance.

`UIManager` also provides a `getSystemLookAndFeelClassName` method as a convenience in identifying the system PLAF. (This is the native windowing system's look and feel.) The following code fragment shows how you would call this method to retrieve the name of the system PLAF's main class, and then pass this name to the `setLookAndFeel` method to establish the system PLAF as the current PLAF.

```
public static void main (String [] args)
{
   try
   {
       String name = UIManager.getSystemLookAndFeelClassName();
       UIManager.setLookAndFeel (name);
   }
   catch (Exception e) { }

   new SwingApplication (); // Create and show the GUI.
}
```

Figure 16.5 shows an application's GUI, rendered using the system PLAF (which just happens to be Windows on the author's computer).

When a Swing program begins running, it might or might not attempt to change its PLAF. If it doesn't (or its attempt is unsuccessful), the Java runtime environment's `lib` directory is examined for a file called `swing.properties`. If this file exists, it is examined for a `swing.defaultlaf` entry. If this entry exists, its value is used to create the default PLAF. However, if this entry is invalid (or doesn't exist), the Java PLAF is chosen as the default startup PLAF.

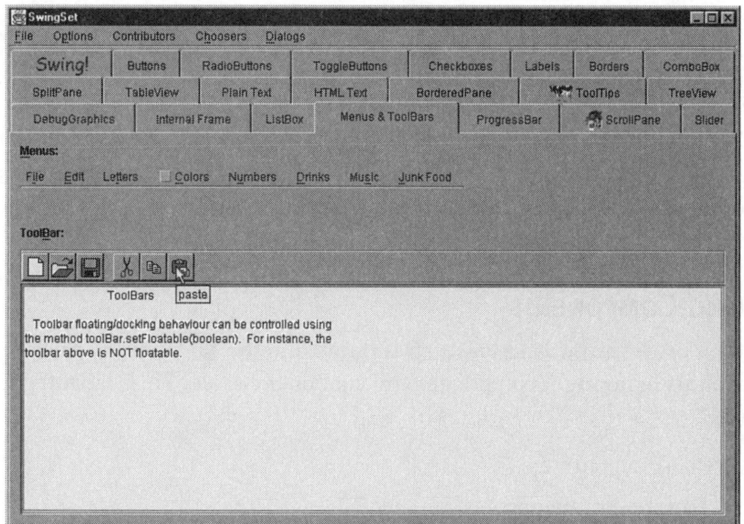

Figure 16.5
As with Motif, an application's GUI, rendered by the Windows PLAF, has a strong 3D appearance. However, unlike Motif, toolbar buttons are placed side by side, with no in-between spacing.

Suppose you want to change a GUI's PLAF, after the GUI is visible. You can make this change by invoking the `updateComponentTreeUI` method (in the `SwingUtilities` class located in the `javax.swing` package). You pass a container as the sole argument, and this method informs all the container's children that the PLAF has changed and that they must replace their UI delegates with the new PLAF's delegates. The following code fragment provides a demonstration:

```
String lnfName = " com.sun.java.swing.plaf.motif.MotifLookAndFeel";
try
{
    UIManager.setLookAndFeel (lnfName);
}
catch (Exception e) {}
SwingUtilities.updateComponentTreeUI (frame); // Assume frame exists.
frame.pack ();
```

Tip

You should resize the container after calling `updateComponentTreeUI` (by calling `pack`), because new UI delegates could reflect views that provide different sizes.

So how is a component made aware that its PLAF has changed? The answer lies in the `updateUI` method that every component inherits from the `JComponent` class. This method is automatically called for each component when a PLAF change occurs. In response, `updateUI` calls `UIManager`'s `getUI` method to return the new delegate, and either the inherited or overridden `setUI` method to establish this new delegate as the current delegate.

As you've seen, Java includes a small handful of PLAFs. Although they are adequate for many situations, suppose that none of these PLAFs meet your needs, and you find yourself in a position where you must create a new PLAF. What do you do? The answer is to check out "Creating an Alternate PLAF" in the "Troubleshooting" section at the end of this chapter.

BUILDING A GUI: COMPONENTS, CONTAINERS, AND LAYOUT MANAGERS

Chapter 14 introduced you to the two-phase GUI building approach. Although this approach was used with the AWT's windowing toolkit, it can also be used with Swing's windowing toolkit. As you learned, the first phase constructs a GUI's look, and is achieved by working with components, containers, and layout managers.

EXPLORING COMPONENTS

Swing provides the `JComponent` class (located in the `javax.swing` package) as the superclass for all its lightweight component and container classes. This class offers the following services:

- PLAF support
- Accessibility support
- ToolTip support
- Improved keystroke handling
- Double-buffered painting structure that supports borders
- Component-specific property support

PLAF has already been discussed. Accessibility will be discussed in the next chapter. As for the other services, you will get an opportunity to learn about them as you work your way through this chapter.

BUTTONS

The `JButton` class (located in `javax.swing` package) represents a new kind of button component. Unlike AWT buttons, this button can be associated with an icon and a *mnemonic*—a key stroke that, when pressed in conjunction with the `Alt` key, results in a button click.

A button can serve as the *default button* (a button that is clicked when either the `Return` or `Enter` key is pressed). Its text can be aligned horizontally or vertically. HTML tags can be used to render the appearance of the button's text (on platforms that offer such support). Finally, a ToolTip can be specified to provide a description of the button's purpose. To see what a pair of Swing buttons look like, check out Figure 16.6.

Figure 16.6's buttons were created from the `ButtonDemo` application. The source code to this application is presented in Listing 16.1.

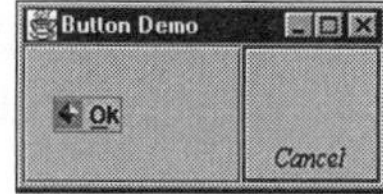

Figure 16.6 Swing's buttons can display icons, and horizontally or vertically aligned and HTML formatted captions.

Listing 16.1 The ButtonDemo Application Source Code

```
// ButtonDemo.java

import javax.swing.*;

import java.awt.*;
import java.awt.event.*;

class ButtonDemo extends JFrame implements ActionListener
{
   ButtonDemo (String title)
   {
      super (title);

      addWindowListener (new WindowAdapter ()
                         {
                             public void windowClosing (WindowEvent e)
                             {
                                System.exit (0);
                             }
                         });

      JButton jb = new JButton ("Ok", new ImageIcon ("bullet.gif"));
      jb.setHorizontalAlignment (SwingConstants.LEFT);
      jb.setToolTipText ("Press Ok to terminate the program.");
      jb.addActionListener (this);

      jb.setMnemonic ('O');

      getContentPane ().add (jb, BorderLayout.CENTER);

      jb = new JButton ("<html><i>Cancel</i></html>");
      jb.setVerticalAlignment (SwingConstants.BOTTOM);
      jb.setToolTipText ("Press Cancel to terminate the program.");
      jb.addActionListener (this);

      jb.setDefaultCapable (true);

      getContentPane ().add (jb, BorderLayout.EAST);

      getRootPane ().setDefaultButton (jb);

      setSize (200, 100);
      setVisible (true);
   }

   public void actionPerformed (ActionEvent e)
   {
```

LISTING 16.1 CONTINUED

```
        if (e.getActionCommand ().equals ("Ok"))
            System.out.println ("OK was pressed.");
        else
            System.out.println ("Cancel was pressed.");

        System.exit (0);
    }

    public static void main (String [] args)
    {
        new ButtonDemo ("Button Demo");
    }
}
```

Note

When you run ButtonDemo, don't forget to make sure that bullet.gif is located in the same directory as ButtonDemo.class. (bullet.gif is included with the rest of this book's source code.)

In ButtonDemo's source code, two of JButton's constructors are called to create buttons. The JButton (String txt, Icon icon) constructor creates a button that displays the characters found in its txt argument and the image found in its icon argument. If only text is required (as in the Cancel button), JButton (String txt) is called.

Note the ImageIcon object that is passed to the Ok button's constructor. The ImageIcon class creates objects that represent icons (because ImageIcon implements the Icon interface). The ImageIcon (String name) constructor is called with the name of an image file. Internally, it uses MediaTracker to preload the image, and is then responsible for painting this image. By passing an ImageIcon to the JButton constructor, you can have an icon appear alongside a button's text.

When you study ButtonDemo, you'll find two references to the SwingConstants interface (located in the javax.swing package). This interface provides a variety of useful position and orientation constants that are used throughout Swing—and also can be used in your programs.

As you work your way through ButtonDemo, you'll come across the getContentPane and getRootPane methods. The getContentPane method returns a reference to a Swing program's content pane, which is used like a panel to store components. The getRootPane method returns a reference to a Swing program's root pane, which contains the content pane, and is required to set the default button. (Content and root panes are explored later in this chapter. For now, keep in mind that you must use a content pane in your Swing applications and applets.)

Caution

Two bugs were discovered when testing `ButtonDemo`. The first bug (which the author refers to as the incredible vibrating button) is related to ToolTips. When you slowly move the mouse pointer into the bottom few pixel rows of either button, these buttons develop a bad case of the shakes, because a ToolTip is being rapidly switched on and off.

The second bug is more ominous. At times, the mnemonic and default button features stop working. You need to reset the computer and re-run the program to get these features to start working again. (These bugs were only discovered when `ButtonDemo` was tested under the Windows version of the Java 2 Platform–Windows 98 to be specific. There is a good chance that they might not show up on your platform. Instead, you'll probably have other bugs to deal with!)

CHECK BOXES

The `JCheckBox` class (located in `javax.swing` package) represents a new kind of check box component. This check box has all the features of an abstract button (because `JCheckBox` indirectly inherits from the `AbstractButton` class), along with a state that can be toggled on or off (because `JCheckBox` directly inherits from the `JToggleButton` class). Figure 16.7 presents a collection of check boxes.

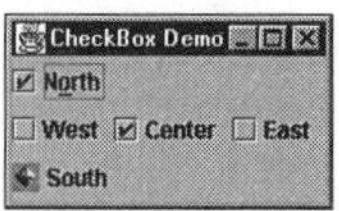

Figure 16.7 As with buttons, Swing's check boxes can be associated with icons.

Figure 16.7's check boxes were created from the `CheckBoxDemo` application. The source code to this application is presented in Listing 16.2.

LISTING 16.2 THE `CheckBoxDemo` APPLICATION SOURCE CODE

```
// CheckBoxDemo.java

import javax.swing.*;

import java.awt.*;
import java.awt.event.*;

class CheckBoxDemo extends JFrame implements ActionListener
{
   CheckBoxDemo (String title)
   {
      super (title);

      addWindowListener (new WindowAdapter ()
                         {
                             public void windowClosing (WindowEvent e)
                             {
                                System.exit (0);
                             }
```

LISTING 16.2 CONTINUED

```
                                 });

        ButtonGroup bg = new ButtonGroup ();

        JCheckBox north = new JCheckBox ("North");
        north.setMnemonic ('o');
        north.addActionListener (this);
        bg.add (north);
        getContentPane ().add (north, BorderLayout.NORTH);

        JCheckBox west = new JCheckBox ("West", true);
        west.addActionListener (this);
        bg.add (west);
        getContentPane ().add (west, BorderLayout.WEST);

        JCheckBox center = new JCheckBox ("Center");
        center.addActionListener (this);
//        bg.add (center);
        getContentPane ().add (center, BorderLayout.CENTER);

        JCheckBox east = new JCheckBox ("East");
        east.addActionListener (this);
        bg.add (east);
        getContentPane ().add (east, BorderLayout.EAST);

        JCheckBox south = new JCheckBox ("South",
                                         new ImageIcon ("bullet.gif"));
        south.addActionListener (this);
        bg.add (south);
        getContentPane ().add (south, BorderLayout.SOUTH);

        pack ();
        setVisible (true);
    }

    public void actionPerformed (ActionEvent e)
    {
        System.out.println (e.getActionCommand ());
    }

    public static void main (String [] args)
    {
        new CheckBoxDemo ("CheckBox Demo");
    }
}
```

When you study `CheckBoxDemo`, you'll notice a `bg` object being created from the `ButtonGroup` class. Check boxes are subsequently added to this object by calling `bg`'s `add` method. (In most cases, your check boxes are not added to button groups.)

`ButtonGroup` has a similar purpose to the AWT's `CheckBoxGroup` class: It groups its components to form a mutually exclusive group (only one of the components in this group can be selected at any point in time). If you recall, AWT's `CheckBoxGroup` class was used to achieve this effect—and create radio buttons. This is no longer needed because Swing introduces a `JRadioButton` class for this purpose. Check boxes placed in a button group still look like check boxes as you can clearly see in Figure 16.7.

The commented out line prevents the center check box from being part of the button group. As a result, this check box and one other check box (from the group) can be simultaneously selected.

Caution

It's not a good idea to associate an image with a check box because the image hides the check box rectangle and check mark.

COLOR CHOOSERS

The `JColorChooser` class (located in `javax.swing` package) represents a tabbed component with three tabs (`Swatches`, `HSB`, and `RGB`) that allow you to choose colors in different ways. After a color has been chosen, the color chooser's selection model fires a change event. By registering a listener, the newly selected color can be used to color one or more components. To see what a color chooser looks like, check out Figure 16.8.

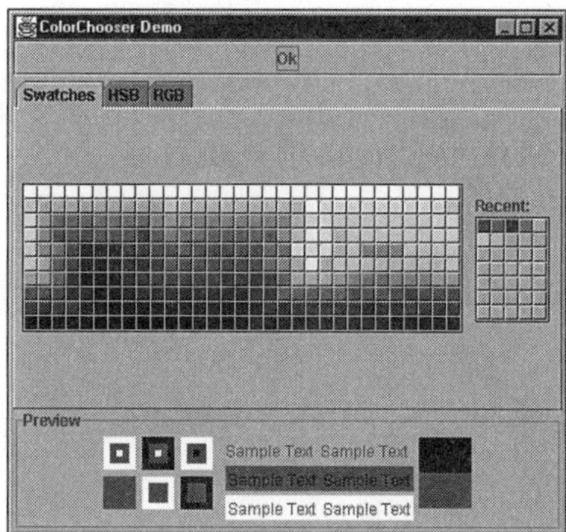

Figure 16.8 Swing's color chooser is useful for selecting a GUI's colors.

Figure 16.8's color chooser and button were created from the `ColorChooserDemo` application. This application's source code is presented in Listing 16.3.

LISTING 16.3 THE `ColorChooserDemo` APPLICATION SOURCE CODE

```
// ColorChooserDemo.java

import javax.swing.*;
import javax.swing.event.*;

import java.awt.*;
import java.awt.event.*;
```

LISTING 16.3 CONTINUED

```
class ColorChooserDemo extends JFrame
{
   ColorChooserDemo (String title)
   {
      super (title);

      addWindowListener (new WindowAdapter ()
                         {
                             public void windowClosing (WindowEvent e)
                             {
                                System.exit (0);
                             }
                         });

      final JButton jb = new JButton ("Ok");

      getContentPane ().add (jb, BorderLayout.NORTH);

      final JColorChooser cc = new JColorChooser (Color.black);

      getContentPane ().add (cc, BorderLayout.SOUTH);

      ChangeListener cl = new ChangeListener ()
                          {
                              public void stateChanged (ChangeEvent e)
                              {
                                 Color nc = cc.getColor ();
                                 jb.setForeground (nc);
                              }
                          };

      cc.getSelectionModel ().addChangeListener (cl);

      pack ();
      setVisible (true);
   }

   public static void main (String [] args)
   {
      new ColorChooserDemo ("ColorChooser Demo");
   }
}
```

In `ColorChooserDemo`, variables `jb` and `cc` are marked `final` because they are local variables that must be accessed from inside an inner class method.

The color chooser's current selection model is retrieved by calling its `getSelectionModel` method. The model's `addChangeListener` method is then called to register the current object as a change listener. When a change event is fired, the listener's `stateChanged` method is called. The color chooser's current color is extracted, by calling `getColor`, and this color is chosen as the button's foreground color. (Change events and listeners will be discussed later in this chapter.)

COMBO BOXES

The `JComboBox` class (located in `javax.swing` package) represents a combo box component from which you can choose a single item. This component operates in one of two modes: non-edit and edit.

In non-edit mode, a combo box behaves like an AWT choice component. An item is displayed, along with a down-arrow button. Clicking this button results in the display of a pop-up menu from which you can choose a different item. Figure 16.9 shows a simple non-edit combo box.

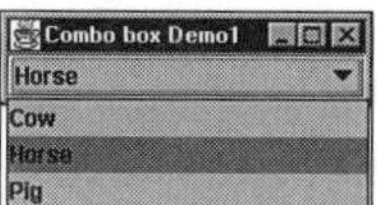

Figure 16.9
Swing's combo box can be used in non-edit mode to select an item from a pop-up list of items.

Figure 16.9's combo box was created from the `ComboBoxDemo1` application. (Notice the absence of the bottom line on the pop-up menu. This appears to be an example of a Swing painting bug. The second time you pull down the combo box, the bottom line appears.) Listing 16.4 presents source code to `ComboBoxDemo1`.

LISTING 16.4 THE `ComboBoxDemo1` APPLICATION SOURCE CODE

```
// ComboBoxDemo1.java

import javax.swing.*;

import java.awt.event.*;

import java.util.*;

class ComboBoxDemo1 extends JFrame
{
   ComboBoxDemo1 (String title)
   {
      super (title);

      addWindowListener (new WindowAdapter ()
                         {
                             public void windowClosing (WindowEvent e)
                             {
                                System.exit (0);
                             }
                         });

      Vector v = new Vector ();
      v.add ("Cow");
      v.add ("Horse");
      v.add ("Pig");
      JComboBox jcb = new JComboBox (v);
```

LISTING 16.4 CONTINUED

```
      getContentPane ().add (jcb);

      setSize (200, 50);
      setVisible (true);
   }

   public static void main (String [] args)
   {
      new ComboBoxDemo1 ("Combo box Demo1");
   }
}
```

Among other constructors, `JComboBox` provides a constructor that takes a `Vector` object argument. This vector serves as the model for the combo box. Before calling the constructor, you would populate the vector with objects that will appear in the combo box.

In edit mode, a combo box uses an editor for entering values. You can choose to enter a value via this editor, or you can select an item from the pop-up menu (by clicking the down-arrow button). The contents of the selected item will then appear in the editor. Figure 16.10 shows a simple edit combo box.

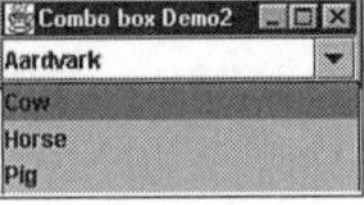

Figure 16.10
Swing's combo box can be used in edit mode to either enter an item (via an editor) or select an item from a pop-up list of items. The selected item subsequently appears in the editor.

Figure 16.10's combo box was created from the `ComboBoxDemo2` application. This application's source code is nearly identical to `ComboBoxDemo1`. The only difference is a call to `JComboBox`'s `setEditable` method with a Boolean `true` value, which changes the combo box from its default non-edit mode to edit mode. This is shown in the following code fragment.

```
jcb.setEditable (true);
```

Swing offers the ability to change the combo box's editor, by calling `JComboBox`'s `setEditor` method. For example, if you wanted to enter a color, you might want to choose the color from a palette of colors, as opposed to typing the color's name.

Furthermore, Swing offers the ability to change the combo box's renderer, by calling `JComboBox`'s `setRenderer` method. The renderer is responsible for rendering the content of each item in a combo box's pop-up menu. A renderer can even render images. Figure 16.11 shows a combo box with items that integrate images with text.

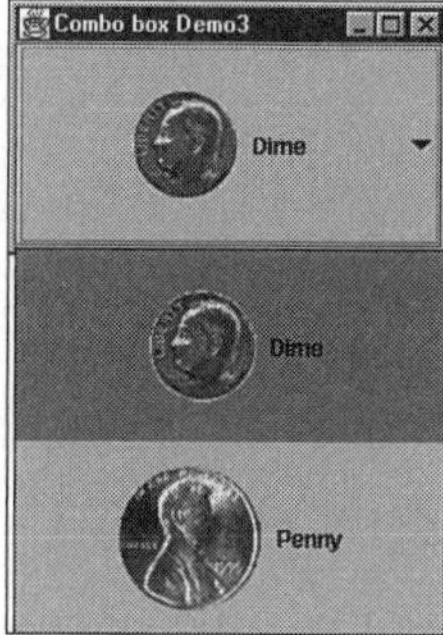

Figure 16.11
A custom rendered combo box can integrate images with text.

Figure 16.11's combo box was created from the `ComboBoxDemo3` application. This application's source code is presented in Listing 16.5.

Listing 16.5 The `ComboBoxDemo3` Application Source Code

```
// ComboBoxDemo3.java

import javax.swing.*;

import java.awt.*;
import java.awt.event.*;

class ComboBoxDemo3 extends JFrame
{
   ImageIcon [] im;

   ComboBoxDemo3 (String title)
   {
      super (title);

      addWindowListener (new WindowAdapter ()
                         {
                             public void windowClosing (WindowEvent e)
                             {
                                System.exit (0);
                             }
                         });

      im = new ImageIcon [2];

      im [0] = new ImageIcon ("dime.gif");
      im [0].setDescription ("Dime");

      im [1] = new ImageIcon ("penny.gif");
      im [1].setDescription ("Penny");

      JComboBox coins = new JComboBox (im);
      ComboBoxRenderer renderer = new ComboBoxRenderer ();
      renderer.setPreferredSize (new Dimension (200, 100));
      coins.setRenderer (renderer);

      getContentPane ().add (coins);
```

LISTING 16.5 CONTINUED

```
      pack ();
      setVisible (true);
   }

   public static void main (String [] args)
   {
      new ComboBoxDemo3 ("Combo box Demo3");
   }
}

class ComboBoxRenderer extends JLabel implements ListCellRenderer
{
   public ComboBoxRenderer ()
   {
      setOpaque (true);
      setHorizontalAlignment (CENTER);
      setVerticalAlignment (CENTER);
   }

   public Component getListCellRendererComponent (JList list,
                                                  Object value,
                                                  int index,
                                                  boolean selected,
                                                  boolean hasfocus)
   {
      if (selected)
      {
          setBackground (list.getSelectionBackground ());
          setForeground (list.getSelectionForeground ());
      }
      else
      {
          setBackground (list.getBackground ());
          setForeground (list.getForeground ());
      }

      ImageIcon icon = (ImageIcon) value;
      setText (icon.getDescription ());
      setIcon (icon);
      return this;
   }
}
```

The `setRenderer` method takes a single argument, which is an object created from a class that implements the `ListCellRenderer` interface. If you check the SDK documentation, you'll see that `ListCellRenderer` provides a single `getListCellRendererComponent` method.

The `getListCellRendererComponent` method returns a component that has been configured to display the specified value. This component is capable of rendering a *cell*—another name for menu item. After the component has been returned, its `paint` method is called (behind the scenes) to render the cell. (This is why the `ComboBoxRenderer` class is derived from `JLabel`, which will be discussed later in this chapter.)

The `getListCellRendererComponent` method takes four arguments: a `JList` argument to identify the combo box or list that contains cells to be rendered; an `Object` that identifies the current item from the combo box pop-up menu (or list menu); an `int` that identifies the cell; a Boolean that identifies the cell's selection state (so that an appropriate highlight can be provided during rendering); and a Boolean that indicates if the cell has focus (so that appropriate focus details can be provided during rendering).

You might be curious about the purpose behind the `setOpaque` method call in the `ComboBoxRenderer` constructor. This method is called to ensure that all pixels are rendered by the component returned from `getListCellRendererComponent`. If `setOpaque` was not called, you would not see the selection highlight because underlying pixels in the nonhighlight color would show through.

FILE CHOOSERS

The `JFileChooser` class (located in `javax.swing` package) provides improved platform-independent modal dialog boxes for choosing files during an open or save operation. (If you recall, the AWT provides a `FileDialog` class for this purpose.) To see what an Open dialog box looks like, check out Figure 16.12.

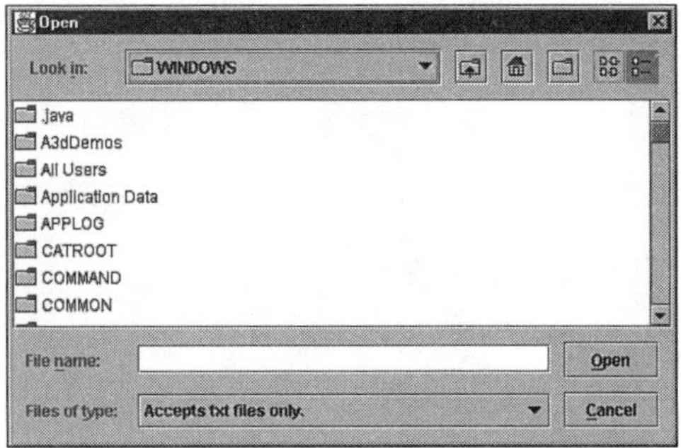

Figure 16.12 Swing's file chooser is configured to serve as an Open dialog box. It can also be configured to serve as a Save dialog box.

Figure 16.12's file chooser was created from the `FileChooserDemo` application. This application's source code is presented in Listing 16.6.

LISTING 16.6 THE `FileChooserDemo` APPLICATION SOURCE CODE

```
// FileChooserDemo.java

import javax.swing.*;
import javax.swing.event.*;
import javax.swing.filechooser.*;

import java.awt.event.*;

import java.io.File;

class FileChooserDemo extends JFrame implements ActionListener
```

LISTING 16.6 CONTINUED

```
{
   FileChooserDemo (String title)
   {
      super (title);

      addWindowListener (new WindowAdapter ()
                         {
                             public void windowClosing (WindowEvent e)
                             {
                                System.exit (0);
                             }
                         });

      JPanel p = new JPanel ();

      JButton jb = new JButton ("Open ...");
      jb.addActionListener (this);
      p.add (jb);

      jb = new JButton ("Save ...");
      jb.addActionListener (this);
      p.add (jb);

      getContentPane ().add (p);

      setSize (200, 65);
      setVisible (true);
   }

   public void actionPerformed (ActionEvent e)
   {
      int retVal;

      JFileChooser fc = new JFileChooser ();

      if (e.getActionCommand ().equals ("Open ..."))
      {
          fc.addChoosableFileFilter (new TextFilter ());
          retVal = fc.showOpenDialog (this);
      }
      else
          retVal = fc.showSaveDialog (this);

      if (retVal == JFileChooser.APPROVE_OPTION)
          System.out.println (fc.getSelectedFile ().getName ());
   }

   public static void main (String [] args)
   {
      new FileChooserDemo ("FileChooser Demo");
   }
}

class TextFilter extends FileFilter
{
```

LISTING 16.6 CONTINUED

```
   // Accept all directories and txt files.

   public boolean accept (File f)
   {
      if (f.isDirectory ())
          return true;

      // Check extension for txt.

      String s = f.getName ();
      int i = s.lastIndexOf ('.');

      if (i > 0 && i < s.length () - 1)
          if (s.substring (i + 1).toLowerCase ().equals ("txt"))
              return true;

      return false;
   }

   public String getDescription ()
   {
      return "Accepts txt files only.";
   }
}
```


Caution

The source code to `TextFilter`'s `accept` method is based on source code presented in the Java Tutorial. However, there is a simpler way to write this method, as demonstrated by the following code fragment.

```
public boolean accept (File f)
{
   return f.isDirectory () || f.getName ().toLowerCase ().endsWith
(".txt");
}
```

`FileChooserDemo` calls the `JFileChooser ()` constructor to create a file chooser. If a user clicks the `Open ...` button, a filter is created to narrow the range of displayable filenames.

The filter is created by calling `JFileChooser`'s `addChoosableFileFilter` method—with a reference to a subclass of the abstract `FileFilter` class (located in the `javax.swing.filechooser` package). The subclass that's chosen is called `TextFilter`—to restrict displayable filenames to those names ending in a `.txt` file extension. `TextFilter` overrides the `accept` and `getDescription` methods.

Before a filename is displayed, the file chooser calls the filter's `accept` method. A `File` object argument, containing the filename, is passed to this method. To retrieve this name, `File`'s `getName` method is called. The extension is examined to see if it's acceptable to the filter. If not, a Boolean `false` value is returned. Otherwise, `true` is returned.

The `getDescription` method is called by the file chooser to return a `String` object, whose contents are displayed in a dialog's `Files of Type` combo box.

To activate an open file chooser dialog box, call `showOpenDialog`. In contrast, call `showSaveDialog` to activate a save file chooser dialog box. These methods cause an appropriate title to be displayed in each dialog box's title bar. Furthermore, they require a single argument that references a `Component` as the dialog box's parent.

Each dialog box returns a user's response to the dialog box as an `int`. If the user accepts the dialog box (by clicking either the `Open` or `Save` button—as appropriate), a value identified by `JFileChooser`'s `APPROVE_OPTION` constant is returned. However, if the user chooses to cancel the dialog box, `CANCEL_OPTION` is returned. Assuming an `APPROVE_OPTION` return value, a call to `getSelectedFile` causes a reference to a `File` object—containing the filename of the approved file—to be returned.

Version 1.3 of the Java 2 Platform Standard Edition adds two new properties to the `JFileChooser` class. These properties include control over accept all files (`*.*`) and button removal. (For more information, check out the file chooser section of the new Swing features in the SDK documentation.)

Note

Properties is a JavaBeans term for data that's manipulated by "get" and "set" methods, which conforms to the JavaBeans design pattern.

LABELS

Swing's `JLabel` class offers richer labels than its counterpart AWT `Label` class. As with buttons, you can create labels that display icons. To see an example, check out Figure 16.13.

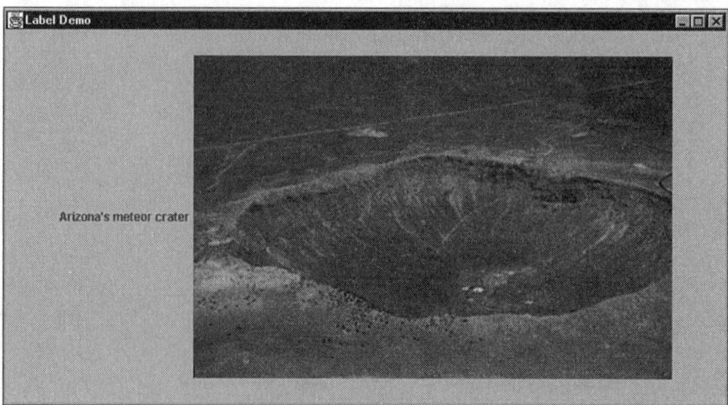

Figure 16.13
Swing's labels can display icons.

Note

Figure 16.13 shows a rather large image being used as an icon. This suggests that the `JLabel` class can be used in place of the AWT's `Canvas` class for displaying images. If you check out the Java Tutorial, you will see that `JLabel` is commonly used for this purpose.

Figure 16.13's label was created from the `LabelDemo` application. This application's source code is presented in Listing 16.7.

LISTING 16.7 THE `LabelDemo` APPLICATION SOURCE CODE

```
// LabelDemo.java

import javax.swing.*;

import java.awt.*;
import java.awt.event.*;

class LabelDemo extends JFrame
{
   LabelDemo (String title)
   {
      super (title);

      addWindowListener (new WindowAdapter ()
                         {
                             public void windowClosing (WindowEvent e)
                             {
                                System.exit (0);
                             }
                         });

      ImageIcon icon = new ImageIcon ("meteorcrater.jpg");

      JLabel jl = new JLabel ("Arizona MeteorCrater", icon,
                              JLabel.CENTER);
      jl.setHorizontalTextPosition (SwingConstants.LEADING);

      getContentPane ().add (jl);

      setSize (750, 400);
      setVisible (true);
   }

   public static void main (String [] args)
   {
      new LabelDemo ("Label Demo");
   }
}
```

`LabelDemo` creates a label combining text and an icon. The label is centered in its container by using `JLabel.CENTER`.

Note

By the way, if you look in the `JLabel` class, you won't find a constant called `CENTER`. This constant is located in the `SwingConstants` interface. Because `JLabel` implements `SwingConstants`, it's legal to specify `JLabel.CENTER`. Alternatively, you could just as easily specify `SwingConstants.CENTER`.

JLabel's `setHorizontalTextPosition` method is called to determine the location of the label's text, relative to the icon. The `LEADING` constant indicates that this text should appear to the left of the icon. (The default is `TRAILING`.)

LISTS

The `Jlist` class (located in `javax.swing` package) represents a list component from which you can choose one or more items. By default, you can choose multiple items. However, it's also possible to create a list from which a user can only choose a single item. Figure 16.14 shows a simple list.

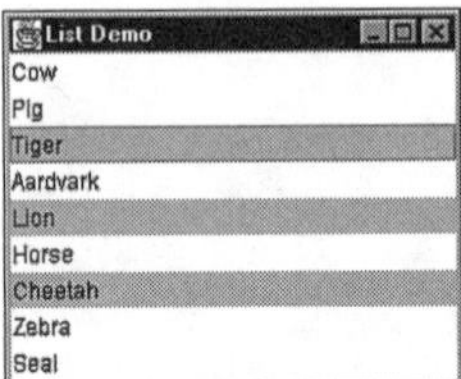

Figure 16.14
Swing's list can be used to select single or multiple items.

Figure 16.14's list was created from an application called `ListDemo`. This application's source code is presented in Listing 16.8.

LISTING 16.8 THE `ListDemo` APPLICATION SOURCE CODE

```
// ListDemo.java

import javax.swing.*;

import java.awt.event.*;

import java.util.*;

class ListDemo extends JFrame
{
   ListDemo (String title)
   {
      super (title);

      addWindowListener (new WindowAdapter ()
                         {
                             public void windowClosing (WindowEvent e)
                             {
                                System.exit (0);
                             }
                         });

      Vector v = new Vector ();
      v.add ("Cow");
      v.add ("Pig");
      v.add ("Tiger");
      v.add ("Aardvark");
      v.add ("Lion");
```

LISTING 16.8 CONTINUED

```
      v.add ("Horse");
      v.add ("Cheetah");
      v.add ("Zebra");
      v.add ("Seal");
      v.add ("Donkey");
      v.add ("Gorilla");
      v.add ("Chimpanzee");
      JList animals = new JList (v);
      animals.setSelectedIndex (0);

      // Uncomment the following line to make it possible to ONLY
      // select a single item at a time.

      // animals.setSelectionMode (ListSelectionModel.SINGLE_SELECTION);

      getContentPane ().add (animals);

      setSize (250, 200);
      setVisible (true);
   }

   public static void main (String [] args)
   {
      new ListDemo ("List Demo");
   }
}
```


`ListDemo` calls the `JList (Vector listData)` constructor to create a list. Internally, `listData` is converted into a `ListModel` object—an object created from a class that implements the `ListModel` interface, and designed to serve as the list's model.

By subclassing the abstract `AbstractListModel` class (located in `javax.swing` package), you can create your own list model and pass it to the `JList (ListModel listData)` constructor. (This class implements `ListModel`.)

Tip

You must explicitly specify the index of a list's highlighted item. If you don't, you won't see a highlighted item when the list is displayed.

You might be wondering why only nine of the twelve items are displayed. The reason is due in part to the use of the `setSize` method, rather than `pack`. If `pack` had been specified, all twelve items would be visible. However, if you had a long list of items (such as 35), not even the use of `pack` would result in all items being displayed. The reason is that lists do not possess an inherit scrolling capability. Scrolling can only be achieved by inserting a list into a scroll pane—a topic that is discussed later in this chapter.

MENUS, POP-UP MENUS, AND TOOLBARS

Menus, pop-up menus, and toolbars are staples of modern GUIs. In Chapter 14, you learned how to use the AWT's various classes to incorporate menus and pop-up menus.

However, toolbars couldn't be explored because the AWT does not support these components. Fortunately, Swing supports toolbars. In fact, Swing provides the following menu and toolbar classes:

- JCheckBoxMenuItem
- JMenuBar
- JMenu
- JMenuItem
- JPopupMenu
- JRadioButtonMenuItem
- JToolBar

As far as menu classes are concerned, you've already had a taste of what they can offer—except for `JRadioButtonMenuItem`. This latter class is used to create objects that represent a group of mutually exclusive menu items.

Suppose you want to create a toolbar. How would you accomplish this task? For an answer, check out the following code fragment:

```
JToolBar tb = new JToolBar ();

JButton jb = new JButton ("D");
jb.addActionListener (this);
tb.add (jb);

jb = new JButton ("S");
jb.addActionListener (this);
tb.add (jb);

getContentPane ().add (tb, BorderLayout.NORTH);
```

As you can see, a toolbar is a collection of buttons. You attach an action listener to each button to handle a toolbar button press event. You then call the toolbar's `add` method to add each button to the toolbar. After you're finished, you can add the toolbar to your program's content pane. Listing 16.9 presents source code to the `MPTDemo` application that demonstrates putting together a toolbar, along with a menu bar, menus, menu items, and a pop-up menu. (For more information, check out the Java Tutorial and SDK documentation.)

LISTING 16.9 THE MPTDemo APPLICATION SOURCE CODE

```
// MPTDemo.java

import javax.swing.*;

import java.awt.*;
import java.awt.event.*;

class MPTDemo extends JFrame implements ActionListener
{
   JPopupMenu pm;
```

Listing 16.9 Continued

```
MPTDemo (String title)
{
   super (title);

   addWindowListener (new WindowAdapter ()
                      {
                          public void windowClosing (WindowEvent e)
                          {
                             System.exit (0);
                          }
                      });

   JMenu plaf = new JMenu ("PLAF");

   pm = new JPopupMenu ();

   JMenuItem mi = new JMenuItem ("Default PLAF");
   mi.addActionListener (this);
   plaf.add (mi);

   mi = new JMenuItem ("Default PLAF");
   mi.addActionListener (this);
   pm.add (mi);

   mi = new JMenuItem ("System PLAF");
   mi.addActionListener (this);
   plaf.add (mi);

   mi = new JMenuItem ("System PLAF");
   mi.addActionListener (this);
   pm.add (mi);

   JMenuBar mb = new JMenuBar ();
   mb.add (plaf);
   setJMenuBar (mb);

   JToolBar tb = new JToolBar ();

   JButton jb = new JButton ("D");
   jb.addActionListener (this);
   tb.add (jb);

   jb = new JButton ("S");
   jb.addActionListener (this);
   tb.add (jb);

   getContentPane ().add (tb, BorderLayout.NORTH);

   jb = new JButton ("Hello World!");
   jb.setPreferredSize (new Dimension (200, 50));
   getContentPane ().add (jb, BorderLayout.SOUTH);

   jb.addMouseListener (new MouseAdapter ()
                        {
                            public void mousePressed (MouseEvent e)
```

LISTING 16.9 CONTINUED

```
                                   {
                                      if (e.isPopupTrigger ())
                                          pm.show (e.getComponent (),
                                                   e.getX (),
                                                   e.getY ());
                                   }

                                   public void mouseReleased (MouseEvent e)
                                   {
                                      if (e.isPopupTrigger ())
                                          pm.show (e.getComponent (),
                                                   e.getX (),
                                                   e.getY ());
                                   }
                               });

      pack ();
      setVisible (true);
   }

   public void actionPerformed (ActionEvent e)
   {
      String s = e.getActionCommand ();

      String lnfName;

      if (s.equals ("D") || s.equals ("Default PLAF"))
          lnfName = UIManager.getCrossPlatformLookAndFeelClassName ();
      else
          lnfName = UIManager.getSystemLookAndFeelClassName ();

      try
      {
          UIManager.setLookAndFeel (lnfName);
      }
      catch (Exception e2) { System.out.println (e2);}

      SwingUtilities.updateComponentTreeUI (this);
      pack ();
   }

   public static void main (String [] args)
   {
      new MPTDemo ("Menu/Pop-up Menu/Toolbar Demo1");
   }
}
```

Caution

You might be wondering why code has been duplicated in `MPTDemo`. For example, why do the `Default PLAF` and `System PLAF` menu items have to be created twice, and a separate action listener attached to each menu item. Unfortunately, if you try to share a single menu item between a `JMenu` and `JPopupMenu`, the `JMenu` will never show its items (at least not when run under Windows 98).

By using JToolBar, you get docking functionality for free. Just grab to the left of the toolbar and drag it to either the top, left, right, or bottom, or outside the window to get a free-standing toolbar.

Note

You can experiment with docking in MPTDemo. However, you will need to resize the window, otherwise the toolbar will be partially hidden by the button when docked to either the left or right of the window. (You might want to change the pack method call to a setSize method call—to create a window of a sufficiently large size.) By the way, because the button occupies the bottom portion of the window, you will not be able to dock the toolbar to the window's bottom.

PROGRESS BARS

When an activity is going to take a long time to complete, many applications use progress bars to show the activity's current status, and to help a user know that the activity is continuing. Figure 16.15 shows a progress bar.

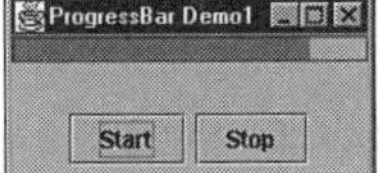

Figure 16.15 Swing's progress bar provides a visual cue to an activity's current status, and lets the user know that an activity is progressing.

Unlike the AWT, Swing provides a progress bar component via its JProgressBar class (located in the javax.swing package). Essentially, JProgressBar displays an integer value within a bounded interval. To create a JProgressBar (with either default or explicit intervals), you would call any of several constructors, as demonstrated by the following code fragment:

```
// Create a horizontal progress bar bounded by 0 and 100 (the default).
JProgressBar jpbar1 = new JProgressBar ();

// Create a horizontal progress bar bounded by 0 and 50.
JProgressBar jpbar2 = new JProgressBar (0, 50);

// Create a vertical progress bar bounded by 20 and 56.
JProgressBar jpbar3 = new JProgressBar (JProgressBar.VERTICAL, 20, 56);
```

After you have a progress bar, you can call the setValue method to update its model (which just happens to be an object created from a class that implements the BoundedRangeModel interface). In turn, the model updates the progress bar's UI delegate so that the current status is visible to users.

You can also call the setMinimum and setMaximum methods to change the progress bar's minimum and maximum bounds. (To learn more about the various methods that are offered by JProgressBar, check out the SDK documentation.)

Figure 16.15's progress bar was created from an application called `ProgressBarDemo1`. This application demonstrates creating a simple progress bar and calling some of its methods. The source code is presented in Listing 16.10.

LISTING 16.10 THE `ProgressBarDemo1` APPLICATION SOURCE CODE

```
// ProgressBarDemo1.java

import javax.swing.*;

import java.awt.*;
import java.awt.event.*;

class ProgressBarDemo1 extends JFrame
{
   JProgressBar pbar;
   ProgressThread pthread;

   ProgressBarDemo1 (String title)
   {
      super (title);

      addWindowListener (new WindowAdapter ()
                         {
                             public void windowClosing (WindowEvent e)
                             {
                                System.exit (0);
                             }
                         });

      pbar = new JProgressBar ();
      getContentPane ().add (pbar, BorderLayout.NORTH);

      JPanel jp = new JPanel ();

      ActionListener l = new ActionListener ()
                         {
                             public void actionPerformed (ActionEvent e)
                             {
                                if (pthread == null ||
                                    !pthread.isAlive ())
                                {
                                    pthread = new ProgressThread (pbar);
                                    pthread.start ();
                                }
                             }
                         };

      JButton jb = new JButton ("Start");
      jb.addActionListener (l);
      jp.add (jb);

      l = new ActionListener ()
          {
              public void actionPerformed (ActionEvent e)
              {
```

Listing 16.10 Continued

```
                 if (pthread != null)
                     pthread.setStop (true);
              }
          };

       jb = new JButton ("Stop");
       jb.addActionListener (l);
       jp.add (jb);

       getContentPane ().add (jp, BorderLayout.SOUTH);

       setSize (200, 100);
       setVisible (true);
   }

   public static void main (String [] args)
   {
      new ProgressBarDemo1 ("ProgressBar Demo1");
   }
}

class ProgressThread extends Thread
{
   JProgressBar pbar;
   boolean stopped;

   ProgressThread (JProgressBar pbar)
   {
      this.pbar = pbar;
   }

   void setStop (boolean state)
   {
      stopped = state;
   }

   public void run ()
   {
      int min = 0;
      int max = 50;

      pbar.setMinimum (min);
      pbar.setMaximum (max);
      pbar.setValue (min);

      for (int i = min; i <= max; i++)
           if (stopped)
               break;
           else
           {
               pbar.setValue (i);
               try
               {
                  Thread.sleep (100);
               }
```

LISTING 16.10 CONTINUED

```
                catch (InterruptedException e) {}
           }
    }
}
```

Progress bars require a background thread to keep them updated, and `ProgressBarDemo1` is no exception. You'll notice that its `setValue` method is called in the thread's `run` method to update the progress bar's model (which also updates the progress bar's UI delegate).

> **Note**
>
> Although thread safety hasn't been discussed, the `setValue` method is one of Swing's few thread-safe methods. As a result, it can be called from other threads. (Many of Swing's methods cannot be called from another thread. Later in this chapter, this threading issue will be addressed.)

In addition to `JProgressBar`, Swing provides the `ProgressMonitor` and `ProgressMonitorInputStream` classes. `ProgressMonitor` is used to automatically display a progress dialog box if a task takes longer than a minimum amount of time. (To get a sense of how this class is used, you'll want to check out the source code to the `ProgressBarDemo2` application, which is included with the rest of this book's source code.) `ProgressMonitorInputStream` is similar to `ProgressMonitor`. However, it's designed for monitoring stream I/O operations. (Streams are discussed in Chapter 21, "Streams, Files, and Serialization.")

RADIO BUTTONS

The `JRadioButton` class (located in `javax.swing` package) represents a radio button. This radio button has all the features of an abstract button (because `JRadioButton` indirectly inherits from the `AbstractButton` class), along with a state that can be toggled on or off (because `JRadioButton` directly inherits from the `JToggleButton` class).

Unlike check boxes, radio buttons are normally added to a button group. Only one of the buttons in this group can be selected. This allows a user to toggle between several possibilities. In contrast, check boxes are not normally added to a button group. Each check box represents a separate element of state and allows a user to toggle between a true or false value. Knowing whether to use check boxes or radio buttons is one of the challenges that faces GUI designers. Figure 16.16 presents a collection of radio buttons.

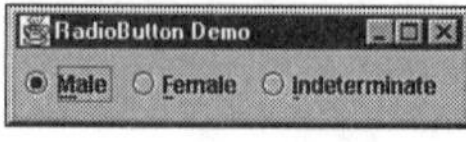

Figure 16.16
Swing's radio buttons are typically organized in button groups.

Figure 16.16's radio buttons were created from the `RadioButtonDemo` application. The source code to this application is presented in Listing 16.11.

LISTING 16.11 THE RadioButtonDemo APPLICATION SOURCE CODE

```
// RadioButtonDemo.java

import javax.swing.*;

import java.awt.event.*;

class RadioButtonDemo extends JFrame
{
   RadioButtonDemo (String title)
   {
      super (title);

      addWindowListener (new WindowAdapter ()
                         {
                             public void windowClosing (WindowEvent e)
                             {
                                System.exit (0);
                             }
                         });

      JRadioButton rb1 = new JRadioButton ("Male");
      rb1.setMnemonic (KeyEvent.VK_M);
      rb1.setActionCommand ("Male");
      rb1.setSelected (true);

      JRadioButton rb2 = new JRadioButton ("Female");
      rb2.setMnemonic (KeyEvent.VK_F);
      rb2.setActionCommand ("Female");
      rb2.setSelected (true);

      JRadioButton rb3 = new JRadioButton ("Indeterminate");
      rb3.setMnemonic (KeyEvent.VK_I);
      rb3.setActionCommand ("Indeterminate");
      rb3.setSelected (true);

      ButtonGroup bg = new ButtonGroup ();
      bg.add (rb1);
      bg.add (rb2);
      bg.add (rb3);

      JPanel jp = new JPanel ();
      jp.add (rb1);
      jp.add (rb2);
      jp.add (rb3);

      getContentPane ().add (jp);

      pack ();
      setVisible (true);
   }

   public static void main (String [] args)
   {
      new RadioButtonDemo ("RadioButton Demo");
   }
}
```

Version 1.3 of the Java 2 Platform Standard Edition corrects an oversight with button groups. In previous versions, you could establish the current button group, by calling `ButtonModel`'s `setGroup` method. However, no one thought to provide a `getGroup` method that returns this group. Adding `getGroup` to `ButtonModel` would result in code being broken. Therefore, a `getGroup` method has been added to the `DefaultButtonModel` class (which is the default model used by buttons, check boxes, and radio buttons). If you create a new button model class, you should provide a `getGroup` method—or risk breaking code.

SLIDERS AND SCROLLBARS

Sliders and scrollbars are similar components. They both allow users to select a value from a range of values. However, sliders are intended for selecting values that don't represent percentages (and display major/minor tick marks and numeric labels), whereas scrollbars are intended for selecting percentages. For example, suppose you have a slider and a scrollbar that both range from 0 to 100. If you select 25 from the slider, you are returning the number 25 from the slider's range. With the scrollbar, 25 refers to 25%. This is a subtle difference, but important enough to warrant two different classes: `JSlider` and `JScrollBar` (located in the `javax.swing` package).

Note

Because `JScrollBar` is similar to the AWT's `Scrollbar` class, and because `Scrollbar` was explored in a previous chapter, `JScrollBar` won't be discussed here.

Figure 16.17 shows a slider (along with a scrollbar).

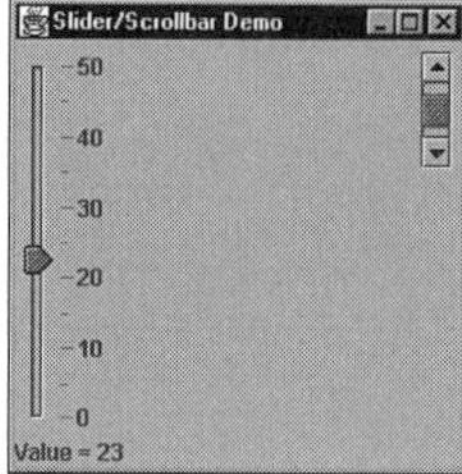

Figure 16.17
Swing's sliders can display major/minor tick marks with numeric labels.

`JSlider` provides several constructors for creating horizontal and vertical sliders. By default, tick marks and labels aren't displayed. The following code fragment calls one of these constructors to create a vertical slider with a bounded interval from 0 to 50, and an initial value of 25:

```
JSlider js = new JSlider (JSlider.VERTICAL, 0, 50, 25);
```

You can call various methods to customize the appearance and behavior of a slider. For example, `setPaintTicks` causes tick marks to be displayed, `setPaintLabels` causes labels to be displayed (only if there is sufficient major tick mark spacing), `setMajorTickSpacing` sets the amount of spacing between major tick marks, `setMinorTickSpacing` sets the amount of spacing between minor tick marks, and `setSnapToTicks` forces the knob to only point to tick marks.

Figure 16.17's slider and scroll bar were created from the `SSDemo` application. This application's source code is presented in Listing 16.12.

LISTING 16.12 THE `SSDemo` APPLICATION SOURCE CODE

```
// SSDemo.java

import javax.swing.*;
import javax.swing.event.*;

import java.awt.*;
import java.awt.event.*;

class SSDemo extends JFrame implements ChangeListener
{
   JLabel sliderValue;

   SSDemo (String title)
   {
      super (title);

      addWindowListener (new WindowAdapter ()
                         {
                             public void windowClosing (WindowEvent e)
                             {
                                System.exit (0);
                             }
                         });

      JSlider js = new JSlider (JSlider.VERTICAL, 0, 50, 25);
      js.setPaintTicks (true);
      js.setPaintLabels (true);
      js.setMajorTickSpacing (10);
      js.setMinorTickSpacing (5);
//      js.setSnapToTicks (true);
      js.addChangeListener (this);

      JPanel jp = new JPanel ();
      jp.add (js);
      getContentPane ().add (jp, BorderLayout.WEST);

      JScrollBar jsb = new JScrollBar (JScrollBar.VERTICAL, 25, 5,
                                       0, 50);

      jp = new JPanel ();
      jp.add (jsb);
      getContentPane ().add (jp, BorderLayout.EAST);

      sliderValue = new JLabel ("Value = 25");
      getContentPane ().add (sliderValue, BorderLayout.SOUTH);

      setSize (250, 250);
      setVisible (true);
   }

   public void stateChanged (ChangeEvent e)
```

LISTING 16.12 CONTINUED

```
   {
      sliderValue.setText ("Value = " + ((JSlider) e.getSource ())
                                             .getValue ());
   }

   public static void main (String [] args)
   {
      new SSDemo ("Slider/Scrollbar Demo");
   }
}
```

`SSDemo` displays a vertical slider, vertical scrollbar, and a label. When you move the slider's knob, a change event is fired which results in the label being updated. (Nothing happens when you move the scrollbar.)

By default, the slider does not snap to ticks. However, you can observe this behavior by uncommenting the `js.setSnapToTicks (true);` method call.

TABLES

One of the application categories that resulted in the success of personal computers is the spreadsheet. Spreadsheets present data in a table-oriented view. Swing's `JTable` class makes it possible to incorporate such tables into your programs. (This class is located in the `javax.swing` package.) Figure 16.18 illustrates a simple two-column table.

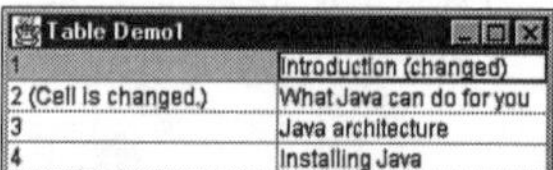

Figure 16.18 Creating tables with Swing is easy.

Listing 16.13 presents source code to the `TableDemo1` application. This application was used to create Figure 16.18's GUI.

LISTING 16.13 THE `TableDemo1` APPLICATION SOURCE CODE

```
// TableDemo1.java

import javax.swing.*;

import java.awt.event.*;

class TableDemo1 extends JFrame
{
   TableDemo1 (String title)
   {
      super (title);

      addWindowListener (new WindowAdapter ()
```

Listing 16.13 Continued

```
                          {
                             public void windowClosing (WindowEvent e)
                             {
                                System.exit (0);
                             }
                          });

      String [][] data =
      {
         { "1", "Introduction" },
         { "2", "What Java can do for you" },
         { "3", "Java architecture" },
         { "4", "Installing Java" },
         { "5", "JDK tools" }
      };

      String [] columnNames = { "Chapter Number", "Chapter Title" };

      JTable jt = new JTable (data, columnNames);

      getContentPane ().add (jt);

      setSize (300, 90);
      setVisible (true);
   }

   public static void main (String [] args)
   {
      new TableDemo1 ("Table Demo1");
   }
}
```


Note

As with `ListDemo`, `TableDemo1` does not display all rows of information. Once again, the reason is due to `JTable`'s lack of support for scrolling. To remedy this situation, the `JTable` would need to be inserted into a scroll pane–a topic that is discussed later in this chapter.

`TableDemo1` creates a table, by calling a `JTable` constructor. For example, `JTable (Object [][] rowData, Object [] columnNames)` is called to establish a two-column table. A two-dimensional array of objects is passed. Each array row contains the data for all columns in a table row. Furthermore, a one-dimensional array of column names is passed to add some class to this table. (These column names will only be displayed if the table is inserted into a scroll pane.)

Although it's not hard to create a basic table, you lose a lot of flexibility. For example, you can modify the data in any of the table's cells. The only way to create a read-only table (amongst other things), is to provide your own table model. As a result, Listing 16.14 presents source code to the `TableDemo2` application, which does just this.

LISTING 16.14 THE TableDemo2 APPLICATION SOURCE CODE

```
// TableDemo2.java

import javax.swing.*;
import javax.swing.event.*;
import javax.swing.table.*;

import java.awt.event.*;

class TableDemo2 extends JFrame implements TableModelListener
{
   TableDemo2 (String title)
   {
      super (title);

      addWindowListener (new WindowAdapter ()
                         {
                             public void windowClosing (WindowEvent e)
                             {
                                System.exit (0);
                             }
                         });


      JTable jt = new JTable (new MyTableModel ());
//      jt.setSelectionMode (ListSelectionModel.SINGLE_SELECTION);
      jt.getModel ().addTableModelListener (this);

      getContentPane ().add (jt);

      setSize (300, 90);
      setVisible (true);
   }

   public void tableChanged (TableModelEvent e)
   {
      System.out.println ("Affected column = " + e.getColumn ());
      System.out.println ("First affected row = " + e.getFirstRow ());
      System.out.println ("Last affected row = " + e.getLastRow ());
   }

   public static void main (String [] args)
   {
      new TableDemo2 ("Table Demo2");
   }
}

class MyTableModel extends AbstractTableModel
{
   private String [][] data =
   {
      { "1", "Introduction" },
      { "2", "What Java can do for you" },
      { "3", "Java architecture" },
      { "4", "Installing Java" },
      { "5", "JDK tools" }
```

LISTING 16.14 CONTINUED

```
   };

   private String [] columnNames =
   {
      "Chapter Number",
      "Chapter Title"
   };

   public int getRowCount ()
   {
      return data.length;
   }

   public int getColumnCount ()
   {
      // Assume that all rows have the same number of columns.
      // As you probably know, it is possible for each row in
      // a Java array to have a different number of columns.

      return data [0].length;
   }

   public Object getValueAt (int row, int column)
   {
      return data [row] [column];
   }

   public boolean isCellEditable (int row, int column)
   {
      return (column == 1) ? false : true;
   }

   public void setValueAt (Object value, int row, int col)
   {
      if (value instanceof String)
      {
          data [row] [col] = (String) value;

          // Must fire a table model event so that views are
          // notified about the change to the table's model.

          fireTableCellUpdated (row, col);
      }
   }
}
```


Note

`TableDemo2` subtly raises the hotly-debated issue of readability versus terseness in source code. If you look at the `isCellEditable` method, you'll notice the `return (column == 1) ? true : false;` statement. This statement could be alternatively specified as `return (column != 1);`. Many developers consider the former statement to be more readable than the second statement–which is considered to be rather terse. The reason the first statement is considered more readable is that its meaning "jumps out at most people,"

> whereas one might need to think for a few moments to comprehend the meaning of the second statement. In some coding shops (where this author has worked), readability was preferred over terseness. Although some developers suggest that readability results in extra compiled code (which can slow down execution), an optimizing compiler can generate the same code for either statement. As a result, there's often no need to resort to terseness.

`TableDemo2` demonstrates quite a few items. First, `JTable`'s `setSelectionMode` method can be called to change a table from the default multiple selection mode (in which multiple rows can be selected) to a single selection mode (in which only one row can be selected).

Second, by creating a `MyTableModel` class that extends the abstract `AbstractTableModel` class (located in the `javax.swing.table` package), and overriding key methods, a new model is established that simplifies table data management. The `isCellEditable` method is one of these overridden methods. This method determines if a cell is editable or read only. When a user moves from cell to cell, this method is called with arguments that identify the current cell. If a Boolean `false` value is returned, the cell is read only. `TableDemo2` ensures that all cells in the second column are read-only by returning false, from `isCellEditable`, when the user is in column 1. (Row and column indices are zero-based.)

Finally, the table's model is retrieved (by calling `getModel`) and its `addTableModelListener` method is called to register the application as a listener to changes in the table's model. So, what changes this model? Look at `MyTableModel` and note the `setValueAt` method. When this method is called, it changes model data. It also calls the model's `fireTableCellUpdated` method to alert all table model listeners, by calling their `tableChanged` methods.

There is so much more that could be said about tables. Cell editors is one example. You would use a cell editor (such as a combo box) to more conveniently select or enter cell data. To learn more, you are encouraged to explore your SDK documenation and the Java Tutorial.

Version 1.3 of the Java 2 Platform Standard Edition makes several improvements to the `JTable` class. These improvements include a performance benefit for tables with many columns, the ability to dynamically change an individual row's height, simplified creation of nonstandard editor components (by way of the `AbstractCellEditor` class), and improved handling of inter-cell spacing. Because of these improvements, quite a few methods have been deprecated. (For more information, check out the table section of the new Swing features in the SDK documentation.)

TEXT

It would be an understatement to say that Swing has enlarged upon the AWT's `TextArea` and `TextField` classes (for working with text). In fact, so much work has been done on enhancing Swing's text component capabilities, that an entire chapter is needed to adequately cover this material. Unfortunately, there just isn't enough room to provide such coverage in this chapter. Therefore, you're strongly encouraged to review the excellent coverage of this material in the Java Tutorial (and SDK documentation).

Swing's text component classes descend from `JTextComponent`. This class identifies what it means to be a text component. As you work through the SDK documentation, you'll encounter `JTextField`, `JTextArea`, `JPasswordField`, `JEditorPane`, and a lot more classes. To give you a small sense of what Swing's text components can do, take a quick look at the `JEditorPane` class.

Have you ever wanted to create a Web browser? If the answer is yes, you'll need to explore Swing's `JEditorPane` class. Not only does `JEditorPane` make it possible to view Web pages, you can also use this class to view RTF (Rich Text Format) files. (Microsoft Word is capable of generating RTF files.) Figure 16.19 shows part of the main Web page from the Java Tutorial rendered by `JEditorPane`.

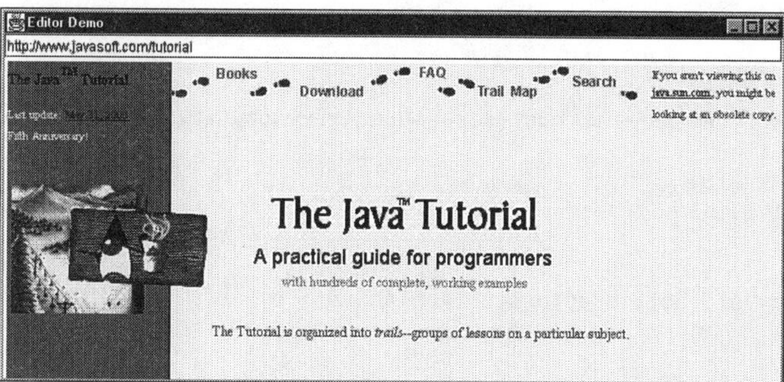

Figure 16.19 Swing's editor pane can be used to view a Web page.

Listing 16.15 presents source code to the `EditorDemo` application. This application was used to provide the GUI in Figure 16.19.

LISTING 16.15 THE `EditorDemo` APPLICATION SOURCE CODE

```
// EditorDemo.java

import javax.swing.*;
import javax.swing.event.*;

import java.awt.*;
import java.awt.event.*;

import java.net.*;

class EditorDemo extends JFrame
                 implements ActionListener, HyperlinkListener
{
   JEditorPane view;
   JTextField commandLine;

   EditorDemo (String title)
   {
      super (title);

      addWindowListener (new WindowAdapter ()
```

LISTING 16.15 CONTINUED

```
                              {
                                 public void windowClosing (WindowEvent e)
                                 {
                                    System.exit (0);
                                 }
                              });

      commandLine = new JTextField ();
      commandLine.addActionListener (this);
      getContentPane ().add (commandLine, BorderLayout.NORTH);

      view = new JEditorPane ();
      view.setEditable (false);
      view.setPreferredSize (new Dimension (400, 400));
      view.addHyperlinkListener (this);

      getContentPane ().add (view, BorderLayout.CENTER);

      pack ();
      setVisible (true);
   }

   public void actionPerformed (ActionEvent e)
   {
      try
      {
         URL url = new URL (e.getActionCommand ());
         view.setPage (url);
         commandLine.setText (url.toExternalForm ());
      }
      catch (MalformedURLException e2)
      {
         System.out.println ("Bad URL: " + e.getActionCommand ());
      }
      catch (java.io.IOException e2) {}
   }

   public void hyperlinkUpdate (HyperlinkEvent e)
   {
      try
      {
         view.setPage (e.getURL ());
         commandLine.setText (e.getURL ().toExternalForm ());
      }
      catch (java.io.IOException e2) {}
   }

   public static void main (String [] args)
   {
      new EditorDemo ("Editor Demo");
   }
}
```

Caution

To run `EditorDemo` from behind a firewall, you could issue the following command line:

```
java -Dhttp.proxyHost=<host> -Dhttp.proxyPort=<port> EditorDemo
```

Replace `<host>` with the appropriate proxy host and `<port>` with the appropriate port.

`EditorDemo` uses two different components: a `JEditorPane` and a `JTextField`. The editor pane displays a Web page, and the text field holds the address of this Web page. To use `EditorDemo`, type an address in the text field and press the `Return` key.

You can travel from Web page to Web page by positioning the mouse pointer over a link.

Note

To force `EditorDemo` to only follow a link when the link is clicked, you need place the following code fragment before the try/catch construct in the `hyperlinkUpdate` method:

```
if (e.getEventType () != HyperLinkEvent.EventType.ACTIVATED)
    return;
```

In response to moving the mouse pointer over a link, the editor pane fires a hyperlink event, which results in a `HyperLinkEvent` object being passed to a hyperlink listener's `hyperLinkUpdate` method. This method calls the editor pane's `setPage` method to establish the new Web page as the current Web page. Furthermore, the address URL's `toExternalForm` method is called to present a user-oriented Web address (for the new Web page) in the text field.

Caution

`JEditorPane` only supports HTML 3.2. As a result, it cannot correctly render Web pages that use more recent HTML tags.

Trees

Trees are important components in modern GUIs, and are popular with programs that display hierarchical data (such as directories and files).

Trees are made up of *nodes* (structures of data). Each node represents either a leaf or a branch. A *leaf* is a distinct element that has no children (subelements). In other words, leaves cannot be *expanded* (opened) and *collapsed* (closed). In contrast, a *branch* is a distinct element that can have children. Furthermore, branches can be expanded and collapsed.

Swing introduces the `JTree` class (located in the `javax.swing` package) for working with trees. Furthermore, Swing provides the `DefaultMutableTreeNode` class to meet most (if not all) of your node-based needs. (This class is located in the `javax.swing.tree` package.)

To give you a small taste for trees, Listing 16.16 presents source code to the `TreeDemo` application.

LISTING 16.16 THE TreeDemo APPLICATION SOURCE CODE

```
// TreeDemo.java

import javax.swing.*;
import javax.swing.event.*;
import javax.swing.tree.*;

import java.awt.event.*;

class TreeDemo extends JFrame implements TreeSelectionListener
{
   TreeDemo (String title)
   {
      super (title);

      addWindowListener (new WindowAdapter ()
                         {
                             public void windowClosing (WindowEvent e)
                             {
                                System.exit (0);
                             }
                         });

      DefaultMutableTreeNode rootNode = createNodes ();
      JTree tree = new JTree (rootNode);
      tree.addTreeSelectionListener (this);
      tree.setRootVisible (true);

      getContentPane ().add (tree);

      setSize (400, 300);
      setVisible (true);
   }

   DefaultMutableTreeNode createNodes ()
   {
      DefaultMutableTreeNode root;
      root = new DefaultMutableTreeNode ("Java");

      DefaultMutableTreeNode resources;
      resources = new DefaultMutableTreeNode ("Resources");

      DefaultMutableTreeNode books;
      books = new DefaultMutableTreeNode ("Books");

      books.add (new DefaultMutableTreeNode ("Java 2 By Example"));
      books.add (new DefaultMutableTreeNode ("Special Edition Using " +
                                             "Java 2 Platform " +
                                             "Standard Edition"));

      resources.add (books);

      DefaultMutableTreeNode magazines;
      magazines = new DefaultMutableTreeNode ("Magazines");

      magazines.add (new DefaultMutableTreeNode ("JavaWorld"));
```

LISTING 16.16 CONTINUED

```
      resources.add (magazines);

      DefaultMutableTreeNode webSites;
      webSites = new DefaultMutableTreeNode ("Web sites");

      webSites.add (new DefaultMutableTreeNode ("Gamelan"));
      webSites.add (new DefaultMutableTreeNode ("Javasoft"));

      resources.add (webSites);

      root.add (resources);

      DefaultMutableTreeNode tools;
      tools = new DefaultMutableTreeNode ("Tools");

      tools.add (new DefaultMutableTreeNode ("JDK"));
      tools.add (new DefaultMutableTreeNode ("Kawa"));
      tools.add (new DefaultMutableTreeNode ("Visual Age for Java"));

      root.add (tools);

      return root;
   }

   public void valueChanged (TreeSelectionEvent e)
   {
      TreePath path;
      path = (TreePath) e.getNewLeadSelectionPath ();

      System.out.println (path);
   }

   public static void main (String [] args)
   {
      new TreeDemo ("Tree Demo");
   }
}
```


`TreeDemo` uses `DefaultMutableTreeNode` to build and connect several nodes into a tree. Furthermore, it registers itself as a listener for tree selection events. When a tree selection event is fired, `TreeDemo`'s `valueChanged` method is called. This method calls `TreeSelectionEvent`'s `getNewLeadSelectionPath` method to obtain the path from the root branch node to the selected branch or leaf node. Figure 16.20 shows `TreeDemo`'s tree with all its branches expanded.

Note

As with `JList` and `JTable`, `JTree` is not inherently scrollable. To remedy this situation, the `JTable` object would need to be inserted into a scroll pane—a topic that is discussed later in this chapter.

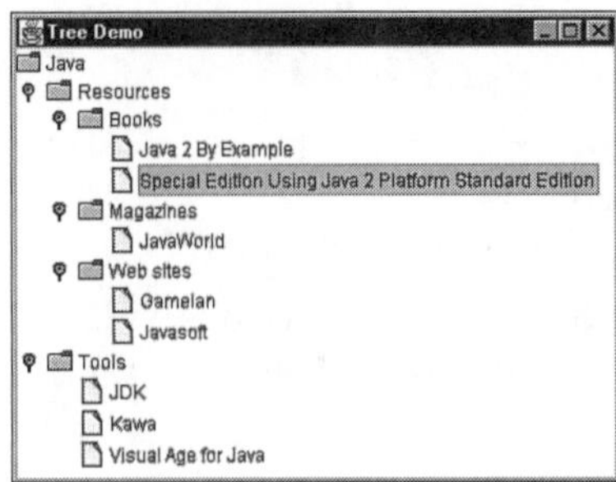

Figure 16.20
Swing's trees make it easier to navigate hierarchies.

Version 1.3 of the Java 2 Platform Standard Edition adds several new properties and methods to the `JTree` class. For example, the new toggle click property can be used for configuring how many mouse clicks are needed to expand and collapse a node. (For more information, check out the tree section of the new Swing features in the SDK documentation. This information can be found online at `http://java.sun.com/j2se/1.3/docs/relnotes/features.html`.)

EXPLORING CONTAINERS

Swing provides four top-level container classes that correspond to the AWT's `Applet`, `Dialog`, `Frame`, and `Window` classes: `JApplet`, `JDialog`, `JFrame`, and `JWindow`. Swing applets use instances of `JApplet` as their top-level containers, whereas Swing applications use `JFrame`. Furthermore, instances of `JDialog` serve as top-level containers for dialog boxes with users, and instances of `JWindow` represent pop-up windows that serve various needs (not met by the other top-level containers). In either case, a dialog box or window must be associated with an applet or frame.

Swing's top-level containers are organized into a series of panes: root pane, layered pane, content pane, and glass pane. The *root pane* manages the layered pane, content pane, and glass pane. The *layered pane* organizes components into a Z-order to handle situations in which components overlap. The *content pane* contains all components except for the menu bar. Finally, the *glass pane* (hidden and transparent by default) can be used to paint content over multiple components and intercept events.

A reference to the root pane can be obtained, by calling a top-level container's `getRootPane` method. You can use this reference to add a default button to a container (among other things). However, as a rule, you'll rarely need to access this pane. (Top-level containers have a `setRootPane` method, but it's protected.)

A reference to the content pane can be obtained by calling a top-level container's `getContentPane` method. (You've already seen quite a few examples of the content pane.) By default, the content pane uses a border layout manager. If you like, you can replace the current content pane by calling `setContentPane`, as the following code fragment demonstrates:

```
JPanel jp = new JPanel ();
setContentPane (jp);
```

A reference to the layered pane can be obtained by calling a top-level container's `getLayeredPane` method. You can also replace the current layered pane by calling `setLayeredPane`. (You create a new layered pane by using the `JLayeredPane` class.)

A layered pane consists of several layers. Each layer represents a Z-order position for handling situations in which components overlap. For example, when you activate a pop-up menu, you don't want an underlying button to appear over the pop-up. (Your users wouldn't be too happy.) By using layers, Swing orchestrates painting so that overlap is properly handled. Table 16.1 presents the various layers (in a back to front manner—the frame content layer is the closest to the back of the Z-order and the drag layer is the closest to the front).

TABLE 16.1 `JLayeredPane`'S VARIOUS LAYERS

Layer Constant	Description
`FRAME_CONTENT_LAYER`	This layer positions the applet's/frame's content pane and menu bar. The root pane adds the menu bar and content pane to its layered pane at this layer.
`DEFAULT_LAYER`	This is the default layer where most components are placed.
`PALETTE_LAYER`	Floating toolbars and palettes use this layer.
`MODAL_LAYER`	Modal internal frame dialog boxes are placed in this layer.
`POPUP_LAYER`	Pop-up menus are placed in this layer, so they can appear over almost everything else.
`DRAG_LAYER`	A component is moved to this layer when dragging, and returned to its own layer when dropped.

A reference to the glass pane can be obtained by calling a top-level container's `getGlassPane` method. You can also replace the current glass pane by calling `setGlassPane`. (The Java Tutorial provides an interesting example of using a glass pane.)

In addition to these panes, there are other panes that can be used for special purposes. These panes include desktop, scroll, tabbed, option, and split.

DESKTOP PANES AND INTERNAL FRAMES

Microsoft Windows 3.0 and 3.1 introduced the world to the idea of multiple document interfaces (MDI). Basically, each document would be placed in a separate window, and the various windows would be managed by a container window. Microsoft decided to abandon this idea when it released Windows 95. However, MDI is still useful.

Swing supports MDI through its `JDesktopPane` and `JInternalFrame` classes (located in the `javax.swing` package). Figure 16.21 shows what a GUI using these classes looks like.

The following code fragment, taken from the `DesktopPaneDemo` program (whose source code is included with the rest of this book's source code), shows how to set up a desktop pane and one internal frame.

```
JDesktopPane desktop = new JDesktopPane ();
JInternalFrame jf1 = new JInternalFrame ("First Window");
JLabel jl = new JLabel ("Label #1");
jf1.getContentPane ().add (jl);
jf1.setSize (150, 75);
jf1.setVisible (true);
desktop.add (jf1);
```

Figure 16.21
Swing's desktop pane and internal frames are used to achieve MDI.

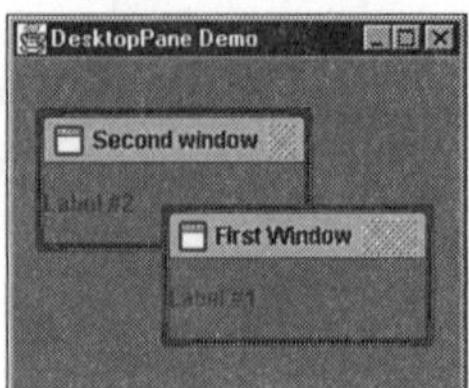

SCROLL PANES AND VIEWPORTS

`JList`, `JTable`, and `JTree` don't scroll their data. Unlike `JComboBox`, there is no inherit scrolling ability in these classes. As a result, if some of the data is not visible, you just can't access it. However, Swing comes to the rescue, by providing a common scrolling component known as a scroll pane.

Scroll panes are created from the `JScrollPane` class. This class works in conjunction with `JViewPort` to manage a container's scrolling needs. Figure 16.22 shows what the `TreeDemo` program would look like with scrollbars.

Note

The program used to generate this figure is called `ScrollPaneDemo3`. It contains the same source code as `TreeDemo`, except for class name changes and some scrolling code. `ScrollPaneDemo3`–and two other scroll pane demo programs that add scrolling to a list and table–are included with this book's source code.

Figure 16.22
Swing's `JScrollPane` and `JViewPort` classes help users access all data.

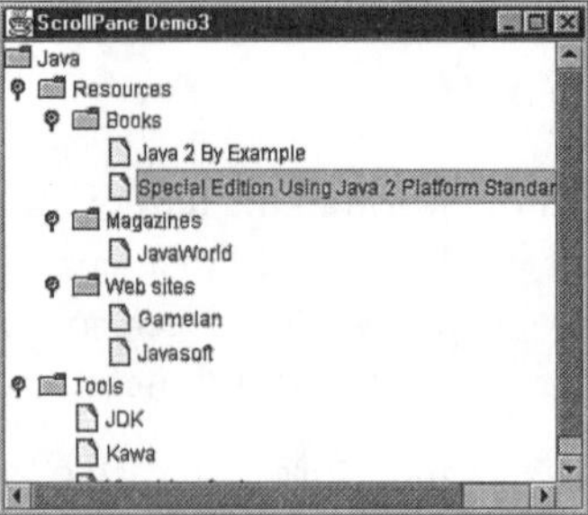

The following code fragment, taken from `ScrollPaneDemo3`, shows how easy it is to add scrolling behavior to a component:

```
JScrollPane jsp = new JScrollPane ();
jsp.setViewportView (tree);
getContentPane ().add (jsp);
```

TABBED PANES

Tabbed panes work like the AWT's card layout manager. They allow you to place components on different tabs and switch from one tab to another. Swing's `JTabbedPane` class (located in the `javax.swing` package) is used to create tabbed panes.

Listing 16.17 presents source code to the `TabbedPaneDemo` program that demonstrates tabbed panes.

LISTING 16.17 THE `TabbedPaneDemo` APPLICATION SOURCE CODE

```
// TabbedPaneDemo.java

import javax.swing.*;

import java.awt.event.*;

class TabbedPaneDemo extends JFrame
{
   TabbedPaneDemo (String title)
   {
      super (title);

      addWindowListener (new WindowAdapter ()
                         {
                             public void windowClosing (WindowEvent e)
                             {
                                System.exit (0);
                             }
                         });

      JTabbedPane tabs = new JTabbedPane (SwingConstants.BOTTOM);
      tabs.addTab ("First tab", new JLabel ("Hello!"));
      tabs.addTab ("Second tab", new JButton ("Goodbye!"));

      getContentPane ().add (tabs);

      setSize (250, 200);
      setVisible (true);
   }

   public static void main (String [] args)
   {
      new TabbedPaneDemo ("TabbedPane Demo");
   }
}
```

`TabbedPaneDemo` calls the `JTabbedPane (int location)` constructor, with a `location` argument set to `SwingUtilities.BOTTOM`, that identifies the bottom of the GUI as the place to display the tab markers. (You can also pass either of `SwingUtilities`' `TOP`, `LEFT`, or `RIGHT` constants.) After the tabbed pane is created, its `addTab` method is called to add a label to the first tab and a button to the second tab. Figure 16.23 shows the resulting GUI.

Figure 16.23
Swing's `JTabbedPane` class can help you manage screen space.

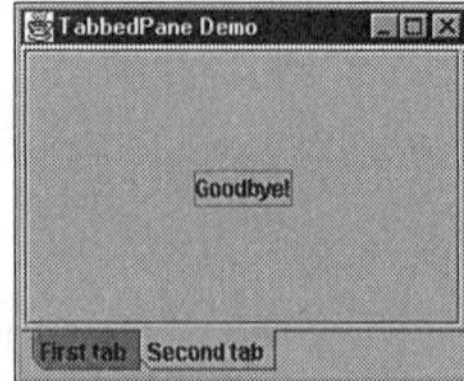

Version 1.3 of the Java 2 Platform Standard Edition adds a pair of methods to the `JTabbedPane` class, making it possible to associate ToolTips with individual tabs. (For more information, check out the tabbed pane section of the new Swing features in the SDK documentation.)

OPTION AND SPLIT PANES

Two panes have not yet been explored: option and split. An option pane (created from the `JOptionPane` class) is used to activate a standard dialog box (such as confirmation, input, and message dialog boxes) by using one of its class methods. For example, the following method displays an error message dialog box (as opposed to warning message or question message dialog boxes):

```
JOptionPane.showMessageDialog (null, "File deleted", "Error",
                               JOptionPane.ERROR_MESSAGE);
```

The `null` argument indicates that the dialog box is independent of a parent component. The `"File deleted"` string serves as the message dialog box's message. The `"Error"` string appears in the dialog box's title bar. Finally, the `ERROR_MESSAGE` constant (one of several) identifies the type of message dialog box.

Each of `JOptionPane`'s `showInputDialog` methods returns a null reference when the user selects the dialog's `Cancel` button.

A split pane (created from the `JSplitPane` class) is used to graphically divide a pair of components. For more information (and examples), consult the SDK documentation and the Java Tutorial.

EXPLORING LAYOUT MANAGERS

There are no restrictions on using the AWT's layout managers with your Swing programs. However, you might prefer using Swing's box layout manager. Box offers features that are similar to the AWT's more complex grid-bag layout manager, but is much easier to use—and respects a component's maximum size and alignment. Furthermore, Swing simplifies the manner in which a component's minimum, preferred, and maximum sizes (along with alignment) are specified.

BOXES

The box layout manager allows multiple components to be laid out horizontally or vertically. When its container is resized, box layout causes horizontally laid out components to stay in a horizontal row and vertically laid out components to stay in a vertical column.

Objects created from the `BoxLayout` class (located in the `javax.swing` package) represent box layout managers. Call the `BoxLayout (Container target, int axis)` constructor to create a box that lays out its components (in the `target` container) along a major axis (specified by the `axis` argument). Either `BoxLayout.X_AXIS` (for laying out components in a horizontal row) or `BoxLayout.Y_AXIS` (for laying out components in a vertical column) can be specified as the `axis` argument. For example, the following code fragment creates a box layout manager that lays out its components in a vertical column:

```
JPanel jp = new JPanel ();
jp.setLayout (new BoxLayout (jp, BoxLayout.Y_AXIS));
```

To see what this looks like, check out Figure 16.24. This figure shows the output from the `BoxLayoutDemo1` application. (This application's source code is included with the rest of the book's source code).

Figure 16.24
Swing's box layout manager can lay out components in a vertical column.

Swing provides a convenient `Box` class that creates containers with a box layout manager. To create this container, call the `Box (int axis)` constructor and identify the major axis via the `axis` argument. This is demonstrated in the following code fragment:

```
Box b = new Box (BoxLayout.X_AXIS);
```

`Box` provides several methods for precisely controlling alignment. These methods create invisible components, known as struts, glues, and rigid areas.

A *strut* is a fixed-width invisible component that forces a certain amount of space between two components. Call `createVerticalStrut` to specify the number of empty pixels that separate two vertical components, or `createHorizontalStrut` to specify the number of empty pixels that separate two horizontal components. The following code fragment uses `createHorizontalStrut` to reserve 10 pixels of empty space between two horizontal components (and assumes that the previous code fragment was just executed):

```
b.add (new JLabel ("First"));
b.add (Box.createHorizontalStrut (10));
b.add (new JLabel ("Second"));
```

A *glue* is an invisible component that expands to fill space between other components. It's typically used in a horizontal box in which components have a maximum width, or a vertical box in which components have a maximum height. Call `createHorizontalGlue` or `createVerticalGlue` to create a glue between two horizontal components or two vertical components. The following code fragment adds horizontal glue between two labels:

```
b.add (new JLabel ("First"));
b.add (Box.createHorizontalGlue ());
b.add (new JLabel ("Second"));
```

Finally, a *rigid area* is an invisible component with a specific width and height. You can depend on this component "wasting" a precise number of pixels in your container. The `createRigidArea` method is called with a `Dimension` argument that specifies the size of a rigid area. The region that's identified by this argument will consist of empty pixels. The following code fragment demonstrates the use of this method to reserve a rigid area of 10×20 pixels:

```
b.add (Box.createRigidArea (new Dimension (10, 20)));
```

To learn more about glues and struts, check out the source code to `BoxLayoutDemo2`, in Listing 16.18.

LISTING 16.18 THE `BoxLayoutDemo2` APPLICATION SOURCE CODE

```
// BoxLayoutDemo2.java

import javax.swing.*;

import java.awt.*;
import java.awt.event.*;

class BoxLayoutDemo2 extends JFrame
{
   BoxLayoutDemo2 (String title)
   {
      super (title);

      addWindowListener (new WindowAdapter ()
                         {
                             public void windowClosing (WindowEvent e)
                             {
                                System.exit (0);
                             }
                         });

      Box box = Box.createHorizontalBox ();
      box.add (Box.createHorizontalStrut (10));
      JButton jb = new JButton ("Left button");
      box.add (jb);
      box.add (Box.createHorizontalGlue ());
      jb = new JButton ("Right button");
      box.add (jb);
      box.add (Box.createHorizontalStrut (10));
```

LISTING 16.18 CONTINUED

```
      getContentPane ().add (box);

      setSize (300, 100);
      setVisible (true);
   }

   public static void main (String [] args)
   {
      new BoxLayoutDemo2 ("Box Layout Demo2");
   }
}
```


`BoxLayoutDemo2` creates a horizontal box layout. The first and last components are invisible struts that are 10 pixels wide. They reserve margins around the left and right edges of the container. A glue component is placed between both labels, so extra space will appear between the labels, and not to the right of the right-most label.

SIZING AND ALIGNMENT

To determine a component's minimum and preferred sizes, the AWT's layout managers call a component's `getMinimumSize` and `getPreferredSize` methods. The only way the AWT lets you specify new minimum and preferred sizes is to subclass a component's class and override these methods. However, Swing's `JComponent` class provides `setMinimumSize` and `setPreferredSize` methods to achieve the same goal—without subclassing.

If you study the `Component` class, you'll discover `getMaximumSize`. This method returns the maximum size of a component. However, it was never called by the AWT's layout managers, so `getMaximumSize` was never used. However, the box layout manager supports maximum sizes, and `JComponent` provides a more convenient `setMaximumSize` method to specify this size.

Figure 16.24 appears to violate what the SDK documentation says about `BoxLayout`. To quote from this documentation, "`BoxLayout` attempts to make all components in the column as wide as the widest component." However, when you look at this figure, these components have different sizes. What's going on?

`BoxLayout` will only draw a component up to its maximum size, and a component's maximum size is generally the same as its preferred size. Therefore, if you want the component to be drawn wider, you must change this maximum size. This task is accomplished by calling `setMaximumSize`. Figure 16.25 shows the resulting GUI from the `BoxLayoutDemo3` application that does just this. (`BoxLayoutDemo3`'s source code is included with the rest of this book's source code.)

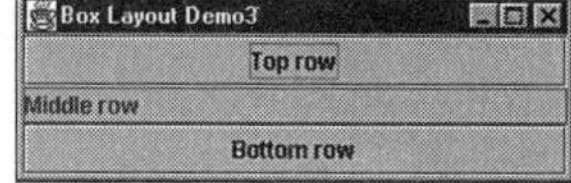

Figure 16.25 Swing's box layout manager stretches its components to their maximum sizes.

While studying `Component`, you'll probably encounter `getAlignmentX` and `getAlignmentY`. These methods return alignment data (as floating point values between 0.0 and 1.0) that indicate how to align components (left, right, centered, or somewhere in between). However, the AWT's layout managers do not use this information, although it's used by box layout to more accurately position components. To eliminate the need for subclassing, `JComponent` provides the `setAlignmentX` and `setAlignmentY` methods to specify this information.

Suppose you want to align three vertical components with the right-hand side of a container. You would call `setAlignmentX` with a `RIGHT_ALIGNMENT` argument for each component. (The `RIGHT_ALIGNMENT` constant is inherited from the `Component` class.) Figure 16.26 shows the resulting alignment. (The source code to the `BoxLayoutDemo4` application that was used to produce this illustration is included with the rest of this book's source code.)

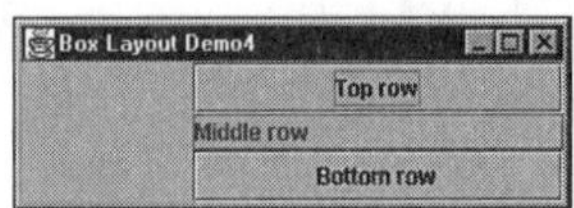

Figure 16.26
Swing's box layout manager can align components in a container.

> **Caution**
>
> All components in a column should be aligned using the same alignment. Otherwise, weird looking GUIs will result. For example, if a column is to consist of three right-aligned components, call `setAlignmentX (RIGHT_ALIGNMENT)` for each component.

Validation, Invalidation, and Revalidation

When a developer begins writing AWT and Swing programs, she is often faced with trying to figure out why the GUI isn't being properly laid out. For example, an AWT label is assigned text (by calling its `setText` method) and this text is truncated. To understand this situation, it's important to have a good understanding of how validation, invalidation, and revalidation work.

In a nutshell, *validation* is the process of making sure that all components are properly sized and laid out in their containers. In contrast, *invalidation* is the process of marking a component and/or a container as being invalid in response to modifying a component (by changing its font, text, and so on). Finally, *revalidation* is a concept (introduced by Swing) that is similar to validation.

Validation is achieved by calling `validate`, and invalidation is a achieved by calling `invalidate`. (As you learned in Chapter 14, the `Component` and `Container` classes have their own versions of these methods.) Finally, revalidation is achieved by calling `JComponent`'s `revalidate` method. Understanding how these methods work will help you understand why your GUIs aren't always laid out according to your desires. You first need to consider `validate` and `invalidate` by investigating AWT code. Then, you will move on to Swing code, where `revalidate` can be explored.

Validation and invalidation will be explored by studying an AWT application called `ValidationDemo1`. This application presents a GUI with a label and two buttons—`Change` and `Restore`. Initially, this label displays `Hello`. If the `Change` button is clicked, the label displays `Hello World`. If `Restore` is clicked, the label reverts to displaying `Hello`. In either case, the following code fragment (taken from `ValidationDemo1`) is executed (it assumes the existence of a `Label` object called `l`):

```
System.out.println ("Label validity: " + l.isValid ());
System.out.println ("Label's container validity: " + isValid ());
System.out.println ("Label's preferred size: " + l.getPreferredSize ());
System.out.println ("Label's minimum size: " + l.getMinimumSize ());
System.out.println ("Label's maximum size: " + l.getMaximumSize ());

if (e.getActionCommand ().equals ("Change"))
    l.setText ("Hello World");
else
    l.setText ("Hello");

if (option != NOTHING)
{
    setSize (getPreferredSize ());

    if (option == SIZE_AND_VALIDATE)
        validate ();
}

System.out.println ("Label validity: " + l.isValid ());
System.out.println ("Label's container validity: " + isValid ());
System.out.println ("Label's preferred size: " + l.getPreferredSize ());
System.out.println ("Label's minimum size: " + l.getMinimumSize ());
System.out.println ("Label's maximum size: " + l.getMaximumSize ());
```

Before studying this code fragment, take a look at Figure 16.27. This figure displays three windows. The top window appears when the program is run without any command arguments. It displays the GUI after the `Change` button is clicked. Notice that the label's text is truncated. The middle window appears when the program is run with a command argument of `s` (for sizing). As you can see, the window has been resized. However, the button's text is still truncated. Finally, the bottom window appears when the program is run with a command argument of `v` (for sizing and validation). In addition to the window being resized, validation ensures that this text is not truncated.

Figure 16.27 `ValidationDemo1`'s GUI is shown when no arguments (top), an `s` argument, and a `v` argument (bottom) are specified.

Whether or not command arguments are specified, assume that a user has just clicked the `Change` button (for the first time and has not clicked the `Restore` button), and that the preceding code fragment is being executed.

The System.out.println method calls output information about the label and its parent container. When this code is first executed, the isValid method calls return a Boolean true value. (At this point, both the label and its container are in a valid state.) Furthermore, the label's preferred and minimum sizes are equal, and the maximum size (which is not used by the AWT, but is included for completeness) suggests that the component can grow to 32,767 by 32,767 pixels (when run under Windows 98).

Because Change was clicked, setText ("Hello World") (in the Label class) is called. (Don't forget, Hello is currently being displayed by the label.)

The setText method assigns its text argument to the label's peer (if it exists, which is the case because the GUI is visible when this method is called.) (The peer has the capability to increase its preferred size by a small margin. However, this isn't enough to prevent text from being truncated at the peer's right edge.) If the label is valid (which is currently the case), its inherited invalidate method (from the Component class) is called.

In response, invalidate sets an internal Boolean valid flag to false, nullifies the label's minimum and preferred sizes, and (assuming there is a parent container and that this container is valid—which is the case on both counts), calls the parent container's invalidate method. (Containers inherit the invalidate method from the Container class. Therefore, it is Container's invalidate method which is just being called.)

The container's invalidate method checks to see if the current layout manager is an instance of a class that implements the LayoutManager2 interface. If this is the case, the layout manager's invalidateLayout method is called to clear out any cached layout information. Upon return, the component layer's invalidate method is called.

Note

Remember: An AWT container is created from the Container class, and this class is a subclass of the Component class. As a result, a Container has a Container class outer layer and a Component class inner layer.

The component layer's invalidate method sets the Boolean valid flag to false (for the label's parent container) and nullifies its minimum and preferred sizes. If the label's parent container has a parent container (and this parent container is valid, which would be the case when the Change button is clicked for the first time), this new parent container's invalidate method is called and the process continues. Otherwise, invalidate exits, the stack is rewound, and execution picks up right after the setText method call.

What happens next depends on the value of the option variable. This variable is assigned a value to indicate whether code that changes the container's size and validates the container executes. It gets its value from parsing a command argument to the ValidationDemo1 program.

Assuming no command arguments were passed to ValidationDemo1, option has a default value of NOTHING. As a result, the container's size and validity are not changed. Therefore, the second group of System.out.println method calls will report the label and container to be invalid. (If you resize the container, both the container and label will be validated. As a result, the first group of `System.out.println` method calls will report both the label and container to be valid when the `Change` button is clicked for a second time.) Note that the label's peer is still showing truncated text.

Assuming the `S` command argument was passed (as in `java ValidationDemo1 S`), `option` is assigned the value `SIZE_ONLY`. As a result, `setSize (getPreferredSize ());` is called.

The container's `getPreferredSize` method is called to return its preferred size. The return value should be `null`, because the previous `invalidate` method call (resulting from the `setText` method call) nullified this size. However, this isn't the case.

The container's `getPreferredSize` method calls an internal `preferredSize` method. This latter method discovers that the preferred size is `null`. As a result, it does one of two things. If there is a layout manager—you haven't called `setLayout (null)`—for this container, the layout manager's `preferredLayoutSize` method is called to return the layout size. Otherwise, the component layer's `preferredSize` method is called to return the preferred size. Because `ValidationDemo1` has not removed any layout managers, `preferredLayoutSize` is called with a reference to the container as its argument.

The `preferredLayoutSize` method calculates the preferred size of its container. To carry out this task, it calls the `getPreferredSize` method for each of the container's components. (In this example, you have two buttons and one label contained in the container. Also, it is the `getPreferredSize` method from the `Component` class—and not the `Container` class—that is called.)

For each button, the `getPreferredSize` method returns the previous preferred size for these components, because they haven't changed their sizes. However, when called for the label, `getPreferredSize` "notices" that the preferred size is `null`. As a result, it returns the peer's preferred size (because there is a peer—the `getMinimumSize` method would be called if there wasn't a peer).

When the peer's text was set during the earlier call to `setText`, it was able to slightly increase the width of the label peer. As a result, the width is a little larger than it was before the `setText` method call. Eventually, through stack rewinding, the original `getPreferredSize` method call returns this value. At this point, the container's `setSize` method is called.

The container inherits its `setSize` method from the `Component` class. When called, this method calls `Component`'s `resize` method—the overloaded version that takes a `Dimension` argument. This `resize` method calls `setSize (d.width, d.height)`—assuming the `Dimension` argument is called `d`. Finally, this `setSize` method calls a second `resize` method that takes two `int` argument (for the width and height).

The `resize` method calls the `setBounds (int x, int y, int width, int height)` method. (The `x` and `y` arguments identify the upper-left corner of the container. They can be ignored in this scenario, because you aren't moving `ValidationDemo1`'s main window around the screen.) In turn, this method calls the `reshape` method with the same four arguments. (You're getting to the good stuff.)

The `reshape` method sets a Boolean `resized` flag to `true`, if the container's new width and height differ from the old width and height. Obviously, this flag will be set to true, because the previous `getPreferredSize` method call returned the peer's new size (after `setText` was called), which differs from the old size.

The `reshape` method ends up calling the peer's `setBounds` method, the component layer's `invalidate` method, the parent container's `invalidate` method (if there is a parent), and then dispatches a component resized event. When this method exits, and the stack unwinds to a return from the `setSize` method call, the container is displayed at the new size (thanks to the call to the peer's `setBounds` method). Note that the label's peer is still showing truncated text.

Assuming the `V` command argument was passed (as in `java ValidationDemo1 V`), `option` is assigned the value `SIZE_AND_VALIDATE`). As a result, the container's `validate` method is called.

In response, `validate` calls the `validateTree` helper method to recursively lay out (by calling the container's overridden `doLayout` method) and validate each contained container and component. (A component is validated by calling its `validate` method, inherited from `Component`.) The `validateTree` method sets the `valid` flag to true for each container, and the component's `validate` method sets the `valid` flag to true for each component. (`Component`'s `isValid` method returns the value of this flag.)

The `doLayout` method calls the `layout` helper method, and this method calls the current layout manager's `layoutContainer` method (assuming the container has a layout manager.) As a result, the label's peer will show nontruncated text.

Although long-winded, you have just been taken on a condensed journey through the AWT's source code. Hopefully, this will help you come to terms with what is happening behind the scenes when a GUI is laid out.

Tip

The `pack` method is a wrapper for `setSize (getPreferredSize ()); validate ();`. Because this method originates in the AWT's `Window` class, is inherited by the AWT's `Frame` class—because `Frame` is derived from `Window`—and because `JFrame` is derived from `Frame`, you can always call `pack` in your Swing applications.

Now that validation and invalidation have been discussed, it's time to focus on Swing's revalidation concept. Revalidation involves automatic calls to `JComponent`'s `revalidate` method when something happens to a Swing component that affects it size (such as setting its text). When this occurs, `revalidate` invalidates the component (or container), by calling `Container`'s `invalidate` method (`JComponent` is derived from `Container`), and queues a validation request for a later time by calling Swing's repaint manager's `addInvalidComponent` method and scheduling a subsequent call to the repaint manager's `validateInvalidComponents` method. (The repaint manager manages repaint requests and is created from Swing's `RepaintManager` class.)

The ValidationDemo2 application (identical to the ValidationDemo1 application except that Swing is being used) demonstrates revalidation. (As with ValidationDemo1, ValidationDemo2's source code is included with the rest of the book's source code.) Figure 16.28 displays ValidationDemo2's windows. (These windows are the Swing equivalents of the three windows shown in Figure 16.27, and were generated in the same manner.)

Figure 16.28 ValidationDemo2's GUI is shown when no arguments (top), an s argument, and a v argument (bottom) are specified.

When you study Figure 16.28, you'll notice that Hello World is not truncated. It's not truncated because JLabel's setText method calls revalidate to validate the label. In turn, this method calls the repaint manager's addInvalidateComponent method, and addInvalidateComponent searches for the highest JComponent container whose isValidateRoot method returns true (which would be the root pane in this example). This root component is used by validateInvalidComponents to call the validate method, starting with the root container and working its way down to the lowest container (with its components), to ensure that all containers and components are resized. However, this does not apply to the JFrame container that contains everything else. As a result, the main window is not resized during revalidation.

Tip

The only way to understand what goes on with Java and the JFC (in general), and concepts such as validation (in particular), is to devise example programs and walk through Java's source code (like you've just done). You might want to consider setting aside some time (now and then) for doing just that. If you do, your skills will definitely increase and your talents will be in demand.

BUILDING A GUI: EVENTS AND LISTENERS

Now that you've learned how to establish a Swing GUI's look, it's time to consider its feel by using events and listeners.

Caution

Don't confuse this use of the phrase "look and feel" with the term PLAF. From a GUI building perspective, "look and feel" refers to the GUI design process.

You've already seen examples of Swing's events and listeners. If you recall, the ColorChooserDemo source code (in Listing 16.3), demonstrated change events and a change listener to respond to selections from a color chart.

Getting to know Swing's events and listeners involves studying the `javax.swing.event` package. You will also want to carefully review the SDK documentation, to learn what events are fired by each component. If you need additional examples, check out Sun's Java Tutorial at `http://java.sun.com/docs/books/tutorial/`.

ODDS AND ENDS

This chapter has focused on building a GUI with Swing's windowing toolkit. Components, containers, layout managers, events, and listeners have been emphasized. However, Swing offers additional capabilities that need to be addressed—beginning with actions.

ACTIONS

Actions simplify working with toolbars and menus, by centralizing their action event handling, text, icons, and enabled state. An action is represented by an action object, created from a class that implements the `Action` interface. For example, the abstract `AbstractAction` class (located in the `javax.swing` package) implements this interface. To create an action, either subclass `AbstractAction` or use an inner class, and override the `actionPerformed` method. The following code fragment demonstrates creating an action from `AbstractAction`:

```
Action open  = new AbstractAction ("Open...", new ImageIcon ("open.gif"))
               {
                   public void actionPerformed (ActionEvent e)
                   {
                      System.out.println ("Open file.");
                   }
               };
```

This code fragment specifies `Open...` as the action's text, and `open.gif` as the file containing its icon. Assuming that this action is registered with either a toolbar button or a menu item, the open action's `actionPerformed` method is called when either that button or menu item is selected. In response, this method sends the `Open file.` string to the standard output device.

To create a toolbar button and register it with an action, call `JToolBar`'s `add` method. This method returns a reference to a newly created button that's registered with an action. You can then use this reference to add a ToolTip to the button, as is done in the following code fragment:

```
JToolBar tb = new JToolBar ();
JButton b = tb.add (open);
b.setToolTipText ("Open a file.");
```

To create a menu item and register it with an action, call `JMenu`'s `add` method. This method returns a reference to a newly created menu item that's registered with an action. You can then use this reference to disable an icon (if one was specified by the action) because you probably wouldn't want to see an icon in the menu. This is demonstrated in the following code fragment:

```
JMenu file = new JMenu ("File");
JMenuItem mi = file.add (open);
mi.setIcon (null);
```

You can enable or disable all components that share an action, by calling `Action`'s `setEnabled` method. For example, by making the following method call, you can disable both the toolbar button and menu item (created in previous code fragments):

```
open.setEnabled (false);
```

Listing 16.19 presents source code to an `ActionDemo1` application that brings these concepts together into a working program.

Listing 16.19 The `ActionDemo1` Application Source Code

```
// ActionDemo1.java

import javax.swing.*;

import java.awt.*;
import java.awt.event.*;

class ActionDemo1 extends JFrame
{
   Action open, save;

   ActionDemo1 (String title)
   {
      super (title);

      addWindowListener (new WindowAdapter ()
                         {
                             public void windowClosing (WindowEvent e)
                             {
                                System.exit (0);
                             }
                         });

      open  = new AbstractAction ("Open...",
                                  new ImageIcon ("open.gif"))
              {
                  public void actionPerformed (ActionEvent e)
                  {
                     System.out.println ("Open file.");
                  }
              };

      save  = new AbstractAction ("Save...",
                                  new ImageIcon ("save.gif"))
              {
                  public void actionPerformed (ActionEvent e)
                  {
                     System.out.println ("Save file.");
                  }
              };
```

LISTING 16.19 CONTINUED

```
      JToolBar tb = new JToolBar ();
      JButton b = tb.add (open);
      b.setToolTipText ("Open a file.");
      b = tb.add (save);
      b.setToolTipText ("Save a file.");

      JMenu file = new JMenu ("File");
      JMenuItem mi = file.add (open);
      mi.setIcon (null);
      mi = file.add (save);
      mi.setIcon (null);

      JMenuBar mb = new JMenuBar ();
      mb.add (file);

      JMenu options = new JMenu ("Options");
      JCheckBoxMenuItem cbmi = new JCheckBoxMenuItem ("Enabled");
      cbmi.setSelected (true);

      ItemListener il = new ItemListener ()
                        {
                            public void itemStateChanged (ItemEvent e)
                            {
                               JCheckBoxMenuItem cbmi;
                               cbmi = (JCheckBoxMenuItem) e.getSource ();
                               boolean selected;
                               selected = e.getStateChange () ==
                                          ItemEvent.SELECTED;
                               open.setEnabled (selected);
                               save.setEnabled (selected);
                            }
                        };

      cbmi.addItemListener (il);
      options.add (cbmi);
      mb.add (options);

      setJMenuBar (mb);

      JPanel p = new JPanel ();
      p.add (tb);

      getContentPane ().add (p, BorderLayout.WEST);

      setSize (200, 100);
      setVisible (true);
   }

   public static void main (String [] args)
   {
      new ActionDemo1 ("Action Demo1");
   }
}
```

Sun has discovered that many developers would prefer to create their own components which are `ActionEvent` sources, and then have a method which connects these components to a particular action. As a result, starting with Version 1.3 of the Java 2 Platform Standard Edition, two new methods were added to the `AbstractButton` class (which is the parent of `JButton`, `JCheckBox`, `JMenu`, `JMenuItem`, and so on): `setAction` and `getAction`. You can call `setAction` after creating a component, which is demonstrated in the following code fragment. (This code fragment is taken from `ActionDemo2.java`; distributed with the rest of this book's source code.)


```
JToolBar tb = new JToolBar ();

JButton b = new JButton ();
b.setToolTipText ("Open a file.");

// The following setText method call must be made after setAction
// to disable text.

b.setText ("");
b.setAction (open);
tb.add (b);

b = new JButton ();
b.setToolTipText ("Save a file.");
b.setAction (save);
b.setText ("");
tb.add (b);

JMenu file = new JMenu ("File");

JMenuItem mi = new JMenuItem ();
mi.setAction (open);
mi.setIcon (null);
file.add (mi);

mi = new JMenuItem ();

// The following setIcon method call must be made after setAction
// to disable icon.

mi.setIcon (null);
mi.setAction (save);
file.add (mi);
```

Before concluding this topic, you might have noticed (after running `ActionDemo1` and `ActionDemo2`), that in `ActionDemo1`, the open and save toolbar buttons don't display the `Open ...` and `Save ...` action text. (This text is displayed on the open and save toolbar buttons in `ActionDemo2`.) It turns out that if you call each button's `getText` method, `null` is returned. However, if you call each button's `getIcon` method, the name of the image file is returned. The rationale for this situation is that toolbar buttons typically display images and not text. As a result, there is no requirement that a toolbar button's `getText` method return a reference to the button's text.

BORDERS

Borders provide edges around components. They "know" how to draw lines, reserve empty space, and supply titles. Furthermore, they are objects created from classes that implement the `Border` interface (located in the `javax.swing.border` package). Figure 16.29 presents the GUI to an application called `BorderDemo`. This GUI illustrates beveled, etched, matted, and titled borders. (The GUI is surrounded by a beveled border.)

Figure 16.29
Swing's borders can make a GUI look more professional.

You create a border by calling one of the `create` methods in the `BorderFactory` class (located in the `javax.swing` package). After you have this border, call a component's `setBorder` method to apply the border to the component. (If you need to identify the current border, you can call the component's `getBorder` method.) For example, the following code fragment establishes a red-lined border around a panel:

```
JPanel p = new JPanel ();
p.setBorder (BorderFactory.createLineBorder (Color.red));
```

Version 1.3 of the Java 2 Platform Standard Edition adds a pair of `createEtchedBorder` methods to `BorderFactory`. These methods create etched borders.

To simplify working with borders, you can take advantage of the numerous border subclasses (such as `EtchedBorder`) of the abstract `AbstractBorder` class (located in the `javax.swing.border` package). For example, you could use the following code fragment to create a red-lined border that's identical to the border created in the previous code fragment:

```
JPanel p = new JPanel ();
p.setBorder (new LineBorder (Color.red));
```

Version 1.3 of the Java 2 Platform Standard Edition adds a new constructor to the `LineBorder` class. This constructor makes it possible to more conveniently create lined borders with rounded corners.

Listing 16.20 presents source code to the `BorderDemo` application. This application demonstrates the simplicity of `AbstractBorder`'s subclasses.

LISTING 16.20 THE `BorderDemo` APPLICATION SOURCE CODE

```
// BorderDemo.java

import javax.swing.*;
import javax.swing.border.*;

import java.awt.*;
import java.awt.event.*;
```

Listing 16.20 Continued

```
class BorderDemo extends JFrame implements ActionListener
{
   BorderDemo (String title)
   {
      super (title);

      addWindowListener (new WindowAdapter ()
                         {
                             public void windowClosing (WindowEvent e)
                             {
                                System.exit (0);
                             }
                         });

//    getRootPane ().setBorder (new EmptyBorder (5, 5, 5, 5));

      getRootPane ().setBorder (new BevelBorder (BevelBorder.LOWERED));

      JLabel jl = new JLabel ("Hello World");
      jl.setBorder (new EtchedBorder ());
      getContentPane ().add (jl, BorderLayout.WEST);

      JButton jb = new JButton ("Isn't this fun!");
      Icon icon = new ImageIcon ("bullet.gif");
      jb.setBorder (new MatteBorder (10, 10, 10, 10, icon));
      getContentPane ().add (jb, BorderLayout.CENTER);

      jl = new JLabel ("Goodbye World");
      jl.setBorder (new TitledBorder ("Title"));
      getContentPane ().add (jl, BorderLayout.EAST);

      pack ();
      setVisible (true);
   }

   public void actionPerformed (ActionEvent e)
   {
      if (e.getActionCommand ().equals ("Ok"))
          System.out.println ("OK was pressed.");
      else
          System.out.println ("Cancel was pressed.");

      System.exit (0);
   }

   public static void main (String [] args)
   {
      new BorderDemo ("Border Demo");
   }
}
```

Note the commented out line in `BorderDemo`'s source code. If this line was not commented out and the line creating the beveled border was commented out, an empty border would be applied to the root pane. The interesting thing about an empty border is that it draws nothing: All underlying pixels show through. If a container with an empty border was resized to a smaller size, the new border area would display some of the pixels from the previously sized container's component(s). This would not make a user very happy. Therefore, it's best to reserve empty borders for nonresizable containers.

Tip

Empty borders are a handy alternative to `Box`'s glues, struts, and rigid areas.

KEYSTROKES AND BINDINGS

An instance of the `KeyStroke` class (located in the `javax.swing` package) represents a key being typed on the keyboard. `KeyStroke` objects are bound to component actions (such as inserting a character into a text field, beeping the speaker, or selecting an item from a combo box's pop-up menu). When the user types keys corresponding to these bound keystrokes, the associated actions are carried out. For example, suppose a user is familiar with WordPerfect. By binding actions (that represent standard editing commands) to those keystrokes that are familiar to WordPerfect users, the user's investment in learning WordPerfect key/command associations can be carried over to a Java-based word processor program.

A `KeyStroke` object represents either a single character (such as `A`), a character and modifier key (such as `Ctrl+A`), a key code (such as `F1`), or a key code and modifier key (such as `Shift+F1`). You obtain a `KeyStroke` object representing a key stroke by calling one of `KeyStroke`'s `getKeyStroke` methods as demonstrated by the following code fragment:

```
KeyStroke ks1 = KeyStroke.getKeyStroke ('B', Event.CTRL_MASK);
KeyStroke ks2 = KeyStroke.getKeyStroke (KeyEvent.VK_B, Event.CTRL_MASK);
KeyStroke ks3 = KeyStroke.getKeyStroke ('B');
```

Java has several techniques for binding keystrokes to actions. The first two techniques involve `JComponent`'s `registerKeyboardAction` methods (for nontext components) and key maps (for text components). Version 1.3 of the Java 2 Platform Standard Edition introduces a third technique that unifies these other two techniques. (This third technique will be examined later.) All three techniques are thoroughly explored in an online article called "Keyboard Bindings in Swing" (located at `http://java.sun.com/products/jfc/tsc/special_report/kestrel/keybindings.html`).

Imagine that you have a text field component, and you want to generate a beep when `Ctrl+B` is pressed. For starters, a text field is associated with an editor kit that serves as the component's controller. This editor kit supplies a list of actions that can be bound to key strokes. If you look in the `DefaultEditorKit` class (located in the `javax.swing.text` package), you'll find a `String` field called `beepAction`. This field names the action that causes a text component to issue a beep.

You can determine if the beep action is supported by the text field by doing the following: Call the text field's `getActions` method to return an array of all supported actions. Search this array for the beep action by calling `Action`'s `getValue` method (with an `Action.NAME` argument that identifies the action's name field) for each array element and comparing the result with the beep action's name. If there is a match, you extract the action, create the key stroke that triggers the action, obtain the text component's key map, and call its `addActionForKeyStroke` method to bind the keystroke to the action. This is all demonstrated in the following code fragment:


```
JTextField jt = new JTextField (20);

Action [] aList = jt.getActions ();
for (int i = 0; i < aList.length; i++)
     if (aList [i].getValue (Action.NAME) == DefaultEditorKit.beepAction)
     {
         Action a = aList [i];

         KeyStroke ks = KeyStroke.getKeyStroke (KeyEvent.VK_B, Event.CTRL_MASK);

         jt.getKeymap ().addActionForKeyStroke (ks, a);
     }
```

Listing 16.21 presents source code to a `BindingDemo1` application that uses a key map to bind the `Ctrl+B` key stroke to a text field's beep action. You can use this application to experiment with discovering text component actions, creating different key strokes, and binding these key strokes to these actions.

LISTING 16.21 THE `BindingDemo1` APPLICATION SOURCE CODE

```
// BindingDemo1.java

import javax.swing.*;
import javax.swing.plaf.*;
import javax.swing.text.*;

import java.awt.*;
import java.awt.event.*;

import java.util.*;

class BindingDemo1 extends JFrame
{
   BindingDemo1 (String title)
   {
      super (title);

      addWindowListener (new WindowAdapter ()
                         {
                             public void windowClosing (WindowEvent e)
                             {
                                System.exit (0);
                             }
                         });
```

LISTING 16.21 CONTINUED

```
      JPanel jp = new JPanel ();

      JLabel jl = new JLabel ("Name:");
      jp.add (jl);

      JTextField jt = new JTextField (20);
      jp.add (jt);

      Action [] aList = jt.getActions ();
      for (int i = 0; i < aList.length; i++)
           if (aList [i].getValue (Action.NAME) ==
               DefaultEditorKit.beepAction)
           {
               Action a = aList [i];

               KeyStroke ks = KeyStroke.getKeyStroke (KeyEvent.VK_B,
                                                      Event.CTRL_MASK);

               jt.getKeymap ().addActionForKeyStroke (ks, a);
           }

      getContentPane ().add (jp);

      pack ();
      setVisible (true);
   }

   public static void main (String [] args)
   {
      new BindingDemo1 ("Binding Demo1");
   }
}
```

Version 1.3 of the Java 2 Platform Standard Edition introduces the `InputMap` and `ActionMap` classes for unifying earlier techniques that bind keystrokes to nontext and text components. These classes support any kind of component.

To get a sense of the power behind these classes, check out the following code fragment (taken from the `BindingDemo2` application, which is practically identical to `BindingDemo1`, and is included with the book's source code), which binds the `Ctrl+B` keystroke to the text field's beep action:

```
KeyStroke ks = KeyStroke.getKeyStroke (KeyEvent.VK_B, Event.CTRL_MASK);
jt.getInputMap ().put (ks, DefaultEditorKit.beepAction);
```

The text field's input map object is obtained by calling the text field's `getInputMap` method. This object contains all the current keystroke/action mappings for this component. By calling the input map's `put` method, an association between the keystroke and beep action is made for the text field.

Note

Actually, there are three tables of mappings: one for the component when it has the focus, one for its ancestor, and one for a descendent component. The "Keyboard Bindings in Swing" article, mentioned earlier, provides an explanation for the existence of three tables.

Unlike input maps, which associate keystrokes with action names, action maps associate action names with action objects. For example, suppose you want to modify a combo box so that when you enter the first few characters of a pop-up menu item and press the down-arrow key, the first matching menu item (the menu item whose first few characters match the characters entered in the editor) is highlighted. To accomplish this task, you need to know which action gets executed when the down-arrow key is pressed. (It was discovered that the `selectNext` action is executed by looking at the source code to the `BasicComboBoxUI` class.)

After you know which action to override, you call the component's `getActionMap` method to return its current action map, and then call the action map's `put` method to replace the existing action. This is demonstrated by the following code fragment:

```
jcb = new JComboBox (v);
jcb.setEditable (true);
jcb.getActionMap ().put ("selectNext", new DownAction ());
```

This code fragment replaces the `selectNext` action object with an object created from the `DownAction` class. The `actionPerformed` method (in this class) will be called when the user presses the `Down Arrow` key, because this key is internally registered to an action called `selectNext`, and the `actionPerformed` method in the object associated with `selectNext` is called when this key is pressed.

How would you introduce a brand new action? For example, suppose you want to erase all characters in the combo box's editor when a user presses `Ctrl+Delete`. The solution is to work with the combo box's current input and action maps. The following code fragment demonstrates:

```
KeyStroke ks = KeyStroke.getKeyStroke (KeyEvent.VK_DELETE, Event.CTRL_MASK);
jcb.getInputMap (JComponent.WHEN_ANCESTOR_OF_FOCUSED_COMPONENT).put (ks,
                 "rubOut");
jcb.getActionMap ().put ("rubOut", new RubOutAction ());
```

This code fragment creates a `KeyStroke` object for the `Ctrl+Delete` key combination. It then calls the combo box's `getInputMap` method to associate this keystroke with a fictional action name called `rubOut`. This name, and an object created from the `RubOutAction` class, are added to the action table. Now, when the `Ctrl` and `Delete` keys are simultaneously pressed, the input map is searched to find the name of the action. This name is then used to search the action map for the action object. If found, its `actionPerformed` method is called and the deletion takes place.

You might be wondering why `WHEN_ANCESTOR_OF_FOCUSED_COMPONENT` is passed as an argument to `getInputMap`. The answer has to do with a combo box consisting of multiple components (a pop-up menu and an editor—in edit mode). For detailed information, check out the "Keyboard Bindings in Swing" article discussed earlier.

To conclude, check out Listing 16.22. This listing presents source code to the `BindingDemo3` application, and demonstrates overriding an existing combo box action and introducing a brand new action.

LISTING 16.22 THE `BindingDemo3` APPLICATION SOURCE CODE

```
// BindingDemo3.java

import javax.swing.*;
import javax.swing.plaf.*;

import java.awt.*;
import java.awt.event.*;

import java.util.*;

class BindingDemo3 extends JFrame
{
   JComboBox jcb;

   BindingDemo3 (String title)
   {
      super (title);

      addWindowListener (new WindowAdapter ()
                         {
                             public void windowClosing (WindowEvent e)
                             {
                                System.exit (0);
                             }
                         });

      JPanel jp = new JPanel ();

      Vector v = new Vector ();
      v.add ("Camaro");
      v.add ("Corvette");
      v.add ("Firebird");
      v.add ("TransAM");
      v.add ("Porsche");
      v.add ("Lamborgini");

      jcb = new JComboBox (v);
      jcb.setEditable (true);

      jcb.getActionMap ().put ("selectNext", new DownAction ());

      KeyStroke ks = KeyStroke.getKeyStroke (KeyEvent.VK_DELETE,
                                             Event.CTRL_MASK);

      jcb.getInputMap (JComponent.WHEN_ANCESTOR_OF_FOCUSED_COMPONENT)
         .put (ks, "rubOut");
      jcb.getActionMap ().put ("rubOut", new RubOutAction ());
```

LISTING 16.22 CONTINUED

```
      jp.setPreferredSize (new Dimension (200, 35));
      jp.add (jcb);
      getContentPane ().add (jp);

      pack ();
      setVisible (true);
   }

   public static void main (String [] args)
   {
      new BindingDemo3 ("Binding Demo3");
   }
}

class DownAction extends AbstractAction
{
   public void actionPerformed (ActionEvent e)
   {
      JComboBox jcb = (JComboBox) e.getSource ();

      ComboBoxUI ui = jcb.getUI ();

      if (ui.isPopupVisible (jcb))
      {
          int i = jcb.getSelectedIndex ();
          if (i < jcb.getModel ().getSize () - 1)
          {
              jcb.setSelectedIndex (i + 1);
              jcb.repaint ();
          }
      }
      else
      {
          int nItems = jcb.getItemCount ();

          ComboBoxEditor cbe = jcb.getEditor ();

          String st; // Search text

          st = ((String) cbe.getItem ()).toUpperCase ();

          for (int i = 0; i < nItems; i++)
          {
               String item = ((String) jcb.getItemAt (i)).toUpperCase ();

               if (item.startsWith (st))
               {
                   jcb.setSelectedIndex (i);
                   break;
               }
          }

          ui.setPopupVisible (jcb, true);
      }
   }
}
```

LISTING 16.22 CONTINUED

```
class RubOutAction extends AbstractAction
{
   public void actionPerformed (ActionEvent e)
   {
      JComboBox jcb = (JComboBox) e.getSource ();

      ComboBoxEditor cbe = jcb.getEditor ();

      cbe.setItem ("");
   }
}
```

PAINTING

Swing GUIs are painted when they are made visible for the first time, or because something changes in a component's state (such as a component becoming invalid and then being resized). Painting begins with the highest component in the containment hierarchy and works its way down to the lowest component. This process is under the control of the AWT's windowing toolkit. (Yes, the AWT's windowing toolkit serves as the foundation for painting Swing components.) However, Swing's repaint manager (identified by the `RepaintManager` class in the `javax.swing` package) and double-buffering logic improve the efficiency of this process and eliminate flicker.

Swing's windowing toolkit forces painting code to execute in the event handling thread. As a result, if it takes too long to handle an event, painting will slow down (and the GUI's appearance will deteriorate). On the other hand, if painting logic takes too long to execute, the GUI will not be very responsive to user interaction.

As you learned in Chapter 12, "Introduction to Java Foundation Classes," a component's (typically overridden) `paint` method is called to perform component-specific painting. However, this changes in Swing. Because `JComponent` overrides `paint` to call the `paintComponent`, `paintBorder`, and `paintChildren` methods, you must not override this method. If you do, you will probably forget to call `paintComponent`, `paintBorder`, and `paintChildren`. The resulting component's UI will suffer.

The `paintComponent` method is the first method called by `paint`. It first calls its superclass `paintComponent` method to ensure that the component's background is painted. (This background is painted if the component's opaque property is true—the result of a call to `JComponent`'s `setOpaque` method with a Boolean `true` argument.)

The `paintBorder` method is called after `paintComponent`, to paint the component's border (if there is a border). (This method must not be overridden or invoked.)

The `paintChildren` method is called after `paintBorder`, to allow child components of the current container component to paint themselves. (Do not override or invoke this method.)

In each of Swing's component classes, the `paintComponent` method calls the component's UI delegate to perform the actual painting. Because a UI delegate is not associated with `JComponent`, the background of any component (whose class extends `JComponent`) will not be painted. However, if you extend another class that has a UI delegate (such as `JLabel`), the background will be painted. (You must override `paintComponent` and call `super.paintComponent` to ensure that a background is painted, if the opaque property is true.) This is demonstrated in the following code fragment:

```
class MyPanel extends JPanel
{
   // ...

   public void paintComponent (Graphics g)
   {
      super.paintComponent (g); // Paint the background.

      // Call Graphics methods to perform custom painting.
   }
}
```


PROPERTIES

When you study the SDK documentation for `JComponent` and its many subclasses, you'll come across the term property. This JavaBeans term refers to the various state items (such as opaque) that are part of a Swing component. Furthermore, by calling `JComponent`'s `putClientProperty` method, you can add your own properties for associating extra information with components. For example, a layout manager can store constraint information in a component.

The `putClientProperty` method is called to store or remove a property. This method takes `Object` key and `Object` value arguments. The key identifies the property. If `null` is passed, the property is removed. (Internally, properties are stored in a hash table.) To obtain the value of a current property, call `getClientProperty`.

When a change is made to one of these properties, a property change event is fired. Listeners can then react to these events and perform component-specific tasks. (For more information on properties, check out the SDK documentation.)

THREADING ISSUES

Unlike the AWT, Swing requires you to take care when working with threads. Apart from a few methods, Swing's methods can only be called from the event-handling thread. (This thread handles Swing and AWT events.) It all boils down to the single-thread rule: After a Swing component is visible (through a call to the `setVisible` method), any code that might affect or depend on a component's state must be executed from the event-handling thread. If you need to execute GUI code from another thread, you should investigate the `invokeAndWait` and `invokeLater` methods, located in the `SwingUtilities` class. (The Java Tutorial shows how to use these methods.)

If one or more of your components are behaving strangely (perhaps as a result of improperly using threads), and you need some help in finding the cause, see "Debugging Swing Components" in the "Troubleshooting" section at the end of this chapter.

TIMERS

Swing provides a `Timer` class (located in the `javax.swing` package) that fires an action event to one or more listeners after a delay. (The ToolTip manager uses this class to determine when to show and hide a ToolTip.) Because a timer's *task* (code executed in the timer's `actionPerformed` method) is executed in the event-handling thread, components can be safely manipulated. However, this task shouldn't take too long to execute, otherwise a GUI's performance will suffer.

Call `Timer (int delay, ActionListener l)` to create a timer that notifies action listener `l` every `delay` milliseconds. (You can add more action listeners by calling `Timer`'s `addActionListener` method.) The newly created timer is in its stopped state. To start the timer, call its `start` method. Conversely, you would call `stop` to terminate the timer. Furthermore, by calling its `isRunning` method, you can find out if a timer is running. To get a sense of how to use a Swing timer, examine Listing 16.23's source code to the `TimerDemo1` application.

LISTING 16.23 THE `TimerDemo1` APPLICATION SOURCE CODE

```
// TimerDemo1.java

import javax.swing.*;

import java.awt.*;
import java.awt.event.*;

class TimerDemo1 extends JFrame
{
   Timer timer;
   int counter;

   TimerDemo1 (String title)
   {
      super (title);

      addWindowListener (new WindowAdapter ()
                         {
                             public void windowClosing (WindowEvent e)
                             {
                                System.exit (0);
                             }
                         });

      ActionListener a = new ActionListener ()
                         {
                             public void actionPerformed (ActionEvent e)
                             {
                                System.out.println ("Counter = " +
                                                    counter);
```

Listing 16.23 Continued

```
                                if (++counter > 10)
                                {
                                    timer.stop ();
                                    System.exit (0);
                                }
                            }
                        };

      timer = new Timer (300, a);
      timer.start ();

      pack ();
      setVisible (true);
   }

   public static void main (String [] args)
   {
      new TimerDemo1 ("Timer Demo1");
   }
}
```

Timers can simplify Swing-based animation. When the next frame is to be drawn, the timer's `actionPerformed` method increments the frame number and calls the `repaint` method on the component whose `paintComponent` method draws the next frame. The source code to a `TimerDemo2` application, which shows how to use a timer to animate an image, is presented in Listing 16.24.

Listing 16.24 The `TimerDemo2` Application Source Code

```
// TimerDemo2.java

import javax.swing.*;

import java.awt.*;
import java.awt.event.*;
import java.awt.image.*;

class TimerDemo2 extends JFrame
{
   final static int WIDTH = 200;
   final static int HEIGHT = 200;

   final static int DIRECTCOLORBACK = 0;
   final static int INDEXCOLORBACK = 1;

   int backType = INDEXCOLORBACK;

   Timer timer;
   int frameNumber = -1;

   TimerDemo2 (String title)
   {
      super (title);
```

LISTING 16.24 CONTINUED

```
addWindowListener (new WindowAdapter ()
                   {
                       public void windowClosing (WindowEvent e)
                       {
                          System.exit (0);
                       }
                   });

int [] pixels = new int [WIDTH * HEIGHT];

Toolkit tk = Toolkit.getDefaultToolkit ();
Image imBack;

if (backType == DIRECTCOLORBACK)
{
    MkDirectColorBackground (pixels, WIDTH, HEIGHT);
    imBack = tk.createImage (new MemoryImageSource (WIDTH,
                                                    HEIGHT,
                                                    pixels,
                                                    0,
                                                    WIDTH));
}
else
{
    IndexColorModel icm;
    icm = MkIndexColorBackground (pixels, WIDTH, HEIGHT);
    imBack = tk.createImage (new MemoryImageSource (WIDTH,
                                                    HEIGHT,
                                                    icm,
                                                    pixels,
                                                    0,
                                                    WIDTH));
}

Image imFront = tk.getImage ("bullet.gif");

final AnimPane ap = new AnimPane (imBack, imFront);

setContentPane (ap);

ActionListener a = new ActionListener ()
                   {
                       public void actionPerformed (ActionEvent e)
                       {
                          frameNumber++;

                          ap.repaint ();
                       }
                   };

timer = new Timer (300, a);

timer.start ();

setSize (WIDTH, HEIGHT);
```

Listing 16.24 Continued

```
      setVisible (true);
   }

   void MkDirectColorBackground (int [] pixels, int w, int h)
   {
      int index = 0;

      for (int y = 0; y < h; y++)
      {
           int numerator = y * 255;
           int b = numerator / h;
           int r = 255 - numerator / h;

           for (int x = 0; x < w; x++)
           {
                int g = x * 255 / w;
                pixels [index++] = (255 << 24) | (r << 16) | (g << 8)
                                   | b;
           }
      }
   }

   IndexColorModel MkIndexColorBackground (int [] pixels, int w, int h)
   {
      Color [] colors = { Color.magenta, Color.green, Color.blue };

      byte [] reds = new byte [colors.length];
      byte [] greens = new byte [colors.length];
      byte [] blues = new byte [colors.length];

      for (int i = 0; i < colors.length; i++)
      {
           reds [i] = (byte) colors [i].getRed ();
           greens [i] = (byte) colors [i].getGreen ();
           blues [i] = (byte) colors [i].getBlue ();
      }

      int stripeSize = w / colors.length;

      int colorIndex;
      int index = 0;

      for (int y = 0; y < h; y++)
           for (int x = 0; x < w; x++)
           {
                if (x < stripeSize)
                    colorIndex = 0;
                else
                if (x < stripeSize * 2)
                    colorIndex = 1;
                else
                    colorIndex = 2;

                pixels [index++] = colorIndex;
           }
```

LISTING 16.24 CONTINUED

```
      IndexColorModel icm;
      icm = new IndexColorModel (8, colors.length, reds, greens, blues);
      return icm;
   }

   class AnimPane extends JPanel
   {
      Image back, front;

      AnimPane (Image back, Image front)
      {
         this.back = back;
         this.front = front;
      }

      //Draw the current frame of animation.

      public void paintComponent (Graphics g)
      {
         super.paintComponent (g);  // Paint space not covered
                                    // by background image.

         int compWidth = getWidth ();
         int compHeight = getHeight ();
         int imgWidth, imgHeight;

         // If you have a valid width and height for the
         // background image, draw this image - centered
         // horizontally and vertically.

         imgWidth = back.getWidth (this);
         imgHeight = back.getHeight (this);

         if (imgWidth > 0 && imgHeight > 0)
             g.drawImage (back,
                          (compWidth - imgWidth) / 2,
                          (compHeight - imgHeight) / 2, this);

         // If you have a valid width and height for the
         // front image, draw it.

         imgWidth = front.getWidth (this);
         imgHeight = front.getHeight (this);

         if (imgWidth > 0 && imgHeight > 0)
         {
             // Compute new horizontal position to fall in component
             // bounds. The larger the multiplier (such as 10), the
             // greater the horizontal distance that's traveled.
```

Listing 16.24 Continued

```
            int x = (frameNumber * 10) % (imgWidth + compWidth)
                    - imgWidth;

            // Center front image vertically.

            int y = (compHeight - imgHeight) / 2;

            // Draw front image.

            g.drawImage (front, x, y, this);
         }
      }
   }

   public static void main (String [] args)
   {
      new TimerDemo2 ("Timer Demo2");
   }
}
```

TimerDemo2 creates a background image in memory. This image uses either a direct color model (if the backType variable is set to DIRECTCOLORBACK) or an index color model (if backType is set to INDEXCOLORBACK). An animation pane, which is nothing more than a subclassed JPanel component, is created and its paintComponent method overridden to paint the background and foreground images. Every 300 milliseconds, the timer calls its actionPerformed method. Each call increments the frameNumber variable and issues a call to the animation pane's repaint method. This call eventually results in a call back to the animation pane's paintComponent method, which uses frameNumber's value to determine the next horizontal location. This value is multiplied by 10 to increase the distance covered during each call. Figure 16.30 shows TimerDemo2's output when the index color background is used.

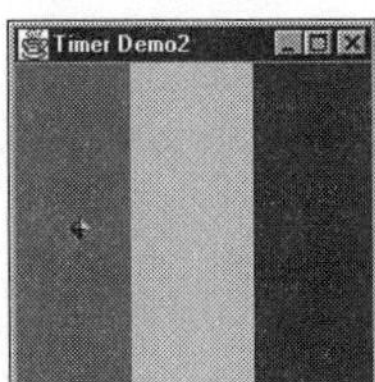

Figure 16.30
Timers can be used to achieve slick-looking Swing animations.

> **Note**
>
> Because Swing painting is double-buffered, the flickering problems that are prevalent with AWT animations don't exist.

TROUBLESHOOTING

CREATING AN ALTERNATE PLAF

How do I create my own PLAF?

Creating your own PLAF is a significant task and not for the faint of heart. Don't even think about writing code until you have a solid understanding of Swing's PLAF architecture. You can obtain this understanding by "surfing" to the following Web page:

`http://manning.spindoczine.com/sbe/files/uts2/Chapter21html/Chapter21.htm`

When you arrive, you'll discover that this Web page contains the contents of Chapter 21 in an online book on Swing. The material being discussed is Swing's PLAF architecture. Not only is the PLAF architecture thoroughly examined, this Web page shows you the source code to an alternate PLAF.

You can learn more about how PLAF works by reading an overview of Swing architecture at the following Web page:

`http://java.sun.com/products/jfc/tsc/articles/architecture/index.html`

This is just one of many useful Swing Connection articles that discusses various aspects of Swing architecture. Enjoy!

DEBUGGING SWING COMPONENTS

How do I find out what is happening to a malfunctioning Swing component?

The `JComponent` class provides a `setDebugGraphicsOptions` method for activating (or deactivating) debugging mode. In this mode, component information is either logged or displayed as a Swing program executes. You can also find out the state of Swing's debugging mode by calling `JComponent`'s `getDebugGraphicsOptions` method.

CHAPTER 17

Accessibility

In this chapter

by Geoff Friesen

WHAT IS ACCESSIBILITY?

When you interact with a computer, you normally input commands by way of a keyboard and mouse, and examine the computer's output by way of a video screen and printer. Unfortunately, many people cannot access a computer by using the conventional keyboard, mouse, video screen, and printer. For example, if a person has no limbs, this person won't be using the keyboard or mouse. Furthermore, a blind person would not have much use for a screen or printer. These people need more accessible computing devices.

You don't have to be physically challenged to benefit from computing devices that are more accessible. For example, suppose you are driving down a busy freeway and you feel a need to adjust your vehicle's environment. Without taking your eyes off the road, wouldn't it be great if you could ask your Java-enabled vehicle to take care of these tasks on your behalf?

When you interact with a computer, you're really interacting with its software. To become more accessible, this software must be written to take into account *assistive technologies*. Assistive hardware and software technologies—such as screen magnifiers, Braille input devices, speech synthesizers, speech recognizers, and so on—are used either in place of or in conjunction with video displays, printers, mice, and keyboards.

To support assistive technologies, Sun Microsystems has created an accessibility framework designed around the `javax.accessibility` package. Classes and interfaces contained in this package are used throughout Swing's components to automate much of this support.

Sun has introduced some AWT accessibility support in version 1.3 of the Java 2 Platform Standard Edition. This has been accomplished by making API changes to the AWT's `Component` and `Container` classes, along with `Component/Container` subclasses. However, in the case of certain AWT classes (such as `Menu` and `List`), this support is limited. (Sun is working to extend this support.) For more information, check out the accessibility framework enhancements in the Java 2 Platform Standard Edition version 1.3 documentation.

Because the accessibility framework is designed to be queried by assistive technologies, you will almost never need to interact with its classes and interfaces. However, if you are designing new Swing components, you should support appropriate accessibility interfaces and classes to ensure that assistive technologies can access information about these components.

HOW DOES ACCESSIBILITY WORK?

An assistive technology needs an entry point into a GUI before it can examine the state of each component. Java's accessibility framework specifies this entry point by enforcing the rule that each component's class implement the `Accessible` interface. For example, the `JButton` class implements `Accessible`.

The `Accessible` interface presents a `getAccessibleContext` method. When called, this method returns an object whose class implements the `AccessibleContext` interface. (Each component class contains an inner class that implements `AccessibleContext`.) After an assistive technology has this object, it can call various methods to learn more about the component.

For example, after a `JButton` object has been created, an assistive technology can call its `getAccessibleContext` method to return an `AccessibleContext` object. It can then call various `AccessibleContext` methods to learn more about the button.

Figure 17.1 illustrates a component's `AccessibleContext` object being obtained by an assistive technology.

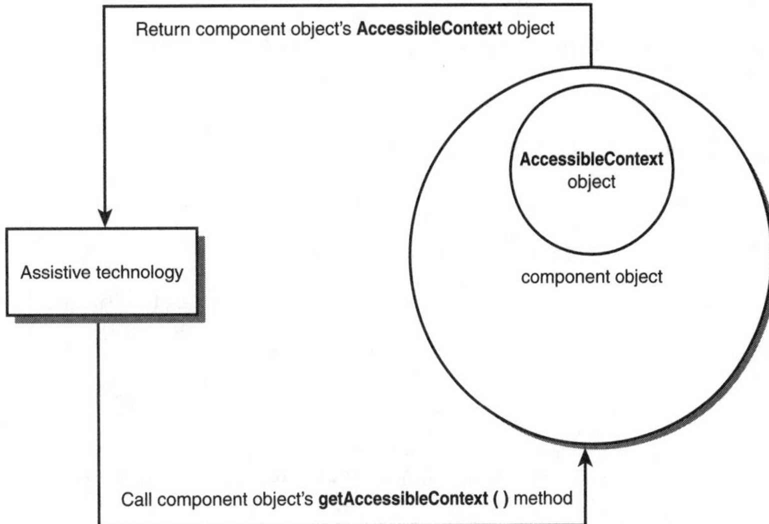

Figure 17.1
A component's `AccessibleContext` object can be obtained by calling `getAccessibleContext`.

The simplest kind of information that an assistive technology can access is a component's name and description. The name is obtained by calling `AccessibleContext`'s `getAccessibleName` method and the description is obtained by calling `AccessibleContext`'s `getAccessibleDescription` method.

An assistive technology can obtain names and descriptions (and other information) by first obtaining an `AccessibleContext` object for the main component—a frame component created from the `JFrame` class for Swing applications or an applet component created from the `JApplet` class for Swing applets. It can then call `AccessibleContext`'s `getAccessibleChildrenCount` method to obtain a count of accessible components contained by the frame or applet.

Each component is obtained by calling `AccessibleContext`'s `getAccessibleChild` method with an index argument (ranging from zero through one less than `getAccessibleChildrenCount`'s return value) that identifies the component. This process can continue recursively until all names and descriptions (and other information) have been obtained. Listing 17.1 presents source code for the `AccessibilityDemo1` application. This application demonstrates obtaining names and descriptions for all components in a GUI.

LISTING 17.1 THE AccessibilityDemo1 APPLICATION SOURCE CODE

```
// AccessibilityDemo1.java

import javax.accessibility.*;

import javax.swing.*;

import java.awt.event.*;

class AccessibilityDemo1 extends JFrame implements ActionListener
{
   JButton jb;

   AccessibilityDemo1 (String title)
   {
      super (title);

      addWindowListener (new WindowAdapter ()
                         {
                             public void windowClosing (WindowEvent e)
                             {
                                System.exit (0);
                             }
                         });

      AccessibleContext ac = getAccessibleContext ();
      ac.setAccessibleDescription ("Accessibility Demo1 description.");

      ac = getRootPane ().getAccessibleContext ();
      ac.setAccessibleName ("Root pane");
      ac.setAccessibleDescription ("Root pane description");

      ac = getGlassPane ().getAccessibleContext ();
      ac.setAccessibleName ("Glass pane");
      ac.setAccessibleDescription ("Glass pane description");

      ac = getLayeredPane ().getAccessibleContext ();
      ac.setAccessibleName ("Layered pane");
      ac.setAccessibleDescription ("Layered pane description");

      ac = getContentPane ().getAccessibleContext ();
      ac.setAccessibleName ("Content pane");
      ac.setAccessibleDescription ("Content pane description");

      JPanel p = new JPanel ();
      ac = p.getAccessibleContext ();
      ac.setAccessibleName ("Panel");
      ac.setAccessibleDescription ("Panel description");

      jb = new JButton ("Press Me");
      jb.addActionListener (this);
      jb.setToolTipText ("Press me for accessibility information.");
      p.add (jb);

      getContentPane ().add (p);
```

Listing 17.1 Continued

```
      setSize (200, 75);
      setVisible (true);
   }

   public void actionPerformed (ActionEvent e)
   {
      dumpInfo (getAccessibleContext ());
   }

   void dumpInfo (AccessibleContext ac)
   {
      System.out.println ("Name = " + ac.getAccessibleName ());
      System.out.println ("Description = " +
                          ac.getAccessibleDescription ());

      int nChildren = ac.getAccessibleChildrenCount ();

      for (int i = 0; i < nChildren; i++)
           dumpInfo (ac.getAccessibleChild (i).getAccessibleContext ());
   }

   public static void main (String [] args)
   {
      new AccessibilityDemo1 ("Accessibility Demo1");
   }
}
```


When you click `AccessibilityDemo1`'s button, the `actionPerformed` method obtains its frame's `AccessibleContext` object, and then calls `dumpInfo` to recursively dump the frame's (and contained components') information to the standard output device. Listing 17.2 presents the output generated by this program.

Listing 17.2 `AccessibilityDemo1`'s Output

```
Name = Accessibility Demo1
Description = Accessibility Demo1 description.
Name = Root pane
Description = Root pane description
Name = Glass pane
Description = Glass pane description
Name = Layered pane
Description = Layered pane description
Name = Content pane
Description = Content pane description
Name = Panel
Description = Panel description
Name = Press Me
Description = Press me for accessibility information.
```

Notice that each component has both a name and description. The button's name is taken from the label passed as an argument to its constructor. However, not all components are given names when created. For example, the root pane, layered pane, glass pane, content pane, and panels are not given names. To assign a name, your code must obtain an `AccessibleContext` for the component and then call its `setAccessibleName` method. Furthermore, because components don't have default descriptions, you must call `setAccessibleDescription` to assign descriptions to components.

But wait! The `setAccessibleDescription` method was not called to assign a description to the button. Where did this description come from when `getAccessibleDescription` was called? The source code holds the answer. Notice the call to `setToolTipText`. Behind the scenes, the accessibility framework is "smart enough" to use the ToolTip text as the button's description. However, if `setAccessibleDescription` is called to assign a description to the button, this description is returned by `getAccessibleDescription` instead of the ToolTip text. (The ToolTip text, as specified by `setToolTipText`, will still appear when the mouse pointer is positioned over the button.)

In addition to a name and description, components can provide other information. This information includes actions, component layout, hypertext and hyperlinks, icons, selections, table attributes, text attributes, and numeric values. If a component provides one or more kinds of this information, its class implements the appropriate interfaces. These interfaces include

- `AccessibleAction`
- `AccessibleComponent`
- `AccessibleHypertext` and `AccessibleHyperlink`
- `AccessibleIcon`
- `AccessibleSelection`
- `AccessibleTable`
- `AccessibleText`
- `AccessibleValue`

`AccessibleContext`'s `getAccessibleAction` method returns an `AccessibleAction` object. After it is obtained, an assistive technology can call `AccessibleAction` methods to find out what actions are supported by the component. Furthermore, it can also tell this component to perform these actions.

`AccessibleAction`'s `getAccessibleActionCount` method can be called to return the number of actions associated with the component. For each action, `getAccessibleActionDescription` can be called to return a description of that action. Furthermore, the action can be performed by calling `doAccessibleAction`.

Note

The `getAccessibleActionDescription` method always returns the literal string `click`, instead of a more appropriate description. A complete implementation of this method is pending because localized strings are required to support internationalization software and work to ensure that these strings are localized has not yet been done. Presumably, this method will be completed when version 1.4 of the Java 2 Platform Standard Edition is released.

To learn more about AccessibleAction, look at the source code for the AccessibilityDemo2 application in Listing 17.3.

Listing 17.3 The AccessibilityDemo2 Application Source Code

```
// AccessibilityDemo2.java

import javax.accessibility.*;

import javax.swing.*;

import java.awt.*;
import java.awt.event.*;

class AccessibilityDemo2 extends JFrame
{
   AccessibilityDemo2 (String title)
   {
      super (title);

      addWindowListener (new WindowAdapter ()
                         {
                             public void windowClosing (WindowEvent e)
                             {
                                System.exit (0);
                             }
                         });

      JToolBar toolBar = new JToolBar ();

      Action a = new AbstractAction ("Demo")
                 {
                    public void actionPerformed (ActionEvent e)
                    {
                       System.out.println ("Action taken.");
                    }
                 };

      JButton b = toolBar.add (a);
      b.setText ("Demo Button");
      b.setToolTipText ("Press me to take action.");

      JMenu mainMenu = new JMenu ("Menu");
      JMenuItem mi = mainMenu.add (a);
      mi.getAccessibleContext ().setAccessibleName ("Menu item");

      JMenuBar mb = new JMenuBar ();
      mb.add (mainMenu);
      setJMenuBar (mb);

      JPanel pane = new JPanel ();
      pane.setLayout (new BorderLayout ());
      pane.setPreferredSize (new Dimension (200, 100));
      pane.add (toolBar, BorderLayout.NORTH);
      setContentPane (pane);
```

LISTING 17.3 CONTINUED

```
        pack ();
        setVisible (true);
    }

    public static void main (String [] args)
    {
        AccessibilityDemo2 ad2;
        ad2 = new AccessibilityDemo2 ("Accessibility Demo2");

        try
        {
            Thread.sleep (5000);
        }
        catch (InterruptedException e) {}

        ad2.dumpActionInfo (ad2.getAccessibleContext ());
    }

    void dumpActionInfo (AccessibleContext ac)
    {
        AccessibleAction aa = ac.getAccessibleAction ();

        if (aa != null)
        {
            String s = ac.getAccessibleName ();
            System.out.println (s);

            int count = aa.getAccessibleActionCount ();

            for (int i = 0; i < count; i++)
            {
                 s = aa.getAccessibleActionDescription (i);
                 System.out.println ("Description = " + s);
            }
        }

        int nChildren = ac.getAccessibleChildrenCount ();

        for (int i = 0; i < nChildren; i++)
             dumpActionInfo (ac.getAccessibleChild (i)
                                 .getAccessibleContext ());
    }
}
```

AccessibilityDemo2 creates a GUI that consists of a menu and a toolbar with a single button. Both the menu and toolbar are associated with an action called Demo. When either the menu's sole menu item or the toolbar's sole button is selected, this action is performed.

AccessibilityDemo2 (as with the rest of the AccessibilityDemo applications) simulates an assistive technology interrogating a GUI's components. This is done by causing its main thread to sleep for 5 or 10 seconds (which allows a user to interact with the GUI) before calling a dump method to recursively search for all components, whose classes implement an appropriate interface.

As far as AccessibilityDemo2 is concerned, the only components of interest are those whose classes implement AccessibleAction. As soon as an appropriate component is found, its accessible name and accessible action description are sent to the standard output device. This information is shown in Listing 17.4.

Listing 17.4 AccessibilityDemo2's Output

```
Menu
Description = click
Menu item
Description = click
Demo Button
Description = click
```


As shown, three components are associated with AccessibleAction objects. These components are identified by their accessible names: Menu (for the JMenu component), Menu item (for the JMenuItem component), and Demo Button (for the JButton component added to the JToolBar). Furthermore, the "most helpful" click description automatically identifies each action.

AccessibleContext's getAccessibleComponent method returns an AccessibleComponent object. After this object is obtained, an assistive technology can call AccessibleComponent methods to find out the onscreen size, position, color, cursor, and so on, of its associated component. Furthermore, these attributes can be changed. To learn more about AccessibleComponent, look at the source code for the AccessibilityDemo3 application in Listing 17.5.

Listing 17.5 The AccessibilityDemo3 Application Source Code

```
// AccessibilityDemo3.java

import javax.accessibility.*;

import javax.swing.*;

import java.awt.*;
import java.awt.event.*;

class AccessibilityDemo3 extends JFrame
{
   AccessibilityDemo3 (String title)
   {
      super (title);

      addWindowListener (new WindowAdapter ()
                         {
                             public void windowClosing (WindowEvent e)
                             {
                                System.exit (0);
                             }
                         });
```

LISTING 17.5 CONTINUED

```
      JPanel p = new JPanel ();
      p.setPreferredSize (new Dimension (200, 50));
      JButton jb = new JButton ("OK");
      p.add (jb);

      getContentPane ().add (p);

      pack ();
      setVisible (true);
   }

   public static void main (String [] args)
   {
      AccessibilityDemo3 ad3;
      ad3 = new AccessibilityDemo3 ("Accessibility Demo3");

      try
      {
          Thread.sleep (5000);
      }
      catch (InterruptedException e) {}

      ad3.dumpComponentInfo (ad3.getAccessibleContext ());
   }

   void dumpComponentInfo (AccessibleContext ac)
   {
      AccessibleComponent ax = ac.getAccessibleComponent ();

      if (ax != null)
      {
          String s = ac.getAccessibleName ();

          if (s != null && s.equals ("OK"))
          {
              System.out.println ("Background color: " +
                                  ax.getBackground ());

              System.out.println ("Cursor: " +
                                  ax.getCursor ());

              Cursor c;
              c = Cursor.getPredefinedCursor (Cursor.WAIT_CURSOR);
              ax.setCursor (c);

              System.out.println ("Foreground color: " +
                                  ax.getForeground ());

              System.out.println ("Location: " +
                                  ax.getLocationOnScreen ());
          }
      }

      int nChildren = ac.getAccessibleChildrenCount ();
```

Listing 17.5 Continued

```
      for (int i = 0; i < nChildren; i++)
           dumpComponentInfo (ac.getAccessibleChild (i)
                                .getAccessibleContext ());
   }
}
```

AccessibilityDemo3 creates a GUI consisting of a single button. After a five-second delay, the main thread calls dumpComponentInfo to recursively search for the OK button's AccessibleComponent object. After the object is found, the background color, cursor, foreground color, and mouse pointer location are displayed. Furthermore, the mouse pointer's cursor is changed to a wait cursor. Listing 17.6 shows this information sent to the standard output device, after a five-second delay.

Listing 17.6 AccessibilityDemo3's Output

```
Background color: javax.swing.plaf.ColorUIResource[r=204,g=204,b=204]
Cursor: java.awt.Cursor[Default Cursor]
Foreground color: javax.swing.plaf.ColorUIResource[r=0,g=0,b=0]
Location: java.awt.Point[x=78,y=28]
```

AccessibleContext's getAccessibleHypertext method returns an AccessibleHypertext object. An assistive technology can query this object to learn about the number of links embedded in a Web page. Furthermore, one of AccessibleHypertext's methods returns an AccessibleHyperlink object, whose methods can be called to obtain link information. Listing 17.7 presents source code for an AccessibilityDemo4 application that demonstrates how to obtain this information.

Listing 17.7 The AccessibilityDemo4 Application Source Code

```
// AccessibilityDemo4.java

import javax.accessibility.*;

import javax.swing.*;
import javax.swing.event.*;

import java.awt.*;
import java.awt.event.*;

import java.net.*;

class AccessibilityDemo4 extends JFrame
                         implements ActionListener, HyperlinkListener
{
   JEditorPane view;
   JTextField commandLine;

   AccessibilityDemo4 (String title)
   {
      super (title);
```

LISTING 17.7 CONTINUED

```
      addWindowListener (new WindowAdapter ()
                         {
                             public void windowClosing (WindowEvent e)
                             {
                                System.exit (0);
                             }
                         });

      commandLine = new JTextField ();
      commandLine.addActionListener (this);
      getContentPane ().add (commandLine, BorderLayout.NORTH);

      view = new JEditorPane ();
      view.setEditable (false);
      view.setPreferredSize (new Dimension (400, 400));
      view.addHyperlinkListener (this);

      getContentPane ().add (view, BorderLayout.CENTER);

      pack ();
      setVisible (true);
   }

   public void actionPerformed (ActionEvent e)
   {
      try
      {
         URL url = new URL (e.getActionCommand ());
         view.setPage (url);
         commandLine.setText (url.toExternalForm ());
      }
      catch (MalformedURLException e2)
      {
         System.out.println ("Bad URL: " + e.getActionCommand ());
      }
      catch (java.io.IOException e2) {}
   }

   public void hyperlinkUpdate (HyperlinkEvent e)
   {
      try
      {
         view.setPage (e.getURL ());
         commandLine.setText (e.getURL ().toExternalForm ());
      }
      catch (java.io.IOException e2) {}
   }

   public static void main (String [] args)
   {
      AccessibilityDemo4 ad4;
      ad4 = new AccessibilityDemo4 ("Accessibility Demo4");

      try
      {
          Thread.sleep (10000);
```

Listing 17.7 Continued

```
      }
      catch (InterruptedException e) {}

      ad4.dumpHypertextInfo (ad4.getAccessibleContext ());
   }

   void dumpHypertextInfo (AccessibleContext ac)
   {
      AccessibleText at = ac.getAccessibleText ();

      AccessibleHypertext ah = null;
      if (at instanceof AccessibleHypertext)
          ah = (AccessibleHypertext) at;

      if (ah != null)
      {
          int nLinks = ah.getLinkCount ();

          for (int i = 0; i < nLinks; i++)
          {
               AccessibleHyperlink ahl = ah.getLink (i);

               int nActions = ahl.getAccessibleActionCount ();

               for (int j = 0; j < nActions; j++)
               {
                    String s = ahl.getAccessibleActionDescription (j);
                    System.out.println ("Action = " + s);
               }
          }

          return;
      }

      int nChildren = ac.getAccessibleChildrenCount ();

      for (int i = 0; i < nChildren; i++)
           dumpHypertextInfo (ac.getAccessibleChild (i)
                                .getAccessibleContext ());
   }
}
```

`AccessibilityDemo4` creates a GUI consisting of command line text field and editor pane components. A uniform resource locator is entered in the command line and the resulting Web page is displayed in the editor pane. Listing 17.8 shows the information that is sent to the standard output device (after 10 seconds have elapsed) when the `dummy.html` file is used. (This file is included with the rest of this book's source code, which you can download from this book's Web site at `www.mcp.com`.)

Listing 17.8 `AccessibilityDemo4`'s Output

```
Action = CNN Web site
Action = PC Magazine Web site
```

Note

Listing 17.8's output was generated by using the `dummy.html` file, which is included with this book's source code. Furthermore, 10 seconds was chosen as being sufficient for interacting with `AccessibilityDemo4`'s GUI, before Listing 17.8's output is automatically generated. You might need to increase this delay to obtain the same results as shown in Listing 17.8. (This advice also applies to the other `AccessibilityDemo` programs shown in this chapter.)

`AccessibleContext`'s `getAccessibleIcon` method returns an `AccessibleIcon` object. An assistive technology can query this object to learn about a component's icons. Listing 17.9 presents source code for the `AccessibilityDemo5` application, which demonstrates `AccessibleIcon`.

LISTING 17.9 THE `AccessibilityDemo5` APPLICATION SOURCE CODE

```
// AccessibilityDemo5.java

import javax.accessibility.*;

import javax.swing.*;

import java.awt.*;
import java.awt.event.*;

class AccessibilityDemo5 extends JFrame
{
   AccessibilityDemo5 (String title)
   {
      super (title);

      addWindowListener (new WindowAdapter ()
                         {
                             public void windowClosing (WindowEvent e)
                             {
                                System.exit (0);
                             }
                         });

      JPanel p = new JPanel ();
      p.setPreferredSize (new Dimension (200, 50));
      JButton jb = new JButton (new ImageIcon ("bullet.gif"));
      p.add (jb);

      getContentPane ().add (p);

      pack ();
      setVisible (true);
   }

   public static void main (String [] args)
   {
      AccessibilityDemo5 ad5;
      ad5 = new AccessibilityDemo5 ("Accessibility Demo5");
```

Listing 17.9 Continued

```
        try
        {
            Thread.sleep (5000);
        }
        catch (InterruptedException e) {}

        ad5.dumpIconInfo (ad5.getAccessibleContext ());
    }

    void dumpIconInfo (AccessibleContext ac)
    {
        AccessibleIcon [] ai = ac.getAccessibleIcon ();

        if (ai != null)
        {
            for (int i = 0; i < ai.length; i++)
            {
                 String s = ai [i].getAccessibleIconDescription ();
                 System.out.println ("Description = " + s);
                 System.out.println ("Width = "
                                     + ai [i].getAccessibleIconWidth ());
                 System.out.println ("height = "
                                     + ai [i].getAccessibleIconWidth ());
            }

            return;
        }

        int nChildren = ac.getAccessibleChildrenCount ();

        for (int i = 0; i < nChildren; i++)
             dumpIconInfo (ac.getAccessibleChild (i)
                             .getAccessibleContext ());
    }
}
```

`AccessibilityDemo5` creates a GUI consisting of a button with an icon. Information about this icon is sent to the standard output device after five seconds have passed. This information is shown in Listing 17.10.

Listing 17.10 `AccessibilityDemo5`'s Output

```
Description = bullet.gif
Width = 15
height = 15
```

`AccessibleContext`'s `getAccessibleSelection` method returns an `AccessibleSelection` object. An assistive technology can query this object to learn about, and modify, the selections in a list, combo box, and so on. To demonstrate `AccessibleSelection`, Listing 17.11 presents source code for the `AccessibilityDemo6` application.

LISTING 17.11 THE AccessibilityDemo6 APPLICATION SOURCE CODE

```
// AccessibilityDemo6.java

import javax.accessibility.*;

import javax.swing.*;

import java.awt.*;
import java.awt.event.*;

import java.util.Vector;

class AccessibilityDemo6 extends JFrame
{
   AccessibilityDemo6 (String title)
   {
      super (title);

      addWindowListener (new WindowAdapter ()
                         {
                             public void windowClosing (WindowEvent e)
                             {
                                System.exit (0);
                             }
                         });

      Vector v = new Vector ();
      v.add ("First item");
      v.add ("Second item");
      v.add ("Third item");
      v.add ("Fourth item");

      JPanel p = new JPanel ();
      p.setPreferredSize (new Dimension (200, 100));
      JList jl = new JList (v);
      jl.setPreferredSize (new Dimension (100, 75));
      p.add (jl);

      getContentPane ().add (p);

      pack ();
      setVisible (true);
   }

   public static void main (String [] args)
   {
      AccessibilityDemo6 ad6;
      ad6 = new AccessibilityDemo6 ("Accessibility Demo6");

      try
      {
          Thread.sleep (5000);
      }
      catch (InterruptedException e) {}

      ad6.dumpSelectionInfo (ad6.getAccessibleContext ());
```

Listing 17.11 Continued

```
   }

   void dumpSelectionInfo (AccessibleContext ac)
   {
      AccessibleSelection as = ac.getAccessibleSelection ();

      if (as != null)
      {
          int count = as.getAccessibleSelectionCount ();

          for (int i = 0; i < count; i++)
          {
               Accessible a = as.getAccessibleSelection (i);
               AccessibleContext ac2 = a.getAccessibleContext ();
               String s = ac2.getAccessibleName ();
               System.out.println ("Name = " + s);
          }

          return;
      }

      int nChildren = ac.getAccessibleChildrenCount ();

      for (int i = 0; i < nChildren; i++)
           dumpSelectionInfo (ac.getAccessibleChild (i)
                                    .getAccessibleContext ());
   }
}
```


`AccessibilityDemo6` creates a GUI consisting of a list with four items. When the program is run, you must select an item from this list before the 5 seconds expires. Listing 17.12 shows that the third item was currently selected when the information was sent to the standard output device (after the passage of five seconds).

Listing 17.12 `AccessibilityDemo6`'s Output

```
Name = Third item
```

`AccessibleContext`'s `getAccessibleTable` method returns an `AccessibleTable` object. An assistive technology can query this object to find out information about a table (such as the number of columns and rows). Listing 17.13 presents source code for an `AccessibilityDemo7` application that shows how to accomplish this task.

Listing 17.13 The `AccessibilityDemo7` Application Source Code

```
// AccessibilityDemo7.java

import javax.accessibility.*;

import javax.swing.*;
```

LISTING 17.13 CONTINUED

```
import java.awt.*;
import java.awt.event.*;

class AccessibilityDemo7 extends JFrame
{
   AccessibilityDemo7 (String title)
   {
      super (title);

      addWindowListener (new WindowAdapter ()
                         {
                             public void windowClosing (WindowEvent e)
                             {
                                System.exit (0);
                             }
                         });

      JPanel p = new JPanel ();
      p.setPreferredSize (new Dimension (200, 200));

      JTable jt = new JTable (10, 3);
      p.add (jt);

      getContentPane ().add (p);

      pack ();
      setVisible (true);
   }

   public static void main (String [] args)
   {
      AccessibilityDemo7 ad7;
      ad7 = new AccessibilityDemo7 ("Accessibility Demo7");

      try
      {
          Thread.sleep (5000);
      }
      catch (InterruptedException e) {}

      ad7.dumpTableInfo (ad7.getAccessibleContext ());
   }

   void dumpTableInfo (AccessibleContext ac)
   {
      AccessibleTable at = ac.getAccessibleTable ();

      if (at != null)
      {
          int nCol = at.getAccessibleColumnCount ();
          System.out.println ("Columns = " + nCol);

          int nRow = at.getAccessibleRowCount ();
          System.out.println ("Rows = " + nRow);
```

Listing 17.13 Continued

```
            return;
        }

        int nChildren = ac.getAccessibleChildrenCount ();

        for (int i = 0; i < nChildren; i++)
             dumpTableInfo (ac.getAccessibleChild (i)
                                  .getAccessibleContext ());
    }
}
```

AccessibilityDemo7 creates a GUI consisting of a 10 row by 3 column table. After a five-second delay, this row/column information is sent to the standard output device, as shown in Listing 17.14.

Listing 17.14 AccessibilityDemo7's Output

```
Columns = 3
Rows = 10
```

AccessibleContext's getAccessibleText method returns an AccessibleText object. An assistive technology can query this object to retrieve text, text attributes (such as font style), and other information (such as text length). This is demonstrated by the AccessibilityDemo8 application, whose source code is presented in Listing 17.15.

Listing 17.15 The AccessibilityDemo8 Application Source Code

```
// AccessibilityDemo8.java

import javax.accessibility.*;

import javax.swing.*;

import java.awt.*;
import java.awt.event.*;

class AccessibilityDemo8 extends JFrame
{
   AccessibilityDemo8 (String title)
   {
      super (title);

      addWindowListener (new WindowAdapter ()
                         {
                             public void windowClosing (WindowEvent e)
                             {
                                System.exit (0);
                             }
                         });

      JPanel p = new JPanel ();
```

LISTING 17.15 CONTINUED

```
      p.setPreferredSize (new Dimension (300, 50));
      JTextField jtf = new JTextField (20);
      jtf.setPreferredSize (new Dimension (100, 20));
      p.add (jtf);

      getContentPane ().add (p);

      pack ();
      setVisible (true);
   }

   public static void main (String [] args)
   {
      AccessibilityDemo8 ad8;
      ad8 = new AccessibilityDemo8 ("Accessibility Demo8");

      try
      {
          Thread.sleep (5000);
      }
      catch (InterruptedException e) {}

      ad8.dumpTextInfo (ad8.getAccessibleContext ());
   }

   void dumpTextInfo (AccessibleContext ac)
   {
      AccessibleText at = ac.getAccessibleText ();

      if (at != null)
      {
          System.out.println ("Caret position = "
                              + at.getCaretPosition ());
          System.out.println ("Selected text = "
                              + at.getSelectedText ());

          return;
      }

      int nChildren = ac.getAccessibleChildrenCount ();

      for (int i = 0; i < nChildren; i++)
           dumpTextInfo (ac.getAccessibleChild (i)
                           .getAccessibleContext ());
   }
}
```

`AccessibilityDemo8` creates a GUI consisting of a single text field component. You can type and select text. After five seconds, information about this text is sent to the standard output device. This information is shown in Listing 17.16.

Listing 17.16 AccessibilityDemo8's Output

```
Caret position = 1
Selected text = bc
```

From the listing, the assistive technology can deduce that the caret is positioned to the right of the first entered character, and that two characters have been selected.

`AccessibleContext`'s `getAccessibleValue` method returns an `AccessibleValue` object. An assistive technology can query this object to retrieve the minimum, current, and maximum values of a component object (such as a scrollbar) that contains numeric data. Listing 17.17 presents source code for the `AccessibilityDemo9` application, which demonstrates retrieving this information.

Listing 17.17 The AccessibilityDemo9 Application Source Code

```
// AccessibilityDemo9.java

import javax.accessibility.*;

import javax.swing.*;

import java.awt.*;
import java.awt.event.*;

class AccessibilityDemo9 extends JFrame
{
   AccessibilityDemo9 (String title)
   {
      super (title);

      addWindowListener (new WindowAdapter ()
                         {
                             public void windowClosing (WindowEvent e)
                             {
                                System.exit (0);
                             }
                         });


      JPanel p = new JPanel ();
      p.setPreferredSize (new Dimension (300, 50));
      JScrollBar jsb;
      jsb = new JScrollBar (Adjustable.HORIZONTAL, 0, 1, 0, 100);
      jsb.setPreferredSize (new Dimension (200, 20));
      p.add (jsb);

      getContentPane ().add (p);

      pack ();
      setVisible (true);
   }

   public static void main (String [] args)
```

LISTING 17.17 CONTINUED

```
   {
      AccessibilityDemo9 ad9;
      ad9 = new AccessibilityDemo9 ("Accessibility Demo9");

      try
      {
          Thread.sleep (5000);
      }
      catch (InterruptedException e) {}

      ad9.dumpValueInfo (ad9.getAccessibleContext ());
   }

   void dumpValueInfo (AccessibleContext ac)
   {
      AccessibleValue av = ac.getAccessibleValue ();

      if (av != null)
      {
          System.out.println ("Minimum value = "
                              + av.getMinimumAccessibleValue ());
          System.out.println ("Current value = "
                              + av.getCurrentAccessibleValue ());
          System.out.println ("Maximum value = "
                              + av.getMaximumAccessibleValue ());

          return;
      }

      int nChildren = ac.getAccessibleChildrenCount ();

      for (int i = 0; i < nChildren; i++)
           dumpValueInfo (ac.getAccessibleChild (i)
                            .getAccessibleContext ());
   }
}
```

`AccessibilityDemo9` creates a GUI consisting of a single scrollbar component. You can move the scrollbar's slider to any desired location within its range. After five seconds, information about the current state of this scrollbar is sent to the standard output device. This information is shown in Listing 17.18.

LISTING 17.18 `AccessibilityDemo9`'S OUTPUT

```
Minimum value = 0
Current value = 48
Maximum value = 100
```

Because Swing components are designed with accessibility in mind, much of the work is automatically done for you. However, there are some things you can do (in addition to assigning names and descriptions) to ensure that your GUI program is as accessible as possible:

- Specify keyboard alternatives where practical. For example, you can call the setMnemonic method on a button or menu item to provide a convenient keyboard alternative. (If a user has no limbs, he won't be able to use a mouse—at least not very effectively. However, by placing a straw between his teeth, the user could still operate the keyboard—to a certain extent.)
- Call setDescription to assign descriptions to all ImageIcon objects. (If a user is blind, a description could be translated into speech when the mouse pointer is moved over the corresponding image.)
- If a label is describing another component (such as a text field), call the label's setLabelFor method to associate this other component with the label. Assistive technologies can then identify this component by calling the label's getLabelFor method.

Tip

In addition to these three guidelines, IBM has established its own set of guidelines for developing accessible applications using 100% pure Java. IBM's guidelines are located at the following Web address:

http://www-3.ibm.com/able/snsjavag.html

To learn more about associating labels with other components, check out the source code for the AccessibilityDemo10 application. This source code is presented in Listing 17.19.

Listing 17.19 The AccessibilityDemo10 Application Source Code

```
// AccessibilityDemo10.java

import javax.accessibility.*;

import javax.swing.*;

import java.awt.*;
import java.awt.event.*;

class AccessibilityDemo10 extends JFrame
{
   JLabel jl;

   AccessibilityDemo10 (String title)
   {
      super (title);

      addWindowListener (new WindowAdapter ()
                         {
                             public void windowClosing (WindowEvent e)
                             {
                                System.exit (0);
                             }
                         });

      JPanel p = new JPanel ();
      p.setPreferredSize (new Dimension (300, 50));
```

LISTING 17.19 CONTINUED

```
        jl = new JLabel ("Name:");
        p.add (jl);
        JTextField jtf = new JTextField (20);
        jtf.getAccessibleContext ().setAccessibleName ("Name-entry");
        p.add (jtf);
        jl.setLabelFor (jtf);

        getContentPane ().add (p);

        pack ();
        setVisible (true);
    }

    public static void main (String [] args)
    {
        AccessibilityDemo10 ad10;
        ad10 = new AccessibilityDemo10 ("Accessibility Demo10");

        try
        {
            Thread.sleep (5000);
        }
        catch (InterruptedException e) {}

        ad10.dumpConnectedInfo (ad10.getAccessibleContext ());
    }

    void dumpConnectedInfo (AccessibleContext ac)
    {
        String s = ac.getAccessibleName ();

        if (s != null && s.equals ("Name:"))
        {
            AccessibleContext ac2;
            ac2 = jl.getLabelFor ().getAccessibleContext ();

            System.out.println ("Label connected to: "
                                + ac2.getAccessibleName ());

            return;
        }

        int nChildren = ac.getAccessibleChildrenCount ();

        for (int i = 0; i < nChildren; i++)
             dumpConnectedInfo (ac.getAccessibleChild (i)
                                  .getAccessibleContext ());
    }
}
```

`AccessibilityDemo10` creates a GUI consisting of label and text field components. The `setLabelFor` method is called to associate the text field with the label. After five seconds, the information shown in Listing 17.20 is sent to the standard output device.

Listing 17.20 AccessibilityDemo10's Output

```
Label connected to: Name-entry
```

Caution

If you don't call `setAccessibleName` to assign a name to the component associated with a label, and this component doesn't display any text, the label's name will be returned when you call `getAccessibleName` for the component associated with the label.

`AccessibilityDemo10` demonstrates a weakness with `setLabelFor` and `getLabelFor`. An assistive technology needs access to the label component so that it can call `getLabelFor` to retrieve the associated text field component. Unless it has access to the label (which isn't possible), it cannot retrieve the associated text field component. (This is why the `JLabel jl` field variable was declared outside `AccessibilityDemo10`'s methods, and used in the `dumpConnectedInfo` method.)

There is a better technique for retrieving associated components. This technique involves `AccessibilityContext`'s `getAccessibleRelationSet` method along with the `AccessibleRelation` and `AccessibleRelationSet` classes.

The `getAccessibleRelationSet` method returns an object created from the `AccessibleRelationSet` class. This object identifies the set of all components associated with another component. For example, a reference to the text field component would be placed in the relation set belonging to the label component.

Each entry in the `AccessibleRelationSet` object is an object that's created from the `AccessibleRelation` class. An `AccessibleRelation` object describes a component that serves as the target of an association between two components. For example, the text field component is the target of the label component. `AccessibleRelation` methods can retrieve this target or change it to another component.

Listing 17.21 presents source code for `AccessibilityDemo11`. This application is equivalent to `AccessibilityDemo10`, except that it uses the new relationship architecture. (The output is the same as the output shown previously in Listing 17.20.)

Listing 17.21 The AccessibilityDemo11 Application Source Code

```
// AccessibilityDemo11.java

import javax.accessibility.*;

import javax.swing.*;

import java.awt.*;
import java.awt.event.*;

class AccessibilityDemo11 extends JFrame
{
   JLabel jl;
```

Listing 17.21 Continued

```
AccessibilityDemo11 (String title)
{
   super (title);

   addWindowListener (new WindowAdapter ()
                      {
                          public void windowClosing (WindowEvent e)
                          {
                             System.exit (0);
                          }
                      });

   JPanel p = new JPanel ();
   p.setPreferredSize (new Dimension (300, 50));
   jl = new JLabel ("Name:");
   p.add (jl);
   JTextField jtf = new JTextField (20);
   jtf.getAccessibleContext ().setAccessibleName ("Name-entry");
   p.add (jtf);

   AccessibleRelation ar = new AccessibleRelation ("connector", jtf);

   AccessibleContext ac = jl.getAccessibleContext ();
   ac.getAccessibleRelationSet ().add (ar);

   getContentPane ().add (p);

   pack ();
   setVisible (true);
}

public static void main (String [] args)
{
   AccessibilityDemo11 ad11;
   ad11 = new AccessibilityDemo11 ("Accessibility Demo11");

   try
   {
       Thread.sleep (5000);
   }
   catch (InterruptedException e) {}

   ad11.dumpConnectedInfo (ad11.getAccessibleContext ());
}

void dumpConnectedInfo (AccessibleContext ac)
{
   AccessibleRelationSet ars = ac.getAccessibleRelationSet ();

   AccessibleRelation ar = null;

   if (ars != null)
       ar = ars.get ("connector");

   if (ar != null)
```

LISTING 17.21 CONTINUED

```
        {
            Object [] o = ar.getTarget ();

            JComponent jc = (JComponent) o [0];

            System.out.println ("Label connected to: "
                                + jc.getAccessibleContext ()
                                    .getAccessibleName ());

            return;
        }

        int nChildren = ac.getAccessibleChildrenCount ();

        for (int i = 0; i < nChildren; i++)
             dumpConnectedInfo (ac.getAccessibleChild (i)
                                  .getAccessibleContext ());
    }
}
```

Now that you've explored how an assistive technology uses the accessibility framework to learn about a GUI's components, you might be wondering how to support the accessibility framework in any new components that you create. To learn how to implement this support, see "Creating Accessible Components" in the "Troubleshooting" section.

UTILITIES

Sun provides several utilities that can help you discover just how accessible your JFC programs really are. These utilities are freely available and can be downloaded from the following address: `http://java.sun.com/products/jfc/#download-access`.

Follow the instructions for downloading and installation. Six utilities are included in the download: `AccessibilityMonitor`, `AWTMonitor`, `Ferret`, `JavaMonitor`, `Linker`, and `Monkey`.

The following sections provide a brief introduction to these utilities. For more information, consult the documentation that is included in the download.

AccessibilityMonitor

`AccessibilityMonitor` monitors all accessible property change events on all nontransient objects. This program automatically starts up when you run JFC programs.

Before `AccessibilityMonitor` can be used, you must do two things:

1. Copy `jaccess.jar` and `jaccess-examples.jar` to your JRE's extensions directory. Under Windows 98, if you've installed SDK 1.3 to your `c:\jdk1.3` directory, your extensions directory should be located at `c:\Program Files\Javasoft\JRE\1.3\lib\ext`.
2. Create or modify the `accessibility.properties` file so that it includes the line `assistive_technologies=AccessibilityMonitor`. (The `accessibility.properties` file is located in the `lib` directory, one level above the JRE's `ext` directory.)

The next time you run a JFC program, AccessibilityMonitor's main window will be displayed. For example, if you run AccessibilityDemo1 and click its button (after checking the Accessibility PropertyChange Events checkbox), AccessibilityMonitor displays information similar to that shown in Figure 17.2.

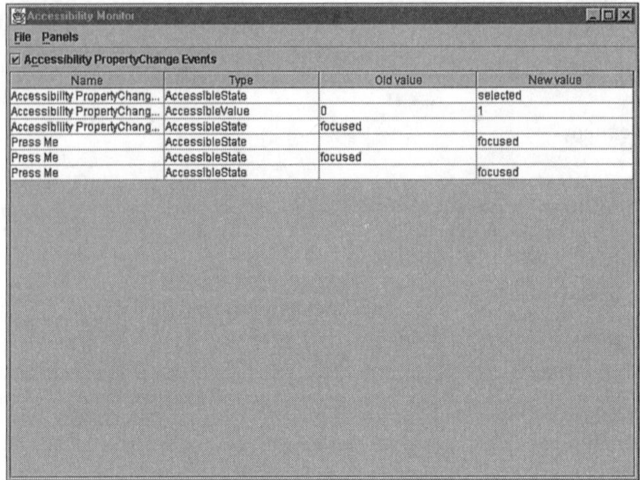

Figure 17.2 AccessibilityMonitor shows AccessibilityDemo1's property change events.

AWTMonitor

AWTMonitor is an AWT program that extracts information common to AWT and Swing components. However, Swing is not required to use AWTMonitor. This program automatically starts up when you run JFC programs.

Before AWTMonitor can be used, you must do two things:

1. Copy jaccess.jar and jaccess-examples.jar to your JRE's extensions directory.
2. Create or modify the accessibility.properties file so that it includes the line assistive_technologies=AWTMonitor.

The next time you run a JFC program, AWTMonitor's main window will be displayed. For example, if you run AccessibilityDemo1 and move the mouse (after checking the Mouse checkbox), AWTMonitor displays information similar to that shown in Figure 17.3.

Ferret

Ferret tracks mouse movements, focus updates, and the movement of a caret in either a text field or a text area. This program automatically starts up when you run JFC programs.

Before Ferret can be used, you must do two things:

1. Copy jaccess.jar and jaccess-examples.jar to your JRE's extensions directory.
2. Create or modify the accessibility.properties file so that it includes the line assistive_technologies=Ferret.

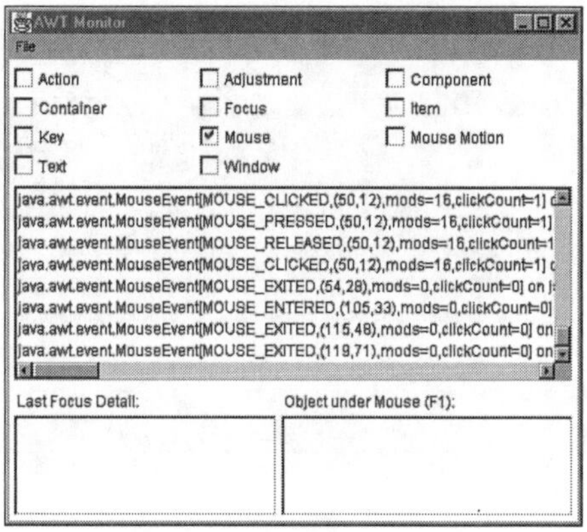

Figure 17.3
`AWTMonitor` shows `AccessibilityDemo1`'s mouse events.

The next time you run a JFC program, `Ferret`'s main window will be displayed. For example, if you run `AccessibilityDemo8` (after choosing `Track Caret` from the `Settings` menu), `Ferret` displays caret information similar to that shown in Figure 17.4.

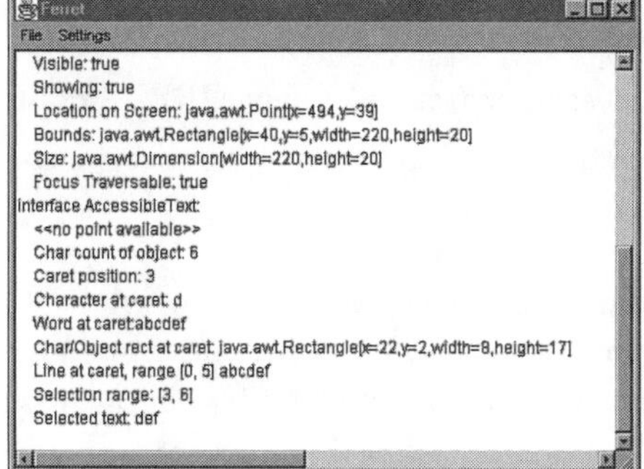

Figure 17.4
`Ferret` shows `AccessibilityDemo8`'s caret information.

`JavaMonitor`

`JavaMonitor` is a Swing program that extracts all kinds of AWT and Swing information. This program automatically starts up when you run JFC programs.

Before `JavaMonitor` can be used, you must do two things:

1. Copy `jaccess.jar` and `jaccess-examples.jar` to your JRE's extensions directory.
2. Create or modify the `accessibility.properties` file so that it includes the line `assistive_technologies=JavaMonitor`.

The next time you run a JFC program, `JavaMonitor`'s main window will be displayed. For example, if you run `AccessibilityDemo1` and click its button (after checking the `Action` checkbox in the `AWT Events` checkbox group from `JavaMonitor`'s main window), `JavaMonitor` displays information similar to that shown in Figure 17.5.

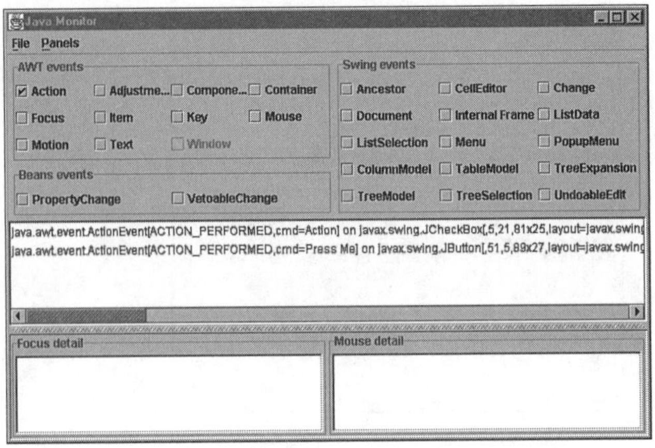

Figure 17.5
`JavaMonitor` shows `Accessibility Demo1`'s action events.

`Linker`

`Linker` captures accessible hypertext information. This program automatically starts up when you run JFC programs.

Before `Linker` can be used, you must do two things:

1. Copy `jaccess.jar` and `jaccess-examples.jar` to your JRE's extensions directory.
2. Create or modify the `accessibility.properties` file so that it includes the line `assistive_technologies=Linker`.

The next time you run a JFC program, `Linker`'s main window will be displayed. For example, if you run `AccessibilityDemo4`, load an HTML document, and press the `F1` function key while the mouse is positioned over this document, `Linker` displays information similar to that shown in Figure 17.6.

Caution

`Linker` is a tricky program to use. For example, during the development of this chapter section, it took several attempts to obtain the hyperlink information. For each attempt, `AccessibilityDemo4` was run and `F1` was pressed, until the information (shown in Figure 17.6) was obtained. To achieve the desired results, you'll have to experiment with this program.

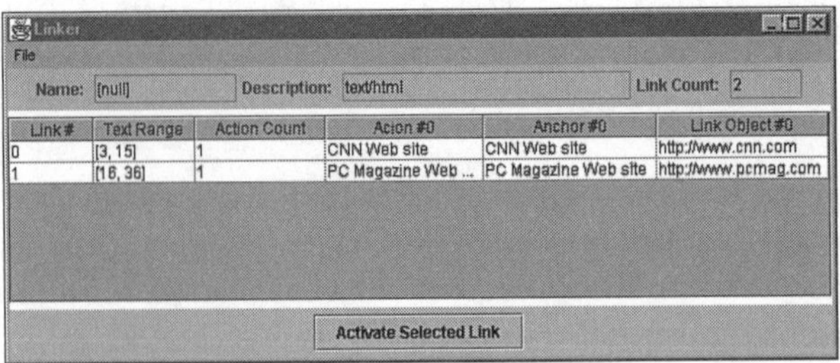

Figure 17.6
`Linker` shows `Accessibility Demo4`'s hyperlink information.

Monkey

Monkey "swings" through a JFC program's component hierarchy. The hierarchy is displayed as both a Component tree and as an Accessible tree in Monkey's window. This program automatically starts up when you run JFC programs.

Before Monkey can be used, you must do two things:

1. Copy jaccess.jar and jaccess-examples.jar to your JRE's extensions directory.
2. Create or modify the accessibility.properties file so that it includes the line assistive_technologies=Monkey.

The next time you run a JFC program, Monkey's main window will be displayed. For example, if you run AccessibilityDemo1, click the Refresh Trees menu item on Monkey's File menu, expand the AccessibiltyDemo1 tree fully, and right-click the Press Me entry in the Accessible Tree hierarchy (selecting AccessibleAction Panel), Monkey displays information similar to that shown in Figure 17.7.

Note

The small Action window appears because the AccessibleAction Panel menu item was selected from the pop-up menu that appeared when Press Me was right-clicked.

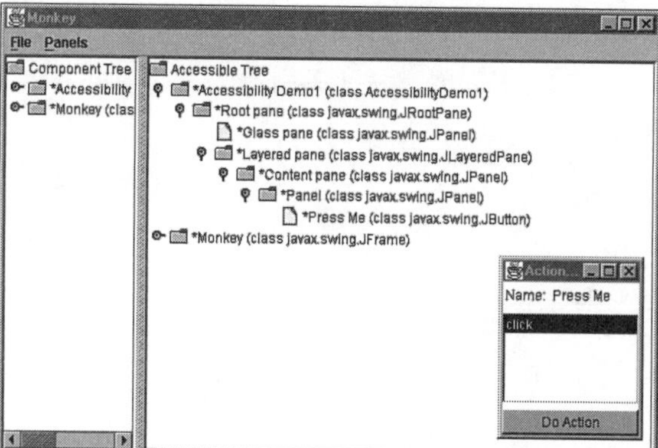

Figure 17.7 Monkey's main window shows AccessibilityDemo1's Component and Accessible trees.

ROBOTS

From time to time, software developers need to automate software execution (as in self-running demos) and testing. In each case, a *robot* (an autonomous program) programmatically delivers events describing keystrokes, mouse clicks, and mouse movements to the program being controlled.

Version 1.3 of the Java 2 Platform Standard Edition introduces a class called Robot. The methods in this class programmatically deliver keystroke and mouse events to the native windowing system's event queue.

To use `Robot`, you must first create an object. For example, the following code fragment creates a `Robot` object.

```
Robot r = new Robot ();
```

After you have a `Robot` object, you can issue method calls. For example, you can send keystroke events by calling `Robot`'s `keyPress` and `keyRelease` methods. Furthermore, you can send mouse events by calling the `mouseMove`, `mousePress`, and `mouseRelease` methods. Additional methods range from retrieving a pixel's color to waiting between events. (For more information, check out the SDK documentation.)

To demonstrate robots, Listing 17.22 presents source code for a `RobotDemo` application.

LISTING 17.22 THE `RobotDemo` APPLICATION SOURCE CODE

```
// RobotDemo.java

import java.awt.*;
import java.awt.event.*;

class RobotDemo extends Frame implements ActionListener
{
   RobotDemo (String title)
   {
      super (title);

      addWindowListener (new WindowAdapter ()
                         {
                             public void windowClosing (WindowEvent e)
                             {
                                System.exit (0);
                             }
                         });

      Panel p = new Panel ();
      Button b = new Button ("Press Me");
      b.addActionListener (this);
      p.add (b);

      add (p);

      setSize (175, 100);
      setVisible (true);
   }

   public void actionPerformed (ActionEvent e)
   {
      try
      {
         Runtime.getRuntime ().exec ("notepad.exe ");
      }
      catch (java.io.IOException e2) { System.out.println (e2);}

      try
      {
         Thread.sleep (1000);
```

Listing 17.22 Continued

```
      }
      catch (InterruptedException e2) {}

      try
      {
         Robot r = new Robot ();

         int [] keys =
         {
             KeyEvent.VK_T,
             KeyEvent.VK_E,
             KeyEvent.VK_X,
             KeyEvent.VK_T,
             KeyEvent.VK_ENTER
         };

         for (int i = 0; i < keys.length; i++)
         {
              r.keyPress (keys [i]);
              r.keyRelease (keys [i]);
         }

         Toolkit tk = Toolkit.getDefaultToolkit ();
         Dimension dim = tk.getScreenSize ();

         r.mouseMove (dim.width / 2, dim.height / 2);
      }
      catch (AWTException e2) {}
   }

   public static void main (String [] args)
   {
      new RobotDemo ("Robot Demo");
   }
}
```


`RobotDemo`'s main thread creates a GUI with a single button. After this button is pressed, `RobotDemo`'s event dispatching thread attempts to launch the `notepad.exe` program on a Windows platform. (If you want to play with `RobotDemo` on some other platform, replace `notepad.exe` with the platform-specific name of a more appropriate program.) After the program is started, `RobotDemo`'s event dispatching thread sleeps for one second.

Caution

The reason for sleeping is to give the program a chance to activate. For slower computers, you might need to increase the sleep interval.

After the event dispatching thread wakes up, it issues keystrokes that spell out the word `text`. A carriage return keystroke is then issued. At this point, the event dispatching thread obtains the screen size and moves the mouse pointer to its center.

Caution

Some platforms require special privileges before a `Robot` object can be created. If these privileges are not present, `Robot`'s constructors are designed to throw an `AWTException` object.

TROUBLESHOOTING

CREATING ACCESSIBLE COMPONENTS

How can I support the accessibility framework in new components, so that assistive technologies can automatically learn about them?

You incorporate accessibility support in a new component's class by using the `AccessibleRole` and `AccessibleState` classes. Sun's online Java Tutorial provides a good demonstration on how to accomplish this task. Check out this demonstration at `http://www.javasoft.com/tutorial/uiswing/misc/access.html`.

CHAPTER 18

Java 2D

In this chapter

by Geoff Friesen

WHAT IS JAVA 2D?

Java 2D enhances the AWT's support for graphics, fonts, colors, and images by introducing additional rendering options, new shapes, improved text management, buffered images, and a uniform rendering model for both screen and printer devices. These enhancements can lead to richer user interfaces and new kinds of Java applications.

The Java 2D API enables the creation of graphics libraries (such as CAD—Computer Assisted Drafting—libraries), special effects libraries for images, and read/write filters for use with the Java Media Framework (JMF). In fact, JMF uses Java 2D to perform its rendering tasks.

Graphics2D

When the time comes for a component to render its appearance, the component's `paint` method is called with a reference to a `Graphics` subclass object that represents a graphics context. However, this object is really a `Graphics2D` object. When accessed via a `Graphics` reference, only `Graphics` methods can be called. If this object is cast to a `Graphics2D` object, all of `Graphics2D`'s methods, along with inherited `Graphics` methods, can be called.

Like `Graphics`, `Graphics2D` is located in the `java.awt` package. To access `Graphics2D` methods, cast the `Graphics` reference to a `Graphics2D` reference, as shown in the following code fragment:

```
public void paint (Graphics g)
{
   Graphics2D g2 = (Graphics2D) g;

   // Java2D stuff
}
```

COORDINATE SYSTEMS

Java 2D works with a pair of coordinate systems: user space and device space. *User space* is a device-independent logical coordinate system that's automatically used by applications. All coordinates passed to Java 2D methods are specified in terms of user space. These coordinates are floating point numbers that represent logical pixel locations, instead of physical locations. For example, you can refer to a logical pixel at (50.392, -45.3). Obviously, these are not the coordinates of a physical pixel. In contrast, *device space* is a device-dependent physical coordinate system that varies with the target rendering device. Device space coordinates are integer values that identify physical pixel locations.

Java 2D automatically converts from user space to device space, by using an *affine transformation* (a mathematical concept whereby straight lines are transformed into straight lines and parallel lines are transformed into parallel lines, but the distance between points and the angles between lines can be altered). The default affine transform maps the origins of both coordinates systems to the upper-left corner, causes x values to increase to the right, and y values to increase to the bottom. However, it's possible to introduce a new transform that changes the location of either origin along with the directions in which x/y increase through positive values. This is accomplished by way of the AffineTransform class (discussed in a later section).

Java 2D maintains compatibility with Graphics methods (such as the drawLine method), by regarding the integer coordinates passed to these methods as device space coordinates. However, Java 2D still uses its affine transform to transform these coordinates into other device space coordinates.

ENVIRONMENTS, DEVICES, AND CONFIGURATIONS

Java 2D identifies three levels of configuration information that support the conversion from user space to device space. This information is encapsulated in objects created from subclasses of the abstract GraphicsEnvironment, GraphicsDevice, and GraphicsConfiguration classes (located in the java.awt package).

GraphicsEnvironment describes the collection of rendering devices visible to a Java application on a particular platform. Rendering devices include screens, printers, and image buffers. GraphicsEnvironment also includes a list of all available fonts. Each GraphicsEnvironment is associated with at least one GraphicsDevice.

GraphicsDevice describes an application-visible rendering device, such as a screen or printer. Each possible configuration of this device is represented by a GraphicsConfiguration subclass object.

GraphicsConfiguration describes a single mode of operation for a GraphicsDevice. For example, a super-VGA screen device can operate in several modes: 640×480×16 colors, 640×480×256 colors, 800×600×256 colors, and so on. Its screen is represented by a GraphicsDevice subclass object, and each of these modes is represented by a GraphicsConfiguration object.

To work with these classes, you first need to get a copy of the local graphics environment, as demonstrated by the following code fragment:

```
GraphicsEnvironment ge;
ge = GraphicsEnvironment.getLocalGraphicsEnvironment ();
```

After you have a graphics environment, a GraphicsDevice subclass object describing the default screen can be obtained by calling getDefaultScreenDevice. Alternatively, you can obtain an array of GraphicsDevice subclass objects describing all available screens by calling getScreenDevices. The following code fragment shows both approaches:

```
GraphicsDevice default = ge.getDefaultScreenDevice ();
GraphicsDevice [] all = ge.getScreenDevices ();
```

If you are more interested in retrieving information about fonts, you can call getAllFonts or getAvailableFontFamilyNames. The getAllFonts method returns an array of Font objects. (Each object describes a font with a one-point size. To create an identical font with a different size, you would call Font's deriveFont method.) The getAvailableFontFamilyNames method returns an array of String objects that contain font family names. Your program might present this information to a user in a list box. Both of these methods are demonstrated in the following code fragment:

```
Font [] fontList = ge.getAllFonts ();
Font f = fontList [0].deriveFont (2.0);
String [] fnames = ge.getAvailableFontFamilyNames ();
```

Listing 18.1 presents source code to a `ListFonts` application that obtains the local graphics environment and an array of all installed fonts, and then prints out the family and font names for each font.

LISTING 18.1 THE `ListFonts` APPLICATION SOURCE CODE

```
// ListFonts.java

import java.awt.*;

class ListFonts
{
   public static void main (String [] args)
   {
      GraphicsEnvironment ge;
      ge = GraphicsEnvironment.getLocalGraphicsEnvironment ();

      Font [] fonts = ge.getAllFonts ();

      for (int i = 0; i < fonts.length; i++)
           System.out.println ("Family = " + fonts [i].getFamily ()
                               + ", " + " Font = "
                               + fonts [i].getFontName ());
   }
}
```

MULTIPLE-SCREEN ENVIRONMENTS

You've probably heard about computers that support multiple screens. In one case, each screen displays different content. In a second case, all screens display the same content. In a third case, these screens are configured into one large virtual desktop. The desktop's upper-left corner is usually located in the upper-left corner of the screen that, in turn, is located in the upper-left corner of a rectangular grid of screens, whereas the desktop's lower-right corner is usually located in the lower-right corner of the screen that, in turn, is located in the lower-right corner of this screen grid.

When two or more screens are used to form a virtual desktop, a *virtual desktop coordinate system* existing outside the bounds of any screen is used to identify the coordinates of a pixel. One of these screens is designated the *primary screen*, and its upper-left corner is located at (`0, 0`). Usually, the primary screen is positioned in the upper-left corner of a rectangular screen grid. If not, the virtual desktop might use negative coordinates. Figure 18.1 illustrates a virtual desktop.

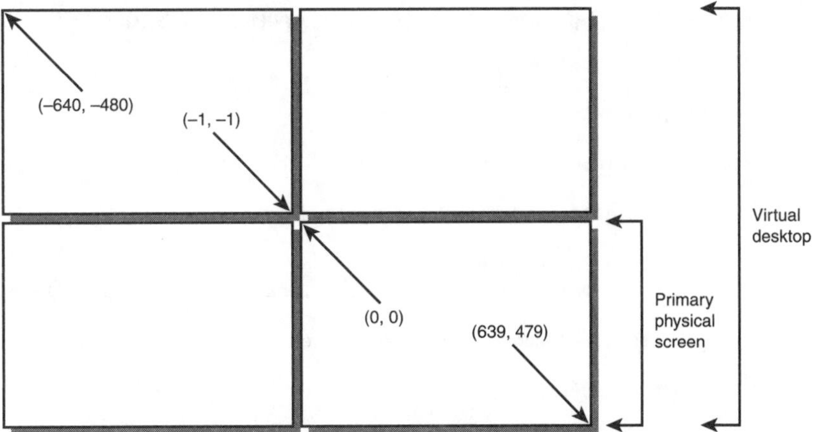

Figure 18.1
A virtual desktop is composed of multiple screens.

NEW TO 1.3

Version 1.3 of the Java 2 SDK supports the use of multiple screens. You can create `Frame`, `JFrame`, `Window`, or `JWindow` objects with a `GraphicsConfiguration` argument that targets a specific screen using one of its configurations (screen dimensions and number of colors). For example, the following code fragment constructs a frame that takes an argument consisting of the default (primary) screen's default graphics configuration:

```
GraphicsEnvironment ge;
ge = GraphicsEnvironment.getLocalGraphicsEnvironment ();

GraphicsDevice gd = ge.getDefaultScreenDevice ();
Frame f = new Frame (gd.getDefaultConfiguration ());
```

You can determine if a screen is the primary screen by calling its default graphics configuration's `getBounds` method and checking for a (0, 0) origin. This is shown in the following code fragment:

```
Rectangle bounds = gd.getDefaultConfiguration ().getBounds ();
Point origin = bounds.getLocation ();
if (origin.x == 0 && origin.y == 0)
    System.out.println ("primary screen");
```

Tip

You can determine if you are working in a multiple-screen environment by doing the following: Obtain an array of all screen devices. For each device, obtain an array of that device's configurations. For each configuration, call its `getBounds` method and examine the origin value. If this value is anything other than (0, 0), you are working in a multiple-screen environment.

Just as `getBounds` returns a screen's origin, it also returns a screen's size. It's possible to obtain the total size of the virtual desktop by taking the union of each `getBounds`' return value for all screens and configurations. Listing 18.2 presents source code to the `MultipleScreenDemo1` application, which shows how this is done.

LISTING 18.2 THE `MultipleScreenDemo1` APPLICATION SOURCE CODE

```
// MultipleScreenDemo1.java

import java.awt.*;

class MultipleScreenDemo1
{
   public static void main (String [] args)
   {
      GraphicsEnvironment ge;
      ge = GraphicsEnvironment.getLocalGraphicsEnvironment ();

      Rectangle vBounds = new Rectangle ();

      GraphicsDevice [] gdArray = ge.getScreenDevices();

      for (int i = 0; i < gdArray.length; i++)
      {
           GraphicsDevice gd = gdArray [i];

           GraphicsConfiguration [] gcArray = gd.getConfigurations ();

           for (int j = 0; j < gcArray.length; j++)
                vBounds = vBounds.union (gcArray [j].getBounds ());
      }

      Point origin = vBounds.getLocation ();
      System.out.println ("Virtual x = " + origin.x);
      System.out.println ("Virtual y = " + origin.y);

      Dimension size = vBounds.getSize ();
      System.out.println ("Virtual width = " + size.width);
      System.out.println ("Virtual height = " + size.height);
   }
}
```

How would you go about writing a program that displays a separate frame on each screen? Listing 18.3 presents source code to the `MultipleScreenDemo2` application that shows how to accomplish this task.

LISTING 18.3 THE `MultipleScreenDemo2` APPLICATION SOURCE CODE

```
// MultipleScreenDemo2.java

import java.awt.*;
import java.awt.event.*;

class MultipleScreenDemo2
{
   public static void main (String [] args)
   {
      GraphicsEnvironment ge;
      ge = GraphicsEnvironment.getLocalGraphicsEnvironment ();
```

LISTING 18.3 CONTINUED

```
      GraphicsDevice [] gdArray = ge.getScreenDevices ();

      for (int i = 0; i < gdArray.length; i++)
      {
           GraphicsDevice gd = gdArray [i];

           GraphicsConfiguration [] gcArray = gd.getConfigurations ();

           for (int j = 0; j < gcArray.length; j++)
           {
                Frame f = new Frame (gdArray [i].
                                     getDefaultConfiguration ());

                Rectangle bounds = gcArray [j].getBounds ();
                int xoffset = bounds.x;
                int yoffset = bounds.y;

                f.addWindowListener (new wClose ());

                f.setTitle ("Screen "+ Integer.toString (i)
                           + ", GC# " + Integer.toString (j));

                f.setSize (200, 200);

                f.setLocation ((j * 50) + xoffset, (j * 60) + yoffset);

                f.setVisible (true);
           }
      }
   }
}

class wClose extends WindowAdapter
{
   public void windowClosing (WindowEvent e)
   {
      System.exit (0);
   }
}
```


When you run `MultipleScreenDemo2` on a computer that uses multiple screens, you'll see a separate frame appearing on each screen. If you are fortunate enough to have a rectangular grid of screens in front of you, you'll see the position of each frame staggered to the right and below the frame appearing on the screen to its immediate left.

THE API

Java 2D is organized into eight packages that contain many classes and interfaces. Although most of these are new, some are AWT classes/interfaces that have been enhanced for use with Java 2D. Table 18.1 presents the names and contents of these packages, along with a list of affected classes and interfaces.

TABLE 18.1 JAVA'S JAVA 2D PACKAGES

Package	Description
java.awt	Classes and interfaces that are general in nature or enhance legacy classes. These include AlphaComposite, BasicStroke, Color, Composite, CompositeContext, Font, GradientPaint, Graphics2D, GraphicsConfiguration, GraphicsDevice, GraphicsEnvironment, Paint, PaintContext, Rectangle, RenderingHints, Shape, Stroke, TexturePaint, and Transparency.
java.awt.color	Classes and interfaces for the definition of color spaces and color profiles. These include ColorSpace, ICC_ColorSpace, ICC_Profile, ICC_ProfileGray, and ICC_ProfileRGB. (Consult the Java 2D user guide to learn more about ICC and color spaces. This guide is part of the Java 2 SDK 1.3 documentation.)
java.awt.font	Classes and interfaces for text layouts and the definition of fonts. These include FontRenderContext, GlyphJustificationInfo, GlyphMetrics, GlyphVector, GraphicAttribute, ImageGraphicAttribute, LineBreakMeasurer, LineMetrics, MultipleMaster, OpenType, ShapeGraphicAttribute, TextAttribute, TextHitInfo, TextLayout, TextLayout.CaretPolicy, TextMeasurer, and TransformAttribute.
java.awt.geom	Classes and interfaces related to the definition of geometric primitives. These include AffineTransform, Arc2D, Arc2D.Double, Arc2D.Float, Area, CubicCurve2D, CubicCurve2D.Double, CubicCurve2D.Float, Dimension2D, Ellipse2D, Ellipse2D.Double, Ellipse2D.Float, FlatteningPathIterator, GeneralPath, Line2D, Line2D.Double, Line2D.Float, PathIterator, Point2D, Point2D.Double, Point2D.Float, QuadCurve2D, QuadCurve2D.Double, QuadCurve2D.Float, Rectangle2D, Rectangle2D.Double, Rectangle2D.Float, RectangularShape, RoundRectangle2D, RoundRectangle2D.Double, and RoundRectangle2D.Float.
java.awt.image	Classes and interfaces for creating and modifying images. These include AffineTransformOp, BandCombineOp, BandedSampleModel, BufferedImage, BufferedImageFilter, BufferedImageOp, ByteLookupTable, ColorConvertOp, ColorModel, ComponentColorModel, ComponentSampleModel, ConvolveOp, DataBuffer, DataBufferByte, DataBufferInt, DataBufferShort, DataBufferUShort, DirectColorModel, IndexColorModel, Kernel, LookupOp, LookupTable, MultiPixelPackedSampleModel, PackedColorModel, PixelInterleavedSampleModel, Raster, RasterOp, RescaleOp, SampleModel, ShortLookupTable, SinglePixelPackedSampleModel, TileObserver, WritableRaster, and WritableRenderedImage. (Some of these classes—such as ColorModel—have been examined to some degree in previous chapters.)

TABLE 18.1 CONTINUED

Package	Description
`java.awt.image.renderable`	Classes and interfaces for producing rendering-independent images. These include `ContextualRenderedImageFactory`, `ParameterBlock`, `RenderableImage`, `RenderableImageOp`, `RenderableImageProducer`, `RenderContext`, and `RenderedImageFactory`.
`java.awt.print`	Classes and interfaces for printing non-Java 2D and Java 2D graphics, text, and images. These include `Book`, `Pageable`, `PageFormat`, `Paper`, `Printable`, `PrinterGraphics`, and `PrinterJob`.
`java.text`	Classes and interfaces for text layout. These include `AttributedCharacterIterator`, `AttributedCharacterIterator.Attribute`, and `AttributedString`.

RENDERING 101

Java 2D's `Graphics2D` methods render shapes, text, and images onto a drawing surface. These shapes can be constructed, either from `Graphics` drawing methods (such as `drawArc`) or from objects created from Java 2D's geometry classes (such as `Ellipse`). (These classes will be explored in an upcoming section.)

In the past, you could only choose one rendering state attribute: the current color. This color attribute would subsequently be used when drawing a shape or text. Furthermore, it would be used to fill a solid shape. In contrast, Java 2D's `Graphics2D` context maintains several state attributes. These state attributes can be divided into the following categories: rendering hint, stroke, paint (also known as fill), transform, clipping path, and composition.

State attributes are specified by creating attribute objects and by calling appropriate `Graphics2D` "set" methods with references to these objects as their arguments.

Note

A `Graphics2D` context holds references to attribute objects: They are not cloned. If your code alters an attribute object that is part of this context, it must call the appropriate "set" method to notify the context.

RENDERING HINT ATTRIBUTES

A rendering hint attribute is used to improve rendering quality, which is often at the expense of rendering speed (because higher quality results in slower rendering speed). These attributes are represented by objects created from the `RenderingHints` class (located in the `java.awt` package).

You can create a new rendering hint by calling the `RenderingHints (RenderingHints.Key key, Object value)` constructor. The `key` argument is one of the constants declared in `RenderingHints`, and serves to identify the new rendering hint. Its value is specified by the `value` argument. This is shown in the following code fragment:

```
RenderingHints rh = new RenderingHints (RenderingHings.KEY_ANTIALIASING,
                                        RenderingHints.VALUE_ANTIALIAS_ON);
```

The antialiasing hint is used to prevent graphics from appearing with jagged edges. These jagged edges result from *aliasing*—a technique of approximating arcs and diagonal lines by turning on the pixels that are closest to the path of the line or curve. *Antialiasing* provides smoother-appearing edges by modifying the intensity of pixels appearing around pixels closest to an arc or line, instead of turning on the closest pixels. However, antialiasing requires additional computing resources and can reduce rendering speed.

After you've created a `RenderingHints` object, you can specify this object as the new rendering hint for the graphics context. You do this by calling the `setRenderingHints` method, as shown in the following code fragment:

```
Graphics2D g2 = (Graphics) g;
g2.setRenderingHints (rh);
```

Alternatively, you could call `Graphics2D`'s `getRenderingHints` method to retrieve the current rendering hints and then modify only those hints that you are interested in by calling the `put` method on the `RenderingHints` object. The following code fragment shows how to achieve this task:

```
RenderingHints rh = g2.getRenderingHints ();
rh.put (RenderingHints.KEY_ANTIALIASING,
        RenderingHints.VALUE_ANTIALIAS_ON);
g2.setRenderingHints (rh);
```

The following types of hints can be specified:

- Alpha interpolation (can be set to default, quality, or speed)
- Antialiasing (can be set to default, on, or off)
- Color rendering (can be set to default, quality, or speed)
- Dithering (can be set to default, disable, or enable)
- Fractional metrics (can be set to default, on, or off)
- Interpolation (can be set to nearest-neighbor, bilinear, or bicubic)
- Rendering algorithms (can be set to default, quality, or speed)
- Text antialiasing (can be set to default, on, or off)

Consult the SDK documentation for more information (such as default values) on these rendering hints. To see the difference between aliasing (the default) and antialiasing, and how to turn on the antialiasing rendering hint, check out the source code to the `RenderingDemo1` applet, which is presented in Listing 18.4.

LISTING 18.4 THE `RenderingDemo1` APPLET SOURCE CODE

```
// RenderingDemo1.java

import java.awt.*;

public class RenderingDemo1 extends java.applet.Applet
{
   public void paint (Graphics g)
   {
      Graphics2D g2 = (Graphics2D) g;

      Font f = new Font ("Arial", Font.PLAIN, 48);
      g2.setFont (f);

      g2.drawString ("Aliased text", 10, 60);

      RenderingHints rh = g2.getRenderingHints ();
      rh.put (RenderingHints.KEY_ANTIALIASING,
              RenderingHints.VALUE_ANTIALIAS_ON);
      g2.setRenderingHints (rh);

      g2.drawString ("Antialiased text", 10, 120);
   }
}
```


`RenderingDemo1` obtains a `Graphics2D` subclass object and sets its font to Arial (which should be available on most platforms). By default, antialiasing is disabled. However, it can be enabled by first obtaining the default rendering hints, replacing the antialiasing attribute's off state with an on state, and restoring the default rendering hints with the antialiasing modification by calling `Graphics2D`'s `setRenderingHints` method. Antialiased text is then displayed, as shown in Figure 18.2.

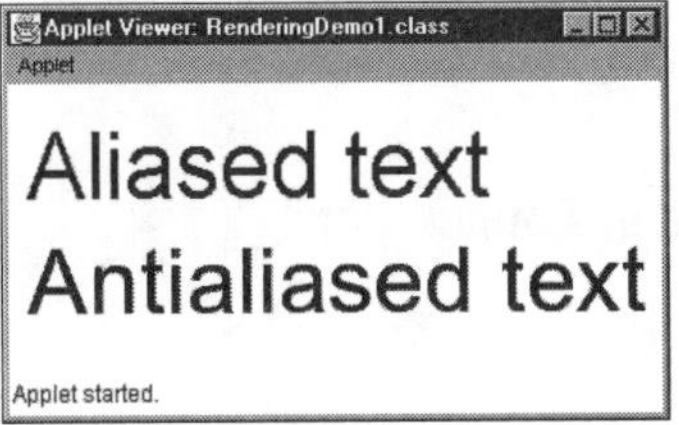

Figure 18.2 Aliased text has a more jagged appearance than antialiased text.

STROKE ATTRIBUTES

A stroke attribute is used to select the outline style of a shape (such as an ellipse or rectangle). Styles range from an *end cap style* (the shape of an unconnected line's endpoints) to a *join style* (the shape of the point where two angled lines meet) to a solid or dashed appearance (or some combination of these styles).

Strokes are represented by objects created from the `BasicStroke` class (located in the `java.awt` package). This class defines the outline attributes of a shape, including the width of the pen used to draw this shape, end caps, joins, and a dashed or solid pattern.

You can create a new stroke by calling the `BasicStroke ()` constructor. The stroke attributes default to a solid line with a width of 1.0 (in the user space coordinate system), a square end cap, a mitered join, and a miter limit of 10.0. (The miter limit is used to limit the trim of a miter join.) The following code fragment shows how to create this stroke:

```
BasicStroke bs = new BasicStroke ();
```

Alternatively, you can specify values for these attributes by calling one of the other `BasicStroke` constructors. For example, the `BasicStroke (float width, int cap, int join)` constructor creates a basic stroke object, whose pen width attribute is specified by `width`, cap style attribute is specified by `cap`, and join style attribute is specified by `join`. (This class contains several constants that can be passed as the `join` and `cap` argument values.) The following code fragment shows how to create a more specific stroke:

```
BasicStroke bs = new BasicStroke (2.0f, BasicStroke.CAP_ROUND,
                                  BasicStroke.JOIN_ROUND);
```

After you've created a `BasicStroke` object, you can specify this object as the new stroke for the graphics context. You do this by calling the `setStroke` method, as shown in the following code fragment:

```
Graphics2D g2 = (Graphics) g;
g2.setStroke (bs);
```

If you like, you can call `Graphics2D`'s `getStroke` method to retrieve the current stroke and extract its attribute settings, as shown in the following code fragment. (It's important to cast `getStroke`'s return value to a `BasicStroke`, because `getStroke` returns a `Stroke` subclass object reference.)

```
Graphics2D g2 = (Graphics) g;
BasicStroke bs = (BasicStroke) g2.getStroke ();
System.out.println (bs.getLineWidth ());
```

Listing 18.5 presents source code to a `RenderingDemo2` applet that demonstrates drawing lines using different end cap styles.

LISTING 18.5 THE `RenderingDemo2` APPLET SOURCE CODE

```
// RenderingDemo2.java

import java.awt.*;

public class RenderingDemo2 extends java.applet.Applet
{
   public void paint (Graphics g)
   {
      Graphics2D g2 = (Graphics2D) g;

      BasicStroke bs = new BasicStroke (16.0f,
                                        BasicStroke.CAP_BUTT,
                                        BasicStroke.JOIN_BEVEL);
      g2.setStroke (bs);
      g.drawLine (30, 20, 270, 20);
```

LISTING 18.5 CONTINUED

```
      bs = new BasicStroke (16.0f,
                            BasicStroke.CAP_ROUND,
                            BasicStroke.JOIN_BEVEL);

      g2.setStroke (bs);
      g.drawLine (30, 50, 270, 50);


      bs = new BasicStroke (16.0f,
                            BasicStroke.CAP_SQUARE,
                            BasicStroke.JOIN_BEVEL);

      g2.setStroke (bs);
      g.drawLine (30, 80, 270, 80);
   }
}
```

Figure 18.3 shows three lines, generated by `RenderingDemo2`, that illustrate end cap styles. The top line illustrates the `BasicStroke.CAP_BUTT` style, which ends unconnected lines with no added decoration. The middle line illustrates the `BasicStroke.CAP_ROUND` style, which ends unconnected lines with a round decoration, which has a radius equal to half of the width of the pen. Finally, the bottom line illustrates the `BasicStroke.CAP_SQUARE` style, which ends unconnected lines with a square projection, that extends beyond the end of the line to a distance equal to half of the line's width.

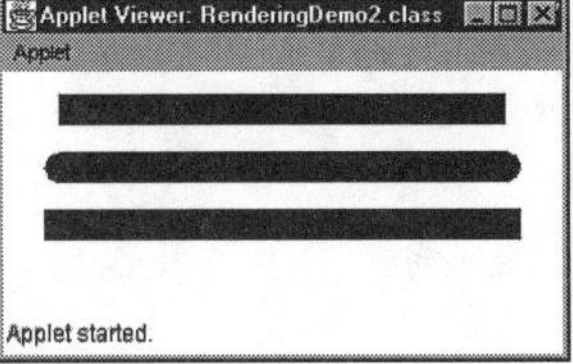

Figure 18.3 A basic stroke's end cap styles include butt (top), round (middle), and square (bottom).

Listing 18.6 presents source code to a `RenderingDemo3` applet that demonstrates drawing pairs of lines using different join styles.

LISTING 18.6 THE `RenderingDemo3` APPLET SOURCE CODE

```
// RenderingDemo3.java

import java.awt.*;
import java.awt.geom.*;

public class RenderingDemo3 extends java.applet.Applet
{
   public void paint (Graphics g)
   {
      Graphics2D g2 = (Graphics2D) g;
```

LISTING 18.6 CONTINUED

```
        RenderingHints rh = g2.getRenderingHints ();
        rh.put (RenderingHints.KEY_ANTIALIASING,
                RenderingHints.VALUE_ANTIALIAS_ON);
        g2.setRenderingHints (rh);

        BasicStroke bs = new BasicStroke (36.0f,
                                          BasicStroke.CAP_BUTT,
                                          BasicStroke.JOIN_BEVEL);
        g2.setStroke (bs);

        GeneralPath path = new GeneralPath ();
        path.moveTo (30.0f, 90.0f);
        path.lineTo (150.0f, 20.0f);
        path.lineTo (270.0f, 90.0f);
        g2.draw (path);

        bs = new BasicStroke (36.0f,
                              BasicStroke.CAP_BUTT,
                              BasicStroke.JOIN_ROUND);

        g2.setStroke (bs);

        path = new GeneralPath ();
        path.moveTo (30.0f, 190.0f);
        path.lineTo (150.0f, 120.0f);
        path.lineTo (270.0f, 190.0f);
        g2.draw (path);

        bs = new BasicStroke (36.0f,
                              BasicStroke.CAP_BUTT,
                              BasicStroke.JOIN_MITER);

        g2.setStroke (bs);

        path = new GeneralPath ();
        path.moveTo (30.0f, 290.0f);
        path.lineTo (150.0f, 220.0f);
        path.lineTo (270.0f, 290.0f);
        g2.draw (path);
    }
}
```

Note

In `RenderingDemo3`, the `GeneralPath` class was used to create a path object that describes a shape from a sequence of lines. `Graphics2D`'s `draw` method was then used to draw this shape. `GeneralPath` was used instead of the `drawLine` method because join styles don't work with `drawLine`. (`GeneralPath` and `draw` will be more fully explained in an upcoming section.)

Figure 18.4 shows three pairs of lines, generated by `RenderingDemo3`, that illustrate join styles. The top pair illustrates the `BasicStroke.JOIN_BEVEL` style, which joins lines by connecting the outer corners of their wide outlines with a straight line. The middle pair illustrates the `BasicStroke.JOIN_ROUND` style, which joins lines by rounding off the corner at a radius of half the line width. Finally, the bottom pair illustrates the `BasicStroke.JOIN_MITER` style, which joins lines by extending their outside edges until they meet.

Figure 18.4
A basic stroke's join styles include bevel (top), round (middle), and miter (bottom).

When you want to create dashed lines, call the `BasicStroke (float width, int cap, int join, float miterLimit, float [] dash, float dashPhase)` constructor. This constructor creates a basic stroke object whose pen width attribute is specified by `width`, cap style attribute is specified by `cap`, join style attribute is specified by `join`, miter limit attribute is specified by `miterLimit`, array of dash and space lengths is specified by `dash`, and dash phase is specified by `dashPhase`. This is demonstrated in the following code fragment.

```
float [] dashSpaceValues = { 20.0, 10.0, 5.0, 10.0 };
BasicStroke bs = new BasicStroke (2.0f, BasicStroke.CAP_ROUND,
                                  BasicStroke.JOIN_ROUND, 0.0f,
dashSpaceValues, 0.0f);
```

The `dash` array contains entries that describe the lengths of dashes and spaces. These entries alternate from dash to space to dash, and so on. The `dashPhase` argument specifies a length offset that determines if the line begins with a dash or a space, along with the length of this dash or space. For example, if the first two entries of the `dash` array are 10 (the length of the first dash) followed by 5 (the length of the first space), and the dash phase is 11, the line is drawn, beginning with the first space. In contrast, (assuming the same `dash` array) if the dash phase is 6, the line is drawn beginning with an initial dash of length 4 (10 minus 6). This shortened dash is followed by a space of length 5. These examples show that the use of a dash phase helps in aligning dashed lines.

In the preceding code fragment, the first entry in the `dashSpaceValues` array specifies the length of the first dash (20.0). The second entry specifies the length of the first space (10.0). The third entry specifies the length of the second dash (5.0). Finally, the fourth entry specified the length of the second space (10.0). A dash phase of 0.0 indicates that the line will begin with the very first dash entry (20.0).

Listing 18.7 presents source code to a `RenderingDemo4` applet that demonstrates drawing lines using an array of dash and space lengths, and a dash phase of zero.

LISTING 18.7 THE `RenderingDemo4` APPLET SOURCE CODE

```
// RenderingDemo4.java

import java.awt.*;

public class RenderingDemo4 extends java.applet.Applet
{
   public void paint (Graphics g)
   {
      Graphics2D g2 = (Graphics2D) g;

      float [] dash = { 20.0f, 10.0f, 5.0f, 10.0f };

      BasicStroke bs = new BasicStroke (8.0f,
                                        BasicStroke.CAP_ROUND,
                                        BasicStroke.JOIN_BEVEL,
                                        0.0f,
                                        dash,
                                        0.0f);
      g2.setStroke (bs);

      g.drawLine (30, 20, 270, 20);
      g.drawLine (270, 20, 270, 305);
      g.drawLine (270, 305, 30, 305);
      g.drawLine (30, 305, 30, 20);
   }
}
```

`RenderingDemo4` creates a dashed rectangle out of four lines. The result is shown in Figure 18.5.

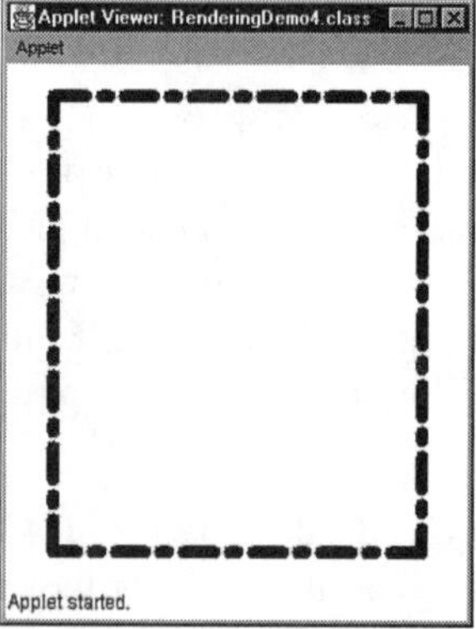

Figure 18.5
A basic stroke can be used to create dashed lines.

Java 2 Version 1.3 introduces a new rendering hint to be used with `BasicStroke` objects. This hint specifies whether lines drawn with a `BasicStroke` attribute are normalized; that is, automatically translated by (0.5, 0.5) from user space to device space.

Normalization is performed so that a line is centered on pixels and exactly covers whole pixels. By completely covering whole pixels, the line looks the same whether or not antialiasing is applied. The translation bias also ensures that the output to a screen and a printer is consistent. However, normalization can produce unexpected results, in some cases. For example, when the coordinate system is scaled up significantly, a stroked line that encloses a filled shape is not exactly centered on the edge of that shape.

`RenderingHints.KEY_STROKE_CONTROL` has been provided, for use in conjunction with `setRenderingHint`, to determine whether normalization should be used. The `RenderingHints.VALUE_STROKE_NORMALIZE` constant indicates that a translation bias should be applied. The `RenderingHints.VALUE_STROKE_PURE` constant indicates that no normalization is performed. Use this constant when you prefer that the rendering of your geometry is accurate, rather than visually consistent. Finally, `RenderingHints.VALUE_STROKE_DEFAULT` indicates that you have no preference whether or not a stroke is normalized. The following code fragment enables normalization:

```
Graphics2D g2 = (Graphics2D) g;
g2.setRenderingHint (RenderingHints.KEY_STROKE_CONTROL,
                     RenderingHints.VALUE_STROKE_NORMALIZE);
```

PAINT ATTRIBUTES

A paint attribute is used to select the interior color style of an enclosed shape (such as an ellipse or rectangle). Before Java 2D, only a solid color paint attribute could be used. However, Java 2D supports a more meaningful paint attribute, using either the *gradient* (gradual change in) paint style or the *texture* (patterned) paint style.

The gradient paint style is represented by an object created from the `GradientPaint` class (located in the `java.awt` package) and the texture paint style is represented by an object created from the `TexturePaint` class (also located in the `java.awt` package). (Because the `TexturePaint` class involves working with buffered images, this class won't be discussed until buffered images are presented.)

You can create a new gradient paint object by calling the `GradientPaint (float x1, float y1, Color c1, float x2, float y2, Color c2)` constructor. This object specifies a paint area ranging from (`x1`, `y1`) to (`x2`, `y2`), with colors that gradually range from `c1` to `c2`. Furthermore, the painting process defaults to being acyclic. In other words, after the endpoint color has been reached, any additional coloring will use that color. The following code fragment demonstrates creating a gradient paint object:

```
GradientPaint gp = new GradientPaint (0.0f, 0.0f, Color.red, 100.0f, 100.0f,
                                      Color.green);
```

Alternatively, you can choose cyclic painting (reverting to the source color when the destination color has been reached, and repeating the gradual change in color) by calling a `GradientPaint` constructor that takes a Boolean argument for specifying cyclic or acyclic painting. For example, `GradientPaint (float x1, float y1, Color c1, float x2, float y2, Color c2, boolean cyclic)` can be called with a Boolean `true` value in its `cyclic` argument to specify cyclic painting.

After you've created a `GradientPaint` object, you can specify this object as the new paint attribute for the graphics context. You do this by calling the `setPaint` method, as shown in the following code fragment:

```
Graphics2D g2 = (Graphics) g;
g2.setPaint (gp);
```

The best way to understand gradient paint is to examine a program that demonstrates this attribute. Therefore, Listing 18.8 presents source code to a `RenderingDemo5` applet, that creates a gradient paint object and then fills a rectangle with this style.

LISTING 18.8 THE `RenderingDemo5` APPLET SOURCE CODE

```
// RenderingDemo5.java

import java.awt.*;

public class RenderingDemo5 extends java.applet.Applet
{
   public void paint (Graphics g)
   {
      Graphics2D g2 = (Graphics2D) g;

      GradientPaint gp = new GradientPaint (0,
                                            0,
                                            Color.red,
                                            getSize ().width,
                                            getSize ().height,
                                            Color.blue);

      g2.setPaint (gp);

      g.fillRect (0, 0, getSize ().width, getSize ().height);
   }
}
```

`RenderingDemo5` performs a gradient paint from red to blue over the entire applet's surface. This paint works its way from the upper-left corner to the lower-right corner. The result is shown in Figure 18.6.

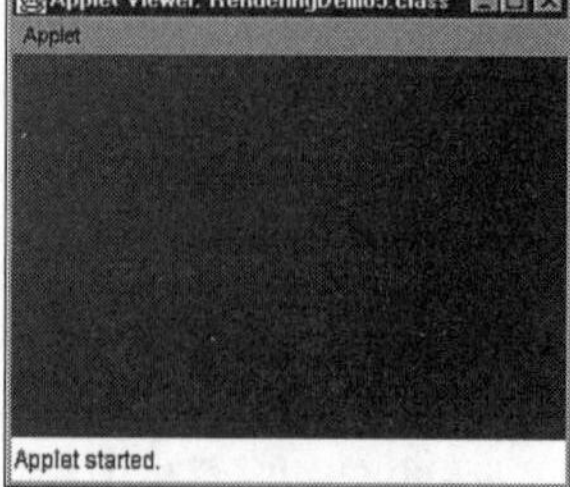

Figure 18.6
A gradient paint fill operation provides a smooth transition from one color to another.

> **Note**
>
> Unfortunately, because Figure 18.6 shows `RenderingDemo5`'s output in black and white, the gradual color change is not easy to see. To get the full effect of this program, you need to run `RenderingDemo5` with a video resolution that is capable of displaying more than 256 simultaneous colors. The same can be said for other figures in this chapter (and other chapters).

The pattern of a gradient paint follows the direction of the line between the two defined points. If these points lie on a horizontal line, a horizontal pattern will emerge. Similarly, if these points lie on a vertical line, a vertical pattern emerges. However, it these points lie on a diagonal line, you will see a diagonal pattern. (A diagonal pattern is shown in Figure 18.6, because the applet's upper-left and lower-right corner points lie on a diagonal line.)

TRANSFORM ATTRIBUTES

A transform attribute is used to convert from user space coordinates to device space coordinates. Each `Graphics2D` context uses a default transform to perform this conversion. To perform additional transformations (such as rotation or scaling), you can chain other transforms to the default transform, by calling `Graphics2D`'s `translate`, `rotate`, `scale`, and `shear` methods. To demonstrate some of these methods, Listing 18.9 presents source code to the `RenderingDemo6` applet.

LISTING 18.9 THE `RenderingDemo6` APPLET SOURCE CODE

```
// RenderingDemo6.java

import java.awt.*;
import java.awt.geom.*;

public class RenderingDemo6 extends java.applet.Applet
{
   public void paint (Graphics g)
   {
      // Draw original rectangle.

      g.fillRect (0, 0, 20, 20);

      Graphics2D g2 = (Graphics2D) g;

      // Tranlate result 50 pixels to the right and 50 pixels down.

      g2.translate (50, 50);

      // Then, rotate result by 30 degrees.

      g2.rotate (30.0 * Math.PI / 180.0);

      // Then, scale result by both x and y by a factor of 2.

      g2.scale (2.0, 2.0);

      g.setColor (Color.red);
```

LISTING 18.9 CONTINUED

```
        // Draw transformed rectangle.

        g.fillRect (0, 0, 20, 20);
    }
}
```

RenderingDemo6 draws a pair of rectangles. The first rectangle is drawn using the default transform. This transform is then changed by chaining translation, rotation, and scaling transforms, in the order of the method calls. This results in a second rectangle being drawn where each point is first translated by 50 units horizontally and vertically, then rotated by 30 degrees, and finally scaled by a factor of 2. The result is shown in Figure 18.7.

Figure 18.7
Rectangles and other shapes can be transformed through translation, rotation, and scaling transforms.

Transformations affect strings of characters in the same manner as shapes. For example, suppose the following code fragment is executed. Where do you think X and Y will appear?

```
Graphics2D g2 = (Graphics2D) g;
g2.translate (80, 60);
g2.drawString ("X", 0, 0);
g2.drawString ("Y", 10, 30);
```

The (0, 0) coordinates passed to the first drawString method will be added to (80, 60). The result is that X will be located 80 pixels from the left-hand side of the drawing surface and its baseline located 60 pixels from the top. Furthermore, the (10, 30) coordinates passed to the second drawString method will be added to (80, 60). As a result, Y will be located 90 pixels from the left-hand side and its baseline will be located 90 pixels from the top of the drawing surface.

More complex transforms can be created by creating objects from the AffineTransform class (located in the java.awt.geom package). You create a new affine transform by calling the AffineTransform () constructor, as shown in the following code fragment:

```
AffineTransform af = new AffineTransform ();
```

The default constructor creates an affine transform initialized to an *identity transform* (a transform that does not affect a transformation from user space to device space). After it's created, you can call various AffineTransform methods to build a more complicated transform, as shown in the following code fragment:

```
AffineTransform transform = new AffineTransform ();
transform.rotate (45.0 * Math.PI / 180.0);
```

This transform is designed to rotate points (around the origin of the user space coordinate system) by 45 degrees in the clockwise direction.

After you've created an `AffineTransform` object, you can specify this object as the new transform attribute for the graphics context. You do this by calling the `setTransform` method, as shown in the following code fragment:

```
Graphics2D g2 = (Graphics) g;
g2.setTransform (at);
```

You can easily undo the current transform by calling `getTransform` to return the current transform, and then by calling `setTransform` to restore this transform, as shown in the following code fragment:

```
Graphics2D g2 = (Graphics) g;

// Save current transform.

AffineTransform original = g2.getTransform ();

// Modify the transform.

g2.translate (100, 100);

// Do stuff with the modified transform.

// Restore the original transform.

g2.setTransform (original);
```


Listing 18.10 presents source code to the `RenderingDemo7` applet, which demonstrates creating and establishing an affine transform.

LISTING 18.10 THE `RenderingDemo7` APPLET SOURCE CODE

```
// RenderingDemo7.java

import java.awt.*;
import java.awt.geom.*;

public class RenderingDemo7 extends java.applet.Applet
{
   public void paint (Graphics g)
   {
      Graphics2D g2 = (Graphics2D) g;

      g.fillRect (100, 50, 100, 100);

      GradientPaint gp = new GradientPaint (100, 50, Color.green,
                                            200, 150, Color.blue);
      g2.setPaint (gp);

      AffineTransform transform = new AffineTransform ();
      transform.rotate (45.0 * Math.PI / 180.0, 100, 50);
      g2.setTransform (transform);
```

LISTING 18.10 CONTINUED

```
      g.fillRect (100, 50, 100, 100);
   }
}
```

RenderingDemo7 draws two rectangles. The first rectangle is transformed by the default transform (an identify transform). This rectangle appears toward the center of the applet's drawing surface. An affine transform is created. Its rotate method is passed a rotation angle along with translation arguments. Essentially, each user space point belonging to the second rectangle will first be translated from that rectangle's origin (100, 50) to the user space coordinate system origin, rotated 45 degrees, and finally translated back to the rectangle's origin. The end result is shown in Figure 18.8.

Note

The paint attribute is also set to a gradient paint style, to distinguish the second rectangle from the first.

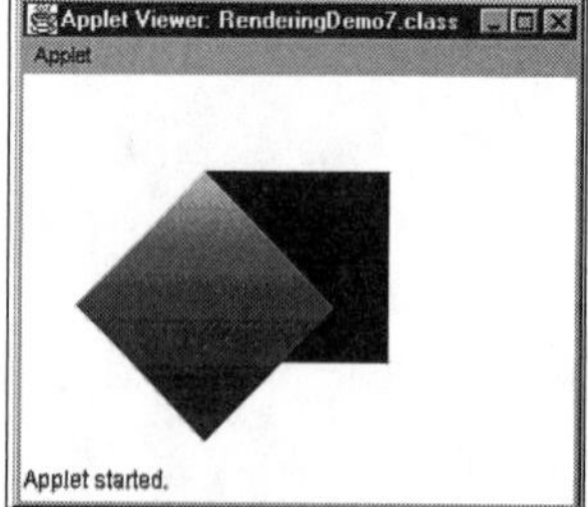

Figure 18.8
A rectangle is rotated and translated by an affine transform.

To wrap up this section, take a quick look at the shear method, found in both the AffineTransform and Graphics2D classes.

The shear method is called to perform a shearing operation. This transform multiplies the (x, y) coordinates by its argument values, to shift the resulting point in a new direction. Listing 18.11 presents source code to the RenderingDemo8 applet that shows this method at work.

LISTING 18.11 THE RenderingDemo8 APPLET SOURCE CODE

```
// RenderingDemo8.java

import java.awt.*;
import java.awt.geom.*;

public class RenderingDemo8 extends java.applet.Applet
{
   Image im;
   boolean shear;
```

LISTING 18.11 CONTINUED

```
   public void init ()
   {
      String imageName = getParameter ("image");
      if (imageName != null)
          im = getImage (getCodeBase (), imageName);

      String shear = getParameter ("shear");
      if (shear.toLowerCase ().equals ("true"))
          this.shear = true;
   }

   public void paint (Graphics g)
   {
      Graphics2D g2 = (Graphics2D) g;

      if (im != null)
      {
          if (shear)
          {
              AffineTransform at = new AffineTransform ();
              at.shear (0.5, 0.5);
              g2.setTransform (at);
          }

          g.drawImage (im, 0, 0, this);
      }
   }
}
```


RenderingDemo8 obtains and draws an image on the applet's drawing surface. If shearing is specified, a shearing transform is created and established. Each point in the subsequently drawn image will have its coordinates multiplied by 0.5. The result is shown in Figure 18.9.

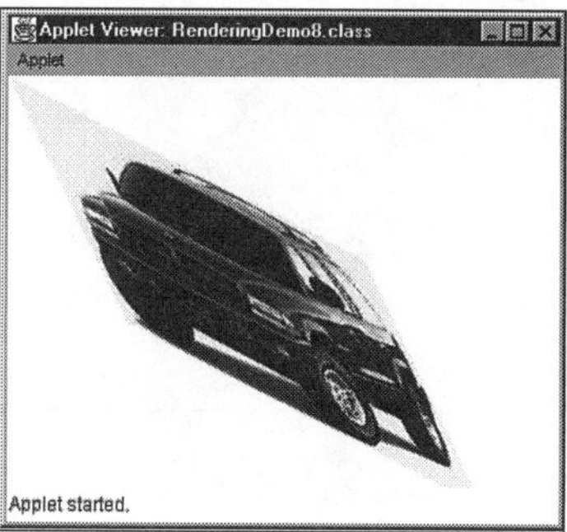

Figure 18.9
A sheared Durango—most unfortunate.

CLIPPING PATH ATTRIBUTES

A clipping path attribute identifies that portion of a drawing surface on which content can appear. Anything outside this path is clipped.

Chapter 13, "Beginning AWT," introduced the setClip method, which is part of the Graphics class. Any object whose class implements the Shape interface can be passed as an argument to this method to define the clipping path. Prior to Java 2D, only rectangular shapes could be passed. However, it's now possible to specify nonrectangular shapes (such as ellipses and even text). What's more, you don't need a Graphics2D reference to establish the current clipping path. To demonstrate, Listing 18.12 presents source code to a RenderingDemo9 applet.

LISTING 18.12 THE RenderingDemo9 APPLET SOURCE CODE

```
// RenderingDemo9.java

import java.awt.*;
import java.awt.geom.*;

public class RenderingDemo9 extends java.applet.Applet
{
   Image im;

   public void init ()
   {
      String imageName = getParameter ("image");
      if (imageName != null)
          im = getImage (getCodeBase (), imageName);
   }

   public void paint (Graphics g)
   {
      int w = getSize ().width;
      int h = getSize ().height;

      g.fillRect (0, 0, w, h);

      Polygon p = new Polygon ();
      p.addPoint (0, 0);
      p.addPoint (w / 2, h);
      p.addPoint (w, 0);

      g.setClip (p);

      if (im != null)
          g.drawImage (im, 0, 0, this);
   }
}
```

RenderingDemo9 creates a polygon from the Polygon class. Because this class implements the Shape interface, a polygon can be used to specify the clipping path. RenderingDemo9's polygon consists of an inverted triangle. When an image is drawn, only that part of the image that fits inside this triangle will be displayed. The rest of this image will be clipped at the triangle's edges. Figure 18.10 shows the resulting clipped image.

Figure 18.10
Polygons and other shapes can be used as clipping paths.

COMPOSITION ATTRIBUTES

A composition attribute determines what color is rendered when two pixels overlap. For example, suppose you have a solid green circle overlapping a solid red circle. Should the overlapped pixels be red, green, or some other color? The right choice of color will determine which circle appears to be on top, along with its level of transparency. The process of determining this color is known as *compositing*.

Note

If you recall, Chapter 13, "Beginning AWT," discussed the `setXORMode` method (located in the `Graphics` class). This method was the only means of compositing pixels in the pre-Java 2D era.

Java 2D provides a pair of interfaces that form the foundation of its compositing model: `Composite` and `CompositeContext`. Furthermore, the `Composite` interface is implemented by the `AlphaComposite` class (located in the `java.awt` package).

Objects created from the `AlphaComposite` class identify *alpha compositing rules*; that is, compositing rules that take the alpha channel of each pixel's color into account. (These rules are a subset of the Porter-Duff rules for alpha compositing as described in T. Porter and T. Duff, "Compositing Digital Images," SIGGRAPH 84, pages 253–259.)

`AlphaComposite` provides constants for eight alpha compositing rules. These constants, along with descriptions, are presented in Table 18.2.

TABLE 18.2 `AlphaComposite` RULES

Rule Constant	Description
`CLEAR`	Both the color and the alpha of the destination are cleared.
`DST_IN`	The part of the destination lying inside of the source replaces the destination.
`DST_OUT`	The part of the destination lying outside of the source replaces the destination.
`DST_OVER`	The destination is composited over the source and the result replaces the destination.
`SRC`	The source is copied to the destination.
`SRC_IN`	The part of the source lying inside of the destination replaces the destination.

TABLE 18.2 CONTINUED

Rule Constant	Description
SRC_OUT	The part of the source lying outside of the destination replaces the destination.
SRC_OVER	The source is composited over the destination.

To create an object that represents an alpha compositing rule, call one of AlphaComposite's two overloaded getInstance static methods. (Each method returns an AlphaComposite object.) After your code has this rule, it can call Graphics2D's setComposite method to specify the new compositing attribute, as shown in the following code fragment:

```
Graphics2D g2 = (Graphics) g;
AlphaComposite ac = AlphaComposite.getInstance (AlphaComposite.SRC_IN);
g2.setComposite (ac);
```

Listing 18.13 presents source code to a RenderingDemo10 applet that demonstrates alpha compositing.

LISTING 18.13 THE RenderingDemo10 APPLET SOURCE CODE

```
// RenderingDemo10.java

import java.awt.*;

public class RenderingDemo10 extends java.applet.Applet
{
   public void paint (Graphics g)
   {
      Graphics2D g2 = (Graphics2D) g;

      RenderingHints rh = g2.getRenderingHints ();
      rh.put (RenderingHints.KEY_ANTIALIASING,
              RenderingHints.VALUE_ANTIALIAS_ON);
      g2.setRenderingHints (rh);

      int [] rules =
      {
         AlphaComposite.CLEAR,
         AlphaComposite.DST_IN,
         AlphaComposite.DST_OUT,
         AlphaComposite.DST_OVER,
         AlphaComposite.SRC,
         AlphaComposite.SRC_IN,
         AlphaComposite.SRC_OUT,
         AlphaComposite.SRC_OVER
      };

      String [] ruleNames =
      {
         "CLEAR",
         "DST_IN",
         "DST_OUT",
         "DST_OVER",
```

LISTING 18.3 CONTINUED

```
            "SRC",
            "SRC_IN",
            "SRC_OUT",
            "SRC_OVER"
        };

        int w = getSize ().width;

        int x = 40, y = 40;

        for (int i = 0; i < rules.length; i++)
        {
             g.setColor (Color.red);
             g.fillOval (x, y, 50, 50);

             Composite old = g2.getComposite ();

             g2.setComposite (AlphaComposite.getInstance (rules [i]));

             g.setColor (Color.green);
             g.fillOval (x + 30, y + 30, 30, 30);

             g2.setComposite (old);

             g.setColor (Color.black);
             g.drawString (ruleNames [i], x, y + 80);

             x += 100;

             if ((x + 100) >= w)
             {
                 x = 40;
                 y += 100;
             }
        }
    }
}
```


RenderingDemo10 exercises all the alpha compositing rules. For each rule, it draws a red circle using the default source over alpha compositing rule, saves the default composite rule, establishes a new alpha compositing rule, draws a green circle that partially overlays the red circle, restores the composite rule, and draws a string of text. The composite rule must be restored prior to drawing the text (and the red circle). If not, this text and circle will not appear for some composite rules. Figure 18.11 shows the compositing results.

As you scan through Figure 18.11, you'll probably start to feel confused. Although some of the compositing results seem intuitive, other are downright weird! The best way to learn how this works is to carefully study the SDK documentation for the AlphaComposite class.

Consider the destination in rule. If you look up the documentation for this rule, you'll discover a pair of formulae that identify the resulting color. Basically, the source color (green) contributes nothing to the resulting color. Furthermore, the destination's color and alpha values are multiplied by the source's alpha value. Because color constants (such as `Color.red`) were used, and these constants are completely opaque (and nonzero) alpha values, the destination color, and alpha values are preserved. Therefore, a green circle does not appear.

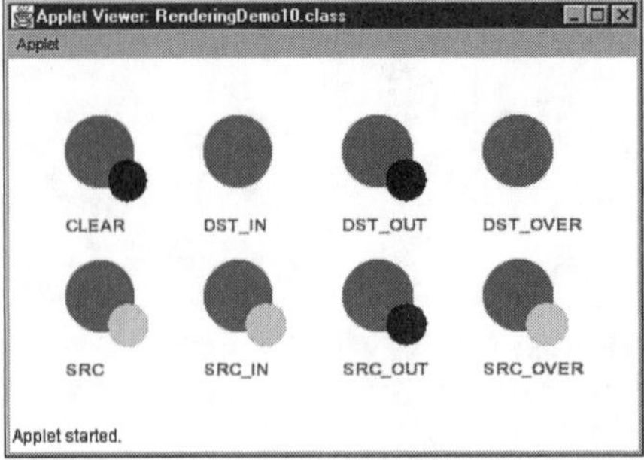

Figure 18.11
Java 2D provides eight alpha compositing rules that determine what colors to use when pixels overlap.

When an `AlphaComposite` object is created, an additional constant alpha value can be specified. This value is multiplied with a source pixel's alpha component to increase its transparency. For example, to create an `AlphaComposite` object that renders source pixels to be 50% transparent, specify an alpha of 0.5. This is shown in the following code fragment:

```
AlphaComposite ac = AlphaComposite.getInstance (AlphaComposite.SRC_OVER, 0.5f);
```

Listing 18.14 presents source code to the `RenderingDemo11` applet. This applet creates an `AlphaComposite` object representing a source over compositing rule. Furthermore, an alpha constant of 0.5 is provided. This constant will be multiplied with each pixel's alpha component to achieve a 50% transparency effect.

LISTING 18.14 THE `RenderingDemo11` APPLET SOURCE CODE

```
// RenderingDemo11.java

import java.awt.*;
import java.awt.geom.*;

public class RenderingDemo11 extends java.applet.Applet
{
  public void paint(Graphics g)
  {
     Graphics2D g2 = (Graphics2D) g;

     g2.setColor (Color.red);
     g2.translate (200, 100);
     g2.rotate ((60 * java.lang.Math.PI) / 180);
     g2.fillRect (0, 0, 100, 100);

     g2.setTransform (new AffineTransform ());  // set to identity

     AlphaComposite ac;
     ac =  AlphaComposite.getInstance (AlphaComposite.SRC_OVER, 0.5f);
     g2.setComposite (ac);
```

LISTING 18.14 CONTINUED

```
      g2.setColor (Color.orange);
      g2.fillRect (150, 50, 100, 100);

      g2.setColor (Color.green);
      g2.fillRect (225, 125, 100, 100);

      g2.setColor (Color.blue);
      g2.fillRect (150, 175, 100, 100);

      g2.setColor (Color.yellow);
      g2.fillRect (75, 125, 100, 100);
   }
}
```

RenderingDemo11 draws a rectangle, rotated by 60 degrees, using the default source over and opaque compositing rule. After this rule is changed to allow for 50% transparency, four rectangles are drawn so that they overlap the original rectangle and each other. The result is shown in Figure 18.12.

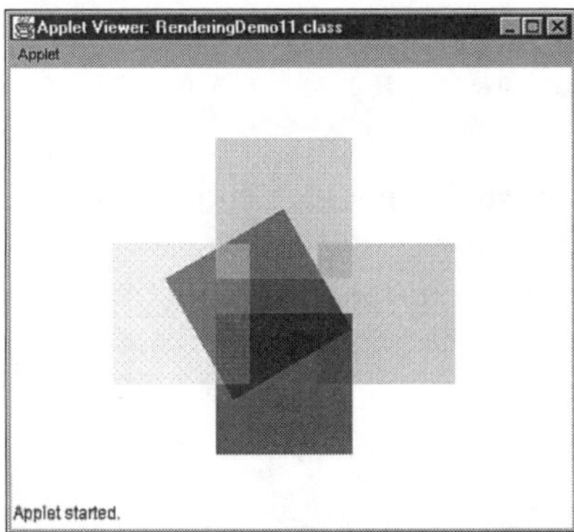

Figure 18.12 Alpha compositing makes it possible to achieve transparency.

SHAPES, TEXT, AND BUFFERED IMAGES

Now that you've seen how Java 2D improves on the AWT's rendering model, it's time to explore Java 2D's shapes, text enhancements, and buffered images.

SHAPES

From a mathematical perspective, shapes are geometric entities (such as circles and rectangles). From Java's perspective, shapes are objects whose classes implement the `Shape` interface.

`Graphics` declares a variety of methods (such as `drawArc` and `fillArc`) for drawing and filling various kinds of shapes. The problem with these methods is that they don't represent shapes in an object-oriented manner. Although they might draw and fill shapes, it's not possible to, say, create an `Arc` object describing an arc and then call `draw (Arc)` to render its outline.

The capability to create objects that represent shapes is very important to some programs (such as CAD programs) that treat shapes as entities instead of pixels. Fortunately, Java 2D solves this problem by providing a variety of geometric classes for creating shapes. Furthermore, Java 2D provides a pair of methods—`draw` and `fill`—that take a single `Shape` argument (via an object whose class implements `Shape`) and draw either an outline or a solid shape.

The geometric classes contain `Float` and `Double` inner classes, whose constructors are called, with single-precision or double-precision user space coordinates (respectively), to create the appropriate shapes. Furthermore, the geometric classes contain a variety of methods for manipulating shapes. These methods will not be covered (for space reasons). If you want to learn more about these methods, consult the SDK documentation.

ARCS

The `Arc2D` class (located in the `java.awt.geom` package) is used to create arc shapes. Each arc is created in a bounding rectangle that identifies its upper-left corner and dimensions. The arc's starting angle and angular extent can be specified (in degrees). Furthermore, the arc's closure type can be specified as either chord, open, or pie. The following code fragment creates an arc:

```
Arc2D arc = new Arc2D.Float (0.0f, 0.0f, 100.0f, 100.0f, 25.0f, 10.0f,
                             Arc2D.CHORD);
```

This arc is created in a bounding box whose upper-left corner is located at (0.0, 0.0) and dimensions are (100.0, 100.0). A start angle of 25.0 degrees and an extent of 10.0 degrees is specified. (The arc will range from 25.0 degrees to 25.0 + 10.0 = 35.0 degrees.) The closure type is *chord*—a straight line drawn from the start of the arc to the end of the arc. Listing 18.15 presents source code to a `ShapeDemo1` applet that demonstrates drawing various kinds of arcs.

LISTING 18.15 THE ShapeDemo1 APPLET SOURCE CODE

```
// ShapeDemo1.java

import java.awt.*;
import java.awt.geom.*;

public class ShapeDemo1 extends java.applet.Applet
{
   public void paint (Graphics g)
   {
      Graphics2D g2 = (Graphics2D) g;

      int w = getSize ().width;
      int h = getSize ().height;

      Arc2D arc = new Arc2D.Double (0.0, 0.0, w, h,
                                    0.0, 60.0, Arc2D.CHORD);

      g2.draw (arc);
```

LISTING 18.15 CONTINUED

```
      arc = new Arc2D.Float (0.0f, 0.0f, w, h,
                             80.0f, 110.0f, Arc2D.PIE);

      g2.fill (arc);

      arc = new Arc2D.Float (0.0f, 0.0f, w, h,
                             210.0f, 130.0f, Arc2D.OPEN);

      g2.draw (arc);
   }
}
```

ShapeDemo1 demonstrates creating Arc2D objects by using either the Float or Double constructors. (You would normally use Float when speed is of the essence and Double when precision is more important.) An arc closed with a chord is drawn from 0 to 60 degrees. This is followed by a pie-shaped arc being drawn from 80 to 190 degrees. Finally, an open arc is drawn from 210 to 340 degrees. These arcs are shown in Figure 18.13.

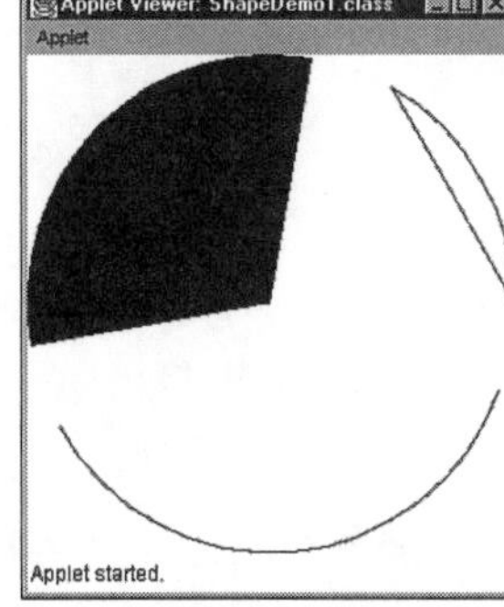

Figure 18.13
Arc2D simplifies the creation of outline or solid arcs.

Note

One item in ShapeDemo1 that you might find curious is the passing of the applet's physical width and height (obtained by calling getSize) to the Arc2D.Double and Arc2D.Float constructors. These constructors (and the other shape constructors) expect a logical width and height. The answer to this riddle is that the default transform's physical width and logical width are identical. (The same is true for physical height and logical height.) If you change the transform to specify a different logical width and/or height, you must use the logical values.

CUBIC CURVES

The CubicCurve2D class (located in the java.awt.geom package) is used to create cubic curves. Each cubic curve is constructed from a start point, an endpoint, and two *control points* (points that determine the shape of the curve). The following code fragment creates a cubic curve:

```
CubicCuve2D cubic = new CubicCurve2D.Double (0.0, 50.0, 50.0, 25.0,
                                              75.0, 75.0, 100.0, 50.0);
```

The start point is located at (0.0, 50.0) and the endpoint is located at (100.0, 50.0). The first control point is located at (50.0, 25.0) and the second control point is located at (75.0, 75.0). Listing 18.16 presents source code to a `ShapeDemo2` applet that demonstrates drawing a cubic curve:

LISTING 18.16 THE `ShapeDemo2` APPLET SOURCE CODE

```
// ShapeDemo2.java

import java.awt.*;
import java.awt.geom.*;

public class ShapeDemo2 extends java.applet.Applet
{
   public void paint (Graphics g)
   {
      int w = getSize ().width;
      int h = getSize ().height;

      CubicCurve2D cubic = new CubicCurve2D.Double (w / 2 - 50,
                                                    h / 2,
                                                    w / 2 - 25,
                                                    h / 2 - 25,
                                                    w / 2 + 25,
                                                    h / 2 + 25,
                                                    w / 2 + 50,
                                                    h / 2);

      // Draw first control point.

      g.drawLine (w / 2 - 25, h / 2 - 25, w / 2 - 25, h / 2 - 25);

      // Draw second control point.

      g.drawLine (w / 2 + 25, h / 2 + 25, w / 2 + 25, h / 2 + 25);

      // Draw the curve.

      Graphics2D g2 = (Graphics2D) g;

      g2.draw (cubic);
   }
}
```

`ShapeDemo2` draws the two control points in addition to the curve. The result is shown in Figure 18.14.

Note

If you are looking for an interactive program that allows you to move the start points, endpoints, and control points of a cubic curve, check out the 2D Graphics trail in the Java Tutorial (`http://www.javasoft.com/tutorial`).

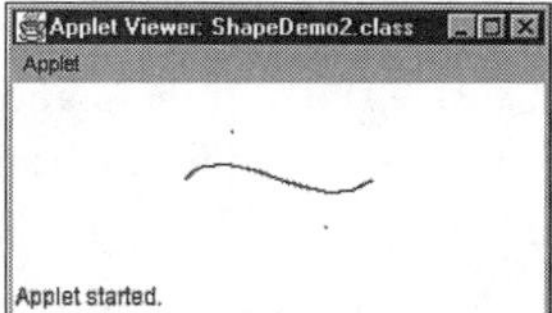

Figure 18.14
A cubic curve's appearance is governed by a pair of control points.

Version 1.3 of the Java 2 SDK introduces two new `CubicCurve2D` methods for solving *cubic equations*—equations of the form `dx^3 + ax^2 + bx + c = 0`. The `solveCubic (double [] eqn)` and `solveCubic (double [] eqn, double [] res)` methods take an `eqn` array of four equation coefficients: `eqn [0]` contains `c`, `eqn [1]` contains `b`, `eqn [2]` contains `a`, and `eqn [3]` contains `d`. A return value of `-1` identifies a constant equation (`b`, `a`, and `d` are 0). Otherwise, this value represents the number of noncomplex *roots* (values of `x` that make the equation evaluate to 0). If a second `res` array is passed, roots are stored in this array. Otherwise, they are stored in `eqn`.

ELLIPSES

The `Ellipse2D` class (located in the `java.awt.geom` package) is used to create ellipses or circles. A circle is drawn when the width and height of the bounding box that contains this shape are equal. The following code fragment creates an ellipse:

```
Ellipse ellipse = new Ellipse.Double (0.0, 50.0, 100.0, 100.0);
```

This ellipse represents a circle drawn in a bounding box whose upper-left corner is located at (0.0, 50.0) and dimensions are (100.0, 100.0). Listing 18.17 presents source code to a `ShapeDemo3` applet that demonstrates drawing ellipses and filling circles.

LISTING 18.17 THE `ShapeDemo3` APPLET SOURCE CODE

```
// ShapeDemo3.java

import java.awt.*;
import java.awt.geom.*;

public class ShapeDemo3 extends java.applet.Applet
{
   public void paint (Graphics g)
   {
      Graphics2D g2 = (Graphics2D) g;

      int w = getSize ().width - 1;
      int h = getSize ().height - 1;

      Ellipse2D ellipse = new Ellipse2D.Double (0.0, 0.0, w, h);
      g2.draw (ellipse);

      ellipse = new Ellipse2D.Double (w / 2, h / 2, w / 4, w / 4);
      g2.fill (ellipse);
   }
}
```

ShapeDemo3 draws a filled circle inside an ellipse's outline, when the applet's width and height are different. Otherwise, a filled circle is drawn inside the outline of another circle. The reason for subtracting 1 from the width and height is to ensure that the right-most column and bottom-most row of pixels that belong to the ellipse are visible. (The ellipse is drawn in a bounding box from (0.0, 0.0) to (0.0 + w, 0.0 + h), and the applet's coordinates range from (0.0, 0.0) to (0.0 + w – 1, 0.0 + h – 1).) Figure 18.15 shows the ellipse and circle.

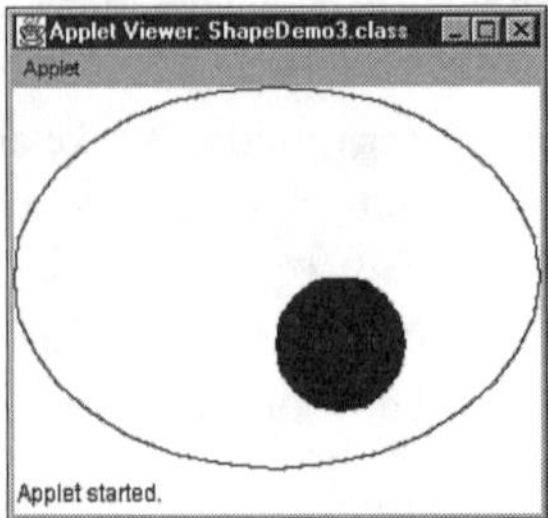

Figure 18.15 Ellipse2D is used to create an outlined ellipse and a filled circle.

GENERAL PATHS

The GeneralPath class (located in the java.awt.geom package) is used to create arbitrary shapes. After you've created a GeneralPath object, you create a shape by calling its moveTo, lineTo—and even curveTo and quadTo (for drawing cubic and quadratic curves, respectively)—methods. The following code fragment creates a general path that defines a triangle:

```
GeneralPath gp = new GeneralPath ();
gp.moveTo (100.0, 100.0);
gp.lineTo (200.0, 0.0);
gp.lineTo (300.0, 100.0);
gp.lineTo (100.0, 100.0);
```

Listing 18.18 presents source code to a ShapeDemo4 applet that demonstrates general paths.

LISTING 18.18 THE ShapeDemo4 APPLET SOURCE CODE

```
// ShapeDemo4.java

import java.awt.*;
import java.awt.geom.*;

public class ShapeDemo4 extends java.applet.Applet
{
   public void paint (Graphics g)
   {
      Graphics2D g2 = (Graphics2D) g;

      int w = getSize ().width - 1;
      int h = getSize ().height - 1;

      GeneralPath gp = new GeneralPath ();
      gp.moveTo (0.0f, h);
      gp.lineTo (w / 2, 0.0f);
```

LISTING 18.18 CONTINUED

```
      gp.lineTo (w, h);
      gp.lineTo (0.0f, h);

      g2.draw (gp);

      g2.scale (0.25, 0.25);
      g2.translate (50.0, 50.0);

      g2.fill (gp);
   }
}
```

ShapeDemo4 uses a general path to define a triangle, whose outline is subsequently drawn. After scaling and translation transforms are chained to the default transform, a smaller filled version of this triangle is drawn. These triangles are shown in Figure 18.16.

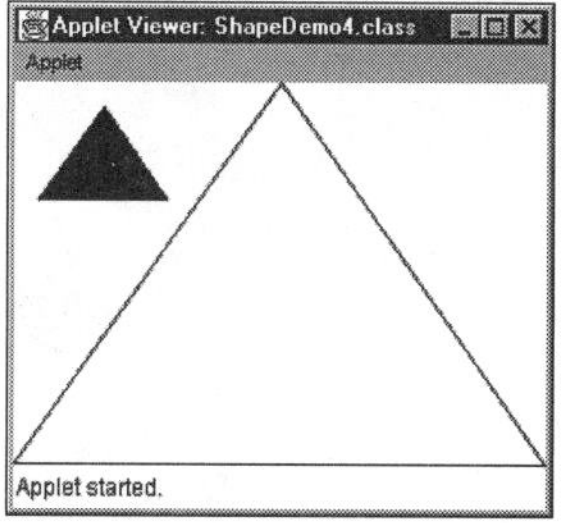

Figure 18.16 Triangles and other shapes can be drawn using a general path.

LINES

The Line2D class (located in the java.awt.geom package) is used to create lines. This is illustrated in the following code fragment, which specifies a diagonal line:

```
Line2D l = new Line2D.Float (0.0f, 0.0f, 20.0f, 20.0f);
```

The line is drawn from (0.0, 0.0) to (20.0, 20.0). Listing 18.19 presents source code to a ShapeDemo5 applet that demonstrates lines.

LISTING 18.19 THE ShapeDemo5 APPLET SOURCE CODE

```
// ShapeDemo5.java

import java.awt.*;
import java.awt.geom.*;

public class ShapeDemo5 extends java.applet.Applet
{
   public void paint (Graphics g)
   {
      Graphics2D g2 = (Graphics2D) g;

      int w = getSize ().width - 1;
      int h = getSize ().height - 1;
```

LISTING 18.19 CONTINUED

```
        for (int i = 0; i < 12; i++)
        {
             double angle = Math.PI / 2 - i * Math.PI / 6;
             double x = Math.cos (angle);
             double y = Math.sin (angle);

             Line2D l = new Line2D.Double (100 + 55.0 * x,
                                           100 - 55.0 * y,
                                           100 + 65.0 * x,
                                           100 - 65.0 * y);

             g2.draw (l);
        }
    }
}
```

ShapeDemo5 uses lines to define the tick marks on a clock face. This is shown in Figure 18.17.

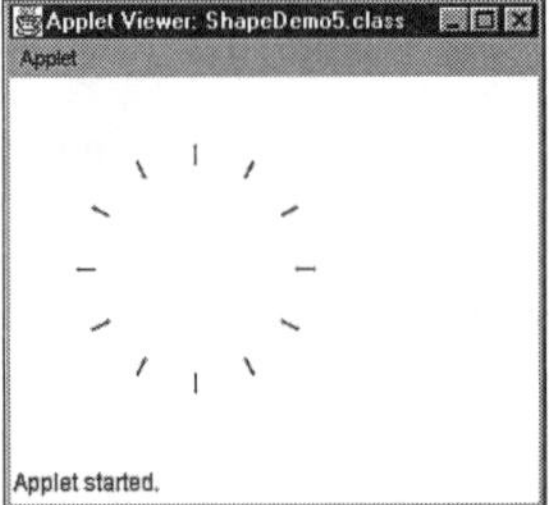

Figure 18.17 Lines created with Line2D can be used to draw the tick marks on a clock face.

POINTS AND DIMENSIONS

Java 2D's Point2D and Dimension2D classes are used to create objects representing user space points and dimensions. You would normally use these classes in programs that treat all graphics as a series of objects, instead of pixels. For example, Point2D can be used to keep track of the points representing a line's endpoints. This is shown in the following code fragment:

```
Line2D l = new Line2D.Double (new Point2D.Double (10.0, 10.0),
                              new Point2D.Double (20.0, 30.0));
```

QUADRATIC CURVES

The QuadCurve2D class (located in the java.awt.geom package) is used to create quadratic curves. Each quadratic curve is constructed from a start point, an endpoint, and one control point. The following code fragment creates a quadratic curve:

```
QuadCuve2D quad = new QuadCurve2D.Double (0.0, 50.0, 50.0, 25.0, 100.0, 50.0);
```

The start point is located at (0.0, 50.0) and the endpoint is located at (100.0, 50.0). The control point is located at (50.0, 25.0). Listing 18.20 presents source code to a `ShapeDemo6` applet that demonstrates drawing a quadratic curve.

LISTING 18.20 THE `ShapeDemo6` APPLET SOURCE CODE

```
// ShapeDemo6.java

import java.awt.*;
import java.awt.geom.*;

public class ShapeDemo6 extends java.applet.Applet
{
   public void paint (Graphics g)
   {
      int w = getSize ().width;
      int h = getSize ().height;

      QuadCurve2D quad = new QuadCurve2D.Double (w / 2 - 50,
                                                 h / 2,
                                                 w / 2 + 25,
                                                 h / 2 + 25,
                                                 w / 2 + 50,
                                                 h / 2);

      // Draw control point.

      g.drawLine (w / 2 + 25, h / 2 + 25, w / 2 + 25, h / 2 + 25);

      // Draw the curve.

      Graphics2D g2 = (Graphics2D) g;

      g2.draw (quad);
   }
}
```

`ShapeDemo6` draws the control point in addition to the curve. The result is shown in Figure 18.18.

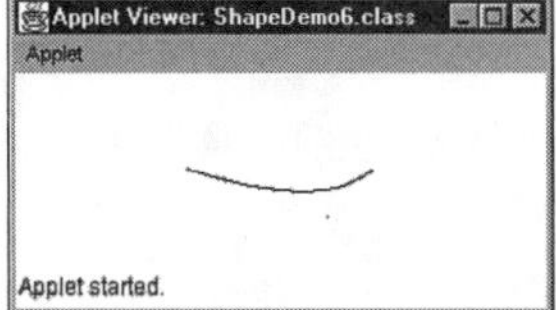

Figure 18.18
A quadratic curve's appearance is governed by a single control point.

Tip

If you are looking for an interactive program that allows you to move the start points, endpoints, and control points of a quadratic curve, check out the 2D Graphics trail in the Java Tutorial (`http://www.javasoft.com/tutorial`).

Version 1.3 of Java 2 introduces two new `QuadCurve2D` methods for solving *quadratic equations*—equations of the form `ax^2 + bx + c = 0`. The `solveQuadratic (double [] eqn)` and `solveQuadratic (double [] eqn, double [] res)` methods take an `eqn` array of three equation coefficients: `eqn [0]` contains `c`, `eqn [1]` contains `b`, and `eqn [2]` contains `a`. A return value of `-1` identifies a constant equation (`b` and `a` are 0). Otherwise, this value represents the number of noncomplex roots. If a second `res` array is passed, roots are stored in this array. Otherwise, they are stored in `eqn`.

RECTANGLES

The `Rectangle2D` class (located in the `java.awt.geom` package) is used to create rectangles. The following code fragment creates a rectangle:

```
Rectangle2D r = new Rectangle2D.Float (0.0f, 0.0f, 20.0f, 20.0f);
```

The upper-left corner is located at (0.0, 0.0) and the dimensions are (20.0, 20.0). Listing 18.21 presents source code to a `ShapeDemo7` applet that demonstrates rectangles.

LISTING 18.21 THE `ShapeDemo7` APPLET SOURCE CODE

```
// ShapeDemo7.java

import java.awt.*;
import java.awt.geom.*;

public class ShapeDemo7 extends java.applet.Applet
{
   public void paint (Graphics g)
   {
      Graphics2D g2 = (Graphics2D) g;

      GradientPaint gp = new GradientPaint (20.0f, 20.0f, Color.blue,
                                            80.0f, 80.0f, Color.green);
      g2.setPaint (gp);

      Rectangle2D r = new Rectangle2D.Double (20.0, 20.0, 60.0, 60.0);
      g2.fill (r);

      gp = new GradientPaint (100.0f, 20.0f, Color.blue,
                              250.0f, 20.0f, Color.green);
      g2.setPaint (gp);

      r = new Rectangle2D.Double (100.0, 20.0, 150.0, 60.0);
      g2.fill (r);

      gp = new GradientPaint (20.0f, 100.0f, Color.blue,
                              20.0f, 200.0f, Color.green);
      g2.setPaint (gp);

      r = new Rectangle2D.Double (20.0, 100.0, 230.0, 100.0);
      g2.fill (r);

   }
}
```

`ShapeDemo7` draws three filled rectangles, with each rectangle being filled with a different gradient paint style. Figure 18.19 shows the resulting rectangles.

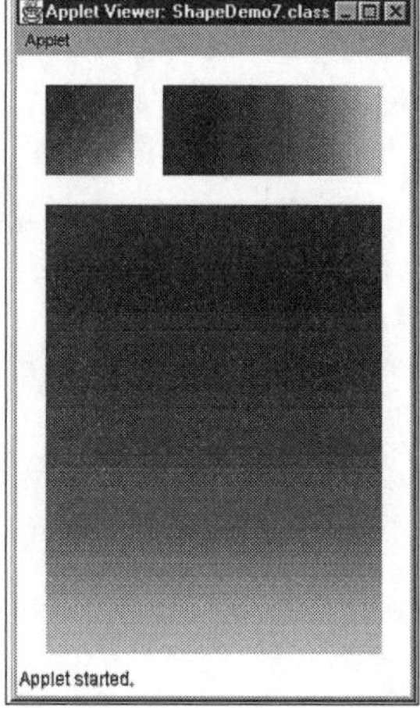

Figure 18.19
`Rectangle2D` is used to create three rectangles, which are subsequently painted with gradient paint styles.

Round Rectangles

The `RoundRectangle2D` class (located in the `java.awt.geom` package) is used to create rectangles with rounded corners. The following code fragment creates a rounded rectangle:

```
RoundRectangle2D r = new RoundRectangle2D.Double (0.0, 0.0, 20.0, 20.0,
                                                  5.0, 5.0);
```

The rectangle is drawn relative to (0.0, 0.0), its dimensions are (20.0, 20.0), and its corner arc width/arc height is specified as (5.0, 5.0). Listing 18.22 presents source code to a `ShapeDemo8` applet that demonstrates rounded rectangles.

Listing 18.22 The `ShapeDemo8` Applet Source Code

```
// ShapeDemo8.java

import java.awt.*;
import java.awt.geom.*;

public class ShapeDemo8 extends java.applet.Applet
{
   public void paint (Graphics g)
   {
      Graphics2D g2 = (Graphics2D) g;

      RoundRectangle2D r = new RoundRectangle2D.Double (10.0, 10.0,
                                                        50.0, 50.0,
                                                        5.0, 5.0);

      g2.draw (r);

      g.setColor (Color.magenta);
```

LISTING 18.22 CONTINUED

```
        r = new RoundRectangle2D.Double (80.0, 10.0, 80.0, 100.0,
                                         20.0, 20.0);
        g2.fill (r);

        GradientPaint gp = new GradientPaint (180.0f, 10.0f, Color.orange,
                                              270.0f, 110.0f, Color.blue);
        g2.setPaint (gp);

        r = new RoundRectangle2D.Double (180.0, 10.0, 90.0, 100.0,
                                         40.0, 60.0);
        g2.fill (r);
    }
}
```

ShapeDemo8 draws three rounded rectangles with different-sized corners. These rectangles are shown in Figure 18.20.

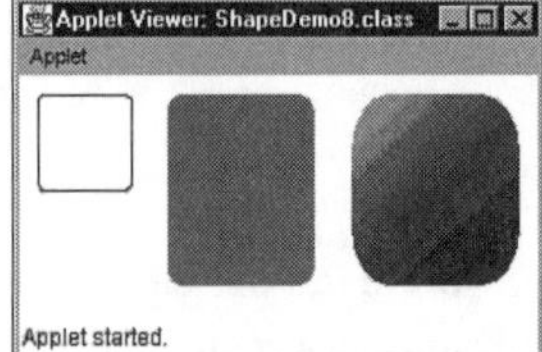

Figure 18.20 Rounded rectangles can have different-sized rounded corners.

CONSTRUCTIVE AREA GEOMETRY

Constructive area geometry (CAG) is the process of creating new geometric shapes out of existing geometric shapes, by performing Boolean operations on these shapes. Operations include Boolean OR (union—the new shape consists of all pixels in the two original shapes), Boolean AND (intersection—the new shape only consists of overlapping pixels), Boolean NOT (subtraction—the new shape only consists of those pixels in one shape that are not in the other shape), and Boolean XOR (exclusive or—the new shape consists only of nonoverlapping pixels).

Java 2D's `Area` class (located in the `java.awt.geom` package) is used to perform CAG. You create an area by calling `Area (Shape shape)`. The `shape` argument is a reference to an object whose class implements the `Shape` interface. This is demonstrated by the following code fragment:

```
Ellipse2D e = new Ellipse2D.Double (10.0, 10.0, 60.0, 60.0);
Area a1 = new Area (e);
```

Before you can perform a Boolean operation, you need to construct another area, as demonstrated by the following code fragment:

```
e = new Ellipse2D.Double (10.0, 50.0, 30.0, 30.0);
Area a2 = new Area (e);
```

When it comes time to perform a CAG operation, call one of Area's CAG methods. The following code fragment calls Area's add method to perform a union:

```
a1.add (a2);
```

The resulting shape is now the union of two ellipses. This shape can be drawn with the draw method, as the following code demonstrates:

```
Graphics2D g2 = (Graphics2D) g;
g2.draw (a1);
```

Listing 18.23 presents source code to a CAGDemo applet that shows how to accomplish various CAG operations.

LISTING 18.23 THE CAGDemo APPLET SOURCE CODE

```
// CAGDemo.html

import java.awt.*;
import java.awt.geom.*;

public class CAGDemo extends java.applet.Applet
{
   public void paint (Graphics g)
   {
      Graphics2D g2 = (Graphics2D) g;

      Ellipse2D e1 = new Ellipse2D.Double (20.0, 20.0, 80.0, 70.0);

      g2.setColor (Color.red);
      g2.fill (e1);

      Ellipse2D e2 = new Ellipse2D.Double (20.0, 70.0, 40.0, 40.0);

      g2.setColor (Color.blue);
      g2.fill (e2);

      g2.setColor (Color.black);
      g2.drawString ("Original", 20, 140);

      g2.translate (110.0, 0.0);

      // Perform union.

      Area a1 = new Area (e1);
      Area a2 = new Area (e2);

      a1.add (a2);

      g2.setColor (Color.orange);
      g2.fill (a1);

      g2.setColor (Color.black);
      g2.drawString ("Union", 20, 140);

      g2.translate (110.0, 0.0);
```

LISTING 18.23 CONTINUED

```
        // Perform intersection.

        a1 = new Area (e1);
        a1.intersect (a2);

        g2.setColor (Color.magenta);
        g2.fill (a1);

        g2.setColor (Color.black);
        g2.drawString ("Intersection", 20, 140);

        g2.translate (110.0, 0.0);

        // Perform subtraction.

        a1 = new Area (e1);
        a1.subtract (a2);

        g2.setColor (Color.gray);
        g2.fill (a1);

        g2.setColor (Color.black);
        g2.drawString ("Subtraction", 20, 140);

        g2.translate (110.0, 0.0);

        // Perform exclusive or.

        a1 = new Area (e1);
        a1.exclusiveOr (a2);

        g2.setColor (Color.green);
        g2.fill (a1);

        g2.setColor (Color.black);
        g2.drawString ("Exclusive Or", 20, 140);
    }
}
```

`CAGDemo` creates two ellipses and draws them without using CAG. Then, `Area`'s `add`, `intersect`, `subtract`, and `exclusiveOr` methods are called to demonstrate CAG operations. The result is shown in Figure 18.21.

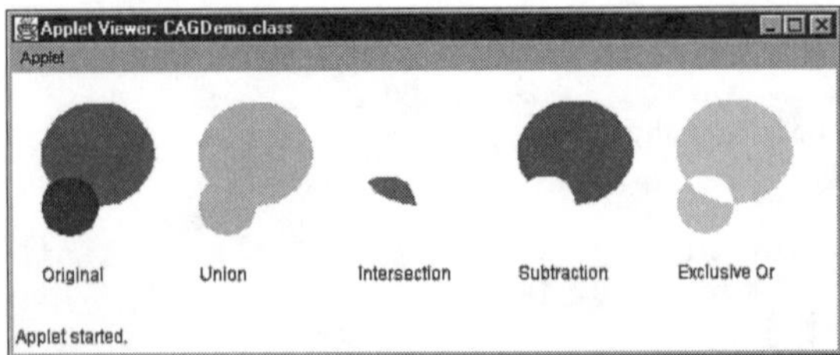

Figure 18.21
CAG operations can be performed on all kinds of shapes, including ellipses.

BOUNDS AND HIT TESTING

A *bounding box* is a rectangle that fully encloses a shape's geometry. Bounding boxes are used to determine whether an object has been selected or "hit" by a user.

The `Shape` interface declares two methods for retrieving a shape's bounding box: `getBounds` and `getBounds2D`. (The `getBounds2D` method returns a `Rectangle2D` object reference instead of a `Rectangle` object reference, providing a higher-precision description of the shape's bounding box.)

`Shape`'s `contains` method is used to determine if a specified point lies in the bounds of the shape. In contrast, its `intersects` method determines if a specified rectangle intersects the shape. For more information on these methods, check out the 2D Graphics trail's hit testing section in the Java Tutorial (`http://www.javasoft.com/tutorial`).

TEXT

Java 2D offers improvements in the areas of text and fonts. For example, a line of text can be measured by using the `LineBreakMeasurer` class, and this text can be laid out by using the `TextLayout` class. Furthermore, a font's attributes (such as its name, size, transform, weight, and posture) can be obtained from its `getAttributes` method, and font measurement information (such as ascent, descent, and leading) can be obtained from a font's `LineMetrics` object. (A `LineMetrics` object is retrieved by calling one of `Font`'s `getLineMetrics` methods.)

ATTRIBUTED STRINGS

Java 2D makes it possible to combine a string of characters with attributes (font size, strikethrough, swap colors, and so on) that describe the appearance of that string. The resulting string is known as an *attributed string*.

Tip

Attributed strings are useful in word processing programs that display formatted text.

The `AttributedString` class (located in the `java.text` package) creates objects that represent attributed strings. This class provides several constructors, including `AttributedString (String s, Map m)`. The `s` argument identifies a string of characters that will be associated with attributes and the `m` argument identifies an object whose class implements the `Map` interface (such as `Hashtable`), which contains these attributes. (Each `Map` entry represents a separate attribute.) To find out how to create an attributed string, take a look at the following code fragment:

```
String s = "The LineBreakMeasurer class allows styled " +
           "text to be broken into lines (or segments) " +
           "that fit within a particular visual " +
           "advance.  This is useful for clients who " +
           "wish to display a paragraph of text that " +
           "fits within a specific width, called the " +
           "wrapping width.";
```

```
Hashtable map = new Hashtable ();
map.put (TextAttribute.SIZE, new Float (18.0f));
map.put (TextAttribute.SWAP_COLORS, TextAttribute.SWAP_COLORS_ON);
map.put (TextAttribute.UNDERLINE, TextAttribute.UNDERLINE_LOW_DASHED);

AttributedString as = new AttributedString (s, map);
```

Attributes have names and values represented by constants in the `TextAttribute` class (located in the `java.awt.font` package). The `SIZE` attribute identifies the size of the string, `SWAP_COLORS` swaps foreground and background colors when displaying the string, and `UNDERLINE` identifies either a solid or a dashed underline to appear under the string's characters.

When an attributed string is created, attributes are applied to all characters in that string. However, it's possible to limit attributes to a select range of characters by calling `AttributedString`'s `addAttributes (MAP map, int beginIndex, int endIndex)` method. Only those attributes specified by `map` will be applied to characters ranging from `beginIndex` to `endIndex - 1`. This is demonstrated by the following code fragment:

```
map = new Hashtable ();
map.put (TextAttribute.POSTURE, TextAttribute.POSTURE_OBLIQUE);
as.addAttributes (map, 4, 21);
```

The `POSTURE` attribute is used to select a regular or italic font face. It is applied to characters located at indexes 0 through 20 (inclusive).

After an attributed string has been created, call its `getIterator` methods to return an `AttributedCharacterIterator` object that can access any character in the string. The following code fragment shows how this is done:

```
AttributedCharacterIterator aci = as.getIterator ();
```

The resulting iterator's methods can be called to retrieve characters and attributes. However, the real power of this iterator is shown when passed to a `LineBreakMeasurer` object—to break this text into lines. A line break measurer is constructed in the following code fragment:

```
LineBreakMeasurer measurer;
measurer = new LineBreakMeasurer (aci, new FontRenderContext (null, false,
                                  false));
```

In addition to an `AttributedCharacterIterator` argument, the line break measurer requires a `FontRenderContext` argument. This latter argument contains information about a graphics device that is needed to correctly measure the text. (Text measurements can vary slightly depending on the device resolution, and attributes such as antialiasing.)

At this point, the attributed string can be drawn and measured so that only complete words appear on each line, as demonstrated by the following code fragment:

```
int startIndex = aci.getBeginIndex ();
int endIndex = aci.getEndIndex ();

measurer.setPosition (startIndex);
```

```
float wrappingWidth = (float) size.width;

float Y = 0.0f;

while (measurer.getPosition () < endIndex)
{
   TextLayout layout = measurer.nextLayout (wrappingWidth);

   Y += layout.getAscent ();

   float X = 0.0f;
   if (!layout.isLeftToRight ())
       X = wrappingWidth - layout.getAdvance ();

   layout.draw ((Graphics2D) g, X, Y);

   Y += layout.getDescent () + layout.getLeading ();
}
```

As you can see, the line break measurer returns a text layout to provide font measurement information for each line of text to be drawn. Furthermore, the text layout's `draw` method is called to render each line of text.

One item that might not be obvious is the call to the text layout's `isLeftToRight` method. This method is called to handle bidirectional text. For English and other written languages that support left-to-right text, text is typically left-justified (and `isLeftToRight` returns a Boolean `true` value). However, other written languages (such as Arabic) right-justify text.

If you're having trouble figuring out how to justify text, see "Justifying Text" in the "Troubleshooting" section at the end of this chapter.

For information and examples of these classes, consult both the Java Tutorial (`http://www.javasoft.com/tutorial`) and the Java 2D Guide—part of the SDK 1.3 documentation.

Caution

When run under Windows 98, the previous code generates intermittent exception access violations. The error message indicates that these violations are detected in native code outside of the JVM. If the problem is not Windows-related, it's resulting from one of the JVM support DLLs.

TRANSFORMING STRINGS

In addition to the two `drawString` methods in the `Graphics` class, there are four `drawString` methods in `Graphics2D`. These new methods support floating-point coordinates. Whether you are calling the `Graphics` `drawString` methods or `Graphics2D` `drawString` methods, the current transform is applied. This means that, among other things, it's now possible to rotate text. Listing 18.24 presents source code to the `TextDemo` applet that shows how this is done.

LISTING 18.24 THE `TextDemo` APPLET SOURCE CODE

```
// TextDemo.java

import java.awt.*;

public class TextDemo extends java.applet.Applet
{
   public void paint (Graphics g)
   {
      Graphics2D g2 = (Graphics2D) g;

      g.drawString ("Non-rotated text", 50, 50);

      // The following rotate method call concatenates three transforms
      // to the default transform. The first transform translates
      // subsequent points to the coordinate system's origin by
      // subtracting 50 from the x coordinate and 60 from the y
      // coordinate. (The assumption is that (50.0, 60.0) is the
      // origin used by subsequent graphics methods.) Then, these
      // points are rotated around the coordinate system's origin,
      // not (50.0, 60.0). Finally, each point is translated back to
      // the (50.0, 60.0) origin.

      g2.rotate (45.0 * Math.PI / 180, 50.0, 60.0);

      // You must still pass (50.0, 60.0) as the origin of the text.

      g2.drawString ("Rotated text", 50.0f, 60.0f);
   }
}
```

`TextDemo`'s output is shown in Figure 18.22.

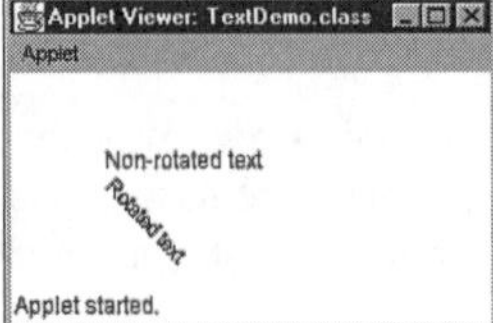

Figure 18.22
Java 2D makes it possible to rotate text.

BUFFERED IMAGES

Java 2D introduces an immediate-mode imaging model that gives you the ability to manipulate and display pixel-mapped images whose data is stored in memory. This data is accessible in a variety of formats, and manipulated by using several types of filtering operations.

Version 1.3 of the Java 2 SDK adds support for PNG (Portable Network Graphics) images—in addition to GIF and JPEG support—to Java 2D's imaging model. (PNG was created as a nonproprietary replacement for GIF—which is proprietary. The PNG format is flexible and extensible.)

The imaging model is based on the BufferedImage class. This class manages an image in memory and provides all necessary methods for interpreting, storing, and rendering pixel data. A BufferedImage object's contents can be rendered, either through a Graphics context or through a Graphics2D context.

At its core, a BufferedImage object is an encapsulation of a Raster object that holds pixel data, and a ColorModel subclass object that holds color information. Furthermore, the Raster object contains a DataBuffer object that stores pixel values, and a SampleModel object that describes how to locate a pixel value in the data buffer. Figure 18.23 illustrates this architecture.

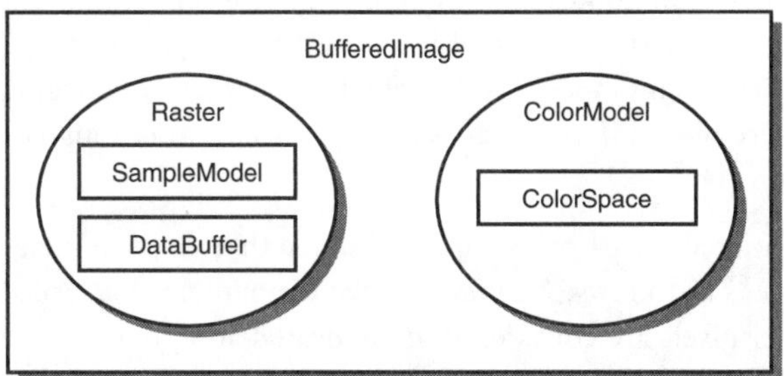

Figure 18.23
A buffered image is composed of a raster and a color model.

A BufferedImage object can be created by calling BufferedImage (int width, int height, int type). The width argument specifies the width of the raster, the height argument specifies its height, and the type argument specifies the type of image. You can choose one of the constants in the BufferedImage class (such as TYPE_INT_RGB) for this argument. The following code fragment creates a buffered image:

```
BufferedImage bi = new BufferedImage (100, 100, BufferedImage.TYPE_INT_RGB);
```

The code fragment creates a buffered image that holds 100 by 100 pixel images. Furthermore, TYPE_INT_RGB specifies that the image has 8-bit RGB color components packed into integer pixels, along with a direct color model that doesn't use alpha components.

After a buffered image has been created, it's empty. You need to populate this image with colored pixels. One way to accomplish this task is to call BufferedImage's setRGB methods. However, a more common technique is to draw an Image subclass object's pixels into the buffered image, as the following code fragment demonstrates:

```
Image im = getImage (getDocumentBase (), "someimage.gif");
MediaTracker mt = new MediaTracker (this);
mt.addImage (im, 0);

try
{
   mt.waitForID (0);
}
catch (InterruptedException e) {}
```

```
BufferedImage bi = new BufferedImage (im.getWidth (this), im.getHeight (this),
BufferedImage.TYPE_INT_RGB);
Graphics bg = bi.createGraphics ();
bg.drawImage (im, 0, 0, this);
```

If you plan to draw an image into a buffered image, you will need to specify the image's width and height as the dimensions of this buffer. You then need to obtain a graphics context associated with the buffer. After you have this context, you can call one of its `drawImage` methods to transfer the pixels to the buffer.

IMAGE PROCESSING

Image processing has been popularized by Adobe Photoshop and other products, because these products simplify the processing of images. Although Java can also process images, its traditional image processing model (as described in Chapter 13, "Beginning AWT") is not so easy to use. Therefore, buffered images provide image-processing capabilities that you'll undoubtedly prefer.

Embossing is a traditional image processing technique that gives an image a metallic look. This technique works as follows: An image is like a mountain. Each pixel represents an elevation, and brighter pixels are considered to be located at higher elevations. When an imaginary light source shines on this "mountain," the "uphills" facing this light source are lit, whereas the "downhills" facing away from the light source are shaded. A light ray can be simulated by scanning source pixels in a specific direction (such as left to right). When the "ray moves uphill," a pixel's color is brightened by the change in elevation from the previous pixel. An embossed image is shown in Figure 18.24.

Figure 18.24 Embossing gives images a metallic look.

To emboss, you start with a completely gray image. For each source image pixel, you examine the pixels to the upper left and lower right, and figure out the maximum change in their red, green, and blue color components. (This change can be either positive or negative.) For example, if green has changed by –5, blue has changed by 10, and red has changed by –100, the maximum change is –100. (The red component changed the most.) Now, you add the amount of change to 128 (the gray level) and create a pixel in the destination image with red, green, and blue values equal to this level. (This level is adjusted so that it isn't less than 0 or greater than 255.)

Listing 18.25 presents source code to an `emboss` method that takes a buffered image source (containing an image) as its argument and creates a new buffered image destination containing an embossed version of the source image. (One of the `setRGB` methods is called to set the pixel values in the destination image.)

LISTING 18.25 THE `emboss` METHOD

```
public BufferedImage emboss (BufferedImage src)
{
   int width = src.getWidth ();
   int height = src.getHeight ();

   BufferedImage dst;
   dst = new BufferedImage (width, height,
                            BufferedImage.TYPE_INT_RGB);

   for (int i = 0; i < height; i++)
        for (int j = 0; j < width; j++)
        {
             int upperLeft = 0;
             int lowerRight = 0;

             if (i > 0 && j > 0)
                 upperLeft = src.getRGB (j - 1, i - 1);

             if (i < height - 1 && j < width - 1)
                 lowerRight = src.getRGB (j + 1, i + 1);

             int redDiff = ((lowerRight >> 16) & 255) -
                           ((upperLeft >> 16) & 255);

             int greenDiff = ((lowerRight >> 8) & 255) -
                             ((upperLeft >> 8) & 255);

             int blueDiff = (lowerRight & 255) -
                            (upperLeft & 255);

             int diff = redDiff;
             if (Math.abs (greenDiff) > Math.abs (diff))
                 diff = greenDiff;
             if (Math.abs (blueDiff) > Math.abs (diff))
                 diff = blueDiff;

             int grayColor = 128 + diff;

             if (grayColor > 255) grayColor = 255;
             else
             if (grayColor < 0) grayColor = 0;

             int newColor = (grayColor << 16) + (grayColor << 8)
                            + grayColor;

             dst.setRGB (j, i, newColor);
        }

   return dst;
}
```

In many cases, image processing is simplified by using existing image operations, known as buffered image ops. These *ops* are objects created from classes that implement the `BufferedImageOp` interface. Classes include `AffineTransformOp`, `BandCombineOp`, `ColorConvertOp`, `ConvolveOp`, `LookupOp`, and `RescaleOp`. For space reasons, only `ConvolveOp` and `LookupOp` will be explored.

Note

The following sections demonstrate various image-processing operations. The code fragments are taken from a large image-processing program called `BufferedImageDemo1`. The code for this program is included with the rest of this book's source code.

CONVOLUTIONS

A *convolution* is an image-processing operation that combines the color of a source pixel with the colors of its immediate neighbors. The resulting color is assigned to the destination pixel. This operation is carried out by using a linear operator that determines what fraction of each source pixel's color contributes to the color of the destination pixel. This operator is known as a *kernel*.

A kernel is like a template moved across an image to perform a convolution on each pixel. The center of the kernel overlays the source pixel being convoluted, whereas kernel values surrounding this center are applied to neighboring pixels.

An *identity kernel* has no effect on a source pixel. The source pixel's color is multiplied by 1.0 and each neighboring pixel's color is multiplied by 0.0. The results are added together and the destination pixel's color is the same as the source pixel's color. The identity kernel can be specified by using the following 3×3 matrix of floating point values:

```
0.0   0.0   0.0
0.0   1.0   0.0
0.0   0.0   0.0
```

The `ConvolveOp` class creates objects that represent various kinds of convolutions. To create a `ConvolveOp` object, call the `ConvolveOp (Kernel kernel)` constructor with a `kernel` argument that identifies the kernel used to perform the convolution.

The `Kernel` class creates objects that represent kernels. Call `Kernel (int width, int height, float [] matrix)` to create a kernel. The `width` argument identifies the number of columns and the `height` argument identifies the number of rows making up the kernel's matrix, whereas the `matrix` argument identifies this matrix.

The following code fragment creates an identity kernel and a `ConvolveOp` object that is handed this kernel in its constructor. (Because the identity kernel is used, this convolution does not change source pixels.)

```
float [] identityKernel =
{
   0.0f, 0.0f, 0.0f,
   0.0f, 1.0f, 0.0f,
   0.0f, 0.0f, 0.0f
```

```
};

BufferedImageOp identityOp =
   new ConvolveOp (new Kernel (3, 3, identityKernel));
```

To perform a convolution, ConvolveOp's filter method must be called. This method takes two arguments—source and destination buffered images—and returns the destination image. (If you pass null as the destination image, filter creates a new buffered image to serve as the destination.) The following code fragment demonstrates how you would call filter on the buffered image that's identified as bi. (The identityOp object is assumed.)

```
BufferedImage clone = identityOp.filter (bi, null);
```

Blurring is a convolution in which equal amounts of a source pixel's color and its neighbors' colors are added together. For a 3×3 matrix, each value would be divided by 9 because there are 9 elements in the matrix. The blurring kernel can be specified by using the following 3×3 matrix:

```
1.0 / 9.0   1.0 / 9.0   1.0 / 9.0
1.0 / 9.0   1.0 / 9.0   1.0 / 9.0
1.0 / 9.0   1.0 / 9.0   1.0 / 9.0
```

Notice that the sum of these values adds up to 1.0. This is quite common with kernels. If the sum does not equal 1.0, the image is either noticeably brightened or darkened.

The following code fragment demonstrates setting up a blurring kernel and performing a blurring operation on the buffered image that's identified as bi:

```
float ninth = 1.0f / 9.0f;

float [] blurKernel =
{
   ninth, ninth, ninth,
   ninth, ninth, ninth,
   ninth, ninth, ninth
};

BufferedImageOp blurOp =
   new ConvolveOp (new Kernel (3, 3, blurKernel));

BufferedImage clone = blurOp.filter (bi, null);
```

The blurring kernel works as follows: Imagine operating in an area that consists of a single color. Each pixel will keep its own color. Now imagine operating in an area of color change. Because neighboring pixels contribute equal amounts of their color, a gradual blending of the source pixel's color and neighboring pixel colors results in a source pixel color that is close to the average of its neighboring pixel colors. This blending results in a blur. Figure 18.25 shows a blurred image.

Edge detection is a convolution in which edges are detected by subtracting neighboring pixel colors from a source pixel's color. Its kernel uses the following matrix. (This is an example in which kernel values do not add up to 1.0. The result is a much darker image.)

```
 0.0   -1.0    0.0
-1.0    4.0   -1.0
 0.0   -1.0    0.0
```

Figure 18.25
A blurring kernel is used to create a blurred image.

The following code fragment demonstrates setting up an edge detection kernel and performing an edge detection operation on the buffered image that's identified as `bi`:

```
float [] edgeKernel =
{
    0.0f, -1.0f,  0.0f,
   -1.0f,  4.0f, -1.0f,
    0.0f, -1.0f,  0.0f
};

BufferedImageOp edgeDetectionOp =
   new ConvolveOp (new Kernel (3, 3, edgeKernel));

BufferedImage clone = edgeDetectionOp.filter (bi, null);
```

The edge detection kernel works as follows: Imagine operating in an area that consists of a single color. Each pixel will end up as a black pixel because the color of the source pixel being convoluted is multiplied by 4.0, whereas the color of each of its neighboring pixels is multiplied by -1.0. Because each neighbor pixel has the same color as the source pixel, the result of the multiplication by 1.0 is one quarter the result of the multiplication by 4.0. When you add all these values together, the result is 0.0 (or black). (The four neighbor pixels that are assigned 0.0 kernel values contribute no color because multiplying by 0.0 results in 0.0, and adding 0.0 to the result doesn't change a thing.) Figure 18.26 shows an edge-detected image.

Figure 18.26
An edge detection kernel emphasizes an image's edges.

Sharpening is a convolution that is the inverse of blurring. If you replace the 4.0 value in the edge kernel with a value of 5.0, you can achieve sharpening. Sharpening works by de-emphasizing the contributions of neighboring pixels. As a result, each source pixel in an area of change stands out from its neighbors. (Of course, in a region of constant color, you wouldn't notice a sharpening effect.)

LOOKUP TABLES

Several kinds of image processing operations (such as inverting, thresholding, and posterizing) can be performed by translating source pixel colors to destination pixel colors through the use of lookup tables. Although you can define separate tables for each of the color components in an RGB color, you will probably only need a single table to process all three components at once. Because each component is represented by an 8-bit value ranging from 0 through 255, a lookup table only needs 256 entries.

The `LookupOp` class creates objects that represent various kinds of lookup operations. To create a `LookupOp` object, call the `LookupOp (LookupTable table, RenderingHints hints)` constructor with a `table` argument that identifies the table of lookup values and a `hints` argument that identifies rendering hints to improve quality. (You can pass `null` as the value of `hints`.)

`LookupTable` is an abstract class that identifies a lookup table. When working with RGB images, you will normally create objects from its `ShortLookupTable` subclass.

By swapping color numbers with their extreme opposites, you can achieve *inverting*. This effect is demonstrated by the following code fragment:

```
short [] invert = new short [256];

for (int i = 0; i < invert.length; i++)
     invert [i] = (short) (255 - i);

BufferedImageOp invertOp =
   new LookupOp (new ShortLookupTable (0, invert), null);

BufferedImage clone = invertOp.filter (bi, null);
```

To create a negative, a pixel's color number is replaced by its opposite color number. This is achieved by subtracting the color number from 255. Figure 18.27 shows the result of inverting.

Figure 18.27 An inverted image results from swapping color numbers with their extreme opposites.

The process of making obvious color changes across developer-defined boundaries is known as *thresholding*. This technique uses a threshold value, minimum value, and maximum value to control the color component values for each source pixel. Component values below the threshold are assigned the minimum value. Values equal to or above the threshold are assigned the maximum value. The following code fragment demonstrates this effect:

```
short [] threshold = new short [256];

for (int i = 0; i < threshold.length; i++)
     threshold [i] = (i < 128) ? (short) 0 : (short) 255;

BufferedImageOp thresholdOp =
   new LookupOp (new ShortLookupTable (0, threshold), null);
```

All color component values less than 128 are mapped to color number 0, and all color component values greater than or equal to 128 are mapped to color number 255. The result is an image with eight colors: black (0, 0, 0), blue (0, 0, 255), green (0, 255, 0), cyan (0, 255, 255), red (255, 0, 0), magenta (255, 0, 255), yellow (255, 255, 0), and white (255, 255, 255). Figure 18.28 shows the result of thresholding.

Figure 18.28
Thresholding uses a threshold value to reduce the number of colors in an image.

By reducing the number of colors in an image, you can achieve an effect known as *posterizing*. This is demonstrated by the following code fragment, which posterizes an image by mapping 256 colors down to 8:

```
short [] posterize = new short [256];

for (int i = 0; i < posterize.length; i++)
     posterize [i] = (short) (i - i % 32);

BufferedImageOp posterizeOp =
   new LookupOp (new ShortLookupTable (0, posterize), null);

BufferedImage clone = posterizeOp.filter (bi, null);
```

This code might not seem very intuitive. However, when you work your way through the expression `i - i % 32`, you discover that all color numbers are mapped to color numbers 0, 32, 64, 96, 128, 160, 192, and 224. (There are only eight resulting colors.) The result of posterizing is shown in Figure 18.29.

Figure 18.29
Posterizing an image results in color reduction. Although posterizing and thresholding are similar color reduction techniques, a posterized image looks more natural than a thresholded image.

TEXTURED PAINTING

Earlier, you were introduced to the gradient paint style. A second paint style (texture paint) was mentioned but not explored because it works in partnership with buffered images. Basically, a texture paint style is used by pens that paint with images, instead of colors.

A texture paint style is represented by an object created from the `TexturePaint` class (located in the `java.awt` package). Call the `TexturePaint (BufferedImage bi, Rectangle2D rect)` constructor to create a texture paint that uses the image contained in `bi` as its texture and the rectangle specified by `rect` as the dimensions of a rectangle in which the texture appears. The following code fragment demonstrates creating a texture paint object:

```
TexturePaint tp = new TexturePaint (bi, new Rectangle2D.Double (0.0, 0.0,
                                    100.0, 100.0));
```

After you've created a `TexturePaint` object, you can specify this object as the new paint attribute for the graphics context. You do this by calling the `setPaint` method, as shown in the following code fragment:

```
Graphics2D g2 = (Graphics) g;
g2.setPaint (tp);
```

The best way to understand texture paint is to examine a program that demonstrates this attribute. Listing 18.26 presents source code to a `BufferedImageDemo2` applet that does just this.

LISTING 18.26 THE `BufferedImageDemo2` APPLET SOURCE CODE

```
// BufferedImageDemo2.java

import java.awt.*;
import java.awt.geom.*;
import java.awt.image.*;

public class BufferedImageDemo2 extends java.applet.Applet
{
   public void paint (Graphics g)
   {
      Graphics2D g2 = (Graphics2D) g;

      RenderingHints rh = g2.getRenderingHints ();
```

LISTING 18.26 CONTINUED

```
      rh.put (RenderingHints.KEY_ANTIALIASING,
              RenderingHints.VALUE_ANTIALIAS_ON);
      g2.setRenderingHints (rh);

      GeneralPath path = new GeneralPath ();
      path.moveTo (60.0f, 0.0f);
      path.lineTo (50.0f, 300.0f);
      path.curveTo (160.0f, 230.0f, 270.0f, 140.0f, 400.0f, 100.0f);

      Image im = getImage (getDocumentBase (), "corvette.jpg");

      MediaTracker mt = new MediaTracker (this);
      mt.addImage (im, 0);

      try
      {
         mt.waitForID (0);
      }
      catch (InterruptedException e) {}

      BufferedImage bi = new BufferedImage (im.getWidth (this),
                                            im.getHeight (this),
                                            BufferedImage.TYPE_INT_RGB);

      Graphics bg = bi.createGraphics ();
      bg.drawImage (im, 0, 0, this);

      Rectangle2D rect = new Rectangle2D.Float (0.0f, 0.0f,
                                                im.getWidth (this),
                                                im.getHeight (this));

      TexturePaint tp = new TexturePaint (bi, rect);
      g2.setPaint (tp);

      BasicStroke stroke;
      stroke = new BasicStroke (100.0f, BasicStroke.CAP_SQUARE,
                                BasicStroke.JOIN_ROUND);
      g2.setStroke (stroke);

      g2.draw (path);
   }
}
```

`BufferedImageDemo2` creates a general path shape that will be drawn on the applet's drawing surface. An image is loaded and converted into a buffered image. Then, a rectangle is created that encompasses the entire buffered image. Together with the buffered image, this rectangle is used to create a texture paint style. After this style has been selected as the graphics context paint attribute, a stroke is created to achieve a pen that draws in wide strokes. Finally, the drawing is then rendered. Figure 18.30 shows the resulting image.

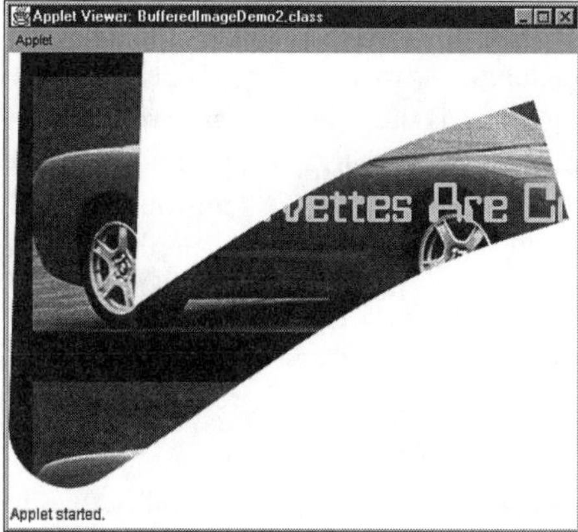

Figure 18.30 A pen can paint an image instead of a color.

PRINTING

The ability to print graphics to a printing device was introduced in Java 1.1. However, it's only through Java 2D that printing has become sophisticated. You can use Java 2D's printing API to perform the following tasks:

- Print Java 2D and AWT graphics (including text and images)
- Control document composition (such as reverse order printing)
- Invoke printer-specific functions (such as stapling)

Note Not all the aforementioned tasks are completely implemented in Version 1.3 of Java 2.

The printing API is located in the `java.awt.print` package. This package contains three interfaces and four classes, which are described in Table 18.3.

TABLE 18.3 PRINTING CLASSES AND INTERFACES

Interface/Class	Description
`Book`	This class provides a representation of a document in which pages might have different page formats and page painters.
`Pageable`	This interface is implemented by classes whose objects represent a set of pages to be printed.
`PageFormat`	This class describes the size and orientation of a page to be printed.
`Paper`	This class describes the physical characteristics of a piece of paper.
`Printable`	This interface is implemented by classes whose objects represent page painters.
`PrinterGraphics`	This interface is implemented by `Graphics` subclass objects that are passed to page painters for rendering pages.
`PrinterJob`	This class is the main class that controls printing.

THE PRINTING FRAMEWORK

The printing API works in conjunction with a printing framework that uses a callback printing model. According to this model, it is the printing framework (and not the application) that controls when pages are printed. Essentially, an application provides information about a document to be printed, and the printing framework informs the application to render each page when needed. (The callback printing model is similar to the callback painting model that was discussed in Chapter 13, "Beginning AWT.")

The printing framework can request a certain page to be rendered multiple times, or request that pages be rendered out of order. It's the application's responsibility to render the correct page, no matter which page is requested.

The callback-printing model offers a higher degree of flexibility than is found in the traditional application-driven model. As an example, the printing framework will ask an application to render pages in reverse order, so that a printer capable of stacking pages in reverse order receives the final stack of pages in nonreverse order.

Another feature of the callback-printing model is that it allows applications to render content to bitmap printers that don't have enough memory to hold an entire page. In this situation, a page is printed as a series of *bands* (small bitmaps). For example, if a printer only has one-fifth the memory required to hold an entire page, this page is divided into five bands and the application is requested to render this page five times, with each rendering producing an appropriate band that is sent to the printer.

JOB CONTROL AND RENDERING

When it comes time to print, an application initiates and manages a printer job on behalf of a user's request. (This request can be specified by selecting an item from a menu, or through some other means). To initiate printing, the application must first obtain a subclass object from the abstract `PrinterJob` class as shown in the following code fragment:

```
PrinterJob job = PrinterJob.getPrinterJob ();
```

Each printer job requires a *page painter* (an object that implements the `Printable` interface) to take care of rendering content. This page painter can be easily created by implementing `Printable`'s solitary `print` method. The following code fragment shows `print`'s signature:

```
int print(Graphics graphics, PageFormat pageFormat, int pageIndex)
```

The `graphics` argument is a reference to an object created from a subclass of `Graphics`. (This object's class implements the `PrinterGraphics` interface. As a result, you can cast `graphics` from `Graphics`—or `Graphics2D`—to `PrinterGraphics`, and then call its `getPrinterJob` method to return the printer job.) The `pageFormat` argument is a reference to a *page formatter* (an object that describes the size and orientation of a page being rendered). Finally, `pageIndex` provides a zero-based index that identifies the page to be rendered. An index of 0 corresponds to the first page, 1 corresponds to the second page, and so on.

The print method returns Printable.PAGE_EXISTS to indicate that a requested page was rendered, or Printable.NO_SUCH_PAGE to indicate that pageIndex was too large, and printing should end.

A page formatter determines whether a page has portrait or landscape orientation. (Portrait is the default.) If portrait orientation is used, a page's x-axis will be aligned with the page's width and the y-axis will be aligned with the page's height. When landscape orientation is used, the x-axis aligns with the page's height and the y-axis aligns with the page's width. PageFormat's getOrientation method returns the current orientation and its setOrientation (int o) method sets this orientation to o. (PageFormat contains PORTRAIT, LANDSCAPE, and REVERSE_LANDSCAPE constants that should be used when specifying the orientation.)

A page formatter contains a Paper object that describes a paper's physical characteristics. PageFormat's setPaper method sets the current paper and its getPaper method retrieves this paper.

Paper's setSize method can be called to set a paper's horizontal and vertical size (in units of 1/72 inches). At any point, its getWidth and getHeight methods can be called to retrieve this size.

Because some printers cannot render content on an entire piece of paper, each Paper object specifies an *imageable area* (the region of a paper on which it's safe to render). This imageable area can be specified by calling Paper's setImageableArea method. At any point, its getImageableX, getImageableY, getImageableWidth, and getImageableHeight methods can be called to return the imageable area's current origin (located in the upper-left corner of the paper) and dimensions (where x values increase to the right and y values increase to the bottom).

Note

PageFormat contains getImageableX, getImageableY, getImageableWidth, and getImageableHeight methods. Although similar to Paper's same-named methods, these methods take orientation into account.

A user can alter page format information by requesting that the application display a page dialog box. (This request can be made from an application's menu item.) To display this dialog box, the application would call PrinterJob's pageDialog method. (The page dialog box is initialized by using the PageFormat argument passed to pageDialog.) If the user clicks the OK button, the PageFormat instance is cloned, altered to reflect the user's selections, and then returned. If the user cancels the dialog box, pageDialog returns the original unaltered PageFormat object. The following code fragment shows how to create a PageFormat object, and then provide a user with an opportunity to modify this format, via a page dialog box:

```
PageFormat pf = new PageFormat ();
pf = job.pageDialog (pf);
```

What comes next depends on the kind of printer job being initiated: a printable or a pageable. In a nutshell, *printables* are simple printer jobs, whereas *pageables* are more complex printer jobs.

For a printable, your code would pass an object, whose class implements the `Printable` interface, to `PrinterJob`'s `setPrintable` method. This provides the printing framework with the location of the `print` method, which it calls when necessary. The following code fragment shows how to accomplish this objective. (It assumes that the current object provides the `print` method.)

```
job.setPrintable (this);
```

This version of the `setPrintable` method assumes that a default page formatter is being used. However, you can specify your own page formatter and pass it to a second version of `setPrintable`, as shown in the following code fragment:

```
job.setPrintable (this, pf);
```

For a pageable, your code would create a `Book` object. It would then call one of `Book`'s two overloaded `append` methods to append a series of instructions for how one or more pages are rendered. Each `append` method call specifies the location of the `print` method (via an object whose class implements `Printable`), the page format to be used, and (optionally) how many pages must be printed using the information passed to the `append` method. After this is done, your code would call `PrinterJob`'s `setPageable` method and pass the `Book` object as this method's solitary argument, so that the printing framework knows the locations of all `print` methods that render the various pages contributing to the pageable. The following code fragment shows how to take care of this task:

```
Book bk = new Book ();
bk.append (this, pf, 2);
job.setPageable (bk);
```

The book, referenced by `bk`, is instructed to print two pages using the page formatter specified by `pf`. Furthermore, the `print` method is located in the current object (that is, the object referenced by `this`).

At this point, your code could specify additional printer job properties, such as the number of copies to print or the name of the job to be displayed on a banner page. To demonstrate, the following code fragment shows how you would specify two copies to be printed, along with a name for this printer job:

```
job.setCopies (2);
job.setJobName ("Resume");
```

The number of copies and job name can be accessed from inside a `print` method by casting its `Graphics` argument to a `PrinterGraphics` argument, calling `PrinterGraphics`' `getPrinterJob` method, and finally calling `getCopies` and `getJobName`—as demonstrated by the following code fragment:

```
PrinterGraphics p = (PrinterGraphics) g;
System.out.println (p.getPrinterJob ().getCopies ());
System.out.println (p.getPrinterJob ().getJobName ());
```

The next task depends on whether the application is designed to be interactive. If interactive, a print dialog box must be displayed. A user can then choose how printing will proceed.

To display this print dialog box, an application calls `PrinterJob`'s `printDialog` method. A user's choices are constrained by the number and format of pages in the printable or pageable. The number of copies, previously specified by `setCopies`, is also displayed. If the user clicks `OK`, `printDialog` returns a Boolean `true` value and printing can continue. However, if the user cancels this dialog box, by clicking the `Cancel` button, `false` is returned and the printer job should be abandoned.

Assuming that the user chose to print, `PrinterJob`'s `print` method is called to perform the actual printing. This method throws a `PrinterException` object if an error, occurring during printing, results in the job being aborted.

The printer job is usually not finished when the `print` method returns. Work is typically still being done by a printer driver, print server, or the printer itself. As a result, the state of the `PrinterJob` subclass object might not reflect the state of the actual job being printed. Furthermore, because the state of a `PrinterJob` subclass object changes during its life, it's illegal to invoke certain methods at certain times. For example, if `setPageable` is called after you've called `print`, the `PrinterJob` subclass object throws an `IllegalStateException` object.

PLAYING WITH PRINTABLES

Printables are the simplest printer jobs. Only a single page painter is required. Furthermore, the application provides a single class that implements the `Printable` interface. When it's time to print, the printing system calls the page painter's `print` method to render a page. Pages are requested in order, beginning at page index 0. However, a page painter might be requested to render a page several times before advancing to the next page. (Remember banding?) After the last page has been printed, the page painter's `print` method will return `Printable`'s `NO_SUCH_PAGE` constant. The following points summarize printable job features:

- All pages use the same page painter and page formatter. If a print dialog box is presented, it will not display the number of pages in the document, because that information isn't available to the printing framework. (Under Windows 98, the print dialog box typically shows 10,000 pages—from 0 to 9,999.)
- The printing framework will always ask the page painter to print each page in indexed order, starting with page index 0. No pages are skipped. For example, if a user wants pages 7 and 8 to be printed, the page painter will be called with page indexes 0 (for page 1) through 7 (for page 8).
- The page painter informs the printing system when the end of the document has been reached.
- All page painters are called in the same thread.
- Some printing systems might not be able to achieve the ideal output. For example, the stack of pages emerging from the printer might be in the wrong order, or the pages might not be collated if multiple copies are requested.

Listing 18.27 presents source code to a `PrintDemo1` application that creates and demonstrates a printable.

LISTING 18.27 THE PrintDemo1 APPLICATION SOURCE CODE

```
// PrintDemo1.java

import java.awt.*;
import java.awt.geom.*;
import java.awt.print.*;

class PrintDemo1 implements Printable
{
   public static void main (String [] args)
   {
      // Get a printer job.

      PrinterJob job = PrinterJob.getPrinterJob ();

      // Specify the printable to be an instance of PrintDemo1.

      job.setPrintable (new PrintDemo1 ());

      // Specify number of copies and job name.

      job.setCopies (2);
      job.setJobName ("Printable");

      // Put up the dialog box.

      if (job.printDialog ())
      {
          // Print the job if the user didn't cancel printing.

          try
          {
             job.print ();
          }
          catch (PrinterException e)
          {
             System.out.println (e);
          }
      }

      System.exit (0);
   }

   public int print (Graphics g, PageFormat pf, int pageIndex)
              throws PrinterException
   {
      // pageIndex 0 corresponds to page number 1.

      if (pageIndex >= 1)
          return Printable.NO_SUCH_PAGE;

      PrinterGraphics p = (PrinterGraphics) g;

      System.out.println (p.getPrinterJob ().getCopies ());
      System.out.println (p.getPrinterJob ().getJobName ());
```

LISTING 18.27 CONTINUED

```
      Graphics2D g2 = (Graphics2D) g;

      double w = pf.getImageableWidth ();
      double h = pf.getImageableHeight ();

      int xo = (int) pf.getImageableX ();
      int yo = (int) pf.getImageableY ();

      Rectangle2D r = new Rectangle2D.Double (xo, yo, w, h);

      g2.setColor (Color.red);
      g2.draw (r);

      for (int x = 0; x + 32 < w; x += 36)
           for (int y = 0; y + 32 < h; y += 36)
      {
           g2.setColor (new Color (rnd (256), rnd (256), rnd (256)));

           Shape s = new Ellipse2D.Double (xo + x + 4, yo + y + 4,
                                           32, 32);

           g2.fill (s);
      }

      return Printable.PAGE_EXISTS;
   }

   int rnd (int limit)
   {
      return ((int) (Math.random () * limit));
   }
}
```


`PrintDemo1` is not that remarkable. When run, its `main` method creates a printer job and gives a user a chance to print this job, by way of a print dialog box. If the user chooses OK, the `print` method is called to print randomly colored circles in a rectangular outline of the imageable area.

The `print` method is called once for each page that the user selects from the print dialog box. The `pageIndex` argument identifies the current page being printed. (The first page is assigned page index 0.) When the `print` method "decides" that there are no more pages to print, `Printable.NO_SUCH_PAGE` is returned. This causes printing to terminate. However, for each successfully printed page, `Printable.PAGE_EXISTS` is returned. (To keep printing pages, you must return `PAGE_EXISTS`.)

PLAYING WITH PAGEABLES

Pageable jobs are more flexible (and complex) than their printable cousins. For example, each page in a pageable job can have a different layout and implementation. The `Book` class is used to manage a pageable job. Through this job, the printing framework is able to determine how many pages need to be printed, along with the page painter and page formatter to be used for each page. Applications (such as word processors) that need to print documents with a planned structure and format should use pageable jobs. The following points summarize pageable job features:

- Different pages can use different page painters and page formatters.
- The printing system can ask page painters to print pages in an arbitrary order and some pages might be skipped. For example, if a user asks to print pages 2 and 3 of a document, the page painter will be called with indices 1 (for page 2) and 2 (for page 3). Page index 0 (for page 1) will be skipped.
- Pageable jobs do not need to know in advance how many pages are in the document. However, unlike printable jobs, they must be able to render pages in any order. There might be gaps in the sequencing and the printing system might request that a page be rendered multiple times before moving to the next page. For example, a request to print pages 2 and 3 of a document might result in a sequence of calls that request pages with indices 2 (for page 3) and 1 (for page 2).

Listing 18.28 presents source code to a `PrintDemo2` application that creates and demonstrates a pageable.

LISTING 18.28 THE `PrintDemo2` APPLICATION SOURCE CODE

```
// PrintDemo2.java

import java.awt.*;
import java.awt.geom.*;
import java.awt.print.*;

class PrintDemo2
{
   public static void main (String [] args)
   {
      // Get a PrinterJob

      PrinterJob job = PrinterJob.getPrinterJob ();

      // Create a landscape page format.

      PageFormat pf = job.defaultPage ();
      pf.setOrientation (PageFormat.LANDSCAPE);

      // Set up a book.

      Book bk = new Book ();
      bk.append (new paintCover (), pf);
      bk.append (new paintContent (), job.defaultPage (), 1);

      // Pass the book to the PrinterJob.

      job.setPageable (bk);

      // Specify the job name.
```

LISTING 18.28 CONTINUED

```
      job.setJobName ("My book");

      // Put up the dialog box.

      if (job.printDialog ())
      {
          // Print the job if the user didn't cancel printing

          try
          {
             job.print ();
          }
          catch (PrinterException e)
          {
             System.out.println (e);
          }
       }

      System.exit (0);
   }
}

class paintContent implements Printable
{
   public int print (Graphics g, PageFormat pf, int pageIndex)
              throws PrinterException
   {
      System.out.println ("Page index = " + pageIndex);

      // pageIndex 1 corresponds to page number 2.

      if (pageIndex > 2)
          return Printable.NO_SUCH_PAGE;

      Graphics2D g2 = (Graphics2D) g;

      double w = pf.getImageableWidth ();
      double h = pf.getImageableHeight ();

      int xo = (int) pf.getImageableX ();
      int yo = (int) pf.getImageableY ();

      Rectangle2D r = new Rectangle2D.Double (xo, yo, w, h);

      g2.setColor (Color.red);
      g2.draw (r);

      for (int x = 0; x + 32 < w; x += 36)
           for (int y = 0; y + 32 < h; y += 36)
      {
           g2.setColor (new Color (rnd (256), rnd (256), rnd (256)));

           Shape s = new Ellipse2D.Double (xo + x + 4, yo + y + 4,
                                           32, 32);
```

LISTING 18.28 CONTINUED

```
            g2.fill (s);
         }

         return Printable.PAGE_EXISTS;
      }

      int rnd (int limit)
      {
         return ((int) (Math.random () * limit));
      }
}

class paintCover implements Printable
{
   Font fnt = new Font ("TimesRoman", Font.ITALIC, 72);

   public int print (Graphics g, PageFormat pf, int pageIndex)
              throws PrinterException
   {
      Graphics2D g2 = (Graphics2D) g;

      double w = pf.getImageableWidth ();
      double h = pf.getImageableHeight ();

      int xo = (int) pf.getImageableX ();
      int yo = (int) pf.getImageableY ();

      Rectangle2D r = new Rectangle2D.Double (xo, yo, w, h);

      g2.setColor (Color.red);
      g2.draw (r);

      PrinterGraphics p = (PrinterGraphics) g2;
      String s = p.getPrinterJob ().getJobName ();
      int x = s.length () / 10;

      g2.setFont (fnt);
      int y = g2.getFont ().getSize () * 5 / 2;

      g2.translate (xo + x, yo + y);

      AffineTransform old = g2.getTransform  ();

      g2.shear (-0.95, 0.0);
      g2.scale (1.0, 3.0);

      g2.setPaint (Color.lightGray);
      g2.drawString (s, 0, 0);

      g2.setTransform (old);

      g2.setPaint (Color.black);
      g2.drawString (s, 0, 0);

      return Printable.PAGE_EXISTS;
   }
}
```

PrintDemo2 creates a pageable with two different page painters. The first page painter renders a cover. It gets the cover's name from the job name. The second page painter paints the content of the book. It uses the same page painter as used by PrintDemo1.

QUICK AND DIRTY PRINTING

Suppose you need to send some text to a printer and don't want to bother with the printing framework. There is a very simple (and nonportable) way in which you can accomplish this task. The trick is to create a PrintWriter object that's attached to a FileWriter object. In turn, the FileWriter object is attached to a printer device. Listing 18.29 contains source code to a PrintDemo3 application that illustrates sending text to a Windows printer device, code named LPT1:.

LISTING 18.29 THE PrintDemo3 APPLICATION SOURCE CODE

```
// PrintDemo3.java

import java.io.*;

class PrintDemo3
{
   static String s = "This paragraph is being sent to the printer.  " +
                     "I'll bet you didn't think there was such an " +
                     "easy way to accomplish this task.  The trick " +
                     "is to create a FileWriter object that's " +
                     "connected to a printer device, and then a " +
                     "PrintWriter object that's connected to the " +
                     "FileWriter.  Obviously, this isn't very " +
                     "portable.";

   public static void main (String [] args)
   {
      try
      {
          FileWriter fw = new FileWriter ("LPT1:");

          PrintWriter pw = new PrintWriter (fw);

          int i, len = s.length ();

          for (i = 0; len > 80; i += 80)
          {
               pw.print (s.substring (i, i + 80));
               pw.print ("\r\n");
               len -= 80;
          }

          if (len > 0)
          {
              pw.print (s.substring (i));
              pw.print ("\r\n");
          }

          pw.close ();
```

LISTING 18.29 CONTINUED

```
         }
         catch (IOException e)
         {
            System.out.println (e);
         }
      }
   }
```

PrintDemo3 outputs the contents of a String object, referenced by s, to the printer attached to LPT1:. It uses a loop to output this string in 80 character lines. After each line is printed, a carriage return character '\r' followed by a new-line character '\n' are output. If not output, some printers (such as HP Deskjet printers) will truncate the line, and you'll only see the first 80 characters of the string.

Caution

Although PrintDemo3's technique will work on many printers, there is no guarantee that it will work on your printer. For example, PrintDemo3 works on an HP Deskjet 970Cse printer, but doesn't work on a Lexmark 3200. Because it's nonportable, you should only use this technique for debugging and experimentation. In other words, don't use it in a production-quality program.

TROUBLESHOOTING

JUSTIFYING TEXT

How do I left-, center-, right-, and equally- (both left and right) justify text using Java 2D's AttributedString, LineBreakMeasurer, *and* TextLayout *classes?*

Sun's online Java 2D text tutorial discusses justification. You can read this tutorial, by pointing your browser to the following Web address:

http://developer.java.sun.com/developer/onlineTraining/Media/2DText/other.html#just

Listing 18.30 presents source code to a Justify application that demonstrates left-, center-, right-, and equality-justification. (Set the justify variable to the appropriate justification constant and watch the results.)

LISTING 18.30 THE Justify APPLICATION SOURCE CODE

```
// Justify.java

import java.awt.*;
import java.awt.font.*;

import java.text.*;

import java.util.*;
```

LISTING 18.30 CONTINUED

```
public class Justify extends java.applet.Applet
{
   final static int LEFT = 0;
   final static int RIGHT = 1;
   final static int CENTER = 2;
   final static int EQUALITY = 3;

   int justify = EQUALITY;

   public void paint (Graphics g)
   {
      Dimension size = getSize ();

      String s = "To plagiarize or not to plagiarize William " +
                 "Shakespeare, that is the question!  Whether " +
                 "'tis nobler in the mind to suffer the lack of " +
                 "ideas for a decent paragraph, or to take arms " +
                 "against Mr. Shakespeare by plagiarizing his work " +
                 "... 'tis a consummation devoutly to be wished!";

      Hashtable map = new Hashtable ();
      map.put (TextAttribute.SIZE, new Float (18.0f));

      AttributedString as = new AttributedString (s, map);

      map = new Hashtable ();
      map.put (TextAttribute.POSTURE, TextAttribute.POSTURE_OBLIQUE);

      as.addAttributes (map, 4, 21);

      AttributedCharacterIterator aci = as.getIterator ();

      int startIndex = aci.getBeginIndex ();
      int endIndex = aci.getEndIndex ();

      LineBreakMeasurer measurer;
      measurer = new LineBreakMeasurer (aci,
                                        new FontRenderContext (null,
                                                               false,
                                                               false));
      measurer.setPosition (startIndex);

      float wrappingWidth = (float) size.width;

      float Y = 0.0f;

      while (measurer.getPosition () < endIndex)
      {
         TextLayout layout = measurer.nextLayout (wrappingWidth);

         Y += layout.getAscent ();

         float X = 0.0f;

         switch (justify)
         {
```

LISTING 18.30 CONTINUED

```
            case LEFT:
                 if (layout.isLeftToRight ())
                     X = 0.0f;
                 else
                     X = wrappingWidth - layout.getAdvance ();
                 break;

            case RIGHT:
                 if (layout.isLeftToRight ())
                     X = wrappingWidth - layout.getVisibleAdvance ();
                 else
                     X = wrappingWidth;
                 break;

            case CENTER:
                 if (layout.isLeftToRight ())
                     X = (wrappingWidth - layout.getVisibleAdvance ())
                         / 2;
                 else
                     X = (wrappingWidth + layout.getAdvance ()) / 2 -
                         layout.getAdvance ();
                 break;

            case EQUALITY:
                 layout = layout.getJustifiedLayout (wrappingWidth);
        }

        layout.draw ((Graphics2D) g, X, Y);

        Y += layout.getDescent () + layout.getLeading ();
      }
   }
}
```

Equality justification requires a developer to do two things: First, an attributed string that is to be justified must not include a `TextAttribute.JUSTIFICATION` attribute with a value set to `TextAttribute.JUSTIFICATION_NONE`. Second, `TextLayout`'s `getJustifiedLayout` method must be called with the width of the justified line. Figure 18.31 shows the result.

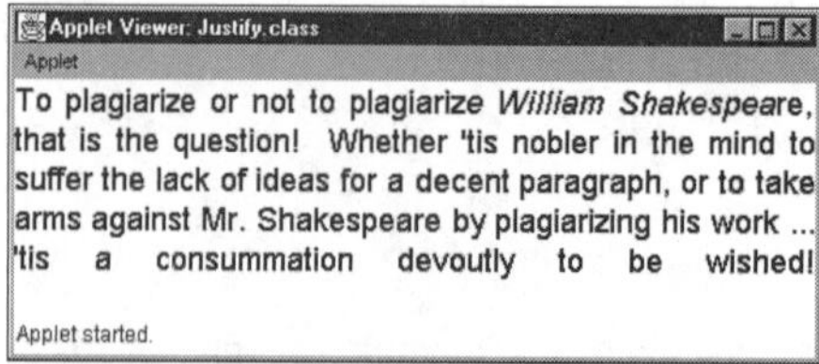

Figure 18.31
Equality justification is used to left- and right-justify text.

Caution

When run under Windows 98, the previous code generates intermittent exception access violations. The error message indicates that these violations are detected in native code outside of the JVM. If the problem is not Windows-related, it's resulting from one of the JVM support DLLs.

CHAPTER 19

Drag and Drop

In this chapter

by Geoff Friesen

WHAT IS DRAG AND DROP?

It's hard to imagine a windowing system that doesn't support drag and drop. This capability makes it possible to drag document icons to trashcan icons and then drop these "documents" into the "trash can." (Obviously, the document files associated with these icons are deleted.) Furthermore, drag and drop supports the copying or moving of file icons from one location to another location in a directory hierarchy. (As you know, the actual files are copied or moved behind the scenes.) Wherever it makes sense to drag an icon to another window, drop this icon onto that window, and perform an operation in the background, drag and drop is used.

Because modern windowing systems support drag and drop, Java must also support this capability, or be found inadequate. Therefore, it's most fortunate for Java that drag and drop has found its way into the JFC—as the Drag and Drop API. This API can be used to perform drag and drop between Java programs or between Java and non-Java programs.

The Drag and Drop API is based on the Data Transfer API that debuted in Java Version 1.1. This API simplifies the transfer of data between Java and non-Java programs or between Java programs. Before exploring the Drag and Drop API, it's important to learn about the Data Transfer API. After that, the Drag and Drop API will be easier to understand.

FIRST COMES DATA TRANSFER

The Data Transfer API is used to develop JFC programs that cut objects to and paste objects from either the system clipboard or a private clipboard. Although almost any kind of object can be cut and pasted (in theory), this API is typically used to cut and paste text strings. As a result, special support for cutting and pasting strings is provided.

The Data Transfer API is located in the `java.awt.datatransfer` package, which contains three interfaces and six classes—described in Table 19.1.

TABLE 19.1 DATA TRANSFER CLASSES AND INTERFACES

Interface/Class	Description
`Clipboard`	This class implements a mechanism for transferring data by way of copy/cut/paste operations.
`ClipboardOwner`	This interface is used by classes whose objects provide data to a clipboard.
`DataFlavor`	Each instance of this class represents a data format for data appearing on a clipboard, during drag and drop, or in a file system.
`FlavorMap`	This interface is used by classes (such as `SystemFlavorMap`) to provide mappings between platform native type names and MIME types (and their associated data flavors).

Table 19.1 Continued

Interface/Class	Description
`MimeTypeParseException`	This class is used to create objects that represent MIME type parsing exceptions. (This class is used internally by `DataFlavor`.)
`StringSelection`	This convenience class is used for transferring `String` objects to a clipboard.
`SystemFlavorMap`	This class is used (by Drag and Drop) to create objects that represent externally configurable flavor maps.
`Transferable`	This interface is used by classes whose objects provide data for a transfer operation.
`UnsupportedFlavorException`	This class is used to create objects that represent unsupported flavor exceptions.

Table 19.1 introduces several concepts that are important to data transfer. These concepts include data flavors, transferables, clipboard owners, and clipboards.

Data Flavors

Data flavors are objects that represent formats in which data can be transferred. These formats tell recipients what kind of data has been sent. Without this knowledge, a recipient would not know how to handle newly received data. For example, is the data formatted as text, image, audio, video, or something else? If text is sent, is this text plain, rich, or Unicode? Furthermore, if an image is sent, is this image GIF, JPEG, PNG, or some other kind? As this example shows, formats are divided into primary types (such as text) and subtypes (such as rich).

Each format corresponds to a MIME (Multipurpose Internet Mail Extensions) type. Although originally developed as a means to identify the various formats of data included in an email message, MIME's usefulness extends into the Data Transfer API.

Each MIME type consists of a primary type and a subtype, with a forward slash character serving as a separator. For example, `text/plain` represents a MIME type. The primary type is `text` and the subtype is `plain`. Furthermore, optional parameters might be present with some MIME types. For example, the `text/plain` MIME type might be followed by a `charset=Unicode` parameter. As a result, the fully qualified MIME type would read `text/plain; charset=Unicode`. (The `charset` parameter is used to differentiate between different kinds of plain text. The `Unicode` value represents text formatted as 16-bit Unicode characters.)

Objects created from the `DataFlavor` class represent data flavors. This class has quite a few methods, which include

- Constructors
- `getHumanPresentableName`

- `getMimeType`
- `getParameter`
- `getPrimaryType`
- `getRepresentationClass`
- `getSubType`
- `isMimeTypeEqual`

`DataFlavor` has several constructors. However, only two of these constructors will be examined. The first constructor has the following signature:

```
DataFlavor (String mimeType, String humanPresentableName)
```

A data flavor corresponding to a MIME type, as specified by the `mimeType` argument, is constructed. A more user-friendly name is provided by the `humanPresentableName` argument. This name can be displayed in a menu to provide a user with a selection of data flavors from which to choose. Furthermore, the resulting data flavor is associated with the default `java.io.InputStream` representation class. (The concept of a representation class will be explained when the next constructor is discussed.) The following code fragment constructs a data flavor using this constructor:

```
DataFlavor df1 = new DataFlavor ("text/plain; charset=ASCII",
                                 "Plain ASCII text");
```

The MIME type is `text/plain; charset=ASCII`, and its human presentable name is `Plain ASCII text`. The representation class is `java.io.InputStream`.

The second constructor has the following signature:

```
DataFlavor (Class representationClass, String humanPresentableName)
```

A data flavor corresponding to a representation class, as specified by the `representationClass` argument, is constructed. This class is used by a recipient to retrieve data by creating an object from this class and calling its methods. As with the previous constructor, a more user-friendly name is provided by the `humanPresentableName` argument. This name can be displayed in a menu to provide a user with a selection of data flavors from which to choose. The following code fragment constructs a data flavor using this constructor:

```
DataFlavor df = new DataFlavor (java.awt.Button.class, "AWT Button");
```

The representation class is `java.awt.Button`, and the human presentable name is `AWT Button`. Assuming that a `Button` object has been transferred to a clipboard, its `getText` method can be called to retrieve the button's text after this object is fetched from the clipboard. The MIME type is `application/x-java-serialized-object`.

Note

The concepts of files and *serialization* (saving objects in files so they can be reconstructed at a later point in time) are used by the Data Transfer API. Because these concepts are discussed at great length in subsequent chapters, they are only briefly referred to in this chapter.

The getHumanPresentableName method returns the human presentable name. It has the following signature:

```
String getHumanPresentableName ()
```

The MIME type is returned by the getMimeType method. It has the following signature:

```
String getMimeType ()
```

A MIME type's parameter is returned by the getParameter method. This method has the following signature:

```
String getParameter (String name)
```

If the parameter, identified by name, is part of a MIME type, its value is returned.

The getPrimaryType method returns a MIME type's primary type. It has the following signature:

```
String getPrimaryType ()
```

The getRepresentationClass method returns the data flavor's representation class. This method has the following signature:

```
Class getRepresentationClass ()
```

A MIME type's subtype is returned by the getSubType method, which has the following signature:

```
String getSubType ()
```

Finally, the current DataFlavor object can be compared to another DataFlavor object, to see if they are identical. Comparison is based on MIME types and performed by the isMimeTypeEqual method. It has the following signature:

```
boolean isMimeTypeEqual (DataFlavor df)
```

If the current data flavor's MIME type matches the MIME type of the df argument, a Boolean true value is returned. Otherwise, false is returned.

To make sense out of these methods, Listing 19.1 presents source code to a DataFlavorDemo1 application.

LISTING 19.1 THE DataFlavorDemo1 APPLICATION SOURCE CODE

```
// DataFlavorDemo1.java

import java.awt.datatransfer.*;

class DataFlavorDemo1
{
   public static void main (String [] args)
   {
      DataFlavor df1 = new DataFlavor ("text/plain; charset=ASCII",
                                       "Plain ASCII text");

      System.out.println ("Mime type: " + df1.getMimeType ());
```

LISTING 19.1 CONTINUED

```
        System.out.println ("Primary type: " + df1.getPrimaryType ());
        System.out.println ("Subtype: " + df1.getSubType ());
        System.out.println ("Parameter: " + df1.getParameter ("charset"));
        System.out.println ("Name: " + df1.getHumanPresentableName ());
        String s = df1.getRepresentationClass ().toString ();
        System.out.println ("Representation class: " + s + "\n");

        DataFlavor df2 = new DataFlavor (java.awt.Button.class,
                                         "AWT Button");

        System.out.println ("Mime type: " + df2.getMimeType ());
        System.out.println ("Primary type: " + df2.getPrimaryType ());
        System.out.println ("Subtype: " + df2.getSubType ());
        System.out.println ("Name: " + df2.getHumanPresentableName ());
        s = df2.getRepresentationClass ().toString ();
        System.out.println ("Representation class: " + s + "\n");

        System.out.println ("df1 equals df2: " +
                            df1.isMimeTypeEqual (df2));
    }
}
```

`DataFlavorDemo1` constructs two data flavors. The first data flavor uses the `text/plain; charset=ASCII` MIME type and is automatically assigned `java.io.InputStream` as its representation class. The second data flavor uses the `application/x-java-serialized-object` MIME type and is assigned `java.awt.Button` as its representation class.

`DataFlavor` includes three predefined data flavor variables that represent common data flavors. These variables include `stringFlavor`, `plainTextFlavor`, and `javaFileListFlavor`.

The `stringFlavor` variable is the data flavor for textual data represented by Java's `String` objects. Its MIME type is `application/x-java-serialized-object`, and its representation class is `java.lang.String`. The `plainTextFlavor` variable is the data flavor for textual data represented by Unicode characters. Its MIME type is `text/plain; charset=unicode`, and its representation class is `java.io.InputStream`. Finally, the `javaFileListFlavor` variable is the data flavor for files represented by Java's `File` objects. Its MIME type is `application/x-java-file-list`, and its representation class is `java.util.List`.

Caution

`plainTextFlavor` has been deprecated because its `InputStream` representation class uses 8-bit bytes to retrieve 16-bit Unicode characters. Instead of using `plainTextFlavor`, `DataFlavor`'s `getReaderForText` method is recommended.

Listing 19.2 presents source code to a `DataFlavorDemo2` application that extracts information from the `stringFlavor`, `plainTextFlavor`, and `javaFileListFlavor` data flavor objects.

LISTING 19.2 THE `DataFlavorDemo2` APPLICATION SOURCE CODE

```
// DataFlavorDemo2.java

import java.awt.datatransfer.*;

class DataFlavorDemo2
{
   public static void main (String [] args)
   {
      DataFlavor df = DataFlavor.stringFlavor;

      System.out.println ("Mime type: " + df.getMimeType ());
      System.out.println ("Primary type: " + df.getPrimaryType ());
      System.out.println ("Subtype: " + df.getSubType ());
      System.out.println ("Name: " + df.getHumanPresentableName ());
      String s = df.getRepresentationClass ().toString ();
      System.out.println ("Representation class: " + s + "\n");

      df = DataFlavor.plainTextFlavor;

      System.out.println ("Mime type: " + df.getMimeType ());
      System.out.println ("Primary type: " + df.getPrimaryType ());
      System.out.println ("Subtype: " + df.getSubType ());
      System.out.println ("Parameter: " + df.getParameter ("charset"));
      System.out.println ("Name: " + df.getHumanPresentableName ());
      s = df.getRepresentationClass ().toString ();
      System.out.println ("Representation class: " + s + "\n");

      df = DataFlavor.javaFileListFlavor;

      System.out.println ("Mime type: " + df.getMimeType ());
      System.out.println ("Primary type: " + df.getPrimaryType ());
      System.out.println ("Subtype: " + df.getSubType ());
      System.out.println ("Name: " + df.getHumanPresentableName ());
      s = df.getRepresentationClass ().toString ();
      System.out.println ("Representation class: " + s);
   }
}
```


Note

To establish a sense of completeness, `DataFlavorDemo2` extracts information using `plainTextFlavor`. However, `plainTextFlavor` is only presented as an illustration. Because this flavor has been deprecated, you should avoid using `plainTextFlavor` in your programs.

Version 1.3 of the Java 2 Platform Standard Edition adds two new methods to `DataFlavor`: `getReaderForText` and `selectBestTextFlavor`.

The `getReaderForText` method takes a single `Transferable` argument and returns a *reader* (a mechanism for reading Unicode character streams by interpreting a stream's contents as a sequence of 16-bit Unicode characters) corresponding to the input stream, based on the

MIME `charset` parameter value. (This works if the representation class is `java.io.InputStream` or a subclass. If the representation class is a reader, the representation class is returned.)

The `selectBestTextFlavor` method takes an array of `DataFlavor` objects (corresponding to text data flavors) as its single argument and attempts to locate the data flavor of highest fidelity. If found, this data flavor is returned. Otherwise, `null` is returned.

TRANSFERABLES

Transferables are objects placed on or retrieved from a clipboard. Their classes implement the `Transferable` interface. `Transferable`'s methods allow transferables to describe their presentations to clipboard readers, and include

- `getTransferData`
- `getTransferDataFlavors`
- `isDataFlavorSupported`

The `getTransferData` method returns an object representing the data retrieved from a clipboard. It has the following signature:

```
Object getTransferData (DataFlavor df)
```

The `df` argument identifies the desired data flavor in which to obtain the data. If the data is no longer available in this data flavor, an `IOException` object is thrown. Furthermore, if the `df` data flavor is not supported, an `UnsupportedFlavorException` object is thrown.

Assuming that the data is available and that the data flavor is supported, this method returns an object created from the data flavor's representation class. Methods can then be called on this object to retrieve the data. However, if the data flavor is `DataFlavor.stringFlavor`, you don't have to call any methods, because this flavor returns an instance of the `String` class. All you need to do is cast from `Object` to `String`. (The `ClipboardDemo1` application—introduced later in this chapter—provides an illustration.)

The `getTransferDataFlavors` method returns an array of `DataFlavor` objects that correspond to all supported data flavors. It has the following signature:

```
DataFlavor [] getTransferDataFlavors ()
```

This array is usually ordered from the most descriptive data flavor (such as a rich text data flavor) to the least descriptive data flavor (such as a plain text data flavor).

The `isDataFlavorSupported` method returns a Boolean that indicates whether a specific data flavor is supported. It has the following signature:

```
boolean isDataFlavorSupported (DataFlavor df)
```

A Boolean `true` value is returned if the transferable supports the data flavor specified by `df`. Otherwise, `false` is returned.

Clipboard Owners

Clipboard owners are objects created from classes that implement the `ClipboardOwner` interface. These objects are responsible for placing transferables on the clipboard. (You'll learn about clipboards very shortly.) When a clipboard owner places a transferable on the clipboard, it becomes the owner of that clipboard. However, if some other clipboard owner places an object on the clipboard, it becomes the new owner and the previous owner loses ownership.

`ClipboardOwner` provides a single method, which has the following signature:

```
void lostOwnership (Clipboard clipboard, Transferable contents)
```

This method is called when a clipboard owner loses ownership of a clipboard (and can be used to prompt a user to keep or remove any data on the clipboard prior to exiting a program). The `clipboard` argument identifies the previously owned clipboard, and `contents` identifies the transferable previously on the clipboard. (In other words, `contents` represents the notified clipboard owner's transferable.)

Clipboards

One of the more intuitive aspects of a windowing system is the concept of a *clipboard*. Most users are familiar with this concept, along with the standard copy/cut/paste metaphor that is used to copy or cut text from one document and paste it into another document. Between copy/cut and paste operations, a clipboard serves as a repository for this text.

In a much broader sense, a clipboard serves as a repository for transferables. These transferables are not limited to text, but can include any other kind of data (such as audio or image data). Only a single transferable can be stored on a clipboard at any given point in time.

Clipboards fall into two categories: *system* and *private*. The system clipboard is used by the underlying windowing system. JFC applications and native programs have access to the system clipboard. You can obtain the system clipboard by calling `Toolkit`'s `getSystemClipboard` method. For example, the following code fragment acquires the system clipboard:

```
Clipboard c = java.awt.Toolkit.getDefaultToolkit ().getSystemClipboard ();
```

Private clipboards are used by the currently running program and have no security restrictions placed on them. (This means that an applet can create and use a private clipboard.) You can obtain a private clipboard by constructing objects from the `Clipboard` class. `Clipboard`'s methods include

- Constructor
- `getContents`
- `getName`
- `setContents`

`Clipboard`'s single constructor has the following signature:

```
Clipboard (String name)
```

The name argument identifies the newly constructed clipboard. The following code fragment constructs a private clipboard:

```
Clipboard c = new Clipboard ("My private clipboard");
```

The getContents method retrieves the current transferable placed on the clipboard, or null if the clipboard is empty. It has the following signature:

```
Transferable getContents (Object requester)
```

The requester argument identifies the object requesting the transferable. However, the concept of a requester is currently not implemented. Therefore, the requester argument is ignored. (It's a good idea to pass this as the requester argument's value. This way, your code will work properly when the requester concept is implemented.)

The getName method returns the name of the clipboard. It has the following signature:

```
String getName ()
```

The name passed to a private clipboard's constructor is returned. However, System is returned if this method is called for the system clipboard.

The setContents method changes the clipboard's contents and owner. It has the following signature:

```
void setContents (Transferable contents, ClipboardOwner owner)
```

The new contents are specified by contents, and the new owner is specified by owner. The previous clipboard owner is notified by a call to its lostOwnership method.

Listing 19.3 presents source code to a ClipboardDemo1 application that demonstrates clipboards, transferables, and data flavors.

LISTING 19.3 THE ClipBoardDemo1 APPLICATION SOURCE CODE

```
// ClipboardDemo1.java

import java.awt.*;
import java.awt.datatransfer.*;
import java.awt.event.*;

import java.io.*;

class ClipboardDemo1 extends Frame
                     implements ActionListener, ItemListener
{
   TextArea ta;
   Checkbox cbFlavor;

   boolean useFlavor = true;

   ClipboardDemo1 (String title)
   {
      super (title);

      addWindowListener (new WindowAdapter ()
```

Listing 19.3 Continued

```
                   {
                       public void windowClosing (WindowEvent e)
                       {
                          System.exit (0);
                       }
                   });

      MenuBar mb = new MenuBar ();

      Menu file = new Menu ("File");
      file.add ("Exit");

      // An action listener is being assigned to
      // the entire menu instead of just a single
      // menu item because there is only one menu
      // item. Swing does not support this capability.

      file.addActionListener (this);

      mb.add (file);

      Menu edit = new Menu ("Edit");
      edit.add ("Paste");

      // An action listener is being assigned to
      // the entire menu instead of just a single
      // menu item because there is only one menu
      // item. Swing does not support this capability.

      edit.addActionListener (this);

      mb.add (edit);

      setMenuBar (mb);

      Panel p = new Panel ();
      CheckboxGroup cbg = new CheckboxGroup ();
      cbFlavor = new Checkbox ("Flavor", true, cbg);
      cbFlavor.addItemListener (this);
      p.add (cbFlavor);
      Checkbox cb = new Checkbox ("Text", false, cbg);
      cb.addItemListener (this);
      p.add (cb);

      add (p, BorderLayout.SOUTH);

      p = new Panel ();
      ta = new TextArea (10, 60);
      ta.setEditable (false);
      p.add (ta);

      add (p, BorderLayout.NORTH);

      pack ();
```

LISTING 19.3 CONTINUED

```
      setVisible (true);
   }

   public void actionPerformed (ActionEvent e)
   {
      if (e.getActionCommand ().equals ("Exit"))
          System.exit (0);

      // Paste is assumed.

      ta.setText ("");

      Toolkit tk = Toolkit.getDefaultToolkit ();
      Clipboard c = tk.getSystemClipboard ();

      Transferable t = c.getContents (this);
      if (t == null)
          return;

      String s = "";

      if (useFlavor)
      {
          DataFlavor [] df = t.getTransferDataFlavors ();

          for (int i = 0; i < df.length; i++)
               s = s + df [i].getHumanPresentableName () + " ("
                     + df [i].getMimeType () + ")\n";
      }
      else
          try
          {
              s = (String) t.getTransferData (DataFlavor.stringFlavor);
          }
          catch (IOException e2) {}
          catch (UnsupportedFlavorException e2) {}
      ta.setText (s);
   }

   public void itemStateChanged (ItemEvent e)
   {
      if (e.getItemSelectable () == cbFlavor)
          useFlavor = true;
      else
          useFlavor = false;
   }

   public static void main (String [] args)
   {
      new ClipboardDemo1 ("Clipboard Demo1");
   }
}
```

ClipboardDemo1 is an AWT application that creates a GUI consisting of a menu bar with two menus, a text area, and a pair of radio buttons that are used to select whether data flavor information or text will be pasted. (The default is data flavor information.) You can select Exit from the File menu to terminate this program, or you can select Paste from the Edit menu to paste either the transferable's data flavor information (if there is a transferable) or the transferable's data (provided that its data flavor corresponds to the string data flavor) from the system clipboard to the text area.

When you select Paste, the actionPerformed method is called. The contents of the text area are erased, and then the system clipboard is obtained (via getDefaultToolkit and getSystemClipboard) along with its transferable (via the getContents method). If no transferable is present, getContents returns null, and this method exits. If getContents returns a reference to a Transferable object, either all data flavors are captured by calling getTransferDataFlavors or the transferable's data is obtained by calling getTransferData.

In the situation where data flavors are retrieved, each data flavor's human presentable name and MIME type are extracted and appended to a String object. Figure 19.1 shows ClipboardDemo1's GUI displaying data flavors.

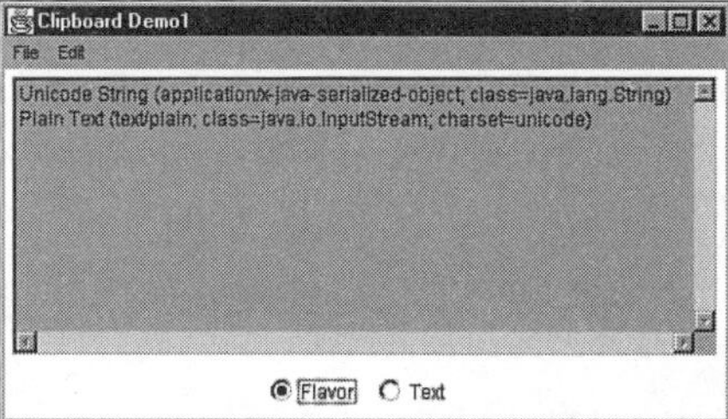

Figure 19.1
The ClipboardDemo1 application displays the transferable's data flavors.

The first displayed data flavor has Unicode String as its human presentable string, whereas the second data flavor is identified as Plain Text.

When data is retrieved, this data is stored in a String object. Figure 19.2 shows ClipboardDemo1's GUI displaying the data (using the string data flavor).

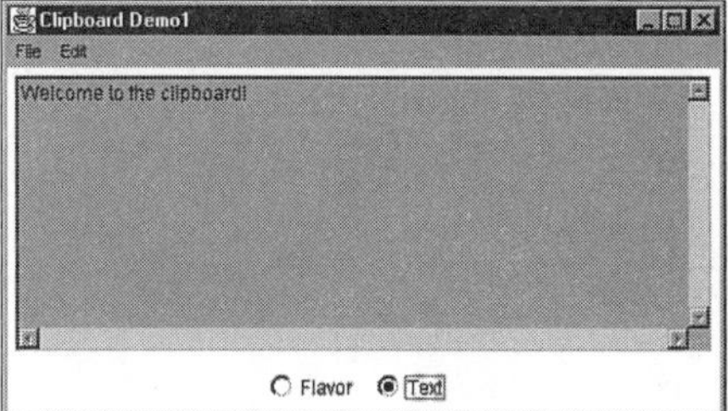

Figure 19.2
The ClipboardDemo1 application displays the transferable's data.

So far, you've seen how data is pasted from the system clipboard. It's time to broaden this knowledge by learning how to copy data to either the system or a private clipboard, as well as learning how to paste this data from a private clipboard. Therefore, Listing 19.4 presents source code to a `ClipboardDemo2` application that demonstrates these tasks.

LISTING 19.4 THE `ClipBoardDemo2` APPLICATION SOURCE CODE

```
// ClipboardDemo2.java

import java.awt.*;
import java.awt.datatransfer.*;
import java.awt.event.*;

import java.io.*;

class ClipboardDemo2 extends Frame
                     implements ActionListener, ItemListener
{
   TextArea ta;
   TextField tf;
   Checkbox cbSystem;

   boolean useSystem = true;

   Clipboard pc = new Clipboard ("Personal");
   Clipboard sc = Toolkit.getDefaultToolkit ().getSystemClipboard ();

   ClipboardDemo2 (String title)
   {
      super (title);

      addWindowListener (new WindowAdapter ()
                         {
                             public void windowClosing (WindowEvent e)
                             {
                                System.exit (0);
                             }
                         });

      MenuBar mb = new MenuBar ();

      Menu file = new Menu ("File");
      MenuItem fileItem = new MenuItem ("Exit");
      fileItem.addActionListener (this);
      file.add (fileItem);

      mb.add (file);

      Menu edit = new Menu ("Edit");
      MenuItem editItem = new MenuItem ("Copy");
      editItem.addActionListener (this);
      edit.add (editItem);
      editItem = new MenuItem ("Paste");
      editItem.addActionListener (this);
      edit.add (editItem);
```

Listing 19.4 Continued

```
      mb.add (edit);

      setMenuBar (mb);

      Panel p = new Panel ();
      CheckboxGroup cbg = new CheckboxGroup ();
      cbSystem = new Checkbox ("System", true, cbg);
      cbSystem.addItemListener (this);
      p.add (cbSystem);
      Checkbox cb = new Checkbox ("Private", false, cbg);
      cb.addItemListener (this);
      p.add (cb);

      add (p, BorderLayout.SOUTH);

      p = new Panel ();
      tf = new TextField (60);
      p.add (tf);

      add (p, BorderLayout.CENTER);

      p = new Panel ();
      ta = new TextArea (10, 60);
      ta.setEditable (false);
      p.add (ta);

      add (p, BorderLayout.NORTH);

      pack ();

      setVisible (true);
   }

   public void actionPerformed (ActionEvent e)
   {
      if (e.getActionCommand ().equals ("Exit"))
          System.exit (0);

      Clipboard c = (useSystem) ? sc : pc;

      if (e.getActionCommand ().equals ("Copy"))
      {
          myTransferable mt = new myTransferable (tf.getText ());
          c.setContents (mt, mt);
          return;
      }

      // Paste is the default.

      try
      {
         Transferable t = c.getContents (this);
         if (t != null)
         {
             String s;
```

LISTING 19.4 CONTINUED

```
             s = (String) t.getTransferData (DataFlavor.stringFlavor);
             ta.setText (s);
          }
       }
       catch (IOException e2) {}
       catch (UnsupportedFlavorException e2) {}

       return;
   }

   public void itemStateChanged (ItemEvent e)
   {
      ta.setText ("");

      if (e.getItemSelectable () == cbSystem)
          useSystem = true;
      else
          useSystem = false;
   }

   public static void main (String [] args)
   {
      new ClipboardDemo2 ("Clipboard Demo2");
   }
}

class myTransferable implements Transferable, ClipboardOwner
{
   private DataFlavor [] dataFlavors =
   {
      DataFlavor.stringFlavor
   };

   private String data;

   myTransferable (String data)
   {
      this.data = data;
   }

   public DataFlavor [] getTransferDataFlavors ()
   {
      // Do not allow caller to modify the flavors.

      return (DataFlavor []) dataFlavors.clone ();
   }

   public boolean isDataFlavorSupported (DataFlavor flavor)
   {
      return (flavor == DataFlavor.stringFlavor) ? true : false;
   }

   public Object getTransferData (DataFlavor flavor)
          throws UnsupportedFlavorException, IOException
```

Listing 19.4 Continued

```
    {
       if (flavor == DataFlavor.stringFlavor)
           return (Object) data;
       else
           throw new UnsupportedFlavorException (flavor);
    }

    public void lostOwnership (Clipboard c, Transferable contents)
    {
       System.out.println ("losing ownership");
    }
}
```

`ClipboardDemo2` is an AWT application that creates a GUI consisting of a menu bar with two menus, a text area, a text field, and a pair of radio buttons that are used to select whether the system or the private clipboard is used. (The default is the system clipboard.) You can select Exit from the File menu to terminate this program, Copy from the Edit menu to copy the contents of the text field to the appropriate clipboard, or Paste from the Edit menu to paste the transferable's data (provided that there is a transferable and that its data flavor corresponds to the string flavor) from the clipboard to the text area.

To take care of copying, `ClipboardDemo2` needs to create an object from a class that implements the `Transferable` and `ClipboardOwner` interfaces. This class is given the name `myTransferable`. When Copy is selected, an object from this class is created and its constructor is given the contents of the text field. These contents are saved in a private `String` variable. Then, the current clipboard's `setContents` method is called to transfer this data to either the system or private clipboard. (You can get away with passing the `myTransferable` variable as both arguments to `setContents` because `myTransferable` is both a transferable and a clipboard owner, by virtue of implementing both interfaces.)

To take care of pasting, the clipboard's `getContents` method is called to return the transferable. If an accessible transferable exists on the clipboard, `getTransferData` is called to return the data in accordance with the string data flavor.

Figure 19.3 shows `ClipboardDemo2`'s GUI displaying text field data copied to the system clipboard and then pasted to the text area.

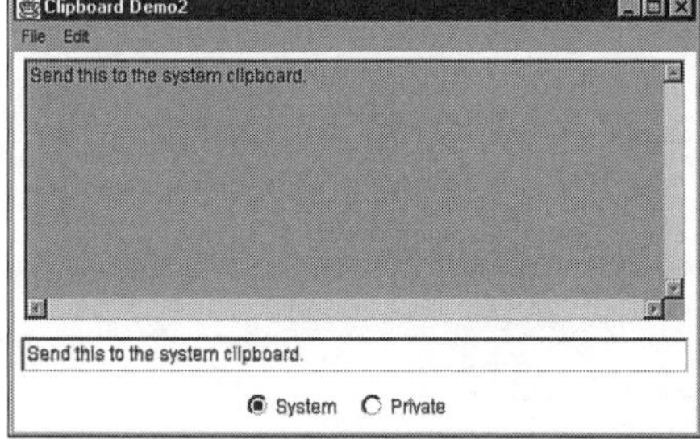

Figure 19.3 The `ClipboardDemo2` application displays text field data pasted from the system clipboard to the text area.

The myTransferable class isn't necessary because the Data Transfer API includes a convenience class called StringSelection. This class behaves identically to myTransferable. To demonstrate StringSelection (and also to provide a Swing alternative), Listing 19.5 presents source code to an application called ClipboardDemo3.

LISTING 19.5 THE ClipBoardDemo3 APPLICATION SOURCE CODE

```
// ClipboardDemo3.java

import javax.swing.*;

import java.awt.*;
import java.awt.datatransfer.*;
import java.awt.event.*;

import java.io.*;

class ClipboardDemo3 extends JFrame implements ActionListener
{
   JTextArea ta;
   JTextField tf;
   JRadioButton rbSystem, rbPrivate;

   boolean useSystem = true;

   Clipboard pc = new Clipboard ("Personal");
   Clipboard sc = Toolkit.getDefaultToolkit ().getSystemClipboard ();

   ClipboardDemo3 (String title)
   {
      super (title);

      addWindowListener (new WindowAdapter ()
                         {
                             public void windowClosing (WindowEvent e)
                             {
                                System.exit (0);
                             }
                         });

      JMenuBar mb = new JMenuBar ();

      JMenu file = new JMenu ("File");
      JMenuItem fileItem = new JMenuItem ("Exit");
      fileItem.addActionListener (this);
      file.add (fileItem);

      mb.add (file);

      JMenu edit = new JMenu ("Edit");
      JMenuItem editItem = new JMenuItem ("Copy");
      editItem.addActionListener (this);
      edit.add (editItem);
      editItem = new JMenuItem ("Paste");
      editItem.addActionListener (this);
      edit.add (editItem);
```

Listing 19.5 Continued

```
      mb.add (edit);

      setJMenuBar (mb);

      JPanel p = new JPanel ();
      rbSystem = new JRadioButton ("System", true);
      rbSystem.addActionListener (this);
      p.add (rbSystem);
      rbPrivate = new JRadioButton ("Private", false);
      rbPrivate.addActionListener (this);
      p.add (rbPrivate);

      ButtonGroup bg = new ButtonGroup ();
      bg.add (rbSystem);
      bg.add (rbPrivate);

      getContentPane ().add (p, BorderLayout.SOUTH);

      p = new JPanel ();
      tf = new JTextField (40);
      p.add (tf);

      getContentPane ().add (p, BorderLayout.CENTER);

      p = new JPanel ();
      ta = new JTextArea (10, 40);
      ta.setEditable (false);
      p.add (ta);

      getContentPane ().add (p, BorderLayout.NORTH);

      pack ();

      setVisible (true);
   }

   public void actionPerformed (ActionEvent e)
   {
      ta.setText ("");

      if (e.getSource () == rbSystem)
      {
          useSystem = true;
          return;
      }

      if (e.getSource () == rbPrivate)
      {
          useSystem = false;
          return;
      }

      if (e.getActionCommand ().equals ("Exit"))
          System.exit (0);

      Clipboard c = (useSystem) ? sc : pc;
```

LISTING 19.5 CONTINUED

```
      if (e.getActionCommand ().equals ("Copy"))
      {
          StringSelection ss = new StringSelection (tf.getText ());
          c.setContents (ss, ss);
          return;
      }

      // Paste is the default.

      try
      {
         Transferable t = c.getContents (this);
         if (t != null)
         {
             String s;
             s = (String) t.getTransferData (DataFlavor.stringFlavor);
             ta.setText (s);
         }
      }
      catch (IOException e2) {}
      catch (UnsupportedFlavorException e2) {}

      return;
   }

   public static void main (String [] args)
   {
      new ClipboardDemo3 ("Clipboard Demo3");
   }
}
```

`ClipboardDemo3` is a Swing application that presents an equivalent GUI to `ClipboardDemo2`. The only real difference (in terms of clipboard functionality) is the use of `StringSelection` instead of `myTransferable` to transfer data using a string data flavor. Figure 19.4 shows `ClipboardDemo3`'s GUI displaying text field data copied to a private clipboard and then pasted to the text area.

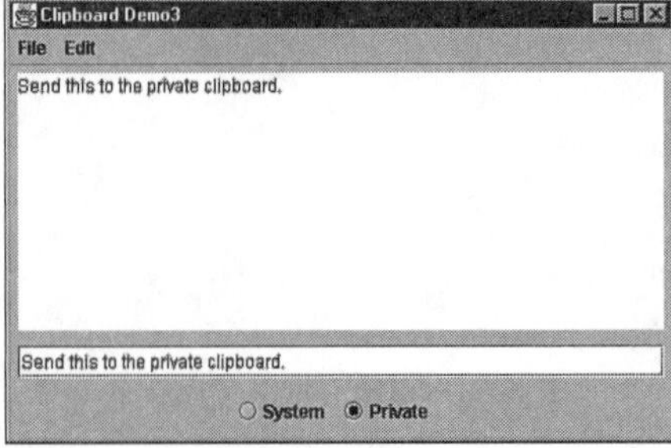

Figure 19.4
The `ClipboardDemo3` application displays text field data pasted from the private clipboard to the text area.

Text field and text area components provide automatic copy, cut, and paste operations. However, there might be situations in which you need to perform these operations in a programmatic fashion. If you're having trouble figuring out how to accomplish this task, see "Programmatically Copying, Cutting, and Pasting" in the "Troubleshooting" section at the end of this chapter.

So far, the discussion has revolved around transferring textual data to the clipboard. However, as you know, other kinds of data (such as images) exist. To give you an idea of what is required in transferring an image to a clipboard, Listing 19.6 presents source code to the `ClipboardDemo4` application.

LISTING 19.6 THE `ClipboardDemo4` APPLICATION SOURCE CODE

```
// ClipboardDemo4.java

import java.awt.*;
import java.awt.datatransfer.*;
import java.awt.event.*;
import java.awt.image.*;

class ClipboardDemo4
{
   static Clipboard c = new Clipboard ("My clipboard");

   public static void main (String [] args)
   {
      int width = 100;
      int height = 100;

      int [] pixels = new int [width * height];

      int index = 0;

      for (int y = 0; y < height; y++)
      {
           int numerator = y * 255;
           int b = numerator / height;
           int r = 255 - numerator / height;

           for (int x = 0; x < width; x++)
           {
                int g = x * 255 / width;
                pixels [index++] = (255 << 24) | (r << 16) | (g << 8)
                                   | b;
           }
      }

      Toolkit tk = Toolkit.getDefaultToolkit ();
      Image im = tk.createImage (new MemoryImageSource (width,
                                                        height,
                                                        pixels,
                                                        0,
                                                        width));

      ImageSelection is = new ImageSelection (im);
      c.setContents (is, is);
```

LISTING 19.6 CONTINUED

```
      Frame f = new Frame ("Clipboard Demo4");

      f.addWindowListener (new WindowAdapter ()
                           {
                             public void windowClosing (WindowEvent e)
                             {
                                System.exit (0);
                             }
                           });

      picture p = new picture (f);

      f.add (p);

      Transferable t = c.getContents (new ClipboardDemo4 ());
      if (t == null)
          return;

      try
      {
          p.draw ((Image)
                  t.getTransferData (ImageSelection.imageFlavor));
      }
      catch (java.io.IOException e) {}
      catch (UnsupportedFlavorException e) {}

      f.pack ();

      f.setVisible (true);
   }
}

class ImageSelection implements Transferable, ClipboardOwner
{
    public static final DataFlavor imageFlavor =
                                 new DataFlavor (java.awt.Image.class,
                                                 "AWT Image");

    private DataFlavor [] flavors =
    {
       imageFlavor
    };

    private Image picture;

    public ImageSelection (Image picture)
    {
       this.picture = picture;
    }

    public DataFlavor [] getTransferDataFlavors ()
    {
       return flavors;
    }
```

LISTING 19.6 CONTINUED

```
    public boolean isDataFlavorSupported (DataFlavor df)
    {
       return imageFlavor.equals (df);
    }

    public Object getTransferData (DataFlavor df)
                  throws UnsupportedFlavorException
    {
       if (df.equals (imageFlavor))
           return picture;
       else
           throw new UnsupportedFlavorException (df);
    }

    public void lostOwnership (Clipboard c, Transferable contents)
    {
       System.out.println ("lost ownership");
    }
}

class picture extends Canvas
{
   private Frame observer;  // The frame window that monitors an image.
   private Image image;     // The current image.

   picture (Frame observer)
   {
      this.observer = observer; // Save the current observer.
      setBackground (Color.lightGray);
   }

   public void draw (Image image)
   {
      this.image = image;            // Save the current image.
      repaint ();                    // Draw the image.
   }

   public Dimension getPreferredSize ()
   {
      // When the layout manager calls picture's getPreferredSize ()
      // method, this method will return a Dimension object that
      // tells the layout manager how much room to reserve for the
      // picture component. Because images are already present in
      // memory (by virtue of being on the clipboard), it's okay to
      // call the Image's getWidth and getHeight methods. However,
      // an 80-pixel border is also provided.

      return new Dimension (image.getWidth (observer) + 80,
                            image.getHeight (observer) + 80);
   }

   public void paint (Graphics g)
   {
      // Determine the upper-left image corner (x, y) coordinates so
      // that the image will be centered.
```

LISTING 19.6 CONTINUED

```
      int x = (getSize ().width - image.getWidth (observer)) / 2;
      int y = (getSize ().height - image.getHeight (observer)) / 2;

      // Draw the image.

      g.drawImage (image, x, y, observer);
   }

   public void update (Graphics g)
   {
      // The inherited update method clears the background prior
      // to calling paint. This results in flicker. The flicker
      // is eliminated by overriding update.

      paint (g);
   }
}
```

`ClipboardDemo4` constructs an image in memory and converts this image into an `Image` object by way of a `MemoryImageSource` producer. This `Image` object is copied to a clipboard and later retrieved.

Because you've seen most of this code in previous chapters, the only new concept is the `ImageSelection` class. This class is modeled after `StringSelection` and introduces a flavor called `imageFlavor`. The idea is to return an `Image` object from the clipboard when `getTransferData` is called.

You cannot use this program (at least not under Windows or Unix) to transfer an image to the system clipboard because that clipboard does not understand the MIME type corresponding to the image flavor. (This is why a private clipboard is created.)

From one perspective, this program is "much ado about nothing." After all, you aren't really accomplishing anything useful by transferring the image to and from the private clipboard. However, imagine creating a drawing program. You could use `ClipboardDemo4`'s `ImageSelection` class, and its metaphor for transferring images to and from a private clipboard, to support clipboard functionality in this drawing program.

`ClipboardDemo4` *shows that textual data isn't the only kind of data that can be copied to and pasted from a private clipboard. An image object can also be copied and pasted. However, you'll be disappointed if you try to copy this image object to the system clipboard. If you're having trouble trying to transfer an image or some other kind of nontextual data to/from the system clipboard, see "Transferring Nontextual Data to/from the System Clipboard" in the "Troubleshooting" section at the end of this chapter.*

THEN COMES DRAG AND DROP

The Drag and Drop API is located in the `java.awt.dnd` package and consists of 4 interfaces and 15 classes. When you first encounter `java.awt.dnd`, you'll probably feel overwhelmed. After all, there's a lot of infrastructure to Drag and Drop. However, after you've learned the basics, this feeling will dissipate.

Drag and Drop uses the concepts of drag sources and drop targets. A *drag source* is an object associated with a component that serves as the source of a drag-and-drop operation. In contrast, a *drop target* is an object associated with a component that serves as the target of a drag-and-drop operation. So what gets dragged (and subsequently dropped)? It turns out that Drag and Drop uses transferables to encapsulate the data being sent from a source to a target. This data is then used by the target to perform a behind-the-scenes operation. For example, when dragging a file from one directory to another, the transferable would contain a filename. The target would use this name to identify the file being copied or moved. Figure 19.5 illustrates components, drag sources, drop targets, and transferables.

Figure 19.5
The fundamental entities of a drag-and-drop operation.

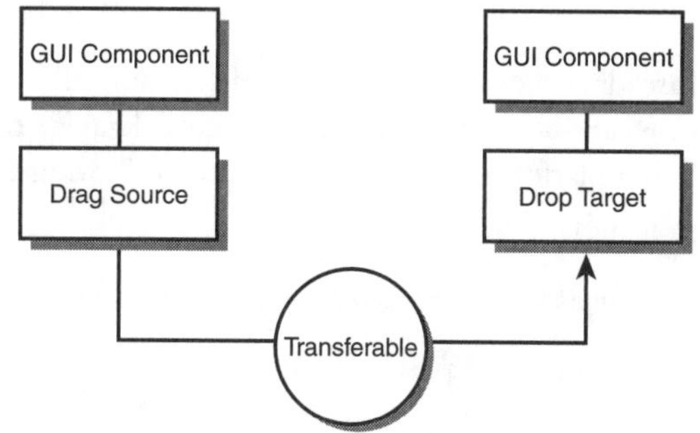

When a drag-and-drop operation is invoked, a particular action is specified. Actions determine what happens to a transferable's data when a drag-and-drop operation has completed and are represented by constants declared in the `DnDConstants` class. These constants (along with descriptions) are presented in Table 19.2.

TABLE 19.2 `DnDConstants` ACTION CONSTANTS

Action Constant	Description
`ACTION_COPY`	The drag source leaves the data intact.
`ACTION_COPY_OR_MOVE`	The drag source performs either a copy or move action, as requested by the drop target.
`ACTION_LINK`	A change to either the drag source or drop target is propagated to the other entity.
`ACTION_MOVE`	The drag source deletes the data upon successful completion of the drop.
`ACTION_NONE`	No action is taken.
`ACTION_REFERENCE`	A synonym for `ACTION_LINK`.

A drag-and-drop operation is initiated with a *gesture* (a platform-dependent mechanism for choosing a copy, move, or link action). For example, under Windows, pressing the left mouse button would initiate a move gesture, whereas pressing this button while simultaneously pressing the Ctrl key would initiate a copy gesture.

To implement drag and drop, the first thing you do is subclass an existing component's class. For example, you might want to subclass `JLabel`. The following code fragment shows the result of this subclassing:

```
class DragLabel extends JLabel
{
   DragLabel (String label, int alignment)
   {
      super (label, alignment);
      // Other stuff
   }

   // More stuff
}
```

You would subsequently introduce a `DragSource` field variable and call `DragSource.getDefaultDragSource` to assign a reference to the default drag source that's associated with the underlying platform. This is shown in the following code fragment:

```
class DragLabel extends JLabel
{
   private DragSource ds = DragSource.getDefaultDragSource ();

   DragLabel (String label, int alignment)
   {
      super (label, alignment);
      // Other stuff
   }

   // More stuff
}
```

At this point, you create a gesture recognizer that responds to gestures. You do this by calling `DragSource`'s `createDefaultDragGestureRecognizer` method and passing it three arguments. The first argument is a reference to the component object. (You can use the reserved word `this`.) The second argument is the desired action (which you specify by using a `DnDConstants` constant). The final argument is a reference to an object whose class implements the `DragGestureListener` interface. (This interface contains a single `dragGestureRecognized` method, which gets called when the drag gesture recognizer detects a gesture.) The following code fragment illustrates what has been achieved thus far:

```
class DragLabel extends JLabel implements DragGestureListener
{
   private DragSource ds = DragSource.getDefaultDragSource ();

   DragLabel (String label, int alignment)
   {
      super (label, alignment);

      int action = DnDConstants.ACTION_COPY_OR_MOVE;
      ds.createDefaultDragGestureRecognizer (this,
                                             action,
                                             this);
   }
```

```
    public void dragGestureRecognized (DragGestureEvent e)
    {
       // ...
    }

    // More stuff
}
```

When dragGestureRecognized gets called, it sends a start dragged message to the drag source. This is accomplished by calling DragGestureEvent's startDrag method. In turn, this method creates a DragSourceContext object to track the state of the operation by listening to a native DragSourceContextPeer. The startDrag method takes three arguments: a cursor, a transferable, and a drag source listener.

The cursor identifies the initial drag cursor and shows the preliminary state of the drag-and-drop operation. You can choose one of DragSource's six predefined cursors, which are presented in Table 19.3.

TABLE 19.3 DragSource'S PREDEFINED CURSORS

Cursor Constant	Description
DefaultCopyDrop	The default Cursor to use with a copy operation indicating that a drop is currently allowed
DefaultCopyNoDrop	The default Cursor to use with a copy operation indicating that a drop is currently not allowed
DefaultLinkDrop	The default Cursor to use with a link operation indicating that a drop is currently allowed
DefaultLinkNoDrop	The default Cursor to use with a link operation indicating that a drop is currently not allowed
DefaultMoveDrop	The default Cursor to use with a move operation indicating that a drop is currently allowed
DefaultMoveNoDrop	The default Cursor to use with a move operation indicating that a drop is currently not allowed

The transferable is an object that encapsulates data being transferred. If you recall, this object provides the data for an operation that will occur behind the scenes, after this object has been dropped.

The drag source listener provides methods, for originators of drag-and-drop operations, that are notified to track the state of a user's gesture and to give "drag over" feedback as the drag-and-drop operation proceeds. These methods include

- dragDropEnd
- dragEnter
- dragExit
- dragOver
- dropActionChanged

The `dragDropEnd` method has the following signature:

```
void dragDropEnd (DragSourceDropEvent e)
```

This method is called to signify that the drag-and-drop operation has completed. The `DragSourceDropEvent` argument's `getDropSuccess` method can be used to determine the termination state. Furthermore, `DragSourceDropEvent`'s `getDropAction` method returns the operation that the `DropTarget` selected (via the argument passed to the `DropTargetDropEvent` `acceptDrop` method) to apply to the drop operation. After this method is complete, the current `DragSourceContext` and associated resources become invalid.

The `dragEnter` method has the following signature:

```
void dragEnter (DragSourceDragEvent e)
```

This method is called as the drag cursor's *hotspot* (that portion of the cursor's icon that a windowing system uses to track the cursor—such as the extreme tip of an arrow icon) enters a drop target. All the following conditions must be true:

- The drag cursor's hotspot initially intersects a drop target's visible GUI component.
- The component has an active `DropTarget` associated with it.
- The `DropTarget's` registered `DropTargetListener` `dragEnter` method has been invoked and returned successfully.

The `dragExit` method has the following signature:

```
void dragExit (DragSourceEvent e)
```

This method is called when the drag cursor's hotspot exits a drop target. *One* of the following conditions must be true:

- The drag cursor's hotspot no longer intersects the drop target's visible GUI component.
- The component that the drag cursor's hotspot intersected, resulting in the previous `dragEnter` invocation, no longer has an active `DropTarget` or `DropTargetListener` associated with it.
- The current `DropTarget`'s `DropTargetListener` has invoked `rejectDrag` since the last `dragEnter` or `dragOver` invocation.
- The drag-and-drop operation is aborted before the hotspot enters the drop target's visible component.

The `dragOver` method has the following signature:

```
void dragOver (DragSourceDragEvent e)
```

This method is called as the drag cursor's hotspot moves over a platform-dependent drop site. *All* the following conditions must be true:

- The drag cursor's hotspot has moved, but still intersects the visible GUI component associated with the previous `dragEnter` invocation.
- The component still has a `DropTarget` associated with it.

- That DropTarget is still active.
- The DropTarget's registered DropTargetListener dragOver method is invoked and returns successfully.
- The DropTarget does not reject the drag via rejectDrag.

Finally, the dropActionChanged method has the following signature:

```
void dropActionChanged (DragSourceDragEvent e)
```

This method is called when the user has modified the drop gesture, as when the state of the input device(s) with which the user is interacting changes. Such devices are typically the mouse buttons or keyboard modifiers.

Caution

> If the startDrag method cannot initiate a drag-and-drop operation, this methods throws a java.awt.dnd.InvalidDnDOperationException object. Your code should gracefully handle this condition so a user isn't left in a confused state as to why he cannot perform a drag-and-drop operation.

After adding support for the start dragged message, the code fragment looks like the following:

```
class DragLabel extends JLabel
                implements DragGestureListener, DragSourceListener
{
   private DragSource ds = DragSource.getDefaultDragSource ();

   DragLabel (String label, int alignment)
   {
      super (label, alignment);

      int action = DnDConstants.ACTION_COPY_OR_MOVE;
      ds.createDefaultDragGestureRecognizer (this,
                                             action,
                                             this);
   }

   public void dragGestureRecognized (DragGestureEvent e)
   {
      try
      {
           Transferable t = new StringSelection (getText ());

           e.startDrag (DragSource.DefaultCopyNoDrop, t, this);
      }
      catch (InvalidDnDOperationException e2)
      {
           System.out.println (e2);
      }
   }

   public void dragDropEnd (DragSourceDropEvent e)
   {
```

```
        System.out.println ("Drag and drop end");

        if (!e.getDropSuccess ())
        {
            System.out.println ("unsuccessful");
            return;
        }

        int action = e.getDropAction ();
        if ((action & DnDConstants.ACTION_MOVE) != 0)
            setText ("");
    }

    public void dragEnter (DragSourceDragEvent e)
    {
        System.out.println ("Entering drop target #2");

        DragSourceContext ctx = e.getDragSourceContext ();

        int action = e.getDropAction ();
        if ((action & DnDConstants.ACTION_COPY) != 0)
            ctx.setCursor (DragSource.DefaultCopyDrop);
        else
            ctx.setCursor (DragSource.DefaultCopyNoDrop);
    }

    public void dragExit (DragSourceEvent e)
    {
        System.out.println ("Exiting drop target #2");
    }

    public void dragOver (DragSourceDragEvent e)
    {
        System.out.println ("Dragging over drop target #2");
    }

    public void dropActionChanged (DragSourceDragEvent e)
    {
        System.out.println ("Drop action changed #2");
    }
}
```

After the `DragLabel` constructor is finished, the `dragEnter` method is invoked when a user moves the mouse cursor over a drop target. In response, the `DragSourceContext` is obtained along with the drop action. If the user has chosen to perform a copy (by simultaneously pressing the Ctrl key and left mouse button—under Windows platforms), the `DefaultCopyDrop` cursor is assigned. Otherwise, the `DefaultCopyNoDrop` cursor is assigned. The `dragOver` method is called while the mouse cursor moves over the drop target. If the user should exit this target, the `dragExit` method is called. If the user should change the drop action (by releasing the Ctrl key), the `dropActionChanged` method is called. Finally, `dragDropEnd` is called when the drop is complete. If successful, and the action was a move action, the label's text is erased.

At this point, you're half finished. You've seen how dragging is done, but still need to see how dropping is accomplished. The component receiving a drop must be registered with a newly created `DropTarget` object. The `DropTarget (Component c, int actions, DropTargetListener dtl)` constructor creates this object and registers the component, identified by `c`, as the drop target. The default acceptable actions are identified by `actions`. Finally, a drop target listener, whose methods are called to provide drop-related notifications, is specified by `dtl`. The following code fragment creates a drop target that corresponds to the previously described drag source:

```
new DropTarget (target, DnDConstants.ACTION_COPY_OR_MOVE, this);
```

The target component is identified by `target`. Because the drag source is designed to initiate copy or move gestures, the target is designed to accept these gestures. This constructor also indicates that the current object (identified by `this`) functions as a drop target listener.

The drop target listener provides methods for destinations of drag-and-drop operations, which are notified to track the state of a user's gesture and to give "drag under" feedback as the drag-and-drop operation proceeds. These methods include

- `dragEnter`
- `dragExit`
- `dragOver`
- `drop`
- `dropActionChanged`

The `dragEnter` method has the following signature:

```
void dragEnter (DropTargetDragEvent e)
```

This method is called (prior to the drag source listener's `dragEnter` method) when the drag cursor's hotspot encounters a drop target.

The `dragExit` method has the following signature:

```
void dragExit (DropTargetEvent e)
```

This method is called (prior to the drag source listener's `dragExit` method) when the drag cursor's hotspot exits the drop target, without dropping.

The `dragOver` method has the following signature:

```
void dragOver (DropTargetDragEvent e)
```

This method is called (prior to the drag source listener's `dragOver` method) as the drag cursor's hotspot moves over a drop target.

The `drop` method has the following signature:

```
void drop (DropTargetDropEvent)
```

This method is called when the drag operation has terminated with a drop on this drop target. The drop method is responsible for undertaking the transfer of data associated with the gesture—its DropTargetDropEvent argument provides a means to obtain a transferable that represents the data being transferred.

From this method, the drop target listener accepts or rejects the drop, via DropTargetDropEvent's acceptDrop or rejectDrop methods.

Subsequent to acceptDrop (but not before), DropTargetDropEvent's getTransferable method can be invoked and data transfer performed, via the returned transferable's getTransferData method.

At the completion of a drop, an implementation of this method is required to signal the success/failure of the drop, by passing an appropriate Boolean to DropTargetDropEvent's dropComplete method.

To wrap up these methods, dropActionChanged has the following signature:

```
void dropActionChanged (DropTargetDragEvent e)
```

This method is called when the user has modified the drop gesture, as when the state of the input device(s) with which the user is interacting changes. Such devices are typically the mouse buttons or keyboard modifiers.

It's time to bring all of this together. Therefore, Listing 19.7 presents source code to the DragDropDemo application. After you spend some time studying this code, you should have a basic idea of how to incorporate drag and drop into your programs.

LISTING 19.7 THE DragDropDemo APPLICATION SOURCE CODE

```
// DragDropDemo.java

import javax.swing.*;

import java.awt.*;
import java.awt.datatransfer.*;
import java.awt.dnd.*;
import java.awt.event.*;

class DragDropDemo extends JFrame
                   implements ActionListener, DropTargetListener
{
   DragLabel source = new DragLabel ("Text", JLabel.CENTER);
   JButton target = new JButton ();

   DragDropDemo (String title)
   {
      super (title);

      addWindowListener (new WindowAdapter ()
                         {
                             public void windowClosing (WindowEvent e)
                             {
                                System.exit (0);
```

LISTING 19.7 CONTINUED

```
                          }
                       });

      source.setForeground (Color.red);
      getContentPane ().add (source, BorderLayout.NORTH);
      target.addActionListener (this);
      getContentPane ().add (target, BorderLayout.SOUTH);
      new DropTarget (target,
                      DnDConstants.ACTION_COPY_OR_MOVE,
                      this);

      setSize (205, 100);

      setVisible (true);
   }

   public void actionPerformed (ActionEvent e)
   {
      JButton b = (JButton) e.getSource ();
      b.setText ("");
      source.setText ("Text");
   }

   public void dragEnter (DropTargetDragEvent e)
   {
      System.out.println ("Entering drop target #1");
   }

   public void dragExit (DropTargetEvent e)
   {
      System.out.println ("Exiting drop target #1");
   }

   public void dragOver (DropTargetDragEvent e)
   {
      System.out.println ("Dragging over drop target #1");
   }

   public void drop (DropTargetDropEvent e)
   {
      System.out.println ("Dropping");

      try
      {
          Transferable t = e.getTransferable ();

          if (e.isDataFlavorSupported (DataFlavor.stringFlavor))
          {
              e.acceptDrop (e.getDropAction ());

              String s;
              s = (String) t.getTransferData (DataFlavor.stringFlavor);

              target.setText (s);
```

LISTING 19.7 CONTINUED

```
                e.dropComplete (true);
            }
            else
                e.rejectDrop ();
        }
        catch (java.io.IOException e2) {}
        catch (UnsupportedFlavorException e2) {}
    }

    public void dropActionChanged (DropTargetDragEvent e)
    {
        System.out.println ("Drop action changed #1");
    }

    public static void main (String [] args)
    {
        new DragDropDemo ("Drag and Drop Demo");
    }
}

class DragLabel extends JLabel implements DragGestureListener,
                                          DragSourceListener
{
    private DragSource ds = DragSource.getDefaultDragSource ();

    public DragLabel (String s, int alignment)
    {
        super (s, alignment);

        int action = DnDConstants.ACTION_COPY_OR_MOVE;
        ds.createDefaultDragGestureRecognizer (this,
                                               action,
                                               this);
    }

    public void dragGestureRecognized (DragGestureEvent e)
    {
        try
        {
            Transferable t = new StringSelection (getText ());

            e.startDrag (DragSource.DefaultCopyNoDrop, t, this);
        }
        catch (InvalidDnDOperationException e2)
        {
           System.out.println (e2);
        }
    }

    public void dragDropEnd (DragSourceDropEvent e)
    {
        System.out.println ("Drag and drop end");

        if (e.getDropSuccess () == false)
        {
```

LISTING 19.7 CONTINUED

```
            System.out.println ("unsuccessful");
            return;
        }

        int action = e.getDropAction ();
        if ((action & DnDConstants.ACTION_MOVE) != 0)
            setText ("");
    }

    public void dragEnter (DragSourceDragEvent e)
    {
        System.out.println ("Entering drop target #2");

        DragSourceContext ctx = e.getDragSourceContext ();

        int action = e.getDropAction ();
        if ((action & DnDConstants.ACTION_COPY) != 0)
            ctx.setCursor (DragSource.DefaultCopyDrop);
        else
            ctx.setCursor (DragSource.DefaultCopyNoDrop);
    }

    public void dragExit (DragSourceEvent e)
    {
        System.out.println ("Exiting drop target #2");
    }

    public void dragOver (DragSourceDragEvent e)
    {
        System.out.println ("Dragging over drop target #2");
    }

    public void dropActionChanged (DragSourceDragEvent e)
    {
        System.out.println ("Drop action changed #2");
    }
}
```


DragDropDemo's GUI consists of a label and a button. The idea is to either move or copy the label's text to this button. If moved, the text disappears from the label and appears on the button. (DragDropDemo is said to be in a moved state.) If copied, a duplicate of the label's text appears on the button. (DragDropDemo is said to be in a copied state.) Click the button to restore DragDropDemo to its initial state.

You can track drag-and-drop operations by studying messages sent to the standard output device. Figure 19.6 shows the initial state (the top window), the moved state (the middle window), and the copied state (the bottom window).

Because Drag and Drop is a rather complicated API, it's good to have a lot of examples. If you are having trouble learning this API and need some additional help, see "Learning More About Drag and Drop" in the "Troubleshooting" section at the end of this chapter.

Figure 19.6
DragDropDemo shows its three states: initial, moved, and copied.

TROUBLESHOOTING

PROGRAMMATICALLY COPYING, CUTTING, AND PASTING

I want to programmatically perform copy, cut, and paste operations on text fields and text areas.

Swing's abstract `JTextComponent` class provides programmatic copy, cut, and paste support through its `copy`, `cut`, and `paste` methods. These methods are inherited by its `JTextField` and `JTextArea` subclasses. When called, each method performs the appropriate operation on the component's associated text model. However, the capability to programmatically copy, cut, and paste is not present in the AWT's `TextComponent`, `TextField`, and `TextArea` classes.

TRANSFERRING NONTEXTUAL DATA TO/FROM THE SYSTEM CLIPBOARD

I want to transfer nontextual data (such as an image), via the system clipboard, between Java and non-Java programs.

The system clipboard, obtained by calling `Toolkit`'s `getSystemClipboard` method, doesn't appear to support the transfer of nontextual data between Java and non-Java programs. After searching a large number of Java-related Web sites and newsgroups, I have yet to uncover a technique for accomplishing this task. However, there is a pair of articles that you might want to investigate. These Microsoft Windows-related articles could help you achieve this objective.

The first article shows how to use the Java Native Interface to access the Microsoft Windows system clipboard. This article is located at `http://www.ddj.com/articles/1996/9617/9617d/9617d.htm`. Although it's rather dated, it might give you some ideas.

The second article shows how to save an image using Microsoft's bitmap format. This JavaWorld article is located at `http://www.javaworld.com/javaworld/javatips/f_jw-javatip60_p.html`.

LEARNING MORE ABOUT DRAG AND DROP

I'm still a little unclear on Drag and Drop.

JavaSoft's Swing Connection contains an introductory "Drag and Drop with Swing" article. This article is located at `http://java.sun.com/products/jfc/tsc/articles/dragndrop/index.html`.

JavaWorld has published a couple of articles that delve deeper into the Drag and Drop API:

- The two-part "How to Drag and Drop with Java 2" provides a comprehensive look at the Drag and Drop API architecture. The first part is located at `http://www.javaworld.com/javaworld/jw-03-1999/jw-03-dragndrop.html`, and the second part is located at `http://www.javaworld.com/javaworld/jw-08-1999/jw-08-draganddrop.html`.
- "Java Tip 97: Add Drag and Drop to Your Jtrees" shows how to add Drag and Drop API support to `JTree` components. This article is located at `http://www.javaworld.com/javaworld/javatips/jw-javatip97.html`.

Rockhopper Technologies has created a FAQ that answers many Drag and Drop API questions. This online FAQ is located at `http://www.rockhoppertech.com/java-drag-and-drop-faq.html`.

CHAPTER 20

JAVA MEDIA FRAMEWORK

In this chapter

by Geoff Friesen

WHAT IS JMF?

Java Media Framework (JMF) is an API for playing, processing, and capturing *media* (audio and video). Furthermore, this API can be used to transmit or receive live media broadcasts, and conduct videoconferences. To accomplish these latter two tasks, JMF uses RTP—Real-time Transport Protocol. (RTP is not discussed in this chapter. If you want to learn about RTP, consult JMF's API guide, which is part of a JMF download's documentation.)

JMF Version 1.0 came into existence a few years ago as the result of a partnership between Sun Microsystems Inc., Silicon Graphics Inc., and Intel Corp. This version was soon followed by JMF Version 1.1, which made minor improvements to the framework. However, JMF 1.0 and 1.1 were limited to media playback. They did not support media processing or media capture. (Conducting videoconferences and transmitting/receiving live media broadcasts were definitely out of the question.) These limitations led Sun, in partnership with IBM Corp., to develop JMF Version 2.0. Although quite successful, JMF 2.0's architecture needed to be improved. Earlier in 2000, Sun completed these improvements, and JMF Version 2.1 arrived. (In spite of changes, Version 2.1 could still benefit from additional improvements.)

DOWNLOADING AND INSTALLING JMF

Contrary to what you might think, JMF is not bundled with version 1.3 of the Java 2 Platform Standard Edition. Instead, it's a standard extension that is downloaded separately from the Javasoft Web site (`http://www.javasoft.com/jmf`).

You have two options when downloading JMF. You can choose cross-platform JMF (which runs on all Java-supported platforms), or you can download a performance pack for either Solaris or Windows. (As this book is being written, a performance pack for Linux has been promised for release in the near future.) The performance pack includes JMF and extensions (that are operating system-specific) for improving the playback quality of media.

The way JMF is installed depends on whether cross-platform JMF or a performance pack was downloaded. If you downloaded cross-platform JMF, you will need to extract all files from an archive. For example, if you chose to download a ZIP file, you would end up unzipping `jmf-2_1-alljava.zip`. However, if you downloaded a performance pack, you must run a program to take care of installation. For example, if you chose the performance pack for Windows, you would end up running `jmf-2_1-win.exe` to install the Windows version of JMF.

THE API

JMF's API consists of 11 packages. The main package is known as `javax.media`, and contains the following subpackages:

- `javax.media.bean.playerbean`
- `javax.media.control`
- `javax.media.datasink`

- javax.media.format
- javax.media.protocol
- javax.media.renderer
- javax.media.rtp
- javax.media.rtp.event
- javax.media.rtp.rtcp
- javax.media.util

After you start to create JMF programs, you might want to know how to obtain this API's version number for those times when your program must run correctly under multiple versions of JMF. The Manager class (located in the javax.media package) contains a getVersion method that returns this version number, as a String object. To demonstrate this method, Listing 20.1 presents source code to the JMFVersion application.

LISTING 20.1 THE JMFVersion APPLICATION SOURCE CODE

```
// JMFVersion.java

import javax.media.*;

class JMFVersion
{
   public static void main (String [] args)
   {
      System.out.println ("Version = " + Manager.getVersion ());
   }
}
```

A LAYERED ARCHITECTURE

JMF presents a layered architecture comprised of a high-level presentation (player) and processing API and a low-level plug-in API. Software developers create applications, applets, or *beans* (components developed with the JavaBeans framework) that interact with this high-level API. In turn, this API interacts with a low-level plug-in API. The plug-in API offers extensibility to JMF's architecture, by way of *plug-ins* (separate code modules, such as demultiplexers, codecs, effect filters, renderers, and multiplexers) that can be integrated into this architecture. JMF's layered architecture is illustrated in Figure 20.1.

MEDIA STREAMS

JMF has been designed to play, process, and capture *media streams* (media flowing from a source to a destination). Each media stream is identified by its *content type* (format). This content type describes the data format of the media stream. For example, MPEG represents the content type of a video stream.

Figure 20.1
JMF's layered architecture is divided into high-level and low-level APIs.

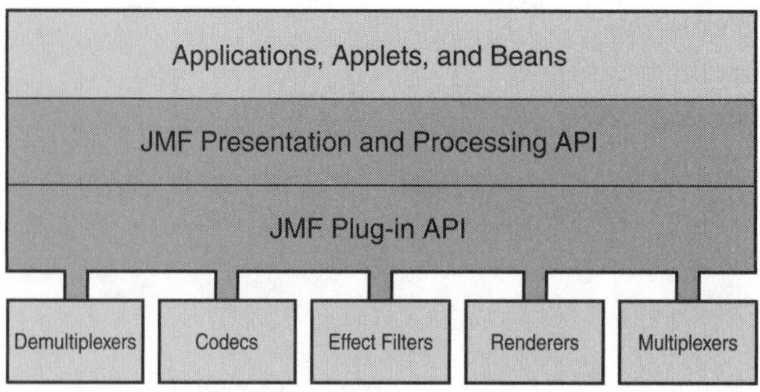

A media stream consists of one or more *tracks* (data channels). Each track represents a separate kind of media to describe an overall experience. For example, QuickTime media might contain an audio track in addition to a video track. Multiple tracks are combined into a single track (for storage or transmission), through a process known as *multiplexing* and individual tracks are recovered (for playback) through *demultiplexing*. Furthermore, the actual structure of a track's media is known as its *format*. For example, Cinepak is a format used by the QuickTime content type.

A media stream is identified by location and access protocol. Either *uniform resource locators* (URLs) or *media locators* (URLs without URL stream handlers) are used for this task. (A *URL stream handler* is an object created from a subclass of the abstract `URLStreamHandler` class. This object can make a connection to a remote computer using a specific access protocol such as HTTP.)

A media stream can be categorized as either a pull stream or a push stream. A *pull stream* is initiated and controlled from the client side. An example of a pull stream is an HTTP media stream originating from a Web server, and initiated and controlled by a Web browser. In contrast, a *push stream* is initiated and controlled from the server side. A media stream originating from a microphone is an example of a push stream.

TIME BASES AND CLOCKS

Time-based media must be played, processed, or captured at a precise rate of time. Otherwise, pauses or jittery behavior will occur. To handle time-based media, JMF uses time bases and clocks. (In most cases, you will never work with these entities. However, to understand JMF, you need to have some comprehension of time bases and clocks.)

A *time base* is an object (created from a class that implements the `TimeBase` interface) that represents a constant ticking source of time (like a crystal oscillator). It is based either on the native system clock or on another hardware clock (such as the hardware clock on an audio card). In any case, a time base can never be stopped or reset. The current time can be returned from this object, either by calling `getNanoseconds` (to return the number of nanoseconds that have elapsed since the system clock was started), or by calling `getTime` (to return an object created from the `Time` class that contains the same time information).

A `Time` object represents a point in time. Its `getNanoseconds` method returns this time in nanoseconds, whereas its `getSeconds` method returns this time in seconds. Finally, its `secondsToNanoseconds` method converts from seconds to nanoseconds.

Objects that decode and render media streams are created from classes that implement the `Clock` interface. Each clock contains a time base that tracks the passage of time as a media stream is presented. This passage is known as *media time*.

A clock's media time represents the current position in a media stream. The beginning of this stream is referred to as media time zero and the end of this stream is the maximum media time for the stream. The *duration* of this stream is the elapsed time from start to finish. In other words, the duration is the length of time taken to present the media stream.

To keep track of the current media time, a clock uses the time base *start-time* (the time that its time base reports when the presentation begins), the media start-time (the position in the media stream where presentation begins), and the *playback rate* (how fast the clock is running in relation to its time base). The rate is a scale factor applied to the time base. For example, 1.0 represents a normal playback rate, whereas 2.0 represents a playback rate that is twice as fast. A negative rate implies that the clock runs in the reverse direction, and can be used to play a media stream in reverse.

When presentation begins, media time is mapped to the time base time. The advancement of the time base time is then used to measure the passage of time. During presentation, the current media time is calculated with the following formula:

```
media time = media start time + (time base time - time base start time) * rate
```

When the presentation stops, media time stops, but the time base time continues to advance. If the presentation is restarted, media time is remapped to the current time base time.

MANAGERS

JMF's interfaces define the behavior and interaction of objects used to play, process, and capture time-based media. Implementations of these interfaces operate within the structure of this framework. By using *managers* (intermediary objects that control key JMF activities), JMF makes it easy to integrate new implementations of key interfaces with existing classes. Managers can be divided into four categories: media managers, package managers, plug-in managers, and capture device managers.

A media manager is created from the `Manager` class. It handles the construction of players, processors, *data sources* (media protocol-handlers that manage the life-cycle of media sources, by providing simple connection protocols), and *data sinks* (objects that read media content delivered by a data source and render the media to some destination). Media managers allow new players, processors, data sources, and data sinks to be seamlessly integrated with JMF. From the client perspective, these objects are always created the same way, whether the requested object is constructed from a default or custom class.

The package manager is created from the `PackageManager` class. It maintains a registry of packages that contain classes for custom players, processors, data sources, and data sinks. When you extend JMF's capabilities with new players, processors, data sources, or data sinks, you must register new package prefixes for these classes with the package manager, so JMF will find them at runtime.

The plug-in manager is created from the `PlugInManager` class. It maintains a registry of available JMF plug-in processing components (such as multiplexers, demultiplexers, codecs, effect filters, and renderers). When you extend JMF's capabilities with new plug-ins, you must register these plug-ins with the plug-in manager to make them available to processors that support the plug-in API.

Tip

You don't have to register a plug-in with the plug-in manager during development. Instead, you can set the `CLASSPATH` environment variable to the location of your plug-in's class (or classes).

Finally, the capture device manager is created from the `CaptureDeviceManager` class. It maintains a registry of available capture devices. If you are writing a program that captures media, this program must query the capture device manager to make sure that an appropriate capture device is present.

PLAYING MEDIA

JMF player programs play audio and video media by routing it to speakers and monitors. These programs present VCR-like controls to give users the opportunity to control stream playback. In many cases, a user can fast forward and rewind media streams (in addition to starting and stopping).

Playing media streams requires *players*, which are objects created from classes that implement the `Player` interface. You can obtain a player by calling one of `Manager`'s `createPlayer` methods. Each player receives a media stream from a data source and renders it at precise moments in time. The rendering destination (such as speakers or monitor) for a specific track depends on the track's format.

A player can be in any one of six states: Unrealized, Realizing, Realized, Prefetching, Prefetched, and Started. When a player has been created but does not know anything about the media it will be playing, the player is said to be in the *Unrealized state*.

When a player's `realize` method is called, the player moves from the Unrealized state into a *Realizing state*. A realizing player determines its resource requirements. During realization, it acquires all its non-exclusive resources. (An exclusive resource is a limited resource—such as a specific hardware device—that can be used by one and only one player at a time.) A realizing player might download its resources over a network. As a result, realizing can be a time-intensive task.

When realizing is finished, the player moves to the *Realized state*. In this state, a player knows what resources it needs and information about the type of media that will be presented. Because a realized player knows how to render its data, it can provide visual components and *controls* (objects—such as audio gain—that control various aspects of a media stream). The player's connections to other objects in the system are in place, but it does not own any resources that would prevent another player from starting.

When the player's `prefetch` method is called, it moves from the Realized state into the *Prefetching state*. A prefetching player is preparing to present its media. During this phase, the player preloads its media data, obtains exclusive resources, and does whatever else is necessary to prepare itself to play. Prefetching might have to recur if a player's media presentation is repositioned, or if a change in the player's rate requires that additional buffers be acquired or alternate processing take place.

When a player finishes prefetching, it moves into the *Prefetched state*. A prefetched player is ready to be started.

A player enters the *Started state*, after its `start` method is called. A started player's time base time and media time are mapped and its clock is running, although the player might be waiting for a particular time to begin presenting its media data. This time is referred to as *latency*.

Figure 20.2 illustrates the various states of a player. At any point in time, the player is in one and only one of these states.

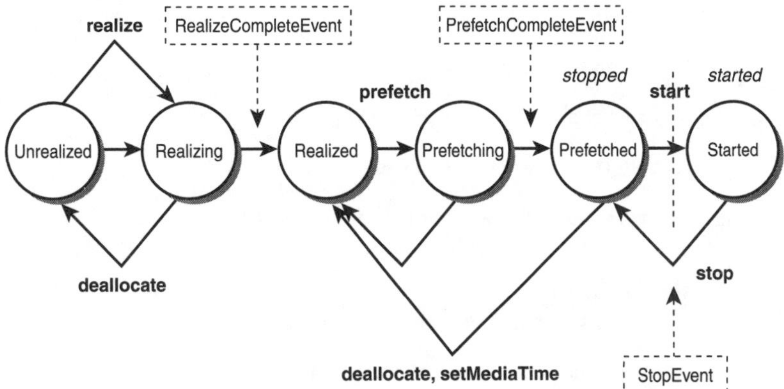

Figure 20.2
A player transitions through six states as it operates.

Method calls that transition a player from one state to another are shown in bold. Furthermore, various events are fired to indicate state transitions. Prior to the Started state, the player is said to be stopped. After the Started state is reached, the player is actively playing media.

To learn more about state transitions, and to see what a simple player looks like, take a look at Listing 20.2. This listing presents source code for a `PlayerDemo1` application, which can play audio and video media streams.

LISTING 20.2 THE `PlayerDemo1` APPLICATION SOURCE CODE

```
// PlayerDemo1.java

import javax.media.*;

import java.awt.*;
import java.awt.event.*;

class PlayerDemo1 extends Frame implements ControllerListener
{
   Component vc;
   Player player;

   PlayerDemo1 (String title, String mediaURL)
   {
      super (title);

      addWindowListener (new WindowAdapter ()
                         {
                             public void windowClosing (WindowEvent e)
                             {
                                player.close ();

                                System.exit (0);
                             }
                         });

      try
      {
         player = Manager.createPlayer (new MediaLocator (mediaURL));
      }
      catch (java.io.IOException e)
      {
         terminate (e.toString ());
      }
      catch (NoPlayerException e)
      {
         terminate ("Could not find a player.");
      }

      if (player == null)
          terminate ("Trouble creating player.");

      player.addControllerListener (this);
      player.prefetch ();
   }

   public void controllerUpdate (ControllerEvent e)
   {
      if (e instanceof ControllerClosedEvent)
          System.exit (0);

      if (e instanceof EndOfMediaEvent)
      {
          player.setMediaTime (new Time (0));
          player.start ();
```

LISTING 20.2 CONTINUED

```
            return;
        }

        if (e instanceof PrefetchCompleteEvent)
        {
            player.start ();
            return;
        }

        if (e instanceof RealizeCompleteEvent)
        {
            vc = player.getVisualComponent ();
            if (vc != null)
                add (vc);

            pack ();
            setResizable (false);
            setVisible (true);
        }
    }

    void terminate (String s)
    {
        System.out.println (s);
        System.exit (-1);
    }

    public static void main (String [] args)
    {
        if (args.length != 1)
        {
            System.out.println ("usage: java PlayerDemo1 url");
            return;
        }

        new PlayerDemo1 ("Player Demo1", args [0]);
    }
}
```


PlayerDemo1's constructor calls Manager's createPlayer method with a MediaLocator argument to create and return a reference to a player. The MediaLocator argument identifies the protocol and location of the source of a media stream. Although similar to uniform resource locators, media locators do not require protocol handlers to be installed. If a player cannot be found, a NoPlayerException object is thrown.

The return value should be a player. Although the documentation does not suggest that createPlayer returns null, a check for null is made, just to be safe. Assuming that a player has been created, its addControllerListener method is called to register PlayerDemo1 as a listener for various controller events. (The player is the controller.) These events are fired for a number of reasons, including player transitions from one state to another. Finally, the player's prefetch method is called to put the player into its Prefetching state.

All the good stuff happens in the `controllerUpdate` method: If something should go wrong and the controller is closed (as indicated by a `ControllerClosedEvent` object), `PlayerDemo1` exits. This might happen if the player does not "understand" a certain format of media. When the end of a media stream is reached (as indicated by an `EndOfMediaEvent` object), the stream is rewound to the beginning, by calling the player's `setMediaTime` method. This is followed by a call to the player's `start` method to restart the stream, which results in a continuous loop. (You don't have to set your player into a continuous loop.) After the player is in its Prefetched state, the only way it can reach its Started state is for its `start` method to be called. This occurs when `controllerUpdate` receives a `PrefetchCompleteEvent` object. When the player has reached its Realized state, a `RealizeCompleteEvent` object is sent to `controllerUpdate`. At this point, the player's `getVisualComponent` method is called to return its visual component. For video streams, this component is a window that contains image frames. For audio streams, `null` will most likely be returned to indicate that there is no visual component. The `pack` method is called to ensure a proper size and layout, `setResizable` is called with a `false` argument to prevent the user from resizing the window, and `setVisible` ensures that both the frame window and visual component are visible.

Figure 20.3 shows an image of the Orion Nebula. This image is part of an MPEG movie that's stored in the `OrionMosaic.mpg` file. To run this movie, you would type the following line in a Microsoft Windows DOS command window (assuming that Microsoft Windows is your operating system):

```
java PlayerDemo1 file:OrionMosaic.mpg
```

Figure 20.3
`PlayerDemo1`'s output shows the Orion Nebula in all its glory.

Wouldn't it be nice if there was some way to replay this movie, without having to stop and restart `PlayerDemo1`? There actually is a way to accomplish this task. Listing 20.3 presents source code for the `PlayerDemo2` application that demonstrates this technique.

LISTING 20.3 THE `PlayerDemo2` APPLICATION SOURCE CODE

```
// PlayerDemo2.java

import javax.media.*;

import java.awt.*;
import java.awt.event.*;

class PlayerDemo2 extends Frame implements ControllerListener
```

Listing 20.3 Continued

```
{
   Component cc, vc;
   Player player;

   PlayerDemo2 (String title, String mediaURL)
   {
      super (title);

      addWindowListener (new WindowAdapter ()
                         {
                             public void windowClosing (WindowEvent e)
                             {
                                player.close ();

                                System.exit (0);
                             }
                         });

      try
      {
         player = Manager.createPlayer (new MediaLocator (mediaURL));
      }
      catch (java.io.IOException e)
      {
         terminate (e.toString ());
      }
      catch (NoPlayerException e)
      {
         terminate ("Could not find a player.");
      }

      if (player == null)
          terminate ("Trouble creating player.");

      player.addControllerListener (this);
      player.prefetch ();
   }

   public void controllerUpdate (ControllerEvent e)
   {
      if (e instanceof ControllerClosedEvent)
          System.exit (0);

      if (e instanceof EndOfMediaEvent)
      {
          player.setMediaTime (new Time (0));
          return;
      }

      if (e instanceof RealizeCompleteEvent)
      {
          vc = player.getVisualComponent ();
          if (vc != null)
              add (vc, BorderLayout.CENTER);
```

LISTING 20.3 CONTINUED

```
         cc = player.getControlPanelComponent ();
         if (cc != null)
             add (cc, (vc != null) ? BorderLayout.SOUTH
                                   : BorderLayout.CENTER);

         pack ();
         setResizable (false);
         setVisible (true);
      }
   }

   void terminate (String s)
   {
      System.out.println (s);
      System.exit (-1);
   }

   public static void main (String [] args)
   {
      if (args.length != 1)
      {
          System.out.println ("usage: java PlayerDemo2 url");
          return;
      }

      new PlayerDemo2 ("Player Demo2", args [0]);
   }
}
```

The difference between `PlayerDemo1` and `PlayerDemo2` is that the player's `getControlPanelComponent` method is called to retrieve a play bar control panel by which you can start, stop, and control playback. This play bar is shown in Figure 20.4, together with a *frame* (a still image) from an MPEG movie of the Cassini spacecraft approaching Saturn.

Figure 20.4
`PlayerDemo2`'s output includes a play bar control panel across the bottom.

Tip

The `getVisualComponent` and `getControlPanelComponent` methods return heavyweight AWT components. Although these components don't cause problems in some Swing programs, they will cause problems in others. (See Chapter 15, "And Then There Was Swing," for examples of various problems that occur when heavyweight AWT components are intermixed with lightweight Swing components.) You can still use these components in Swing programs, if you first call `Manager`'s `setHint` method with

LIGHTWEIGHT_RENDERER and Boolean (true) arguments. This argument causes Manager to try and create a player with a renderer that interoperates with lightweight components. As an example, you can set this hint, after creating a player, as follows:

```
Manager.setHint (Manager.LIGHTWEIGHT_RENDERER,
                 new Boolean (true));
```

One big problem with downloading media over the Internet is that it can take quite a while—especially if you are using a modem. Some kind of progress indicator would help users know what's happening. Fortunately, JMF includes a special component, called a progress bar, for indicating the current state of a download. This component is included in Listing 20.4's PlayerDemo3 source code.

LISTING 20.4 THE PlayerDemo3 APPLICATION SOURCE CODE

```
// PlayerDemo3.java

import javax.media.*;

import java.awt.*;
import java.awt.event.*;

class PlayerDemo3 extends Frame implements ControllerListener
{
   Component cc, pbar, vc;
   Player player;

   PlayerDemo3 (String title, String mediaURL)
   {
      super (title);

      addWindowListener (new WindowAdapter ()
                         {
                             public void windowClosing (WindowEvent e)
                             {
                                player.close ();

                                System.exit (0);
                             }
                         });

      try
      {
         player = Manager.createPlayer (new MediaLocator (mediaURL));
      }
      catch (java.io.IOException e)
      {
         terminate (e.toString ());
      }
      catch (NoPlayerException e)
      {
         terminate ("Could not find a player.");
      }
```

LISTING 20.4 CONTINUED

```
      if (player == null)
          terminate ("Trouble creating player.");

      player.addControllerListener (this);
      player.prefetch ();
   }

   public void controllerUpdate (ControllerEvent e)
   {
      if (e instanceof CachingControlEvent)
      {
          CachingControlEvent cce = (CachingControlEvent) e;
          CachingControl cc = cce.getCachingControl ();
          long cc_progress = cce.getContentProgress ();
          long cc_length = cc.getContentLength ();

          if (pbar == null)
              if ((pbar = cc.getControlComponent ()) != null)
              {
                  add (pbar, BorderLayout.NORTH);
                  pack ();
              }

          if (cc_progress == cc_length && pbar != null)
          {
              remove (pbar);
              pbar = null;
              pack ();
          }

          return;
      }

      if (e instanceof ControllerClosedEvent)
          System.exit (0);

      if (e instanceof EndOfMediaEvent)
      {
          player.setMediaTime (new Time (0));
          return;
      }

      if (e instanceof RealizeCompleteEvent)
      {
          vc = player.getVisualComponent ();
          if (vc != null)
              add (vc, BorderLayout.CENTER);

          cc = player.getControlPanelComponent ();
          if (cc != null)
              add (cc, (vc != null) ? BorderLayout.SOUTH
                                    : BorderLayout.CENTER);

          pack ();
          setResizable (false);
          setVisible (true);
```

LISTING 20.4 CONTINUED

```
      }
   }

   void terminate (String s)
   {
      System.out.println (s);
      System.exit (-1);
   }

   public static void main (String [] args)
   {
      if (args.length != 1)
      {
          System.out.println ("usage: java PlayerDemo3 url");
          return;
      }

      new PlayerDemo3 ("Player Demo3", args [0]);
   }
}
```

Each time an image is downloaded off the Internet, the player fires a `CachingControlEvent` object to the listener. This event's `getCachingControl` method returns a caching control object that describes the current state of the download. Its `getContentLength` method returns the length of the download, whereas the event's `getContentProgress` method returns the current location in the download. Finally, the caching control's `getProgressBarComponent` retrieves an AWT progress bar component. This progress bar is shown in Figure 20.5.

Figure 20.5 `PlayerDemo3`'s output includes a progress bar–shown as the "Loading media" indicator at the top of the window.

Caution

Although you can click the progress bar's pause and resume button to pause and resume the download, you should not click the play button when the download is paused. If you do, the program will most likely lock up. (This is an example of JMF's unpredictable behavior.) Furthermore, you should also avoid pressing the play button during download. (Experiments have shown that pressing Play while downloading can result in unpredictable behavior.) It's okay to press Play once download is complete.

PROCESSING MEDIA

JMF processor programs manipulate media. After manipulation, the results can be played back to a user, or delivered to some other destination (such as a file). These programs typically present controls to perform various processing operations.

Processing involves working with demultiplexers, multiplexers, codecs, effect filters, and renderers. As previously mentioned, *demultiplexers* extract individual tracks from a media stream, whereas *multiplexers* combine individual tracks into a single media stream. *Codecs* (compressors/decompressors) perform compression and decompression operations on individual tracks. Effect *filters* modify track data to achieve special effects. *Preprocess effect filtering* occurs before a codec processes a track. In contrast, *postprocess effect filtering* occurs after a codec has processed a track. (Normally, preprocess effect filtering is used.) Finally, *renderers* are output devices (such as speakers and monitors). Some renderers can *composite* (overlay) one track of data over another track. For example, a renderer could overlay a video track with a track that consists of text.

Processing media streams requires *processors*—objects created from classes that implement the `Processor` interface. You can obtain a processor by calling one of `Manager`'s `createProcessor` methods. (Because the `Processor` interface extends `Player`, a processor is nothing more than a player with processing capability.)

A processor adds two additional transition states to the six player states: Configuring and Configured. While in the *Configuring state*, a processor gathers the information it needs to construct `TrackControl` objects for each track. A `TrackControl` object is created from a class that implements the `TrackControl` interface. A processor provides `TrackControl` to query, control, and manipulate a track's data.

After it's finished configuring, the processor moves into the *Configured state* and posts a `ConfigureCompleteEvent` object. After this state has been reached, you can set the processor's output content type (by calling its `setContentDescriptor` method) and `TrackControl` options. When you're finished specifying these options, you can call `realize` to move the processor into the Realizing state and begin the realization process.

Figure 20.6 illustrates the various states that a processor can be in at any point in its duration.

Suppose you wanted to create a processor that would play a movie from a negative perspective. In other words, you want to see each frame's negative. Listing 20.5 presents source code to a `ProcessorDemo` application that creates a processor with a negative effect filter for achieving this task.

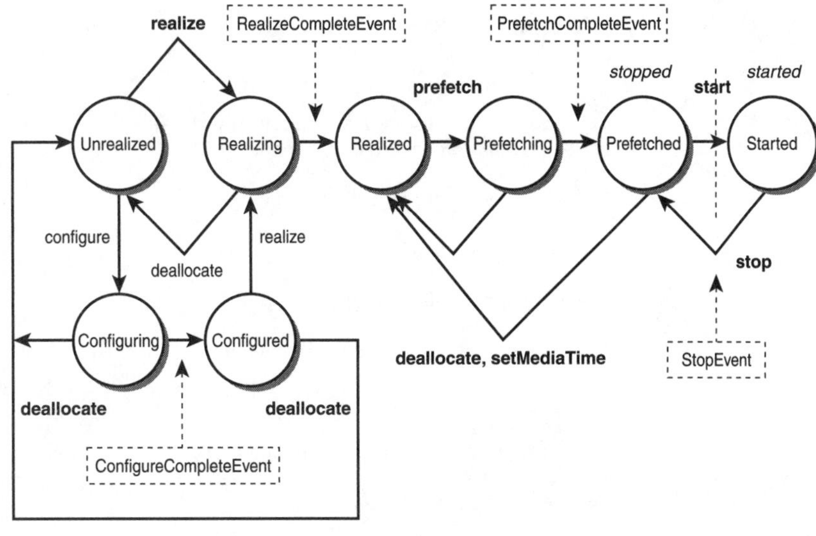

Figure 20.6
Unlike players, a processor transitions through eight states as it operates. The two new states are Configuring and Configured.

LISTING 20.5 THE ProcessorDemo APPLICATION SOURCE CODE

```
// ProcessorDemo.java

import javax.media.*;
import javax.media.control.*;

import java.awt.*;
import java.awt.event.*;

class ProcessorDemo extends Frame implements ControllerListener
{
   Component cc, vc;
   TrackControl [] tc;
   Processor processor;

   ProcessorDemo (String title, String mediaURL)
   {
      super (title);

      addWindowListener (new WindowAdapter ()
                         {
                             public void windowClosing (WindowEvent e)
                             {
                                processor.close ();

                                System.exit (0);
                             }
                         });
```

LISTING 20.5 CONTINUED

```
      try
      {
         MediaLocator ml = new MediaLocator (mediaURL);
         processor = Manager.createProcessor (ml);
      }
      catch (java.io.IOException e)
      {
         terminate (e.toString ());
      }
      catch (NoProcessorException e)
      {
         terminate ("Could not find a processor.");
      }

      if (processor == null)
          terminate ("Trouble creating processor.");

      processor.addControllerListener (this);

      processor.configure ();

      while (processor.getState () != Processor.Configured);

      processor.setContentDescriptor (null);

      TrackControl [] tc = processor.getTrackControls ();

      if (tc.length > 0)
      {
          Codec [] c = new Codec [1];
          c [0] = new NegativeEffect ();

          try
          {
             tc [0].setCodecChain (c);
          }
          catch (UnsupportedPlugInException e2)
          {
             terminate (e2.toString ());
          }
      }

      processor.realize ();
   }

   public void controllerUpdate (ControllerEvent e)
   {
      if (e instanceof ControllerClosedEvent)
          System.exit (0);

      if (e instanceof EndOfMediaEvent)
      {
          processor.setMediaTime (new Time (0));
          return;
      }
```

Listing 20.5 Continued

```
        if (e instanceof RealizeCompleteEvent)
        {
            vc = processor.getVisualComponent ();
            if (vc != null)
                add (vc, BorderLayout.CENTER);

            cc = processor.getControlPanelComponent ();
            if (cc != null)
                add (cc, (vc != null) ? BorderLayout.SOUTH
                                      : BorderLayout.CENTER);

            pack ();
            setResizable (false);
            setVisible (true);
        }
    }

    void terminate (String s)
    {
        System.out.println (s);
        System.exit (-1);
    }

    public static void main (String [] args)
    {
        if (args.length != 1)
        {
            System.out.println ("usage: java ProcessorDemo url");
            return;
        }

        new ProcessorDemo ("Processor Demo", args [0]);
    }
}
```

`ProcessorDemo` calls `configure` to transition to the Configured state. However, it might take some time before this state is reached. Therefore, `ProcessorDemo` enters a busy-wait by repeatedly calling its `getState` method to interrogate the current state. After the Configured state has been reached, it exits the busy-wait.

By passing `null` to its `setContentDescriptor` method, the processor indicates that it will function as a player—a user will be able to view processed output. If track controls are present, a negative effect object (created from the `NegativeEffect` class) will be added to a chain of codecs for the first track. (The assumption is that the first track is a video track.) This is accomplished by calling `TrackControl`'s `setCodecChain` method. (If you examine JMF's documentation, you'll discover that an effect filter is a special kind of codec.) The processor then calls its `realize` method to enter the Realizing state. The resulting output is shown in Figure 20.7.

Figure 20.7
ProcessorDemo's output shows a negative of a frame taken from the OrionMosaic.mpg movie.

To achieve a negative effect, ProcessorDemo requires a separate class called NegativeEffect. The source code for this effect filter is presented in Listing 20.6.

LISTING 20.6 THE NegativeEffect EFFECT FILTER SOURCE CODE

```
// NegativeEffect.java

import javax.media.*;
import javax.media.format.*;

public class NegativeEffect implements Effect
{
   /** effect name **/

   private static String EffectName = "NegativeEffect";

   /** chosen input format **/

   protected RGBFormat inputFormat;

   /** chosen output format **/

   protected RGBFormat outputFormat;

   /** supported input formats **/

   protected Format [] supportedInputFormats;

   /** supported output formats **/

   protected Format [] supportedOutputFormats;

   /** initialize the formats **/

   public NegativeEffect ()
   {
      supportedInputFormats = new Format []
      {
         new RGBFormat ()
      };

      supportedOutputFormats = new Format []
      {
```

LISTING 20.6 CONTINUED

```
        new RGBFormat ()
     };
  }

  /** get the resources needed by this effect **/

  public void open () throws ResourceUnavailableException
  {
     System.out.println ("open");
  }

  /** free the resources allocated by this effect **/

  public void close ()
  {
     System.out.println ("close");
  }

  /** reset the effect **/

  public void reset ()
  {
     System.out.println ("reset");
  }

  /** no controls for this simple effect **/

  public Object [] getControls ()
  {
     System.out.println ("getControls");

     return new Controls [0];
  }

  /** return the control based on a control type for the effect **/

  public Object getControl (String controlType)
  {
     System.out.println ("getControl [controlType = "
                         + controlType + "]");

     try
     {
        Class cls = Class.forName (controlType);

        Object cs [] = getControls ();

        for (int i = 0; i < cs.length; i++)
        {
             if (cls.isInstance (cs [i]))
                 return cs [i];
        }

        return null;
     }
```

LISTING 20.6 CONTINUED

```
      catch (Exception e)
      {
         // no such controlType or such control

         return null;
      }
   }

   /************** format methods *************/

   /** set the input format **/

   public Format setInputFormat (Format input)
   {
      System.out.println ("setInputFormat [input = " + input + "]");

      // the following code assumes valid format

      inputFormat = (RGBFormat) input;

      return (Format) inputFormat;
   }

   /** set the output format **/

   public Format setOutputFormat (Format output)
   {
      System.out.println ("setOutputFormat [output = " + output + "]");

      // the following code assumes valid format

      outputFormat = (RGBFormat) output;

      return (Format) outputFormat;
   }

   /** get the input format **/

   protected Format getInputFormat ()
   {
      System.out.println ("getInputFormat");

      return inputFormat;
   }

   /** get the output format **/

   protected Format getOutputFormat ()
   {
      System.out.println ("getOutputFormat");

      return outputFormat;
   }

   /** supported input formats **/
```

LISTING 20.6 CONTINUED

```
public Format [] getSupportedInputFormats ()
{
   System.out.println ("getSupportedInputFormats");

   return supportedInputFormats;
}

/** output Formats for the selected input format **/

public Format [] getSupportedOutputFormats (Format in)
{
   System.out.println ("getSupportedOutputFormats [in = " + in
                       + "]");

   if (in == null)
       return supportedOutputFormats;

   if (!(in instanceof RGBFormat))
       return new Format [0];

   RGBFormat irf = (RGBFormat) in;

   RGBFormat orf = (RGBFormat) in.clone ();

   return new Format [] { orf };
}

/** return effect name **/

public String getName ()
{
   System.out.println ("getName");

   return EffectName;
}

/** do the processing **/

public int process (Buffer inBuffer, Buffer outBuffer)
{
   // == prolog

   Object o1 = inBuffer.getData ();
   int inLength = inBuffer.getLength ();
   int inOffset = inBuffer.getOffset ();

   if (!(o1 instanceof short []) && ! (o1 instanceof int []))
       return BUFFER_PROCESSED_FAILED;

   Object o2 = outBuffer.getData ();

   if (o2 != null)
   {
       if (!(o2 instanceof short []) && !(o2 instanceof int []))
           return BUFFER_PROCESSED_FAILED;
   }
```

LISTING 20.6 CONTINUED

```
        else
        {
            if (o1 instanceof short [])
                outBuffer.setData (new short [inLength]);
            else
                outBuffer.setData (new int [inLength]);

            o2 = outBuffer.getData ();
        }

        int outOffset = outBuffer.getOffset ();

        // == main

        if (o1 instanceof short [])
        {
            short [] inData = (short []) o1;
            short [] outData = (short []) o2;

            for (int i = 0; i < inLength; i++)
                 outData [outOffset++] = (short) ~inData [inOffset++];
        }
        else
        {
            int [] inData = (int []) o1;
            int [] outData = (int []) o2;

            for (int i = 0; i < inLength; i++)
                 outData [outOffset++] = ~inData [inOffset++];
        }

        outBuffer.setFormat (outputFormat);
        outBuffer.setLength (inLength);
        outBuffer.setOffset (0);

        return BUFFER_PROCESSED_OK;
    }
}
```

`NegativeEffect` implements the `Effect` interface (directly), along with the `Codec`, `PlugIn`, and `Controls` interfaces (indirectly). As a result, it must supply a variety of methods. To learn more about these methods, check out Chapter 6, "Extending JMF," in the *Java Media Framework API Guide*. This chapter discusses these methods in the context of building an effect filter. (The *Java Media Framework API Guide*, and the rest of the JMF documentation, is part of the JMF download.)

After you become comfortable with JMF, you'll probably want to explore some advanced topics, including how to seek to a specific frame in a movie, wrap a movie around a 3D image, and generate a movie from a series of JPEG images. If you're not sure how to make this happen, check out "JMF Solutions" in the "Troubleshooting" section at the end of this chapter.

CAPTURING MEDIA

JMF capture programs are designed to capture time-based media from a live source for processing and playback. For example, audio can be captured from a microphone and a video capture card can be used to capture video from a camera. These programs usually provide controls that enable users to manage the capture process. For example, a capture control panel might provide controls that enable a user to specify the encoding type and data rate of a media stream being captured, as well as controls that allow the capture process to be started and stopped.

In essence, a capture program must determine if a certain capture device (such as a microphone and audio card, or a video camera/TV tuner and video capture card) is present before it can proceed. This is accomplished by first calling the capture device manager's `getDeviceList` method to return a `Vector` of `CaptureDeviceInfo` objects that correspond to a certain capture device format, and then choosing an appropriate object from this `Vector`.

After a capture device has been obtained, the capture program creates a processor to handle the capture process. Usually, a data sink is also created to route captured media to some kind of destination (such as a file). To demonstrate the capture of live audio from a microphone, Listing 20.7 presents source code to a `CaptureDemo` application.

LISTING 20.7 THE `CaptureDemo` APPLICATION SOURCE CODE

```
// CaptureDemo.java

import javax.media.*;
import javax.media.control.*;
import javax.media.datasink.*;
import javax.media.format.*;
import javax.media.protocol.*;

import java.awt.*;
import java.awt.event.*;

import java.io.*;

import java.util.*;

class CaptureDemo extends Frame
                  implements ActionListener, DataSinkListener
{
   StateHelper sh;
   Processor processor;
   DataSink filewriter = null;

   CaptureDemo (String title)
   {
      super (title);

      Panel p = new Panel ();
```

LISTING 20.7 CONTINUED

```
        Button b = new Button ("Start");
        b.addActionListener (this);
        p.add (b);

        b = new Button ("Stop");
        b.addActionListener (this);
        p.add (b);

        add (p);

        CaptureDeviceInfo di = null;

        AudioFormat a = new AudioFormat (AudioFormat.LINEAR,
                                         8000, 16, 1);

        Vector deviceList;
        deviceList = CaptureDeviceManager.getDeviceList (a);

        if (deviceList.size () > 0)
            di = (CaptureDeviceInfo) deviceList.firstElement ();
        else
            terminate ("Could not find 44,100 Hz 16-bit audio device.");

        try
        {
            processor = Manager.createProcessor (di.getLocator ());
        }
        catch (IOException e)
        {
            terminate (e.toString ());
        }
        catch (NoProcessorException e)
        {
            terminate ("Could not find processor.");
        }

        // Create a helper to ensure certain states are reached.

        sh = new StateHelper (processor);

        // Configure the processor

        if (!sh.configure (10000))
            terminate ("Could not configure processor.");

        // Set the output content type.

        FileTypeDescriptor f;
        f = new FileTypeDescriptor (FileTypeDescriptor.BASIC_AUDIO);
        processor.setContentDescriptor (f);

        // Realize the processor.

        if (!sh.realize (10000))
            terminate ("Could not realize processor.");
```

LISTING 20.7 CONTINUED

```
      setSize (200, 60);
      setResizable (false);
      setVisible (true);
   }

   public void actionPerformed (ActionEvent e)
   {
      String cmd = e.getActionCommand ();

      ((Component) e.getSource ()).setEnabled (false);

      if (cmd.equals ("Start"))
      {
          // Get the processor's output data source.

          DataSource source = processor.getDataOutput ();

          // Create a File protocol MediaLocator with the location of
          // the file, to which the data is to be written.

          MediaLocator dest = new MediaLocator ("file:out.au");

          // Create a datasink to perform file writing. Add a data
          // sink listener to wait for an end of stream event. Open
          // the sink to ensure that it is writable.

          try
          {
             filewriter = Manager.createDataSink (source, dest);
             filewriter.addDataSinkListener (this);
             filewriter.open ();
          }
          catch (NoDataSinkException e2)
          {
             terminate ("Could not create data sink.");
          }
          catch (IOException e2)
          {
             terminate (e2.toString ());
          }

          // If the Processor implements StreamWriterControl, you can
          // call setStreamSizeLimit to set a limit on the size of the
          // file that is written.

          StreamWriterControl swc = (StreamWriterControl)
                        processor.getControl ("javax.media.control." +
                                              "StreamWriterControl");

          // Set limit to 5MB.

          if (swc != null)
              swc.setStreamSizeLimit (5000000);

          // Start the data transfer.
```

LISTING 20.7 CONTINUED

```
          try
          {
             filewriter.start ();
          }
          catch (IOException e2)
          {
             System.out.println (e2);
          }

          processor.start ();

          return;
       }

       processor.stop ();

       processor.close ();
    }

    public void dataSinkUpdate (DataSinkEvent e)
    {
       if (e instanceof EndOfStreamEvent)
       {
           filewriter.close ();

           System.exit (0);
       }
    }

    void terminate (String msg)
    {
       System.out.println (msg);
       System.exit (-1);
    }

    public static void main (String [] args)
    {
       new CaptureDemo ("Capture Demo");
    }
}

class StateHelper implements javax.media.ControllerListener
{
    Player player = null;

    boolean configured = false;
    boolean realized = false;
    boolean prefetched = false;
    boolean failed = false;
    boolean closed = false;

    public StateHelper (Player p)
    {
       player = p;
       p.addControllerListener (this);
    }
```

LISTING 20.7 CONTINUED

```
public boolean configure (int timeOutMillis)
{
   long startTime = System.currentTimeMillis ();

   synchronized (this)
   {
      if (player instanceof Processor)
          ((Processor) player).configure ();
      else
          return false;

      while (!configured && !failed)
      {
         try
         {
             wait (timeOutMillis);
         }
         catch (InterruptedException ie)
         {
         }

         if (System.currentTimeMillis () - startTime > timeOutMillis)
             break;
      }
   }

   return configured;
}

public boolean realize (int timeOutMillis)
{
   long startTime = System.currentTimeMillis ();

   synchronized (this)
   {
      player.realize ();

      while (!realized && !failed)
      {
         try
         {
             wait (timeOutMillis);
         }
         catch (InterruptedException ie)
         {
         }

         if (System.currentTimeMillis () - startTime > timeOutMillis)
             break;
      }
   }

   return realized;
}
```

LISTING 20.7 CONTINUED

```
   public boolean prefetch (int timeOutMillis)
   {
      long startTime = System.currentTimeMillis ();

      synchronized (this)
      {
         player.prefetch ();

         while (!prefetched && !failed)
         {
            try
            {
                wait (timeOutMillis);
            }
            catch (InterruptedException ie)
            {
            }

            if (System.currentTimeMillis () - startTime > timeOutMillis)
                break;
         }
      }

      return prefetched && !failed;
   }


   public void close ()
   {
      synchronized (this)
      {
         player.close ();

         while (!closed)
         {
            try
            {
                wait (100);
            }
            catch (InterruptedException ie)
            {
            }
         }
      }

      player.removeControllerListener (this);
   }

   public synchronized void controllerUpdate (ControllerEvent ce)
   {
```

LISTING 20.7 CONTINUED

```
        if (ce instanceof RealizeCompleteEvent)
            realized = true;
        else
        if (ce instanceof ConfigureCompleteEvent)
            configured = true;
        else
        if (ce instanceof PrefetchCompleteEvent)
            prefetched = true;
        else
        if (ce instanceof ControllerErrorEvent)
            failed = true;
        else
        if (ce instanceof ControllerClosedEvent)
            closed = true;
        else
            return;

        notifyAll();
    }
}
```

`CaptureDemo` uses a `StateHelper` class to do its job. Objects created from this class (which is similar to the `StateHelper` class in the JMF API guide) monitor certain transition events, and help `CaptureDemo` determine when its Configured and Realized states have been reached. The approach taken by `StateHelper` makes use of Java's synchronization mechanism for multiple threads, together with its `wait` and `notifyAll` methods. The sole benefit is to prevent the busy-wait that was used by `ProcessorDemo`. (Although busy-waits are simpler, they consume microprocessor clock cycles and can slow down JVM performance.)

`CaptureDemo` presents a GUI that consists of a `Start` button and a `Stop` button (see Figure 20.8). Click `Start` to begin recording and `Stop` to finish. After `Start` is clicked, speak into the microphone. After `Stop` is clicked, `CaptureDemo` exits. The resulting audio is stored in a file called `out.au` in the current directory. Unfortunately, when tested under Windows 98, the quality of the sound capture is very poor. This is not a function of `CaptureDemo`, as the same poor quality results when using the JMStudio tool to capture audio.

Note

JMStudio and another tool called JMFRegistry are included with the JMF performance pack download. JMStudio demonstrates JMF's features and JMFRegistry works with the package and plug-in managers to register package prefixes for player, processor, data source, data sink, and plug-in classes.

Figure 20.8
CaptureDemo's GUI consists of `Start` and `Stop` buttons.

TROUBLESHOOTING

JMF SOLUTIONS

How can I wrap a movie around a 3D image, seek to a specific frame, generate a movie from a series of JPEG images, add Swing support, and so on?

A movie can be wrapped around a 3D image (such as a cylinder) by creating a Java3D renderer plug-in that integrates with the rest of JMF. For a complete description of this solution (along with source code), please visit Sun's Java3D Renderer Web page (`http://java.sun.com/products/java-media/jmf/2.1/solutions/DemoJMFJ3D.html`).

It's possible to seek to a specific frame by using JMF's `FramePositioningControl` class (located in the `javax.media.control` package). A complete description of a solution (as well as source code) that uses this class is available at Sun's Frame Seeking inside a Movie Web page (`http://java.sun.com/products/java-media/jmf/2.1/solutions/Seek.html`).

If you want to generate a movie from a series of JPEG images, you'll need to create a custom `PullBufferDataSource`, which is then used to create a processor. Information on how to achieve this task is located at Sun's Generating a Movie File from a List of (JPEG) Images Web page (`http://java.sun.com/products/java-media/jmf/2.1/solutions/JpegImagesToMovie.html`).

Earlier in this chapter, a tip was presented that discussed supporting Swing components. To learn more about this support, check out Sun's Using JMF in Swing Web page (`http://java.sun.com/products/java-media/jmf/2.1/solutions/SwingJMF.html`).

In addition to the aforementioned solutions, Sun has provided a Web page index to a comprehensive online set of JMF solutions to a wide variety of JMF problems. To visit this index, go to `http://java.sun.com/products/java-media/jmf/2.1/solutions/`.

PART III

I/O

CHAPTER 21

Streams, Files, and Serialization

In this chapter

by Chuck Cavaness

WHAT ARE STREAMS?

Most computer programs accept some form of input and generate some type of output. That is, after all, basically what a computer is useful for. Every computer language must have a way of dealing with input and output; otherwise, it would be impossible to write a useful program. The input could come from a file on disk, data sent over the network, or even another program. This is true of the output as well.

Most information used within a computer program flows from the input source through the computer program and then possibly on to an output destination. This idea of data flow leads to the term *stream*. A stream is nothing more than a flow of data through some channel. Input streams direct data from the outside world—a keyboard or a file, for instance—into the computer. Output streams direct data toward output devices, such as the computer screen, file, or even another computer program. Because streams are general in nature, a basic stream does not specifically define which devices the data flows from or to. Just like a wire carrying electricity that is being routed to a light bulb, TV, or dishwasher; a basic input or output stream can be directed to or from many different sources.

The Java API features a rich set of classes that represents everything from a general input or output stream to a sophisticated stream that uses data from a random-access file. In this chapter, you learn how to use these important classes.

In general, there are streams for a variety of sources including access to common file system functions (such as file and directory creation, removal, and renaming, as well as directory listing). The input and output streams can be connected to files, network sockets, or internal memory buffers.

The `java.io` package also contains a number of stream filters that enable you to access stream data in a variety of different formats. You can also create your own filters to add more functionality to the Java programming language.

WORKING WITH THE STREAM CLASSES

The `java.io` package provides different input and output streams for reading and writing data. There are also two separate sets of stream classes. Prior to JDK 1.1, the input and output classes only supported 8-bit byte streams. Starting with JDK 1.1, 16-bit Unicode character streams were also being supported. This was very important because character streams have these important characteristics:

- They can deal with any character in the Unicode set.
- They use buffering internally.
- Internationalization is easier because they don't rely on a specific encoding.

The byte and character streams are really a distinct set of classes. Most of the functionality for byte streams is located in the base `InputStream` and `OutputStream` classes. The functionality for character streams is located in the abstract base classes `java.io.Reader` and java.io.Writer. It's actually pretty easy to remember which streams are for byte data and which are for character data. The byte-related streams end with an InputStream or OutputStream. The streams that are for character data end with Reader or Writer.

Most of the functionality for byte streams also exists in the character stream. Both have input and output streams and both have specialized subclasses. When deciding on which stream you need to use in a program, first determine whether you are dealing with binary or character data. After that, you can focus your decision on either the byte stream classes or the character stream classes exclusively. Character streams are dealt with a little later in this chapter. For now, take a look at byte streams.

READING AND WRITING DATA USING BYTE STREAMS

There are many different types of streams within the Java API. Each type of stream within the Java API is represented by a different Java class or interface. The InputStream and OutputStream classes represent the simplest of the byte stream classes. These two classes provide general streaming capabilities for byte data. Java uses these base classes to derive other classes that are more specifically oriented toward a certain type of input or output. You can find all the various stream classes in the java.io package. Here are a few of the available streams for byte data:

- **BufferedInputStream**—A basic buffered input stream
- **DataInputStream**—An input stream for reading primitive data types
- **FileInputStream**—An input stream used for basic file input
- **ByteArrayInputStream**—An input stream whose source is a byte array
- **StringBufferInputStream**—An input stream whose source is a string
- **LineNumberInputStream**—An input stream that supports line numbers
- **PushbackInputStream**—An input stream that allows a byte to be pushed back onto the stream after the byte is read
- **PipedInputStream**—An input stream used for inter-thread communication
- **SequenceInputStream**—An input stream that combines two other input streams
- **PrintStream**—An output stream for displaying text
- **BufferedOutputStream**—A basic buffered output stream
- **DataOutputStream**—An output stream for writing primitive data types
- **FileOutputStream**—An output stream used for basic file output
- **FilterInputStream**—An abstract input stream used to add new behaviors to existing input stream classes
- **FilterOutputStream**—An abstract output stream used to add new behaviors to existing output stream classes
- **ByteArrayOutputStream**—An output stream whose destination is a byte array
- **PipedOutputStream**—An output stream used for inter-thread communication.

There are too many stream classes to be covered thoroughly in a single chapter. An entire book could be written on Java I/O alone. For that reason, this chapter covers the most useful of the stream classes. Before getting into the specialized byte stream classes, here's a brief introduction of the abstract base byte stream classes that describes the behavior that all the byte stream classes inherit.

THE `InputStream` CLASS

The `InputStream` class represents the basic input stream. As such, it defines a set of methods that all input streams need. Table 21.1 lists these methods, without their parameters.

TABLE 21.1 METHODS OF THE `InputStream` CLASS

Method	Description
`read()`	Reads data into the stream
`skip()`	Skips over bytes in the stream
`available()`	Returns the number of bytes immediately available in the stream
`mark()`	Marks a position in the stream
`reset()`	Returns to the marked position in the stream
`markSupported()`	Returns a boolean value indicating whether the stream supports marking and resetting
`close()`	Closes the stream

If you are getting an incorrect number when using the `available` *method. See "Using the* `available()` *Method" in the "Troubleshooting" section at the end of the chapter.*

The `read` method is overloaded in the class, providing three methods for reading data from the stream. The methods' signatures look like this:

```
int read()
int read(byte b[])
int read(byte b[], int off, int len)
```

The most basic method for getting data from any `InputStream` object is the `read` method:

```
public abstract int read() throws IOException
```

The `read` method reads a single byte from the input stream and returns it. This method performs what is known as a *blocking read*, which means that it waits for data if there is none available. So, when a datasource doesn't have any data to be read yet, the method will wait until a byte becomes available before returning. One example of this situation is when the stream is on a network and the next byte of data might not have arrived yet. You want to be careful with this situation, however, because it can cause similar problems to the synchronization problems discussed back in Chapter 11, "Threads," if you are not careful.

→ **See** "Threads," **p. 259**

When the stream reaches the end of a file, this method returns a negative 1.

Note that to be able to return 8 bits of data (a byte) and still have –1 only occur when the stream is at an end, the values are actually returned as if they were generated from an unsigned byte. That is, if you write a –1 into a stream, it will actually get read back in as an integer with a value of 255. Fortunately, casting that `int` back to a byte will return the value to –1.

Note

This `read` method is the most important because it is the method that actually grabs data from the native source. All the other methods use this one to perform their work.

This `read()` method

```
public int read(byte[] bytes) throws IOException
```

fills an array with bytes read from the stream and returns the number of bytes read. It is possible for this method to read fewer bytes than the array can hold, because there might not be enough bytes in the stream to fill it. When the stream reaches the end of the file, the read method also returns a negative one (–1). You will always receive all the bytes in the stream before you hit the end of the file. In other words, if 50 bytes are left in the stream and you ask to read 100 bytes, this method returns the 50 bytes, and then the next time it is called, it returns –1, if the stream is at an end.

This version of the `read()` method

```
public int read(byte[] bytes, int offset, int length) throws IOException
```

fills an array starting at position `offset` with up to `length` bytes from the stream. It returns either the number of bytes read or –1 for end of file.

The `read` method always blocks (it sits and waits without returning) when there is no data available. To avoid blocking, you might need to ask ahead of time exactly how many bytes you can safely read without blocking. The `available` method returns the number of bytes that can be read with the stream being blocked:

```
public int available() throws IOException
```

You can skip over data in a stream by passing the `skip` method the number of bytes you want to skip over:

```
public long skip(long n)
```

The `skip` method actually uses the `read` method to skip over bytes, so it will block under the same circumstances as `read`. It returns the number of bytes it skipped or –1 if it hits the end of file.

Some input streams enable you to place a bookmark of sorts at a point so that you can return to that location later. The `markSupported` method returns true if the stream supports marking:

```
public boolean markSupported()
```

The `mark` method marks the current position in the stream, so you can back up to it later:

```
public synchronized void mark(int readLimit)
```

The `readLimit` parameter in the `mark` method sets the maximum number of bytes that can be read from the stream before the mark is no longer set. In other words, you must tell the stream how many bytes it should let you read before it forgets about the mark. Some streams might need to allocate memory to support marking, and this parameter tells them how big to make their arrays.

If you set a mark in a stream, you can reposition the stream back to the mark by calling the `reset` method:

```
public synchronized void reset() throws IOException
```

After you are done with a stream, it's very important to always close the stream. You can do this with the `close` method like this:

```
public void close() throws IOException
```

Although streams usually get closed at garbage collection time, it's good practice and much safer to close all your open resources when you are finished with them. On the majority of operating systems, the number of files you can have open at one time is limited. Therefore, you should close your streams when you are finished with them to free up system resources immediately without waiting for garbage collection.

THE `OutputStream` CLASS

The counterpart to `InputStream` is the `OutputStream` class, which provides the basic functionality for all output streams. Table 21.2 lists the methods defined in the `OutputStream` class, along with their descriptions.

TABLE 21.2 METHODS OF THE `OutputStream` CLASS

Method	Description
`write()`	Writes data to the stream
`flush()`	Forces any buffered output to be written
`close()`	Closes the stream

Rather than being a source of data like the input stream, an output stream is a recipient of data. The most basic method of an `OutputStream` object is the `write` method.

```
public abstract void write(int b) throws IOException
```

writes a single byte of data to an output stream.

```
public void write(byte[] bytes) throws IOException
```

writes the entire contents of the bytes array to the output stream. This version of the `write()` method

```
public void write(byte[] bytes, int offset, int length) throws IOException
```

writes `length` bytes from the `bytes` array, starting at position `offset`.

Depending on the type of stream, you might need to occasionally flush the stream if you need to be sure that the data written on the stream has been delivered. Flushing a stream does not destroy any information in the stream; it just makes sure that any data stored in internal buffers is written out onto whatever device the stream might be connected to. To flush an output stream, call the `flush` method:

```
public void flush() throws IOException
```

As with the input streams, you should close output streams when you are done with them by calling the `close` method.

READING AND WRITING BYTE ARRAYS

There are many situations in which you have to read or write a byte array to a file, memory, or even a network socket. The `ByteArrayInputStream` and `ByteArrayOutputStream` classes are designed to make it easy to read and write byte arrays, respectively. Both classes inherit from the base stream classes, but are designed specifically for byte arrays.

`ByteArrayInputStream` is designed for holding an internal byte array and then streaming in the bytes using the `read` method on the class. The class has two constructors:

```
ByteArrayStream(byte[] buf )
ByteArrayStream(byte[] buf, int offset, int length)
```

`ByteArrayOutputStream` is specifically designed for written bytes. The class's internal buffer can grow as the bytes are written into it. The data can be obtained by using the `toByteArray()` or `toString()` method. The `ByteArrayOutputStream` class also has two constructors:

```
ByteArrayOutputStream()
ByteArrayOutputStream(int size)
```

The `size` argument in the second constructor sets up a buffer with a specified size, in bytes.

READING AND WRITING FILES

The `FileInputStream` and `FileOutputStream` classes are designed to read and write bytes from a file in the file system. Both classes have several constructors that can use a filename represented by a `String`, a `java.io.File` argument, or a `FileDescriptor`. After an instance is created, you can read in the bytes from the file using the standard `read` method.

Note

If you have binary data that you need to read or write from a file, a `FileInputStream` or `FileOutputStream` class is probably a good one to use. However, if you need to read or write text to or from a file, a better choice is one of the reader or writer classes that you'll see later in this chapter.

STREAM BUFFERING

The `BufferedInputStream` and `BufferedOutputStream` classes offer byte streams that have internal buffering capabilities. This allows you to programmatically mark a certain position in the buffer stream using the mark method and then return to that position later using the reset method.

Buffered streams help speed up your programs by reducing the number of reads and writes on system resources. Suppose you have a program that is writing one byte at a time. You might not want each write call to go out to the operating system, especially if it is writing to a disk. Instead, you want the bytes to be accumulated into big blocks and written out in bulk. The BufferedInputStream and BufferedOutputStream classes provide this functionality. When you create them, you can provide a buffer size:

```
public BufferedInputStream(InputStream in)
public BufferedInputStream(InputStream in, int bufferSize)
public BufferedOutputStream(OutputStream out)
public BufferedOutputStream(OutputStream out, int bufferSize)
```

The BufferedInputStream class tries to read as much data into its buffer as possible in a single read call; the BufferedOutputStream class calls the write method only when its buffer fills up, or when flush is called.

FILTERING STREAMS

One of the most powerful aspects of streams is that you can chain one stream to the end of another. The basic input stream, for example, only provides a read method for reading bytes. If you want to read strings and integers, you can attach a special data input stream to a general input stream and suddenly have methods for reading strings, integers, and even floats. The FilterInputStream and FilterOutputStream classes provide the capability to chain streams together. The FilterInputStream and FilterOutputStream classes don't provide any new methods, however. Their big contribution is that they are "connected" to another stream. The constructors for the FilterInputStream and FilterOutputStream classes take InputStream and OutputStream objects as parameters:

```
public FilterInputStream(InputStream in)
public FilterOutputStream(OutputStream out)
```

Because these classes are themselves instances of InputStream and OutputStream, they can be used as parameters to constructors to other filters, enabling you to create long chains of input and output filters.

The DataInputStream class, discussed later in this chapter, is a useful filter that enables you to read strings, integers, and other simple types from an input stream. In addition, the LineNumberInputStream filter automatically counts lines as you read input. You can chain these filters together to read data while counting the lines:

```
LineNumberInputStream lineCount = new LineNumberInputStream( System.in );
DataInputStream dataIn = new DataInputStream( lineCount );
```

PRINT STREAMS

The PrintStream class and its only subclass, LogStream, provide the capability to print or log data more conveniently than other stream classes. You also can set these classes to be automatically flushed after data is written. `PrintStream` never throws an exception. Rather it sets a internal flag that can be tested with the `checkError` method.

REDIRECTING STANDARD INPUT/OUTPUT

To support the standard input and output devices (usually the keyboard and screen), Java defines two stream objects that you can use in your programs without having to create stream objects of your own. The `System.in` object (instantiated from the `InputStream` class) enables your programs to read data from the keyboard, whereas the `System.out` object (instantiated from the `PrintStream` class) routes output to the computer's screen. You can use these stream objects directly to handle standard input and output in your Java programs, or you can use them as the basis for other stream objects you might want to create.

These streams, like other streams, can be redirected to cause the input and output to be read from or written to something other than the default source. The default behavior for these two streams in shown in Listing 21.1.

Listing 21.1, for example, is a Java application that accepts a line of input from the user and then displays the line onscreen.

LISTING 21.1 SOURCE CODE FOR `IOApp.java`

```
import java.io.*;

class IOApp
{
  public static void main(String args[])
  {
    String inputStr = "";
    byte buffer[] = new byte[255];
    System.out.println("Type a line of text. Type 'exit' to quit the program.");

    // Keep looping until the user types exit
    while( inputStr.indexOf( "exit" ) == -1 )
    {
      try
      {
        System.in.read(buffer, 0, 255);
        inputStr = new String( buffer );

        System.out.print("The line you typed was: ");
        System.out.println(inputStr);
      }
      catch ( IOException ex )
      {
        System.out.println( ex );
      }
    }
  }
}
```

To redirect these streams to another source, you can create a new stream that wraps one of the `System.in` or `System.out` streams and does something different with it. For example, you could take the `System.out` stream and redirect it to a file. Listing 21.2 shows how this could be done.

LISTING 21.2 SOURCE CODE FOR `RedirectExample.java`

```
import java.io.*;
import java.sql.Timestamp;

class RedirectExample
{
  // Change this path if you are using Unix or want another path
  public static final String FILE = "c:\\systemin.txt";

  public static void main(String args[])
  {
    try
    {
      // Create a file output stream and set the append = true flag
      FileOutputStream outStr = new FileOutputStream( FILE, true );
      // Create a print stream so that you can connect to System.out
      PrintStream printStream  = new PrintStream( outStr );

      // Tell System.out to redirect to the printStream that you've created
      System.setOut( printStream );

      // Print out some text. It should not go to the console, but to the
      // text file created above.
      Timestamp now = new Timestamp( System.currentTimeMillis() );
      System.out.println( now.toString() + ": This is text that should go to the
file" );

      // Close the open Resources
      outStr.close();
      printStream.close();
    }
    catch( FileNotFoundException ex )
    {
      ex.printStackTrace();
      System.exit( -1 );
    }
    catch( IOException ex )
    {
      ex.printStackTrace();
      System.exit( -1 );
    }
  }
}
```

USING READERS AND WRITERS

Now it's time to talk about the character stream classes that are present in the `java.io` package. If you remember from the previous discussion, these are used for 16-bit Unicode characters. The abstract base classes of all the Reader and Writer classes are, not surprisingly, java.io.Reader and java.io.Writer.

These classes have the default behavior to read and write 16-bit character streams. There are similarities between the types of subclasses available underneath the byte stream super class and the subclasses available under the character stream super class. So, you should be able to do exactly the same types of things with character streams that you can do with byte streams. With character streams, however, you will notice new methods to make dealing with String objects much easier than the byte streams.

USING BufferedReader AND BufferedWriter

The BufferedReader and BufferedWriter classes provide behavior for buffering of data for better efficiency. These classes are more examples of stream classes that are constructed using other stream classes. Here's a code fragment using BufferedWriter that wraps or "decorates" a FileWriter instance. Then a PrintWriter wraps the BufferedWriter for more convenient methods:

```
PrintWriter out = null;
out = new PrintWriter(new BufferedWriter(new FileWriter("foo.out")));
```

USING THE LineNumberReader

The LineNumberReader class is used to keep track of the line number as it reads in character data. A line is terminated by a linefeed (\n), a carriage return (\r), or a carriage return followed by a linefeed.

The LineNumberReader enables you to track the current line number of an input stream. As usual, you create a LineNumberReader by passing it the input stream you want it to filter:

```
public LineNumberReader(new InputStreamReader(InputStream inStream))
```

The getLineNumber method returns the current line number in the input stream:

```
public int getLineNumber()
```

By default, the lines are numbered starting at 0. The line number is incremented every time an entire line has been read. You can set the current line number with the setLineNumber method:

```
public void setLineNumber(int newLineNumber)
```

Listing 21.3 shows a program that prints the contents of standard input along with the current line number.

LISTING 21.3 SOURCE CODE FOR PrintLines.java

```
import java.io.*;

// This class reads lines from standard input (System.in) and
// prints each line along with its line number.

public class PrintLines extends Object
```

LISTING 21.3 CONTINUED

```
{
  public static void main(String[] args)
  {
    // Set up a line number input filter to count the line numbers
    LineNumberReader lineCounter = new LineNumberReader( new InputStreamReader(
System.in ) );

    String nextLine = null;
    System.out.println( "Type any text and press return. Type 'exit' to quit the
program." );
    try
    {
      // Keep going until exit is typed
      while ( (nextLine = lineCounter.readLine()).indexOf( "exit") == -1 )
      {
        // If readLine returns null, you've hit the end of the file
        if (nextLine == null) break;

        // Print out the current line number followed by the line
        System.out.print(lineCounter.getLineNumber());
        System.out.print(": ");
        System.out.println(nextLine);
      }
    }
    catch (Exception done)
    {
      done.printStackTrace();
    }
  }
}
```

USING `InputStreamReader` AND `OutputStreamReader`

These classes are used to bridge the gap between the byte stream classes and the character stream classes. They act as sort of a middle wrapper between the two distinct sets of streams. Listing 21.4 shows an example using the `System.in` stream.

LISTING 21.4 SOURCE CODE FOR `InputStreamReaderExample.java`

```
import java.io.*;

class InputStreamReaderExample
{
  public static void main(String args[])
  {

    System.out.println("Type a line of text. Type 'exit' to quit the program.");

    // Create the middle stream wrapper
    InputStreamReader in = new InputStreamReader( System.in );
    // Create a buffered reader around the InputStreamReader
    BufferedReader reader = new BufferedReader( in );
```

Listing 21.4 Continued

```
    String data = null;
    try
    {
      // Keep looping until the user hits just return
      while( (data = reader.readLine()).indexOf( "exit" ) == -1 )
      {
        System.out.print("The line you typed was: ");
        System.out.println( data );
      }
    }
    catch ( IOException ex )
    {
      System.out.println( ex );
    }
  }
}
```

PrintWriter Class

You probably noticed in Listings 21.1 and 21.2 a method called `println`, which is not a part of the `OutputStream` class. To provide for more flexible output on the standard output stream, the `System` class derives its output-stream object from the `PrintWriter` class, which provides for printing values as text output. Table 21.3 lists the methods of the `PrintWriter` class, along with their descriptions.

Table 21.3 Basic Methods of the PrintWriter Class

Method	Description
`write()`	Writes data to the stream
`flush()`	Flushes data from the stream
`checkError()`	Flushes the stream, returning errors that occurred
`print()`	Prints data in text form
`println()`	Prints a line of data (followed by a newline character) in text form
`close()`	Closes the stream

As with many of the methods included in the stream classes, the `write`, `print`, and `println` methods are overloaded many times and come in several versions. The `write` method can write `Strings`, partial `Strings`, single `chars`, or whole `char` arrays, whereas the `print` and `println` methods can display almost any type of data onscreen. The various method signatures look like this:

```
void write(int c)
void write(char c[], int off, int len)
void write(String s)
void write(String s,int off,int len)
void print(Object obj)
void print(String s)
```

```
void print(char s[])
void print(char c)
void print(int i)
void print(long l)
void print(float f)
void print(double d)
void print(boolean b)
void println()
void println(Object obj)
void println(String s)
void println(char s[])
void println(char c)
void println(int i)
void println(long l)
void println(float f)
void println(double d)
void println(boolean b)
```

If you are not seeing an exception that you are expecting using `PrintWriter` *or* `PrintStream`*. See "Exceptions Thrown by the* `PrintStream` *and* `PrintWriter` *Classes" in the "Troubleshooting" section at the end of the chapter.*

WORKING WITH FILES

Now that you've had an introduction to the stream classes, you can put your knowledge to work. Perhaps the most common use of I/O—outside of retrieving data from the keyboard and displaying data onscreen—is file I/O. Any program that wants to retain its status (including the status of any edited files) must be capable of loading and saving files. Java provides several classes—including `File`, `FileDescriptor`, `RandomAccessFile`, `FileInputStream`, `FileOutputStream`, `FilePermission`, `FileReader`, and `FileWriter`—for dealing with files. In this section, you examine these classes and get a chance to see how they work.

CREATING FILES

If you need to obtain information about a file, you should create an object of Java's `File` class. This class enables you to query the system about everything from the file's name to the time it was last modified. You can also use the `File` class to make new directories, as well as to delete and rename files. Create a `File` object by calling one of the class's three constructors, whose signatures are as follows:

```
File(String path)
File(String path, String name)
File(File dir, String name)
```

The first constructor creates a `File` object from the given full pathname (for example, `C:\CLASSES\MYAPP.JAVA`). The second constructor creates the object from a separate path and a file. The third creates the object from a separate path and filename, with the path being associated with another `File` object.

The `File` class features a full set of methods that gives your program a lot of file-handling options. Table 21.4 lists these methods along with their descriptions. The parameters are not shown here in this listing. In some cases, there is more than one version of a method with the same name. The difference is the number and type of arguments the each version expects. Check the JavaDocs for the exact arguments expected by the method.

TABLE 21.4 METHODS OF THE `File` CLASS

Method	Description
`getName()`	Gets the file's name (as a `String`).
`getPath()`	Gets the file's path (as a `String`).
`getAbsolutePath()`	Gets the file's absolute path (as a `String`).
`getAbsoluteFile()`	Gets the file's absolute path (as a `File`).
`getCanonicalPath()`	Gets the file's canonical path (as a `String`).
`getCanonicalFile()`	Gets the file's canonical path (as a `File`).
`getParent()`	Gets the file's parent directory (as a `String`).
`getParentFile()`	Gets the file's parent directory (as a `File`).
`exists()`	Returns true if the file exists, false otherwise.
`createNewFile()`	Creates a new file, but only if the file does not already exist (returns true if the file was created).
`createTempFile()`	Creates a temporary file. The file's name is created first, by name (`String` pattern, the directory, and then by using the pattern to create a unique `File` directory) (returns a `File`).
`deleteOnExit()`	Requests that this file be deleted when the VM exits.

Note

This is only successful when the Virtual Machine exits normally, not by abnormal exits.

Method	Description
`canWrite()`	Returns true if the file can be written to.
`canRead()`	Returns true if the file can be read.
`setReadOnly()`	Sets the file so that it is read-only.
`isFile()`	Returns true if the file is valid.
`isDirectory()`	Returns true if the directory is valid.
`isAbsolute()`	Returns true if the filename is absolute.
`isHidden()`	Tests to see if the file is hidden. (Returns true if it is.)
`lastModified()`	Returns the time the file was last changed, represented as the number of milliseconds since 00:00:00 GMT, January 1, 1970.
`setLastModified()`	Sets the time when the file was last modified. The time should be represented as the number of milliseconds since 00:00:00 GMT, January 1, 1970.

TABLE 21.4 CONTINUED

Method	Description
`length()`	Returns the number of bytes in the file.
`mkdir()`	Makes a directory represented by this file. (Returns true if successful.)
`mkdirs()`	Makes a directory represented by this file, and any required but nonexistent parent directories.(Returns true if successful.)
`renameTo(File dest)`	Renames the file to the indicated file.
`list()`	Gets a list of files in the directory. (Returns an array of strings.)
`listFiles()`	Gets a list of files in the directory. (Returns an array of files.)
`listRoots()`	Gets a list of the root directories for the current system. A Windows or Macintosh computer would have one root for each drive; a Unix machine has one root (/). (Returned as an array of files.)
`delete()`	Deletes the file. (Returns true if successful.)
`hashCode()`	Gets a hash code for the file.
`equals()`	Compares the file object with another object. (Returns true if they are equal.)
`toString()`	Gets a string containing the file's path.
`toURL()`	Returns an URL object equivalent to the file.

If you are having trouble with the `File` class. See "Understanding the Use of the `File` Class" in the "Troubleshooting" section at the end of the chapter.

CREATING TEMPORARY FILES

Temporary files are useful for a variety of purposes in many programs. To create a temporary file, you can use the static `createTemporaryFile` method in the `File` class. In Listing 21.5, a temporary file is created by passing in the name of the prefix and suffix of the file that you want to create. The string should contain the first several letters of the filename (minimum three characters), followed by an extension. The VM will insert a four- or five-digit number that is guaranteed to be unique within this instance of the VM. If you do not provide an extension, it is automatically assigned the value of `.tmp`. You have to put the "." in the suffix for it to be added as an extension.

LISTING 21.5 SOURCE CODE FOR `CreateTempFile.java`

```
import java.io.*;

public class CreateTempFile
{
    public static void main(String args[])
    {
        try
        {
          File tempFile = File.createTempFile( "myfile", ".tmp" );
```

Listing 21.5 Continued

```
            FileOutputStream fout = new FileOutputStream(tempFile);
            PrintStream out = new PrintStream(fout);
            out.println("Place this test string in the temp file");
        }
        catch ( IOException ex )
        {
            System.out.println("There was a problem creating/writing to the temp
file");
            ex.printStackTrace();
        }
    }
}
```

After you run the `CreateTempFile` program in Listing 21.5, you should see a file called `myfileXXXXX.tmp` in your system's temp directory (where the `X`s are actually numbers). There is also a constructor that will allow you to assign a directory location for the temporary file.

Reading and Writing Files

If your file-reading needs are relatively simple, you can use the `FileInputStream` class, which is a simple input-stream class derived from `InputStream`. This class features all the methods inherited from the `InputStream` class. To create an object of the `FileInputStream` class, you call one of its constructors, of which there are three, as shown:

```
FileInputStream(String name)
FileInputStream(File file)
FileInputStream(FileDescriptor fdObj)
```

The first constructor takes a `String` as the argument and uses this `String` to create a `FileInputStream` object. The second constructor creates the object from a `File` object, and the third creates the object from a `FileDescriptor` object.

As you might have guessed, the counterpart to the `FileInputStream` class is `FileOutputStream`, which provides basic file-writing capabilities. Besides `FileOutputStream`'s methods, which are inherited from `OutputStream`, the class features three constructors, whose signatures look like this:

```
FileOutputStream(String name)
FileOutputStream(File file)
FileOutputStream(FileDescriptor fdObj)
```

The first constructor here also takes a `String` as the argument and creates a `FileOutputStream` object with the given filename, whereas the second constructor creates the object from a `File` object. The third constructor creates the object from a `FileDescriptor` object.

Random File Access

At this point, you might think that Java's file-handling capabilities are scattered throughout a lot of different classes, making it difficult to obtain the basic functionality you need to read, write, and otherwise manage a file. But Java's creators are way ahead of you. They created the `RandomAccessFile` class for those times when you really need to get serious about your file handling. By using this class, you can do just about everything you need to do with a file.

You create a `RandomAccessFile` object by calling one of the class's two constructors, whose signatures are as follows:

```
RandomAccessFile(String name, String mode)
RandomAccessFile(File file, String mode)
```

The first constructor creates a `RandomAccessFile` object from a string containing the filename and another string containing the access mode (`r` for read and `rw` for read and write). The second constructor creates the object from a `File` object and the mode string.

After you have the `RandomAccessFile` object created, you can call on the object's methods to manipulate the file. Table 21.5 lists those methods.

TABLE 21.5 METHODS OF THE `RandomAccessFile` CLASS

Method	Description
`close()`	Closes the file
`getFD()`	Gets a `FileDescriptor` object for the file
`getFilePointer()`	Gets the location of the file pointer
`length()`	Gets the length of the file
`read()`	Reads data from the file
`readBoolean()`	Reads a boolean value from the file
`readByte()`	Reads a byte from the file
`readChar()`	Reads a `char` from the file
`readDouble()`	Reads a double floating-point value from the file
`readFloat()`	Reads a `float` from the file
`readFully()`	Reads data into an array, completely filling the array
`readInt()`	Reads an `int` from the file
`readLine()`	Reads a text line from the file
`readLong()`	Reads a long `int` from the file
`readShort()`	Reads a short `int` from the file
`readUnsignedByte()`	Reads an unsigned byte from the file
`readUnsignedShort()`	Reads an unsigned short `int` from the file
`readUTF()`	Reads a `UTF` string from the file
`seek()`	Positions the file pointer in the file
`skipBytes()`	Skips over a given number of bytes in the file

TABLE 21.5 CONTINUED

Method	Description
`write()`	Writes data to the file
`writeBoolean()`	Writes a boolean to the file
`writeByte()`	Writes a byte to the file
`writeBytes()`	Writes a string as bytes
`writeChar()`	Writes a `char` to the file
`writeChars()`	Writes a string as `char` data
`writeDouble()`	Writes a double floating-point value to the file
`writeFloat()`	Writes a `float` to the file
`writeInt()`	Writes an `int` to the file
`writeLong()`	Writes a long `int` to the file
`writeShort()`	Writes a short `int` to the file
`writeUTF()`	Writes a UTF string

Listing 21.6 is a Java application that takes a filename on the command line and then reads and displays the text file using a `RandomAccessFile` object.

LISTING 21.6 SOURCE CODE FOR `RandomAccessExample.java`

```
import java.io.*;

class RandomAccessExample
{
  public static void main( String[] args )
  {
    if ( args.length != 1 )
    {
      System.out.println( "Usage: java RandomAccessExample <textfile>" );
      System.exit( 0 );
    }

    String fileName = args[0];
    try
    {
      // Create a random access file for read only
      RandomAccessFile file = new RandomAccessFile( fileName, "r");
      long filePointer = 0;
      long length = file.length();

      // Keep going through the file until you reach the length of the file
      while ( filePointer < length )
      {
        String s = file.readLine();
        System.out.println(s);
        filePointer = file.getFilePointer();
```

LISTING 21.6 CONTINUED

```
        }
      }
      catch ( IOException ex )
      {
        ex.printStackTrace();
      }
    }
  }
```

FILE SECURITY

When you start reading and writing to a disk from a networked application, you have to consider security issues. Because the Java language is used especially for creating Internet-based applications, security is even more important. No user wants to worry that the Web pages he's currently viewing are capable of reading from and writing to his hard disk. For this reason, the Java system was designed to allow the user to set system security from within his Java-compatible browser and determine which files and directories are to remain accessible to the browser and which are to be locked up tight.

In most cases, the user disallows all file access on his local system, thus completely protecting his system from unwarranted intrusion. In fact, the default setting on all current browsers disallows access to the local system, and until recently, even volunteering access to the file system was not possible. This tight security is vital to the existence of applets because of the way they are automatically downloaded onto a user's system behind the user's back, as it were. No one would use Java-compatible browsers if he feared that such use would open his system to any sort of tampering.

Java standalone applications, however, are a whole different story. Java applications are no different from any other application on your system. They cannot be automatically downloaded and run the way applets are. For this reason, standalone applications can have full access to the file system on which they are run. The file-handling examples in this chapter, then, are incorporated into Java standalone applications.

DIRECTORY OPERATIONS

Although most of the methods in the `File` class can be used on both files and directories, the `list` method is only for use in a directory:

```
public String[] list()
```

The `list` method returns an array of the names of all the files contained within the directory. You can also set up a filename filter for the `list` method, which enables you to select only certain filenames:

```
public String[] list(FilenameFilter filter)
```

The `FilenameFilter` interface defines a single method, `accept`, that returns true if a filename should be included in the list:

```
public abstract boolean accept(File dir, String name)
```

Listing 21.7 shows an object that implements a filename filter that allows only files ending with `.java`.

LISTING 21.7 SOURCE CODE FOR `JavaFilter.java`

```
import java.io.*;

// This class implements a filename filter that only allows
// files that end with .java

public class JavaFilter extends Object implements FilenameFilter
{
     public JavaFilter()
     {
     }

     public boolean accept(File dir, String name)
     {
       // Only return true for accept if the file ends with .java
       return name.endsWith(".java");
     }
}
```

Listing 21.8 shows a program that uses the `JavaFilter` to list out all the `.java` files in the current directory.

LISTING 21.8 SOURCE CODE FOR `JavaList.java`

```
import java.io.*;

public class JavaList
{
  public static void main( String[] args )
  {
    if ( args.length != 1 )
    {
      System.out.println( "Usage: java RandomAccessExample <directory>" );
      System.exit( 0 );
    }

    String dir = args[0];
    // Create a File instance for the current directory
    File currDir = new File( dir );

    // Get a filtered list of the .java files in the current directory
    String[] javaFiles = currDir.list( new JavaFilter() );

    // Print out the contents of the javaFiles array
    for (int i=0; i < javaFiles.length; i++)
    {
      System.out.println(javaFiles[i]);
    }
  }
}
```

DELETING FILES ON EXIT

There is one additional feature commonly used with temporary files, but which can be applied to any file. The `deleteOnExit` method was added to JDK 1.2 which allows you to schedule a file to be deleted when the VM exits. This is useful if, for instance, you are creating a file within your program, but don't want to leave it on the system after the program quits.

Caution

There are two cautions you need to be aware of with this method. First, after you schedule a file to be deleted, it can't be unscheduled. The second is that the `deleteOnExit` method is effective only if the VM exits normally, such as by `System.exit(0)`. If the system crashes, or there is some other form of abnormal crash, the VM will not be able to delete the file.

Listing 21.9 shows how `CreateTempFile.java` in Listing 21.5 would be modified to delete the file when the system exits. Notice that when you run `CreateTempFile2.java`, you see a file in the temp directory before the system exits, but afterwards the file is gone.

LISTING 21.9 SOURCE CODE FOR `CreateTempFile2.java`

```
import java.io.*;

public class CreateTempFile2
{
  public static void main( String[] args )
  {
    try
    {
      File tempFile = File.createTempFile( "myfile" , ".tmp" );
      FileOutputStream fout = new FileOutputStream(tempFile);
      PrintStream out = new PrintStream(fout);
out.println("Place this test string in the temp file");
      tempFile.deleteOnExit();
    }
    catch ( IOException ex )
    {
      System.out.println("There was a problem creating/writing to the temp file"
);
    }
System.out.println("Until you hit 'Enter' there is a temp file on the system");
    try
    {
      System.in.read();
    }
    catch( IOException ex )
    {
      ex.printStackTrace();
    }
    System.exit(0);
  }
}
```

OBJECT STREAMS

When Sun added Remote Method Invocation (RMI) to Java, it also added the capability to stream arbitrary objects. The `ObjectInput` and `ObjectOutput` interfaces define methods for reading and writing any object, in the same way that `DataInput` and `DataOutput` define methods for reading and writing primitive types. In fact, the `ObjectInput` and `ObjectOutput` interfaces extend the `DataInput` and `DataOutput` interfaces, respectively. The `ObjectInput` interface adds a single input method for reading in an object:

```
public abstract Object readObject()
throws ClassNotFoundException, IOException
```

Similarly, the `ObjectOutput` interface adds a single `output` method:

```
public abstract void writeObject(Object obj)
throws IOException
```

The two interfaces have a few other methods for dealing with the stream. These other methods define behavior that classes that implement these two interfaces must provide. The other methods on these two interfaces deal with determining the number of bytes available, reading and writing bytes, and flushing and closing the stream.

The `ObjectOutputStream` implements a stream filter that enables you to write any object to a stream, as well as any primitive type. Like most stream filters, you create an `ObjectOutputStream` by passing it an `OutputStream`:

```
public OutputStream(OutputStream outStream)
```

You can use the `writeObject` method to write any object to the stream:

```
public final void writeObject(Object ob)
```

The `writeObject` method can throw a `ClassMismatchException`, `MethodMissingException`, or `IOException`.

Because the `ObjectOutputStream` is a subclass of `DataOutputStream`, you can also use any of the methods from the `DataOutput` interface, such as `writeInt` or `writeUTF`.

Listing 21.10 shows a program that uses `writeObject` to stream a date and hash table to a file.

LISTING 21.10 SOURCE CODE FOR `WriteObject.java`

```
import java.io.*;
import java.util.*;

// This class writes out a date object and a hash table object
// to a file called "writeme" using an ObjectOutputStream.

public class WriteObject
{
  public static void main( String[] args )
  {
    // Create a hash table with a few entries
```

LISTING 21.10 CONTINUED

```
    Hashtable writeHash = new Hashtable();
    writeHash.put("Leader", "Moe");
    writeHash.put("Lieutenant", "Larry");
    writeHash.put("Stooge", "Curly");

    try
    {
      // Create an output stream to a file called "writeobject.txt"
      FileOutputStream fileOut = new FileOutputStream( "writeobject.txt" );

      // Open an output stream filter on the file stream
      ObjectOutputStream objOut = new ObjectOutputStream( fileOut );

      // Write out the current date and the hash table
      objOut.writeObject( new Date() );
      objOut.writeObject( writeHash );

      // Close the stream
      objOut.close();
     }
     catch ( IOException ex )
     {
        ex.printStackTrace();
     }
   }
}
```

The `ObjectInputStream`, as you might have guessed, implements a stream filter for the `ObjectInput` interface. You create an `ObjectInputStream` by passing it the input stream you want it to filter:

```
public ObjectInputStream(InputStream inStream)
```

The `readObject` method reads an object from the input stream:

```
public final Object readObject()
throws MethodMissingException, ClassMismatchException
     ClassNotFoundException, StreamCorruptedException, IOException
```

You can also use any of the methods from the `DataInput` interface on an `ObjectInputStream`.

Listing 21.11 shows a program that uses `readObject` to read the objects written to the `"writeobject.txt"` file by the example in Listing 21.10.

LISTING 21.11 SOURCE CODE FOR `ReadObject.java`

```
import java.io.*;
import java.util.*;

// This class opens up the file "writeme" and reads two
// objects from it. It makes no assumptions about the
// types of the objects, it just prints them out.

public class ReadObject extends Object
```

LISTING 21.11 CONTINUED

```
{
  public static void main(String[] args)
  {

    try
    {
      // Open an input stream to the file "writeme"
      FileInputStream fileIn = new FileInputStream( "writeobject.txt" );

      // Create an ObjectInput filter on the stream
      ObjectInputStream objIn = new ObjectInputStream(fileIn);

      // Read in the first object and print it
      Object ob1 = objIn.readObject();
      System.out.println(ob1);

      // Read in the second object and print it
      Object ob2 = objIn.readObject();
      System.out.println(ob2);

      // Close the stream
       objIn.close();
    }
    catch( ClassNotFoundException ex )
    {
      ex.printStackTrace();
    }
    catch( IOException ex )
    {
      ex.printStackTrace();
    }
  }
}
```

TROUBLESHOOTING

UNDERSTANDING THE USE OF THE `File` CLASS

Whenever I create a `File` instance, I can't figure out how to read or write to the file.

The `File` class represents a filename, not an actual file object. It is really immutable. To read or write, you will need to use one of the `stream` classes or the `reader/writer` classes. The `File` classes can be used for certain operations such as renaming a file.

USING THE `available()` METHOD

When I use the `available()` method on the `InputStream` class, it does not return the correct number that I expect.

The `available()` method does not necessarily guaranteed to return the maximum number of bytes available without blocking.

EXCEPTIONS THROWN BY THE PrintStream AND PrintWriter CLASSES

I'm using a PrintStream *or a* PrintWriter *and even though there's no problem, they are not throwing exceptions.*

Both the PrintStream and PrintWriter classes will not throw any exceptions. You must check for errors by calling the checkError method.

CHAPTER 22

Object Serialization

In this chapter

by Chuck Cavaness

What Is Object Serialization?

To this point, you've been working with objects and ways to manipulate those objects through the methods defined on them. You have created an application, started it, and instantiated some objects. When that application exited, those objects—or really the state of those objects—was lost. To keep that from happening, you need to learn how to save that state for later retrieval.

The term for saving the state of an object to an external source so that it can be constructed later is usually known as *persistence*. In other words, you will want to ensure that the object persists over a longer life cycle than just the execution of an application. Later when you learn about JDBC and Databases, you'll also get more detail about how to persist an object state to a database. However, a database is not needed for every application. Some applications have no need to persist object states after the exit of the application. For some applications, installing and creating a database is a giant overkill. For those types of applications, you really need a smaller method of persisting object states. This is one place that Object serialization can help.

Another use of Object serialization is that it allows an application to communicate objects across a network and be reconstituted back into an object on the other side (discussed further in Chapter 23, "Communications and Networking"). Object serialization is the tool that was added to Java to allow you to fully use the Object Oriented Programming nature of Java and write those objects you've labored to produce to a file or other stream so that they can be persisted or shared with other applications.

To understand object serialization, first look at how you would persist an object to a file so that it can be read back in later. This approach assumes that you have one or more objects that needed to be persisted and a database is too much. Normally when you open a stream to and from a client program, the odds are good that you are sending/receiving some type of primitive data types, such as an `int` or a byte. Persisting an object in this manner means that for each attribute that is within the object, it needs to be manually written out to the file. If an object has a reference to another object or a collection of objects, it gets extremely complicated very quickly.

If you really wanted to, you could write generalized methods to handle some of the redundant work, but you would still be faced with some problems. Fortunately, object serialization enables you to grab an object a whole class at a time.

If you need to store or send complete object instances to a file or over the network, object serialization makes this an easy chore to perform.

How Object Serialization Works

The key to object serialization is to store enough data about the object to be able to reconstruct it fully. Furthermore, to protect the user (and programmer), the object must have a "fingerprint" that correctly associates it with the legitimate object from which it was made. This fingerprint is actually the class name and signature of the class, the values of the object's fields and arrays, and the closure of any other objects referenced from the initial objects. Non-transient and static fields are not serialized. That probably sounds like a lot of work and things to write out. Fortunately, the handling of all of this complexity is taken care of by the Java Virtual Machine, and the Java developer just needs to call the appropriate write methods. This normally is as easy as calling something like this:

```
writeObject( someObject );
```

It's not necessary, however, for the serialization routines to store the methods of a class. The class code is assumed available any time these elements are required. In other words, when you store an instance of the class Date, you are not also storing the methods for that class. It's assumed that you are using the same Date class to reconstitute the object that was used to serialize it.

Object serialization can take advantage of using streams to make the writing out of objects even easier (you learned about streams in Chapter 21, "Streams, Files, and Serialization") However, only objects supporting the `java.io.Serializable` interface can be written to streams. When an object is written out to a stream or to the network, it's critical that it be read back in the exact sequence that it was written out or the object will not be able to be reconstructed. So if multiple objects are written out, they must be read in the same order. This method is easier than writing the attributes of an object out, because you don't have to keep track of which attribute was written out and in which order. Also, the type of attribute must be tracked if you simply write the attributes of an object out. Using object serialization, this is all handled for the developer. It's as easy as calling the `writeObject` and `readObject` methods.

Note

If you are a C or C++ programmer, you're probably used to accomplishing much of object serialization by taking the pointer to a class or struct, doing a `sizeOf()`, and writing out the entire class. Java does not support pointers or direct-memory access, so this technique will not work in Java, and object serialization is required.

DEALING WITH OBJECTS WITH OBJECT REFERENCES

Objects frequently refer to other objects by declaring instance variables that reference the other class. For example, in the `TestObject` class in Listing 22.3, a `nextNode` private instance variable is a reference to an object of type `TestObject`. To persist an object, it is also necessary to persist the objects that these objects reference. Of course, the reference objects might also refer to yet even more objects. So, as a rule, to serialize an object completely, you must store all the information for that object, as well as every object that is reachable by the object, including all the recursive objects.

NEW TO 1.3

Prior to SDK 1.3, Strings longer than 64K could not be serialized. That is no longer a problem with the SDK 1.3 version. There has also been several performance improvements for serialization within the 1.3 version. The improvements revolved around removing unnecessary synchronization/method call overhead during serialization. These two improvements alone make serialization more attractive than the previous editions.

LISTING 22.1 SOURCE CODE FOR TestObject.java

```
public class TestObject
{
  // Private instance variables
  private int x;
  private int y;
  private float angle;
  private String name = null;
  private TestObject nextNode = null;

  // Constructor
  public TestObject (int x, int y, float angle, String name,
➥TestObject nextNode)
{
    super();
    this.x = x ;
    this.y = y;
    this.angle= angle;
    this.name = name;
    this.nextNode = nextNode;
  }
}
```

OBJECT SERIALIZATION EXAMPLE

This simple examples of serialization stores and retrieves an instance of the Date class to and from a file. To do this without object serialization, you would probably do something on the order of `getTime()` and write the resulting long integer to the file. However, with object serialization the process is much easier.

Listing 22.2 shows a utility class called `OurDateUtility` that has two static methods: `writeDateToFile` and `readDateFromFile`. These methods write and read a Date object using serialization. Remember, to serialize an object to a stream, the class must be serializable. Fortunately, if you look at the Date class, it implements the Serializable interface already. One important thing to watch is that all the data within the class must be serializable. If the attributes are primitives, you don't have to worry. If the attributes are references to other objects, make sure those other objects are serializable.

LISTING 22.2 OurDateUtility.java—UTILITY CLASS FOR DATE SERIALIZATION

```
import java.util.Date;
import java.io.*;

public class OurDateUtility
{
  /**
   * Static utility method that takes an instance of the Date class and a
   * filename and serializes the Date instance to the file
*/
  public static void writeDateToFile( Date dateInstance, String fileName )
  {
```

LISTING 22.2 CONTINUED

```
    try
    {
      // Create the object stream on an output file stream
      FileOutputStream fileStream =
new FileOutputStream( fileName, false );

      ObjectOutputStream objectStr =
new ObjectOutputStream( fileStream );
      // write out the object
      objectStr.writeObject( dateInstance );

      // Close the resources
      objectStr.close();
      fileStream.close();
    }
    catch( FileNotFoundException ex )
    {
      ex.printStackTrace();
      System.out.println( "Could not create the file for some reason" );
      System.exit(-1);
    }
    catch( IOException ex )
    {
      ex.printStackTrace();
      System.out.println(
 "There was a problem writing the object to the stream" );
System.exit(-1);
    }
  }
  /**
   * Static utility method that takes a filename and deserializes
* a date instance from it and returns the Date instance
   */
  public static Date readDateFromFile( String fileName )
  {
    Date dateFromFile = null;
    try
    {
      // Create an Object input stream on an input file stream
      FileInputStream in = new FileInputStream( fileName );
      ObjectInputStream objectInStr = new ObjectInputStream( in );
      // read in the object
      Object obj = objectInStr.readObject();

      // Double check that it is the right type before casting
      if ( obj instanceof Date )
      {
        dateFromFile = (Date)obj;
      }
    }
    catch( ClassNotFoundException ex )
    {
      ex.printStackTrace();
    }
    catch( FileNotFoundException ex )
    {
```

LISTING 22.2 CONTINUED

```
        ex.printStackTrace();
      }
      catch( IOException ex )
      {
        ex.printStackTrace();
      }
      return dateFromFile;
    }
  }
```

Look at the code in Listing 22.2. First, notice that the program creates a `FileOutputStream`. To do any serialization to a file, it is first necessary to declare a `FileOutputStream` to which you will attach the `ObjectOutputStream`.

After you have established a stream, you must create an `ObjectOutputStream` with it. The `ObjectOutputStream` contains all the necessary methods to serialize any primitive or object and to write it to the stream.

Listing 22.3 shows a test class that uses the `OurDateUtility` class to perform serialization.

LISTING 22.3 `OurDateUtilityTest.java`—A CLASS FOR TESTING `OurDateUtility`

```
import java.util.Date;

public class OurDateUtilityTest
{
  public static final String DATE_FILE = "datefile.dat";

  public static void main(String[] args)
  {
    // Create an instance of the Date class and print out its value
    Date aDate = new Date( System.currentTimeMillis() );

    System.out.println( "Serializing date: " + aDate.toString() );
    // Call the utility class to serialize it

    OurDateUtility.writeDateToFile(
 aDate, OurDateUtilityTest.DATE_FILE );

    // Deserialize the Date object from the file and print its value
    Date dateFromFile =
 OurDateUtility.readDateFromFile( OurDateUtilityTest.DATE_FILE );
if ( dateFromFile != null )
    {
      System.out.println(
 "Deserializing date: " + dateFromFile.toString() );
    }
  }
}
```

When you run the `OurDateUtilityTest` class, the output should look similar to this:

```
C:\jdk1.3se_book\classes>java OurDateUtilityTest
Serializing date: Tue Jul 11 20:31:05 PDT 2000
Deserializing date: Tue Jul 11 20:31:05 PDT 2000

C:\jdk1.3se_book\classes>
```

The actual date value will be different, but hopefully the value that was serialized to the file is the same after being deserialized.

If you experience a `ClassNotFoundException` *during the deserialization process, see "*`ClassNotFoundException` *Thrown During Deserialization" in the "Troubleshooting" section at the end of this chapter.*

The file that was created to hold the serialized object is called `datefile.dat`. Note that the name could have been any legal file named for the operating system. It didn't have to have an extension of `.dat`, it could have been anything. It should still be on the file system. The file is not removed by deserializing the object or by the utility class. If you open the file with a text editor, you will see something that looks mostly like garbage. However, a closer inspection reveals that this file contains several interesting things. The text that looks like garbage characters is actually what the serialization used to store information about the class, such as the value of the fields and the class signature that was discussed earlier.

READING AND WRITING YOUR OWN OBJECTS

You can also customize your objects to have the capability to be serialized just as you did with the `Date` class.

Listing 22.4 shows the source code for serializing an example class called `Employee`. Because all the data within the class can be serialized, all you had to do in this case was to implement the `java.io.Serializable` interface.

LISTING 22.4 SOURCE CODE FOR `Employee.java`

```
public class Employee implements java.io.Serializable
{
  // Private instance variables for an employee
  private String firstName = null;
  private String lastName = null;
  private float payRate;
  private int hoursWorked;

  // Constructor
  public Employee( String first, String last, float rate, int hours )
  {
    super();
    firstName = first;
    lastName = last;
    payRate = rate;
    hoursWorked = hours;
  }
```

LISTING 22.4 CONTINUED

```
  // Override the toString() method from object to display an employee
  public String toString()
  {
    StringBuffer strBuf = new StringBuffer( "First: " );
    strBuf.append( getFirstName() );
    strBuf.append( " Last: " );
    strBuf.append( getLastName() );
    strBuf.append( " Rate: " );
    strBuf.append( getPayRate() );
    strBuf.append( " Hours: " );
    strBuf.append( getHoursWorked() );

    return strBuf.toString();
  }

  // Public Getters for the object's state
  public String getFirstName()
  {
    return firstName;
  }

  public String getLastName()
  {
    return lastName;
  }

  public float getPayRate()
  {
    return payRate;
  }

  public int getHoursWorked()
  {
    return hoursWorked;
  }
}
```

A `toString()` method, which is actually inherited from the `Object` class, was implemented in the `Employee` class. This provides an easy way to display an instance of the `Employee` as a string.

Listing 22.5 shows the source code for a class to test the Employee class shown previously.

LISTING 22.5 SOURCE CODE FOR `EmployeeTest`

```
import java.io.*;

public class EmployeeTest
{
  // Used to keep from hard-coding the filename in multiple places
  public static final String EMPLOYEE_FILE = "employees.dat";

  public static void main(String[] args)
  {
```

Listing 22.5 Continued

```
    // Create a few employees
    Employee employee1 =
new Employee( "Zachary", "Cavaness", 10.25f, 40 );

    Employee employee2 =
new Employee( "Joshua", "Cavaness", 10.25f, 40 );

    Employee employee3 =
 new Employee( "Tracy", "Cavaness", 21.50f, 40 );

    try
    {
      // Create the File and Object streams to serialize to the file
      FileOutputStream out =
 new FileOutputStream( EmployeeTest.EMPLOYEE_FILE );
ObjectOutputStream objOutStr = new ObjectOutputStream( out );
      objOutStr.writeObject( employee1 );
      objOutStr.writeObject( employee2 );
      objOutStr.writeObject( employee3 );

      // close the open resources
      objOutStr.close();
      out.close();
    }
    catch( FileNotFoundException ex )
    {
      System.out.println( "Could not create the employee file" );
      System.exit(-1);
    }
    catch( IOException ex )
    {
      System.out.println( "Could not serialize the employees" );
      System.exit(-1);
    }

    // Read the employees back in
    try
    {
      Object obj = null;
      // Create the file and object streams
      FileInputStream in = new FileInputStream( EmployeeTest.EMPLOYEE_FILE );
      ObjectInputStream objInStr = new ObjectInputStream( in );

      // In this example, you keep going until the EOFException is
      // raised and then you catch that exception and stop
while( true )
      {
        obj = objInStr.readObject();
        System.out.println( obj );
      }
    }
    catch( EOFException ex )
    {
      System.out.println( "All records have been read in" );
    }
    catch( FileNotFoundException ex )
```

LISTING 22.5 CONTINUED

```
    {
      System.out.println( " Could not open the file " + EmployeeTest.EMPLOYEE_FILE
);
    }
    catch( IOException ex )
    {
      System.out.println( "Could not serialize the employees" );
    }
    catch( ClassNotFoundException ex )
    {
      System.out.println(
 "Could not find the class definition for serialized class" );
}
  }
}
```

The `EmployeeTest` class is used to test the serialization of the `Employee` class from Listing 22.4. It performs a similar process as in the `OurDateUtility` class from before. It serializes objects using file and object streams. Here's the output from running the `EmployeeTest` class:

```
C:\jdk1.3se_book\classes>java EmployeeTest
First: Zachary Last: Cavaness Rate: 10.25 Hours: 40
First: Joshua Last: Cavaness Rate: 10.25 Hours: 40
First: Tracy Last: Cavaness Rate: 21.5 Hours: 40
All records have been read in

C:\jdk1.3se_book\classes>
```

CUSTOMIZING OBJECT SERIALIZATION

Sometimes it is useful, or even necessary, to control how an individual object is serialized. If for instance you want to encrypt the data values held by the object's attributes, you would not want to use the default serialization mechanisms.

To override how an object is serialized or deserialized, you must implement two methods in your class with these exact signatures:

```
private void writeObject(java.io.ObjectOutputStream out)
     throws IOException
 private void readObject(java.io.ObjectInputStream in)
     throws IOException, ClassNotFoundException;
```

You might have noticed that the Serializable interface does not define any methods. If you look back at the `Employee` class from listing 22.4, no methods had to be implemented when you made the `Employee` class implement the Serializable interface. Because `writeObject()` and `readObject()` are not in the Serializable interface, the serialization system calls these methods by using Reflection. *Reflection* essentially allows programs to access methods and constructors of components based on knowing their signature. Reflection is generally a complicated API, and for most of your programs, you won't need to be concerned with actually getting Reflection to work. However, you do need to know that Reflection requires the signatures of the methods to be exact. Therefore, it is critical that you use exactly these signatures. Failure to make the methods private will cause the serialization mechanism to use its default algorithms, which is not what you want when implementing these two methods.

➔ **See** Chapter 28, "Reflection," **p. 977**

If your classes subclass another class, they do not need to be concerned with calling `super.writeObject()` or `super.readObject()` on the parent object. You also don't need to be concerned about how subclasses will serialize the class, because each portion of the object will be handled separately by the serialization mechanism.

On the other hand, if you want to use the default mechanism within the `writeObject()` method, you can do so by calling `out.defaultWriteObject()`. Or from the `readObject()` method, you can call `in.defaultReadObject()`. This method uses the default serialization mechanism to write out the part of object that can be serialized. Then you can handle the specifics in a custom manner.

Listing 22.6 contains a class called `User` that implements the `readObject` and `writeObject` methods. The class does this so that it can encrypt the string values for the username and password values for an object. The encryption routine just reverses the values before writing out the data and then reverses them back after reading them in. This obviously does not provide an ounce of real encryption, but it's not the point of the example.

Listing 22.6 Source Code for `User.java`

```
import java.io.*;

public class User implements Serializable
{
  // Private instance variables
  private String userName = null;
  private String password = null;

  // Constructor
  public User( String name, String passwd )
  {
    super();
    userName = name;
    password = passwd;
  }

  //Public accessors
  public String getUserName()
  {
    return userName;
  }

  public void setUserName( String name )
  {
    userName = name;
```

LISTING 22.6 CONTINUED

```
  }

  public String getPassword()
  {
    return password;
  }

  public void setPassword( String passwd )
  {
    password = passwd;
 }

  // Implement the necessary writeObject method for handling the
  // serialization of this object other than the default way
  private void writeObject( ObjectOutputStream out ) throws IOException
  {
    String userNameEncrypted = encryptStr( getUserName() );
    String passwordEncrypted = encryptStr( getPassword() );
    out.writeObject( userNameEncrypted );
    out.writeObject( passwordEncrypted );
  }

  // Implement the necessary readObject method for handling the
  // serialization of this object other than the default way
  private void readObject( ObjectInputStream in )
    throws IOException, ClassNotFoundException
  {
    String userNameEncrypted = (String)in.readObject();
    String passwordEncrypted = (String)in.readObject();
    setUserName( decryptStr( userNameEncrypted ));
    setPassword( decryptStr( passwordEncrypted ));
  }

  // Extremely simple encryption routine just to show the point
  // of something being done with the data
  public String encryptStr( String normalStr )
  {
    StringBuffer buf = new StringBuffer( normalStr );
    buf.reverse();
    return buf.toString();
  }

  // Simple decryption routine
  public String decryptStr( String encryptStr )
  {
    StringBuffer buf = new StringBuffer( encryptStr );
    buf.reverse();
    return buf.toString();
  }

  // Override the toString() method from Object to pretty print a User object
  public String toString()
  {
    StringBuffer strBuf = new StringBuffer( "User: " );
    strBuf.append( getUserName() );
```

Listing 22.6 Continued

```
    strBuf.append( " Password: " );
    strBuf.append( getPassword() );
    return strBuf.toString();
  }
}
```

Listing 22.7 is a class called `UserTest` that can be used to test the serialization of the User class. It creates several instances of the `User` class and serializes them to a file. It then reads them back in and prints out the objects to the console.

Listing 22.7 Source Code for `UserTest.java`

```
import java.io.*;

public class UserTest
{
  // Constant for the user data filename
public static final String USER_DATA_FILE = "users.dat";

  public static void main(String[] args)
  {
    // Create a couple of User objects
    User user1 = new User( "User1", "foobar" );
    User user2 = new User( "admin", "admin" );
    User user3 = new User( "guest", "guest" );

    try
    {
      // Create the streams to write the objects out
      // Notice there is really no difference here. The real
      // difference is in the User class
      FileOutputStream out = new FileOutputStream( USER_DATA_FILE );
      ObjectOutputStream objOutStr = new ObjectOutputStream( out );
      objOutStr.writeObject( user1 );
      objOutStr.writeObject( user2 );
      objOutStr.writeObject( user3 );
      // Read the users back in
      FileInputStream in = new FileInputStream( USER_DATA_FILE );
      ObjectInputStream objInStr = new ObjectInputStream( in );
      // Print all of the User's out
      while( true )
      {
        System.out.println( objInStr.readObject() );
      }
    }
    catch( EOFException ex )
    {
      System.out.println( "All records have been read" );
    }
    catch( FileNotFoundException ex )
    {
      System.out.println( "Could not find the file " + USER_DATA_FILE );
    }
    catch( IOException ex )
```

LISTING 22.7 CONTINUED

```
    {
      System.out.println(
 "There was a problem with serialization of the users" );
}
    catch( ClassNotFoundException ex )
    {
      System.out.println( "Could not find the User class definition" );
    }
  }
}
```

Running the `UserTest` class produces this output:

```
C:\jdk1.3se_book\classes>java UserTest
User: User1 Password: foobar
User: admin Password: admin
User: guest Password: guest
All records have been read

C:\jdk1.3se_book\classes>
```

USING THE `Transient` KEYWORD

In the previous example, the user's login and password were written out to the file. Although the encryption routine was primitive, even the better encryption routines can be broken in some amount of time. There are techniques that have been around for a while that enable encryption routines to be broken in a relative amount of time. The real question here is whether the password field should even be written out. What if there are other fields that are sensitive that should not be serialized? Fortunately, that's where the `transient` keyword can help. By declaring a field as `transient`, the value will not be serialized along with the rest of the object.

Note

If you have written your own serialization using the approach from Listing 22.8, you must make sure that you don't write out the fields that you don't want to be serialized. The `transient` keyword will not prevent it in this case. You must handle it manually.

Listing 22.8 is almost exactly the same as the `Employee` class from Listing 22.4. The only change was adding the `transient` keyword to the `payRate` attribute so that it will not be serialized out to the file. The name of the class has also been renamed to `PrivateEmployee` to keep the two classes separate for comparison.

LISTING 22.8 SOURCE CODE FOR `PrivateEmployee.java`

```
public class PrivateEmployee implements java.io.Serializable
{
  // Private instance variables for an employee
  private String firstName = null;
```

LISTING 22.8 CONTINUED

```
  private String lastName = null;
  transient private float payRate;
  private int hoursWorked;

  // Constructor
  public PrivateEmployee( String first, String last, float rate, int hours )
  {
    super();
    firstName = first;
    lastName = last;
    payRate = rate;
    hoursWorked = hours;
  }

  // Override the toString() method from object to display an employee
  public String toString()
  {
    StringBuffer strBuf = new StringBuffer( "First: " );
    strBuf.append( getFirstName() );
    strBuf.append( " Last: " );
    strBuf.append( getLastName() );
    strBuf.append( " Rate: " );
    strBuf.append( getPayRate() );
    strBuf.append( " Hours: " );
    strBuf.append( getHoursWorked() );

    return strBuf.toString();
  }

  // Public Getters for the object's state
  public String getFirstName()
  {
    return firstName;
  }

  public String getLastName()
  {
    return lastName;
  }

  public float getPayRate()
  {
    return payRate;
  }

  public int getHoursWorked()
  {
    return hoursWorked;
  }
}
```

The `EmployeeTest` class from before has been changed to use the new `PrivateEmployee` class. Listing 22.9 shows this new test class.

LISTING 22.9 SOURCE CODE FOR PrivateEmployeeTest.java

```
import java.io.*;

public class PrivateEmployeeTest
{
  // Used to keep from hard-coding the filename in multiple places
  public static final String EMPLOYEE_FILE = "employees.dat";

  public static void main(String[] args)
  {
    // Create a few employees
    PrivateEmployee employee1 =
new PrivateEmployee( "Zachary", "Cavaness", 10.25f, 40 );

    PrivateEmployee employee2 =
new PrivateEmployee( "Joshua", "Cavaness", 10.25f, 40 );

    PrivateEmployee employee3 =
 new PrivateEmployee( "Tracy", "Cavaness", 21.50f, 40 );

    try
    {
      // Create the File and Object streams to serialize to the file
      FileOutputStream out =
 new FileOutputStream( EmployeeTest.EMPLOYEE_FILE );
ObjectOutputStream objOutStr = new ObjectOutputStream( out );
      objOutStr.writeObject( employee1 );
      objOutStr.writeObject( employee2 );
      objOutStr.writeObject( employee3 );

      // close the open resources
      objOutStr.close();
      out.close();
    }
    catch( FileNotFoundException ex )
    {
      System.out.println( "Could not create the employee file" );
      System.exit(-1);
    }
    catch( IOException ex )
    {
      System.out.println( "Could not serialize the employees" );
      System.exit(-1);
    }

    // Read the employees back in
    try
    {
      Object obj = null;
      // Create the file and object streams
      FileInputStream in =
 new FileInputStream( PrivateEmployeeTest.EMPLOYEE_FILE );
ObjectInputStream objInStr = new ObjectInputStream( in );

      // In this example, you keep going until the EOFException is
      // raised and then you catch that exception and stop
```

LISTING 22.9 CONTINUED

```
while( true )
      {
        obj = objInStr.readObject();
        System.out.println( obj );
      }
    }
    catch( EOFException ex )
    {
      System.out.println( "All records have been read in" );
    }
    catch( FileNotFoundException ex )
    {
      System.out.println( "Could not  open the file " +
PrivateEmployeeTest.EMPLOYEE_FILE );
    }
    catch( IOException ex )
    {
      System.out.println( "Could not serialize the employees" );
    }
    catch( ClassNotFoundException ex )
    {
      System.out.println(
  "Could not find the class definition for serialized class");
}
  }
}
```

The only changes from the previous test class are that references to `EmployeeTest` have been changed to `PrivateEmployee` and the actual name of the test class was changed to `PrivateEmployeeTest`. Other than those two changes, the test class is the same. Running the `PrivateEmployeeTest` class, the output should look like this:

```
First: Zachary Last: Cavaness Rate: 0.0 Hours: 40
First: Joshua Last: Cavaness Rate: 0.0 Hours: 40
First: Tracy Last: Cavaness Rate: 0.0 Hours: 40
All records have been read in

C:\jdk1.3se_book\classes>
```

Notice that the rate values are 0.0 for all three users. This is because the rate was never serialized to the file and when the deserialization occurred, the `payRate` attribute was set to the initial values for the float primitive, which is 0.0.

USING THE EXTERNALIZABLE INTERFACE

The `java.io.Externalizable` interface can be used when an object must have complete control over how the object is serialized or externalized to be consistent with the interface name. The two methods that must be implemented are `readExtenal` and `writeExternal`. The method signatures are in Listing 22.10.

Listing 22.10 Method Signatures for the `java.io.Externalizable` Interface

```
public void readExternal(ObjectInputin)
                throws IOException,
                       ClassNotFoundException;

public void writeExternal(ObjectOutputout)
                throws IOException;
```

The Externalizable interface supercedes the Serializable interface. If a class implements both the Externalizable and Serializable interface, the Externalizable will be used over the Serializable to perform the externalization.When an Externalizable object is reconstructed, an instance is created using the public no-arg constructor, and then the `readExternal` method called. If an object is a subclass of another object, it must coordinate with the superclass to have the state inherited from the superclass.

TROUBLESHOOTING

`ClassNotFoundException` THROWN DURING DESERIALIZATION

If you are trying to deserialize a file or stream back into an object or set of objects and a `ClassNotFoundException` is thrown.

The SDK 1.3 has improved `Exception` reporting for serialization. Instead of a generic `Exception` being thrown during a deserialization process, a more descriptive exception will be thrown. In most cases, it will be a `ClassNotFoundException`. This exception is raised when a stream being deserialized contains one or more classes that can't be found in the system CLASSPATH. The Exception will now correctly report the exact class can't find during the deserialization process. You need to make sure that all of the classes contained within the stream being deserialized are in the system CLASSPATH. Usually, the problem is not with the high-level classes, but with another class that one of these high-level classes reference through an instance variable.

CHAPTER 23

Communications and Networking

In this chapter

OVERVIEW OF NETWORK COMMUNICATIONS

Despite all its other merits, the rapid embrace of Java by the computing community is primarily due to its powerful integration with Internet networking. The Internet revolution has forever changed the way the personal computer is used, empowering individuals to gather, publish, and share information in a vast resource with millions of participants. Building on this foundation, Java could be the next major revolution in computing.

The Java execution environment is designed so that applications can be easily written to efficiently communicate and share processing with remote systems. The standard Java API within the java.net package provides much of this functionality. As a foundation for this chapter on Java and network communications, there are some fundamentals that should be understood before the discussion goes too far. The fundamentals revolve mainly around the design of the Internet network protocol suite: TCP/IP.

TCP/IP is a suite of protocols that interconnects the various systems on the Internet. TCP/IP provides a common programming interface for diverse and foreign hardware. The suite supports the joining of separate physical networks implementing different network media. TCP/IP makes a diverse, chaotic, global network such as the Internet possible.

Models provide useful abstractions of working systems, ignoring fine detail while enabling a clear perspective on global interactions. Models also facilitate a greater understanding of functioning systems and provide a foundation for extending that system. Understanding the models of network communications is an essential guide to learning TCP/IP fundamentals. Although there are several communication protocols that are used to communicate over the Internet and intranets, TCP/IP and UDP are the focus in this chapter.

TCP/IP ARCHITECTURE

There are four levels to understanding how Java applications communicate over the network using TCP. Figure 23.1 shows these levels in their simplest form.

When viewed as a layered model, TCP/IP is usually seen as being composed of four layers, each playing a specific role:

Application Layer—The Application Layer enables network applications to communicate clearly. In a client/server system, the client application knows how to request services, and the server knows how to appropriately respond. Protocols that implement this layer include HTTP, FTP, and Telnet.

Transport Layer—The Transport Layer enables network applications to obtain messages over clearly defined channels and with specific characteristics. The two protocols within the TCP/IP suite that generally implement this layer are Transmission Control Protocol (TCP) and User Datagram Protocol (UDP).

Network Layer—The Network Layer enables information to be transmitted to any machine on the contiguous TCP/IP network, regardless of the different physical networks that intervene. Internet Protocol (IP) is the mechanism for transmitting data within this layer.

Link Layer—The Link Layer consists of the low-level protocols used to transmit data to machines on the same physical network. Protocols that aren't part of the TCP/IP suite, such as Ethernet, Token Ring, FDDI, and ATM, implement this layer.

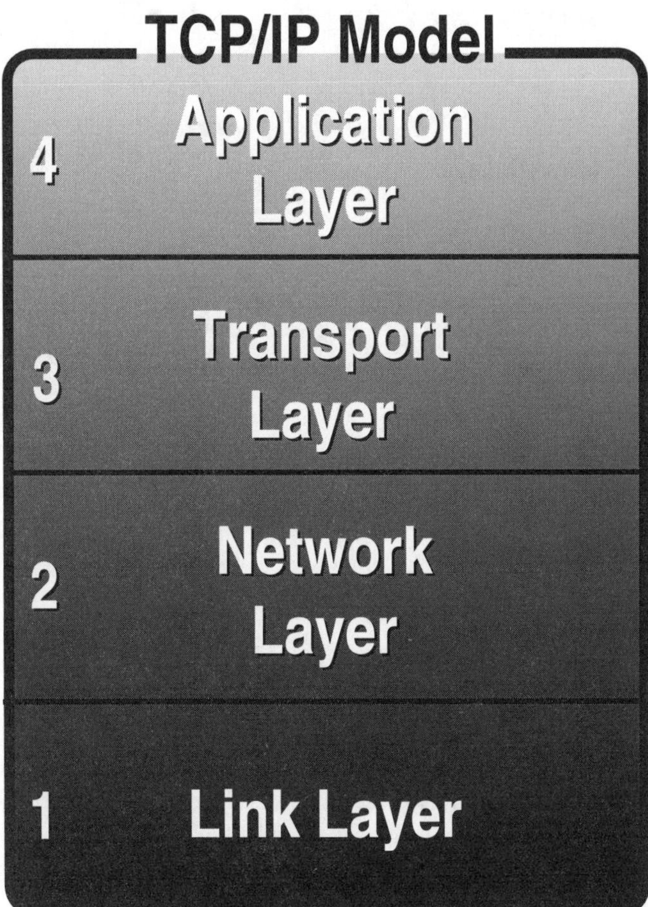

Figure 23.1
The TCP/IP network model can be broken down into four layers.

Data within these layers is usually encapsulated with a common mechanism: protocols have a header that identifies meta-information—such as the source, destination, and other attributes—and a data portion that contains the actual information. The protocols from the upper layers are encapsulated within the data portion of the lower ones. When traveling back up the protocol stack, the information is reconstructed as it is delivered to each layer. Figure 23.2 shows this concept of encapsulation.

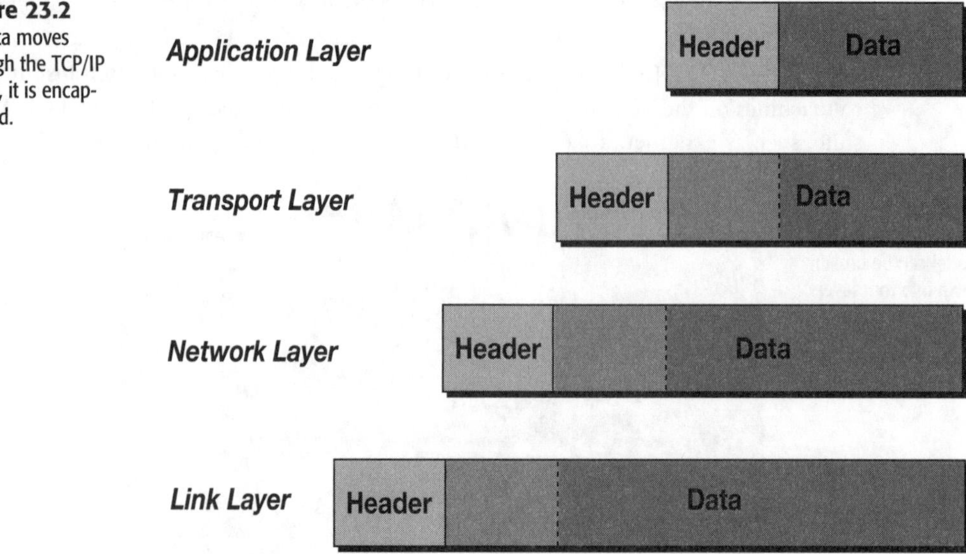

Figure 23.2
As data moves through the TCP/IP layers, it is encapsulated.

TCP/IP PROTOCOLS

Three protocols are most commonly used within the TCP/IP scheme, and a closer investigation of their properties is warranted. Understanding how these three protocols (IP, TCP, and UDP) interact is critical to developing network applications.

INTERNET PROTOCOL (IP)

IP is the keystone of the TCP/IP suite. All data on the Internet flows through IP packets, the basic unit of IP transmissions. IP is a connectionless, unreliable protocol. As a *connectionless* protocol, IP does not exchange control information before transmitting data to a remote system. Data packets are merely sent to the destination with the expectation that they will be treated properly. IP is *unreliable* because it does not retransmit lost packets or detect corrupted data. These tasks must be implemented by higher-level protocols, such as TCP.

IP defines a universal addressing scheme called IP addresses. An IP address is a 32-bit number, and each standard address is unique on the Internet. Given an IP packet, the information can be routed to the destination based upon the IP address defined in the packet header. IP addresses are generally written as four numbers, between 0 and 255, separated by a period (for example, 124.148.157.6).

Although a 32-bit number is an appropriate way to address systems for computers, humans understandably have difficulty remembering them. Thus, a system called the *Domain Name System* (DNS) was developed to map IP addresses to more intuitive identifiers and vice versa. You can use `www.netspace.org` instead of 128.148.157.6.

It is important to realize that these domain names are not used or understood by IP. When an application wants to transmit data to another machine on the Internet, it must first translate the domain name to an IP address using the DNS. A receiving application can perform a reverse translation, using the DNS to return a domain name given an IP address. There is not a one-to-one correspondence between IP addresses and domain names: a domain name can map to multiple IP addresses, and multiple IP addresses can map to the same domain name.

Caution

Even more important to note is that the entire body of DNS data cannot be trusted. Varied systems through the world are responsible for maintaining DNS records. DNS servers can be tricked, and servers can be set up that are populated with false information.

TRANSMISSION CONTROL PROTOCOL (TCP)

Most Internet applications use TCP to implement the transport layer. TCP provides a reliable, connection-oriented, continuous-stream protocol. These characteristics are described here:

- **Reliable**—When TCP segments, the smallest unit of TCP transmissions, are lost or corrupted, the TCP implementation will detect this and retransmit necessary segments.
- **Connection-oriented**—TCP sets up a connection with a remote system by transmitting control information, often known as a handshake, before beginning a communication. At the end of the connection, a similar closing handshake ends the transmission.
- **Continuous-stream**—TCP provides a communications medium that allows for an arbitrary number of bytes to be sent and received smoothly; after a connection has been established, TCP segments provide the application layer the appearance of a continuous flow of data.

Because of these characteristics, it is easy to see why TCP would be used by most Internet applications. TCP makes it easy to create a network application, freeing you from worrying how the data is broken up or about coding error-correction routines. However, TCP requires a significant amount of overhead and perhaps you might want to code routines that more efficiently provide reliable transmissions, given the parameters of your application. Furthermore, retransmission of lost data might be inappropriate for your application, because such information's usefulness might have expired. In these instances, UDP serves as an alternative. A later section of this chapter, "User Datagram Protocol (UDP)," describes this protocol.

An important addressing scheme that TCP defines is the port. Ports separate various TCP communications streams that are running concurrently on the same system. For server applications, which wait for TCP clients to initiate contact, a specific port can be established from where communications will originate. These concepts come together in a programming abstraction known as sockets. This is the discussion of the next section.

WORKING WITH SOCKETS

Sockets are a programming abstraction that isolates your code from the low-level implementations of the TCP/IP protocol stack. TCP sockets enable you to quickly develop your own custom client/server applications. Although the URL classes described later in this chapter are useful with well-established protocols, sockets allow you to develop your own modes of communication.

Sockets, as a programming interface, were originally developed at the University of California at Berkeley as a tool to easily accomplish network programming. Originally part of UNIX operating systems, the concept of sockets has been incorporated into a wide variety of operating environments, including Java.

WHAT IS A SOCKET?

A *socket* is a handle to a communications link over the network with another application. A TCP socket uses the TCP protocol, inheriting the behavior of that transport protocol. Four pieces of information are needed to create a TCP socket:

- The local system's IP address
- The TCP port number the local application is using
- The remote system's IP address
- The TCP port number to which the remote application is responding

The original TCP specification, RFC 793, used the term socket to mean the combination of a system's IP address and port number. A pair of sockets identified a unique end-to-end TCP connection. In this discussion, the term socket is used at a higher level, and a socket is your interface to a single network connection.

Sockets are often used in client/server applications. A centralized service waits for various remote machines to request specific resources, handling each request as it arrives. For clients to know how to communicate with the server, standard application protocols are assigned well-known ports. On UNIX operating systems, ports below 1,024 can only be bound by applications with super-user (for example, root) privileges; thus, for control, these well-known ports lie within this range by convention. Some well-known ports are shown in Table 23.1.

TABLE 23.1 WELL-KNOWN TCP PORTS AND SERVICES

Port	Service
7	Echo Server
21	FTP
23	Telnet

Table 23.1 Continued

Port	Service
25	SMTP (Standard Mail Transfer Protocol)
79	Finger
80	HTTP

For many application protocols, you can merely use the Telnet application to connect to the service port and then manually emulate a client. This might help you understand how client/server communications work.

Client applications must also obtain, or bind, a port to establish a socket connection. Because the client initiates the communication with the server, such a port number could conveniently be assigned at runtime. Client applications are usually run by normal, unprivileged users on UNIX systems, and thus these ports are allocated from the range above 1,024. This convention has held when migrated to other operating systems, and client applications are generally given a dynamically allocated or ephemeral port above 1,024.

Because no two applications can bind the same port on the same machine simultaneously, a socket uniquely identifies a communications link. Realize that a server can respond to two clients on the same port, because the clients will be on different systems and/or different ports; the uniqueness of the link's characteristics are preserved. Figure 23.3 illustrates this concept.

Figure 23.3 shows a server application responding to three sockets through port 80, the well-known port for HTTP. Two sockets are communicating with the same remote machine, although the third is to a separate system. Note the unique combination of the four TCP socket characteristics.

Figure 23.3 also shows a simplified view of a client-server connection. Many machines are configured with multiple IP interfaces—they have more than one IP address. These distinct IP addresses allow for separate connections to be maintained. Thus, a server might have an application accept connections on port 80 for one IP address while a different application handles connections to port 80 for another IP address. These connections are distinct. The Java socket classes, described within the next section, "Java TCP Socket Classes," allow you to select a specific local interface for the connection.

Java has a number of classes that allow you to create socket-based network applications. The two classes you use include `java.net.Socket` and `java.net.ServerSocket`. The `Socket` class acts as one-side in machine-to-machine connection. There is a socket on each side of the connection. The `ServerSocket` class waits for connections from client `Socket's` and then communicates to that `Socket` using a different client `Socket`. That's the second socket in a machine-to-machine communication. Don't worry if you are still confused. It will become more apparent shortly.

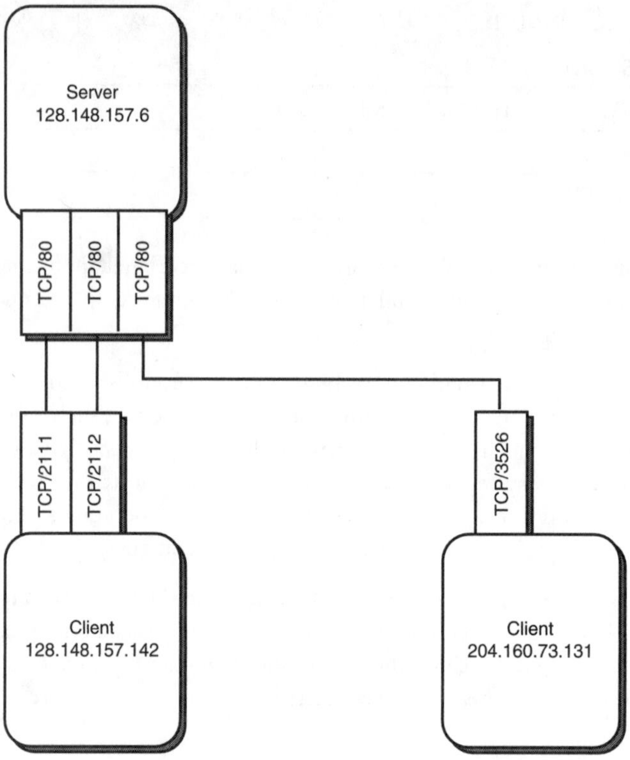

Figure 23.3
Many clients can connect to a single server through separate sockets.

CLIENT SOCKETS

As stated previously, the `Socket` class is used for normal two-way socket communications. The actual work of the `Socket` class is performed by an instance of the `SocketImpl` class. By changing the implementation class for the `Socket`, an application can change the behavior of the underlying communication. This might be necessary for an application that needs to communicate through a company firewall.

There are several constructors for the `Socket` class. They differ in the number and type of parameters each one takes. There's also one that takes a `SocketImpl` as a parameter to use a user-defined implementation rather than the default behavior. To get started, take a look at an example.

The `Socket` class has methods that allow you to read and write through the socket `getInputStream` and `getOutputStream` methods. To make applications simpler to design, the streams these methods return are usually decorated by another `java.io` object, such as `BufferedReader` or `PrintWriter`, respectively. Both `getInputStream` and `getOutputStream` throw an `IOException`, which should be caught. Here's an example that uses the `Socket` class. Listing 23.1 shows a client program that connects to an echo server running somewhere on the Internet. An echo server is a program that after a client is connected, just sends back exactly the text that is sent to it. Echo servers usually listen on port 7.

Note

You might have to find a different host to run this example if the one listing in the source no longer supports an echo server. You can find some by searching on the Internet, or just try some well-known sites. Usually, most educational institutions have an echo server running. You can change the host for this example by modifying the static final variables listed at the top of the source code.

Listing 23.1 Source Code for EchoClientExample.java

```
import java.net.*;
import java.io.*;

public class EchoClientExample
{
  public static final String HOST = "www.gatech.edu";
  public static final int PORT = 7;

  // Default Constructor
  public EchoClientExample()
  {
    super();
  }

  public void testEcho()
  {
    try
    {
      // Get connected to an echo server somewhere, they are usually on
      // port 7 of a well known server
      Socket socket = new Socket( HOST, PORT );
      // Create a reader and stream for reading the data from the echo server
      BufferedReader input = new BufferedReader( new
InputStreamReader(socket.getInputStream()));
      // Create a writer and stream for writing to the echo server
      PrintWriter output = new PrintWriter( socket.getOutputStream(), true);
      // Send some text to the echo server
      System.out.println( "Sending Hello to the echo server" );
      output.println( "Hello" );
      // Get the message from the echo server
      System.out.println( input.readLine() + " from the echo server" );
      // Close the socket
      socket.close();
    }
    catch(UnknownHostException ex)
    {
      System.err.println("Unknown host: " + ex);
      System.exit(1);
    }
    catch(IOException excpt)
    {
      System.err.println("Failed I/O: " + excpt);
      System.exit(1);
    }
  }
```

LISTING 23.1 CONTINUED

```
  public static void main(String[] args)
  {
    EchoClientExample example = new EchoClientExample();
    example.testEcho();
  }
}
```

Listing 23.2 shows the output generated from the `EchoClientExample` program.

LISTING 23.2 OUTPUT FOR `EchoClientExample.java`

```
C:\jdk1.3se_book\classes>java EchoClientExample
Sending Hello to the echo server
Hello from the echo server
C:\jdk1.3se_book\classes>
```

If you are trying to connect using a socket and are having trouble, see "Can't Connect to a Socket" in the "Troubleshooting" section at the end of this chapter.

Remember to close the `Socket` class when you are finished using it. You will also want to close any input or output streams that you have opened to use with the `Socket`.

SERVER SOCKETS

There's nothing special about the program in Listing 23.1. Using the `Socket` class is just that easy. The `Socket` class is really only half of it. What if you wanted to support an echo server on your site? An echo server, as its name implies, is a server program. The `Socket` class is used by clients, whereas the `ServerSocket` is to be used for TCP server programs.

The basic function of a `ServerSocket` is to listen and wait for a client `Socket` to establish a connection and then create a separate `Socket` instance on the server side to handle the connection with the client. After the `ServerSocket` handles the hand shaking with the client and a connection is established, the `ServerSocket` goes back to listening for other clients to connect.

As mentioned before, the actual work of both the `Socket` and the `ServerSocket` classes is performed by a class called `SocketImpl` and its subclasses. The `SocketImpl` class is abstract and is provided by a vendor. By default, you use the standard Sun implementation of the `SocketImpl` class. You can however change out the `SocketImpl` implementation, which acts as a socket factory, to tunnel or go through a local firewall for example. In most cases, you'll want to stick with the default implementation.

`ServerSocket` has three constructors:

```
public ServerSocket(int port) throws IOException;

public ServerSocket(int port, int backlog) throws IOException;

public ServerSocket(int port, int backlog, InetAddress localAddr) throws
IOException;
```

The first constructor creates a listening socket at the port specified, allowing for the default number of 50 clients waiting in the connection queue. The second constructor enables you to change the length of the connection queue, allowing greater or fewer clients to wait to be processed by the server. In either case, if the number of clients requesting a connection exceeds the queue size, the connection will be refused.

The final constructor allows you to specify a local interface to listen for connections. This is in case your machine has multiple IP addresses, this constructor allows you to provide services to specific IP addresses. Should you use the first two constructors on such a machine, the `ServerSocket` will accept connections to any of the machine's IP addresses.

Note

If you specify a port value of 0 in any three of the constructors, a `Socket` is created on any free port that the server selects.

Remember to close the `Socket` class when you are finished using it. You will also want to close any input or output streams that you have opened.

After creating a `ServerSocket`, the `accept` method can be used to wait for a client to connect. The `accept` method blocks until a client connects, and then returns a `Socket` instance for communicating to the client. *Blocking* is a programming term that means a routine enters an internal loop indefinitely, returning only when a specific condition occurs. The condition in the case of the `accept` method is that a client attempts to make a connection. When a client requests a connection to the server program, the `accept` method will unblock and continue executing the program.

The application in Listing 23.3 creates a `ServerSocket` at port 7, waits for client connections, and then opens streams through which communication can take place after a client connects. The server will just echo any text that is sent to it. This example is simplistic, but this is basically what an echo server does.

LISTING 23.3 SOURCE CODE FOR `EchoServer.java`

```
import java.net.*;
import java.io.*;

public class EchoServer
{
  public static final int PORT = 7;

  // Default Constructor
  public EchoServer()
  {
    super();
  }

  public void startEcho()
  {
    try
    {
```

LISTING 23.3 CONTINUED

```
      // Create a Server Socket on the
      ServerSocket server = new ServerSocket( PORT );
      // Wait for a single client to connect
      System.out.println( "Waiting on a client to connect" );
      Socket clientSocket = server.accept();

      System.out.println(
         "Client requested a connection to the echo server" );
      BufferedReader input =
        new BufferedReader(
           new InputStreamReader( clientSocket.getInputStream() ));

      PrintWriter output =
          new PrintWriter( clientSocket.getOutputStream(), true);

      // Get the data from the client
      String msg = input.readLine();
      System.out.println( "Client sent " + msg );

      // Send the data back to the client
      output.println( msg );

      System.out.println( "echo server exiting..." );
      clientSocket.close();
    }
    catch( IOException ex )
    {
      System.err.println( "Failed I/O: " + ex );
      System.exit( 1 );
    }
  }

  public static void main(String[] args)
  {
    EchoServer echoServer = new EchoServer();
    echoServer.startEcho();
  }
}
```

You can use the `EchoClientExample` from Listing 23.1 to test this `EchoServer` example. You will just need to change the `HOST` value at the top of the `EchoClientExample` source code. You can change it to `localhost`, which is your machine where the `EchoServer` program should be listening.

The example in Listing 23.2 only handles a single client and exits after the client sends some initial data, but you can add some looping and change the manner in which the server program handles the client to almost make this a full-fledged echo server program. To handle the client `Socket` properly, you would probably want to create a `ClientHandler` class that extends `Thread` and just echoes back everything the client sends until the client exists. This would be very easy to write.

Note

The socket classes in the Java API provide a convenient stream interface by using your host's TCP implementation. Within the SDK, a subclass of the abstract class `SocketImpl` performs the interaction with your machine's TCP. It is possible to define a new `SocketImpl` that could use a different transport layer than plain TCP. You can change this transport layer implementation by creating your own subclass of `SocketImpl` and defining your own `SocketImplFactory`. However, in this chapter, it is assumed that you are using the SDK socket implementation, which uses TCP.

COMPRESSING DATA WHEN USING SOCKETS

By default, the data that is sent through or over a socket is just raw data. You send the data by acquiring either the input or output stream on the socket and using it or wrapping it in another type of stream such as a `BufferedReader` or `PrinterWriter`.

The term *network traffic* represents all the data that is being sent over the network. Some of this data is used for control, such as verifying that a host is alive. Most of the data is just application data that is being used by all the network applications that are communicating with each other. The amount of network traffic is always a concern for network administrators and also programmers trying to do performance tuning on an application.

Unfortunately, the core Java language provides no behavior to compresses the data. However, you can use your own algorithm or a third-party algorithm to compress your application data before sending through one of the output streams and then uncompress it on the other side. This is not needed for small amounts of data, but if your application is sending large amounts of information back and forth between components, you might consider it.

SENDING OBJECTS ACROSS THE NETWORK USING SOCKETS

You saw earlier how easy it is to create a client `Socket` and a `ServerSocket` and then send data between the two using sockets. What about sending objects between the two using sockets? Can it be done? Fortunately, it can, and it's almost as easy as sending primitive data. There is one thing that hasn't been discussed yet and that's an application rotocol.

An *application protocol* is the understood messaging structure that goes on between the client and server sides. From the server side standpoint, the client can send all the data that it wants, but unless the server knows what to do with it ahead of time, the act is pretty much meaningless. There has to be an agreed upon structure in the communication. This is not referring to the underlying communication protocol, but a syntax protocol between the client and server. For example, suppose you have an application that allows two clients to connect to a server and play a game of Tic Tac Toe against each other. Someone needs to go first, both sides need to know which one is going to go first, and then each side has to understand when it's their turn. The server and client need to agree on the message that each one will send to convey certain pieces of information. Consider when a client sends a move to the server. The server needs to be able to determine which move the client made or the entire game will not function correctly and no one will want to play it. That's the level of communication that the server and client sides need.

Take a look at how you might communicate for the game Tic Tac Toe. The entire game isn't built in this example, instead you'll see a small section of the game: sending a move to the server. First, look at the information that needs to be sent to the server to indicate the client's move. Following is the board that will be used. The numbers along the side and top indicate the row and column, respectively.

Row/Column

_0_|_1_|_2_

_1_|___|___

2 | |

Here's the information that the client will send to the server to indicate the client's next move:

```
clientId: int - Just an id representing this client
row: int - Which row this move is selecting
column: - Which column this move is selecting
```

You can look at the board differently and come up with a different application protocol. Look at this board design to see the difference:

_0_|_1_|_2_

_3_|_4_|_5_

6 | 7 | 8

This difference in the two boards indicates a difference in application design and also in the application protocol that was mentioned earlier. There are many different ways an application protocol can be designed. You must use good object-oriented analysis and design in selecting which one is best suited for the particular application.

For the example here, the second of the two boards is used. You might have a class that represents the board, `TicTacToeBoard`. Listing 23.4 shows what the class might look like.

LISTING 23.4 `TicTacToeBoard.java`

```
public class TicTacToeBoard
{
  private String[] board = new String[9];

  public TicTacToeBoard()
  {
    super();
```

LISTING 23.4 CONTINUED

```
  }

  public boolean isWinning()
  {
    // The algorithm here to see if any combination is a winner
  }

  public TicTacToeMoveResult addNewMove( TicTacToeMove nextMove )
  {
    // validate the move for the client and return a result
  }
}
```


This is a simple representation of what the board class might actually need to be, but it's a good start. You can use the following information to indicate the client's next move:

```
clientId: int - Just an id representing this client
index: int - The index into the String array
```

You need to design an object that represents the client's next move. You might be wondering why an object is needed when the information about the next move is only a few pieces of data. In some cases, that might be the correct thinking, but you must also consider whether there might be any other pieces of information sent later. This is where an understanding of the application and analysis and design techniques comes into play. For now, let's assume that you have decided to use an object to represent the move. Listing 23.5 shows what the object might look like.

LISTING 23.5 TicTacToeMove.java

```
public class TicTacToeMove implements java.io.Serializable
{
  String playerId = null;
  int index;

  public TicTacToeMove( String id, int moveIndex )
  {
    super();
    playerId = id;
    index = moveIndex;
  }

  public String getPlayerId()
  {
    return playerId;
  }

  public int getIndex()
  {
    return index;
  }
}
```

Objects that are going to be *marshaled* (sent) across the network must implement java.io.Serializable interface. Refer to chapter 22, "Object Serialization," for a complete description of Object Serialization.

So now that you have identified the object that the client will send to indicate its move, what happens if the client sends an invalid move? Suppose the opponent is already positioned in the square that the client requested in the move. The server, which is also acting as the umpire, must inform the client to select a different move. The server could return a String telling the client that it's invalid. But where would you keep the list of valid Strings that can be returned for a particular situation? The problem with this approach is that you end up with a bunch of so-called magic values all over the code that really don't have any meaning to the problem you are trying to solve. This is why an application protocol is very important. You must decide ahead of time what messages and information the client and the server will send back and forth in all the possible scenarios.

Ideally, what you need every TicTacToeMove object that is sent to the server to return a TicTacToeMoveResult object. Listing 23.6 shows what the board class might look like.

LISTING 23.6 TicTacToeBoard.java

```
public class TicTacToeMoveResult
{
  TicTacToeBoard board = null;
  boolean validMove;
  boolean winningMove;

  // Default Constructor
  public TicTacToeMoveResult()
  {
    super();
  }

  public TicTacToeBoard getBoard()
  {
    return board;
  }

  public boolean wasValidMove()
  {
    return validMove;
  }

  public boolean wasWinningMove()
  {
    return winningMove;
  }
}
```

Notice that an instance called TicTacToeBoard is referenced in the TicTacToeMoveResult class. Every time a client sends a move, the client would be expecting an instance of this class to see what the latest board looks like. That establishes a protocol. The protocol is to make a move, get a move result object back. This way the client can figure out if your move was valid and a winning move. Obviously the opponent would also have to get some type of notice of the client's move. This object could be modified slightly to accommodate both clients.

Obviously, plenty of details have been omitted about building a complete game here, but the idea is still valid. You can't have a client and server start sending data back and forth and expect each side to know exactly what to do with it or even really what sort of data to expect. This is where the protocol is absolutely necessary. Spending the time up front during design will pay off big during the construction phase.

Sending Objects Using Sockets

In chapter 22, you learned about object serialization. In that chapter, you saw how you could serialize objects to streams and then de-serialize the objects later. What if you wanted to send complete objects over the network, rather than just primitive data or strings? This can be done using the `Socket` classes already covered and the `ObjectInputStream` and `ObjectOutputStream` classes as shown in the following example. The following example which is contained in Listing 23.7 and 23.8 is similar to the echo server that was shown in the previous example; except this echo server takes an object that both the client and the server are familiar with. The client sends an `EchoObject` (see Listing 23.9) and the server prints out some information from that object.

Note

The object that is being sent across the network must implement the `java.io.Serializable` interface, as discussed in Chapter 22.

Listing 23.7 Source Code for EchoObjectServer.java

```
import java.net.*;
import java.io.*;

public class EchoObjectServer
{
  public static final int PORT = 7;

  // Default Constructor
  public EchoObjectServer()
  {
    super();
  }

  public void startEcho()
  {
    Socket clientSocket = null;

    try
    {
      // Create a Server Socket on the
      ServerSocket server = new ServerSocket( PORT );
      // Wait for a single client to connect
```

LISTING 23.7 CONTINUED

```
      System.out.println( "Waiting on a client to connect" );
       clientSocket = server.accept();

      System.out.println(
         "Client requested a connection to the echo object server" );

      ObjectInputStream input =
          new ObjectInputStream( clientSocket.getInputStream() );

      PrintWriter output =
          new PrintWriter( clientSocket.getOutputStream(), true);

      output.println( "Echo Object Server received an echo object" );

      Object obj = input.readObject();
      if ( obj instanceof EchoObject )
      {
        EchoObject echoObj = (EchoObject)obj;
        StringBuffer buf = new StringBuffer( "Client Name: " );
        buf.append( echoObj.getClientName() );
        buf.append( " sent msg: " );
        buf.append( echoObj.getMsg() );

        System.out.println( buf.toString() );
      }
      else
      {
        System.out.println( "Unknown data sent" );
      }

      System.out.println( "echo server exiting..." );

      clientSocket.close();
    }
    catch( ClassNotFoundException ex )
    {
      System.out.println( "Unknown object type sent" );
      System.exit( -1 );
    }
    catch( IOException ex )
    {
      System.err.println( "Failed I/O: " + ex );
      System.exit( -1 );
    }

  }

  public static void main(String[] args)
  {
    EchoObjectServer echoServer = new EchoObjectServer();
    echoServer.startEcho();
  }
}
```

LISTING 23.8 SOURCE CODE FOR EchoObjectClient.java

```
import java.net.*;
import java.io.*;

public class EchoObjectClient
{
  public static final String HOST = "localhost";
  public static final int PORT = 7;

  // Default Constructor
  public EchoObjectClient()
  {
    super();
  }

  public void testEcho()
  {
    try
    {
      // Get connected to an echo server somewhere, they are usually on
      // port 7 of a well known server
      Socket socket = new Socket( HOST, PORT );

      // Create a reader and stream for reading the data from the echo server
      BufferedReader input =
           new BufferedReader(
                    new InputStreamReader(socket.getInputStream()));

      // Create a writer and stream for writing to the echo server
      ObjectOutputStream output =
        new ObjectOutputStream( socket.getOutputStream() );

      // Send some text to the echo server
      EchoObject obj = new EchoObject( "CLIENT 1", "Hello there server" );

      output.writeObject( obj );
      // Get the message from the echo server

      System.out.println(
           input.readLine() + " from the echo object server" );

      // Close the socket
      socket.close();
    }
    catch(UnknownHostException ex)
    {
      System.err.println("Unknown host: " + ex);
      System.exit(1);
    }
    catch(IOException excpt)
    {
      System.err.println("Failed I/O: " + excpt);
      System.exit(1);
    }
  }
```

LISTING 23.8 CONTINUED

```
  public static void main(String[] args)
  {
    EchoObjectClient example = new EchoObjectClient();
    example.testEcho();
  }
}
```

LISTING 23.9 SOURCE CODE FOR EchoObject.java

```
public class EchoObject implements java.io.Serializable
{
  private String clientName = null;
  private String msg = null;

  // Default Constructor
  public EchoObject( String client, String data )
  {
    super();
    clientName = client;
    msg = data;
  }

  // Public Accessor for Client Name
  public String getClientName()
  {
    return clientName;
  }
  // Public Accessor for Msg
  public String getMsg()
  {
    return msg;
  }
}
```

Listing 23.10 shows the output from the `EchoObjectServer` program that received an `EchoObject` from the client.

LISTING 23.10 OUTPUT FROM EchoObjectServer

```
C:\jdk1.3se_book\classes>java EchoObjectServer
Waiting on a client to connect
Client requested a connection to the echo object server
Echo Object Server received an echo object
Client Name: CLIENT 1 sent msg: Hello there server
echo server exiting...

C:\jdk1.3se_book\classes>
```

OBTAINING HOSTNAME AND IP ADDRESS INFORMATION

Often when dealing with network applications, it's necessary to figure out the IP address of some remote host. The `InetAddress` class represents an Internet Protocol (IP) address.

The `InetAddress` class contains an Internet host address. Internet hosts are identified one of two ways:

- Name
- Address

We have already discussed how a name is associated with an IP address back in the section "TCP/IP Architecture."

As a refresher, when you make a connection to `www.javasoft.com`, your system needs to find out the numeric address for JavaSoft. It will use a service called Domain Name Service, or DNS.

You might have noticed that Internet host names are usually a number of names that are separated by periods. These separate names represent the domain a host belongs to. `netcom5.netcom.com`, for example, is the host name for a machine named `netcom5` in the `netcom.com` domain. The `netcom.com` domain is a subdomain of the `.com` domain. A `netcom.edu` domain could be completely separate from the `netcom.com` domain, and `netcom5.netcom.edu` would be a totally different host. Again, this is not too different from phone numbers. The phone number 404-555-1017 has an area code of 404, for example, which could be considered the Atlanta domain. The exchange 555 is a subdomain of the Atlanta domain, and 1017 is a specific number in the 555 domain, which is part of the Atlanta domain. Just as you can have a `netcom5.netcom.edu` that is different from `netcom5.netcom.com`, you can have an identical phone number in a different area code, such as 212–555–1017.

The important point to remember here is that host names are only unique within a particular domain. Don't think that your organization is the only one in the world to have named its machines after The Three Stooges, *Star Trek* characters, or characters from various comic strips.

There are no constructors for the `InetAddress` class. If you need a new instance, you have to use one of the static methods on the class. The three ways to get an instance of the class from the `InetAddress` class itself are

```
static InetAddress getByName(String host)

static InetAddress[] getAllByName(String host)

static InetAddress getLocalHost()
```

The `getByName` method determines the IP address of a host using the host's name. The `getAllByName` method returns an array of `InetAddresses` if the host has multiple ones. One reason that the host might have multiple IPs is if there are multiple network cards on the host machine. The final method creates an instance of the `InetAddress` class for the `localhost`, which is the machine that the method is executed on. Listing 23.11 shows an example using all three methods.

LISTING 23.11 SOURCE CODE FOR `InetAddressExample.java`

```
import java.net.*;

public class InetAddressExample
{
  // Default Constructor
  public InetAddressExample()
  {
    super();
  }

  public void doExample()
  {
    try
    {
      // Use the getByName method
      System.out.print( "Using getByName(): " );
      System.out.println( InetAddress.getByName( "www.sun.com" ) );

      // Use the getAllByName method
      // This host is used because it has several IPs for this hostname
      System.out.println( "Using getAllByName()" );
      InetAddress[] addresses = InetAddress.getAllByName( "www.microsoft.com" );
      int size = addresses.length;
      for( int i = 0; i < size; i++ )
      {
        System.out.println( addresses[i] );
      }

      // Use the get LocalHost method
      System.out.print( "Using getLocalHost(): " );
      System.out.println( InetAddress.getLocalHost() );
    }
    catch( UnknownHostException ex )
    {
      ex.printStackTrace();
    }
  }

  public static void main(String[] args)
  {
    InetAddressExample example = new InetAddressExample();
    example.doExample();
  }
}
```

Listing 23.12 shows the output from Listing 23.11.

Listing 23.12 Output from the InetAddressExample

```
C:\jdk1.3se_book\classes>java InetAddressExample
Using getByName(): www.sun.com/192.18.97.195
Using getAllByName()
www.microsoft.com/207.46.230.219
www.microsoft.com/207.46.130.14
www.microsoft.com/207.46.130.149
www.microsoft.com/207.46.131.137
www.microsoft.com/207.46.230.218
Using getLocalHost(): ccavane01/24.92.158.120

C:\jdk1.3se_book\classes>
```


You've seen how you can get an instance of the `InetAddress` class using the static methods on the class itself, but there other ways as well. On the `Socket` and `ServerSocket` classes, there are several methods that return an instance of the `InetAddress` class. Both the `Socket` and `ServerSocket` classes have a method called `getInetAddress`. This method on the `ServerSocket` class returns an address that represents the local address of the `ServerSocket`. The method on the `Socket` class returns the address that the `Socket` is connected to. As mentioned previously in this chapter, the `InetAddress` is a parameter to several of the constructors in both classes.

User Datagram Protocol (UDP)

For many Internet developers, UDP (User Datagram Protocol) is used much less often than TCP. UDP does not isolate you as neatly from the details of implementing a continuous network communication. For many Java applications, however, choosing UDP as the tool to create a network linkage might be the most prudent option.

Programming with UDP has significant ramifications. Understanding these factors will guide and educate your network programming efforts.

UDP is a good choice for applications in which communications can be separated into discrete messages, where a single query from a client might invoke a single response from a server. Time-dependent data is particularly suited to UDP. UDP requires much less overhead, but the burden of engineering any necessary reliability into the system is your responsibility. For instance, if clients never receive responses to their queries, it's perfectly possible and legitimate with UDP; you might want to program the clients to retransmit the request or perhaps display an informative message indicating communication difficulties.

UDP Socket Characteristics

UDP behaves very differently than TCP. UDP is described as unreliable, connectionless, and message-oriented. A common analogy that explains UDP is that of communicating with postcards.

A dialogue with UDP must be translated into small messages that fit within a small packet of a specific size, although some packets can hold more data than others. When you send out a message, you can never be certain that you will receive a return message. Unless you do receive a return message, you have no idea if your message was received. Your message could have been lost en route, the recipient's confirmation could have been lost, or the recipient might be ignoring your message.

The postcards you will be exchanging between network programs are referred to as *datagrams*. Within a datagram, you can store an array of bytes. A receiving application can extract this array and decode your message, possibly sending a return datagram response.

As with TCP, you program in UDP using the socket programming abstraction. However, UDP sockets are very different from TCP sockets. Extending the postcard analogy, UDP sockets are much like creating a mailbox.

A mailbox is identified by your address, but you don't construct a new one for each person to whom you will be sending a message. (However, you might create a new mailbox to receive newspapers, which shouldn't go into your normal mailbox.) Instead, you place an address on the postcard that indicates to whom the message is being sent. You place the postcard in the mailbox, and it is (eventually) sent on its way.

When receiving a message, you could potentially wait forever until one arrives in your mailbox. After one arrives, you can read the postcard. Meta-information appears on the postcard that identifies the sender through the return address.

With UDP, you can also address a datagram to a subnet instead of a specific machine on the network. This will cause the datagram to be sent to everyone on the subnet. This might be an easy to send a broadcast message that a server is going down.

As the previous analogies suggest, UDP programming involves the following general tasks:

- Creating an appropriately addressed datagram to send
- Setting up a socket to send and receive datagrams for a particular application
- Inserting datagrams into a socket for transmission
- Waiting to receive datagrams from a socket
- Decoding a datagram to extract the message, its recipient, and other meta-information

JAVA UDP CLASSES

The `java.net` package has the tools that are necessary to perform UDP communications. For sending and/or receiving datagrams, Java provides the `DatagramPacket` class.

To create a datagram to send to a remote system, there are two constructors that can be used:

```
DatagramPacket(byte[] buf, int length, InetAddress addr, int port);

DatagramPacket(byte[] buf, int offset, int length, InetAddress address, int port);
```

The `buf` argument is an array of bytes that encodes the data of the message, while `length` is the length of the byte array to place into the datagram. This factor determines the size of the datagram. The `address` argument is an `InetAddress` object, which stores the IP address of the intended recipient. The port argument identifies which `port` the datagram should be sent to on the receiving host.

To receive a datagram, you must use another one of two of the other `DatagramPacket` constructors in which the incoming data will be stored. The two constructors are


```
DatagramPacket(byte[] buf, int offset, int length);
```

```
DatagramPacket(byte[] buf, int length);
```

The `buf` argument is the byte array into which the data portion of the datagram will be copied. The `length` argument is the number of bytes to copy from the datagram into the array corresponding to the size of the datagram. If `length` is less than the size of the UDP datagram received by the machine, the extra bytes will be silently ignored by Java.

Programming with TCP sockets relieves you from breaking your data down into discrete chunks for transmission over a network. When creating a UDP-based client/server protocol, you must specify some expected length of the datagrams or create a means for determining this at runtime.

According to the TCP/IP specification, the largest datagram possible contains 65,507 bytes of data. However, a host is only required to receive datagrams with up to 548 bytes of data. Most platforms support larger datagrams of at least 8,192 bytes in length.

Large datagrams are likely to be fragmented at the IP layer. If, during transmission, any one of the IP packets that contains a fragment of the datagram is lost, the entire UDP datagram will be silently lost.

Note

You must design your application with the datagram size in mind. It is prudent to limit this size to a reasonable length. The actual length will vary according to the platform, network bandwidth available, and your particular application.

After a datagram has been received, you can read that data. Other methods allow you to obtain meta-information regarding the message:

```
public int getLength();
public byte[] getData();
public InetAddress getAddress();
public int getPort();
```

The `getLength` method is used to obtain the number of bytes contained within the data portion of the datagram. The `getData` method is used to obtain a byte array containing the data received. `getAddress` provides an `InetAddress` object identifying the sender, whereas `getPort` indicates the UDP port used.

Performing the sending and receiving of these datagrams is accomplished with the `DatagramSocket` class, which creates a UDP socket. Three constructors are available:

```
public DatagramSocket() throws IOException;
public DatagramSocket(int port) throws IOException;
public DatagramSocket(int port, InetAddress localAddr) throws IOException;
```

The first constructor allows you to create a socket at an unused ephemeral port, generally used for client applications. The second constructor allows you to specify a particular port, which is useful for server applications. As with TCP, most systems require super-user privileges to bind UDP ports below 1024. The final constructor is useful for machines with multiple IP interfaces. You can use this constructor to send and listen for datagrams from one of the IP addresses assigned to the machine. On such a host, datagrams sent to any of the machine's IP addresses are received by a `DatagramSocket` created with the first two constructors, whereas the last constructor obtains only datagrams sent to the specific IP address.

Just as regular sockets rely on the `SocketImpl` class for the implementation of the socket behavior, the `DatagramSocket` class relies on the `DatagramSocketImplFactory` class for its implementation.

You can use this socket to send properly addressed `DatagramPacket` instances created with the first constructor described by using this `DatagramSocket` method:

```
public void send(DatagramPacket p) throws IOException;
```

After a `DatagramPacket` has been created with the second constructor described, a datagram can be received:

```
public synchronized void receive(DatagramPacket p) throws IOException;
```

Note that the `receive` method blocks until a datagram is received. Because UDP is unreliable, your application cannot expect `receive` ever to return unless a timeout is enabled. Such a timeout, named the `SO_TIMEOUT` option from the name of the Berkeley sockets API option, can be set with this method from the `DatagramSocket` class:

```
public synchronized void setSoTimeout(int timeout) throws SocketException;
```

The `timeout` argument is a value in milliseconds. If set to 0, the `receive` method exhibits an infinite timeout—the default behavior. When greater than 0, a subsequent `receive` method invocation waits only the specified timeout before an `InterruptedIOException` is thrown.

Your host's UDP implementation has a limited queue for incoming datagrams. If your application cannot process these datagrams rapidly enough, they are silently discarded. Neither the sender nor the receiver is notified when datagrams are dropped from a queue overflow. Such is the unreliable nature of UDP.

After communications through the UDP socket are completed, that socket should be closed:

```
public synchronized void close();
```

A Datagram Example

In this section, you learn how to create a basic UDP client and server that broadcasts and received messages to one another. The idea here a simple tool that where network users can send messages out to everyone on the network or to specific users. However, for this example you are just going to start up a client program and then send messages to the client program from a server program. The reason for this is you don't want to send messages out to the entire Internet. Remember that it was said earlier that if you send a message to a subnet, then everyone might possibly receive that message. You don't want that to happen. Of course if they don't have the client program, it wouldn't happen anyway. You do have to be careful of this sort of accident when dealing with network applications.

The `BroadcasterClient` application in Listing 23.13 starts up and listens for UDP messages on a certain port. When it receives a message, it prints out who sent it and what the message is.

Listing 23.13 shows the Java code used to implement the BroadcasterClient.

Listing 23.13 Source Code for `BroadcasterClient.java`

```
import java.io.*;
import java.net.*;
import java.util.*;
import java.text.*;

public class BroadcasterClient extends Thread
{
  // Set a default listener port
  private int listenerPort = 59;
  private DatagramSocket listenerSocket = null;
  private static int MAX_PACKET_SIZE = 1000;

  // Default Constructor
  public BroadcasterClient()
  {
    super();
  }

  // Alternate Constructor to Override Port
  public BroadcasterClient( int newPort )
  {
    // overide port setting
    listenerPort = newPort;
  }

  public void run()
  {
    byte[] buffer = new byte[ MAX_PACKET_SIZE ];
    // Create a packet to hold the data when it arrives

    DatagramPacket infoPacket =
        new DatagramPacket( buffer, MAX_PACKET_SIZE );
```

LISTING 23.13 CONTINUED

```
    try
    {
      listenerSocket = new DatagramSocket( this.listenerPort );
    }
    catch( Exception ex )
    {
      System.out.println(
           "Problem creating socket on port: " + listenerPort );
      System.exit( -1 );
    }

    // do an infinite loop
    while( true )
    {
      try
      {
        System.out.println( "Waiting on broadcasts..." );
        // Setting this value to 0 causes it to be an infinite timeout
        listenerSocket.setSoTimeout( 0 );
        listenerSocket.receive( infoPacket );

        // What address sent the packet
        InetAddress fromAddress = infoPacket.getAddress();
        // Get the message within the packet
        byte[] msg = infoPacket.getData();

        System.out.println( "Received broadbast from " + fromAddress );
        System.out.println( new String(msg) );
      }
      catch( IOException ex )
      {
        // Print the exception and try to keep going
        ex.printStackTrace();
      }
    }
  }

  public static void main( String[] args )
  {
    BroadcasterClient client = null;
    int argLength = args.length;
    // Make sure the correct number of args were passed
    if ( argLength > 1 )
    {
      System.out.println( "Usage: java BroadcasterClient <port>" );
      System.exit( 0 );
    }

    if ( argLength == 0 )
      client = new BroadcasterClient();

    if ( argLength == 1 )
    {
      int port = 0;
```

Listing 23.13 Continued

```
      String arg = args[0];
      try
      {
        port = Integer.parseInt( arg );
      }
      catch( Exception ex )
      {
        System.out.println(
          "Invalid port specified on the command line:arg" );
        System.exit( -1 );
      }

      client = new BroadcasterClient( port );
    }

    // Listen for messages
    client.start();
}
```


One thing to notice in Listing 23.13 is the use of the `setSoTimeout` method. This causes the `BroadcasterClient` to wait infinitely and not timeout while waiting for a broadcast message.

Starting the `BroadcasterClient` Application

The `BroadcasterClient` class uses a default port in which to listen for UDP messages on. You can use this default or pass in another port if the default port is in use by another application. For running our example, the default port should be fine.

The `BroadcasterClient` will sit and listen for broadcasts indefinitely. You'll notice an infinite loop in the `run` method in Listing 23.13. To stop the `BroadcasterClient` application, you'll need to press Ctrl+C. When a broadcast message is received, it is printed out and then the application goes back to listening for more.

Now you will need the application that initiates the broadcasts. Listing 23.14 shows the `BroadcasterServer` class. This class sends a message in the form of a `DatagramPacket`. Once the message is broadcasted out, the `BroadcasterServer` ends. Again, for this example, the messages will only be broadcasted to the localhost.

Listing 23.14 shows the `BroadcasterServer` application.

Listing 23.14 Source Code for `BroadcasterServer.java`

```
import java.io.*;
import java.net.*;
import java.util.*;
import java.text.*;

public class BroadcasterServer
{
  // Set a default listener port
  private int senderPort = 59;
```

LISTING 23.14 CONTINUED

```
// set a 10 second UDP timeout
private static final int TIMEOUT = 10000;
private DatagramSocket senderSocket = null;
private static int MAX_PACKET_SIZE = 255;

// Default Constructor
public BroadcasterServer()
{
  super();
}

// Alternate Constructor to Override Port
public BroadcasterServer( int newPort )
{
  // overide port setting
  senderPort = newPort;
}

public void sendBroadcast( String msg )
{
  // Determine the actual size of the message
  int msgSize = msg.length();

  // Create a byte to hold the message
  byte[] buffer = new byte[ msgSize ];
  buffer = msg.getBytes();

  try
  {
    // For this example, just send it to the local host
    InetAddress addr = InetAddress.getLocalHost();

    // Create the packet of information
    DatagramPacket infoPacket =
      new DatagramPacket( buffer, msgSize, addr, this.senderPort );

    senderSocket = new DatagramSocket();

    // Send the packet and clean up the resources
    senderSocket.send( infoPacket );
    senderSocket.close();
  }
  catch( Exception ex )
  {
    System.out.println( "Problem creating socket on port: " + senderPort );
    System.exit( -1 );
  }
}

public static void main( String[] args )
{
  BroadcasterServer server = null;
  int argLength = args.length;
  // Make sure the correct number of args were passed in
  if ( argLength != 2 )
```

Listing 23.14 Continued

```
    {
      System.out.println( "Usage: java BroadcasterClient <port> <message>" );
      System.exit( 0 );
    }

    int port = 0;

    String arg = args[0];
    String msg = args[1];

    try
    {
      // Try to parse the port string into an int
      port = Integer.parseInt( arg );
    }
    catch( Exception ex )
    {
      System.out.println( "Invalid port specified on the command line:arg" );
      System.exit( -1 );
    }

    server = new BroadcasterServer( port );
    // Broadcast the data out
    server.sendBroadcast( msg );
  }
}
```


Starting `BroadcasterServer`

To broadcast a message to the clients, just start the application and pass in the port number and the message on the command line. Remember, the message will probably have to have double quotes around it when you pass it in on the command line. Here's an example of starting the `BroadcasterServer`:

```
java BroadcasterServer 59 "What time are we going to lunch?"
```

Multicasting

Internet Protocol (IP) is the means by which all information on the Internet is transmitted. UDP datagrams are encapsulated within IP packets to send them to the appropriate machines on the network.

Most uses of IP involve unicasting. *Unicasting* is sending a packet from one host to another. However, IP is not limited to this mode and includes the capability to multicast. With *multicasting*, a message is addressed to a targeted set of hosts. One message is sent, and the entire group can receive it.

Multicasting is particularly suited to high-bandwidth applications, such as sending video and audio over the network, because a separate transmission need not be established (which could saturate the network). Other possible applications include chat sessions, distributed data storage, and online, interactive games. A client searching for an appropriate server on the network can use multicasting. It can send a multicast solicitation, and any listening servers could contact the client to begin a transaction.

To IP multicasting, a certain range of IP addresses is set aside solely for this purpose. These IP addresses are class D addresses, those within the range of 224.0.0.0 and 239.255.255.255. Each of these addresses is referred to as a multicast group. Any machine that has joined that group receives any IP packet addressed to that group. Group membership is dynamic and changes over time. To send a message to a group, a host need not be a member of that group.

When a machine joins a multicast group, it begins accepting messages sent to that IP multicast address. Extending the previous analogy from the "User Datagram Protocol (UDP)" section, joining a group is similar to constructing a new mailbox that accepts messages intended for the group. Each machine that wants to join the group constructs its own mailbox to receive the same message. If a multicast packet is distributed to a network, any machine that is listening for the message has an opportunity to receive it. That is, with IP multicasting, there is no mechanism for restricting which machines on the same network can join the group.

Multicast groups are mapped to hardware addresses on interface cards. Thus, IP multicast datagrams that reach an uninterested host can usually be rapidly discarded by the interface card. However, more than one multicast group maps to a single hardware address, making for imperfect hardware-level filtering. Some filtering must still be performed at the device driver or IP level.

Multicasting has its limitations, however—particularly the task of routing multicast packets throughout the Internet. A special TCP/IP protocol, Internet Group Management Protocol (IGMP), is used to manage memberships in a multicast group. A router that supports multicasting can use IGMP to determine if local machines are subscribed to a particular group; such hosts respond with a report about groups they have joined using IGMP. Based on these communications, a multicast router can determine if it is appropriate to forward on a multicast packet.

Caution

Realize that there is no formal way of reserving a multicast group for your own use. Certain groups are reserved for particular uses, assigned by the Internet Assigned Numbers Authority (IANA).

Other than avoiding a reserved group, there are few rules to choosing a group. The groups from 224.0.0.0 through 224.0.0.225 should never be passed on by a multicast router, restricting communications using them to the local subnet. Try picking an arbitrary address between 224.0.1.27 and 224.0.1.225.

If you happen to choose a group already being used, those other machines will disrupt your communications. Should this occur, quit your application and try another address.

Besides the multicast group, another important facet of a multicast packet is the time-to-live (TTL) parameter. The TTL is used to indicate how many separate networks the sender intends the message to be transmitted over. When a router forwards a packet on, the TTL within the packet is decremented by one. When a TTL reaches zero, the packet is not forwarded further.

Choose a TTL parameter as small as possible. A large TTL value can cause unnecessary bandwidth use throughout the Internet. Furthermore, you are more likely to disrupt other multicast communications in diverse areas that happen to be using the same group.

If your communications should be isolated to machines on the local network, choose a TTL of 1. When communicating with machines that are not on the local network, try to determine how many multicast routers exist along the way and set your TTL to one more than that value.

The *Multicast Backbone*, or MBONE, is an attempt to create a network of Internet routers that are capable of providing multicast services. However, multicasting today is by no means ubiquitous. If all participants reside on the same physical network, routers need not be involved, and multicasting is likely to prove successful. For more distributed communications, you might need to contact your network administrator.

JAVA MULTICASTING

The Java `MulticastSocket` class is the key to using this powerful Internet networking feature. `MulticastSocket` allows you to send or receive UDP datagrams that use multicast IP. To send a datagram, you use the default constructor:

```
public MulticastSocket() throws IOException;
```

Then you must create an appropriately formed `DatagramPacket` addressed to a multicast group between 224.0.0.0 and 239.255.255.255. After it is created, the datagram can be sent with the `send` method, which requires a TTL value. The TTL indicates how many routers the packets should be allowed to go through. Avoid setting the TLL to a high value, which could cause the data to propagate through a large portion of the Internet. Here is an example:

```
int multiPort = 2222;
int ttl = 1;
InetAddress multiAddr = InetAddress.getByName("239.10.10.10");
byte[] multiBytes = new byte[256];
DatagramPacket multiDatagram = new DatagramPacket(multiBytes, multiBytes.length,
multiAddr,multiPort);
MulticastSocket multiSocket = new MulticastSocket();
multiSocket.send(multiDatagram, ttl);
```

To receive datagrams, an application must create a socket at a specific UDP port. Then, it must join the group of recipients. Through the socket, the application can then receive UDP datagrams:

```
MulticastSocket recei7veSocket = new MulticastSocket(multiPort);
receiveSocket.joinGroup(multiAddr);
receiveSocket.receive(multiDatagram);
```

When the `joinGroup` method is invoked, the machine now pays attention to any IP packets transmitted along the network for that particular multicast group. The host should also use IGMP to appropriately report the usage of the group. For machines with multiple IP addresses, the interface through which datagrams should be sent can be configured:

```
receiveSocket.setInterface(oneOfMyLocalAddrs);
```

To leave a multicast group, the `leaveGroup` method is available. A `MulticastSocket` should be closed when communications are done:

```
receiveSocket.leaveGroup(multiAddr);
receiveSocket.close();
```

As is apparent, using the `MulticastSocket` is similar to using the normal UDP socket class `DatagramSocket`. The essential differences are

- The `DatagramPacket` must be addressed to a multicast group.
- The `send` method of the `MulticastSocket` class takes two arguments: a `DatagramPacket` and a TTL value.
- To begin listening for multicast messages after creating the `MulticastSocket` instance, you must use the `joinGroup` method.
- The `receive` method is used just as with the `DatagramSocket` to obtain incoming messages; however, there is no method to set a timeout, such as `setSoTimeout` in `DatagramSocket`.

World Wide Web Overview

There's no sense spending a lot of time explaining that the World Wide Web (WWW) has had exponential growth over past several years. Just about everyone has at least heard about `www.this` or `www.that`. It's really inescapable. It's gone from a tool designed primarily for researchers to share their research information, to a completely new paradigm for business exploration and channeling goods and services. Along with this explosion in Internet development, Java has been moving right along at the same speed and has become an extremely critical component to the future of Internet development. This is not to claim that Java is the only language that is or will be used for development of e-business on the Net, but it is and will remain a dominant technology as the growth continues.

Understanding the Request/Response Scenario

If you are new to Internet development or at least development using the Web, the first thing to understand is that Web development is a different paradigm that most of what you are probably familiar with. Especially because most of the business-to-business communication is taken place through protocols such as HTTP/S and the length that a company must go to in order to provide security as well as fast response times.

This section will not go through a lengthy discussion on what makes developing Web-based applications different from the rest. That type of information belongs in a book by itself. However, you do need to understand that most Web-based development involves a request made by a client using a protocol such as HTTP and that there is a server that fulfills that request in the form of a response. That is different from other distributed development because as soon as the client receives the response from the server, the connection is usually gone. In other words, no state is maintained from call to call. There are exceptions to this rule, but in general, after a response is returned to the client, the server forgets about the client. This is a big difference from the way things normally work.

USING THE URL CLASSES

Before jumping into the classes that are provided by the Java core API for dealing with URLs and the Web, you need to understand what is being referred to as URLs.

WHAT ARE URLS?

The primary classification of URLs is the scheme, which usually corresponds to an application protocol. Schemes include HTTP, FTP, Telnet, and Gopher. The rest of the URL syntax is in a format that depends on the scheme. A colon separates these two portions of information:

```
scheme-name:scheme-info
```

Thus, while `mailto:chuckcavaness@yahoo.com` indicates "send mail to user 'chuckcavaness' at the machine yahoo.com," `ftp://chuckcavaness@foobar.org` means "open an FTP connection to foobar.org and log in as user chuckcavaness."

Although IP addresses uniquely identify systems on the Internet, and ports identify TCP or UDP services on a system, URLs provide a universal identification scheme at the application level. Anyone who has used a Web browser is familiar with URLs; however, their complete syntax might not be self-evident. URLs were developed to create a common format of identifying resources on the Web, but they were designed to be general enough to encompass applications that predated the Web by decades. Similarly, the URL syntax is flexible enough to accommodate future protocols.

Most URLs conform to a general format that follows this pattern:

```
scheme-name://host:port/file-info#internal-reference
```

`Scheme-name` is a URL scheme such as HTTP, FTP, or Gopher. `host` is the domain name or IP address of the remote system. `port` is the port number on which the service is listening; because most application protocols define a standard port, unless a non-standard port is being used, the port and the colon that delimits it from the host are omitted. `file-info` is the resource requested on the remote system, which often is a file. However, the file portion might actually execute a server program and it usually includes a path to a specific file on the system. The `internal-reference` is usually the identifier of a named anchor within an

HTML page. A named anchor enables a link to target a particular location within an HTML page. Usually this is not used, and this token with the # character that delimits it is omitted.

CREATING A URL OBJECT

The URL class enables you to easily create a data structure containing all the necessary information to obtain the remote resource. After a URL object has been created, you can obtain the various portions of the URL according to the general format. The URL object also enables you to obtain the remote data.

The URL class has six constructors that can be used:

```
URL(String spec) throws MalformedURLException;

URL(String protocol, String host, int port, String file) throws
MalformedURLException;

URL(String protocol, String host, int port, String file,URLStreamHandler handler)
throws MalformedURLException;

URL(String protocol, String host, String file) throws MalformedURLException;

URL(URL context, String spec) throws MalformedURLException;

URL(URL context, String spec, URLStreamHandler handler) throws
MalformedURLException;
```

The first constructor is the most commonly used and enables you to create a URL object with a simple declaration like

```
URL myURL = new URL("http://www.yahoo.com/");
```

The other constructors allow you to specify explicitly the various portions of the URL. The last two constructors enable you to use relative URLs. A relative URL only contains part of the URL syntax; the rest of the data is completed from the URL to which the resource is relative. This will often be seen in HTML pages, where a reference to `other.html` means "get other.html from the same machine and directory where the current document resides."

Here are examples of a few of the constructors mentioned previously:

```
URL firstURLObject = new URL("http://www.yahoo.com/");
URL secondURLObject = new URL("http","www.yahoo.com","/");
URL thirdURLObject =  new URL("http","www.yahoo.com",80,"/");
URL fourthURLObject = new URL(firstURLObject,"text/suggest.html");
```

The first three statements create URL objects that all refer to the Yahoo! Main page, although the fourth creates a reference to `"text/suggest.html"` relative to Yahoo's home page (such as `http://www.yahoo.com/text/suggest.html`). All these constructors can throw a `MalformedURLException`, which you will generally want to catch. The example shown later in this section illustrates this. Note that after you create a URL object, you can't change the resource that it points to. You will need to create a new URL object.

Several new access methods have been added to the URL class to make it more consistent with the URL defined in the IETF specification, RFC2396. The new methods are

- `public String getAuthority()`
- `public String getPath()`
- `public String getQuery()`
- `public String getUserInfo()`

Creating a URL Connection

Java provides a powerful and elegant mechanism for creating network client applications, allowing you to use relatively few statements to obtain resources from the Internet. The `java.net` is the primary package that contains the necessary Java classes, of which the two most important are the `URL` and `URLConnection` classes.

Now that you've created a URL object, you will want to actually obtain some useful data. You can either read directly from the `URL` object or obtain a `URLConnection` instance from it.

Reading directly from the `URL` object requires less code, but it is much less flexible, and it only allows a read-only connection. This is limiting, as many Web services enable you to write information that will be handled by a server application. The URL class has an `openStream` method that returns an `InputStream` object through which the remote resource can be read byte-by-byte.

Handling data as individual bytes is cumbersome, so you will often want to embed the returned `InputStreamReader` like a `BufferedReader`, allowing you to read the input line-by-line. This coding strategy is often referred to as using a decorator, as the `DataInputStream` decorates the `InputStream` by providing a more specialized interface. Listing 23.15 shows how to go about this while using a URL object to obtain an HTML page from a Web site and print out the HTML page to the console.

Listing 23.15 Source Code for `PrintURLPage.java`

```
import java.net.*;
import java.io.*;

public class PrintURLPage
{
  // Default Constructor
  public PrintURLPage()
  {
    super();
  }

  // Read the HTML page
  public void printHTMLPage( String urlStr )
  {
    URL url = null;
    BufferedReader reader = null;
    String data = null;
```

LISTING 23.15 CONTINUED

```
    try
    {
      // Create the URL object
      url = new URL( urlStr );
      // Decorate the input stream with something easier to use
      reader = new BufferedReader( new InputStreamReader(url.openStream()) );

      // Keep reading lines until there are no more to read
      while( (data = reader.readLine()) != null )
      {
        // Just write out the text to the console
        System.out.println( data );
      }
    }
    catch( MalformedURLException ex )
    {
      ex.printStackTrace();
    }
    catch( IOException ex )
    {
      ex.printStackTrace();
    }
  }

  // Start the example
  public static void main( String args[] )
  {
    if ( args.length == 0 )
    {
      System.out.println( "Usage: java PrintURLPage http://<url>" );
      System.exit( 0 );
    }

    // Get the url passed in on the command line
    String url = args[0];

    PrintURLPage f = new PrintURLPage();

    // Get and print the URL passed in
    f.printHTMLPage( url );
  }
}
```

Listing 23.15 will print out the HTML page to any available URL that is passed in on the command line. You must prefix the URL that is passed in with the HTTP protocol before the URL or a `MalformedURLException` will be thrown. Test the example out by running it with these URL's like this:

```
java PrintURLPage http://www.yahoo.com
java PrintURLPage http://www.cnn.com
```

Reading and Writing to a URL Connection

Another more flexible way of connecting to the remote resource is by using the `openConnection` method of the `URL` class. This method returns a `URLConnection` object that provides a number of powerful methods that you can use to customize your connection to the remote resource.

For example, unlike the `URL` class, a `URLConnection` enables you to obtain both an `InputStream` and an `OutputStream`. This has a significant impact upon the HTTP protocol, whose access methods include both `GET` and `POST`. With the `GET` method, an application merely requests a resource and then reads the response. The `POST` method is often used to provide input to server applications by requesting a resource, writing data to the server with the HTTP request body, and then reading the response. To use the `POST` method, you can write to an `OutputStream` obtained from the `URLConnection` prior to reading from the `InputStream`. If you read first, the `GET` method will be used and a subsequent write attempt will be invalid.

If you are using the HTTP protocol, you will actually get an instance of a subclass of the `URLConnection` when you call the `openConnection()` method. The subclass naturally is called `HttpURLConnection`.

Also in SDK 1.3SE, there are other enhancements such as client-side support for http `keepalives`. The SDK also is reported to do a better job at URL parsing by following the RFC2396 more closely.

An Example: Building a World Wide Web Graph

Now that you've learned the basics of Java networking, it would be nice to do something actually useful. As you know, there are millions of Web sites available on the Internet. Each site probably refers to many others sites and you could, if you really wanted to, construct a graph of all the connected Web sites present on the Internet. Of course, doing all of them would take some time, but nonetheless is possible.

The example in Listing 23.16 is a program that takes a URL as an argument and searches for all the URL links that come off the page. This application does not recursively go down into the URL links it finds, but it would not take much to add that functionality and therefore build a huge realistic graph of Web sites.

Listing 23.16 Source Code for `URLLinkExample.java`

```
import java.net.*;
import java.io.*;
import java.util.*;

public class URLLinkExample
{
```

LISTING 23.16 CONTINUED

```
  // Default Constructor
  public URLLinkExample()
  {
    super();
  }

  // Does the token have a "http:" substring within it
private boolean hasMatch( String token )
  {
    return token.indexOf( "http:" ) != -1;
  }

  // Trim the string to something respectful to print out
  private String trimURL( String url )
  {
    String tempStr = null;
    int beginIndex = url.indexOf( "http" );
    int endIndex = url.length();
    tempStr = url.substring( beginIndex, endIndex );
    endIndex = tempStr.indexOf( '"' );
    if ( endIndex == -1 )
      endIndex = tempStr.length();
    return tempStr.substring( 0, endIndex );
  }

  // Go through all the text returned from a Web site and search for links
  public Collection searchURL( String urlString )
  {
    URL url = null;
    URLConnection conn = null;
    String nextLine = null;
    StringTokenizer tokenizer = null;
    Collection urlCollection = new ArrayList();

    try
    {
      // Get a new URL object on the url string passed in
      url = new URL( urlString );
      // open the connection
      conn = url.openConnection();
      conn.setDoOutput( true );
      // Complete the connection
      conn.connect();
      BufferedReader reader =
           new BufferedReader(
                   new InputStreamReader( conn.getInputStream() ));

      // Go through all the text and check it for being a link to another page
      while( (nextLine = reader.readLine()) != null )
      {
        // Create a tokenizer on each text line
        tokenizer = new StringTokenizer( nextLine );
        while( tokenizer.hasMoreTokens() )
        {
          String urlToken = tokenizer.nextToken();
```

LISTING 23.16 CONTINUED

```
          // If the token is a link, add it to a collection
          if ( hasMatch( urlToken) )
            urlCollection.add( trimURL( urlToken ) );
        }
      }
    }
    catch( MalformedURLException ex )
    {
      ex.printStackTrace();
    }
    catch( IOException ex )
    {
      ex.printStackTrace();
    }
    return urlCollection;
  }

  public static void main(String[] args)
  {
    if( args.length != 1 )
    {
      System.out.println( "Usage: java URLLinkExample <url>" );
      System.exit( -1 );
    }

    // Get the url from the command line arguments
    String url = args[0];
    System.out.println( "Searching web site: " + url );
    URLLinkExample example = new URLLinkExample();
    Collection urlCollection = example.searchURL( url );

    // Print out the candidate links
Iterator iter = urlCollection.iterator();
    while( iter.hasNext() )
    {
      System.out.println( iter.next() );
    }
  }
}
```


Listing 23.17 and 23.18 shows the output when you run the application with a few sample URL test sites.

LISTING 23.17 OUTPUT FOR THE `URLLinkExample` APPLICATION

```
C:\jdk1.3se_book\classes>java URLLinkExample http://www.netvendor.com
Searching web site: http://www.netvendor.com
http://www.crn.com/Components/Search/Article.asp?ArticleID=19596
http://www.crn.com/Components/Search/Article.asp?ArticleID=19596
http://www.iwvaluechain.com/Features/advatorialjuly.asp
http://www.iwvaluechain.com/Features/advatorialjuly.asp
http://www.ibm.com/e-business/casestudies/
http://atlanta.bbb.org/

C:\jdk1.3se_book\classes>
```

LISTING 23.18 OUTPUT FOR THE `URLLinkExample` APPLICATION

```
C:\jdk1.3se_book\classes>java URLLinkExample http://www.javasoft.com
Searching web site: http://www.javasoft.com
http://search.java.sun.com/query.html
http://www1.ecorpstore.com/consumer/javawear/
http://developer.java.sun.com/servlet/SessionServlet?url=http://developer.java.s
un.com/developer/bugParade/index.jshtml
http://reseller.sun.com:8003/
http://industry.java.sun.com/javanews/more/by_industry/0,2162,
http://192.18.97.137/testdev/javanews/
http://industry.java.sun.com/jug/by_country/0,2236,
http://industry.java.sun.com/jug/by_state/0,2248,
http://industry.java.sun.com/jug
http://developer.java.sun.com/developer/earlyAccess/j2sdk13/index.html
http://sun.com/software/embeddedjava/
http://www.sun.com/developers/techdays
http://forum.java.sun.com
http://forum1.java.sun.com
http://forum.java.sun.com/forum?folderBy@1.8aUZa1ZRa4G^
http://forum.java.sun.com/forum?folderBy@1.8aUZa1ZRa4G^0@.ee75dd0!skip=574
http://forum.java.sun.com/forum?folderBy@1.8aUZa1ZRa4G^0@.ee76e9a!skip=729
http://forum.java.sun.com/forum?folderBy@14.MagBa2p1acQ^0@.ee777e1!skip=57
http://java.sun.com/products/ejb/2.0.html
http://developer.java.sun.com/developer/community/
http://204.160.241.24/javanews/classes
http://www.sun.com/presents/discussions/j2ee/index.html
http://www.sun.com/MySun/
http://www.sun.com/products-n-solutions/
http://www.sun.com/
http://www.iplanet.com/
http://www.javaworld.com/index.html
http://www.artima.com/jini/
http://www.hotdispatch.com/java.html
http://www.flashline.com/
http://www.componentsource.com/java/
http://theserverside.com/
http://www.jguru.com/portal/
http://www.javareport.com/
http://www.jars.com/
http://www.gamelan.com
http://www.sys-con.com/java/index2.html
http://www.dynamicdiagrams.net/mapa/cgi-bin/help.tcl?db=javasoft&dest=http://jav
a.sun.com/
http://www.att.com/tollfree/international/dialguide/
http://www.sun.com
http://www.sun.com
http://www.sun.com/share/text/termsofuse.html
http://www.sun.com/privacy

C:\jdk1.3se_book\classes>
```

HTTP AND SSL

If you are trying to get an HTTPS connection using Java and are having trouble, see "Can't Get HTTPS Connection" in the "Troubleshooting" section at the end of this chapter.

SSL is a protocol that runs on top of a TCP/IP connection. When a client `Socket` attempts to make a connection with a server socket that is listening on a secure port, such as the standard SSL port 443, there is some extra communication that takes place between the server and the client. The main thing that is decided between the two sides is how they are going to encrypt the data that is sent back and forth between them. This is not always successful, because the two sides can support various algorithms and they might not have an algorithm in common and therefore are unable to communicate with one another. When they do have an algorithm in common, the rest of the communication is basically the same.

From the Java programmer's viewpoint, it's pretty easy. There is some setup involved to communicate on a port other than the default 80, but basically, after a SSL communication is established, it's like any other stream that a client can write to.

There are various ways to communicate via HTTPS with the core Java API, but it becomes a headache to get all of it set up for this. Fortunately, Sun has introduced the Java Secure Socket Extensions. It's not part of the core API, but it will be probably in the next release. You have to download it separately, but after you have it, things get pretty easy. You can get the latest version at

```
http://developer.java.sun.com/developer/earlyAccess/jsse/index.html
```

Note

To download the JSSE, you will have to become a member of the Java Developer Connection. It's free to join and this will also give you access to beta products earlier than the standard site will release them.

JAVA SECURE SOCKET EXTENSION PACKAGE OVERVIEW

Listing 23.19 is basically the example from Listing 23.15, which just prints out the page found at a given URL. The difference in this example is that it is reading the page from a site that is using SSL. This example does the handshaking with the server and negotiates an encryption algorithm and then gets the text.

Note

You will need to have all three JSSE jar files included in your system CLASSPATH for this example to work correctly.

LISTING 23.19 SOURCE CODE FOR `PrintHTTPSUrlPage` APPLICATION

```
import javax.net.ssl.*;
import java.io.*;
import java.net.*;
import java.security.*;


public class PrintHTTPSUrlPage
{

  public static void main(String args[]) throws Exception
  {

    System.setProperty("java.protocol.handler.pkgs",
"com.sun.net.ssl.internal.www.protocol");
    Security.addProvider( new com.sun.net.ssl.internal.ssl.Provider());

    // Notice the https protocol here
    URL url = new URL("https://www.verisign.com" );
    URLConnection conn = url.openConnection();
    conn.connect();

    BufferedReader reader = new BufferedReader( new InputStreamReader(
conn.getInputStream() ) );
    String data = null;

    // Keep reading lines until there are no more to read
    while( (data = reader.readLine()) != null )
    {
      // Just write out the text to the console
      System.out.println( data );
    }
  }
}
```

If your HTTPS connection takes a long time to connect, see " Using JSSE Takes Forever" in the following "Troubleshooting" section.

TROUBLESHOOTING

CAN'T CONNECT TO A SOCKET

Whenever I attempt to make a socket connection, I get an exception.

Most of the time, the reason that you can't connect to a port is either there is another application listening on that port that doesn't understand your protocol, or the application that you are trying to connect to isn't running.

CAN'T GET HTTPS CONNECTION

Whenever I try to connect to a site using the HTTPS protocol, I get a MalformedURLException.

This is a common problem that comes up regularly on the newsgroups. You need to be using the Java Secure Socket Extension library and make sure that the JAR files for JSSE are properly installed in your systemCLASSPATH.

USING JSSE TAKES FOREVER

When using JSSE, it seems to take forever for the connection to take place.

Unfortunately that's the normal behavior right now. What is taking so long is the handshaking that is going on between the client and server. They are trying to negotiate the algorithm that they will use to exchange information. Hopefully, it will speed up with newer versions of JSSE, but it will always have some overhead. That's the price we pay for the additional security.

CHAPTER 24

USING INTERNATIONALIZATION

In this chapter

by Chuck Cavaness

WHAT IS INTERNATIONALIZATION?

Internationalization is the process of designing an application so that it can be adapted to various languages and regions without software changes. Of course, the goal is to design your Java applications so that there is no need for software changes to support new locales or regions. Although the tools and API's exist, it's also important that you plan up front if you need to support internationalization features in your application. It's much harder to add it in after the software is built.

Note

Sometimes the term internationalization is abbreviated as i18n, because there are 18 letters between the first "i" and the last "n."

Typically, when a developer writes an application, not much attention is given to where geographically the program will be run. The typical scenario is that an application is built with the assumption that it will only be ran from a single country, but then usually after the program is built, a decision is made that it will need to support other regions or countries. Writing an application for a single location is commonly referred to as a myopic program. A *myopic program* is only suited to one locale.

A *locale* is a region (usually geographic, but not necessarily so) that shares customs, culture, and language. Usually, the standard program is localized for one specific locale and is virtually unusable outside that locale without major alteration to the software. This violates a fundamental principle of OOP design, because the program is no longer portable or reusable. The process of isolating the culture-dependent code (text, pictures, and so on) from the language-independent code (the actual functionality of the program) is called *internationalization*. After a program has been through this process, it can easily be adapted to various locales with a minimal amount of effort. The Java language has built-in support for internationalization, which makes writing portable code easier.

JAVA SUPPORT FOR INTERNATIONALIZATION

Internationalization required several changes to the Java language. With early versions of the Java language, writing internationalized code required extra effort and was substantially more difficult than writing myopic code. Latest versions of the Java language seek to make writing internationalized code easier than its locale-specific counterpart. Internationalization support mainly comes from the following three packages:

- **`java.util`**—Includes the `Locale`, `TimeZone`, and `ResourceBundle` classes. A `Locale` class encapsulates certain information about a locale, but does not provide the actual locale-specific operations. Rather, affected methods can now be passed a `Locale` object as a parameter that will alter their behavior. If no `Locale` is specified, a default `Locale` is taken from the environment. This package also provides support for `ResourceBundles`, objects that encapsulate locale-sensitive data in a portable, independent way.

- **java.io**—All the classes in java.io that worked with InputStreams and OutputStreams have corresponding classes that work with class Reader and Writer. Readers and Writers work like Streams, except they are designed to handle 16-bit Unicode characters instead of 8-bit bytes.
- **java.text**—A package that provides support for manipulating various kinds of text. This includes collating (sorting) text, formatting dates and numbers, and parsing language-sensitive data.

THE Locale CLASS

An internationalized program can display information differently throughout the world. For example, the program will display different messages in Paris, Tokyo, and New York. If the localization process has been fine-tuned, the program will display different messages in New York and London to account for the differences between American and British English. The internationalized program identifies the appropriate language and region of its end users by referencing a particular Locale object.

A Locale object encapsulates just enough information about a specific locale to uniquely identify the locale's region. When a locale-sensitive method is passed a Locale object as a parameter, it attempts to modify its behavior for that particular locale. A Locale is initialized with a language code, a country code, and an optional variant code. These three things define a region, although you need not specify all three. For example, you could have a Locale object for American English, California variant. If you ask the Calendar class what the first month of the year is, the Calendar tries to find a name suitable for Californian American English. Because month names are not affected by what state you are in, the Calendar class has no built-in support for Californian English, and it tries to find a best fit. It next tries American English, but because month names are constant in all English-speaking countries, this fails as well. Finally, the Calendar class returns the month name that corresponds to the English Locale. This best-fit lookup procedure allows the programmer complete control over the granularity of internationalized code.

You create a Locale object using the following syntax:

```
Locale theLocale = new Locale("en", "US");
```

en specifies English, and US specifies United States. These two-letter codes are used internally by Java programs to identify languages and countries. They are defined by the ISO-639 and ISO-3166 standards documents, respectively. More information on these two documents can be found at

```
http://www.ics.uci.edu/pub/ietf/http/related/iso639.txt
http://www.chemie.fu-berlin.de/diverse/doc/ISO_3166.html
```

Table 24.1 shows a few of the default language codes supported by the Java language. This is not the complete list, but are the codes probably used most often.

TABLE 24.1 A SAMPLING OF THE LANGUAGE CODES SUPPORTED BY JAVA

Code	Description
`de`	German
`en`	English
`fr`	French
`ja`	Japanese
`jw`	Javanese
`ko`	Korean
`zh`	Chinese

SUPPORTED LOCALES

Currently, Java supports the language and country combinations, shown in Table 24.2, in all its locale-sensitive classes, such as `Calendar`, `NumberFormat`, and so on. This list might change in the future, so be sure to check the documentation in the `docs/guide/intl` directory under your SDK installation root directory with future versions.

TABLE 24.2 LOCALES SUPPORTED BY THE SDK

Locale	Country	Language
`da_DK`	Denmark	Danish
`de_AT`	Austria	German
`de_CH`	Switzerland	German
`de_DE`	Germany	German
`el_GR`	Greece	Greek
`en_CA`	Canada	English
`en_GB`	United Kingdom	English
`en_IE`	Ireland	English
`en_US`	United States	English
`es_ES`	Spain	Spanish
`fi_FI`	Finland	Finnish
`fr_BE`	Belgium	French
`fr_CA`	Canada	French
`fr_CH`	Switzerland	French
`fr_FR`	France	French
`it_CH`	Switzerland	Italian

TABLE 24.2 CONTINUED

Locale	Country	Language
it_IT	Italy	Italian
ja_JP	Japan	Japanese
ko_KR	Korea	Korean
nl_BE	Belgium	Dutch
nl_NL	Netherlands	Dutch
no_NO	Norway	Norwegian (Nynorsk)
no_NO_B	Norway	Norwegian (Bokmål)
pt_PT	Portugal	Portuguese
sv_SE	Sweden	Swedish
tr_TR	Turkey	Turkish
zh_CN	China	Chinese(Simplified)
zh_TW	Taiwan	Chinese (Traditional)

You can also get a List of the installed Locale's programmatically by using the `getAvailableLocales` method on the `Locale` class. The method is static and returns an array of `Locale` objects. Here's an example of how you can use the method:

```
public void getAvailableLocales()
  {
    Locale[] availableLocales = Locale.getAvailableLocales();
    int size = availableLocales.length;
    for ( int i = 0; i < size; i++ )
    {
      Locale aLocale = availableLocales[i];
      System.out.println( aLocale.getDisplayName() );
    }
  }
```

Programmers can also create their own custom `Locales` by specifying a unique sequence of country, language, and variant. You can use an underscore character to separate multiple variants. To create a variant of Californian American English running on a Windows machine, use the following code:

```
Locale theLocale = new Locale("en", "US", "CA_WIN");
```

Remember that methods that do not understand this particular variant will try to find a best fit match, in this case probably `en_US`.

The two-letter abbreviations listed here are not to be displayed to the user; they are meant only for internal representation. For display purposes, use one of the `Locale` methods listed in Table 24.3. You will notice that these methods are generally overloaded so that you can get the parameter either for the current locale or the one specified.

TABLE 24.3 `Locale` DISPLAY METHODS

Method Name	Description
`getDisplayCountry()`	
`getDisplayCountry(Locale)`	Country name, localized for default `Locale`, or specified `Locale`.
`getDisplayLanguage()`	
`getDisplayLanguage(Locale)`	Language name, localized for default `Locale`, or specified `Locale`.
`getDisplayName()`	
`getDisplayName(Locale)`	Name of the entire `Locale`, localized for default `Locale`, or specified `Locale`.
`getDisplayVariant()`	
`getDisplayVariant(Locale)`	Name of the `Locale`'s variant. If the localized name is not found, this returns the variant code.

These methods are useful when you want to have a user interact with a `Locale` object. Here's an example of using the getDisplayLanguage() method:

```
//Set default Locale to American English
Locale.setDefault( new Locale("en", "US") );
//Create locale for Japan
Locale japanLocale = new Locale("ja", "JP");
System.out.println( japanLocale.getDisplayLanguage() );
System.out.println( japanLocale.getDisplayLanguage( Locale.FRENCH ) );
```

This code fragment prints out the name of the language used by `japanLocale`. In the first case, it is localized for the default `Locale`, which has been conveniently set to American English. The output would therefore be `Japanese`. The second print statement localizes the language name for display in French, which yields the output `Japonais`.

All the `Locale` "display" methods use this same pattern. Almost all Internationalization API methods allow you to explicitly control the `Locale` used for localization, but in most cases, you'll just want to use the default `Locale`.

Another thing to note in the preceding example is the use of the static constant `Locale.FRENCH`. The `Locale` class provides a number of these useful constants, each of which is a shortcut for the corresponding `Locale` object. A list of these objects is shown in Table 24.4.

TABLE 24.4 `Locale` STATIC OBJECTS

Constant Name	Locale	Shortcut For
`CANADA`	English Canada	`new Locale("en", "CA", "")`
`CANADA_FRENCH`	French Canada	`new Locale("fr", "CA", "")`
`CHINA SCHINESE PRC`	Chinese (Simplified)	`new Locale("zh", "CN", "")`

Table 24.4 Continued

Constant Name	Locale	Shortcut For
`CHINESE`	Chinese Language	`new Locale("zh", "", "")`
`ENGLISH`	English Language	`new Locale("en", "", "")`
`FRANCE`	France	`new Locale("fr", "FR", "")`
`FRENCH`	French Language	`new Locale("fr", "", "")`
`GERMAN`	German Language	`new Locale("de", "", "")`
`GERMANY`	Germany	`new Locale("de", "DE", "")`
`ITALIAN`	Italian Language	`new Locale("it", "", "")`
`ITALY`	Italy	`new Locale("it", "IT", "")`
`JAPAN`	Japan	`new Locale("jp", "JP", "")`
`JAPANESE`	Japanese Language	`new Locale("jp", "", "")`
`KOREA`	Korea	`new Locale("ko", "KR", "")`
`KOREAN`	Korean Language	`new Locale("ko", "", "")`
`TAIWAN TCHINESE (Traditional Chinese)`	Taiwan	`new Locale("zh", "TW", "")`
`UK`	Great Britain	`new Locale("en", "GB", "")`
`US`	United States	`new Locale("en", "US", "")`

Packaging Locale-Sensitive Data

The `Locale` class allows you to easily handle `Locale`-sensitive methods. However, most programs (especially applets and GUI-based applications) require the use of `Strings`, data, and other resources that also need to be localized. For instance, most GUI programs have `OK` and `Cancel` buttons. This is fine for the United States, but other locales require different labels for these buttons. In Germany, for instance, you might use `Gut` and `Abbrechen` instead. Traditionally, information such as this was included in the source code of an application, which can lead to many problems when trying to simultaneously support many localized versions of one program. To solve this problem, Java provides a way to encapsulate this data into objects called `ResourceBundles` that are loaded upon demand.

Resource Bundles

A `ResourceBundle` conceptually represents a set of `Locale`-specific information. In reality, the specific data for the resource bundle can be stored in a class or in a text file. The `ResourceBundle` base class provides functionality for locating and instantiating the correct `ResourceBundle` for a given locale. `ResourceBundles` are loaded according to the name of the `ResourceBundle` being referenced and the bundles must follow a strict naming convention to be loaded properly. For example, if you have a class called `LabelBundle` that extends

ResourceBundle and contains the names of all GUI labels you use in an application. The class called LabelBundle provides default information; LabelBundle_fr provides French labels; LabelBundle_ge_GE provides German labels; and LabelBundle_en_US_MAC provides Macintosh-specific American English labels. You request a ResourceBundle using the following static method:

```
ResourceBundle static getResourceBundle(String baseName, Locale locale);
```

You can leave off the Locale parameter and the getResourceBundle method will use the default Locale instance. The getResourceBundle method searches for a class that matches baseName, plus certain attributes of the specified Locale. There is a specific search pattern that is used to find the closest match to the Bundle you request:

```
bundleName + "_" + localeLanguage + "_" + localeCountry + "_" + localeVariant
bundleName + "_" + localeLanguage + "_" + localeCountry
bundleName + "_" + localeLanguage
bundleName + "_" + defaultLanguage + "_" + defaultCountry + "_" + defaultVariant
bundleName + "_" + defaultLanguage + "_" + defaultCountry
bundleName + "_" + defaultLanguage
bundleName
```

In this example, if you request the baseName LabelBundle with a fr_FR_WIN (French language, France, Windows platform) Locale, the getResourceBundle() method performs the following steps:

1. Searches for the class LabelBundle_fr_FR_WIN, which fails because you have defined no such class.
2. Searches for the class LabelBundle_fr_FR, which also fails because you did not define a France-only Bundle.
3. Searches for class LabelBundle_fr. This succeeds and returns the class with this name. However, if this search had failed (if you had not supplied a French-language Bundle), the search would have continued, using the language, country, and variant codes supplied in the default Locale.

Now that you understand the naming convention used with ResourceBundles, take a look at how they are created. The simplest form of ResourceBundles extends the ResourceBundle class directly, and then overrides one method:

```
Object handleGetObject(String key)
```

This method returns an object that corresponds to the specified key. These keys are internal representations of the content stored in the ResourceBundle and should be the same for all localized versions of the same data. An extremely simple version of your LabelBundle might be defined as follows:

```
class LabelBundle extends ResourceBundle
{
 public Object handleGetObject(String key)
 {
  if( key.equals("OK") )
   return "OK";
```

```
  else if( key.equals("Cancel") )
   return "Cancel";

  // Other labels could be handled here

  return null; // If the key has no matches, always return null
 }
}
```

Other versions of the same bundle might return values translated into different languages. You can see, however, that this method of handling key-value pairs is inefficient if you have more than a few keys. Luckily, Java provides two subclasses of `ResourceBundle` that can make life easier:

- `ListResourceBundle`
- `PropertyResourceBundle`

ListResourceBundles

`ListResourceBundles` use an array of two-element arrays to store the key-value pairs used earlier. All you have to do is override the default `getContents` method , like this:

```
class LabelBundle extends ListResourceBundle
{
  static final Object[][] labels = {
  {"OK", "OK"},
  {"Cancel", "Cancel"},
  ("AnotherKey", "Another Value"}
  //More key-value pairs can go here
  };

  public Object[][] getContents()
  {
    return labels;
  }
}
```

You could also provide your own similar functionality using a hash table, but that's only worthwhile if you want the contents to change dynamically over time.

PropertyResourceBundle

`PropertyResourceBundles` are created as needed from predefined "property" files stored on disk. These are usually used for system wide settings, or when large amounts of data need to be stored in a key-value pair. `PropertyResourceBundles` are built from files with the same name as the corresponding class file, but with the `.properties` extension instead. To implement the `LabelBundle_de_DE` class, you might provide a file called `LabelBundle_de_DE.properties` with the following content:

```
OK=Gut
Cancel=Abbrechen
```

Contents are always specified in the form `key=value` and are assumed to be `Strings` (although they can be cast into other appropriate objects). This functionality is based on the `java.util.Properties` class. See Chapter 10, " Data Structures and Java Utilities," for more information on the `java.util.Properties` class. There is no need to define a Java class when you are using `PropertyResourceBundle's`. All you need to do is create the properties file (which should be just a plain text file), and make sure the properties file is located somewhere in your system `CLASSPATH`. This makes it kind of nice because the values can be changed without having to recompile code.

Note

Although the examples given here all deal with `String` objects, `ResourceBundles` can store objects of any type, including Dates, Applets, GUI elements, or even other `ResourceBundles`.

Accessing `ResourceBundles` as previously mentioned, you load `ResourceBundles` by name using the static method `getResourceBundle`. Assuming this succeeds (it throws an exception otherwise), you can then query individual values within the bundle using the `getObject` method. Of course, this also usually requires an explicit cast to the kind of object you want, so you need to know this information ahead of time. As a matter of convenience, `ResourceBundle` also provides the following methods that return already-cast objects:

- `String[] getStringArray(String key)`
- `Enumeration getKeys()`
- `Object getObject(String key)`
- `getString(String key)`

CALENDAR AND TIME ZONE SUPPORT

Since version 1.1 of the JDK, the `Date` class has been used as just a wrapper around a date or time instance. It can represent dates or times with millisecond precision. However, you need more when it comes to working with internationalized dates or times. For this, you need to use the `java.util.Calendar` class and its subclass `java.util.GregorianCalendar`. You also can make use of the `java.util.TimeZone` class to represent time zone offsets and to help in calculating daylight savings. Together, these classes provide a rich library to aid in date and time calculations. The following sections look at each one briefly.

`Calendar` CLASS

The `java.util.Calendar` class is an abstract class that provides culture-independent methods for manipulating the epoch, century, year, month, week, day, and time in various ways. Because the `Calendar` class is abstract, it relies on the subclasses to provide functionality based on a particular calendar system. The only subclass provided by the Java language itself is the `java.util.GregorianCalendar` class, which provides sophisticated functionality for the world's most popular calendar system. Future releases might include support for various lunar, seasonal, or other calendar systems. An adjunct to the `Calendar` class, which is not usually used directly by the programmer, is the `TimeZone` (and `SimpleTimeZone`) class, which allows dates and times to be properly adjusted for other time zones.

The `Date`, `Calendar`, and `TimeZone` classes provide a large amount of functionality that most programmers will never need to know about. You don't need to understand the intricacies of temporal arithmetic to make use of these classes; they all contain default methods that allow you to get the current time and date, and display it in a `Locale`-sensitive way. By merely using the provided methods, your programs will become localized by default, requiring no added effort on your part.

Note

There are too many methods in these classes to discuss here. If you are interested, a simple example of the `Calendar` and `Date` classes interacting is provided in the example at the end of the chapter. For a more complete discussion of the available methods, you should consult the Java API documentation directly.

INTERNATIONALIZATION FORMATTING

In most cases, the work that must be done to provide support for internationalization of a Java application is in the formatting of output data for a specific locale. Numbers, dates, and other text can all require formatting before they are displayed. Java provides a set of easy to use classes for formatting data based on standard locale formatting rules. The support for internationalization formatting is provided through the `Format` class and its specialized set of format classes.

`Format` CLASS

The `java.text.Format` class is an abstract base class that provides support for formatting dates, times, numbers, and other locale sensitive objects into strings and also for parsing strings back into the corresponding objects. The three main subclasses are

- **`DateFormat`**—Format and parse date and times in a locale-sensitive way.
- **`NumberFormat`**—Format and parse numerical data in a locale-sensitive way.
- **`MessageFormat`**—Format and parse string messages in a language-independent way.

`Date` AND `Time` FORMATTING

`Date` and `Time` are stored internally in a locale-independent manner. To produce a locale-sensitive date or time, the date and/or time must be formatted specifically for a particular locale where it is being used. The same internally stored date would be displayed differently for two distinct locales. The following two lines show an example of the same date for two different locales:

```
November 3, 1997 (English)
3 novembre 1997 (French)
```

The DateFormat class is actually an abstract class. It has several static methods for getting locale-sensitive formats for date and times. A concrete subclass of DateFormat is SimpleDateFormat and is probably used more than any other class for formatting date and times. It has functionality to format a Date object to a string and also to parse a string into a Date object. The SimpleDateFormat provides a set of patterns that will be used when formatting or parsing a Date or date String object. A summary of that set of patterns is provided here:

Symbol	Meaning	Presentation	Example
G	era designator	(Text)	AD
y	year	(Number)	1996
M	month in year	(Text & Number)	July & 07
d	day in month	(Number)	10
h	hour in am/pm (1~12)	(Number)	12
H	hour in day (0~23)	(Number)	0
m	minute in hour	(Number)	30
s	second in minute	(Number)	55
S	millisecond	(Number)	978
E	day in week	(Text)	Tuesday
D	day in year	(Number)	189
F	day of week in month	(Number)	2 (2nd Wed in July)
w	week in year	(Number)	27
W	week in month	(Number)	2
a	am/pm marker	(Text)	PM
k	hour in day (1~24)	(Number)	24
K	hour in am/pm (0~11)	(Number)	0
z	time zone	(Text)	Pacific Standard Time
'	escape for text	(Delimiter)	
‘’	single quote single quote	(Literal) (Literal)	`'' '

A pattern is constructed using these symbols and then the pattern is applied when formatting a Date object or parsing a date String. Here are some examples of using these patterns to format date and time strings:

Format Pattern	Result
"yyyy.MM.dd G 'at' hh:mm:ss z"	1996.07.10 AD at 15:08:56 PDT
"EEE, MMM d, ''yy"	Wed, July 10, '96
"h:mm a"	12:08 PM
"hh 'o''clock' a, zzzz"	12 o'clock PM, Pacific Daylight Time
"K:mm a, z"	0:00 PM, PST
"yyyyy.MMMMM.dd GGG hh:mm aaa"	1996.July.10 AD 12:08 PM

Listing 24.1 shows an example of how to use a custom format. Here it is used to format a `Timestamp` object into a certain format. This format pattern is hard-coded here, but it easily be put into a `ResourceBundle` to make it easier to change.

LISTING 24.1 USING A CUSTOM FORMAT PATTERN

```
import java.sql.Timestamp;
import java.text.DateFormat;
import java.text.SimpleDateFormat;

public class CustomDateFormat
{
  // Default Constructor
  public CustomDateFormat()
  {
    super();
  }

  public void printTimestamp( Timestamp ts, String formatPattern )
  {
    SimpleDateFormat dateFormat = new SimpleDateFormat( formatPattern );
    dateFormat.applyPattern( formatPattern );
    String timeStampStr = dateFormat.format( ts );
    System.out.println( timeStampStr );
  }

  public static void main(String[] args)
  {
    CustomDateFormat example = new CustomDateFormat();

    // Create a custom format pattern string
    String pattern = "EEE, MMM d, ''yy";

    // Create a Timestamp object
    Timestamp ts = Timestamp.valueOf( "2000-09-10 15:30:20.000" );
    example.printTimestamp( ts, pattern );
  }
}
```

Although you can use these patterns to generate a `SimpleDateFormat` instance, you are encouraged to create a date-time formatter with `getTimeInstance`, `getDateInstance`, or `getDateTimeInstance` methods in the `DateFormat` class. Each of these class methods can return a date/time formatter initialized with a default format pattern. You can thenuse the `format` method as before to format a Date to the proper `Locale` string.

LISTING 24.2 USING THE DEFAULT DATE FORMAT

```
import java.sql.Timestamp;
import java.text.DateFormat;
import java.text.SimpleDateFormat;

public class DefaultDateFormat
{
  // Default Constructor
  public DefaultDateFormat()
  {
    super();
  }

  public void printTimestamp( Timestamp ts )
  {
    DateFormat dateFormat = DateFormat.getDateTimeInstance();
    String timeStampStr = dateFormat.format( ts );
    System.out.println( timeStampStr );
  }

  public static void main(String[] args)
  {
    DefaultDateFormat example = new DefaultDateFormat();

    // Create a Timestamp object
    Timestamp ts = Timestamp.valueOf( "2000-09-10 15:30:20.000" );
    example.printTimestamp( ts );
  }
}
```

NUMBER FORMATTING

The `java.text.NumberFormat` class and the concrete subclass `DecimalNumberFormat` give the Java programmer the ability to parse and format numerical data in a language-specific manner. As stated before, the data is stored internally in a locale-neutral format and then can be formatted depending on the current locale.

With the `DecimalNumberFormat` class, differences in the way decimal point data is displayed in various Locales can easily be handled with little. For example, the code in Listing 24.3 prints out a decimal number in all the available Locales. If you wanted to print out the information just for the default Locale, you could get an instance of a `DecimalFormat` object by using the static `getInstance` method on the `NumberFormat` class.

LISTING 24.3 USING THE DecimalFormat CLASS

```
import java.util.Locale;
import java.text.NumberFormat;

public class DecimalFormatExample
{

  public DecimalFormatExample()
  {
  }

  public void formatDecimalNumber( Locale aLocale, double aDecimalNumber )
  {
    NumberFormat format = NumberFormat.getInstance( aLocale );
    System.out.println( aLocale.getDisplayName() + " " + format.format
➥( aDecimalNumber ) );
  }

  public static void main(String[] args)
  {
    DecimalFormatExample example = new DecimalFormatExample();

    // Create a decimal number
     double aDecimalNumber = -7143.65;

    // Get the installed Locales
    Locale[] availableLocales = NumberFormat.getAvailableLocales();
    int size = availableLocales.length;
    for( int i = 0; i < size; i++ )
    {
      Locale aLocale = availableLocales[i];

      // Skip language-only locales
      if( aLocale.getCountry().length() != 0 )
        example.formatDecimalNumber( aLocale, aDecimalNumber );
    }
  }
}
```


MESSAGE FORMATTING

The `java.text.MessageFormat` class provides a way to concatenate messages in a language-neutral manner. Although it can be used for non-internationalized applications just as well, its use can save time in internationalized application that need to dynamically concatenate messages at runtime. For example, say that you need to print out a message to the user of how many files are contained on a particular drive and we want to be able to print the same message in both English and German.

Ideally, the display strings would come from a `ResourceBundle` and we would just load the correct `ResourceBundle` depending on the `Locale`. The example in Listing 24.4 shows how you might go about doing this task. In this example however, we don't utilize a `ResourceBundle`, but rather have the format strings in the main method. This is to keep the example simple. The only difference between this example and one using a `ResourceBundle` is with a ResouceBundle, you just need to read in the correct pattern from the `Bundle` and pass it to the `formatMessage` method in the example class. Here is Listing 24.4.

LISTING 24.4 AN EXAMPLE USING THE `MessageFormat` CLASS

```
import java.text.MessageFormat;

public class MessageFormatExample
{
  // Default Constructor
  public MessageFormatExample()
  {
    super();
  }

  public void formatMessage( String pattern, Object[] tokens )
  {
    MessageFormat msgFormatter = new MessageFormat( pattern );
    System.out.println( msgFormatter.format( pattern, tokens ) );
  }

  public static void main(String[] args)
  {
    MessageFormatExample example = new MessageFormatExample();

    // Create a English pattern for the MessageFormat object to use
    String englishPattern = "The disk {0} contains {1} files.";

    // Create a French Pattern for the MessageFormat Object to use
    String frenchPattern = "Il y a {0} fichiers sur le disque {1}.";

    // Create the token array and initialize it
    Object[] tokens = {"C", "3"};

    // Format the English version
    example.formatMessage( englishPattern, tokens );

    // Format the French version
    example.formatMessage( frenchPattern, tokens );
  }
}
```

Here is the output for Listing 24.4.

```
C:\jdk1.3se_book\classes>java MessageFormatExample
The disk C contains 3 files.
Il y a C fichiers sur le disque 3.

C:\jdk1.3se_book\classes>
```

The top message that is printed out from Listing 24.4 is obviously for an English locale, whereas the bottom one is for a French locale. Notice that in both cases, the number of files is 3 and the drive letter is C.

Again, the pattern format should probably be stored in a resource bundle and the data can be inserted into the message dynamically. The `MessageFormat` class uses a pattern to figure out where to insert the data into the message. Look at one of the patterns from the previous Listing. Here's the English `Locale` pattern from the Listing in 24.4:

```
"The disk {0} contains {1} files."
```

Remember that this message should come from a `ResourceBundle` and represents the English locale. The French equivalent pattern looks like this:

```
"Il y a {0} fichiers sur le disque {1}."
```

Notice that the data that's being inserted into each message is the same. Only the message itself is different. When you call the `format` method on the `MessageFormat` class, you can pass an object array. The number `0` and `1` that you see in these patterns are indexes into the `object[]` that was passed in.

Remember in the beginning of this section, you read that the `MessageFormat` could be used for situations other than internationalization. There are no locale-specific methods or functionality in the `MessageFormat` class. You just need to set up the locale-specific strings in `ResourceBundles` and then use them accordingly.

The `MessageFormat` class can also be used in other areas of Java application design. Suppose you need to send email messages to different users wherein only a certain portion of the email was specific to a user. You could set up a `MessageFormat` pattern for this and then just substitute the dynamic information for each user into the appropriate template. The `MessageFormat` class is really flexible and makes this type of application programming easy to do.

CHARACTER SET CONVERTERS

Characters can be represented as binary numbers. This is normally referred to as an *encoding scheme*. The most common scheme used for English text is called the ISO Latin-1 encoding. The set of characters supported by any one encoding is said to be its character set, which includes all possible characters that can be represented by the encoding. Usually, the first 127 codes of an encoding correspond to the almost universally accepted ASCII character set, which includes all the standard characters and punctuation marks. Nevertheless, most encoding schemes can vary radically, especially because some, such as Chinese and Japanese encoding schemes, have character sets that bear little resemblance to the English set.

The SDK 1.3 supports the encodings shown in Table 24.4. The Java 2 Runtime Environment, 1.3 Standard Edition, for Windows comes in two different versions: US-only and international. The US-only version only supports the encodings shown in table 24.4. The international version (which includes the `lib/i18n.jar` file) supports the encodings shown in Table 24.4 and many more. In fact, too many to list here. For the encodings supported in the i18n.jar, see the internationalization documentation under the `JAVA_HOME/docs/guide/intl directory`.

TABLE 24.4 STANDARD JAVA CHARACTER ENCODINGS	
`ASCII`	American Standard Code for Information Interchange
`Cp1252`	Windows-Latin-1
`ISO8859_1`	ISO 8859-1, Latin alphabet No. 1
`UnicodeBig`	Sixteen-bit Unicode Transformation Format, big-endian byte order, with byte-order mark
`UnicodeBigUnmarked`	Sixteen-bit Unicode Transformation Format, big-endian byte order
`UnicodeLittle`	Sixteen-bit Unicode Transformation Format, little-endian byte order, with byte-order mark
`UnicodeLittleUnmarked`	Sixteen-bit Unicode Transformation Format, little-endian byte order
`UTF8`	Eight-bit Unicode Transformation Format
`UTF-16`	Sixteen-bit Unicode Transformation Format, byte order specified by a mandatory initial byte-order mark

READERS AND WRITERS

Character streams make heavy use of character set converters. They hide the underlying complexity of the conversion process, making it easy for Java programs to be written without knowledge of the internationalizing process. Again, you see that programs are internationalized by default.

The advantages of using character streams over byte streams are many. Although character streams have the added overhead of doing character conversion on top of byte reading, they also allow for more efficient buffering. Byte streams are designed to read information one byte at a time, whereas character streams read one buffer at a time. According to Sun, this fact, combined with a new efficient locking scheme, more than compensates for the speed loss caused by the conversion process. Every input or output stream in the old class hierarchy now has a corresponding `Reader` or `Writer` class that performs similar functions using character streams (see Table 24.5).

TABLE 24.5 INPUT/OUTPUT STREAMS AND CORRESPONDING `Reader` AND `Writer` CLASSES (FROM SUN MICROSYSTEMS, INC.)

Byte Stream Class Character Stream	**Corresponding Class (`Reader`/`Writer`)**	**Function (`InputStream`/ `OutputStream`)**
`InputStream`	`Reader`	Abstract class from which all other classes inherit methods, and so on
`BufferedInputStream`	`BufferedReader`	Provides a buffer for input operations
`LineNumberInputStream`	`LineNumberReader`	Keeps track of line numbers

TABLE 24.5 CONTINUED

Byte Stream Class Character Stream	Corresponding Class (Reader/Writer)	Function (InputStream/ OutputStream)
ByteArrayInputStream	CharArrayReader	Reads from an array
N/A	InputStreamReader	Translates a byte stream into a character stream
FileInputStream	FileReader	Allows input from a file on disk
FilterInputStream	FilterReader	Abstract class for filtered input
PushbackInputStream	PushbackReader	Allows characters to be pushed back into the stream
PipedInputStream	PipedReader	Reads from a process pipe
StringBufferInputStream	StringReader	Reads from a String
OutputStream	Writer	Abstract class for character-output streams
BufferedOutputStream	BufferedWriter	Buffers output, uses platform's line separator
ByteArrayOutputStream	CharArrayWriter	Writes to a character array
FilterOutputStream	FilterWriter	Abstract class for filtered character output
N/A	OutputStreamWriter	Translates a character stream into a byte stream
FileOutputStream	FileWriter	Translates a character stream into a byte file
PrintStream	PrintWriter	Prints values and objects to a Writer
PipedOutputStream	PipedWriter	Writes to a PipedReader
N/A	StringWriter	Writes to a String

The impact of these changes is actually quite minor if you're developing new programs. All you have to do is remember to use Reader and Writer classes where before you used InputStream and OutputStream. The biggest change you'll have to worry about relates to the DataInputStream and PrintStream, which used to be the classes of choice for receiving text from input and sending text to output. The DataInputStream.readLine method has been deprecated—you should use BufferedReader.readLine instead. Furthermore, you can no longer instantiate a new PrintStream object, although you can still use pre-existing PrintStreams (such as System.out) for debugging purposes. To output line-terminated strings, you should use the PrintWriter class instead. The main offshoot of this is that all code that is used to communicate with the DataInputStream and PrintStream classes (which includes much Socket, File, and Piped code) will have to be updated to use the proper Reader and Writer classes. To make this easier, Java provides classes called InputStreamReader and OutputStreamWriter, which are used to create a new Writer or

Reader based on a byte stream. This makes the Reader/Writer system compatible with all the other classes that currently use byte streams (such as URL, Socket, File, and so on).

THE java.text PACKAGE

The most advanced and complex Internationalization API features are found in the java.text package. They include many classes for formatting and organizing text in a language-independent way. You have already seen some of the classes and features in the previous sections of this chapter. To refresh your memory, date formatting can be problematic for programmers. In America, dates are written in month-day-year order, but in Europe, dates are written in day-month-year order. This makes interpreting a date like 10/2/97 difficult: Does this represent October 2, 1997 or February 10, 1997? One goal of the classes within the java.text package is parsing and formatting text properly based on the correct Locale so that the data is always parsed and formatted correctly. A second but still very important goal of the java.text package is to reduce the amount of work a Java developer has to do to accomplish goal number 1. The classes within the java.text package don't necessary deal with internationalization features directly although they are designed to deal with text, dates, numbers, and messages in a manner independent of natural languages. As we saw with the MessageFormat example from Listing 24.4, these classes can assist the developer in building internationalization into your Java applications.

Text collating , on the other hand, is the process of sorting text according to particular rules. In English, sorting in alphabetical order is relatively easy because English lacks many special characters (such as accents) that could complicate things. In French, however, things are not so simple. Two words that look very similar (like péché and pêche) have entirely different meanings. Which should come first alphabetically? And what about hyphenation or punctuation characters? The Java Collation class provides a way of defining language-specific sort criteria in a robust, consistent manner.

Text boundaries can also be ambiguous across languages. Where do words, sentences, and paragraphs begin and end? In English, a period generally marks the end of a sentence and a space defines the boundary for a word, but this is not always the case. The BreakIterator and CharacterIterator classes can intelligently break up text into various subunits based on language-specific criteria. Java comes with built-in support for some languages, but you can always define your own set of rules, as well. The BreakIterator works by returning the integer index of boundaries that occur within a String, as demonstrated by the example in Listing 24.5, which breaks up a String by words:

LISTING 24.5 AN EXAMPLE OF USING THE BreakIterator CLASS.

```
import java.text.BreakIterator;
import java.util.Locale;

public class BreakIteratorExample
{
  // Default Constructor
```

LISTING 24.5 CONTINUED

```
  public BreakIteratorExample()
  {
    super();
  }

  public void breakString( String stringToExamine, Locale aLocale )
  {
    // Create a BreakIterator for the string
    BreakIterator boundary = BreakIterator.getWordInstance( aLocale );
    boundary.setText(stringToExamine);

    // Setup the start of the sentence
    int start = boundary.first();

     for (int end = boundary.next();
      end != BreakIterator.DONE;
          start = end, end = boundary.next())
    {
      String subStr = stringToExamine.substring(start,end);
      System.out.println( subStr );
    }

  }

  public static void main(String[] args)
  {
    BreakIteratorExample example = new BreakIteratorExample();
    example.breakString( "This is a test.", Locale.US );
  }
}
```

This snippet of code prints out each word on its own line. Although this example is trivial, text boundaries can be extremely important, especially in GUI applications that require text selection, intelligent word wrapping, and so on.

AN EXAMPLE: InternationalizationTest

To better understand how all this fits together, take a look at this simple Java application that makes use of several of the features discussed in this chapter.

The simple application takes up to three command-line parameters that specify a locale and uses this information to

- Display some information about the default locale and the one entered.
- Try to load a `ResourceBundle` corresponding to the specified locale and print out what the `Bundle` contains.
- Display the date, localized to the specified locale.

Besides the main application class called `InternationalizationTest.java`, the program requires three other files. The three files are `.properties` files that correspond to three supported locales. They will get converted into `PropertyResourceBundles` automatically by the virtual machine when they are loaded. The property files must be in the `CLASSPATH` for them to be found and loaded properly by the `ClassLoader`. As long as the `ResourceBundles` and `.properties` files are available via `CLASSPATH`, you don't need a separate `ClassLoader` to load them. If you were making an applet, on the other hand, you would need a `ClassLoader` to load the classes across the Internet. You can use the same `ClassLoader` instance that loaded the applet like this:

```
ClassLoader loader = this.getClass().getClassLoader();
```

Listing 24.6 provides the complete listing of `InternationalizationTest`.

LISTING 24.6 `InternationalizationTest.java`

```
import java.util.*;
import java.lang.*;
import java.text.DateFormat;

class InternationalizationTest extends Object
{

  public static void main(String args[])
  {
    // Declare variables to hold the three parameters
    String lang = "";
    String country = "";
    String variant = "";

    // Make sure the user passes the language variable on the command line
    if ( args.length == 0 )
    {
      System.out.println("You must specify at least one parameter");
      System.exit(1);
    }

    int argsSize = args.length;
    // There was at least the language passed in
    lang = args[0];

    // Need to check the other two to see if they were passed in
    if ( argsSize > 1 )
      country = args[1];

    if ( argsSize > 2 )
      variant = args[2];

    // Get the locale for the specific locale variables
    Locale locale = new Locale( lang, country, variant );

    // Get the Default Locale
    Locale defaultLocale = Locale.getDefault();

    // Print out the Locale information to the console
```

LISTING 24.6 CONTINUED

```
    System.out.println(
 "Default Locale is: "+ defaultLocale.getDisplayName() );
    System.out.println("You have selected Locale: "+ locale.getDisplayName() );
    System.out.println("Default language, localized for your locale is: " +
            defaultLocale.getDisplayLanguage( locale ) );
    System.out.println(
"Default country name, localized: " + defaultLocale.getDisplayCountry( locale ) );


    // Get a resource bundle based on the passed in locale
    ResourceBundle bundle = null;
    try
    {
      bundle = ResourceBundle.getBundle( "TestBundle", locale );
      System.out.println( "Resources available are: ");
      System.out.println("OK Label: " + bundle.getString("OK_LABEL") );
      System.out.println("Cancel Label: " + bundle.getString("CANCEL_LABEL") );
    }
    catch( MissingResourceException e)
    {
      System.out.println( "No resources available for that locale." );
    }

    // Display date and time information based on the locale instance
    DateFormat myFormat =
DateFormat.getDateTimeInstance(DateFormat.FULL, DateFormat.FULL, locale);
    Calendar myCalendar = Calendar.getInstance( locale );
    System.out.println(
"The localized date and time is: " +  myFormat.format( myCalendar.getTime() ) );
   }
}
```


Listing 24.7 through 24.9 are the provided property files for the three supported locales. If you needed to support more locales, all you would have to do is provide a `.properties` file with the locale name and put the `OK_LABEL` and `CANCEL_LABEL` values in the file. This is why Java internationalization is so easy if it's done correctly. It takes little or no software changes to support new locales.

Note You should always have a base resource bundle in case a locale that is not supported is passed in. In this example, the properties file called `TestBundle.properties` is the default case.

If you are having trouble in your application when it's trying to locate the `.properties` file(s), see "Finding the `.properties` Files" in the "Troubleshooting" section at the end of the chapter.

LISTING 24.7 `TestBundle_en_US.properties`

```
OK_LABEL=OK
CANCEL_LABEL=Cancel
```

LISTING 24.8 `TestBundle_de_DE.properties`

```
OK_LABEL=Gut
CANCEL_LABEL=Abbrechen
```

LISTING 24.9 `TestBundle.properties`

```
OK_LABEL=Okay
CANCEL_LABEL=Forget about it!
```

Figures 24.1, 24.2, and 24.3 show output from the `InternationalizationTest` program.

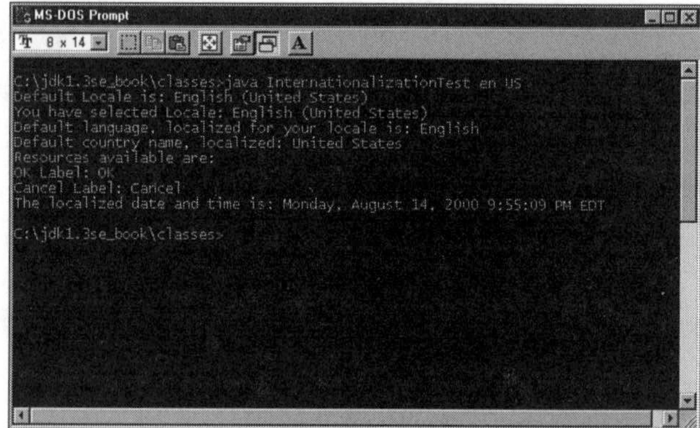

Figure 24.1
Output from Listing 24.6 using the American English Locale.

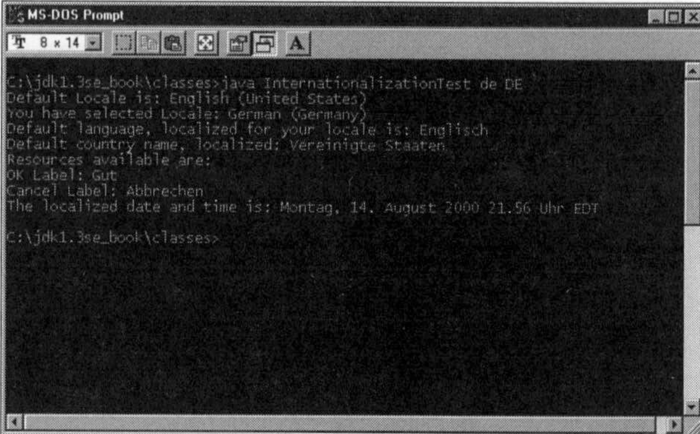

Figure 24.2
Output from Listing 24.6 using the German Locale.

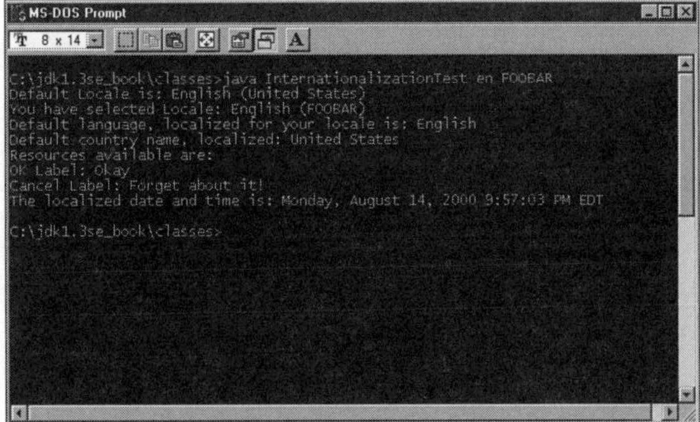

Figure 24.3
Output from Listing 24.6 using the Default English Locale.

Here's one final important note on adding internationalization to your Java applications. As with most everything else in designing software applications, the most important time to think about internationalization for your Java applications in before you start coding your applications. The cost to design and programming is always much less earlier in the process. If you think that your application might have to support other locales, go ahead and plan to use the Java internationalization features early so you don't find yourself ripping your program apart later to add it in.

TROUBLESHOOTING

FINDING THE `.properties` FILES

I've defined a properties file, but my application can't find the file when the getResourceBundle method is called.

When using `.properties` files for your resource bundles, make sure they are in your system `CLASSPATH`. Otherwise, you will get a `MissingResourceException` when calling the `getBundle` method on the `ResourceBundle` class. Because the key/value pairs are loaded dynamically, there is no way for the compiler to check to see if you are referencing invalid keys. When you call the `getObject` or `getString` methods on a `ResoureBundle`, you might also get a `MissingResourceException`. You should handle this by always having a default value for the key.

CHAPTER 25

JAR Files

In this chapter

By *Chuck Cavaness*

USING JAR FILES

Java introduced Java Archive files (JAR files) back in JDK 1.1. JAR files bundle multiple files into a single deployable archive file that can be used in Java applications and/or applets. JAR files provide many valuable features for Java applications. Some of the features are

- Bundling
- Compression
- Portability
- Versioning
- Security
- Decreased Download Time

Each of these features is described in more detail in the following sections.

BUNDLING

A complex applet or application might consist of dozens or hundreds of Java classes, each stored in a separate class file (recall that each public class must be stored in a separate file). For applets, the Web browser makes an HTTP connection to load each file, as needed, from the server. Establishing an HTTP connection entails overhead, and if the class files are small, as they typically are, much of the time spent loading an applet can be spent establishing the multiple HTTP connections required to load all the class files.

For Java applications, bundling aids in application distribution. Because there can be many class files and/or resources within a single JAR file, an entire application can be contained exclusively within a JAR. If you need to redistribute a newer version of your software, just install the new JAR file over the older version.

Note

JAR files can contain any type of file, class files, images, HTML pages, and even other JAR files.

COMPRESSION

JAR files, like CAB files, are compressed. For example, using the `TicTacToe` directory located in the `JAVA_HOME/demo/applets` directory is about 40.2KB in a standard SDK 1.3 installation. If you JAR the entire contents of that directory, the JAR file is approximately 29KB. That's about a 28% compression rate. Not bad, but it's obviously dependent on the type of the files. Usually, graphics are already compressed, so their compression is not so hot. The point is that it compresses files and resources and can greatly reduce the size of the distribution.

Portability

The JAR file utilities are part of Java's core API. As long as there is a current version of Java for that platform, JAR files will port to that platform.

Versioning

Since JDK 1.2, JAR files have had the capability to contain meta-information about the contents of the JAR itself. This meta-data is stored in a file called MANIFEST.MF. This file has to be in a directory within the JAR file called META-INF. (Notice, the name of the file and directory are uppercase.)

By using the manifest file, a JAR file can record information about what files are in the JAR, what version each file is, who the vendor was, and so on. You'll hear more about the manifest file shortly.

Security

JAR files can be signed digitally so that users can download them as trusted pieces of an application. This is very important for applications or applets that are downloaded over the Web. It's also important for users who don't allow code to execute if they don't know where it came from.

Decreased Download Time

Because a single JAR file can contain multiple files and be compressed, their download times are reduced dramatically.

Some Differences Between ZIP and JAR Formats

The JAR file format was really introduced in the JDK 1.1 version. Although there was little to do with JAR files in 1.0.2, it wasn't until the JDK 1.1 when JAR files started to become the preferred method of packing classes.

Most of the literature that was produced a few years ago had to do with how JAR files could be used in Applets. This was mainly due to the increased download speed because of the manner in which HTTP downloads files. However, now entire applications are being distributed in JAR file formats as described in the "Using JAR Files" section previously.

Although the JAR file format is based on the ZIP file format, there are some differences between ZIP files and JAR files when it comes to using one or the other in Java applications. Although in earlier versions of Java, ZIP files were used for things such as packing the Java libraries in the classes.zip file, JAR files are used almost exclusively in most applications today. You'll notice that Sun distributes the Java libraries now as JAR files. Look in the lib directory under your Java installation directory. You should see an rt.jar file under the JAVA_HOME/jre/lib and probably the tools.jar file in the JAVA_HOME/lib directory. That's not to say that you won't come across the occasional third-party Java tool that uses ZIP files. This is okay, because there is still support in the core Java APIs for the ZIP file format.

The real differences revolve around security and the manifest file. Use JAR files for packaging your applications to take advantage of the benefits mentioned previously.

WHEN TO USE JARS

You should consider using a JAR archive for your applications if any of the following apply:

- You want to decrease your applet's loading time, especially if your applet consists of many files.
- You want to simplify the distribution of your application or make it more portable.
- Your applet or application needs to be authenticated as trusted code.
- You have meta-information such as version information that you want to associate with the application files.

CREATING AND VIEWING A JAR

The JARJARJ tool allows you to create, list, and extract files from JAR archives. It deliberately resembles the Unix tar tool, both in function and in usage. Like other tools in the SDK, the JAR tool is implemented as a Java application, making it portable to any platform supporting Java.

The `jar` command is used from the command line exclusively. There are many options that you provide to the `jar` command, depending on what you are trying to do. You can type just `jar` on the command line to see the options. For a detailed look at the options, see Appendix B, "SDK Tools."

To create a new JAR file, you can use the `c` option with the `jar` command. Options can be appended together. When creating a new JAR file, most often you want use `cvf`. The `c` option tells the `jar` command to create a new archive. The `v` option tells jar command to output verbose diagnostic messages to the console while it is working so you can see what is being added. The `f` option tells `jar` command to create an archive file of the given name. Take a look at this example:

```
jar cvf foo.jar *.class images
```

The name of the new JAR file must come after the `f` option. This command, when run from the command line, creates a new JAR archive named `foo.jar` in the current directory. The archive will contain all the class files in the current directory, as well as the complete images directory and all its contents, assuming those directories existed.

As an example, open up a console window and change to the `JAVA_HOME/demo/applets/TicTacToe` directory. This directory should be under your JDK 1.3 home installation directory. Listing 25.1 shows the directory contents of the directory.

LISTING 25.1 LISTING OF THE TicTacToe DIRECTORY

```
C:\jdk1.3\demo\applets\TicTacToe>dir

 Volume in drive C has no label
 Volume Serial Number is 07D0-0606
 Directory of C:\jdk1.3\demo\applets\TicTacToe

.              <DIR>        06-15-00  3:54p .
..             <DIR>        06-15-00  3:54p ..
TICTAC~1 CLA          3,900  06-02-00  1:11p TicTacToe.class
TICTAC~1 JAV          8,020  06-02-00  1:11p TicTacToe.java
EXAMPL~1 HTM            424  06-02-00  1:11p example1.html
AUDIO          <DIR>        06-15-00  3:54p audio
IMAGES         <DIR>        06-15-00  3:54p images
         3 file(s)         12,344 bytes
         4 dir(s)      23,087.70 MB free


C:\jdk1.3\demo\applets\TicTacToe>
```

For purposes here, create a new JAR file containing everything in this directory and the entire audio and images subdirectories as well. Call the new JAR file `ourtest.jar` and create it in the current directory. You'll use this file later, so don't delete it right away.

PART III CH 25

Caution

Be careful when creating a new JAR file; if one already exists with the same name as the new one being created, the old one will be overwritten.

Type the following command and run it from the `TicTacToe` directory, which should be located at `JAVA_HOME/demo/applets` directory:

```
jar cvf ourtest.jar *
```

Notice that when directories are listed as input files to the JAR tool, their contents are added to the archive and the directory names are preserved. Also, notice that directories are processed recursively. You didn't have to tell it anything special to recursively process into the audio or images directory. Listing 25.2 shows the output when you run the command.

LISTING 25.2 CREATING A NEW JAR FILE

```
C:\jdk1.3\demo\applets\TicTacToe>jar cvf ourtest.jar *
added manifest
adding: audio/(in = 0) (out= 0)(stored 0%)
adding: audio/beep.au(in = 4032) (out= 3572)(deflated 11%)
adding: audio/ding.au(in = 2566) (out= 2055)(deflated 19%)
adding: audio/return.au(in = 6558) (out= 4401)(deflated 32%)
adding: audio/yahoo1.au(in = 7834) (out= 6985)(deflated 10%)
adding: audio/yahoo2.au(in = 7463) (out= 4607)(deflated 38%)
adding: example1.html(in = 424) (out= 238)(deflated 43%)
```

LISTING 25.2 CONTINUED

```
adding: images/(in = 0) (out= 0)(stored 0%)
adding: images/cross.gif(in = 157) (out= 160)(deflated -1%)
adding: images/not.gif(in = 158) (out= 161)(deflated -1%)
adding: TicTacToe.class(in = 3900) (out= 2247)(deflated 42%)
adding: TicTacToe.java(in = 8020) (out= 2971)(deflated 62%)

C:\jdk1.3\demo\applets\TicTacToe>
```

When the JAR tool creates a new archive, it automatically adds a manifest file to the archive. In most cases, this will suffice. However, if you need to add your own manifest file and have the JAR tool use that, you can do so by specifying the m option.

LISTING ARCHIVE CONTENTS

The JAR tool can also list the contents of a JAR archive without changing the contents. For example, run the following command from the directory where you created the `ourtest.jar` from before:

```
jar tvf ourtest.jar
```

It will list the contents of the `ourtest.jar` file that was just created. Note that you will have to run this command from the directory where the `ourtest.jar` was written. Listing 25.3 shows the contents of the JAR file.

LISTING 25.3 DISPLAY OF THE JAR FILE CONTENTS

```
C:\jdk1.3\demo\applets\TicTacToe>jar tvf ourtest.jar
     0 Thu Jul 13 22:24:18 PDT 2000 META-INF/
    68 Thu Jul 13 22:24:18 PDT 2000 META-INF/MANIFEST.MF
     0 Thu Jun 15 15:54:36 PDT 2000 audio/
  4032 Fri Jun 02 13:11:22 PDT 2000 audio/beep.au
  2566 Fri Jun 02 13:11:22 PDT 2000 audio/ding.au
  6558 Fri Jun 02 13:11:22 PDT 2000 audio/return.au
  7834 Fri Jun 02 13:11:22 PDT 2000 audio/yahoo1.au
  7463 Fri Jun 02 13:11:22 PDT 2000 audio/yahoo2.au
   424 Fri Jun 02 13:11:22 PDT 2000 example1.html
0 Thu Jun 15 15:54:36 PDT 2000 images/
   157 Fri Jun 02 13:11:22 PDT 2000 images/cross.gif
   158 Fri Jun 02 13:11:22 PDT 2000 images/not.gif
  3900 Fri Jun 02 13:11:22 PDT 2000 TicTacToe.class
  8020 Fri Jun 02 13:11:22 PDT 2000 TicTacToe.java

C:\jdk1.3\demo\applets\TicTacToe>
```

Notice that a manifest file has been added to the archive automatically. See the "Manifest File" section later in this chapter for more information.

Note

Because JAR files are based on ZIP files, you don't have to use the command line to view the contents of a JAR file. You can also use the WinZip tools to view a JAR file. Just be careful not to modify the contents or corrupt it in any way. This might cause problems for applications that need to read it later. Otherwise, it's a handy way to view contents.

If you are having trouble with opening a JAR file using the WinZip application, see "Can't View a JAR File Using the WinZip™ Program" in the "Troubleshooting" section at the end of this chapter.

EXTRACTING FILES FROM AN ARCHIVE

Finally, the JAR tool can extract files from an archive file. For example, to extract the TicTacToe.class file from the ourtest.JAR file, type the following:

```
C:\jdk1.3\demo\applets\TicTacToe>jar xvf ourtest.jar TicTacToe.class
extracted: TicTacToe.class

C:\jdk1.3\demo\applets\TicTacToe>
```

You can also use the x option to extract a single file within a subdirectory of the JAR archive. You just need to specify the full path. So if you wanted to extract just the cross.gif file from the images directory within the ourtest.JAR, you would need to specify the following command:

```
C:\jdk1.3\demo\applets\TicTacToe>jar xvf ourtest.jar images/cross.gif
extracted: images/cross.gif

C:\jdk1.3\demo\applets\TicTacToe>
```


UPDATING A JAR FILE

You can update the files within the JAR file by using the -u option on the jar command like this:

```
jar uf jar-file input-file(s)
```

input-file(s) is a space-separated list of one or multiple files that need to be added to the JAR file. If a file already exists in the JAR, it will be overwritten.

You can also update the manifest file by using the um option. For example, you can do the following to merge a new manifest file with an existing one:

```
jar umf manifest jar-file
```

The file manifest contains changes that you want to merge into the manifest that exists in the JAR-file. The next section gives more information about the manifest file.

THE MANIFEST FILE

The first entry in any JAR file is a collection of meta-information about the archive. The JAR tool generates this meta-information automatically and stores it in a top-level directory named META-INF. This directory always contains what is known as the manifest file, META-INF/MANIFEST.MF (see Listing 25.3). Use the following command to extract the manifest file:

```
C:\jdk1.3\demo\applets\TicTacToe>jar xvf ourtest.jar META-INF/MANIFEST.MF
extracted: META-INF/MANIFEST.MF

C:\jdk1.3\demo\applets\TicTacToe>
```

Listing 25.3 shows the contents of the manifest file from ourtest.jar file.

LISTING 25.3 MANIFEST FILE MANIFEST.MF OF ourtest.jar

```
Manifest-Version: 1.0
Created-By: 1.3.0 (Sun Microsystems Inc.)
```

The manifest file that is created automatically by the JAR tool doesn't contain much information. There are many parameters that can be added to take advantage of special features of JAR files. The following list summaries the most important features:

- Applications Bundled as JAR Files
- Package Sealing
- Package Versioning
- Download Extensions

APPLICATIONS BUNDLED AS JAR FILES

If you bundle your entire application as a JAR file, there has to be some way to indicate which class file contains the main method that is the entry point to your application. You can do this by putting the following line into the manifest file:

```
Main-Class: classname
```

classname is the fully qualified name of the class with the main method.

PACKAGE SEALING

You can seal one or more packages within the JAR file. This ensures that all the classes within the sealed package must be present within the JAR file. You do this my putting the following line in the manifest file for each package that needs to be sealed:

```
Name: CompanyName/Package1/
Sealed: true
```

PACKAGE VERSIONING

You can also define versioning information for a package within a JAR file. You need to define the versioning information underneath the package name within the manifest file. For example, the java.util package can be versioned like this:

```
Name: java/util/
Specification-Title: "Java Utility Classes"
```

```
Specification-Version: "1.2"
Specification-Vendor: "Sun Microsystems, Inc."
Implementation-Title: "java.util"
Implementation-Version: "build57"
Implementation-Vendor: "Sun Microsystems, Inc."
```

Programs can use the methods available in the `java.lang.Package` to programmatically get the version information from a JAR file. In this way, an application can check to see which version of an application or package is loaded in the application.

Download Extension

Download extensions provide a way for manifest files to reference JAR files other than the one that the manifest file belongs to. This usually introduces itself it terms of the Java Extension mechanism that was introduced in the JDK 1.2 version. This enables custom APIs that are outside of the standard Java APIs to be referenced by the manifest file.

Reading and Writing JAR Files

The JDK 1.2 introduced several classes and packages to interact specifically with JAR files. These have been continued and also enhanced in the SDK 1.3. The classes and packages that deal with ZIP files are still in the core API as well.

The classes within the `java.util.jar` package can be used to read and write JAR files. Because the JAR file format is based on the standard ZIP file format, the package contains several classes that extend the classes found in the `java.util.zip` package.

Two other classes can be used in conjunction with reading and writing JAR files. They are `java.net.URLClassLoader` and `java.net.JarURLConnection`.

The `java.net.JarURLClassLoader` class is used to load classes and other resources from a search path of URL's that contain JAR files and directories. If a URL ends with a `/`, that URL is assumed to be a directory. Otherwise, it's assumed to be a JAR file that is opened and accessed accordingly. This class is helpful if you need to access a JAR file remotely or over a HTTP URL.

The `java.net.JarURLConnection` class extends `java.net.URLConnection` and provides a connection to a JAR file or an entry within the JAR file.

By using the previous classes and the classes within the `java.util.jar` package, you can imagine developing an application that is bundled completely as a JAR file. Using the manifest as stated earlier, you can specify the main class to start the application. Using the `JarURLConnection` class and the `URLClassLoader`, an application can reference an application bundled within a JAR and start that application. Suppose you have an application bundled within a JAR file called `MyApp.jar`. If the manifest file specifies the main class of the application, you could execute something like the following example:

```
java ApplicationLoader http://www.host.com/MyApp.jar
```

The ApplicationLoader class could get a connection to the remote JAR file and open up the JAR file for reading. The ApplicationLoader could then use the classes available in the java.util.jar package to determine the main class and call the main method on that class to start the application.

ADDING A JAR TO YOUR Classpath

Although Appendix A, "Installing the SDK and Getting Started," describes installation of the SDK and touches on ensuring that the JAR files are in your System CLASSPATH, you should understand how to add other JAR files to your CLASSPATH. These other JAR files could be your own JAR files for you application or a third-party vendor's JAR files. The good news is that it's no different than adding the JAR files for the SDK. You can specify them by appending them to your system CLASSPATH after the JAR files from the SDK. When adding JAR files, however, keep in mind that if you have a class that exists in two different JAR files, or even one JAR file and then a directory that contains Java class files, the first class of that name a Java application reads will be loaded. Of course, if you use packages, the problem is not so likely to occur. Packages can help resolve this problem if two different developers use the same name for a class, but put the classes into a different package name.

You can also append JAR files on the command line when running your applications. You can do this by using the "cp option when executing the java command. Here's an example that works on Windows:

```
java "cp %CLASSPATH%;test1.jar;test2.jar SomeApplication
```

This command tells the virtual machine to append the test1.jar and test2.jar files to the system classpath and then run the application using the SomeApplication class.

Of course, the format of the search path is different for different platforms. On Unix, instead of a semicolon, you must use a colon.

JARS AND SECURITY

As mentioned earlier, one of the main benefits of a JAR file is that it can be digitally signed. This allows potential users of the JAR file to inspect it and verify that it is a valid JAR file from one of the user's "trusted" sources. This gives JAR files a little more freedom to access system resource that normally would not be allowed.

By signing the JAR file with your particular signature, users that trust you will be able to inspect the signature and see that it came from you and then trust the JAR file. This is called verification.

It is possible to detect deliberate corruption of the files in a JAR archive. To do so, the JAR archive must be signed digitally. A digital signature is stronger than a physical one; it is harder to forge, the signer cannot repudiate it, and the signed document cannot be modified.

PRIVATE KEYS, PUBLIC KEYS, AND CERTIFICATES

To sign a JAR archive, you must first create a private key, a public key, and a certificate. The public and private keys are paired pieces of data used to create digital signatures and to encrypt data. A certificate is a guarantee by one entity, usually a trusted public organization, that another entity's public key is valid. (In this case, more specifically, a certificate conforms to the X.509 standard. The combination of a public key and a certificate can be used confidently to verify a digital signature.)

keytool

`keytool` handles the creation and management of identities, public and private keys, and certificates. The details of key and certificate creation and management are beyond the scope of this chapter.

The `keytool` program creates files called `keystore` databases. These databases are actually files that reside on the machine creating them and contain the certificates that you have created or used.

`keytool` itself has a variety of parameters, used to specify the manipulation of a key. However, this section just looks at one scenario, generating a key. To do this, you need to know several things. First, you need an alias by which this key will be known. For this example, use `myalias`. Next, you need a distinguishing name by which you will be known. This name is part of the X.509 standard for specifying your name and follows this format:

```
CN=commonName OU=organizationUnit O=organizationName L=locality,
➥Name S=stateName C=country
```

Each of these fields helps spell out who you are; for example, my distinguishing name might be

```
"CN=Chuck Cavaness, OU=QUE, O=Macmillan Publishing, L=Atlanta,
➥S=Georgia, C=US"
```

Now you can use both of these values to generate a new key:

```
C:\jdk1.3se_book>keytool -genkey -dname "CN=Chuck Cavaness, OU=QUE, O=Macmillan
➥Publishing, L=Atlanta, S=Georgia, C=US" -alias myalias
```

As you probably already guessed, the `-genkey` command tells `keytool` that you are generating a new key, `-dname` specifies distinguishing name, and `-alias` specifies the alias you will be using. Note that the alias is case sensitive, so `myalias` is not the same alias as `MyAlias`.

When you run `keytool` like this, you are prompted to enter a password for the `keystore` and a password for your new key. These passwords will be required each time you use the key later down the road. The following examples use `foobar` for both passwords.

Note

The `keytool` may take some time to complete. It could be as long as 30 seconds. Give it enough time to complete.

Caution

Don't forget, you should write down the password somewhere that is secure. You must remember the password or you will have to generate a new key. This could be a problem if you have JAR files signed and need to change them later.

You could also have specified the key password on the command line using the `-storepass` `-keypass` parameters

In general, the parameters for generating a key are

```
keytool -genkey {-alias alias} {-keyalg keyalg} {-keysize keysize}
 {-sigalg sigalg} [-dname dname] [-keypass keypass] {-validity valDays}
 {-keystore keystore} [-storepass storepass] {-v}
```

jarsigner

Now that you have generated a key, you can digitally sign your JAR file. Signing a file is useful so that you and users of the file can be sure that you are the person who sent the file and that it hasn't been tampered with.

Before you can sign the JAR file, you need to know a couple of details. First, you need to know the alias for the key you want to use. Next, you need to know the `-keystore` password and the private key password for the key you will be using. Finally, you optionally need to know the location of the `keystore` file. If you've left it in the default location, you don't need this, but if you've moved it elsewhere, you need to specify that information. See Appendix B for more information on the `jarsigner` options. Do a search on the name "`keystore`" and see where it put the key database file.

Using the key that you created under the `keytool` section, you can now sign a JAR file. Use the `ourtest.jar` file from the earlier example. If you deleted that JAR file, recreate it or create a new one using the methods that were discussed before. Here's an example of signing the JAR file:

Note

The `jarsigner` may take some time to complete. It could be as long as 30 seconds. Give it enough time to complete.

```
C:\jdk1.3\demo\applets\TicTacToe>jarsigner -storepass foobar -keypass foobar our
➥test.jar myalias
```

When you sign the JAR file, it adds two files to the manifest for the file. The first file is an `.SF` file. The `.SF` file contains information similar to the manifest file that is always included with a JAR file. However, the `.SF` file's digest doesn't include the hash of the binary data in the file (as the manifest's does), but rather a hash of the data in the manifest. This locks in the manifest information.

The second file is a .DSA file. The .DSA file contains a signature of the .SF file and also contains, encoded inside it, a copy of the .SF file and a certificate authenticating the public key corresponding to the private key used for signing.

Fortunately, you should never have to know any of those details. However, you should know that both files, by default, are named via the first eight characters in the alias; so in this case, you would have Myalias.DSA and Myalias.SF. Using the alias allows you to sign a JAR file more than once and chain these signatures together, resulting in an .SF and .DSA file for each person who signed the file.

jarsigner has a number of additional options that you can use, depending on your particular situation, as outlined in Table 25.1.

TABLE 25.1 jarsigner OPTIONS

Option	Description
-keystore file	Specifies the keystore (database file) location. By default, this file refers to .keystore in the user's home directory. This directory is specified by the user.home system property. For Windows systems, user.home is the path specified by concatenating the HOMEDRIVE and HOMEPATH environment variables if they produce a valid path; otherwise, it is the root of the SDK installation directory.
-storepass password	Specifies the keystore password. You need this password only when signing a JAR file, not when verifying it. If you fail to specify this command option, you are prompted to enter it. Normally, you should not specify this password on the command line for security reasons.
-keypass password	Specifies the password for the individual key entry. You need this password only when signing a JAR file, not when verifying it. If you fail to specify this command option, you will be prompted to enter it. Normally, you should not specify this password on the command line for security reasons. Note: The keypass password can be the same as the keystore password. If it is, the keypass is not required.
-sigfile file	Specifies the base filename for the .SF and .DSA files. If none is specified, the first eight characters of the alias (converted to uppercase) are used.
-signedjar file	Specifies the name to be used for the signed JAR file (output). If this is not specified, the new JAR file contains the same name as its source (and overwrites it).
-verify	Specifies that you want to verify the signatures in the file. This is basically the opposite of signing the file. Assuming the verification was successful, jar verified will be displayed. If an unsigned JAR file is verified, or one is signed with an unsupported algorithm (for example, RSA when you don't have an RSA provider installed), the following is displayed: jar is unsigned. (signatures missing or not parsable).

TABLE 25.1 CONTINUED

Option	Description
`-ids`	This option can be used only if the `-verify` and `-verbose` options are also used. If they are, the distinguished names of the JAR file `signer(s)` and the alias name for the `keystore` entry are also displayed.
`-verbose idOrSigner`	Puts `jarsigner` into verbose mode. In this mode, the signer outputs additional information as the signing or verification progresses.

WHEN TO USE JARS

As you have seen, using JAR files in an application or applet have many advantages over multiple class files or the standard ZIP file format. When deciding whether to package or bundle a set of class files or resources as a JAR, here are some questions to ask:

- Is the user of the JAR file concerned about security on his system?
- Can the application or applet be bundled?
- Does the application need to take advantage of compression?
- Does the application or applet need to be versioned?
- Is download time an issue?

Obviously, there are probably other criteria to use when trying to decide on creating a JAR file out of an application or applet. Each system is different and has different requirements and constraints. However, by using JAR files wherever possible, you will be able to take advantage of the Java core language more and use some of the best features for deployment, execution, and security.

TROUBLESHOOTING

CAN'T VIEW A JAR FILE USING THE WINZIP PROGRAM

If you are trying to click on a JAR file from within Windows explorer and it's not working, that's because the `.jar` extension has not been assocated with the `WinZip` program yet.

The way to fix this is to view your folder/file options under the menu on the Windows Explorer. Select the file types tab. Add a new extension for `.jar` files and associate it the WinZip program. You must already have the `WinZip` application on your machine. If you don't, you can download it from the `http://www.winzip.com` Web site. If you already have a `.jar` file extension in the file types list, you just need to add an association to the `WinZip` application for the `.jar` extension.

PART IV

DATABASES

CHAPTER 26

JDBC 2.0 Fundamentals

In this chapter

by Chuck Cavaness

WHAT IS THE JDBC?

This chapter is an introduction to using Java database connectivity (JDBC). JDBC is a part of the core Java APIs and provides cross-platform, cross-database access to databases from Java programs.

JDBC is based on Microsoft's open database connectivity (ODBC). The idea of basing JDBC design on ODBC is that because ODBC is so popular with ISVs (independent software vendors) as well as users, implementing and using JDBC will be easier for database practitioners who have earlier experience with ODBC. Also, Sun and Intersolv have developed a JDBC-ODBC bridge layer to take advantage of the ODBC drivers available in the market. So with the JDBC APIs and the JDBC-ODBC bridge, you can access and interact effectively with almost all databases from Java applets and applications. From a developer's point of view, JDBC is the first standardized effort to integrate relational databases with Java programs. JDBC has opened all the relational power that can be mustered to Java applets and applications. In this chapter and the next, you take an in-depth look at the JDBC classes and methods.

Java Database Connectivity is a set of relational database objects and methods for interacting with SQL data sources. The JDBC API's are part of core API, and thus are a part of all Java Virtual Machine (JVM) implementations.

Even though the objects and methods are based on the relational database model, JDBC makes no assumption about the underlying data source or the data storage scheme. You can access and retrieve audio or video data from many sources and load into Java objects using the JDBC APIs. The only requirement is that there should be a JDBC implementation for that source. The JDBC Version 2.0 specification available at `http://java.sun.com/products/jdbc` includes the latest information available on JDBC. As of the writing of this book, the public review of the JDBC 3.0 specification was just about to be released.

JDBC 2.0 OVERVIEW

The JDBC APIs have been around for quite a while with the Java language. However, since the JDBC 2.0 was introduced as part of the core in SDK 1.2, it has been getting more use by Internet developers for connecting to large relational databases.

The JDBC 2.0 API includes many new features in the `java.sql` package as well as the new standard extension package `javax.sql`. New features in the `java.sql` package include enhancements such as support for SQL3 data types, scrollable result sets, programmatic updates, and batch updates. All these features or enhancements help make the core JDBC package support newer technologies in today's databases and also increase performance across any type of database that is supported by JDBC.

Features in the new JDBC standard Extension API include connection pooling and the capability to connect to a wider range of data sources such as files and spread sheets. Some of the features in both packages include enhancements to support the Enterprise JavaBeans (EJB) specification. JDBC is a required feature of J2EE. Although Enterprise JavaBeans and distributed technologies are out of scope for this book, more information on EJB and Java enterprise technologies can be found at `http://java.sun.com/j2ee`.

Features found in the Standard Extension package will be discussed in the next chapter. This chapter focuses on the core JDBC 2.0 features.

JDBC Drivers

JDBC drivers provide the necessary communication layer to allow your Java applications to communicate with the database. The drivers use an underlying transport layer such as TCP/IP to communicate with the database. As you will see, how your applications talk to the driver and how the driver talks with the database is dependent on several factors, including the database vendor and the type of driver that you select.

JDBC drivers come in four distinct types. Each type is better suited for a particular type of application of network architecture.

Note

There have been many debates about which driver gives better performance and there are some very clear guidelines about choosing a particular type. However, there still are a few subjective factors that have to be considered by the application developers based on their particular needs and situation. It also should be noted that there have been several benchmarks done on JDBC drivers to see which one is the fastest. You can more information about drivers and performance starting from the Sun JDBC site at `http://java.sun.com/products/jdbc`.

The best place to start looking for a driver, after you understand the types, is the Sun JDBC site at `http://java.sun.com/products/jdbc`. You can find plenty of information about JDBC drivers and their purposes. You can also find a list of vendors that have JDBC drivers and all the information about each vendor and driver.

To probably best understand the driver type for your applications, you need to have a clear understanding of what separates one driver type from the other. The four JDBC driver types are examined separately in the following sections.

Type I

Type I JDBC drivers are referred to as a JDBC-ODBC bridge. The ODBC in this name refers to the Open Database Connectivity supported by the Windows platform. All the JDBC calls made by a Java application that is using a Type I driver are translated into ODBC calls and sent to the ODBC driver. Each host application that is making the JDBC calls must have an ODBC driver as well as the JDBC driver installed. Figure 26.1 shows a typical JDBC-ODBC environment.

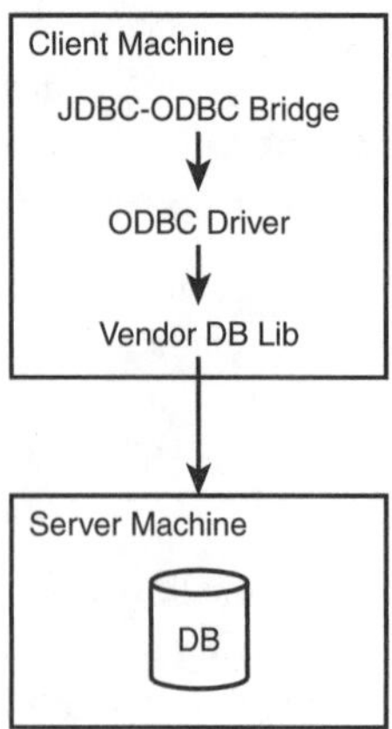

Figure 26.1
A typical Type I JDBC driver environment.

There are ODBC drivers for almost any database that is being used and also can be used for text files or Excel spreadsheets if you find the need. The setup to use this driver type is straightforward, but an ODBC datasource must be set up through the ODBC application on the Windows control panel. Because Windows is the only operating system to support ODBC, this type of driver only works for the Windows platform.

For small applications, especially ones that need to talk with databases such as Microsoft Access, this is probably the best way to go. However for large-scale applications, this probably would not be your best choice. The reason is that performance will most likely suffer due to database calls being translated through the ODBC layer in both directions. This will have a negative impact on performance and will not scale sufficiently for large applications.

The other problem with this type of driver is that the host application must have a DSN setup on each machine that needs to access the database; this does not work well for applets. Because applets are downloaded onto a host machine, there's no guarantee that the machine will have an ODBC connection set up correctly.

A small benefit of using this type of driver is that if you need to support multiple database vendors, you can install the different ODBC drivers and an application can just change between the different DSN names set up for each database vendor.

Type II

Type II drivers are considered Native-API/Partly Java drivers. This is because the JDBC calls that an application makes are translated into the native database API calls for a particular database such as Sybase, Oracle, or Informix. There are Type II drivers for just about any relational database in use today.

Type II drivers perform better than Type I drivers because there is no ODBC layer that the calls must pass through. After the JDBC calls are translated into the native database language call, the call can go directly to the database without having to be translated by any other layer.

The downside to this type of driver is that software for each specific database platform must be loaded onto the machine accessing the database. For the Windows platform, this is usually in the form of some DLL files. This has been known to present some problems if you need to support multiple databases on a single machine, because you might have DLL conflicts.

It also can become a problem of maintenance. If your application is shipped and installed on customer machines, some additional software must be installed for each database platform that your application needs to support.

Figure 26.2 shows a typical Type II environment.

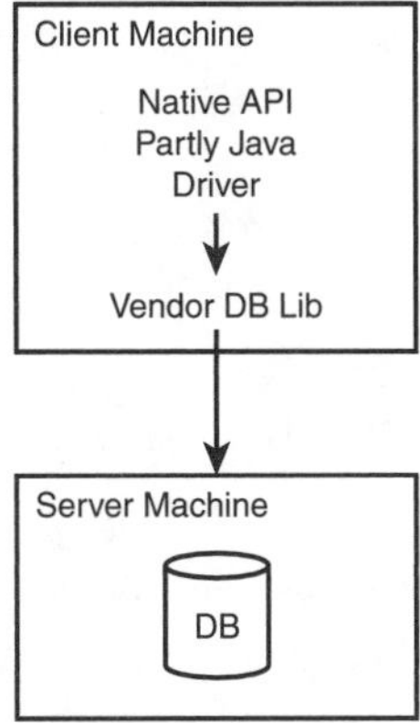

Figure 26.2
A typical Type II JDBC driver environment.

TYPE III

The Type III JDBC driver can be called a Net-protocol/All Java driver. They are also sometimes referred to as three-tier drivers. This is because JDBC calls are sent using a DBS vendor-independent protocol to a middle server where they are then translated to a vendor-dependent access method. Figure 26.3 shows a typical Type III environment.

These types of drivers are popular for both intranet and Internet applications. They usually offer very good performance when compared to Type I or Type II and allow for more flexibility when it comes to feature set. These drivers typically have features such as connection pooling, logging, and caching enabled in the middle server piece. They also can perform additional security features, such as encryption, that other drivers might not be able to handle directly.

As a downside, it usually takes a little more work to install due to the middle server that must also be running for an application to communicate with the database. There also can be a little performance degradation due to the middle server. However, this is vendor dependent.

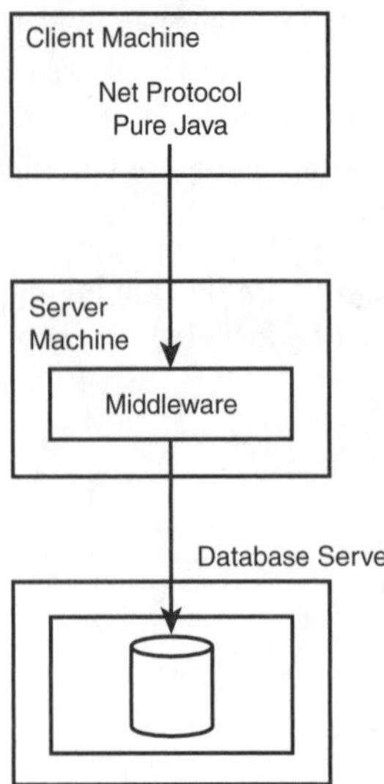

Figure 26.3
A typical Type III JDBC driver environment.

TYPE IV

Type IV JDBC drivers are usually called either native drivers or All Java drivers. The Type IV driver converts the JDBC calls into the native database protocol for the specific database. Therefore, you will need a different Type IV driver for each database platform you need to support.

Type IV drivers, like Type III, usually give significantly better performance when compared to Type I or Type II drivers. Unlike Type III drivers however, the installation and distribution of applications using a Type IV driver is extremely easy. There is no additional software or middle server that must be installed for an application to communicate with the database. Only the driver needs to be downloaded, usually in the form of a JAR file, and the application can then use the driver to connect to the database. Figure 26.4 shows the typical Type IV environment.

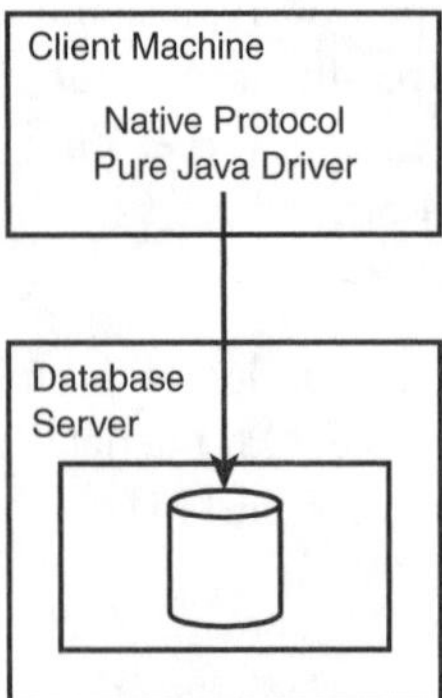

Figure 26.4
A typical Type IV JDBC driver environment.

Type III and Type IV drivers are becoming the drivers that more and more Internet developers are choosing for the reasons mentioned previously. Type IV is typically easier to use, but again you must have a driver for each database that you need to support.

It was mentioned early and it bears repeating here that all these drivers and their associated performance factors are very database vendor dependent. It should not automatically be assumed that a Type III driver would out perform another type of driver. You should also get specific benchmarks or perform the benchmarks of various drivers against your specific application.

SETTING UP A DATABASE

For the rest of this chapter and Chapter 27, "Advanced JDBC 2.0," a database had to be selected to use for the examples. As you know, there are many to pick from. Some of the relational databases have been around for a long time and have a large share of the market. However, there are a few new vendors in the market and the price is just right for using one of these for the purposes of this book. The problem with some of these newer databases is that they don't fully support the JDBC 2.0 driver functionality.

So, the Oracle8i Lite database from Oracle will be used for these examples.Oracle also now has a version called Oracle8i Personal Edition. This version will also run on Windows98 as well as Windows NT, Linux, and other Unix platforms. You can choose one of these databases or select one of your favorites to use along with the examples in this book. Just be sure that there is a JDBC 2.0 compliant driver for the database before using it.

Note

The download size of Oracle Lite and Personal Edition is quite large. The Personal Edition is approximately 200 MB. Unless you have a fast Internet connection, you might want to get a CD from Oracle or use a different database.

You can download a developer copy from the following URL:

```
http://technet.oracle.com/software/index.htm
```

or you can start from the main Oracle site at

```
http://www.oracle.com
```

Oracle8i supports the Windows, Linux, and several of the UNIX platforms such as Solaris. If you already have another database such as Informix, Sybase, or Microsoft SQL Server, you are welcome to use that along with the examples in this and the next chapter. If you are going to be using a different database as you follow along, you must ensure that you download a JDBC 2.0 driver for your specific database. It doesn't matter which JDBC driver type it is, just ensure that the JDBC driver you are using supports the full JDBC 2.0 features or you will not be able to run all the upcoming examples.

The same schema will be used throughout the two database chapters. If you choose Oracle8i Lite, the schema has already been created for you and populated with some sample data. If you are using another database, you should create the schema on your particular database. Also, when you get to the part about setting up a JDBC driver, you will need to read the specific documentation for the driver that you will be using. The steps to set up a JDBC driver for the Oracle8i Lite database are discussed later.

Caution

You can use whichever database you are most comfortable with. Just be sure that it supports transactions and you can find a JDBC 2.0 driver for it. Many vendors say that they support the full 2.0, but when you attempt to execute a 2.0 feature, it prints a message saying, "That 2.0 feature not yet supported."

You get the JDBC 2.0 driver for Oracle8i Lite with the same download. When you run the installer for the database, it will create a datasource with the name "POLITE". This is the reference that you will use to connect to the database later.

Note

Even though the install will create a datasource during the installation process, this is not a TYPE I driver, it is a TYPE II.

For installation of the Oracle8i Lite database, refer to the documentation that is provided with the download. There are several tools that are provided with the Oracle install. You can use these to check your installation and to view the sample data that is provided. Again, refer to the database documentation for any problems with the database itself.

SETTING UP THE EXAMPLE DATABASE SCHEMA

A database schema must be selected for the rest of this chapter and the next. If you have ever designed or used a database schema, you know that there are good schema designs and bad ones. There are complete college degrees given for creating good database designs. This book doesn't spend any time analyzing the example schema for being properly or improperly "*normalized.*" In short, normalization is database term for a database that has had all the redundant and duplicate meta-data definitions removed and relocated for optimal consistency. There are a series of tests that can be applied to any database to test to what degree the database has been normalized. Normalization by itself does not guarantee a good database design. It is just way to help get there in the beginning of the design.

The example schema used here is for purposes of this book and it's being used just as it is. There also won't be much explanation about SQL or database details such as VARCHAR. If you need a refresher on either of these topics, read the documentation for your particular database before going any further with this chapter.

Tables 26.1, 26.2, and 26.3 show the tables and columns that the examples will use. Because a schema and sample data is provided by the Oracle install, those tables are used for the examples. Some columns are not listed and will not be used throughout the examples, because they don't add any necessary information.

Note

If you choose to use another database, you will need to create these tables in that database and populate them with some sample data.

Note

Creating tables and schema is something normally done by a Database Administrator. If you don't know how to do this or are having trouble, check the documentation that comes with your database.

TABLE 26.1 `Customer` **TABLE**

Column Name	Column Type
CUSTID	NUMBER NOT NULL (PK)
NAME	VARCHAR(45) NOT NULL
ADDRESS	VARCHAR(40)
CITY	VARCHAR(30)
STATE	VARCHAR(2)
ZIP	VARCHAR(9)
PHONE	VARCHAR(9)
REPID	NUMBER

The `(PK)` *for* `CUST_NO` *indicates that it is the primary key of the table.*

TABLE 26.2 `Emp` **(EMPLOYEE) TABLE**

Column Name	Column Type
EMPNO	NUMBER NOT NULL (PK)
ENAME	VARCHAR(10)
JOB	VARCHAR(9)
MGR	NUMBER
HIREDATE	TIMESTAMP
SAL	NUMBER
COMM	NUMBER
DEPTNO	NUMBER NOT NULL

TABLE 26.3 SalaryHistory TABLE

Column Name	Column Type
EMPID	NUMBER (PK)
DATE	DATE (PK)
SALARY	VARCHAR(10)

Caution

The column name DATE above in the Salary History table was chosen to make a point. Although Oracle Lite allowed me to name the column with this name, in other databases, this is a reserved word. Not to mention that the name is not very informative to begin with. Make sure to choose good names when naming your schema.

Note that there are two columns in the Salary History table that make up the primary key. This is called a composite primary key and is made up of two or more columns in the table. Because an employee hopefully will have many salary change records, the column EMP_NO will not be unique. This is why an additional primary key is used along with the EMP_NO column to help ensure uniqueness. With this schema design, an employee could only have one salary history record per Timestamp value, but the likelihood of that happening is extremely small.

INSTALLING AND USING A JDBC DRIVER

The installation of a JDBC driver varies according to the type of driver that is being used. Oracle8i Lite provides a Type II driver. It uses an ODBC datasource setup to locate and communicate with the database. Although this TYPE II driver uses an ODBC configuration, it is different from the JDBC-ODBC Bridge of the type I.

After all the pieces are installed, it's a good idea to test the database connection outside of your Java applications to be sure everything is correct. Oracle8i Lite provides a utility called SQL*Plus that can get a connection to an Oracle8i Lite database and issue SQL commands. The utility will prompt you for three input fields; username, password, and host string. For username, you can use SYSTEM. The password can be any string, and for host string, use ODBC:POLITE. If everything is set up correctly, you should see the screen shown in Figure 26.5.

You can issue SQL commands and see the results. For example, to select all the rows in the EMP table, type `select * from EMP;` and press Enter. The results should match those seen in Figure 26.6.

Note

If you are using another database, your sample data will probably not match these results.

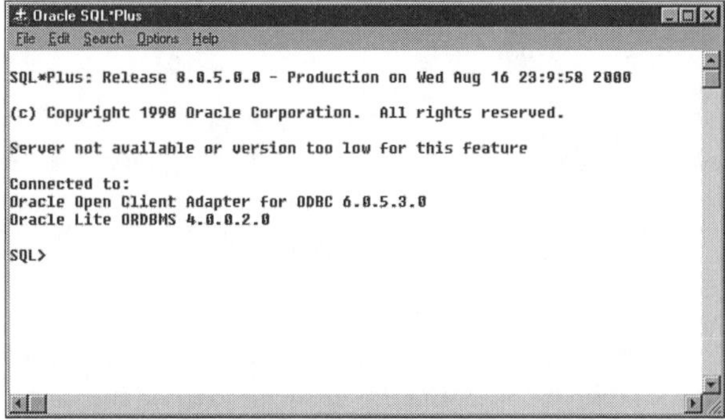

Figure 26.5
A SQL Plus connection is successful when you are presented with the SQL command prompt.

```
Oracle Open Client Adapter for ODBC 6.0.5.3.0
Oracle Lite ORDBMS 4.0.0.2.0

SQL> select * from EMP;

    EMPNO ENAME      JOB              MGR HIREDATE         SAL       COMM    DEPT
--------- ---------- --------- --------- ---------- --------- --------- -------
     7839 KING       PRESIDENT           1981-11-1       5000
     7698 BLAKE      MANAGER        7839 1981-05-0       2850
     7782 CLARK      MANAGER        7839 1981-06-0       2450
     7566 JONES      MANAGER        7839 1981-04-0       2975
     7654 MARTIN     SALESMAN       7698 1981-09-2       1250       1400
     7499 ALLEN      SALESMAN       7698 1981-02-2       1600        300
     7844 TURNER     SALESMAN       7698 1981-09-0       1500          0
     7900 JAMES      CLERK          7698 1981-12-0        950
     7521 WARD       SALESMAN       7698 1981-02-2       1250        500
     7902 FORD       ANALYST        7566 1981-12-0       3000
     7369 SMITH      CLERK          7902 1980-12-1        800
     7788 SCOTT      ANALYST        7566 1982-12-0       3000
     7876 ADAMS      CLERK          7788 1983-01-1       1100
     7934 MILLER     CLERK          7782 1982-01-2       1300

14 rows selected.

SQL>
```

Figure 26.6
SQL returns results from the query in a tabular format.

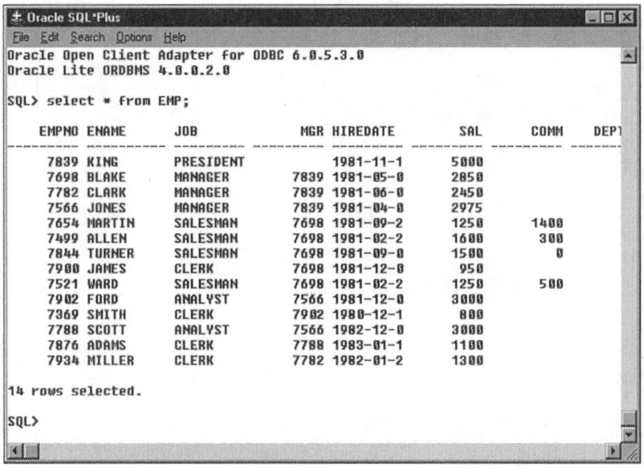

There are several JAR files included in the Oracle8i Lite installation. You will want to add `OLITE40.JAR` to your system CLASSPATH before attempting to connect to the databases. This jar file can be found in the `<DRIVE>:\orawin95\LITE\CLASSES` directory.

Note

The default login for Oracle8i Lite is either `SYSTEM` with no password or you can also use `SCOTT` as the username and `TIGER` as the password. The username and password of SCOTT and TIGER are the defaults for the Oracle demo database.

For any programs with installation of the database and/or driver JAR file, check the user documentation that came with the installations or the newsgroups.

JDBC URLs

A Uniform Resource Locator (URL) provides a standard way of locating a resource on the Internet. It's very much like an address. The first part of an URL specifies the protocol used. The rest of the URL gives information for locating the resource using the protocol mentioned at the beginning of the URL.

A JDBC URL is a way to specify a database so that the application or applet will use it to make the connection. JDBC driver vendors have some flexibility when establishing what the URL format will be for their driver. Of course, there are standards that must be followed to some extent. The standard format of a JDBC URL looks like this:

```
jdbc:<subprotocol>:<subname>
```

Notice that a colon must separate each section. The protocol for a JDBC URL is always `jdbc`. The subprotocol is the name of the driver being used or the name of the database. A well known subprotocol is `odbc`. For example, to access a database through the JDBC-ODBC Bridge, you could use something like this:

```
jdbc:odbc:my_access_database
```

The subname section is a way to identify the database for the JDBC URL. The general format for this usually looks something like this:

```
//hostname:port/subsubname
```

Applications that need to access a database over the Internet or the physical network could specify the logical hostname of an IP address and a port to connect. It would probably also specify the name of the database instance that it wanted to connect to.

Keep in mind that each JDBC driver vendor will specify the exact format for the URL. Check the documentation for your driver to find the exact format.

For Oracle8i Lite, use the following URL format to connect to the database. Substitute the drive letter and/or database name for your specific needs.

```
jdbc:polite:POLITE
```

The `<subname>` part of this URL is the datasource name that was created in the ODBC configuration.

If you are having trouble with the JDBC URL, see "Setting Up the Correct JDBC URL" in the "Troubleshooting" section at the end on this chapter.

CONNECTING TO THE DATABASE

Connecting to a database using JDBC can be divided into two steps. The first involves loading the JDBC driver and the second step is actually making the connection. Each step is described individually in the following sections.

LOADING THE DRIVER

A JDBC driver is loaded using the Class.forName method. The single argument to the method is the name of the driver that you want to load. This may seem a little confusing at first.You need to figure out what the driver class name is from the driver documentation and thencall the `forName` method. The `forName("className")` method initializes and loads an instance of the named class and returns the `Class` object for the class specified by the argument to the `forName` method.

Caution

When using the `forName` method on the `Class` object, you must catch a `ClassNotFound` exception.

Listing 26.1 shows an example of loading the Oracle8i Lite driver for use with the Oracle8i Lite database.

LISTING 26.1 LOADING A JDBC DRIVER

```
try
  {
    Class.forName ( "oracle.lite.poljdbc.POLJDBCDriver"  );
  }
  catch ( ClassNotFoundException ex )
  {
    System.out.println ( "Oracle driver not found in class path" );
    System.out.println ( ex.getMessage () );
  }
```

Listing 26.1 is obviously not a complete listing meant to compile, but shows an example of how to load the Oracle8i Lite JDBC driver.

Some of the older documentation that you might find referred developers to create an instance of the driver and register it with the `DriverManager`. Calling the *`forName()`* method will do this for you when you call it with a driver classname. Creating an instance of the driver doesn't really hurt anything. It's just redundant work.

If you are having trouble loading the JDBC driver, see "Finding the JDBC Driver Class" in the "Troubleshooting" section at the end on this chapter.

MAKING THE CONNECTION

The second part of getting a connection to a database is actually making the driver establish the connection. As with the first step, this is easy to do. The hardest part of this step is using the correct JDBC URL.

As mentioned in a previous section, the URL specifies everything the driver needs to know to make a connection to the database. You should use one of the three `getConnection()` methods on the `java.sql.DriverManager` class to actually perform the connection process. The three different methods are listing here for convenience:

```
static Connection getConnection(String url);
static Connection getConnection(String url, Properties info);
static Connection getConnection(String url, String user, String password);
```

Notice that the three methods return a single instance of a `Connection` object. A `Connection` is really a Java interface from the `java.sql` package that represents a session with a database.

The only differences between the three methods are the additional parameters for specifying either a Properties instance or two strings for user and password. Depending on the specific URL format for your JDBC driver, you will need to use a certain `getConnection()` method. If for example, the URL format for your driver has the user and password specified in the URL itself, you probably can get away with using the first method format, otherwise you might have to use the second or third. The second format that has an instance of the `Properties` class as the second parameter, can be used to set key/value pairs that are then used by the driver to establish a connection. An example of a key/value pair might be `user-name="SCOTT"` and `password="tiger"`. Some of the older driver URLs did not support having the username and password values in the URL itself. You needed to set them in the `Properties` instance and pass the `Properties` instance along with the URL in the `getConnection()` method.

Take a look at a complete example that establishes a connection to Oracle. Listing 26.2 shows a class called `DatabaseManager`, which is responsible for creating and returning instances of the `Connection` interface on which other Java classes can make SQL calls. This class will be reused throughout the examples in this chapter, so it's a good idea to become familiar with its operation. The `DatabaseManager` has all the information it needs to connect to the database, including the complete JDBC URL. Later, you'll learn the good points and the bad points about a design like this.

Note

The example `POLITE` database that comes with the Oracle Lite installation is used in the following example.

LISTING 26.2 SOURCE CODE FOR `DatabaseManager.java`

```
import java.sql.*;
import java.util.*;

public class DatabaseManager
{
  // These properties could come from a system configuration file
  static private String urlHeader = "jdbc:polite:";
  static private String databaseName = "POLITE";
  static private String user = "SYSTEM";
  static private String password = "";
  static private String driverName = "oracle.lite.poljdbc.POLJDBCDriver";

  public static Connection getConnection()
  {
    // Define the local Connection instance that gets returned
    Connection conn = null;

    try
    {
      // Load the JDBC driver
      Class.forName( driverName );
      // Get an instance of the Connection. Really the Connection is an
      // interface that some class implements.
```

LISTING 26.2 CONTINUED

```
      // Concat the three parts together to build the full URL
String databaseURL = urlHeader + databaseName;
      conn = DriverManager.getConnection( databaseURL, user, password );
    }
    catch( ClassNotFoundException ex )
    {
      // The JDBC driver class could not be found
      ex.printStackTrace();
      System.exit( -1 );
    }
    catch( SQLException ex )
    {
      // A sql exception occurred, for now just print out the stack trace
      ex.printStackTrace();
    }

    return conn;
  }
}
```

Listing 26.3 shows the class that is used to test the `DatabaseManager` class from Listing 26.2.

LISTING 26.3 SOURCE CODE FOR `DatabaseConnectTest.java`

```
import java.sql.*;

public class DatabaseConnectTest
{
  public static void main(String[] args)
  {
    // Get an instance of a Connection from the DatabaseManager
    // who is performing Creator pattern here by creating instances of
    // a class that implements the Connection interface.
    Connection conn = DatabaseManager.getConnection();
    if ( conn != null )
    {
      System.out.println( "Connection attempt was successful!" );

      try
      {
        conn.close();
      }
      catch( SQLException ex )
      {
        ex.printStackTrace();
        System.out.println( "Problem closing the connection" );
      }
    }
  }
}
```

There's not much output for this example. It should look like the output in Listing 26.4.

LISTING 26.4 `DatabaseConnectTest` **OUTPUT**

```
C:\jdk1.3se_book\classes>java DatabaseConnectTest
Connection attempt was successful!

C:\jdk1.3se_book\classes>
```

Let's take a closer look at the `DatabaseManager` class from Listing 26.2 and see exactly what it's doing. The first thing to notice about this class is it defines some private static variables that contain information about the database that it will connect to. As this is a very easy and simple way to handle the connection information, it's not very flexible. If one or more of the connection values changes, then the software would need to be recompiled. It's probably not a great solution. A better solution would be to read it from a `java.util.Properties` file. It will do for now.

The next interesting thing to notice in the case takes place just inside the try block. This is where the database driver class is loaded and a connection is established to the database. Notice that you must catch a `ClassNotFoundException`, just in case the driver is not in the system CLASSPATH.

Finally, if a connection was established it is returned to the back to the caller. Otherwise, null will be returned. The `DatabaseConnectTest` class in Listing 26.3 checks to see if the connection that was returned is null. It prints out some information either way.

Another thought is that because the time it takes to actually get the connection to the database is considerable, you might want to create a pool of database connections when the system starts and then use the connections when a client asks for them. When the client is finished, it hands it back to the `DatabaseManager`, which would recycle it by putting it back into the pool of connections. This concept and several others are discussed in the next chapter in the sections about connection pooling.

READING DATA USING JDBC

As you saw in the previous example, a `Connection` represents a session to a database. When it becomes necessary to read data from the database, the instance of the `Connection` is used, but indirectly. The main class that is used in conjunction with the Connection class is the `java.sql.Statement` class.

THE `Statement` CLASS

The `Statement` class is used to execute static SQL statements and possibly read the results that were returned by the query. As the name implies, the `Statement` class represents a single SQL statement that needs to be executed against the database. You don't create a new instance of the `Statement` class directly. You use the instance of the connection as sort of a `Statement` Factory. You do this by calling the `createStatement` method that exists on the `Connection` class. This method will return an instance of the `Statement` class that you can use to execute SQL statements.

There are several other similar methods that also exist on the `Connection` class that are used for such things as creating an instance of a `java.sql.PreparedStatement`. A `PreparedStatement` is used for preparing a SQL statement for execution at a later time. This is more efficient that creating a new statement each time.

You'll see more of this class and others later in the "Using Prepared Statements" section.

For now, take a look at an example using the `Statement` class. The following example shows how to read a set of records from the employee database and display those records to the console. The `DatabaseManager` class from the previous example is reused throughout the examples to make it easier and more consistent when acquiring the initial connection to the database.

Note

You will see that creating a `DatabaseManager` type of class for your Java applications that access the database to be a very valuable idea. The complete functionality might be slightly different for various applications, but it makes sense to isolate the connection creation to a factory type of object. This makes it easier in the future if you have to support different databases, because all the connection information is located in one area, which tends to decrease the coupling your application has on any particular database platform.

Listing 26.5 shows the class called `ReadEmployeeRecords`. This class gets a connection to the database through the `DatabaseManager` class and then reads all the `Employee` records in the database. It then iterates through the records, printing out certain pieces of information about each employee. Listing 26.6 shows the source code for `Employee.java` that is used within the `ReadEmployeeRecords.java` example.

Listing 26.5 Source Code for `ReadEmployeeRecords.java`

```
import java.sql.*;

public class ReadEmployeeRecords
{
  // Private reference to an instance of the Connection
  private Connection conn = null;

  // Default Constructor
  public ReadEmployeeRecords( Connection connection )
  {
    conn = connection;
  }

  // Public method to read all the records for the employees
  public void readRecords()
  {
    // SQL Statement to get all the employees
    String READ_EMPLOYEE_SQL_STMT = "SELECT * FROM EMP";
    Statement stmt = null;
    ResultSet rs = null;
```

LISTING 26.5 CONTINUED

```
    try
    {
      stmt = getConnection().createStatement();
      stmt.execute( READ_EMPLOYEE_SQL_STMT );
      rs = stmt.getResultSet();
    }
    catch( SQLException ex )
    {
      ex.printStackTrace();
    }

    // Call the public method to print the employees out
    printEmployeeRecords( rs );
  }

  // Private accessor for the connection
  private Connection getConnection()
  {
    return conn;
  }

  // Use the ResultSet and print the records to the console
  public void printEmployeeRecords( ResultSet rs )
  {
    try
    {
      // While there are more records to read from the ResultSet
      while( rs.next() )
      {
        // Get the data by using the column index from the table.
        // Could also have used the column names like
        // rs.getString( "firstName" );
        //
        String nbr = rs.getString( 1 );
        String name = rs.getString( 2 );
        String job = rs.getString( 3 );
        String mgr = rs.getString( 4 );
        Timestamp hireDate = rs.getTimestamp(5);

        Employee employee = new Employee( nbr, name, job, mgr, hireDate );

        System.out.println( employee.toString() );
      }
    }
    catch( SQLException ex )
    {
      ex.printStackTrace();
    }
  }

  // Method to start this class and test the examples
  public static void main(String[] args)
  {
    // Use the previous DatabaseManager
    Connection conn = DatabaseManager.getConnection();
    ReadEmployeeRecords reader = new ReadEmployeeRecords( conn );
```

LISTING 26.5 CONTINUED

```
    reader.readRecords();

    // Always make sure to close the connection when you are finished
    try
    {
      conn.close();
    }
    catch( SQLException ex )
    {
      ex.printStackTrace();
    }
    catch( Exception ex )
    {
      ex.printStackTrace();
    }
  }
}
```

LISTING 26.6 SOURCE CODE FOR Employee.java

```
import java.sql.Timestamp;

public class Employee implements java.io.Serializable
{
  // Private instance variables for an employee
  private String employeeNbr = null;
  private String name = null;
  private String job = null;
  private String mgr = null;
  private Timestamp hireDate = null;

  // Constructor
  public Employee( String nbr, String name, String job,
  String mgr, Timestamp hiredDate )
{
    super();
    employeeNbr = nbr;
    this.name = name;
    this.job = job;
    this.mgr = mgr;
    this.hireDate = hiredDate;
  }

  // Override the toString() method from object to display an employee
  public String toString()
  {
    StringBuffer strBuf = new StringBuffer();
    strBuf.append( "ID: " );
    strBuf.append( getEmployeeNbr() );
    strBuf.append( " -" );
    strBuf.append( " Name: " );
    strBuf.append( getName() );
    strBuf.append( " -" );
    strBuf.append( " Job: " );
```

LISTING 26.6 CONTINUED

```
    strBuf.append( getJob() );
    strBuf.append( " -" );
    strBuf.append( " Mgr: " );
    strBuf.append( getMgr() );

    strBuf.append( " -" );
    strBuf.append( " Hire Date: " );
    if ( getHireDate() != null )
    {
      strBuf.append( getHireDate().toString() );
    }
    return strBuf.toString();
  }

  // Public Getters for the object's state
  public String getEmployeeNbr()
  {
    return employeeNbr;
  }

  public String getName()
  {
    return name;
  }

  public String getJob()
  {
    return job;
  }

  public String getMgr()
  {
    return mgr;
  }

  public Timestamp getHireDate()
  {
    return hireDate;
  }
}
```

Listing 26.7 shows the output when you run the previous `ReadEmployeeRecords.java` example.

LISTING 26.7 `ReadEmployeeRecords.java` **OUTPUT**

```
C:\jdk1.3se_book\classes>java ReadEmployeeRecords
ID: 7839 - Name: KING      - Job: PRESIDENT - Mgr: null - Hire Date:
➥ 1981-11-17 00:00:00.0
ID: 7698 - Name: BLAKE     - Job: MANAGER   - Mgr: 7839 - Hire Date:
➥ 1981-05-01 00:00:00.0
ID: 7782 - Name: CLARK     - Job: MANAGER   - Mgr: 7839 - Hire Date:
➥ 1981-06-09 00:00:00.0
```

LISTING 26.7 CONTINUED

```
ID: 7566 - Name: JONES      - Job: MANAGER   - Mgr: 7839 - Hire Date:
➥ 1981-04-02 00:00:00.0
ID: 7654 - Name: MARTIN     - Job: SALESMAN  - Mgr: 7698 - Hire Date:
➥ 1981-09-28 00:00:00.0
ID: 7499 - Name: ALLEN      - Job: SALESMAN  - Mgr: 7698 - Hire Date:
➥ 1981-02-20 00:00:00.0
ID: 7844 - Name: TURNER     - Job: SALESMAN  - Mgr: 7698 - Hire Date:
➥ 1981-09-08 00:00:00.0
ID: 7900 - Name: JAMES      - Job: CLERK     - Mgr: 7698 - Hire Date:
➥ 1981-12-03 00:00:00.0
ID: 7521 - Name: WARD       - Job: SALESMAN  - Mgr: 7698 - Hire Date:
➥ 1981-02-22 00:00:00.0
ID: 7902 - Name: FORD       - Job: ANALYST   - Mgr: 7566 - Hire Date:
➥ 1981-12-03 00:00:00.0
ID: 7369 - Name: SMITH      - Job: CLERK     - Mgr: 7902 - Hire Date:
➥ 1980-12-17 00:00:00.0
ID: 7788 - Name: SCOTT      - Job: ANALYST   - Mgr: 7566 - Hire Date:
➥ 1982-12-09 00:00:00.0
ID: 7876 - Name: ADAMS      - Job: CLERK     - Mgr: 7788 - Hire Date:
➥ 1983-01-12 00:00:00.0
ID: 7934 - Name: MILLER     - Job: CLERK     - Mgr: 7782 - Hire Date:
➥ 1982-01-23 00:00:00.0
C:\jdk1.3se_book\classes>
```

You might have noticed that when you retrieve data from the database, instead of just printing out the data, an Employee class is built. The reason this was done instead of just printing it out has to do with object oriented systems and specifically Object-to-Relational Mapping frameworks. You'll learn more about this later in this chapter and the next chapter, but just know that there is a method and a purpose to the madness.

After a `Statement` is created from the connection instance and the `execute` method is called on the `Statement`, a `ResultSet` object is associated with the `Statement` object. The `ResultSet` object is explained next.

THE `ResultSet` CLASS

You can think of a `ResultSet` as a table of data that represents the result after executing a database query. It's considered a table because there can be multiple rows and usually there are multiple columns. Each column in the `ResultSet` represents a table column from the database. In the simple SQL statement that was executed in the *`ReadEmployeeRecords.java`* example from Listing 26.5, the `ResultSet` represents all the columns in the `EMP` table and all the rows from the table.

A `ResultSet` can be thought of as an open view to a set of data. It's open because the `ResultSet` maintains a cursor to a specific row in the data that was returned from the `Statement` execution. The cursor initially points to a position before the first row in the set of data and then can be moved around by calling the various methods in the `ResultSet` class. It wouldn't make sense to have it point to the first row, because there might be no data returned from the execution. You must use the *`next`* method to move to the first row. The *`next`* method moves the cursor to the next row in the set.

The next method returns a boolean value. It returns true if the row is valid and false if there are no more rows to read. You can see from the ReadEmployeeRecords example, iterating through the records in done by putting the next in a while loop and then iterating until the method returns false, which causes the while loop to end. There are other methods in the ResultSet that allow the cursor to be placed at a certain row. The default behavior of the ResultSet is to only allow moving forward through the rows and never backward. However, with the JDBC 2.0 API, you can setup a ResultSet to move both forward and backward. There are also new methods that allow the ResultSet to be updatable, rather than a read-only view as it was in the 1.0 JDBC API. These new features are discussed more in the next chapter.

As you probably noticed, the next method does not retrieve the data from the ResultSet. It is used only for positioning within the set of rows. To retrieve the actual data that exists in the ResultSet, you have to use one of the many getXXX methods defined in the ResultSet class. There is a method for just about any type that can be stored in the database.

TABLE 26.4 getXXX METHODS IN java.sql.ResultSet CLASS

Return Type	Method	Parameter
Array	getArray	(int index)
Array	getArray	(String name)
InputStream	getArray	(int index)
InputStream	getAsciiStream	(String name)
BigDecimal	getBigDecimal	(int index)
BigDecimal	getBigDecimal	(String name)
InputStream	getBinaryStream	(int index)
InputStream	getBinaryStream	(String name)
Blob	getBlob	(int index)
Blob	getBlob	(String name)
boolean	getBoolean	(int index)
boolean	getBoolean	(String name)
byte	getByte	(int index)
byte	getByte	(String name)
byte[]	getBytes	(int index)
byte[]	getBytes	(String name)
Reader	getCharacterStream	(int i)
Reader	getCharacterStream	(String name)

TABLE 26.4 CONTINUED

Return Type	Method	Parameter
Clob	getClob	(int index)
Clob	getClob	(String name)
Date	getDate	(int index)
Date	getDate	(String name)
Double	getDouble	(int index)
Double	getDouble	(String name)
float	getFloat	(int index)
float	getFloat	(String name)
int	getInt	(int index)
int	getInt	(String name)
long	getLong	(int index)
long	getLong	(String name)
Ref	getRef	(int index)
Ref	getRef	(String name)
Short	getShort	(int index)
Short	getShort	(String name)
String	getString	(int index)
String	getString	(String name)
Time	getTime	(int index)
Time	getTime	(String name)
Timestamp	getTimestamp	(int index)
Timestamp	getTimestamp	(String name)
InputStream	getUnicodeStream	(int index)
InputStream	getUnicodeStream	(String name)

There are two ways to use the `getXXX` methods. First, you can specify the column name that you want to retrieve. For example, if you have a column in the `EMP` table called `EMPNO` of type `varchar`, you can get the value by doing this:

```
String employeeNbr = rs.getString( "EMPNO" );
```

You can also get the value by specifying the index of the column. So, if the column `EMPNO` was the first column in the `ResultSet` that was returned, you can also do this:

```
String employeeNbr = rs.getString( 1 );
```

Caution

You have to be careful when using the column index approach. The index that the column is in the `ResultSet` might be completely different from the index of the column in the table. This is because the `ResultSet` might have a couple of columns from different tables and the column indexes will not be the same as they are when the column is in its own table.

The JDBC documentation recommends that the index approach be used to obtain the best efficiency. If there are multiple columns with the same name in the `ResultSet`, the first encountered will be returned. Remember, the `ResultSet` can represent columns across several tables and there is a chance that there are two columns with the same name. Also, when using the `getXXX` that takes the column name, the name parameter is case insensitive.

Note

Although the column index works fine, it may be a better approach to use the column name over the index. This is mainly a debugging issue. It will be easier to find an error using:

```
String.employeeNbr = rs.getString("WRONG_NAME")
```

than it will be to see

```
String.employeeNbr = rs.getString(2)
```

There are many `getXXX` methods that return a type for just about every Java primitive and several Java object types such as the `String` class. You have to be careful to use the correct `getXXX` method for the type of `Object` or primitive that will be returned. If you use the incorrect one, an `SQLException` might be raised. In some cases, the type can be converted. For example, if you have a `VARCHAR` value of `2` and you use a `getInt` method, the value might be converted to an `int` value of `2`. The `getString` might correctly convert all the standard SQL types to a valid `String`. It's recommended in most cases if you are not sure of the database type, to use the `getString` method to retrieve the data from the `ResultSet`.

Other methods such as the *`getInt()`* can actually retrieve any of the numeric or character types. The data will be converted to an `int`. For example, if the database type is a `varchar`, JDBC will attempt to parse an `int` out of the value. If it can't, it will throw an `SQLException`.

WRITING DATA USING JDBC

In most applications in which you need to read data from the database, you often need to insert or update data in the database as well. You can do this using the same manner as before, except that the SQL statement must be changed to actually perform the insert or update. Using the `CUSTOMER` table for this, you can create a new customer record in the database. Then you can read it back out and update some fields.

As mentioned, the Java classes that you need to use to accomplish this were discussed in the last example. The primary classes that you will need are the `Connection`, `Statement`, and `ResultSet` classes.

Note

If you are using Oracle8i Lite to follow along, go into the ODBC configuration for the `POLITE` datasource and turn the AutoCommit selection to On. Otherwise, when you write your data, you will have to call `commit` on it before it will become persistent. You will use this type of feature later, but handle it with JDBC, not an ODBC configuration option. If you are using another database, you are probably already set the correct way.

Listing 26.8 shows the source code for the `Customer.java` class that is used in the `NewCustomerExample.java` in Listing 26.9. This example shows how to insert a new `Customer` record into the database using JDBC. Then it updates a field in the new `Customer` record and updates the record into the database. Listing 26.10 shows the output when the example is executed.

LISTING 26.8 SOURCE CODE FOR `Customer.java`

```
public class Customer
{
  // Default Constructor
  public Customer()
  {
    super();
  }

  // Private Instance Variables
  private String id;
  private String name;
  private String city;
  private String state;
  private String zip;

  // Public Accessors
  public String getId()
  {
    return id;
  }

  public void setId( String custId )
  {
    id = custId;
  }

  public void setName( String newName )
  {
    name = newName;
  }

  public String getName()
  {
    return name;
  }

  public void setCity( String city )
  {
    this.city = city;
```

LISTING 26.8 CONTINUED

```
  }

  public String getCity()
  {
    return city;
  }

  public void setState( String state )
  {
    this.state = state;
  }

  public String getState()
  {
    return state;
  }

  public void setZip( String zip )
  {
    this.zip = zip;
  }

  public String getZip()
  {
    return zip;
  }

  // Return a String that clients can use to insert an instance of this
  // class into the database.
public String getInsertSQL()
  {
    StringBuffer sqlBuf = new StringBuffer( "INSERT INTO CUSTOMER (" );
    sqlBuf.append( "CUSTID, NAME, CITY, STATE, REPID, ZIP ) " );
    sqlBuf.append( " VALUES ( " );
    sqlBuf.append( getId() );
    sqlBuf.append( "," );

    sqlBuf.append( "'" );
    sqlBuf.append( getName() );
    sqlBuf.append( "'," );

    sqlBuf.append( "'" );
    sqlBuf.append( getCity() );
    sqlBuf.append( "'," );

    sqlBuf.append( "'" );
    sqlBuf.append( getState() );
    sqlBuf.append( "'," );

    sqlBuf.append( 1 );
    sqlBuf.append( "," );

    sqlBuf.append( "'" );
    sqlBuf.append( getZip() );
    sqlBuf.append( "')" );
```

Listing 26.8 Continued

```
    return sqlBuf.toString();
  }

  // Return a string that clients can use to get all the Customer records
  public static String getReadAllSQL()
  {
    return "SELECT CUSTID, NAME, CITY, STATE, ZIP FROM CUSTOMER";
  }

  // Return a SQL update String for this instance. Notice that this is done
  // very inefficiently because all the fields are being updated regardless of
  // whether they have changed. There are better ways to do it
  //. Because customer number was assigned, this field will not be updated
  // . It would cause big referential integrity problems if
  // it was updated.
  public String getUpdateSQL()
  {
    StringBuffer sqlBuf = new StringBuffer( "UPDATE CUSTOMER SET " );

    sqlBuf.append( "NAME='" );
    sqlBuf.append( getName() );
    sqlBuf.append( "', CITY='");
    sqlBuf.append( getCity() );
    sqlBuf.append( "', STATE='");
    sqlBuf.append( getState() );
    sqlBuf.append( "', ZIP='");
    sqlBuf.append( getZip() );
    sqlBuf.append( "' WHERE CUSTID = " );
    sqlBuf.append( getId() );

    return sqlBuf.toString();
  }

  // Override the default toString method to output something of your own
  public String toString()
  {
    StringBuffer buf = new StringBuffer();
    buf.append( "ID: " );
    buf.append( getId() );
    buf.append( " Name: " );
    buf.append( getName() );
    buf.append( " City: " );
    buf.append( getCity() );
    buf.append( " State: " );
    buf.append( getState() );
    buf.append( " Zip: " );
    buf.append( getZip() );

    return buf.toString();
  }
}
```

Listing 26.9 is a class that is used to insert a `Customer` record into the database. The class gets a database connection and then creates a new instance of a `Customer` object. Listing 26.8

previously shows the `Customer` class that is used. After the Customer is inserted into the database, the ZIP code field of the `Customer` object is modified and an `updateCustomer` method is called causing the `Customer` record that inserted previously to be updated with the new ZIP code. Listing 26.10 shows all of the Customer records in the database, including the new one that was just inserted and updated.

LISTING 26.9 SOURCE CODE FOR `NewCustomerExample.java`

```
import java.sql.*;

public class NewCustomerExample
{
  // Private Instance variable for the Connection
  private Connection conn = null;

  // Default Constructor
  public NewCustomerExample( Connection connection )
  {
    super();
    conn = connection;
  }

  public Customer insertNewCustomer( Customer aCustomer ) throws SQLException
  {
    // Local variable for the Statement object
    Statement stmt = null;
    ResultSet rs = null;

    // Create a Statement object from the Connection
    stmt = getConnection().createStatement();

    // Get the highest customer id and increment it by 1 for the next id
    String maxCustomerNbrSQL = "SELECT MAX(CUSTID) FROM CUSTOMER";
    rs = stmt.executeQuery( maxCustomerNbrSQL );
    rs.next();
    int maxNbr = rs.getInt( 1 );
    aCustomer.setId( String.valueOf( maxNbr + 1 ) );

    // Ask the Customer for its insert sql statement
    String sql = aCustomer.getInsertSQL();
    stmt.executeUpdate( sql );

    // return the customer instance with the customer number set
    return aCustomer;
  }

  // A method to update an existing customer in the database
  public void updateCustomer( Customer cust )
  {
    // Local variable for the Statement object
    Statement stmt = null;
    ResultSet rs = null;
    try
    {
      String sql = cust.getUpdateSQL();
```

Listing 26.9 Continued

```
      // Put a line here so that you can read the output better
      System.out.println("");
      System.out.println( sql );
      // Create a Statement object from the Connection
      stmt = getConnection().createStatement();
      stmt.executeUpdate( sql );
    }
    catch( SQLException ex )
    {
      ex.printStackTrace();
    }
  }

  public void printAllCustomers()
  {
    // Local variable for the Statement object
    Statement stmt = null;
    ResultSet rs = null;
    try
    {
      // Create a Statement object from the Connection
      stmt = getConnection().createStatement();
      // Ask the Customer for its insert sql statement
      String sql = Customer.getReadAllSQL();
      rs = stmt.executeQuery( sql );

      while( rs.next() )
      {
        Customer cust = new Customer();

        String id = rs.getString( 1 );
        String name = rs.getString( 2 );
        String city = rs.getString( 3 );
        // Had to do this because the database type was a char and
        // there were too many spaces at the end for it to print out
        // and look reasonable. This is a bad thing, but necessary for the
        // example here in this book.
        if ( city != null )
          city = city.substring( 0, 15 );

        String state = rs.getString( 4 );
        String zip = rs.getString( 5 );

        cust.setId( id );
        cust.setName( name );
        cust.setCity( city );
        cust.setState( state );
        cust.setZip( zip );

        System.out.println( cust.toString() );
      }
    }
    catch( SQLException ex )
    {
      ex.printStackTrace();
```

LISTING 26.9 CONTINUED

```
      }
    }

    // Private accessor for the connection
    private Connection getConnection()
    {
      return conn;
    }

    public static void main(String[] args)
    {
      try
      {
        // Use the previous DatabaseManager to acquire a connection
        Connection conn = DatabaseManager.getConnection();
        NewCustomerExample example = new NewCustomerExample( conn );
        // Create a new Customer object to be inserted into the database
        // Notice you don't have to populate the customer nbr field because the
        // database is set up to do that for you

        Customer cust = new Customer();
        cust.setName( "Josh Alan" );
        cust.setCity( "Snellville" );
        cust.setState( "GA" );
        cust.setZip( "12345" );

        // Call the insert method so that the customer will be inserted
        example.insertNewCustomer( cust );
        // Print the customer records, including the one just inserted
        example.printAllCustomers();
        // Update a field in the customer
        cust.setZip( "54321" );
        example.updateCustomer( cust );
        // Print the records out again. The zip for the one that was
        // just added should be 54321, not 12345
        example.printAllCustomers();

        // Always be sure to close the connection when you are finished
        conn.close();
      }
      catch( SQLException ex )
      {
        ex.printStackTrace();
      }
      catch( Exception ex )
      {
        ex.printStackTrace();
      }
    }
  }
```

LISTING 26.10 OUTPUT FROM `NewCustomerExample.java`

```
C:\jdk1.3se_book\classes>java NewCustomerExample

ID: 100 Name: JOCKSPORTS                                   City: BELMONT
➥ State: CA Zip: 96711
ID: 101 Name: TKB SPORT SHOP                               City: REDWOOD
➥ CITY    State: CA Zip: 94061
ID: 102 Name: VOLLYRITE                                    City:
➥ BURLINGAME      State: CA Zip: 95133
ID: 103 Name: JUST TENNIS                                  City:
➥ BURLINGAME      State: CA Zip: 97544
ID: 104 Name: EVERY MOUNTAIN                               City:
➥ CUPERTINO       State: CA Zip: 93301
ID: 105 Name: K + T SPORTS                                 City: SANTA
➥ CLARA     State: CA Zip: 91003
ID: 106 Name: SHAPE UP                                     City: PALO
➥ ALTO        State: CA Zip: 94301
ID: 107 Name: WOMENS SPORTS                                City:
➥ SUNNYVALE       State: CA Zip: 93301
ID: 108 Name: NORTH WOODS HEALTH AND FITNESS SUPPLY CENTER City: HIBBING
➥ State: MN Zip: 55649
ID: 109 Name: Josh Alan                                    City:
➥ Snellville      State: GA Zip: 12345

UPDATE CUSTOMER SET NAME='Josh Alan', CITY='Snellville', STATE='GA',
➥ ZIP='54321' WHERE CUSTID = 109
ID: 100 Name: JOCKSPORTS                                   City: BELMONT
➥ State: CA Zip: 96711
ID: 101 Name: TKB SPORT SHOP                               City: REDWOOD
➥ CITY    State: CA Zip: 94061
ID: 102 Name: VOLLYRITE                                    City:
➥ BURLINGAME      State: CA Zip: 95133
ID: 103 Name: JUST TENNIS                                  City:
➥ BURLINGAME      State: CA Zip: 97544
ID: 104 Name: EVERY MOUNTAIN                               City:
➥ CUPERTINO       State: CA Zip: 93301
ID: 105 Name: K + T SPORTS                                 City: SANTA
➥ CLARA     State: CA Zip: 91003
ID: 106 Name: SHAPE UP                                     City: PALO
➥ ALTO        State: CA Zip: 94301
ID: 107 Name: WOMENS SPORTS                                City:
➥ SUNNYVALE       State: CA Zip: 93301
ID: 108 Name: NORTH WOODS HEALTH AND FITNESS SUPPLY CENTER City: HIBBING
➥ State: MN Zip: 55649
ID: 109 Name: Josh Alan                                    City:
➥ Snellville      State: GA Zip: 54321
```

Notice that because an update was done, another "Josh Alan" record was not added, but the ZIP for the existing one was updated and written back out to the database.

USING PREPARED STATEMENTS

Up to this point, a `java.sql.Statement` class has been used to execute the SQL statements against the database. This is not very efficient if you will be executing the same SQL statements more than a couple of times because the SQL statement must be compiled each time it is sent to the database. The database does not understand the SQL string and is not able to execute it in the string format. It must turn the SQL string into something that it can understand and execute.

The `java.sql.PreparedStatement` can help with this because it will compile the SQL statement one time and then you can send the `PreparedStatement` to the database without the database having to compile it each time. This increases performance because the statement is, in effect, precompiled.

The SQL statements have also been used without parameters in the previous examples. You can also pass parameters to the SQL statements and then reuse the same statement and pass different parameters in to it. Although you can use the `PreparedStatement` on a SQL statement that does not take parameters, you generally should be passing parameters to it. This will allow for better performance and reuse.

Look at an example using a `PreparedStatement`. For this example, the `PreparedStatement` is supplied that takes two input parameters. One input parameter will be a CUSTID, which is the primary key of the customer table. The second is a REPID. The example will update the customer's rep id with the new value.

Remember that in the previous example in Listing 26.9, an update SQL string was used that was returned by the Customer class to perform the update. The update string had to be built each time and executed. It also had to be compiled each time it was executed. If you wanted to update several customers, this would be very inefficient.

This example is pretty basic, but it shows the basics of using the `PreparedStatement` with parameters. Notice that question marks in the `UPDAATE_SQL` static `String`. These question marks are replaced by actual values during execution of the `PreparedStatement`. You should also notice that a `PreparedStatment` is given a SQL `String` when it is created. It uses this `String` to precompile the `Statement` that will be executed. This is why the performance is better; the SQL String has already been compiled into something native that can be executed. Only the parameters for the questions marks need to be passed in. Listing 26.11 shows the complete example.

LISTING 26.11 SOURCE CODE FOR `UpdateCustomerRepID.java`

```
import java.sql.*;

public class UpdateCustomerRepID
{
  // Private instance variables for the connection and the prepared statement
  private Connection connection = null;
```

LISTING 26.11 CONTINUED

```
  private PreparedStatement stmt = null;

  // The SQL to be used for the PreparedStatement. The question marks are
  // for the input parameters that will be passed in
  private static String UPDATE_SQL =
"UPDATE CUSTOMER SET REPID = ? WHERE CUSTID = ?";

  // Default Constructor
  public UpdateCustomerRepID( Connection conn ) throws SQLException
  {
    super();
    connection = conn;
    // Create the instance of the PreparedStatement for this class
    stmt = connection.prepareStatement( UpdateCustomerRepID.UPDATE_SQL );
  }

  // Public Accessor for the PreparedStatement
  public PreparedStatement getStatement()
  {
    return stmt;
  }
  // Public Accessor for the Connection
  public Connection getConnection()
  {
    return connection;
  }

  // Print out all the Customers to the console
  public void printAllCustomers()
  {
    // Local variable for the Statement object
    Statement stmt = null;
    ResultSet rs = null;
    try
    {
      // Create a Statement object from the Connection
      stmt = getConnection().createStatement();
      // Ask the Customer for its insert sql statement
      String sql = "SELECT CUSTID, REPID FROM CUSTOMER";
      rs = stmt.executeQuery( sql );

      while( rs.next() )
      {
        String id = rs.getString( 1 );
        String repId = rs.getString( 2 );

        System.out.println( "CUSTID: " + id + " REPID: " + repId );
      }
    }
    catch( SQLException ex )
    {
      ex.printStackTrace();
    }
  }
```

LISTING 26.11 CONTINUED

```
  // This method performs the update through the PreparedStatement
  public void updateCustomerRepId( String customerNumber,
     int repId )
   throws SQLException
{
    stmt.setInt( 1, repId );
    stmt.setString( 2, customerNumber );
    stmt.executeUpdate();
  }

  // The main method for this example
  public static void main(String[] args)
  {
    try
    {
      // Use the previous DatabaseManager class to acquire a connection
      Connection conn = DatabaseManager.getConnection();

      // Create an instance of the example class
      UpdateCustomerRepID example = new UpdateCustomerRepID( conn );

      System.out.println( "Before running the update on the records." );
      example.printAllCustomers();

      Statement custStatement = conn.createStatement();
      ResultSet rs = custStatement.executeQuery( Customer.getReadAllSQL() );
      while( rs.next() )
      {
        // Get the customer number(id) from the record
        String customerNumber = rs.getString( 1 );
        // Set the phone number to all zero's
        int repId = 1;
        // Execute the PreparedStatement
        example.updateCustomerRepId( customerNumber, repId );
      }
      System.out.println( "After running the update on the records." );
      example.printAllCustomers();

      // Always be sure to close the connection when you are finished
      conn.close();
    }
    catch( SQLException ex )
    {
      ex.printStackTrace();
    }
  }

}
```

Here is the output from running the `UpdateCustomerRepID` example in Listing 26.12.

LISTING 26.12 OUTPUT FROM UpdateCustomerRepID.java

```
C:\jdk1.3se_book\classes>java UpdateCustomerRepID
Before running the update on the records.
CUSTID: 100 REPID: 7844
CUSTID: 101 REPID: 7521
CUSTID: 102 REPID: 7654
CUSTID: 103 REPID: 7521
CUSTID: 104 REPID: 7499
CUSTID: 105 REPID: 7844
CUSTID: 106 REPID: 7521
CUSTID: 107 REPID: 7499
CUSTID: 108 REPID: 7844
CUSTID: 109 REPID: 1
After running the update on the records.
CUSTID: 100 REPID: 1
CUSTID: 101 REPID: 1
CUSTID: 102 REPID: 1
CUSTID: 103 REPID: 1
CUSTID: 104 REPID: 1
CUSTID: 105 REPID: 1
CUSTID: 106 REPID: 1
CUSTID: 107 REPID: 1
CUSTID: 108 REPID: 1
CUSTID: 109 REPID: 1

C:\jdk1.3se_book\classes
```

As mentioned earlier, this example is simple. How often would you want to set all the values in a column to the same value? Hopefully, the point comes across, however, that you don't need to create a new `Statement` each time. You can use a `PreparedStatement` and pass parameters to it. This will increase performance because the statement is precompiled. This also potentially reduces the number of objects in memory.

USING TRANSACTIONS

There are times when you have multiple statements that depend on one another successfully completing before another statement should execute. For example, in the employee database that you are working with, if an employee's salary is updated in the `EMPLOYEE` table, you also need to update that in the `SALARYHISTORY` table. If the update to the `EMPLOYEE` table fails, you don't want to go through with the update to the `SALARYHISTORY` table or you will have invalid data in the database. This is known as a *data integrity* problem.

The best way to ensure that this happens in the correct manner is to wrap these two updates in a *transaction*. A transaction is a set of one or more statements that work together as a unit. Either all the statements complete or they all fail. This is typical behavior in most real-world applications and especially in Internet applications. If a user's online order isn't saved to the database, you don't want to bill the users credit card.

To begin a transaction, you need to turn off the auto-commit mode on the connection instance. For example, you would need to do this:

```
connection.setAutoCommit(false);
```

Assuming that the connection instance was a live instance, then any statements executed after this method call would not be automatically committed to the database. Only after the `commit` was called would the statements be executed against the database. You can also cause the statements to be committed by setting the auto commit back to true like this:

```
connection.setAutoCommit(true);
```

Note

Note that when the auto commit mode is `true`, which is the connection default, that every statement is a transaction with only the statement in the transaction.

If an `SQLException` is thrown during execution of the `commit` of a transaction, the `rollback` method should be called on the transaction. The `rollback()` method ensures that all data that was updated by the statements in the transaction will be undone. The `SQLException` might or might not give you enough information about why the execution failed, but it's a good idea to call the `rollback` and start the transaction all over again if possible. Otherwise, you might just provide a message back to the client explaining what happened. One possible explanation is that someone else acquired a lock on the table or record that the transaction tried to update. In this case, you will have to `rollback` your transaction and get updated data and start the transaction over again.

Look at an example using the `EMP` and `SALARYHISTORY` explanation from before. In Listing 26.13, you will cause the update to intentionally fail. There has been a constraint put on the column `SAL` in the `EMP` table. It must be greater than 0. In this example, two statements are part of the transaction. The first one is valid, but the second one will cause the transaction to fail because the check constraint rule on the `SAL` column is not met. So when the transaction is committed, the database will rollback the transaction and neither statement will be committed to the database.

Note

By default, the constraint on the SAL column is not in the database already. You will need to add a constraint on this column to ensure that all values in this column are greater than zero. View the database documentation on how to setup this constraint.

LISTING 26.13 `EmployeeSalaryTransactionExample.java`

```
import java.sql.*;

class EmployeeSalaryTransactionExample
{
  // Private instance variables for the connection and the prepared statement

  private Connection connection = null;
```

Listing 26.13 Continued

```
  // Default Constructor
  public EmployeeSalaryTransactionExample( Connection conn )
  {
    super();
    connection = conn;
  }

  // Public Accessor for the Connection
  public Connection getConnection()
  {
    return connection;
  }

  // Method to update the EMPLOYEE and SALARY_HISTORY tables
  public void updateEmployeeSalary( int employeeId, double oldSalary, double
newSalary )
  {
    try
    {
      // Start the transaction by turning off auto commit
      getConnection().setAutoCommit( false );

      // Set up the first statement, which is valid
      String sqlString2 = "INSERT INTO SALARYHISTORY (EMPID, DATE, SALARY )";
      sqlString2 = sqlString2 + " VALUES( ?, ?, ? )";
      PreparedStatement stmt2 = getConnection().prepareStatement( sqlString2 );
      stmt2.setInt( 1, employeeId );
      Timestamp ts = new Timestamp( System.currentTimeMillis() );
      stmt2.setTimestamp( 2, ts );
      stmt2.setDouble( 3, newSalary );
      // This statement should not really execute until
    // the commit of the transaction
      stmt2.executeUpdate();

      // Set up the second statement which should fail because of database
      // constraints on the salary value. The salary must be greater than 0
      String sqlString1 = "UPDATE EMP SET SAL = ? WHERE EMPNO = ?";
      PreparedStatement stmt1 =
      getConnection().prepareStatement( sqlString1 );
      stmt1.setDouble( 1, newSalary );
      stmt1.setInt( 2, employeeId );
      stmt1.executeUpdate();

      // Attempt to commit the transaction
      getConnection().commit();
    }
    catch( SQLException sqlException )
    {
      try
      {
        // There was a problem, so roll back the changes
        System.out.println(
        "Database Transaction Failed...Rolling back the changes" );
        sqlException.printStackTrace();
        getConnection().rollback();
      }
```

LISTING 26.13 CONTINUED

```
      catch( Exception ex )
      {
        ex.printStackTrace();
      }
    }
  }

  // Main method to test this class
  public static void main(String[] args)
  {
    try
    {
      // Use the previous DatabaseManager class to acquire a connection
      Connection conn = DatabaseManager.getConnection();

      // Create an instance of the example class
      EmployeeSalaryTransactionExample example =
new EmployeeSalaryTransactionExample( conn );

      // Get the first employee record and use it for this example
      Statement stmt = conn.createStatement();
      ResultSet rs = stmt.executeQuery( "SELECT EMPNO, SAL FROM EMP" );

      // Just interested in the first record for this example.
    // Make sure there is at least one record
      // at least one record
      if ( rs.next() )
      {
        int employeeId = rs.getInt( 1 );
        double oldSalary = rs.getDouble( 2 );

        // Close the result set since you don't need it anymore
        rs.close();

        // This is being set to a negative number so that
      // it will fail because the database column has a constraint
      // that it has to be greater than zero.
        double newSalary = -10.00;
        example.updateEmployeeSalary( employeeId, oldSalary, newSalary );
      }
      else
      {
        System.out.println( "There were 0 employee records in the database" );
      }

      // Always be sure to close the connection when you are finished
      conn.close();
    }
    catch( SQLException ex )
    {
      ex.printStackTrace();
    }
  }
}
```

Listing 26.14 can be used to test the transaction rollback example from Listing 26.13.

LISTING 26.14 EXCEPTION STACKTRACE FROM LISTING 26.13

```
C:\jdk1.3se_book\classes>java EmployeeSalaryTransactionExample
Database Transaction Failed...Rolling back the changes
java.sql.SQLException: [POL-4317] Check constraint is violated
        at
oracle.lite.poljdbc.POLJDBCPreparedStatement.jniExecute(Native Method
)
        at oracle.lite.poljdbc.POLJDBCPreparedStatement.executeInt(Unknown Sourc
e)
        at oracle.lite.poljdbc.POLJDBCPreparedStatement.executeUpdate(Unknown So
urce)
        at EmployeeSalaryTransactionExample.updateEmployeeSalary(EmployeeSalaryT
ransactionExample.java:46)
        at EmployeeSalaryTransactionExample.main(EmployeeSalaryTransactionExampl
e.java:96)

C:\jdk1.3se_book\classes>
```

As expected, the transaction fails because of the constraint on the `SAL` column value. Remember to always rollback the changes when a transaction fails or otherwise you might leave the database integrity in an unknown condition.

GETTING METADATA FROM THE DATABASE

The public Java interface called `java.sql.DatabaseMetaData` defines methods that allow the JDBC developer to obtain detailed pieces of information about the database as a whole. There are many, many methods contained within this interface. Because it is an interface, there must be a concrete class that implements the interface so that the methods can be called. This concrete class is the `Connection` class itself. You can call the `getMetaData` method on a `Connection` object and obtain the metadata for the database that the `Connection` is connected to. After you have the metadata, you can query for just about anything that you want to know about the database. The example in Listing 26.15 shows some of the information that can be obtained through the `DatabaseMetaData` interface.

LISTING 26.15 SOURCE CODE FOR `MetaDataExample.java`

```
import java.sql.*;

public class MetaDataExample
{

  // Default Constructor
  public MetaDataExample()
  {
    super();
  }
```

LISTING 26.15 CONTINUED

```
    // Just a convenience print method
    public void print( String txt )
    {
      System.out.println( txt );
    }

    // Main method for this example
    public static void main(String[] args)
    {
      try
      {
        // Acquire a connection from the DatabaseManager
        Connection conn = DatabaseManager.getConnection();

        MetaDataExample example = new MetaDataExample();
        // Get the MetaData
        DatabaseMetaData metaData = conn.getMetaData();

        // Get driver information
        example.print( "Driver Information" );
        example.print( metaData.getDriverName() );
        example.print( metaData.getDriverVersion() );
        example.print( "" );

        // Get schema information
        example.print( "Schemas" );
        ResultSet schemas  = metaData.getSchemas();
        while( schemas.next() )
        {
          example.print( schemas.getString(1) );
        }
        example.print( "" );

        // Get table information
        example.print( "Tables" );
        ResultSet tables  = metaData.getTables( "", "", "", null );
        while( tables.next() )
        {
          example.print( tables.getString(3) );
        }
        // Always close the open resources
        conn.close();
      }
      catch( Exception ex )
      {
        ex.printStackTrace();
      }
    }
  }
```

Listing 26.16 Output from `MetaDataExample.java`

```
C:\jdk1.3se_book\classes>java MetaDataExample
Driver Information
oracle.lite.poljdbc.POLJDBCDriver
OLite 4.0

Schemas
SYSTEM
SCOTT

Tables
BONUS
CUSTOMER
DEPT
DUMMY
EMP
INVENTORY
ITEM
ORD
PRICE
PRODUCT
PRODUCT_COMPOSITION
SALARYHISTORY
SALGRADE
T_EMP
SALES

C:\jdk1.3se_book\classes>
```

Note

There might be some variation in your output based on the database vendor and version. You might also have to use a name/string pattern and null for the other parameters in the `getTables()` method in Listing 26.15. Check your driver and vendor documentation for more information on the variations.

Again, there are so many methods that you can use to obtain information about the database that they can't all be mentioned here. You can review the documentation for the `DatabaseMetaData` interface for additional details.

Using Stored Procedures

For a secure, consistent, and manageable multi-tier client/server system, the data access should allow the use of stored procedures. Stored procedures centralize the business logic in terms of manageability and running the query. Java applets or applications running on clients with limited resources cannot be expected to run huge queries. JDBC allows the use of stored procedures by way of the `CallableStatement` class.

A CallableStatement object is created by the prepareCall method in the Connection object. The prepareCall method takes a string as the parameter. This string, called an escape clause, is of the form

```
{[? =] call <stored procedure name> [<parameter>,<parameter> ...]}
```

The CallableStatement class supports parameters. These parameters are of the OUT kind to receive data from a stored procedure or the IN kind to pass values into a stored procedure. The parameter marker (question mark) must be used for the return value (if any) and any output arguments because the parameter marker is bound to a program variable in the stored procedure. In other words, a database stored procedure can receive values through the parameters of a CallableStatement, and may also return results through those same parameters or by a separate return value. Like a PreparedStatement, a question mark identifies the place where parameters are inserted, and in addition can also mark the place where values are returned.

Input arguments can be either literals or parameters. For a dynamic parameterized statement, the escape clause string takes the form

```
{[? =] call <stored procedure name> [<?>,<?> ...]}
```

If there are any OUT parameters, they must be registered using the registerOutparameter method (see Table 26.5) before the call to the executeQuery, executeUpdate, or execute methods.

TABLE 26.5 CallableStatement—OUT PARAMETER REGISTER METHODS

Return Type	Method Name	Parameter
void	registerOutParameter	(int parameterIndex, int sqlType)
void	registerOutParameter	(int parameterIndex, int sqlType, int scale)

When the executeQuery method is called, the escape clause is translated into a form that the database can use to execute the named stored procedure. After the stored procedure is executed, the DBMS returns the result value to the JDBC driver. The return value is accessed by using the methods in Table 26.6.

TABLE 26.6 CallableStatement PARAMETER ACCESS METHODS

Return Type	Method Name	Parameter
boolean	getBoolean	(int parameterIndex)
byte	getByte	(int parameterIndex)
byte[]	getBytes	(int parameterIndex)
java.sql.Date	getDate	(int parameterIndex)
double	getDouble	(int parameterIndex)

Table 26.6 Continued

Return Type	Method Name	Parameter
`float`	`getFloat`	`(int parameterIndex)`
`int`	`getInt`	`(int parameterIndex)`
`long`	`getLong`	`(int parameterIndex)`
`java.lang.Bignum`	`getBignum`	`(int parameterIndex, int scale)`
`Object`	`getObject`	`(int parameterIndex)`
`short`	`getShort`	`(int parameterIndex)`
`String`	`getString`	`(int parameterIndex)`
`java.sql.Time`	`getTime`	`(int parameterIndex)`
`java.sql.Timestamp`	`getTimestamp`	`(int parameterIndex)`
Miscellaneous Functions		
`boolean`	`wasNull`	`()`

In the JDBC call, you create a `CallableStatement` object with the `?` symbol as a placeholder for parameters, and then connect Java variables to the parameters as shown in Listing 26.17. (This example is not complete or meant to execute.)

Listing 26.17 Example Method Executing a Stored Procedure

```
public double getEmployeeStartSalary( Connection connection,
 String employeeId ) throws SQLException
{
  //Create a Callable Statement object.
  CallableStatement cStmt =
connection.prepareCall( "{call getEmployeeStartSalary(?,?)}" );

  // Set the IN parameter for the stored procedure
cstmt.setString(1, employeeId );

  // Register the OUT parameter for the stored procedure
cStmt.registerOutParameter( 2,java.sql.Types.DOUBLE );

  // Now you are ready to call the stored procedure
  cStmt.executeQuery();

  // Get the OUT parameter from the registered parameter
  // Note that you get the result from the CallableStatement object
  double salary = cStmt.getDouble( 2 );
return salary;

}
```

TROUBLESHOOTING

SETTING UP THE CORRECT JDBC URL

The attempt at creating a database connection using a JDBC driver fails.

Because each JDBC driver vendor has flexibility to use a slightly different JDBC URL, you can never really guess at the format of the URL. As mentioned earlier in this chapter, the URL has the following format:

```
jdbc:<subprotocol>:<subname>
```

Remember that a colon must separate each section. The protocol for a JDBC URL is always jdbc. The subprotocol and the subname is the part that will vary across vendors. It usually depends also on the driver type that the driver implements as well. The best advice is to read the documentation thoroughly when setting up the database URL. There really is no standard way except to read the documentation.

The other thing that might go wrong is the actual connection to the database. Make sure you are providing the username and password in the format that the driver needs. Remember there are three `getConnection()` methods that get the username and password from different places. Check the documentation as to which the driver is expecting.

FINDING THE JDBC DRIVER CLASS

When loading a database driver using the `Class.forName` *method, a* `ClassNotFoundException` *is thrown.*

The cause of this problem is most always that the driver is not in your system CLASSPATH. The best thing to do is to "echo" or "cat" the system CLASSPATH at the command line and see if the driver is in your CLASSPATH. The driver can be inside a JAR or ZIP file, so look for that file if it is. Remember, you can open a JAR or ZIP file and look to see if the class is in there. You might need to do this to make sure you are loading the correct JAR or ZIP file. Sometimes a vendor will provide multiple JARs. One can be a larger development JAR file, whereas another one is built for distribution and contains fewer class files.

CHAPTER 27

ADVANCED JDBC 2.0

In this chapter

by *Chuck Cavaness*

NEW FEATURES IN JDBC 2.0 API

The JDBC 2.0 includes many new features in the `java.sql` package as well as the `javax.sql` Standard Extension Package. This section discusses three of the new features from the core 2.0 API and a later section briefly describes a few features found in the Standard Extension Package. The JDBC 2.0 core APIs found in the `java.sql` package is available as part of the standard SDK 1.3 download. The Optional Package APIs, which are within the `javax.sql` package, are available as a separate download. You can download the Optional Package at the following URL:

`http://java.sun.com/products/jdbc/download.html`

The new JDBC 2.0 core features discussed in this chapter are

- Scrollable `ResultSets`
- Updatable `ResultSets`
- Batch Updates

Caution

Be careful when choosing a JDBC 2.0 driver. Some driver vendors report that their drivers are JDBC 2.0 compliant, but when you start testing some of the newer 2.0 features, you get an exception that says that 2.0 feature is not yet implemented. Always understand which features are implemented and which ones are not for a particular driver or database.

USING SCROLLABLE `ResultSets`

In some of the previous examples with `ResultSet` objects that were returned from statement executions, the results were moved through forward one row at a time. With the JDBC 2.0 API, you can also move backward. There are also methods that move the cursor to a particular row in the `ResultSet`. Having a cursor that can move to a particular row is useful when you have a record in the `ResultSet` that needs to be updated. There are other benefits to the bidirectional movement of the cursor in a `ResultSet`. You'll see some of those benefits in the examples. `ResultSets` are not scrollable by default. You need to set up a `ResultSet` that is scrollable.

Caution

There is some overhead in setting up and using a scrollable `ResultSet`, so make sure you really need one before using it. Otherwise, just use a standard `ResultSet` that moves only in the forward direction.

To create a scrollable `ResultSet` object, you need to specify two new parameters to the `createStatement` method on the `Connection` class. Both parameters are required, and the order is important here. The first parameter is the scroll type. The options are

- `TYPE_FORWARD_ONLY`
- `TYPE_SCROLL_INSENSITIVE`
- `TYPE_SCROLL_SENSITIVE`

The TYPE_FORWARD_ONLY constant is the default for a ResultSet when no type is specified. This is a ResultSet that has a cursor that can only move forward. Using one of the other constants creates a scrollable ResultSet. Using the TYPE_SCROLL_INSENSITIVE constant creates a ResultSet that is not sensitive to changes made to it while it remains open, whereas the TYPE_SCROLL_SENSITIVE constant sets up a ResultSet that is sensitive to changes while it's open. Of course, when the ResultSet is closed and then reopened, it will always reflect the changes.

The second parameter that must be used determines whether the ResultSet is updatable or read-only. Here is a code fragment that shows how to set up a scrollable ResultSet:

```
Statement stmt = con.createStatement(
                        ResultSet.TYPE_SCROLL_INSENSITIVE,
                        ResultSet.CONCUR_READ_ONLY);

ResultSet srs = stmt.executeQuery("SELECT * FROM EMPLOYEES");
```

Caution

Because both parameters are int primitives, the compiler will not complain when you have them backward. Make sure that you have the order correct or you might not actually get a scrollable ResultSet.

The driver or database that you are using might not support scrollable ResultSets. In that case, you will get the default ResultSet, which is forward scrolling and read-only. Make sure to check with the database vendor and JDBC driver vendor to see whether they support this feature. If you attempt to use one of the new JDBC 2.0 features that is not supported, you will get an SQLException and probably a message saying that it's not yet supported.

You can also determine programmatically whether the ResultSet is scrollable. When you create a scrollable ResultSet as describe previously, you can use the getType method on the ResultSet instance. The method returns an int value. The possible values are

- 1003 means ResultSet.TYPE_FORWARD_ONLY
- 1004 means ResultSet.TYPE_SCROLL_INSENSITIVE
- 1005 means ResultSet.TYPE_SCROLL_SENSITIVE

In the previous examples, the next method was used to scroll through the ResultSet in the forward direction to the next row, if there was one. As you can may have guessed, to go backward one row, you can use the previous method. As with the forward scrolling ResultSet, the cursor is still positioned before the first row with a scrollable ResultSet. Here is a code fragment using the previous method. This fragment assumes that the ResultSet is scrollable:

```
while ( rs.previous() )
{
  String name = rs.getString( "EMP_NO" );
  String salaryStr = rs.getString( "EMP_SALARY" );
  System.out.println( name + " - " + salaryStr );
}
```

Now, take a look at a complete example using a scrollable `ResultSet`. However, before you do that, you need to know about JDBC version 2.0 compatibility. The JDBC Type II driver for Oracle8i Lite doesn't support some of these new features introduced in JDBC 2.0. There is an alternative that is used for this example. That alternative is the JDBC-ODBC Bridge from Sun. This Bridge is a Type I driver that will allow you to connect to any ODBC datasource and make JDBC calls on it. The performance is not that great because a Type I driver is being used, but it does support these new JDBC 2.0 features.

The changes you need to make to use the new driver affect only the `DatabaseManager` class that you have been using from the previous JDBC chapter. This is why it is nice to isolate the database connection management code. The only changes to switch to the newer driver are contained with the `DatabaseManager` class. Listing 27.1 shows the new `DatabaseManager` class that uses the JDBC-ODBC Bridge.

LISTING 27.1 SOURCE CODE FOR NEW `DatabaseManager.java`

```
import java.sql.*;
import java.util.*;
import sun.jdbc.odbc.*;

public class DatabaseManager
{
  static private String urlHeader = "jdbc:odbc:";
  static private String databaseName = "POLITE";
  static private String user = "SYSTEM";
  static private String password = "";
  static private String driverName = "sun.jdbc.odbc.JdbcOdbcDriver";


  public static Connection getConnection()
  {
    // Define the local Connection instance that gets returned
    Connection conn = null;

    try
    {
      // Load the JDBC driver
      Class.forName( driverName );
      // Get an instance of the Connection. Really the Connection is an
      // interface that some class implements.

      // Concat the three parts together to build the full URL
      String databaseURL = urlHeader + databaseName;
      conn = DriverManager.getConnection( databaseURL, user, password );
    }
    catch( ClassNotFoundException ex )
    {
      // The JDBC driver class could not be found
      ex.printStackTrace();
      System.exit( -1 );
    }
    catch( SQLException ex )
    {
      // A sql exception occurred, for now just print out the stack trace
```

Listing 27.1 Continued

```
      ex.printStackTrace();
    }

    return conn;
  }
}
```

In Listing 27.1, the only changes that have to be made are the `urlHeader String` and the `driverName String`. This is why it's nice to isolate the necessary database parameters. The JDBC-ODBC Bridge driver comes with the SDK so you will not have to download a different driver.

Listing 27.2 shows the `ScrollableResultSetExample` using the new `DatabaseManager` to scroll backward through the Employee records in the database.

Listing 27.2 Source Code for `ScrollableResultSetExample.java`

```
import java.sql.*;

public class ScrollableResultSetExample
{
  // Private reference to an instance of the Connection
  Connection connection = null;

  // Default Constructor
  public ScrollableResultSetExample( Connection conn )
  {
    super();
    connection = conn;
  }

  // Private accessor for the connection
  private Connection getConnection()
  {
    return connection;
  }

  // Print out the Employee Records backwards using a scrollable
  // ResultSet
  public void printEmployeeRecordsBackwards()
  {
    Statement stmt = null;
    ResultSet rs = null;

    try
    {
      // Get a scrollable ResultSet
      Connection conn = getConnection();
      stmt = conn.createStatement(
                                   ResultSet.TYPE_SCROLL_INSENSITIVE,
                                   ResultSet.CONCUR_READ_ONLY );

      // Get some fields from the employee table
```

LISTING 27.1 CONTINUED

```
      String sqlQuery =
 "SELECT EMPNO, EName, Job, MGR, HIREDATE FROM EMP";

      rs = stmt.executeQuery( sqlQuery );

      // Move the cursor directly to the last position in the ResultSet
      // You can't do this like this before JDBC 2.0
      rs.last();

      // Move the cursor backwards through the ResultSet
      while( rs.previous() )
      {
        String nbr = rs.getString( 1 );
        String name = rs.getString( 2 );
        String job = rs.getString( 3 );
        String mgr = rs.getString( 4 );
        Timestamp hireDate = rs.getTimestamp( 5 );

        // Create a new Employee using the data
        Employee emp = new Employee( nbr, name, job, mgr, hireDate );
        // Call the Employee's default toString() method
        System.out.println( emp.toString() );
      }

      rs.close();
    }
    catch( SQLException ex )
    {
      ex.printStackTrace();
    }
  }

  public static void main(String[] args)
  {
     // Use the previous DatabaseManager
    Connection conn = DatabaseManager.getConnection();
    ScrollableResultSetExample example =
new ScrollableResultSetExample( conn );

    example.printEmployeeRecordsBackwards();

    // Always make sure to close the connection when you are finished
    try
    {
      conn.close();
    }
    catch( SQLException ex )
    {
      ex.printStackTrace();
    }
    catch( Exception ex )
    {
      ex.printStackTrace();
    }
  }
}
```

Listing 27.3 shows the output from `ScrollableResultExample`.

Listing 27.3 Output for `ScrollableResultSetExample`

```
C:\jdk1.3se_book\classes>java ScrollableResultSetExample
ID: 7876 - Name: ADAMS      - Job: CLERK     - Mgr: 7788 - Hire Date: 1983-01-12
 00:00:00.0
ID: 7788 - Name: SCOTT      - Job: ANALYST   - Mgr: 7566 - Hire Date: 1982-12-09
 00:00:00.0
ID: 7369 - Name: SMITH      - Job: CLERK     - Mgr: 7902 - Hire Date: 1980-12-17
 00:00:00.0
ID: 7902 - Name: FORD       - Job: ANALYST   - Mgr: 7566 - Hire Date: 1981-12-03
 00:00:00.0
ID: 7521 - Name: WARD       - Job: SALESMAN  - Mgr: 7698 - Hire Date: 1981-02-22
 00:00:00.0
ID: 7900 - Name: JAMES      - Job: CLERK     - Mgr: 7698 - Hire Date: 1981-12-03
 00:00:00.0
ID: 7844 - Name: TURNER     - Job: SALESMAN  - Mgr: 7698 - Hire Date: 1981-09-08
 00:00:00.0
ID: 7499 - Name: ALLEN      - Job: SALESMAN  - Mgr: 7698 - Hire Date: 1981-02-20
 00:00:00.0
ID: 7654 - Name: MARTIN     - Job: SALESMAN  - Mgr: 7698 - Hire Date: 1981-09-28
 00:00:00.0
ID: 7566 - Name: JONES      - Job: MANAGER   - Mgr: 7839 - Hire Date: 1981-04-02
 00:00:00.0
ID: 7782 - Name: CLARK      - Job: MANAGER   - Mgr: 7839 - Hire Date: 1981-06-09
 00:00:00.0
ID: 7698 - Name: BLAKE      - Job: MANAGER   - Mgr: 7839 - Hire Date: 1981-05-01
 00:00:00.0
ID: 7839 - Name: KING       - Job: PRESIDENT - Mgr: null - Hire Date: 1981-11-17
 00:00:00.0
```

Note

The type of message that you will see when your JDBC driver does not implement a JDBC 2.0 feature will vary among vendors. Some print out a nice message that the particular 2.0 feature is not implemented yet, and some print out just a stack trace like this:

```
Exception in thread "main" java.lang.AbstractMethodError
at
ScrollableResultSetExample.printEmployeeRecordsBackwards
➥(ScrollableResultSetExample.java:31)
at
ScrollableResultSetExample.main
➥(ScrollableResultSetExample.java:68)
```

Just beware that all vendors are not clear as to what the actual problem is.

As mentioned before, you can also jump to a specific row within the `ResultSet`. There are several convenience methods that take the cursor to regularly traversed rows. The convenience methods are

- `first()`
- `last()`

- beforeFirst()
- afterLast()

You can also use the absolute method to move the cursor to the row number indicated in the argument passed in to it. So, performing this method call on a scrollable ResultSet

```
rs.absolute(1)
```

will move the cursor to the first record. If the rowIndex parameter is a positive number, the cursor starts from the beginning of the ResultSet, whereas a negative number will start from the end of the ResultSet. So passing a (-1) into the absolute method will move the cursor to the last row in the ResultSet.

You can also use the relative method on the ResultSet, which will cause the cursor to move that many rows from the current position. A positive index number will cause the cursor to move forward, whereas a negative number will move the cursor backward.

To check to see which row the cursor is currently at, you can use the getRow method. This method returns the row index of the current position. There are also convenience methods that allow you to find the location more directly. The methods are

- isFirst()
- isLast()
- isBeforeFirst()
- isAfterLast()

All these methods return true or false depending on the actual position. Take a look at another example using some of these new methods. Listing 27.4 shows a class called MovingCursorExample that shows the various methods for moving the cursor to starting positions other than the first row.

LISTING 27.4 SOURCE CODE FOR MovingCursorExample.java

```
import java.sql.*;

public class MovingCursorExample
{
  // Private reference to an instance of the Connection
  Connection connection = null;

  // Default Constructor
  public MovingCursorExample( Connection conn )
  {
    super();
    connection = conn;
  }

  // Private accessor for the connection
  private Connection getConnection()
  {
```

Listing 27.4 Continued

```
    return connection;
  }

  // Print out the Employee Records backwards using a scrollable
  // ResultSet
  public void performExample()
  {
    Statement stmt = null;
    ResultSet rs = null;

    try
    {
      // These two variables are used throughout this example
      String name = null;
      int cursorPosition = 0;

      // Get a scrollable ResultSet
      Connection conn = getConnection();
      stmt = conn.createStatement(
                                   ResultSet.TYPE_SCROLL_INSENSITIVE,
                                   ResultSet.CONCUR_READ_ONLY );

      // Get some fields from the employee table
      String sqlQuery =
          "SELECT EMPNO, EName, Job, MGR, HIREDATE FROM EMP";

      rs = stmt.executeQuery( sqlQuery );


      // Count the rows
      int rowSize = 0;
      while( rs.next() )
      {
        rowSize++;
      }

      System.out.println( "Number of Rows in ResultSet is: " + rowSize );
      if ( rowSize == 0 )
      {
        System.out.println( "Since there are no rows, exiting..." );
        System.exit( 0 );
      }


      // Go to the halfway point in the ResultSet
      cursorPosition = Math.round( rowSize /  2 );

      System.out.println( "Moving to position: " + cursorPosition );
      // Get the name at the halfway position
      rs.absolute( cursorPosition );
      System.out.println( "Name: " + rs.getString( 2 ) );

      // Try to go back one row relative from the current position
      rs.relative( -1 );
```

LISTING 27.4 CONTINUED

```
        cursorPosition = rs.getRow();
        System.out.println( "Moving to position: " + cursorPosition );
        System.out.println( "Name: " + rs.getString( 2 ) );

        System.out.println( "Moving to the first row" );
        // Move to the first row backwards, one row at a time
        while( !rs.isFirst() )
        {
          rs.previous();
        }
        System.out.println( "Name: " + rs.getString( 2 ) );

        rs.close();
      }
      catch( SQLException ex )
      {
        ex.printStackTrace();
      }
    }


    public static void main(String[] args)
    {
       // Use the previous DatabaseManager
      Connection conn = DatabaseManager.getConnection();
      MovingCursorExample example = new MovingCursorExample( conn );
      example.performExample();

      // Always make sure to close the connection when you are finished
      try
      {
        conn.close();
      }
      catch( SQLException ex )
      {
        ex.printStackTrace();
      }
      catch( Exception ex )
      {
        ex.printStackTrace();
      }
    }
  }
```

Listing 27.5 shows the output from the `MovingCursorExample`.

LISTING 27.5 OUTPUT FROM `MovingCursorExample.java`

```
C:\jdk1.3se_book\classes>java MovingCursorExample
Number of Rows in ResultSet is: 14
Moving to position: 7
Name: TURNER
Moving to position: 6
Name: ALLEN
```

LISTING 27.5 CONTINUED

```
Moving to the first row
Name: KING

C:\jdk1.3se_book\classes>
```

USING UPDATABLE ResultSets

Another new feature in the JDBC 2.0 is the capability to update rows in a `ResultSet`. Rather than relying on update statements, you can update the current `ResultSet`. Take a look at how you might have updated a column prior to the JDBC 2.0 API. The following code fragment shows an SQL statement being executed just like in the previous examples:

```
stmt.executeUpdate(
    "UPDATE EMPLOYEE SET SALARY = 45000 " +
    "WHERE EMP_NO = '2719'");
```

Doing the same thing using the JDBC 2.0 API would look like the following:

```
rs.absolute(5);
rs.updateFloat("SAL", 45000.00f);
rs.upateRow();
```

The previous fragment is assuming that the fifth record in the `ResultSet` is the employee record that needs to be updated, but you should get the idea.

The current row in the `ResultSet` is affected by the update, so you need to move the cursor to the appropriate position before updating any column values. There are many different `updateXXX` methods in the `ResultSet` to use. The `updateXXX` methods generally take two parameters. The first one is the column to update, and the second is the value to update it to. As before, you can specify either the column index or the column name in the first parameter field. The effect will not take place on data in the database until the `updateRow` method is called. If you move the cursor to another row before calling `updateRow`, the update changes will be lost.

If you need to cancel the changes that you have made using the `updateXXX` methods, you can call the `cancelRowUpdates` method. However, this must be called before `updateRow` or the changes will take effect on the database. You can also call the `RefreshRow` method to cause the current row to refresh the data from the database. By default, a `ResultSet` is not updatable. As with the scrollable `ResultSet`, you must inform the API that you want an updatable `ResultSet`. Here is a code fragment showing you how to do this:


```
Statement stmt = con.createStatement(
              ResultSet.TYPE_SCROLL_SENSITIVE,
              ResultSet.CONCUR_UPDATABLE );
```

Notice that you can also create a scrollable `ResultSet` at the same time. You don't need a scrollable `ResultSet` to do updates on it, but generally you will want to move the cursor around to update different rows.

As with the scrollable `ResultSet`, you can check to make sure that you have an updatable `ResultSet`. You do this by calling the `getConcurrency` method on the `ResultSet`. The `getConcurrency` method will return one of these two values:

- `1007` indicates the `ResultSet` is `CONCUR_READ_ONLY`.
- `1008` indicates the `ResultSet` is `CONCUR_UPDATABLE`.

Listing 27.6 shows an example of using the updatable `ResultSet`.

LISTING 27.6 SOURCE CODE FOR `UpdateEmployeeExample1.java`

```
import java.sql.*;

public class UpdateEmployeeExample1
{
  // Private reference to an instance of the Connection
  Connection connection = null;

  // Default Constructor
  public UpdateEmployeeExample1( Connection conn )
  {
    super();
    connection = conn;
  }

  // Private accessor for the connection
  private Connection getConnection()
  {
    return connection;
  }

  // Print out the Employee Records backwards using a scrollable
  // ResultSet
  public void updateEmployees()
  {
    Statement stmt = null;
    ResultSet rs = null;

    try
    {
      // Get a scrollable ResultSet
      Connection conn = getConnection();
      stmt = conn.createStatement(
                                  ResultSet.TYPE_SCROLL_SENSITIVE,
                                  ResultSet.CONCUR_UPDATABLE );


      // Get some fields from the employee table
      String sqlQuery =
        "SELECT EMPNO, EName, Job, MGR, HIREDATE FRO

M EMP";

      rs = stmt.executeQuery( sqlQuery );
```

LISTING 27.6 CONTINUED

```
while( rs.next() )
      {
        Timestamp ts = new Timestamp( System.currentTimeMillis() );
        rs.updateTimestamp( "HIREDATE", ts );

        // Cause the update changes to be made persistent
       rs.updateRow();
      }


      rs.first();
      while( rs.next() )
      {
        String name = rs.getString( 2 );
        Timestamp hireDate = rs.getTimestamp( 5 );
        System.out.println( "Name: " + name + " Hire Date: " + hireDate );
      }

      rs.close();
    }
    catch( SQLException ex )
    {
      ex.printStackTrace();
    }
  }

  public static void main(String[] args)
  {
     // Use the previous DatabaseManager
    Connection conn = DatabaseManager.getConnection();
    UpdateEmployeeExample1 example = new UpdateEmployeeExample1( conn );
    example.updateEmployees();

    // Always make sure to close the connection when you are finished
    try
    {
      conn.close();
    }
    catch( SQLException ex )
    {
      ex.printStackTrace();
    }
    catch( Exception ex )
    {
      ex.printStackTrace();
    }
  }
}
```

The new features in the JDBC 2.0 API also allow you to insert and delete rows using an updatable `ResultSet`. This removes the necessity of having to use `Insert` or `Delete` SQL statements in your application, for the most part. Listing 27.7 shows an example of inserting a new employee and then deleting it back out of the database.

LISTING 27.7 SOURCE CODE FOR InsertAndDelete.java

```
import java.sql.*;

public class InsertAndDelete
{
  // Private reference to an instance of the Connection
  Connection connection = null;

  // Default Constructor
  public InsertAndDelete( Connection conn )
  {
    super();
    connection = conn;
  }

  // Private accessor for the connection
  private Connection getConnection()
  {
    return connection;
  }

  // Insert and Delete a new Employee Record
  public void insertAndDelete()
  {
    Statement stmt = null;
    ResultSet rs = null;

    try
    {
      // Get a scrollable ResultSet
      stmt = getConnection().createStatement( ResultSet.TYPE_SCROLL_SENSITIVE,
                                              ResultSet.CONCUR_UPDATABLE );

      // Get some fields from the employee table
      rs = stmt.executeQuery( "SELECT * FROM EMP" );

      //Move the cursor to where you need to insert a new row
      rs.moveToInsertRow();

      // Even though an insert is being performed, the
      // update methods have to be used
      rs.updateInt( "EMPNO", 3100 );
      rs.updateTimestamp(
      "HIREDATE", new Timestamp(System.currentTimeMillis()));
      rs.updateString( "SAL", "35.00" );
      rs.updateInt( "DEPTNO", 10 );
      // Cause the update changes to take effect
      rs.insertRow();

      // Move to the last row and delete it
      rs.last();
      rs.deleteRow();

      // Close the connection
      rs.close();
    }
```

LISTING 27.7 CONTINUED

```
    catch( SQLException ex )
    {
      ex.printStackTrace();
    }
  }

  public static void main(String[] args)
  {
     // Use the previous DatabaseManager
    Connection conn = DatabaseManager.getConnection();
    InsertAndDelete example = new InsertAndDelete( conn );
    example.insertAndDelete();

    // Always make sure to close the connection when you are finished
    try
    {
      conn.close();
    }
    catch( SQLException ex )
    {
      ex.printStackTrace();
    }
    catch( Exception ex )
    {
      ex.printStackTrace();
    }
  }
}
```

USING BATCH UPDATES

A *batch update* is when a set of update statements are queued up and executed together against the database. In some situations, this can increase performance of a database application. Whether it increases performance for your particular application depends on several factors such as how many transactions or update statements are being requested and how long each one is taking.

Prior to JDBC 2.0, each update statement was executed by itself. Even if it was part of a transaction of other update statements, the updates were done one by one. With JDBC 2.0, the `Statement` class has the capability to add a SQL command to a batch and then execute the entire batch as a set.

To add a new SQL command to the batch, you can call the `addBatch` method on the `Statement` class like this:

```
Statement stmt = conn.createStatement();
stmt.addBatch("INSERT INTO EMP ( EMPNO ) " + "VALUES( 2346 )");
```

To execute the commands in the batch, just call the `executeBatch` method like this:

```
int [] updateCount = stmt.executeBatch();
```

You should always perform a batch inside a transaction to properly handle errors. Remember, to do this you will need to turn off `autoCommit` by calling the `setAutoCommit(false)` on the `Connection` class. Listing 27.8 shows a complete example of performing a batch update.

Note

Batch updates cannot be done for SQL statements that return a `ResultSet`.

LISTING 27.8 SOURCE CODE FOR `BatchUpdateExample.java`

```
import java.sql.*;

public class BatchUpdateExample
{
  // Private reference to an instance of the Connection
  Connection connection = null;

  // Default Constructor
  public BatchUpdateExample( Connection conn )
  {
    super();
    connection = conn;
  }

  // Private accessor for the connection
  private Connection getConnection()
  {
    return connection;
  }

  // Print out the Employee Records backward using a scrollable
  // ResultSet
  public void batchUpdates()
  {
    Statement stmt = null;
    ResultSet rs = null;

    try
    {
      // Start a transaction
      getConnection().setAutoCommit( false );

      stmt = getConnection().createStatement();
      stmt.addBatch( "UPDATE EMP SET JOB = 1" );
      stmt.addBatch( "UPDATE EMP SET HIREDATE = '15-DEC-1999'" );

      // Submit the batch of commands for this statement to the database
      stmt.executeBatch();

      // Commit the transaction
      getConnection().commit();
    }
    catch( SQLException ex )
    {
```

Listing 27.8 Continued

```
        ex.printStackTrace();
      }
    }

    public static void main(String[] args)
    {
      // Use the previous DatabaseManager
      Connection conn = DatabaseManager.getConnection();
      BatchUpdateExample example = new BatchUpdateExample( conn );
      example.batchUpdates();

      // Always make sure to close the connection when you are finished
      try
      {
        conn.close();
      }
      catch( SQLException ex )
      {
        ex.printStackTrace();
      }
      catch( Exception ex )
      {
        ex.printStackTrace();
      }
    }
}
```

Listing 27.9 shows the output after the example in Listing 27.8 is finished executing. All the job id's and `hireDate` values are the same. This is because the two batch update statements did not provide a `where` clause. They just updated every record.

Listing 27.9 Output for `BatchUpdateExample.java`

```
C:\jdk1.3se_book\classes>java BatchUpdateExample
7839:1:1999-12-15 00:00:00.000000
7698:1:1999-12-15 00:00:00.000000
7782:1:1999-12-15 00:00:00.000000
7566:1:1999-12-15 00:00:00.000000
7654:1:1999-12-15 00:00:00.000000
7499:1:1999-12-15 00:00:00.000000
7844:1:1999-12-15 00:00:00.000000
7900:1:1999-12-15 00:00:00.000000
7521:1:1999-12-15 00:00:00.000000
7902:1:1999-12-15 00:00:00.000000
7369:1:1999-12-15 00:00:00.000000
7788:1:1999-12-15 00:00:00.000000
7876:1:1999-12-15 00:00:00.000000

C:\jdk1.3se_book\classes>
```

If you are having trouble with your JDBC driver in that it doesn't support the new 2.0 features, see "JDBC 2.0 Feature Not Implemented" in the "Troubleshooting" section at the end of this chapter.

USING THE JDBC OPTIONAL PACKAGE

The JDBC Optional Package (formerly known as the Standard Extension API) adds functionality that mostly applies if you are building distributed applications in which multiple clients are accessing remote databases. However, there is some functionality that applies generally to all JDBC development.

As mentioned before, the core JDBC API resides in the `java.sql` package. The `optional` package resides in the `javax.sql` package alone. The `optional` package includes four new high-level features:

- `RowSets`
- Connection pooling
- Distributed transactions
- Datasource

RowSets

A `RowSet` object is designed to be a container for a collection or set of rows. The `RowSet` is not provided by the driver implementation, but rather is implemented on top of a driver. This means it can be implemented by anyone who needs one, and the object can be implemented in many different ways depending on the needs of the application.

`RowSet` is a Java interface that extends the `java.sql.ResultSet` interface. Therefore, `RowSet` can perform all the functionality of the `ResultSet` interface like the `getXXX` and `updateXXX` methods. With the JDBC 2.0 Optional Package functionality, `RowSet` is a `JavaBean`. This means that you can set and get the properties of the `RowSet` object as well as add listeners to the `RowSet` obect.

A `RowSet` object is not limited to where it gets the data to populate itself. It can come from a relational database or from a tabular data source. Once the `RowSet` has the data, it can be serialized over the network to a remote client. A client can deal with the `RowSet` object just like it was connected to the data source itself. Once a client has modified the data, the `RowSet` object can be sent back across the network. The `RowSet` can reconnect to the data source and upload the data. This makes it ideal for thin client implementations.

CONNECTION POOLING

Connection pooling was mentioned briefly in the previous JDBC chapter. It's a mechanism to allow reuse of database connections. Because the time it takes to get a connection to the database is substantial, reusing connections can save time and speed up performance.

Usually, a connection pooling is created when the application is first started. Normally, you can specify how many connections to start with in the pool, the maximum number of connections the pool should grow to, and how many to increment each time more are needed. The logic for maintaining the pool of connections is not very complicated. When a client needs a connection, it is taken from the pool. Once a client is finished with the connection, it is placed back in. If a client never releases the connection or fails to release the connection within a certain amount of time, the client is usually reclaimed back into the pool forcibly.

This sounds like more work than it's worth, but the timesavings for not having to create connections when a client needs one is more than worth it in performance. Connection pooling can be done at various levels, and it also depends on what type of driver your application is using. Type III JDBC drivers most always have connection pooling within the middle tier. This is one reason that they can offer increased performance over Type I and II drivers.

Distributed Transactions

Distributed transactions really deal with more Enterprise technologies that are better covered in *Special Edition Using Java 2, Enterprise Edition* by Mark Wutka (Que, 2001). Although the first two features are also important in Enterprise applications, they do have context in general JDBC development.

Distributed transactions are used more often in Enterprise applications where data must be inserted or read from different heterogeneous persistent stores. These persistent stores may be relational databases, legacy databases, or even ERP systems. Dealing with a distributed transaction is usually very transparent to a developer. The main difference is the boundary of where the transaction begins and ends. In our previous examples of dealing with transactions, all the transaction statements were located in our code. This is because all the transaction operations were going to the same database. If we needed to operate on other databases as well and either commit the entire operation or roll it all back, we could solve this with a distributed transaction.

For example, let's say that we went out on the Internet to buy a book. During the ordering process, we select a book and then enter our credit card for payment. If the credit card authorization server crashes while the system is processing our credit card, the entire operation better roll back. The business does not want the book shipped to me if I did not pay for it. The system that processes the payment might be different from the fulfillment service, and the two need to participate in the same transaction or the business might not be very profitable.

DataSource

Throughout the examples in this and the previous JDBC chapter, a class has been used called `DatabaseManager` that was developed in the JDBC examples within this book. It abstracted the database connection for any client that needed a connection. Well, you can do better than having that level of abstraction by using a `Datasource` interface to acquire connections to a database.

A client can use a JNDI naming service to locate a `Datasource` object that it can then use to work with the database. The client stores enough information on how to locate the `Datasource`, and after it has the `Datasource` object, it can do whatever it needs to do against the database. The client does not need to know about driver names, URLs, or any other connection information.

The following code fragment gives you an idea of how you can get a `Connection` from JNDI:

```
Context ctx = new InitialContext();
DataSource ds = (DataSource)ctx.lookup("jdbc/EmployeeDB");
Connection con = ds.getConnection("Scott", "tiger");
```

The first line acquires the initial context to the JNDI naming service. After it has the initial context, it can then get a reference to an object within the naming service. In this case, that object is a `Datasource` object. The `jdbc/EmployeeDB` parameter that you see in the lookup method gives kind of a unique name to each object within the naming service. There is sort of a hierarchical structure about the names. You can think of it as a tree or directory structure to get a mental picture of how it looks. To get more information on JNDI, check out this URL:

`http://java.sun.com/products/jndi/`

After the client has located a `Datasource` object, it can then get connections as before by passing only minimal information, such as username and password. The `Datasource` hands the client a `Connection` instance that the client is free to access the database with. The main issue with this approach is the time that it takes to get the initial context to the `JNDI` naming service. The amount of time varies across JNDI vendors. The other real issue that some developers complain about is the complexity of learning another technology such as `JNDI`. Of course, after you understand it, it becomes easier to use it.

One other advantage to using a `Datasource` is that the actual underlying data source can be anything from a relational database to a spreadsheet. Information about the underlying data source is stored within the `JNDI Datasource` object. This makes it very portable. A client does not need to worry about which machine a spreadsheet file is on, because the client can get that information from the `Datasource` once it has acquired a reference to it through JNDI.

> **Note**
>
> You may also want to read the database vendor's documentation. Some databases like Oracle 8i allow an application to obtain a Datasource without using JNDI. For example, you can instantiate an `OracleDataSource()` without JNDI and use it to access the database. Check the documentation for your database to see if it offers this feature.

You should be aware that these and many other features in general with Java are defined by Sun specifications, but are actually implemented by various third-party vendors. It's up to the vendor's implementation to adhere to the specification. Most of the time, a vendor will adhere to the specification, but sometimes you'll find a vendor who doesn't completely adhere to a specification. As we learned earlier, many vendors claim to have a JDBC driver that is 2.0 compliant, but in actuality they do not support all of the features.

Within Java, there are places where interfaces are defined like we found in the `java.sql` package. `ResultSet` is just a Java interface. It needs a concrete implementation for it to work. A vendor provides a set of classes that make up the driver and also provides implementations classes defined by the specification. It's up to the vendor how they implement some piece of functionality. The specification from Sun is a guideline for the vendor, but there is usually enough room for the vendor to be different from another vendor. You have to understand that all things being equal, implementations will vary according to a particular vendor.

Note

There are other features that are available, such as logging JDBC error messages. You can find more about these other features available in the Optional Package API at the following site:

`http://java.sun.com/products/jdbc/`

UNDERSTANDING OBJECT-TO-RELATIONAL MAPPING FRAMEWORKS

When you begin developing applications using JDBC, you will want to pay close attention to the design. In the previous chapter, several examples were used that persisted Java objects to a relational database. The knowledge of how to store the objects in the database was placed either in a method or in the class itself. In some cases, SQL commands were added to `Insert` or `Update` data in the database. Although using SQL directly to interact with the database will almost always work, it can become a maintenance nightmare. Although these approaches worked in the simple examples that were presented in this and the previous chapter, there are issues with both approaches, especially for larger real-world applications.

It's true that for some applications, using SQL directly is probably a satisfactory approach. For some small applications, you can argue that maintenance of the SQL will not be an issue. Some, on the other hand, might argue that you never want to have the knowledge of SQL commands in your business objects. The point is that there should be some sort of "Layered" design used in which your business objects contain nothing but pure business logic and the knowledge of how to persist the objects resides in a data layer or database-mapping layer.

This data layer can take the form of other objects or maybe something lighter that is used at runtime by the business objects; the business objects can delegate the persistence to this data layer.

The issues with performing SQL directly in the business objects revolve mainly around the problem of software maintenance and object-oriented design. The question is how do you design a Java database application in which the system knows how to persist the Java objects in an application without the objects having too much knowledge about which datastore they are being persisted to? This was referred to earlier as *decoupling* the application from a specific database or implementation.

For example, what if you have an application with Java objects that know how to read and write their state to the database. Suppose further that the SQL to read and write the objects was located throughout your Java objects. What happens when the schema changes? It can become difficult to track down the correct places that need to change along with the schema. Remember back in the previous JDBC chapter when you had to switch to the JDBC-ODBC Bridge? Because the database configuration information was isolated from the classes, it made it easy to change the configuration. In fact, that configuration information could have been read in from an XML file and used at runtime. In that case, all you would have had to do is edit a text file and no software changes would have been necessary. That's the ultimate goal here—to reduce the software changes that are necessary when the underlying database configuration changes whether the change is the JDBC URL, the database schema, or even the database vendor.

One way to fix this problem might be to always keep the SQL inside the class that will be using it. For example, what if you have a class called `Employee` and this class contains all the SQL that it needs to persist itself to some datastore? When the underlying schema changes for this class, you would know where to go to fix the SQL. This helps the problem a little. The modifications would always need to be made in the class or classes that are directly affected by the database changes. There still is a problem with this solution, however. Any time the column names or fields change, you must recompile Java code. In some cases, this might be okay because, if there are new fields, you probably need to add the attributes to the Java class anyway. What if just one of the column names changes or the table name changes? You must change Java code and then recompile. The problem is that the changes usually have cascading effects. So, a single database change can turn into several software changes.

As you can see, there are various ways that you can keep abstracting out the database knowledge and move it further and further away from the actual Java code. This leads to the discussion of Object-to-Relational Mapping (ORM) frameworks. Whether you are designing a small single-user database application or a large multi-client application, one issue will always come up during design, "How are you going to access the database with the Java objects?" You need a strategy for mapping the object model to the relational model in order for Java objects to become persistent to the database. The problem is that you need to take an object model and flatten it out for the relational database to deal with. You need to do this in a manner that will be relatively easy to maintain and scalable if the number of database calls becomes high.

ORM frameworks are like any other framework in the Java world. They provide a set of classes that can be used and extended in your Java applications. ORM frameworks are specific to giving the Java objects access to a database in a way that makes it easier for the developer to interact with the database. In most cases, the developer is interacting with an API above JDBC. So it's usually even more object oriented. For example, to save an object instance of `Employee`, all you might have to do is something like this:

```
Employee newEmployee = new Employee();
newEmployee.setFirstName( "Linda" );
newEmployee.setLastName( "Lee" );
// Set some more required fields
newEmployee.save();
```

This code is a little fictitious, but there are some frameworks that do it this way. You don't interact with JDBC, but rather a higher-level API that uses JDBC in it. The details of where the attributes of `Employee` go in the database are taken care of through the mapping that was done during design. The framework classes could also handle issues such as using the native sequencing of the database to provide a new *unique identifier* (UID) for the `Employee` record. Also, there's the issue of objects that reference other objects. Suppose the `Employee` class referenced an `Address` and `Phone Number` class. The framework could handle saving these child classes when the `Employee` was saved. It could also update the foreign keys from the `Employee` table to the `Address` and `Phone Number` table. Here's what the code might look like:

```
Employee newEmployee = new Employee();
newEmployee.setFirstName( "Linda" );
newEmployee.setLastName( "Lee" );
// Set some more required fields for Employee

// Create and set the address for this employee
Address addr = new Address( "3275 Main", "Snellville", "GA" );
NewEmployee.addAddress( addr );

// Create and set a phone number object
PhoneNumber phone = new PhoneNumber( "770", "123-4567", "x1234" );
NewEmployee.addPhone( phone );

// Save the employee which also saves the children objects automatically
newEmployee.save();
```

There are many Java ORM frameworks available. Some are open-source projects that are available for free, and then there are some that are downright expensive. Not all of them are created equal either. When evaluating them, you have to look at the list of features that each provides and do the usual buy-versus-build analysis on what you get with the framework against what it would cost for you to build in that functionality. There are too many features to list all of them here, but here's a brief list of Java ORM frameworks and where to find out more about them:

Name	Location
TOPLink	`http://www.webgain.com`
CocoBase	`http://www.thoughtinc.com`
Poet	`http://www.thoughtinc.com`
Java Blend	`http://www.sun.com/software/javablend`

This list is by no means complete. Each vendor provides different features and functionality.

As stated earlier, ORM deals with mapping `Objects` to relational databases. Unless you are using an `Object` database or some of the newer features of databases such as Oracle, objects need to be flattened out before they can be persisted into a relational database. *Flattening* means taking all the object's attributes and storing them horizontally into a database record. You also need to maintain the references an object has to other objects.

When attempting to map classes to a database, there are several ways this mapping can be done. First, a class can map directly to a table by itself. Secondly, it can be mapped to multiple tables. Or several classes can be mapped to a single table. This really depends on the physical design that you are mapping to. The process usually involves performing a good logical object-oriented design, without any thought of what the physical will be. This is done based on good OO analysis and design methods. Then, usually a data architect who understands how logical and efficient physical models should be built, goes off and designs the database schema. Finally, the two worlds need to be combined so that the objects can be persisted in the physical and then be reconstituted back into the object model later.

There are many things to consider, and it does get a little complicated depending on the size and complexity of the design. Some things are easy to figure out, such as mapping attributes and columns. Other areas are not easy, such as inheritance and aggregate objects. Each ORM vendor supports these a little differently, so make sure when choosing a vendor that it supports all the design features you need. For example, does the vendor's ORM framework support one-to-one, one-to-many, and many-to-many relationships? Does it have some kind of easy-to-use GUI builder to help with the mappings, which can get confusing? Even more serious issues should be considered, such as whether the ORM provides connection pooling and caching. It really all depends on what you are looking for in an ORM and how much money and time you have to invest in choosing one. The newsgroups are a great source of information for ORM frameworks because many people have used them or are in the process of evaluating them. So, many questions can be answered by reading the various newsgroups.

TROUBLESHOOTING

JDBC 2.0 FEATURE NOT IMPLEMENTED

When I try to use a 2.0 feature, I get an error message and/or a stack trace saying that the feature is not implemented.

If you find yourself in a situation where one or more JDBC 2.0 features are not implemented for your driver or database, unfortunately there's not a great deal you can do. The first thing to do is check with the driver and database vendor to see if there's an update that supports the feature or features that are missing. If that doesn't work, you can check around to see if there is another vendor that provides a driver that does implement the new features. For the bigger databases, such as, Oracle or Microsoft SQL Server, usually more than one vendor provides drivers.

You might have to change the type of driver that you are using to find one that supports the features you need. This might cause some performance risks, but if the features are important enough to your application, it's probably a good tradeoff.

PART V

Component Development

CHAPTER 28

Reflection

In this chapter

by Brian Keeton

WHAT IS REFLECTION?

According to Sun, *Reflection* is an API that supports introspection of the classes and objects in the current JVM. Essentially, the key word in this definition is *introspection*. If you're new to Java, this is probably not a term you are familiar with, especially in a software sense. Using Reflection, you can take an object at runtime, such as an `ArrayList` instance, examine it, and fully describe it. The information you can obtain about an object includes details about its class and about that unique object itself. As far as its class, you can learn which classes it extends, interfaces it implements, methods it provides, and fields it has. After you know this, you can determine the values held by the fields for the particular instance you are examining. The important part is that you can do this without knowing anything about the object in advance, not even that it's an `ArrayList`.

Reflection is a powerful tool, but it is not something you need in a typical application. Most of the time, you will have full knowledge at compile time of the classes you are using. This has been true for every example in the preceding chapters of this book. The need for Reflection arises when this knowledge is not available. Typically this is the case when extreme flexibility is required in how an application interacts with objects as they are created. Most of the examples of Reflection that you will see in practice are related to development tools, such as debuggers and GUI layout tools. Here, Reflection is a natural fit for querying an object so that its attributes can be displayed or its properties configured for a specific use. Reflection also plays a key role in supporting other parts of the Java API such as JavaBeans (see Chapter 29, "JavaBeans").

KEY CLASSES OF THE REFLECTION API

To accomplish the task of introspection, the Java API provides `java.lang.Class` and several classes in the `java.lang.reflect` package, including `Constructor`, `Method`, and `Field`. These classes are used to obtain information about their respective characteristics from an object. The following sections introduce you to the three key classes in the `java.lang.reflect` `package`. This discussion covers the major methods of each class (refer to the Java API documentation for a complete listing). Examples later in the chapter build on this introduction to the Reflection API to demonstrate how you use these classes in conjunction with `java.lang.Class` to support runtime discovery in your programs.

THE `Constructor` CLASS

A `Constructor` instance provides information about a particular class constructor and allows you to call that constructor to instantiate an object. If you know the name of a class and the parameter lists of its constructors prior to runtime, you don't need to use `Constructor` to create an instance. As you've seen starting in Chapter 7, "Classes," you only need to use the `new` operator and specify the constructor name and arguments in that case. However, if you are writing a program that is required to load a class that is not known prior to runtime and create instances of it using constructors that accept arguments, it is `Constructor` that makes this possible.

Note

You can access no-argument constructors to create an object using the `newInstance` method of `Class` instead of using `Constructor`. This approach is discussed later in the chapter.

You'll see later how to obtain a `Constructor` instance for a class, but for now, look at the methods that are available to you once you have a reference to such an instance. First, a `Constructor` object allows you to query it for the associated constructor's class and the constructor name.

```
public Class getDeclaringClass()
public String getName()
```

Beyond its name, you can learn more about a constructor's signature using methods that report the modifiers and exceptions included in its declaration.

```
public int getModifiers()
public Class[] getExceptionTypes()
```

The integer value returned by `getModifiers` can be decoded by calling static methods, such as `isPublic`, provided by `java.lang.reflect.Modifier`. The `Class` array returned by `getExceptionTypes` includes an entry for each exception listed in the `throws` clause of the constructor you are inspecting.

The more interesting `Constructor` methods are those that allow you to instantiate an object. First, you can discover the parameter types, in their declared order, found in the constructor's parameter list.

```
public Class[] getParameterTypes()
```

Using this knowledge, you can create an object using `Constructor` by calling its `newInstance` method.

```
public Object newInstance( Object[] initargs )
  throws InstantiationException, IllegalAccessException,
         IllegalArgumentException, InvocationTargetException
```

This method accepts an array of parameters and passes them to the associated constructor to perform the instantiation. The exceptions declared as thrown represent the possible problems that might occur, such as an attempt to call a constructor without having the required access, a mismatch of passed parameters with the parameter list, or an attempt to instantiate an abstract class. You'll see the `newInstance` method used in the later examples.

THE `Method` CLASS

A `Method` instance provides information about a particular method declared by a class or interface. Similar to `Constructor`, `Method` is useful when you need to call a method that is not known to your program until runtime. Given that methods and constructors have much in common, the set of methods declared by `Method` is nearly the same as the set declared by `Constructor`. The first difference results from the fact that methods, unlike constructors, can return a value. Reflection allows you to determine a method's return type using getReturnType declared in Method.

```
public Class getReturnType()
```

The other difference addressed by Method is that you call a method on a particular instance (or its class if it's static), where a constructor is instead used to create an instance. In place of newInstance, Method declares invoke to support method calls using Reflection.

```
public Object invoke( Object targetObj, Object[] args )
  throws IllegalAccessException, IllegalArgumentException,
         InvocationTargetException
```

When you call invoke, you pass the instance on which to invoke the method and an array of method arguments. If the method you want to invoke is static, you can pass null for the target object.

THE Field CLASS

A Field instance provides information about a class or instance field declared by an interface or class. Field allows you to dynamically discover the characteristics of a field, query its value, and even change its value. Similar to the other classes you've seen so far, Field supports getDeclaringClass, getModifiers, and getName methods to provide access to basic information. Somewhat like the getReturnType method of the Method class, Field allows you to determine the declared type of an associated field.

```
public Class getType()
```

The remaining methods of Field are mostly related to retrieving and setting a field's value. This can be done in a manner that is either general or specific with respect to type. First, look at the general methods.

```
public Object get( Object targetObj )
  throws IllegalArgumentException, IllegalAccessException

public void set( Object targetObj, Object newValue )
  throws IllegalArgumentException, IllegalAccessException
```

In these methods, the targetObj parameter is the object whose field is to be accessed. This parameter is ignored for static fields, so you can pass null in that situation. As implied by the signatures, get returns the value of the field for the target object and set assigns the value of the argument newValue to the corresponding field. These methods treat the field type generically as Object, but you can also use methods that work with a field using a more specific type. These methods take the following form, where *Type* is one of Boolean, Byte, Char, Double, Float, Int, Long, or Short and *primitiveType* is the primitive type corresponding to *Type*.

```
public primitiveType getType( Object targetObj )
  throws IllegalArgumentException, IllegalAccessException

public void setType( Object targetObj, primitiveType newValue )
  throws IllegalArgumentException, IllegalAccessException
```

SECURITY CONSIDERATIONS

Reflection involves substantial discovery at runtime about code that has been loaded into the virtual machine. For an application such as an integrated development environment (IDE), virtually every aspect of a class must be accessible through Reflection to satisfy the needs of the program. However, from earlier chapters, you have seen that access to, and knowledge of, the methods and fields of a class are restricted through the use of access specifiers. Some of the uses of Reflection require that these restrictions be suspended, but this is done in a secure way.

The Java 2 security mechanisms are central to allowing or disallowing Reflection access to a requestor.

The Java 2 security model prevents classes that don't have access to methods, fields, constructors, and so on from being able to see them. In particular, the `checkMemberAccess` method of `SecurityManager` has the capability to grant or refuse access to the nonpublic members of a class. For example, when a method is called on a class that would cause an instance of the `Method` class to be created (the `Method`, `Field`, and `Constructor` classes do not have public constructors and can only be instantiated by `java.lang.Class`), it first queries the `SecurityManager` to determine if providing the requesting class what it is asking for is allowed. Say you have a scenario in which the object `Requestor` wants to know what constructors are available in the class `Provider`. To do this, you might create two classes like those in Listing 28.1.

LISTING 28.1 `Requestor` **CLASS REQUESTS CONSTRUCTOR INFORMATION FROM THE** `Provider` **CLASS**

```
/*
* Requestor
*/
import java.lang.reflect.*;
public class Requestor {
  public void requestConstuctors() {
    try {
      // load the Provider class and use Reflection
      // to get an array of constructor information
      Constructor con[]= Class.forName("Provider").getDeclaredConstructors();
      for (int x=0; x<con.length; x++)
        System.out.println("Constructor " + x + " = " + con[x]);
    }
    catch (ClassNotFoundException ce) {
      // Class.forName was unable to load Provider.class
      System.out.println("Could not locate class");
    }
    catch (SecurityException se) {
      // Reflection permission was not granted
      System.out.println("Not allowed to get class info");
    }
  }

  public static void main(String args[]) {
```

LISTING 28.1 CONTINUED

```
    // construct a Requestor and ask it for the
    // constructors declared by Provider
    Requestor req = new Requestor();
    req.requestConstuctors();
  }
}

/*
 *  Provider
*/
class Provider {
  public Provider(String s) {
  }

  private Provider(int i) {
  }
}
```

After you compile these classes, which should be placed in a source file named `Requestor.java`, you can then run the `Requestor` program. The output you get looks like this:

```
Constructor 0 = private Provider(int)
Constructor 1 = public Provider(java.lang.String)
```

The implementation of `requestConstructors` in Listing 28.1 introduces the static `forName` method of `Class`. This method instructs the class loader to load the class or interface with the name given by its argument and then returns a corresponding `Class` object. As shown here, the `getDeclaredConstructors` method of `Class` returns all constructors declared in a class, regardless of access restriction. This assumes of course that the required permissions exist.

Note

`Class` is not restricted to representing only classes. One of its instances could also represent an interface, an array, a primitive type, or the keyword `void`. Every class must have at least one constructor, so if `getDeclaredConstructors` returns an empty array as its result, the `Class` instance being used must be associated with one of the other supported entities. To determine this at runtime, you can call the `isInterface`, `isArray`, and `isPrimitive` methods of `Class` that each return a `boolean` result.

If you have trouble inspecting the characteristics of a `Class` instance, see "No Class Members Reflected" in the "Troubleshooting" section at the end of this chapter.

This type of information about a class could not be retrieved in Java without Reflection. Under other languages, such as C/C++, access to methods can be accomplished using method pointers. Because Java has no pointers, it's necessary to have the Reflection model to gain access to methods at runtime.

The example in Listing 28.1 shows a `catch` clause for a `SecurityException`. This is not a checked exception, so this `catch` is not required, but it's included to illustrate what is happening. Notice that `Requestor` was able to access a `private` constructor. This requires the approval of the SecurityManager. If this request had been denied, a SecurityException would have been thrown.

The complete details of the Java 2 security model are beyond the scope of this chapter, but some of the details here do illustrate some of the core concepts. Java security is largely permissions based. The access a class has to a particular method of another class is determined by the permissions it has.

The permission suppressAccessChecks of the ReflectPermission class is the one that is most interesting within this discussion. A class that has this permission grants Reflection privileges to classes that would not have them by default. Classes are given this permission through the use of a policy file. The other key class related to Reflection and security is AccessibleObject, which is the superclass of Field, Method, and Constructor. This class allows a reflected object to be used in a manner that suppresses all normal access checks. For more information on the Java 2 security model, refer to Sun's documentation available at http://java.sun.com/security/.

CREATING A CLASS KNOWING ONLY THE LIST OF CONSTRUCTORS

After you have retrieved the constructors associated with a class, it is also possible to use them to instantiate an object. Listing 28.2 shows a simple example of how to do this.

LISTING 28.2 Requestor CREATES A Provider WITHOUT KNOWING THE CONSTRUCTOR DETAILS IN ADVANCE

```
/*
 * Requestor
 */
import java.lang.reflect.*;
public class Requestor {

  // Return an array of Provider instances that
  // includes an instance created with each
  // constructor declared by the class
  public static Provider[] constructProvider() {

    Provider[] prov = null;
    try {
      // load the class and retrieve its constructors
      Class cl = Class.forName("Provider");
      Constructor[] con = cl.getDeclaredConstructors();

      // allocate the Provider array based on the
      // number of constructors found
      prov = new Provider[con.length];
      for (int i=0; i<con.length; i++) {
        // get parameter info for the constructor
        Class param[] = con[i].getParameterTypes();
        // create an array to hold the number of
```

LISTING 28.2 CONTINUED

```
        // parameters required by this constructor
        Object paramValues[] = new Object[param.length];
        // look at each parameter type
        for (int x=0; x<param.length; x++) {
          if (!param[x].isPrimitive()) {
            System.out.println("param:" + param[x]);
            // create an object of this parameter type
            // using its no-argument constructor
            paramValues[x] = param[x].newInstance();
          }
        }
        // the parameter array has been loaded, so create
        // an object using this Provider constructor
        prov[i] = (Provider)con[i].newInstance(paramValues);
      }
    }
    catch (InvocationTargetException e) {
      System.out.println("Could not get class info");
    }
    catch (Exception e) {
      System.out.println("Exception during construction");
    }
    // return the array of Providers
    return prov;
  }

  public static void main(String args[]) {
    // create a Provider instance from each constructor
    Provider[] prov = Requestor.constructProvider();
    for (int i=0; i<prov.length; i++) {
      // display the Provider's one attribute to see which
      // constructor it was created by
      System.out.println("Created provider with attribute: " +
        prov[i].attribute);
}
  }
}

/*
 * Provider
 *   A simple class with one field and two constructors
 */
class Provider{
    String attribute;
    // Declare a no-argument constructor
    public Provider(){
        attribute = "Not specified";
    }

    // Declare a single-argument constructor
    public Provider(String s){
        attribute = s;
    }
}
```

This example cheats somewhat by taking advantage of the fact that the single-argument constructor of `Provider` expects a `String`, which can be constructed with a no-argument constructor.

Creating a Class Instance

Perhaps the most important aspect of Java demonstrated in Listing 28.2 is that you are not limited to a single approach for creating an instance of a class. The most common method is to use the `new` operator introduced in Chapter 7 to instantiate a class by specifying a constructor to call, as in the following:

```
String string1 = new String();
String string2 = new String("My String");
```

As you have begun to see in this chapter, there are other mechanisms for instantiating a class as well. For example, the `forName` and `newInstance` methods of `Class` provide a way to instantiate a class using its no-argument constructor:

```
Class stringClass = Class.forName("java.lang.String");
String string3 = stringClass.newInstance();
```

As shown here, `forName` loads a `Class` object based on a specified name. An already accessible class is used in the example, but this approach is most often used for classes that are not known until runtime. For example, you might have several classes that implement a particular interface and want to defer the decision of which implementation to use until runtime. The `forName` method allows you to provide the class name as a parameter, perhaps as a command line argument, to your program that can be used to load the class dynamically. Assuming the class has a no-argument constructor, the `newInstance` method of `Class` can then be used to create an instance.

As first shown in Listing 28.2, `Class` and `Constructor` can also be used to instantiate a class using a constructor that accepts parameters. The following example shows how this can be done to construct a `String` instance using the constructor that accepts another `String as an argument`:

```
// get the String class object
Class stringClass = Class.forName("java.lang.String");
// build a one-element array that holds the class of the
// constructor parameter
Class[] parameterType = { String.class };
// find the constructor that accepts a String as an argument
Constructor con = stringClass.getConstructor( parameterType );
// build a one-element array that holds the argument
Object[] parameter = { "My String" };
// use Reflection to call the desired constructor
String string4 = (String)con.newInstance( parameter );
```

The example in Listing 28.2 works, but it's not practical. After all, it's not often that all you want to do is construct an object without assigning any useful information to it. This concept is more meaningful when you want to instantiate an object that has a constructor of a form that you expect. For example, if you were to build up an API that includes a superclass with a constructor that accepts several parameters, each class that extends it should probably declare a constructor that accepts the same parameter list so that the parameters can be passed on to the superclass during instantiation.

As an example, look at a factory approach for building subclass instances where the superclass constructor requires a single parameter. In this case, the superclass and its constructor parameter type are the `Car` and `TireSpecification` classes shown in Listing 28.3.

LISTING 28.3 A Car WITH A TireSpecification

```
public class TireSpecification {
  float treadDepth;
  float diameter;
}

public class Car {
  TireSpecification tires;
  public Car (TireSpecification tires){
    this.tires = tires;
   }
}
```

The other details of these classes are left out to put the focus only on what is necessary to work with the `Car` constructor. Based on these declarations, the class `Car` needs to receive a `TireSpecification` object from some source whenever an instance is created. When you create subclasses to represent specific car models, say `BMW_540i` and `Volvo_V70`, you will need to obtain this same information and provide it to the superclass constructor as shown in Listing 28.4.

LISTING 28.4 BMW_540i AND Volvo_V70 SUBCLASS CONSTRUCTORS

```
public class BMW_540i extends Car {
  public BMW_540i(TireSpecification tires) {
    super(tires);
  }
}

public class Volvo_V70 extends Car {
  public Volvo_V70(TireSpecification tires) {
    super(tires);
  }
}
```

If every program that uses the subclasses of `Car` has knowledge of them in advance, those programs can access the constructors for classes such as `BMW_540i` and `Volvo_V70` to create instances as needed. The drawback is that this requires code to be changed whenever a new type of car is defined, even though some programs might not exercise any behavior unique to a particular subclass. You might think that this sounds like a problem that could be addressed with polymorphism or an interface, but neither of these works when dealing with constructors. Reflection does offer a solution is this case, however. Given that every subclass declares a constructor that accepts a `TireSpecification`, you can use Reflection to make the programs that use `Car` subclasses aware of new car types dynamically. Such an approach is shown in Listing 28.5.

LISTING 28.5 CarShop CREATES Car INSTANCES USING REFLECTION

```
/*
 * CarShop
 */
import java.lang.reflect.*;

public class CarShop {
  Car carList[];

  public CarShop( String[] carTypes ) {
    // create a car of each specified type
    carList = new Car[carTypes.length];
    for ( int i=0; i<carTypes.length; i++ ) {
      carList[i] = createCar(carTypes[i], new TireSpecification());
    }
  }

  public Car createCar(String carName, TireSpecification tires) {
    Car newCar = null;
    try {
      Object constructorParam[] = new TireSpecification[1];
      constructorParam[0]= tires;

      // get the class name for the car that you want
      Class carClass = Class.forName(carName);

      // create an array of Classes, and use this
      // array to find the constructor that you want
      Class parameters[] = new Class[1];
      parameters[0]= TireSpecification.class;
      Constructor  con = carClass.getDeclaredConstructor(parameters);

      // create a car instance for the carList
      newCar = (Car)con.newInstance(constructorParam);
    }
    catch (Exception e) {
      System.out.println("Error creating " + carName);
    }
    return newCar;
  }

  // supply names of the car types as command line arguments
  public static void main( String args[] ) {
    // create a car shop that contains the specified car types
    CarShop shop = new CarShop( args );
    for ( int i=0; i<shop.carList.length; i++ ) {
      System.out.println( shop.carList[i] );
    }
  }
}
```

Listing 28.5 should be saved as `CarShop.java` and it should be executed using the command

```
java CarShop BMW_540i Volvo_V70
```

In this example, the most important operation is obviously the `createCar` method. Look at each of the steps, starting with the creation of the constructor parameters. These two lines place the `TireSpecification` provided to the method into a single element array.

```
Object constructorParam[] = new TireSpecification[1];
constructorParam[0]= tires;
```

As you saw earlier, the method `newInstance` of `Constructor` accepts an array of objects for its parameter list. Given that the constructors of `Car` and its subclasses accept a single parameter of type `TireSpecification`, `constructorParam` now holds all that is necessary.

The next step is to obtain a `Class` instance associated with the type of car being created. This is done using the name of the class:

```
Class carClass = Class.forName(carName);
```

Now the desired constructor for the class can be obtained using the `getDeclaredConstructor` method of `Class`. The whole point here is to take advantage of the fact that every `Car` subclass should have a constructor that accepts a `TireSpecification`. The `getDeclaredConstructor` method accepts an array of classes and attempts to find a constructor whose parameters match the class types and order represented in this array.An array is passed in with a single element containing the `TireSpecification` class:

```
Class parameters[] = new Class[1];
parameters[0]= TireSpecification.class;
Constructor  con = carClass.getDeclaredConstructor(parameters);
```

The correct constructor is then used to create the specified type of car:

```
newCar = (Car)con.newInstance(constructorParam);
```

You might be questioning all the effort when a BMW could have been created much easier using:

```
newCar = new BMW_540i(tires);
```

This seems true, but to really account for this situation you would need a conditional expression that looked like the following:

```
if (carName.equals("BMW_540i"))
  newCar = new BMW_540i(tires);
else if (carName.equals("Volvo_V70"))
  newCar = new Volvo_V70(tires);
```

Each time you add a new car, you would have to go back in and add another conditional statement. With Reflection, this isn't necessary. Instead, new car types can be used by `CarShop` by doing nothing more than including the name of the new `Car` subclass as one of the command line arguments to the program.

Inspecting a Class for Its Methods

The previous examples have focused on constructors, but Reflection also allows you to discover the regular methods a class declares. This functionality is again provided by `java.lang.Class`.

Obtaining a List of Methods

Going back to the `Requestor/Provider` example used in Listing 28.1, a few simple changes allow the methods of a class to be queried and displayed along with its constructors. Listing 28.6 shows the necessary modifications.

Listing 28.6 Reflection Reveals Methods as Well as Constructors

```
/*
 * Requestor
 */
import java.lang.reflect.*;
public class Requestor {
  public void requestConstuctors() {
    try {
      // load the Provider class and use Reflection
      // to get an array of constructor information
      Class provClass = Class.forName("Provider");
      Constructor con[] = provClass.getDeclaredConstructors();
      for (int x=0; x<con.length; x++)
        System.out.println("Constructor " + x + " = " + con[x]);

      // get an array of Provider method information
      Method meth[] = provClass.getDeclaredMethods();
      for (int x=0; x<meth.length; x++)
        System.out.println("Method " + x + " = " + meth[x]);

    }
    catch (ClassNotFoundException ce) {
      // Class.forName was unable to load Provider.class
      System.out.println("Could not locate class");
    }
    catch (SecurityException se) {
      // Reflection permission was not granted
      System.out.println("Not allowed to get class info");
    }
  }

  public static void main(String args[]) {
    // construct a Requestor and ask it for the
    // constructors and methods declared by Provider
    Requestor req = new Requestor();
    req.requestConstuctors();
  }
}
```

LISTING 28.6 CONTINUED

```
/*
 *  Provider
 */
class Provider {
  String attribute;

  // construct with a String to assign to the attribute
  public Provider(String s) {
    attribute = s;
  }

  // construct with an int to assign to the attribute
  private Provider(int i) {
    attribute = String.valueOf(i);
  }

  // set the attribute String
  public void setAttribute(String attribute) {
    this.attribute = attribute;
  }

  // get the attribute String
  public String getAttribute() {
    return attribute;
  }
}
```

Now, when you compile `Requestor.java` and run it, the output you see should look like this:

```
Constructor 0 = private Provider(int)
Constructor 1 = public Provider(java.lang.String)
Method 0 = public void Provider.setAttribute(java.lang.String)
Method 1 = public java.lang.String Provider.getAttribute()
```

As you can see, the underlying `toString` operation for the `Method` class reports the same information as does the one for `Constructor` with the addition of the method return type. One point to note about `getDeclaredMethods` is that it only returns the methods declared by the class or interface being reflected and not any of its superclasses or superinterfaces.

This does not mean, however, that if you override or overload a method, you won't be able to detect it because it was obtained through inheritance. You will see these methods. Overloaded methods are actually new, so they are not obtained through inheritance; and overridden methods are included in the methods list because there is a new implementation for them in the subclass that is unique to that class.

Instead of `getDeclaredMethods`, you can call `getMethods` to access the methods declared in a class or interface plus those it inherits. As with `getConstructors`, this method only returns the `public` methods.

USING getDeclaredMethod() TO INVOKE A METHOD

As you might have guessed, just like with the constructor example, invoking a method for the sake of invoking it isn't useful. The only exception might be to support the needs of a debugger, but this type of requirement is rare for most programmers.

Like its constructor counterpart, getDeclaredMethods has a sibling method, getDeclaredMethod, which obtains a specific method based on its name and parameter list:

```
public Method getDeclaredMethod(String name, Class parameterTypes[])
```

You might notice that getDeclaredMethod takes an additional parameter compared to getDeclaredConstructor. It is necessary to specify a parameter list in both cases, but all constructors share the same name, so the name parameter is only needed here.

Notice that the method name and the parameter list are all that are needed to differentiate a method from any others. Remember that differences in the modifiers, return types, or exceptions thrown by two methods are not enough for them to be recognized by the compiler as two legal declarations. They must differ in name or parameter list as well. Here, getDeclaredMethod takes advantage of this fact and only requires you to provide the minimum information necessary to locate a specific method.

If no method matches the signature you pass to getDeclaredMethod, a NoSuchMethodException is thrown. This is a checked exception, so you need to enclose any calls to this method in a try-catch block.

Now let's go back to the car example and add a method to each subclass as shown in Listing 28.7.

LISTING 28.7 THE Car EXAMPLE WITH METHODS ADDED

```
class Car {
  TireSpecification tires;
  boolean running;
  public Car (TireSpecification tires){
    this.tires = tires;
   }
}

class BMW_540i extends Car {
  public BMW_540i(TireSpecification tires) {
    super(tires);
  }

  public boolean start() {
    running = true;
    System.out.println("The 540i is now running");
    return true;
  }
}

class Volvo_V70 extends Car {
  public Volvo_V70(TireSpecification tires) {
```

LISTING 28.7 CONTINUED

```
    super(tires);
  }

  public boolean start() {
    running = true;
    System.out.println("The V70 is now running");
    return true;
  }
}
```

In Listing 28.7, both the `BMW_540i` and `Volvo_V70` classes have had a `start` method added. If you're thinking ahead, a better design here is obviously to declare this method in `Car` and take advantage of polymorphism, but this example is a little harder to illustrate a point. Given that, you need to add a method to the `CarShop` class to allow it to start either type of car. Listing 28.8 shows the addition of the `startCar` method for this purpose.

LISTING 28.8 THE COMPLETE `CarShop` CLASS

```
/*
 * CarShop
 */
import java.lang.reflect.*;

public class CarShop {
  Car carList[];

  public CarShop( String[] carTypes ) {
    // create and start a car of each specified type
    carList = new Car[carTypes.length];
    for ( int i=0; i<carTypes.length; i++ ) {
      carList[i] = createCar(carTypes[i], new TireSpecification());
      startCar( carList[i] );
    }
  }


  public Car createCar(String carName, TireSpecification tires) {
    Car newCar = null;
    try {
      Object constructorParam[] = new TireSpecification[1];
      constructorParam[0]= tires;

      // get the class name for the car that you want
      Class carClass = Class.forName(carName);

      // create an array of Classes, and use this to
      // array to find the constructor that you want
      Class parameters[] = new Class[1];
      parameters[0]= TireSpecification.class;
      Constructor  con = carClass.getDeclaredConstructor(parameters);

      // create a car instance for the carList
      newCar = (Car)con.newInstance(constructorParam);
```

LISTING 28.8 CONTINUED

```
    }
    catch (Exception e) {
      System.out.println("Error creating " + carName);
    }
    return newCar;
  }

  public void startCar(Car theCar) {
    try {
      // Define a zero-length Class array to represent
      // the empty parameter list of the start method
      Class parameters[] = new Class[0];
      Class carType = theCar.getClass();
      Method meth = carType.getDeclaredMethod("start", parameters);

      // invoke the method on the specified car
      meth.invoke(theCar,parameters);
    }
    catch (Exception e) {
      System.out.println("Error starting car: " + e);
    }
  }

  // supply names of car types as command line arguments
  public static void main( String args[] ) {
    // create a car shop that contains the specified car types
    CarShop shop = new CarShop( args );
    for ( int i=0; i<shop.carList.length; i++ ) {
      System.out.println( shop.carList[i] );
    }
  }
}
```

Now when you execute this application, it should notify you that both car types are running. The `invoke` method (of the `Method` class), used here to execute `start`, requires two parameters. One of these is the array of parameters required to invoke the method, just as a parameter array was used in the `newInstance` method of `Constructor`. However, `invoke` also needs to know which object the method is being called upon, so the method call also includes an instance of the class associated with the method. If the object is not an instance of the class that declared the method, an exception is thrown.

Going back to Listing 28.8, notice that to obtain the method `start`, you need to be operating directly on the class `BMW_540i` or `Volvo_V70`, and not on an instance of either of these classes. This is easy to manage because `java.lang.Object` defines a `getClass` method that returns the `Class` associated with an object.

Now let's revisit the earlier observation that this particular problem could have been solved with an interface or an overridden method. Neither of these approaches requires retrieving a method and invoking it through Reflection. The approach used in this example is obviously more complex. Although true here, you will not always have the information at compile time to implement a method call. You'll see in Chapter 29 that JavaBeans programming relies on Reflection to make properties of a bean accessible to code that knows nothing about it until runtime. With the capability to invoke methods like this with Reflection, you have added flexibility in how method calls are specified. In particular, `getDeclaredMethod` can be used to provide another method with a reference to a method that behaves somewhat like a method pointer in other languages.

This means the portion of the method signature that becomes important is the parameter list and not necessarily the method name. This approach allows you to create multiple methods, which provide similar functionality, without the need to enforce an inheritance hierarchy or even a shared set of method signatures declared in an interface.

As with `getDeclaredMethods`, `getDeclaredMethod` has a counterpart in `getMethod`. This method accepts the same two parameters as `getDeclaredMethod` but only returns a method that matches the specified criteria if the method is `public`.

INVOKING METHODS THAT ACCEPT PRIMITIVE TYPES AS PARAMETERS

One limitation of the examples so far is that you have not seen how to invoke any methods or constructors that accept a primitive type as a parameter. For instance, consider the `NewCar` in Listing 28.9.

LISTING 28.9 `NewCar` HAS A CONSTRUCTOR THAT ACCEPTS AN `int`

```
public class NewCar{
  int numTires;
  public NewCar(int numTires) {
     this.numTires = numTires;
  }

  public int getTireCount(){
    return numTires;
  }
}
```

To create an instance of `NewCar`, you must provide an `int` to the constructor. The `getDeclaredContructor` method, however, requires an array of `Class` objects to locate a specific constructor based on its parameter list. How do you get the class for an `int`? It's actually a simple construct built into the language. You can obtain a class object representing any primitive type by appending `.class` to the name of the type (for example, `int.class`).

After you locate a constructor that requires a primitive type as a parameter, the next challenge is to provide an argument to use with `newInstance` given that it also works only with objects. You have probably already guessed that you need to use the wrapper classes from `java.lang`. In this example, `java.lang.Integer` can be used to pass an `int` argument. Listing 28.10 shows how to instantiate a `NewCar` this way.

Listing 28.10 `TestNewCar` Creates an Instance of the `NewCar` Class.

```
import java.lang.reflect.Constructor;

public class TestNewCar{
  public static void main(String args[]) {
    try {
      Class car = Class.forName("NewCar");

      // create the array of parameter types and find the constructor
      Class param[] = {int.class};
      Constructor con = car.getDeclaredConstructor(param);

      // use a wrapper class to hold the int argument 4
      Object values[] = {new Integer(4)};

      // create an instance of the class
      NewCar carObj = (NewCar)con.newInstance(values);
      System.out.println("The car has " + carObj.getTireCount() + " tires");
    }
    catch (Exception e){
      System.out.println("Something went wrong while instantiating NewCar");
      e.printStackTrace(System.err);
    }
  }
}
```

Accessing the Declared Fields of a Class

With constructors and methods covered, that leaves fields as the major remaining aspect of class Reflection. As you might have guessed, the methods used in this endeavor are `getDeclaredFields`, `getDeclaredField`, `getFields`, and `getField`. This section focuses on `getDeclaredFields` and `getDeclaredField`. The other two forms differ from these only in that they reflect superclasses and superinterfaces, and return only `public` fields.

In the previous `Provider` class, there was already a field named `attribute`, so you can modify `Requestor` slightly to access it, as shown in Listing 28.11.

Listing 28.11 Requestor Application That Gets Fields

```
/*
 * Requestor
 */
import java.lang.reflect.*;
public class Requestor {
  public void requestConstuctors() {
    try {
      // load the Provider class and use Reflection
      // to get an array of constructor information
      Class provClass = Class.forName("Provider");
      Constructor con[] = provClass.getDeclaredConstructors();
      for (int x=0; x<con.length; x++)
        System.out.println("Constructor " + x + " = " + con[x]);
```

Listing 28.11 Continued

```
      // get an array of Provider method information
      Method meth[] = provClass.getDeclaredMethods();
      for (int x=0; x<meth.length; x++)
        System.out.println("Method " + x + " = " + meth[x]);

      // get an array of Provider field information
      Field field[] = provClass.getDeclaredFields();
      for (int x=0; x<field.length; x++)
        System.out.println("Field " + x + " = " + field[x]);
    }
    catch (ClassNotFoundException ce) {
      // Class.forName was unable to load Provider.class
      System.out.println("Could not locate class");
    }
    catch (SecurityException se) {
      // Reflection permission was not granted
      System.out.println("Not allowed to get class info");
    }
  }

  public static void main(String args[]) {
    // construct a Requestor and ask it for the
    // constructors, methods, and fields declared by Provider
    Requestor req = new Requestor();
    req.requestConstuctors();
  }
}

/*
 *  Provider
 */
class Provider {
  String attribute;

  // construct with a String to assign to the attribute
  public Provider(String s) {
    attribute = s;
  }

  // construct with an int to assign to the attribute
  private Provider(int i) {
    attribute = String.valueOf(i);
  }

  // set the attribute String
  public void setAttribute(String attribute) {
    this.attribute = attribute;
  }

  // get the attribute String
  public String getAttribute() {
    return attribute;
  }

}
```

The resulting output now includes an entry for the `String` field `attribute`:

```
Constructor 0 = private Provider(int)
Constructor 1 = public Provider(java.lang.String)
Method 0 = public void Provider.setAttribute(java.lang.String)
Method 1 = public java.lang.String Provider.getAttribute()
Field 0 = java.lang.String Provider.attribute
```

An additional use of `Field` is that it provides a number of accessor and mutator methods that you can use to query the value of a field or set it. These methods all accept an `Object` parameter that specifies the class instance to which the operations are applied.

UTILITY METHODS

The preceding sections have focused on the aspects of Reflection you are most likely to use. Namely, locating a constructor, creating an instance, locating and invoking a method, and locating a field. The other methods in `Class`, `Constructor`, `Method`, and `Field` provide additional utilities for object discovery that are important, but probably not as widely used.

Besides the methods already covered, `Class` allows you to query an entity for information about its position in the class hierarchy. This includes learning the interfaces implemented by a class or extended by an interface (`getInterfaces`), or the superclass of any class (`getSuperclass`). You can also get the name of an entity, the modifiers included in its declaration, and its package assignment. The need for this level of detail is not widespread, but it is invaluable in tools such as the class browsers found in many IDE applications.

The `java.lang.reflect` package also includes the `Array` class. This class consists solely of static methods that are available for dynamically creating and accessing arrays of any primitive or object type.

IMPLEMENTING AN INTERFACE USING A PROXY

Java 1.3 added the capability to dynamically create a proxy class at runtime that implements one or more interfaces. The `Proxy` class and the `InvocationHandler` interface were added to the `java.lang.reflect` package to support this functionality. With this capability, you can create a proxy that delegates the method calls associated with the interfaces it implements to a class that implements `InvocationHandler`. This interface defines a single method:

```
public Object invoke(Object proxy, Method method, Object[] args)
  throws Throwable
```

You obtain a proxy to work with an `InvocationHandler` using a static method of the `Proxy` class:

```
public static Object newProxyInstance(ClassLoader loader, Class[] interfaces,
    InvocationHandler h) throws IllegalArgumentException
```

The object returned by `newProxyInstance` can then be cast to any of the interfaces assigned as part of its creation. Calls are made to the proxy and then redirected to its `InvocationHandler`.

The subject of dynamic proxies is somewhat complex, so let's look at an example implementation. A natural use for a proxy is when you need to wrap one or more existing classes with some additional functionality. A typical approach for doing this is to first define an interface that includes each method of interest in the class to be wrapped. You can then declare a wrapper class that implements this same interface and delegates the execution of each method call to an instance of the original class. Any additional functionality can be executed by each wrapper class method either before or after the delegate's method is called. By coding to an interface, you can substitute the wrapper class for the original wherever the new functionality is needed.

This delegation approach works well, but it can be tedious to implement all the wrapper methods if an interface is substantial in size. The problem grows if the new functionality applies to multiple classes that are not related through inheritance or interface; this leads to the creation of many wrapper classes. Dynamic proxies offer a more flexible approach in this case.

The example in Listing 28.12 shows how a new capability can be added to classes that implement a particular interface. For this example, an existing interface and class were selected, namely `Set` and `HashSet`. The proxy created offers the capability to selectively allow or disallow calls to the methods defined by `Set` that remove elements from the collection. The `DisallowRemoveSet` class implements `InvocationHandler` by passing method calls to a delegate `Set`. If the method call would remove an element from the set, and this option is currently disabled, the call is rejected by throwing an `UnsupportedOperationException`.

LISTING 28.12 DYNAMIC PROXY CREATION

```
import java.lang.reflect.*;
import java.util.*;
/*
 * Implement InvocationHandler to turn on and off the ability
 * to disable the methods in Set that remove elements from the
 * collection
 */
class DisallowRemoveSet implements InvocationHandler {
  private Set delegate;
  private boolean disallowRemove = true;

  public DisallowRemoveSet(Set delegate) {
    this.delegate = delegate;
  }

  public void setDisallowRemove(boolean disallowRemove) {
    this.disallowRemove = disallowRemove;
  }

  public Object invoke( Object proxy, Method meth, Object[] args )
    throws Throwable {
    if ( disallowRemove && (meth.getName().startsWith("remove") ||
     meth.getName().equals("retainAll") || meth.getName().equals("clear")) ) {
      // trying to remove when the option is disabled
      throw new UnsupportedOperationException(
```

LISTING 28.12 CONTINUED

```
        "Set does not allow element removal");
}
    // method call okay, send it on to the delegate Set implementation
    return meth.invoke(delegate, args);
  }
}

public class SetProxyExample {
  public static void main(String[] args) {
    Set delegate = new HashSet();
    Class[] setInterface = new Class[] { Set.class };
    DisallowRemoveSet handler = new DisallowRemoveSet(delegate);

    // create a proxy that wraps a HashSet implementation of the Set
    // interface with a DisallowRemoveSet
    Set setProxy = (Set)Proxy.newProxyInstance( Thread.currentThread().
      getContextClassLoader(), setInterface, handler );

    // build a set with 5 elements
    String[] data = new String[] {"A","B","C","D","E"};
    setProxy.addAll( Arrays.asList(data) );

    try {
      System.out.println("Enable removes and call for first data entry");
      handler.setDisallowRemove(false);
      setProxy.remove( data[0] );

      handler.setDisallowRemove(true);
      System.out.println("Disable removes and call for second data entry");
      setProxy.remove( data[1] );
    }
    catch (UnsupportedOperationException e ) {
      System.out.println("Exception thrown: " + e.getMessage());
    }
  }
}
```

The program in Listing 28.12, which should be saved as `SetProxyExample.java`, creates a proxy that implements `Set` using the `Proxy.newProxyInstance` method. This proxy is then used to add elements to the underlying set. Two removals are then attempted, one with the option to remove elements allowed and the other with it disallowed. If you execute the application, you'll get the following output:

```
Enable removes and call for first data entry
Disable removes and call for second data entry
Exception thrown: Set does not allow element removal
```

One of the strengths of this approach is that, even though this example used `HashSet` as the interface implementation, the same functionality would be obtained if another implementation of `Set` were substituted. The `InvocationHandler` does not impose any requirements on the implementation classes, so the existing class hierarchy is not intruded upon in any way.

TROUBLESHOOTING

REFLECTION PERMISSION DENIED

You get a runtime error that says you do not have permission to perform a requested Reflection operation.

Reflection often includes requests that conflict with the access restrictions assigned to a class and its members. If you need to perform Reflection that is not by default granted by the `SecurityManager`, you need to explicitly grant the appropriate permission. This is typically done by adding the following entry to the associated policy file, which is the means used within the Java security architecture to specify the security policy in effect at runtime:

```
permission java.lang.reflect.ReflectPermission "suppressAccessChecks";
```

The default policy is determined by the `java.policy` file in the `lib\security` directory underneath your JRE directory (for example, `c:\Program Files\JavaSoft\JRE\1.3\lib\security`). For more information on the use of policy files, refer to Sun's documentation available at `http://java.sun.com/docs/books/tutorial/ext/security/policy.html`.

NO CLASS MEMBERS REFLECTED

You query a `Class` object for its fields and methods, but nothing is returned.

Remember that a `Class` object does not necessarily represent a class, or even an interface. A `Class` instance might also represent an array, a primitive type, or even the keyword `void`. You should use the `isArray`, `isInterface`, and `isPrimitive` methods to determine more information about an instance when in doubt.

CHAPTER 29

JavaBeans

In this chapter

by Brian Keeton

SELF-CONTAINED COMPONENTS

The specification of JavaBeans adds to the Java platform the capability to create a complete application by linking together a set of self-contained components. Microsoft's Visual Basic and Borland's Delphi are both examples of applications that allow users to build full-blown applications by combining independent components. The success and popularity of these two applications alone speak volumes to the success of this style of application building.

Just as with other models, there is no restriction on the size or complexity of a JavaBeans component. In principle, JavaBeans components (or just Beans) can range from widgets and controls to containers and applications. The philosophy behind JavaBeans is to provide easy-to-implement functionality for the former, while allowing enough flexibility for the latter. In the spirit of this philosophy, you'll see how to create and use fairly simple Beans. However, after you finish reading this chapter, you'll have learned enough to create larger and more complex Beans, if you choose to do so.

IMPORTANT CONCEPTS IN COMPONENT MODELS

JavaBeans provides a platform-neutral component architecture. This is in contrast to platform-specific component architectures such as COM for the Windows platform. A COM component written to be placed inside a corresponding container such as Microsoft Word cannot be used in containers based on other component architectures. Because JavaBeans is an architecture-neutral specification, Beans can be placed into any container for which a bridge exists between JavaBeans and the container's component architecture. This means that a JavaBean can be used in containers as diverse as Microsoft Word, Internet Explorer, and Lotus Notes, among others. To accomplish this seemingly impossible feat, the JavaBeans specification adopts features common with the other popular component models. In particular, these features include the following:

- Component fields or properties
- Component methods or functions
- Events and intercommunication
- State persistence and storage

Note

If you are familiar with component models already, you don't necessarily need to read this section. You can jump right into the next section, "The Basics of Designing a JavaBean."

COMPONENT FIELDS OR PROPERTIES

For a component to be useful, it has to have a set of properties that defines its state. For example, if you were to design a component that displayed some text, one of the properties of that component might be the foreground color of the font. Another property might be the type and size of the font. Taken as a whole, the set of properties that make up a component also defines its state. For example, if the properties of one component completely match that of another, they are in the same state.

Properties are often used to define not only the appearance but also the behavior of components. This is because a component need not have any appearance at all. For example, a component in a spreadsheet might calculate the interest earned on some earnings column. If that component is not capable of displaying the data, it probably shouldn't have any properties associated with appearance. It is likely, however, that it will have a property that defines the current interest rate.

Properties can range from Boolean values, to strings, to arrays, to other components. They can also be interdependent. Following the same example given previously, a component that displays the earnings column might want to be notified if the interest rate property of the other component changes.

COMPONENT METHODS OR FUNCTIONS

The API, so to speak, of a component is the collection of methods or functions that it contains that other components and containers can call. There has to be some way for a container to modify a component's properties, notify it of an event, or execute some functionality.

The various component models differ in how they make the properties and methods of their components available to other components. Because entire books have been written on how this is implemented for different models, it's clear that this is a common feature of component models. This topic will be discussed as it relates to JavaBeans in the section on introspection later in the chapter.

EVENTS AND INTERCOMMUNICATION

A component by itself is a lonely component. Although some components might have extensive functionality and many properties, in the true spirit of a component, it should be the most useful when exercised in conjunction with other components. So if two components are sitting together in a container, how do they talk? How does one let the other know when it has done something the other really ought to know about?

The method by which most components communicate is through event transmission. One component (or the container) undergoes some action causing it to generate an event. For example, an event is generated when you click a button. Depending on the model, the component will notify the container, the interested components, or both of the events. At the same time, the objects in the environment also act on events delivered to them. For example, the File dialog box displays itself when it hears that you just clicked a Browse button.

STATE PERSISTENCE AND STORAGE

It is important for components to remember their state. This is so common that you might not even recognize it. When you open an application and it remembers the size and position of its window when it was last closed, it is maintaining (to some degree) a persistent state.

Also important is the capability to store and retrieve components. Sun Microsystems, Inc., likes to call this *packaging*. This is especially important in a distributed environment where the components are likely to be served up over a network.

THE BASICS OF DESIGNING A JAVABEAN

All good programmers recognize the importance of the design phase in programming. Thus, you'll start out by addressing how to design a Bean. As you will learn later, the way in which you design your Bean directly affects the way it behaves in containers. For example, the names you choose for the methods should follow specific design specifications. If you start from the beginning with these rules in mind, allowing your Bean to participate in introspection does not require any additional programming on your part. The concept of introspection was introduced in Chapter 28, "Reflection," but you'll see more of how it relates to JavaBeans a little later.

Designing a Bean consists of the following steps:

1. Specifying the Bean's properties
2. Specifying the events the Bean generates or responds to
3. Defining which properties, methods, and events the Bean exposes to other Beans or to its container
4. Deciding miscellaneous issues, such as whether the Bean has its own Customization dialog box or whether it requires some prototypical state information

You'll start by designing some Beans. For the sake of a simple example, assume that you are developing two Beans; one Bean allows text to be entered into it, and the other displays some text. You can imagine how these Beans might be useful. By placing these two Beans into a container, you can use one to enter text that the other will then display. What types of properties do you think these Beans need to have? What events are these Beans interested in hearing about? What events do these Beans generate? Do these Beans expose all their properties and events, or just some? At this point, you might not know the answers to these questions. The process is the important concept here; the details will become clearer as you progress through the chapter. Regardless, the first thing any Bean needs is a name. In this chapter, the sample Beans will be called `TextDisplayer` and `TextReader`.

SPECIFYING THE BEAN'S PROPERTIES

The `TextDisplayer` and `TextReader` Beans definitely need to have a property defining the text they hold. For example, say that the `TextDisplayer` Bean also contains properties defining the background color, font, and font color. The `TextReader` Bean also contains a property that defines how many columns of characters it can display. Table 29.1 lists the `TextDisplayer` Bean's properties and the Java types that will be used to implement them. Table 29.2 lists the `TextReader` Bean's properties and the Java types that will be used for them.

TABLE 29.1 THE TextDisplayer BEAN'S PROPERTIES AND JAVA TYPES

Property Name	Java Type
OutputText	java.lang.String
BGColor	java.awt.Color
TextFont	java.awt.Font
FontColor	java.awt.Color

TABLE 29.2 THE TextReader BEAN'S PROPERTIES AND JAVA TYPES

Property Name	Java Type
InputText	java.lang.String
Width	int

SPECIFYING THE EVENTS THE BEAN GENERATES OR RESPONDS TO

The TextDisplayer Bean must respond to an event specifying that its text should change. Specifically, it must update its OutputText property and redraw itself. The TextReader Bean doesn't need to respond to any events, but it must generate (or fire) an event when the user changes its InputText property. This type of event is called a PropertyChangeEvent, for obvious reasons.

PROPERTIES, METHODS, AND EVENT EXPOSURE

Because these Beans are particularly simple, you don't need to hide anything from the Beans' container or the other Beans interested in them. JavaBeans provides a mechanism for you that will use the names of your methods to extract the names and types of your properties and events. Rest assured that you will learn how this works as you go along. Later in the chapter, you'll learn how to explicitly define what information in a Bean is exposed to its environment.

INITIAL PROPERTY VALUES AND BEAN CUSTOMIZERS

To keep this example simple, assume that your Beans do not need any prototypical information (you'll define default values for all their properties) and that they do not have their own Customization dialog box. This means that your Beans have a predefined state when they're instantiated and that they use the standard PropertyEditors for their properties. If you were designing a Bean that displays an HTML page, for example, specifying default values might not be possible. You would need to know what file to display when the Bean is instantiated. Table 29.3 shows your TextDisplayer Bean's properties and the default values it will hold. Likewise, Table 29.4 is for the TextReader Bean.

TABLE 29.3 DEFAULT PROPERTY VALUES FOR THE `TextDisplayer` BEAN

Property Name	Default Value
`OutputText`	`"TextDisplayer"`
`BGColor`	`java.awt.Color.white`
`TextFont`	`Courier, normal, 12`
`FontColor`	`java.awt.Color.black`

TABLE 29.4 DEFAULT PROPERTY VALUES FOR THE `TextReader` BEAN

Property Name	Default Value
`InputText`	`""` (an empty string)
`Width`	`40`

At this point, you've designed your Beans enough to begin coding. This will be an additive process because you haven't learned how to make the Beans do anything yet. You'll see the relevant pieces of code as you build the example. In Figure 29.1, you can see your Beans hard at work inside the BeanBox. The BeanBox is a JavaBeans container that you can download from Sun's Web site; it's included in the BDK, or Beans Development Kit.

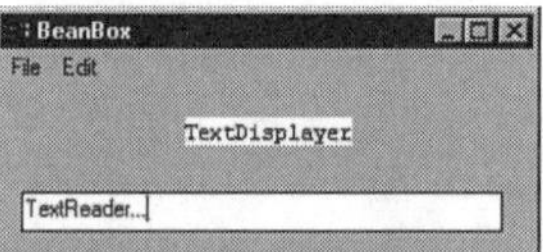

Figure 29.1
Sun's BeanBox shows the `TextDisplayer` and `TextReader` Beans.

Right now, the Beans are completely isolated. Because you haven't given the Beans any functionality yet, this is about as good as it gets. The preliminary code needed to instantiate and draw the `TextDisplayer` Bean is shown in Listing 29.1. Notice that there is no class hierarchy required for a Bean. It is not necessary for a Bean to extend any particular superclass, although it must implement the `Serializable` interface (or extend a class such as `Canvas` that does).

LISTING 29.1 `TextDisplayer.java`—PRELIMINARY CODE FOR THE `TextDisplayer` BEAN

```
import java.awt.*;
import java.beans.*;
public class TextDisplayer extends Canvas implements PropertyChangeListener {
   // default constructor for this Bean. This is the constructor that an
   // application builder (such as Visual Basic) would use.
   public TextDisplayer() {
      this( "TextDisplayer", Color.white,
            new Font( "Courier", Font.PLAIN, 12 ),
            Color.black );
   }
```

LISTING 29.1 CONTINUED

```
   // custom constructor for this Bean. This is the constructor you would
   // likely use if you were going to do all your coding from scratch.
   public TextDisplayer( String OutputText, Color BGColor, Font TextFont,
                         Color FontColor ) {
      this.OutputText = OutputText;
      this.BGColor = BGColor;
      this.TextFont = TextFont;
      this.FontColor = FontColor;

      setFont( TextFont );          // set the Canvas's font.
      setBackground( BGColor );     // set the Canvas's background color.
      setForeground( FontColor ); // set the Canvas's foreground color.
   }

   // this Bean's properties.
   protected String OutputText;
   protected Color BGColor, FontColor;
   protected Font TextFont;

   // override the Canvas's paint method to display the text
   public void paint( Graphics g ) {
     // simplistic implementation to display a string
     g.drawString( OutputText, 10, 20 );
   }

   // implement the PropertyChangeListener interface
   public void propertyChange( PropertyChangeEvent evt ) {
     // add code here to respond to a change in a bound property
   }
}
```

The `draw` method implementation in Listing 29.1 is obviously not as robust as you would want for a reusable component, but it's adequate for demonstrating how the Bean works. You might have also noticed that you have specified that your Bean implement an interface called `PropertyChangeListener`. This is so that the `TextDisplayer` Bean can update its `OutputText` property by receiving an event through its `propertyChange` method. How that works will be discussed in more detail later in the chapter. The preliminary code needed to instantiate your `TextReader` Bean is shown in Listing 29.2.

LISTING 29.2 `TextReader.java`—PRELIMINARY CODE FOR THE `TextReader` BEAN

```
import java.awt.*;
import java.awt.event*;
import java.beans.*;
public class TextReader extends TextField {
   // default constructor for this Bean. This is the constructor that an
   // application builder (such as Visual Basic) would use.
   public TextReader() {
      this( "", 40 );
   }

   // custom constructor for this Bean. This is the constructor that you
   // would likely use if you were doing your coding from scratch.
```

LISTING 29.2 CONTINUED

```
   public TextReader( String InputText, int Width ) {
      super( InputText, Width );
      this.InputText = InputText;
      this.Width = Width;
      setEditable( true );

      // update the InputText property when the enter key is
      // pressed within the TextField
      this.addActionListener( new ActionListener() {
        public void actionPerformed( ActionEvent e ) {
          setInputText(getText());
        }
      });
   }

   // this Bean's properties.
   protected String InputText;
   protected int Width;

   // getter method for the InputText property.
   public synchronized String getInputText() {
     return InputText;
   }

   // setter method for the InputText property.
   public synchronized void setInputText( String newText ) {
      String oldText = InputText;
      InputText = newText;
      setText( InputText );
// uncomment this statement after the Listing 29.4 additions are made
//    changeAgent.firePropertyChange( "inputText", new String( oldText ),
//                                    new String( newText ) );
}
```

CREATING AND USING PROPERTIES

Previously in Figure 29.1, notice that the `TextDisplayer` Bean displayed itself with a white background and black text. It did so because that's how you set its properties in the default constructor. If you had set the `FontColor` property to red, it would have displayed the text in red. If the properties of a component cannot be changed by another Bean (or any other class that uses it), the usefulness of the Bean is reduced, as well as the reusability. For example, if you used the `TextDisplayer` Bean in an accounting package, you would need to change the Bean's `FontColor` property to red to indicate a negative value. So how do you let other Beans know that they can set (or read) this property? If you're coding from scratch, you can look at the documentation for the Bean. But what if you're in an application builder? Luckily, there's a way to do this without incurring any extra coding on your part. You'll see how that works a little later.

Two types of properties are supported by JavaBeans: single-value and indexed. In addition, properties can also be bound or constrained. A *single-value property* is a property for which there is only one assigned value at a time. As the name suggests, an *indexed property* has several values, each of which has a unique index. If a property is bound, it means that some other Bean is dependent on that property. In the continuing example, the `TextReader` Bean's `InputText` property is bound to the `TextDisplayer` Bean; the `TextReader` must notify the `TextDisplayer` whenever its `InputText` field changes. A property is constrained if it must check with other components before it can change.

Note

Constrained properties cannot change arbitrarily. One or more components might not allow the updated value.

SINGLE-VALUE PROPERTIES

All properties are accessed by calling methods on the owning Bean instance. Readable properties have a `getter` method used to read the value of the property. Writable properties have a `setter` method used to change the value of a property. These methods are not constrained to returning the value of a field declared within a Bean; they can also perform calculations and return some other value. All the properties the Beans have in the examples here are single-value.

At this point, you're ready to start talking about introspection. The method by which other components learn of your Bean's properties depends on a few things. In general, however, this process is called *introspection*. In fact, the class `java.beans.Introspector` is the class that provides this information for other components. The `Introspector` class traverses the class hierarchy of a particular Bean. If it finds explicit information provided by the Bean, it uses that. However, it uses design patterns to implicitly extract information from those Beans that do not provide information. Note that this is what happens to your Beans in the example. Specific design rules should be applied when defining accessor methods so that the `Introspector` class can do its job. If you choose to use other names, you can still expose a Bean's properties, but it requires you to supply a `BeanInfo` class. For more about what a `BeanInfo` class is, see the "Introspection: Creating and Using `BeanInfo` Classes" section later in this chapter. Here are the design patterns you should use:

```
public void set<PropertyName>( <PropertyType> value );
public <PropertyType> get<PropertyName>();
public boolean is<PropertyName>();
```

Note that the last pattern is an alternative `getter` method for Boolean properties only. `setter` methods are allowed to throw exceptions if they so choose. The accessor methods for the `TextDisplayer` Bean are shown in Listing 29.3. Notice that all the accessor methods have been declared as synchronized. Even though nothing serious could happen in this Bean, you should always assume that your Beans are running in multithreaded environments. Using synchronized accessor methods helps prevent race conditions from forming. `TextReader` requires a similar set of accessor methods for its properties.

LISTING 29.3 TextDisplayer.java—THE ACCESSOR METHODS FOR THE PROPERTIES IN THE TextDisplayer BEAN

```
public synchronized String getOutputText() {
   return( OutputText );
}

public synchronized void setOutputText( String text ) {
   OutputText = text;
   // force a paint
   Graphics g = getGraphics();
   if ( g != null ) {
     update(g);
   }
}

public synchronized Color getBGColor() {
   return( BGColor );
}

public synchronized void setBGColor( Color color ) {
   BGColor = color;
   setBackground( BGColor );   // set the Canvas's background color.
   repaint();
}

public synchronized Font getTextFont() {
   return( TextFont );
}

public synchronized void setTextFont( Font font ) {
   TextFont = font;
   setFont( TextFont );        // set the Canvas's font.
}

public synchronized Color getFontColor() {
   return( FontColor );
}

public synchronized void setFontColor( Color color ) {
   FontColor = color;
   setForeground( FontColor ); // set the Canvas's foreground color.
   repaint();
}
```

Figure 29.2 shows you what the property sheet of Sun's BeanBox shows for your `TextDisplayer` Bean. Notice that you can see the properties of the parent class, too. Your Bean inherits from `java.awt.Canvas`, which inherits from `java.awt.Component`, which inherits from `java.lang.Object`. The additional properties that you see are from the `java.awt.Component` class. This illustrates the principal drawback of using the automatic JavaBeans introspection methods. In your own Beans, this might be the motivation for providing a `BeanInfo` class. Again, more on that is in the "Introspection: Creating and Using `BeanInfo` Classes" section later in this chapter.

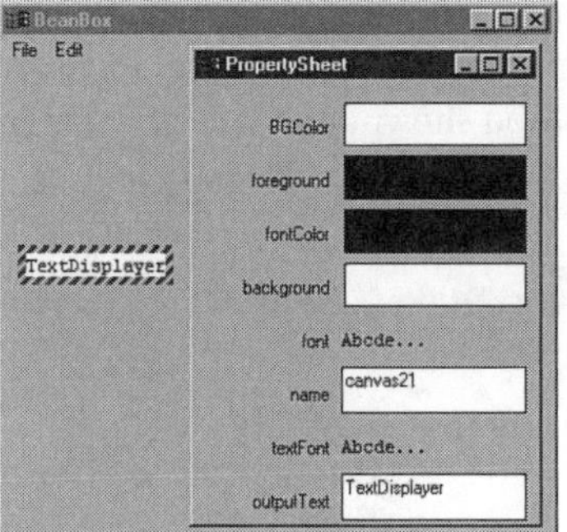

Figure 29.2
The `PropertySheet` of Sun's BeanBox showing the Bean's exposed properties. Notice the properties of the parent class.

Indexed Properties

An indexed property takes on multiple values simultaneously and can be treated as an array. You read or write the values associated with an indexed property by specifying an integer index or working with the entire array at once. The design patterns for indexed properties are as follows:

```
public <PropertyType> get<PropertyName>( int index );
public void set<PropertyName>( int index, <PropertyType> value );
public <PropertyType>[] get<PropertyName>();
public void set<PropertyName>( <PropertyType>[] value );
```

To illustrate, assume there is a `Meal` property that consists of an array of `Courses`:

```
public Course getMeal( int course );
public void setMeal( int course, Course dish );
public Course[] getMeal();
public void setMeal( Course[] dishes );
```

Bound Properties

As the programmer, you can decide which of your Bean's properties can be bound to other components. To provide bound properties in your Beans, you must define the following methods:

```
public void addPropertyChangeListener( PropertyChangeListener l );
public void removePropertyChangeListener( PropertyChangeListener l );
```

To provide this functionality on a per-property basis, the following design pattern should be used:

```
public void add<PropertyName>Listener( PropertyChangeListener l );
public void remove<PropertyName>Listener( PropertyChangeListener l );
```

Beans wanting to bind to other components' properties should implement the `PropertyChangeListener` interface, which consists of the following method:

```
public void propertyChange( PropertyChangeEvent evt );
```

Whenever a bound property in a Bean is updated, it must call the `propertyChange()` method in all the components that have registered with it. The class java.beans.PropertyChangeSupport is provided to help you with this process. The code in Listing 29.4 shows you what is required in the TextReader Bean to allow its InputText property to be bound. The setInputText method shown here was included previously in Listing 29.2, but the call to firePropertyChange can now be uncommented.

LISTING 29.4 TextReader.java—CODE REQUIRED TO MAKE THE InputText PROPERTY OF THE TextReader BEAN A BOUND PROPERTY

```
// setter method for the InputText property.
public synchronized void setInputText( String newText ) {
   String oldText = InputText;
   InputText = newText;
   setText( InputText );
   changeAgent.firePropertyChange( "inputText", new String( oldText ),
                                   new String( newText ) );
}

// these two methods allow this Bean to have bound properties.
public void addPropertyChangeListener( PropertyChangeListener l ) {
   changeAgent.addPropertyChangeListener( l );
}

public void removePropertyChangeListener( PropertyChangeListener l ) {
   changeAgent.removePropertyChangeListener( l );
}

protected PropertyChangeSupport changeAgent =
  new PropertyChangeSupport( this );
```

After you make the Listing 29.4 changes to TextReader, you can implement the propertyChange method of TextDisplayer that was declared previously in Listing 29.1. You should implement this method to respond to changes in the TextReader InputText property as follows:

```
// implement the PropertyChangeListener interface
public void propertyChange( PropertyChangeEvent evt ) {
  // only interested in the inputText property of TextReader
  if ( evt.getPropertyName().equals("inputText") ) {
    // display the new value of the TextReader property
    setOutputText( (String)evt.getNewValue() );
  }
}
```

Notice that this method refers to the property name as "inputText" even though we declared the TextReader property using the identifier InputText. In general, the rules used to extract property names based on getter and setter method declarations produce names that begin with a lowercase letter. The exception to this rule occurs when an accessor method contains a property name that begins with two or more uppercase letters. For example, getToolKitName corresponds to a property named toolKitName, but getGUIToolKitName corresponds to a property named GUIToolKitName.

If you have trouble configuring a bound property, see "Bean Events Are Not Propagated" in the "Troubleshooting" section at the end of this chapter.

CONSTRAINED PROPERTIES

The process for providing constrained properties in your code is also fairly straightforward. You must define the following methods in your Bean:

```
public void addVetoableChangeListener( VetoableChangeListener l );
public void removeVetoableChangeListener( VetoableChangeListener l );
```

Just as with bound properties, you can make individual properties constrained using the following design pattern:

```
public void add<PropertyName>Listener( VetoableChangeListener l );
public void remove<PropertyName>Listener( VetoableChangeListener l );
```

Beans intended to constrain other components' properties should implement the `VetoableChangeListener` interface, which consists of the following method:

```
public void vetoableChange( PropertyChangeEvent evt ) throws
PropertyVetoException;
```

Whenever a constrained property in a Bean is updated, it must call the `vetoableChange()` method in all the components that have registered with it. If a registered component disapproves of the property change, it can throw a `PropertyVetoException` to request that the previous value be retained instead. There is also a support class to help make this process easier. Use the class `java.beans.VetoableChangeSupport` to help manage your vetoable properties. The code in Listing 29.5 shows you what is required in the `TextReader` Bean to allow its `Width` property to be constrained.

LISTING 29.5 `TextReader.java`—CODE REQUIRED TO MAKE THE `Width` PROPERTY OF THE `TextReader` BEAN A CONSTRAINED PROPERTY

```
// setter method for the Columns property.
public synchronized void setWidth( int newWidth )
throws PropertyVetoException {
   int oldWidth = Width;
   vetoAgent.fireVetoableChange( "width", new Integer( oldWidth ),
                                 new Integer( newWidth ) );
   // no one vetoed, so change the property.
   Width = newWidth;
   setColumns( Width );
   Component p = getParent();
   if ( p != null ) {
      p.invalidate();
      p.doLayout();
   }
   changeAgent.firePropertyChange( "width", new Integer( oldWidth ),
                                   new Integer( newWidth ) );
}

// getter method for the Columns property.
public synchronized int getWidth() {
   return Width;
```

LISTING 29.5 CONTINUED

```
    }

    // these two methods allow this Bean to have constrained properties.
    public void addVetoableChangeListener( VetoableChangeListener l ) {
       vetoAgent.addVetoableChangeListener( l );
    }

    public void removeVetoableChangeListener( VetoableChangeListener l ) {
       vetoAgent.removeVetoableChangeListener( l );
    }

    protected VetoableChangeSupport vetoAgent =
      new VetoableChangeSupport( this );
```

In this particular example, the `Width` property is bound and constrained. A property does not have to be bound to be constrained. For example, to make the `Width` property constrained but not bound, you would remove the following line from Listing 29.5:

```
changeAgent.firePropertyChange( "width", new Integer( oldWidth ),
                                         new Integer( newWidth ) );
```

USING EVENTS TO COMMUNICATE WITH OTHER COMPONENTS

The whole idea behind the JavaBeans component model is to provide a way to create reusable components. To do this, Beans must be able to communicate with the other Beans in their environment and with their container. This is accomplished by means of `Listener` interfaces. You've already seen some of this with the `PropertyChangeEvent` from the last section. This section goes into more detail about how `Listeners` work.

Beans use the same event-handling scheme as AWT and Swing. This means that if your Bean needs to hear about events coming from another Bean, it must register itself with that Bean. To do this, it must implement the `Listener` interface for the event of interest. At the same time, if your Bean is no longer interested in hearing about some other Bean's event, it must unregister itself with that Bean. Any event that a Bean wants to fire must inherit from the `java.util.EventObject` class. For simple events, the `java.util.EventObject` class itself could be used; however, as with `java.lang.Exception`, using child classes provides clarity and is preferred. All `Listener` interfaces must inherit from the `java.util.EventListener` interface, and the same subclassing convention applies. The event handling method of a `Listener` interface should follow the design pattern for introspection as shown here:

```
void <EventOccuranceName>( <EventObjectType evt );
```

Note that `<EventObjectType>` must inherit from `java.util.EventObject`. Here is an example of an event handler for a `DinnerServedListener` interface:

```
// DinnerServedEvent inherits from
// java.util.EventObject.
void dinnerServed( DinnerServedEvent evt );
```

There is no restriction preventing an event-handler method from throwing an exception. In addition, any one `Listener` interface can have any number of related event handlers.

There are two types of events that components can listen for: multicast events and unicast events.

MULTICAST EVENTS

Multicast events are the most common types of events. The `PropertyChangeEvent`, which you have already been exposed to, is a multicast event because there can be any number of listeners. In that example, you had `addPropertyChangeListener()` and `removePropertyChangeListener()` methods, which allowed other components to register with the Bean as being interested in hearing when a bound property changed. The process is the same for any other type of multicast event, and the registration methods should follow the design pattern for introspection as shown here:

```
public synchronized void add<ListenerType>( <ListenerType> listener );
public synchronized void remove<ListenerType>( <ListenerType> listener );
```

The keyword `synchronized` is not actually part of the design pattern. It is included as a reminder that race conditions can occur, especially with the event model, and precautions must be taken.

UNICAST EVENTS

Unicast events don't occur nearly as often as their counterpart, but they're just as useful. Unicast events can have only one listener. If additional components attempt to listen to the unicast event, a `java.util.TooManyListenersException` will be thrown. The following design pattern should be used when declaring unicast events:

```
public synchronized void add<ListenerType>( <ListenerType> listener ) throws
   java.util.TooManyListenersException;
public synchronized void remove<ListenerType>( <ListenerType> listener );
```

EVENT ADAPTERS

In some cases, it might be necessary to build an event adapter class that can transfer an event to a component. This comes into play especially for an application builder because the application doesn't know until runtime how the components will be linked together or how they will interact with each other's events.

An event adapter intervenes in the normal event-handling scheme by intercepting the events normally meant for another component. For example, assume that a user places a button and a text box in an application builder. If the user wants the text box to fill with the word "Pressed" when the button is pressed, the application builder can use an event adapter to call a method containing the user-generated code needed to do it. Here's how it will eventually work:

1. The event adapter registers with the event source. In other words, it calls an `addSomeEventListener()` method on the event source component.

2. The event source component fires an event by calling the event adapter's event-handler method, `someEvent()`. Keep in mind that the event source component doesn't care whether it's calling an event adapter or a true event listener. At this point, with the event fired, it can continue with its business.
3. The event adapter calls the specific user-designed method on the final target component.
4. The code in the user-designed method fills in the text box component with the "Pressed" text.

Sometimes it helps to see some code. Listing 29.6 contains some pseudocode you can examine to see how an event adapter is written. The code in the example builds off the procedure listed previously. You won't be able to compile this code (notice the class keywords have been changed to pseudoclass), but it serves as an example you can build off of in your own Beans.

LISTING 29.6 `AdaptorExample.java`—PSEUDOCODE SHOWING HOW TO IMPLEMENT AN `Adapter` CLASS; THIS CODE MIGHT BE GENERATED BY AN APPLICATION BUILDER

```
// this pseudoclass example uses a unicast mechanism to keep things simple.

public interface SomeEventListener extends java.util.EventListener {
   public someEvent( java.util.EventObject e );
}

public pseudoclass button extends java.awt.Button {
   public void synchronized addSomeEventListener( SomeEventListener l )
                                throws java.util.TooManyListenersException {
      if ( listener != null ) {
         listener = l;
      } else throw new java.util.TooManyListenersException;
   }

   private void fireSomeEvent() {
      listener.someEvent( new java.util.EventObject( this ) );
   }

   private SomeEventListener listener = null;
}

public pseudoclass eventAdaptor implements SomeEventListener {
   public eventAdaptor( TargetObject target ) {
      this.target = target;
   }

   someEvent( java.util.EventObject e ) {
      // transfer the event to the user generated method.
      target.userDefinedMethod();
   }

   private TargetObject target;
```

LISTING 29.6 CONTINUED

```
}

public pseudoclass TargetObject {
   public TargetObject() {
      adaptor = new eventAdaptor( this );
   }

   public userDefinedMethod() {
     // user generated code goes here.
   }

   private eventAdaptor adaptor;
}
```

INTROSPECTION: CREATING AND USING BeanInfo CLASSES

You've already seen in the preceding sections and in the two Beans you designed how to use design patterns to facilitate automatic introspection. You also saw that the automatic introspection mechanism isn't perfect. If you look back at Figure 29.2, you'll see an example of this. Introspection is probably the most important aspect of JavaBeans because without it a container can't do anything with a Bean other than display it. As you become proficient at designing your own Beans, you'll find that you sometimes need to provide additional introspection information for the users of your Beans. In the case of your Beans, this is to hide the parent class's properties to clear up ambiguities.

The `java.beans.Introspector` class, as discussed earlier in the chapter, does all the pattern analysis to expose the properties, methods, and events that a component has. As a first step, however, this class looks to see whether a `BeanInfo` class is defined for the Bean it's inspecting. If it finds one, it doesn't do any pattern analysis on the areas of the Bean for which the `BeanInfo` class supplies information. This means that you can selectively choose which information you want to provide and which information you want to be derived from analysis. To show how this is done, you'll design a `BeanInfo` class for our `TextDisplayer` Bean.

The first thing you need to do is define what information you'll provide and what you'll leave up to the `Introspector` class to analyze. For the sake of example, say that you'll choose to provide the properties of your Bean, and you'll let the `Introspector` class use analysis to expose the events and methods. Table 29.5 shows the names of the `TextDisplayer` Bean's properties and the user-friendly names you want to display. With that information defined, you can start working on your `BeanInfo` class, `TextDisplayerBeanInfo.class`. Notice how you appended "`BeanInfo`" to the class name. That's an introspection design pattern; the `Introspector` class looks for `BeanInfo` information by appending "`BeanInfo`" to the class name of the Bean it's currently analyzing.

TABLE 29.5 THE TextDisplayer BEAN'S PROPERTIES AND USER-FRIENDLY NAMES

Property Name	User-Friendly Name
OutputText	"Text String"
BGColor	"Background Color"
TextFont	"Text Font"
FontColor	"Text Color"

All BeanInfo classes must implement the java.beans.BeanInfo interface. At first glance, that seems difficult; there are eight methods in the java.beans.BeanInfo interface! But remember the Introspector class has a set procedure for the way it looks for information. For the sake of clarity, that procedure is shown in the following list:

1. The Introspector class looks for a BeanInfo class for the Bean it's analyzing.
2. If a BeanInfo class is present, each method in the BeanInfo class is called to find out whether it can provide any information. The Introspector class will use implicit analysis to expose information for which the BeanInfo class denies any knowledge (returns a null value). If no BeanInfo class is found, the Introspector class will use implicit analysis for all the methods in the java.beans.BeanInfo interface.
3. The Introspector class then checks to see whether it has obtained explicit information for each of the methods in the BeanInfo interface. If it hasn't, it steps into the parent class (if one exists) and starts the process over for only those methods that it had to use analysis on.
4. When the Introspector class has information from a BeanInfo class for all the methods in the java.beans.BeanInfo interface, or when there are no more parent classes to explore, the Introspector class returns its results.

To make your life easier as a programmer, Sun has provided a prebuilt class, java.beans.SimpleBeanInfo, which returns a null value for all the BeanInfo methods. That way, you can inherit from that class and only override the methods you choose. Listing 29.7 shows the BeanInfo class for the TextDisplayer Bean. Notice how you only override the getPropertyDescriptors() method. The parent class returns null for all the other methods in the java.beans.BeanInfo interface.

LISTING 29.7 TextDisplayerBeanInfo.java—THE ENTIRE BeanInfo CLASS FOR THE TextDisplayer BEAN SHOWING HOW TO PROVIDE PROPERTY INFORMATION

```
import java.beans.*;

public class TextDisplayerBeanInfo extends SimpleBeanInfo {
   // override the getPropertyDescriptors method to provide that info.
   public PropertyDescriptor[] getPropertyDescriptors() {
      PropertyDescriptor[] properties = new PropertyDescriptor[4];

      try {
```

LISTING 29.7 CONTINUED

```
            properties[0] = new PropertyDescriptor( "Text String",
               BeanClass, "getOutputText", "setOutputText" );
            properties[1] = new PropertyDescriptor( "Text Color",
               BeanClass, "getFontColor", "setFontColor" );
            properties[2] = new PropertyDescriptor( "Text Font",
               BeanClass, "getTextFont", "setTextFont" );
            properties[3] = new PropertyDescriptor( "Background Color",
               BeanClass, "getBGColor", "setBGColor" );
         } catch( IntrospectionException e ) {
            return( null ); // exit gracefully if you get an exception.
         }

         return( properties );
      }

      private Class BeanClass = TextDisplayer.class;
   }
```

Take a second to look at the `try-catch` clause in Listing 29.7. Notice how you return a `null` value if you catch a `java.beans.IntrospectionException`. If you catch this exception, it usually means that you've provided an incorrect `getter` or `setter` method name. You should always return a `null` value if you catch this exception so that the `Introspector` class can still analyze your Bean. You should be able to extend this example to override the other methods in the `java.beans.BeanInfo` interface. Figure 29.3 shows the `PropertySheet` window of Sun's BeanBox for your `TextDisplayer` Bean. Notice how the user-friendly names for the properties have been used, and the parent class's properties are gone. Sweet success!

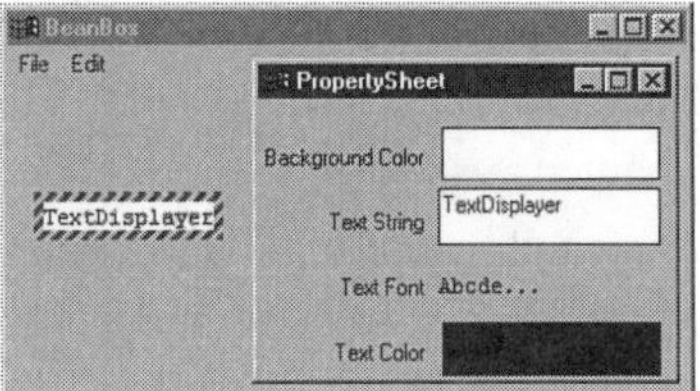

Figure 29.3
The `PropertySheet` window of Sun's BeanBox shows the user-friendly names for the properties in the `TextDisplayer` Bean.

CUSTOMIZATION: PROVIDING CUSTOM `PropertyEditors` AND GUI INTERFACES

So far, you have seen how to create a Bean; how to expose its properties, methods, and events; and how to tweak the introspection process. You might have noticed from the figures that the properties of a Bean have a `PropertyEditor`. For example, look back at Figure 29.3. In the `PropertySheet` window, next to the `"Text String"` label, there's a `TextField` component already filled with the value of the `OutputText` property. You didn't supply any code for this component, so how did Sun's BeanBox know to provide it? The answer is that the BeanBox application asked the `java.beans.PropertyEditorManager` what the default `PropertyEditor` was for an object of type `java.lang.String` and displayed it.

Just because PropertyEditors and Customizers require a GUI environment doesn't mean a Bean can't function without one. For example, a Bean designed to run on a server might not use (or need) a GUI environment at all. The java.beans.Beans class and the java.beans.Visibility interface allow Beans to exhibit different behavior in GUI and non-GUI environments.

PropertyEditors AND THE PropertyEditorManager

The class java.beans.PropertyEditorManager provides default PropertyEditors for the majority of the Java class types. So, if you use only native Java data types and objects, you're all set. But what if you design a Bean that has a property for which there's no default PropertyEditor? You'll run into this problem any time you design a custom property type. For those cases where there is no default PropertyEditor, you have to provide your own. Actually, you could redesign all the default PropertyEditors, too, if you choose, but you would only do this in rare cases, so this won't be discussed here. This means that you have to provide an additional class, by appending Editor to the class name, that the PropertyEditorManager can use. In most cases, you provide a subclass of java.awt.Component. The property sheet for your component will then pop up your custom PropertyEditor to allow your custom property to be edited. You won't actually design a custom PropertyEditor here because the majority of Beans won't require it, but an explanation of how to do it will be included. The requirements of a PropertyEditor are as follows:

1. Custom PropertyEditors must inherit from java.awt.Component so that they can be displayed in a property sheet. Note that this could mean inheriting from an AWT component such as java.awt.TextField.
2. Custom PropertyEditors must derive their class name by postfixing Editor to the property class name unless they register themselves with the PropertyEditorManager for their container (see step 3). For example, the PropertyEditor for a custom property type CustomProperty.class must be named CustomPropertyEditor.class.
3. For custom PropertyEditors that do not follow the standard naming convention in step 2, the custom property type must register itself with the container's PropertyEditorManager by calling the registerEditor() method.
4. Custom PropertyEditors always must fire a PropertyChange event to update the custom property. This is a must! Otherwise, the container has no way of knowing to update the component.

You can provide your own property sheet; in fact, for complex Beans, this is absolutely imperative. Property sheets by nature are simple and relatively not user-friendly. The following section discusses how to override the property sheet mechanism to provide your own customization dialog boxes.

CUSTOMIZATION EDITOR

All application builders have to implement some method of customizing the Beans placed into their containers. Thus, the PropertyEditor mechanism and the idea of a property sheet were born. But what about the special cases where a Bean can be customized several different ways, or there are dozens of properties? The solution to this problem is called *customizers*. Bean developers can optionally supply customizer classes with their Beans to be used in place of standard property sheets. Even though the property sheet mechanism works just fine for the `TextReader` Bean, you'll create a customizer class anyway, to learn how it's done.

To implement a customizer class, a Bean must also provide a `BeanInfo` class. The class name of a Bean's customizer class is determined from a call to the `getBeanDescriptor()` method of the `java.beans.BeanInfo` interface. This is a little bit different from what you've encountered so far. There is no default introspection design pattern for customizers; you must provide a `BeanInfo` class, even if the only information it provides is a `BeanDescriptor`. In fact, this is what you do for the `TextReaderBeanInfo.class` shown in Listing 29.8. Notice how the class inherits from `java.beans.SimpleBeanInfo`; the parent class implements the `java.beans.BeanInfo` class, and you override the `getBeanDescriptor()` method so that it returns something meaningful.

LISTING 29.8 `TextReaderBeanInfo.java`—THE `BeanInfo` CLASS FOR THE `TextReader` BEAN SHOWING HOW TO PROVIDE CUSTOMIZER CLASS INFORMATION

```
import java.beans.*;

public class TextReaderBeanInfo extends SimpleBeanInfo {
   // override the getBeanDescriptor method to provide a customizer.
   public BeanDescriptor getBeanDescriptor() {
      return( new BeanDescriptor( BeanClass, CustomizerClass ) );
   }

   private Class BeanClass = TextReader.class;
   private Class CustomizerClass = TextReaderCustomizer.class;
}
```

Although there isn't a design pattern for it, it's customary to name a customizer class by postfixing `Customizer` to the class name. Notice that you named the `TextReader` customizer `TextReaderCustomizer.class`. This is a good habit to get into.

The programmer has a tremendous amount of freedom when designing customizer classes. There are only two restrictions: The class must inherit from `java.awt.Component`, so that it can be placed in a `Panel` or `Dialog`, and it must implement the `java.beans.Customizer` interface. The customizer class is given a reference to the target component through a call to the `setObject()` method. After this point, what the customizer class does is its business, for the most part. Remember, however, that you'll be required (by the compiler) to acknowledge constrained properties because their accessor methods might throw `PropertyVetoExceptions`. Finally, the `java.beans.Customizer` interface includes functionality for `PropertyChangeListeners`. Because the Bean's container might register itself as a listener with the customizer class, any property updates should be followed by a call to `firePropertyChange()`. The easiest way to do this is by using a `java.beans.PropertyChangeSupport` class as was done when discussing bound properties earlier.

Listing 29.9 shows most of the code for the `TextReaderCustomizer` class. Some of the AWT-specific code was removed for clarity. Take a look at the `handleEvent()` method. This method is called by AWT when the user enters data. Notice how you were forced to catch `ProperyVetoExceptions` for the `setWidth()` method? You can also see how the `PropertyChangeListener` methods are used appropriately. Figure 29.4 shows what the customizer looks like when called up from within Sun's BeanBox.

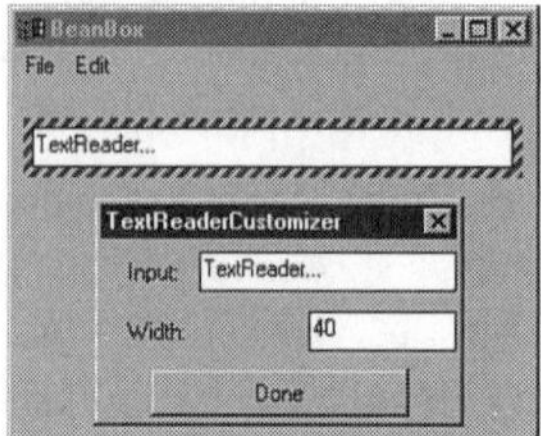

Figure 29.4
Sun's BeanBox shows the `TextReader` Bean and its customizer dialog box.

LISTING 29.9 `TextReaderCustomizer.java`—THE CODE FROM `TextReaderCustomizer.java` SHOWING HOW TO IMPLEMENT A CUSTOMIZER CLASS

```
import java.awt.*;
import java.beans.*;
public class TextReaderCustomizer extends Panel implements Customizer {
   public TextReaderCustomizer() {
      setLayout( new BorderLayout() );
   }

   public void setObject( Object target ) {
      component = (TextReader)target;
      // generate the User Interface (code removed for clarity)
   }

   public void processEvent( AWTEvent event ) {
      if ( event.getID() == Event.KEY_RELEASE &&
       event.getSource() == InputText ) {
         String old_text = component.getInputText();
         String text = InputText.getText();
         component.setInputText( text );
         changeAgent.firePropertyChange( "inputText", old_text, text );
      } else if ( event.getID() == Event.KEY_RELEASE &&
       event.getSource() == Width ) {
         int old_width, width;
         old_width = component.getWidth();
         try {
            width = Integer.parseInt( Width.getText() );
            try {
               component.setWidth( width );
               changeAgent.firePropertyChange( "width",
                 new Integer( old_width ), new Integer( width ) );
            } catch( PropertyVetoException e ) {
               // do nothing... wait for acceptable data.
            }
         } catch( NumberFormatException e ) {
            // do nothing... wait for better data.
```

LISTING 29.9 CONTINUED

```
            }
        }
        super.processEvent( event );
    }

    public void addPropertyChangeListener( PropertyChangeListener l ) {
        changeAgent.addPropertyChangeListener( l );
    }

    public void removePropertyChangeListener(PropertyChangeListener l) {
        changeAgent.removePropertyChangeListener( l );
    }

    private TextReader component;
    private TextField InputText, Width;
    private PropertyChangeSupport changeAgent =
        new PropertyChangeSupport( this );
}
```

PROVIDING ALTERNATIVE BEHAVIOR IN NON-GUI ENVIRONMENTS

Unfortunately, a GUI interface is not always available to a Bean. The most likely reason for this is that the Bean is being run in the background or on a server. Whatever the case, Beans that need to provide alternative or additional behavior in non-GUI environments can do so by using the `java.beans.Beans` class and the `java.beans.Visibility` interface.

The static methods `isDesignTime()` and `isGuiAvailable()` in the `java.beans.Beans` class can be used to check whether the Bean is being used in an application builder and a GUI environment is available. The method `isDesignTime()` returns true if the Bean is in an application builder and false if not. The method `isGuiAvailable()` returns true if a GUI environment is available to the Bean, and false if not.

Just because a GUI environment is available doesn't necessarily mean a container wants a Bean to use it. Similarly, a container might want to know whether a Bean isn't using the GUI environment, or even whether it needs one. A Bean and its container can communicate these things by implementing the `java.beans.Visibility` interface. The vast majority of Beans have no need for this interface, and it isn't necessary to implement it unless a Bean plans to use it. There are four methods in the interface:

`public abstract boolean avoidingGui()`

This method is called by a container to ask whether a Bean is currently avoiding the GUI environment. A Bean should return true for this method if it is actively avoiding the GUI environment. Notice that this is not the same as indicating that it doesn't need the GUI environment. For example, a container might use this information to free up resources being used by the GUI environment if a call to this method returns true.

`public abstract void dontUseGui()`

This method is called by the container to tell the Bean that even though a GUI environment might be available, the Bean shouldn't use it. For example, a container using a Bean on a server would call this method to tell the Bean there's no point in using the GUI environment. If a Bean chooses to comply with this method (and it should), the Bean should return true for subsequent calls to `avoidingGui()`.

```
public abstract boolean needsGui()
```

This method is called by the container to ask whether a Bean absolutely has to have a GUI environment. If a Bean can function in a non-GUI environment, it should return false. Note that it's safe to return true and then never use the GUI environment, but it's not safe to return false and use it anyway.

```
public abstract void okToUseGui()
```

This method is called by a container to tell a Bean that a GUI environment is available and the Bean can use it. This method might also be called after `dontUseGui()` to indicate that a previously unavailable GUI environment is available again. Note that a call to this method in no way implies that a Bean should use the GUI environment, for example, if it wasn't planning to.

BEAN PACKAGING

If you want an application builder to access the Beans you develop, you have to package them in a JAR file (see Chapter 25, "JAR Files"). When you create a JAR for this purpose, it must contain the class files that support your Beans and a manifest file that identifies each Bean included in the archive. The JAR might also include optional support files for each Bean. These optional files include any associated `BeanInfo` or `PropertyEditor` classes, HTML documentation that describes the Bean's use, a serialized instance that can be used to initialize the Bean, and any required resource files (for example, image or sound files).

For the example Beans, you might create a JAR with a manifest file like the following:

```
Name: TextReader.class
Java-Bean: True

Name: TextDisplayer.class
Java-Bean: True

Name TextDisplayerBeanInfo.class
Design-Time-Only: True

Name: TextReaderInfo.class
Design-Time-Only: True
```

You identify each Bean in the JAR with an entry in the manifest that includes the `Java-Bean` tag. The `Design-Time-Only` tag identifies entries that are required only by the application builder and are not needed at runtime. This tag is shown used with the `BeanInfo` classes. If a Bean has dependencies on other class files or resources, you identify those with the `Depends-On` tag to make it known to the builder tool which files are required to deploy and use a Bean.

ENTERPRISE JAVABEANS

Although this book is targeted toward the Java 2 Standard Edition (J2SE), a brief crossover into the enterprise side is necessary to make some terminology clear. With the increasing emphasis on server-side Java development, you will likely hear the term Enterprise JavaBeans, or EJB, as often, if not more so, than JavaBeans itself. Both technologies are based on components, but their uses are quite different. EJB is a component model for building and deploying Java in a distributed multitier environment. This technology extends the JavaBeans component model to support server components.

PARTITIONING YOUR APPLICATIONS

Modern object-oriented designs typically split application design into three pieces. These pieces are the user interface, the business logic, and the data. Client/server applications combine the user interface and business logic code of an application, but multitier applications split the functionality of a system into three or more pieces. In either case, the persistent data used by the system is maintained by a database management system (DBMS), which the application communicates with but isn't actually part of the application itself. In a multitier architecture, the client application contains only user interface functionality. The business logic is implemented in one or more middle tiers by components deployed on a corresponding number of servers.

The result of moving the business and data logic to a server is that your application can take advantage of the power of multithreaded and multiprocessing systems. In addition, server components can pool and share scarce resources across users and even applications. As system demands increase, components that are heavily used can be replicated and distributed across multiple systems. This means that there is almost no limit to the scalability of a multitier system. As system resources become overtaxed, you can replicate another system to handle more of the load. In addition to providing enhanced performance, this replication can be used for redundancy. Redundant systems help to eliminate any single points of failure, which is of great concern for Internet applications that are expected to be available around the clock.

SERVER COMPONENTS

EJBs fill the role of server components in multi-tier applications. Although different from standard JavaBeans in many ways, EJBs are still reusable software building blocks that can be assembled to efficiently create new applications. Because you always develop EJBs to run on a server, they never have a visual appearance. They instead are created to manage persistent data and to provide functionality that can be exposed to multiple client applications simultaneously.

Beyond reuse, the EJB architecture provides a framework that frees you from coding intricate transaction management and security logic for each application you develop. You might instead focus on the business logic required by your systems while taking advantage of a robust and scalable infrastructure that is capable of being run on every platform supported by Java.

The subject of EJB goes well beyond this brief introduction. The important point here is that you understand the differences between standard JavaBeans and EJBs. You should take a look at the Java 2 Enterprise Edition (J2EE) information on Sun's Web site to go more in depth on the subject.

TROUBLESHOOTING

BEAN PROPERTIES ARE NOT DETECTED

The set of Bean properties reported by an application builder is incomplete.

Unless you're using a `BeanInfo` class or a `Customizer`, application builders and similar tools determine a Bean's properties based on method name patterns. For example, defining an integer field named `fontSize` in a Bean class isn't sufficient to have it recognized as a property. You need to declare appropriate `setter` and `getter` methods with the following signatures:

```
public void setFontSize( int value )
public int getFontSize()
```

BEAN EVENTS ARE NOT PROPAGATED

Changes in the bound properties of a Bean are not reflected in a dependent Bean.

The key to responding to property changes in a Bean is to implement the `PropertyChangeListener` interface. You implement this interface in a dependent Bean by providing a `propertyChange` method to respond to events. For this method to be called, you must also register the dependent Bean as a listener with the Bean of interest by calling its `addPropertyChangeListener` method. That Bean must make a `firePropertyChange` call whenever a bound property is modified. Verify that your implementation of `propertyChange` is checking for the correct property name when events are received.

APPENDIX 

Installing the SDK and Getting Started

In this appendix

by Chuck Cavaness

GETTING THE SDK 1.3SE

You can download the SDK 1.3SE right off the Sun's Web site (`http://java.sun.com/j2se/1.3/`). You will have to decide which version you need, because there are three versions that you can download depending on which platform you plan to do your development on. Although Java code is portable, the development tools take advantage of the underlying platform that the code is being developed and run on for performance and other requirements. The download sizes are large, so make sure you have a decent Internet connection and free disk space for the download. Table A.1 shows the size of the download files for each of the platforms available.

TABLE A.1 SDK 1.3 DOWNLOAD SIZES PER PLATFORM

Platform	Download Size
Windows	~30MB
Linux	~40MB
Solaris(SPARC)	~36MB
Solaris(Intel)	~34MB

These files are large, but get even larger when installed. For example, the size of the Windows installation is approximately 150MB, so make sure that you have enough free disk space to download and install.

Caution

At the time of this writing, the Linux version of the Java 2 SDK version 1.3 is only available as a release candidate. The general release is expected before the end of the year assuming the release candidate goes well. This is important if you plan to use the 1.3 version in production applications.

If your Internet connection is limited, certain platforms allow you to split up the download into smaller chunks of the much larger installation file. For example, the Windows version allows you to download multiple files a few at a time; each file is 1.44MB or less. This will help in case you don't have time to sit and wait for 30MB to download. Besides, some Internet service providers (ISP) terminate connections after a certain time has elapsed, so this might be your only hope.

Unfortunately, if you want the documentation (which most do), you must download and install it separately. You can find these downloads at the following URL:

`http://java.sun.com/j2se/1.3/docs.html`

Caution

When installing the documentation, make sure you specify the root directory of where you installed the SDK. If you put the documentation somewhere else, the URL links in the documentation might not work.

Note

Make sure you download the full version of the SDK (SDK 1.3SE) and not just the runtime version (J2RE 1.3). The runtime version does not contain the development tools.

INSTALLING THE SDK 1.3SE

Installing the Java SDK 1.3SE is different for each platform. Make sure you select the installation instructions for the platform you are installing the SDK on.

INSTALLING THE SDK FOR WINDOWS

The SDK installation for the Windows platform is consists of running the self-installing executable to unpack and install the SDK onto your computer. If you downloaded the Windows installation multiple install files, read this next section carefully. If you have a single executable file, jump to "Starting the Windows Installation."

CONCATENATING THE MULTIPLE INSTALLATION FILES

Because the files are split into multiple installation files, you need to rebuild these files back into a single Windows executable. To do this, you will have to use the `copy` command on DOS or the `cp` command on Unix. If you type `copy /?` at a DOS command line, you can get all the options for the `copy` command.

You will be copying or appending all the small single installation files into one large executable file. Here is the command:

```
C:\>  copy /b j2sdk1_3_0-win-a.exe +
j2sdk1_3_0-win-b.exe + j2sdk1_3_0-win-c.exe +
j2sdk1_3_0-win-d.exe + j2sdk1_3_0-win-e.exe +
j2sdk1_3_0-win-f.exe + j2sdk1_3_0-win-g.exe +
j2sdk1_3_0-win-h.exe + j2sdk1_3_0-win-i.exe +
j2sdk1_3_0-win-j.exe + j2sdk1_3_0-win-k.exe +
j2sdk1_3_0-win-l.exe + j2sdk1_3_0-win-m.exe +
j2sdk1_3_0-win-n.exe + j2sdk1_3_0-win-o.exe +
j2sdk1_3_0-win-p.exe + j2sdk1_3_0-win-q.exe +
j2sdk1_3_0-win-r.exe + j2sdk1_3_0-win-s.exe +
j2sdk1_3_0-win-t.exe + j2sdk1_3_0-win-u.exe +
j2sdk1_3_0-win-v.exe + j2sdk1_3_0-win-w.exe
j2sdk1_3_0-win.exe
```

The `/b` in the first line informs the `copy` command that you are dealing with binary files. The `+` is the appending option. This is all just a single command. The problem is that all this might not fit in your DOS command window. You can copy all this into a batch file and then execute the batch file. You can also copy a few files into a temp file and then copy all the temp files together.

You should first try to copy all this from a DOS shell and see if it will allow you type this much. Of course, if you misspell a line, it's hard to fix it and go back. You can turn on doskey by typing `doskey` from a DOS shell. This will allow you to repeat commands by using the up- and down arrows. Using the arrows brings up the previous commands that were typed. This only works while that DOS shell is opened. If you want it to last across sessions, put it into your `autoexec.bat` file.

After you have copied all the smaller files into a single executable file, go on to the next section, "Starting the Windows Installation."

STARTING THE WINDOWS INSTALLATION

Before you run the self-installing executable, first make sure that the size of file is correct. It could have been corrupted while downloading or if you had to append the smaller files into a single executable, you could have had a problem or missed a file. Change to the directory where you downloaded or created the single large installation executable file. Type `DIR` in that directory and look at the size of the file. Among other potential files, you should see the following file and size:

```
j2sdk1_3_0-win.exe  30,916,766 bytes
```

If the file size is different, there might be a problem, and you need to either perform the download again, or if you copied the smaller files into a large one, perform the copy operation again.

If you don't see the file, find the directory where you downloaded or copied the large file.

If the file size is correct, start the self-installing executable by double-clicking the file or using Start, Run.

The Java splash screen appears and starts unpacking the files. Click the Next button and then accept the license agreement. The next screen asks you for a destination directory. It's best just to accept the default location, which is `c:\jdk1.3`. This will help the document installation process and improve consistency among your development. If you are running other versions of the SDK, this will also help identify which version is where.

After you accept the destination directory or specify a new one, the files are copied onto your computer. At the end of the installation, the install program might ask permission to reboot your computer so that changes to the reg database can take effect. These changes mostly deal with setting up the uninstall in case you need to uninstall the SDK later.

The directory tree for the SDK should be similar to this assuming you accepted the default installation directory of jdk1.3. Only the top level of the tree is shown in the following code sample:

```
C:\jdk1.3>dir

 Volume in drive C has no label
 Volume Serial Number is 07D0-0606
 Directory of C:\jdk1.3

.              <DIR>         07-19-00 11:04p .
..             <DIR>         07-19-00 11:04p ..
UNINST   ISU        112,684  07-19-00 11:05p Uninst.isu
BIN            <DIR>         07-19-00 11:04p bin
README   TXT          5,063  06-02-00  1:10p README.txt
```

```
LICENSE             10,637  06-02-00   1:10p LICENSE
COPYRI~1               945  06-02-00   1:10p COPYRIGHT
README~1 HTM        18,374  06-02-00   1:10p readme.html
JRE           <DIR>         07-19-00  11:04p jre
LIB           <DIR>         07-19-00  11:04p lib
INCLUDE       <DIR>         07-19-00  11:04p include
INCLUD~1      <DIR>         07-19-00  11:04p include-old
DEMO          <DIR>         07-19-00  11:04p demo
SRC      JAR    19,565,690  06-02-00   1:11p src.jar
DOCS          <DIR>         07-19-00  11:16p docs
         6 file(s)     19,713,393 bytes
         9 dir(s)       22,191.14 MB free

C:\jdk1.3>
```


Note

Remember, the previous directory shows the docs directory. This is not installed by the SDK installer. The docs installation is a separate download and should be installed in the base directory of the SDK.

Throughout this appendix, the term `<JAVA_HOME>` refers to the base directory for the SDK installation. In the previous directory tree, this would be the drive letter and the `jdk1.3` directory. So for example, if the previous directory tree was installed on your c drive, your `<JAVA_HOME>` would be:

```
C:\jdk1.3
```

After the computer reboots, go to the "Testing the Java Compiler and JVM" section later in this chapter to ensure that the SDK installation is correct.

→ **See** "Testing the Java Compiler and JVM," **p. 1034**

INSTALLING THE SDK FOR SOLARIS

Installing the SDK 1.3SE is a little more difficult than the Windows installation. Actually, this really depends on which platform you are more comfortable with, which is probably Solaris for you because you are reading this section. The truth is that it isn't that much more difficult; it's just not as GUI friendly as the Windows self-installing executable.

Probably the most important thing to do before installing the SDK 1.3SE is to make sure you have all the necessary Solaris patches for your particular version of Solaris. This list and the patches themselves can usually be found at the following Web address:

```
http://developer.java.sun.com/developer/earlyAccess/j2sdk13/install-patches.html
```

If for some reason this address changes, go to the main Sun site at `http://www.sun.com` and follow the links to the particular Solaris operating system that you are using. We'll assume for these instructions that all the required patches have been applied to the operating system.

There are two installation formats available for Solaris:

- A self-extracting binary file
- A `.tar.Z` file

The self-extracting file allows a user to specify to which directory the SDK is installed. This would probably be good if you were the only one using the SDK. You have the flexibility to put it into a local directory. This also might be a good idea if you are evaluating the SDK 1.3SE and don't want to give everyone access to it until a later time.

The `.tar.Z` file contains Solaris packages that can be installed with the standard `pkgadd` utility. Normally this has to be done by someone with root privilege, so if you are not root or are not able to get root privilege, this option is probably not available to you and you should choose the first installation format.

Caution

> The SDK 1.3SE for the Solaris platform is packaged to be the default Java installation. It will overwrite previous installations of Java and make them unavailable for users. If you don't want to overwrite the previous version of Java installed, either use the self-extracting format or specify the –R option on the `pkgadd` utility to specify a non-default directory.

USING THE SELF-EXTRACTING INSTALLATION FORMAT

Follow these steps to use the self-extracting installation feature:

1. As with any download, first check the file size before installing to make sure that the download file was not corrupted. The file sizes should be

Filename	File Size
`j2sdk1_3_0beta_refresh-solsparc.bin`	24,871,111 bytes
`j2sdk1_3_0beta_refresh-solx86.bin`	23,241,953 bytes

   If the file sizes are different, try downloading the files again to ensure that they were not corrupted somehow during the download process.

2. Make sure the binary file has execute permissions. For either the Sparc or Intel platform, use the `chmod` command by executing the command

   ```
   chmod +x <filename>
   ```

   substituting in the correct filename.

3. Change to the directory where you want the SDK to be installed.

4. Run the binary self-extracting file by typing the name of the file. The name of the directory will probably be something like `j2sdk1_3_0beta_refresh`, but it can be renamed to anything you like after installation is completed. However, you should probably use a standard naming convention, such as SDK 1.3SE, so you will be able to quickly determine which version of the SDK is installed where.

USING THE `.tar.Z` INSTALLATION FORMAT

Use the following steps to install the SDK using the `.tar.Z` format:

1. As mentioned previously, check the size of the file that you downloaded.

Filename	File Size
`j2sdk1_3_0beta_refresh-solsparc.tar.Z`	35495284 bytes
`j2sdk1_3_0beta_refresh-solx86.tar.Z`	33291889 bytes

2. After you are comfortable that the download was not corrupted and you have the correct file size, extract the contents of the compressed `tar` file by typing the following:

   ```
   zcat <filename>.tar.Z | tar -xf
   ```

   Substitute the correct filename depending on your platform.

   This should create four packages (`SUNWj2dem`, `SUNWj2dev`, `SUNWj2man`, and `SUNWj2rt`) along with some other files such as the product license, `README`, and release documentation.
3. Become root by executing a `su` command or logging in as root from the shell.
4. Execute the `pkgadd` command. This should look something like this:

   ```
   # pkgadd -d . SUNWj2rt SUNWj2dev SUNWj2man SUNWj2dem
   ```

This will install the SDK into the `/usr/java1.3` directory. You can now remove all the `tar` files and extracted directories. Exit the root shell and test the installation.

INSTALLING THE JDK FOR LINUX

As with the Windows installation, you have the option of downloading small pieces of the installation in sizes of 1.44MB or less and then concatenating the small files into a single large file or you can download one large installation file. This option is to support users who don't have access to superfast Internet connections and might have to split up the download over several download sessions or connections.

There are also two installation formats as in the Solaris installation; however, Linux installation formats are different. For Linux, the two installation formats are

- A self-extracting binary file
- RPM file for RedHat

Determine which format you want to use. Either will work, but if you are using RedHat, you should probably choose that format. Remember to check the file sizes before starting installation. This is especially important if you downloaded the smaller files and then rejoined them.

If you download the smaller files, you need to concatenate the files into a single large file by using the `cat` command. Either download all the smaller files into the same directory or move them to the same directory after you finish downloading them. After you have all the smaller files downloaded, change to the directory where the multiple smaller files reside. Then, use `cat` to concatenate the files together like this:

```
% cat j2sdk-1_3_0-beta_refresh-linux-* > j2sdk-1_3_0-beta_refresh-linux.tar.gz
```

Or you can use this command for the RPM format:

```
% cat j2sdk-1_3_0-beta_refresh-linux-* > j2sdk-1_3_0-beta_refresh-linux.rpm
```

Be sure you end the filename with the `.tar.gz` extension or the `.rpm` extension, depending on which format you downloaded.

USING THE SELF-EXTRACTING INSTALLATION FORMAT

Follow these steps to use the self-extracting installation:

1. Change to the directory in which you want to install Java 1.3SE. If you plan to install it in a place for all users to access it, remember that you must first become root. Otherwise, change to a local directory where you have write permissions. The installation will create a directory called `jdk1.3` in the directory you select, so make sure to rename any directory that might be present with the same name. Otherwise it will be overwritten.
2. Extract the contents of the files using the following two utilities:
   ```
   % gunzip j2sdk-1_3_0-beta_refresh-linux.tar.gz
   % tar xvf j2sdk-1_3_0-beta_refresh-linux.tar
   ```
3. You can now delete the self-extracting installation file if you want, but it might be a good idea to place it somewhere in case you need to reinstall it.

USING THE RPM INSTALLATION FORMAT

If you need to concatenate the smaller files into the large single installation file, make sure you have already done that by following the previous instructions. Then, follow these steps to use the RPM installation:

1. Become root by executing the `su` command or by logging in as root in a shell.
2. Run the `RPM` command to install the packages. You can do this by executing the following command:
   ```
   % rpm -iv j2sdk-1_3_0-beta_refresh-linux.rpm
   ```
3. Exit the root shell.

TESTING THE JAVA COMPILER AND JVM

Now that you have hopefully made it through the installation process without any issues, you need to be sure the installation was successful. The two main things that you need to test are the Java compiler and the Java Virtual Machine. These tools are necessary to compile and run your applications. Before you get there however, you need to be sure that the two environment variables that you'll need are setup correctly. Let's look at each one separately.

THE PATH ENVIRONMENT VARIABLE

When you want to run a Java application or use the SDK tools, the operating system needs to be able to locate the `java` command to execute the program. You can specify this by fully qualifying the directory where the SDK tools are installed, which is in the \bin directory under the base directory for the SDK 1.3 installation.

The other option is to add the \bin directory to the system PATH variable. This approach allows you to run the SDK command from any directory. To do this on a Windows platform, just add the <<JAVA_HOME>>\bin directory to your PATH variable in the autoexec.bat (for Win95/98/2000) or the system environment properties (for WinNT). The <JAVA_HOME> variable is the base directory where the SDK was installed. On Unix, you can add the PATH variable to the .login so that it will be set each time you log in.

THE CLASSPATH ENVIRONMENT VARIABLE

The CLASSPATH variable is the single way to tell applications and SDK tools where to locate user and system classes. It must be set correctly. If it isn't, the compiler, interpreter, and other SDK tools and user applications will not be able to find the class files they need to run.

The CLASSPATH variable contains class file directories, JAR files, and ZIP files. You should separate each one of the directories or JAR/ZIP files by a separator character depending on the platform. For Windows, the separator is a ";" character, for Unix and Linux, use a ":" character.

Another important question is what directories or JAR files are required to be in the CLASSPATH. For the SDK 1.3, you should have a minimum of two JAR files in the CLASSPATH. The two JAR files are the <<JAVA_HOME>>\jre\lib\rt.jar file and the <JAVA_HOME>\lib\tools.jar file. You will also probably have other JAR files and or directories as you develop your applications.

There are two methods to setting the variable. One method is to set the CLASSPATH variable each time you run an application by specifying the -cp or -classpath option for the java or javac commands. The second alternative is to set the system CLASSPATH once and then there is not much need to set it when starting your applications or using the Java tools. A good approach is to set the CLASSPATH variable with the SDK necessary JAR files and then use the -cp or -classpath options when running your applications. This way, you will not have to worry about changing the system CLASSPATH very often. Most developers use batch or shell scripts to execute Java applications and set the CLASSPATH variables in there. You can add JAR files and directories to the system CLASSPATH by using the environment variable to reference the system CLASSPATH variable. For example, on the Windows platform, here is an example of starting an application:

```
java -classpath %CLASSPATH%;c:\classfiledir;c:\another.jar
```

On UNIX machines, the CLASSPATH variable is a colon-separated list of directories, JAR files, and/or ZIP files.

```
setenv CLASSPATH .:/users/java/:/usr/local/jdk1.3/jre/lib/rt.jar:
➥/usr/local/jdk1.3/lib/tools.jar
```

This command can be put in your `.login` file, so it's set properly every time you log in. If you are the system administrator, you probably want to make this `CLASSPATH` variable available to all users.

On the Windows platform, it's a semicolon-separated list of directories in the form

```
set CLASSPATH=.;C:\users\dac\classes;C:\jdk1.3\jre\lib\rt.jar;
➥c:\jdk1.3\lib\tools.jar
```

This line can be put in your `AUTOEXEC.BAT` file so that the `CLASSPATH` is set properly every time you boot your machine.

The first period points the `CLASSPATH` at the current working directory, which is quite helpful if you don't feel like typing in full pathnames every time you want to do something with the Java program you're working on at a given moment.

APPENDIX 

SDK Tools

In this appendix

by Chuck Cavaness

SDK TOOLS REFERENCE

This appendix covers all the tools included in the Java Software Developer's Kit. You'll learn about each tool, what it does, all its associated options, and the environment variables it references. If you're just beginning to program in Java, this appendix can serve as an introduction to the tools of the SDK. If you're a hard-core Java hacker, this appendix will be more of a reference, so you don't have to waste precious time looking through man pages or HTML documents. Either way, browsing this appendix gives you a good idea of what the SDK tools can do and how to make them do it.

APPLETVIEWER

Applets are programs written in Java that are designed to run embedded in an HTML document, just like a Web page. Under most circumstances, they don't have the capability to run by themselves. The AppletViewer tool is a small program that lets you run applets without having to launch a Web browser each time you want to test your applet code. It's a quick and easy way to test your applets as you're developing them.

You call the AppletViewer with the following command:

```
appletviewer <options> URLs...
```

The `URLs` in the command line are the Uniform Resource Locators to HTML files that contain applet tags (such as `http://www.javasoft.com/index.html`). Alternatively, if you're in a directory that has an HTML file that references an applet, you can call AppletViewer by typing in the name of the HTML file that contains the applet tag. The following option is available:

Option	Description
`-debug`	Starts the AppletViewer in the Java debugger.
`-encoding`	Specifies character encoding used by HTML files.

With the SDK 1.3, the HotSpot client Virtual Machine is the default virtual machine. It provides increased performance over the previous class virtual machine. However, you can still invoke the classic virtual machine with the AppletViewer by providing an addition parameter like this:

```
appletviewer -classic URL
```

`URL` is the HTML file that contains the `APPLET` tag. By default, the HotSpot virtual machine will be used unless this additional parameter is specified.

The Applet menu in the AppletViewer window enables you to set a number of different functions. Those menu options are as follows:

- **Restart**—Restarts the applet using the current settings.
- **Reload**—Reloads the applet. Changes in the class file are applied upon reload.

- **Stop**—Causes the `stop()` method of the applet to be called and halts the applet. Note that the applet is not destroyed in this example as it is with Reload.
- **Save**—Saves the serialized state of the applet.
- **Start**—Starts the applet. This is useful when the Stop option has been used. If the applet has not been stopped, it has no action.
- **Clone**—Duplicates the current applet, using the same settings to create another AppletViewer instance.
- **Tag**—Shows the HTML applet tag that is used to run the current applet, as well as any parameters that are passed to the applet from the HTML tag.
- **Info**—Shows special information about the applet, which is set within the applet's program.
- **Edit**—This doesn't appear to do anything; it has been grayed out since the first beta.
- **Print**—Causes the applet's PrintGraphics to be sent to a printer.
- **Character Encoding**—Specifies the character encoding for the HTML files.
- **Properties**—Shows the AppletViewer security properties. These settings enable you to configure AppletViewer for a network environment that includes a firewall proxy, or an HTTP proxy, using the relative proxy server and proxy port boxes. The Network Access box allows you to select the type of network access that AppletViewer is allowed. The choices are No Network Access, Applet Host (default), and Unrestricted. The Class Access box enables you to choose what kind of access—Restricted or Unrestricted—you want AppletViewer to have on other classes.
- **Close**—Closes the AppletViewer window and terminates the applet.
- **Quit**—Closes the AppletViewer window and terminates the applet.

java—THE JAVA INTERPRETER

The Java interpreter is what you use to run your compiled Java application.

The syntax for the interpreter is

```
java [-options] class [args...]
```

where `class` only includes the name of the class and not the extension (`.class`). If the class belongs to a package, the class name should include the fully qualified package name with the class. The standard Java interpreter options are listed in Table B.1.

TABLE B.1 JAVA INTERPRETER OPTIONS

Option	Description
`-cp dirs or jars/zips`	`java` looks for class files in the specified directories, `DIRS`. For multiple directories, a colon (in UNIX) or semicolon (in DOS) is used to separate each directory. `JAR` files and/or `ZIP` files can also be specified, separated also by the separator character mentioned previously. `-classpath` is also supported for backward compatibility.

Table B.1 Continued

Option	Description
`-help or -?`	Displays all the options.
`-version`	Displays the version of the SDK that is used to compile the source code and then exits.
`-showversion`	Similar to the `-version` command. It will show the version information, but continue to execute any additional commands.
`-verbose`	Enable verbose output.

Caution

The Java interpreter also includes nonstandard options that are used less frequently. There are no guarantees that these will be supported in future releases of Java, so use this carefully.

Option	Description
`-Xdebug`	Used with remote Java files that are to be debugged later with the `jdb` tool. The interpreter generates a password for you, which is used in the `jdb`'s password option (see the section "`jdb`—The Java Debugger" later in this chapter).
`-Xprof`	Outputs `cpu` profiling data.
`-Xnoclassgc`	Disables class garbage collection.
`-Xmx val`	Sets the maximum Java heap size to the value specified by `val`. (Use the letters `m` and `k` to specify megabytes or kilobytes for the value of `val`.)
`-Xms val`	Sets the initial Java heap size to the value specified by `val`. (Use the letters `m` and `k` to specify megabytes or kilobytes for the value of `val`.)

javac—The Java Compiler

The `javac` program is the tool you use to compile `.java` files into class files that can be run by the interpreter. The command is executed like this:

```
javac <options> <sourcefiles>
```

Table B.2 lists the Java compiler options.

Table B.2 Java Compiler Options

Option	Description
`-g`	Generates all debugging information.
`-g:none`	Doesn't generate any debugging information.
`-verbose`	Outputs messages that describe what the compiler is doing.
`-deprecation`	Outputs source locations where deprecated API's are being used.

TABLE B.2 CONTINUED

Option	Description
`-classpath <path>`	Overrides the default `CLASSPATH` environment variable and specifies a new path to look up classes. Make certain you always include library classes, such as `jdk1.2\jre\rt.jar`.
`-d <directory>`	Specifies the directory to place the resulting class files in. Note the directory specifies the root location.
`-nowarn`	Turns off warnings. When this is turned off, the compiler does not generate any warning messages. Note: This option is available in JDK 1.1 and above, but not in JDK 1.0.
`-O`	Turns optimization on. This causes all `static`, `final`, and `private` methods to be placed inline. Although this can result in faster performance, it might also cause your class files to become larger.
`-target <release>`	Generates class files for a specific VM.
`-sourcepath`	Specifies where to find input source files.

javap—THE JAVA DISASSEMBLER

The Java disassembler is used to disassemble Java bytecode that has already been compiled. After disassembling the code, information about the member variables and methods is printed. The syntax for the Java disassembler is

```
javap <options> <classes>
```

Multiple classes can be disassembled. Use a single space to separate each class. The options available for the disassembler are shown in Table B.3.

TABLE B.3 javap OPTIONS

Option	Description
`-c`	Disassembles the source file and displays the bytecodes produced by the compiler.
`-l`	Prints the local variable tables.
`-public`	Shows only public classes and members.
`-protected`	Shows protected and public classes and members.
`-package`	Prints out private, protected, and public member variables and methods. (By default, `javap` uses this option.)
`-private`	Shows all classes and members.
`-s`	Prints internal type signatures.
`-verbose` works.	Prints stacks, local variables, and member methods as the `javap`

Table B.3 Continued

Option	Description
`-classpath <pathlist>`	Looks for class files in the specified directories. For multiple directories, a colon (UNIX) or semicolon (DOS) is used to separate each directory. For example, on a DOS machine the CLASSPATH might look like `set CLASSPATH=.;C:\users\dac\classes;C:\tools\java\ classes`.

The javadoc Tool (Documentation Generator)

The `javadoc` tool creates an HTML file based on the tags that are embedded in the `/** */` type of comments within a Java source file. These HTML files are used to store information about the classes and methods that you can easily view with any Web browser.

Here is the format of the `javadoc` command:

```
javadoc [options] [ packagenames ] [sourcefiles] [classnames] [@files]
```

`javadoc` was actually used by the creators of the SDK to create the Java API Documentation. The `javadoc` homepage can be found at

`http://java.sun.com/products/jdk/javadoc/index.html`

Many options can be used by the `javadoc` command. Tables B.4 and B.5 attempt to describe the most important options. For a complete list, type `javadoc` on the command line.

Table B.4 javadoc Options

Option	Description
`-verbose`	Outputs message about what `javadoc` is doing.
`-d directory`	Specifies the directory where `javadoc` stores the generated HTML files. For example, `javadoc -d C:\usrs\dac\public_html\doc java.lang`.
`-classpath <pathlist>`	Looks for class files within the specified directories or JAR files.. For multiple directories, a colon (UNIX) or semicolon (DOS) is used to separate each directory. For example, on a DOS machine, the CLASSPATH might look like `set CLASSPATH=.;C:\users\dac\classes;C:\tools\java\classes`.
`-sourcefile <pathlist>`	Specifies in colon-separated directories the list of files to use.
`-nodeprecated`	Causes `javadoc` to ignore `@depreciated` paragraphs.
`-author`	Causes `javadoc` to use the `@author` paragraphs.
`-noindex`	Causes `javadoc` not to create an index file.
`-notree`	Causes `javadoc` not to create a tree file.

TABLE B.5 javadoc TAGS

Tag	Description
`@see class`	Puts a See Also link in the HTML file to the class specified by `class`.
`@see class#method`	Puts a See Also link in the HTML file to the method specified by `method`.
`@param param descr`	Describes method arguments.
`@version ver`	Specifies the version of the program.
`@author name`	Includes the author's name in the HTML file.
`@return descr`	Describes a method's return value.
`@exception class`	Creates a link to the exceptions thrown by the class specified by `class`.

jdb—THE JAVA DEBUGGER

The Java debugger is the debugging tool for the Java environment and is completely command-line driven. You can use the debugger to debug files located on your local system or files that are located on a remote system. For remote Java files, the `jdb` must be used with the `-host` and `-password` options described in the table of options. The `jdb` also consists of a list of commands that are not covered in this appendix. See Table B.6 for information regarding `jdb` options.

TABLE B.6 jdb OPTIONS

Options	Description
`-host hostname`	Tells the `jdb` where the remote Java program resides. hostname is the name of the remote computer (such as `well.com` or `sun.com`).
`-password password`	Passes the password for the remote Java file to the `jdb`, issued by the Java interpreter using the `-debug` option.

APPENDIX

SDK 1.3 Performance Improvements

In this appendix

by Chuck Cavaness

GENERAL PERFORMANCE IMPROVEMENTS

The Java platform is arguably becoming the programming language of choice for Internet development. In fact, it has been used successfully for Internet development for quite a few years now. Still, many questions have been raised about the seriousness of Java within mainstream software application development. Most of the issues have centered on the language feature set and the performance measurement when compared with other languages such as C++. The number and type of features that are a part of the core language has been growing since the first version was released. Some still argue that there is more work to do on this front. The truth is that it might never be the language that everyone wants it to be. It never will be C++ or Smalltalk. From all accounts, it was never designed to be a replacement for these languages and therefore the comparisons are sometimes not justified.

The other questions arise regarding the performance of Java when compared to other major languages such as C++. Most of the performance comparisons made on Java compare it to this language in particular. Keep in mind that most people compare the features of the two languages as if C++ and Java are in exactly the same language class. Although both languages are widely used and offer rich libraries and object-oriented features, the languages are very different. This is especially true with respect to how the languages are compiled.

As you probably heard, Java is designed to be very portable. In other words, source code that is compiled on a Windows machine can run on a Solaris machine without any additional compilation. This can happen because the `.class` files that are created when the source is compiled are not dependent on any particular operating system. Each operating system that supports Java has what is called a virtual machine. This *virtual machine* is an intermediary between the bytecode that makes up the Java application and the operating system that the application depends on for resources. Inside the virtual machine, there is something called the interpreter. The *interpreter* analyzes the bytecodes in the application and helps translate them into something the operating system can execute.

In the past, this has generally meant taking a huge performance hit for the additional level of interaction by the virtual machine and the interpreter to gain more portability. This happens because some additional dynamic compilation and security checking must happen when the application runs, rather than being performed during the compilation process. When Java was first introduced, and even with the 1.2 release, there still was a substantial performance loss due to this dynamic compilation. The Just In Time (JIT) compiler attempted to alleviate this by compiling the bytecode the first time a bytecode was accessed and then using this compiled version rather than using the interpreter to evaluate the bytecode on-the-fly. This helped with some aspects, but introduced overhead at startup time, because the JIT compiler usually compiled the bytecode up-front or when the first access to the code happened, thus causing detectable pauses in execution of an application. The JIT was a major step forward, but more had to be done.

With the release of the SDK 1.3, the performance of the virtual machine has been dramatically increased, primarily due to the new HotSpot technology. This is discussed in detail in the next section. If you want to understand HotSpot, you should skip this section for now and come back to it later.

Before getting into the HotSpot technology discussion, there are a few general enhancements that are unrelated to the HotSpot and focus more on common performance issues that developers have dealt with in previous version of Java. These enhancements involve pieces of the Java language that are used extensively and can make a difference in most "real-world" applications. There are four general performance enhancements that typically affect all real-world programs. These general enhancements also are examples of changes that have been made throughout the SDK 1.3 version. This list is not an exhaustive list, but rather examples from different areas of the language. The four enhancements are

- Reduce Memory Footprint Associated with Strings
- JAR File Memory Usage Reduction
- Performance Enhancements in BigInteger
- Swing Class Loading

Each one of these is discussed in a little more detail in the following sections.

Reduce Memory Footprint Associated with Strings

Strings are used for almost every application you can imagine, especially business type applications. If you have ever run a memory profile on a Java application, you might have actually passed out from all the instances of the `String` class loaded in memory. Each object instance loaded has to use some memory for the representation and the `String` instances are no exception. Besides the memory footprint, there is also a performance issue with all these instances in memory. The `garbage` collection system has to work overtime trying to figure out if these instances can be collected and the memory they are taking up regained. There have been improvements in the overall internal structures to help with this and to reduce the size and frequency of creation of these new instances.

JAR File Memory Usage Reduction

The way JAR files are indexed in memory has been improved so that the memory cost of loading a JAR file has been greatly reduced. The class libraries in `rt.jar`, for example, occupied about 420KB of memory when loaded in version 1.2, but require only about 100KB in version 1.3.

Performance Enhancements in `BigInteger`

Previously, implementation for the `BigInteger` class was based on an underlying C library. The new implementation performs all standard operations much faster than the old implementation. The speed-up realized in the new implementation can be as much as 5x or more, depending on the operation being performed and the length of the operands.

Swing Class Loading

In version 1.2 and before, if an application used any of the classes from the `Swing` libraries, these classes were loaded into memory regardless of whether they were accessed right away. In version 1.3, loading of some of the `Swing` classes is delayed until they are actually needed by the runtime environment. The delay improves startup time of applications that use the `Swing` libraries.

Introduction to HotSpot Technology

Version 1.3 is leaps and bounds better than previous versions thanks to the new HotSpot technology that has been introduced in this new version. The new version includes the Java HotSpot Client virtual machine (Client VM) and the HotSpot Server virtual machine (Server VM). The Client VM is tuned to maximize performance on client systems, improving performance in areas of startup time and memory footprint. The Server VM is tuned to maximize performance of program execution speed and is aimed at server applications that are less concerned with startup and memory footprint. The HotSpot Server VM is a separate download for the Windows platform. You can download the HotSpot Server VM 2.0 at the following Web site:

```
http://java.sun.com/products/hotspot/2.0/download.html
```

What Makes HotSpot Better?

The HotSpot performance engine, which is encapsulated in both the Client- and Server VM, has dramatic improvements in just about all possible areas: from its fast thread synchronization techniques to its more reliable and faster performance garbage collection. Take a look at several new performance features of the HotSpot performance engine:

- On-the-Fly Adaptive Compilation
- Method Inlining
- Improved and Redesigned Object Layout
- Fast and Fully Accurate Garbage Collection
- Fast Thread Synchronization

On-the-Fly Adaptive Compilation

HotSpot takes advantage of the 80/20 rule that exists for more real-world applications. That is that most real-world applications spend 80% of time in 20% of the code. This simple assumption allows the adaptive compilation to work.

What happens is that when a Java application using the HotSpot technology is loaded, an interpreter starts running the bytecode. While it starts running the code, it looks for sections of the application that seem to be getting more attention than other areas. These areas are commonly known as *hot spots*. These hot spots are actually compiled after the interpreter detects them. After they are compiled, the compiled versions are used rather than the interpreted bytecode. This ensures that the sections of the application that are being executed over and over get the most attention from the compiler. With the JIT compiler, all code was compiled when accessed, regardless of how often it was accessed. This meant that sections of the application that were rarely used, were getting as much attention as the hot spots.

There are several benefits to this performance feature. First, programs generally start up faster because there is less compilation being performed at the start of the application run compared to JIT-type compilers. Secondly, compilation tends to be spread out over the life of the application. This has the effect of reducing the noticeable pauses with previous compilers and interpreters.

Finally, because less time is spent on compiling the entire application, more time can be spent optimizing the code. For example, more information can be obtained for optimizes like method inlining, which is talked about in the next section.

Method Inlining

Method inlining is when the compiler notices that a method call is being made that can be handled in a different way and makes changes to the execution instructions. These changes do not change the basic implementation or outcome of the method call, but reduce the overhead when making the method call.

For example, suppose you have a method that just decrements an argument passed in to the method. The compiler can detect this method and just decrement one from the argument instead if making the method call. This will increase the speed of the application, because the act of setting up the method call, making the call, and getting a return takes time and memory to execute. Remember, method inlining is trying to reduce the time it takes to execute instructions.

The problem with method inlining lies in a benefit of using Java as an object-oriented language. In Java, a base class can implement a method. Then subclasses of the base class can override that method. Because classes can be loaded dynamically, the virtual machine can never be 100% sure which class will implement the method at runtime. This is sometimes referred to as *Dynamic Dispatch*.

The HotSpot virtual machines uses what is known as *dynamic deoptimizaton*. This means that if the code has already been compiled and the virtual machine detects that something has changed with respect to that code, the virtual machine will revert to the interpreted code. If the application continues to execute that section of code, it will then be recompiled and go on to use the compiled version until something else changes with it.

Improved and Redesigned Object Layout

The HotSpot virtual machine also has removed the concept of handles, which was a level of indirection used to access objects in memory. In previous versions of the virtual machine, a table of handles was maintained. These handles, among other things, maintained a pointer to an object. If object X had a conceptual reference to object Y, what really was going on was that object X had a reference to a table entry that then pointed to object Y. The purpose of this level of indirection was to allow for faster pointer updates. Imagine if 10 objects pointed to object Y and then object Y changed, only the table entry would have to change. If instead all 10 objects pointed to object Y directly, then each of the 10 pointers to object Y would have to change. This was primarily done in earlier versions to help the garbage collector quickly find unreferenced objects and to more easily move objects around to prevent fragmentation.

However, because of the nature of the garbage collection process, each object basically had to be traversed anyway and this process turned out not to be much slower than the table and handle method. So with the HotSpot virtual machine, direct pointers are used to reference objects instead of handles. This is similar to the way the C language handles object references, and the speed is much faster.

Fast and Fully Accurate Garbage Collection

Prior to the 1.3 release of the HotSpot virtual machine, the garbage collection process was a "conservative" or partially accurate collector. This means that the virtual machine would err on the side of thinking something had a valid reference to an object. This approach is must easier to implement than a fully accurate garbage collector because it really didn't need to keep accurate records of which objects were alive and which were dead. If it couldn't figure it out, the collector would assume that an object had a reference to it, causing it not to be collected.

One of the major problems with this approach is that memory leaks can happen because some objects that have no references to it might not be collected if the garbage collector gets confused. Also, a conservative garbage collector needs to use handles to refer to objects because when it moves objects around, it needs to know about all the live and dead objects. This might not be the case with a conservative collector due to the problems that were mentioned before.

With the release of the HotSpot 2.0 virtual machine, the garbage collector is a fully accurate model. This means that it is aware at all times which objects are inaccessible and can be reclaimed. It is also aware which objects can be relocated so that memory can be compacted and fragmentation can be reduced or removed.

Other garbage collector features within the virtual machine increase functionality and performance. These features mainly deal with objects that are long-lived and are still being referenced. The virtual machine separates the short-lived objects and the long-lived objects. This helps because if an object is around for awhile, chances are that it will stay around longer. The virtual machine deals with these objects differently than ones that are constantly being created and then unreferenced.

Fast Thread Synchronization

The HotSpot virtual machine offers a "fully preemptive" thread model using the host operating system's thread model. In previous versions of the virtual machine, a single native thread might have been multiplexed to handle multiple Java threads.

The problem this caused was that if one of the Java threads is blocked for I/O or some other reason, all the other Java threads were also blocked and prevented from doing any work. In the new version of the HotSpot virtual machine, each Java thread maps to a single native OS thread. In this case, if a Java thread is blocked waiting on I/O, it can be preempted and another thread can execute.

There are also some optimizations done for threads that enter a synchronized method uncontested. The performance for this access is improved due to assumptions and optimizations done by the virtual machine.

JAVA HOTSPOT CLIENT VIRTUAL MACHINE

The HotSpot Client VM serves as a replacement for both the "classic" and the JIT compilers that were used in previous SDK's. The HotSpot Client VM uses the previously mentioned HotSpot technology developed by Sun. The Client- and the Server VM are very similar except that the Client VM has been tuned especially for faster startup times, which makes it more suitable for client environments.

The Client VM also takes advantages of other features of the HotSpot technology such as

- Adaptive Compiler
- Improved Garbage Collection
- Faster Thread Synchronization

Keep in mind that client applications tend to use native libraries to handle hardware intensive operations such as graphics or I/O. The HotSpot technology is not able to help much in this area. In this case, it's really up to the native libraries and hardware performance directly.

Also, client applications tend to do one thing repeatedly such as show a graphics screen and allow the user to press a button. The main features of the HotSpot technology will not be able to help in this area much. Its primary benefits come into play where a "hot" section of code is being executed over and over, which typically happens on a server application. It can help in startup time because not all the code is being compiled as in earlier versions of the virtual machine.

THE JAVA APPLICATION LAUNCHER

The Java application launcher is used to launch Java applications and is launched when you type

```
java SomeClassFile
```

on the command line. By default with the SDK 1.3, the HotSpot Client VM is used. If you need to run the classic virtual machine from 1.2, you can specify a "`-classic`" option and that virtual machine will be used instead of the HotSpot Client VM. This might be necessary for some development tools that use a different class loader for debugging. You would do something like this to use the classic virtual machine:

```
java -classic SomeClassFile
```

Java HotSpot Server Virtual Machine 2.0

The Java HotSpot Server VM is based on the same HotSpot technology as the Client VM. The only real difference is that it has a different compiler that is more suited for its role on a server application.

The 2.0 version is advertised to be a whopping 30% faster than the 1.0.1 version. The HotSpot Server VM must be downloaded separately from the standard SDK download. There is a version already available for the Windows platform and for Solaris. There is a release candidate for Linux with a full release for Linux expected later in Fall of 2000. For more information on the HotSpot 2.0 version, check out the Web site at `http://java.sun.com/products/hotspot/`.

Applet Deployment Improvements

There have also been improvements in the areas of applets. The four main improvements are

- Applet Caching Control
- Fast Loading of Applet Support Classes
- Jar Indexing
- Automatic Installation of Extensions

Applet Caching Control

Most applications in the past that used applets have relied on the browser cache to keep the applet from being downloaded each time it's referenced. The applet was stored in the browser cache and the cache's applet was used instead when the application referenced the applet instead of downloading it again. However, there was a problem with this method because if the applet was large and the cache for the browser was full, the applet could be removed and would have to be downloaded again if it was referenced by the application.

With the 1.3 version, the applet deployer can decide that the applet should stay around longer and thus make the applet *"sticky."* This causes the applet to stick around in a secondary cache on the client machine. The only time that the applet is downloaded again after the initial time is if the server were to have a newer version available for the client. This new secondary cache is provided by the Java plug-in.

Fast Loading of Applet Support Classes

JAR files containing support classes for applets can now be placed in the Java 2 Runtime Environment/Plug-in `lib/applet/` directory. This reduces startup time for large applets by allowing applet classes to be preloaded from the local file system by the applet class loader, providing the same protections as if they had been downloaded over the net.

JAR Indexing

Instead of the class loader having to search linearly through all the resources in the CLASSPATH, the class loader is able to use the `INDEX.LIST` file that can be generated by the jar utility to create a lookup of supporting files and/or resources. This helps decrease the time it takes to locate files within `JARS` and decrease the overall startup time for applications, especially applets.

Automatic Installation of Extensions

Version 1.3 of the Java 2 Platform introduces support for an expanded set of JAR-file manifest attributes that enables applets to specify version and vendor information for the optional packages that they require. The manifests of JAR-packaged applets can specify a URL at which the latest version of the optional package the Java Plug-in can download if

- The needed optional package is not already installed in the Java runtime environment
- The optional package is installed but has an out-of-date version number
- The optional package is installed but is not from a specified vendor

APPENDIX 

Java Resources

In this appendix

by Chuck Cavaness

WEB SITES

Keeping on top of resources for something that changes as rapidly as the Java world is a daunting task, to say the least. As a result, any listing of Java resources is going to be obsolete before it's completed.

Rather than a comprehensive listing of every site that mentions Java (AltaVista search returns more than hundreds of thousands of hits on the word "java"), this list provides information on a few of the ever-expanding number of Java Web sites as well as data on good places to look for more Web sites. So, these sites are by no means the totality of what's out there—this is a starting point for you to begin your Java reference bookmark lists. These sites are in no particular order and have no other qualification beyond the fact that Java programmers of all levels should find them useful in some way.

Site Name: Sun's Home Page

Site URL: `http://java.sun.com/`

Sun's home page hosts the Java 2 SDK Standard Edition Documentation and is probably the best place to start when looking for Java resources. You can find extensive documentation on the Java API, the SDK, and the Java language itself. You can download the latest versions of the SDK and other Java-related tools. Anyone serious about programming in Java should explore this site fully and return frequently. You can also find timely information that you can't find anywhere else.

Site Name: Earthweb's developer.com

Site URL: `http://www.gamelan.com/`

Originally known as Gamelan (pronounced "gamma-lahn"), this is the granddaddy of all Java resource sites offering a huge listing of just about anything available on the Web for Java. From its extensive applet collection to its listing of other outside Java resources, Gamelan is a great place to start browsing to see what other Java programmers are up to.

Site Name: Focus on Java

Site URL: `http://java.about.com/compute/java/`

In Focus on Java's Java Guide, John Zukowski offers a vast collection of exceptional information on Java. John hand picks the best Java tidbits, identifies the best books and tools, and provides insight into the disparate directions Java is headed. His resource collection is a library of Java resources categorized by type.

Site Name: Java Applet Rating Service (JARS)

Site URL: `http://www.jars.com/`

The main focus of JARS is to provide ratings for Java applets that are available on the World Wide Web. Each applet is reviewed by a panel of independent judges, including some of this book's authors, who base the rating on a set of criteria. If an applet achieves specified totals for its rating, distinction might be recognized by the following JARS awards:

- Top 1% Web Applet
- Top 5% Web Applet
- Top 25% Web Applet
- Top 10 Web Applet (of the month)
- Top 100 Web Applet (of the month)

In addition, applets with publicly available source code are further acknowledged, and a link to the source is provided when possible.

JARS.com is a great site for checking out other programmers' applets and seeing how yours stacks up against the rest of the world.

Site Name: The Java Boutique

Site URL: `http://javaboutique.internet.com/`

The Java Boutique has many URL listings, along with applets, reviews, forums, how-to articles, and many other interesting features.

Site Name: Java Developer's Journal

Site URL: `http://www.javadevelopersjournal.com/java/`

Java Developer's Journal has free Java courses, a free three-month trial subscription to its Java Developer's Journal magazine, free software, and so on. This site includes product reviews, which can help when you want to buy software.

Site Name: Java Developers Connection

Site URL: `http://java.sun.com/jdc`

This site is a free resource from Sun providing up-to-date material and prerelease software. A must visit for any serious Java developer.

Site Name: Java Lobby

Site URL: `http://www.javalobby.com or http://www.javalobby.org`

The Java Lobby is a group of Java developers dedicated to insuring the "Write Once Run Anywhere" promise of Java. The group lobbies to make sure that Java is always kept pure.

Site Name: Java Resources from Netscape

Site URL: `http://developer.netscape.com/library/documentation/javalist.html`

Java Resources from Netscape offers a comprehensive listing of Java technical information for use with its products. At this site, you can find multiple listings and third-party listings covering just about anything you might want to know about Java.

Site Name: Java World

Site URL: `http://www.javaworld.com/`

A monthly online magazine, *Java World* is IDG's magazine for the Java community. Here you find informative links to resources and how-to's. You can search for specific information and check out its "Nuts & Bolt's" section for great information on software usage.

Site Name: JavaBeans Site

Site URL:

The root of all JavaBeans information is this wonderful site that includes information and links to a variety of information on JavaBeans and JavaBeans projects.

Site Name: Swing Connection

Site URL: `http://java.sun.com/products/jfc/swingdoc-current/`

This site is the home of the Swing (JFC) project offering timely tips and techniques on using JFC, as well as information about upcoming features.

Site Name: Team Java

Site URL: `http://www.teamjava.com/`

Team Java is intended to assist Java consultants by providing information regarding available jobs, news, educational materials, and other useful Java resources. Team Java also has an applet-of-the-day service called Java the Hut. Overall, this site is very useful for people who use, or plan to use, Java in a professional environment. Even weekend Java warriors will find this site useful.

Site Name: IBM alphaWorks Site

Site URL: `http://www.alphaworks.ibm.com/`

This site is managed by IBM Java people and has a tremendous amount of downloads for the Java platform. These downloads include tools to help design, develop, and deploy Java applications. Spend some time there browsing the available downloads.

NEWSGROUPS

Usenet newsgroups can be a great source of information. They can also be a major pain when people stop being helpful and start arguing about whatever they feel like arguing about. If you're familiar with Usenet, and feel comfortable using it, these newsgroups are a valuable asset. If you're not familiar with Usenet news, it's best to just observe for a while, get a feel for the system, stay out of flame wars, and read the FAQ before starting to post.

With that said, the many Usenet newsgroups on Java worth mentioning are as follows:

- **`comp.lang.java`**—Java language and programming.
- **`comp.lang.java.advocacy`**—Java proponents speak out.
- **`comp.lang.java.announce`**—Java products and other services announced (moderated).
- **`comp.lang.java.beans`**—JavaBeans discussions and programming.

- **comp.lang.java.databases**—Java database programming.
- **comp.lang.java.gui**—Graphical interface tips and help.
- **comp.lang.java.help**—General help with the Java language and programming.
- **comp.lang.java.machine**—Java virtual machine discussions.
- **comp.lang.java.programmer**—Java programmer help.
- **comp.lang.java.security**—Java security discussions.
- **comp.lang.java.softwaretools**—Discussion of Java tools to help you be more productive.
- **alt.www.hotjava**—HotJava World Wide Web browser.

Be aware that not all news servers make the `alt.` hierarchy of newsgroups available to its subscribers. If you have trouble locating it, contact your news administrator.

If your ISP does not support newsgroups, you can use a web version by going to `http://www.deja.com/usenet`.

MAILING LISTS

In addition to the mailing list administered by Java-SIG and run by various smaller groups, a few lists are run out of Sun. The main list URL is `java-interest@java.sun.com`.

This is an extremely high-traffic group, with more than 20,000 subscribers and dozens of posts every day. The list isn't moderated, so this isn't a place for you if you're easily overwhelmed.

You can subscribe to the list by sending the words `subscribe java-interest` in the body of your message to this `majordomo@java.sun.com`.

There are really too many mailing lists to mention and they would probably fill an entire book. The best way to find out which lists are out there is to go the Sun site at `www.javasoft.com` and do a search for a mailing list that discusses the Java topic you are interested in.

INDEX

Symbols

A

B

C

D

E

F

G

H

I

K

M

N

O

Q

R

T

V

W

X-Z